MUSEUM OF BROADCAST COMMUNICATIONS

Encyclopedia of

TELEVISION

SECOND EDITION

MUSEUM OF BROADCAST COMMUNICATIONS

Encyclopedia of TELEVISION

SECOND EDITION

Volume 3
M–R

Horace Newcomb
EDITOR

FITZROY DEARBORN
New York • London

Published in 2004 by
Fitzroy Dearborn
An imprint of the Taylor & Francis Group
270 Madison Avenue
New York, New York 10016

First published by
Fitzroy Dearborn Publishers
70 East Walton Street
Chicago, Illinois 60611
U.S.A.

Library of Congress Cataloging-in-Publication Data:

Encyclopedia of television / Museum of Broadcast Communications ; Horace
Newcomb, editor.—2nd ed.
    p. cm.
  Includes bibliographical references and index.
  ISBN 1-57958-394-6 (set : alk. paper) -- ISBN 1-57958-411-X (v. 1 :
alk. paper) -- ISBN 1-57958-412-8 (v. 2 : alk. paper) -- ISBN
1-57958-413-6 (v. 3 : alk. paper) -- ISBN 1-57958-456-X (v. 4 : alk.
paper)
  1. Television broadcasting--Encyclopedias. I. Title: Encyclopedia of
television. II. Newcomb, Horace. III. Museum of Broadcast
Communications.
  PN1992.18.E53 2005
  384.55'03--dc22
                    2004003947

Contents

Advisory Board

Alphabetical List of Entries

Volume 1

Volume 2

Volume 3

Volume 4

M

Magic Roundabout, The

France/U.K. Children's Entertainment

The Magic Roundabout was a long-running animation for preschool children that became a cult classic. The five-minute program was first broadcast in the 1960s, shown at the end of the British Broadcasting Corporation's (BBC's) weekday children's programs. *The Magic Roundabout* offered an assortment of colorful, toylike characters for children and a dry and witty script for adults. A revival on Channel 4 in the 1990s brought *the Magic Roundabout* to a new generation of fans.

Despite being considered a national institution in the United Kingdom, *The Magic Roundabout* was discovered in France by Doreen Stephens, the head of the BBC's Family Programs. French animator Serge Danot's *Le Manège Enchanté* had been running on French television for a couple of years. Danot built the sets and shot the puppets one frame at a time to create a three-dimensional animation. Eric Thompson, father of actress Emma and a presenter on the BBC preschool program *Playschool,* was chosen as writer and narrator for the English version. Rather than translating Danot's script, Thompson chose to rename the characters and write new scripts. First appearing on the BBC in 1965, *The Magic Roundabout* was shown just before the 5:55 P.M. main early-evening news bulletin on BBC 1, which meant that many adults caught the program while waiting for the news. At the start of a new series in October 1967, *Radio Times* (the BBC listings magazine) described the series as a "favorite with children from two to ninety-two."

The first few programs introduced the basic storyline. Mr. Rusty is unhappy because his roundabout (fairground carousel with horses) has fallen into disrepair, and the children no longer visit. A magical jack-in-the-box, called Zebedee, appears one day and, using his magic, repairs the roundabout. On the sound of the music from Mr. Rusty's barrel organ, the roundabout turns, and the children return to play. Zebedee offers one of the children a special gift: a visit to a magic garden. The rest of the series follows this child, a young girl named Florence, and her encounters with the odd assortment of characters that inhabit the magic garden. The remaining episodes were short interactions between the characters, the program starting with the roundabout and often ending with Zebedee bounding into the frame, announcing, "Time for bed!"

In addition to Florence, the main characters were Dougal, a long-haired orange dog with a fondness for lumps of sugar; Brian, a yellow snail; Ermintrude, a pink cow with red spots who wore a hat; and Dylan, a floppy-eared rabbit who wore clothes, carried a guitar, and spent most of the time sleeping propped against a tree. There were also two elderly characters, Mr. McHenry, the gardener who rode a tricycle, and the previously mentioned Mr. Rusty. The garden was home to two-dimensional trees and flowers that spun like pinwheels. Aired in black and white, it was not until 1970 that the bright colors of Danot's designs could be seen in their true splendor on British television.

If the bright designs of the characters and scenery appealed to its younger viewers, then it was Thompson's commentary, with frequent references to topical issues and personalities, that appealed to the older viewers. One of the most often quoted pieces of dialogue from the series was Dougal's manifesto when standing before Parliament: "I'm in favor of the four-day week, the 47-minute hour and the 30-second minute. This gives a lot of time for lying about in the sun and eating" (a comment on the British government's introduction of the three-day week).

As is the case with many cult programs, rumors abounded about subliminal messages in the program. Most of the rumors that surrounded *The Magic Roundabout* centered on drugs; the psychedelic garden was an acid trip, Dougal's favorite sugar lumps were LSD, and Dylan was in fact named after Bob Dylan. All these ideas were officially dismissed but added to the cult status of the program. The BBC was inundated with complaints in October 1966, when the network moved *The Magic Roundabout* to the earlier time of 4:55, which meant that fewer working adults would be able to view it. The BBC bowed to public pressure and moved it back to the later slot several weeks later. Even though Danot had stopped production of the series in 1972, *The Magic Roundabout* remained on the BBC, with reruns, until 1977. (Danot resumed production of the series in 1980 with 55 new episodes.)

Eric Thompson died in 1982, so when Channel 4 purchased rights to the new episodes in 1992, the actor Nigel Planer (best known in the United Kingdom for his role as Neil the hippy in *The Young Ones*) took over the role of narrator, writing the new scripts along with his brother Roger. Shown as one of Channel 4's early-morning children's programs, Planer's version remained faithful to the earlier version (even carrying the credit line "with grateful acknowledgement to Eric Thompson"). The programs continued to refer to current affairs, personalities, and topics well beyond the comprehension of its preschool audience. The series ran on Channel 4 until 1994, with reruns still being shown to the present day.

Danot made a feature length version of the program, *Pollux et Le Chat Bleu* (Pollux was the original French name for Dougal). Eric Thompson narrated an English version, *Dougal and the Blue Cat,* which was released in Britain in 1972. A stage production of the program toured the United Kingdom in 1993.

KATHLEEN LUCKEY

Programming History
BBC 1965–77 Weekdays 5:50
Channel 4 1992–94 Weekdays 7:37

Credits (English version)
Created by Serge Danot
For BBC (written and narrated by Eric Thompson)
For Channel 4 (written by Nigel and Roger Planer)
Narrated by Nigel Planer
Produced/directed by Brendan Donnison
Executive producer Lucinda Whiteley
A Lyps Inc. Production for Channel 4 and ABTV

Further Reading

Cook, William, "Time for Bed Again," *New Statesman and Society* (March 8, 1996)
Home, Anna, *Into the Box of Delights: A History of Children's Television,* London: BBC Books, 1993
Law, Phyllida, Emma Thompson, and Sophie Thompson, *The Adventures of Dougal,* London: Bloomsbury, 1998
Macksey, Serena, "His Life as a Dog, My Life as a Cow," *The Independent* (May 22, 1998)
Matthews, John, "Magic Roundabout: The Trip That Never Was," *Classic Television,* 5 (June/July 1998)

Magid, Frank N. *See* **Frank N. Magid Associates**

Magnum, P.I.

U.S. Detective Program

A permutation of the hard-boiled detective genre, *Magnum, P.I.* aired on the Columbia Broadcasting System (CBS) from 1980 through 1988. Initially, the network had the series developed to make use of the extensive production facilities built during the 1970s in Hawaii for the successful police procedural *Hawaii Five-O* and intended the program to reflect a style and character suited to Hawaiian glamour. For the first five years the series was broadcast, it ranked in the top 20 shows for each year.

The series was set in the contemporary milieu of 1980s Hawaii, a melting pot of ethnic and social groups. Thomas Magnum, played by Tom Selleck, is a former naval intelligence officer making his way as a private investigator in the civilian crossroads between Eastern and Western cultures. In charge of the security for the estate of the never-seen author Robin Masters, Magnum lives a relatively carefree life on the property. A friendly antagonism and respect exists between Magnum and Jonathan Higgins III (John Hillerman), Masters's overseer of the estate. Though both men come from military backgrounds, Magnum's free-wheeling style often clashes with Higgins's more mannered British discipline. In addition, two of Magnum's former military buddies round out the regular cast. T.C., or Theodore Calvin (Roger Mosely), operates and owns a helicopter charter company, a service that comes in handy for many of Magnum's cases. Rick Wright (Larry Manetti), a shady nightclub owner, often provides Magnum with important information through his links to the criminal element lurking below the vibrant tropical colors of the Hawaiian paradise.

Though originally dominated by an episodic narrative structure, *Magnum, P.I.* moved far beyond the simple demands of stock characters solving the crime of the week. Without using the open-ended strategy developed by the prime-time soap opera in the 1980s, the series nevertheless created complex characterizations by building a cumulative text. Discussion of events from previous episodes would continually pop up, constructing memory as an integral element of the series franchise. While past actions might not have an immediate impact on any individual weekly narrative, the overall effect was to expand the range of traits that characters might invoke in any given situation. For the regular viewer of the series, the cumulative strategy offered a richness of narrative, moving beyond the simpler whodunit of the hard-boiled detective series that populated American television in the 1960s and 1970s.

Part of the success of *Magnum, P.I.* stemmed from the combination of familiar hard-boiled action and exotic locale. Just as important perhaps, the series was one of the first to regularly explore the impact of the Vietnam War on the American cultural psyche. Many of the most memorable episodes deal with contemporary incidents triggered by memories and relationships growing out of Magnum's past war experiences. In-

Magnum P.I., Tom Selleck, 1980–88.
Courtesy of the Everett Collection

deed, the private investigator's abhorrence of discipline and cynical attitude toward authority seem to stem from the general mistrust of government and military bureaucracies that came to permeate American society in the early 1970s.

On one level, Magnum became the personification of an American society that had yet to deal effectively with the fallout from the Vietnam War. By the end of the 1980s, the struggle to deal with the unresolved issues of the war erupted full force into American popular culture. Before Magnum began to deal with his psychological scars in the context of the 1980s, network programmers apparently believed that any discussion of the war in a series would prompt viewers to tune it out. With the exception of Norman Lear's *All in the Family* in the early 1970s, entertainment network programming acted, for the most part, as if the war had never occurred. However, *Magnum, P.I.*'s success proved programmers wrong. Certainly, the series' success opened the door for other dramatic series that were able to examine the Vietnam War in its historical setting. Series such as *Tour of Duty* and *China Beach,* though not as popular, did point out that room existed in mainstream broadcasting for discussions of the emotional and political wounds that had yet to heal. As Thomas Magnum began to deal with his past, so too did the American public.

Critics of the show often point out, however, that in dealing with this past, the series recuperated and reconstructed the involvement of the United States in Vietnam. While some aspects of the show seem harshly critical of that entanglement, many episodes justify and rationalize the conflict and the U.S. role. As a result, *Magnum, P.I.* is shot through with conflicting and often contradictory perspectives, and any "final" interpretation must take the entire series into account rather than concentrate on single events or episodes. The construction of this long-running narrative, riddled as it is with continuously developing characterizations, ideological instability, and multilayered generic resonance, illustrates many aspects of commercial U.S. television's capacity for narrative complexity as well as some of its most vexing problems and questions. Perhaps it is *Magnum, P.I.*'s narrative and ideological complexity that has ensured the series' ongoing success as a syndicated programming staple.

RODNEY A. BUXTON

See also **Action Adventure Shows; Detective Programs; Vietnam on Television**

Cast

Thomas Sullivan Magnum	Tom Selleck
Jonathan Quayle Higgins III	John Hillerman
T.C. (Theodore Calvin)	Roger E. Mosley
Rick (Orville Wright)	Larry Manetti
Robin Masters	
(voice only) 1981–85	Orson Welles
Mac Reynolds	Jeff MacKay
Lt. Tanaka	Kwan Hi Lim
Lt. Maggie Poole	Jean Bruce Scott
Agatha Chumley	Gillian Dobb
Asst. District Attorney,	
Carol Baldwin	Kathleen Lloyd
Francis Hofstetler ("Ice Pick")	Elisha Cook Jr.

Producers

Donald P. Bellisario, Glen Larson, Joel Rogosin, John G. Stephens, Douglas Benton, J. Rickley Dumm, Rick Weaver, Andrew Schneider, Douglas Green, Reuben Leder, Chas. Floyd Johnson, Nick Thiel, Chris Abbot

Programming History

150 episodes; 6 2-hour episodes
CBS

December 1980–	
August 1981	Thursday 9:00–10:00
September 1981–	
April 1986	Thursday 8:00–9:00
April 1986–June 1986	Saturday 10:00–11:00
June 1986–August 1986	Tuesday 9:00–10:00
September 1986–May 1987	Wednesday 9:00–10:00
July 1987–February 1988	Wednesday 9:00–10:00
June 1988–September 1988	Monday 10:00–11:00

Further Reading

Anderson, Christopher, "Reflections on *Magnum, P.I.,*" in *Television: The Critical View,* edited by Horace Newcomb, New York: Oxford University Press, 1976; 4th edition, 1987

Flitterman, Sandy, "Thighs and Whiskers: The Fascination of *Magnum, P.I.,*" *Screen* (1985)

Haines, Harry W., "The Pride Is Back: Rambo, Magnum, P.I., and the Return Trip to Vietnam," in *Cultural Capacities of Vietnam: Uses of the Past and Present,* edited by Peter Mowies and Peter Ehrenhaus, Norwood, New Jersey: Ablex, 1990

Meyers, Richard, *TV Detectives,* San Diego, California: A.S. Barnes, 1981

Newcomb, Horace, "Magnum: The Champagne of TV," *Channels of Communication* (May–June 1985)

Malone, John C. (1941–)

U.S. Telecommunications Executive

John C. Malone is the chairman of Liberty Media Corporation. Prior to its acquisition by AT&T in 1999, he was the chief executive officer of Telecommunications, Inc. (TCI), until that time the largest operator of cable systems in the United States. Malone oversaw TCI's phenomenal growth from the time of his arrival at the company in 1973 and in the process came to be regarded as one of the most powerful people in the television industry. He has been praised by many for his outstanding business acumen and his technological foresight, but at the same time he has also acquired a less flattering reputation for his hardball style of business practice. Among those who have been openly critical of Malone in this latter vein is Albert Gore Jr., who once dubbed Malone the "Darth Vader" of the cable industry.

Malone began his career at AT&T Bell Labs in the mid-1960s before moving on to become a management consultant for McKinsey and Company in 1968. He received his Ph.D. in industrial engineering from Johns Hopkins University in 1969 and soon joined the General Instrument Corporation, where he became president of its Jerrold cable equipment division. It was here that he first established ties to many of the cable industry's pioneers. In 1972 he turned down an offer from Steve Ross of Warner Communications to head its fledgling cable division, opting instead to leave the East Coast to accept an offer from TCI founder Bob Magness to run the small cable company from its Denver, Colorado, headquarters.

Malone joined TCI just before it fell into very difficult times. Malone's first major success at TCI was in negotiating a restructuring of the company's heavy debt load. Once freed from the burden of this debt, Malone embarked on a conservative growth strategy for TCI. Rather than attempting to expand its holdings by building large urban cable systems at great expense, as many other cable companies did in the late 1970s, Malone focused TCI's growth efforts on gaining franchise rights in smaller communities, where the costs to build the systems would be far less onerous. The wisdom of Malone's strategy soon became evident. TCI was able to grow without encountering the exceedingly high costs associated with building capital-intensive urban cable systems, and in the early 1980s it

was able to purchase several existing large-market systems, such as those in Pittsburgh, Pennsylvania, and St. Louis, Missouri, at bargain prices from companies that had financially overextended themselves in the construction process.

As TCI grew throughout the 1980s, so did its power within the television industry. The company invested heavily in programming services and eventually came to hold stakes in more than 25 different cable networks under the arm of its Liberty Media subsidiary. However, TCI's success was sometimes overshadowed by the public's perception of it as a heavy-handed com-

John C. Malone.
Photo courtesy of John Malone

pany that occasionally would resort to bullying tactics to achieve its desired ends. For instance, in TCI's earlier days, some of its systems were known to replace entire channels of programming for days at a time, leaving these channels blank except for the names and home telephone numbers of local franchising officials. The strategy aimed to gain leverage in franchise negotiations. Fairly or not, Malone came to personify TCI and its negative public image.

Despite the company's poor public relations record, few would deny that Malone and TCI were among the most powerful forces shaping the television industry in the late 20th century. Like William S. Paley of the Columbia Broadcasting System (CBS) and David Sarnoff of the Radio Corporation of America (RCA) an earlier era, Malone exercised great control over what American television viewers would or would not see. At TCI's peak, nearly one in four cable subscribers in the United States was served by a TCI system, and these viewers were directly affected by the decisions Malone made. Even those who were not TCI subscribers felt Malone's influence because access to the critical mass of viewers represented by TCI's cable systems was crucial to any programmer's success. Programmers needed carriage on TCI systems in order to gather the audience numbers that provide solid financial status. Malone assumed the position of a gatekeeper, wielding enormous influence over the entire television marketplace, which explains another nickname that was sometimes applied to him: "The Godfather" of cable television.

Malone first hinted at his ultimate ambitions for TCI when he attempted to merge the company with the regional telephone operator Bell Atlantic in 1993. Although the deal was scuttled only four months after it was announced, it foreshadowed Malone's eventual plans for TCI's place in the future television marketplace. In 1999 Malone was able to successfully negotiate the purchase of TCI and its programming arm, Liberty Media, by AT&T for a staggering $54 billion. The acquisition allowed AT&T to assume a central position within the cable television industry, while Malone was able to command top dollar for TCI shareholders in exchange for what were, in many instances, older cable systems with infrastructures that were technologically inferior to those of many other cable services. In the meantime, Malone stayed on after the acquisition as Liberty Media's chairman.

AT&T struggled in the cable operations business, and the relationship between Malone and AT&T Chairman Michael Armstrong grew increasingly rocky until 2001, when AT&T divested its stake in Liberty Media and agreed to sell its cable systems to Comcast Corp. With its newly found freedom from AT&T, Malone led Liberty Media into a new round of asset acquisition, most notably by reentering the cable operations business by buying stakes in European cable systems. In so doing, Malone gave every indication of his intention to be as dominant a force in shaping the 21st century's global telecommunications marketplace as he was in influencing the direction of U.S. television in the last quarter of the 20th century.

DAVID GUNZERATH

See also **Cable Networks; United States: Cable Television**

John Malone. Born in Milford, Connecticut, March 7, 1941. Educated at Yale University, New Haven, Connecticut, Phi Beta Kappa, B.S. in electrical engineering and economics, 1963, and M.S. in industrial management, 1964; Johns Hopkins University, Baltimore, Maryland, Ph.D. in industrial engineering, 1969. Married Leslie; two children. Began professional career in economic planning and research and development with Bell Telephone Laboratories/AT&T, 1963; worked as management consultant for McKinsey and Co., 1968; group vice president, General Instrument Corporation, 1970; former president, cable equipment division, Jerrold Electronics Corporation (a General Instrument Corporation subsidiary); president and chief executive officer, TeleCommunications Inc., Denver, Colorado, 1973–99; chairman, Liberty Media Corporation, since 1990. Chair emeritus, Cable Television Laboratories. Board member, Bank of New York; the CATO Institute; Discovery Communications, Inc.; USANi, LLC; UnitedGlobalCom, Inc.; and Cendant Corp. Recipient: TVC Magazine Man of the Year Award, 1981; Wall Street Transcript's Gold Award for the cable industry's best chief executive officer, 1982, 1985, 1986, and 1987; NCTA Vanguard Award, 1983; Wall Street's Transcript Silver Award, 1984 and 1989; Women in Cable's Betsy Magness Fellowship Honoree; University of Pennsylvania Wharton School Sol C. Snider Entrepreneurial Center Award of Merit for Distinguished Entrepreneurship; American Jewish Committee Sherrill C. Corwin Human Relations Award; Communications Technology Magazine Service and Technology Award; Financial World CEO of the Year Competition, 1993; Johns Hopkins University Distinguished Alumnus Award, 1994. Honorary degree: Doctor of Humane Letters, Denver University, 1992.

Further Reading

"Another TBS Network Envisioned by Malone," *Broadcasting* (May 11, 1987)

Auletta, Ken, *The Highwaymen: Warriors of the Information Superhighway,* New York: Random House, 1997

Chen, Christine, "Liberty Media's Surprising Reach," *Fortune* (September 17, 2001)

Davis, Lawrence J., *The Billionaire Shell Game: How Cable Baron John Malone and Assorted Corporate Titans Invented a Future Nobody Wanted,* New York: Doubleday, 1998

"Malone Looks to the Future with Cable Labs," *Broadcasting* (June 5, 1989)

"Malone Paints Rosy Picture for IRTS," *Broadcasting* (March 20, 1989)

"Malone Urges Creation of Bandwidth Manager; TCI Wants Vendors to Come Up with a Residential Communications Gateway Unit," *Broadcasting & Cable* (August 15, 1994)

Mehta, Stephanie, "The Island of Dr. Malone," *Fortune* (July 24, 2000)

Mermigas, Diane, "John Malone Making His Way in Europe," *Electronic Media* (March 5, 2001)

Moshavi, Sharon D., "TCI's Malone: Cable Nearing Compression Revolution," *Broadcasting* (March 18, 1991)

Roberts, Johnnie L., "Time's Uneasy Pieces," *Newsweek* (October 2, 1995)

Samuels, Gary, "You Gotta Consolidate, You Gotta Swap" (interview), *Forbes* (December 19, 1994)

Weinberg, Neil, "Taking Liberty," *Forbes* (October 18, 1999)

Mama

U.S. Domestic Comedy/Drama

Mama, which aired from 1949 to 1957 on the Columbia Broadcasting System (CBS), proves that television was capable of complex characterizations in the series format even early in its history. A weekly family comedy-drama based on Kathryn Forbes's *Mama's Bank Account* as well as its play and film adaptations *I Remember Mama, Mama* would best be described today as "dramedy." Unfortunately, except for its last half season, when it was filmed, the program aired live, with kinescope recordings prepared for West Coast broadcasts. Consequently, it is unavailable in the repetitive reruns that have made other domestic situation comedies from the 1950s (including many, such as *Father Knows Best,* that it influenced) familiar to several generations of viewers.

Each episode dramatized, with warmth and humor, the Hansen family's adventures and everyday travails in turn-of-the-20th-century San Francisco. The working-class Norwegian family included Mama, Papa (a carpenter), and children Katrin, Nels, and Dagmar. Mama's sisters and an uncle were semiregular characters. Although earlier incarnations of the Forbes material had focused on the relationship between Mama and Katrin, the television series centered episodes on all the characters, a technique made available and almost demanded by the production of a continuing series.

The stories might revolve around Dagmar's braces, Nels starting a business, or the children buying presents for Mama's birthday. The entire family would contribute to the drama's resolution, however, and images of them sitting down to a cup of Maxwell House

coffee—the show's longtime sponsor—would frame each episode of the show. As George Lipsitz points out, it was common for the dramatic solutions to in-

Mama, Peggy Wood, Judson Laire, 1949–57.
Courtesy of the Everett Collection

volve some kind of commodity purchase, not surprising given the commercial basis of American network television and the consumer culture of the postwar United States. What is surprising is how often the show foregrounded the contradictions of this consumer culture in which everyone does not have access to the desired goods. Dramatic tension often resulted from the realization that Mama's endeavors provided the foundation for the achievements of individual family members. It was not uncommon for Papa and the Hansen children to have to come to terms with the value of Mama's work.

The program's complex treatment of cultural tensions resulted not only from Forbes's original material but also from the contributions of head writer Frank Gabrielson, director-producer Ralph Nelson (a Hollywood liberal of Norwegian descent who went on to direct the film *Lilies of the Field*), and a distinguished cast. Peggy Wood, who incarnated Mama, was a versatile stage and film actress who had starred in operetta and Shakespeare and is probably best known to today's audiences for her Oscar-nominated role as Mother Superior in *The Sound of Music.* (Mady Christians, who starred in the role of Mama on Broadway, was not considered for the television role because she was blacklisted.) Dick Van Patten played Nels and would later star in television's *Eight Is Enough* in the 1970s. Robin Morgan, who played Dagmar from 1950 to 1956, became a well-known feminist activist and writer. Not surprisingly, she attributes to *Mama* many of her early lessons in feminine power.

MARY DESJARDINS

See also **Comedy, Domestic Settings; Family on Television**

Cast

Marta Hansen (Mama)	Peggy Wood
Lars Hansen (Papa)	Judson Laire
Nels	Dick Van Patten
Katrin	Rosemary Rich
Dagmar (1949)	Iris Mann
Dagmar (1950–56)	Robin Morgan
Dagmar (1957)	Toni Campbell
Aunt Jenny	Ruth Gates
T.R. Ryan (1952–56)	Kevin Coughlin
Uncle Chris (1949–51)	Malcolm Keen
Uncle Chris (1951–52)	Roland Winters
Uncle Gunnar Gunnerson	Carl Frank
Aunt Trina Gunnerson	Alice Frost
Ingeborg (1953–56)	Patty McCormack

Producers

Carol Irwin, Ralph Nelson, Donald Richardson

Programming History

CBS

July 1949–July 1956	Friday 8:00–8:30
December 1956–March 1957	Friday 8:00–8:30

Further Reading

Lipsitz, George, "Why Remember Mama? The Changing Face of a Woman's Narrative?" in *Time Passages: Collective Memory and American Popular Culture,* Minneapolis: University of Minnesota Press, 1990

Man Alive

Canadian Religious/Information Program

A critically acclaimed, nondenominational program that the show's executive producer, Louise Lore, describes as "a religious program for a post-Christian age," *Man Alive* is one of Canada's longest-running information programs. Begun in 1967 amid a renewed sense of theological activism inspired by the reforms of Vatican II, *Man Alive* takes its name and inspiration from a St. Irnaeus quote: "the glory of God is man

fully alive." From a format that concentrated on theological issues, the show's focus has broadened considerably in its 30 seasons.

Man Alive has profiled and interviewed many of the world's most important religious figures, from Mother Teresa to the Dalai Lama and Archbishop Desmond Tutu. An October 8, 1986, interview with the Aga Khan was this religious leader's first formal North

Man Alive.
Photo courtesy of National Archives of Canada/CBC Collection

American interview. He had declined previous requests from such well-known shows as the Columbia Broadcasting System's (CBS's) *60 Minutes* in favor of *Man Alive* because of the show's reputation for balance and the relaxed, soft-spoken interviewing style of the show's host, Roy Bonisteel. Many *Man Alive* interviews were marked by their candidness and honesty, as in the case of Archbishop Tutu, who related how Jackie Robinson and Lena Horne were his boyhood heroes.

Bonisteel, the show's host for 22 seasons and so identified with it that many mistake him for a minister, is a journalist by training. He had been producing radio shows for the United Church of Canada in the mid-1960s, when he was approached to be the host of the new television program. By the time he left, he had become the longest-running host of any information program in Canada. He was succeeded by Peter Downie, former cohost of the Canadian Broadcasting Corporation's (CBC's) *Midday* current affairs program in the fall of 1989. *Man Alive* observed its 25th anniversary with a one-hour special in February 1992 that celebrated not only its longevity but also the diversity of its programming.

Throughout its history, the show has consistently provided programming that appeals to a broad audience, and this has been one of the keys to its success. It has delved into a variety of topics, from UFOs to the threat of nuclear war, from father–son relationships to life in a maximum-security hospital for the criminally insane. Nor has it avoided controversial and unpopular subjects, such as the Vatican bank scandal, sexual abuse in the church, or aid to El Salvador. Some of the show's most critically acclaimed episodes have been those that have chronicled very personal human dramas, such as the story of David McFarlane, who met the challenges presented by his Down syndrome to star in a television drama, or the story of the Rubineks, Holocaust survivors, and their moving return to Poland after 40 years. Despite the changing nature of television audiences and serious budgetary constraints, *Man Alive* continues the tradition of providing an informative and well-balanced examination of relevant social issues and contemporary ethical questions.

MANON LAMONTAGNE

Hosts
Roy Bonisteel (1967–89)
Peter Downie (1989–)

Executive Producers
Leo Rampen (1967–85); Louise Lore (1985–)

Programming History
CBC

October 1967–March 1968	Sunday 5:00–5:30
November 1968–March 1978	Monday 9:30–10:00
October 1979–March 1980	Tuesday 10:30–11:00
October 1980–March 1983	Sunday 10:30–11:00
October 1983–March 1984	Sunday 10:00–10:30
October 1984–March 1987	Wednesday 9:30–10:00
October 1987–	Tuesday 9:30–10:00

Further Reading

Bonisteel, Roy, *In Search of Man Alive,* Toronto: Totem, 1980
Bonisteel, Roy, *Man Alive: The Human Journey,* Toronto: Collins, 1983

The Man from U.N.C.L.E./The Girl from U.N.C.L.E.

U.S. Spy Parody

The Man from U.N.C.L.E., which aired on the National Broadcasting Company (NBC) from September 1964 to January 1968, has often been described as television's version of James Bond, but it was much more than that. It was, quite simply, a pop culture phenomenon. Although its ratings were initially poor early in the first season, a change in time period and cross-country promotional appearances by its stars, Robert Vaughn and David McCallum, helped the show build a large and enthusiastic audience.

At the peak of its popularity, *The Man from U.N.C.L.E.* was telecast in 60 countries and consistently ranked in the top ten programs on U.S. television. Eight feature-length films were made from two-part episodes and profitably released in the United States and Europe. *TV Guide* called it "the cult of millions." The show received 10,000 fan letters per week, and Vaughn and McCallum were mobbed by crowds of teenagers as if they were rock stars. *U.N.C.L.E.* was also a huge merchandising success, with images of the series' stars and its distinctive logo (a man standing beside a skeletal globe) appearing on hundreds of items, from bubble gum cards to a line of adult clothing.

The show had a little something for everyone. Children took it seriously as an exciting action adventure. Teenagers enjoyed its hip, cool style, identifying with and idolizing its heroes. More mature viewers appreciated the tongue-in-cheek humor and the roman à clef references to such real-life political figures as Mahatma Gandhi and Eva Peron, interpreting it as a metaphor for the struggle common to all nations against the forces of greed, cruelty, and aggression.

The Man from U.N.C.L.E. redefined the television spy program, introducing into the genre a number of fresh innovations. Notably, the show broke with espionage tradition and looked beyond the cold war politics of the time to envision a new world order. The fictional United Network Command for Law Enforcement was multinational in makeup and international in scope, protecting and defending nations regardless of size or political persuasion. For example, a third-season

episode, "The Jingle Bells Affair," showed a Soviet premier visiting New York during Christmastime, touring department stores and delivering a speech on peaceful coexistence at the United Nations, 22 years before Mikhail Gorbachev actually made a similar trip.

The show also broke new ground in reconceptualizing the action adventure hero. Prompted by a woman at the British Broadcasting Corporation (BBC) he once met who complained that the leads in U.S. series were all big, tall, muscular, and, well, American, producer Norman Felton (*Eleventh Hour* and *Dr. Kildare*) de-

The Man from U.N.C.L.E., David McCallum, Robert Vaughn, Leo G. Carroll, 1964–68.
Courtesy of the Everett Collection

The Girl from U.N.C.L.E., Stefanie Powers, 1966–67.
Courtesy of the Everett Collection

cided to vary the formula. His series, developed with Sam Rolfe (co-creator of *Have Gun—Will Travel*) teamed a U.S. agent, Napoleon Solo (Vaughn), with a Soviet one, Illya Kuryakin (McCallum). Each week they were sent off on their missions (called "affairs") by their boss, Alexander Waverly, a garrulous, craggy, pipe-smoking spymaster played by Leo G. Carroll.

Neither the suave Solo nor the enigmatic Kuryakin were physically impressive. They were instead intelligent, sophisticated, witty, charming, always polite, and impeccably well tailored. Sometimes they made mistakes, and often they lost the battle before they won the war.

What made *U.N.C.L.E.* truly appealing was the way it walked a fine line between the real and the fanciful, juxtaposing elements that were both surprisingly fantastic and humorously mundane. For example, as they battled bizarre threats to world peace, such as trained killer bees, radar-defeating bats, hiccup gas, suspended-animation devices, and earthquake machines, the agents also worried about expense accounts, insurance policies, health plans, and interdepartmental gossip.

While the series showed that heroic people had ordi-

nary concerns, it also demonstrated that ordinary people could be heroic. During the course of each week's affair, at least one civilian or "innocent" was inevitably caught up in the action. These innocents were average, everyday people—housewives, stewardesses, secretaries, librarians, schoolteachers, college students, tourists, even some children—people very much like those sitting in *U.N.C.L.E.*'s viewing audience. At the start of the story, they often complained of their boring, unexciting lives—lives to which, after all the terror and mayhem was over, they were only too happy to return.

By contrast, *U.N.C.L.E.*'s villains were fabulously exotic and larger than life. In addition to the usual international crime syndicates, Nazi war criminals, and power hungry dictators, U.N.C.L.E. also battled THRUSH, a secret society of mad scientists, megalomaniac industrialists, and corrupt government officials who held the Nietzschean belief that because of their superior intelligence, wealth, ambition, and position, they were entitled to rule the world. A number of prominent actors and actresses guest starred each week as either villains or innocents, including Joan Crawford, George Sanders, Kurt Russell, William Shatner and Leonard Nimoy (who appeared together pre–*Star Trek* in "The Project Strigas Affair"), and Sonny and Cher.

The *U.N.C.L.E.* formula was so successful that it spawned a host of imitators, including a spin-off of its own, *The Girl from U.N.C.L.E.,* in 1966. Starring Stefanie Powers as female agent April Dancer and Noel Harrison (son of Rex) as her British sidekick, Mark Slate, *The Girl from U.N.C.L.E.* took its cue from the wild campiness of the then-popular *Batman* rather than from its parent show. Although it featured many of the same elements of *Man,* including a specially designed gun and other advanced weaponry and the supersecret headquarters hidden behind an innocent tailor shop, *Girl*'s plots were either absurdly implausible or downright silly, and the series lasted only a year.

By its third season, *The Man from U.N.C.L.E.* had also become infected by the trend toward camp, and though the tone was readjusted to be more serious in the fourth season, viewers deserted the show in droves. Once in the top ten, the series dropped to 64th in the ratings and was canceled midseason, to be replaced by *Rowan and Martin's Laugh-In.*

This was not the end of *U.N.C.L.E.,* however. Because of concerns about violence voiced by parent–teacher groups, the series was not widely syndicated, and reruns did not appear until cable networks began to air them in the 1980s. Nevertheless, *The Man from U.N.C.L.E.* was not forgotten. Nearly every spy program that appeared during the ensuing decades borrowed from its various motifs (naming spy organizations with an acronym has become a genre cliché). For example, *Scarecrow and Mrs. King* expanded the premise of *U.N.C.L.E.*'s original pilot episode into an entire series. Even nonespionage programs as diverse as *thirtysomething, Star Trek: Deep Space Nine,* and *Seinfeld* continued to make references to it.

In 1983 Vaughn and McCallum reunited to play Solo and Kuryakin in a made-for-TV movie *Return of the Man from U.N.C.L.E.: The Fifteen Years Later Affair.* Three years later, the stars again reunited for an homage episode of *The A-Team* titled "The Say U.N.C.L.E. Affair."

In the early 1990s, Felton and Rolfe negotiated with Turner Broadcasting (TNT) to make a series of made-for-cable U.N.C.L.E. movies, but the project stalled when Rolfe died in 1993. Subsequently, John Davis Productions optioned the property in order to produce a feature-length film for theatrical release. Development, however, has not moved beyond the scripting stage. In 1996, there were plans for Vaughn and McCallum to play villains on a spy-spoof series, *Mr. and Mrs. Smith,* but the short-lived series was canceled before such an episode could be filmed. Eventually, only McCallum appeared as a villain in an episode that aired in the United Kingdom.

CYNTHIA W. WALKER

See also **Spy Programs**

Cast

Napoleon Solo	Robert Vaughn
Illya Kuryakin	David McCallum
Mr. Alexander Waverly	Leo G. Carroll
Lisa Rogers (1967–68)	Barbara Moore

Producers

Norman Felton, Sam H. Rolfe, Anthony Spinner, Boris Ingster

Programming History

104 episodes
NBC

September 1964–December 1964	Tuesday 8:30–9:30
January 1965– September 1965	Monday 8:00–9:00
September 1965–September 1966	Friday 10:00–11:00
September 1966–September 1967	Friday 8:30–9:30
September 1967–January 1968	Monday 8:00–9:00

Further Reading

Anderson, Robert, *The U.N.C.L.E. Tribute Book,* Las Vegas, Nevada: Pioneer, 1994

Heitland, John, *The Man from U.N.C.L.E. Book: The Behind-the-Scenes Story of a Television Classic,* New York: St. Martin's Press, 1987

Javna, John, *Cult TV,* New York: St. Martin's Press, 1985

Paquette, Brian, and Paul Howley, *The Toys from U.N.C.L.E.,* Worchester, Massachusetts: Entertainment, 1990

Worland, Rick, "The Cold War Mannerists: *The Man from U.N.C.L.E.* and TV Espionage in the 1960s," *Journal of Popular Film and Television* (winter 1994)

Mann, Abby (1927–)

U.S. Writer

Abby Mann's television and film writing career has spanned six decades and earned him widespread critical acclaim and numerous prestigious industry awards in the United States and abroad. He has received an Academy Award and New York Film Critics Award for his screenplay for *Judgment at Nuremberg* (1961) and Emmys for *The Marcus-Nelson Murders* (1973, the *Kojak* pilot), *Murderers Among Us: The Simon Wiesenthal Story* (1989), and *Indictment: The McMartin Trial* (1995).

Mann's made-for-television movies (a television genre in which he is widely acknowledged as a leading practitioner) have covered a breadth of subjects. His most daring (and controversial) scripts have offered viewers a withering critique of the functioning of the U.S. criminal justice system. Although some critics

Abby Mann in the 1970s.
Courtesy of the Everett Collection

have argued that Mann has, on occasion, selectively marshaled facts and taken "polemical" positions in his portrayal of his subjects, almost all have expressed admiration for his exhaustive investigative research and his rich dramatic portrayal of character. Most important, few have questioned the factual basis for his arguments.

Mann, the son of a Russian-Jewish immigrant jeweler, grew up in the 1930s in East Pittsburgh, Pennsylvania, a predominantly Catholic, working-class neighborhood he describes as a "tough steel area." As a Jewish youth in these surroundings, Mann felt himself an outsider. Perhaps this in part explains the persistent preoccupation, in his scripts, with the working poor and racial minorities: outsiders who are trapped in a social system in which prejudice, often institutionalized in the police and judicial apparatus, is used to deprive them of their rights.

This recurrent overarching theme is developed in stories focusing on the forced signing of criminal confessions; inadequate police and district attorney investigation of murder cases involving victims who are minorities, poor, or both; judicial and police officials who protect their reputations and careers, when confronted with evidence of possible miscarriage of jus-

tice, by refusing to reopen cases in which innocent persons, often minorities, have been convicted; the possibility that law enforcement officials conspired in the assassination of Martin Luther King Jr.; the failure of union leaders to fight adequately for the rights of their workers; the greed and questionable ethics of some members of the legal, medical, and mental health professions; and the sensationalized coverage of murder cases by the media, who tend to prejudge cases according to their perception of general public sentiment.

Mann began his professional writing career in the early 1950s, writing for the National Broadcasting Company's (NBC's) *Cameo Theater* and for the noted anthology series *Studio One, Robert Montgomery Presents,* and *Playhouse 90.* His script for the celebrated film drama *Judgment at Nuremberg* (1961), recounting the Nazi war crimes trials, was originally produced for *Playhouse 90.* Mann moved to Hollywood as production on the feature film version began. Other successful film scripts quickly followed, including *A Child Is Waiting* (1963), directed by John Cassavetes, which offered one of the first sympathetic film portrayals of the care and treatment of mentally challenged children, and a screen adaptation of Katherine Anne Porter's novel *Ship of Fools* (1965), the story of the interlocking lives of passengers sailing from Mexico to pre-Hitler Germany, directed by Stanley Kramer (who had directed *Judgment at Nuremberg*).

Mann returned to television writing in 1973 with the script for *The Marcus-Nelson Murders,* which launched Universal Television's popular *Kojak* series. Universal approached Mann about doing a story based on the 1963 brutal rape and murder of Janice Wylie and Emily Hoffert, two young, white professional women living in midtown Manhattan. George Whitmore, a young black man who had previously been arrested in Brooklyn for the murder of a black woman, signed a detailed confession for the Wylie and Hoffert murders. Whitmore later recanted his confession, claiming that he was beaten into signing it. Mann visited Whitmore in jail in New York before agreeing to write the screenplay, and he became convinced not only that Whitmore was innocent but also that some top officials in the Manhattan and Brooklyn district attorneys' offices had ignored Whitmore's alibi that he was in Seacliff, New Jersey (50 miles from New York City), at the moment of the murders. After the airing of *The Marcus-Nelson Murders,* for which Mann won an Emmy and a Writers Guild Award, Whitmore was released from prison.

Although he was not involved in the production of *Kojak,* Mann was unhappy with the treatment of the series by its producer, Universal Television, which, he argued, reframed the police melodrama as a formulaic cops-and-robbers potboiler, whereas in *The Marcus-Nelson Murders* he had sought to show that law enforcement officials should be monitored.

In his next television project, Mann cast his critical gaze on one of the most sacrosanct institutions in the United States: the medical profession. *Medical Story,* an anthology series produced by Columbia, premiered on NBC in 1975 and had a brief four-month run. Mann was the series creator and also served as co–executive producer.

Mann made his directorial debut with *King,* a six-hour docudrama on the life of civil rights leader Martin Luther King Jr. He had wanted to do a feature film on King while King was still alive but was unable to raise the necessary financing. Ironically, unforeseen circumstances brought the project to fruition in 1978, ten years after King's death. The central figure in *The Marcus-Nelson Murders,* George Whitmore, had claimed that he was watching King's "I Have A Dream" speech on television when the murders were committed. Mann asked King's widow, Coretta Scott King, for the rights to use the film clip of King's speech in *The Marcus-Nelson Murders,* which she granted. She then asked Mann if he were still interested in the piece on King's life. Encouraged by Mrs. King's continued interest, Mann pursued the project. In doing research on the script, Mann uncovered information that led him to believe that a conspiracy involving the Memphis, Tennessee, police and fire departments may have been responsible for King's death. The conspiracy theory focused on the reassignment, just prior to the assassination, of a black police officer and two black firefighters who had been stationed in a firehouse overlooking the motel where King was shot despite numerous threats of assassination while King was in Memphis.

Reporter Mark Lane assisted Mann in his investigation of the circumstances surrounding the King assassination. The research resulted in an official House of Representatives inquiry into whether a conspiracy had indeed been involved in the assassinations. As a result, Mann was publicly maligned by the Memphis police and fire chiefs.

For *Skag,* his next television project, which aired on NBC in 1980, Mann returned to the steel mills of the suburbs surrounding Pittsburgh. He developed the concept and wrote the script for the three-hour pilot and was given "complete freedom" by NBC President Fred Silverman. Starring Karl Malden as Pete "Skag" Skagska, *Skag* was a unflinching, realistic portrait of a middle-aged steelworker who had worked hard all his life but, when afflicted by a stroke, found himself suddenly "expendable" because he was no longer able to provide food for the table or perform sexually with his wife. *Skag* also dealt with the larger social issues of steelworkers' unhealthy working conditions and the failure of their unions to fight for their rights. Steelworkers' unions bitterly attacked *Skag,* calling Mann "anti-union." With this series, however, Mann was attempting to draw attention to a class of Americans who until the 1980s were grossly underrepresented in prime-time television drama, a fictional world populated largely by white, white-collar, middle-aged male protagonists.

While the premiere episode won critical praise and high ratings, viewership for *Skag* rapidly declined, and the series ended its run after six weeks on the air. Mann, who was involved in the first two regular series episodes, attributed the series' failure to uneven directing of some of the subsequent episodes and artistic interference from the show's star, Malden.

Mann's direct involvement with *Medical Story* and *Skag* convinced him that the process involved in producing series television inevitably led to too many compromises, both ideological, as politically controversial themes became "muddled," and creative, as strong pilots were followed by aesthetically weak regular series episodes. For these reasons, he decided in the 1980s to focus his artistic energy exclusively on made-for-television movies over which he had greater artistic control.

The Atlanta Child Murders aired on the Columbia Broadcasting System (CBS) in 1985. The notorious Atlanta, Georgia, case involving multiple murders of black children focused on Wayne Williams, a black who was accused of recruiting young boys for his homosexual father, using them sexually along with his father, and then murdering them. Mann was urged by prominent black leaders in Atlanta not to take on the project because, they argued, the additional publicity generated by a television movie focusing on an accused black mass murderer would, in the end, only further damage the black community. Mann initially withdrew from the proposed project, but he attended the Williams trial and was disturbed by the courtroom proceedings, which revealed to him the inadequate investigation into the murders of victims who belonged to poor minority families, the introduction of potentially unreliable evidence, and the sensationalized media coverage of the trial.

Mann, the only writer able to speak to Wayne Williams in prison after his conviction, raised doubts about the case, arguing that the judicial system itself was on trial, as was a society that neither had compassion for the victims during their lives nor did justice for them after their deaths. Critics praised the dramaturgy of *The Atlanta Child Murders,* but some questioned Mann's doubts about both the propriety of the courtroom proceedings and Williams's guilt, arguing that, after all, the Georgia supreme court had upheld Williams's conviction. After seeing the television movie, prominent defense attorneys Alan Dershowitz, William Kunstler, and Bobby Lee Cook agreed to join in a pro bono defense of Williams, but, according to Mann, once the publicity died down, they did not pursue the appeal to reopen the case.

Mann's more recent made-for-television movies premiered on Home Box Office (HBO), which he found to be much more supportive of his often-contentious stands on controversial social issues than were the commercial broadcast networks, who felt they must avoid the inherent commercial risks of alienating significant sectors of their mass audience. Most recent among these HBO films was *Indictment: The McMartin Trial,* created by Mann and his wife Myra. The film won an Emmy and a Golden Globe in 1995. Once again, Mann questioned the workings of the judicial system. This case involved the McMartin preschool in Manhattan Beach, California, at which it was alleged that seven preschool teachers had molested 347 children over the course of a decade. Most people in Los Angeles were convinced of the veracity of the charges, which were supported by the accounts of hundreds of children who attended the school. Mann became intrigued by the case when charges against five of the defendants were dropped. The two remaining defendants, Peggy Buckey, the school superintendent, and her son, Ray, were still under arrest. Buckey's daughter argued on *The Larry King Show* that the Los Angeles district attorney was continuing with the prosecution of her mother and brother because they had been kept in jail so long that the district attorney could not admit his error without losing face. As Mann investigated the case, he once again confronted the seamy side of the justice system: informers who supposedly heard confessions saying so only because they had made financial deals to their own advantage, greedy parents who were suing to get damages, and prosecutors who withheld crucial evidence and selectively ignored facts to advance their own careers by obtaining a conviction. Mann was also intent on exploring the important psychological question regarding the ease with which children can be led by manipulative adults into admitting events that never occurred.

Ultimately, despite two trials, no one was convicted in the McMartin case. *Indictment* produced very strong reactions among viewers. According to Mann, "People seem...obsessed by it. I suppose they realize that they have watched and believed stories that were as incredible as the Salem witch hunt." Reaction to the television film had a direct impact on the Manns as well. On the day production on *Indictment* began, their house was burned to the ground. Undeterred, Mann has continued to write. In 2001 *Judgment at Nuremberg* was adapted for the stage and appeared on Broadway.

HAL HIMMELSTEIN

See also **Anthology Drama; "Golden Age" of Television;** *Playhouse 90; Studio One*

Abby Mann. Born in Philadelphia, Pennsylvania, 1927. Educated at Temple University, Philadelphia, and New York University. Married: Myra. Gained fame as television writer for *Robert Montgomery Presents, Playhouse 90, Studio One,* and *Alcoa-Goodyear Theatre.* Recipient: Academy Award; two Emmy Awards; Golden Globe Award; Writers Guild Award.

Television Series

1948–58	*Studio One*
1950–55	*Cameo Theatre*
1950–57	*Robert Montgomery Presents*
1956–61	*Playhouse 90*
1973–78	*Kojak*
1975–76	*Medical Story*
1980	*Skag*

Made-for-Television Movies

1973	*The Marcus-Nelson Murders* (executive producer, writer)
1975	*Medical Story* (executive producer, writer)
1979	*This Man Stands Alone* (executive producer)
1980	*Skag* (executive producer, writer)
1985	*The Atlanta Child Murders* (executive producer, writer)
1989	*Murderers Among Us: The Simon Wiesenthal Story* (co–executive producer)
1992	*Teamster Boss: The Jackie Presser Story* (executive producer)
1995	*Indictment: The McMartin Trial* (writer)
2002	*Whitewash: The Clarence Bradley Story* (writer)

Television Miniseries

1978	*King* (director, writer)

Films

Judgment at Nuremberg, 1961; *A Child Is Waiting,* 1963; *Ship of Fools,* 1965; *The Detectives,* 1968;

Report to the Commissioner, 1975; *War and Love,* 1985.

Stage
Judgment at Nuremberg, 2001.

Further Reading

O'Connor, John J., "McMartin Preschool Case: A Portrait of Hysteria," *New York Times* (May 19, 1995)
Shales, Tom, "Tipping the Scales of Justice," *Washington Post* (May 20, 1995)

Mann, Delbert (1920–)

U.S. Director, Producer

Like many directors of television's "golden age," Delbert Mann came from a theatrical background. While studying political science at Vanderbilt University, Mann became involved with a Nashville, Tennessee, community theater group where he worked with Fred Coe, who went on to produce the alternating anthology program *Philco-Goodyear Television Playhouse.* Mann received a masters of fine arts degree in directing from Yale School of Drama and then worked as a director/producer at the Town Theatre (Columbia, South Carolina) and as a stage manager at the Wellesley Summer Theater. When he first went to New York, Mann worked as a floor manager and assistant director for the National Broadcasting Company (NBC).

In 1949 Mann began directing dramas for *Philco-Goodyear Television Playhouse,* where he was one of a stable of directors that included Vincent Donahue, Arthur Penn, and Gordon Duff. During the 1950s, Mann also directed productions for *Producers' Showcase, Omnibus, Playwrights '56, Ford Star Jubilee,* and *Ford Startime.* Although he worked almost exclusively on anthology series, Mann also directed live episodes of *Mary Kay and Johnny,* one of the first domestic sitcoms.

Mann is perhaps most often identified with the *Philco-Goodyear Television Playhouse* (and subsequent film) production of Paddy Chayefsy's *Marty,* which has been praised by critics as one of the most outstanding original dramas produced by Fred Coe and the *Philco-Goodyear Television Playhouse.* Although the production did not receive outstanding reviews when it first aired on May 24, 1953, it was one of the first television plays to receive any major press coverage and more than one line in a reviewer's column. When Mann directed the film version of *Marty* two years later, he was awarded the Academy Award for Best Director, and the film won the Palm d'Or at the Cannes Film Festival and Academy Awards for Best Picture, Actor, and Screenplay and earned four other Oscar nominations for Best Supporting Actor, Supporting Actress, Cinematography, and Art Direction.

Many of Mann's works tackled social issues, such as the plight of the elderly in *Ernie Barger Is Fifty,* which aired on August 9, 1953, as part of *The Goodyear The-*

Delbert Mann.
Photo courtesy of Delbert Mann

atre series. However, the director contends that, at the time, the teleplays were not thought of in terms of their social issues—they were simply stories about people and "just awfully good drama."

Mann's theatrical training was a tremendous influence on his television work, as he tended to use a static camera and actors staged within the frame. At Coe's direction, close-ups were used only to emphasize something or if there was a dramatic reason for doing so. The use of the static camera is particularly effective in the *Marty* dance sequence, which Mann filmed with one camera and no editing. Actors were carefully choreographed to turn to the camera at the exact moment when they needed to be seen. Combined with the crowded, relatively small set, the static camera focused the audience's attention on the characters and their sense of uneasiness in the situation. Chayefsky later credited the success of *The Bachelor Party* (October 11, 1953) to Mann's direction, noting that, through simple stage business and careful balancing of scenes, Mann was able to illustrate the emptiness of life in the small town and the protagonist's increasing depression.

Many of Mann's works are period pieces based on the director's own love of history, which he tried to recreate accurately. But historical context is secondary to the personal relationships in the story. Broadcast on April 24, 1973, in the era of anti-Vietnam protests, *The Man Without a Country* is a patriotic story of love of country and flag intended to stir a sense of nationalism during the Civil War and, simultaneously, the intimate story of one man's oppression.

Mann shifted to filmmaking in the 1960s but periodically returned to television to pursue more personal, people-oriented stories in made-for-television films. Productions such as *David Copperfield* (March 15, 1970) and *Jane Eyre* (March 24, 1971) allowed him to, once again, tell stories of personal relationships in a historical setting.

Mann returned to his live television roots for the productions of *All the Way Home* (December 21, 1981) and *Member of the Wedding* (December 20, 1982) for NBC's *Live Theater Series*. These productions differed from live television in the 1950s in that they were staged as a theatrical production in a theater rather than a studio and were filmed with a live audience in order to show their reaction to the piece.

Mann has been nominated for three additional Emmy Awards for directing: *Our Town* (*Producers' Showcase*, 1955), *Breaking Up* (American Broadcasting Company [ABC], 1977), and *All Quiet on the Western Front* (Columbia Broadcasting System [CBS], 1979).

SUSAN R. GIBBERMAN

See also **Chayefsky, Paddy; Coe, Fred; "Golden Age" of Television;** *Goodyear Playhouse; Omnibus; Philco Television Playhouse*

Delbert Mann. Born in Lawrence, Kansas, January 30, 1920. Educated at Vanderbilt University, Nashville, Tennessee, B.A. 1941; Yale University, New Haven, Connecticut, M.F.A. Married Ann Caroline Gillespie, 1942; children: David Martin, Frederick G., Barbara Susan, and Steven P. Served as first lieutenant in U.S. Air Force during World War II: B-24 pilot and squadron intelligence officer, 1944–45. Worked as director of Town Theater, Columbia, South Carolina, 1947–49; stage manager, Wellesley Summer Theater, 1947–48; director, *Philco-Goodyear Playhouse,* 1949–55; began film directing career with *Marty,* 1954; freelance film and television director, since 1954. Honorary degree: L.L.D., Northland College, Ashland, Wisconsin. Former member, board of governors, Academy of Television Arts and Sciences; former cochair, Tennessee Film, Tape and Cinema Commission; former president, Directors Guild Educational Benevolent Foundation, Cinema Circulus; former lecturer, Claremont McKenna College; board of trustees, Vanderbilt University, since 1962. Member: Directors Guild of America (president, 1967–71).

Television Series

1948–55	*Philco-Goodyear Television Playhouse*
1949	*Mary Kay and Johnny*
1949	*Lights Out*
1950	*The Little Show*
1950	*Waiting for the Break*
1950	*Masterpiece Theatre*
1954–56, 1957, 1959	*Omnibus*
1955	*Producers Showcase*
1956	*Ford Star Jubilee*
1956	*Playwrights '56*
1958	*DuPont Show of the Month*
1958–59	*Playhouse 90*
1959	*Sunday Showcase* (also producer)

Made-for-Television Movies

1968	*Heidi*
1968	*Saturday Adoption*
1970	*David Copperfield*
1971	*Jane Eyre*
1972	*She Waits* (also producer)
1972	*No Place to Run*
1973	*The Man Without a Country*
1974	*The First Woman President* (also producer)

1974	*Joie* (also producer)
1975	*A Girl Named Sooner*
1976	*Francis Gary Powers: The True Story of the U-2 Spy Incident*
1977	*Breaking Up*
1977	*Tell Me My Name*
1978	*Love's Dark Ride*
1978	*Tom and Joann*
1978	*Thou Shalt Not Commit Adultery*
1978	*Home to Stay*
1979	*All Quiet on the Western Front*
1979	*Torn Between Two Lovers*
1980	*To Find My Son*
1981	*All the Way Home*
1982	*Bronte*
1982	*The Member of the Wedding*
1983	*The Gift of Love*
1984	*Love Leads the Way*
1985	*A Death in California*
1986	*The Last Days of Patton*
1986	*The Ted Kennedy Jr. Story*
1987	*April Morning* (also coproducer)
1991	*Ironclads*
1992	*Against Her Will: An Incident in Baltimore* (also coproducer)
1993	*Incident in a Small Town* (also coproducer)
1994	*Lily in Winter*

Films

Marty, 1954; *The Bachelor Party,* 1956; *Desire Under the Elms,* 1957; *Separate Tables,* 1958; *Middle of the Night,* 1959; *The Dark at the Top of the Stairs,* 1960; *The Outsider,* 1960; *Lover Come Back,* 1961; *That Touch of Mink,* 1962; *A Gathering of Eagles,* 1962; *Dear Heart,* 1963; *Quick Before It Melts* (also producer), 1964; *Mister Buddwing* (also producer), 1965; *Fitzwilly,* 1967; *Kidnapped,* 1972; *Birch Interval,* 1976; *Night Crossing,* 1982.

Opera

Wuthering Heights, 1959.

Plays

A Quiet Place, 1956; *Speaking of Murder,* 1957; *Zelda,* 1969; *The Glass Menagerie,* 1973.

Further Reading

Averson, Richard, and David Manning White, editors, *Electronic Drama: Television Plays of the Sixties,* Boston: Beacon Press, 1971

Hawes, William, *The American Television Drama: The Experimental Years,* Tuscaloosa: University of Alabama Press, 1986

Kindem, Gorham, editor, *The Live Television Generation of Hollywood Film Directors: Interviews with Seven Directors,* Jefferson, North Carolina: McFarland, 1994

Miner, Worthington, *Worthington Miner,* Metuchen, New Jersey: Scarecrow Press, 1985

Nudd, Donna Marie, "Jane Eyre and What Adaptors Have Done to Her," Ph.D. diss., University of Texas at Austin, 1989

Shales, Tom, "When Prime Time Meant Live: NBC and Delbert Mann Revive a Golden Age," *Washington Post* (December 20, 1982)

Skutch, Ira, *Ira Skutch: I Remember Television: A Memoir,* Metuchen, New Jersey: Scarecrow Press, 1989

Snider, Gerald Edward, "*Our Town* by Thorton Wilder: A Descriptive Study of Its Production Modes," Ph.D. diss., Michigan State University, 1983

Squire, Susan, "For Delbert Mann, All the Problems of Live TV Are Worth It," *New York Times* (December 19, 1982)

Stempel, Tom, *Storytellers to the Nation: A History of American Television Writing,* New York: Continuum, 1992

Sturcken, Frank, *Live Television: The Golden Age of 1946–1958 in New York,* Jefferson, North Carolina: McFarland, 1990

Wicking, Christopher, and Tise Vahimagi, *The American Vein: Directors and Directions in Television,* New York: Dutton, 1979

Wilk, Max, *The Golden Age of Television: Notes from the Survivors,* New York: Delacorte Press, 1976

Mansbridge, Peter (1948–)

Canadian Broadcast Journalist

Peter Mansbridge serves as anchor for *The National,* the flagship nightly newscast of the Canadian Broadcasting Corporation (CBC), and all CBC news specials. He is also host of *Mansbridge: One-on-One,* on CBC's 24-hour news network, Newsworld. His lengthy career with the CBC has made him one of Canadian media's most familiar figures, synonymous with "the corporation." The prominence to which Mansbridge has risen, however, began in a somewhat unorthodox fashion.

Peter Mansbridge.
Photo courtesy of National Archives of Canada/CBC Collection

In what is now Canadian news media folklore, a local CBC radio producer "discovered" Mansbridge in 1968 as he was making a public address announcement in an airport while working as a freight manager for a small airline in Churchill, Manitoba. Mansbridge turned the resulting position as a disc jockey into one as a newscaster, simultaneously transforming himself into a journalist despite his lack of formal training or apprenticeship. From this unlikely beginning, Mansbridge moved quickly through the ranks of CBC television news, beginning with a one-year stint in 1972 with the CBC Winnipeg station as a local reporter,

followed by another one-year position as the Saskatchewan-based reporter for the CBC national newscast. From 1976 to 1980, Mansbridge held a spot on the prestigious parliamentary bureau in the nation's capital. Anchor status commenced with the *Quarterly Report* (co-anchored by Barbara Frum), a series of special reports concerning issues of an urgent, national nature that aired four times a year. Beginning in 1985, Mansbridge anchored the newly formed national weekly *Sunday Report.*

Mansbridge's nationwide prominence was secured in 1988, when he accepted the enviable position of chief correspondent and anchor of the flagship CBC broadcast *The National,* a weekday 10:00 P.M. newscast (22 minutes long) that was followed by the highly respected current affairs and documentary broadcast *The Journal.* The status attributed to this anchor position was reflected in the public interest created by the events that preceded Mansbridge's assumption of the job. Amid much press speculation, Mansbridge was offered in 1987 a co-anchor position in the United States, opposite Kathleen Sullivan on *CBS This Morning,* for a salary reputed to be five to six times his earnings with the CBC. It was expected that Mansbridge would follow the familiar exodus of Canadian broadcast journalists to the United States, where the level of national and international experience of many Canadian journalists is highly valued. This emigration has included journalists such as Don Miller, Don McNeill, Robert MacNeil, Morley Safer, and Peter Jennings. In a last-minute, much-publicized effort to stop Mansbridge from leaving Canada, the current chief anchor of *The National,* Knowlton Nash, stepped down early to offer his position to Mansbridge. Nash and Mansbridge were consequently heralded as patriots and, moreover, managed to promote the turnover of anchors.

Despite the respectable audience numbers drawn under Mansbridge's leadership, *The National* was moved in 1992 to CBC's all-news network, Newsworld. Mansbridge assumed the role of anchor (originally co-anchored by Pamela Wallin) on CBC's *Prime Time News.* This new broadcast was part of a controversial decision to move the national evening news from the 10:00 P.M. to the 9:00 P.M. time slot. In 1995, network executives decided to reverse their previous scheduling move and return the news/current affairs hour to 10:00, with the entire hour now titled *The National* and with Mansbridge continuing his role as newscast anchor. The revamped program currently airs on both the CBC and Newsworld.

During his tenure as CBC's star anchor, Mansbridge has covered many of the key events that have attracted public attention in Canada, including federal elections and leadership campaigns, the Gulf War, the Charlottetown Referendum, and the events of Tiananmen Square. Coverage of these and other stories has garnered Mansbridge eight Gemini Awards (Academy of Canadian Cinema and Television). Mansbridge's style of presentation is understated and sober but sufficiently amiable to attract viewers in the increasingly entertainment-oriented news media. His understated delivery, in combination with his appearance (once described as "bland good looks"), makes Mansbridge's presentation and persona consistent with the standard among Canadian broadcast journalists.

Although the CBC has historically placed a great deal of emphasis on news and current affairs programming, this was particularly evident during the years of Mansbridge's rise within the corporation in the 1980s. The reduced resources made available to the broadcaster, in addition to the challenges of broadcasting in the increasingly multichannel media system, demanded a renewed focus by the CBC on this area in which it was traditionally strong. The CBC's subsequent commitment to news has been evident in the continuing production of quality news programming and has assisted Mansbridge in developing a particularly strong profile within the industry.

KEITH C. HAMPSON

See also **Canadian Television Broadcasting in English;** *National, The/The Journal*

Peter Mansbridge. Born in London, England, 1948. Educated in Ottawa. Married: Wendy Mesley (divorced). Served in the Royal Canadian Navy, 1966–67. Disc jockey and newscaster, CBC Radio, Churchill, Manitoba, 1968; reporter, CBC Radio, Winnipeg, 1972; reporter, CBC Television News, 1973; reporter, *The National,* Saskatchewan, 1975; assigned to the Parliamentary Bureau in Ottawa, 1976–80; co-anchor, *Quarterly Report,* and anchor, *Sunday Report,* from 1985; anchor, *The National,* since 1988; anchor of CBC's *Prime Time News,* 1992–95. Recipient: eight Gemini Awards, including Gordon Sinclair Award.

Television Series

1972–85	*CBC News* (reporter)
1985–88	*Quarterly Report* (co-anchor)
1985–88	*Sunday Report* (anchor)
1988–92, 1995–	*The National* (anchor)
1992–95	*Prime Time News* (anchor)
1999–	*Mansbridge: One on One*

Marchant, Tony (1959–)

British Writer

Tony Marchant is one of British television's most distinctive dramatic writers. Just one of his screenplays (the comedy of transsexual love, *Different for Girls*), has had a theatrical release; otherwise, throughout his career, he has maintained a commitment to television drama as both the equal of cinema and the "true writer's medium." He has also fought against the market-led ideology of drama commissioning in the 1990s and the drive to deliver audiences by means of standardized generic formulae. In 1999, the year that he received the British Academy of Film and Television Arts (BAFTA) Dennis Potter Award for Television Drama, he spoke up for what he called "the singular and eccentric voice" of the writer. Two dramas broadcast in that year perhaps embody the range encompassed by that voice. In *Kid in the Corner,* he drew on his own experience as the parent of a boy with learning difficulties to deliver a deeply intimate account of a couple's relationship with a son suffering from attention deficit hyperactivity disorder (ADHD), while in *Bad Blood* he traced the moral disintegration of a surgeon, desperate to adopt a Romanian boy, through the increasingly surreal metaphor of vampirism.

Marchant began his career in the fringe theater at the start of the 1980s, when, inspired by the "do it yourself" directness of punk music, he produced a string of plays for the Theatre Royal in London's Stratford East. Although rooted in his East End working-class experience, however, his was not the stereotypical voice of disaffected youth. *Welcome Home,* about soldiers returning from the Falklands conflict to attend a friend's funeral, carefully juggled opposing ideological views, while *Raspberry* explored two women's differing experiences on a hospital gynecological ward. While at Stratford East, Marchant first worked with Adrian Shergold, the director who was to become one of his principal collaborators on television and whose filming would bring to his work a potent rhythmic and visual style.

It was with a screen version of *Raspberry,* produced by the British Broadcasting Corporation (BBC) in 1984, that Marchant moved into writing for television. The play was well received, and he followed it over the next five years with a string of single dramas on socially resonant topics ranging from money dealing in the London foreign exchange (*The Moneymen*) to the struggle by a mother to bring to justice the people responsible for her son's death from a drug overdose (*Death of a Son*). In 1989 the BBC broadcast his first serial, the three-part *Take Me Home*. It is the story of a passionate and ultimately doomed affair between a middle-aged man, forced into redundancy and now working as a minicab driver, and the young wife of a successful computer programmer. Set against the high-tech sterility of a British "new town," the story provided a potent metaphor of social and spiritual isolation in a culture imbued with the apparent virtues of success and prosperity. This was followed by two further three-part dramas, *Goodbye Cruel World,* about a woman suffering from an unspecified and incurable form of motor neuron disease and her husband's campaign to set a charity on her behalf, and *Into the Fire,* in which a hitherto upstanding businessman's involvement in insurance fraud to save his company leads to the death of a young employee and a relationship with the boy's mother. In each work, one can begin to recognize Marchant's characteristic preoccupation with motives and principles and his engagement with serial drama as a means of following through the complex ethical ramifications of impulsive but socially induced actions.

It is this concern, amplified into a sweeping narrative of epic proportions, that permeates what could be considered Marchant's masterpiece. The eight-episode serial *Holding On* was inspired by sources as diverse as Charles Dickens's *Our Mutual Friend* and Robert Altman's multistranded film *Short Cuts* and was commissioned by the BBC on the back of the success enjoyed by Peter Flannery's *Our Friends in the North.* Its setting is London and its subject the city and the connections that lie, dark and unrecognized, between the disparate lives of its inhabitants. The violent death of a young woman at the hands of a schizophrenic provides the catalyst for a dark journey through cause and effect, culpability and guilt, involving a range of characters who either were linked to the victim and the perpetrator or witnessed the event. Marchant's vision of corrupted social responsibility is embodied in the central story of a tax inspector lured into bribery by the millionaire whom he is investigating for fraud, while the London Underground replaces Dickens's River Thames as the metaphoric thoroughfare ominously linking the lives of the characters.

Marchant was subsequently commissioned to dramatize Dickens's *Great Expectations,* to which he brought a contemporary sense of the preoccupation with social class, and Dostoyevsky's *Crime and Punishment,* another tale of unraveling guilt. For the BBC's series of modern adaptations of *The Canterbury Tales,* his version of *The Knight's Tale* transposed Chaucer's story of courtly love into a gripping account of the rivalry between two prisoner friends for the love of a continuing-education language tutor, revealing poetic passion, tenderness, and honor in a seemingly brutalized world. A similar reversal of expectation permeates *Never, Never,* a story of the relationship between a loan shark debt collector and a young woman living on an inner-London estate. Here, as in *Swallow,* where a woman addicted to antidepressants battles with a pharmaceutical company, and *Passer-By,* which follows the terrible consequences of a man's decision to ignore the appeal of a woman in distress, Marchant creates a modern social fable that has not only a wider political resonance but, at its core, a deeply intimate story of goodness and hope. His characters are on journeys, the ends of which are never predictable but that invariably entail an encounter with moral and social responsibility. "I'm sure it has something to do with the fact that I was brought up a Catholic," he admits in an interview article by Louise Bishop, published in *Television* in May 1998. "I have to admit that a lot of the stuff I write is to do with redemption and guilt."

JEREMY RIDGMAN

Tony Marchant. Born in London, England, July 11, 1959. Left school at age 18; unemployed, then worked in local office of Department of Employment. British Theatre Association Award, Most Promising Playwright (1983); Recipient: Royal Television Society Writer's Award for *Goodbye Cruel World* (1992) and *Holding On* (1997); British Academy of Film and Television Arts TV Awards, Best Drama Serial (1998) for *Holding On* and Dennis Potter Award (2000).

Television Series

1989	*Take Me Home*
1992	*Goodbye Cruel World*
1993	*Westbeach* (3 episodes)
1993	*Lovejoy* ("God Helps Those")
1996	*Into the Fire*
1997	*Holding On*
1999	*Great Expectations*
1999	*Bad Blood*
1999	*Kid in the Corner*
2000	*Never, Never*
2001	*Swallow*
2002	*Crime and Punishment*
2004	*Passer By*

Television Plays

1984	*Raspberry*
1985	*Reservations*
1988	*The Moneymen*

Stage Plays

Remember Me?, 1980; *Thick As Thieves*, 1981; *Stiff*, 1982; *The Lucky Ones*, 1982; *Raspberry*, 1982; *Welcome Home*, 1983; *Lazydays Ltd*, 1984; *Speculators*, 1987; *The Attractions*, 1987.

Further Reading

Bishop, Louise, "London Calling," *Television* (May 1998)

Davies, John, "How to Be Good? An Interview with Tony Marchant, Television Playwright," *Critical Quarterly*, 44, no. 3 (October 2002)

Towner, Angus, "The World According to Marchant," *Television Today* (January 16, 1992)

Marcus Welby, M.D.

U.S. Medical Drama

Marcus Welby, M.D., which aired on the American Broadcasting Company (ABC) from late September 1969 through mid-May 1976, was one of the most popular doctor shows in U.S. television history. During the 1970 television year, it even ranked number one among all TV series, according to the Nielsen Television Index. As such, it was the first ABC program to take the top program slot for an entire season. The Nielsen data suggested that *Marcus Welby, M.D.* was viewed regularly in about one of every four U.S. homes that year.

The program was created by David Victor, who had been a producer on the hit *Dr. Kildare* television series during the 1960s. Victor took a centerpiece of the basic doctor-show formula (the older physician-mentor tutoring the young man) and transferred it from the standard hospital setting to the suburban office of a general practitioner. The sicknesses that Marcus Welby and his young colleague Steven Kiley dealt with—everything from drug addition to rape, from tumors to autism—ran the same wide gamut that hospital-based medical shows had covered. In fact, many of the patients ended up in the hospital, and Welby even moved his practice to a hospital toward the end of the show's run. Nevertheless, *Marcus Welby, M.D.* was different from other shows of its era, such as *Medical Center* and *The Bold Ones*. Those shows stressed short-term illnesses that paralleled or ignited certain unrelated personal problems. *Welby*, on the other hand, dealt consistently with long-term medical problems that were tied directly to the patient's psyche and interpersonal behavior. Acute episodes of the difficulty often sparked movement toward a cure, but only after Welby or Kiley uncovered the root causes of the behavioral problems.

In one case, for example, Dr. Welby and Dr. Kiley become concerned about Enid Cooper, a counselor in an orphanage, when they learn that she is addicted to pills. The doctors are unable to persuade the young woman to give them up. Then, under the influence of pills, Enid is responsible for a car accident in which one of her charges is hurt. That allows Welby to move her toward conquering her addiction.

This emphasis on the psyche and medicine was celebrated by Robert Young, who played Marcus Welby. Young suffered from chemical imbalances in his body that led him toward depression and alcoholism. To fight those difficulties, he had developed an approach to life that mirrored the holistic health philosophy that he now acted out as a TV doctor. People who worked with him on the set said that it was often hard to tell where Young stopped and Welby began, so closely did the actor identify with his role. Viewers seemed to have that difficulty, too. Young received thousands of letters asking for advice on life's problems.

In choosing topics to deal with in the program itself, *Welby*'s producers and writers benefited from a softening in the U.S. television networks' rules regarding what was acceptable on TV in the early 1970s. The relaxation came about partly because of increased network competition for viewers in their 20s and 30s and partly as a result of new demands for openness and the questioning of authority that the social protests of the

Marcus Welby, M.D., Robert Young, 1969–76.
Courtesy of the Everett Collection

late 1960s brought. It allowed David Victor to initiate stories, such as one on venereal disease, that he could not get approved for *Dr. Kildare.*

The show did ignite public controversies. One episode called "The Outrage" centered on the rape of a teenage boy by a male teacher. It ignited one of the first organized protests against a TV show by gay activists. More general were complaints by the rising women's rights movement that Marcus Welby's control over the lives of his patients (many of whom were women) represented the worst aspects of male physicians' paternalistic attitudes.

While scathing, such opposition made up a rather small portion of the public discussion of the series over its seven-year prime-time life. More consistent was the controversy over *Welby*'s impact on physicians' images. With previous doctor shows, the concern of physicians was to cultivate as favorable an image as possible. Now some physicians worried that Welby's incredibly solicitous and loyal bedside manner was leading their patients to question why they did not act toward them as Welby would. Was it true, as writer-physician Michael Halberstam contended in the *New York Times Magazine,* that the series could not help "but make things better for American doctors and their patients"? Or was it the case, as others claimed, that *Welby* was among the factors contributing to the rise of malpractice actions against physicians?

The debate marked the first time that the physicians' establishment got involved in a large-scale argument over whether fictional images that were positive actually had negative effects on their status. The argument would continue about other doctor shows in the coming years. But to Robert Young, Marcus Welby incarnate, it was a nonissue. According to an article in *McCall's* magazine, a doctor said to Young at a convention of family physicians, "You're getting us all into hot water. Our patients tell us we're not as nice to them as Doctor Welby is to his patients." Young did not mince words. "Maybe you're not," he replied.

JOSEPH TUROW

See also **Young, Robert**

Cast

Dr. Marcus Welby	Robert Young
Dr. Steven Kiley	James Brolin
Consuelo Lopez	Elena Verdugo
Myra Sherwood (1969–70)	Anne Baxter
Kathleen Faverty (1974–76)	Sharon Gless
Sandy Porter (1975–76)	Anne Schedeen
Phil Porter (1975–76)	Gavin Brendan
Janet Blake (1975–76)	Pamela Hensley

Producers

David Victor, David J. O'Connell

Programming History

172 episodes
ABC
September 1969–May 1976   Tuesday 10:00–11:00

Further Reading

Turow, Joseph, *Playing Doctor: Television, Storytelling, and Medical Power,* New York: Oxford University Press, 1989

Market

Broadcasting is inherently a medium of fixed location, and because of its dependence on direct-wave radiation, television broadcasting is particularly so. In the United States, because of the dominance of advertising, these fixed locations have come to be called "markets." Additionally, the term "market" may refer to a group of people of interest to broadcasters and/or advertisers for business reasons. Indeed, the term is increasingly used in this manner throughout the world, as more and more television systems become supported by advertising revenue or other commercial underwriters.

The broadcast television signal operates by direct-wave radiation; the signal waves must travel in a straight line from the transmitting to the receiving antenna. Even if transmitters could operate with unlimited power, television broadcasting operates in a geography fixed by the horizon of the curve of the Earth's surface. As the signal radiates outward from a transmitting antenna, it produces a more or less round geographical coverage pattern, with a radius of about 60 miles for VHF (very high frequency) stations and about 35 miles for UHF (ultrahigh frequency) stations. The coverage contour can be distorted by hills and mountains that block the signal, increased by antenna height, or added to by translators that rebroadcast the signal at another frequency in another location or by retransmission on cable television systems.

Reflecting the inherent "locatedness" of television broadcasting, the Federal Communications Commission (FCC) allocates channels and assigns licenses to facilities in communities. The word "market" has come to be the designator of those communities, reflecting the degree to which advertising dominates television in the United States. Anyone doing any type of business in an area may of course refer to that area or the people living in it as a market, placing the boundaries wherever sensible for the business in question. This practice includes the operators of commercial television. (The operators of noncommercial television facilities have less reason to use the word "market," although it is increasingly applied in this arena.) In the business of television, these geographically outlined markets are formally defined by the ratings companies, among which Nielsen Media Research dominates.

Markets are defined by Nielsen as designated market areas (DMAs) in a manner essentially the same that the Arbitron company, which is no longer in the business of providing television ratings, once defined areas of dominant influence (ADIs). Both acronyms are still commonly used and designate essentially the same thing.

DMAs are defined by county or, in some cases, parts of counties (for convenience, counties will suffice in this discussion). Every county in the United States is assigned to one and only one DMA. Each DMA is named after the city that defines its center, such as the Chicago DMA or the Des Moines (Iowa) DMA. Each county is assigned to that DMA for which the most-watched television stations are broadcast. So, for example, Los Angeles County is assigned to the Los Angeles DMA because the television stations that the people in Los Angeles County watch most often are located in Los Angeles County. Orange County is also assigned to the Los Angeles DMA because the most frequently watched television stations by viewers in Orange County are also located in Los Angeles County.

Such a system of categories, in which every county in the United States is assigned to one and only one DMA, is considered mutually exclusive and exhaustive. Such systems have formal advantages. The key benefit here is the simple arithmetic for manipulating numbers associated with the categories. Since none of the markets overlap, numbers associated with any of them can be added together to describe a market that would be defined as the aggregate of the smaller markets. Since no area is left out of the system of market definitions, the sum of all of them defines the national market. This eases the calculation of ratings and other data for local, regional, or national markets and for syndicated, cable, and network television shows available in different areas.

In addition to these formal uses of the term "market," as Nielsen's DMA or regional or national aggregates of DMAs, there are various other uses for the term in the television business. One of the most common is in phrases such as "the African-American market," "the Hispanic market," "the youth market," or "an upscale market." These are extensions of the use of demographics to define types of people of interest to advertisers and other businesspeople. In either usage, the term remains a clear marker of the commercial aspects of the U.S. television industry, in which buying and selling—of both programs and audiences—is a central component.

ERIC ROTHENBUHLER

See also **Advertising; Call Signs/Letters; Frank N. Magid Associates; Ratings; Share**

Further Reading

Bagdikian, Ben H., *The Media Monopoly,* Boston: Beacon Press, 1992

Bogart, Leo, *Commercial Culture: The Media System and the Public Interest,* New York: Oxford University Press, 1995

Compaine, Benjamin, et al., editors, *Who Owns the Media? Concentration of Ownership in the Mass Communication Industry,* New York: Harmony Books, 1979

Multimedia Audiences, New York: Mediamark Research, 1986

Study of Media and Markets, New York: Simmons Market Research Bureau, 1990

Turow, Joseph, *Media Systems in Society: Understanding Industries, Strategies, and Power,* New York: Longman, 1992

Marketplace

Canadian Consumer Affairs Program

Marketplace, which went on the air in 1972, is a weekly half-hour, prime-time consumer news show on the Canadian Broadcasting Corporation (CBC). It has won many national and international awards, including the Gemini in 1994 as Canada's best information program. The format, which has changed little over its history, involves a pair of hosts introducing segments on product testing, service evaluation, fraudulent practices, and trends in consumer advocacy. The show's audience has held up well for more than four decades—it remains one of the CBC's most highly rated shows—and it is regarded by many in the CBC as the benchmark by which other public affairs programs should be judged.

The first producer, Dodi Robb, with consumer reporter Joan Watson (from CBC Radio) and broadcaster George Finstad as hosts, had a mandate to inform consumers about questionable sales practices and inferior products. From the beginning, the show treated consumer information as hard news, but it gradually expanded its mandate to include investigative reports with particular attention to public health and safety. According to *Globe and Mail* television writer John Haslett Cuff, the program is "a veritable gadfly in the hard-sell marketplace of consumer television." It is "routinely monitored ... by manufacturers and government regulatory agencies and frequently copied by American newsmagazine programs such as *60 Minutes* and *20/20.*" Although it does put defenders of commercial practices and products on the "hot seat," *Marketplace* has an earnest quality that distinguishes it from the "ambush journalism" sometimes practiced by U.S. public affairs producers.

The program not only gets headlines; as one reviewer put it, it also gets results. Laws have been amended, new regulations adopted, and consumer guidelines imposed as a result of *Marketplace* reports. Its major contributions include the banning of urea formaldehyde foam insulation (UFFI) and lawn darts, warnings on soda pop bottles that sometimes explode on store shelves, prosecution of retailers for false advertising (leading in one case to a fine of $1 million), new standards for bottled drinking water and drinking fountains, new regulations for children's nightwear (to make the clothing less flammable), and new designs for children's cribs. From tests for bacteria content in supermarket hamburger (an early report) to checks on the safety of furnaces and long-haul tractor-trailers, the program has

Marketplace.
Photo courtesy of CBC Television

used its small staff—relying on independent laboratories for tests—to considerable effect. More recent investigations include the safety of rebuilt air bags, lead in children's jewelry, and toxic waste. It has examined both specific consumer and larger issues of public health and safety. Despite lawsuits and threats of suits (and other pressures), the show has retained its probing quality. The longest-serving hosts, Joan Watson and Bill Paul, became leading consumer advocates.

Reviewers have commented that the tough-minded consumer advocacy practiced by *Marketplace* is the kind of programming that public broadcasters, somewhat insulated from commercial considerations, should be providing. It is unlikely that the show would have had the same effectiveness and longevity in private-sector television. Its producers attribute consistent good ratings to its focus on the personal concerns of its audience, which derives in part from careful attention to the thousands of letters it receives from viewers each year, many of which have led to *Marketplace* investigations. Freedom from commercial pressures may also be significant. Recently, *Marketplace* has made its reports available on its website (http://www.cbc.ca/consumers/market).

FREDERICK J. FLETCHER AND ROBERT EVERETT

Hosts
George Finstad
Joan Watson
Harry Brown
Bill Paul
Christine Brown
Norma Kent
Jim Nunn
Jacquie Perrin
Erica Johnson

Producers
Dodi Robb, Bill Harcourt, Jock Ferguson, Murray Creed, Joe Doyle

Programming History
CBC
October 1972–

Further Reading

Miller, Mary Jane, *Turn Up the Contrast: CBC Television Drama Since 1952,* Vancouver: University of British Columbia Press, 1987
Stewart, Sandy, *Here's Looking at Us: A Personal History of Television in Canada,* Toronto: CBC Enterprises, 1986

Married...with Children

U.S. Situation Comedy

Married...with Children (*MWC*), created by Michael Moye and Ron Leavitt, premiered as one of the new FOX Broadcasting Company's Sunday series in 1987. Moye and Leavitt had previously produced *The Jeffersons,* a long-running comedy about a black entrepreneur who becomes wealthy and moves his family to an almost all-white New York City neighborhood. Set in Chicago, their new show was a parody of American television's tendency to create comedies dealing with relentlessly perfect families. Their program was immediately termed "antifamily."

At the time of *MWC*'s appearance, the top-rated U.S. television series was *The Cosby Show.* In the *Cosby* version of family, an African-American doctor and his attorney-wife raise their college-bound offspring in an upper-middle-class environment. Instead of such faultless people, Moye and Leavitt presented

"patriarch" Al Bundy (Ed O'Neil), whose family credo is, "when one of us is embarrassed, the others feel better about ourselves." In *MWC,* almost every character is amusingly tasteless and satirically vulgar.

Bundy is a luckless women's shoe salesman who hates fat women, tries to relive his days as a high school football hero, and does almost anything to avoid having sex with his stay-at-home, bon-bon-eating spouse, Peggy (Katey Sagal). Peg loves to shop, and her ability to buy always exceeds Al's capacity to earn. She refuses to cook, and the Bundys must take desperate measures to stay fed, frequently searching beneath the sofa cushions for crumbs of food. After one family funeral, the Bundys steal the deceased man's filled refrigerator. Peggy's clothes are too tight, her hair is too big, her makeup is too thick, and her heels are too high. She wants sex as much as Al avoids it.

Married . . . with Children, Christina Applegate, David Faustino, Katey Sagal, Ed O'Neill, 1987–97.
©20th Century Fox/Courtesy of the Everett Collection

The Bundy's stereotypically beautiful, dumb-blonde daughter, Kelly (Christina Applegate), is a frequent target of their naive con artist son, Bud (David Faustino). Moye and Leavitt created Kelly in the guise of Sheridan's Mrs. Malaprop; she can never manage to find the right word, and her verbal confusions are felicitous. According to Bud, Kelly will have sex with any available male. In one episode, Kelly acquires backstage passes to a rock concert and announces she is just one paternity suit away from a Caribbean home. The Bundys think Bud has no chance of ever attracting a date; running jokes mention his collection of inflatable rubber women. All characters have a common failing: none exercises good judgment.

In *MWC,* Moye and Leavitt not only lampooned *Cosby* but also parodied its creator, Marcy Carsey. The other continuing characters in the series were the Bundy's upscale next-door neighbors. In the initial seasons, the neighbors were Marcy (Amanda Bearse) and Steve Rhoades (David Garrison). Garrison was a series regular from 1987 to 1990 and made frequent guest appearances after Steve and Marcy split. Then, in the 1991 season, Marcy remarried, to a man named Jefferson D'Arcy—giving her the moniker Marcy D'Arcy. Marcy and her husbands serve as a device to entice and challenge the Bundy clan, then put them

down. Marcy is a banker and activist for almost any cause that will defeat Al's current get-rich-quick scheme. She marries Jefferson (Ted McGinley) while drunk and discovers him in her bed the next morning. He has no career, although he has claimed to be a clever criminal, now living in the witness protection program.

The show had a small, loyal following until February 1989, and the producers had a history of arguments over taste and language with FOX's lone, part-time network censor. One episode, "A Period Piece," in which the Bundy and Rhoades families go camping, was delayed one month in the broadcast schedule because it focused on the women's menstrual cycles. Two months later, the episode scheduled for February 19, 1989, "I'll See You in Court," was pulled from the schedule and never aired on the FOX network. The episode involves sexual videotapes of Marcy and Steve that Al and Peggy view when they rent a sleazy motel room. When both couples realize their activity at the motel was broadcast to other rooms, they sue. The jury chooses to compensate the couples for their performance quality, with Al and Peggy getting no money.

That same winter, two weeks after "A Period Piece," an episode titled "Her Cups Runneth Over" led to a social stir. The segment features Peggy's need for a new brassiere, coinciding with her birthday. Al and Steve travel to a lingerie shop in Wisconsin, where an older male receptionist wears nothing below his waist but panties, a garter belt, stockings, and spike-heeled shoes. Steve fingers leather-fringed falsies attached to the nipples of one near-naked mannequin; women flash Al and Steve, although the nudity is not shown on camera.

One television viewer, Terry Rakolta, from the wealthy Detroit, Michigan, suburb of Bloomfield Hills, took offense at the show after the brassiere episode. She saw her children watching the program and found both the language and the partial nudity unacceptable for a program airing during a time when children made up a large portion of the audience. Rakolta acted by writing to advertisers and asking them to question the association of their products with *MWC*'s content. She also brought her cause to national television news shows.

In March 1989, Rakolta said on *Nightline*, "I picked on *Married...with Children* because they are so consistently offensive. They exploit women, they stereotype poor people, they're anti-family. And every week that I've watched them, they're worse and worse. I think this is really outrageous. It's sending the wrong messages to the American family."

Rakolta had mixed success. Some advertisers, including major movie studios and many retail stores, refused to buy commercials on the new FOX network (prime-time telecasts had started less than two years earlier). Media brokers cited a bad connotation with FOX programming. *Newsweek* magazine featured a front-page story on "Trash TV," questioning the standards of taste in prime-time television. Both *MWC* and tabloid news shows such as *A Current Affair* were primary examples.

However, the greater effect of Rakolta's campaign was strongly positive for FOX. Among the fledgling network's greatest problems at the time of the controversy was limited viewer awareness. Many viewers simply did not know that a fourth network existed. Related to this was the fact that a small, mostly homogeneous viewing group comprised FOX's entire audience. Moreover, many FOX stations had weak UHF (ultrahigh frequency) signals that were difficult to receive. Rakolta's complaints garnered substantial national publicity, and this seemed to assist the network in solving many of its difficulties. After *Nightline, Good Morning America, The Today Show,* and most other national and local news shows featured the controversy over *MWC,* viewer awareness rose dramatically. People purposely sought out their local FOX affiliates, and *MWC* became a success.

By April 1989, *MWC* had reached a 10 rating, according to Nielsen's national measurements, the highest rating of any FOX show to that date. FOX began charging the same amount for commercials in *MWC* that the Columbia Broadcasting System (CBS) asked for *60 Minutes*. The comedy began intermittently winning its time slot.

By 1995 the show had become the longest-running situation comedy currently programmed on network television, on the air as long as the classic comedy *Cheers*. In its final years, *MWC* no longer pushed new boundaries of good taste, and the jokes became routine and expected, even when still funny.

The show did, however, have an extremely lucrative afterlife in daily syndication, running strongly for years in many markets. In Los Angeles, FOX's station KTTV ran the program twice each weekday in the prime-time access hour. Daily viewership for the show continues to be strong, and with 11 seasons of episodes to add variety to off-network reruns, *MWC* is likely to consistently remain one of the most successful properties in the history of television syndication. At the end of its run on June 9, 1997, the program's off-network earnings were estimated to be more than $400 million.

During its long run, the show won no awards, but the actors were recognized for their performances. The Hollywood Foreign Press nominated the show for seven Golden Globe Awards: one for the program as Best TV-Series—Comedy/Musical, four for Katey Sagal's acting, and two for Ed O'Neill. American Comedy Award nominations also went to Sagal (three) and O'Neill (one).

JOAN GIGLIONE

Cast

Al Bundy	Ed O'Neill
Peggy Bundy	Katey Sagal
Kelly Bundy	Christina Applegate
Bud Bundy	David Faustino
Steve Rhoades (1987–90)	David Garrison
Marcy Rhoades D'Arcy	Amanda Bearse
Jefferson D'Arcy (1991–97)	Ted McGinley

Producers

John Maxwell Anderson, Calvin Brown Jr., Vince Cheung, Kevin Curran, Pamela Eells, Ralph Farquhar, Ellen L. Fogle, Katherine Green, Richard Gurman, Larry Jacobson, Ron Leavitt, Stacie Lipp, Russell Marcus, Ben Montanio, Michael G. Moye, Arthur Silver, Sandy Sprung, Marcy Vosburgh, Kim Weiskopf

Programming History

262 episodes
FOX
April 1987–October 1987   Sunday 8:00–8:30

October 1987–July 1989	Sunday 8:30–9:00
July 1989–August 1996	Sunday 9:00–9:30
September 1996–January 1997	Saturday 9:00–9:30
January 1997–June 1997	Monday 9:00–9:30

Further Reading

American Broadcasting Company, "Steamy TV" (transcript), *Nightline* (March 2, 1989)

Block, Alex Ben, *Outfoxed*, New York: St. Martin's Press, 1990
Impoco, Jim, "The Bundys Meet the Censors at FOX," *U.S. News and World Report* (September 11, 1995)
Lowry, Brian, "Married…with Few Regrets As Series Ends After 11 Years," *Los Angeles Times* (April 27, 1997)
Stuller, Joan, "Fox Broadcasting Company: A Fourth Network Entry Within the Broadcasting Marketplace," Masters thesis, California State University, Northridge, 1989

Marshall, Garry (1934–)

U.S. Producer, Writer, Actor

Garry Marshall was the executive producer of a string of sitcoms that helped the American Broadcasting Company (ABC) win the ratings race for the first time in the network's history in the late 1970s. While Norman Lear's Tandem Productions and Grant Tinker's MTM Enterprises had put the Columbia Broadcasting System (CBS) on top in the early part of the decade, by the end of the 1978–79 season, four of the five highest-rated shows of the year were Marshall's.

Marshall became a comedy writer during the last years of television's "golden age." He started out as an itinerant joke writer for an assortment of TV comics and eventually secured a staff writing position on *The Joey Bishop Show*. There he met Jerry Belson, with whom he would go on to write two feature films, a Broadway play, and episodes for a variety of TV series, including *The Dick Van Dyke Show, The Lucy Show,* and *I Spy*. The last project Marshall and Belson did together was the most successful of their partnership. *The Odd Couple,* a series they adapted from the Neil Simon play in 1970, would run for five seasons and have a major impact on Marshall's comic style.

Rather than forming his own independent production company, which had become standard procedure for producers at the time, Marshall remained at Paramount to make a succession of hit situation comedies for ABC. *Happy Days* debuted as a series in January 1974, and by the 1976–77 season, it was the most popular show on TV. Set in Milwaukee, Wisconsin, in the 1950s and centered around a teenager (Ron Howard), his family, and his friends, *Happy Days* generated three spin-offs, all of which Marshall supervised. *Laverne and Shirley* featured two working-class women (Penny Marshall and Cindy Williams), whose antic schemes were reminiscent of those portrayed on *I Love Lucy*. Viewers were introduced to the frenetic young comic Robin Williams in *Mork and Mindy,* a series about an alien (Williams) who comes to Earth to study human behavior by moving in with an all-American young woman (Pam Dawber). *Joanie Loves Chachi* followed two of the younger characters from *Happy Days* as they struggled to make it as rock-and-roll musicians.

While Norman Lear had used such shows as *All in the Family* and *Maude* to explore contemporary social issues such as racism, the women's movement, and the war in Vietnam, Marshall's shows were usually more concerned with less timely, personal issues, such as blind dates, making out, and breaking up. Lear, Tinker, and others had attracted young audiences with "relevant" programming earlier in the decade; Marshall attracted even younger ones with lighter, more escapist fare, most of it set in the supposedly simpler historic past. In an interview reprinted in *American Television Genres* (1985), Marshall recalled that, after producing the adult-oriented *Odd Couple,* he had been anxious to make shows "that both kids and their parents could watch." When he gave a speech on accepting the Lifetime Achievement Prize given at the American Comedy Awards in 1990, Marshall said, "If television is the education of the American people, then I am recess." Not surprisingly, four of Marshall's sitcoms were adapted into Saturday morning cartoons.

Marshall continued to borrow from *The Odd Couple* throughout his career. Over and over again, he employed the comic device of coupling two distinctly different characters: the hip and the square on *Happy Days,* the earthling and the Orkan on *Mork and Mindy,*

Garry Marshall, 1999.
©*Robert Hepler/Everett Collection*

the rich and the poor on *Angie,* and, later, the business-man and the prostitute in the movie *Pretty Woman.* In 1982 he brought a short-lived remake of *The Odd Couple* to ABC, this time with African Americans Ron Glass and Demond Wilson playing the parts of Felix and Oscar.

By the mid-1980s, Marshall had turned his attention to directing, producing, and occasionally writing feature films, including *Young Doctors in Love* (1982), *The Flamingo Kid* (1984), *Nothing in Common* (1986), *Overboard* (1987), *Beaches* (1989), *Pretty Woman* (1990), *Frankie and Johnny* (1991), *Runaway Bride* (1999), and *The Princess Diaries* (2001). He also began appearing on screen occasionally, most notably in a recurring role on *Murphy Brown.*

Marshall's television tradition was carried on by Thomas L. Miller and Robert L. Boyett, two alumni of Marshall's production staff. Their youth-oriented series, such as *Perfect Strangers, Full House,* and *Fam-*

ily Matters, became staples of ABC's lineup in the later 1980s and early 1990s.

ROBERT J. THOMPSON

See also **Comedy, Domestic Settings;** *Happy Days;* **Producer in Television;** *Laverne and Shirley*

Garry Marshall. Born in New York City, November 13, 1934. Educated at Northwestern University, B.S. in journalism, 1956. Married: Barbara; children: one son and two daughters. Served in the U.S. Army during the Korean War, writing for *Stars and Stripes* and serving as a production chief for the Armed Forces Radio Network. Worked as a copy boy and briefly as a reporter for the New York *Daily News,* 1956–59; wrote comedy material for Phil Foster and Joey Bishop; drummer in his own jazz band; successful stand-up comedian and playwright; in television from late 1950s, starting as writer for *The Jack Paar Show;* prolific television writer through 1960s, creator and executive producer for various television series from 1974; also active creatively in films and stage.

Television Series

1959–61	*The Jack Paar Show* (writer)
1961–65	*The Joey Bishop Show* (writer)
1961–64	*The Danny Thomas Show* (writer)
1961–66	*The Dick Van Dyke Show* (writer)
1962–68	*The Lucy Show* (writer)
1965–68	*I Spy* (writer)
1966–67	*Hey Landlord* (creator, writer, director)
1970–75	*The Odd Couple* (executive producer, writer, director)
1972–74	*The Little People* (*The Brian Keith Show*) (creator, executive producer)
1974–84	*Happy Days* (creator, executive producer)
1974	*Blansky's Beauties* (creator, executive producer)
1976–83	*Laverne and Shirley* (creator, executive producer)
1978	*Who's Watching the Kids?* (creator, executive producer)
1978–82	*Mork and Mindy* (creator, executive producer)
1979–80	*Angie* (creator, executive producer)
1982–83	*Joanie Loves Chachi* (creator, executive producer)
1982–83	*The New Odd Couple* (executive producer)
1988–98	*Murphy Brown* (actor)

Made-for-Television Movie

1972   *Evil Roy Slade* (creator, executive producer)

Television Special

1979   *Sitcom: The Adventures of Garry Marshall*

Films

How Sweet It Is (writer-producer), 1968; *The Grasshopper,* 1970; *Young Doctors in Love* (also executive producer, director), 1982; *The Flamingo Kid* (also co-writer), 1984; *Nothing in Common,* 1986; *Overboard,* 1987; *Beaches,* 1988; *Pretty Woman,* 1990; *Frankie and Johnnie,* 1991; *Psych-Out* (actor), 1968; *Lost in America,* 1985; *Jumpin' Jack Flash,* 1986; *Soapdish,* 1991; *A League of Their Own,* 1992; *Hocus Pocus,* 1993; *The Other Sister,* 1999; *Runaway Bride,* 1999; *The Princess Diaries,* 2001; *Raising Helen,* 2004; *The Princess Diaries 2,* 2004.

Stage

The Roost (writer, with Jerry Belson), 1980; *Wrong Turn at Lungfish* (writer, with Lowell Ganz; also director, actor), 1992.

Publication

Wake Me When It's Funny: How to Break into Show Business and Stay There, 1995

Further Reading

Kaminsky, Stuart, with Jeffrey H. Mahan, *American Television Genres,* Chicago: Nelson-Hall, 1985

Marc, David, and Robert J. Thompson, *Prime Time, Prime Movers: From I Love Lucy to L.A. Law—America's Greatest TV Shows and the People Who Created Them,* Boston: Little, Brown, 1992

Newcomb, Horace, and Robert S. Alley, *The Producer's Medium: Conversations with Creators of American TV,* New York: Oxford University Press, 1983

Martin, Quinn (1922–1987)

U.S. Producer

Quinn Martin, among the most prolific and consistent television producers, helped to create and control some of television's most successful and popular series from the 1950s through the 1970s. At various times in the 1960s and 1970s, Martin simultaneously had as many as four series on various networks.

Martin's early television career consisted of writing and producing for many shows at Ziv Television and at Desilu Productions. He produced the *Desilu Playhouse* two-hour television movie "The Untouchables," which served as the basis for the series. Under Martin, *The Untouchables* became a huge hit for the American Broadcasting Company (ABC). Martin left after the first two seasons to form his own production company, QM Productions. The first series from QM, *The New Breed,* was unusual for Martin in that it was unsuccessful. During the years at Desilu and the first years of QM, Martin surrounded himself with a cadre of writers, directors, and producers who would later ably serve him when he was juggling the production schedules of several series. Alan Armer, George Eckstein,

Walter Grauman, and John Conwell are but a few of the names to appear again and again in the credits of QM productions.

QM and Martin entered into an era of considerable success in the 1960s. Among the shows to come from QM during this period were *The Fugitive, Twelve O'clock High, The FBI,* and *The Invaders,* all broadcast on ABC. Indeed, the relationship between QM and ABC was enormously beneficial to both despite repeated charges that they rode to their mutual successes on a wave of violent programming that began with *The Untouchables* and continued as a central stylistic feature in QM programs.

It was also during this period that two aspects of Martin's approach to television production emerged. First was the QM segmented-program format: a teaser; an expository introduction that often employed the convention of a narrator; a body broken into acts I, II, III, and IV; and an epilogue, using an off-screen narrator to explain or offer insight into the preceding action. So recognizable did this convention become that it was

Quinn Martin, 1965.
Courtesy of the Everett Collection/CSU Archives

parodied in the 1982 sitcom *Police Squad.* Second, Martin compartmentalized his productions. This was done not only out of necessity, resulting from the volume of television being produced by the company, but also because of the trusted individuals with whom Martin populated QM. At QM, the writers, producers, and postproduction supervisors had very well defined tasks and would rarely stray beyond the parameters established by Martin. John Conwell, casting director and assistant to Martin for years, often referred to Martin as "Big Daddy" because of his paternalistic approach to production.

Additionally, as John Cooper reports, Alan Armer credited Martin with changing the face of the telefilm by moving from the soundstage to the outdoors and by ensuring authenticity by employing night-for-night shooting, as described in *The Fugitive* (see Cooper). Too often producers would save a few dollars by simply darkening film footage shot during the day to simulate nighttime. Not Quinn Martin. He made money, and he spent money. In 1965 *Television Magazine* quoted Martin as saying that the 10 percent he would have paid an agent (if he had retained one) was simply rolled back into production.

The successes of QM and Martin continued well into the 1970s. Preeminent and longest running among the QM shows of this era were *The Streets of San Francisco, Cannon,* and *Barnaby Jones,* itself a spin-off of *Cannon.* Martin had at least a half dozen other series in prime time during the 1970s. During this period, virtually every QM show dealt with law enforcement and crime.

Since the first days of *The Untouchables,* Martin had been criticized for using excessive violence in his productions. A new criticism was now mounted against Martin's work because of the subject matter. Critics claimed that Martin's shows enforced the dominant ideology of the inherent value of law and order. They suggested that the bulk of Martin's work legitimized a right-wing, conservative agenda. As Horace Newcomb and Robert Alley indicate in *The Producer's Medium,* Martin openly acknowledged his fondness for authority and his positive presentation of institutions of police powers—individual, state, and federal (see Newcomb and Alley).

Martin sold QM Productions to Taft Broadcasting around 1978. Part of the agreement required Martin to leave television production for five years and not to compete with Taft. Martin became an adjunct professor at Warren College of the University of California, San Diego. In the late 1980s, Martin became president of QM Communications, which developed motion pictures for Warner Brothers. He died in 1987, leaving a production legacy of 17 network series, 20 made-for-television movies, and a feature film, *The Mephisto Waltz.* No one has yet surpassed his streak of 21 years with a show in prime time.

JOHN COOPER

See also **Arnaz, Desi;** *The FBI; The Fugitive;* **Producer in Television;** *The Untouchables;* **Westinghouse-Desilu Playhouse**

Quinn Martin. Born Martin Cohn in New York City, May 22, 1922. Educated at University of California, Berkeley, B.A. 1949. Married: 1) Madelyn Pugh, 1958; child: Michael; 2) Muffet Webb, 1961; children: Jill and Cliff. Served in U.S. Army Air Corps during World War II. Began career as apprentice editor, MGM; worked as film editor, writer, and head of postproduction for various studios, including Universal, 1950–54; writer and executive producer, Desilu Productions' *Jane Wyman Theater, The Desilu Playhouse,* and *The Untouchables,* 1957–59; founder, president, and chief executive officer, QM Productions, 1960–78; sold QM Productions to Taft Broadcasting, 1978; chair of the board, Quinn Martin Films; president, Quinn Martin Communications Group, 1982–87; adjunct professor of drama and in 1983 endowed the Quinn Martin Chair of Drama, Warren College, University of California, San Diego; president, Del Mar Fair Board, with jurisdiction over Del Mar Race Track, 1983–84; president, La Jolla Playhouse, California, 1985–86. Trustee: Buckley School, North Hollywood, California; La Jolla Playhouse. Recipient: TV Guide Award, 1963–64; Emmy Award, 1964. Died in Rancho Santa Fe, California, September 6, 1987.

Television Series

1955–58	*The Jane Wyman Theater* (writer)
1958	*The Desilu Playhouse* (writer)
1959–63	*The Untouchables*
1961–62	*The New Breed*
1963–67	*The Fugitive*
1964–67	*Twelve O'clock High*
1965–74	*The FBI*
1967–68	*The Invaders*
1970–71	*Dan August*
1971–76	*Cannon*
1972–73	*Banyon*
1972–77	*The Streets of San Francisco*
1973–80	*Barnaby Jones*
1974	*Nakia* (coproducer)
1974–75	*The Manhunter*
1975	*Caribe*
1976	*Bert D'Angelo/Superstar*
1976–77	*Most Wanted*
1977	*Tales of the Unexpected*

Made-for-Television Movies (selected)

1970	*House on Greenapple Road*
1971	*Face of Fear*
1971	*Incident in San Francisco*
1974	*Murder or Mercy*
1974	*Attack on the 5:22*
1975	*The Abduction of St. Anne*
1975	*Home of Our Own*
1975	*Attack on Terror*
1976	*Brinks: The Great Robbery*
1978	*Standing Tall*

Film

The Mephisto Waltz, 1971.

Further Reading

Barnouw, Erik, *Tube of Plenty: The Evolution of American Television,* New York: Oxford University Press, 1975; 2nd revised edition, 1990

Cooper, John, *The Fugitive: A Complete Episode Guide, 1963–1967,* Ann Arbor, Michigan: Popular Culture Ink, 1994

Marc, David, and Robert J. Thompson, *Prime Time, Prime Movers: From I Love Lucy to L.A. Law—America's Greatest TV Shows and the People Who Created Them,* Boston: Little, Brown, 1992

Newcomb, Horace, and Robert S. Alley, *The Producer's Medium: Conversations with Creators of American TV,* New York: Oxford University Press, 1983

Robertson, Ed, *The Fugitive Recaptured,* Los Angeles: Pomegranate, 1993

Marx, Groucho (1890–1977)

U.S. Comedian

Although often remembered as the quipping leader of the team of brothers who starred in anarchic film comedies of the 1930s and 1940s, Groucho Marx reached a far larger audience through his solo television career. As the comic quizmaster of the long-running *You Bet Your Life,* Marx became an icon of 1950s television, maintaining a weekly presence in the Nielsen top ten for most of the decade.

The familiar Groucho persona served as a comedic anchor for the popular quiz-show format when the 60-year-old Marx made the transition to television in 1950. Groucho replaced his trademark greasepaint mustache with a real one, but his attributes were otherwise unchanged. The show simply let Groucho be Groucho. He unleashed his freewheeling verbal wit in repartee with contestants, scattered good-natured insults at his willing participants, and lived up to his billing as "TV's King Leer" by greeting female guests with his characteristic raised eyebrows and waggling cigar. Groucho's personality and gift for gab drove the program, with the quiz playing only a minor role. So immediate was his success in the medium that Groucho received an Emmy as Outstanding Television Personality of 1950 and was on the cover of *Time* a year later.

Groucho Marx.
Courtesy of the Everett Collection

Groucho's move to TV was not surprising, but the magnitude of his success was. Like many of early television's "vaudeo" stars, he was a show business veteran with roots in vaudeville and an established presence on national radio. However, his radio career had been erratic. He lacked a successful show of his own until program packager John Guedel brought *You Bet Your Life* to ABC Radio in 1947. Guedel modeled the show on his other popular series, *People Are Funny* and *House Party,* which featured host Art Linkletter interacting with audiences. The format showcased Groucho's talents well. He gained a large listenership and moved to the more powerful Columbia Broadcasting System (CBS) after two seasons. Like other radio hits, *You Bet Your Life* moved into television.

A pilot was made at CBS with Groucho simply filmed performing one of his radio episodes. A bidding war for Groucho's services ensued (the star later wrote that he chose the National Broadcasting Company [NBC] over CBS because CBS's William Paley displeased him by trying to appeal to their Jewish solidarity). *You Bet Your Life* remained a staple of NBC's Thursday night TV lineup for 11 seasons and played on the network's radio stations each Wednesday until 1957. Television episodes were different editions of performances aired on radio the previous evening.

The show's idiosyncratic production methods had as much to do with the nature of Groucho's performance style as they did with the logistics of working in two media simultaneously. Both the radio and the television version of *The Groucho Show* (as it was retitled in its final season) were somewhat pioneering in that they were recorded and edited for later broadcast. Visually, the TV edition was quite static, using a single set: Groucho sitting on a stool chatting with contestants. A multicamera system used two cameras to film the interviews from each of four angles, including a slave camera on Groucho. The look was simple, but the setup allowed the producers to edit and sharpen Groucho's performances. He could venture into risqué banter, knowing that anything too blue for broadcast could be cut. Dull bits of his unrehearsed, hour-long interviews were deleted, leaving only the comic highlights for the 30-minute telecasts.

Putting the program on film (and paying a star's salary) gave *You Bet Your Life* a higher production cost than other game shows. The investment was returned, however, by both high ratings and the ability to repeat episodes. During the 13-week summer hiatus, NBC aired *The Best of Groucho,* helping to innovate the programming convention of the rerun. When production ceased in 1961, *The Best of* telefilms also went straight into daily syndication for several years.

Throughout its run, *You Bet Your Life*'s formula remained unchanged. Announcer and straight man George Fenneman began, "Here he is: the one, the only...," prompting the studio audience to shout "Groucho!" The quizmaster previewed the week's "secret woid," and a wooden duck (in Groucho guise) descended with $100 whenever the word was spoken. Male and female contestants were paired up to talk with Groucho, who often played matchmaker. The show recruited entertaining, oddball contestants as well as celebrities. Many performed vaudeville-style numbers, making *You Bet Your Life* as much a variety show as a talk or quiz program. After each interview, Groucho posed trivia questions. Winners received modest amounts of money, while losers received a consolation prize for answering a variation of Groucho's famous query, "Who's buried in Grant's Tomb?"

The routine thrived because of Groucho's rapport with guests. He was a living encyclopedia of showbiz patter, gags, and lyrics and possessed a genuine gift for witty ad libs. Yet his material was more scripted than it appeared. A staff of writers provided teleprompted jokes. Working off these, Groucho maintained a palpable spontaneity, never meeting with the screened contestants before the show.

While *You Bet Your Life* was Groucho's greatest contribution to television, he was a popular TV raconteur until the latter years of his life. After a short-lived series revival on CBS (*Tell It to Groucho*) and appearances on British TV in the early 1960s, he hosted variety programs, did cameos, and sat in on panel shows. However, he found his most comfortable niche as a talk show personality with an intellectual edge. His acerbic manner fit well with fringe late-night programming, such as Les Crane's controversial talk show (on its 1964 premiere Groucho served as a metacritic to political dialogue among William F. Buckley, John Lindsay, and Max Lerner). Of more lasting importance, Groucho served as an interim host for *The Tonight Show* when Jack Paar stepped down, and he introduced Johnny Carson when he debuted as host. Groucho also developed a famous friendship with *Tonight Show* writers Dick Cavett and Woody Allen, thereby influencing a new generation of TV and film comedians.

In the 1970s, Groucho's celebrity was revived by a surprisingly successful resyndication of *You Bet Your Life* (though later imitations of it by Buddy Hackett and Bill Cosby flopped). Books, films, and records by and about Groucho also sold well. His popularity extended to both those nostalgic for a past era and those who made his antiauthority comedy style part of the younger counterculture.

This contradiction was appropriate for the performer who was simultaneously an insightful intellectual critic and a pop icon. Groucho is attributed with a memorable put-down of television: "I find television very educational. The minute somebody turns it on, I go into the library and read a good book." Yet, in true contrarian fashion, when promoting his own show's premiere, he added a seldom-quoted rejoinder : "Now that I'm a part of television, or 'TV' as we say out here on the Coast, I don't mean a word of it."

DAN STREIBLE

Groucho Marx. Born Julius Henry Marx in New York City, October 2, 1890. Married: 1) Ruth Johnson, 1922 (divorced, 1942); children: Miriam and Arthur; 2) Catherine Gorcey, 1945 (divorced, 1950); child: Melinda; 3) Eden Hartford, 1953 (divorced, 1969). With brothers Chico, Harpo, and Zeppo, formed comedy team, the Marx Brothers, successful in film comedies; served as host for radio and television game show *You Bet Your Life.* Recipient: Emmy Award, 1950. Died in Los Angeles, California, August 19, 1977.

Television Series
1950–61   *You Bet Your Life (The Groucho Show)*
1962   *Tell It to Groucho*

Films
The Cocoanuts, 1929; *Animal Crackers,* 1930; *Monkey Business,* 1931; *Horsefeathers,* 1932; *Duck*

Soup, 1933; *A Night at the Opera,* 1935; *A Day at the Races,* 1937; *The King and the Chorus Girl,* 1937; *Room Service,* 1938; *At the Circus,* 1939; *Go West,* 1940; *The Big Store,* 1941; *A Night in Casablanca,* 1946; *Copacabana,* 1947; *Mr. Music,* 1950; *Love Happy,* 1950; *Double Dynamite,* 1951; *A Girl in Every Port,* 1952; *Will Success Spoil Rock Hunter?,* 1957; *The Story of Mankind,* 1957; *Skidoo,* 1968.

Radio
You Bet Your Life, 1947–57.

Stage
Minnie's Boys (co-author), 1970.

Publications

Beds, 1930
Many Happy Returns: An Unofficial Guide to Your Income-Tax Problems, 1942
Time for Elizabeth: A Comedy in Three Acts, with Norman Krasna, 1949
Groucho and Me, 1959
Memoirs of a Mangy Lover, 1963
The Groucho Letters, 1967
The Marx Bros. Scrapbook, with Richard J. Anobile, 1973
The Groucho Phile: An Illustrated Life, 1976
The Secret Word Is Groucho, with Hector Arce, 1976
Love, Groucho: Letters from Groucho Marx to His Daughter Miriam, edited by Miriam Marx Allen, 1992

Further Reading

Arce, Hector, *Groucho,* New York: Putnam, 1979
Chandler, Charlotte, *Hello, I Must Be Going: Groucho and His Friends,* Garden City, New York: Doubleday, 1978
Gehring, Wes D., *Groucho and W.C. Fields: Huckster Comedians,* Jackson: University Press of Mississippi, 1994
Groucho, London: Gollancz, 1954
Kanfer, Stefan, editor, *The Essential Groucho: Writings by, for, and about Groucho Marx,* New York: Vintage, 2000
Marx, Arthur, *Son of Groucho,* New York: D. McKay, 1972
Marx, Arthur, *My Life with Groucho: A Son's Eye View,* London: Robson, 1988
Marx, Arthur, *Arthur Marx's Groucho: A Photographic Journey,* Pomona, California: Phoenix Marketing Services, 2001
Marx, Arthur, and Robert Fisher, *Groucho: A Life in Revue,* New York: S. French, 1988
National Broadcasting Company, *Educational Television and Groucho Marx,* New York: NBC, 1957
Oursler, Fulton, "My Dinner with Groucho: It Came with Japes and Tears, Everything but the Duck," *Esquire* (June 1989)
Stoliar, Steve, *Raised Eyebrows: My Years Inside Groucho's House,* Los Angeles, California: General Publishing Group, 1996
Tyson, Peter, *Groucho Marx,* New York: Chelsea House, 1995

Mary Tyler Moore Show, The

U.S. Situation Comedy

The Mary Tyler Moore Show premiered on the Columbia Broadcasting System (CBS) in September 1970 and during its seven-year run became one of the most-acclaimed television programs ever produced. The program represented a significant change in the situation comedy, quickly distinguishing itself from typical plot-driven storylines filled with narrative predictability and unchanging characters. As created by the team of James Brooks and Allan Burns, *The Mary Tyler Moore Show* presented the audience with fully realized characters who evolved and became more complex throughout their life on the show. Storylines were character based, and the ensemble cast used this approach to develop relationships that changed over time.

The program starred Mary Tyler Moore, who had previously achieved success as Laura Petrie on *The Dick Van Dyke Show*. As Mary Richards, a single woman in her 30s, Moore presented a character different from other single TV women of the time. She was not widowed or divorced or seeking a man to support her. Rather, the character had just emerged from a live-in situation with a man whom she had helped through medical school. He left her on receiving his degree, and she relocated to Minneapolis, Minnesota, determined to "make it on her own." This now common concept was rarely depicted on television in the early 1970s despite some visible successes of the women's movement.

Mary Richards found a job in the newsroom of fictional television station WJM, the lowest-rated station in its market, and there she began her life as an independent woman. She found a "family" among her co-workers and her neighbors. Among her at-work friends were Lou Grant (Ed Asner), the crusty news director; Murray Slaughter (Gavin MacLeod), the cynical news writer; Ted Baxter (Ted Knight), the supercilious anchorman; and, later, Sue Ann Nivens (Betty White), the man-hungry "Happy Homemaker." Sharing her apartment house were Rhoda Morgenstern (Valerie Harper), Mary's best friend, and Phyllis Lindstrom (Cloris Leachman), their shallow landlady. This ensemble pushed the situation comedy genre in new directions and provided the show with a fresh feel and look.

The "workplace family," while not new to television sitcoms (*Our Miss Brooks* and *The Gale Storm Show* were among earlier incarnations of this subgenre), was redefined in *The Mary Tyler Moore Show*. Here were characters easily defined by traditional familial qualities—Lou as the father figure, Ted as the problem child, Rhoda as the family confidante, and Mary as the mother/daughter around whom the entire situation revolved. But the special nature of these relationships gave the show its depth and humor. Never static, each character changed in ways previously unseen in the genre. One of the best examples occurred when Lou divorced his wife of many years. His adjustment to the transition from married to divorced middle-aged man provided rich comic moments but also allowed viewers to see new depths in the character, glimpse behind the gruff facade into Lou's vulnerability, and grow closer to him. This type of evolution occurred with all the cast members, providing writers with constantly shifting perspective on the characters. From those perspectives, new storylines could be developed, and these fresh approaches helped renew a genre grown weary with repetition and familiar techniques.

Similarly, the program set the standard for a new subgenre of situation comedy: the working-woman sitcom. Beginning as a determined but uncertain independent woman, Mary Richards came to represent what has since become a convention in this type of comedy. Unattached and not reliant on a man, Mary never rejected men as romantic objects or denied her hopes to one day be married. Unlike Rhoda, however, Mary did not define her life through her search for "Mr. Right." Rather, she dated several men and even spent the night with a few of them (another new development in TV sitcoms). Working-woman sitcoms since, including *Kate and Allie* and *Murphy Brown*, owe a debt to Mary Richards.

The program became an anchor of CBS's Saturday night schedule and, along with *All in the Family, M*A*S*H, The Bob Newhart Show,* and *The Carol Burnett Show,* was part of one of the strongest nights of programming ever presented by a network. From September 1970 until its final airing in September 1977, *The Mary Tyler Moore Show* was usually among the top 20 shows. It garnered three Emmy Awards as

The Mary Tyler Moore Show, Mary Tyler Moore, Gavin MacLeod, Ed Asner, Ted Knight, Betty White, Georgia Engel, 1970–77.
Courtesy of the Everett Collection

Outstanding Comedy Series (in 1975, 1976, and 1977). Moore, Asner, Harper, Knight, and White all won Emmys for their performances, and the show's writing and directing were similarly honored several times.

The show was the first from MTM Productions, the company formed by Moore and her then husband, Grant Tinker. MTM went on to produce an impressive list of landmark situation comedies and dramas, including *The Bob Newhart Show, Newhart, The White Shadow, Hill Street Blues, St. Elsewhere,* and *L.A. Law.* The characters from *The Mary Tyler Moore Show* provided the focus for several successful spin-offs in the 1970s: *Rhoda, Phyllis,* and *Lou Grant.* The latter was significant in that it represented the successful continuation and transformation of a character across genre lines. In the new show, Asner played Grant as a news-

paper editor in a serious, hour-long, issue-oriented drama. MTM Productions developed a reputation, begun in *The Mary Tyler Moore Show,* for creating what became known as "quality television," television readily identifiable by its textured, humane, and contemporary themes and characters.

Traits of *The Mary Tyler Moore Show* have become standard elements of many situation comedies since its airing. Because numerous writers and directors worked at MTM (and on *The Mary Tyler Moore Show* in particular) and then moved on to develop their own productions, the program's influence is notable in sitcoms such as *Taxi, Cheers,* and *Night Court.*

The Mary Tyler Moore Show was also one of the first sitcoms to bring closure to its story. In its last episode in 1977, the entire WJM news staff, with the exception of the very expendable Ted Baxter, was fired. Mary's neighbors Rhoda and Phyllis had departed previously for their own programs. Now the rest of her "family" was being broken up. Ironically, television brought them together, and now the vagaries of television were separating them—in the "real" world as well as in their own fictional context. In the final moments, Mary, Lou, Murray, Ted, Ted's wife Georgette, and Sue Ann mass together in a teary group hug and exit. Then Mary turns out the lights in the newsroom for the last time. It was a fitting conclusion to a program that had become very comfortable and very real in ways few other programs ever had.

GEOFFREY HAMMILL

See also **Asner, Ed; Brooks, James L.; Burns, Allan; Comedy, Domestic Settings; Comedy, Workplace; Family on Television; Gender and Television;** *Lou Grant;* **Moore, Mary Tyler; Tinker, Grant; Workplace Programs**

Cast

Mary Richards	Mary Tyler Moore
Lou Grant	Edward Asner
Ted Baxter	Ted Knight
Murray Slaughter	Gavin MacLeod
Rhoda Morgenstern (1970–74)	Valerie Harper
Phyllis Lindstrom (1970–75)	Cloris Leachman
Bess Lindstrom (1970–74)	Lisa Gerritsen
Gordon (Gordy) Howard (1970–73)	John Amos
Georgette Franklin Baxter (1973–77)	Georgia Engel
Sue Ann Nivens (1973–77)	Betty White
Marie Slaughter (1971–77)	Joyce Bulifant
Edie Grant (1973–74)	Priscilla Morrill
David Baxter (1976–77)	Robbie Rist

Producers

James L. Brooks, Alan Burns, Stan Daniels, Ed Weinberger

Programming History

168 episodes
CBS

September 1970–December 1971	Saturday 9:30–10:00
December 1971–September 1972	Saturday 8:30–9:00
September 1972–October 1976	Saturday 9:00–9:30
November 1976–September 1977	Saturday 8:00–8:30

Further Reading

Alley, Robert S., and Irby B. Brown, *Love Is All Around: The Making of The Mary Tyler Moore Show,* New York: Delta, 1989

Bathrick, Serifina, "*The Mary Tyler Moore Show:* Women at Home and at Work," in *MTM: "Quality Television,"* edited by Jane Feuer, Paul Kerr, and Tise Vahimagi, London: British Film Institute, 1984

Dow, Bonnie, "Hegemony, Feminist Criticism, and *The Mary Tyler Moore Show,*" *Critical Studies in Mass Communication* (September 1990)

Rabinovitz, Lauren, "Sitcoms and Single Moms: Representations of Feminism on American TV," *Cinema Journal* (Fall 1989)

M*A*S*H

U.S. Comedy

*M*A*S*H,* based on the 1970 movie of the same name directed by Robert Altman, aired on the Columbia Broadcasting System (CBS) from 1972 to 1983 and has become one of the most-celebrated television series in the history of the television medium. During its initial season, however, *M*A*S*H* was in danger of being canceled because of low ratings. The show reached the top-ten program list the following year and never fell out of the top-20 rated programs during the remainder of its run. The final episode of *M*A*S*H* was a two-and-a-half-hour special that attracted the largest audience to ever view a single television program episode.

In many ways, the series set the standard for some of the best programming to appear later. The show used multiple plotlines in half-hour episodes, usually

*M*A*S*H,* Larry Linville, Loretta Swit, Alan Alda, McLean Stevenson, Wayne Rogers, William Christopher, Gary Burghoff, Jamie Farr, 1972–83.
©*20th Century Fox/Courtesy of the Everett Collection*

with at least one story in the comedic vein and another dramatic. Some later versions of this form—for example, *Hooperman* (American Broadcasting Company [ABC], 1987–89) and *The Days and Nights of Molly Dodd* (National Broadcasting Company [NBC], 1987–89)—would be known as the "dramedy," half-hour programs incorporating elements of both comedy and drama. Other comedies would forgo the more serious aspects of *M*A*S*H* but maintain its focus on character and motive, whereas some dramatic programming, such as *St. Elsewhere* and *Moonlighting,* would draw on the mixture of elements to distinguish themselves from more conventional television.

*M*A*S*H* was set in South Korea, near Seoul, during the Korean War. The series focused on the group of doctors and nurses whose job was to heal the wounded who arrived at this "Mobile Army Surgical Hospital" by helicopter, ambulance, or bus. The hospital compound was isolated from the rest of the world. One road ran through the camp; a mountain blocked one perimeter and a minefield the other. Here the wounded were patched up and sent home—or back to the front. Here, too, the loyal audience came to know and respond to an exceptional ensemble cast of characters.

The original cast assumed roles created in Altman's movie. The protagonists were Dr. Benjamin Franklin "Hawkeye" Pierce (Alan Alda) and Dr. "Trapper" John McIntyre (Wayne Rogers). Pierce and McIntyre were excellent surgeons who preferred to chase female nurses and drink homemade gin to operating and who had little, if any, use for military discipline or authority. As a result, they often ran afoul of two other medical officers, staunch military types, Dr. Frank Burns (Larry Linville) and senior nurse Lieutenant Margaret "Hot Lips" Houlihan (Loretta Swit). The camp com-

mander, Lieutenant Colonel Henry Blake (McLean Stevenson), was a genial bumbler whose energies were often directed toward preventing Burns and Houlihan from court-martialing Pierce and McIntyre. The camp was actually run by Corporal Walter "Radar" O'Reilly (Gary Burghoff), the company clerk who could spontaneously finish Blake's sentences and hear incoming helicopters before they were audible to other human ears. Other regulars were Corporal Max Klinger (Jamie Farr), who, in the early seasons, usually dressed in women's clothing in an ongoing attempt to secure a medical (mental) discharge, and Father Francis Mulcahy (William Christopher), the kindly camp priest who looked out for an orphanage.

In the course of its 11 years, the series experienced many cast changes. Trapper John McIntyre was "discharged" after the 1974–75 season because of a contract dispute between the producers and Rogers. He was replaced by Dr. B.J. Hunnicutt (Mike Farrell), a clean-cut family man quite different from McIntyre's lecherous doctor. Frank Burns was given a psychiatric discharge in the beginning of the 1977–78 season and was replaced by Dr. Charles Emerson Winchester (David Ogden Stiers), a Boston blueblood who disdained the condition of the camp and tent mates Pierce and Hunnicutt. O'Reilly's departure at the beginning of the 1979–80 season was explained by the death of his fictional uncle, and Klinger took over the company clerk position.

Perhaps the most significant change for the group occurred with the leave-taking of Henry Blake. His exit was written into the series in tragic fashion. As his plane was flying home over the Sea of Japan, it was shot down and the character killed. Despite the "realism" of this narrative development, public sentiment toward the event was so negative that the producers promised never to have another character depart the same way. Colonel Sherman Potter (Harry Morgan), a doctor with a regular-army experience in the cavalry, replaced Blake as camp commander and became both more complex and more involved with the other characters than Blake had been.

Although set in Korea, both the movie and the series *M*A*S*H* were initially developed as critiques of the Vietnam War. As that war dragged toward conclusion, however, the series focused more on characters than situations—a major development for situation comedy. Characters were given room to learn from their mistakes, to adapt, and change. Houlihan became less the rigid military nurse and more a friend to both her subordinates and the doctors. Hawkeye changed from a gin-guzzling skirt chaser to a more "enlightened" male who cared about women and their issues, a reflection of Alda himself. Radar outgrew his youthful innocence, and Klinger gave up his skirts and wedding dresses to assume more authority. This focus on character rather than character type set M*A*S*H apart from other comedies of the day, and the style of the show departed from the norm in many other ways as well in terms of both its style and its mode of production.

While most other contemporary sitcoms took place indoors and were produced largely on videotape in front of a live audience, M*A*S*H was shot entirely on film on location in southern California. Outdoor shooting at times presented problems. While shooting the final episode, for example, forest fires destroyed the set, causing a delay in filming. The series also made innovative uses of the laugh track. In early seasons, the laugh track was employed during the entire episode. As the series developed, the laugh track was removed from scenes set in the operating room. In a few episodes, the laugh track was removed entirely, another departure from sitcom conventions.

The most striking technical aspect of the series is found in its aggressively cinematic visual style. Instead of relying on straight cuts and short takes, episodes often used long shots, with people and vehicles moving between the characters and the camera. Tracking shots moved with action and changed direction when the story was "handed off" from one group of characters to another. These and other camera movements, wedded to complex editing techniques, enabled the series to explore character psychology in powerful ways and to assert the preeminence of the ensemble over any single individual. In this way, M*A*S*H seemed to be asserting the central fact of war, that individual human beings are caught in the tangled mesh of other lives and must struggle to retain some sense of humanity and compassion. This approach was grounded in Altman's film style and enabled M*A*S*H to manipulate its multiple storylines and its mixture of comedy and drama with techniques that matched the complex, absurd tragedy of war itself.

M*A*S*H was one of the most innovative sitcoms of the 1970s and 1980s. Its stylistic flair and narrative mix drew critical acclaim, while the solid writing and vitally drawn characters helped the series maintain high ratings. The show also made stars of it performers—none more so than Alda, who went on to a successful career in film. The popularity of M*A*S*H was quite evident in the 1978–79 season. CBS aired new episodes during prime time on Monday and programmed reruns of the series in the daytime and on Thursday late night, giving the show a remarkable seven appearances on a single network in a five-day period. The series produced one unsuccessful spin-off, After M*A*S*H, which aired from 1983 to 1984. The true popularity of M*A*S*H can still be seen, for the series is one of the most widely syndicated series throughout the world. Despite the historical setting, the characters and issues in this series remain fresh, funny, and compelling in ways that continue to stand as excellent television.

JEFF SHIRES

See also **Alda, Alan; Gelbart, Larry; Vietnam on Television; War on Television**

Cast

Capt. Benjamin Franklin Pierce (Hawkeye)	Alan Alda
Capt. John McIntyre (Trapper John) (1972–75)	Wayne Rogers
Lt. (later Major) Margaret Houlihan (Hot Lips)	Loretta Swit
Maj. Frank Burns (1972–77)	Larry Linville
Cpl. Walter O'Reilly (Radar) (1972–79)	Gary Burghoff
Lt. Col. Henry Blake (1972–75)	McLean Stevenson
Father John Mulcahy (pilot only)	George Morgan
Father Francis Mulcahy	William Christopher
Dr. Sydney Friedman	Alan Arbus
Cpl. Maxwell Klinger (1973–83)	Jamie Farr
Col. Sherman Potter (1975–83)	Harry Morgan
Capt. B.J. Hunnicutt (1975–83)	Mike Farrell
Maj. Charles Emerson Winchester (1977–83)	David Ogden Stiers
Lt. Maggie Dish (1972)	Karen Philipp
Spearchucker Jones (1972)	Timothy Brown
Ho-John (1972)	Patrick Adiarte
Ugly John (1972–73)	John Orchard
Lt. Leslie Scorch (1972–73)	Linda Meiklejohn
Gen. Brandon Clayton (1972–73)	Herb Voland
Lt. Ginger Ballis (1972–74)	Odessa Cleveland
Nurse Margie Cutler (1972–73)	Marcia Strassman
Nurse Louise Anderson (1973)	Kelly Jean Peters
Lt. Nancy Griffin (1973)	Lynette Mettey
Various Nurses (1973–77)	Bobbie Mitchell
Gen. Mitchell (1973–74)	Robert F. Simon
Nurse Kellye (1974–83)	Kellye Nakahara
Various Nurses (1974–78)	Patricia Stevens
Various Nurses (1976–83)	Judy Farrell
Igor (1976–83)	Jeff Maxwell
Nurse Bigelow (1977–79)	Enid Kent

Sgt. Zale (1977–79)   Johnny Haymer
Various Nurses (1978–83)   Jan Jordan
Various Nurses (1979–83)   Gwen Farrell
Various Nurses (1979–81)   Connie Izay
Various Nurses (1979–80)   Jennifer Davis
Various Nurses (1980–83)   Shari Sabo
Sgt. Luther Rizzo (1981–83)   G.W. Bailey
Roy (1981–83)   Roy Goldman
Soon-Lee (1983)   Rosalind Chao
Various Nurses (1981–83)   Joann Thompson
Various Nurses (1992–83)   Deborah
                                       Harmon

Producers

Larry Gelbart, Gene Reynolds, Burt Metcalf, John Rappaport, Allan Katz, Don Reo, Jim Mulligan, Thad Mumford, Dan Wilcox, Dennis Koenig

Programming History

251 episodes
CBS

September 1972–September 1973	Sunday	8:00–8:30
September 1973–September 1974	Saturday	8:30–9:00
September 1974–September 1975	Tuesday	8:30–9:00
September 1975–November 1975	Friday	8:30–9:00
December 1975–January 1978	Tuesday	9:00–9:30
January 1978–September 1983	Monday	9:00–9:30

Further Reading

Alda, Arlene, and Alan Alda, *The Last Days of M*A*S*H,* Verona, New Jersey: Unicorn, 1983

Budd, Mike, and Clay Steinman, "*M*A*S*H* Mystified: Capitalization, Dematerialization, Idealization," *Cultural Critique* (fall 1988)

Clauss, Jed, *M*A*S*H: The First Five Years, 1972–1977: A Show by Show Arrangement,* Mattituck, New York: Aeonian, 1977

Dennison, Linda T., "In the Beginning...." (interview with Larry Gelbart), *Writer's Digest* (April 1995)

Freedman, Carl, "History, Fiction, Film, Television, Myth: The Ideology of *M*A*S*H,*" *The Southern Review* (winter 1990)

Heard, A., "The *M*A*S*H* Era," *The New Republic* (April 4, 1983)

Kalter, Suzy, *The Complete Book of M*A*S*H,* New York: Abrams, 1984

Marc, David, "The World of Alda and 'Hawkeye,'" *Television Quarterly* (fall 1988)

Reiss, David S., *M*A*S*H: The Exclusive, Inside Story of TV's Most Popular Show,* Indianapolis, Indiana: Bobbs-Merrill, 1983

Sawyer, Corinne Holt, "'If I Could Walk That Way, I Wouldn't Need the Talcum Powder': Word-Play Humor in *M*A*S*H,*" *Journal of Popular Film and Television* (spring 1983)

Sawyer, Corinne Holt, "Kilroy Was Here—But He Stepped Out for a Minute! Absentee Characters in Popular Fiction (with Particular Attention to *M*A*S*H*)," *Journal of Popular Culture* (fall 1984)

Winther, Marjorie, "*M*A*S*H,* Malls, and Meaning: Popular and Corporate Culture in *In Country,*" *Lit: Literature Interpretation Theory* (1993)

Mass Communication

The term "mass communication" is used in a variety of ways that, despite the potential for confusion, are usually clear from the context. These include (1) reference to the activities of the mass media as a group, (2) the use of criteria of "massiveness" to distinguish among media and their activities, and (3) the construction of questions about communication as applied to the activities of the mass media. Significantly, only the third of these uses does not take the actual process of communication for granted.

"Mass communication" is often used loosely to refer to the distribution of entertainment, arts, information, and messages by television, radio, newspapers, magazines, movies, recorded music, the Internet, and associated media. This general application is appropriate only as designating the most common features of such otherwise disparate phenomena as broadcast television, cable, video playback, theater projection, recorded song, radio talk, advertising, and the front page, editorial page, sports section, and comics page of the newspaper. In this usage, "mass communication" refers to the activities of the media as a whole and fails to distinguish among specific media, modes of communication, genres of text or artifact, production or reception situations, or any questions concerning actual communication. The only analytic purpose served is to distinguish mass communication from interpersonal, small-group, and other face-to-face communication situations.

Various criteria of massiveness can also be brought to bear in analyses of media and mass communication situations. These criteria may include size and differentiation of audience, anonymity, simultaneity, and the nature of influences among audience members and between the audience and the media.

Live television spectaculars of recent decades may be the epitome of mass communication. These include such serious events as the funerals of John Fitzgerald Kennedy, Martin Luther King Jr., or Princess Diana and entertainment spectaculars such as the Olympic Games, the Super Bowl, and the Academy Awards. These transmissions are distributed simultaneously and regardless of individual or group differences to audiences numbering in several tens or even a few hundreds of millions. Outside their own local groups, members of these audiences know nothing of each other. They have no real opportunities to influence the television representation of the events or the interpretation of those representations by other audience members.

By contrast, the audience for most cable television channels is much smaller and more differentiated from other audience groups. The audience for newspapers, magazines, and movies is less simultaneous, as well as smaller and more differentiated, and holds out the potential for a flow of local influences as people talk about articles and recommend movies. The audience for Internet web pages and downloadable files may be so thoroughly distributed in time and space that there is never more than one audience member at a time. Yet the audience members for streaming files of Internet radio or TV may be having experiences very similar to broadcast radio or TV audiences, even if there are fewer of them, more widely dispersed. When television shows prompt viewers to check their web pages, these programs are trying to steer the audience in a way that would reduce its unpredictability and hence one aspect of its massiveness. Compared to a letter, phone call, conversation, group discussion, or public lecture, all these media produce communication immensely more massive on every criteria.

All the criteria used in defining mass communication are potentially confused when one is engaged in a specific research project or critical examination. The most confounding problem is encountered when determining the level of analysis. Should the concern be with a single communication event or with multiple events but a single communication channel? Should the focus be on multiple channels but a single medium? Does the central question concern a moment in time or an era, a community, a nation, or the world?

Radio provides an excellent example of the importance of these choices. Before television, network radio was the epitome of mass communication; it was national, live, and available and listened to everywhere. Today it is difficult to think of radio this way because the industry no longer works in the same manner. Commercial radio stations depend on local and regional sources of advertising income. Essentially, all radio stations are programmed to attract a special segment of a local or regional audience, and even when programming national entertainment materials, such as popular songs, stations emphasize local events, personalities, weather, news, and traffic in their broadcast talk. Radio is an industry characterized by specialized channels, each attracting relatively small, relatively differentiated audiences. However, the average home in the United States has five and half radios, more than twice the number of televisions. Cumulatively, the U.S. audience for radio is just as big, undifferentiated, and anonymous as that for television, and because radio is normally live and television is not, the reception of radio communication is more simultaneous than that of television. Is radio today, then, a purveyor of mass communication? It depends on whether the concern is with the industry as a whole or with the programming and audience of a particular station.

Most uses of the term "mass communication" fall into one of these first two categories, either to refer to the activities of the mass media as a whole or to refer to the massiveness of certain kinds of communication. Both uses have in common that they take issues of communication for granted and instead place emphasis on size, on the massiveness of the distribution system and the audience. Attention is given to what are called the "mass media" because they are the institutional and technological systems capable of producing mass audiences for mass-distributed "communications." Communication, then, ends up implicitly defined as merely a kind of object (message, text, artifact) that is reproduced and transported by these media. For some purposes, this may be exactly the right definition. However, it diminishes our ability to treat communication as a social accomplishment, as something people do, rather than as an object that gets moved from one location to another. If communication is something people do, then it may or may not be successful, may or may not be healthy and happy. If communication means "to share," for example, rather than "to transmit," then what, if anything, of importance is shared when people watch a television show?

Scholars of mass communication are often more interested in communication as a social accomplishment than they are in the media as mass-distribution systems. This interest is based on an intellectual independence from existing habits of terminology and, most important, independence from media institutions as they exist. The term "mass," however it may be defined, is then treated as a qualification on the term "communication," however it may be defined. Such intellectual exercises, of course, can work out in a great variety of ways, but a few examples will suffice.

At one extreme, if "communication" is defined so that interaction between parties is a necessary criterion, as in "communication is symbolic interaction," and "mass" is defined as an aggregate of *non*interacting entities, then "mass communication" is an oxymoron and an impossibility. At the opposite extreme, if the term "mass communication" is defined as involving *any* symbolic behavior addressed "to whom it may concern," then choices of clothing, furniture, and appliance styles, body posture, gestures, and any other publicly observable activity may well count as mass communication. Both of these extremes may seem like mere intellectual games, but they are important precisely because their intellectuality frees them of the practical constraints under which we operate in other realms. The contribution of such intellectual games is precisely to stimulate new thinking. Perhaps pausing to consider the idea that mass communication may be an impossibility could help us understand some of the paradoxes and incoherencies of contemporary American culture.

Consider a third example in which we use a model of communication to evaluate industry practices. Definitions of "mass communication" that take communication for granted and focus simply on the massiveness of the medium are always in danger of implicitly adopting, or certainly failing to question, the assumed criteria of evaluation already used in industries. In commercial television, as in any of the other commercial media, what is assumed is that television is a business. The conventions of the industry are to evaluate things solely in business terms. Is this television show good for business? Would increasing network news to an hour be a good business decision? Would noncommercial, educational programming for children be a successful business venture? In such an environment, it is an important intervention to point out that these industries are communicators as well as businesses. As such, they can and should be held to communicative standards. The public has a right to ask whether a tele-

vision show is good for communication, whether an hour of network news would be a successful form of communication, and whether there is a communication need for noncommercial, educational children's programming. As the terms of the questions shift, so, of course, may the answers. Becoming aware of such possibilities begins with being sensitive to the definitions of such terms as "mass communication."

ERIC ROTHENBUHLER

See also **Advertising; Americanization; Audience Research; Cable Networks; Market; Narrowcasting; Political Processes and Television; Public Interest, Convenience, and Necessity; Satellite; United States: Cable Television**

Further Reading

Beniger, James R., "Toward an Old New Paradigm: The Half-Century Flirtation with Mass Society," *Public Opinion Quarterly* (1987)

Blum, Eleanor, *Basic Books in the Mass Media,* Urbana: University of Illinois Press, 1980

Curran, James, and Michael Gurevitch, editors, *Mass Media and Society,* London and New York: Edward Arnold, 1991

Dominick, Joseph R., *The Dynamics of Mass Communication,* 5th edition, New York: McGraw-Hill, 1996

Gitlin, Todd, *Media Unlimited: How the Torrent of Images and Sounds Overwhelms Our Lives,* New York: Metropolitan Books, 2001

Hamelink, Cees J., and Olga Linne, editors, *Mass Communication Research: On Problems and Policies: The Art of Asking the Right Questions,* Norwood, New Jersey: Ablex, 1994

Jensen, Joli, *Redeeming Modernity: American Media Criticism as Social Criticism,* Newbury Park, California: Sage, 1990

Katz, Elihu, "Communication Research Since Lazersfeld," *Public Opinion Quarterly* (1987)

Lorimer, Rowland, with Paddy Scannell, *Mass Communications: A Comparative Introduction,* Manchester, England: Manchester University Press, 1994

Mass Communication Review Yearbook, Newbury Park, California: Sage, 1980–

McQuail, Denis, *Mass Communication Theory: An Introduction,* London and Newbury Park, California: Sage, 1987

Meyrowitz, Joshua, *No Sense of Place: The Impact of Electronic Mass Media on Social Behavior,* New York: Oxford University Press, 1985

Rosengren, Karl Erik, editor, *Media Effects and Beyond: Culture, Socialization and Lifestyles,* London and New York: Routledge, 1994

Schramm, Wilber Lang, *Mass Communications: A Book of Readings,* Urbana: University of Illinois Press, 1960

Sterling, Christopher H., *Mass Communication and Electronic Media: A Survey Bibliography,* Washington, D.C.: George Washington University, 1983

Turow, Joseph, *Media Systems in Society: Understanding Industries, Strategies, and Power,* New York: Longman, 1992

Turow, Joseph, *Media Today: An Introduction to Mass Communication,* Boston: Houghton Mifflin, 1999

Mastermind

U.K. Quiz Show

Mastermind, a long-running quiz show of an unusually challenging academic character, was first screened by the British Broadcasting Corporation (BBC) in 1972 and defied all expectations to become staple peak-time viewing over the next 25 years. Made for next to nothing and generally filmed on location in a university setting, no one guessed at the outset that the program would break out of the cult niche to which it seemed fated (give its initial late-night viewing time) and, in short order, overtake even the long-established rival *University Challenge.*

The structure of the quiz was relatively straightforward, with four "contenders" (rather than "contestants") being given two minutes to answer as many questions as they could about a topic of their own choosing. These specialist subjects varied from the relatively conventional ("British moths," "English cathedrals" or "the works of Dorothy L. Sayers") to the more esoteric (such as "old time music hall" or "the Buddhist sage Niciren"). The general rule was that any subject was admissible as long as it was of a broadly academic nature and wide enough to provide scope for a torrent of exacting questions. After the specialist rounds, each of the four contenders were tested for a further two minutes in a similar fast-paced round of general knowledge questions, which seemed to get more difficult as the round wore on. The series as a whole was run on a knockout system, with highest scorers (and highest-scoring losers) progressing to later stages of the tournament. Winners were required to choose different specialist subjects when reappearing but were allowed to return to an earlier topic if they managed to get as far as the grand final. The eventual winner of the competition was presented with a special cut-glass bowl to take home.

The challenge facing the contenders was vastly intensified by the intimidating atmosphere that characterized the program. As well as having to maintain concentration in such daunting surroundings, participants were required to sit in an isolated pool of light in an intimidating black leather chair at the total mercy of the quizmaster. Audiences maintained complete silence as each contender faced a barrage of questions designed to reveal the depth (or lack thereof) of their knowledge. Even the opening title music, a piece by Neil Richardson titled "Approaching Menace," was

suitably threatening. The forbidding atmosphere of the program, with its spotlighted victim seated in a darkened room and exposed to intellectual torture, owed much to its creator, BBC producer Bill Wright. Wright had been a prisoner of war during World War II, and his idea for the program came out of his experience of interrogation by the German Gestapo, who had accused him of being a spy.

The presenter throughout the entire duration of the program was the Icelandic-born Scottish journalist Magnus Magnusson, who was already well known as a broadcaster on a variety of cultural topics. His politely sympathetic manner offered contenders some crumbs of reassurance, but once the stopwatch started, there was nowhere to retreat from his relentless inquisition. On occasion, it all proved too much, and some participants caved in completely, barely registering a score in the face of such pressure—acutely embarrassing, but certainly making for memorable television. One luckless participant in 1990 ended up with a record-low score of just 12 points. Magnusson's catchphrases "I've started, so I'll finish" (a mantra recited whenever the buzzer ending the round sounded in the middle of a question) and the formulaic reply "Pass" mouthed by participants when they did not know the answer were readily absorbed into everyday language.

Though initially considered to be too high-brow for peak-time audiences, the program escaped its late-night slot through a happy accident. When a Galton and Simpson comedy series called *Casanova '73* was removed from the schedule at short notice after BBC 1 Controller Bill Cotton Jr. and Director of Programs Alasdair Milne found opening episodes of the latter too offensive to be shown, *Mastermind* was put on in its peak-time slot as a short-term emergency replacement. The response was immediate, and the program's right to a permanent place in the peak-time schedule was recognized. By 1974 *Mastermind* was topping the ratings alongside *The Generation Game.* By 1978 it was attracting audiences of 20 million.

Thus established, the program was henceforth run on an annual basis (with the single exception of 1982, when no contest was held). Despite the lack of big cash prizes and the fearsome grilling they stood to face, hundreds of people auditioned for the show each season. They came from a wide range of backgrounds, by no means all academic. Winners over the years ranged from Sir David Hunt (1977), who was a former ambassador to Brazil, to London taxi driver Fred Housego (1980), who capitalized on his newfound fame to appear in further quizzes and other programs, and train driver Christopher Hughes (1983). All winners automatically became members of the Mastermind Club, which staged annual reunions and a quiz of quizzes chaired by Magnusson himself. One exceptional Christmas show featured Magnusson himself in the chair, going through the ordeal he had presided over for so many years. Afterward, he freely admitted how demanding it was to be a contender and how much he admired those who had been through it before him.

The series was finally deemed to have run out of steam in 1997, after 25 years, and ended after a final contest filmed at St. Magnus Cathedral in Orkney. As well as all the usual spin-offs in the form of board games, books, and so forth, the program's legacy may be detected in many subsequent shows, notably those in which contenders are asked seriously challenging questions in tense, hushed surroundings.

In November 2001, the black leather chair was dusted off once more for a revived version of the show to be screened on Discovery Channel, with Clive Anderson inheriting the post of quizmaster.

In June 2003, *Mastermind* was brought back on the air, showing on BBC 2 and hosted by John Humphrys.

DAVID PICKERING

See also **Quiz and Game Shows;** *University Challenge*

Producers
Bill Wright, Roger Mackay, Peter Massey, David Mitchell

Programming History
BBC 1
1972–97
Hosted by Magnus Magnusson
Discovery Channel
November 2001–
BBC 2
June 2003–

Further Reading
Magnusson, Magnus, *I've Started so I'll Finish,* London: Little, Brown, 1997

Maude

U.S. Situation Comedy

Maude, the socially controversial, sometimes radical sitcom featuring a strong female lead character played by Bea Arthur, ran on the Columbia Broadcasting System (CBS) from 1972 to 1978. Like its predecessor *All in the Family, Maude* was created by Norman Lear's Tandem Productions. Maude Findlay was first introduced as Edith's liberal, outspoken cousin from suburban Tucahoe, New York, on an episode of *All in the Family* in 1972 before spinning off later that year to her own series set in upper-middle-class Tucahoe, where she lived with her fourth husband, Walter Findlay, her divorced daughter Carol, and Carol's young son Phillip. The Findlays also went through three housekeepers during the run of the series, the first of whom, Florida Evans, left in 1974 to her own spin-off, *Good Times.* These three shows, among others, comprised a cadre of 1970s Norman Lear urban sitcoms

that raised social and political issues and dealt with them in a manner as yet unexplored in television sitcoms. *Maude* enjoyed a spot in the top-ten Nielsen ratings during its first four seasons despite being subjected to day and/or time changes in the CBS schedule that continued throughout the entire run of the program.

Like many of Lear's productions, *Maude* was a character-centered sitcom. Maude Findlay was opinionated like Archie Bunker, but her politics and class position were completely different. Strong willed, intelligent, and articulate, the liberal progressive Maude spoke out on issues raised less openly on Lear's highly successful *All in the Family.* While questions of race, class, and gender politics reverberated throughout both series, certain specific issues, such as menopause, birth control, and abortion, were more openly confronted on

Maude, Bea Arthur, 1972–78.
Courtesy of the Everett Collection

Maude. In a two-part episode that ran early in the series, the 47-year-old Maude finds out that she is pregnant and decides, with her husband Walter, that she would have an abortion, which had just been made legal in New York State. Part 2 of the double episode also deals with men and birth control, as Walter considers getting a vasectomy. Thousands of viewers wrote letters in protest of the episode because of the abortion issue. In other episodes, Maude gets a facelift; Walter's business goes bankrupt, and he deals with the resulting bout with depression; in yet another program, Walter confronts his own alcoholism. The realism of *Maude,* though conforming to the constraints of the genre, made it one of the first sitcoms to create a televisual space where highly charged, topical issues and sometimes tragic contemporary situations could be discussed.

Maude represented a change in television sitcoms during the early 1970s. Many 1960s sitcoms reflected the context and values of white middle America, where gender and family roles were fixed and problems encountered in the program rarely reached beyond the confines of nuclear family relationships. Despite variations on that theme in terms of alternative families (*Family Affair* and *My Three Sons*) and an added su-

pernatural element (*Bewitched* and *I Dream of Jeannie*), the context was middle to upper middle class, mostly suburban, and white. However, cultural upheaval in the 1960s, the political climate of the early 1970s, shifting viewer demographics, and the maturation of television itself were responsible for a departure from the usual fare. By the early 1970s, a growing portion of the viewing audience, baby boomers, were open to new kinds of television, having come of age during the era of the civil rights movement, Vietnam protests, and various forms of consciousness raising. However, the changing tastes of the audience and the social climate of the early 1970s cannot by themselves account for the rise of socially conscious television during this period. The sitcom had also matured, and producers such as Norman Lear, familiar generally with American humor and specifically with the rules of television sitcom, decided to make television comedy that was more socially aware. Like *All in the Family, Maude* set out to explode the dominant values of the white middle-class domestic sitcom, with its traditional gender roles and nonwhite stereotypes, by openly engaging in debates where various political points of view were embodied in the sitcom characters.

Such debates were the staple of *Maude* throughout its six-year run. In an early episode, Maude hires Florida Evans, a black woman, to be housekeeper. Maude goes out of her way to prove her progressive attitude to Florida by insisting the housekeeper act as if she is one of the family. Florida, along with Walter and Carol, points out to Maude the foolishness of her extreme behavior. In the end, Maude recognizes her underlying condescension toward Florida, who, as witty and outspoken as Maude, retains her dignity and decides to remain as the Findlay housekeeper on her own terms. The interaction between Maude and Florida in this episode was a comment on the issues and attitudes about race that stemmed from the civil rights efforts of the 1960s. Maude's attitudes and behavior were indicative of white liberal politics during a time when race relations in the United States were being reconfigured.

Another reconfiguration was taking place within the arena of women's rights. In one of the final episodes of the show, Maude is given the opportunity to run for the New York state senate, but Walter refuses to consider the possibility. He offers Maude an ultimatum, and after mulling over her decision, she decides to let Walter leave. This episode, like many others, reflected a feminist sensibility emerging within the country and can be viewed as a platform for discussions about the changing roles of women and the difficulties they encountered as they were faced with new challenges and more choices. Maude's character agonized over the conflict between tradition and her own career aspirations.

The show's ratings began to fall after its fourth season, and by 1978, Bea Arthur announced that she would leave the show. The end of *Maude* marked another shift in the domestic sitcom, away from open political debate and toward a renewal of the safer, more traditional family-centered sitcoms of an earlier period in television history.

KATHERINE FRY

See also All in the Family; **Arthur, Beatrice; Gender and Television; Lear, Norman**

Cast

Maude Findlay	Beatrice Arthur
Walter Findlay	Bill Macy
Carol	Adrienne Barbeau
Phillip (1972–77)	Brian Morrison
Phillip (1977–78)	Kraig Metzinger
Dr. Arthur Harmon	Conrad Bain
Vivian Cavender Harmon	Rue McClanahan
Florida Evans (1972–74)	Esther Rolle
Henry Evans (1973–74)	John Amos
Chris (1973–1974)	Fred Grandy
Mrs. Nell Naugatuck (1974–77)	Hermione Baddeley
Bert Beasley (1975–77)	J. Pat O'Malley
Victoria Butterfield (1977–78)	Marlene Warfield

Producers

Norman Lear, Rod Parker, Bob Weiskopf, Bob Schiller

Programming History

142 episodes
CBS

September 1972–September 1974	Tuesday 8:00–8:30
September 1974–September 1975	Monday 9:00–9:30
September 1975–September 1976	Monday 9:30–10:00
September 1976–September 1977	Monday 9:00–9:30
September 1977–November 1977	Monday 9:30–10:00
December 1977–January 1978	Monday 9:00–9:30
January 1978–April 1978	Saturday 9:30–10:00

Further Reading

Cowan, Geoffrey, *See No Evil: The Backstage Battle over Sex and Violence on Television,* New York: Simon and Schuster, 1979

Feuer, Jane, "Genre Study and Television," in *Channels of Discourse: Television and Contemporary Criticism,* edited by Robert C. Allen, Chapel Hill: University of North Carolina Press, 1987

Hamamoto, Darrell Y., *Nervous Laughter: Television Situation Comedy and Liberal Democratic Ideology,* New York: Praeger, 1989

Himmelstein, Hal, *Television Myth and the American Mind,* Westport, Connecticut: Praeger, 1994

Marc, David, *Comic Visions: Television Comedy and American Culture,* Boston: Unwin Hyman, 1989; 2nd edition, Malden, Massachusetts: Blackwell Publishers, 1997

Maverick

U.S. Western

A subversive western with a dark sense of humor, *Maverick* soared to sixth place in the Nielsen ratings during its second season with a 30.4 share, and it won an Emmy Award for Best Western Series in 1959. Produced by Warner Brothers (WB) and starring the then relatively unknown James Garner as footloose frontier gambler Bret Maverick, soon to be joined by Jack Kelly as Bret's brother Bart, this hour-long series followed the duplicitous adventures and, more often, mis- adventures of the Mavericks in their pursuit of money and the easy life.

Starting out as a straight western drama (the first three episodes, "The War of the Silver Kings," "Point Blank," and "According to Hoyle," were directed by feature western auteur Budd Boetticher), the series soon developed a comedy streak after writer Marion Hargrove decided to liven up his script-writing work by inserting the simple stage direction: "Maverick

Maverick, James Garner, 1981–82.
Courtesy of the Everett Collection

their repertoire for evading difficult moments was the collection of "Pappyisms" that corrupted their speech. When all else failed, for example, they were likely to quote their mentor's excuse: "My old Pappy used to say, 'If you can't fight 'em, and they won't let you join 'em, best get out of the county.'"

Following the success of *Cheyenne* on the American Broadcasting Company (ABC) from its premiere in 1955, the network asked WB's TV division to give them another hour-long western program for their Sunday evening slot. *Maverick* premiered on September 22, 1957, and pretty soon won over the viewers from the powerful opposition of the Columbia Broadcasting System's (CBS's) *The Ed Sullivan Show* and the National Broadcasting Company's (NBC's) *The Steve Allen Show,* two programs that had been Sunday night favorites from the mid-1950s. With Garner alone starring in early episodes, WB found that it was taking eight days to film a weekly show. They decided to introduce another character, Bret's brother, in order to keep the production on schedule. This strategy resulted in a weekly costarring series when Jack Kelly's Bart was introduced in the "Hostage" episode (November 10, 1957). With separate production units now working simultaneously, WB managed to supply a steady stream of episodes featuring either Bret or Bart on alternate weeks. Occasionally, both Maverick brothers were seen in the same episode, usually when they teamed up to help each other out of some difficult situation or to outwit even more treacherous characters than themselves.

The series also reveled in colorful characters as well as presenting wild parodies of other TV programs of the period. During the early seasons, recurring guest characters popped in and out of the plots to foil or assist the brothers: Dandy Jim Buckley (played by Efrem Zimbalist, Jr.), Gentleman Jack Darby (Richard Long), Big Mike McComb (Leo Gordon), and Bret's regular antagonist, the artful conwoman Samantha Crawford (Brewster). Among the more amusing episodes were "Gun-Shy" (second season), a send-up of *Gunsmoke* featuring a hick character called Mort Dooley; "A Cure for Johnny Rain" (third season), spoofing Jack Webb's *Dragnet* with Garner doing a deadpan Joe Friday voice-over; "Hadley's Hunters" (fourth season), which had Bart enlist the help of Ty Hardin (*Bronco*), Will Hutchins (*Sugarfoot*), Clint Walker (*Cheyenne*), and John Russell and Peter Brown (*Lawman*)—all playing their respective characters from the WB stable of western TV series (and with Edd "Kookie" Byrnes from WB's *77 Sunset Strip* as a blacksmith); and "Three Queens Full" (fifth season), a wicked parody of *Bonanza* in which the Subrosa Ranch was run by Joe Wheelwright and his three sons, Moose, Henry, and

looks at him with his beady little eyes." Other scriptwriters then followed suit. Garner, in particular, and Kelly joined in with the less-than-sincere spirit of the stories, and *Maverick* took a unique turn away from the other, more formal and traditional WB-produced westerns then on the air (*Lawman, Colt .45, Cheyenne,* and *Sugarfoot*).

The series was created by producer Roy Huggins and developed out of a story (co-written with Howard Browne) in which Huggins tried to see how many TV western rules he could get away with breaking; the script, ironically, was filmed as an episode of the "adult" *Cheyenne* series ("The Dark Rider") and featured guest star Diane Brewster as a swindler and practiced cheat, a role she was later to take up as a recurring character, gambler Samantha Crawford, during the 1958–59 season of *Maverick*. "*Maverick* is *Cheyenne,* a conventional western, turned inside out," said Huggins. "But with *Maverick* there was nothing coincidental about the inversion." The Maverick brothers were not heroes in the traditional western sense. They were devious, cowardly cardsharps who exploited easy situations and quickly vanished when faced with potentially violent ones. A popular part of

Small Paul. In addition, two other episodes ("The Wrecker" and "A State of Siege") were loose adaptations of Robert Louis Stevenson stories, albeit translated into the *Maverick* vein.

In 1960 actor James Garner and his WB studio bosses clashed when Garner took out a lawsuit against the studio for breach of contract arising out of his suspension during the January–June writers' strike of that year. To justify its suspension of Garner, WB tried to invoke the force majeure clause in Garner's contract; this clause dictated that if forces beyond the control of the studio (i.e., the writers' strike) prevented it from making films, the studio did not have to continue paying actors' salaries. It had been no secret at the time that Garner had wanted to be released from his contract ("Contracts are completely one-sided affairs. If you click, [the studio] owns you," he stated). Finally, in December 1960, the judge decided in favor of Garner. During the course of the testimony, it was revealed that during the strike WB had obtained—under the table—something in the number of 100 TV scripts and that at one time the studio had as many as 14 writers working under the pseudonym of "W. Hermanos" (Spanish for "brothers").

Garner then went on to a successful feature film career but returned to series television in the 1970s with *Nichols* (1971–72) and the popular *The Rockford Files* (1974–80). He appeared as a guest star along with Jack Kelly in the 1978 TV movie/pilot *The New Maverick,* which produced the short-lived *Young Maverick* (1979–80) series, minus Garner; he also starred in the title role of *Bret Maverick* (1981–82), which he coproduced with WB. A theatrical film version, *Maverick,* was produced in 1994 with Mel Gibson starring as Bret Maverick and Garner appearing as Bret's father; Richard Donner directed the WB release.

As a replacement for Garner in the fourth season of the original series, WB brought on board Roger Moore, as cousin Beauregard, a Texas expatriate who had lived in England (a WB contract player, Moore had been transferred from another WB western series, *The Alaskans,* which had run only one season from 1959). When Moore departed after just one season, another Maverick brother, Robert Colbert's Brent Maverick, a slight Garner/Bret look-alike, was introduced in the spring of 1961 to alternate adventures with Bart. Colbert stayed only until the end of that season, leaving the final (and longest-remaining) Maverick, Jack Kelly, to ride out the last *Maverick* season (1961–62) alone, except for some rerun episodes from early seasons.

The series came to an end after 124 episodes, and with it a small-screen western legend came to a close. Perhaps the ultimate credit for *Maverick* should go to creator-producer Roy Huggins for the originality to steer the series clear of the trite and the ordinary and for not only trying something different but also executing it with a comic flair.

TISE VAHIMAGI

See also **Garner, James; Huggins, Roy; Westerns**

Cast

Bret Maverick (1957–60)	James Garner
Bart Maverick	Jack Kelly
Samantha Crawford (1957–59)	Diane Brewster
Cousin Beauregard Maverick (1960–61)	Roger Moore
Brent Maverick (1961)	Robert Colbert

Producers

Roy Huggins, Coles Trapnell, William L. Stuart

Programming History

124 episodes
ABC

September 1957–April 1961	Sunday 7:30–8:30
September 1961–July 1962	Sunday 6:30–7:30

Further Reading

Anderson, Christopher, *Hollywood TV: The Studio System in the Fifties,* Austin: University of Texas Press, 1994

Barer, Burl, *Maverick: The Making of the Movie and the Official Guide to the Television Series,* Boston, Massachusetts: Tuttle, 1994

Hargrove, Marion, "This Is a Television Cowboy?" *Life* (January 19, 1959)

Heil, Douglas, "Auterism and the Television Scriptwriter," *Creative Screenwriting,* 2 (autumn 1995)

Heil, Douglas, "Marion Hargrove: On Writing for *Maverick* and *The Waltons*," *Creative Screenwriting,* 3 (summer 1996)

Jackson, Ronald, *Classic TV Westerns: A Pictorial History,* Secaucus, New Jersey: Carol, 1994

MacDonald, J. Fred, *Who Shot the Sheriff?: The Rise and Fall of the Television Western,* New York: Praeger, 1987

Marsden, Michael T., and Jack Nachbar, "The Modern Popular Western: Radio, Television, Film, and Print," in *A Literary History of the American West,* Fort Worth: Texas Christian University Press, 1987

Robertson, Ed, *Maverick, Legend of the West,* Los Angeles, California: Pomegranate Press, 1994

Strait, Raymond, *James Garner: A Biography,* New York: St. Martin's Press, 1985

West, Richard, *Television Westerns: Major and Minor Series, 1946–1978,* Jefferson, North Carolina: McFarland, 1987

Woolley, Lynn, Robert W. Malsbary, and Robert G. Strange, Jr., *Warner Bros. Television: Every Show of the Fifties and Sixties Episode-by-Episode,* Jefferson, North Carolina: McFarland, 1985

Yoggy, Gary A., *Riding the Video Range: The Rise and Fall of the Western on Television,* Jefferson, North Carolina: McFarland, 1995

Max Headroom

U.S. Science Fiction Program

Max Headroom was one of the most innovative science fiction series ever produced for American television, an ambitious attempt to build on the cyberpunk movement in science fiction literature. The character of Max Headroom, the series' unlikely cybernetic protagonist, was originally introduced in a 1984 British television movie, produced by Peter Wagg and starring Canadian actor Matt Frewer. The American Broadcasting Company (ABC) brought the series to U.S. television in March 1987, refilming the original movie as a pilot but recasting most of the secondary roles. The ABC series attracted critical acclaim and a cult following but lasted for only 14 episodes. The anarchic and irreverent Max went on to become an advertising spokesman for Coca-Cola and to host his own talk show on the Cinemax cable network.

The original British telefilm appeared just one year after the publication of William Gibson's *Neuromancer,* the novel that brought public attention to the cyberpunk movement and introduced the term "cyberspace" into the English language. Influenced by films such as *The Road Warrior* and *Bladerunner,* the cyberpunks adopted a taut, intense, and pulpy writing style based on brisk yet detailed representations of a near future populated by multinational corporations, colorful youth gangs, and computer-hacker protagonists. Their most important theme was the total fusion of human and machine intelligences. Writers such as Gibson, Bruce Sterling, Rudy Rucker, and Pat Cadigan developed a shared set of themes and images that were freely adopted by *Max Headroom.*

Set "20 minutes in the future," *Max Headroom* depicts a society of harsh class inequalities, where predators roam the street looking for unsuspecting citizens who can be sold for parts to black-market "body banks." Max inhabits a world ruled by Zic-Zac and other powerful corporations locked in a ruthless competition for consumer dollars and television rating points. In the opening episode, Network 22 dominates the airwaves through its use of blipverts, which compress 30 seconds of commercial information into three seconds. Blipverts can cause neural overstimulation and (more rarely) spontaneous combustion in more sedate viewers. Other episodes center around the high crime of zipping (interrupting a network signal) and

neurostim (a cheap burger pack giveaway that hypnotizes people into irrational acts of consumption). We encounter blanks, a subversive underground of have-nots who have somehow dodged incorporation into the massive data banks kept on individual citizens.

At the core of this dizzying and colorful world is Edison Carter, an idealistic Network 24 reporter who takes his portable minicam into the streets and the boardrooms to expose corruption and consumer exploitation, which, in most episodes, lead him back to the front offices of his own network. Edison's path is guided by Theora Jones, his computer operator, whose hacker skills allow him to stay one step ahead of the security systems—at least most of the time—and Bryce Lynch, the amoral boy wonder and computer wizard. Edison is aided in his adventures by Blank Reg, the punked-out head of a pirate television operation, BigTime Television. Edison's alter ego, Max Headroom, is a cybernetic imprint of the reporter's memories and personality who comes to "life" within computers, television programs, and other electronic environments. There he becomes noted for his sputtering speech style, his disrespect for authority, and his penchant for profound non sequiturs.

Critics admired the series' self-reflexivity, its willingness to pose questions about television networks and their often unethical and cynical exploitation of the ratings game, and its parody of game shows, polit-

Max Headroom, Matt Frewer, 1987.
Courtesy of the Everett Collection

ical advertising, televangelism, news coverage, and commercials. Influenced by Music Television (MTV), the series' quick-paced editing and intense visual style were also viewed as innovative, creating a televisual equivalent of the vivid and intense cyberpunk writing style. This series' self-conscious parody of television conventions and its conception of a "society of spectacle" was considered emblematic of the "postmodern condition," making it a favorite of academic writers as well. Their interest was only intensified by Max's move from science fiction to advertising and to talk television, where this nonhuman celebrity (commodity) traded barbed comments with other talk show–made celebrities, such as Doctor Ruth, Robin Leach, Don King, and Paul Shaffer. Subsequent series, such as Oliver Stone's *Wild Palms* or *VR,* have sought to bring aspects of cyberpunk to television, but none have done it with *Max Headroom*'s verve, imagination, and faithfulness to core cyberpunk themes.

HENRY JENKINS

Cast

Edison Carter/	
Max Headroom	Matt Frewer
Theora Jones	Amanda Pays
Ben Cheviot	George Coe
Bryce Lynch	Chris Young
Murray	Jeffrey Tambor
Blank Reg	William Morgan Sheppard
Dominique	Concetta Tomei
Ashwell	Hank Garrett
Edwards	Lee Wilkof
Lauren	Sharon Barr
Ms. Formby	Virginia Kiser

Producers
Phillip DeGuere, Peter Wagg, Brian Frankish

Programming History
ABC

March 1987–May 1987	Tuesday 10:00–11:00
August 1987–	
October 1987	Friday 9:00–10:00

Further Reading

Berko, Lili, "Simulation and High Concept Imagery: The Case of Max Headroom," *Wide Angle: A Film Quarterly of Theory, Criticism, and Practice* (1988)

Kerman, Judith B., "Virtual Space and Its Boundaries in Science Fiction Film and Television: Tron, 'Max Headroom' and Wargames," in *The Celebration of the Fantastic: Selected Papers from the Tenth Anniversary International Conference on the Fantastic in the Arts,* edited by Donald E. Morse, Marshall Tymn, and Bertha Csilla, Westport, Connecticut: Greenwood, 1992

Lentz, Harris M., *Science Fiction, Horror, and Fantasy Film and Television Credits, Supplement 2, Through 1993,* Jefferson, North Carolina: McFarland, 1994

Long, Marion, "Paradise Tossed," *Omni* (April 1988)

Roberts, Steve, *Max Headroom: The Picture Book of the Film,* New York: Random House, 1986

Staiger, Janet, "Future Noir: Contemporary Representations of Visionary Cities," *East-West Film Journal* (December 1988)

McDonald, Trevor (1939–)

British Broadcast Journalist

Trevor McDonald is the comforting face of nighttime news. As Big Ben chimes ten o'clock, McDonald looks up from his news desk and, with considerable gravitas, reads out the news headlines for Independent Television News (ITN). Although this act is undertaken in newsrooms across Britain, he occupies a very particular position in the media firmament. McDonald not only is one of the most respected elder statesmen of news broadcasting, regardless of race, but also has been an abidingly positive role model for countless young black Britons growing up in a society where

skin color still matters. He was born in Trinidad and came to Britain in 1969 to work for the British Broadcasting Corporation (BBC) World Service, joining ITN a few years later as its first black reporter. McDonald has quietly got on with doing his job, courting neither controversy nor fame but a settled life doing what he does best. Because of his extreme visibility as, still, one of a few black media professionals who are regularly on television, he has been criticized for not using his privileged position more overtly to combat racism and discrimination. However, as he argued in the *Ra-*

dio Times, although he is aware of "racial undercurrents in this country...I have been very lucky and found none at all."

His most important contribution to television is probably his exemplary professionalism as a black newscaster and journalist who manifests a positive role to younger generations, in counterpoint to many of the more stereotyped media portraits of black communities in Western societies. He also offers a professional image to those who know nothing of black people other than their vicarious experiences of television. As evidence to his illustrious career, he was awarded TRIC's "Newscaster of the Year" and, in 1993, Order of the British Empire. He was knighted in 1999. Although he will probably retire in 2005, Sir Trevor's enduring appeal among ITV's news watchers has enabled him to sign a new contract that once again makes him the face of ITN's revived *News at Ten* bulletin.

KAREN ROSS

Trevor Mcdonald. Born in San Fernando, Trinidad, August 16, 1939. Attended schools in Trinidad. Married: 1) Josephine (divorced); 2) Sabrina; children: Timothy, Jamie, and Joanne. Reporter, local radio, Trinidad, 1959; announcer, sports commentator, and assistant program manager; joined Trinidad Television, 1962; producer for the Caribbean Service and World Service in London, BBC, 1969; reporter, ITN, 1973–78; sports correspondent, ITN, 1978–80; diplomatic correspondent, ITN, 1980–82; diplomatic correspondent and newscaster, *Channel 4 News,* 1982–87; diplomatic editor, *Channel 4 News,* 1987–89; newscaster, ITN's *News at 5.40,* 1989–90; newscaster, ITN's *News at Ten* since 1990. Order of the British Empire, 1992; knighted 1999. Recipient: TRIC Newscaster of the Year, 1993.

Television (selected)

1982–89	*Channel 4 News*
1989–90	*News at 5.40*
1990–	*News at Ten*

Publications

Viv Richards—A Biography, 1984
Clive Lloyd—A Biography, 1985
Queen and Commonwealth, 1986
Fortunate Circumstances (autobiography), 1993

McGovern, Jimmy (1949–)

British Writer

As the creator of *Cracker,* the writer Jimmy McGovern made one of the most influential contributions to British television drama in the 1990s, fundamentally shifting the locus of the crime series from action and consequence toward psychology and motivation. Elsewhere, his work has encompassed a broad generic range while retaining a powerful and distinctive voice, exploring themes of guilt, loss, and working-class identity. Underlying these concerns is a disconcerting sense of moral ambiguity and a readiness to challenge an audience's liberal assumptions on such taboos as racism, sexism, and homophobia. McGovern uses television, he admits, as "a kind of confessional" (Butler, p. 22).

Born into a working-class Catholic family in Liverpool, the fifth of eight children, and educated at a Jesuit-run grammar school, McGovern moved through a succession of jobs before deciding in his early 20s to train as schoolteacher. His brief teaching career (at Quarry Bank Comprehensive, the school earlier attended by John Lennon) would later provide the basis for the serial *Hearts and Minds,* about an idealistic probationary teacher struggling to inspire his pupils while battling professional demoralization and cynicism. It was while teaching that he began to submit plays to local theaters and radio and, through this, met the producer Phil Redmond, who was setting up *Brookside,* the house soap opera for the new Channel 4. Over the next seven years, he wrote approximately 80 scripts for the series and, on leaving, had a small stock of stories that he had been unable to introduce but that he now began to develop. The idea for a story about a Catholic priest surfaced in his early single drama, *Traitors,* an account of the Gunpowder Plot of 1605 focusing on the dilemma of a priest who opposes the plan but, because he has heard of it through a confession, is powerless to act on his concerns. McGovern returned to this event in 2004 with *Gunpowder, Treason and Plot,* a sweeping historical account, backed by a large budget and a cast led by Robert Carlyle (whose early career is closely linked to McGovern's work) as King James I. The moral dilemma of *Traitors* was also at the center of *Priest,* originally written as a serial but produced by the British Broadcasting Corporation (BBC) as a single film and given a limited theatrical release in which an inner-city priest struggled with his own homosexuality and with the knowledge, again gleaned through confession, that one of his parishioners is being abused by her father.

A further story idea from *Brookside* was to produce one of the most compelling threads in McGovern's later work. In 1989, 94 soccer fans, supporters of the Liverpool Football Club, were crushed to death and a further 170 seriously injured on an overcrowded terrace at the Sheffield Wednesday ground at Hillsborough. For McGovern, the significance underlying this tragedy lay not only in the culpability of the police and the conduct of the subsequent enquiry but also in the contempt displayed toward the Liverpool crowd by the tabloid press and in particular the *Sun* newspaper. McGovern's storyline involving a commemorative burning of the *Sun* was ruled out of *Brookside,* but his anger over the event and his reflection on the class prejudices that it revealed would form the basis of one of the most powerful episodes of *Cracker,* in which a working-class young man began a campaign of murders to avenge the Hillsborough victims, transforming himself into the image of a shaven-headed delinquent as a response to the institutional stereotyping of his class. Having met some of the bereaved families during the making of this episode, McGovern went on to confront the impact of the event and its aftermath in the drama documentary *Hillsborough.* As well as exploring the political question of institutional responsibility (and contributing to the campaign for a public inquiry into the event), the play found its dramatic core in the lives of three families and in the emotional fallout of grief, pain, and self-reproach that follows sudden and violent bereavement.

Although McGovern claimed to have felt restricted by the overriding concern for factual accuracy in writing drama documentary, he twice returned to the form. *Dockers* was an account of a lengthy but largely unpublicized strike in 1995 by Liverpool dockworkers against deteriorating working conditions that had resulted in hundreds of men being fired and replaced. In concentrating on the effect of the political upheaval on family relationships and friendships, it drew much of its insight from McGovern's co-authorship with a writing workshop made up of men and women involved in

the original dispute. Sunday commemorated the 30th anniversary of the "Bloody Sunday" shooting of demonstrators in Northern Ireland in 1972. McGovern's deeply emotional account, told through the lives of a small group of young men and women and again highlighting themes of family, friendship, and loss, contrasted tellingly with the spare, documentary style of Paul Greengrass's *Bloody Sunday,* which was released in the same week.

The chain of grief and recrimination that follows a sudden death runs through *The Lakes.* As McGovern himself had once done, a young Liverpudlian, Danny, arrives to work in a seemingly peaceful rural community and, when the community is torn apart by the drowning of three young girls, becomes the scapegoat for the guilt and feuding that lurks beneath the surface. At one level, the serial opens up to examination a particular aspect of class conflict in British society; at another, it is concerned with one of McGovern's most personal themes, the guilt and emotional wreckage produced by addiction. He had written about drug addiction in the early play *Needle,* but in *The Lakes,* as in *Cracker,* the compulsion is gambling, a habit from which McGovern suffered in his early adulthood and which here feeds Danny's sense of implication in the guilt felt at the loss of the girls and threatens his redemptive relationship with a young woman from the community.

McGovern writes from the depths of his own emotional experience. In the character of Fitz from *Cracker,* the brilliant but deeply flawed forensic psychologist, he has created one of the most resonant figures of British television drama. Fitz's intellectual acuity and mordant wit, his obsessiveness, and his instinctive ability to winkle a confession out of his suspect are rooted not only in the ability to identify with the criminal mind but also in a knowledge of his own guilt as gambler, drinker, chauvinist, and liar. Yet there is a political dimension to this lapsed figure, embodied in the idea of what McGovern has described as "post-Hillsborough man" (Day-Lewis, p. 67), a haunting sense of intellectual cynicism born out of the erosion of moral certainty in Britain during the ideologically evacuated period of the 1980s.

JEREMY RIDGEMAN

*See also **Cracker; Hillsborough;** Redmond, Phil*

Jimmy McGovern. Born in Liverpool, England, 1949. Educated St. Francis Xavier Grammar School, Liverpool. Worked as laborer, bus conductor, and insurance clerk, then trained as schoolteacher; taught three years, Liverpool. Early plays written for local theater and BBC Radio, then six years as scriptwriter on soap opera *Brookside*. After three single dramas, had major success with crime series *Cracker*. Several other series and single dramas or films for television (some with theatrical release). British Academy of Film and Television Arts TV Award, Best Single Drama (1997), for *Hillsborough;* Edgar Allan Poe Award, Best TV Series (1995, 1997), for *Cracker;* Royal Television Society Television Award, Best Drama Serial (1994), for *Cracker,* and Writers' Award (1995) for *Hearts and Minds* and *Go Now;* Writers' Guild of Great Britain Award, Best TV Drama Series (1996), for *Cracker,* and Best TV Play or Film (1997), for *Hillsborough.*

Television Series

1983–89	*Brookside*
1990	*El C.I.D.,* "A Proper Copper," "Christmas Spirit," "Piece of Cake"
1993–95	*Cracker*
1995	*Hearts and Minds*
1997	*The Lakes*
1999	*The Lakes* (series 2)
2004	*Gunpowder, Treason and Plot*

Television Plays

1990	*Traitors*
1990	*Needle*
1991	*Gas and Candles*
1995	*Priest*
1995	*Go Now*
1996	*Hillsborough*
1999	*Dockers*
2002	*Liam*
2002	*Sunday*

Stage Plays

The Hunger, Taig, True Romance, City Echoes, Block Follies

Further Reading

Ansorge, Peter, *From Liverpool to Los Angeles: On Writing for Theatre, Film and Television,* London: Faber and Faber, 1997

Brundson, Charlotte, "Structures of Anxiety: Recent British Television Crime Fiction," in *British Television: A Reader,* Oxford: Oxford University Press, 2000

Butler, Robert, "The Man Who Raped Sheila Grant," *Independent on Sunday* (February 5, 1995)

Day-Lewis, Sean, *Talk of Drama: Views of the Television Dramatist Then and Now,* Luton: University of Luton Press/John Libbey Media, 1998

Jeffries, Stuart, "The Sinner Repents," *Guardian* (August 22, 1997)

Wood, David, "Jimmy Jewel," *Broadcast* (August 15, 1997)

McGrath, John (1935–)

British Writer, Director

John McGrath's career was marked by an absolute commitment to working-class politics in theater, film, and television. McGrath's theatrical career spans London's Royal Court and the Liverpool Everyman to his own 7:84 Theatre Company ("7% of the population own 84% of the wealth"), while his film credits extend from Russell's *Billion Dollar Brain* to rewrites on FOX's *Adventures of Robin Hood.* His TV career opened with Kenneth Tynan's formative arts program *Tempo,* while his 1963 Granada documentary *The Entertainers* won critical plaudits. With Troy Kennedy Martin and John Hopkins, McGrath shaped the British Broadcasting Corporation's (BBC's) *Z Cars* into the breakthrough cop drama of the 1960s, fired by moral uncertainty and Royal Court grittiness. McGrath hallmarked the series with a profound compassion for his protagonists, instituting a concern for real lives among the social problems that were already, however comfortably, addressed by earlier genre offerings. The use of 16-millimeter film allowed for actual locations, and the shift from received pronunciation to the vernacular of his native Merseyside opened the way, notably in Stratford Johns's performance as Inspector Barlow, for subsequent generations of tough cop stories. McGrath took the combination of entertainment formula and social concern that distinguished much of the best of the BBC's output in the 1960s to his work as producer and director for BBC 2 experimental dramas by, among others, *Johnny Speight, Edna O'Brien,* and his own adaptation, with Ken Russell, of *The Diary of a Nobody* in the style of a silent comedy. Continuing to work in theater, he eventually amassed over 40 scripts, one of which became a successful movie, *The Bofors Gun,* directed by Jack Gold, a chilling account of class war and military service.

Appalled by bureaucracy and mismanagement in the arts, he resigned from the 7:84 Theatre Company, which he had founded, in 1981. In 1984, he started Freeway Films, dedicated to producing programs and features for his adopted homeland in Scotland. Characteristically committed to social causes, to political entertainment, and to the immediacy of performance (whose demise, with the rise of videotape, he has not ceased to mourn), Freeway began to produce, largely for Channel 4, a series of programs, including *Poets and People,* in which leading poets read their work to audiences with whom they felt particular affinities in housing estates and clubs. *Sweetwater Memories,* based on McGrath's military service in Suez, opened a more personal vein in his writing, expanded on in the 1986 three-part series *Blood Red Roses,* coproduced with Lorimar and subsequently cut for theatrical release. *Roses* follows the life of Bessie MacGuigan from life in the rural hinterlands with her disabled father, through unsuccessful marriage to a Communist Party activist, to trades unionism among the women workers of East Kilbride.

The remarkable trilogy on Scottish history and English colonialism—*There Is a Happy Land, Border Warfare,* and *John Brown's Body*—is a record of the epic productions performed at Glasgow's Tramway Theatre. In 1992 McGrath provided an election broadcast for the Labour Party, some of whose themes are picked up in 1993's *The Long Roads,* a picaresque romance that anchors a dissection of contemporary mores in the reviving romance of an elderly couple visiting their children, scattered through Thatcher's Britain.

Despite major illness, McGrath completed the feature *Mairi Mhor* in 1994 and remained fiercely active in theater and film as well as television. Unlike some of his more famous theatrical contemporaries, he retained a commitment to regionalism (and to nationalism in the case of Scotland), turning to television as the most effective way of bringing the power of drama to the widest audience. McGrath died in January 2002.

SEAN CUBITT

See also ***Z Cars***

John Peter McGrath. Born in Birkenhead, Cheshire, England, June 1, 1935. Attended Alun Grammar School, Mold, Wales; St. John's College, Oxford (Open Exhibitioner), 1955–59, Dip. Ed. Served in British Army (national service), 1953–55. Married: Elizabeth MacLennan in 1962; two sons and one daughter. Worked on farm in Neston, Cheshire, 1951; play reader, Royal Court Theatre, London, and writer for the theater, 1958–61; writer and director for BBC Television, 1960–65; founder and artistic director, 7:84 Theatre Company, 1971–88; continued to write for stage, television, and films; director, Freeway Films, since 1983; Channel 4 Television, London, since 1989. Judith E. Wilson Fellow, Cambridge University, 1979.

Television Series

1961	*Bookstand* (also director)
1962	*Z Cars* (also director)
1963	*Tempo*
1964	*Diary of a Young Man* (with Troy Kennedy Martin)

Television Specials (selection)

1961	*The Compartment* (director)
1963	*The Fly Sham* (director)
1963	*The Wedding Dress* (director)
1964	*The Entertainers* (also director)
1965	*The Day of Ragnarok* (also director)
1966	*Diary of a Nobody* (with Ken Russell)
1972	*Bouncing Boy*
1977	*Once upon a Union*
1978	*Z Cars: The Final Episode* (director)
1979	*The Adventures of Frank* (also director)
1984	*Sweetwater Memories*
1986	*Blood Red Roses* (also director)
1987	*There Is a Happy Land*

Films

Billion Dollar Brain, 1967; *The Bofors Gun,* 1968; *The Virgin Soldiers* (with John Hopkins and Ian La Frenais), 1969; *The Reckoning,* 1970; *Blood Red Roses,* 1986 (director); *The Dressmaker,* 1989; *Carrington,* 1995 (producer).

Stage

A Man Has Two Fathers, 1958; *The Invasion* (with Barbara Cannings), 1958; *The Tent,* 1958; *Why the Chicken,* 1959; *Tell Me Tell Me,* 1960; *Take It,* 1960; *The Seagull,* 1961; *Basement in Bangkok,* 1963; *Events While Guarding the Bofors Gun,* 1966; *Bakke's Night of Fame,* 1968; *Comrade Jacob,* 1969; *Random Happenings in the Hebrides,*

1970; *Sharpeville Crackers,* 1970; *Unruly Elements,* 1971; *Trees in the Wind,* 1971; *Soft or a Girl,* 1971; *The Caucasian Chalk Circle,* 1972; *Prisoners of the War,* 1972; *Underneath,* 1972 (also director); *Sergeant Musgrave Dances On,* 1972; *Fish in the Sea,* 1972; *The Cheviot, the Stag, and the Black, Black Oil,* 1973 (also director); *The Game's a Bogey,* 1974 (also director); *Boom,* 1974 (also director); *Lay Off,* 1975 (also director); *Little Red Hen,* 1975 (also director); *Oranges and Lemons,* 1975 (also director); *Yobbo Nowt,* 1975 (also director); *The Rat Trap,* 1976 (also director); *Out of Our Heads,* 1976 (also director); *Trembling Giant,* 1977; *The Life and Times of Joe of England,* 1977 (also director); *Big Square Fields,* 1979; *Joe's Drum,* 1979 (also director); *Bitter Apples,* 1979; *If You Want to Know the Time,* 1979; *Swings and Roundabouts,* 1980 (also director); *Blood Red Roses,* 1980 (also director); *Nightclass,* 1981 (also director); *The Catch,* 1981; *Rejoice!,* 1982; *On the Pig's Back* (with David MacLennan), 1983; *The Women of the Dunes,* 1983; *Women in Power,* 1983; *Six Men of Dorset,* 1984; *The Baby and the Bathwater: The Imperial Policeman,* 1984; *The Albannach,* 1985; *Behold the Sun,* 1985; *All the Fun of the Fair* (with others), 1986; *Border Warfare,* 1989; *John Brown's Body,* 1990; *Watching for Dolphins,* 1991; *The Wicked Old Man,* 1992; *The Silver Darlings,* 1994.

Publications

Events While Guarding the Bofors Gun, 1966
Random Happenings in the Hebrides, 1972
Bakke's Night of Fame, 1973
The Game's a Bogey, 1975
Little Red Hen, 1977
Fish in the Sea, 1977
Yobbo Nowt, 1978
Joe's Drum, 1979
Two Plays for the Eighties, 1981
The Cheviot, the Stag, and the Black, Black Oil, 1981
A Good Night Out: Popular Theatre: Audience, Class and Form, 1981
The Bone Won't Break: On Theatre and Hope in Hard Times, 1990

Further Reading

Ansorge, Peter, *Disrupting the Spectacle,* London: Pitman, 1975
Bigsby, C.W.E., "The Politics of Anxiety," *Modern Drama* (December 1981)
Craig, Sandy, editor, *Dreams and Deconstructions,* Ambergate, Derbyshire, England: Amber Lane Press, 1980
Itzin, Catherine, *Stages in the Revolution,* London: Eyre Methuen, 1980

McKay, Jim (1921–)

U.S. Sportscaster

There are few commentators with accolades to match those of Jim McKay or whose career is marked by an equally impressive list of broadcasting "firsts." In 1947 McKay was the first on-air television broadcaster seen and heard on the airwaves of Baltimore, Maryland. Twenty-one years later, in 1968, McKay earned distinction as the first sports commentator honored with an Emmy Award. McKay built on his reputation of excellence and went on to receive a total of 13 Emmy Awards and further distinguished himself as the first and only broadcaster to win Emmy Awards for both sports and news broadcasting, as well as for writing.

McKay's first reporting job was with the *Baltimore Evening Sun.* In 1947 the *Sun*'s leadership invested in Baltimore's first TV station, WMAR-TV, and McKay was chosen as that station's first on-camera personality. McKay did everything but run WMAR-TV—functioning as the station's producer, director, writer, and news and sports reporter. His reputation as a hardworking and skillful journalist earned him an opportunity to host a New York City–based Columbia Broadcasting System (CBS) variety show, and McKay became a strong presence in the largest media market in the world. Although CBS gave McKay his broadcasting break, it was ABC Sports, under the leadership

Jim McKay.
Courtesy of Jim McKay

of Roone Arledge, that provided McKay the opportunity to flourish. During the 1950s, McKay covered events ranging from international golf and horse-racing events to college football. McKay and American Broadcasting Company (ABC) colleague Howard Cosell, gave ABC the most comprehensive sports programming available on television.

In fact, McKay's assignment as an Olympic commentator would make McKay one of the most recognizable sports personalities throughout the world. His most memorable Olympic Games were those at Munich, where his experience as a seasoned reporter was put to the test. While preparing to take a swim on his first day off at the games, McKay received word that gunshots were fired in the Olympic Village. He ran to the ABC studio, threw clothes on over his swimsuit, and for the next 16 hours delivered to the world award-winning coverage of the Black September terrorists' attack on Israeli athletes in Munich's Olympic Village.

McKay received two Emmy Awards for his work during the 1972 games, one for his coverage of the games and the other for his reporting on the terrorism. He was also the 1972 recipient of the George Polk Memorial Award, given annually to the one journalist whose work represents the most significant and finest reporting of the year. The Munich coverage was also recognized with his receipt of the Officer's Cross Order of Merit, bestowed by the former West German Federal Republic.

Although ABC lost the Olympics contract following the 1988 games, the National Broadcasting Company (NBC) invited McKay to cross network lines and join its 2002 Olympic coverage as a special correspondent. This historic crossover marked McKay's 12th time to report on the Olympic Games. It is no wonder why McKay is known as "Mr. Olympics" throughout the television industry.

McKay is perhaps best known for his role as host for *ABC's Wide World of Sports,* which began with McKay as its host in 1961. Now, some 35 years later, *ABC's Wide World* is the most successful and longest-running sports program in the history of television. Through his work with *ABC's Wide World,* McKay became the first American television sports reporter to enter the People's Republic of China during China's policy of isolationism.

McKay's pioneering work in the field has not gone unrecognized. His multiple Emmy Awards are a tribute not only to his excellence but also to his versatility. In fact, among his most impressive Emmy is one from 1988, given for his opening commentary scripts of ABC Sports' coverage of the 1987 Indianapolis 500, the British Open, and the Kentucky Derby; a 1990 Award, another first, for Lifetime Achievement in Sports; and a 1992 Emmy for his sports special *Athletes and Addiction: It's Not a Game.*

In addition to his role on *Wide World,* McKay anchors most major horse-racing events, such as the Kentucky Derby, the Preakness Stakes, and the Belmont Stakes. In 1987, McKay was chosen as a member of the Jockey Club, horse racing's governing body. McKay and his wife, Margaret, are steadfast supporters of Maryland's horse-racing industry and culture. He is founder of the Maryland Million, a million-dollar horse-racing spectacular for Maryland thoroughbreds. They are also part owners of the Baltimore Orioles baseball team.

JOHN TEDESCO

***See also* Arledge, Roone; Sports on Television; Sportscaster**

Jim McKay. Born James Kenneth McManus in Philadelphia, Pennsylvania, U.S.A., September 24, 1921. Educated at Loyola College, Baltimore, Maryland, B.A. 1943. Married: Margaret Dempsey, 1948; children: Mary Edwina and Sean Joseph. Served in U.S. Navy, 1943–46. Reporter, *Baltimore Evening Sun,* 1946–47; writer-producer-director, Baltimore Sunpapers' WMAR-TV, 1947–50; variety show host, sports commentator, CBS-TV, 1950–61; host, *ABC*

Wide World of Sports, 1961; television commentator, all Olympiads, 1960–88; founder and chair, Maryland Million horse-racing program, from 1986. H.H.D., Loyala College, 1981. Recipient: 13 Emmy Awards; George Polk Memorial Award, 1973; Federal Republic of Germany Officer's Cross Order of Merit, 1974; Olympic Medal, Austria, 1977; Thoroughbred Breeders of Kentucky Engelhard Award, 1978, 1990; Maryland Racing Writers Humphrey S. Finney Award, 1985; named to Sportscasters Hall of Fame, 1987; National Turf Writers Award, 1987; Peabody Award, 1989; U.S. Olympic Hall of Fame, 1989; Television Academy Hall of Fame, 1995; Medal of Olympic Order, the highest award of the International Olympic Committee, 1998.

Television Series

1950	*The Real McKay*
1955	*Make the Connection* (moderator)
1957–60	*The Verdict Is Yours* (actor)
1958–59	*This Is New York*
1961–	*ABC's Wide World of Sports*

Television Special

1992	*Athletes and Addiction: It's Not a Game*

Publications

My Wide World, 1973
The Real McKay, 1998

Further Reading

Considine, T., *The Language of Sport,* New York: World Almanac Publications, 1982
Gunther, Marc, *The House That Roone Built: The Inside Story of ABC News,* Boston: Little, Brown, 1994
Spence, Jim, *Up Close and Personal: The Inside Story of Network Television Sports,* New York: Atheneum, 1988
Sugar, Bert Randolph, *"The Thrill of Victory": The Inside Story of ABC Sports,* New York: Hawthorn, 1978

McKern, Leo (1920–2002)

Australian Actor

Trained and critically acclaimed in theater, a successful character actor in movies, Australian performer Leo McKern made his most indelible mark in television. In the mind of many audiences, he became irrevocably intertwined with the title character of *Rumpole of the Bailey,* the irascible British barrister created by author John Mortimer. Starring as the wily, overweight, jaded but dedicated defense attorney for seven seasons, McKern brought an intelligent, acerbic style to the character that was applauded by critics, audiences, and creator Mortimer. The actor's performance thus ascribed qualities to the character just as the character was inscribed on McKern's acting persona. More than once McKern vowed he would not return to the series because of the inevitable typecasting. Yet he was always persuaded otherwise by Mortimer, who himself vowed that no one but McKern would play the role of Horace Rumpole.

The program, which began in 1978 in the United Kingdom and was soon exported to the United States via the Public Broadcasting Service's (PBS's) *Mystery!* series, featured McKern as an attorney who profoundly believed in a presumption of innocence, the validity of the jury system, and the importance of a thorough defense. It was a position unabashedly in support of civil liberties. In the course of each show, Rumpole typically dissected the stodgy and inefficient machinations of fellow barristers, judges, and the legal system in Britain. His resourcefulness and unorthodoxy matched that of the title character in U.S. television's *Perry Mason,* but with his askew bow tie and white wig, his sidelong looks and interior monologues, Rumpole was more colorful and complicated.

As the program was shown around the world through 1996, McKern could not escape what he called the "insatiable monster" of television, which blotted out memories of earlier performances. However, that did not stop the Australian periodical *The Bulletin* from naming McKern one of Australia's top 55 "human assets" in 1990. And, in fact, television did offer McKern another distinctive, if more transitory, role much earlier than Rumpole. In *The Prisoner,* a British drama aired in the United Kingdom and the United States in the late 1960s, McKern was one of the first authority figures to repress the series' hero.

Leo McKern.
Courtesy of Leo McKern

The Prisoner, still a cult classic dissected on many websites and Internet chat groups, was created by the then enormously popular actor Patrick McGoohan and was intended as an indictment of authoritarian subjugation of the individual. In the title role, McGoohan was kept prisoner in a mysterious village by the state, represented most forcefully by the person in charge of the village, who was called Number 2. Engaging in a battle of wills and wits with Number 6 (McGoohan), Number 2 typically died at episode's end, to be replaced by a new Number 2 in the next show. McKern played Number 2 in the series' second program, "The Chimes of Big Ben," and helped set the tone of serious banter and political conflict. His character, killed at the end of the episode, was resurrected the next season at the end of the series in two episodes, "Once upon a Time" and "Fallout," to demonstrate a change of position in favor of the hero and opposed to the state. Not completely unlike Rumpole, McKern's Number 2 was a system insider who understood principles better than the rest of the establishment (if only belatedly).

With its use of fantastic technology to keep Number 6 from escaping, *The Prisoner* was ostensibly a science fiction program. The science fiction motif also in-

formed a TV guest appearance McKern made some years later in the U.S. program *Space: 1999,* which aired in 1975. In that episode, "The Infernal Machine," McKern was again part of a larger entity, this time not the "state" but a living spacecraft. As the companion of "Gwent," McKern mediated with human beings (notably Martin Landau and Barbara Bain, recent *Mission: Impossible* veterans) on a lunar station. His character was slightly cynical, critical, bantering, and attached to the entity he served, like the later Rumpole. Among McKern's decades of television experience, these roles were notable on three levels: their connection to general recurring themes; their development of a recognizable, familiar character function; and their demonstration of the actor's particular talents. For instance, the "Companion" episode on *Space 1999* evoked both the "Companion" episode on the original 1967 *Star Trek,* in which Glenn Corbet's character was kept alive by fusion with an alien presence, and the Trill character of "a symbiotic fusion of two species" on *Star Trek: Deep Space Nine.* In addition, the threatening power of the state and of technology of *The Prisoner* prefigured a reliable theme of the popular 1990s program *The X-Files.*

The Rumpole role is the one most connected with a number of recurring character functions on television. The deep commitment covered by a veneer of cynicism is a staple of police officers and other investigators throughout U.S. television history. The belief in the civil liberties of the individual is the core of lawyer programs such as *Perry Mason* of the 1960s and *Matlock* of the 1990s. The rumpled insider, "only by virtue of superior competence," was the essence of *Columbo* of the 1970s. The British Rumpole is a rather more complex example of a U.S. television perennial.

However well written it might be, the Rumpole role would not have the cachet it has among fans if not for the actor. Critics cited McKern's intelligence, energy, and remarkably flexible baritone as the heart of the character. McKern's varied, multimedia career—from movies such as the lightweight Beatles' *Help!* to the epic *Lawrence of Arabia* to plays such as *Othello*—may not be remembered by most fans, but the depth of talent required for such diversity is critically acknowledged in reviews of *Rumpole of the Bailey.*

IVY GLENNON

See also **Rumpole of the Bailey**

Leo McKern. Born Reginald McKern in Sydney, Australia, March 16, 1920. Attended Sydney Technical High School. Married: Joan Alice Southa (Jane Holland), 1946; children: Abigail and Harriet. Engineering apprentice, 1935–37; commercial artist, 1937–40; served in Australian Army Engineering Corps,

1940–42; debut as actor, 1944; settled in the United Kingdom, 1946; participated in tour of Germany, 1947; appeared at Old Vic Theatre, London, 1949–52 and 1962–63, at the Shakespeare Memorial Theatre, Stratford-upon-Avon, 1952–54, and at the New Nottingham Playhouse, 1963–64; has appeared in numerous films and television productions, including the popular *Rumpole of the Bailey* series, 1978–92. Officer of the Order of Australia, 1983. Died in Bath, England, July 23, 2002.

Television Series

1955	*The Adventures of Robin Hood* (two episodes)
1967–68	*The Prisoner* (three episodes)
1975	*Space: 1999* (one episode)
1978–92	*Rumpole of the Bailey*
1983	*Reilly: Ace of Spies*

Made-for-Television Movies

1967	*Alice in Wonderland*
1979	*The House on Garibaldi Street*
1980	*Rumpole's Return*
1985	*Murder with Mirrors*
1992	*The Last Romantics*

Television Specials (selected)

1965	*The Tea Party*
1968	*On the Eve of Publication*
1983	*King Lear*
1985	*Monsignor Quixote*

1988	*The Master Builder*
1993	*A Foreign Field*

Films (selected)

All for Mary, 1955; *X—the Unknown,* 1956; *Time Without Pity,* 1957; *The Mouse That Roared,* 1959; *Mr. Topaze,* 1961; *The Day the Earth Caught Fire,* 1962; *Lawrence of Arabia,* 1962; *Hot Enough for June,* 1963; *A Jolly Bad Fellow,* 1964; *King and Country,* 1964; *The Amorous Adventures of Moll Flanders,* 1965; *Help!,* 1965; *A Man for All Seasons,* 1966; *Nobody Runs Forever,* 1968; *Decline and Fall...of a Birdwatcher!,* 1968; *Ryan's Daughter,* 1971; *Massacre in Rome,* 1973; *The Adventure of Sherlock Holmes' Smarter Brother,* 1976; *The Omen,* 1976; *Candleshoe,* 1977; *Damien: Omen II,* 1978; *The Blue Lagoon,* 1980; *The French Lieutenant's Woman,* 1983; *Ladyhawke,* 1984; *The Chain,* 1985; *Travelling North,* 1986; *On Our Selection,* 1995; *Molokai: The Story of Father Damien,* 1999.

Stage (selected)

Toad of Toad Hall, 1954; *Queen of the Rebels,* 1955; *Cat on a Hot Tin Roof,* 1958; *Brouhaha,* 1958; *Rollo,* 1959; *A Man for All Seasons,* 1960; *The Thwarting of Baron Bolligrew,* 1965; *Volpone,* 1967; *The Wolf,* 1973; *The Housekeeper,* 1982; *Number One,* 1984; *Boswell for the Defence,* 1989, 1991; *Hobson's Choice,* 1995.

Publication

Just Resting, 1983

McLuhan, Marshall (1911–1980)

Canadian Media Theorist

Marshall McLuhan was perhaps one of the best-known media theorists and critics of this era. A literary scholar from Canada, McLuhan became entrenched in American popular culture when he decided that this was the only way to understand his students at the University of Wisconsin. Until the publication of his best-known and most popular works, *The Gutenberg Galaxy: The Making of Typographic Man* (1962) and *Understanding Media: The Extensions of Man* (1964), McLuhan led a very ordinary academic life. His polemic prose (a style frequently compared to that of James Joyce) irritated many and inspired some. However cryptic, McLuhan's outspoken and often outrageous philosophies of the "electric media" roused a popular discourse about the mass media, society, and culture. The pop culture motto "The medium is the message (and the massage)" and the term "global village" are pieces of what is known affectionately (and otherwise) as "McLuhanism."

Marshall McLuhan.
Photo courtesy of Nelson/Marshall McLuhan Center on Global Communications

McLuhan was a technological determinist who credited the electronic media with the ability to exact profound social, cultural, and political influences. Instead of offering a thoughtful discourse regarding the positive or negative consequences of electric media, McLuhan preferred instead to pontificate about its inevitable impact, which was neither good nor bad but simply was. McLuhan was primarily concerned that people acknowledge and prepare for the technological transformation. He argued that people subscribe to a "rear-view mirror" understanding of their environment, a mode of thinking in which they do not foresee the arrival of a new social milieu until it is already in place. In McLuhan's view, instead of "looking ahead," society has tended to cling to the past. He wrote, "We are always one step behind in our view of the world," and we do not recognize the technology that is responsible for the shift.

McLuhan first began to grapple with the relationship between technology and culture in *The Mechanical Bride: Folklore of Industrial Man* (1951). However, he did not elaborate on their historical origins until the publication of *The Gutenberg Galaxy,* which traces the social evolution of modern humanity

from tribal society. In his theory, this process encompasses four stages.

McLuhan defines tribal society as dependent on the harmonious balance of all senses. Tribal society was an oral culture; members used speech (an emotionally laden medium) to communicate. As a result, nonliterate societies were passionate, involved, interdependent, and unified. The "acoustic space" that enveloped tribal society was eroded by the invention of the phonetic alphabet. McLuhan credits phonetic literacy for the dissolution of tribal society and the creation of "Western Man."

Literacy inspired a more detached, linear perspective; the eye replaced the ear as the dominant sensory organ. Western Man evolved into "Gutenberg Man" with the arrival of the printing press in the 16th century. According to McLuhan, the printing press was responsible for such phenomena as the industrial revolution, nationalism, and perspectivity in art. The printing press eventually informed a "Mechanical Culture."

The linearity and individualization characteristic of Mechanical Culture has been usurped by electric media. This process began with the invention of the telegraph. McLuhan considers the electric media as extensions of the entire nervous system. Television is perhaps the most significant of the electric media because of its ability to invoke multiple senses. Television, as well as future technologies, have the ability to "retribalize," that is, to re-create the sensory unification characteristic of tribal society.

In perhaps his most popular work, *Understanding Media: The Extensions of Man,* McLuhan elaborates on the sensory manipulation of the electric media. Like most of his writing, *Understanding Media* has been criticized for its indigestible content and often paradoxical ideas. Ironically, it was this work that first captured the minds of the American public and triggered McLuhan's metamorphosis from literary scholar into pop culture guru.

Understanding Media contains the quintessential McLuhanism, "The medium is the message." McLuhan explains that the content of all electric media is insignificant; it is instead the medium itself that has the greatest impact on the sociocultural environment. This perspective has been contested by representatives of various schools in mass communication—in particular, empirical researchers have rejected McLuhan's grand theorizing, whereas critical cultural theorists have argued that McLuhan undermines their agenda by discounting the power relationships inherent in and perpetuated by media content.

However, many judge McLuhan's thesis to have certain merit. His focus on the "televisual experience" and the role of the medium within contemporary life has inspired much popular culture research. Within this same framework, some theorists ponder the impact of newer technologies, such as the Internet and high-definition television.

In *Understanding Media,* McLuhan proposes a controversial frame for judging media: "hot" and "cool." These categorizations are puzzling, and contemporary technology may render them obsolete. In simplest terms, "hot" is exclusive, and "cool" is inclusive. Hot media are highly defined; there is little information to be filled in by the user. Radio is a hot medium; it requires minimal participation. Cool media, by contrast, are less defined and thus highly participatory because the user must "fill in the blanks." Television is the ultimate "cool" medium because it is highly participatory. This categorization is extremely problematic to those who consider television viewing a passive activity.

To illustrate this concept, McLuhan analyzed the Kennedy–Nixon debates of 1960. Those who watched the debates on television typically judged Kennedy the winner; according to McLuhan, this televisual victory was due to the fact that Kennedy exuded an objective, disinterested, "cool" persona. However, Nixon, better suited for the "hot" medium of radio, was considered victorious by those who had listened to the debates on radio.

The McLuhanism with the loudest echo in contemporary popular culture is the concept of the "global village." It is a metaphor most invoked by the telecommunications industry to suggest the ability of new technologies to link the world electronically. McLuhan's once-outrageous vision of a postliterate society, one in which global consciousness was shaped by technology instead of verbalization, has been partially realized by the Internet. For McLuhan, television begins the process of retribalization through its ability to transcend time and space, enabling the person in New York, for example, to "experience" a foreign culture across the globe.

McLuhan contemplated the profound impact of electronic technology on society. Loved or loathed, his opinions penetrated academic, popular, and corporate spheres. Within the context of popular culture theorizing, McLuhan's commentaries will remain part of history. Mass communication researchers continue to explore the relationship between media and society. In doing so, they delineate the significance of television in global culture and amplify the ideas McLuhan contributed to this discourse.

SHARON ZECHOWSKI

Marshall McLuhan. Born Herbert Marshall McLuhan in Edmonton, Alberta, Canada, July 21, 1911. Educated at University of Manitoba, B.A. 1933, M.A. 1934; Trinity Hall, Cambridge, B.A. 1936, M.A. 1939, Ph.D. 1942. Married: Corinne Keller Lewis, 1939; children: Eric, Mary Colton, Teresa, Stephanie, Elizabeth O'Sullivan, Michael. Instructor, University of Wisconsin, Madison, 1936–37; instructor of English, St. Louis University, Missouri, 1937–44; associate professor of English, Assumption College, Windsor, Ontario, 1944–46; instructor, 1946–52, professor of English, St. Michael's College, University of Toronto, 1952–79; chair, Ford Foundation seminar on culture and communications, 1953–60; cofounder, *Explorations* magazine, 1954, co-editor, 1954–59, editor, 1964–79; director, media studies for U.S. Office of Education and the National Association of Education Broadcasters, 1959–60; director, Toronto University's McLuhan Centre for Culture and Technology, 1963–66, 1969–79; editor, *Patterns of Literary Criticism* series, 1965–69; consultant, Johnson, McCormick and Johnson, public relations, Toronto, 1966–80; Albert Schweitzer Professor in the Humanities, Fordham University, Bronx, New York, 1967–68; consultant, Responsive Environments Corporation, New York, 1968–80; consultant, Vatican Pontifical Commission for Social Communications, 1973; Eugene McDermott Professor, University of Dallas, Texas, 1975; Pound Lecturer, 1978; fellow, Royal Society of Canada, 1964. D.Litt.: University of Windsor, 1965; Assumption University, 1966; University of Manitoba, 1967; Simon Fraser University, 1967; Grinnell College, 1967; St. John Fisher College, 1969; University of Western Ontario, 1971; University of Toronto, 1977; LL.D.: University of Alberta, 1971; University of Toronto, 1977. Recipient: Canadian Governor-General's Prize, 1963; Niagara University Award in culture and communications, 1967; Young German Artists Carl Einstein Prize, West Germany, 1967; Companion, Order of Canada, 1970; President's Award, Institute of Public Relations, Great Britain, 1970; Assumption University Christian Culture Award, 1971; University of Detroit President's Cabinet Award, 1972. Died in Toronto, Ontario, Canada, December 31, 1980.

Films

This Is Marshall McLuhan, 1968; *Annie Hall* (cameo as himself), 1977.

Recording

The Medium Is the Massage, 1967.

Publications

The Mechanical Bride: Folklore of Industrial Man, 1951

Selected Poetry of Tennyson (editor), 1956

Explorations in Communications (editor with Edmund Carpenter), 1960

The Gutenberg Galaxy: The Making of Typographic Man, 1962

Understanding Media: The Extensions of Man, 1964

Voices of Literature, vols. 1–4 (editor with R.J. Schoeck), 1964–70

The Medium Is the Massage: An Inventory of Effects, with Quentin Fiore, 1967

Through the Vanishing Point: Space in Poetry and Painting, with Harley Parker, 1968

War and Peace in the Global Village: An Inventory of Some of the Current Spastic Situations That Could Be Eliminated by More Feedforward, with Quentin Fiore, 1968

Counterblast, 1969

The Interior Landscape: Selected Literary Criticism of Marshall McLuhan, 1943–1962, edited by E. McNamara, 1969

Culture Is Our Business, 1970

From Cliché to Archetype, with Wilfred Watson, 1970

Take Today: The Executive as Dropout, with Barrington Nevitt, 1972

The City as Classroom, with Eric McLuhan and Kathy Hutchon, 1977

Letters of Marshall McLuhan (edited by Matie Molinaro et al.), 1987

Media Research: Technology, Art, Communication (edited by Michael A. Moos), 1997

Further Reading

Benedetti, Paul, and Nancy DeHart, editors, *Forward Through the Rearview Mirror: Reflections on and by Marshall McLuhan,* Scarborough, Ontario: Prentice Hall Canada, 1996; Cambridge, Massachusetts: MIT Press, 1997

Crosby, Harry H., and George R. Bond, editors, *The McLuhan Explosion: A Casebook on Marshall McLuhan and Understanding Media,* New York: American Book Company, 1968

Curtis, James M., *Culture As Polyphony: An Essay on the Nature of Paradigms,* Columbia: University of Missouri Press, 1978

Day, Barry, *The Message of Marshall McLuhan,* London: Lintas, 1967

Duffy, Dennis, *Marshall McLuhan,* Toronto: McClelland and Stewart, 1969

Finkelstein, Sidney Walter, *Sense and Nonsense of McLuhan,* New York: International Publishers, 1968

Genosko, Gary, *McLuhan and Baudrillard: The Masters of Implosion,* London and New York: Routledge, 1999

Gordon, W. Terrence, *Marshall McLuhan: Escape into Understanding: A Biography,* New York: Basic Books, 1997

Gordon, W. Terrence, *McLuhan for Beginners,* London and New York: Writers and Readers, 1997

Kroker, Arthur, *Technology and the Canadian Mind: Innis/McLuhan/Grant,* New York: St. Martin's Press, 1985

Levinson, Paul, *Digital McLuhan: A Guide to the Information Millennium,* New York: Routledge, 1999

Marchand, P., *Marshall McLuhan: The Medium and the Messenger,* New York: Ticknor and Fields, 1989

Miller, Jonathan, *Marshall McLuhan,* London: Fontana, 1971; New York: Viking, 1971

Rosenthal, Raymond, editor, *McLuhan: Pro and Con,* Funk and Wagnalls, 1968

Sanderson, F., and F. Macdonald, *Marshall McLuhan: The Man and His Message,* Golden, Colorado: Fulcrum, 1989

Stearns, Gerald Emanuel, editor, *McLuhan: Hot and Cool,* New York: Dial Press, 1967; London: Penguin, 1968

Theall, Donald F., *The Medium Is the Rear View Mirror: Understanding McLuhan,* Montreal: McGill-Queens University Press, 1971

McQueen, Trina (1943–)

Canadian Broadcast Journalist, News Executive

In her 27 years with the Canadian Broadcasting Corporation (CBC), Trina McQueen's singularly successful career has constituted a series of "firsts" for women. In 1991 she became vice president of English television news and current affairs and of CBC Newsworld (the all-news cable channel), the first and only woman to hold such a high-ranking position at the Canadian network.

The following year, McQueen was made vice president of regional broadcasting operations, which included equity in portrayals across all broadcast services and foreign bureaus. This move was widely regarded as a demotion as well as a backward step for the future of high-level female broadcast executives. The network, however, denied that charge, and McQueen remained uncomplaining even after her departure. The only other female vice president, however, Donna Logan, who was head of English-language CBC Radio, was also demoted, leaving the executive suite all male. McQueen had been opposed to the changes being initiated by the head office to move the successful flagship nightly 10:00 news *The National* to the all-news cable channel Newsworld. The switch also involved canceling the acclaimed in-depth nightly documentary news series that followed, *The Journal,* and launching *Prime Time News* at 9:00 P.M. CBC brass brought in news head Tim Kotcheff from rival network CTV to implement the changes, which proved to be disastrous.

McQueen's quiet, soft-spoken, and tactful negotiating manner combines with a toughness attested to by longtime colleagues. She has been called "something of a Patton in Pollyanna's clothing." It was reported that McQueen lost a power struggle for the position of senior vice president of TV services to fast-rising wunderkind Ivan Fecan in a management arrangement in which their duties, previously carried out by vice president Denis Harvey, were split into two vice president jobs. McQueen oversaw a thousand people and more than 200 hours of information programming per week in her position.

McQueen began in journalism at the entry level, parlaying student jobs on newspapers to a stint with the *Journal* (Ottawa). From there, she became the first female reporter for CTV's local Toronto station, CFTO, and cohost for CTV's current affairs magazine show, *W5.* When CTV execs indicated that a woman would not be hired as a national reporter, McQueen quit and joined the public network, CBC, in 1967. There she became the first female on-camera reporter for *The National* news. After nine years as reporter, producer, and assignment editor, she became the first female executive producer of *The National* in 1976 when she was 33.

Having grown up watching *The National* in Belleville, Ontario, she has said that it was a glorious dream job for her. She presided over a virtual revolution of the news, replacing the old guard with the then-new faces of Hike Duffy, Peter Mansbridge, and Knowlton Nash. She guided the new management through the 1980 Quebec referendum and two federal elections in addition to daily news stories. She also stood up to the chauvinists' stereotypes of women in news and won respect and success.

McQueen returned to news, after nine years in CBC administration, as director of news and current affairs. It was a time of huge budget cuts that decimated jobs,

regional CBC stations, and employee morale. Then as vice president, she also became manager of the CBC broadcast center, the new downtown facility that gathered together the disparate TV and radio production entities that had inhabited various spaces throughout Toronto. In addition, she was head of English network finances and human resources.

In 1993, when the federal government handed down more budget cuts for CBC, as it had every year since 1985, McQueen decamped for a job in the private sector. She became vice president and general manager of the newly created Discovery Channel, Canada, largely owned by Labatt Communications, Inc., the entertainment arm of the giant beer conglomerate, which produces shows on science, technology, nature, the environment. and world cultures. In 1999, however, McQueen returned to CTV in the role of vice president. She was eventually promoted to president and then chief operating officer. In this capacity, she was responsible for overseeing the CTV network of 27 local stations, seven cable channels, and three production companies. McQueen retired in 2002, although she continues to work and perform volunteer activities through her company, Hutton-Belleville Inc. She is chair of the board of the Governor-General's Performing Arts Awards. McQueen is also a professor at Carleton University. In 2003, McQueen was chosen to lead the International Jury at the 24th Banff Television Festival.

JANICE KAYE

See also **National/The Journal**

Trina McQueen. Born Catherine Janitch in Canada, 1943. Educated at Carleton University, Ottawa, Ontario, Canada. Summer relief reporter for CBC National News, 1967; reporter, *Journal,* Ottawa; reporter, CFTO-CTV, Toronto; cohost, *W5* magazine show, CTV; reporter, producer, and editor, *The National,* from 1967, and executive producer, 1976; vice president, news and current affairs and Newsworld cable news service, CBC, 1991, and vice president of regional broadcasting, 1992; general manager and vice president, Discovery Channel, 1993. Named vice president, then president and chief operating officer, of CTV, 1999. Retired in 2002. Member: Canadian Broadcasters Hall of Fame and Canadian News Hall of Fame. Recipient of Lifetime Achievement Awards from the Canadian Journalism Foundation and the Academy of Canadian Cinema and Television.

Media Conglomerates

The conglomeration of the media has greatly affected the structure of the television industry worldwide, but especially in the United States. The U.S. television industry is now largely contained within large, diversified, transnational media conglomerates that own interests ranging from Internet services, outdoor advertising, magazines, and book publishing to video games, theme parks, film, and music as well as television interests such as programming, broadcast stations, broadcast networks, cable networks, and cable operators. In the past, from the late 1950s until the early 1980s, three broadcast networks dominated U.S. television (the National Broadcasting Company [NBC], the Columbia Broadcasting System [CBS], and the American Broadcasting Company [ABC]). In the 2000s, however, there are four major broadcast networks in the United States, including FOX, three minor broadcast networks (The WB, United Paramount Network [UPN], and PAX), and over 100 cable and satellite networks (or programming services). However, most of these networks are subsidiaries of a few large media conglomerates. NBC is a subsidiary of General Electric, CBS is owned by Viacom, the Walt Disney Company owns ABC, and FOX is part of the News Corporation. These conglomerates also own cable and/or satellite television programming services. For example, Disney also owns the Entertainment and Sports Network (ESPN) and Disney as well as interests in the Lifetime, E!, A&E, and the History Channel cable networks; Viacom owns cable programmers Music Television (MTV), Video Hits 1 (VH1), The Nashville Network (TNN), Nickelodeon, and Showtime; and News Corporation holdings include FX, FOX News, and FOX Sports as well as satellite services British Sky Broadcasting (BskyB) and StarTV. Thus, although programming outlets have greatly diversified, ownership has consolidated, creating a new form of postnetwork-era television oligopoly. Instead of three major networks gathering a 90 percent share of prime-time audiences as in the network era, today a handful of media conglomerates utilize their affiliated broadcast and cable programming services to aggregate over 80 percent of prime-time audiences. How and why have media conglomerates become so dominant in the television and entertainment industries? What follows is a brief overview of the broad trends that have contributed to conglomeration, some specific

rationales for media and entertainment conglomeration, and summary descriptions of key major media conglomerates.

Beginning in the mid-1980s, a spate of major mergers have reshaped the structure of the media and entertainment industries: News Corporation acquired 20th Century-Fox (1985); Sony bought CBS Records (1987) and Columbia Pictures (1989); Time merged with Warner (1989); Universal was acquired first by Matsushita (1990), then by Seagram (1996), then by Vivendi (2000), then by General Electric (2003); Viacom acquired Paramount (1994); Westinghouse bought CBS (1995), which was later acquired by Viacom (2000); Disney bought CapCities/ABC (1995); and America Online (AOL) merged with Time Warner (2001). Three broad trends contributed to this surge of media conglomeration. First, increasing economic globalization expanded foreign markets for entertainment products as well as attracting capital investment in U.S. entertainment firms from investors in Japan, Australia, Canada, France, and Germany. Second, in order to stimulate increased investment and technological innovation within the media and communications industries, policymakers in the United States and Europe have dismantled many of the regulatory standards that had governed the media industries for the previous half century. The Telecommunications Act of 1996, for example, relaxed many rules concerning cross-ownership of media and dropped limits on single-firm ownership of multiple media outlets (ownership caps). Policymakers expected that the subsequent wave of consolidations and mergers among telephony, cable, broadcasting, and film companies would stimulate increased investment in new technologies and lower prices for consumers. Underlying these policy changes were expectations concerning the direction and rate of technological change, the third broad trend affecting conglomeration. New delivery technologies, including VCRs, cable, satellite, and the networking potential of the Internet, have opened new markets for entertainment products. Digitization, the conversion of data into computer code, has expanded as computing power has increased and computing costs have decreased. However, digitization is a two-edged sword for the entertainment industries. Digitization provides cost efficiencies because copying and transferring data is easier and more accurate, yet it is precisely that ease and accuracy that threatens to undermine the entertainment industries' control over intellectual property rights. Consequently, while technological change promises to open new markets for entertainment, it also threatens already existing markets. Thus, firms that own interests in both "new" and "old" media technologies expect to reap the advantages of diversification through conglomeration or, at the least, survive the forthcoming upheavals wrought by technological change.

However, in addition to the overall economic, political, and technological factors affecting the media's industrial structure, the entertainment industry is itself a risky business, subject to high product failure rates and shifting audience tastes. Success rates in the entertainment industries are extremely low: only about 20 to 30 percent of films, roughly 10 percent of music recordings, and approximately 5 percent of television pilots return a net profit. The high profit rates of a small number of entertainment products (the "hits") must subsidize the costs incurred in the production of the majority of unprofitable entertainment products. Thus, entertainment firms engage in a number of risk management strategies to survive these long odds, including overproduction and high marketing expenditures. A key risk management strategy is for a firm to grow through mergers and acquisitions, the fastest way to gain market share and market power. Market power through mergers can increase a firm's ability to negotiate favorable terms with competitors, set prices, and reduce competition, all of which improve a firm's ability to weather the high product failure rates of entertainment.

Mergers may be characterized as either horizontal, vertical, or conglomerate. Horizontal integration is when a firm acquires or merges with firms in the same business, for example, when local television stations merge into a station group. Vertical integration occurs when a firm merges with its suppliers or buyers, or up and down the product chain of production, distribution, and exhibition. For example, in the 1960s, the networks (program distributors) vertically integrated upstream into program production (program suppliers) and downstream into program syndication (program resales), thus controlling programming at each stage of its product life. Conglomerate mergers occur when a firm acquires a company that is neither in the same business nor a direct supplier or buyer, as, for example, when the major newspaper publisher News Corporation acquired the 20th Century-Fox film studio. The horizontal, vertical, and conglomerate merger strategies are all intended to create greater efficiencies of scale and scope by consolidating overhead and administrative costs, cutting out intermediaries, and guaranteeing smoother production chains.

Some conglomerates may be characterized as loosely conglomerated because their subsidiaries are in unrelated fields. For example, General Electric, the conglomerate that owns NBC and the entity formerly known as Universal or Vivendi/Universal, also owns companies that make aircraft engines, medical systems, power plants, and plastics as well as financial services companies, none of which are directly involved in the television business. However, most media conglomerates are not loose but what Thomas Schatz calls "tightly diversified": they have a tight focus on media and entertainment yet are diversified across fields such as film, television, music, book publishing, theme parks, and online services as well as being vertically integrated into production, distribution, and exhibition. Tightly diversified conglomerates can cross-collateralize losses from one business with gains in another, cross-promote entertainment products across different media, and sell products on multiple distribution platforms (film, video, broadcast, and cable).

Most tightly diversified media conglomerates are formed with at least one of the three following rationales. One rationale is to create "content synergies," that is, to build entertainment "franchises" that can be repurposed into multiple products including films, television programs, videos, DVDs, books, comics, toys, video games, theme park rides, music soundtracks, and so on. The *Star Trek* franchise, for example, based on a television series, expanded to include additional television series (*Next Generation* and *Enterprise*), films, books, games, and merchandise. *Star Trek*'s conglomerate owner, Viacom, produces, distributes, and promotes these through its various holdings (Paramount, UPN, and Simon and Schuster). Other television programs converted into franchises include *Mission Impossible, The Flintstones,* and *The Brady Bunch,* which have been resold on home video, pay-per-view cable, premium cable, and broadcast television. Owning and controlling a variety of content producers and distributors enables a conglomerate to capture the majority of the revenues from these multiple product extensions.

A second major rationale for tight diversification is to ensure distribution for a production company or to ensure a supply of content for a distribution outlet. For example, after losing key scheduling slots for its children's programming on the FOX network, Disney ensured that its programming would continue to be distributed on network television by acquiring Cap-Cities/ABC. Likewise, Viacom acquired Paramount in part to guarantee a steady supply of films for its cable network Showtime and then launched the broadcast network UPN in 1995 to ensure a distribution outlet for its Paramount-produced program *Star Trek.* This type of vertical integration between film studios and television distributors cut across previously existing ownership boundaries between film and television companies.

A third major rationale for tight diversification is to secure content for new distribution technologies or to acquire software for hardware. For example, Sony acquired Columbia Pictures and CBS Records in part to gain control of films, programs, and music for distribution on the consumer electronics technologies it manufactures. In the early 1980s, Sony's Betamax home video technology had lost the market to the competing VHS technology in part because Hollywood film studios refused to license the rights to major films to Sony for use on Betamax video. Acquiring Columbia Pictures and CBS Records, now both renamed Sony, protects Sony's hardware products from failing solely because they lack the rights to film, television, and music content. Each of these rationales for conglomeration is intended to strengthen a firm's performance in high-risk environments; however, none can guarantee the ultimate outcome.

Time Warner

Time Warner, at the time of this writing the largest media conglomerate, was created in 2001 when the online services provider AOL parlayed its highly valued stock into a friendly takeover of the "old media" company Time Warner. Time Warner controls major television interests, including one of the largest U.S. cable operators, Time Warner Cable. Warner Bros. Television and its fellow subsidiaries produce programming shown on a variety of broadcast and cable networks, including *Friends, ER, Gilmore Girls, The West Wing, Everybody Loves Raymond, The Drew Carey Show, Six Feet Under,* and *Smallville.* Although Time Warner created the WB broadcast network in a joint venture with Tribune Broadcasting in order to gain a broadcast network foothold, it is more dominant in cable networks. Home Box Office (HBO), originally a Time company, pioneered programming distribution by satellite, becoming one of the first and most successful nationally distributed pay cable programmers. In 1995 Time Warner acquired the Turner networks (Turner Network Television, Turner Broadcasting System, Turner Classic Movies, and Cable News Network) to become the conglomerate dominant in both cable networks and cable systems. The Turner, Cable News Network (CNN), and HBO networks are also distributed in Asia and Europe. Time Warner's other cable networks include Cinemax and the Cartoon Network.

Time Warner is also dominant in film (Warner Bros. and New Line), music (Warner Music Group), and publishing (Time/Life). However, a key element in its conglomeration strategy was to meld Time Warner's cable operating systems (then second largest in the United States) with AOL's top brand name in online services. By aggregating the more than 100 million subscribers to AOL Time Warner's Internet services, cable systems, premium cable networks, and the *Time* magazine group (including *People, Sports Illustrated, In Style,* and *Entertainment Weekly*), the merger was expected to create a base for launching new entertainment technology services, such as video-on-demand, interactive television, and broadband Internet. However, by 2003, as Time Warner's stock price suffered severe declines, the merger was heavily criticized by investors for pursuing the aim of media convergence at the cost of its core businesses. In that year, "AOL" was dropped from the corporate name.

Viacom

CBS spun off Viacom in 1971 when the Federal Communications Commission (FCC) required the major networks to divest their vertically integrated program production and syndication subsidiaries. As Viacom expanded, acquiring cable networks MTV, Nickelodeon, and VH1 from Warner in the mid-1980s, it was then absorbed by Sumner Redstone's holding company, National Amusements, in 1987. Redstone led Viacom's battle for control over Paramount Communications, which succeeded, bringing Paramount Studios and Simon and Schuster publishers into the Viacom conglomerate. Paramount has produced numerous television programs, including every *Star Trek* series, *JAG, Frasier,* and *That's Life;* other subsidiaries, Viacom Productions and Spelling Productions, have produced *Sabrina, Charmed, 7th Heaven,* and *Beverly Hills 90210.* In 1995 Viacom launched the minor broadcast network UPN in part to guarantee broadcast exposure for its expensive *Star Trek* series. Viacom also controls premium cable networks Showtime and The Movie Channel and basic cable networks Black Entertainment Television, Comedy Central, and Spike as well as owning an interest in the Sundance Channel. However, despite these strengths in cable programming, Viacom divested its cable operating systems in 1995 because the maintenance and upgrading of cable systems were too capital intensive. Instead, in 2000, Viacom surprised observers by acquiring a major stake in the "old media" of broadcasting by buying its former parent company CBS and its subsidiaries, including Infinity Broadcasting (one of the largest radio station groups) and CBS Radio. With 34 owned-and-operated television stations, one major and one minor broadcast network, and major cable networks that are top rated in their demographic categories, Viacom is one of the most dominant conglomerates in the television industry. Viacom's holdings also include theater chains in Canada and Europe, Famous Music publishing, the Viacom Outdoor advertising group, theme parks (Great America and Star Trek: The Experience), and the video retailer Blockbuster.

The Walt Disney Co.

Founder Walt Disney had diversified his animation production company into merchandising, theme parks (Disneyland), and television production (*The Wonderful World of Disney*) by the 1950s in part to survive the competition with the major Hollywood studios. This tightly diversified firm was almost broken apart and sold in the early 1980s, until an investor installed Michael Eisner as chief executive officer to revive the Disney brand. Disney has remained focused on film (Disney, Touchstone, Hollywood Pictures, Miramax, Buena Vista, and Dimension), television production (Walt Disney Television, Buena Vista Television, and Network Television Production), and theme parks (Disney World and Paris and Tokyo Disneylands). By acquiring CapCities/ABC, Disney became a major television distributor as well, gaining a national network plus ten owned-and-operated stations. Disney has also invested in cable networks, including Disney, Toon Disney, Family Channel, and SoapNet as well as having interests in the ESPN networks, Lifetime, E!, A&E, and the History Channel. Walt Disney TV International includes channels in Europe and Asia. Disney also owns the ABC Radio Network, Radio Disney, and ESPN Radio. Disney has interests in music (Buena Vista Music Group), book publishing (Disney and Hyperion), and sports teams (Anaheim Angels and Anaheim Mighty Ducks) as well as numerous Internet investments (Walt Disney Internet Group).

News Corporation

Originating as an Australian newspaper group, News Corporation, under the leadership of Rupert Murdoch, has diversified aggressively. Having acquired the film and television studio 20th Century-Fox in 1985, News Corporation launched the fourth major broadcast network, FOX, in 1986. As the first conglomerate to integrate a film studio and broadcast network, its FOX network exploited those synergies, airing 20th Century-Fox Television productions such as *The Simpsons* and *The X-Files*. For competing networks, 20th Century-Fox produced programs such as *Buffy the Vampire Slayer, Dharma and Greg, Judging Amy,* and *Roswell.* News Corporation, like Viacom, pushed the regulatory limits on ownership caps of local television stations by acquiring several station groups and helped precipitate a debate on the appropriateness of ownership caps in an era of cable and satellite television. Although News Corporation does not own any U.S. cable operators and only a few cable networks (FX and FOX News), it is an international presence in satellite television, which is more prevalent than cable in Europe and Asia. News Corporation controls the majority interest in the satellite services BSkyB (Europe), StarTV (Asia), SkyPerfecTV (Japan), Sky Latin America, and Sky Brazil and at this writing is planning to merge with the largest U.S. direct broadcast service, DirecTV. News Corporation has also invested in sports (Los Angeles Dodgers), Internet services (FOX Interactive), music (FOX Music), and one of the world's largest publishing companies (HarperCollins) as well as hundreds of magazines and newspapers in the United States, the United Kingdom, and Australia (*New York Post, The Times, The Sun, TV Guide,* and *The Weekly Standard*).

Sony

Headquartered in Japan, Sony is barred from owning any U.S. broadcast stations or networks; however, its Columbia Tri Star Television subsidiary is a major producer of network and syndicated programs, including *Bewitched, Seinfeld, Dawson's Creek, The King of Queens, Family Law, Ricki Lake,* and soap operas *Days of Our Lives* and *The Young and the Restless.* Sony's other media interests include its film studio (Sony, formerly Columbia Pictures), theater chains, Japan Sky Broadcasting, Sony Online Entertainment, and its major music group, Sony Music Entertainment, which includes the former CBS Records. Only a small proportion of Sony's revenues derive from its media holdings; Sony is primarily an electronics manufacturing company (Trinitron, Walkman, and PlayStation). Sony's game box, PlayStation, was designed as a multimedia entertainment appliance for games, DVDs, CDs, and Internet access in order to present a possible alternative to interactive television or PC appliances. The principal purpose of Sony's investments in media production and distribution is to support its consumer electronics manufacturing interests.

NBC-Universal

Vivendi Universal was a French-based conglomerate that was originally in the water, construction, waste management, and real estate business. Under the leadership of Jean-Marie Messier, it expanded into European telephony (Cegetel and SFR) and cable and film interests (Canal Plus) and by 2000 had acquired the Universal holdings then owned by Seagram, a Canadian beverage company. Having gained control of the Universal film studios and theme park as well as the single largest music company in the world, Universal Music Group, Vivendi also recaptured the Universal television production and distribution interests by agreeing to repurchase USA Networks (including cable networks USA and the Sci-Fi Channel) back from Barry Diller, who had bought them from Seagram. In 2003 Vivendi Universal agreed to sell the Universal film and television interests to General Electric, which has merged them with its NBC holdings (including Bravo, Telemundo, MSNBC, and CNBC). Historically, Universal Television had been one of the largest producers of television programs throughout the network era (*Kojak, Magnum, P.I.,* and *Miami Vice*). Recent Universal television programs include *Just Shoot Me* and *The Steve Harvey Show*. By integrating Universal's massive film and television production subsidiaries with NBC's broadcast and cable networks, General Electric joins the other fully vertically integrated media conglomerates.

In summary, media conglomerates are structured to take advantage of diversification as well as the efficiencies and synergies of integration. However, the rewards of such efficiencies are sometimes outweighed by the costs of unwieldy diversification, internal competition, and debt service. Since entertainment is difficult to produce efficiently, media conglomeration is more often a means toward market domination and negotiating leverage with fellow oligopolistic competitors. The largest media conglomerates account for up to 90 percent of the U.S. markets for film, television, and music, thus creating production and distribution bottlenecks that keep smaller competitors in check.

Investors have cyclically valued and devalued conglomeration, as can be seen in the peaking and crashing of the merger waves of the 1890s, 1920s, and 1960s. For example, many of the conglomerates that were formed in the 1960s were broken up by leveraged buyouts during the 1980s. Corporate raiders discovered that selling conglomerates piecemeal provided greater returns than keeping conglomerates whole. Consequently, the structures of the previously mentioned media conglomerates may undergo yet another round of restructuring if investment markets are devalued, if there is a long-term economic downturn, or if policymakers decide to discourage conglomeration by enforcing new regulatory standards. However, given that conglomeration does provide advantages of scale and diversification in the highly volatile business of entertainment, media conglomeration is likely to remain a key risk management strategy for the time to come. The ultimate impact of media conglomeration on cultural and democratic processes is problematic. Hence, it is essential that viewers, audiences, and consumers learn more as to how and why media conglomeration occurs in order to more effectively engage as citizens in the political processes that shape the regulatory standards affecting the structure of the media industries.

CYNTHIA B. MEYERS

See also **AOL Time Warner; Mergers and Acquisitions; News Corporation, Ltd; Sony Corporation; Vivendi Universal**

Further Reading

Barnouw, Erik, et al., *Conglomerates and the Media,* New York: New Press, 1997

Compaine, Benjamin M., and Douglas Gomery, *Who Owns the Media?* 3rd edition, Mahwah, New Jersey: Lawrence Erlbaum Associates, 2000

Croteau, David, and William Hoynes, *The Business of Media,* Thousand Oaks, California: Pine Forge Press, 2001

Herman, Edward S., and Robert W. McChesney, *The Global Media,* London: Cassell, 1997

Schatz, Thomas, "The Return of the Hollywood Studio System," in *Conglomerates and the Media,* edited by Erik Barnouw et al., New York: New Press, 1997

Woodhull, Nancy J., and Robert W. Snyder, eds., *Media Mergers,* New Brunswick, New Jersey: Transaction Publishers, 1998

Media Events

In contrast to the routine array of genres that characterizes everyday television, media events have a disruptive quality. They have the power of interrupting social life by canceling all other programs. But while always characterized by live broadcasting, the term "media events" evokes at least three different realities. In some cases, the notion is used in connection with major news events (televised wars and assassinations). In other cases, the notion is used in reference to what Victor Turner would call "social dramas": protracted crises whose escalation progressively monopolizes public attention. Thus, the O.J. Simpson trial or

Elizabeth II as the Queen arrived for the coronation ceremony, her husband is to her left, June 2, 1953.
Courtesy of the Everett Collection

the Anita Hill–Clarence Thomas controversy are television equivalents of a genre whose most famous example—the Dreyfus affair—had immense consequences for the nature of the French public sphere. Finally, one may speak of media events concerning expressive events: television ceremonies that typically last a few hours or, at most, a few days. This essay focuses on media events of the third sort, events that are consciously integrative and deliberately constructed with a view of orchestrating a consensus. They are public rituals, emotional occasions. The broadcast does not include the assassinations but the ensuing funerals, not social dramas but their ritualized outcomes.

Forming a relatively coherent television "genre," these ceremonial events share semantic features. They celebrate consensus, "history in the making," acts of will, and charismatic leaders. Formally, they disrupt television syntax. They cancel the rule of "schedules," interrupt the flows of programming, and monopolize many (if not all) channels while they themselves are broadcast "live" from remote locations. In terms of their pragmatics, they are viewed by festive communities. Audiences prepare themselves for the event, gather, dress up, and display their emotions.

Like all "genres" but more explicitly than most, media events can be considered contracts. Thus, each particular event results from negotiations among three major partners. First, organizers propose that a given situation be given ceremonial treatment. Second, broadcasters will transmit but also restructure the event. Third, audiences will validate the event's ceremonial ambition or denounce it as a joke. In order for a media event to trigger a collective experience, each of these partners must actively endorse it. No broadcasting organization can unilaterally decide to mount a ceremonial event. This decision is generally that of national, supranational, or religious institutions. The authority invested in such institutions is what turns events that are essentially gestures into more than gesticulations. It is what makes them media events and not, as Daniel Boorstin would put it, "pseudoevents."

Yet television is not utterly subservient to these institutions. In the ceremonial politics of modern democracies, it stands as a powerful partner whose mediation is necessary, given the scale of audiences. Television is also a partner whose performance is controlled by professional standards. As opposed to earlier "information ceremonies," media events can hardly dispense with the presence of journalists. They cannot be confined to what Jürgen Habermas calls a "public sphere of representation." Thus, negotiations on the pertinence of an event, discussions on the nature of the script, and the option of mocking or ignoring it all distinguish democratic ceremonies from those of regimes where organizers control broadcasters and audiences.

Beyond the generic features they all share, media events vary in terms of (1) the institutionalization or improvisation of the ceremonial event, (2) the temporal orientation of the ceremony, and (3) the nature of the chosen script. This last point is essential, given the organizational complexity of media events and the multiplicity of simultaneous performance involved. Coordination is facilitated by the existence of major dramaturgical models or scripts. Three such scripts can be identified: coronations, contests, and conquests.

The script of coronations is by no means exclusive to monarchic contexts. It characterizes all the rites of passage of the great: inaugurations, funerals, and acceptance (or resignation) speeches. Coronations are celebrations of norms, reiterations of founding myths. They invite ceremonial audiences to manifest their loyalty to these norms and to the institutions that uphold them.

Contests stress the turning points of the democratic curriculum. They celebrate the very existence of a forum open to public debate. Whether they are regularly scheduled (e.g., presidential debates) or mounted in response to political crises, contests are characterized by their dialogic structure, by their focus on argumentation, and by their insistence on procedure. They point to the necessity of interpreting and debating the norms. They are celebrations of pluralism, of the diversity of legitimate positions. Contests call for reflexivity. They invite their audiences to an attitude of deliberation.

Conquests are probably the most consequential of media events. They are also the rarest. They take the form of political or diplomatic initiatives aiming at a swift change in public opinion on a given subject. Rendered possible by the very stature of their protagonists—Egypt's Anwar Sadat going to Jerusalem or Pope John Paul II visiting Poland—conquests reactivate forgotten aspirations. They are attempts at rephrasing a society's history, at redefining the identity of its members. They call on their audiences to be "conquered" by the paradigm change that the ceremonial actor is trying to implement, to suspend skepticism. Conquests celebrate the redefinition of norms.

All three major ceremonial scripts address the question of authority and of its legitimating principle. In the case of coronations, this principle is "traditional." In the case of contests, it belongs to the "rational-legal" order. As for conquests, they stress "charismatic" authority. This helps us understand the political distribution of media events. Coronations are to be found everywhere, for there are no societies without traditions. Unless they are faked (and they often are), contests can emerge only in pluralistic societies. The charismatic dynamics of conquests is always subversive, making them hardly affordable to those societies that are afraid of change.

Compared to the types of public events that were prevalent before the emergence of media events, the latter introduce at least two major transformations. These transformations affect both the nature of the events and that of ceremonial participation.

Televised ceremonies are examples of events that exist but do not need to "take place." These events have been remodeled in order not to need a territorial inscription any longer. The scenography of former public events was characterized by the actual encounter, on a specifiable site, of ceremonial actors and their audiences. That scenography has been replaced by a new mode of "publicness" inspired by cinema and based on the potential separation (1) between actors (2) of actors and audiences.

A second transformation affects ceremonial participation. This transformation turns the effervescent crowds of mass ceremonies into domestic audiences. Instead of mobilizing expressive publics, the media event is celebrated by small groups. A monumental but distant celebration triggers a multitude of microcelebrations. Leading to a typically "diasporic ceremoniality," the immensity of television audiences translates collective events into intimate occasions.

Television ceremonies or media events are necessary inasmuch as they are among the few means available to individuals that assist and enable them to imagine the societies in which they live. Dismissing them as "political spectacles" would lead to two errors: on the one hand, that of presupposing that the mediation they offer is superfluous; on the other, that of believing that the absence of political spectacle is an ideal and a distinctive sign of modern democracies.

Democracies are distinct from authoritarian or totalitarian regimes but not in terms of the presence or absence of a political ceremoniality. Democracies differ from other regimes by the nature—not the existence—of the ceremonies staged in their midst. Democratic media events should therefore be differentiated from other television events that are undoubtedly endowed with a ceremonial dimension but are neither consensual nor contractually derived. For example, the events of terrorism are expressive events, enacted statements, and forms of discourse. Their reception by some of their audiences often involves celebration. However, these forms of discourse receive no validation from the institutions of the center or from those of civil society. They differ form other ceremonial statements by not being submitted to a process of legitimation that transforms them into full-size events. Violence is what distinguishes terroristic events from milder exercises in public relations, from other types of "pseudoevents." In a word, there are many repertoires of media events, and the study of consensual, democratically inspired, negotiated media events must be set in the context of other, rougher media events that are dissentious, imposed, and deliberately antagonistic.

DANIEL DAYAN

Further Reading

Alexander, Jeffrey C., editor, *Durkheimian Sociology: Cultural Studies,* Cambridge and New York: Cambridge University Press, 1988

Benjamin, Walter, "Theses on Philosophy of History," in his *Illuminations,* edited by Hannah Arendt and translated by Harry Zohn, New York: Harcourt Brace and World, 1968; London: Cape, 1970

Benjamin, Walter, "The Work of Art in Age of Mechanical Reproduction," in his *Illuminations,* edited by Hannah Arendt and translated by Harry Zohn, New York: Harcourt Brace and World, 1968; London: Cape, 1970

Boorstin, Daniel, *The Image: A Guide to Pseudo Events in America,* New York: Harper and Row, 1964

Cardiff, D., and P. Scannell, "Broadcasting and National Unity," in *Impacts and Influences: Essays on Media Power in the Twentieth Century,* edited by James Curran, Anthony Smith, and Pauline Wingate, London and New York: Methuen, 1987

Chiasson, Lloyd, Jr., editor, *The Press on Trial: Crimes and Trials as Media Events,* Westport, Connecticut: Greenwood Press, 1997

Dayan, Daniel, and E. Katz, "Television Events and Instant History," in *Television: An International History,* edited by Anthony Smith, Oxford and New York: Oxford University Press, 1995; 2nd edition, edited by Anthony Smith and Richard Paterson, 1998

Edelman, Murray Jacob, *Constructing the Political Spectacle,* Chicago: University of Chicago Press, 1988

Geertz, Clifford, "Center, Kings, and Charisma," in *Culture and Its Creators: Essays in Honor of Edward Shils,* edited by Joseph Ben-David and Terry Nichols Clark, Chicago: University of Chicago Press, 1980

Greenberg, Bradley S., and Edwin B. Parker, editors, *The Kennedy Assassination and the American Public: Social Communication in Crisis,* Stanford, California: Stanford University Press, 1965

Handelman, Don, *Models and Mirrors: Towards an Anthropology of Public Events,* Cambridge and New York: Cambridge University Press, 1990

Hobsbawm, Eric, and Terence Ranger, editors, *The Invention of Tradition,* Cambridge and New York: Cambridge University Press, 1983

Lang, Gladys Engel, *The Battle for Public Opinion: The President, the Press, and the Polls During Watergate,* New York: Columbia University Press, 1983

Lang, Gladys Engel, and Kurt Lang, *Politics and Television,* Chicago: Quadrangle Books, 1968

Lukes, S., "Political Ritual and Social Integration," *Sociology* (1975)

MacAloon, John J., editor, *Rite, Festival, Spectacle, Game: Rehearsals Toward a Theory of Cultural Performance,* Chicago: University of Chicago Press, 1984

Scannell, P., "Media Events: A Review Essay," *Media, Culture, and Society* (1995)

Shils, E., and M. Young, "The Meaning of the Coronation," *Sociological Review* (1953)

Turner, Victor W., *The Ritual Process: Structure and Anti-Structure,* Chicago: Aldine Publishers, and London: Routledge and Kegan Paul, 1969

Wark, McKenzie, *Virtual Geography: Living with Global Media Events,* Bloomington: Indiana University Press, 1994

Medic

U.S. Medical Drama

Medic, U.S. television's first doctor drama to center on the skills and technology of medicine, aired at 9:00 P.M. on the National Broadcasting Company (NBC) from mid-September 1954 through mid-November 1956. The half-hour drama became known for an emphasis on medical realism that its creator and principal writer, James Moser, brought to the episodes. Advertisements for the series asserted that it "made no compromise with truth," and journalistic articles about the show repeated that theme. A *Look* magazine article in 1954 discussed Moser's "well-documented scripts" and emphasized that "details are checked, then double-checked." *TV Guide* called the program "a new kind of TV shocker" and added that it was "telling the story of the medical profession without pulling any punches."

Medic was not the first television series about medicine or physicians. Both *The Doctor* and *City Hospital* had aired, on NBC and the Columbia Broadcasting System (CBS), respectively, during the 1952–53 television season. *Medic* is important because, much more than those two, it helped shape the approach that producers and networks took to doctor shows for the next few decades. The program was in large part an anthology of medical cases. They were introduced by Dr. Konrad Styner, played by Richard Boone, who narrated the case and often participated in it.

James Moser had picked up his interest in the details of professions as a writer on Jack Webb's hit *Dragnet* radio series, which prided itself on straightforwardly presenting the facts of police cases. Moser's interest in a TV series about medicine had been stirred through a stint writing the *Doctor Kildare* radio show, through his creation of an NBC radio pilot about medicine with Jack Webb that did not go to series, and through watching his best friend, an intern at Los Angeles County Hospital, make rounds on a wide array of complex problems. Moser was aware of the strong popularity that medical dramas such as *Dr. Kildare* and *Doctor Christian* had enjoyed in the movies and on radio during the 1940s. He felt, however, that those and other previous stories about medicine had not gone deeply enough into the actual ways modern medicine healed.

Consequently, the emphasis in *Medic* was on portraying physicians' approaches to their patients accurately; subplots and nuances of characterization were minimal. Because Moser wanted accuracy and because the program's first sponsor, Dow Chemical, gave the show a relatively small budget that precluded fancy sets, he sought permission from the Los Angeles Country Medical Association (LACMA) to film in actual hospitals and clinics. In return for their commitment to open doors for the show, LACMA physicians required that Moser and his executive producer sign a contract that gave the association control over the medical accuracy of every script.

As it turned out, Moser's positive attitude toward modern medicine meant that LACMA did not have to

Medic, Richard Boone as Dr. Konrad Styner, 1954–56
Courtesy of the Everett Collection

worry about *Medic*'s treatment of health care's basic setting, characters, and patterns of action. Nevertheless, at a time of growing anxiety about physicians' power in the larger society, the LACMA committee members insisted that the physician's image in the show fit organized medicine's ideal image. They even considered what a doctor drove and how he spoke (the physician was almost always a man). Cars that were too expensive and language with slang or contractions were ruled out. This close involvement by organized medicine in the creation of doctor shows was the beginning of a relationship between organized medicine and doctor-show producers that lasted with few exceptions through the 1960s.

Medic's first episode revolved around a difficult birth in which the mother died and the child lived; an actual birth was filmed and televised. Other stories dealt with such subjects as manic depression and corneal transplants. Critics generally received the programs enthusiastically, but the series got mediocre ratings against the hit *I Love Lucy.* Two controversies in the second year, along with those mediocre ratings, seem to have persuaded NBC executives to cancel the series. The first controversy revolved around an episode that showed a cesarean birth, incision and all. Learning about the episode before it was broadcast, Cardinal Spellman of the New York Archdiocese argued that such subjects were not for exposure on television. He persuaded NBC to delete the operation, much to Moser's public anger.

The second controversy did not become public but further soured the relationship between Moser and network officials. It centered on a *Medic* episode about a black doctor choosing between staying in the big city where he trained or going home to practice in a small southern town. In an era still steaming with antiblack prejudice and crackling with tension over a recent U.S.

Supreme Court decision that mandated integration in schools and other places, executives from southern affiliates considered the *Medic* episode a firebrand. They told the network that they would not air the episode, and NBC decided to shelve it.

Such flare-ups notwithstanding, *Medic* impressed many television producers and network officials of its day for its innovative blending of documentary and dramatic traditions. Its legacy would be the stress on clinical realism that medical series following it adopted. In the 1960s, doctor shows melded that emphasis on realism with a greater concern than *Medic* showed regarding the personality of the physicians, the predicaments of their patients, and even some social issues. James Moser's next show after *Medic, Ben Casey,* contributed strongly to this evolution in television's dramatic portrayal of medicine.

JOSEPH TUROW

See also **Boone, Richard; Workplace Programs**

Cast

Dr. Konrad Styner   Richard Boone

Producers

Frank LaTourette, Worthington Miner

Programming History

59 episodes
NBC
September 1954–November 1956   Monday
                                             9:00–9:30

Further Reading

Turow, Joseph, *Playing Doctor: Television, Storytelling, and Medical Power,* New York: Oxford University Press, 1989

Medical Video

Television has been used in medicine since early in the medium's history. In 1937, well before more common uses of television were in place, an operation performed at Johns Hopkins University Hospital was shown over closed-circuit television. From that time, use of television and video has grown to become an integral part of the medical profession and health care industries. Most hospitals have a video division, and

advances in technology are regularly incorporated into medical video. In some instances, as with the practice of endoscopy, video equipment first developed for medicine later finds additional use in the television industry. The use of video in health care falls into four general categories: medical training, telemedicine, patient care and education, and public information.

Surgeon performing laparoscopic surgery using laparoscopic television camera.
Courtesy of University of Iowa Hospitals and Clinics

The first regular instructional use of television in medicine came in 1949, when television equipment was installed at the University of Kansas Medical Center to teach surgery. Using a mirror and a camera mounted above the patient, the incision area could be viewed in detail by many more students than could otherwise be accommodated and without affecting the sterile environment. With the introduction of videotape recording, procedures could be recorded and reviewed later. This innovation allowed for notable or exceptional cases to be archived and no longer restricted observation to physical presence at the time of surgery. Television is especially important for training in situations where the field of operation is small, such as in dentistry or microsurgery. In these instances, television provides a view otherwise visible only to the doctor.

Beyond formal training in schools, television is also important in the continuing education of health care providers. By the early 1960s, broadcast stations (sometimes with the signal scrambled) were being used along with closed-circuit networks to distribute programs to physicians in broad geographic areas. This application has continued to take advantage of available technologies, and medical programs are provided to health care providers through videocassettes or a variety of wired and wireless networks. The opportunities presented by the introduction of cable television and satellite receivers led to many attempts to offer programming aimed at physicians, often sponsored by pharmaceutical advertisers. However, such ventures as the Hospital Satellite Network, Lifetime Medical Television, American Medical Television, and Medical News Network all failed to attract a large enough target audience (although those services available over cable television often attracted a number of

lay viewers), and all had ceased operations by the mid-1990s.

"Telemedicine" (or "telehealth") refers to the use of telecommunication systems to practice medicine and provide health care when geographic distance separates doctor and patient. The first documented use of this method came in 1959 as part of a demonstration project where closed-circuit, two-way interactive television was used to provide mental health consultations between the Nebraska state mental hospital and the Nebraska Psychiatric Institute more than 100 miles away in Omaha. In telemedicine, a nurse, nurse practitioner, or physician assistant is typically present with the patient to assist, while the physician is in another location. For example, examination rooms specially equipped with television cameras and monitors allow for remote diagnostics and consultations between physicians.

During the 1970s, several U.S. programs made use of the National Aeronautics and Space Administration's Applied Technology Satellites to improve health care availability in Alaska, the Appalachian region, and the Rocky Mountain states, where access to physicians and health care facilities was extremely limited. These and similar strategies have been developed further with the use of satellites, fiber-optic and coaxial cables, and microwave technologies, which can connect medical facilities across towns or even around the world. Such networks have important implications for developing nations, offering the possibility of access to higher-quality health care, often at a reduced cost. As technology improves, new uses for television continue to be developed. In 2001, using a high-speed video cable connection and robotics, surgeons in New York City successfully removed the gallbladder of a 68-year-old woman in Strasbourg, France. Although the video signal traveled a round-trip distance of more than 14,000 kilometers, the speed of the connection was such that the surgeon's movements appeared on his video screen within 155 milliseconds. With the development and growth of the Internet, telemedicine is increasingly adjusting to take advantage of the opportunities, although television continues to play an important role in "telehealthcare." An added benefit of telemedicine is that once the video networks are established, they can also be used for administrative aspects of medicine, such as for teleconferences or other meetings.

Although hardly as dramatic as long-distance surgery, patient care and education can also be greatly improved through the use of television. For example, educational videos can explain such matters as surgical procedures before they are performed and proper posthospital home care. Television is also used in patient surveillance—for example, in intensive care units—so that several areas can be monitored from a central nurses' station. Video can also contribute to psychiatric examinations by allowing behavior to be observed without intruding or introducing outside stimuli.

Public information applications of television have enabled hospitals and other health care providers to aim programs at broader communities. The same equipment used for education and training can also be used in preparing materials for public outreach. Not only do hospitals produce video news releases that are provided to local television outlets, but some also syndicate their own "health segments" to national or regional broadcast stations. There are even examples of hospitals that produce their own telethons to raise research funds, often for diseases that afflict children.

As it has in so many other arenas, the convergence of video and computers is having an impact in medicine in areas such as picture archival and communication systems (PACS). Many medical technologies, such as magnetic resonance and ultrasound imagers, filmless radiology, and CT scanners, generate digital images, and PACS then integrate the images with other clinical information so that all relevant patient data are available through the computer network. The Veterans Administration Medical Centers in the United States have 22 Veterans Integrated Service Network Telemedicine Networks that enable images and other data to be shared in such areas as radiology, pathology, cardiology, dermatology, dentistry, and nuclear medicine, among others. The use of video, then, in conjunction with computers and as a technology in its own right will continue to be an important part of the health care field.

J.C. TURNER

Further Reading

Bashshur, R.L., P.A. Armstrong, and Z.I. Youssef, editors, *Telemedicine: Explorations in the Use of Telecommunications in Health Care,* Springfield, Illinois: Charles C. Thomas, 1975

Dan, B.B., "Information Lives; Medical Television Dies," *The Lancet,* 346, no. 8985 (November 11, 1995)

Davis, A., "Medical PACs Here at Last: Image Integration, Economics Make It Real," *Advanced Imaging* (May 1995)

Edworthy, S.M., "Telemedicine in Developing Countries: May Have More Impact Than in Developed Countries," *British Medical Journal,* 323 (September 8, 2001)

Hudson, H.E., *Telemedicine: Some Findings from the U.S. Experience* (report prepared for Bureau for Technical Assistance, Educational and Human Resources), Washington, D.C.: Agency for International Development, 1977

Judge, R.E., and M.T. Romano, editors, *Health Science Television: A Review,* Ann Arbor: University of Michigan Medical Center, 1966

Larkin, M., "Transatlantic, Robot-Assisted Telesurgery Deemed a Success," *The Lancet,* 358, no. 9287 (September 29, 2001)

Perednia, D.A., and A. Allen, "Telemedicine Technology and Clinical Applications," *Journal of the American Medical Association,* 273, no. 6 (February 8, 1995)

Meet the Press

U.S. Public Affairs/Interview

Meet the Press, the longest-running television series in the United States, consistently generates headlines from its interviews with world-renowned guests including national political leaders, foreign heads of state or government, and Nobel Prize winners.

Meet the Press premiered on television on the National Broadcasting Company (NBC) on November 6, 1947. This exceptionally successful program was the first to bring Washington politics into American living rooms. It also was a pioneer in color TV. In 1954 it aired in color as a "test" program. Since NBC was ahead in the development of color technology, that test was likely the first color telecast by any network; six years later, *Meet the Press* became the first NBC program to air regularly in color.

Lawrence E. Spivak first debuted *Meet the Press* as a 1947 radio program to promote his magazine *American Mercury.* After *Meet the Press* moved to television, Spivak continued to serve as producer, regular panelist, and later moderator. He retired from the series in November 1975.

Meet the Press originally aired in a 30-minute, live press conference format, with a panel of newspaper journalists interviewing a political news maker. On September 20, 1992, *Meet the Press* expanded to a one-hour interview program. According to Kathleen

Hall Jamieson, interview programs are successful because neither the follow-up by the reporter nor the length of the candidates' answers is artificially constrained. *Meet the Press*'s contemporary format consists of two or three interview segments with guests of national and international importance followed by a roundtable discussion. Interviews are conducted in the studio, on location, or via satellite. (In fact, on September 19, 1965, *Meet the Press* became the first network television to broadcast a live satellite interview.) In the present-day version, two or three journalists join host Tim Russert during the initial questioning periods and the roundtable discussion.

Russert joined *Meet the Press* as moderator on December 8, 1991. He came to the program with a thorough understanding of Capitol Hill politics, having previously served as counselor to New York Governor Mario Cuomo and as special counsel and chief of staff to U.S. Senator Daniel Patrick Moynihan. He also is well aware of how journalists cover politics. He has served as senior vice president and Washington, D.C., bureau chief for NBC since December 1988. He also serves as a contributing anchor for MSNBC and as a political analyst for the *NBC Nightly News with Tom Brokaw* and for the *Today* show.

According to a former NBC producer, "Tim has an enormous amount of power right now to make and influence [government] policy on *Meet the Press*." On *Meet the Press*, questions are asked of political personalities in hopes of moving the political process forward or, at least, moving it along. Russert has interviewed almost every major political figure of the 1990s and the early 21st century. As of 2002, Bob Dole had been the most frequent guest on *Meet the Press*, with 56 appearances over his career as a congressman, senator, Republican National Committee chair, vice presidential candidate, and presidential nominee. Although a topic of frequent discussion on the program, Senator Hillary Rodham Clinton has never appeared on or accepted an interview for *Meet the Press*.

Meet the Press emerged early on as a leading program for providing political accountability. In fact, President John F. Kennedy was fond of calling it the "51st state." *Meet the Press* has become the most quoted news program in the world. When the show premiered, it aired on Wednesday nights after 10 P.M. Later, it was moved to Monday, then to Saturday. In the mid-1960s, *Meet the Press* found its niche as a daytime Sunday program. In 2002 it aired via network feed on Sundays from 9 to 10 A.M. The national audience has grown more than 40 percent, making it the most-watched Sunday morning interview program in 2002.

The 2002 executive producer of *Meet the Press* is Nancy Nathan, with Betsy Fischer serving as the show's senior producer. The program originates from Washington, D.C., but the show travels when world events become major news. Sites have included the Republican and Democratic national conventions, the 1993 Bill Clinton–Boris Yeltsin summit in Vancouver, the 1990 Helsinki summit, the 1989 United States–Soviet summit on the island of Malta, and the 1989 economic summit of industrialized nations in Paris.

Whether in Washington, D.C., or on location at an event of political importance, the discussions aired on *Meet the Press* often generate headlines in other media outlets. Today, *Meet the Press* continues to engage viewers in the political process.

LORI MELTON MCKINNON

See also **News, Network**

Further Reading

Brown, Les, editor, *The New York Times Encyclopedia of Television,* New York: Times Books, 1977

Brown, Les, editor, *Les Brown's Encyclopedia of Television,* New York: Zoetrope, 1982

Flander, J., "NBC's Tim Russert: The Insider," *Columbia Journalism Review* (1992)

Jamieson, Kathleen Hall, *Dirty Politics: Deception, Distraction, and Democracy,* New York: Oxford University Press, 1992

Pokorny, Heidi, *Meet the Press* (research report), New York: NBC News Information, 1994

Pokorny, Heidi, *Timothy J. Russert: Moderator, Meet the Press; Senior Vice President and Washington Bureau Chief, NBC News* (research report), New York: NBC News Information, 1994

Terrace, V., editor, *The Complete Encyclopedia of Television Programs 1947–1976,* New York: Barnes, 1976

Melodrama

One of television's most diverse program types, the melodramatic genre encompasses an extensive variety of aesthetic formats, settings, and character types. Melodramatic formats include the series, consisting of self-contained episodes, each with a classic dramatic structure of conflict/complication/resolution in which central and supporting characters return week after week; the serial, which features a continuing storyline, carried forward from program to program (this is typical of soap opera, both daytime and prime time); the anthology, a nonepisodic program series constituting an omnibus of different self-contained programs, related only by subgenre, and featuring different actors and characters each week (important examples include *The Twilight Zone,* a science fiction anthology, and *Alfred Hitchcock Presents,* a mystery anthology); and repertory, a nonepisodic series consisting of different programs featuring a group of actors who appear each week but in different roles (very rare on television, the repertory is best represented by *The Richard Boone Show*). Settings include the hostile western frontier of *Gunsmoke* and *Have Gun, Will Travel* and its urban analog—the mean streets of *East Side/West Side* and, more recently, *Hill Street Blues;* the gleaming corporate office towers of *Dallas* and *L.A. Law;* the quiet suburban enclaves in which *Marcus Welby, M.D.* made house calls in the 1970s; the ostentatious exurban chateaus of *Falcon Crest* and the numerous wealthy criminals outsmarted by the proletarian cop *Columbo*; and the high-pressure, teeming workplace peopled by dedicated professionals such as the newspaper reporters in *Lou Grant.* The seemingly endless variety of "heroic" and "villianous" character types in television melodrama, whose weekly travails and romantic interests ground the dramaturgy, are drawn from the rich store of historical legend, the front pages of today's broadsheets and tabloids, and the future projections of science fiction and science fantasy: cowboys, sheriffs, bounty hunters, outlaws, pioneers/settlers, police, mobsters, sleuths, science fiction adventurers and other epic wanderers, spies, corrupt entrepreneurs, doctors, lawyers, and intrepid journalists.

Television melodrama has its direct roots in the early 19th-century stage play in which romantic, sensational plots and incidents were mixed with songs and orchestral music. The word "melodrama" evolved from the Greek "melos," meaning song or music, and "drama," a deed, action, or play, especially tragedy. In tragedy, the hero is isolated from society so that he or she may better understand his or her own and the society's moral weakness; but once enlightened, the hero cannot stave off the disaster embedded in the social structure beyond the hero's control. In contrast, the melodramatic hero is a normative character representing incorporation into society. Northrop Frye, in *Anatomy of Criticism* (1957), described a central theme in melodrama as "the triumph of moral virtue over villainy, and the consequent idealizing of the moral views assumed to be held by the audience." Since melodrama exists within a mass-cultural framework, it could, according to Frye, easily become "advance propaganda for the police state" if it were taken seriously. Frye sidesteps this fear by positing that the audience does not take such work seriously.

Peter Brooks, in *The Melodramatic Imagination* (1976), finds melodrama acting powerfully in society, reflecting the socialization of the deeply personal. Brooks sees in the melodramatic aesthetic unremitting conflict; possibly disabling, excessive enactment; and ultimately clarification and cure. It is, according to Brooks, akin to our experience of nightmare, where virtue is seemingly helpless in the face of menace. "The end of the nightmare is an awakening brought about by confrontation and expulsion of the villain, the person in whom evil is seen to be concentrated, and a reaffirmation of the society of 'decent people.'"

Melodrama demands strong justice, while tragedy, in contrast, often includes the ambivalence of mercy in its code. Melodrama provides us with models of clear resolution for highly personalized, intensely enacted conflict. Television melodrama may be considered a contemporary substitute for traditional forms of social control—the rituals of organized religion and, before that, of "primitive mythologies"—that provided easily understandable models of "primal, intense, polarized forces." It is thus a powerfully conservative social artifact—a public ceremonial ritual, repositioned in politics and economics, drawing us into both the prescriptions and the proscriptions of mainstream cultural values.

The hero is central to melodrama. In classical Greek dramaturgy, the term applied to an individual of superhuman strength, courage, or ability who was favored by the gods. In antiquity, the hero was regarded as an immortal intermediary between the gods and ordinary people—a demigod who was the offspring of a god or goddess and a human being. Later, the heroic class came to include mortals of renown who were deified because of great and noble deeds or for firmness or greatness of soul in any course of action they undertook. The hero was distinguished by extraordinary bravery and martial achievement. Many heroes were boldly experimental or resourceful in their actions. Punishment of those who violated social codes was harsh.

The world in which the classic hero operated was a world of heightened emotional intensity—a harsh world in which the norm included unending tests of both physical and moral strength and the constant threat of death. The hero represented a carefully defined value system in which good triumphed over evil in the end and in which the actions of the hero, with the assistance of the gods, produced order and stability out of chaos.

Heroes are "social types." As Orrin Klapp notes in *Heroes, Villains, and Fools: The Changing American Character* (1962), heroes offer "roles which, though informal, have become rather well conceptualized and in which there is a comparatively high degree of consensus." Drawn from a cultural stock of images and symbols, heroes provide models people try to approximate. As such, Klapp argues, heroes represent "basic dimensions of social control in any society."

Reflecting the increasingly technocratic nature of contemporary American society, many "workplace" melodramas on television have featured what Gary Edgerton (1980) has termed the "corporate hero"—a team of specialists which acts as a unit. The corporate hero derives his or her identity from the group. He or she is more a distinct "talent" than a distinct personality. Heroism by committee emphasizes the individual's need to belong to a group and to interact. The composite corporate hero tends to reinforce the importance of social institutions in maintaining social order. When violence is employed to this end, as in police or spy melodrama, it is corporatized, becoming less a personal expression for the corporate hero than for the traditional individual hero. Major examples of the corporate hero in television melodrama include *Mission: Impossible, Charlie's Angels, Hill Street Blues,* and *L.A. Law.*

Heroes could not exist on the melodramatic stage without their dramaturgical counterparts—villains and fools. While heroes exceed societal norms, villains, in contrast, are negative models of evil to be feared, hated, and ultimately eradicated or reformed by the actions of the hero; villains threaten societal norms. Fools, on the other hand, are models of absurdity, to be ridiculed; they fall far short of societal norms.

Within the television melodrama, these social types operate as images or signs, constructed according to our society's dominant values, reinforcing commonly held beliefs regarding the proper ordering of social relations.

The aesthetic structure of television melodrama, as a form of popular storytelling, is clearly linked to its dramaturgical predecessors. It employs rhythmic patterns in its scene and act progression analogous to the metrical positions in the poetic line of the mnemonically composed classical Greek epic poetry. As in the grand opera of the 19th century, television melodrama is organized into a series of distinct acts, each generally signifying a change in either time or place, and linked by orchestral transitions. Superfluous exposition is eliminated. The spectator is offered a series of intense highlights of the lives of the protagonists and antagonists. Orchestral music introduces actions, provides a background for plot movement, and reinforces moments of heightened dramatic intensity. Television melodrama, like grand opera, is generally constructed to formula. Plot dominates, initiating excitement and suspense by raising for its protagonists explicit questions of self-preservation and implicit questions of preservation of the existing social order.

In 19th- and 20th-century literature, melodrama came to signify "democratic drama." Critics condemned the form as sensational, sentimental entertainment for the masses. Rural-type melodrama—with its beautiful, virtuous, impoverished heroine; its pure hero; its despicable villain who ties the heroine to the railroad tracks; and the rustic clown who aids the hero (wonderfully satirized in the television cartoon "Dudley Do-Right of the Royal Canadian Mounties," originally a segment of *The Bullwinkle Show*)—gave way to city melodrama focusing on the seamy underworld and to suspenseful crime dramas, such as those of Agatha Christie.

Television melodrama has drawn freely from all these precursors both structurally and conceptually. Highly segmented plots developed in four 12-minute acts, each with a climax, and a happy ending usually encompassed in an epilogue in which moral lessons are conveyed to the audience (a function assumed by the "chorus" in classical Greek drama), carried along by background music and stress peaks of action and emotional involvement. Suspense and excitement are heightened by a sense of realism created through sophisticated if formulaic visualizations (car chases being obvious examples). Characterizations are generally unidimensional, employing eccentric protagonists and antagonists made credible by good acting. Ideologically, the plot elements reinforce conventional morality.

The rhythm of the commercial television melodrama depends on a predictable structure motivated by the flow of the sequence of program segment, music, and commercial. As suspense builds and the plot thickens, viewers are carried forward at various crucial junctures by a combination of rapid visual cutting and an intense buildup of the orchestral background music and ambient sound that create a smooth transition to the often frenetic, high-pitched commercials. This rhythm produces a flow that the audience implicitly understands and accepts as a genre convention in the context of the pecuniary mechanisms that define the regime of commercial television.

Raymond Williams, in *Television: Technology and Cultural Form,* refers to melodramatic structuration as commodified "planned flow." By cutting down on exposition or establishing sequences that tend toward lengthy and deliberate characterizations, the purveyors of melodrama are able to break their tales into shortened, fast-paced, and often unconnected simple sequences that make the commercial breaks feel natural to viewers.

The production imperatives of television-series melodrama reinforce Williams's concept of the commodification of flow. Noted producer/writers Richard Levinson and William Link (*Columbo, Mannix,* and *Murder, She Wrote* and made-for-television movies *The Execution of Private Slovik, The Storyteller,* and *That Certain Summer*) described these production procedures in *Stay Tuned* (1983). The network commits itself to a new television series in mid-April. The series premieres in early September, leaving four and a half months' lead time for producers to hire staff (including writers and directors), prepare scripts, and begin shooting and editing. It takes four weeks, under the best conditions, to complete an episode of a melodrama; with luck, four shows will be "in the can" by the season's premiere, with others in varying stages of development (at any time during the process, many series episodes will be in development simultaneously, one being edited, another shot, and another scripted). By October, the initial four episodes will have been aired, and the fifth will be nearly ready. If the show is renewed at mid-season, the producer will need as many as 22 episodes for the entire season. By December, there will be but a matter of days between the final edit and the airing of an episode, as inevitable delays shorten the turnaround time. In addition to normal time problems, there are problems with staff. Levinson and Link cite the frequent problem of having a good freelance writer in demand who agrees to write for one producer's shows as well as those of other producers. The writer with a track record will be juggling an outline for one show, a first draft for another, and a "notion" for a third.

In the frenzied world of the daytime soap opera, actors get their scripts the night before the taping, begin run-through rehearsals at 7:30 the next morning, do three rehearsals before taping, and tape between 3:30 and 6:00 that afternoon. This hectic ritual is repeated five days a week.

The prime-time melodrama production process is driven by shortcuts, scattered attention, and occasional network interference in content, created by the fear of viewer response to potentially controversial material that may range from questionable street language, however dramatically appropriate, to sexual taboos (proscriptions change over time as standards of appropriateness change in the wider culture). Simplicity, predictability, and safety become the norms that frame the creation and production of television melodrama. Planned flow, the melodrama's highly symbolic heroic ideal, its formal conventions, and its reinforcement of the society's dominant values at any given cultural moment render the genre highly significant as a centrist cultural mechanism stressing order and stasis.

Perhaps because it is such a staple—and stable—form of television, melodrama has become a central feature of almost any other program formations in the medium, leading to "blurred" genres modified by melodramatic conventions. Thus, police procedurals such as *NYPD Blue* or *Third Watch* focus as often on the private tribulations of characters as on their professional activities, though the two types of event frequently intertwine and influence each other. One of the more notable examples of this genre blending and bending was *Buffy the Vampire Slayer,* which modified a comic-adventure theatrical release into a compelling exploration of the lives of teens and young adults, providing powerful and poignant moments, such as in the episode in which Buffy's mother dies.

The use of melodrama as a modifying factor even altered the concept of planned flow when cable channels began to produce serialized programming based on familiar genres. Home Box Office's (HBO's) *The Sopranos, OZ,* and *The Wire* have been cited as among the most complex offerings in television history, each of them trading on viewer knowledge of "mafia stories," "prison stories," or "police procedurals," richly embroidered with melodramatic overtones. Indeed, it is likely that the sense of these basic story forms has now been altered by these uninterrupted, randomly available narratives, "rewritten" in melodramatic form.

HAL HIMMELSTEIN

See also Alfred Hitchcock Presents; Buffy the Vampire Slayer; Charlie's Angels, Dallas; East Side/West Side; Gunsmoke; Have Gun, Will Travel; Hill Street Blues; L.A. Law; Lou Grant; Marcus Welby, M.D.;

Mission: Impossible; NYPD Blue; The Sopranos; The Twilight Zone

Further Reading

Bratton, Jacky, Jim Cook, and Christine Gledhill, editors, *Melodrama: Stage, Picture, Screen,* London: British Film Institute, 1994

Brooks, Peter, *The Melodramatic Imagination,* New Haven, Connecticut: Yale University Press, 1976

Frye, Northrop, *Anatomy of Criticism,* Princeton, New Jersey: Princeton University Press, 1957

Himmelstein, Hal, *Television Myth and the American Mind,* Westport, Connecticut: Praeger, 1984; 2nd edition, 1994

Klapp, Orrin E., *Heroes, Villains, and Fools: The Changing American Character,* Englewood Cliffs, New Jersey: Prentice Hall, 1962

Landy, Marcia, editor, *Imitations of Life: A Reader on Film and Television Melodrama,* Detroit, Michigan: Wayne State University Press, 1991

Levinson, Richard, and William Link, *Stay Tuned,* New York: Ace, 1983

Lozano, Elizabeth, "The Force of Myth on Popular Narratives: The Case of Melodramatic Serials," *Communication Theory* (August 1992)

Newcomb, Horace, *TV: The Most Popular Art,* New York: Anchor Press/ Doubleday, 1974

Oglesbee, Frank W., "Doctor Who: Televized Science Fiction as Contemporary Melodrama," *Extrapolation* (Summer 1989)

Thorburn, David, "Television Melodrama." In *Television as a Cultural Force,* edited by Richard Adler and Douglass Cater. New York: Praeger, 1976

Williams, Raymond, *Television: Technology and Cultural Form,* New York: Schocken, 1975

Mercer, David (1928–1980)

British Writer

David Mercer, an innovative and controversial writer for television, stage, and film, was a key figure in the development of television drama in Britain during the 1960s and 1970s. Although he often said he got into television by accident, his television plays first established his reputation and offered a powerful and personal exploration of the possibilities of the medium. Published soon after transmission, Mercer's screenplays sparked lively critical and political debates.

Mercer came from a northern working-class family, but his interest in the arts and in politics began after World War II, when he was able to take advantage of the extension of new educational opportunities. This experience was central to his first television play, *Where the Difference Begins* (1961), originally written for the stage but accepted for broadcast by the British Broadcasting Corporation (BBC). The "difference" in the title referred to the younger generation's break with traditional socialist values. Mercer followed up with two more plays, *A Climate of Fear* (1962) and *The Birth of a Private Man* (1963), which dealt with characters struggling to sustain a left-wing political vision in the new "affluent" society.

Although Mercer's early work showed the influence of the "kitchen sink" realism that had swept through British theater, literature, and cinema in the late 1950s, he soon joined other BBC writers and producers to challenge what Troy Kennedy-Martin called the prevailing "naturalism" of television drama. In Mercer's case, the result was a new verbal and visual freedom: instead of talking heads and colloquial speech patterns, the plays used condensed, witty, articulate dialogue with striking, often subjective or allegorical images. An example of such imagery occurs at the end of *The Birth of a Private Man,* when Colin Waring, whose private life had disintegrated in the face of his political uncertainties, dies at the Berlin Wall in a hail of bullets from both sides.

This antinaturalist style was recognized as an imaginative use of the medium but disturbed critics of all political persuasions. Conservatives objected to Mercer's self-professed Marxist position, liberals found the plays too explicit and lacking in subtlety, while orthodox left-wing critics questioned the emphasis on the problems of Socialism—the compromises of the British postwar Labour governments, the revelations about Stalin's atrocities, and the failures of Communism in Eastern Europe. The plays may be Marxist in their stress on the need for a political revolution, but the revolutionary impulse is usually blocked and becomes internalized as psychological breakdown. However, the impulse also emerges in Mercer's pleasure in breaking the rules of television drama, as he did emphatically in *A Suitable Case for Treatment* (1962), a broad farce in which the main character indulges in "mad" visions of a retreat to the jungle away from the complexities of his political and personal life. Mercer later wrote the screenplay for the successful film version of this play, *Morgan: A Suitable Case for Treatment* (1966), directed by Karel Reisz.

The motif of "madness" in Mercer's plays has much in common with the antipsychiatry philosophy of R.D. Laing, who claimed that schizophrenia is an essentially sane response to a mad society. Laing was extremely influential in the 1960s, and he expressed great interest in Mercer's work, acting as consultant on one of his most powerful television plays, *In Two Minds* (1967), a documentary-style drama that traces the causes of a young woman's schizophrenia to her oppressive family life. The play was directed by Ken Loach, who also directed the 1971 film version *Family Life* (*Wednesday's Child* in the United States), based on Mercer's screenplay.

Mercer himself likened his plays to rituals exploring the tensions and contradictions of fragmented personalities and ambiguous truths. They explore the relationships of the political and the personal in a society that encourages conformity, inhibiting individual expression. He felt that television gave him greater freedom of expression than was possible in the commercial theater or cinema, but he did continue to work in other media. His influence can be seen in the work of a younger generation of writers, such as Trevor Griffiths, David Hare, and Stephen Poliakoff, who have also drawn on the resources of television, theater, and film to produce a powerful body of work dealing with the intersection of personal and political pressures in contemporary Britain.

JIM LEACH

David Mercer. Born in Wakefield, Yorkshire, England, June 27, 1928. Educated at King's College, Newcastle-upon-Tyne; Durham University, B.A. with honors, 1953. Married twice; one daughter. Served in Royal Navy, 1945–48. Laboratory technician, 1942–45; lived in Paris, 1953–54; supply teacher, 1955–59; teacher, Barrett Street Technical College, 1959–61; television dramatist, from 1961; screenwriter, from 1965. Recipient: Writers Guild Award for Television Play, 1962, 1967, 1968; *Evening Standard* Award, 1965; BAFTA Award, 1966; French Film Academy César Award, for screenplay, 1977; Emmy Award, 1980. Died August 8, 1980.

Television Plays

1961	*Where the Difference Begins*
1962	*A Climate of Fear*
1962	*A Suitable Case for Treatment*
1963	*The Buried Man*
1963	*The Birth of a Private Man*
1963	*For Tea on Sunday*
1963	*A Way of Living*
1965	*And Did Those Feet?*
1967	*In Two Minds*
1968	*The Parachute*
1968	*Let's Murder Vivaldi*
1968	*On the Eve of Publication*
1970	*The Cellar and the Almond Tree*
1970	*Emma's Time*
1972	*The Bankrupt*
1973	*You and Me and Him*
1973	*An Afternoon at the Festival*
1973	*Barbara of the House of Grebe*
1974	*The Arcata Promise*
1974	*Find Me*
1976	*Huggy Bear*
1977	*A Superstition*
1977	*Shooting the Chandelier*
1978	*The Ragazza*
1980	*A Rod of Iron*

Films

90 Degrees in the Shade (English dialogue), 1965; *Morgan: A Suitable Case for Treatment* (film version of *In Two Minds*), 1966; *Family Life* (film version of *In Two Minds*), 1972; *A Doll's House* (with Michael Meyer), 1973; *Providence,* 1978.

Radio

The Governor's Lady, 1960; *Folie a Deux,* 1974.

Stage

The Governor's Lady, 1960; *The Buried Man,* 1962; *Ride a Cock Horse,* 1965; *Belcher's Luck,* 1966; *White Poem,* 1970; *Flint,* 1970; *After Haggerty,* 1970; *Blood on the Table,* 1971; *Let's Murder Vivaldi,* 1972; *In Two Minds,* 1973; *Duck Song,* 1974; *The Arcata Promise,* 1974; *Cousin Vladimir,* 1978; *Then and Now,* 1979; *No Limits to Love,* 1980.

Publications

"Huggy Bear" (short story), *Stand* (Summer 1960)
"Positivist" (short story), *Stand* (Autumn 1960)
"Folie a Deux" (short story), *Stand* (Winter 1960)
The Governor's Lady (play), 1962
"What Television Has Meant in the Development of Drama in Britain," with Lewis Greifer and Arthur Swinson, *Journal of the Society of Film and Television Arts* (Autumn 1963)
The Generations: A Trilogy of Plays. (includes *Where the Difference Begins, A Climate of Fear, The Birth*

of a Private Man), 1964; as *Collected TV Plays I,*
1981
"Style in Drama: Playwright's Postscript," *Contrast*
(Spring 1964)
"The Long Crawl Through Time," in *New Writers III,*
1965
"An Open Letter to Harold Wilson," *Peace News*
(February 1965)
Three TV Comedies (includes *A Suitable Case for
Treatment, For Tea on Sunday, And Did Those
Feet*), 1966
"The Meaning of Censorship: A Discussion," with
Roger Manvell, *Journal of the Society of Film and
Television Arts* (Autumn 1966)
Ride a Cock Horse, 1966
*The Parachute with Two More TV Plays: Let's Murder
Vivaldi, In Two Minds,* 1967
Belcher's Luck, 1967
After Haggerty, 1970
Flint, 1970
On the Eve of Publication and Other Plays (television
plays; includes *The Cellar and the Almond Tree,
Emma's Time*), 1970
On the Eve of Publication: Scripts 8 (June 1972)
Let's Murder Vivaldi in *The Best Short Plays 1974,*
edited by Stanley Richards, 1974
The Bankrupt and Other Plays (includes *You and Me
and Him, An Afternoon at the Festival, Find Me*),
1974
Duck Song, 1974
Huggy Bear and Other Plays (includes *The Arcata
Promise, A Superstition*), 1977
Cousin Vladimir, with *Shooting the Chandelier,* 1978

Then and Now, with *The Monster of Karlovy Vary,*
1979
Collected TV Plays 1–2 (includes *Where the Difference Begins, A Climate of Fear, The Birth of a Private Man, A Suitable Case for Treatment, For Tea
on Sunday, And Did Those Feet, The Parachute,
Let's Murder Vivaldi, In Two Minds*), 1981
No Limits to Love, 1981

Further Reading

"David Mercer on Why He Writes the Plays He Does," *The
Times* (London) (July 27, 1966)
Gordon, Giles, "Interview," in *Behind the Scenes: Theatre and
Film Interviews from the Transatlantic Review,* edited by
Joseph McCrindle, London: Pitman, 1971
Itzin, Catherine, *Stages in the Revolution: Political Theatre in
Britain Since 1968,* London: Eyre Methuen, 1980
Jarman, Francis, with John Noyce and Malcolm Page, *The
Quality of Mercer: A Bibliography of Writings by and About
the Playwright David Mercer,* Brighton, United Kingdom:
Smoothie, 1974
Jones, D.A.N., "Mercer Unmarxed," *Listener* (May 14, 1970)
Madden, Paul, editor, *David Mercer: Where the Difference Be-
gins,* London: British Film Institute, 1981
McCrindle, Joseph F., editor, *Behind the Scenes: Theater and
Film Interviews,* New York: Holt, Rinehart and Winston,
1971
McGrath, John, "TV Drama: The Case Against Naturalism,"
Sight and Sound (Spring 1977)
Mustafa, Khalid El Mubarek, "David Mercer," in *British Televi-
sion Drama,* edited by George W. Brandt, Cambridge: Cam-
bridge University Press, 1981
Taylor, John Russell, *Second Wave British Drama for the Seven-
ties,* London: Methuen, 1971
Taylor, John Russell, "David Mercer and the Mixed Blessings
of Television," *Modern Drama* (December 1981)

Mercer, Rick (1969–)

Canadian Actor, Writer, Political Satirist

Rick Mercer is one of Canada's most respected television writers and performers, and his career has successfully melded the quintessentially Canadian
traditions of sketch comedy and political satire. But his
contribution to the social and cultural landscape of
Canada goes far beyond his considerable ability to entertain. Whether directed toward the perceived social
and political arrogance of mainland Canada toward his
home province of Newfoundland or contained within a

wicked send-up of the network television production
industry, Mercer's satire not only is informed by social
and political issues but also unmercifully dismantles
them, revealing the underlying pretensions, contradictions, and absurdities. In 2000, for example, while still
appearing as a regular on the Canadian Broadcasting
Corporation's (CBC's) news satire *This Hour Has 22
Minutes,* Mercer called for a national referendum to
decide the issue of whether ultraconservative prime-

ministerial candidate Stockwell Day should be forced to change his first name to Doris. Mercer justified the position by citing Day's own platform, which included support for staging a national referendum whenever as few as 3 percent of Canadians called for one.

The roots of Mercer's irreverent and antiestablishment comedy lay in Newfoundland, both Mercer's birthplace and home to the legendary CODCO comedy troupe. His early stage work found him in the same local theaters as several of CODCO's founding members, including Mary Walsh and Cathy Jones, with whom Mercer would later work on the long-running CBC production *This Hour Has 22 Minutes*. Mercer broke onto the national scene in the early 1990s, writing and performing several critically acclaimed one-man plays that established the foundations for his career as a "professional ranter."

Mercer's eight years on *This Hour Has 22 Minutes* (named for the legendary Canadian public affairs program *This Hour Has Seven Days*), built his reputation as Canada's most indignant and incisive comic actor. But if its 1960s predecessor was often considered controversial for topics and approaches to stories that explored the boundaries of journalistic autonomy, *This Hour Has 22 Minutes* pushed the envelope even further by pointedly subverting some of Canada's most entrenched public institutions, including broadcast journalism itself. Mercer's contributions were among the show's most subversive and the most popular. One of the Mercer trademarks was "Streeters," two-minute tirades shot in grainy black-and-white film on the Halifax, Nova Scotia, waterfront, which featured an outraged Mercer venting the collective spleen of every Canadian who had ever been angered by the duplicity of federal politicians or the petty tyranny of bank tellers.

"Talking to Americans" would take Mercer's angry-young-man act on the road. As a regular segment on *This Hour Has 22 Minutes,* "Talking to Americans" had Mercer traveling to major U.S. cities and recruiting unsuspecting victims to participate in seemingly benign "man on the street" interviews that collected American opinions on Canada's geography, politics, and culture. Topics ranged from whether Canada should be forced to outlaw the polar bear slaughter in Toronto (though no polar bears live in this cosmopolitan urban center of some 2.5 million people) to whether Americans should embark on a bombing campaign against Bouchard (not a place but a person: Lucien Bouchard, the former leader of the Bloc Quebecois, the party advocating separation from Canada for French-speaking Quebec). The dismal failure of even American politicians to grasp fundamental facts about Canada emerged in the now infamous

"Jean Poutine" episode. At a press event held by then–presidential candidate George W. Bush, Mercer asked the Texas Republican to comment on the support for his presidential run pledged by Canada's prime minister, Jean Poutine. Bush's unfortunate public failure to recall that the Canadian leader's real name is Jean Chretien was compounded only by the fact that "poutine" is actually a fast-food item, popular in Quebec, consisting of french fries covered in gravy and melted cheese curds. *This Hour Has 22 Minutes'* cameras captured the entire episode, much to the delight of the perpetually marginalized Canadian television audience.

An hour-long "Talking to Americans" compilation special gained the highest ratings in Canadian broadcasting history for a comedy show, while a text-based version of *Streeters* was published in 1998. Mercer's eight years on *This Hour* would also net him 12 Gemini Awards for writing and performing as well as several Canadian Comedy Awards. He has also won regional awards in Canada for journalism and for contributions to the arts in Atlantic Canada.

While Mercer has proven his mettle as a stage actor, political satirist, news commentator, and news maker, in 1998 he turned his talents to writing and starring in a situation comedy. *Made in Canada* gleefully lampoons the Canadian private television production industry. Richard Strong, Mercer's character, is head of production (a position earned by drugging and framing his brother-in-law and boss) at "Pyramid/Prodigy Productions," where unbridled office politics and sleazy corporate competition provide the backdrop for Mercer's character's quest to destroy his enemies while churning out lamentably bad Canadian television for American syndication. Mercer has called the role a modern-day Richard III and characteristically subverts television convention by engaging the viewer in playful side commentary made directly into the camera. During the 2001–02 season, *Made in Canada* boasted cameos from a virtual "Who's Who" of Canadian film and television actors, journalists, and media industry executives, all of whom seemed only too happy to be in on the joke that the series makes of the Canadian private TV industry.

But if Mercer's career sometimes appears as a quixotic campaign to use television and journalism to expose the many flaws and ironies in Canadian political, social, and cultural life, it is also redolent with a seemingly sincere fondness and curiosity about the nation's cultural heritage and institutions. As the host of *It Seems Like Yesterday* for Canada's History Television Network, Mercer narrates half-hour retrospectives looking at newsworthy weeks in 20th-century history, emphasizing events and matters of particular importance to Canadians. In 1992 *Secret Nation* brought Mercer together with a collection of fellow Newfoundland artists, writers, and actors in a deft mystery exploring a fictional British-Canadian plot to sabotage a referendum, forcing Newfoundland into confederation with the rest of Canada in the 1940s. Mercer also routinely lends his considerable talents to hosting awards shows and CBC specials, appearing as a special guest on children's programs and at comedy festivals.

JODY WATERS

See also **CODCO**

Rick Mercer. Born October, 17, 1969, St. John's, Newfoundland, Canada. Began career as a writer and performer in local theater in St. John's as a teenager, later going on to work with founders of Newfoundland's famed CODCO theater troupe. First two one-man shows, *Show Me the Button, I'll Push It,* and *I've Killed Before; I'll Kill Again* became Canada-wide hits in the early 1990s. Debuted on television in 1993 on the news satire *This Hour Has 22 Minutes.* Departed in 2001 to write and star in *Made in Canada.* Hosted the Canadian Juno Awards in 2001, the East Coast Music Awards in 1998 and 1999, and the Gemini Awards in 2000.

Television Series

1993–2001	*This Hour Has 22 Minutes* (writer and performer)
	It Seems Like Yesterday
1998–	*Made in Canada* (writer and performer)

Television Specials

1996	*CBC New Year's Eve Comedy Special* (with cast of *This Hour Has 22 Minutes*)
1997	*CBC New Year's Eve Comedy Special* (with cast of *This Hour Has 22 Minutes*)
1998	East Coast Music Awards
1999	East Coast Music Awards
2000	Gemini Awards
2001	Canadian Juno Awards
2001	"Talking to Americans"

Stage

Show Me the Button, I'll Push It, 1991; *I've Killed Before; I'll Kill Again,* 1992; *A Good Place to Hide,* 1995

Film

1992	*Secret Nation*
1991	*Understanding Bliss*

Publications

Streeters, 1998.

Further Reading

Coulter, Diane, "Canucks Are Full of Yuks at Yankee Blunders," *Christian Science Monitor* (June 20, 2001)

Gessell, Paul, "Much More Than 22 Minutes of Fame for Mercer," *Ottawa Citizen* (December 29, 1997)

Pevere, Geoff, "This Column Has 30 Days," *Canadian Forum* (June 1998)

Pevere, Geoff, and Greg Dymond, "The Rock's Revenge: Codco and This Hour Has 22 Minutes," in *Mondo Canuck: A Canadian Pop Culture Odyssey,* by Geoff Pevere and Greg Dymond, Scarborough, Ontario: Prentice Hall Canada, Inc., 1996

Toth, Derrick, "Election Year a Bonus for 22 Minutes," *Vancouver Sun* (October 16, 2000)

Mergers and Acquisitions

Mergers and acquisitions have been a constant theme in the U.S. television business since its commercial beginnings. The vast majority of the dominant companies have been built by taking over other enterprises. For example, all four of the original television networks developed as products of mergers. No better example can be found than the complex formation of the American Broadcasting Company (ABC). During World War II, when the federal government forced the National Broadcasting Company (NBC) to divest itself of one of its two radio networks, Edward Nobel's Lifesavers company acquired the NBC Blue network and renamed it ABC. For nearly a decade, ABC struggled and would probably have not made a major impact in television had not it been acquired by another company, United Paramount Theaters, in 1952. Leonard

Goldenson, then head of United Paramount, took control of the merged units and sold movie theaters to finance the creation of ABC Television.

During this same early period, another television company, Dumont, was able to mount a TV network largely because it had been acquired by Hollywood's Paramount Pictures, and even the NBC and Columbia Broadcasting System (CBS) television networks, usually thought of as secure corporate entities, relied on mergers to increase their stable of owned-and-operated television stations. As the three-network oligopoly of ABC, CBS, and NBC solidified its position in the American news and entertainment contexts and in the wake of specific Federal Communications Commission (FCC) rulings on the allocation of spectrum space, the television industry appeared to be established and unchanging. Through the 1960s and 1970s, the "Big Three" TV networks acquired few TV properties, and the only big news in the late 1960s was an "almost merger" as ITT tried and failed to take control of ABC. The FCC carefully investigated that proposed deal, and the delay caused the parties to abandon the merger. CBS and NBC were satisfied to acquire ancillary entertainment units, from baseball teams to book publishers.

The stability of the three major TV network empires was shattered in the mid-1980s, a time when the television business was changing rapidly. Cable and home video made major inroads into the landscape dominated by terrestrially based broadcasters. Longtime owners, such as William Paley of CBS, began to ponder retirement, and perhaps most significantly, the FCC lowered the level of its threatened opposition to proposed deals.

In 1986 General Electric (GE) purchased the Radio Corporation of America (RCA) at a price in excess of $6 billion and thus acquired NBC. GE, one of the biggest corporations in the world, immediately sold off the NBC Radio network and stations as well as RCA manufacturing. GE's stripped-down NBC then began to expand into cable television, a move most strongly exemplified by its acquisition of shares of the CNBC, Bravo, American Movie Classics (AMC), and A&E cable television networks.

Also in 1986, Laurence Tisch and his Loews investment company took over CBS. Earlier, as Ted Turner attempted a hostile bid for CBS, longtime CBS chief Paley looked for a "white knight" to save his beloved company and in October 1985 asked Tisch to join the CBS board of directors to thwart the Atlanta-based broadcaster. The following year, Tisch took full control and, to no one's surprise, systematically began to sell everything CBS owned in order to concentrate on television. First to go was CBS Educational and Profes-

sional Publishing, which included Holt, Rinehart and Winston, one of the country's leading publishers of textbooks, and W.B. Saunders, a major publisher of medical books. Next Tisch picked up $2 billion from the Sony Corporation of Japan for CBS's Music Group, one of the world's dominant sellers of popular music.

ABC was the third of the Big Three to be merged into another company. By the early 1980s, Leonard Goldenson had transformed ABC into the top TV network, but he had passed his 80th birthday and wanted out of the day-to-day grind of running a billion-dollar corporation. In 1986 Capital Cities, backed by Warren Buffett's Berkshire Hathaway investment group, bought ABC for $3.5 billion. Capital Cities had long ranked as a top group-owner of television stations, and through the late 1980s and into the 1990s, the new "CapCities," led by chief executive officer Thomas Murphy, moved ABC into cable television, most notably by taking control of the cable sports network ESPN (Entertainment and Sports Network).

At this same time, the cable television industry was also in the process of consolidating. Giant companies were created through acquisitions and mergers based on the core of the cable television operation: the local franchise. To take advantage of economies of operation, corporations merged cable franchises under single corporate umbrellas, creating "multiple system operators." No two corporations did this better than Time Warner and TeleCommunications, Inc. (TCI).

Time Warner was formed by the merger of two communications giants in 1989; its assets approached $20 billion, and yearly revenues topped $10 billion. While the colossus covered all phases of the mass media, its heart was a vast nationwide collection of cable franchises. However, this merger to end all mergers also included Warner Brothers (one of Hollywood's major studios, a leading home video distributor, and one of the world's top six major music labels) and Time's vast array of publishing interests, from magazines as well known as *Time, Fortune,* and *Sports Illustrated* to Time-Life Books. In 1995 Time Warner acquired Turner Broadcasting (which had itself acquired other film libraries, production companies, and cable entities), making an already vast empire ever larger.

From the outside, to challenge the Big Three networks and these vast cable corporations, came Rupert Murdoch and his News Corporation Ltd. From a confederation of independent stations around the United States, Murdoch fashioned the FOX television network. He began by taking over the Hollywood studio 20th Century-Fox and thus obtaining a steady source of programming. Next he acquired the most powerful nonnetwork collection of television stations, Metromedia, for well in excess of $1 billion. These six over-the-air television stations, plus a score more in smaller markets that Murdoch would later acquire as legal ownership maximums increased, could reach nearly one-third of homes in the United States. As a capstone, Murdoch spent well in excess of $1 billion for *TV Guide,* the magazine that was best able to promote his new television empire.

In 1990, with the Time Warner merger settled, Rupert Murdoch on scene as a new player, and the new owners for each of the Big Three TV networks, it seemed it would be well into the next century before the television industry in the United States would experience another important wave of mergers. Instead, a frenzy of acquisition came in 1995, far sooner than anyone expected. That summer, Disney acquired Capital Cities/ABC, adding not only a famous TV network but also a score of FM and AM radio stations and two dozen newspapers to the entertainment and theme park company. Within a month, Tisch sold CBS to Westinghouse. At the time, Westinghouse stood as a major manufacturer of industrial equipment in the United States with but a single division owning and operating television and radio stations. (Later in 1995 came the previously mentioned acquisition of Turner Broadcasting by Time Warner.)

A cornerstone event in the history of mergers and acquisitions in the television business had taken place. Critics stood up and asserted that this takeover wave had created a very real threat: a few corporations controlling television, the most important communications medium of the late 20th century. Before 1995, analysts had associated TV networks with one part of the business (distribution run from New York) and Hollywood with another (production of prime-time entertainment). The 1995 merger movement changed all that, consolidating all economic functions into single corporations. Indeed, critics argued that the television industry seemed on the verge of domination by one unit: "The ABC-CBS-NBC-FOX-Disney-Westinghouse-News Corp Entertainment and Appliance Group."

A primary concern for critics of such alliances is the reduction in forms of social and cultural expression. They cite various form of vertical integration—including the unification of production, distribution, and presentation of mediated material—as serious threats to experimentation, variation, and diversity among social and cultural groups. Profit margins, rather than the needs and aspirations of groups and individuals, determine what is produced and exhibited. Moreover, because most of the major participants in the giant, newly merged media corporations also have international interests, critics point to the possibility of a reduction in cultural diversity, forms of expression, and

dissemination of information on a global scale. Indeed, the model of consolidation and merger outlined here in the context of the United States is equally significant among a shrinking handful of European and Asian media conglomerates. Control of communication- and media-based corporations throughout the world, then, is scrutinized as a form of extraordinary political, economic, social, and cultural power.

The wave of mergers continued through the end of the 20th century and the early 2000s. The biggest came in January 2000, when America Online (AOL) merged with Time Warner. This deal lasted only three years, as AOL could never provide a synergistic thrust to the benefit of Time Warner. In August 2003, "AOL" was dropped from the company name.

The second-largest deal came in September 2003, when NBC took control of Hollywood's Universal studios. Therefore, at that point in time, all four major networks (NBC, CBS, ABC, and FOX) were vertically integrated with movie and television studios in a merger worth an estimated $42 billion.

Mergers and acquisitions will continue in the future as corporate players try to anticipate what it means to operate in the new world of 500 channels and the Internet. Future media mergers will most likely take one of three forms.

First, corporations and companies not directly involved in the television industry will wish to enter into mergers with television companies or acquire them. This was exemplified by the Westinghouse takeover of CBS, continuing a trend that started in the mid-1980s with GE taking over NBC. More often than not (and surely in the case with Westinghouse), the outside corporate entity acquires the television company because it is struggling and seeking to reinvent itself.

Second, there will be an increase in vertical integration. Disney, a "software producer," acquired ABC, a top distributor of video, in part to enable Disney to gain a guaranteed market for its future products.

The third merger strategy will be corporate diversification. Corporate chief executive officers will seek to spread risk over as many media enterprises as possible in order to hedge bets in an ever-changing media marketplace. With divisions devoted to all forms of the mass media, the diversified corporation can survive through future recessions and ride the technological wave of the future, whatever direction it may take.

It is likely that mergers and acquisitions will always be a central activity in the television business as companies maneuver to become the dominant player in one media segment. Television, whether defined by networks (distributors) or Hollywood studios (producers), has long been comprised of small, exclusive clubs. As long as television remains a major industry, outsiders will attempt to buy in, current players will struggle to protect what they have, and all will strive to minimize risk. Simply put, it is cheaper to merge with and acquire other companies than to start new companies from scratch, a fact as true in the days of Sarnoff, Paley, and Goldenson as it is today.

DOUGLAS GOMERY

See also **American Broadcasting Company; Columbia Broadcasting System; FOX Broadcasting Company; Hollywood and Television; Media Conglomerates; National Broadcasting Company; Time Warner; Turner Broadcasting Systems; Networks: United States**

Further Reading

Adalian, Josef, "NBC Says: I believe in U," *Variety* (December 8, 2003)

Bruck, Connie, *Master of the Game: Steve Ross and the Creation of Time Warner,* New York: Simon and Schuster, 1994

Clurman, Richard M., *To the End of Time: The Seduction and Conquest of a Media Empire,* New York: Simon and Schuster, 1992

Compaine, Benjamin M., et al., *Who Owns the Media? Concentration of Ownership in the Mass Media Industry,* White Plains, New York: Knowledge Industry Publications, 1979; 3rd edition, as *Who Owns the Media? Competition and Concentration in the Mass Media Industry,* by Compaine and Douglas Gomery, Mahwah, New Jersey: Lawrence Erlbaum Associates, 2000

Flower, Joe, *Prince of the Magic Kingdom: Michael Eisner and the Re-Making of Disney,* New York: John Wiley, 1991

Golberg, Robert, and Gerald Jay Goldberg, *Citizen Turner: The Wild Rise of an American Tycoon,* New York: Harcourt Brace, 1995

Goldenson, Leonard H., *Beating the Odds: The Untold Story Behind the Rise of ABC: The Stars, Struggles, and Egos That Transformed Network Television by the Man Who Made It Happen,* New York: Scribner's, 1991

Gomery, Douglas, "A Marriage Made in Cyberspace," *American Journalism Review* (March 2000)

Greenwald, John, "Hands Across the Cable: The Inside Story of How Media Titans Overcame Competitors and Egos to Create a $20 Billion Giant," *Time* (October 2, 1995)

MacDonald, J. Fred, *One Nation Under Television: The Rise and Decline of Network TV,* New York: Pantheon, 1990; revised edition, Chicago: Nelson-Hall, 1994

Paley, William S., *As It Happened: A Memoir,* Garden City, New York: Doubleday, 1979

Shawcross, William, *Rupert Murdoch: Ringmaster of the Information Circus,* London: Chatto and Windus, 1992; as *Murdoch,* New York: Simon and Schuster, 1993; revised edition, as *Murdoch: The Making of a Media Empire,* New York: Simon and Schuster, 1997

Smith, Sally Bedell, *In All His Glory: The Life of William S. Paley, The Legendary Tycoon and His Brilliant Circle,* New York: Simon and Schuster, 1990

Thomas, Laurie, and Barry Litman, "Fox Broadcasting Company: Why Now? An Economic Study of the Rise of the Fourth Broadcast 'Network,'" *Journal of Broadcasting and Electronic Media* (1991)

Winans, Christopher, *The King of Cash: The Inside Story of Laurence A. Tisch and How He Bought CBS,* New York: John Wiley, 1995

Messer, Don (1910–1973)

Canadian Musician, Television Performer

Don Messer was the star of his own music variety program, *Don Messer's Jubilee,* which ran on the Canadian Broadcasting Corporation (CBC), Canada's public broadcaster, from 1958 to 1969. The program featured the "Down-East" fiddling style of Messer and his band as well as a medley of old-time favorite folk songs sung by the show's two lead singers, Marge Osborne and Charlie Chamberlain. During its run, it was one of the most popular television programs in Canada, and in the mid-1960s it ranked second only to *Hockey Night in Canada* in national ratings.

Don Messer's Jubilee, like many early television programs, had its roots in radio. In 1934, Messer formed a band, the Lumberjacks, in his native province of New Brunswick; along with lead singer Charlie Chamberlain, he developed the musical format and style that he would later translate to television. In 1939, he moved to Prince Edward Island, where the band was joined by Marge Osborne. They changed the band's name to the Islanders. His television career began locally in the Maritimes in 1957. One year later, *Don Messer's Jubilee* was broadcast nationally as a summer replacement for the country-and-western music show *Country Hoedown. Jubilee* was an instant success and remained consistently in the top ten throughout its run. The show's popularity was so strong that its Canadian ratings in 1961 were even higher than the formidable *Ed Sullivan Show.*

The show's success, according to Messer himself, lay in its sincerity and simplicity. The show's style contrasted sharply with the more "showbiz" variety programs that were being made in Canada's larger urban centers, which more often than not emulated the more appealing U.S. programs. *Jubilee* offered its Canadian viewers a "made-in-Canada" variety show. It reflected what one commentator called "an echo of our country and people as they used to be in simpler days."

Don Messer was shy and retiring and rarely spoke in front of the cameras, preferring to let the show's announcer introduce the songs. The two lead singers appeared more ordinary and down-home than glamorous and glitzy. The show's set, format, and staging were simple, straightforward, and inexpensive to produce. Settings were often fixed, and a "book" (two flats hinged together) was often used to provide variety. *Jubilee*'s appeal was largely among Canada's far-flung rural population, reaching nearly one-half of Canadian farm homes, and its greatest appeal was among the fishing population of the Maritimes.

The decision to cancel the show in 1969 in favor of a "younger look" brought such a storm of protest that the CBC board of directors decreed that in the future such popular shows were not to be canceled without justifiable reasons. Attempts were quickly made to revive the show on Hamilton's local television station CHCH, but without its national time slot, *Jubilee* quickly lost its magic. Don Messer passed away three years later on March 26, 1973.

The appeal of *Don Messer's Jubilee* has survived to this day. Since the 1970s, it has come to symbolize the "made-in-Canada" music variety show. Many artists have had successful television careers using the formula and sincere style that Messer pioneered. Shows such as *The Tommy Hunter Show,* a country-western music program; *The Irish Rovers,* featuring Irish folk music; and *Rita MacNeill and Friends,* starring another Maritime musician, have carved out successful programs based on Messer's own conviction that musicians wish to be judged only on their ability to make music rather than the glitz and glamour of their programming. In the mid-1980s, John Gray, composer and songwriter of the stage play *Billy Bishop Goes to War,* revived a stage play based on the television show as a celebration of a Canadian cultural treasure.

MANON LAMONTAGNE

Don Messer. Born in Tweedside, New Brunswick, Canada, 1910. Fiddler since age of seven; formed group, the New Brunswick Lumberjacks, with Charlie Chamberlain, and made first radio appearance, 1934; regular radio and television appearances on CBC; host, maritime regional musical variety program. Died March 26, 1973.

Television Series

1958–69   *Don Messer's Jubilee* (host/performer)

Further Reading

"Fiddling with the Past," *Globe and Mail* (April 20, 1994)
Sellick, L., *Canada's Don Messer,* Kentville, Nova Scotia: Kentville, 1969

Mexico

The first experimental television transmission in Mexico—from Cuernavaca to Mexico City—was arranged by Francisco Javier Stavoli in 1931. Stavoli purchased a Nipkow system from Western Television in Chicago with funding from the ruling party, the Mexican Revolutionary Party, which became the current Institutional Revolutionary Party. In 1934 Guillermo Gonzalez Camarena built his own monochromatic camera; by 1939 Gonzalez Camarena had developed a trichromatic system, and in 1940 he obtained the first patent for color television in the world. In 1942, after Lee deForest traveled to meet with him in order to buy the rights, he secured the U.S. patent under description of the Chromoscopic Adaptors for Television Equipment. In 1946 Gonzalez Camarena also created XE1GGC-Channel 5, Mexico's first experimental television station, and started weekly transmissions to a couple of receivers, built by Gonzalez Camarena himself, installed at the radio stations XEW and XEQ and at the Mexican League of Radio Experimentors. The first on-air presenter was Luis M. Farias, and the group of actors and actresses performing in those transmissions were Rita Rey, Emma Telmo, Amparo Guerra Margain, and Carlos Ortiz Sanchez. Gonzalez Camarena also built the studio Gon-Cam in 1948, which was considered the best television system in the world in a survey done by Columbia College of Chicago.

In 1949, another broadcasting pioneer, Romulo O'Farrill, obtained the concession for XHTV-Channel 4, the first commercial station in Mexico, which was equipped with an RCA system. XHTV made the first remote-control transmission in July 1950 from the Auditorium of the National Lottery—a program televising a raffle for the subscribers of O'Farrill's newspaper, *Novedades*. The first televised sports event, a bullfight, was transmitted the following day. In September 1950, with the firm Omega and the automobile-tire manufacturer Goodrich Euzkadi as the first advertisers, XHTV made the first commercial broadcast, the State of the Union Address of President Miguel Aleman Valdes.

By the late 1980s, the entire telecommunications infrastructure in Mexico consisted of 10,000 miles of microwaves with 224 retransmitting stations and 110 terminal stations, the Morelos Satellite System with two satellites and 232 terrestrial links, 665 AM radio stations and 200 FM radio stations, 192 television stations, and 72 cable systems.

From the time of the earliest experiments, the television system in Mexico has been regulated by article 42 of the Mexican Constitution, which stipulates state ownership of electromagnetic waves transmitted over Mexican territory. This law is supplemented by article 7 of the 1857 Constitution, which deals with freedom of the press, a perspective that became more restrictive as article 20 of the 1917 Constitution. In 1926 the Calles administration produced the Law of Electrical Communications. And the first document that specifically addresses the television industry, the "decree which sets the norms for the installation and operation of television broadcasting stations," was drafted by the Aleman administration in 1950. The current Federal Law of Radio and Television was originally formulated in 1960 during the Lopez Mateos administration, introducing limits to advertising. This law was drastically altered in 2002 by the Fox administration, complying with the proposals of private broadcasters.

Even within the structure of these regulations, television in Mexico has been dominated by a handful of powerful individuals and family groups. The most significant of these is the Azcarraga family. Television station XEW began operations in 1951 under the direction of Emilio Azcarraga Vidaurreta, who already owned the radio station with the same call letters, one of 13 radio stations under his ownership in the northern part of the country. Azcarraga had strong links with the U.S. conglomerate Radio Corporation of America (RCA) and had been the founding president of the

Chamber of the Radiobroadcast Industry in 1941. He was also influential in the creation of the Interamerican Radiobroadcasting Association and, with Goar Mestre of Cuba, was considered one of the two most powerful media barons in Latin America. XHGC was founded in 1952 by Gonzalez Camarena, who was considered a protégé of Azcarraga and had worked as a studio engineer in his radio stations. Telesistema Mexicano was born in 1954 with the integration of XEW-TV, XHGC-TV, and, a year later, XHTV.

Although these stations and systems operated under the laws requiring state ownership of the airwaves, in 1950 Mexico adopted a commercial model of financial support. This decision came two years after, and despite the conclusions of, the report issued by the Television Committee of the National Fine Arts Institute. The report criticized the commercial model of the American television industry, favoring instead the public television system of the United Kingdom. The Television Committee had been formed at the request of President Aleman and was chaired by Salvador Novo, who was assisted by Gonzalez Camarena. In the judgment of the committee, commercial programming was the "simple packaging of commodities with no other aspiration." Later, Novo would characterize Mexican radio as "spiritual tequila" and television as the "monstrous daughter of the hidden intercourse between radio and cinema."

In 1973, 23 years after having committed to this model of commercial support, Television Via Satellite, S.A. (Televisa), was created as a result of the fusion of Telesistema Mexicano and Television Independiente de Mexico (TIM). TIM was the media outlet of the Monterrey Group, the most powerful industrial group in the country, and consisted of XHTM-TV (which started in 1968), two more stations in the interior, and the additional 15 television stations of Telecadena Mexicana, S.A. This network was founded by film producer Manuel Barbachano Ponce in 1965 and was purchased by TIM in 1970. The fusion of Telesistema and TIM was preceded by strong criticisms of programming and advertising by several public officials, including President Luis Echeverria, in 1972.

Emilio Azcarraga Jean became the president of Televisa after the death of Emilio Azcarraga Milmo in 1997, its founding and only president, except for a short period in 1986 and 1987, when Miguel Aleman Velasco—son of the president who opted for the commercial model—replaced him. In addition to its dominant role in the television industry, Televisa has operations in sectors as diverse as the recording industry, soccer teams (America, the winningest team in the country's history; Necaxa; and Real San Luis), a sports stadium with a capacity for 114,000 spectators, a publishing house, newspapers, billboard advertising companies, Cablevision, a cable television system, film studios, video stores, and direct broadcast satellite, among others. Moreover, the Televisa empire extends beyond the boundaries of Mexico. Televisa's board has a new look after the exit of the Aleman, O'Farrill, Diez Barroso, and Canedo families and the entrance new names, such as Asuncion Aramburuzabala, cice chairwoman; Alfonso De Angoitia, chief financial officer; Raul Rodriguez, chief executive officer of radio; and Pablo Vazquez, chief executive officer of Innova. Besides the strategic alliance with Carlos Slim, the wealthiest businessperson in Mexico, the list of foreign stockholders now includes Bill Gates, who holds a 7 percent share.

The first experience of Televisa outside its home country was the creation of what is known today as Univision, a system of Spanish-language television operations in the United States. The move of Azcarraga to the United States coincided with a new strategy to grow internationally while diversifying in the national market. The original operation started in 1960 as Spanish International Network Sales (SIN) with stations in San Antonio and Los Angeles and three more besides the affiliates. The link between Televisa and SIN/SICC was in a hiatus for some time after a lawsuit focused on Azcarraga's potential violation of U.S. regulations preventing foreign citizens from holding controlling interests in U.S. media industries. Within a matter of years, however, Televisa not only recovered Univision but also added Panamsat in 1985 and made substantial investments in Chile, Peru, Spain, and Venezuela. Tele Futura was recently added to the cable channel Galavision as U.S. outlets linked to Univision.

After being dominated by Televisa for 23 years, a duopoly emerged with TV Azteca as the competitor. The quasi monopoly of Televisa in the Mexican television industry was broken in 1994, when the Salinas administration privatized a media package that included Channels 7 and 13 as well as a chain of film theaters. The winning bid was presented by Ricardo Salinas Pliego, president of the electronics manufacturer Elektra and the furniture chain Salinas y Rocha. Salinas Pliego won the bid despite having no experience in the broadcast industry, a qualification required by rules issued by the federal government. Among those who lost the bid were families with a long history in the broadcast industry, such as the Sernas and the Vargas families. Some of these irregularities were coupled with the revelation by Raul Salinas de Gortari—brother of Carlos Salinas de Gortari and the main suspect in the assassination of Jose Francisco Ruiz Massieu—that he had engaged in financial transactions with Salinas Pliego shortly before and after the privatization. The

revelation of this information by Televisa (quoting U.S. newspapers and newscasts) caused a war of accusations between Televisa and the Salinas Pliego group, a war that calmed down after the intervention of the secretary of the interior and President Ernesto Zedillo himself.

Televisa had experienced a similar conflict in 1995 with Multivision, the wireless cable firm owned by the Vargas family. Multivision asked for the nullification of several dozens of new concessions of stations given to Televisa at the end of the Salinas administration. Televisa counterattacked by accusing Multivision of receiving concessions for wireless cable and other services without following correct procedures. After initiating mutual lawsuits, Televisa and Multivision reached a truce with the mediation of the secretary of the interior. The most spectacular conflict, however, occurred between TV Azteca and CNI-Channel 40 when the former took over the transmission facilities of Mount Ciquihuite of the latter with an armed commando in December 2002 because of some disagreements about the interpretation of a programming contract. The Fox administration waited ten days before reacting. A judge gave the facilities back to CNI and imprisoned eight employees of TV Azteca after the federal authorities appeared to be afraid of acting forcefully against TV Azteca.

In addition to these private, commercially supported television systems, a smaller, public system is also in place. The first public television station was Channel 11, started in 1958 by the Instituto Politecnico Nacional (National Polytechnical Institute). In 1972 the Echeverria administration created Television Rural del Gobierno Federal, which later became Television de la Republica Mexicana, and purchased 72 percent of the stock of XHDF-Channel 13 through SOMEX. It later added Channels 7 and 22 and became Instituto Mexicano de Television (Imevision). Although Imevision was owned and operated by the government, it emulated the programming of Televisa. The Salinas administration privatized Imevision, which became TV Azteca, and handed XEIMT-Channel 22 to a group of scholars, artists, and intellectuals.

Although there were some cable television operations in the northern state of Sonora by the late 1950s, the industry has been dominated by Televisa through Cablevision since its creation in 1970. This operation has had its main competitor from direct broadcast satellite delivery, primarily from Multivision, owned by the Vargas family. Multivision has greater market penetration and offers more channels than its counterparts in countries such as the United States. In 1996 Televisa created a joint venture with News Corporation, Rede Globo (Brazil), and TeleCommunications,

Inc. (TCI), to create a direct broadcast satellite service for Latin America. Multivision became part of the rival operation DirecTV, along with the Cisneros Organization (Venezuela) and Television Abril (Brazil). There have been talks to merge both satellite services in the near future.

Much of Televisa's dominance in Mexican television comes from its role as a production and distribution company. It provides over 12,000 hours of television programming each year, of which only 13 percent are imports. Media scholar Florence Toussaint says that the soul of Televisa resides in its programming. She points out that the organization offers an apparent diversity through the four channels (Channels 2, 4, 5, and 9 in Mexico City), with 118 titles in 455 hours each week. Toussaint argues, however, that among and within all these programs, a singular discourse is being elaborated, one that propagates a determinate view of the world. Plurality, she suggests, is not its goal, and all the different shows in the various genres are, in fact, similar. This is especially true of the soap operas (*telenovelas*), the main programming form of Mexican television. (The production and distribution of melodramatic *telenovelas* places Televisa among the top five exporters of television programming in the world; the programs are exported not only to the Americas but also to countries that include China and Russia.) This particular genre can be seen to prescribe the gender roles and the aspirations that the social classes should have. Bourgeois values and symbols are the ideal, the goal, and the measure of failure or success.

Different critical perspectives move away from this analysis, which assumes a passive audience. The alternative points of view, influenced by British and American cultural studies and the works of Jesus Martin-Barbero, Nestor Garcia Canclini, Jorge Gonzalez, Guillermo Orozco, and Rossana Reguillo, point out specificities of Latin American popular culture found in the form. *Telenovelas,* for example, were modeled after *radionovelas,* the primary of example of which, *El Derecho de Nacer* (The Right to Be Born), was broadcast at the beginning of the television era in the 1950s. Although the first *telenovela* in its current format was *Senda Prohibida* (Forbidden Road), other forms of television drama appeared as early as 1951, starting with the detective program *Un muerto en su tumba* (A Dead Man in His Tomb). The first serial drama was *Los Angeles de la Calle* (Street Angels), which ran from 1952 to 1955.

Telenovelas expanded to prime time and included male viewers as part of the target audience in 1981 with Colorina. Besides the melodrama, there are other subgenres in the *telenovela*—the historical, the educa-

tional, and the political—all of which, despite the explicit differences, have a melodramatic subtext. The first antecedent to this strategy of subgenres was *Maximiliano y Carlota* (1956) and was fully initiated with *La Tormenta* (The Storm) in 1967. Educational *telenovelas* began in 1956 with a story focused on adult education, *Ven conmigo* (Come with Me). For the new television network, TV Azteca, one of the most successful programs among audiences and critics has been the political telenovela *Nada Personal* (Nothing Personal) produced by Argos. TV Azteca suffered a big blow when Argos signed an agreement with Televisa's Cablevision to launch Channel 46-Zoom TV.

Before the privatization of TV Azteca, Channel 2, with a programming based around *telenovelas,* had the highest ratings in prime time at 26.8 (a 47 percent audience share), followed by Channels 5 and 4, with a younger target audience, with 17.3 (30.3 percent share) and 8.7 rating (15.2 percent share), respectively. TV Azteca, then Imevision, had a rating of 2.5 (4.3 percent share) and 1.8 (3.1 percent share) for Channels 13 and 7, respectively. By the summer of 2003, Televisa prime-time audience share amounted to 69.6 percent, airing 85 of the 100 most popular programs. In 2002, Televisa won the ratings war in every single genre and continued in 2003 to lead the reality show *Big Brother II.* Even after the departure of Jacobo Zabludovsky after a quarter of a century of being the most widely recognized journalist and media personality, Televisa's newscast, now led by Joaquin Lopez Doriga, doubles the ratings of TV Azteca.

These historical developments and the complex structures of the Mexican television system have been the subject of considerable critical analysis. Most examinations of the Mexican television industry adopt a liberal pluralist approach. They claim that the relation between the authorities and the television monopoly has been fruitful for both parties, especially for the latter. They also stress that in this relation, the interests of the masses have been overlooked. Few critics have taken the simple view that the government and broadcasting have identical objectives, but most do argue that the different administrations have been tolerant and weak, allowing the monopoly greater benefits than its contributions to Mexican society. These analyses focus on several central themes. They cite ownership of media industries and management of news and information, criticizing the historical quasi-monopoly and the progovernment bias of Televisa's newscasts. TV Azteca proved to be even more biased than its competitor with the coverage of the 2000 presidential campaign. Both networks did it again the following year, when they failed to cover the Zapatista "Tour" and spectacular entrance to Mexico City. The two firms became strange bedfellows by organizing a "peace concert" a few days before the Zapatista arrival.

The Mexican system of broadcasting has developed out of the shifting balance between the state, private investors, and outside interests, originating in the postrevolutionary period (1920–40) when foreign capital and entrepreneurs alike were looking for new investment opportunities. Whether the situation remains the same—whether the same groups remain in control of media industries in Mexico in the face of new technological developments—remains to be seen.

EDUARDO BARRERA

See also **Telenovela**

Further Reading

Hernández, O., and E. McAnany, "Cultural Industries in the Free Trade Age: A Look at Mexican Television," in *Fragments of a Golden Age: The Politics of Culture in Mexico Since 1940,* edited by G. Joseph, A. Rubenstein, and E. Zolov, Durham, North Carolina: Duke University Press, 2001

Rodriguez, A., "Control Mechanisms of National News Making," in *Questioning the Media: A Critical Introduction,* edited by J. Downing, A. Mohammadi, and A. Sreberny-Mohammadi. Thousand Oaks, California: Sage, 1990; 2nd edition, 1995

Sinclair, J., *Latin American Television: A Global View,* Oxford: Oxford University Press, 1999

Miami Vice

U.S. Police Drama

Miami Vice earned its nickname of "MTV cops" through its liberal use of popular rock songs and a pulsating, synthesized music track created by Jan Hammer. Segments of the program closely resembled music videos, as quickly edited images, without dialogue, were often accompanied by contemporary hits such as Tina Turner's "What's Love Got to Do with It?" As with music-oriented films such as *Flashdance* (1983) and *Footloose* (1984), *Miami Vice* was a program that could not have existed before Music Television (MTV) began popularizing the music video in 1981.

Originally aired from 1984 to 1989, *Miami Vice* incorporated both current music and musicians (e.g., Phil Collins, Ted Nugent, Glenn Frey, and Sheena Easton), dressed its undercover police officers in stylish fashions, and imbued every frame with an aura of moral decay. It succeeded in making previous police programs, such as *Dragnet,* look stodgy and old-fashioned.

In *Miami Vice,* the city of Miami, Florida, was virtually a character in its own right. Each week's episode began with a catalog of Miami iconography: sunbaked beach houses, Cuban-American festivals, women in bikinis, and postmodern, pastel-colored cityscapes. Executive producer Michael Mann insisted that significant portions of the program be shot in Miami, which helped give *Miami Vice* its distinctive look. In this tropical environment, two detectives in the vice department combated drug traffickers, broke up prostitution and gambling rings, solved vice-related murders, and cruised the city's underground in expensive automobiles.

Don Johnson and Philip Michael Thomas played the program's protagonists, James "Sonny" Crockett and Ricardo "Rico" Tubbs, respectively. They were supported by Edward James Olmos as their tough, taciturn lieutenant and Michael Talbott, John Diehl, Saundra Santiago, and Olivia Brown as their colleagues on the squad. The program's narratives circulated among these characters, but Crockett was at its center, and Johnson received the lion's share of the press about *Miami Vice.*

Miami Vice was less about the solving of mysteries then it was a contemporary morality play. Indeed, Crockett and Tubbs were often inept detectives—mistakenly arresting the wrong person for a crime. Instead of *Columbo*-like problem solving, the program stresses the detectives' ethical dilemmas. Each week, these temptable men were situated in a world of temptations. They were conversant in the language of the underworld, skilled in its practices, and prepared to use both for their own ends. It would not take much for them to cross the thin line between their actions and those of the drug lords and gangsters. One such ethical dilemma frequently posed on the show was the issue of

Miami Vice, Don Johnson, Philip Michael Thomas, 1984.
Courtesy of the Everett Collection

vigilante justice. Were the detectives pursuing the evil-doers out of commitment to law and order or to exact personal revenge? Often it was very hard to distinguish the lawbreakers from the law enforcers. Indeed, one *Miami Vice* season ended with Crockett actually becoming a bona fide gangster—his ties to law enforcement neatly severed by a case of amnesia.

The *Miami Vice* world's moral ambiguity linked it to the hard-boiled detective stories of Raymond Chandler and Dashiell Hammett and characters such as Sam Spade and Philip Marlowe as well as the film noir genre of the theatrical cinema. Television, with its demand for a repeatable narrative format, could not match the arch fatalism of these antecedents (a protagonist could not die at the end of a episode, as they often do in hard-boiled fiction), but *Miami Vice* adapted the cynical tone and world-weary attitude of hard-boiled fiction to 1980s television. Moreover, one of the most striking aspects of *Miami Vice* was its visual style, which borrowed heavily from the film noir.

As *Film Comment* critic Richard T. Jameson has commented, "It's hard to forbear saying, every five minutes or so, 'I can't believe this was shot for televi-

sion!'" *Miami Vice* was one of the most visually stylized programs of the 1980s, and it drew its stylistic inspiration from the cinema's film noir. It incorporated unconventional camera angles, high-contrast lighting, stark black-and-white sets, and striking deep focus to generate unusually dynamic, imbalanced, noir compositions that could have been lifted from *Double Indemnity* (1944) or *Touch of Evil* (1958). *Miami Vice* looked quite unlike anything else on television at the time.

Miami Vice (along with *Hill Street Blues* and *Cagney and Lacey*) was one of the groundbreaking police programs of the 1980s. Its influence can be tracked in the moral ambiguity of *NYPD Blue,* the visual experimentation of *Homicide: Life on the Street,* and the flawed police inspector Don Johnson plays in *Nash Bridges.* Moreover, *Miami Vice*'s incorporation of music video components has become a standard component of youth-oriented television and cinema.

JEREMY G. BUTLER

See also **Police Programs**

Cast

Detective James "Sonny" Crockett	Don Johnson
Detective Ricardo Tubbs	Philip Michael Thomas
Lieutenant Martin Castillo	Edward James Olmos
Detective Gina Navarro Calabrese	Saundra Santiago
Detective Trudy Joplin	Olivia Brown
Detective Stan Switek	Michael Talbott
Detective Larry Zito (1984–87)	John Diehl
Izzy Moreno	Martin Ferrero
Caitlin Davies (1987–88)	Sheena Easton

Producers

Michael Mann, Anthony Yerkovich, Mel Swope

Programming History

108 episodes; 3 2-hour episodes
NBC

September 1984	Sunday 9:00–11:00
September 1984– May 1986	Friday 10:00–11:00
June 1986–March 1988	Friday 9:00–10:00
April 1988–January 1989	Friday 10:00–11:00
February 1989–May 1989	Friday 9:00–10:00
June 1989–July 1989	Wednesday 10:00–11:00

Further Reading

Butler, Jeremy G., "*Miami Vice:* The Legacy of Film Noir," *Journal of Popular Film and Television* (Fall 1985)

Grodal, Torben Kragh, "Potency of Melancholia: *Miami Vice* and the Postmodern Fading of Symbolic Action," *The Dolphin* (1989)

Inciardi, James A., and Juliet L. Dee, "From the Keystone Cops to *Miami Vice:* Images of Policing in American Popular Culture," *Journal of Popular Culture* (Fall 1987)

King, Scott Benjamin, "Sonny's Virtues: The Gender Negotiations of *Miami Vice*," *Screen* (Autumn 1990)

Ross, Andrew, "Masculinity and *Miami Vice:* Selling In," *Oxford Literary Review* (1986)

Rutsky, R.L., "Visible Sins, Vicarious Pleasures: Style and Vice in *Miami Vice*," *SubStance: A Review of Theory and Literary Criticism* (1988)

Schwichtenberg, Cathy, "Sensual Surfaces and Stylistic Excess: The Pleasure and Politics of *Miami Vice*," *Journal of Communication Inquiry* (Fall 1986)

Seewi, Nurit, *Miami Vice: Cashing In on Contemporary Culture? Towards an Analysis of a U.S. Television Series Broadcast in the Federal Republic of Germany,* Heidelberg: Winter, 1990

Microwave

Microwave technology has been used extensively by the broadcast and cable television industries as well as in other telecommunications applications since the early 1950s. Today, microwaves are employed by telecommunications industries in the form of both terrestrial relays and satellite communications.

Microwaves are a form of electromagnetic radiation, with frequencies ranging from several hundred megahertz to several hundred gigahertz and wavelengths ranging from approximately 1 to 20 centimeters. Because of their high frequencies, microwaves have the advantage of being able to carry more information than ordinary radio waves and are capable of being beamed directly from one point to another. In addition to their telecommunications applications (which include telephony and computer networking as well as television), microwaves are used in cooking, police radar, and certain military applications.

Microwave is a "line-of-sight" technology (i.e., because a microwave transmission cannot penetrate the Earth's surface, it will not extend beyond the horizon); therefore, long-distance terrestrial transmission of messages is accomplished via a series of relay points known as "hops." Each hop consists of a tower (often atop a mountain) with one antenna (typically a parabolic antenna) for receiving and another for retransmitting. Hops typically are spaced at 25-mile intervals.

Prior to the widespread use of communications satellites in television industries, terrestrial microwave relays frequently were used to deliver programming from broadcast networks to their affiliates or to deliver special-event programming, such as sports, to local stations. Beginning in the 1950s, terrestrial microwave relays were employed to supplement expensive telephone land lines for long-distance transmission of programming. Microwave mobile units (vans with microwave transmitters attached) have also been used in television news reporting since the late 1950s.

Microwave technology was critical to the development of the community antenna television (CATV) industry. Before microwave technology became available in the early 1950s, local CATV systems were limited in channel selection to those stations that could be received over the air via tall "master" antennas. In such situations, a CATV system could flourish only within 100 to 150 miles of the nearest broadcast television markets. Microwave relays, however, made it possible for CATV systems to operate many hundreds of miles from television stations. The new technology thus was a boon to remote communities, especially in the western United States, which could not have had television otherwise.

Microwave also introduced the possibility for CATV operators to select which broadcast signals they would carry, sometimes allowing them to bypass closer signals in order to provide their customers with more desirable programming—perhaps from well-funded stations in large cities. For this reason, it was microwave technology above all that prompted the earliest efforts by the Federal Communications Commission (FCC) to regulate CATV. By the late 1950s, some concern had been voiced by broadcasters as to the legality of the retransmission—and, in effect, sale—of their signals by CATV systems and CATV-serving microwave outfits. The most notable of these complaints resulted in the U.S. Supreme Court case *Carter Mountain Transmission Co. v. FCC* (1962). In 1965 and 1966, respectively, the FCC issued two bodies of regulation to govern the rapidly growing CATV industry. Both of these focused primarily on the legalities of microwave-delivered CATV programming.

The rules did very little, however, to curtail the growth of CATV (more widely known as "cable television" by the late 1960s), and microwave continued to play a key role. Throughout the United States, the signals of several independent television stations, some of which have become cable "superstations," were delivered to cable systems by microwave. In addition, in late 1972 and early 1973, Home Box Office (HBO) began serving customers in the Northeast via two existing microwave relay networks.

Historically, then, terrestrial microwave technology accomplished many of the television programming tasks for which communication satellites are used today. Terrestrial relays still exist and serve many important functions for television. In recent years, they have also been enlisted for nontelevision applications, such as computer networking and the relaying of long-distance telephone messages. Some companies that began as terrestrial microwave outfits have also diversified into satellite program delivery.

MEGAN MULLEN

See also **Cable Television: United States; Distant Signal; Low Power Television; Translators**

Further Reading

CATV Operator's Handbook, Blue Ridge Summit, Pennsylvania: TAB Books, 1973

Cheung, Steven, and Frederic H. Levien, *Microwaves Made Simple,* Dedham, Massachusetts: Artech, 1985

Midwest Video Case

In the 1979 case of *FCC v. Midwest Video Corp.,* the U.S. Supreme Court held that the Federal Communications Commission (FCC) did not have the statutory authority to regulate public access to cable television. The legal decision, known more simply as the Midwest Video Case, marks the first time the Supreme Court refused to extend the FCC's regulatory power to the cable industry. In May 1976, the FCC used its rulemaking authority to regulate the public's access to cable television "air" time and production facilities. Under the rules, cable television systems with 3,500 or more subscribers were required to upgrade to at least 20 channels by 1986 and set aside up to four of those channels exclusively for low-cost access by community, educational, local governmental, and leased-access users. Cable operators would have had to make channel time and studios available on a first-come, first-served basis to virtually anyone who applied and without discretion or control over programming content.

At an FCC hearing and, later, before the District of Columbia Court of Appeals, Midwest Video and other cable systems objected to the FCC's regulatory intervention into their operations, arguing, among other claims, that the commission's cable access rules were beyond the scope of the agency's jurisdiction as set forth in the Communications Act of 1934. Citing more than a decade of favorable legal precedent, the FCC rejected the cable industry's position as an overly narrow interpretation of the commission's jurisdiction.

Although the Communications Act did not explicitly grant cable television jurisdiction to the FCC, the Supreme Court had previously held in 1968 that FCC regulations that are "reasonably ancillary to the effective performance of the Commission's various responsibilities for the regulation of television broadcasting" fell within the commission's mandate. In that case, *United States v. Southwestern Cable Co.,* the Court upheld FCC rules that required cable systems to retransmit the signals of local broadcast stations and seek prior FCC approval before making certain programming decisions. Similarly, in a 1972 case known as *United States v. Midwest Video Corp.,* the nation's highest court upheld FCC rules that required cable systems with 3,500 or more subscribers to create original programming and provide studio facilities for the production and dissemination of local cable programs.

Arguing specifically that the intent of the 1976 public access rules was no different than the programming rules at issue in the 1972 Midwest Video Case, the FCC maintained that controlling public access to cable was just a logical extension of its broadcasting authority. The Supreme Court, however, disagreed. Although the Court suggested that the public access rules might violate cable operators' First Amendment rights to free speech and Fifth Amendment protections against the "taking" of property without due process of law, the justices declined to make a broad constitutional ruling. Instead, the Court distinguished the public access rules from the FCC's previous cable rules by declaring the public access rules to be in violation of section 3(h) of the Communications Act of 1934, which limits the FCC's authority to regulate "common carriers."

Unlike broadcasters, common carriers are communication systems that permit indiscriminate and unlimited public access. Although the FCC has authority to regulate common carriers such as telephone networks and citizens band (CB) radio, it is expressly prohibited from subjecting broadcasters to common-carrier rules under section 3(h). Because the Court ruled that public control of local cable access would have, in effect, turned cable systems into common carriers, Midwest Video and the cable industry prevailed, at least as a matter of federal law. In the wake of the Midwest Video Case's narrow ruling, state and local authorities were still free to pass ordinances mandating set-asides for public access channels as a precondition for the granting or renewal of a cable franchise in a specific community.

MICHAEL M. EPSTEIN

See also **Cable Television: United States; Distant Signal; Federal Communications Commission**

Further Reading

Garay, Ronald, *Cable Television: A Reference Guide to Information,* New York: Greenwood, 1988
Ginsburg, Douglas H., Michael H. Botein, and Mark D. Director, *Regulation of the Electronic Mass Media: Law and Policy for Radio, Television, Cable, and the New Video Technologies,* St. Paul, Minnesota: West, 1991
Streeter, T., "The Cable Fable Revisited: Discourse, Policy, and the Making of Cable Television," *Critical Studies in Mass Communication* (1987)
United States v. Midwest Video Corp., 406 U.S. 649, 1972 (Midwest Video Case I)
United States v. Midwest Video Corp., 440 U.S. 689, 1979 (Midwest Video Case II)

Miller, J.P. (James Pinckney) (1919–2001)

U.S. Television Writer

J.P. Miller began writing for television during that time in the 1950s when a playwright fortunate enough to see his work performed on a live network drama literally could become an overnight sensation. For Miller, that night was October 2, 1958, when the Columbia Broadcasting System (CBS) broadcast a live production of his play "The Days of Wine and Roses" during its prestigious drama series *Playhouse 90.* By the following morning, the newspapers already had heralded his ascension to the elite ranks of television playwrights, ensuring that his name would be forever linked with those of Paddy Chayefsky, Reginald Rose, Rod Serling, Horton Foote, Gore Vidal, and Tad Mosel. An Emmy nomination followed, along with a lucrative offer from Hollywood for the film rights and an opportunity to write the film adaptation, which eventually became a 1962 movie directed by Blake Edwards and starring Jack Lemmon and Lee Remick.

If J.P. Miller's name is not recalled as quickly as that of other television playwrights of his era, it is because he was never as prolific as his colleagues or as eager to carve out a place in the television and movie industries. He was ambivalent about the business, unwilling

to compromise, perhaps even spoiled by his early taste of freedom under the guidance of producer Fred Coe. After his initial burst of success on television and an inevitable courtship by the movie industry, he returned to New Jersey, where he spent 40 years working out of his home, satisfied to write intermittently for movies, television, and the stage while devoting much of his energy to his own novels. Unlike most writers able to sustain long careers in television, Miller never wrote for episodic television series or aspired to become a producer. He was a playwright who wrote individual television plays—not series episodes—and this craft, honed in the live dramas of the 1950s, did not translate easily to the conditions of the television industry after 1960. Still, Miller returned repeatedly to television, where he earned three more Emmy nominations and received the Emmy Award in 1969 for his *CBS Playhouse* teleplay "The People Next Door." From the beginning of his career to the end, Miller specialized in scripts that were stark and somber, melancholy reminders that America is often a land of opportunities lost. It is a unique and unlikely vision for a writer who survived nearly four decades in television.

J.P. Miller.
Photo courtesy of Sophie Miller Solarino

After World War II (during which he served as a lieutenant, earning a Purple Heart), Miller enrolled in the Yale drama school, which he attended for only a year before moving back to Houston. While in Houston, Miller divorced his first wife and then remarried, failed as a salesman of furnaces and real estate, and never strayed far from his dream of a career as a writer. Soon he moved his young family back to New York, where they lived in a small apartment in Queens. By day, Miller sold refrigeration for air conditioners; by night, he wrote plays that no one would read. Around this time, however, a friend who was a television repairman brought Miller a used television set that was missing its cabinet.

Miller discovered the quality of writing on *Philco-Goodyear Television Playhouse,* which was an expression of the taste of its producer, Fred Coe, who also had studied at the Yale drama school. By commissioning original plays from writers such as Chayefsky, Mosel, and Foote, Coe nurtured a dramatic form influenced by the breakthrough work of Arthur Miller and Tennessee Williams but suited to the scale of early television: intimate family dramas set in ethnic urban neighborhoods or forgotten communities in the rural South in which traditional cultures collide with the forces of modernity. Miller watched and made notes for his first television play.

"A Game of Hide and Seek," Miller's first television play, told of two southern sisters who had grown apart since the day years earlier when the younger sister had married an apparently wealthy stranger and moved away. When the prodigal sister returns home, abandoned and penniless, she hides her misfortune from the older sister, who is blind, until the older sister touches her suitcase and discovers that it is held together by rope. Miller delivered the script to Yale classmate Bob Costello, who had become one of Coe's assistant producers. Coe immediately purchased the script, assigning it to his star director, Arthur Penn, and casting the stage actress Mildred Dunnock.

Miller's first notable success came with the play "The Rabbit Trap," the story of a long-suffering engineer at a construction firm who stands up to his bullying boss and quits the job in order to spend more time with his son. This austere critique of corporate America caught the attention of the movie studios, which were on the lookout for New York talent, and Miller was brought to Hollywood to write the adaptation, an experience that he soon came to regret when he discovered how powerless he was to affect the outcome of the film. Writers in the movie industry enjoyed neither the autonomy nor the influence they were accorded under Fred Coe's benevolent patronage.

While Miller toiled as a screenwriter in Hollywood, fortunes faded for the live television drama. Westerns and private-detective series filmed in Hollywood climbed the ratings, and retailers for companies such as Goodyear and Philco began to pressure the corporate headquarters to sponsor programs more cheerful than the bleak dramas that had become Fred Coe's trademark. With ratings slipping, Philco pulled its sponsorship from *Television Playhouse* in 1955, and Fred Coe eventually left the National Broadcasting Company (NBC) and landed at CBS, where he became one of the producers for *Playhouse 90,* the last remaining prestige drama on television. It was in this capacity that Coe lured Miller back to television, and the result was "The Days of Wine and Roses," a pinnacle of live television drama and very nearly the swan song for the genre.

With prime-time television utterly dominated by filmed series and the live television drama all but forgotten by 1960, Miller turned to screenwriting once again, writing *The Young Savages* (1961) for director John Frankenheimer, adapting his own *The Days of Wine and Roses* (1962), and working with director Fred Zinneman on *Behold a Pale Horse* (1964). From this Hollywood sojourn, Miller saved enough money to purchase a measure of independence. He married for the third time (to the woman with whom he would live for the rest of his life), bought a farmhouse in New Jersey, and began work on his first novel, *The Race for Home* (1968), a Depression-era tale that takes place in a thinly disguised version of the Gulf coast town where he was raised. He returned to television in the late 1960s, when CBS asked Fred Coe to resurrect the anthology drama format in *CBS Playhouse,* an ambitious, short-lived series of plays written for television.

Miller wrote "The People Next Door" as an unacknowledged companion piece to *The Days of Wine and Roses*. In this version, a suburban couple (Lloyd Bridges and Kim Hunter) struggle to understand their drug-addicted teenage daughter (Deborah Winters). Miller received an Emmy Award for Outstanding Writing Achievement in Drama and later wrote the feature film adaptation.

Throughout the 1970s and 1980s, Miller charted his own course, alternating between writing novels and movies and miniseries for television. As he channeled his energies into fiction (eventually writing three more novels), he stopped writing original material for television and became a specialist in "true-life" movies and miniseries, including an Emmy-nominated script for *The Lindbergh Kidnapping Case* (1976) and *Helter Skelter* (1976), an adaptation of Vincent Bugliosi's book about the Charles Manson case (which was the top-rated miniseries of the season). His final work for television, the Emmy-nominated 1989 miniseries *I Know My First Name Is Steven*, written with Cynthia Whitcomb, was based on the real-life abduction of a young boy who spent seven years living with his captor before finally escaping and being reunited with his family.

CHRISTOPHER ANDERSON

J.P. Miller. Born in San Antonio, Texas, December 18, 1919. Son of Rolland James and Rose Jetta (Smith) Miller. Married: 1) Ayers Elizabeth Fite, May 16, 1942 (divorced, 1947); children: James Pinckney Jr.; 2) Juanita Marie Currie, November 29, 1948 (divorced, 1962); children: John R., Montgomery A.; 3) Julianne Renee Nicolaus, November 20, 1965; children: Lia Marie, Anthony Milo, Sophie Jetta. Education: Rice Institute (now Rice University), B.A. in modern languages, 1941; studied drama at Yale University, 1946–47, and at American Theatre Wing, 1951–53. Military service: U.S. Navy, 1941–46; served in Pacific theater; became lieutenant; received Presidential Unit Citation and Purple Heart. Worked as playwright for live television dramas, 1954–59; as freelance screenwriter, playwright, novelist, 1959–2001. Memberships: Dramatists Guild, PEN, Academy of Motion Picture Arts and Sciences, Authors Guild, Authors League of America, Writers Guild of America—West. Died in Stockton, New Jersey, November 1, 2001.

Television Series (writer)

1954	*Man Against Crime* (wrote one episode)
1954–55	*Philco-Goodyear Television Playhouse* (teleplays: "A Game of Hide and Seek," "Old Tasselfoot," "Somebody Special," "The Catamaran," "The Rabbit Trap," "The Pardon-Me Boy")
1955	*Producer's Showcase* (teleplay: "Yellow Jack")
1956	*Playwright's '56* (teleplay: "The Undiscovered Country")
1958	*Kraft Mystery Theatre* (teleplay: "A Boy Called Ciske")
1958–59	*Playhouse 90* (teleplays: "The Days of Wine and Roses," "The Dingaling Girl"
1968	*CBS Playhouse* (teleplay: "The People Next Door")

Made-for-Television Movies (writer)

1972	*Your Money or Your Wife*
1976	*The Lindbergh Kidnapping Case*
1980	*Gauguin the Savage*

Miniseries (writer)

1976	*Helter Skelter*
1989	*I Know My First Name Is Steven* (with Cynthia Whitcomb)

Feature Films (writer)

1959	*The Rabbit Trap*
1961	*The Young Savages*
1962	*The Days of Wine and Roses*
1964	*Behold a Pale Horse*
1970	*The People Next Door*

Novels

1968	*The Race for Home*
1973	*Liv*
1984	*The Skook*
1995	*Surviving Joy*

Awards

Emmy Award for outstanding achievement in drama, Academy of Television Arts and Sciences, 1969, for teleplay *The People Next Door;* Mystery Writers of America Awards, 1974, for television movie, *Your Money or Your Wife,* and Edgar Allan Poe Award, 1977, for television miniseries adaptation of the book *Helter Skelter;* Emmy Award nomination for best writing of a single dramatic program, 1959, for "The Days of Wine and Roses," *Playhouse 90;* Emmy Award nomination for outstanding writing in a special program, 1976, for *The Lindbergh Kidnapping Case;* Emmy Award nomination (with Cynthia Whitcomb) for outstanding writing in a miniseries or special, 1989, for *I Know My First Name Is Steven.*

Further Reading

Gould, Lewis L., editor, *Watching Television Come of Age: The New York Times Reviews by Jack Gould,* Austin: University of Texas Press, 2002

Kisseloff, Jeff, *The Box: An Oral History of Television, 1920–61,* New York: Viking, 1995
Krampner, John, *The Man in the Shadows: Fred Coe and the Golden Age of Television,* New Brunswick, New Jersey: Rutgers University Press, 1997

Milton Berle Show, The

U.S. Comedy-Variety Show

During his multifaceted rise as a performer, Milton Berle first appeared on television in a 1929 experimental broadcast in Chicago when he emceed a closed-circuit telecast before 129 people. In the commercial-TV era, he appeared in 1947 on DuMont station WABD (in Wanamaker's New York City department store) as an auctioneer to raise money for the Heart Fund. In the following year, he would come to television in a far more prominent manner and through the new medium rise to the status of a national icon. He would become known as "Mr. Television," the first star the medium could call its own. Skyrocketing to national prominence in the late 1940s, he was also the first TV personality to suffer overexposure and burnout.

Berle began his professional career at age five, working in motion pictures at Biograph Studios in Fort Lee, New Jersey. He appeared as the child on Marie Dressler's lap in Charlie Chaplin's *Tillie's Punctured Romance* (1914), was tossed from a train by Pearl White in *The Perils of Pauline* (1914), and appeared in some 50 films with stars such as Douglas Fairbanks, Mabel Normand, and Marion Davies. Berle's first stage role was in 1920, in Shubert's Atlantic City, New Jersey, revival of *Floradora,* which eventually moved to Broadway. Soon after, a vaudeville sketch with Jack Duffy launched Berle's career as a comedian. Signed as a replacement for Jack Haley at the Palace, Berle was a smash hit and was held over ten weeks. He then headlined in top nightclubs and theaters across the country, returning to Broadway in 1932 to star in *Earl Carroll's Vanities,* the first of several musical shows in which he appeared.

Berle's reputation for stealing material from other comedians was already part of his persona by this time, engineered in part as a publicity ploy; Walter Winchell labeled him "The Thief of Bad Gags." Berle debuted on radio in 1934, and during the 1940s he hosted several shows, including the comedy-variety

The Milton Berle Show.
Courtesy of the Everett Collection

show *Texaco Star Theater*. He remained on radio (including the radio version of *Texaco*) until the 1948–49 season, and he was also very successful as a writer of Tin Pan Alley fare. His many songs include "Sam, You Made the Pants Too Long."

On June 8, 1948, Berle reprised his role from radio, serving as host for the premiere episode of the TV version of *The Texaco Star Theater*. However, the show as yet had no set format and rotated several emcees during the summer of 1948. Originally signed to a four-week contract, Berle was finally named permanent host for the season premiere that fall. He and the show were an immediate smash, with ratings as high as 80 the first season. Ad-libbing at the end of a 1949 episode, Berle called himself "Uncle Miltie," endearing himself to kids and creating a permanent moniker. The show received a 1949 Emmy for Best Kinescope Show (the Television Academy was then a West Coast entity in the era before coast-to-coast linkup), and Berle won as Most Outstanding Kinescoped Personality. For the next eight years, the nation seemingly shut down on Tuesday evenings during Berle's time slot. The name of the program changed in 1953 to the *Buick-Berle Show*, becoming known from 1954 as *The Milton Berle Show*.

These shows were pitched at an aggressive, anything-for-a-laugh level, which perfectly suited Berle's comic style and profile. This approach also tended to make his programs very visual. Slapstick routines, outrageous costumes (Berle often appeared in drag), and various ludicrous skits became trademarks of his television humor. Audiences across the United States wanted to see what Berle would do next, and he quite obviously thrived on this anticipation. From his malaprop greetings (e.g., "Hello, ladies and germs") to the frenetic, relentless pacing of his jokes and rejoinders and even in his reputation for stealing and recycling material, Berle presented himself as one part buffoon and one part consummate, professional entertainer, a kind of veteran of the Borscht Belt trenches. However, even within his shows' sanctioned exhibitionism, some of Berle's behavior could cross the line from affability to effrontery. At its worst, the underlying tone of the Berle programs could appear to be one of contempt should the audience not respond approvingly. In some cases, the program exhibited a surprising degree of self-consciousness about TV itself; Texaco's original commercial spokesman, Sid Stone, would sometimes hawk his products until driven from the stage by a cop. However, the uneven balance of excess and decorum proved wildly successful.

Featuring such broad and noisy comedy but also multiple guest stars and (for the time) lavish variety-show production values, Berle's shows are credited with spurring the sale of TV sets in the United States, especially to working-class homes. When he first went on the air, less than 500,000 sets had been sold nationwide; when he left *The Milton Berle Show* in 1956, after nearly 500 live shows, that number had increased to nearly 30 million. Berle was signed to an unprecedented $6 million, 30-year exclusive contract with the National Broadcasting Company (NBC) in 1951, guaranteed $200,000 per year in addition to the salaries from his sponsors. Renegotiated in 1966, his annual payments were reduced to $120,000, but Berle could work on other networks.

After his Tuesday night run ended in 1956, Berle hosted three subsequent series and made many appearances on other comedy and variety shows. He received numerous tributes as a television pioneer. In dramatic roles, he received an Emmy nomination for "Doyle Against the House," an episode of *The Dick Powell Show* (1961), and was notable in his role as a blind survivor of an airplane crash in the first American Broadcasting Company (ABC) movie of the week, *Seven in Darkness* (1969). He guest starred on many television series, including *The Big Valley,* and when he was 87 years old, he was nominated for an Emmy Award for his guest role as a former vaudeville star afflicted with Alzheimer's disease on the FOX drama *Beverly Hills 90210.* Doyen of the famous comedians' fraternity, the Friars Club, Berle also sporadically appeared on stage through the 1990s. However, it is the early Berle shows that remain the expression of Mr. Television, the expression of a medium that had not yet set its boundaries in such rigid fashion. In those earlier moments, huge numbers of Americans could settle themselves before the screen, welcome their outrageous "Uncle" into the living room, leave him behind for a week, and know that he would return once again when asked.

MARK WILLIAMS

See also **Berle, Milton**

Regular Performers
Milton Berle
Fatso Marco (1948–52)
Ruth Gilbert (1952–55)
Bobby Sherwood (1952–53)
Arnold Stang (1953–55)
Jack Collins (1953–55)
Milton Frome (1953–55)
Irving Benson (1966–67)

Orchestras
Alan Roth (1948–55)
Victor Young (1955–56)

Billy May (1958–59)
Mitchell Ayres (1966–67)

Producers
Ed Cashman, Milton Berle, Edward Sobol, Arthur
  Knorp, Ford Henry, William O. Harbach, Nick
  Vanoff, Bill Dana

Programming History
NBC
June 1948–June 1956   Tuesday 8:00–9:00

October 1958–May 1959   Wednesday
                                              9:00–9:30
ABC
September 1966–January 1967   Friday 9:00–10:00

Further Reading

Berle, Milton, with Haskel Frankel, *Milton Berle: An Autobiography,* New York: Delacorte, 1974
"Milton Berle: Television's Whirling Dervish," *Newsweek* (May 16, 1949)
Sylvester, Robert, "The Strange Career of Milton Berle," *Saturday Evening Post* (March 19, 1949)

Minder

British Crime Comedy/Drama

A long-running and perennially popular comedy-drama series focusing on the exploits of a wheeler-dealer and his long-suffering bodyguard and right-hand man, *Minder* was the brainchild of veteran TV scriptwriter Leon Griffiths. Griffiths, who had been active in television since the 1950s, also wrote for the cinema, including the screenplays for the hard-hitting crime dramas *The Grissom Gang* and *The Squeeze.* It was one of his film scripts, also called *Minder,* that gave rise to the series. Griffiths's screenplay was a humorless and tough gangland story that his agent felt would be difficult to sell in Britain, so Griffiths shelved the project.

Later, however, that same agent suggested that two of the characters from the script—a wily, small-time London crook and his uneducated but streetwise "minder" (East London slang for "bodyguard")—would work well for a television series. Griffiths wrote a treatment for a series featuring the two characters and took the idea to Euston Films (a division of Thames Television), a group he knew was looking for a follow-up to their successful, tough, London-based police series *The Sweeney.* ("Sweeney" was also London slang, actually cockney rhyming slang, "Sweeney Todd: Flying Squad," a special quick-response unit of the Metropolitan Police.) At Euston, script consultant Linda Agran and producers Verity Lambert, Lloyd Shirley, and George Taylor quickly decided that the series had all the ingredients they were looking for—and there was a general consensus that *Sweeney* star Dennis Waterman would be right for the character of the minder, Terry McCann.

Waterman, however, had his reservations and was worried about immediately following *The Sweeney* with another London-based crime series, but after reading the treatment and the initial scripts, he was persuaded by the difference and the humor of the piece. The true potential of the project was fully realized, however, only with the casting of George Cole as Terry McCann's employer, Arthur Daley. Cole had been active in film and television for many years and

Minder.
Courtesy of © Fremantle Media Enterprises

in his early days had specialized in playing "spivs" (shady characters specializing in black marketeering and other illegal activities). He had become a respected actor over the years, with a wide repertoire, but the character of Arthur Daley was like one of his earlier spiv incarnations grown up.

Although the production may have initially been perceived as a vehicle for Waterman, the casting of Cole and the rapport between them ensured that the series became more balanced. Cole fitted the roguish persona perfectly, and, as the series progressed, with generous support from Waterman, he turned Arthur Daley into a TV icon.

Originally, the series was to have been located in the East End of London, but it was found to be more convenient to shoot in South London. The location changed, but the patois remained that of the cockney-influenced East End. Arthur was always known as "Arfur" because of the cockney habit of pronouncing "th" as "f," and much of the flavor of the series came from the colorful slang, some traditional and some invented. Although some cockney rhyming slang was widely known throughout Britain, *Minder* (along with other shows set in the area, such as the British Broadcasting Corporation's [BBC's] *Only Fools and Horses*) introduced many lesser-known examples to the population as a whole. Soon every *Minder* aficionado knew that "getting a Ruby down your Gregory" meant going out for an Indian meal (popular 1950s singing star Ruby Murray providing a rhyme for "curry"; "Gregory Peck" rhyming with "neck") and that "trouble on the dog" meant your spouse was calling ("trouble and strife": "wife"; "dog and bone": "phone"). As the series went from strength to strength and the character of Arthur Daley captured the imagination of a generation, East London slang became trendy, and cod cockneys (or mockneys) could be found throughout the country.

The early episodes of *Minder* have the emphasis firmly on drama, although there is humor in the dialogue and from the character of Arthur Daley, who seems to haunt the fringes of the plot while Terry McCann gets involved at the sharp end. Daley is devious, cowardly, and exploitative, as opposed to McCann's straightforwardness, courage, and loyalty. Most plots hinge round a problem, created by Daley's greed, that is solved by McCann. But McCann almost always suffers in some way: losing a girlfriend, being involved in a fight, or not getting paid. Daley usually thrives, managing somehow to emerge from the scrape with body unscathed and bank account intact or, more often than not, somewhat inflated. Brushes with the law are commonplace, as are confrontations with "nastier" villains. The local police are endlessly trying to "feel Arfur's collar" (arrest him), but Terry is the only one who actually goes to prison.

Later in the show's run, reacting to the positive feedback from the public, the show shifted slightly but noticeably more toward humor. Scripts tapped the comedic potential of Arthur Daley, and his schemes became wilder and more outrageous, while the regular policemen who dogged him became more caricatured and less threatening. Recurring characters in the series included Patrick Malahide as the long-suffering Detective Sergeant Chisholm and Glynn Edwards as Dave the barman at Arthur's private drinking club, the Winchester.

Finally, in 1991, Dennis Waterman had had enough of *Minder* and left to head a new series. He was replaced by Gary Webster as Arthur's nephew Ray. Ray was a different character from Terry, well educated and well dressed. But he could handle himself well in a fight and was perfectly suited to the role of assistant and bodyguard to his uncle. Initially, he was in awe of Arthur, and Daley took full advantage of this. Soon Ray saw the light and became much more difficult to manipulate. Arthur, however, rose to the challenge and still seemed to get his own way. Webster's involvement gave the series a new lease of life, and the scripts for his episodes seemed as sharp and as witty as when the program had first begun.

Through the run of the series, jokey episode titles were used, usually a pun on a film or other TV series ("The Beer Hunter," "On the Autofront," and "Guess Who's Coming to Pinner," an area to the north of London).

Minder was yet another example of a television program bringing forth a character that seemed bigger than the show. The name "Arthur Daley" is used in Britain as an example of a wheeler-dealer in the same way that Archie Bunker's name came to be synonymous with bigotry in the United States. Daley may be a villain, but he is very much perceived as a hero, someone getting away with foiling the system. In the show's rare satirical moments, Daley would align himself with Margaret Thatcher, seeing himself as the prime example of the help-yourself society that Thatcher advocated, a man of the 1980s.

DICK FIDDY

See also **Cole, George; Lambert, Verity; Waterman, Dennis**

Cast

Arthur Daley	George Cole
Terry McCann	Dennis Waterman
Dave	Glynn Edwards

Des	George Layton	January 1982–April 1982	13 episodes
Det. Sgt. Chisholm	Patrick Malahide	January 1984–March 1984	11 episodes
Sgt. Rycott	Peter Chi	September 1984–December 1984	10 episodes
Maurice	Anthony Valentine	September 1985–October 1985	6 episodes
Det. Insp. Melsip Troughton	Michael	December 1985	Christmas special
Ray Daley	Gary Webster	December 1988	Christmas special
Det. Sgt. Morley	Nicholas Day	January 1989–February 1989	6 episodes
DC Park	Stephen Tompkinson	September 1991– November 1991	12 episodes
		December 1991	Christmas special
		January 1993–April 1993	13 episodes

Producers

Verity Lambert, Johnny Goodman, Lloyd Shirley, George Taylor, Ian Toynton

Programming History

96 60-minute episodes; 1 120-minute special; 1 90-minute special
ITV

October 1979–January 1980	11 episodes
September 1980–December 1980	13 episodes

Further Reading

Armstrong, John, "Obituary: Leon Griffiths," *The Independent* (February 13, 1994)
Bradbury, Malcolm, "Requiem for an Old Rogue," *Daily Mail* (October 9, 1993)
Buss, Robin, "Minder," *Times Educational Supplement* (November 8, 1991)
Truss, Lynne, "Television Workhorses Finally Put Out to Grass," *The Times* (March 10, 1994)

Miner, Worthington (1900–1982)

U.S. Producer, Director

Worthington Miner had an outstanding career in both the theater and television; he also worked for a brief period as a producer of feature films. At the age of 39, Miner abandoned his successful career as a theater director to enter the fledgling television industry, becoming general director of television at the Columbia Broadcasting System (CBS) on August 28, 1939. His work in television has been recognized by his contemporaries and followers as crucial in creating the foundations of modern television.

The Federal Communications Commission (FCC) allowed limited commercial-television broadcasting to begin in July 1941 despite the outbreak of war and legal battles over technical issues that had delayed the introduction of television in the United States. For the first ten weeks, Miner produced and directed the entire 15-hour weekly schedule at CBS and eight to ten hours a week thereafter until the war forced live television off the air in late 1942.

It was not until the regular television schedule returned in 1948 that Miner developed his first major success, *The Toast of the Town,* emceed by Ed Sullivan. This program, later under the title *The Ed Sullivan Show,* went on to run for 23 seasons. It was followed closely by the much-acclaimed *Studio One,* which Miner produced and often wrote and directed as well. He also produced *The Goldbergs* and the award-winning children's program *Mr. I. Magination,* both well-known examples from the "Golden Age" of television.

It has been said by insiders that the real "Mr. Television" was not Milton Berle (as he was called in the 1950s) but Miner. This judgment stems primarily from Miner's development of the basic techniques used in television. In addition to being a major creative force as a writer, producer, and director, Miner is credited with establishing many crew positions and assigning production responsibilities to those positions, which are still in use today. Working in an untried medium and drawing on his technical and operational experience in the theater, Miner developed new staging practices and created camera techniques that exploited the limited technical and financial resources available to television during its earliest stages of growth.

In contrast to his famed counterpart, producer Fred Coe at the National Broadcasting Company (NBC), who developed a stable of television writers, Miner concentrated on the technical and aesthetic problems of mounting and broadcasting a production, particularly from a directorial point of view. In the process, he discovered what became known as "Miner's Laws," which were adopted by directors throughout the television industry. He fostered the directing talents of such luminaries as Franklin Schaffner, George Roy Hill, Sidney Lumet, and Arthur Penn, all of whom went on to fame in television and other media.

In 1952, as a result of a contract dispute, Miner left CBS for NBC. His hopes for achievements there were dashed with the firing of creative head Pat Weaver; Miner languished under NBC's employ. Despite producing two series, *Medic* and *Frontier,* and a few stunning successes with the drama anthology *Play of the Week* (most notably Eugene O'Neill's *The Iceman Cometh*), Miner left television in 1959. He was disappointed with the direction the medium had taken.

Miner's achievements in television cannot be overestimated. He did not change the face of television; he created it. No one in his time had an equal grasp of both the creative and the technical dimensions of the television medium. Many, if not all, of his ideas remain in use today, warranting the statement that Miner was a true television pioneer.

KEVIN DOWLER

See also **Anthology Drama;** *The Ed Sullivan Show;* *The Goldbergs;* **"Golden Age" of Television;** *Medic;* **Schaffner, Franklin**

Worthington Miner. Born in Buffalo, New York, November 13, 1900. Educated at Kent School in Connecticut; Yale University, New Haven, Connecticut, 1922; Cambridge University, 1922–24. Married: Frances Fuller; children: Peter, Margaret, and Mary Elizabeth. Served in U.S. Army with the 16th Field Artillery, 4th Division, during World War I; served in army in occupied Germany, 1918–19. Faculty member, Department of English, Yale University, 1924; acted in stage plays, 1925; assistant to producers of Broadway plays, 1925–29; directed plays, 1929–39; writer and director, RKO Radio Pictures, 1933–34; program development department, CBS, 1939–42; manager, CBS television department, 1942–52; worked for NBC, from 1952; left NBC to become a freelance producer; worked in motion pictures. Died in New York City, December 11, 1982.

Further Reading

Hawes, William, *The American Television Drama: The Experimental Years,* Tuscaloosa: University of Alabama Press, 1986

Kindem, Gorham, editor, *The Live Television Generation of Hollywood Film Directors: Interviews with Seven Directors,* Jefferson, North Carolina: McFarland, 1994

Miner, Worthington, *Worthington Miner: Interviewed by Franklin J. Schaffner,* Metuchen, New Jersey: Scarecrow Press, 1985

Skutch, Ira, *Ira Skutch: I Remember Television: A Memoir,* Metuchen, New Jersey: Scarecrow Press, 1989

Stempel, Tom, *Storytellers to the Nation: A History of American Television Writing,* New York: Continuum, 1992

Sturcken, Frank, *Live Television: The Golden Age of 1946–1958 in New York,* Jefferson, North Carolina: McFarland, 1990

Wicking, Christopher, and Tise Vahimagi, *The American Vein: Directors and Directions in Television,* New York: Dutton, 1979

Wilk, Max, *The Golden Age of Television: Notes from the Survivors,* New York: Delacorte Press, 1976

Miniseries

A miniseries is a narrative drama designed to be broadcast in a limited number of episodes. If the distinction is maintained between "series" (describing a group of self-contained episodes) and "serial" (a group of interconnected episodes), the term "miniseries" is an acknowledged misnomer, for the majority of broadcast material presented in the genre is in fact produced in serial form. There are, of course, exceptions. *Boys from the Blackstuff* (1982), for example, consisted of five narratively independent but interlocking episodes that culminate in a final resolution. The miniseries may also be seen as an extended telefilm divided into episodes. David Shipman provides a useful analysis of this approach and its central question, "When is a movie not a movie?" in his discussion of *The Far Pavilions.*

Whatever the overall approach, the miniseries, at its best, offers a unique televisual experience, often dealing with harrowing and difficult material structured into an often transformative narrative. The time lapse between episodes allows occasion for the audience to assimilate, discuss, and come to terms with the difficulties of the narrative. The extended narrative time offered by serialization makes possible the in-depth exploration of characters, their motivations and development, and the analysis of situations and events. However, the conclusive narrative resolution of the series also allows for evaluation and reflection.

The actual number of episodes differentiating a miniseries from a "regular" series or serial is a matter of dispute. Leslie Halliwell and Philip Purser argue in *Halliwell's Television Companion* that miniseries tend to appear in four to six episodes of various lengths. In contrast, Stuart Cunningham defines the miniseries as "a limited-run program of more than two [installments] and less than the thirteen-part season or half-season block associated with serial or series programming." From a British perspective, the majority of home-produced drama would, in the postderegulation era, now fit into Cunningham's definition. Very few drama productions, apart from continuous serials (soap operas), extend beyond seven episodes.

The term "miniseries" covers a broad generic range of subjects and styles of narration that seem to differ from one national broadcast culture to another. Australia produces a large number of historical miniseries—for example, *Bodyline* (1984) and *Cowra Breakout* (1985)—that dramatically document aspects of Australian history. The United States has produced both historical miniseries, such as *Holocaust* (1978), and serializations of "blockbuster" novels, such as *The Thorn Birds* (1983). Britain tends toward literary classics (*Pride and Prejudice* [1995]) and serializations of "blockbusters" (*The Dwelling Place* [1994]).

Francis Wheen suggests that the form developed in the United States in response to the success of the imported *The Forsyte Saga* (1967), which was an expensive adaptation of John Galsworthy's historical epic novel. The success of this serialization demonstrated that finite stories were popular and that they could provide a boost to weekly viewing figures while imparting on the network/channel a reputation for exciting programming. The potential of the miniseries was significantly promoted, Wheen suggests, by *Roots,* which built up an exclusive culture over its eight consecutive nights on the American Broadcasting Company (ABC)

in January 1977. Americans who did not watch the program felt excluded from the dominant topic of conversation and from one of the major cultural interventions of the era.

It is significant that miniseries are generally part of late-evening, prime-time viewing, the space made available for the privileged viewing of "irregular" material, whether it be contemporary feature films, miniseries, or other forms. This scheduling is important because the high production costs of miniseries can be recovered only through exposure to the largest, most lucrative, and most attentive audiences and because the material dealt with is often either of difficult and potentially upsetting or of a sexually explicit nature not deemed suitable for children.

Miniseries are usually high capital investment ventures. It is interesting to note here that in the United States, the ABC network's introduction of the miniseries in 1976 coincided with the arrival of programmer Fred Silverman from the Columbia Broadcasting System (CBS) and was part of his strategy to revive ailing audience figures. Similarly, in the United Kingdom, Granada's investment in *Prime Suspect* coincided with the franchise bids in British commercial broadcasting.

The miniseries is almost invariably based on the work of an established writer, whether this is a classic literary source (the British Broadcasting Corporation's [BBC's] 1995 adaptation of Jane Austen's *Pride and Prejudice*), a popular blockbuster, (Shirley Conran's *Lace* [1985]), or the work of a renowned television writer (Lynda La Plante's *Prime Suspect* [1991]). Institutionally, the author's name is seen as a valuable investment that is often sought in an attempt to guarantee a prestige audience in the "desirable social categories." For the audience, the author's name provides a set of expectations of potential pleasures and an indication of production quality. The writer's name, then, is an important part of the packaging of the series. Given the condensed period of broadcasting associated with the miniseries format, it is important to attract viewers at the first opportunity, for, unlike a continuous serial or seasonal series, the miniseries cannot accrue an audience over an extended period. Authorial identity thus distinguishes the miniseries from the unattributed flow of soap operas, crime series, and situation comedies.

Charlotte Brunsdon, discussing the literary sources of television fictions, argues that "British culture having a predominantly literary bias, middlebrow literature legitimates the 'vulgar' medium of television (whereas high literature might offend as being too good for TV). Adaptations gain prestige for their literariness." Although one should recognize that producers and broadcasting institutions do intentionally exploit the prestige lent by literary sources, it is difficult to support the term "middlebrow," which is central to Brunsdon's statement, in relation to the miniseries. The authors of miniseries range from the Whitbread Prize winner Jeanette Winterson (*Oranges Are Not the Only Fruit,* 1990) to Jackie Collins (*Hollywood Wives,* 1985), neither of which seem to fit the "middlebrow" category.

One clear link between these two adaptations, however, is their implied autobiographical character. Indeed, the representation of actual lives and experiences is central to a range of miniseries. The approach taken may be autobiographical, as in Dennis Potter's *The Singing Detective* (1986). It may be biographical, as in Jane Campion's *An Angel at My Table* (1991), depicting the early life experiences of Janet Frame, or in Central Television's *Kennedy* (1983), focusing on the life and impact of the U.S. president on the 20th anniversary of his death. Or the approach may present dramatizations enacting significant moments in history, as in the Australian miniseries *Vietnam* (1987), depicting the resettlement of Vietnamese refugees from the Vietnamese and Australian perspectives, or in Alan Bleasdale's *Boys from the Blackstuff* (1982), exploring the experience of working-class life in recession-hit Liverpool.

This relation to "real life" seemed to be one of the strengths and appeals of the miniseries until the 1990s, when the format became increasingly used for the crime genre. In Britain, this shift in representation is evident in *Prime Suspect*. The first miniseries (1991) was written by La Plante and based on the experiences of a senior woman police officer (DCI Jackie Malton of the London Metropolitan Police Force). However, the following *Prime Suspect* miniseries developed as generic sequels rather than dramatizations of actual events. Subsequently, miniseries have been publicized in terms of the popular actors who play the lead roles, the crimes portrayed, and the originality of the content of their stories. *In Deep* (BBC, 2002) features undercover police officers played by Nick Berry and Stephen Tompkinson. *Outside the Rules* focused on the work of a psychiatrist in a high-security hospital, played by Daniela Nardini.

Since 1976, when the U.S. television network ABC broadcast a 12-hour serialized adaptation of Irwin Shaw's *Rich Man, Poor Man,* miniseries have constituted some of the most popular programs in television history. ABC's broadcast of Alex Haley's *Roots* drew an audience of 80 million Americans for the final episode. However, miniseries have also provided some of the most derided programming, as evidenced in Richard Corliss's commentary on *Princess Daisy* (1983): "Not even trash can guarantee the happy ending, and, alas, it happened to Jane Doe: *Princess Daisy* proved a small-screen bust." Conversely, miniseries have often been among the most critically acclaimed of television offerings. *The Singing Detective* "was inspiring," according to Joost Hunniger, "because it showed us the dynamic possibilities of television drama."

MARGARET MONTGOMERIE

See also **Amerika; Boys from the Blackstuff; Boys of St. Vincent; Brideshead Revisited; Day After; Forsyte Saga; Holocaust; I, Claudius; Jewel in the Crown; Pennies from Heaven; Rich Man, Poor Man; Singing Detective; Six Wives of Henry VIII; The Thornbirds; Tinker Tailor Soldier Spy; Upstairs, Downstairs; Women of Brewster Place**

Further Reading

Brandt, George W., editor, *British Television Drama in the 1980s,* Cambridge: Cambridge University Press, 1993

Cantor, Muriel, and Suzanne Pingree, *The Soap Opera,* Beverly Hills, California: Sage, 1983

Cunningham, Stuart, "Textual Innovation in the Australian Historical Mini-Series," in *Australian Television: Programs, Pleasures, and Politics,* edited by John Tulloch and Graeme Turner, Sydney and Boston: Allen and Unwin, 1989

Eaton, Mary, "A Fair Cop? Viewing the Effects of Canteen Culture in *Prime Suspect* and *Between the Lines,*" in *Crime and the Media: The Post-Modern Spectacle,* edited by David Kidd-Hewitt and Richard Osborne, London and East Haven, Connecticut: Pluto Press, 1995

Farber, Stephen, "Making Book on TV," *Film Comment* (November–December 1982)

Halliwell, Leslie, and Peter Purser, *Halliwell's Television Companion,* London: Paladin, 1987

Kozloff, Sarah, "Narrative Theory and Television," in *Channels of Discourse Re-Assembled,* edited by Robert C. Allen, Chapel Hill: University of North Carolina Press, 1992

Lewallen, Avis, "*Lace:* Pornography for Women?," in *The Female Gaze: Women as Viewers of Popular Culture,* edited by Margaret Marshment and Larraine Gamman, London: Women's Press, 1988

Shipman, David, "The Far Pavilions," *Films and Filming* (January 1984)

Tulloch, John, *Television Drama: Agency, Audience and Myth,* London: Routledge, 1990

Wheen, Francis, *Television,* London: Century, 1985

Williams, Raymond, *Television, Technology, and Cultural Form,* London: Fontana, 1974

Minow, Newton (1926–)

U.S. Attorney, Media Regulator

Newton Minow is one of the most controversial figures ever to chair the Federal Communications Commission (FCC). Appointed in 1961 by President John F. Kennedy, Minow served only two years, but during that time he stimulated more public debate over television programming than any other chair in the history of the commission.

Trained at Northwestern University Law School, Minow's public career began with his involvement in the administration of Illinois Governor Adlai Stevenson during the 1950s. At a very young age, Minow became a leading figure both on the governor's staff and in his presidential campaigns of 1952 and 1956. Through the latter efforts, Minow became acquainted with members of the Kennedy circle and in 1960 worked for the Kennedy presidential bid, becoming close friends with the president's brother, Robert Kennedy. Reportedly, the two men frequently talked at length about the increasing importance of television in the lives of their children. It therefore came as little surprise that after the election, Minow eagerly pursued the position of FCC chair. Some observers nevertheless considered the appointment unusual, given his lack of experience with the media industry and with communication law.

Appointed chair at the age of 34, Minow lost little time mapping out his agenda for television reform. In his first public speech at a national convention of broadcasting executives, Minow challenged industry leaders to "sit down in front of your television set when your station goes on the air and stay there without a book, magazine, newspaper, profit-and-loss sheet, or rating book to distract you—and keep your eyes glued to that set until the station signs off. I can assure you that you will observe a vast wasteland." Sharply critical of excessive violence, frivolity, and commercialism, Minow's remarks sparked a national debate over the future of television. Although similar criticisms about television and popular culture had circulated widely during the late 1950s, Minow became the first chair of the FCC to specifically challenge the content of television programming and to urge significant reform. His characterization of the medium as a "vast wasteland" quickly became ubiquitous, especially in newsprint headlines and cartoons. During his

two years in office, it was estimated that, other than the president, Minow generated more column inches of news coverage than any other federal official.

In part, Minow's criticisms of television were linked to broader anxieties about consumerism, child rearing, and suburban living. Many social critics during this period worried that middle-class Americans had "gone soft" and lost their connection to public life. In an inaugural address that focused exclusively on foreign policy, President Kennedy implored Americans to revive their commitment to the urgent struggle for freedom around the globe. Shortly thereafter, Minow framed his critique of television along similar lines, arguing that the medium had become a form of escapism

Newton Minow.
Photo courtesy of Newton Minow/Lisa Berg

that threatened the nation's ability to meet the challenge of global Communism. Moreover, he worried about the increasing export of Hollywood programming overseas and the impact it would have on perceptions of the United States among citizens of other countries. In the months following the speech, Minow advocated the diversification of programming with particular emphasis on educational and informational fare. Confronted by powerful opposition among industry executives, he nevertheless continued to chide network programmers in speeches, interviews, and public appearances.

Although the Minow FCC never drafted specific programming guidelines, some argued that Minow employed a form of "regulation by raised eyebrow" that helped stimulate the production of programs favored by the FCC. Indeed, during the early 1960s, network news grew from adolescence to maturity, and many credit Minow for helping foster its growth. He especially was seen as a champion network documentary, a genre of programming that placed particular emphasis on educating the public about cold war issues. Many critics nevertheless contend that, beyond news, little changed in prime-time television during the Minow years, and some have suggested that, overall, the Minow FCC enjoyed few tangible policy accomplishments.

While that may have been true in the short run, the FCC chair played a leading role in the passage of two pieces of legislation that would have important long-term effects. The first was the All Channel Receiver Act of 1962, which required that all television sets sold in the United States be capable of picking up UHF (ultrahigh frequency) stations in addition to the VHF (very high frequency) stations that then dominated the medium. By the end of the 1960s, this law significantly increased the number of television stations and allowed the American Broadcasting Company (ABC) network to achieve national coverage, making it truly competitive with the National Broadcasting Company (NBC) and the Columbia Broadcasting System (CBS).

Second, Minow crafted the passage of legislation that ushered in the era of satellite communications. Under his leadership, various factions within the electronics and communications industries agreed to a pie-sharing arrangement that resulted in the organization of the Communications Satellite Corporation (Comsat) and ultimately the International Telecommunications Satellite Consortium (INTELSAT). Created with an eye toward attaining a strategic advantage over the Soviet Union, these U.S.-controlled organizations dominated the arena of satellite communications throughout the 1960s and much of the 1970s.

Shortly after the passage of these key pieces of legislation, Minow resigned from the FCC and returned to a lucrative private law practice, later becoming a partner in one of the most powerful communications law firms in the United States, Sidley and Austin. He remains an influential figure both in the media industry and in policy circles, and in 2001 he helped launch a campaign to get the federal government to fund the digitization of collections possessed by public and nonprofit institutions, making those resources available for free to the public via the Internet.

MICHAEL CURTIN

See also **All Channel Legislation; Communications Satellite Corporation; Federal Communications Commission; Quiz and Game Shows; Quiz Show Scandals; Networks: United States**

Newton (Norman) Minow. Born in Milwaukee, Wisconsin, January 17, 1926. Northwestern University, B.S. 1949; J.D. 1950. Married: Josephine Baskin, 1949; children: Nell, Martha, and Mary. Served in U.S. Army, 1944–46. Admitted to Wisconsin Bar, 1950; Illinois Bar, 1950; worked with firm of Mayer, Brown and Platt, Chicago, 1950–51 and 1953–55; law clerk to Chief Justice Fred M. Vinson, 1951–52; administrative assistant to Illinois Governor Adlai Stevenson, 1952–53, special assistant to Stevenson in U.S. presidential campaigns, 1952, 1956; partner, Stevenson, Rifkind and Wirtz, Chicago, New York City, and Washington, D.C., 1955–61; chair, Federal Communications Commission, 1961–63; executive vice president, general counsel, and director, *Encyclopaedia Britannica,* Chicago, 1963–65; partner, Sidley and Austin, Chicago, 1965–91; of counsel, from 1991; board of governors, Public Broadcasting Service, 1973–80, chair of the board, 1978–80; past chair, Chicago Educational TV, now honorary chair; chair, publications review board, Arthur Andersen and Company, 1974–83; chair of the board of overseers, Jewish Theological Seminary, 1974–77; cochair, presidential debates, League of Women Voters, 1976, 1980; professor of communications policy and law, Annenberg Program, Northwestern University, from 1987. Board of directors: Foote, Cone and Belding Communications Inc.; Tribune Company; Sara Lee Corporation; AON Corporation; Manpower, Inc. Trustee: Notre Dame University, 1964–77, from 1983; Mayo Foundation, 1973–81. Trustee, past chair of board, Rand Corporation; chair, board of trustees, Carnegie Corp. of New York; Chicago Orchestral Association, 1975–87, life trustee from 1987; Northwestern University, 1975–87, life trustee, from 1987. Honorary degrees: LL.D., University of Wisconsin, and Brandeis Univer-

Minow, Newton

sity, 1963; LL.D., Northwestern University, 1965; LL.D., Columbia College, 1972; LL.D., Governors State University, 1984; LL.D., DePaul University, 1989; LL.D., RAND Graduate School, 1993. Member: Fellow, American Bar Foundation; American Academy of Arts and Sciences; American Bar Association; Illinois Bar Association; Chicago Bar Association. Recipient: Peabody Award, 1961; Northwestern University Alumni Association Medal, 1978; Ralph Lowell Award, 1982.

Publications

Equal Time: The Private Broadcasters and the Public Interest, 1964
Presidential Television, with John Bartlow Martin and Lee M. Mitchell, 1973
For Great Debates, 1987

How Vast the Wasteland Now, 1991
Abandoned in the Wasteland: Children, Television, and the First Amendment, with Craig L. LaMay, 1995
"A Digital Gift to the Nation," with Lawrence K. Grossman, *Carnegie Reporter* (Fall 2001)

Further Reading

Baughman, James, *Television's Guardians: The FCC and the Politics of Programming, 1958–1967,* Knoxville: University of Tennessee Press, 1985
Curtin, Michael, "Beyond the Vast Wasteland," *Journal of Broadcasting and Electronic Media* (Spring 1993)
Curtin, Michael, *Redeeming the Wasteland: Television Documentary and Cold War Politics,* New Brunswick, New Jersey: Rutgers University Press, 1995
Watson, Mary Ann, *The Expanding Vista: American Television in the Kennedy Years,* New York: Oxford University Press, 1990

Mirren, Helen (1945–)

British Actor

Helen Mirren is probably best known to American television audiences as Detective Chief Inspector Jane Tennison, the complicated and obsessive homicide and vice detective of *Prime Suspect.* However, Mirren, who began her acting career playing Cleopatra and Lady Macbeth in Royal Shakespeare Company productions of the 1960s and 1970s, has appeared in more than 30 productions for British, Australian, and American television. These have included film or taped versions of Royal Shakespeare productions, original television plays, and dramatic adaptations of literary classics (e.g., the British Broadcasting Corporation's [BBC's] serialization of Balzac's *Cousin Bette,* which eventually appeared in the United States on the Public Broadcasting Service's [PBS's] *Masterpiece Theater*) produced by Granada, Thames, and other companies for the BBC, ITV, and Channel 4 in Britain and such American television series as *Twilight Zone* (the 1980s version) and *The Hidden Room* (Lifetime cable production).

The stage training that Mirren received in her teens and 20s encouraged her to embrace diverse roles and risky projects on stage, television, and screen (including a couple of notorious X-rated European art films).

As with many such classically trained British actors, her breathtaking acting range and frequent appearances in every dramatic media made stardom elusive. *Prime Suspect,* first aired on British television in 1991, finally made this 25-year acting veteran an important international star. When it was broadcast on the American PBS series *Mystery!* in 1992, it became that show's highest-rated program, won an Emmy, and made Mirren, according to some television journalists and executives, PBS's "pin-up woman" of the decade. Four *Prime Suspect* series have followed.

Critical consensus attributes the success of the television series to the collaboration of Mirren and writer Lynda La Plante, who created Jane Tennison as a composite of several female police detectives she interviewed. La Plante did not want to compromise their integrity by making Tennison's character too "soft," so she considered casting critical to the success of her vision of the character and these professional women. La Plante found that Mirren had the kind of presence and "great weight" the writer believed crucial to the character: "[Mirren's] not physically heavy, but she has a strength inside her that is unusual.... There's a stillness to her, a great tension and intelligence in her face."

1504

Helen Mirren.
Photo courtesy of Helen Mirren

Mirren has claimed that she likes Tennison because she is "unlikable." The complexity of Mirren's performance resides in how she conveys this unlikability while still making us sympathetic to Tennison's ideals and vulnerability. The character is clearly discriminated against because of her gender, and she knows it, but her own behavior, especially in personal relationships, is not beyond reproach. The tension that La Plante admires in Mirren's face also permeates the stiff posture Mirren adopts for the character, the quick pace of her walk, the intense drags she takes on a cigarette, and the determination of her gum chewing. Tennison, that unlikable yet sympathetic character, is given life in Mirren's world-weary eyes, which do not betray emotion to her colleagues, except when she lashes out in often justifiable anger. In private, however, the eyes express the losses suffered by a successful woman in a masculine public sphere.

Throughout the 1990s, Mirren continued to play strong, even eccentric characters on British and American television. *Losing Chase* (1996) is the story of a woman whose nervous breakdown becomes a way to opt out of a life as wife and mother. She learns to respond to others again when she falls in love with another woman. In the British miniseries *The Painted Lady* (later aired in the United States on PBS's *Masterpiece Theater*), Mirren played a faded rock star turned sleuth. The decade ended with her Emmy Award–winning performance as cult novelist and radical individualist Ayn Rand in Showtime's *Passion of Ayn Rand* (1999). Yet Mirren continues to be identified with Jane Tennison of *Prime Suspect*. For a time, Universal was working with Britain's Granada Productions on a theatrical feature, but Paramount had rights to the property in 1999, when it allowed them to lapse back to author Lynda La Plante. Mirren had responded strongly to rumors that she was not being considered for the film role because she was "too old" to attract a wide audience (Meryl Streep allegedly refused the role because Mirren was so closely associated with it), but it is unclear to what extent the casting controversy had to do with the feature film industry's decision to withdraw from the project. This much is clear: although American and British television made strides in the 1980s and 1990s in depicting strong, complex women in law enforcement, for many viewers and critics Mirren's performance finally enabled "a real contemporary woman [to break] through the skin of television's complacency."

MARY DESJARDINS

See also **La Plante, Lynda;** *Prime Suspect*

Helen Mirren. Born Helen Mironoff in London, England, July 26, 1945. Married Taylor Hackford, 1997. Established reputation as stage actress as Cleopatra with the National Youth Theatre, 1965; subsequently appeared with the Royal Shakespeare Company (RSC) and in Africa with Peter Brook's International Centre of Theatre Research, from 1972; returned to RSC, 1974; has also appeared in numerous films and won acclaim as a television performer, notably in the series *Prime Suspect*, 1991– . Recipient: three British Academy of Film and Television Arts Awards; Cannes Film Festival Best Actress Award, 1984; Emmy Award, 1999; Screen Actors Guild Award, 2002.

Television Series and Miniseries

1971	*Cousin Bette*
1979	*The Serpent Son*
1991–	*Prime Suspect*
1997	*Painted Lady*
2002	*Georgetown*

Made-for-Television Movies

1974	*Coffin for the Bride*
1987	*Cause Célèbre*
1996	*Losing Chase*
1999	*The Passion of Ayn Rand*
2002	*Door to Door*
2003	*The Roman Spring of Mrs. Stone*
2004	*Pride*

Television Specials

1968	*A Midsummer Night's Dream*
1974	*The Changeling*
1975	*The Apple Cart*
1976	*The Collection*

1978	*As You Like It*
1979	*The Quiz Kid*
1979	*Blue Remembered Hills*
1981	*Mrs. Reinhard*

Films

Herostratus, 1967; *Age of Consent*, 1970; *Savage Messiah*, 1972; *O Lucky Man*, 1973; *Caligula*, 1979; *SOS Titanic*, 1979; *Hussy*, 1979; *The Fiendish Plot of Dr. Fu Manchu*, 1980; *The Long Good Friday*, 1980; *Excalibur*, 1981; *Cal*, 1984; *2010*, 1984; *White Nights*, 1985; *The Mosquito Coast*, 1986; *Heavenly Pursuits*, 1987; *People of the Forest* (narrator), 1988; *The Cook, the Thief, His Wife, and Her Lover*, 1989; *When the Whales Came*, 1989; *The Comfort of Strangers*, 1990; *The Gift*, 1990; *Bethune: The Making of a Hero*, 1989; *Where Angels Fear to Tread*, 1991; *The Madness of King George*, 1994; *The Hawk*, 1994; *Some Mother's Son*, 1996; *Critical Care*, 1997; *The Prince of Egypt* (voice), 1998; *Teaching Mrs. Tingle*, 1999; *Greenfingers*, 2000; *Happy Birthday* (also director), 2000; *The Pledge*, 2001; *Gosford Park*, 2001; *No Such Thing*, 2001; *Last Orders*, 2001; *Calendar Girls*, 2003; *The Clearing*, 2004; *Raising Helen*, 2004.

Stage (selection)

Antony and Cleopatra, 1965; *Troilus and Cressida*, 1968; *Much Ado About Nothing*, 1968; *Richard III*, 1970; *Hamlet*, 1970; *Two Gentlemen of Verona*, 1970; *Miss Julie*, 1971; *The Conference of Birds*, 1972; *Macbeth*, 1974; *Teeth 'n' Smiles*, 1974; *The Bed Before Yesterday*, 1976; *Henry VI, Parts 1, 2, and 3*, 1977; *Measure for Measure*, 1979; *The Duchess of Malfi*, 1980; *The Faith Healer*, 1981; *Antony and Cleopatra*, 1983; *The Roaring Girl*, 1983; *Extremities*, 1984; *Two Way Mirror*, 1988; *Sex Please, We're Italian*, 1991; *A Month in the Country*, 1994; *Antony and Cleopatra*, 1998; *Orpheus Descending*, 2000; *Dance of Death*, 2001.

Further Reading

Ansen, David, "The Prime of Helen Mirren," *Newsweek* (May 16, 1994)

Lambert, Pam, "A Good Woman Detective Is Hard to Find," *New York Times* (January 19, 1992)

Wieder, Judy, "Chasing Rainbows," *The Advocate* (July 23, 1996)

Wolcott, James, "Columbo in Furs," *The New Yorker* (January 25, 1993)

Miss Marple

British Mystery Program

Miss Marple, the spinster detective who is one of the most famous characters created by English crime writer Agatha Christie, has been portrayed by a number of actresses in films and on television. In the cinema, Margaret Rutherford portrayed a rumbustious Miss Marple in the 1960s, and Angela Lansbury contributed a performance in *The Mirror Crack'd* before moving on to a similar role in the U.S. television series *Murder, She Wrote*. In Britain, however, certainly the most famous Miss Marple has been Joan Hickson, who starred in a dozen television mysteries over the course of a decade.

Between 1984 ("The Body in the Library") and 1992 ("The Mirror Crack'd"), the British Broadcasting Corporation (BBC), in association with the U.S. A&E network and Australia's Seven network, produced an irregular series of 12 Miss Marple mysteries. The elderly, deceptively delicate Joan Hickson starred in each of these as the amateur detective from the bucolic village of St. Mary Mead.

By conventional critical judgment, Agatha Christie's stories are often flawed. The plots can hinge on contrived and dated gimmicks: in "A Murder Is Announced," it is supposedly a shock that a character called Pip, for whom everyone is searching, is a woman, Philippa. The stories often end with an abruptly descending deus ex machina, as the heroine makes huge intuitive leaps, based on no clues ("4:50 from Paddington") or on clues that only she knows and that have been kept from the audience (the characters' marriages in "The Body in the Library"). Despite this, the television programs have attractive

Joan Hickson (1906–98) as Jane Marple in *The Mirror Crack'd,* TV, 1992.
Courtesy of the Everett Collection

elements that kept them popular over the years of their production.

The BBC's *Miss Marple* is a good example of a "heritage" production, with all the pleasures that implies. The term "heritage television" sums up a certain attitude toward the past that developed in Britain during the 1980s, when a mixture of a new Victorianism in moral standards and an increasingly frenetic late-capitalistic commodification led to two tendencies. The first was an attraction to a particularly sanitized version of England's past. The second capitalized on the first with various moves toward rendering that past easily consumable—in television programs, films, bedsheets, jams and preserves, and so on. The BBC's *Miss Marple* stories are prime examples of "heritage" production. They are set mostly in a rural past. English architecture is featured, and country mansion houses proliferate. As is typical for BBC programs, the "production values" are impeccable, and the programs look beautiful—costumes, houses and decor, cars, hairstyles, and makeup could all be described as "sumptuous."

As a celebration of English culture, "heritage" also demands that the program be as faithful as possible to their source material. Thus, the BBC's Miss Marple does not chase the villains herself as Margaret Rutherford does in her films, nor are the titles of the books altered to make them more sensational, as has occurred in other productions (the novel *After the Funeral* had been made into the 1963 film *Murder at the Gallop,* for example).

Another "heritage" aspect of the program is the morality that structures and underlies the mysteries. Miss Marple is the model of decorum, not only just and good but also polite and correct. And although Miss Marple herself claims that "in English villages.... You turn over a stone, you have no idea what will crawl out," there is in fact very little of a sordid underside in these narratives. There may be murders, but the motives are rarely squalid: mostly greed, sometimes true love. There are dance hostesses but no prostitutes; there is blackmail, but it is never about anything really shameful. Indeed, these murders are themselves peculiarly decorous, always meticulously planned, and rarely messy.

In addition to these "heritage" aspects, Hickson's performance is another of the particularly attractive aspects of the series. Her frail physical appearance contrasts both with her intensely blue eyes and with the way she dominates the scenes in which she appears. Her apparent scattiness, staring absentmindedly over people's shoulders as they talk to her, is delightful. It is believable both that people would ignore her, thinking her to be just "a little old lady," and simultaneously that she is very much in control of the situation.

Miss Marple offers a female-oriented version of detective mythology. Not only does the program present a range of roles for older women (unusual enough in television drama), but it also celebrates a nontraditional approach to investigation. In several of the stories, the traditional strong-arm techniques of police investigation advance the plot only very slightly. Miss Marple takes over; her investigative methods involve no violence, threats, or intimidation. Rather, gossip forms the most powerful of her tools. The very term "gossip" is a way of denigrating forms of speech that have typically been taken up by women. In these stories, gossip moves the narrative forward. In "4:50 from Paddington," for example, Miss Marple knows that the family needs a housekeeper; she says, "They're always needing a housekeeper. The father is particularly difficult to get on with." This enables Miss Marple to send her own agent into the household. It is gossip that unfailingly allows her to solve the mysteries. The character's standard technique is to equate the circumstances of the mystery with representative archetypes she has encountered in the course of her village life. Such a comparison of types provides her with an infallible guide to people's characters, actions, and intentions.

In another departure from more typical detective narratives, at the denouements, Miss Marple is never involved in any physical chase or fight. Although she solves the mystery (through observation, a few polite questions, and a bit of knitting), Miss Marple has very little physical impact on the progress of the narrative. She is often peripheral rather than central. In some stories, female aides act as her physical stand-ins: but at the denouement of the stories, when television narrative convention demands some crisis and excitement, Miss Marple herself is little involved. Although she may engineer a denouement, as in "4:50 from Paddington," she is not involved in the chase that follows. Rather, it is policemen and good male characters who become involved in car chases and leap through glass windows.

The particular pleasures of this very British television production ensures its appeal even when new programs are no longer being produced, and its wide circulation, through syndication on several continents, attests to its continuing popularity.

ALAN MCKEE

Cast

Miss Marple   Joan Hickson

Programming History

12 irregularly produced and scheduled episodes
BBC
Episodes and first dates of broadcast:

"The Body in the Library"	December 26, 27, 28, 1984
"The Moving Finger"	February 21, 22, 1985
"A Murder Is Announced"	February 28 and March 1, 2, 1985
"A Pocketful of Rye"	March 7, 8, 1985
"The Murder at the Vicarage"	December 25, 1986
"Sleeping Murder"	January 11 and 18, 1987
"At Bertram's Hotel"	January 25 and February 2, 1987
"Nemesis"	February 8 and 15, 1987
"4:50 from Paddington"	December 25, 1987
"Caribbean Mystery"	December 25, 1989
"They Do It with Mirrors"	December 29, 1991
"The Mirror Crack'd"	December 27, 1992

Further Reading

Conroy, Sarah, "The Spinster's New Yarns," *Washington Post* (December 10, 1987)

Dunne, Colin, "I'll Miss Her Awfully, Says the Actress She Made a TV Star," *Mail on Sunday* (December 27, 1992)

Terry, Clifford, "Cast Carries PBS Whodunit," *Chicago Tribune* (January 1, 1987)

Mission: Impossible

U.S. Espionage/Adventure Series

Bob Johnson's taped words commissioning the Impossible Mission Force (IMF) with another assignment became synonymous with the techno-sophistry of *Mission: Impossible,* "This tape will self-destruct in five seconds." They were as often cited as the title itself and the opening visual and aural motifs: a match striking into flame and Lalo Schifrin's dynamic theme music.

The program ran for 168 episodes between 1966 and 1973 on the Columbia Broadcasting System (CBS), returning for another 35 episodes on the American Broadcasting Company (ABC) between 1988 and 1990 (shot in Australia for financial and location rea-

sons). Movie versions starring Tom Cruise were released in 1996 and 2000. The original executive producer for the TV series, Bruce Geller, wanted to deploy "the Everyman-superman" in a "homage to team work and good old Yankee ingenuity." The leader of the force was expected to choose a team to deal with each given task, usually comprised of a technical expert, a strongman, a female model, and a man of disguise. Major actors at different moments in the series included Peter Graves (head of the IMF after the first season and through the revived series), Barbara Bain (model), Greg Morris (technical expert), Peter Lupus (muscle bound), and Martin Landau (disguise artist).

Mission: Impossible, Greg Morris, Peter Graves, Martin Landau, Barbara Bain, Peter Lupus, 1966–73.
Courtesy of the Everett Collection

By the time the program first began, TV producers were under intense pressure to include black characters in positive roles. *Mission* was held up in the *TV Guide* of the 1960s as a paragon of virtue for its representation of African Americans, with the character of Barney Collier hailed as one of television's "New Negro figures." However, *Mission: Impossible* did not avoid criticism for making its token African American a "backdoor" technical expert, one-dimensional and emotionless.

The instructions to writers of the first series read:

> The tape message contains the problem. An enemy or criminal plot is in existence; the IMF must counter it. The situation must be of enough importance and difficulty that only the IMF could do it. The villains (as here and later portrayed) are so black, and so clever that the intricate means used to defeat them are necessary. Very commonly, but not inevitably, the mission is to retrieve a valuable item or man, and/or to discredit (eliminate) the villain or villains...avoid names of actual countries as well as mythical Balkan kingdoms by being vague. This

is not a concern at early stages of writing: use real names if it's easier.

The force would accept its assignment and devise a means to carry out the task in an extremely complex way. Some aspect of the plan would go awry, but the team would improvise and survive.

The IMF was a U.S. espionage group, private sector but public spirited, that "assisted" Third World countries, opposed domestic organized crime, and acted as a spy for the government. Because its enemies were great and powerful, the force required intricacy and secrecy ("covertness"). At the very time that the famous words were being intoned in each disembodied, taped assignment ("Should you...be caught or killed, the secretary will disavow any knowledge of your actions"), real-life U.S. Assistant Secretary of Defense Arthur Sylvester was supporting covert operations. The program's considerable overseas sales (69 countries and 15 dubbed versions by its third season) were said to have given many viewers around the world an exaggerated impression of the abilities of the Central Intelligence Agency (CIA).

David Buxton describes *Mission* as an exemplar of the 1960s British/American "pop series." These paeans to the fun of the commodity—to the modernity of design, fashion, and knowingness—leavened the performance of quite serious service to the nation. They had an ideological minimalism, open to a range of interpretations anchored only in the need to preserve everyday "Americanness," in the most general sense of the term. The opening tape's "promise" of official disavowal in the event of failure established entrepreneurial initiative as a basis for action and gave an alibi for minimizing additional references to politics. Instead, episodes could be devoted to a scientifically managed, technical private sphere. The IMF represented an efficient allocation of resources because of its anonymously weightless and depersonalized division of labor and an effective tool of covert activity as a consequence of its distance from the official civilities of diplomacy. This effect was achieved stylistically through a visual quality normally associated with the cinema: numerous changes in diegetic space, lighting that could either trope film noir or action-adventure, rapid cutting, and few lengthy reaction shots.

The first *Mission* was valorized by many critics for its plots. It was unusual for American television drama to have episodes with overlapping and complex storylines at the expense of characterization. Following each program's twists became a talisman for the cognoscenti. The inversion of heroism, whereby treachery, theft, kidnapping, and destruction were qualities of "good" characters, made the series seem both intellectually and politically subversive. Once new people were introduced in a segment, they immediately underwent bewildering transformations that problematized previous information about their psyches, politics, and conduct. Geller's fantasy was that performers be just that: figures performing humanness, infinitely plastic, and ready to be redisposed in a moment. The series lasted much longer than its many spy-theme counterparts on network television through the 1960s, perhaps as a consequence of this decentered, subjectless approach.

Each episode of the original *Mission* cost $225,000, for which CBS paid $170,000. Geller was shooting nearly 50,000 feet of film per screen hour, more than twice the average, and spent 30 percent longer than the norm doing so. Special-effects and writing costs also went far beyond studio policy, in part to make for the feature film look that was a key factor in the program's success. Geller instilled a knowing self-reflexivity into the series. He became renowned for the remark that "nothing is new except in how it's done."

A 150-day strike in 1988 by members of the Writers Guild of America over creative and residual rights payments cast Hollywood's attention toward remakes and toward Australia, where the $5,000 (Australian) cost of a TV script compared favorably to the U.S. figure of $21,000 (Australian). Paramount decided to proceed with plans to bring back *Mission,* a reprise that it had attempted intermittently over almost a decade. Four old scripts were recycled, and new ones were written after the industrial action had concluded. *Mission* offered a built-in "baby-boomer" audience and the opportunity to avoid California unions. This attitude produced a very formulaic remake.

Consider the IMF's efforts to smuggle dissidents out of Eastern Europe ("The Wall"). Posing as a Texan impresario keen to hire a chess player and a magician, Graves is accused by a KGB officer of making "capitalist offers." He replies good naturedly that, "business is business the world over." And so it is, when his team is able to grant U.S. citizenship as it pleases while supposedly remaining independent of affiliation to any particular state. The IMF (ironically sharing an acronym with a key tool of First World economic power, the International Monetary Fund) establishes a sphere of the "other" that is harsh and repressive compared to the IMF's own goodness and light. These spheres represent state socialism and capitalism, respectively, as captured by a close-up of the East German Colonel Barty's highly polished boot grinding a little girl's lost doll into the mud as he arrests her defecting family. The shooting script calls for Graves to have a "broad American smile" to contrast him with a "slow, unfriendly" East German. The cut from unpleasantness at the Berlin Wall to Jim playing golf fully achieves the establishment of a lifestyle and polity distinctiveness, illustrating the IMF's efforts to assist elements "behind the Wall" that favor a new political and economic openness. In his remark to a ravaged Ilse Bruck in act 3, Graves's patriarchal condescension is as much geopolitical as gendered: "You're a very brave girl, Ilse. But we're still in East Berlin and you'll have to call on all your reserves to help us get back to the West." Indeed she would.

TOBY MILLER

See also **Action Adventure Programs; Spy Programs**

Cast (1966–1973)

Daniel Briggs (1966–67)	Steven Hill
James Phelps (1967–73)	Peter Graves
Cinnamon Carter (1966–69)	Barbara Bain
Rollin Hand (1966–69)	Martin Landau
Barney Collier	Greg Morris
Willie Armitage	Peter Lupus
Paris (1969–71)	Leonard Nimoy
Doug (1970–71)	Sam Elliot
Dana Lambert (1970–71)	Lesley Ann Warren
Lisa Casey (1971–73)	Lynda Day George
Mimi Davis (1972–73)	Barbara Anderson

Producer

Bruce Geller

Programming History

171 episodes
CBS

September 1966–January 1967	Saturday 9:00–10:00
January 1967–September 1967	Saturday 8:30–9:30
September 1967–September 1970	Sunday 10:00–11:00
September 1970–September 1971	Saturday 7:30–8:30
September 1971–December 1972	Saturday 10:00–11:00
December 1972–May 1973	Saturday 10:00–11:00

Cast (1988–1990)

Jim Phelps	Peter Graves
Nicholas Black	Thaao Penghis
Max Harte	Antony Hamilton
Grant Collier	Phil Morris
Casey Randall (1988–89)	Terry Markwell

Shannon Reed (1989–90)
The Voice on the Disk

Jane Badler
Bob Johnson

Producers
Michael Fisher, Walter Brough

Programming History
ABC

October 1988–January 1989	Sunday 8:00–9:00
January 1989–July 1989	Saturday 8:00–9:00
August 1989	Thursday 9:00–10:00
September 1989–December 1989	Thursday 8:00–9:00
January 1990–February 1990	Saturday 8:00–9:00
May 1990–June 1990	Saturday 8:00–9:00

Further Reading

Beatie, Bruce A., "The Myth of the Hero: From *Mission: Impossible* to Magdalenian Caves," in *The Hero in Transition*, edited by Ray B. Browne and Marshall W. Fishwick, Bowling Green, Ohio: Bowling Green University Popular Press, 1983

Buxton, David, *From The Avengers to Miami Vice: Form and Ideology in Television Series,* Manchester, United Kingdom: Manchester University Press, 1990

Lewis, Richard Warren, "Is This Mission Possible? The IM Force Struggles to Overcome Cast Changes, Power Plays, Hollywood Intrigue," *TV Guide* (1969)

Miller, Toby, "*Mission: Impossible* and the New International Division of Labour," *Metro-Media and Education Magazine* (autumn 1990)

Miller, Toby, "Mission Impossible: How Do You Turn Indooroopilly into Africa?," in *Queensland Images in Film and Television,* edited by Jonathan Dawson and Bruce Molloy, St. Lucia, Australia: University of Queensland Press, 1990

White, Patrick J., *The Complete Mission: Impossible Dossier,* New York: Avon, 1991

Mr. Bean. *See* **Atkinson, Rowan**

Mister Rogers' Neighborhood. *See* **Rogers, Fred McFeely**

Monkees, The

U.S. Musical Situation Comedy

The Monkees, a situation comedy about a struggling rock-and-roll band of the same name, originally aired on the National Broadcasting Company (NBC) from 1966 to 1968. During its 58-episode run, the program was awarded an Emmy for Outstanding Comedy Program in 1967. The show's popularity has continued, with reruns being broadcast on the Columbia Broadcasting System (CBS) from 1969 to 1973 and on Music Television (MTV), Nick at Nite, and other cable and syndicated venues since the 1980s.

Inspired by the success of the two Beatles films directed by Richard Lester, the show was aimed at 1960s American youth culture. Considerable controversy surrounded the show because the band, four young

The Monkees, Peter Tork, Mickey Dolenz, Michael Nesmith, Davy Jones, 1966–68.
Courtesy of the Everett Collection

men who "portrayed themselves," was "manufactured" by Raybert Productions. In 1965 an advertisement appeared in *Daily Variety,* a major U.S. trade publication for the film and television industry, requesting responses from "4 insane boys aged 17–21." More than 400 individuals replied.

Though Michael Nesmith and Peter Tork, two of the young men selected for the program, had some previous musical experience, the other two, Davy Jones and Mickey Dolenz, had none. Several recordings, closely tied to the series, were released and became commercial successes. Then it also became widely known that the actors did not play their own musical instruments—on the recordings or in the series. The controversy rising from this "revelation" was further exacerbated when the actors embarked on a concert tour. Despite these issues, the Monkees became teen idols, sold millions of records, and were heavily merchandised.

The show was innovative in both form and content, violating the conventions of realist television. Episodes were characterized by self-reflexive techniques such as distorted focus, direct address of the camera, the incorporation of outtakes and screen tests, fast and slow-motion effects, and continuity errors. In all, however, the television version of "psychedelic" cinema was tamed for the domestic medium, and the boys generally engaged in wholesome, if quirky, fun.

"Monkee Mania" experienced a renewal in the 1980s, when the program was rerun on MTV. The popularity of the show with contemporary youth audiences has led to reissue of recordings; fan conventions, magazines, and websites; and several concert tours by three of the original members (Dolenz, Jones, and Tork).

FRANCES GATEWARD

See also **Music on Television**

Cast (as themselves)
Davy Jones
Mike Nesmith
Peter Tork
Mickey Dolenz

Producers
Robert Rafelson, Ward Sylvester

Programming History
58 episodes
NBC
September 1966–August 1968   Monday 7:30–8:00

Monkhouse, Bob (1928–2003)

British Comedian

Bob Monkhouse was one of British television's most prolific performers, indelibly etched on the minds of the public as the smooth, wise-cracking host of countless game shows. Initially a stand-up comic, Monkhouse's early years were spent writing gags for himself and other performers. He made a number of guest appearances on TV shows before he and then writing partner Denis Goodwin finally landed their own television series in 1953 with *Fast and Loose,* a comedy sketch show. With the arrival of Britain's commercial channel in 1955, Monkhouse was able to diversify. He and coproducer Jonathan Routh fooled members of the public with various scams in the British version of *Candid Camera.*

Always a fan of the great silent comedians, Monkhouse paid tribute to some of the men who had inspired him in 1966 with *Mad Movies.* He also continued a punishing schedule of nightclub appearances, before becoming a host of ATV's Sunday night variety show, *The London Palladium Show,* in 1967.

However, it was not until late 1967 that Monkhouse became associated with ATV's *The Golden Shot,* the series that made him a truly household name. Initially presented by Canadian Jackie Rae, this game show featured members of the audience who, to win prizes, guided, via the telephone, a blindfolded marksman to fire a crossbow into a target. In later stages of the game, the audience members were firing the crossbows themselves. From the start, Monkhouse was determined that he should be the presenter, and he even went to the expense of having a telerecording made of the episode in which he made a guest appearance so that Lew Grade, head of ATV, could see how Monkhouse could rescue what was then a fading show. Monkhouse also instigated the show's catchphrase, used when asking the studio hand to load the bolt: "Bernie, the bolt."

Monkhouse did indeed rescue the program, not only enlivening it with his wise-cracking comedy but also changing the format, simplifying it, and making it more visually appealing and exciting. Thus began a career as a host of game and quiz shows. In 1975 ATV adapted the American program *Hollywood Squares,* which was hosted by Monkhouse as *Celebrity Squares.* Once again, he was the fast-talking, ad-libbing host par

excellence. He hosted numerous game shows, including *Family Fortunes, $64,000 Question, Bob's Full House, Bob Says Opportunity Knocks,* and *Wipe Out.* However, while thoroughly professional and able to put contestants at their ease, Monkhouse had a reputation for being smarmy and often played on this aspect of his persona.

In 1993 Monkhouse diversified into straight drama with a role in Yorkshire Television's *All or Nothing at All,* which also starred comedian Hugh Laurie. It was a proficient performance. In 2000 he lent his voice to the lead character in the animated series *Aaagh! It's the Mr. Hell Show.* A darkly comic cartoon, this program

Bob Monkhouse.
Courtesy of the Everett Collection

has aired in the United States and Canada as well as in the United Kingdom.

Throughout his television career, Monkhouse continued his stand-up comedy act in nightclubs across England, and in recent years he had something of a renaissance and made a comeback as a TV comic, having been "rediscovered" by a younger generation of comics along with the likes of Ken Dodd and the late Frankie Howerd. He is probably deserving of "cult" status. The culmination of his return to comic form was the 1995–96 series *Bob Monkhouse on the Spot*, scheduled late Saturday evening on the mainstream British Broadcasting Corporation network BBC 1 and billed as a version of his cabaret act. This was a raunchier and racier Monkhouse than the TV public was used to seeing, and because the programs were recorded close to transmission, they were filled with topical gags.

Monkhouse's television career spanned half a century, and he generally received top billing in his TV ventures. Monkhouse passed away on December 29, 2003.

Pamela Rostron

Bob Monkhouse. Born in Beckenham, Kent, England, June 1, 1928. Attended Dulwich College. Married: 1) Elizabeth, 1949 (divorced, 1972); children: Abigail, Gary, and Simon; 2) Jacqueline, 1973. Trained as a cartoon film animator with Gaumont British; started performing as comedian while member of the Royal Air Force, 1947–49; formed successful writing partnership with Denis Goodwin; became BBC's first contract comedian, performing on the *Work Wonders* radio show, 1949; starred in own radio show, 1949–83; starred in first television series, 1953; built up reputation as major cabaret attraction worldwide; host and guest performer on many BBC and ITV programs. Officer of the Order of the British Empire, 1993. Recipient: Top Comedian in Cabaret, 1981, 1987; After-Dinner Speaker of the Year, 1989. Died December 29, 2003.

Television Series (selected)

1954–55	*Fast and Loose*
1956	*Do You Trust Your Wife?*
1957	*Bury Your Hatchet*
1957–58	*Early to Braden* (writer only)
1958–63	*The Bob Monkhouse Hour*
1960–67	*Candid Camera*
1964	*The Big Noise*
1967	*The London Palladium Show*
1967–71, 1974–75	*The Golden Shot*
1975–79, 1993–94	*Celebrity Squares*
1978–81	*I'm Bob, He's Dickie!*
1979	*Bonkers*
1979–83	*Family Fortunes*
1983–86	*Bob Monkhouse Tonight*
1984–90	*Bob's Full House*
1987–89	*Bob Says Opportunity Knocks*
1990–93	*The $64,000 Question*
1991	*Bob's Your Uncle*
1993	*All or Nothing at All*
1994	*An Audience with Bob Monkhouse*
1995–96	*Bob Monkhouse on the Spot*
1996–	*The National Lottery Live*
1997	*What a Performance!*
1998–	*Wipe Out*
2000	*Aaagh! It's the Mr. Hell Show* (voice of Mr. Hell)

Television Specials (selected)

1956	*The Bob Monkhouse Show*
1957	*Beat Up the Town*
1957	*Cyril's Saga* (writer only)
1958	*The Bob Monkhouse Show*
1966	*Mad Movies*
1967	*Bug*
1969	*Friends in High Places*
1972	*The Bob Monkhouse Comedy Hour*
1972	*The Bob Monkhouse Disturbance*
1973	*The Bob Monkhouse Offensive*
1973	*The Bob Monkhouse Breakdown*
1994	*An Audience with Bob Monkhouse*
1998	*Bob Monkhouse on Campus*

Films

Secret People, 1951; *All in Good Fun*, 1956; *Carry on Sergeant*, 1958; *Dentist in the Chair*, 1960; *Dentist on the Job*, 1961; *She'll Have to Go*, 1962; *A Weekend with Lulu*, 1962; *Thunderbirds Are Go*, 1966; *Up the Junction*, 1967; *The Bliss of Mrs. Blossom*, 1968; *Simon Simon*, 1970; *Out of Order*, 1983.

Radio (selected)

Work Wonders, 1949; *Hello Playmates* (also co-writer), 1954; *Punchline; Bob Hope's 80th Anniversary; Mr. Rodgers and Mr. Hammerstein; Mostly Monkhouse; In the Psychiatrist's Chair.*

Stage (selected)

Start Time with Bob; Aladdin; Boy from Syracuse; Come Blow Your Horn.

Publications

Just a Few Words: The Complete Speakers' Handbook, 1988, revised edition, 1998

Crying with Laughter (autobiography), 1993

Monty Python's Flying Circus

British Sketch Comedy/Farce/Parody/Satire Series

Monty Python's Flying Circus first appeared on the British Broadcasting Corporation's BBC 1 on October 5, 1969. It was a new type of program for the national channel, and its appearance at the end of the decade seemed fitting. The show was created by six young men (Graham Chapman, John Cleese, Terry Gilliam, Eric Idle, Terry Jones, and Michael Palin) whose ideas of comedy and television were clearly nontraditional. *Monty Python*'s style—free form, nonlinear, deeply sarcastic, satirical, and anarchic—seemed somehow to reflect the times. It mocked all conventions that proceeded it, particularly the conventions of television.

The last episode aired on the BBC on December 5, 1974, after the production of 45 installments. The first 39 were titled *Monty Python's Flying Circus*. The final six episodes, all created without Cleese, who had tired of the show, were called *Monty Python*. In addition, the team produced two shows for German television, each running 50 minutes. The second of these two shows, which consisted mostly of new material, was shown in England on BBC 2 in 1973. The Pythons expanded into other media as the result of their TV success. They created four Python movies (*And Now for Something Completely Different, Monty Python and the Holy Grail, Monty Python's Life of Brian,* and *Monty Python's Meaning of Life*), several audio recordings, and several books relating to the programs and films. In England and North America, the group also performed several live stage shows comprised of various sketches and songs from the television program.

Of the cast, all but Gilliam were Englishmen who developed their interest in comedy while students at university (Palin and Jones at Oxford; Chapman, Cleese, and Idle at Cambridge). Gilliam was an American from California via Minnesota. Although he did appear on camera occasionally, Gilliam's primary contribution to the TV shows was his eclectic animation, which usually served, in various ways, to link the sketches.

Each of the British members of the troupe had previous television and stage experience as writers and performers. Their pre-Python credits included the satirical *That Was the Week That Was, The Frost Report* (with David Frost, a regular target of the group's arrows), *Do Not Adjust Your Set,* and *The Complete and Utter History of Britain.* The cross-pollination of talent during these days eventually brought the future Pythons together. They approached the BBC with a program idea, and it was accepted, not without some trepidation by the network. When Gilliam was brought into the group to provide animation, Monty Python was formed.

The programs reflect the influence of several British radio programs from the 1950s—most notably *The Goon Show,* which featured, among others, Peter Sellers. The energy and disregard for rules that hallmarked *The Goon Show* are clearly evident in the *Python* TV show. In turn, *Monty Python's Flying Circus* has exercised its own influence on such television programs as *Saturday Night Live, SCTV, Kids in the Hall,* and *The Young Ones.* The essential disrespect for authority that links each of these programs can ultimately be traced through the Pythons back to *The Goon Show.*

The content of *Monty Python's Flying Circus* was designed to be disconcerting to viewers who expected to see typical television fare. This was obvious from the very first episode. The opening "discussion" featured a farmer who believes his sheep are birds and that they nest in trees. This bit was followed by a conversation between two Frenchmen who consider the commercial potential of flying sheep. Just as viewers thought they were beginning to understand the flow of the show, it cut to a shot of a man behind a news desk announcing, "And now for something completely different," and the scene shifted to a totally unrelated topic. The thread might return to a previous sketch, but more often there was no closure, only more fragmented scenes. Interspersed throughout were Gilliam's animations, often stop-action collages in which skulls opened to reveal dancing women or various body parts were severed. The macabre and disorienting were basic elements of the show.

Opening title sequences were not always found at the beginning of the program, frequently appearing instead midway through the show or even later. In one installment, there were no opening titles. Another element of the opening sequence was the "It's" man, a scruffy old sort who would be seen running, eventually reaching the camera. As he breathlessly croaks, "It's...," the scene would shift dramatically. The theme music (Sousa's "Liberty Bell March") was chosen because, among other reasons, it was free from copyright fees.

Monty Python's Flying Circus, John Cleese, Graham Chapman, Terry Jones, Eric Idle, Michael
Palin (in front), 1969–74 TV Series.
Courtesy of the Everett Collection

Several of the sketches from the series became fa-
vorites of fans but not necessarily of the performers.
"The Ministry of Silly Walks" virtually became
Cleese's signature, much to his displeasure, and "The
Dead Parrot Sketch" had to be repeated any time
Cleese and Palin appeared together. The group's por-
trayal of middle-aged women (known as Pepperpots
among the group) was a popular recurring theme as
well. "Mr. Nudge," "The Spanish Inquisition," "The
Upper-Class Twit of the Year," "The Lumberjack
Song," and "Scott of the Antarctic" are among the bits
that have remained fan favorites.

Monty Python's Flying Circus began appearing in the
United States on Public Broadcasting Service (PBS)
stations in 1974. Its popularity grew, and it quickly became a cult favorite. Several commercial stations, having noticed it on the public stations, also began to air

the program. The American Broadcasting Company
(ABC) purchased the rights to the six-episode fourth
year of *Monty Python,* but when the show was aired,
the episodes had been censored and edited to fit the restrictions of American commercial TV. The group went
to court to prevent further cuts, but ABC was able to air
the second show with only a minor disclaimer. As a result of the case, the Pythons gained ownership of the
copyright outside Great Britain.

Individual members of the group have gone on to
acclaim in film and television. As writers, producers,
directors, and performers, all carry with them residual
elements of *Monty Python.* Graham Chapman died in
1989.

GEOFFREY HAMMILL

See also **Cleese, John; Palin, Michael**

Cast
Graham Chapman
John Cleese
Terry Gilliam
Eric Idle
Terry Jones
Michael Palin

Producer
John Howard Davies

Programming History
45 30-minute episodes
BBC
October 1969–January 1970
September 1970–December 1970
October 1972–January 1973
October 1974–December 1974

Further Reading

"And Now for Something Completely Different...," *The Economist* (October 20, 1990)
Clifford, Andrew, "Caught in the Act," *New Statesman and Society* (September 29, 1989)
Hewison, Robert, *Monty Python: The Case Against Irreverence, Scurrility, Profanity, Vilification, and Licentious Abuse,* New York: Grove, 1981
Johnson, Kim, *The First 20 Years of Monty Python,* New York: St. Martin's Press, 1989
Johnson, Kim, *Life (Before and) After Monty Python: The Solo Flights of the Flying Circus,* New York: St. Martin's Press, 1993
McCall, Douglas L., *Monty Python: A Chronological Listing of the Troupe's Creative Output, and Articles and Reviews About Them,* Jefferson, North Carolina: McFarland, 1991
Perry, George C., *Life of Python,* Boston: Little, Brown, 1983
Schmidt, William E., "Still Zany, Python and Cult Turn 25," *New York Times* (September 18, 1994)

Moonlighting

U.S. Detective Comedy/Drama

Moonlighting, an hour-long episodic series that aired on the American Broadcasting Company (ABC) from 1985 to 1989, signaled the emergence of "dramedy" as a television genre. After the series finished its first season in a ratings tie for 20th place, it rose to 9th place in 1986–87 and tied for 12th place the following season (in which only 14 new episodes were made). The innovative qualities of the program were noted by its nomination, for the first time in the 50-year history of the Directors Guild of America, for both Best Drama and Best Comedy.

Produced by Glen Gordon Caron, *Moonlighting* featured high-fashion model Maddie Hayes (played by real-life former high-fashion model Cybill Shepherd) and fast-talking private eye David Addison (played by then-unknown Bruce Willis). The series' story began after Maddie's business manager embezzled most of her fortune, leaving her with her house and the Blue Moon Detective Agency, designed by the wily accountant as nothing more than a tax write-off and consisting of detective David Addison and secretary Agnes Dipesto (played by Allyce Beasley). The romantic tension between David, a smart, slovenly, party animal and womanizer, and the beautiful, haute couture–

attired, snobbish Maddie lasted for two seasons. After this point, complications on and off the set led to a plotline in which Maddie juggled relationships with David and another suitor, briefly married a third man, had the marriage annulled, and suffered a miscarriage.

The series' importance lies not so much in its convoluted plots as in its unique and sustained fusion of elements characteristically associated with two distinct genres into the emergent genre of dramedy. On the one hand, *Moonlighting* clearly exhibits the semantic features of television drama: serious subject matter dealing with incidents of sufficient magnitude that it arouses pity and fear; rounded, complex central characters who are neither thoroughly admirable nor despicable; textured lighting—both the hard "tele-noir" and diffused lighting accompanied by soft camera focus; multiple exterior and interior settings; and single-camera shooting on film. On the other hand, the series combines the "serious" elements with the syntactic features of television comedy. These comedic features include a four-part narrative structure (consisting of the situation, complication, confusion, and resolution); the metatextual practices of verbal self-reflexivity, musical self-reflexivity, and intertextuality; repetition

Moonlighting, Bruce Willis, Cybill Shepherd, 1985–89.
Courtesy of the Everett Collection

(i.e., the doubling, tripling, and compounding of the same action or incident until the repetition itself becomes humorous); witty repartee; hyperbolic coincidence; and a governing benevolent moral principle within which the violent, confused, often ironic dramas of good and evil and seriousness and silliness were played out.

A full appreciation of the sophistication of *Moonlighting* involves a level of cultural literacy (both popular and classic) rarely required by prime-time television series, which was one reason the series drew accolades from critics early on. Titles of *Moonlighting* episodes intertextually referenced the narrative premises as well as titles, authors, and even visual techniques of films, novels, dramas, poems, and plays from the 16th century through the present (e.g., "It's a Wonderful Job," "The Dream Sequence Always Rings Twice," "Atlas Belched," "Brother, Can You Spare a Blonde," "Twas the Episode Before Christmas," and "The Lady in the Iron Mask"). Another episode titled "Atomic Shakespeare" provided a feminist version of "The Taming of the Shrew," performed, except for the bookend scenes, entirely in iambic pentameter. Additionally, in many episodes, protagonists Maddie and David break the theatrical "fourth wall" convention with self-reflexive references to themselves as actors in a television program or to the commercial nature of the television medium. Such metatextual practices are techniques of defamiliarization that, according to certain formalist critical theories, epitomize the experience and purpose of art; they jar viewers out of the complacent, narcotic-like pleasure of familiar forms

and invite them to question and appreciate the artistic possibilities and limitations of generic forms. *Moonlighting's* use of these metatextual practices signifies its recognition of the traditions that have shaped it as well as its self-conscious comments on its departure from those traditions; thus, the series displays characteristics typically attributed to works regarded as highly artistic.

The series' artistry in fusing the genre features of drama and comedy in such a way that it was both popular and critically acclaimed paved the way for such other innovative "dramedic" ventures as *Frank's Place, Northern Exposure, Sports Night,* and *Ally McBeal. Moonlighting* also led a number of critics to declare that, with *Moonlighting,* American television had finally come of age as an art form.

LEAH R. VANDE BERG

See also **Detective Programs; Dramedy**

Cast

Maddie Hayes	Cybill Shepherd
David Addison	Bruce Willis
Agnes Dipesto	Alice Beasley
Herbert Viola (1986–89)	Curtis Armstrong
Virginia Hayes (1987–88)	Eva Marie Saint
Alex Hayes (1987–88)	Robert Webber
MacGilicuddy (1988–89)	Jack Blessing

Producers

Glenn Gordon Caron, Jay Daniel

Programming History

65 episodes
ABC

March 1985	Sunday 9:00–11:00
March 1985–April 1985	Tuesday 10:00–11:00
April 1985–September 1988	Tuesday 9:00–10:00
December 1988–February 1989	Tuesday 9:00–10:00
April 1989–May 1989	Sunday 8:00–9:00

Further Reading

Caldwell, John Thornton, "Masquerade," in his *Televisuality: Style, Crisis, and Authority in American Television,* New Brunswick, New Jersey: Rutgers University Press, 1995

Finnerman, G.P., "*Moonlighting:* Here's Looking at You Kid," *American Cinematographer* (April 1989)

Joyrich, Lynne, "Tube Tied: Reproductive Politics and *Moonlighting,*" in *Modernity and Mass Culture,* edited by James Naremore and Patrick Brantlinger, Bloomington: Indiana University Press, 1991

Radner, Hilary, "Quality Television and Feminine Narcissism: The Shrew and the Covergirl," *Genders,* 8 (1991)

Sunila, J., "Focus: More Wordplay, I Pray," *Emmy* (April/May 1987)

Vande Berg, Leah R., "Dramedy: *Moonlighting* as an Emer-

gent Generic Hybrid," *Communication Studies,* 40 (1989)

Williams, J.P., "The Mystique of *Moonlighting:* 'When You Care Enough to Watch the Very Best,'" *Journal of Popular Film and Television,* 16 (1988)

Moonves, Leslie R. (1949–)

U.S. Media Executive, President and CEO of CBS Television

Leslie R. Moonves, as president and chief executive officer of Viacom's CBS entertainment division, changed programming for U.S. network television during the 1990s. Moonves found that alternative television shows, when mixed into a traditional schedule of situation comedies and dramas, could succeed against the emergence of burgeoning competing media.

Moonves has made a career of creating successful programming for broadcast television. Often, network executives in the 1990s ascended to their leadership positions after climbing a ladder of successive jobs inside one company. For many of Moonves's contemporaries, such as Robert Iger of the American Broadcasting Company (ABC), the path to upper management included earlier jobs at one network in program development, show scheduling, daytime programming, or production administration. Moonves, however, worked at studios that produced series for network airing. The Columbia Broadcasting System (CBS) recruited him to become its entertainment president when Moonves presided over Warner Brothers television division. At the time, Warner Brothers was a chief supplier for ABC, CBS, and the National Broadcasting Company (NBC), with more than 20 programs on prime-time schedules.

Moonves began his tenure at CBS at a time when new media technologies had caused the erosion of broadcasters' audience shares. After Congress passed the Cable Communications Act of 1984 and videocassette recorders became standard household appliances, marketplace competition forced television programmers to accept smaller audiences. To lead CBS, Moonves had to create a new identity, find a younger audience, and yet still entertain a mass audience that would seek out CBS for news, sports, entertainment, and children's programming.

Moonves's reinvention of CBS blended unscripted reality programs such as *Survivor* and *The Amazing Race* into a nightly prime-time lineup dominated by stalwarts such as *Everybody Loves Raymond, Touched by an Angel,* and *60 Minutes.* This mix has kept CBS ahead in the ratings race in the face of challenges by ABC's fad game show *Who Wants to Be a Millionaire,* FOX's younger focus, and NBC's aging lineup of quality programming. Where other broadcast programmers attempted to deal with lost audiences and advertising dollars by finding fast fixes or by staying loyal to old programming concepts, Moonves succeeded by trailblazing with new show concepts, pretesting most show episodes with audience focus groups before those episodes aired, and closely managing staff, including personally evaluating contestants before casting completed for CBS's unscripted adventure programs.

Moonves had initially chosen acting as a career path. He attended Bucknell University. As a senior, he became interested in acting. In 1971, after graduating with a degree in Spanish, he moved to New York City and studied with Sanford Meisner at New York's Neighborhood Playhouse School of the Theatre. When Moonves's acting career was not immediately successful, he moved to Los Angeles, where he won roles in television programs such as *Gemini Man, Cannon,* and *The Six Million Dollar Man.*

Eventually, he became a development executive with Gregory Harrison's Catalina Productions. The company operated the Coast Playhouse and later produced movies for television. In 1981 Moonves and Catalina produced a stage version of "The Hasty Heart." The production moved to the Los Angeles Music Center's Ahmanson Theatre. That year, the play won several Los Angeles Drama Critic Circle Awards, including Best Production of the Year. Showtime filmed and cablecast the play.

Through his friendship with Warren Littlefield, Moonves changed his emphasis to television production and became a development executive at Saul Ilson

Productions. Moonves served as vice president for development before moving to 20th Century-Fox Television as vice president of movies and miniseries. Next, Moonves joined Lorimar as executive vice president for creative affairs and was promoted to president of television production. In 1988 Lorimar merged with Warner Brothers Studios. While at Lorimar, Moonves was responsible for the development and production of the shows, overseeing *Dallas* and *Knots Landing* while developing dramas such as the critically acclaimed but viewer-ignored *I'll Fly Away* and *Max Headroom* and the sitcom *Full House.*

Moonves left the presidency at Warner Brothers Television for the entertainment president position at CBS in July 1995. He was promoted to his current post in April 1998.

While keeping his network ahead, Moonves has found time to devote to television's future. In November 1999, the National Association for the Advancement of Colored People (NAACP) reported that television characters do not emulate national racial and ethnic diversity. Moonves represented CBS at those hearings and testified that he recognized the problem and would work to correct it. In February 2000, Moonves signed a contract with the NAACP, promising to create a greater numbers of realistic roles for African Americans and to expand the roles of African Americans at CBS. That year, CBS went forward with the medical drama *City of Angels,* with a predominantly African-American cast and production team. CBS aired 23 episodes of the hospital series before its cancellation.

President Clinton appointed Moonves cochair of the Advisory Committee on the Public Interest Obligations of Digital Television Broadcasters (also known as the Public Interest Council). The committee was designed to study and make recommendations on the public interest responsibilities accompanying broadcasters' receipt of digital television licenses. The committee completed its recommendations in 1998 and advised broadcasters to meet digital public interest obligations by voluntarily airing nightly, five-minute candidate discourses beginning a month prior to every election.

When Viacom merged with CBS, Moonves's influence grew, as he was promoted to chief executive officer. Next, Viacom merged its Paramount Studios television production unit with CBS, placing it under Moonves's command. In December 2001, Viacom placed a second television network under Moonves's control. After the Federal Communications Commission changed its dual ownership rules in April 2001, the company had the right to operate Paramount's TV network, the United Paramount Network (UPN), alongside CBS. Moonves now oversees UPN as well.

Moonves serves on the board of directors of Viacom, Americans for the Arts National Policy Board, the Los Angeles Free Clinic, and the board of governors of the annual Banff Television Festival. He is a member of President Clinton's Advisory Committee on the Arts, the board of directors of the Los Angeles Free Clinic, and both the executive committee and board of governors of the Academy of Television Arts and Sciences. He serves on the board of trustees of the Entertainment Industries Council, the Motion Picture Association of America's Executive Committee on Television Violence, and the board of governors of the UCLA Center for Communications Policy. He is a trustee of the National Council for Families and Television and is past president of the Hollywood Radio and Television Society.

JOAN GIGLIONE

See also **Columbia Broadcasting System (CBS)**

Leslie R. Moonves. Born October 6, 1949. Attended Bucknell University, B.A. Spanish, 1971. Married: Nancy, 1979; children: Adam, Sara, and Michael. Named vice president, Lorimar Productions, 1985. Named head of creative affairs, Lorimar Television, 1988. Promoted to president, 1989. Named president of Warner Brothers Television, 1993. Appointed to presidency of CBS Entertainment and executive vice presidency, CBS/Broadcast Group, 1995. Named President and chief executive officer of CBS Television, 1998. Recipient: Bucknell University's Achievement in Chosen Profession Award, 2002; International Radio and Television Society Award for Significant Achievement, 1999; Los Angeles Sports & Entertainment Commission 2nd Annual Award of Excellence, 2001; Bucknell's Academy of Artistic Achievement Award, 1995; Casting Society of America Career Achievement Award and Caucus for Producers, Writers and Directors Executive of the Year Award, 1993.

Moore, Garry (1915–1993)

U.S. Television Personality

Garry Moore, genial host of numerous successful network television programs throughout the 1950s and 1960s, played a major role in making the medium acceptable to American viewers during its early decades. During his long broadcast career, Moore appeared regularly during prime-time hours as well as other time periods; like Arthur Godfrey, he hosted prominent daytime and weekly evening shows, which contributed to his immense popularity. His programs were frequently among the top-ten prime-time programs. As a comedian, Moore combined genial humor with a pleasant personality and a relaxed style that made him a favorite with audiences.

Moore originally worked as a network radio comedian and writer known by his real name, Thomas Garrison Morfit. Because Morfit was difficult to pronounce, an on-air contest to select a stage name was conducted. Beginning in 1940, he became known to the listening audience as Garry Moore.

In 1949 CBS Radio originated *The Garry Moore Show,* a daily one-hour variety program produced in Hollywood. Network programmers recognized a successful radio personality in Moore, and given the need for programming talent on its young television network, the Columbia Broadcasting System (CBS) provided the opportunity for Moore to host a variety television show in New York. When *The Garry Moore Show* was introduced on CBS Television in 1950, Moore established a distinctive on-air identity with his crew-cut hair and bow tie–wearing image. His physical appearance enhanced his casual demeanor and easygoing conversational style, which became familiar to home viewers.

Moore's initial telecasts followed a somewhat checkerboard scheduling pattern. Beginning as a 30-minute evening series, live Monday through Friday, *The Garry Moore Show* made its television debut in June 1950. By August, the program changed to one night per week and expanded to an hour in length. For its fall 1950 lineup, CBS scheduled Moore weekday afternoons, a move that lasted eight years. By 1951 *The Garry Moore Show* reportedly was the second-largest revenue source for CBS, and for a time the network could not accommodate all the potential sponsors awaiting the opportunity to advertise on the program.

Moore's daytime program format was flexible but generally included humorous skits, singing, monologues, and studio-audience interaction. Regular performers were featured along with special guests. Supporting Moore with the various program segments were singers Denise Lor and Ken Carson and announcer and sidekick Durward Kirby. Comedians Don Adams, George Gobel, Don Knotts, and Jonathan Winters made their earliest television appearances on Moore's show, contributing to the entertaining tone and boosting their individual careers. *The Garry Moore Show* remained on the air until mid-1958, when Moore voluntarily relinquished his hosting duties owing to the exhausting work schedule. By the 1958 fall season, Moore returned to CBS, hosting a weekly evening program, again called *The Garry Moore Show.*

The Garry Moore Evening Show, Garry Moore, 1951.
Courtesy of the Everett Collection

The hour-long evening series followed a format similar to Moore's daytime variety program. During its six-year run, *The Garry Moore Show* introduced comedian Carol Burnett, who later starred in her own successful CBS show during the 1960s and 1970s. Other comedic and musical talents regularly appearing on the Moore nighttime variety show included Durward Kirby, Marion Lorne, and Dorothy Loudon. Allen Funt's "Candid Camera" became a regular segment on the program. Another popular weekly feature was a lengthy nostalgia segment known as "That Wonderful Year." Given the grueling work required to produce the show, Moore decided to discontinue the program in 1964. He reappeared in 1966 as host of yet another weekly *Garry Moore Show* variety series, but after five months of competition with *Bonanza,* CBS canceled the show because of poor ratings.

In addition to hosting several variety shows, Garry Moore moderated two television panel quiz programs, *I've Got a Secret* and *To Tell the Truth.* He began a 12-year reign as moderator of Goodson-Todman Productions' *I've Got a Secret* in 1952. This popular CBS prime-time program featured celebrity panelists who tried to guess the secret of ordinary and celebrity contestants. Panel members appearing through the years included Bill Cullen, Jayne Meadows, Henry Morgan, Faye Emerson, and Betsy Palmer. *I've Got a Secret* was among the A.C. Nielsen top-20 television programs for seven years. It remained one of the most popular panel programs ever on television. Goodson-Todman sold *I've Got a Secret* to CBS and Moore in 1959, and he continued to moderate the show until 1964.

To Tell the Truth, also from Goodson-Todman, was moderated for a decade by Bud Collyer before it was taken over by Moore when the program went into syndication in 1969. Another half-hour celebrity panel show, the object of *To Tell the Truth* was to determine which of three contestants was telling the truth. Regular panelists included Orson Bean, Bill Cullen, Kitty Carlisle, and Peggy Cass. Moore left the program and television for good in 1977, when he developed throat cancer. The wit, charm, and personality, so much a part of Moore, influenced numerous television hosts both during and following his long career. He died from emphysema in 1993 at age 78.

DENNIS HARP

See also I've Got A Secret; **Talk Shows**

Garry Moore. Born Thomas Garrison Morfit in Baltimore, Maryland, January 31, 1915. Married: 1) Eleanor Borum Little, 1939 (died, 1974); children: John Mason Morfit and Thomas Garrison Morfit; 2) Mary Elizabeth De Chant, 1975. Writer and actor, radio station WBAL, Baltimore, 1935–38; news announcer and sports commentator, radio station KWK, St. Louis, Missouri, 1939; star and writer, NBC Blue Network's *Club Matinee,* 1939–43; New York emcee, NBC's *Everything Goes,* 1942; costar and writer, *Jimmy Durante–Garry Moore Show,* 1943–48; host, NBC's *Take It or Leave It,* 1948–50; star, CBS radio show *Garry Moore Show,* 1949–50; star, CBS-TV's *Garry Moore Show,* 1950–58, 1958–64, 1966–67; moderator, *I've Got a Secret,* 1952–64; substitute host, *Arthur Godfrey's Talent Scouts,* 1953; host, syndicated television quiz show *To Tell the Truth,* 1969–77. Member: National Academy of Television Arts and Sciences. Died on Hilton Head Island, South Carolina, November 28, 1993.

Television Series

1950–58, 1958–64, 1966–67	*The Garry Moore Show*
1952–64	*I've Got a Secret*
1969–77	*To Tell the Truth*

Radio

Club Matinee, 1939–43; *Jimmy Durante–Garry Moore Show,* 1943–48; *Godfrey's Talent Scouts,* 1946 *Take It or Leave It,* 1948–50; *The Garry Moore Show,* 1949–50.

Further Reading

Blumenthal, Norman, *The TV Game Show Book,* New York: Pyramid, 1975

DeLong, Thomas A., *Quiz Craze: America's Infatuation with Game Shows,* New York: Praeger, 1991

Fabe, Maxine, *TV Game Shows,* Garden City, New York: Doubleday, 1979

Graham, Jefferson, *Come on Down!!!: The Game Show Book,* New York: Abbeville, 1988

Schwartz, David, Steve Ryan, and Fred Wostbrock, *The Encyclopedia of TV Game Shows,* New York: Zoetrope, 1987

Moore, Mary Tyler (1936–)

U.S. Actor

Mary Tyler Moore's most enduring contributions to television are in two classic sitcoms, *The Dick Van Dyke Show* (1961–66) and *The Mary Tyler Moore Show* (1970–77), although she has appeared in the medium in a variety of roles both before and after these series. Her first on-camera television work was as a dancer, and it was as "Happy Hotpoint," a singing and dancing fairy, that she first caught the public eye. Her first regular series role as Sam, the receptionist on *Richard Diamond, Private Detective,* was notable primarily because it featured only her dancer's legs and voice.

As Laura Petrie, the beautiful, talented, and not-so-typical suburban housewife married to comedy writer Rob (Dick Van Dyke) on *The Dick Van Dyke Show,* Moore earned critical praise (and Emmy Awards) as she laid the foundation for the wholesome but spunky identity that would mark her television career. Though she lacked their experience in television comedy, Moore was no mere "straight woman" to comedians Van Dyke, Carl Reiner, Morey Amsterdam, and Rose Marie; she managed to stake out her own comic identity as a lovely and competent housewife who was frequently thrown a curve by her husband's unusual friends and career. Thanks to the show's explorations of the Petries' courtship (they met while he was in the military and she a USO dancer), Moore was able to display on the show her talents as both dancer and singer as well as comedic actor. While *The Dick Van Dyke Show* stopped production in 1966, it appeared in reruns on the Columbia Broadcasting System's (CBS's) daytime lineup until 1969, keeping Moore's perky persona in the public eye as she sought film roles and stage work for the remainder of the decade.

On the basis of Moore's popularity in *The Dick Van Dyke Show,* CBS offered her a 13-episode contract to develop her own series starting in 1970. Moore and her then-husband Grant Tinker, a production executive at 20th Century-Fox at the time, used the opportunity to set up their own production company, MTM Enterprises, to produce the show. Following the success of *The Mary Tyler Moore Show,* MTM went on to produce a number of the most successful and critically praised series of the 1970s and 1980s, with Moore's contributions limited mainly to input on her own show(s) and the use of her initials.

On *The Mary Tyler Moore Show,* Moore played Mary Richards, a 30-something single woman "making it on her own" in 1970s Minneapolis, Minnesota. MTM first pitched her character to CBS as a young divorcée, but CBS executives believed that her role as Laura Petrie was so firmly etched in the public mind that viewers would think that she had divorced Dick Van Dyke (and that the American public would not find a divorced woman likable), so Richards was rewritten as a woman who had moved to the big city after ending a long affair. Richards lands a job working in the news department of fictional WJM-TV, where Moore's all-American spunk plays off against the gruff boss Lou Grant (Ed Asner), world-weary writer Murray Slaughter (Gavin MacLeod), and pompous anchorman Ted Baxter (Ted Knight). In early seasons, her

Mary Tyler Moore.
Courtesy of the Everett Collection

all-male work environment is counterbalanced by a primarily female home life, where again her character contrasts with her ditzy landlady Phyllis Lindstrom (Cloris Leachman) and her New York–born neighbor and best friend, Rhoda Morgenstern (Valerie Harper). Both the show and Moore were lauded for their realistic portrayal of "new" women in the 1970s whose lives centered on work rather than family and for whom men were colleagues rather than just potential mates. While Mary Richards's apologetic manner may have undermined some of the messages of the women's movement, she also put a friendly face on the potentially threatening tenets of feminism, naturalizing some of the decade's changes in the way women were perceived both at home and at work.

After *The Mary Tyler Moore Show* ended its seven-year, award-winning run, Moore appeared in several short-running series, including her attempt to revive the musical variety show *Mary* (1978), which is best remembered for a supporting cast that included the then-unknown David Letterman, Michael Keaton, and Swoosie Kurtz. Moore's later stage, feature film, and made-for-television movie efforts have represented successful efforts to break with the perky Laura Petrie/Mary Richards persona. In the Academy Award–winning *Ordinary People* (1980), for example, Moore's performance contrasts the publicly lovable suburban housewife—a Laura Petrie–type facade—with her character's private inability to love and nurture her grief-stricken family; in *Flirting with Disaster* (1996), she steals scenes as Ben Stiller's vain adoptive mother. Moore won a special Tony Award for her performance as a quadriplegic who wanted to end her existence in *Whose Life Is It, Anyway?* And on television, she has played everything from a breast cancer survivor in *First, You Cry* to the troubled Mary Todd Lincoln in *Gore Vidal's Lincoln* to a villainous orphanage director in *Stolen Babies*. Still, Mary Richards continues to define Moore. In 2001 she and Valerie Harper renewed their on-screen friendship in *Mary and Rhoda*, a made-for-television movie featuring their *Mary Tyler Moore Show* characters. Originally pitched as a new series, Moore, Harper, and the American Broadcasting Company (ABC) opted out of a long-term commitment despite the show's high ratings. Another sign of Mary Richards's enduring appeal came in 2001, when the city of Minneapolis and the cable network TV Land unveiled a bronze statue of "Richards" tossing her famous beret into the air, as Moore did on the opening credits of *The Mary Tyler Moore Show*. In recent years, Moore has devoted much of her attention to work for the Juvenile Diabetes Research Foundation, the American Diabetes Association, and various animal rights organizations.

SUSAN MCLELAND

See also **The Dick Van Dyke Show; Gender and Television;** *The Mary Tyler Moore Show;* **Tinker, Grant**

Mary Tyler Moore. Born in Brooklyn, New York, December 29, 1936. Married: 1) Richard Meeker, 1955 (divorced, 1962), child: Richard (deceased); 2) Grant Tinker, 1963 (divorced, 1981); 3) Robert Levine, 1983. Began television career as "Happy Hotpoint," dancing performer in appliance commercials, 1955; costarred in *The Dick Van Dyke Show*, 1961–66; television guest appearances, 1960s and 1970s; cofounder, with Tinker, of MTM Enterprises; starred in *The Mary Tyler Moore Show*, 1970–77. Recipient: numerous Emmy Awards; Golden Globe Award; named to Academy of Television Arts and Sciences Hall of Fame, 1987.

Television Series

1959	*Richard Diamond, Private Detective*
1961–66	*The Dick Van Dyke Show*
1970–77	*The Mary Tyler Moore Show*
1978	*Mary*
1979	*The Mary Tyler Moore Hour*
1985–86	*Mary*
1988	*Annie McGuire*
1995	*New York News*

Made-for-Television Movies

1979	*Run a Crooked Mile*
1984	*Heartsounds*
1985	*Finnegan Begin Again*
1988	*Gore Vidal's Lincoln*
1990	*Thanksgiving Day*
1990	*The Last Best Year*
1993	*Stolen Babies*
1995	*Stolen Memories: Secrets from the Rose Garden*
1997	*Payback*
2001	*Mary and Rhoda* (also producer)
2001	*Like Mother, Like Son: The Strange Story of Sante and Kenny Kimes*
2002	*Miss Lettie and Me*
2003	*The Gin Game*
2003	*Blessings*

Television Specials

1969	*Dick Van Dyke and the Other Woman, Mary Tyler Moore*
1974	*We the Women* (host and narrator)
1976	*Mary's Incredible Dream*
1978	*CBS: On the Air* (cohost)
1978	*How to Survive the 70s and Maybe Even Bump into Happiness* (host)

1991	*Funny Women of Television*
1991	*The Mary Tyler Moore Show:*
	The 20th Anniversary Show
1998	*Three Cats from Miami and Other*
	Pet Practitioners
1998	*CBS: The First Fifty Years*

Films

X-15, 1961; *Thoroughly Modern Millie*, 1967; *What's So Bad About Feeling Good?*, 1968; *Don't Just Stand There!*, 1968; *Change of Habit*, 1970; *Ordinary People*, 1980; *Six Weeks*, 1982; *Just Between Friends*, 1986; *Flirting with Disaster*, 1996; *Keys to Tulsa*, 1997; *Reno Finds Her Mom*, 1997; *Labor Pains*, 2000; *Cheaters*, 2001.

Publication

After All, 1995

Further Reading

Alley, Robert, and Irby B. Brown, *Love Is All Around: The Making of The Mary Tyler Moore Show*, New York: Delta, 1989

Bonderoff, Jason, *Mary Tyler Moore: A Biography*, New York: St. Martin's Press, 1986

Hingley, Audrey T., "Mary Tyler Moore: After All," *Saturday Evening Post* (November–December 1995)

Moore, Roger (1927–)

British Actor

Roger Moore settled into acting by 1948, appearing in small roles on British television, radio, and repertory theater. In 1953 Moore went to Hollywood, where he secured an MGM contract, appearing in minor roles in four features over the next two years. He moved to Warner Brothers and appeared in several features, including *The Sins of Rachel Cade*. In 1958 Moore returned to England for a year to star in the television series, *Ivanhoe*, a coproduction between Screen Gems of America and Sydney Box. The series was part of a historical cycle in British television in the late 1950s, and the *Ivanhoe* series was an admirable effort in the genre. The series was loosely based on the chivalric exploits of Ivanhoe during the time of Prince John with the hero drawn from the novel by Sir Walter Scott. As the figure of the title, Moore was suitably dashing, an energetic defender of the weak and the poor and a nobleman to boot.

Back in Hollywood with Warners in 1959, Moore was given a starring role in the television series *The Alaskans*. Moore played Silky Harris, an adventurer, and already the suave sophistication that became a later trademark was in evidence. The series was a variation on the one-hour western series that Warners had been successfully churning out for several years, but *The Alaskans* lasted only one season.

Moore was then cast in the western series *Maverick* (1960). Cousin Beau, played by Moore, was sophisticated and upper class but, unfortunately, lacked the comic touch of the original star, James Garner, who had left the series. After one season on *Maverick*, Moore left the series, which folded a year later.

Moore returned to feature films. He made three more features for Warners, including a western, *Gold for Seven Sinners* (1961), a western vehicle for Clint Walker, the former star of *Cheyenne*, which was partly shot in Italy. Moore stayed two years in Italy, where he made two Italian films.

After nearly ten years in film and television, Moore was cast in the role of the Saint in the eponymous television series in 1961. The role perfectly fit his persona of a sophisticated Englishman with more than a modicum of intelligence, cunning, and toughness. While

Roger Moore.
Courtesy of the Everett Collection

some appearances in earlier U.S. television anthology drama series, such as *Alfred Hitchcock Presents,* had Moore playing such a figure, nothing in his previous starring roles had capitalized on this side of Moore's screen personality. *The Saint* expanded considerably on the type over seven years, through 114 filmed hours as well as two telefeatures. The series was produced in Britain by ITC/ATV and was based on the novels by Leslie Charteris. The Saint was a kind of modern Robin Hood who used wealth, cunning, and sophistication to help bring to justice criminals that the law had been unable to catch. *The Saint* taught Moore his trade and made him a large income. He became owner of a textile mill, a director of the Faberge perfume operation, and co-owner of a film production company, Barmoore, which produced later episodes of *The Saint.* The series also gave him a chance to try his hand at directing. All together, he directed eight hour-long episodes of *The Saint* and two hour-long episodes of his next television series, *The Persuaders.*

This latter series was a kind of spin-off to *The Saint* as far as Moore's role was concerned. However, he no longer played solo, being teamed with fading screen idol Tony Curtis. *The Persuaders* was produced by a company of Sir Lew Grade and ran for 24 hour-long episodes in the 1971–72 season. The attempt to enlist audience loyalties on both sides of the Atlantic was obvious enough; nevertheless, the series had sufficient action and adventure, usually in exotic locales, to keep audiences happy and make the series popular. But it did little to advance Moore's career after the achievement of *The Saint.* The real break came in 1973, when Moore was cast as the second James Bond. Chosen over actor Michael Caine, Moore's casting as Bond was in line with the screen persona that had been elaborated over 15 years in television. Moreover, the work in television had given Moore a fame and popularity beyond anything Caine could muster from his film work in the previous ten years.

The Bond role meant that Moore was now an international star who no longer needed to play in television, but the general pattern of his career is a familiar and instructive one regarding the younger medium. Moore decided on an acting career just as television was displacing feature films as the most popular form of screen entertainment. Television taught him his trade as an actor, allowing him the opportunity over several series to elaborate a screen personality that would later stand him in good stead. After a long television apprenticeship, he finally graduated to big-budget feature films, where he has worked ever since. The other significant feature of his career is the paradox that this British star was in fact a product of the international television and film industries, if not the American industry.

ALBERT MORAN

See also **Maverick**

Roger Moore. Born in London, England, October 14, 1927. Attended Royal Academy of Dramatic Art, London. Married: 1) Doorn van Steyn (divorced, 1953); 2) Dorothy Squires, 1953 (divorced, 1969); 3) Luisa Mattioli; children: Geoffrey, Christian, and Deborah. Film cartoonist and model from the age of 16, before training as an actor; made film debut, 1945; after National Service, worked as film actor; made television debut in *Ivanhoe,* 1958–59; television performer and star, from 1960s; subsequently concentrated on film career, notably in seven films as James Bond. Recipient: Golden Globe World Film Favorite Award, 1980.

Television Series

1958–59	*Ivanhoe*
1959–60	*The Alaskans*
1957–62	*Maverick*
1962–69	*The Saint*
1971–72	*The Persuaders*
2002	*Alias* (guest appearance)

Made-for-Television Movies

1977	*Sherlock Holmes in New York*
1992	*The Man Who Wouldn't Die*

Films

Caesar and Cleopatra, 1945; *The Last Time I Saw Paris,* 1954; *Interrupted Melody,* 1955; *The King's Thief,* 1955; *Diane,* 1955; *The Miracle,* 1959; *The Sins of Rachel Cade,* 1961; *Gold of the Seven Saints,* 1961; *Rape of the Sabines,* 1961; *No Man's Land,* 1961; *Crossplot,* 1969; *The Man Who Haunted Himself,* 1970; *Live and Let Die,* 1973; *The Man with the Golden Gun,* 1974; *Gold,* 1974; *That Lucky Touch,* 1975; *Shout at the Devil,* 1976; *Street People,* 1976; *The Spy Who Loved Me,* 1977; *The Wild Geese,* 1978; *Escape from Athena,* 1979; *Moonraker,* 1979; *North Sea Hijack,* 1980; *Sunday Lovers,* 1980; *The Sea Wolves,* 1980; *Cannonball Run,* 1981; *For Your Eyes Only,* 1982; *The Naked Face,* 1983; *Octopussy,* 1983; *A View to a Kill,* 1985; *Bed and Breakfast,* 1989; *Bullseye!,* 1989; *Fire, Ice and Dynamite,* 1990; *The Quest,* 1995; *Spice World,* 1997; *Boat Trip,* 2002, *Victor,* 2003.

Publication

James Bond Diary, 1973.

Further Reading

Owen, Gareth, and Oliver Bayan, *Roger Moore: His Films and Career,* London: Robert Hale Ltd, 2002.

Morecambe and Wise

British Comedy Act

Morecambe and Wise, a comic duo who developed their act in variety shows in provincial theaters, became the popular stars of a long-running series that had a major influence on the development of British television comedy. Born Eric Bartholomew and Ernest Wiseman, they adopted their stage names when they first teamed up in 1941, making their debut as a double act at the Liverpool Empire. They were both 15 and had already gained experience working separately on the music-hall circuit. Eric took his new name from the Lancashire seaside town where he was born, and, since Ernie came from Yorkshire, their northern working-class origins remained a clear but unobtrusive part of their appeal.

After a break for national service, the act was reconstituted in 1947 and went through a number of changes before developing the format that made them stars. They started out by imitating comic routines from the films of Bud Abbott and Lou Costello, with fake American accents and Eric in the role of the straight man. It was not until they reversed their roles that their ability to create characters out of the traditional roles of comedian and straight man began to bring them recognition.

A few radio engagements preceded their first attempt to break into the emerging television field. Their first television series, called *Running Wild,* was broadcast by the British Broadcasting Corporation (BBC) in 1954 but was a short-lived failure. *The Morecambe and Wise Show* first appeared on ATV in 1961 and transferred to BBC 2 in 1968. Scripts were written by Sid Green and Dick Hills, who often appeared in small parts in the sketches. The series was briefly interrupted when Eric suffered a heart attack in 1969 but returned to renewed acclaim, with Eddie Braben as the new scriptwriter.

Their success led to several invitations to appear at Royal Command Performances, and they also made a number of guest appearances in the United States on *The Ed Sullivan Show.* Their three feature films, *The Intelligence Men* (1965), *That Riviera Touch* (1966), and *The Magnificent Two* (1967), were often funny but failed to achieve either the inspiration or the popular success of the television series.

The originality of their show stemmed ironically from its refusal to deny its theatrical origins. The two stars appeared on stage, introduced their guests (who often appeared with them in short comic sketches), ended the show with a song-and-dance number, and then returned for a curtain call. The jokes were usually old or dependent on excruciating puns and double entendres. Their impact came from the contrast between the apparent weakness of the material and the valiant efforts of the comedians to make it funny. The show provided the pleasures of familiarity amid the rapid social and cultural changes of the 1960s and 1970s; however, the familiar was always somehow skewed because of the performers' evident desire to succeed in the contemporary world.

The comic personae of Morecambe and Wise also reflected this tension between the familiar and the modern. Their appearance was mined for recurring

Morecambe & Wise, Eric Morecambe (w/glasses), Ernie Wise, 1967.
Courtesy of the Everett Collection

jokes about Eric's horn-rimmed spectacles and Ernie's alleged wig and "short fat hairy legs." Gestures and catchphrases were also repeated, as when Eric expressed aggression by placing the flat of his hand under Ernie's chin and challenging him to "get out of that." Yet their relationship offered an unfamiliar twist on the conventional double act. Predictably, Ernie was the one with aspirations, in his case a desire to become a serious writer, while Eric was slow on the uptake, constantly exasperating his partner through his failure to understand or his refusal to take things seriously. However, Eric was also quite cunning and clearly had the ultimate authority, slyly deflating all pretensions.

Although there had been many double acts in the British music-hall tradition, they have been a rarity in British television, with only Peter Cook and Dudley Moore achieving a success at all comparable to Morecambe and Wise in a show, *Not Only but Also...,* clearly indebted to their predecessors. The blend of stand-up comedy and sketches in *The Morecambe and Wise Show* was probably influenced by the American *Burns and Allen Show,* which relied more heavily on situation comedy and may have in turn influenced the zanier and more fragmented comedy of *Rowan and Martin's Laugh-In.*

Eric died in 1984 and Ernie in 1999, but the pair continue to be fondly remembered. A tribute show, *The*

Play What I Wrote, written by and starring Sean Foley and Hamish McColl and directed by Kenneth Branagh, opened in London's West End in September 2001. It opened at the Lyceum Theatre in New York in March 2003.

JIM LEACH

Cast
John Bartholomew
Ernest Wisemen

Programming History
ITV (1961–68)
BBC (1968–78)
ITV (1978–84)

Further Reading

McCann, Graham, *Morecamb and Wise,* London: Fourth Estate Classic House, 1999
Midwinter, Eric, *Make 'Em Laugh: Famous Comedians and Their Worlds,* London: George Allen and Unwin, 1979
Morecambe, Eric, and Ernie Wise, *Eric and Ernie: The Autobiography of Morecambe and Wise,* London: W.H. Allen, 1972
Tynan, Kenneth, *The Sound of Two Hands Clapping,* London: Cape, 1975; New York: Holt, Rinehart and Winston, 1975

Morning Television Programs

Morning shows are informal and relaxed, some complete with living room sets, sofas, and coffee tables. Regular hosts are present in most shows as the familiar, foundational, conversational link to the audience. But the programs also sometimes include guest news anchors and sports and weatherpersons from affiliate stations, making that link to the audience even more intimate. Whatever the combination of hosts (usually three), they interact with light and cheerful banter. Within the past decade, the hosts of morning shows have remained fairly consistent with a balance of male and female anchors. *Good Morning America* is hosted at present by Charles Gibson and Diane Sawyer; *The Early Show* by Harry Smith, Hannah Storm, Julie Chen, and Rene Syler, and *Today* by Katie Couric and Matt Lauer. The FOX Network does not seem to be a major competitor in this field. Most cable networks are unaffected by the morning time slot and run a variety

of shows ranging from cartoons to religion. The only exception to this type of programming is the Cable News Network (CNN), which hosts a news show titled *Live at Daybreak.* It probably can be regarded as a major competitor, as it provides abbreviated national and world news segments.

News stories from the previous day are often followed the next morning with related but less formal stories and celebrity interviews and discussion. When national disasters occur—hurricanes, earthquakes, plane crashes—the whole show may be dominated by news coverage of those events. Sometimes the morning anchors and crew go on location in order to feature a particular city or event. On such occasions, organizers, political leaders, dignitaries, and VIPs are interviewed on site. National weather reports are interspersed with sponsored announcements, birthday wishes, and other less formal moments, and the pro-

Today (The Today Show), Matt Lauer, Katie Couric, Willard Scott, Bryant Gumbel, Gene Shalit,
1997.
Courtesy of the Everett Collection

grams are formatted in such a way that local station breaks can be accommodated with ease. These breaks are important because they allow affiliates to provide local news, sports, and weather and to insert local commercials.

Morning shows are constructed in a style best termed as "modular programming": short, unconnected segments are presented with no relationship between them. Modules rarely exceed four minutes, and most are shorter. This program design is based on programmer and producer perceptions of viewer activities—preoccupied with preparations for the day and unable to devote much time or attention to any one segment of the program.

In recent years, morning shows have returned to one of their earliest strategies and have begun to include live audiences in their format. Two approaches to audience participation have been introduced. The first enables people in the street to look into the studio from the outside. At times, these spectators can be distracting, raising signs and waving arms, presumably to attract attention from viewers "back home." But they

can be shut out by means of a mechanized cyclorama. This "fish bowl concept" was an aspect of the early years of *Today,* when Dave Garroway and the chimpanzee J. Fred Muggs were featured. On occasion, the hosts move outside to where people are standing on the sidewalk, interviewing a few selected visitors. The second approach to audience involvement includes a captive audience within the studio, similar to conventional talk shows. Inside the studio, the audience can be controlled much more easily, and consequently their behavior is more predictable and subdued.

The first network "early day" shows followed the patterns of successful radio programming and were not in the morning at all. In 1948 the National Broadcasting Company (NBC) scheduled *Tex and Jinx,* one of the popular morning radio talking couples, at the network's then-earliest hour of 1:00 P.M., and the Columbia Broadcasting System (CBS) showed, half an hour later, *Missus Goes A-Shopping,* a game show with popular radio host John Reed King. In the fall of 1948, Dumont, the weakest network, actually dared, before noon, a miscellany of variety and informational shows

Today Show, 1952–present, Barbara Walters, Hugh Downs, Joe Garagiola, late 1960s–early 1970s.
Courtesy of the Everett Collection

that survived until 1950 and were then forgotten. These earliest shows, however, also provided a chance for technical experiment. In August 1951, CBS offered at 10:30 A.M., an hour when hardly anyone would be watching, their own married couple, Mike Wallace and Buff Cobb, in *Two Sleepy People,* the first regularly scheduled network color show (the video portion of the signal could not be received by conventional black-and-white sets).

In 1952 the efforts to produce a successful morning show finally began to work. On January 7, Arthur Godfrey began simulcasting his popular radio show *Arthur Godfrey Time,* which proved just as popular on television, where it lasted until 1959. A week later (and also a week late), the greatest morning experiment began. *Today* began producing three hours a day (only two were broadcast in each time zone). When writer-producer Larry Gelbart attempted in an interview to define what "real television" was, he said "real televi-

sion might have been the early *Today* show, with Dave Garroway standing in a window doing a show that no one had ever seen before, something that wasn't borrowed from radio or the stage or motion pictures or newspapers."

Today was one of the creations of NBC executive Sylvester "Pat" Weaver, who had carefully considered the needs of various special audiences and devised the responses that became *Your Show of Shows,* the prime-time variety show; *Tonight,* for the "sophisticated" late-night viewer; and *Today,* to address a range of viewers from those preparing to leave for work to the "homemaker" readying children for school and her own daily activities. In March 1954, *Home* with Arlene Francis began broadcasting—Weaver's more specialized solution for the late-morning audience. Although influential on the design of succeeding daytime magazine shows, *Home* itself lasted only until 1957. In later decades, however, suggesting that Weaver's strategies were appropriate, shows similar to *Home* abounded in late-morning times. They were often surrounded by popular game shows such as *Strike It Rich, The Price Is Right, Concentration,* and the early years of *Jeopardy!* In the 1960s and 1970s, reruns of evening shows were popular in late morning, and in recent decades, syndicated confrontation shows, such as those hosted by Jerry Springer and Geraldo Rivera, have flourished. The occasional variety show, such as David Letterman's 1980 program, or even the rare soap opera, such as *The Guiding Light,* have also been programmed as morning offerings.

But it is the history of *Today* and the responses to it by other networks that has anchored the history of the morning genre. During its first year, *Today* had neither great audience nor critical success, although it achieved frequent mention in the news because of its window onto Rockefeller Center and its efforts to interview former President Harry Truman on his early morning New York walks. In its second year, the chimpanzee J. Fred Muggs joined the cast, and viewership, especially among families and children, began to increase.

In 1954 the American Broadcasting Company (ABC) entered the morning competition for a short time with a simulcast of its long-term popular radio show, Don McNeill's *Breakfast Club,* which failed on TV after a year. In direct competition with *Today,* CBS began a remarkable morning variety show. *The Morning Show,* as it was called, had as its successive hosts for the three years it was on the air: Walter Cronkite, Jack Paar, Johnny Carson for a time as guest host, John Henry Faulk (until he was blacklisted), Dick Van Dyke, and Will Rogers Jr. Illustrating the wide range of viewers it sought to attract, the show's regulars included Charles Collingwood, the Baird puppets, singers Merv Griffin and Edie Adams, and, as a writer, Barbara Walters. The show challenged *Today* with every strategy applicable to the variety-talk formulas—then finally gave up. In 1955 CBS substituted *Captain Kangaroo* for the second hour of *The Morning Show.* For over 25 years, the Captain remained in place, appealing to younger audiences but using many of *Today*'s segmented structure by programming regular visits by guests such as Dr. Joyce Brothers and Bill Cosby.

By the 1960s, it had become apparent that competition for the broadest possible morning audience would have to use a mix very similar to that created by Weaver for *Today.* Beginning in 1963 with a 25-minute show hosted by Mike Wallace, the CBS news division attempted to experiment with a response that was "not quite the same as" *Today.* In 1987 the CBS entertainment division briefly intruded on this process with the failed *Morning Program,* but CBS News returned in November 1987 with its final and continuing response to date: a full two-hour *CBS This Morning.* ABC did not begin its first serious challenge to *Today* until 1975, first with the short-lived *A.M. America* and then the still-continuing *Good Morning, America,* which became identified with its host, David Hartman, from 1976 to 1985 and has since had a succession of hosts.

Over the past four and a half decades, then, there have been continuous attempts and strategies for "balancing" the early morning newsmagazine formula. Garroway delivered entertainment, John Chancellor presented serious news, and Hugh Downs and Barbara Walters became a chatting couple. CBS focused on the newsroom, while ABC, with David Hartman, moved toward the living room. But many of the forms stayed constant: for example, the five-minute break for local news, the cheery weatherperson, and the occasional visit to other locales. There was also a gradual expansion of the format into the 6:00 A.M. to 7:00 A.M. hour.

In the 1990s, as the number of available channels vastly increased, an expanding variety of specialized choices in the morning made NBC's *Today,* ABC's *Good Morning, America,* and *CBS This Morning* appear to be venerable institutions that have withstood the test of time. However, cable television news and talk shows, which take advantage of low production costs and flexibility, may become even stronger competitors for the network morning programs in the future. If this is the case, the attempts will most likely follow patterns established by continuous trials in the network arena, trials that have resulted in some of the most familiar and regularized moments "brought to us" by television.

In the early 2000s, a variety of morning shows competed with the traditional programs. Three major competitors were *American Morning* on CNN, with Soledad O'Brien and Bill Hemmer; *Fox and Friends,* with anchors E.D. Hill and Brian Kilmeade; and MSNBC's *Imus in the Morning.* Of these three new offerings, *Fox and Friends* is by far the most popular, based on audience shares. It is estimated that *Fox and Friends* has 1.2 million viewers, *American Morning* 753,000, and *Imus in the Morning* 364,000.

Competition from cable and the Internet and shrinking evening revenues have led the major networks to value the morning program slot more highly than ever. The morning is regarded as an extremely lucrative time slot (*Today* cleared $100 million in profits last year). Many of the morning television program studios have received expensive face-lifts, complete with giant Astrovision screens, bright lights, and custom-made windows offering excellent background views.

In October 2002, *Today* earned a rating of 4.6, *Good Morning America* had a household rating of 3.4 and *The Early Show* had a rating of 2.1.

RICHARD WORRINGHAM AND RODNEY A. BUXTON

See also **Couric, Katie; Talk Shows**

Further Reading

"Before and After: How the War on Terrorism Has Changed The News Agenda, Network Television, June to October 2001," Project for Excellence in Journalism

Graham, Tim, "Objectivity and Morning TV News," *The World & I* (June 1999)

"Invisible Donna Reappears on Morning Shows: CBS Host Praises Political Ascent of 'Unapologetic Liberal,'" Media Research Center-Campaign 2000 Media Reality Check (August 14, 2000), http://secure.media research.org/Campaign2000/mrc/2000814pm.html

Johnson, Peter, "Fox Wakes Up Morning TV (Fox & Friends)," *USA Today* (August 18, 2003)

Motion Picture Association of America

Based in Washington, D.C., the Motion Picture Association of America (MPAA) has long served as the formal political representative for the major Hollywood studios. These studios (including Time Warner's Warner Brothers, Viacom's Paramount, Rupert Murdoch's 20th Century-Fox, Sony's Columbia, Seagram's Universal, and the Disney conglomerate) create and market the majority of television's fictional fare, from comedies and dramas in prime time to the talk and game shows that fill rest of the day. In the MPAA, they join together to work on common concerns. To the public, this objective is most clearly manifest in the MPAA's movie ratings; for the television business, the MPAA grapples with thousands of proposed and actual regulations by foreign and domestic governments.

Headed since 1966 by former White House staff member Jack Valenti, the MPAA lobbies the Federal Communications Commission and the U.S. Congress. Through the U.S. Department of State and the Office of the U.S. Trade Representative, the association argues for free trade of television programs around the world.

The MPAA was formed by major Hollywood companies in 1922 as the Motion Picture Producers and Distributors Association (MPPDA). Both before and after the name change to the Motion Picture Association of America, the main activity of the association has been political, and the companies have always hired well-connected Washington insiders to represent their interests in the capital.

The first head was President Warren G. Harding's brilliant campaign manager, Will H. Hays. In his day, Hays became famous for the MPPDA production code, a set of moralistic restrictions governing the content of motion pictures. Hays retired in 1945 and never had to deal with issues concerning television.

Hays's successor was a former head of the U.S. Chamber of Commerce, Eric Johnston. It was Johnston who, beginning in the 1950s, first had to grapple with television, opposing the minimalist trade restrictions then being proposed by nations worldwide, restrictions that would work against his Hollywood corporate clients. Johnston preached free-trade policies that would enable Hollywood to move its filmed and video products into every country around the globe. In so doing, he became a leading advocate for the establishment of the European Common Market, which would create a single body of trade officials to deal with rather than a different set in each country.

Johnston died in August 1963. Ralph Hetzel served as interim head until 1966, when the moguls of the Hollywood studios persuaded White House assistant and Texan Jack Valenti to take the job. Since then, Valenti has had to deal with the coming of cable television and the rise of home video. He has had to adjust to Japanese purchases of the Columbia and Universal studios and to the opening of the former Soviet Union, eastern Europe, and China as vast new television and movie markets. Despite all these changes and many others, his Hollywood employers have grown ever more powerful and the MPAA ever more influential in the television industry.

From his Washington, D.C., office a couple of blocks from the White House, Valenti exercises this power most visibly by inviting Washington power brokers to his lush headquarters. There, stars greet senators, members of Congress, foreign dignitaries, and government regulators. Glitter in workaholic Washington has been always in short supply, and the MPAA has always been its leading provider in the nation's capital. Valenti asks nothing on these occasions; they serve to keep open the lines of communication on Capitol Hill, into the White House, and through embassies based in Washington.

Valenti has long functioned as the capital's highest-paid and most effective lobbyist. Throughout the 1980s, for example, he consistently beat back moves to overturn regulations giving the Hollywood production community complete control over the rerun market for former hit network television shows. These "Financial Interest and Syndication" (Fin-Syn) rules had been put in place by President Richard M. Nixon as his revenge against the television networks. Under the Fin-Syn rules, networks could share only minimally in profits from television's secondary markets. Valenti made sure the rules were retained and enforced far longer than anyone expected and therefore created millions of dollars in additional profits for his Hollywood studio clients.

If necessary, Valenti took his case directly to the president of the United States. When officials working in the administration of President Ronald Reagan proposed the elimination of the Fin-Syn rules, Valenti asked Universal Studio's head Lew Wasserman to pay a visit to the president. Before becoming head of Universal, Wasserman had been Reagan's Hollywood talent agent. Valenti and Wasserman convinced the president, who long railed against unnecessary governmental regulations, to retain the Fin-Syn rules and to reverse orders issued by his underlings.

Valenti and the MPAA have also long battled against any rules that restricted Hollywood's TV exports. The protracted international negotiations that led to a new General Agreement on Trade and Tariffs (GATT) treaty, for example, were held up so that Valenti could remove television from the negotiating table and block a French proposal for quotas restricting television imports. It was Valenti who stood beside U.S. Trade Representative Mickey Kantor at a February 1995 news conference when a new U.S.–China trade accord was announced. This historic agreement protected television shows from rampant piracy in China, then the largest remaining potential market for television in the world.

In September 2001, Valenti turned 80 years old. During the previous decade, his energy never diminished as he dealt successfully with various issues. He directed the commission that developed parental guidance ratings for television and oversaw legislation requiring the V-chip (which allows users to block access to programming on the basis of its rating) to be placed in all new television sets sold in the United States. The accomplishment of such crucial tasks relied on Valenti's proven success as a negotiator and were undertaken to satisfy—or appease—various critics of television, including powerful congressional figures. He continued to press for opening markets for television around the world and was particularly successful in China.

The Hollywood-based corporate members of the MPAA under Hays, Johnston, and Valenti have long enjoyed considerable political power at home and abroad, as the MPAA has effectively leveraged the prestige of the film and television business to extract favors and win influence. Following in this hallowed tradition will present a sizable challenge for Valenti's eventual successor.

DOUGLAS GOMERY

See also **Financial Interest and Syndication Rules**

Further Reading

Ayscough, Suzan, "Clash Of Cultures: Canadians vs. MPAA," *Variety* (August 19, 1991)
Bromley, Carl, "The House That Jack Built," *The Nation* (April 3, 2000)
Corliss, Richard, "Berating Ratings," *Film Comment* (September–October 1990)
Gray, Timothy, "Ratings Still Rankle After All These Years," *Variety* (January 10, 1994)
Jessell, Harry A., "Valenti Stumps Against European Quotas," *Broadcasting* (November 12, 1990)
McClintock, Pamela, "At 80, Valenti Rates an R for Resilient," *Variety* (July 16–22, 2001)
Valenti, Jack, "Ownership Concentration in Cable Held Threat to Programming Diversity," *Television-Radio Age* (September 15,1986)
Wharton, Dennis, "MPAA Blasts Free-Trade Agreement," *Variety* (September 14, 1992)
Williams, Michael, "Deep Thaw in Beaune: U.S., French Bury GATT Hatchet," *Variety* (November 6, 1995)

The Movie Network

Canadian Pay-TV Channel

The Movie Network (TMN) is eastern Canada's English-language pay-TV motion picture channel. Part of Astral Media, TMN is supported entirely through subscriber fees, as collected by local cable operators. It operates 24 hours a day and specializes in unedited and uninterrupted movies. Home Box Office (HBO) and Cinemax are the principal models for TMN, though, as with all Canadian broadcasting services, TMN must comply with Canadian Radio-television and Telecommunications Commission (CRTC)–imposed licensing criteria, which include Canadian-content quotas.

TMN first received its license in 1982 after considerable public and governmental debate. Similar services in the United States had been successful, but the CRTC and others expressed concern about the impact pay-movie channels would have on Canadian culture. Was the market substantial enough for the proposed services to survive? Or would they become yet another vehicle for the importation of inexpensive U.S. film and made-for-cable products? Despite the recent rapid expansion of specialty channels and the parallel rise of multiple feature film services through cable and satellite delivery, both concerns were initially borne out.

In 1982 the CRTC awarded licenses to a number of pay-TV channels. C Channel, the service devoted to Canadian culture, lasted only five months and collapsed with insufficient viewer support to cover its costs. Star Channel, serving the Atlantic region, went bankrupt shortly thereafter. When the smoke had cleared, only First Choice (to be renamed The Movie Network in 1993), SuperChannel, and Super Ecran (which served the French-language market) were left. TMN operates east of the Manitoba/Ontario border, while SuperChannel operates in the west, thus giving them de facto regional monopolies.

As expected, the remaining movie channels began to ask for reduced Canadian-content requirements, arguing that programming "control" was necessary to their survival. The CRTC complied, and starting in 1986, the channels were required only to show 20 percent Canadian programming overall; their expenditures on Canadian content were reduced from 45 to 20 percent of subscriber revenue. TMN's financial support for Canadian production was almost $7.5 million (Canadian) in 1988–89 and just under $10 million in 1992–93. This amount dropped dramatically to $1.4 million by 2000–01. In 1993 TMN was showing 30 percent Canadian content in prime time and 25 percent otherwise. While TMN remains primarily a carrier of popular U.S. films, it has become a key source of sales for Canadian film and television producers. TMN's Foundation to Underwrite New Drama for Pay-TV

The Movie Network is a trademark of Astral Broadcasting Group Inc.

(FUND) competition awards interest-free loans for scripts at various stages of development.

In 1992 TMN became the first network in North America to offer "multiplexing." Through digital video compression technology, TMN subscribers receive an additional three channels (TMN2, TMN3, and TMN4) at no extra cost. These channels show what is essentially a reorganized broadcast schedule based on that of the main TMN. Multiplexing intends to provide additional choice and convenience to the subscribing customer by multiplying the number of showings of a film and the number of start times.

Through their common parent company, Astral Media, TMN operates in conjunction with Viewer's Choice Canada Pay Per View and Moviepix, which specializes in films from decades past. Astral sees the common ownership of these pay-TV channels as a way to ensure that they complement one another in the relatively small Canadian market. Critics, however, see this as a concentration of media venues that has contributed to the creation of a tiny powerful media elite in Canada.

CHARLES ACLAND

Further Reading

Ellis, David, *Split Screen: Home Entertainment and the New Technologies,* Toronto: Lorimer, 1992

Movie Professionals and Television

A 1944 editorial in the industry magazine *Televiser* questioned whether a motion picture director could approach a new medium such as television without "cynicism." The article warned that film people have been overtly critical of television production without any appreciation of the technique and aesthetics of the small screen. The tension between film and television has been a constant for more than 50 years, but both art forms have been enriched by the often-contentious dialogue.

In the early years of television's history, motion picture executives were acutely aware of the economic threat posed by an entertainment medium in the home and drew up strategies to challenge this incursion by the broadcast industry. Paramount first considered owning a chain of television stations and then tested a system of pay television, 20th Century-Fox and Warner Brothers collaborated on plans to develop theater television in the early 1950s, and in 1949 Columbia, under the leadership of Ralph Cohn, a former B-movie producer, organized Screen Gems to produce television commercials. Moguls tried to make moviegoing a spectacular experience, exploiting widescreen and stereophonic technologies. But it was the "eager and imaginative minds" of television who would create a dramatic form and then have a major impact on the motion pictures.

Television first defined its identity with the production of live dramas on such anthology series as *Studio One* (1948–58), *Kraft Television Theatre* (1947–58), and *Playhouse 90* (1956–61). Critics contended that the immediacy of television brought forth a special relationship between the spectator and the play. The productions were orchestrated by a generation of young directors with some training in theater and film who wedded the character studies of writers such as Paddy Chayefsky and Rod Serling to the inward method-trained acting styles of Paul Newman, Kim Hunter, James Dean, and many other disciples of Konstantin Stanislavski. When *Marty* received the Academy Award in 1955, it was the first time a script that originated on television (*Goodyear Playhouse,* 1953) was adapted by the large screen; in both instances, the partnership of Chayefsky and director Delbert Mann brought the material to life. Television talent was now welcome with open arms in Hollywood, and such TV-originated productions as *The Miracle Worker* and *Days of Wine and Roses* became award-winning films. The most prominent of the television directors journeyed to film, bringing the same psychological realism to the large screen. Among the key directors (with their signature movies in parentheses) whose work defined the new maturity of 1960s Hollywood were John Frankenheimer (*The Manchurian Candidate* [1962] and *Seven Days in May* [1964]), George Roy Hill (*The World of Henry Orient* [1964] and *Butch Cassidy and the Sundance Kid* [1969]), Sidney Lumet (*Long Day's Journey into Night* [1962] and *The Pawnbroker* [1964]), Robert Mulligan (*To Kill a Mockingbird* [1962] and *Baby, the Rain Must Fall* [1965]), Arthur

Penn (*The Miracle Worker* [1962], which he also directed on television, *Bonnie and Clyde* [1967]), and Franklin Schaffner (*The Best Man* [1964] and *Patton* [1970]). These directors, once again melding text and performance as they had on television but with a larger budget, constituted the first wave of new talent that rejuvenated American cinema after the studio system had broken down.

As live television received critical legitimacy on the East Coast, independent companies on the West Coast, including Jerry Fairbanks Productions, the Hal Roach Studios, and Ziv Television Programs, produced films for television, reels that could be cycled from one local station to another in the earliest version of "syndicated" TV. These budget-conscious producers often employed forgotten Hollywood veterans to give luster to their equivalent of the B movie. Jerry Fairbanks, a freelance cameraman and producer of an Academy Award–winning short, hired an established Hollywood name, Edmund Lowe (the suave silent film star of *What Price Glory*), for his Dumont series *Front Page Detective* (1951–53). Hal Roach Jr., a former Laurel and Hardy director, asked Charles Barton, the Universal director of Abbott and Costello comedies, to oversee the translation of the radio program *Amos 'n' Andy* to a visual medium (1951–53). For television's biggest hit of the 1950s, *I Love Lucy* (1951–61), producers Desi Arnaz and Jess Oppenheimer requested Fritz Lang's cinematographer, Karl Freund, to devise a technique for filming with three cameras before a live audience.

Film studios and guilds took immediate notice of the employment possibilities of television. Members of the Directors Guild of America received their name in the title for the 1955 series *Screen Directors Playhouse*. Many Hollywood legends, including John Ford, Leo McCarey, and George Stevens, made half-hour dramas for the *Playhouse*. The newly appointed president of the American Broadcasting Company (ABC), Leonard Goldenson (formerly head of the United Paramount Theaters), and executives at Warner Brothers determined how to financially recycle popular film genres each week on television and employed unsung directors to oversee production. Richard Bare, who had directed such forgettable movies as *Smart Flaxy Martin* (1949) and *Girls Don't Talk* (1958), was in part responsible for the resurgence of the western on television with the success of his *Cheyenne* (1955–63). By the mid-1950s, more than 40 percent of Hollywood's directors, actors, editors, and cameramen worked on television projects. Even cult directors, such as Ida Lupino, Phil Karlson, and Jacques Tourneur, brought their offbeat sensibilities to television.

Television became genuinely respectable for the film industry when the most recognizable director of

Alfred Hitchcock.
Courtesy of the Everett Collection

all time, Alfred Hitchcock, hosted an anthology series for ten years, beginning in 1955. Hitchcock's agent, Lew Wasserman, who would later run Universal, masterminded *Alfred Hitchcock Presents,* which featured the droll introduction by the "Master of Suspense" and then a macabre tale, evocative of the director's dark spirit. Hitchcock directed 18 episodes for *Presents* and two programs for other series. Working three days with an efficient supporting team, Hitchcock was able to explore his familiar themes of duplicity and murder, and he employed most of his TV crew to produce his cinema masterpiece, *Psycho* (1960).

Dramatic series, produced by Hollywood studios, afforded young talent the means to helm their own productions and, occasionally, develop personal themes. Robert Altman directed a variety of genres for television, including westerns (*Bonanza*), detective stories (*Hawaiian Eye*), and war stories (*Combat*). Later, in the 1970s, he would subvert the formulaic rules he learned in those three genres in the films *McCabe and Mrs. Miller* (1971), *The Long Goodbye* (1973), and *M*A*S*H* (1970), respectively. Other well-known directors also learned generic conventions that would come in handy in their film careers. Sam Peckinpah di-

Steven Spielberg, directing Joan Crawford.
Copyright by Universal City Studios, Inc. Courtesy of MCA Publishing Rights, a Division of MCA Inc.

rected episodes of *Route 66, Have Gun—Will Travel, Gunsmoke,* and *The Westerner,* which he also created. Blake Edwards created the pilots for *Richard Diamond* and *Peter Gunn,* which he later brought to the large screen. Michael Ritchie's quirky adventures for *Run for Your Life* and *The Outsider* laid a groundwork for the films *The Candidate* (1972) and *Smile* (1975).

In the mid-1960s, the studios worked with the networks to develop movies made especially for television. The first proposed television movie, *The Killers,* was directed by Don Siegel and starred Ronald Reagan and Angie Dickinson, but it was deemed too violent for television and was released theatrically in 1964. Two network executives, Barry Diller and Michael Eisner, refined the scope and concerns of the television movie and later became two of the most powerful moguls in Hollywood. Directors were able to impart a distinctive vision on the TV movie, which often yielded assignments to the large screen. Steven Spielberg, who had directed episodes of *Columbo* and *Owen Marshall,* received acclaim for the visual audacity of his made-for-television movie *Duel* (1971). Michael Mann, after stints as a writer on *Police Story* and *Vega$,* first attracted notice as writer and director of the TV prison drama *The Jericho Mile* (1979), which led to his 1983 feature *Thief.* Many directors

have shuttled back and forth between movies and television and have delivered their most personal work on the small screen, including Buzz Kulik (*Brian's Song* [1971]), John Korty (*The Autobiography of Miss Jane Pitman* [1974]), Joseph Sargent (*Amber Waves* [1980]), and especially Lamont Johnson (*That Certain Summer* [1972], *The Execution of Private Slovik* [1974], and *Off the Minnesota Strip* [1980]).

The man most responsible for adult comedy on television, Norman Lear, had left television in the late 1950s to become a film director. His film work—including *Come Blow Your Horn* (1963), *The Night They Raided Minsky's* (1968), and *Cold Turkey* (1971)—never matched his satirical temperament, which found its perfect outlet in the situation comedy *All in the Family* (1971–83). Lear did not return to film, but two influential comedy producers, James Brooks and Garry Marshall, have found creative success in both media. The same mixture of drama and comedy that Brooks brought to *The Mary Tyler Moore Show* (1970–77) was evident in his films *Starting Over* (1979), *Terms of Endearment* (1983), *Broadcast News* (1987), and *As Good As It Gets* (1997). Marshall's fondness for mismatched pairs, exemplified by Felix and Oscar in *The Odd Couple* (1970–75) and Ritchie and the Fonz in *Happy Days* (1974–84), has also been apparent in such films of his as *Nothing in Common* (1986) and *Pretty Woman* (1990). Lear and Marshall also mentored other directorial careers. Their comic rhythms have also been brought to the screen by their leading actors, Rob Reiner of *All in the Family,* Ron Howard of *Happy Days,* and Penny Marshall of *Laverne and Shirley.*

Feature film directors have had a presence in other TV genres. Several of television's most exemplary musical programs were crafted by directors who afterward rarely ventured into that genre again. Jack Smight, known for his mystery films *Harper* (1966) and *No Way to Treat a Lady* (1968), directed two of the definitive jazz programs, the smoky *The Sound of Jazz* with Billie Holiday and the very cool *The Sound of Miles Davis.* Norman Jewison, who began his career in British and Canadian television, directed Judy Garland's only duet with Barbra Streisand. Fred De Cordova, who earlier had directed *Bedtime for Bonzo* (1951) with Ronald Reagan and then TV series for George Burns and Jack Benny, produced for 20 years the most popular talk show of all time, *The Tonight Show Starring Johnny Carson.*

As live television affected Hollywood in the 1950s, so too did Music Television (MTV) in the 1980s. The music video disrupted the linear narrative and put a primacy on the visual, making the video creator a new hero in Hollywood. British director Julien Temple journeyed from videos for Culture Club and the Rolling Stones to his first feature, *Absolute Beginners* (1986). David Fincher used Fritz Lang's film *Metropolis* as the source of inspiration for his Madonna's video "Express Yourself" and later reworked the noir genre in his textured *Seven* (1995). Videos have borne the established director's imprint as well, including John Landis and Martin Scorcese's extended narratives for Michael Jackson's "Thriller" and "Bad"; John Sayles and Brian De Palma's different deconstructions of the Bruce Springsteen phenomenon, as working-class hero and lumbering icon, respectively; and Spike Lee's energetic "Hip Hop Hooray" video for Naughty by Nature. Spike Jonze transferred the offbeat, surreal sensibility of his videos for Weezer and Fatboy Slim to his feature film directorial debut, *Being John Malkovich* (1999). Quick cuts and eye-grabbing visuals have also been the domain of the TV commercials, and three graduates of British advertising—Ridley Scott, Alan Parker, and Adrian Lyne—have invigorated the look of popular film.

In 1984 Michael Mann returned to television and brought the MTV synthesis of image and music to series television in his stylishly innovative *Miami Vice*. During the rest of the 1980s, a niche was reserved for "designer television," usually series originated by film auteurs. Spielberg produced his own series, *Amazing Stories* (1985–87), and enlisted Scorcese, Robert Zemeckis, and Paul Bartel to contribute supernatural tales. Altman also returned, this time to cable television, and satirized American politics with Garry Trudeau in *Tanner '88* (1988), a project that was conceived in video to match the look of network news. Network executives also went to cult directors for ideas to entice a mainstream audience beginning to turn to cable. Sayles, a leader in the independent film movement, created *Shannon's Deal* (1990–91), a series focusing on an imperfect lawyer who dropped out of corporate practice. The avant-garde David Lynch of *Blue Velvet* (1986) fame unleashed some of the most surreal and unsettling images ever seen on network television in his video noir *Twin Peaks* (1990–91); a decade later, Lynch reconfigured one of his rejected television pilots into an award-winning film, the dreamscape *Mulholland Drive* (2001). Some of the traveling went the other way, as quality TV producers sought to make it among cineastes. Edward Zwick, who brought suburban angst to prime time with *thirtysomething* (1987–91), *My So-Called Life* (1994–95), and *Once and Again* (1999–2002), directed several epic adventures for the big screen—including *Glory* (1989), *Legends of the Fall* (1994), and *Courage Under Fire* (1996). Gregory Hoblit, who was the directorial eye behind many Steven Bochco productions,

David Lynch.
Courtesy of the Everett Collection

was successful with his 1996 urban thriller *Primal Fear,* no doubt leading the way for other directors of such visually compelling series as *E.R.* and *NYPD Blue* to try their hand at film directing. In a career of generic surprises, Quentin Tarrantino—who auditioned *Pulp Fiction* star John Travolta by playing with him the board game of Travolta's sitcom *Welcome Back, Kotter*—directed the 1994 season finale of the mainstream medical melodrama *E.R.*

Many foreign directors have used television to explore alternative forms of storytelling. Ingmar Bergman of Sweden has been interested in television's ability to weave a narrative over time, and in one of his most celebrated works, *Scenes from a Marriage* (1974), he chronicles the emotional upheavals of an ostensibly perfect union over six episodes. Rainer Werner Fassibinder created two works that also utilized television's expansive narrative: a Marxist soap opera, *Eight Hours Are Not a Day* (1972), and his 15-hour epic of the Weimar years, *Berlin Alexanderplatz* (1980), based on Alfred Doblin's novel. One of the fathers of the new wave, Jean Luc-Godard, has created a series of meditative essays on the history of cinema for

French television. Roberto Rossellini, one of the pioneers of Italian neorealism, used television to create a series of stylized historical portraits from Socrates to Louis XIV. Ken Russell produced a series of wildly expressionistic dramatized biographies on such artists as Elgar, Isadora Duncan, and Delius for the British Broadcasting Corporation that served as a template for his even more flamboyant films, including *The Music Lovers* (1970) and *Lisztomania* (1975). Before becoming an internationally recognized director, Kryzsztof Kieslowski received his training in Polish television; in the late 1980s, he returned to his mentoring medium to explore dramatically the contemporary relevance of the Ten Commandments in a multipart series, *Decalogue* (1988), now considered one of his masterworks.

Many screenwriters have found the more permissive atmosphere of television since the 1990s conducive for character development and narrative complexity. After his gimmicky idea of a "Valley girl" superhero received only a lukewarm reception in the film version of *Buffy the Vampire Slayer* (1992), Joss Whedon adapted the story to become an exploration of evil and female empowerment in a television series with the same name (1997–2003). Aaron Sorkin forsook his career as a screenwriter of such quality films as *A Few Good Men* (1992) and *The American President* (1995) to produce weekly television, most notably his study of the intricacies of the U.S. presidency in the iconic series *The West Wing* (1999–). Having received an Academy Award for his screenplay of *American Beauty* (1999), Alan Ball decided to continue his dissection of middle-class dysfunction as creator and executive producer of the HBO drama *Six Feet Under* (2001–).

For more than two decades, the lines between television and film have been blurred structurally and aesthetically. Most film studios now own some type of television network, and talent flows freely between the two media. Barry Levinson extended the tapestry of his cinematic Baltimore, Maryland, trilogy (*Diner* [1982], *Tin Men* [1987], and *Avalon* [1990]) to television with the equally visual *Homicide: Life on the Street* (1993–99), also set in Baltimore. No longer is film the arena for spectacle and television the home of the close-up. In fact, films screens have been shrinking in the multiplexes, and the television monitor dominates a home's entertainment room. Such films as Thomas Vinterberg's *The Celebration* (1998) and Spike Lee's *Bamboozled* (2000) were shot on digital video and transferred to film for theatrical projection. Director John Frankenheimer, who mastered live television in the 1950s and feature film during the 1960s through the 1980s, triumphed again through the 1990s and the first years of the 21st century, this time as creator of successful made-for-cable movies, including *Against the Wall* (1994), *Andersonville* (1996), and dramatic portraits of George Wallace (*George Wallace* [1997]) and Lyndon Johnson (*Path to War* [2002]). His career proved that both film and television, whatever the reigning technology, offer unique opportunities for creative expression.

RON SIMON

See also **Anthology Drama; Brooks, James L;** *Buffy the Vampire Slayer;* **Chayefsky, Paddy; Frankenheimer, John; "Golden Age" of Television; Johnson, Lamont; Kureshei, Hanif; Lear, Norman; Mann, Delbert; Marshall, Garry; Reagan, Ronald; Rose, Reginald; Serling, Rod; Schaffner, Franklin;** *Twin Peaks; Warner Brothers Presents*

Further Reading

Anderson, Christopher, *Hollywood TV: The Studio System in the Fifties,* Austin: University of Texas Press, 1994

Balio, Tino, editor, *Hollywood in the Age of Television,* Boston: Unwin Hyman, 1990

Boddy, William, *Fifties Television: The Industry and Its Critics,* Urbana: University of Illinois Press, 1990

Frankenheimer, John, and Charles Champlin, *John Frankenheimer: A Conversation with Charles Champlin,* Burbank, California: Riverwood, 1995

Hilmes, Michele, *Hollywood and Broadcasting,* Champaign: University of Illinois Press, 1990

Lafferty, William, "Television Film and Hollywood: The Beginnings," in *Columbia Pictures Television: The Studio and the Creative Process,* New York: Museum of Broadcasting, 1987

Marc, David, and Robert J. Thompson, *Prime Time, Prime Movers: From I Love Lucy to L.A. Law—America's Greatest TV Shows and the People Who Created Them,* Boston: Little, Brown, 1992

McCarty, John, and Brian Kelleher, *Alfred Hitchcock Presents,* New York: St. Martin's Press, 1985

McGilligan, Patrick, *Robert Altman Jumping off the Cliff,* New York: St. Martin's Press, 1984

Thompson, Robert J., *Television's Second Golden Age,* New York: Continuum, 1996

Wicking, Christopher, and Tise Vahimagi, *The American Vein: Directors and Directions in Television,* New York: Dutton, 1979

Movies on Television

The most popular programming form in U.S. television has been the presentation of motion pictures. During the latter third of the 20th century, most people viewed films not in theaters but on television, whether on broadcast television, cable television, or home video. Beginning with *The Late Show* in the mid-1950s and *Saturday Night at the Movies* during the early 1960s, the screening of feature films gradually became one of television's dominant programming forms.

Movie presentation on broadcast TV actually began in the late 1940s, when British companies rented films to new TV stations. Minor Hollywood studios (in particular Monogram and Republic) joined in this process, delivering approximately 4,000 titles to television stations before the end of 1950. Most of the films were genre works such as westerns or B-grade fare. The repeated showings of these low-budget offerings served to remind movie fans of the extraordinary number of treasures resting comfortably in the vaults of the major Hollywood studios: MGM, RKO, Paramount, 20th Century-Fox, and Warner Brothers.

The dominant Hollywood studios finally agreed to tender their vast libraries of film titles to television because eccentric millionaire Howard Hughes, owner of RKO, had run his studio into the ground. By late in 1953, it was clear Hughes had to do something to salvage RKO, and so few industry observers were surprised in 1954 when he agreed to sell RKO's older films to the General Tire and Rubber Company to be presented on its independent New York television station. By 1955 the popularity of *Million Dollar Movie* made it clear that film fans would abandon theaters to curl up and watch a reshowing of their past cinematic favorites.

Thereafter, throughout the mid-1950s, all the major Hollywood companies released their pre-1948 titles to television. For the first time in the 60-year history of film, a national audience was able to watch, at their leisure, a broad cross section of the best and worst of Hollywood "talkies." Silent films were only occasionally presented, usually in the form of compilations of the comedies of Charlie Chaplin or Buster Keaton.

By the mid-1960s, innumerable "Early Shows," "Late Shows," and "Late, Late Shows" dotted TV schedules. For example, by one count, more than 100 classic black-and-white films aired each week on New York City television stations, with fewer movies being broadcast in less populous cities. But with color television becoming a more dominant presence, the three TV networks wished to book newer, Technicolor Hollywood feature films. The network with the most invested in color, the National Broadcasting Company (NBC), thus premiered, at the beginning of the 1961–62 TV season, the first prime-time series of recent films as *Saturday Night at the Movies.* Ratings were high, and the other two major networks, the Columbia Broadcasting System (CBS) and the American Broadcasting Company (ABC), seeing how poorly their shows fared against *Saturday Night at the Movies,* quickly moved to set up their own "Nights at the Movies." Early in 1962, ABC, then a distant third in the ratings, moved to first with a midseason replacement, *Sunday Night at the Movies.* CBS, the longtime ratings leader in network television, did not join in the trend until September 1965.

Soon thereafter, television screenings of recent Hollywood movies became standard practice. In 1968 nearly 40 percent of all television sets in use at the time tuned in to Alfred Hitchcock's *The Birds* (theatrical release date, 1963). Recent feature films regularly attracted blockbuster television ratings, and when *Gone with the Wind* was shown in two parts in early November 1976, half the nation's television-owning homes tuned in.

By the early 1970s, American viewers could choose from ten separate "movie night" programs each week. It soon became clear that there was an imbalance between the many scheduled movies showings on network television and the relatively small amount of new product being aired. Hollywood knew this, and the studios began to charge higher and higher prices for TV screenings. For the widely viewed September 1966 telecast of *The Bridge over the River Kwai,* the Ford Motor Company paid nearly $2 million to be the sole sponsor.

Network executives found a solution: make movies aimed for a television premiere. The networks began making made-for-television movies in October 1964, when NBC aired *See How They Run,* starring John Forsythe. However, the historical turn came in 1966, when NBC contracted with MCA's Universal studios to create a regular series of "world premiere" movies made for television. The initial entry of this continuing effort was *Fame Is the Name of the Game,* inauspiciously presented on a Saturday night in November 1966.

The Winds of War.
Photo courtesy of Dan Curtis Productions, Inc.

By the early 1970s, made-for-television motion pictures had become a mainstay of network programming. Profits proved substantial. A typical movie made for television cost $750,000, far less than what Hollywood was demanding for rental of its recent blockbusters. The ratings were phenomenal. Few expected that millions would tune in for *Brian's Song* (1971), *Women in Chains* (1972), *The Waltons' Thanksgiving Story* (1973), or *A Case of Rape* (1974), but such fare regularly outdrew what were considered the biggest films of the era: *West Side Story* (1961; 1972 premiere on network television), *Goldfinger* (1964; 1972 premiere on network television), and *The Graduate* (1967; 1973 premiere on network television).

ABC led the way in made-for-television movies. The *ABC Movie of the Week* had premiered in the fall of 1969, placed on the schedule by the young executive Barry Diller, then head of prime-time programming at ABC, later a founder of the FOX television network. During the 1971–72 television season, the series was composed entirely of movies made for televi-

sion and finished as the fifth-highest series of the year. TV movies also began to earn praise for the upstart ABC; for *Brian's Song,* the network earned five Emmys, a prestigious George Foster Peabody Award, and citations from the National Association for the Advancement of Colored People (NAACP) and the American Cancer Society.

Made-for-television movies made it possible to deal with topical or controversial material not deemed appropriate for regularly scheduled network series. Celebrated actors and actresses who did not wish to work in series television would agree to be featured in miniseries. Running over several nights, miniseries such as *Holocaust* (1978), *Shogun* (1980), *The Thorn Birds* (1983), *Fresno* (1986), and *Lonesome Dove* (1989) drew large audiences during key rating-measurement periods. In 1983 ABC presented *Winds of War* on six successive February evenings for a total of 18 hours at a cost of production of nearly $40 million. This miniseries required more than 200 days to shoot from a script of nearly 1,000 pages. *Winds of War,* starring

Something for Joey, Marc Singer, Jeff Lynas, 1977.
Courtesy of the Everett Collection

Robert Mitchum and Ali McGraw, more than returned its sizable investment in this key sweeps month by capturing half the total viewing audience and selling out all its advertising spots at $300,000 per minute.

Six years earlier, ABC's miniseries *Roots* had aired for eight consecutive nights in January 1977. An estimated 130 million households tuned in to at least one episode, with approximately 80 million Americans watching the final episode of this docudrama, breaking the TV ratings record set just a year earlier by *Gone with the Wind.* Thus, *Roots* created for network television an event that was the equal of any blockbuster theatrical film.

However, even as *Roots* was setting records, the TV marketplace was changing. In the late 1970s and early 1980s, pay TV, particularly in the form of Time's Home Box Office (HBO), drew millions to its uncut screenings of films, free of advertisement breaks. Later in the 1980s, home video spread to the vast majority of homes in the United States, allowing film fans to watch their favorites—uncut, uninterrupted, and whenever they liked. Theatrical features began to have so much exposure on pay TV and home video that they ceased to be as valuable on network evening showcases, and made-for-television films came to fill more

and more of the time reserved for network "Nights at the Movies."

There was change on the local level as well. The number of independent television stations doubled in the 1980s, and all used movies to help fill their schedules. Independents developed movie libraries by contracting with Hollywood studios for five-year rentals and aired acquired titles as many times as possible during that period. Researchers told executives of independent stations that movies tended to draw a larger-than-average share of valued female watchers, in particular those from the 18- to 34-year-old and 18- to 49-year-old age-groups so prized by advertisers.

By the 1990s, in an average week, a film fan could choose among hundreds of titles scheduled on TV. Reliance on television for the presentation of motion pictures extracted a high price in terms of viewing conditions. The dimensions of a standard television image are constructed on a four-by-three ratio, while the standard image for motion pictures made after 1953 is much wider. To accommodate the larger image on TV, the wide-screen film is cut off at the sides. Panning-and-scanning companies reedit the wide-screen film so that the action shifts to the center of the frame, but the fan misses any subtlety at the edges.

Of course, films need not be panned and scanned. One could reduce the image for television until all of it fits; in practice, this technique of letterboxing fills the empty space above and below with a black matte. During the 1980s, there was a great deal of lip service paid to letterboxing, but movie watchers en masse in the United States did not seem to care for it. Fans seemed to prefer that the TV frame be filled, with the primary action in the center of the screen. In the early 2000s, the increasingly pervasive adoption of wide-screen television technology and the popularity of wide-screen TVs addressed this problem.

However, the biggest complaint from the average television viewer of motion pictures has long concerned the interruption of the movie by advertisements. To fit the formulaic slots of television, a station or network shows but 90 minutes of film for a two-hour slot. Stories of how television companies cut films to fit the program length are legendary. It is said that Fred Silverman, when he was a lowly film editor at WGN-TV in Chicago, solved the problem of fitting in the 96-minute *Jailhouse Rock* in a 90-minute slot by cutting all of Elvis Presley's musical numbers. Indeed, the key attraction of pay TV and then home video was the elimination of interruptions for advertising.

Just when experts declared that, in an age of pay TV and home video, blockbuster movies shown on network television could not draw an audience, NBC offered *Jurassic Park.* The box office hit, widely available on home video for less than $15, was shown on Sunday, May 7, 1995, at the beginning of a key sweeps month. Advertisers paid $650,000 for each 30-second advertising slot, and more than one in four television households in the United States tuned in.

In the early 2000s, broadcast networks and cable channels continued to present feature films and made-for-television movies. Indeed, the latter represented a common strategy for cable channels in their moves to create original programming that could replace material previously aired on network television or produced for other venues. The music channel Video Hits 1 (VH1) produced feature-length films based on performer biographies, whereas the sports channel Entertainment and Sports Network (ESPN) made movies about athletes and coaches. The Court Channel produced dramatic representations of legal battles. A&E produced mysteries based on Nero Wolfe novels. Turner Network Television (TNT) produced westerns and thrillers. At the same time, HBO, Showtime, and Cinemax continued to produce original movies as regular additions to their schedules of previously run theatrical features.

Meanwhile, a new technology for watching films on TV, the digital video disc (DVD), grew in popularity, with one in four U.S. households owning a DVD player in 2001 and various distributors phasing out their VHS stocks altogether. While it is too early to tell whether VHS-format videocassettes and DVD will exist side by side in most households or whether DVD will replace VHS as the preferred means to play movies on television, the popularity and ease of home movie viewing will surely remain a common aspect of the uses of television.

DOUGLAS GOMERY

See also **American Movie Classics; Cable Networks: Channel Four;** *FilmFour/Film on Four;* **Home Box Office (HBO); Miniseries; Movie Networks; Movie Professionals and Television; Programming; Showtime Network**

Further Reading

Chambers, Everett, *Producing TV Movies,* New York: Prentice Hall, 1986

Edgerton, Gary, "High Concept, Small Screen," *Journal of Popular Film and Television* (fall 1991)

Forkan, James P., "For Independents, Movies Remain Prime-Time Priority," *Television-Radio Age* (December 26, 1988)

Marill, Alvin H., *Movies Made for Television: The Telefeature and the Mini-Series, 1964–1979,* Westport, Connecticut: Arlington House, 1980

Rapping, Elayne, *The Movie of the Week: Private Stories/Public Events,* Minneapolis: University of Minnesota Press, 1992

Tobenkin, David, "Movies Still Rolling in Syndication: New Packages Belie Rumor of Genre's Failing Health," *Broadcasting & Cable* (January 23, 1995)

Moyers, Bill

U.S. Broadcast Journalist

For more than 30 years, Bill Moyers has established a brand of excellence in broadcast journalism. Moyers is one of the chief inheritors of the Edward R. Murrow tradition of "deep-think" journalism. He worked alternately on the Columbia Broadcasting System (CBS) and the Public Broadcasting Service (PBS) in the 1970s and early 1980s and has since appeared almost exclusively on PBS, and throughout this career his achievements have been principally in the areas of investigative documentary and long-form conversations with some of the world's leading thinkers. Moyers, who had been a print journalist, an ordained Baptist minister, a press secretary to President Lyndon Johnson, and a newspaper publisher before coming to television in 1970, gained public and private-foundation support to produce some of television's most incisive investigative documentaries. Each was delivered in the elegantly written and deceptively soft-spoken narrations that came, Moyers has said, out of the storytelling traditions of his east Texas upbringing. Whereas Murrow had taken on Joseph McCarthy on *See It Now* and the agribusiness industry in his famous *Harvest of Shame* documentary, Moyers examined the failings of constitutional democracy in his 1974 *Essay on Watergate* and exposed governmental illegalities and cover-up during the Iran Contra scandal. He has looked at issues of race, class and gender; analyzed the power that media images hold for a nation of "consumers," not citizens; and explored virtually every aspect of American political, economic, and social life in his documentaries.

Bill Moyers.
Photo courtesy of Bill Moyers and Lawrence Ivy

Equally influential were Moyers's *World of Ideas* series. Again, Murrow had paved the way in his transatlantic conversations with political leaders, thinkers, and artists on his *Small World* program in the late 1950s, but Moyers used his own gentle, probing style to talk to a remarkable range of articulate intellectuals on his two foundation-supported interview series on PBS. In discussions that ranged from an hour to, in the case of mythology scholar Joseph Campbell, six hours on the air, Moyers brought to television what he called the "conversation of democracy." He spoke with such social critics as Noam Chomsky and Cornel West; writers such as Nigerian novelist Chinua Achebe, Mexican poet and novelist Carlos Fuentes, and American novelist Toni Morrison; and social analysts including philosopher Mortimer Adler and University of Chicago sociologist William Julius Wilson. Moyers engaged voices and ideas that had been seldom if ever heard on television, and, in many instances, the transcribed versions of his series became best-selling books as well (*The Power of Myth,* 1988; *The Secret Government,* 1988; *A World of Ideas,* 1989; *A World of Ideas II,* 1990, *Healing and the Mind,*

1992). Joseph Campbell's *The Power of Myth* was on the *New York Times* best-seller list for more than a year and sold 750,000 copies within the first four years of its publication.

Moyers's television work has been as prolific as his publishing record. In all, he produced more than 600 hours of programming (filmed and videotaped conversations and documentaries) between 1971 and 1989, which comes out to 33 hours of programming a year, or the equivalent of more than half an hour of programming a week for 18 years. Moyers broadcast another 125 programs between 1989 and 1992, working with a series of producers—27 of them on the first two *World of Ideas* series alone. He formed his own company, Public Affairs Television, in 1986 and began to distribute his own shows.

By the early 1990s, Moyers had established himself as a significant figure of television talk, his power and influence providing him access to corridors of power and policy. In January 1992, he was invited for a rare overnight visit with president-elect Bill Clinton to discuss the nation's problems before the Clinton inaugural. A survey of the video holdings of a single large state university at the end of the 1990s showed almost 100 holdings bearing Moyers's name. By this time, he had also received 67 prizes and awards in recognition of his work.

Working closely with his wife, Judith Davidson, as creative collaborator and president of the Public Affairs Television production company, Moyers has continued his prolific output into the 21st century. In January 2002, he began hosting a new weekly PBS series, *Now with Bill Moyers,* which covers stories from angles and with the kind of perspectives and depth that viewers have come to expect from this veteran writer, publisher, and broadcast journalist.

Over his long career, Moyers has become one of the few broadcast journalists who might be said to approach the stature of Murrow. If Murrow founded broadcast journalism, then Moyers has significantly extended its traditions.

BERNARD M. TIMBERG

See also **Documentary; Murrow, William R.**

Bill Moyers. Born in Hugo, Oklahoma, U.S.A., June 5, 1934. Educated at North Texas State College; University of Texas at Austin, B.A. in journalism, 1956; University of Edinburgh, Scotland, 1956–57; Southwestern Baptist Theological Seminary, Fort Worth, Texas, B.D., 1959. Married: Judith Suzanne Davidson, 1954; children: William Cope, Alice Suzanne, and John Davidson. Personal assistant to Senator Lyndon Johnson, 1960–61; associate director of public affairs, 1961–62, and deputy director, 1963, Peace Corps; special assistant to President Johnson, 1963–67, press secretary, 1965–67; publisher, *Newsday,* 1967–70; producer and editor, *Bill Moyers' Journal,* PBS, 1971–76, 1978–81; anchor, *USA: People and Politics,* 1976; chief correspondent, *CBS Reports,* 1976–78; senior news analyst, CBS News, 1981–86; executive editor, Public Affairs Programming Inc., since 1986. Honorary doctorate, American Film Institute. Recipient: more than 30 Emmy Awards; Ralph Lowell medal for contribution to public television; Peabody Awards, 1976, 1980, 1985–86, 1988–90, 1999; DuPont Columbia Silver Baton Award, 1979, 1986, 1988; Gold Baton Award, 1991; George Polk Awards, 1981, 1986; Humanitas Award, 1978, 1986, 1995.

Television Series (selected)

1971–76,	
1977–81	*Bill Moyers' Journal*
1971–72	*This Week*
1976–78	*CBS Reports*
1982	*Creativity with Bill Moyers*
1983	*Our Times with Bill Moyers*
1984	*American Parade* (renamed *Crossroads*)
1984	*A Walk Through the 20th Century with Bill Moyers*
1987	*Moyers: In Search of the Constitution*
1988	*Bill Moyers' World of Ideas*
1988	*The Power of Myth* (with Joseph Campbell)
1990	*Amazing Grace*
1991	*Spirit and Nature with Bill Moyers*
1993	*Healing and the Mind with Bill Moyers*
1995	*The Language of Life with Bill Moyers*
2000	*On Our Own Terms: Moyers on Dying*
2002	*Now with Bill Moyers*

Publications

Listening to America, 1971
Report from Philadelphia, 1987
The Secret Government, 1988
The Power of Myth, 1988
A World of Ideas, 1989
A World of Ideas II, 1990
Healing and the Mind, 1992
The Language of Life: A Festival of Poets, 1995
Genesis: A Living Conversation, 1996
Sister Wendy in Conversation with Bill Moyers, 1997
Fooling with Words: A Celebration of Poets and Their Craft (editor), 1999

Further Reading

Burns, Ken, "'Moyers: A Second Look': More Than Meets the Eye," *New York Times* (May 14, 1989)
"Dialogue on Film: Bill Moyers," *American Film* (June 1990)
Timberg, Bernard, and Robert Erler, *Television Talk: A History of the Talk Show,* Austin: University of Texas Press, 2002
Zurawik, David, "The Following Myth Is Made Possible by a Grant from Bill Moyers," *Esquire* (October 1989)

MSNBC

Cable News Service

MSNBC is a 24-hour, advertising-supported cable and online news service. Envisioned as a fully integrated cable television and Internet-based interactive product, MSNBC is a joint venture between Microsoft and the National Broadcasting Company (NBC). While the slower-than-expected convergence of television and computing has made MSNBC's promise of a unified service difficult to fulfill, MSNBC's entry helped invigorate the 24-hour cable news category and advanced the development of interactive news. MSNBC.com has become the number one news and information website in the United States. The MSNBC cable network has been described as "confused" because of an unsettling churn of program offerings and is an also-ran in its competition for viewers with Cable News Network (CNN) and the FOX News Channel (FNC).

Announced with much fanfare in December 1995, the partnership's financial arrangement called for Microsoft to pay $220 million for 50 percent of NBC's *America's Talking* cable network that was converted to MSNBC, plus $250 million for the network's annual costs. Well funded and armed with NBC's news-gathering and Microsoft's technology resources, MSNBC launched on July 15, 1996.

MSNBC online's challenges included attracting Internet users to the site and initiating untested interactive video technology to a mass audience. The website's rollout, supported by cross promotion on Microsoft's websites and NBC's television outlets, has been highly successful. MSNBC.com was named the number one general news site on the Web by Internet ratings service PC Meter just eight months after its introduction. It has held that distinction in Jupiter Media Metrix's Internet ratings for many months since, including all of 1999 and 2000.

MSNBC.com's leadership position is built on technological and content advantages. The site began with text, graphics, and audio programming. A relaunch in August 1997 improved navigability and added technical capabilities that enabled streaming video news, which has grown in importance as work and more recently home environments have upgraded to broadband Internet access. Alliances with the websites of dozens of local television and print media, plus respected national outlets such as *Newsweek* and the *Washington Post,* have increased the depth and breadth of the site's content. Highly successful at attracting an audience, MSNBC.com's financial future is less clear amid the severe post–September 11, 2001, downturn in the online advertising market.

MSNBC cable launched in a respectable 22.5 million cable television homes with support from outdoor and print advertising, plus cross-platform promotion on the NBC broadcast network and Microsoft websites. MSNBC's acceptance by cable system operators was an early concern, but carriage of the fledgling network grew steadily as agreements were sealed with major cable system operators such as TeleCommunications, Inc. (now AT&T Broadband) and Time Warner Cable.

Programming the network with content cable news viewers find compelling has proved to be more difficult. Hoping to attract younger, Generation X viewers, the network's initial strategy was to feature well-known NBC News talent on a hip, Starbucks-style set, complete with brick wall and open metalwork. Daytime news coverage was anchored by John Gibson, Jodi Applegate, and John Seigenthaler. Prime-time programming centered on three shows, *The News with Brian Williams; The Site,* a youth-oriented new media and technology program; and *InterNight,* a talk show alternatively hosted by Katie Couric, Bob Costas, Tom Brokaw, and others. This schedule was supplemented by repeats of current shows and repurposed content from NBC News.

To fill out its schedule in its first year, a deal was made to simulcast Don Imus's syndicated radio show weekday mornings. The network began recycling NBC's *Dateline* shows, and *Time and Again,* hosted by Jane Pauley, was created around repackaged NBC programming and old news footage. In addition, John Hockenberry joined MSNBC from the American Broadcasting Company (ABC) to host *Edgewise* on weekends.

By August 1997, MSNBC was reaching 38 million cable households, and viewership was growing, in part because of the death on August 31 of Diana, Princess of Wales. Nielsen Media Research reported that third-quarter 1997 prime-time ratings for MSNBC averaged 99,000 households compared with 24,000 and 766,000 for FNC and CNN, respectively.

Under growing pressure to build its audience, MSNBC continued molding its program lineup in its second year by pulling the critically acclaimed show *The Site* and recruiting Keith Olbermann of the Entertainment and Sports Network's (ESPN's) Sports Center and Charles Grodin to host their own shows. The network also went "tabloid" with extended coverage and discussion of sensational stories such as the death of JonBenet Ramsey and the sexual activities of broadcaster Marv Albert.

Cable system carriage continued apace, and after two years MSNBC was reaching 42 million households. Competition for viewers among the cable news networks was intensifying, and by January 1999, amid the Monica Lewinsky scandal and President Clinton's impeachment trial, rival FNC's prime-time household viewership surpassed MSNBC's. MSNBC was already reworking its schedule to offset FNC's fast-growing audience. Keith Olbermann's *Big Show* was canceled. John McLaughlin of *The McLaughlin Group* and Oliver North were recruited to host *McLaughlin Special Report* and *Equal Time,* respectively.

In April 1999, MSNBC turned to Mullen Advertising, based in Wenham, Massachusetts, for aid in attracting 25- to 44-year-old viewers. Nevertheless, at its three-year anniversary, MSNBC's viewership remained a concern to be addressed by yet more programming changes. A prime-time magazine-type tabloid series, *Special Edition,* debuted with a segment profiling serial killers. *Headlines & Legends with Matt Lauer,* a biography show, was introduced in an attempt to build prime-time appointment viewing.

By January 2000, 52 million cable households could watch MSNBC, and, as hoped, the network was attracting youthful viewers with an average age of 50 years old compared with 58 for CNN and 56 for FNC. Apparently, attracting a younger audience did little to address MSNBC's audience shortfall. October 2000's audience ratings showed that MSNBC still trailed its competitors in prime-time and total day average audience.

The 2000 presidential election and its aftermath benefited all three cable news networks. Viewership was up, and advertising was easier to sell, even with the weakening U.S. economy. MSNBC turned profitable late in 2000, but its second-quarter 2001 prime-time viewership averaged just 247,000 homes. FNC averaged 436,000 households and CNN 483,000.

The September 11, 2001, terrorist attacks on the Pentagon and World Trade Center fixated the nation and drove viewership higher. News of anthrax scares and the search for Osama bin Laden in Afghanistan helped retain viewers, but to keep them without a constant stream of breaking news, the cable news services turned to established personalities. CNN lured Paula Zahn from FNC to anchor news. Geraldo Rivera joined FNC as a war correspondent. MSNBC's entry in this competition was relative unknown Ashleigh Banfield, who attracted notice while covering the 2000 presidential election and earned recognition for her September 11 coverage when she kept reporting at the north tower of the World Trade Center as it collapsed. Unseasoned, irreverent, and fashionable, Banfield was given her own prime-time show, *A Region in Conflict,* that has taken her to Afghanistan and the Middle East.

For all of 2001, MSNBC reached on average a mere 382,000 prime-time homes versus CNN's 816,000 and FNC's 675,000. FNC's ability to attract viewers further surprised its competitors when it beat CNN in total day and prime-time ratings for January 2002. Ever in search of a programming solution to its viewership quandary, MSNBC hired Alan Keyes, former conservative presidential candidate and author, to host *Alan Keyes Is Making Sense.* On the other end of the political spectrum, in April 2002, MSNBC signed a contract with former talk show mainstay Phil Donahue to host a prime-time current events program. *Donahue* had its debut in July 2002, but it was canceled after six months on the air, having consistently placed low in the ratings.

Now available in over 74 million households, MSNBC's average prime-time audience is less than half of FNC's and CNN's. MSNBC also trails distantly in viewership within the coveted 25-to-54 age-group. FNC has distinguished itself as a commentator-driven, viewpoint network, while CNN has long been a reporter-driven news-gathering service. Despite years of programming adjustments, MSNBC continues to struggle with no clear editorial direction.

RANDY JACOBS

See also **Cable News Network (CNN); FOX Broadcasting Company**

Further Reading

Gunther, Marc, "CNN Envy," *Fortune* (July 8, 1996)
Kurtz, Howard, "On MSNBC, Sleaze to Please?," *Washington Post* (October 10, 1997)
McClellan, Steve, "MSNBC Has Leg Up in News Race," *Broadcasting & Cable* (April 29, 1996)
Moss, Linda, "Fox Outduels MSNBC over Impeachment," *Multichannel News* (February 8, 1999)
Rutenberg, Jim, "At MSNBC, a Young Anchor for Younger Viewers," *New York Times* (October 29, 2001)
Tedesco, Richard "Audio, Video Boosting 'Net News," *Broadcasting & Cable* (August 25, 1997)

MTV

U.S. Cable Network

MTV (Music Television) is the oldest and most influential U.S. cable network specializing in music-related programming. It was launched on August 1, 1981, with the words "Ladies and gentlemen, rock and roll," spoken by John Lack, one of the creators of MTV. This introduction was immediately followed by a music video for the song "Video Killed the Radio Star," by the Buggles. The song title proved somewhat prophetic, as MTV greatly transformed the nature of music-industry stardom over the next several years. At the same time, MTV became a major presence in the cable-TV industry and the American cultural landscape.

One of the earliest and greatest cable success stories, MTV was established by Warner Amex Satellite Entertainment Company (WASEC) after extensive marketing research. The key to MTV's viability, at least initially, was the availability of low-cost programming in the form of music videos. Originally, these were provided free by record companies, which thought of them as advertising for their records and performers.

MTV presented one video after another in a constant "flow" that contrasted with the discrete individual programs found on other television networks. Clips were repeated from time to time according to a light, medium, or heavy "rotation" schedule. In this respect, MTV was like top-40 radio (it even had video jockeys, or VJs, similar to radio disk jockeys). Moreover, it soon became apparent that MTV could "break" a recording act, just as radio had done for decades.

The visual portion of a video usually consists of live concert footage or, more commonly, lip synching and pantomimed instrument playing by the recording artist(s). Dancing is also very common. In many cases, there is also a dramatic or narrative concept, sometimes grounded in the song lyrics. The "acting" in a concept video is usually done by the musician(s), although in some cases (e.g., "Crazy" and "Cryin'" by Aerosmith), the video cuts away from the band to actors who act out a drama inspired by the lyrics. The combination of elliptical storylines, record-as-soundtrack, lip synching, and direct address to the camera seemed so novel in the early 1980s that music video was often referred to as a new art form. The content of the new art was sometimes bold (and controversial) in its treatment of sex, violence, and other sensitive topics.

Many of the earliest MTV videos came from Great Britain, where the tradition of making promo clips was fairly well developed. One of the earliest indications of MTV's commercial importance was the success of the British band Duran Duran in the U.S. market. This band had great visual appeal and made interesting videos but was not receiving radio airplay in the United States as of 1981. In markets where MTV was available, the network's airing of Duran Duran's videos made the band immediately popular. Ultimately, MTV proved to be immensely important to the careers of numerous artists, including Madonna, Michael Jackson, Prince, Peter Gabriel, U2, N'Sync, and Britney Spears as well as Duran Duran.

Andrew Goodwin identifies three phases in the history of MTV. The real ascendance of the network began in 1983 with phase 2, the so-called second launch, when MTV became available in Manhattan and Los Angeles. Phase 3 began in 1986, following Viacom's purchase of MTV from Warner Amex and the departure of Robert Pittman as the network's president and chief executive officer. Pittman had been largely responsible for leading MTV down the programming path of flow and narrowcasting. By 1986, however, MTV's ratings were in decline as a result of a too-narrow musical palette.

Throughout its so-called third phase, MTV diversified its musical offerings, most notably into rap, dance music, and heavy metal. To some extent, these genres were segregated into their own program slots (*Yo! MTV Raps, Club MTV,* and *Headbangers' Ball,* respectively). At the same time, the move toward discrete programs increasingly became a move away from music video. In the process, MTV became more like a full-service network, offering news, sports, sitcoms, documentaries, cartoons, game shows, and other traditional TV fare. Often these programs were also musical in some sense (*Beavis and Butt-Head*), but sometimes they were not (reruns of *Speed Racer*).

We might now identify a fourth phase in MTV's history, dating from the late 1990s, when MTV itself became a sort of "flagship" network among a stable of branded subsidiaries. Even before this, much of the musical content displaced from MTV, especially soft rock and other "adult" music, had landed on Video Hits 1 (VH1), a second video channel owned by parent company MTV Networks (which, in turn, is a subsidiary of Viacom). Launched in 1985, VH1 quickly acquired a reputation as "video valium" for yuppies. For several years, the channel had an indistinct image and languished in the shadow of MTV, but makeovers in 1989 and (especially) 1994 raised the younger network's profile. By 1994, VH1 was playing slightly harder music and "breaking" recording artists, such as Melissa Etheridge. Meanwhile, MTV continued to play innovative videos on programs such as *Amp* and *120 Minutes,* but these programs aired at odd hours. Nonmusical programs such as *The Real World,* which debuted in 1992 and gave birth to the "reality" genre, sometimes seemed to threaten MTV's identity as a music network.

By about 1998, MTV was again emphasizing music, but its most popular program, *Total Request Live,* or *TRL,* treated videos as raw material to be talked over and covered up by all manner of graphics and inserts. By this time, sister network VH1 was also relying more on traditionally packaged programs, such as *Behind the Music* and *Pop Up Video* (which, along with *Beavis and Butt-Head,* paved the way for *TRL*-style "vandalizing" of video clips). Flow and format, the original ideas behind MTV (and VH1), had by now become secondary components, at best, in the programming philosophy of both networks. These changes were perhaps best exemplified on MTV in the surprise 2002 hit *The Osbournes,* a program that seemed to meld multiple aspects of the channel's history. Focused on the "family life" of notorious rocker Ozzy Osbourne, his wife, and two of their children, the series combined a fascination with music and musicians, the "inside views" developed with *The Real World,* and the (perhaps unintended) blankness of *Beavis and Butt-Head.* Following an initial run and tough negotiations with the family, the series was renewed for two more seasons and by then had led to copycat programming on other networks.

With home satellite reception and digital cable on the rise, MTV launched M2 (also called MTV2) in 1996. The new channel was very similar to what MTV had originally been. It played music videos in a continuous flow, with only occasional interruptions for video jockey patter, promos, and the like. In the early 2000s, MTV Networks exploited the original flow idea even further by launching VH1 Classic Rock (which specialized in 1980s videos) and MTVX (which played mostly hard rock videos). Despite their forays into nonmusical programming, MTV and VH1 are by far the most important outlets for music-video programming in the United States. They have achieved almost a monopoly status, one that has caught the attention of scholars (especially Jack Banks), record companies, and the government. Many competing music-video programs and networks have fallen by the wayside or have been absorbed by Viacom. Most recently, Viacom bought its last remaining major U.S. competitors in music-video programming: Country Music Television (CMT) and The Nashville Network (TNN, subsequently renamed The National Network) in 1997 and Black Entertainment Television (BET) in 2000.

Music video and MTV are major ingredients of television programming internationally. MTV Europe, launched in 1987, was followed by an Asian service in 1991 and MTV Latino in 1993. VH1 established a European service in 1994. In 2001 an international satellite directory listed more than 20 MTV channels worldwide, along with 7 VH1 services and 3 MTV2 channels.

Both economically and aesthetically, MTV has wrought major changes in the entertainment industries. By combining music with television in a new way, MTV has charted a path for both industries (and movies as well) into a future of postmodern synergy.

GARY BURNS

See also **Beavis and Butt-Head; Music on Television; Pittman, Robert**

Further Reading

Banks, Jack, *Monopoly Television: MTV's Quest to Control the Music,* Boulder, Colorado: Westview Press, 1996
Denisoff, R. Serge, *Inside MTV,* New Brunswick, New Jersey: Rutgers University Press, 1988
Goodwin, Andrew, *Dancing in the Distraction Factory: Music Television and Popular Culture.* Minneapolis: University of Minnesota Press, 1992
Hoye, Jacob, editor, *MTV Uncensored,* New York: Pocket Books, 2001
Kaplan, E. Ann, *Rocking Around the Clock: Music Television, Postmodernism, and Consumer Culture,* New York: Methuen 1987
Lewis, Lisa A., *Gender Politics and MTV: Voicing the Difference,* Philadelphia, Pennsylvania: Temple University Press, 1990
Reiss, Steven, and Neil Feineman, *Thirty Frames per Second: The Visionary Art of the Music Video,* New York: Harry N. Abrams, 2000

MuchMusic

Canadian Music Television Programming Service

MuchMusic, a 24-hour Canadian music television station and satellite-to-cable programming service, was launched nationally in September 1984. In a satellite-to-cable structure that relied for its success on the massive penetration of cable coverage of urban Canada, MuchMusic was part of the Canadian Radio-television and Telecommunications Commission (CRTC)–regulated introduction of specialty services on cable two years after the introduction of pay television to Canada. Similar to its U.S. counterpart Music Television (MTV), MuchMusic was instrumental in setting the national agenda of Canadian popular music tastes. The predominant format of the station was and continues to be video clips of artists or music videos received from record companies free of charge. A French sister station, MusiquePlus, was established in 1986, primarily for the Quebec market.

Stylistically, MuchMusic bears the marks of its creative origin. The station's managing team was connected to the syndicated *New Music* program (1978–) developed and sold by Citytv of Toronto. The executive producer of the New Music program and the original owner and manager of Citytv in Toronto was Moses Znaimer. Along with John Martin, Znaimer designed the "live" emphasis of the set of MuchMusic that has made MuchMusic so distinctively different from both MTV and most of the rest of Canadian television. The set of MuchMusic is the actual video paraphernalia of a television station and is inherently "studioless." Between their introductions of new videos, the video jockeys, or VJs, negotiate themselves around the various machines, lights, and screens to chat with the technicians and producers. Indeed, because of this exposure, technicians have even moved into before-the-camera roles. The intention behind this design is to structure an environment that resonates with the youthfulness and exuberance of popular music itself. The set, which often moves with portable cameras to exterior locations, produces a sense of immediacy and spontaneity that, through its weekly reach, has captured the sought-after demographic of youths and young adults in Canada.

MuchMusic is owned and operated by CHUM Limited of Toronto, and the name itself is a play on the corporate name. CHUM operates the only private radio network in Canada and has successfully owned and operated a number of music-oriented radio stations. CHUM also is the owner of Citytv (purchased in 1981 from Znaimer), a Toronto based free-to-air UHF (ultra-high frequency) station that has been distributed by cable to most of southern Ontario, the most heavily populated region of Canada. Its background in music broadcasting allowed CHUM to successfully win the license of the first and only English-language music television station in Canada. The facilities of Citytv in Toronto served as the first home for MuchMusic.

Self-titled "the nation's music station," MuchMusic gradually moved to a format that allowed it to target and promote itself like other television services. Originally a flow service that resembled radio in its seamless quality, MuchMusic relied on its mixed rotation of video clips and the personalities of the VJs to maintain the audience. Later, however, the station began making identifiable programs that would at least allow it to garner the free publicity of listings in TV program guides and to sell portions of time for specific advertisers. It still maintains eight hours of programming, which is taped and repeated three times to fill the 24-hour schedule. In the 1980s, these programming blocks included the *Pepsi Powerhour* and the singly sponsored *Coca-Cola Countdown.* The "spotlight" feature also transformed the mix of rotations of current music into a half-hour retrospective on an individual artist's or group's career. To coordinate with a slightly different demographic of daytime listeners, MuchMusic programmed a show called *MushMusic,* which showcased softer and more romantic ballads. Other programs also coordinated with and competed with the rest of television. A late-night weekend program called *City Limits* attempted to showcase the more avant-garde, alternative visuals and music. In a more prime-time evening slot, a shorter segment, *Combat du Clip,* was programmed; here a returning favorite video clip faced a challenger clip.

MuchMusic's license requirements have posed questions about what kinds of programming are included under the definition of music. In the mid-1980s, MuchMusic was not allowed to show movies, even those with a musical theme or premise. It was likewise questionable whether television programs such as *The Partridge Family* or *The Monkees* could be shown on the station. In recent years, there has been a relaxation of what constitutes music programming, and this shift has allowed MuchMusic a freer hand in organizing a schedule that maintains its key marketing demographics of youth and young adult. Regulatory requirements have demanded, however, that a greater range of musical material be part of the national music television station. Hence, MuchMusic programmed the country music half-hour *Outlaws and Heroes.* The CRTC has likewise continued to maintain that the station must stick close to its license mandate: its top-rated program of 1993, the cartoon series *Ren and Stimpy,* did not meet a minimum musical-content rule and was ordered removed. With the advent of new digital channels, these regulations have been in constant flux, and MuchMusic continues to expand its presence through multichanneling its content.

From its inception, MuchMusic has also provided a percentage of its revenues (currently 5 percent of its gross revenues) for the production of Canadian independent music videos. The production company Videofact Foundation produces clips for emerging popular music groups in both English and French and spent $6 million to produce 820 videos in its first ten years. The production of Canadian sources allows MuchMusic easily to surpass its 10 percent Canadian-content quota established in consultation with the CRTC. This connection to a national popular culture is differently constructed than that produced by public broadcasters such as the Canadian Broadcasting Corporation (CBC). MuchMusic's stance is thus more outward than inward looking. It has actively sought out other markets for its program package. Currently, it is available to more than 4 million cable subscribers through various services in the United States. It has a reach that includes both the United Kingdom and parts of Latin America. The station has been negotiating for inclusion on direct broadcast satellite services for greater coverage of a complete North America. The station format/concept has been sold to New Zealand, and MuchMusic has showcased well in Europe, often outdrawing its more established rival, MTV.

MuchMusic has continued to brand its success with its national youth audience, and it has exported that strategy internationally with equal financial rewards. Contained under the Much brand are specialty and digital channels that cater to specific musical tastes. Thus, relatively new stations, such as MuchmoreMusic, and digital channels, such MuchLoud and MuchVibe, continue to extend the MuchMusic niche of television focused on music and youth across Canada.

P. DAVID MARSHALL

See also **Citytv; Music on Television; Znaimer, Moses**

Further Reading

Flint, Joe, "MuchMusic Confirms Rainbow Coalition," *Variety* (May 24, 1994)

Marshall, David, "Videomusic: The Converging Interests of Promotional Culture," in *Watching All the Music,* edited by Gareth Sansom, Montreal: McGill University Press, 1987

Pawlett, Steve, "Ten Years of MuchMusic," *Cablecaster* (September 1994)

Turbide, Diane, "The Show Moves On: MuchMusic and TSN Bid for New Viewers," *Maclean's* (September 4, 1989)

Munroe, Carmen

British Actor

Carmen Munroe is one of Britain's leading black actresses. Born in Guyana (then British Guiana), she went to Britain in 1951 and gained early acting experience with the West Indian Students' Drama Group. Munroe made her professional stage debut in 1962 and later played major roles in London's West End theater, including Jean Genet's *The Blacks* (1970). When she played Orinthia, the king's mistress, in George Bernard Shaw's *The Apple Cart* (1970), she said it was the first time she had been cast in a leading role not written for a black actress. Since the 1970s, Munroe has played an important part in the development of black theater in Britain, scoring a personal triumph in 1987 as the overzealous pastor of a Harlem "storefront" church in James Baldwin's *The Amen Corner.* In 1993, she won a best actress award from *Time Out* magazine for Alice Childress's *Trouble in Mind.*

In 1965 Munroe made an early television appearance in *Fable.* In this controversial British Broadcasting Corporation (BBC) drama, writer John Hopkins reversed apartheid and located it in Britain so that black people ran the country and whites were subjected to enforced population-movement and pass laws. However, this innovative and highly charged play did not have the reception anticipated from audiences. Viewers were put off, while critics thought the play heavy-handed and moralistic.

In 1967 Munroe was featured in an episode of *Rainbow City,* one of the first British television series to include a black actor in a leading role. Since that time,

she has demonstrated her acting range in numerous other appearances, with roles in a mixture of populist dramas and situation comedies, as well as impressive single dramas. They include *Doctor Who* (1967), *In the Beautiful Caribbean* (1972), *Ted* (1972), *Shakespeare's Country* (1973), *General Hospital* (1974), *The Fosters* (1976), *A Black Christmas* (1977) with Norman Beaton, *Mixed Blessings* (1978), *A Hole in Babylon* (1979), *Rumpole of the Bailey* (1983), and *The Hope and the Glory* (1984).

In 1989 Munroe was in *Desmond's,* one of Channel 4's most successful situation comedy programs. Costarring Norman Beaton as the proprietor of a barbershop in south London, *Desmond's* has been one of the few British television series to feature an almost entirely black cast. For five years, this appealing series won critical acclaim and awards for its humorous exploration of the conflict between the views of young British-born blacks and the values of the older generation who grew up in the Caribbean.

In between her appearances in *Desmond's,* Munroe took part in *Ebony People* (1989), sharing her experiences of the acting world with a studio audience, and *Black and White in Colour* (1992), a documentary tracing the history of black people in British television. In 1992, Munroe gave an outstanding performance as Essie Robeson in a BBC play called *A Song at Twilight.* This emotional drama, shown in the anthology series *Encounters,* explored an imaginary meeting in 1958 between British socialist radical Aneurin Bevan and the black American singer and militant activist Paul Robeson. Another recent role for Munroe was in the two-part drama *The Final Passage* (1996), a story of blacks emigrating from the Caribbean to Britain in the late 1950s.

STEPHEN BOURNE

See also **Beaton, Norman;** *Black and White in* **Color; Desmond's**

Carmen Munroe. Born in Guyana (then British Guiana); immigrated to Britain, 1951. Trained with West Indian Students' Drama Group. Worked in television, since 1959; stage debut, *Period of Adjustment,* 1962; has appeared or starred in numerous television series; cofounder, Talawa Theatre Company, 1985. Recipient: *Time Out* award, 1993.

Television Series (selected)
1971	*You're Only Young Twice*
1971	*Ace of Wands*
1974	*General Hospital*
1974	*Play School*
1976–77	*The Fosters*
1989–95	*Desmond's*
1996	*The Final Passage*

Television Plays
1965	*Fable*
1977	*A Black Christmas*

1992	*A Song at Twilight*
1993	*Great Moments in Aviation*

Television Documentary
1992	*Black and White in Colour*

Films
Naked Evil, 1966; *All Neat in Black Stockings,* 1968; *The Chain,* 1985; *Shades of Fear,* 1993.

Radio (selected)
Obeah, 1989.

Stage (selected)
Period of Adjustment, 1962; *There'll Be Some Changes Made,* 1970; *The Blacks,* 1970; *The Apple Cart,* 1970, *Trouble in Mind; El Dorado; A Raisin in the Sun; The Amen Corner,* 1987; *Alas, Poor Fred* (director); *Remembrance* (director); *The Odyssey,* 2001.

Further Reading

Bourne, Stephen, *Black in the British Frame: Black People in British Film and Television 1896–1996,* London and Washington, D.C.: Cassell, 1996; second edition, as *Black in the British Frame: The Black Experience in British Film and Television,* London: Continuum, 2001

Pines, Jim, editor, *Black and White in Colour: Black People in British Television Since 1936,* London: British Film Institute, 1992

Muppet Show, The

U.S. Syndicated Comedy/Variety Program

From its first broadcast in 1976 to its 1981 finale, *The Muppet Show* was groundbreaking television. A syndicated variety show starring a troupe of puppets, it became more popular than anyone but its creator, Jim Henson, could have imagined. During its five seasons of inspired insanity, it was broadcast in more than 100 countries.

The wonderful children's show *Sesame Street,* also starring Henson's Muppets, had been broadcast since late 1969. For Henson, its success was a mixed blessing, as network executives began to see the Muppets strictly as children's entertainment. *The Muppet Show*

proved that Henson's innovative puppets could appeal equally to children and adults. Its setting, Muppet Theater, allowed onstage sketches and songs as well as backstage antics. Except for Kermit the Frog, a *Sesame Street* favorite, *The Muppet Show* featured an entirely new cast of Muppets: Fozzie Bear, the lovably inept comic and Kermit's second banana; Miss Piggy, a glamorous, Rubenesque starlet and Kermit's would-be love interest; Gonzo the Great, a buzzardlike creature with a chicken fetish; Rowlf, the imperturbable piano-playing dog; Statler and Waldorf, two geriatric hecklers; The Electric Mayhem, the ultracool house

The Muppet Show, Gonzo, Kermit the Frog, Scooter, Fozzie Bear, Miss Piggy, Camilla, Animal, Dr. Teeth, Rowlff, Dr. Bunsen, Statler & Waldorf, Beaker, 1976–81.
Courtesy of the Everett Collection

band; and Scooter, hired as Kermit's gofer because his uncle owned the theater. The show also featured countless other Muppets, from a 12-inch rat named Rizzo to a seven-foot monster named Sweetums.

But Kermit was undeniably the glue that held these lunatics together. As producer/host of Muppet Theater, Kermit had the considerable task of keeping guests and Muppets happy, fending off Miss Piggy's advances, bolstering Fozzie's confidence after another joke fell flat, and tolerating Gonzo's bizarre stunts. As performed by Henson, Kermit was the lone sane creature in the asylum, the viewers' bridge to world of *The Muppet Show,* a small, green Everyman (Everyfrog) just trying to do his job in the midst of gleeful craziness.

The partnership between Henson and Frank Oz produced such puppet pairs as Miss Piggy and Kermit, *Sesame Street*'s Ernie and Bert, and Kermit and Fozzie Bear. The two also teamed up for the Swedish Chef, a Muppet with Henson's voice and Oz's hands, with hilarious results. Oz's nasal boom was a perfect counterpoint to Henson's gentle voice, and the two performers complemented each other well. Other *Muppet Show* puppeteers included Richard Hunt (Sweetums, Scooter, Statler, and Beaker), Dave Goelz (Gonzo and Dr. Bunsen Honeydew), Jerry Nelson (Floyd Pepper and Lew Zealand), and Steve Whitmire (Rizzo the Rat).

Both backstage and onstage, lunacy ruled at Muppet Theater. Memorable sketches included pig Vikings pillaging towns while singing the Village People's "In the Navy," one creature devouring another while singing "I've Got You Under My Skin," and the great ballet dancer Rudolf Nureyev in a pas de deux with a human-size lady pig.

Often, the guest stars were the perfect catalyst for Muppet nuttiness. The frequently starstruck Miss Piggy swooned at guest Christopher Reeve's every move; in another episode, she locked Kermit in a trunk because guest Linda Ronstadt showed too much interest in the little green host. Guest Gene Kelly thought he had been invited just to watch the show; he stayed backstage chatting with the rats until Kermit finally convinced him to perform "Singin' in the Rain" on a near-perfect replica of the film's street set. Victor Borge and Rowlf the Dog played a piano duet. Diva Beverly Sills gave Gonzo a lesson in the fine art of balancing a spoon on one's nose.

During the first season, writes Christopher Finch in his book *Jim Henson: The Works,* guest stars were mostly personal friends of Henson or his manager, Bernie Brillstein. But by the third season, popular performers were practically lining up to appear with the beloved puppets. *The Muppet Show*'s guest roster reads like a "Who's Who" of late 1970s performers, most notably Roger Moore, John Cleese, Harry Belafonte, Dizzy Gillespie, Lynn Redgrave, Diana Ross, Alice Cooper, Julie Andrews, George Burns, Joel Grey, Steve Martin, Ruth Buzzi, and both Candice and Edgar Bergen.

The Muppets' TV history starts long before *Sesame Street.* From 1955 to 1961, Henson's *Sam and Friends,* a five-minute live show, aired twice nightly on WRC-TV in Washington, D.C. *Sam and Friends* afforded Kermit's debut; it also featured several Muppets that did not make the cut for *The Muppet Show.* In 1961, the Muppets began making regular guest appearances on the National Broadcasting Company's (NBC's) *Today.* The following year, Rowlf made his debut in a Purina dog food commercial; in 1963, the affable canine began regular appearances on *The Jimmy Dean Show.* The Muppets also made regular appearances on *The Ed Sullivan Show* from 1966 to 1971. In 1975, the year Henson formed an agreement with Lord Lew Grade to produce 24 episodes of *The Muppet Show,* Henson also created an entirely new set of Muppets that were featured on *Saturday Night Live* in its first season.

During *The Muppet Show*'s heyday in 1979, *The Muppet Movie* was released in the United States, beginning the Muppets' transition from TV to film. Several movies featured *The Muppet Show* cast, including *The Great Muppet Caper, The Muppets Take Manhattan, The Muppets' Christmas Carol,* and *The Muppets' Treasure Island.* Henson also produced several other TV shows featuring the Muppets after *The Muppet Show* ended: *Fraggle Rock,* focusing on an underground community of fun-loving Fraggles, hardworking Doozers, and odious Gorgs; *The Storyteller,* which aired only in England; *Muppet Babies,* a children's cartoon featuring baby versions of *The Muppet Show*'s cast; and several other short-lived productions.

On May 16, 1990, Jim Henson died suddenly after a short illness. He was 54 years old. The Jim Henson Company continues to produce Muppet-related projects for film, television, and the stage. Frank Oz has enjoyed a notable career as a film director, while Kermit, Miss Piggy, and other Muppet characters regularly appear on talk shows and other television programs as well as in films.

JULIE PRINCE

See also **Henson, Jim; Sesame Workshop**

Puppeteers
Jim Henson
Frank Oz
Richard Hunt
Dave Goelz

Jerry Nelson
Erin Ozker (1976–77)
Louise Gold (1979–81)
Kathryn Muller (1980–81)
Steve Whitmire (1980–81)

Muppet Characters
Kermit the Frog (Henson)
Miss Piggy (Oz)
Zoot (Goelz)
Fozzie Bear (Oz)
Gonzo (Goelz)
Sweetums (Hunt)
Sam the Eagle (Oz)
The Swedish Chef (Henson and Oz)
Dr. Teeth (Henson) and the Electric Mayhem
Floyd (Nelson)
Animal (Oz)
Capt. Link Heartthrob (Henson)
Dr. Strangepork (Nelson)
Wayne and Wanda (1976–77)
Rowlf (Henson)
Dr. Bunsen Honeydew (Goelz)
Statler and Waldorf (Hunt and Henson)
Scooter (Hunt)
Beauregard (Goelz) (1980–81)

Pops (Nelson) (1980–81)
Lew Zealand (Nelson) (1980–81)
Janice (Hunt)
Rizzo the Rat (Whitmire) (1980–81)

Musical Director
Jack Parnell

Producers
Jim Henson, Jon Stone, Jack Burns

Programming History
120 30-minute episodes
Syndicated
1976–1981

Further Reading

Finch, Christopher, *Of Muppets and Men: The Making of The Muppet Show,* New York: Knopf, 1981
Finch, Christopher, *Jim Henson: The Works: The Art, the Magic, the Imagination,* New York: Random House, 1993
Henson, Jim, *The Sesame Street Dictionary: Featuring Jim Henson's Sesame Street Muppets,* New York: Random House, 1980
"Jim Henson: Miss Piggy Went to Market and $150 Million Came Home" (interview), *American Film* (November 1989)

Murder, She Wrote

U.S. Mystery

Murder, She Wrote, starring Angela Lansbury as amateur sleuth and mystery writer Jessica Fletcher, has been the only significant dramatic series on American television to feature an older woman in the sole leading role. Lansbury, who has received Oscar nominations and Tony Awards over her long film and stage career, started the series at age 58 and is now probably most widely recognized for her television character.

Creators Richard Levinson, William Link, and Peter S. Fischer brought with them a combined résumé from *Columbo, Mannix, Alfred Hitchcock Presents,* and *Ellery Queen.* In *Murder, She Wrote,* they created a classical mystery program set in the fictional seaside village of Cabot Cove, Maine. The program quickly became one of the Columbia Broadcasting System's (CBS's) most successful offerings and among the most

expensive for it to produce. It frequently placed first among the network's lineup in the Nielsen ratings and was a champion in its time slot, 8:00 P.M. Sundays. It finished in the Nielsen top ten during most of its run. The series' final episode, "Death by Demographics," served as an oblique comment on the network's decision to shift the program from its comfortable time slot to Thursday evenings, when it was forced to do battle against the runaway "must-see" TV hit, *Friends.*

The series narrative remained fairly stable. Widowed Jessica Fletcher, a retired high school English teacher, became a best-selling mystery author after her nephew, Grady, sent a manuscript to a book publisher. She quickly became world famous and affluent, but she maintains the rambling, old house that she and her longtime husband, Frank, shared in Cabot Cove. Jes-

Murder She Wrote, Angela Lansbury, 1984–96.
Courtesy of the Everett Collection

Murder, She Wrote's formula is true mystery: Jessica encounters several people displaying animosity toward a mean person. An innocent person, often a friend or relative of Jessica's, publicly threatens or criticizes the bully. The audience sees the bully murdered, but the killer's identity is hidden. The authorities accuse Jessica's ally, based on circumstantial evidence. Jessica notices—and the camera lingers on—details that seem inconsequential but later prove central to the solution. She investigates, uncovering various means, motives, and opportunities and eliminating suspects. A few minutes before the program ends, she suddenly realizes the last piece of the puzzle and announces that she knows who the killer is. She confronts the killer privately, in a group, or with authorities observing off camera. Almost always, the killer confesses, and Jessica presents the person to the police. A final scene often shows Jessica sharing a good-natured exchange with someone, often the wrongly accused friend.

Coincidences abound. Nephew Grady (Michael Horton) is arrested for murder on several occasions, and Jessica always proves him innocent. In fact, each of the many times Jessica's family members or old, "dear friends" is introduced, one becomes involved in a murder. Tiny Cabot Cove is the site of about 50 of the more than 250 murders Jessica solves. Rarely is a suspect been shown in touch with a lawyer; Jessica always happens to be on the scene when a murder has just taken place and makes time in her schedule to solve the crime. She usually happens upon the body herself. The police never get it right. Her friend is almost always innocent. Jessica is always present when crucial evidence comes to light.

Despite the formulaic nature of the program, the notion that violent death can invade even the quiet world of Jessica Fletcher connects it to old meanings of the mystery genre. The world, as the profession of the mystery writer demonstrates, is not a safe place. The wisdom and acute mental capacity of this older woman are weapons in an ongoing struggle for order.

On the professional rather the fictional level, Lansbury's involvement with the series changed over time. In the 1989–90 season, CBS persuaded her to stay with the show after she announced plans to leave. The network cut demands on her time, and Lansbury made only brief appearances in several episodes. She addressed the viewer directly to introduce the evening's mystery, involving, for example, her sleuthing "friends," Harry McGraw or Dennis Stanton. And she often returned at the end of the hour, explaining how the mystery was solved. In the following 1992 season, however, Lansbury was back in force assuming the role of executive producer. Her sons and brother were also involved in the production.

sica remains close to old friends in the village, including Dr. Seth Haslett, played by character actor William Windom. A few cast changes occurred; most significantly, Tom Bosley, who portrayed bumbling Sheriff Amos Tupper, left after four seasons to pursue his own mystery series. Familiar former television stars and unknown character actors appeared as guests on the program.

In the earlier seasons, a matronly Jessica frequently bicycled across town, boiled lobsters, planned fishing trips on a friend's trawler, or dropped in at the beauty parlor. She wore conservative pantsuits and spoke with an occasional New England influence. Her signature was her ancient manual typewriter, and the opening credits showed her tapping merrily away on one of her mystery novels. Gradually, the character evolved. The manual typewriter eventually shared time in the opening sequence with Jessica's personal computer (which, itself, was involved in two mysteries). Jessica added a second residence, a Manhattan apartment, and the character became more glamorous in appearance, coinciding with Lansbury's own personal makeover in the 1988–89 season.

However, *Murder, She Wrote* skewed toward older audiences, especially older women, and advertisers will pay much more to attract younger viewers. In the 1994–95 season, the show charged lower advertising rates than competitors, such as *Lois and Clark,* appearing in the same time slot on the rival American Broadcasting Company (ABC). *Lois and Clark* attracted fewer viewers but was watched by more young viewers, hence the higher advertising rate.

At a time when less traditional programs, such as the quirky, more serial *Northern Exposure* and the offbeat *Seinfeld,* were attracting favorable critical notices, *Murder, She Wrote* did not. It attracted instead large numbers of viewers with its combination of a highly ritualistic formula and its progressive treatment of a 60-plus heroine played by a popular star. Jessica Fletcher is, significantly, an *amateur,* unlike James Rockford or Thomas Magnum. However, although unfailingly well behaved, she displays a worldliness about modern life, and she has a career that contributes to her vitality. These elements distinguish her from Agatha Christie's Miss Marple character, to whom she has often been compared.

Since her involvement in *Murder, She Wrote,* Lansbury, the actor, has spoken out on occasion against the tendency for network television to propagate a "masculine mystique" and unfairly favor programs oriented toward younger audiences. (In its Sunday time slots, *Murder, She Wrote* followed another long-running successful program on CBS, *60 Minutes,* which has also collected large numbers of older viewers.) Because portrayals of older people on American television have traditionally infrequent and unflattering (in such silly roles as Fred Sanford of *Sanford and Son, Designing Women*'s dotty Bernice, and some of the women of *The Golden Girls*), Lansbury's Jessica Fletcher is especially significant. She has demonstrated that competent, glamorous older women can draw large prime-time audiences. As a result, *Murder, She Wrote* was one of CBS's most valued programs.

KAREN E. RIGGS

See also **Lansbury, Angela**

Cast

Jessica Beatrice Fletcher	Angela Lansbury
Sheriff Amos Tupper (1984–88)	Tom Bosley
Grady Fletcher (1985–90)	Michael Horton
Dr. Seth Hazlitt (1985–96)	William Windom
Mayor Sam Booth (1986–96)	Richard Paul
Sheriff Mort Metzger (1989–96)	Ron Masak
Dennis Stanton (1990–91)	Keith Michell
Robert Butler (1990–91)	James Sloyan
Lt. Perry Catalano (1990–91)	Ken Swofford
Rhoda (1990–91)	Hallie Todd
Dr. Raymond Auerbach (1991–96)	Alan Oppenheimer

Producers

Peter S. Fischer, Anthony J. Magro, J. Michael Straczynski, Peter Lansbury, Angela Lansbury

Programming History

261 episodes
CBS

September 1984–May 1991	Sunday 8:00–9:00
June 1991–July 1991	Sunday 9:00–10:00
July 1991–May 1996	Sunday 8:00–9:00

Further Reading

Allman, Kevin, "Auntie Angela" (interview), *The Advocate* (September 22, 1992)

Riggs, Karen, *Mature Audiences: Television in the Lives of Elders,* New Brunswick, New Jersey: Rutgers University Press, 1998

Smith, Wallace E., "'Cabot Cove,' California: TV Intrigue on Mendocino Coast," *American West* (December 1988)

Waters, Harry F., "A New Golden Age: The Over-55 Set Flexes Its Wrinkles on Prime Time," *Newsweek* (November 18, 1985)

Murdoch, Rupert K.

U.S./Australian Media Executive

Rupert K. Murdoch is the controlling shareholder and chief executive of News Corporation, Ltd. (News Corp), one of the largest and most powerful media companies in the world. In this position, Murdoch has become perhaps the world's leading media mogul. His bold style, unconventional and visionary approach, and willingness to aggressively assume great risks have made him a figure both admired and disdained throughout the world. His company owns properties on four continents that produce and distribute products in television; films; book, newspaper, and magazine publishing; and online data services.

Murdoch began his rise to the status of media baron in a relatively modest way. He inherited his father's newspaper holdings in 1952, which, after estate taxes, consisted of two small Australian papers, the *Adelaide News* and *Sunday Mail.* Murdoch was quickly able to reverse the unprofitable states of these newspapers, and he used the new profits to acquire other media properties, thereby exhibiting the fundamental growth strategy that would come to characterize his career. By the late 1960s, Murdoch expanded his newspaper and magazine empire to include British newspaper holdings, first acquiring London's *The News of the World* in 1968 and soon thereafter *The Sun.* It was the transformation of *The Sun* into a sensationalized tabloid (which, most notoriously, included a regular "Page Three" feature of photos of topless women) that sealed Murdoch's reputation as a media owner who was willing to pander to his audience's worst instincts in exchange for commercial acceptance, a label that has dogged Murdoch throughout his career. However, it must be noted that such fears have sometimes proven to be unfounded, as was the case following Murdoch's 1981 purchase of the revered London *Times,* which largely retained the stoic editorial character for which it was well known.

In the 1970s, Murdoch entered the U.S. media market by purchasing newspapers and magazines, and he also started the supermarket tabloid *The Star.* However, it was not until the mid-1980s that Murdoch began to make his mark on American television. His purchase of Metromedia's independent television stations from John Kluge in 1985 came on the heels of his acquisition of the 20th Century-Fox studio. Murdoch saw the situation as a rare opportunity to purchase a group of choice television stations in the largest U.S. markets, thereby ensuring a distribution vehicle for his new studio's programs. The combined moves allowed Murdoch to initiate the most serious effort to establish a fourth broadcast television network since the demise of Dumont in the mid-1950s and culminated in the establishment of the FOX Broadcasting Company.

Despite his career's many successes, Murdoch's empire nearly collapsed in 1990. Unfavorable conditions in the financial markets, combined with deep losses by some of News Corp's start-up operations, such as British Sky Broadcasting (BSkyB), and the company's extremely heavy short-term debt load (the result of many costly acquisitions, such as *TV Guide,* which News Corp purchased in 1988 from Walter Annenberg's Triangle Publications) brought the company to the brink of financial ruin. While Murdoch was able to renegotiate the terms of his agreements, which avoided the disaster, News Corp's financial problems

Rupert K. Murdoch.
Photo courtesy of Rupert Murdoch

temporarily placed Murdoch in the unusual position of being unable to aggressively expand his holdings. In fact, he was forced to shed some nonessential assets, including most of his U.S. magazine titles. It was only a relatively short time, however, before the company's financial picture improved significantly and Murdoch was able to once again resume his familiar patterns of acquisition, as he did when he purchased a controlling interest in Asia's Star-TV direct broadcast satellite service in 1993.

As perhaps befits a man with such a great level of power and influence, Murdoch has often found himself at the center of political firestorms. He became widely scorned by labor organizations and pro-labor politicians around the world because of his hard-line tactics in battling the British newspaper workers' unions in the mid-1980s. His 1985 purchase of the Metromedia television stations required him to become an American citizen to comply with Federal Communications Commission (FCC) restrictions on foreign ownership of U.S. television stations; many felt he received inordinately preferential treatment by the Reagan administration in expediting the citizenship process. His FOX television network was able to avoid complying with the FCC's "Financial Interest and Syndication" (Fin-Syn) rules—first by airing fewer hours of programming than were stipulated in the legal definition of a "network" and later by receiving a temporary FCC waiver of the rules—an action the other three broadcast networks vigorously opposed. In addition, Murdoch was the specific target of a 1988 effort by Senator Edward Kennedy (at the time a frequent target of Murdoch's *Boston Herald* newspaper) to revoke another FCC ruling, one that waived cross-ownership restrictions that would have prevented Murdoch from owning both newspapers and television stations in New York and Boston. The end result of Kennedy's efforts was that Murdoch eventually sold the *New York Post* (he later would receive a new waiver that allowed him to reacquire the struggling paper in 1993) and put Boston's WFXT-TV into an independent trust.

A mid-1990s political storm held the potential to be the most costly that had ever surrounded Murdoch. Nearly ten years after he had become a U.S. citizen and after many millions of dollars had been invested in the FOX network and its owned-and-operated stations, questions arose related to Murdoch's avoidance of the FCC's restrictions on foreign ownership of television stations. The National Association for the Advancement of Colored People (NAACP), which was seeking to block the purchase of a Philadelphia, Pennsylvania, television station by FOX, asked the FCC to investigate whether it was Murdoch who owned the FOX stations, as he and News Corp claimed, or whether

Australian-based News Corp was the legal owner, which would be in violation of the rules. The National Broadcasting Company (NBC) joined the NAACP in asking the FCC to pursue the investigation but eventually withdrew from the complaint after gaining access for their programming on Murdoch's Star-TV service in Asia. However, the NAACP continued to pursue the issue.

Murdoch's media empire continued to grow and flourish as the new century approached. News Corp expanded its holdings of sports-related properties, most notably adding the Los Angeles Dodgers Major League Baseball franchise (along with its valuable real estate holdings) in 1998, and it also obtained full control over Liberty Media's regional cable sports channels in 1999, which added to FOX Sports' dominant presence in the sports television field. Murdoch also positioned his company for the future by merging *TV Guide* with Gemstar International Group in 2000, which effectively put News Corp at the very center of the burgeoning field of interactive television services. With the purchase of a major share of the Italian pay-cable service Telepiu from beleaguered French conglomerate Vivendi in the summer of 2002, Murdoch expanded his European holdings as well as his stake in pay-television services that could carry FOX productions. A rare failed effort occurred earlier that year when Murdoch attempted to merge his satellite operations with direct-to-home provider DirecTV. He lost out to rival Charles Ergen, owner of the other major satellite provider, EchoStar.

Murdoch also spent these years preparing for the ultimate succession of his children to News Corp leadership posts. His sons, Lachlan and James, were groomed for high-level positions within the organization, as was his daughter, Elisabeth, who left News Corp in 2000 to start her own independent production company. Younger son James has been in charge of News Corp's new media efforts and, at the time of this writing, is chief executive at Star TV, the group's Asian satellite broadcaster. Lachlan, who is most often considered to be his father's heir apparent, has led the company's print and publishing operations in Australia and New York and was named deputy chief operating officer of News Corporation, Ltd, in 2000.

Rupert Murdoch has been one of the most successful international entrepreneurs of his time and a lightning rod for controversy in many parts of the world. While other global media companies, such as AOL Time Warner and Bertelsmann AG, possess power and influence comparable to that of News Corp, Murdoch often appears to stand alone among the ranks of modern media moguls. This is because, unlike those other companies, News Corp is clearly identified as a corporate arm that is strongly controlled by a single individual. It is therefore fair to say that his absolute control over News Corp, with its holdings of some of the world's most pervasive and influential media properties, makes Murdoch perhaps the single most powerful media magnate ever.

DAVID GUNZERATH

See also **Annenberg, Walter; Australia; Australian Production Companies; Berlusconi, Silvio; Bertelsmann AG; British Sky Broadcasting; Cable Networks; Diller, Barry; FOX Broadcasting Company; News Coroporation, Ltd; Star-TV; Time Warner; United States: Cable**

Rupert K(eith) Murdoch. Born in Melbourne, Victoria, Australia, March 11, 1931. Attended Oxford University, England. Married: 1) Anna Maria Torv, 1967 (divorced, 1999); children: Prudence, Elisabeth, Lachlan, James; 2) Wendi Deng, 1999; child: Grace. Spent two years in London as subeditor with the *Daily Express,* 1950–52; inherited father's newspaper holdings, 1952, and returned to Australia to run *The Adelaide News* and *Sunday Mail;* acquired more Australian newspapers and expanded to England in 1968, buying *The News of the World* and *The Sun;* purchased *San Antonio Express–News,* 1973, and the *New York Post,* 1976; his News International organization subsequently bought the *New York Magazine, The Star,* the London *Times,* the *Sunday Times,* the *Boston Herald,* the *Chicago Sun-Times,* television stations, book publishing companies, and airline, oil, and gas concerns; purchased 20th Century-Fox and independent U.S. television stations from Metromedia, 1985, and established FOX Broadcasting Network; took U.S. citizenship, 1985; sold *New York Post* to conform with Federal Communications Commission regulations,

1988; acquired Triangle Publications, including *TV Guide,* 1988; founded Sky satellite television network, 1989; Sky absorbed rival British Satellite Broadcasting to become British Sky Broadcasting, 1990; bought controlling interest in Asia's Star-TV, 1993. Director, News International plc, since 1969; chief executive, since 1979, and chair, since 1991, News Corporation Ltd; chair and chief executive, 20th Century-Fox, since 1992.

Further Reading

Belfield, Richard, Christopher Hird, and Sharon Kelly, *Murdoch: The Decline of an Empire,* London: MacDonald, 1991

Block, Alex Ben, *Outfoxed,* New York: St. Martin's Press, 1990

Brooks, Richard, "Murdoch: A Press Baron Re-Born," *Toronto Star* (September 12, 1993)

Consoli, John, "Fox Buys the Henhouse," *Mediaweek* (March 23, 1998)

Consoli, John, "Murdoch: Give Me Liberty!" *Mediaweek* (April 5, 1999)

Cromie, Ali, "Inside Story: Murdoch's Succession," *The Guardian* (October 29, 1994)

Farhi, Paul, "Murdoch, All Business: The Media Mogul Keeps Making Bets amid Strains in His Global Empire," *Washington Post* (February 12, 1995)

Kiernan, Thomas, *Citizen Murdoch,* New York: Dodd Mead, 1985

la Franco, Robert, "Rupert's on a Roll," *Forbes* (July 6, 1998)

Leapman, Michael, *Arrogant Aussie: The Rupert Murdoch Story,* Secaucus, New Jersey: Little Stuart, 1985

Melvern, Linda, *The End of the Street,* London: Methuen, 1986

Mermigas, Diane, "News Corp.: The Next Generation" (interview), *Electronic Media* (January 22, 2001)

Rohm, Wendy Goldman, *The Murdoch Mission: The Digital Transformation of a Media Empire,* New York: John Wiley, 2002

Shawcross, William, *Rupert Murdoch: Ringmaster of the Information Circus,* London: Chatto and Windus, 1992; as *Murdoch,* New York: Simon and Schuster, 1993; revised edition, as *Murdoch: The Making of a Media Empire,* New York: Simon and Schuster, 1997

Murphy Brown

U.S. Situation Comedy

Since its premier in 1988, *Murphy Brown* appeared in the same 9:00–9:30 P.M. slot on the Columbia Broadcasting System's (CBS's) Monday night schedule, serving as something of an anchor in that network's perennial battle against the male-oriented *Monday Night Football* on the American Broadcasting Company (ABC). The show focused on life behind the scenes at the fictional television series *FYI* (For Your Information). *FYI* was represented as a tough, talk-oriented investigative news program, perhaps a little like another CBS mainstay, *60 Minutes.* From its beginnings, *Murphy Brown* established itself as one of

Murphy Brown.
Photo courtesy of CBS Worldwide, Inc.

television's premier ensemble comedies, exploring life among the reporters, producers, staff, and friends of *FYI*. However, there is no question that, as the title implies, this ensemble was built around its central character.

As played by Candice Bergen, Murphy Brown was one of the most original, distinctive female characters on television. Smart, determined, and difficult, she did not suffer fools gladly. Her ambition and stubbornness frequently got her into trouble, and she often acted a little foolishly herself.

But what set Murphy apart from so many other female sitcom characters was that when she got into a ridiculous mess, it was not because she was a woman. It was because she was Murphy. She was a crack reporter yet managed to get herself banned from the White House during both the George H.W. Bush and the Bill Clinton administrations. When a corrupt judge fell silent during an interview, Murphy finished grilling him—even though he was dead.

Although Murphy acted tough, Bergen showed viewers the character's vulnerable side as well. Wracked with guilt after the judge's death, Murphy toned down her interviewing style (for a while). And she was genuinely hurt when she did not get an invitation to George H.W. Bush's inaugural ball. All these

character developments and revelations built on the fact that the show's pilot introduced Murphy as she returned to the *FYI* set after drying out at the Betty Ford Clinic. The central character, the star of *FYI,* was presented from the very beginning as a recovering alcoholic, vulnerable and flawed. All her foibles and eccentricities were presented in this context, adding richness and depth to the portrayal.

Indeed, throughout the show's run, all the characters and their relationships developed beyond what is typical for a sitcom. The original ensemble included Corky Sherwood (Faith Ford), a Louisiana girl and former Miss America who took a few journalism classes in college but was hired mainly for her looks; Frank Fontana (Joe Regalbuto), ace investigative reporter and irrepressible skirt chaser with a mortal fear of commitment; Jim Dial (Charles Kimbrough), the rigid, serious, eminently competent anchorman; Miles Silverberg (Grant Shaud), a new Harvard graduate, producing *FYI* was his first "real" job; Eldin Bernecky (Robert Pastorelli), a house painter who worked continually on Murphy's townhouse until her son, Avery, was born, at which time he became Avery's nanny; and Phil (Pat Corley), the all-knowing owner of Phil's Bar, hangout for the *FYI* team.

As a running gag, Murphy also had a parade of secretaries, most of whom were inept and lasted only one episode. A few examples: a young African-American man who spoke only in hip-hop slang, a crash-test dummy, a bickering married couple, and a mental patient. Naturally, whenever Murphy found a good secretary, he or she left by the end of the episode.

Initially, some characters were two-dimensional. Miles existed only to run around acting tense and to annoy Murphy, a 40-year-old woman with a 25-year-old boss. In the pilot, Murphy tells him, "I just can't help thinking about the fact that while I was getting maced at the Democratic Convention in 1968, you were wondering if you'd ever meet Adam West." Corky was a stereotypical southern beauty queen, more interested in appearances than in reporting.

However, as the series progressed, Miles became a competent producer and manager. He grew to be fully capable of holding his own against Murphy, who still tended to underestimate him. And Corky, too, became more a friend than an annoyance to Murphy. A failed marriage tarnished the southern belle's fairy-tale life, making Corky more human and giving her more in common with Murphy. Murphy's feminism and ambition also began to rub off on the younger woman.

Beneath the facade of the serious anchorman, Jim Dial was a warm, caring person, more liberal than he seemed. In a first-season flashback, we see Murphy's

1977 *FYI* audition; she is dressed like "Annie Hall" and sports a wildly curly mane. Network executives want to hire a more "professional" woman, but Jim convinces them to hire Murphy. Frank, the skirt chaser, never chased Murphy or Corky. Frank and Murphy were a TV rarity: a man and a woman who are close friends, with no sexual tension.

Murphy Brown's plots often parodied actual news events. In the second-season episode "The Memo That Got Away," a high school journalist hacks into *FYI*'s computer system and finds an uncomplimentary memo Murphy has written about her co-workers. A similar, real-life incident occurred when a memo written by *Today* anchor Bryant Gumbel was leaked. In a seventh-season episode, *Murphy Brown* lampoons the O.J. Simpson trial circus with a story about an astronaut accused of murdering his brother.

Real-life events came head to head with *Murphy Brown* in the summer of 1992, when Vice President Dan Quayle criticized unwed mothers as violating "family values." To support his argument, he pointed to the entertainment industry as site of flawed morals. As a specific example, he singled out the fictitious Murphy, who had given birth to son Avery, out of wedlock, in the 1991–92 season finale. Producer Diane English responded to Quayle with her own analysis of the social and cultural conditions, and the exchanges escalated into a national event, a topic for much discussion in the news and on the late-night television talk shows. In the fall 1992 season premier, the series presented an episode devoted to the controversy. In "I Say Potatoe, You Say Potato" (a reference to the vice president's much-publicized misspelling), Murphy takes Quayle to task, introducing several hardworking, one-parent families on *FYI*.

In 1993 the character of Peter Hunt was added to the cast. Appearing in occasional episodes, Hunt was played by Scott Bakula and became Murphy's new love interest. In the seventh season, two additional characters were added: Miller Redfield (Christopher Rich), an idiot anchorman on another network show, and McGovern (Paula Korologos), a former Music Television (MTV) personality hired to bring "youth appeal" to *FYI*. Miller was stereotypically handsome and stupid and was often played against Peter Hunt's "real" journalistic style. McGovern had more potential; the writers resisted the "slacker" stereotype usually pinned on her generation and instead made her a miniature Murphy, with one exception—she was politically conservative. This fact never failed to annoy Murphy who, in one episode, cut McGovern's report to less than a minute because she (Murphy) did not like its political slant. McGovern complained to Corky, who offered this advice:

Corky: When I want Murphy to leave me alone, I just let her think she's getting her way.
McGovern: But she *is* getting her way!
Corky: Right. But I don't care, as long as she leaves me alone!

In the 1994 season, veteran comedian Garry Marshall joined the cast as Stan Lansing, head of the network. The following year Paul Reubens (aka Pee-wee Herman) appeared as Lansing's fawning (and scheming) nephew. Lily Tomlin became a regular on the series in the ninth season, playing *FYI*'s new executive producer. The presence of new cast members added a fresh energy to the other characters and the stories, helping to ensure that *Murphy Brown* would continue to have its way with comedy and social commentary. Other characters (Miles, Eldin, and Phil), however, departed the program before its tenth and final season in 1997–98. That season focused on Murphy's struggle with breast cancer and concluded with her recovery and the *FYI* cast deciding to leave the air.

JULIE PRINCE

Cast

Murphy Brown	Candice Bergen
Jim Dial	Charles Kimbrough
Frank Fontana	Joe Regalbuto
Corky Sherwood	Faith Ford
Miles Silverberg (1988–95)	Grant Shaud
Phil (1988–96)	Pat Corley
Eldin Bernecky (1988–94)	Robert Pastorelli
Carl Wishnitski (1988–93)	Ritch Brinkley
John, the stage manager	John Hostetter
Gene Kinsella (1988–92)	Alan Oppenheimer
Peter Hunt (1993–)	Scott Bakula
Avery Brown (1994–)	Dyllan Christopher
Stan Lansing (1994–)	Garry Marshall
Miller Redfield (1995–)	Christopher Rich
Andrew J. Lansing, III	Paul Reubens

Producers

Diane English, Joel Shukovsky, Gary Dontzig, Steven Peterman

Programming History

247 episodes
CBS
November 1988–May 1998   Monday 9:00–9:30

Further Reading

Alley, Robert S., and Irby B. Brown, *Murphy Brown: Anatomy of a Sitcom,* New York: Dell, 1990

Benzel, Jan, "Murphy's Choices," *New York Times* (May 31, 1992)

Kolbert, Elizabeth, "Flap over *Murphy Brown:* Art Is Bigger Than Life," *New York Times* (September 23, 1992)

Mandese, Joe, "Advertisers Vote for *Murphy Brown,*" *Advertising Age* (September 7, 1992)

Mandese, Joe, "*Murphy Brown* Flap 'Irresponsible': Producer

Diane English Sees Her Creation as Sensitive 'Real Person,'" *Advertising Age* (September 21, 1992)

"Team of English and Shukovsky Make *Murphy* Work," *Broadcasting* (March 5, 1990)

"An Unmarried Woman and a Political Fight," *U.S. News and World Report* (June 1, 1992)

Zoglin, Richard, "Sitcom Politics," *Time* (September 21, 1992)

Murphy, Thomas S.

U.S. Media Executive

Thomas S. Murphy was chair and chief executive officer of Capital Cities/ABC until 1996, when Disney bought the company and Murphy retired. Murphy built Capital Cities/ABC into a multi-billion-dollar international media conglomerate. In addition to leading Capital Cities from its days as a small television holding company to its position as a media empire, Murphy distinguished himself as a responsible corporate citizen by emphasizing public service.

After service in the U.S. Navy, a Harvard M.B.A., and five years at Kenyon and Eckhardt and at Lever Brothers, Murphy began his broadcasting career with a little help from his father's friends. The legendary broadcaster Lowell Thomas, Thomas's business manager Frank Smith, and a few other investors started Hudson Valley Broadcasting. They needed a station manager and turned to their friend's ambitious son. In 1954, at the age of 29, Murphy assumed duties as the first employee and station manager at WROW-TV in Albany, New York. This station and its sister radio station, WROW-AM, were the Hudson Valley Broadcasting Company. After nearly three years of red ink, the station saw a profit. As the company evolved into Capital Cities and eventually into Capital Cities/ABC, it consistently made money. One share of the company in 1957 cost $5.75; in 1996, that investment would be worth more than $12,000.

In 1960 chair Frank Smith moved Murphy to New York City as executive vice president of Capital Cities. In 1964 Murphy was named president. With Smith's death in 1966, Murphy became chair and chief executive officer. Three cornerstones of Murphy's management philosophy were fiscal responsibility, decentralized local responsibility, and social responsibility. Additionally, he always tried to hire people smarter than himself. Murphy attributed much of his success to what he learned from Smith.

For the next two decades, Murphy led Capital Cities during a time of fantastic growth. In 1985 Capital Cities became the minnow that swallowed the whale when it announced that it was merging with the highly visible American Broadcasting Company (ABC). This was the largest merger to date of media companies. Capital Cities/ABC reclaimed this record about ten years later when it merged with the Disney Company.

Murphy will be remembered not only for his business acumen and ability to expand Capital Cities but

Thomas S. Murphy.
Courtesy of the Everett Collection

also for his firm belief in the importance of public service. In 1961 the company received national attention and a Peabody Award for its nonprofit, exclusive television coverage of Israel's trial of the Nazi war criminal Adolf Eichmann. Murphy continued that level of dedication to public service throughout the early years of the company and into the era of Capital Cities/ABC. The company played a significant role in public service campaigns for "Stop Sexual Harassment," PLUS Literacy, the Partnership for a Drug-Free America, and others. The company also practiced significant internal and external public service with its own Substance Abuse Assistance Program, Corporate Diversity in Management skills bank, Management Initiatives Program to expand minority representation in editorial management, Broadcast Management Training Program for women and minorities, the Advanced Management Training Program for Women, the Women's Advisory Committee, the Capital Cities/ABC Foundation, and the Volunteer Initiatives Program, serving as a clearinghouse for volunteerism. In retirement, Murphy has pursued his public service interests as a trustee of the Inner-City Scholarship Fund, the Lymphoma Research Foundation of America, New York University, and the Madison Square Boys and Girls Club and as a member of the Board of Overseers of Harvard College. In 1998 he was elected board chair of Save the Children.

GUY E. LOMETTI

Thomas S. Murphy. Born in Brooklyn, New York, U.S.A., May 31, 1925. Cornell University, B.S. 1945; Harvard University, M.B.A. 1949. Married. Served in U.S. Navy. Executive positions with Kenyon and Eckhardt, 1949–51; with Lever Brothers Company, 1951–54; with Capital Cities Communications, Inc., New York City, from 1954, executive vice president 1961–64, president, 1964–72, chief executive officer, 1966–90, chair, from 1966; initiated acquisition of Triangle Broadcasting, 1971; initiated merger with ABC to form Capital Cities/ABC, 1986. Board member: The Walt Disney Company, Columbia/HCA Healthcare Corp., Doubleclick Inc., and Smith Barney's International Advisory Board.

Further Reading

Forbes, Malcolm S., "Mighty CEOs Who Are Also All-Round Nice Guys Are Rare," *Forbes* (December 11, 1989)

Hawver, W., *Capital Cities/ABC, the Early Years: 1954–1986, How the Minnow Came to Swallow the Whale,* Radnor, Pennsylvania: Chilton, 1994

Landler, Mark, "Creators of the Big Deal, Capital Cities' Tandem Team," *New York Times* (August 1, 1995)

West, Don, "Broadcaster's Broadcaster" (interview), *Broadcasting & Cable* (November 13, 1995)

Murrow, Edward R.

U.S. Broadcast Journalist

Edward R. Murrow is the most distinguished and renowned figure in the history of American broadcast journalism. He was a seminal force in the creation and development of electronic news gathering as both a craft and a profession. Murrow's career began at the Columbia Broadcasting System (CBS) in 1935 and spanned the infancy of news and public affairs programming on radio through the ascendancy of television in the 1950s, as it eventually became the nation's most popular news medium. In 1961 Murrow left CBS to become director of the U.S. Information Agency for the new Kennedy administration. By that time, his peers were already referring to a "Murrow legend and

tradition" of courage, integrity, social responsibility, and journalistic excellence, emblematic of the highest ideals of both broadcast news and the television industry in general.

David Halberstam has observed in *The Powers That Be* that Murrow was "one of those rare legendary figures who was as good as his myth." Murrow was apparently driven by the democratic precepts of modern liberalism and the more embracing Weltanschauung of the American Protestant tradition. In Alexander Kendrick's *Prime-Time: The Life of Edward R. Murrow,* for example, Murrow's brother, Dewey, describes the intense religious and moral tutelage of his mother

Edward R. Murrow.
Courtesy of the Everett Collection

and father: "they branded us with their own consciences." Murrow's imagination and the long-term effects of his early home life impelled him to integrate his parents' ethical guidelines into his own personality to such an extensive degree that Murrow became the virtual fulfillment of his industry's public service aspirations.

Murrow's rich, full, and expressive voice first came to the attention of the U.S. listening public in his many rooftop radio broadcasts during the Battle of Britain in 1939. In words evocative of the original founding fathers of the United States, Murrow frequently used the airwaves to revivify and popularize many democratic ideals—such as free speech, citizen participation, the pursuit of truth, and the sanctification of individual liberties and rights—that resulted from a broader liberal discourse in England, France, and the United States. Resurrecting these values and virtues for a mass audience of true believers during the London Blitz was high drama—the opposing threat of totalitarianism, made real by Nazi bombs, was ever present in the

background. Murrow's persona was thus established, embodying the political traditions of the Western democracies and offering the public a heroic model on which to focus their energies.

Murrow, of course, was only one of many heroes to emerge from World War II, but he became the eminent symbol for broadcasting. The creation of the Murrow legacy and tradition speaks both to the sterling talent of the man himself and to the enormous growth and power of radio during the war years. Murrow hired a generation of electronic journalists at CBS, such as Eric Sevareid, Charles Collingwood, and Howard K. Smith, among many others, for whom he set the example as their charismatic leader. As late as 1977, more than a decade after Murrow's death, Dan Rather wrote in his autobiography *The Camera Never Blinks* that "it was astonishing how often his [Murrow] name and work came up. To somebody outside CBS it is probably hard to believe. Time and again I heard someone say, 'Ed wouldn't have done it that way.'"

Murrow's initial foray into television was as the on-camera host of the seminal news and public affairs program *See It Now* (1951–57). This series was an adaptation of radio's popular *Hear It Now,* which was also coproduced by Murrow and Fred W. Friendly. *See It Now* premiered in a half-hour format on November 18, 1951, opening with Murrow's characteristic restraint and directness: "This is an old team trying to learn a new trade." By April 20, 1952, *See It Now* had been moved to prime time, where it stayed until July 1955, typically averaging around 3 million viewers. After that point, *See It Now* was expanded to an hour but telecast more irregularly on a special-events basis.

Through the course of its run, *See It Now* was awarded four Emmys for Best News or Public Service Program. Many of its broadcasts were duly considered breakthroughs for the medium. For example, "This is Korea...Christmas 1952" was produced on location "to try to portray the face of the war and the faces of the men who are fighting it." Murrow's most-celebrated piece was his March 9, 1954, telecast, in which he engaged Senator Joseph R. McCarthy in a program "told mainly in [McCarthy's] own words and pictures." In the aftermath of this episode, the descriptions of Edward R. Murrow and his tradition quickly began to transcend the more secular cast that appeared in response to his championing of democratic action and principles in Britain during World War II. In his review of the now legendary McCarthy program, for instance, *New York Times* TV critic Jack Gould reflected an ongoing canonization process when he wrote that "last week may be remembered as the week that broadcasting recaptured its soul."

Murrow also produced lighter, less controversial fare for television. His most popular success was his hosting of *Person to Person,* from 1953 to 1961, where he chatted informally with a wide array of celebrities every Friday during prime time. Murrow remained with this program through the 1958–59 season, "visiting" in their homes such people as Harry Truman, Marilyn Monroe, and John Steinbeck. Murrow, in fact, won an Emmy for the Most Outstanding Personality in all of television after *Person to Person*'s inaugural season. He received four other individual Emmys for Best News Commentator or Analyst as well, with the last coming in 1958, the year he excoriated the broadcasting industry in a speech before the Radio and Television News Directors Association (RTNDA) for being "fat, comfortable, and complacent" and television for "being used to detract, delude, amuse, and insulate us."

The tragedy of Murrow's rapid enervation at CBS after this latest tumult was implicit in his apparent need to ascribe higher motives to his own profession. Murrow had long reveled in his role as broadcasting's Jeremiah. His urgent and inspirational style of presentation fit the life-and-death psychological milieu of a world war, as it was later appropriate for the McCarthy crisis. By 1958, however, the viewing public and the television industry were less inclined to accept yet another of his ethical lambastes, especially since his RTNDA speech was directed at them and their shortcomings. As the business of TV grew astronomically during the 1950s, Murrow's priorities fell progressively out of step. His vision of television as "the world's greatest classroom" increasingly appeared more and more like a quaint vestige of a bygone era, especially to his bosses and a younger generation at the network.

There is still a small plaque in the lobby of CBS headquarters in New York City that bears the image of Murrow and the inscription, "He set standards of excellence that remain unsurpassed." During his 25-year career, Murrow made more than 5,000 broadcasts; and more than anyone else, he invented the traditions of television news. Murrow and his team essentially created the prototype of the TV documentary with *See It Now* and later extended the technological reach of electronic news gathering in *Small World* (1958–59), which employed simultaneous hookups around the globe to facilitate unrehearsed discussion among several international opinion leaders. Most of Murrow's *See It Now* associates were reassembled to produce *CBS Reports* in 1961, although Murrow was only an infrequent participant in this new series. Over the years, he had simply provoked too many trying situations for CBS, and the network's hierarchy made a conscious decision to reduce his profile. There is an apparent irony between Edward R. Murrow's life and the way that he is subsequently remembered today: the industry that finally had no place for him now holds Murrow up as their model citizen, the "patron saint of American broadcasting."

GARY R. EDGERTON

See also **Army-McCarthy Hearings; Columbia Broadcasting System; Cronkite, Walter; Documentary; Friendly, Fred W.; News, Network; Paley, William S.; *Person to Person; See It Now;* Sevareid, Eric; Smith, Howard K.; Talk Shows**

Edward R. Murrow. Born Egbert Roscoe Murrow in Greensboro, North Carolina, U.S.A., April 25, 1908. Attended Stanford University and the University of Washington; graduated from Washington State College, 1930. Married: Janet Huntington Brewster, 1934; one son. Served as assistant director, Institute of International Education, 1932–35; began career with CBS as director of talks and education, 1935; director, CBS's European Bureau in London, 1937; during World War II, hired and trained distinguished corps of war correspondents, including Eric Sevareid, Howard K. Smith, Charles Collingwood, and Richard C. Hottelet; vice president and director of public affairs, CBS, 1946; resigned to return to radio broadcasting, 1947; narrated and produced *Hear It Now* radio series, 1950–51; brought series to television as *See It Now,* 1952–58; began *Person to Person* television program, 1953; moderated and produced *Small World* television series, featuring discussions among world figures, 1958–60; appointed by President John F. Kennedy to head U.S. Information Agency in 1961, and remained in post until 1964. Recipient: nine Emmy Awards. Died in New York, April 27, 1965.

Television Series

1952–57	*See It Now* (host)
1953–61	*Person to Person* (host)
1958–60	*Small World* (moderator and producer)

Radio

Hear It Now (host and coproducer), 1950–51.

Publications

So This Is London, 1941

In Search of Light: The Broadcasts of Edward R. Murrow, 1938–1961, edited with Edward Bliss Jr., 1967

"Call It Courage: Act on Your Knowledge" (transcript), *Vital Speeches* (November 15, 1993)

Further Reading

Edgerton, Gary, "The Murrow Legend as Metaphor: The Creation, Appropriation, and Usefulness of Edward R. Murrow's Life Story," *Journal of American Culture* (Spring 1992)

Edward R. Murrow Papers, 1927–1965: A Guide to the Microfilm Edition, Sanford, North Carolina: Microfilming Corp. of America, 1982

Halberstam, David, *The Powers That Be,* New York: Knopf, 1979

Kendrick, Alexander, *Prime-Time: The Life of Edward R. Murrow,* Boston: Little, Brown, 1969

Lichello, Robert, *Edward R. Murrow, Broadcaster of Courage,* Charlottesville, New York: SamHar Press, 1971

Persico, Joseph E., *Edward R. Murrow: An American Original,* New York: McGraw-Hill, 1988

Persico, Joseph E., "The Broadcaster and the Demagogue," *Television Quarterly* (spring 1989)

Smith, Robert, *Edward R. Murrow: The War Years,* Kalamazoo, Michigan: New Issues Press, 1978

Sperber, A.M., *Murrow: His Life and Times,* New York: Freundlich, 1986

Wald, Malvin, "Shootout at the Beverly Hills Corral: Edward R. Murrow Versus Hollywood," *Journal of Popular Film and Television* (fall 1991)

Music Licensing

Music licensing is the process through which television outlets and producers acquire permission to use copyrighted music in their programming and productions. A music copyright actually consists of a bundle of ownership rights. The four principal parts of this bundle are (1) the *publication right,* authority to copy or publish the musical work; (2) the *mechanical (recording) right,* authority to make audio copies of the work; (3) the *synchronization right,* authority to synchronize recordings of the work with film or video; and (4) the *performance right,* authority to perform the work publicly. Two additional facets of music copyright are (5) *grand dramatic rights,* which involve the use of the composition in a dramatic performance such as a stage play, an opera, or a video representation of the "story" of a song, and (6) the *master-use license (dubbing right),* which pertains to the re-recording of a particular artist's rendition of the music. The first five of these rights emanate from the original composer and publisher of the work. The master-use license is held by the record company that released the particular artist's interpretation of the composition.

While all six of these elements may come into play in the production of a film or video project, it is the performance right that is of overwhelming importance in the public transmission of television programming. In the United States (and elsewhere through agreements with reciprocal agencies), three licensing organizations administer performance rights for virtually all musical compositions still under copyright. These three organizations are the American Society of Composers, Authors and Publishers (ASCAP), Broadcast Music Incorporated (BMI), and the much smaller SESAC (formerly, the Society of European Stage Authors and Composers).

ASCAP, the oldest of the three, was born of a 1913 restaurant meeting of composer Victor Herbert and eight publisher and composer associates who sought some mechanism to ensure that they would be paid for the public performance of their work. ASCAP began licensing broadcast stations to play the music of its member composers and publishers in 1923, when it signed a one-year $500 license with AT&T's WEAF (New York). Perceiving themselves to be at ASCAP's mercy when it came to the use of music in their programming, broadcasters formed the National Association of Broadcasters (NAB) to negotiate with ASCAP on behalf of the entire radio industry. (The NAB sub-

Courtesy of ASCAP

Courtesy of BMI

sequently became U.S. commercial broadcasting's major trade association and lobbying agency.)

BMI was created by the broadcast industry in 1940 in reaction to what stations perceived to be a large and unjustified increase in ASCAP's licensing rates. Until BMI could build its own catalog, many stations that had refused to renew their ASCAP licenses could play nothing but tunes by Stephen Foster and other vintage music no longer under copyright. BMI soon signed affiliation agreements with Latin American, country, western, "race music" (black), and later rock-and-roll composers—musical genres that ASCAP had largely ignored.

SESAC was founded in 1931 by music publishing executive Paul Heinecke, with a catalog consisting primarily of European concert and operatic music. SESAC later dropped its full name in favor of the acronym and expanded its scope to encompass concert band, gospel, religious, and country music, opening a major office in Nashville, Tennessee, in 1964. SESAC is the only one of the three performance-rights organizations also to administer the mechanical and synchronization rights on behalf of its member composers and publishers.

Virtually from its inception, radio performance-rights licensing was accommodated via a "blanket license." Stations paid the rights agency an annual fee based on either gross receipts (ASCAP and BMI) or market size, power, and hours of operation (SESAC). This license allowed the stations to play as much of the licensing organization's music as they wished. This same business arrangement subsequently was extended to the new medium of television. As in radio, television-station rate negotiations with ASCAP and BMI are handled by an all-industry committee supported by voluntary station contributions. Because far less SESAC music is played on television, the dollars

that organization receives are much lower, and stations deal with it separately.

Since 1950, the broadcast television networks have secured their own blanket licenses for the music in the programming and commercials they distribute to their affiliates. Even if they are network affiliates, stations still have needed their own blanket licenses to cover the music included in the syndicated series, local programs, and nonnetwork commercials they air. Since 1970, broadcasters have fought a number of legal battles in an attempt to reduce overlapping license coverage and bring greater flexibility and economy to the performance-rights clearance process. In 1970 the Columbia Broadcasting System (CBS) initiated an antitrust suit against ASCAP and BMI in order to secure the option of a "per use" alternative to the blanket license. However, in 1981, the U.S. Supreme Court reaffirmed the dismissal of the case. Four years later, television stations lost a similar skirmish over "per program" rates that tended to make this option far more costly than the blanket license.

Nevertheless, new licensing alternatives began to emerge. Following a series of legal maneuvers, ASCAP/BMI and television broadcasters began, in 1987, to negotiate a more economically realistic per-program license option. Six years and several judicial proceedings later, the parties had substantially agreed to a feasible per-program license structure. This paved the way for stations more actively to purchase or lease their own music libraries for use in local productions and commercials—thus greatly shortening the list of programs for which they would have to pay an ASCAP or BMI fee. At the same time, major program syndicators such as King World began selling stations the rights to the music contained in their series for a small additional fee. Such "source cleared" deals are expected to become more and more common as stations seek to further reduce their ASCAP and BMI per-program payments. Meanwhile, in a 1992 cable television decision, the Supreme Court affirmed the right of cable networks to obtain the same blanket "through to the viewer" license that had been available to the broadcast networks since 1950. This greatly lessened the performance-rights liability of cable system operators. As a result of negotiations between the National Cable Television Association Music License Committee and the three performance-rights holders, local cable systems can now obtain blanket licenses to cover music used on local-origination channels as well as in locally inserted commercials and promotional announcements.

Local broadcast station blanket rates for ASCAP are determined through negotiations with the broadcasters' Television Music License Committee. An industry-wide flat fee is set in these negotiations. This fee is divided among all defined television markets according to market size. The market fee, in turn, is spread among stations in that market on the basis of the household ratings achieved by each. Annual adjustments are made on the basis of changes in the consumer price index and number of stations in each area. BMI and SESAC fees follow a similar pattern and, essentially, are indexed to the ASCAP-negotiated figure.

An additional simmering controversy involves musicians and some recording companies. These interests sporadically have lobbied Congress to enact legislation that would require an additional performance-rights fee to be paid to the performers of a piece of music. The television industry counters that performers already have been compensated through existing rights mechanisms and have handsomely profited from the exposure with which television has provided them.

PETER B. ORLIK

See also **Music on Television**

Further Reading

Berk, Lee Eliot, *Legal Protection for the Creative Musician,* Berkeley, California: Berklee Press Publications, 1970

"Broadcasters to Press Fight to Send Out Copyright Music," *New York Times* (April 26, 1923)

Emma, Thomas, "Music Clearance," *Video Systems* (September 1993)

Foisie, Geoffrey, "ASCAP Decision Music to TV Stations," *Broadcasting & Cable* (March 8, 1993)

Foisie, Geoffrey, "Making Sense of Music Licensing," *Broadcasting & Cable* (March 29, 1993)

Goldblatt, Cristina, *The Songwriter's Handbook,* Hollywood, California: American Song Festival, 1974

Granville, Elizabeth, "TV Music Licensing in Wake of 'Buffalo,'" *Broadcasting* (May 20, 1985)

"Profile: Alice Heinecke Prager," *Broadcasting* (September 11, 1972)

Shemel, Sidney, and M. William Krasilovsky, *The Business of Music,* New York: Billboard Publishing, 1964

Tobenkin, David, "King World Negotiates Own Music Rights," *Broadcasting & Cable* (May 30, 1994)

Zimmerman, Barbara, "The Music Business Targets Corporations," *Video Systems* (May 1991)

Music on Television

The antecedents for music's presence in television may be found in film and radio. Most television music (like film music) is nondiegetic: it is heard by viewers and listeners but not on-screen performers. This ubiquitous "background" music is added after shooting has been completed and is used to create moods, fill spaces, provide rhythm, and link the production to other cultural texts. Television music also draws on the tradition of radio, which initially presented in featured performances and variety shows, then later through disc jockey selections and chart shows. Musicians who appear on television sometimes play live but more often mime performance (or "lip-synch") to their sound recordings either in the studio or on music videos. Therefore, music *on* or *in* television encompasses a wide range of practices. Though television has become increasingly music driven on a global basis, the particular distribution of styles, techniques, and discourses about music and television has depended on the institutional histories and cultural contexts of both television and music in different localities.

In the United States, variety shows based in the vaudeville tradition dominated the first two decades of television because of their broad appeal and low production costs. Yet music frequently was considered an afterthought during television's early years. In 1948 only 17 stations were on the air. Programming was produced largely on a local basis, and talent and material often were in short supply. Labor unions also played a significant role in determining how music was used on television in the late 1940s. Under the leadership of James Petrillo, the American Federation of Musicians (AFM) instigated freezes on all music recording in 1942 and 1948, and the AFM banned "live" music on television until the spring of 1948. The union also ordered that all programs with featured or background music must be broadcast "live" before they were syndicated via kinescopes, and these kinescopes were banned from airing on any station not affiliated with the originating station. This arrangement favored networks over independent stations and allowed the powerful AFM to strengthen its control of the music industry. The union also prohibited its members from recording for television films until 1950, when the AFM negotiated a system of royalty payments from television producers to musicians (although no such royalty system existed in the film industry). Television music also was hampered by disagreements between program producers and music publishers. Producers sought a broadened general license fee for music use rather than a special license, while the major music publishing concern, the American Society of Composers, Authors and Publishers (ASCAP), demanded three times the rate it received for film music.

The networks were concerned with "cultural uplift" during the late 1940s and early 1950s, and they viewed "high culture" as a way to add cultural legitimacy to the new medium. The National Broadcasting Company (NBC) had telecast a Metropolitan Opera presentation of "Pagliacci" on March 10, 1940, and all three networks featured classical music and opera on a semiregular basis. NBC aired three telecasts of the NBC Orchestra in 1948, and the American Broadcasting Company (ABC) telecast an adaptation of "Othello" on November 29 of that year. The NBC Opera Theater began regular telecasts in 1950 with four programs and continued to air opera specials through 1950s and early 1960s. The network also aired an experimental color broadcast of "Carmen" on October 31, 1953. Producers faced a number of problems with adapting opera to television. The NBC presentations were sung in English and frequently condensed into one-hour programs, arousing the ire of some critics. Early televised operas also were criticized for incessant camera panning and close-ups. A reviewer for *Musical America* described a December 1952 closed-circuit telecast of "Carmen" by New York's Metropolitan Opera to 27 cities: "The relentlessness of the camera in exposing corpulence and other less attractive physical features of some of the performers aroused hilarity among the more unsophisticated viewers, of whom there were, perforce, very many."

The networks also showcased classical music in specials and limited-run series throughout the early 1950s. In 1951 ABC's Chicago affiliate (WENR-TV) became the first station to regularly televise an orchestra, and NBC aired *Meet the Masters,* a classical music series, that spring. The network continued to air occasional telecasts of the NBC Symphony Orchestra, and the Columbia Broadcasting System (CBS) countered with specials featuring the Philadelphia Orchestra. The classical music series "Voice of Firestone" had originated in 1928 on radio; in June 1954, it jumped to television on ABC. Other network programs presented a grab bag of "high culture." CBS's *Omnibus* debuted in 1952 with support from the Ford Foundation. Although it won numerous awards, the program moved to ABC and NBC because of poor ratings. *Omnibus* was canceled in 1959, and the Ford Foundation's experience with the program led them to provide the seed money for American public television. Classical music and opera performers also made occasional appear-

ances on network variety shows, particularly CBS's *Toast of the Town.* NBC musical specials in 1951 showcased the works of Richard Rogers and Irving Berlin, and NBC continued to air lavish musical presentations throughout the decade.

Music was an integral part of amateur talent shows, which ran on all three networks through the 1950s. The most successful of these, *Ted Mack's Original Amateur Hour,* was adapted from radio's *Major Bowes' Original Amateur Hour.* Dumont began telecasting the series in 1948, and it aired on various networks until 1970. Music also was featured in the context of game shows. Celebrities rated records on KNXT's *Juke Box Jury,* which was carried by ABC in 1953 and later syndicated. Other musical game shows included ABC's *So You Want to Lead a Band* and NBC's *Musical Chairs,* which aired in 1954 and 1955, respectively, as well as *Name That Tune,* which ran on NBC and later CBS from 1953 to 1959 and was briefly revived in syndication in the mid-1970s.

Singers often hosted summer replacement shows in the early 1950s. In 1950 Kate Smith and Sammy Kaye hosted replacement shows on NBC while CBS countered with several summer series hosted by Perry Como, Vaughn Monroe, and Frank Sinatra. ABC configured much of its prime-time schedule around music, particularly after Lawrence Welk joined the network in July 1955. Welk, who began telecasting his performances in June 1949, remains perhaps the most popular musical performer in television history. By featuring performers such as Welk, Guy Lombardo, Paul Whiteman, Fred Waring, and Perry Como, networks targeted older audiences (at the time, "teenagers" as a demographic group were of little use to network advertisers).

Television producers in the late 1940s and early 1950s relied on older popular songs, or "standards," and avoided songs without proven audience appeal. In addition, ASCAP's outright hostility to television led producers to use songs licensed by Broadcast Music Association (BMI), many of which were older and in the public domain. Exposing new music largely was relegated to independent stations. This pattern paralleled postwar developments in the recording industry in which small, independent labels distributed new genres, such as rhythm and blues and country music. Independent television stations were particularly strong on the West Coast because weak network links, and remote-band broadcasts provided inexpensive filler for broadcast schedules. KTLA-TV in Los Angeles featured five orchestra shows each week in the early 1950s, including Spade Cooley's hugely popular western program, while KLAC-TV countered with the *Hometown Jamboree* hillbilly program. KLAC also challenged the color barrier by presenting a black singer, Hadda Brooks, regularly in 1949.

"Video deejay" programming provided another economical means of filling airtime. Al Jarvis had created the radio deejay program at Los Angeles's KWAB-AM in the early 1930s, and in the winter of 1950 Jarvis began daily broadcasts of records, interviews, horse-racing results, and "daily religious periods" at KLAC. NBC began airing Wayne Howell's deejay show nationally on Saturday afternoons, and by the end of 1950 video deejays were firmly established in New York, Chicago, and Los Angeles as well as secondary markets such as San Francisco, Miami, Louisville, Philadelphia, Detroit, and Cleveland (where pioneering rock-and-roll deejay Alan Freed held forth late at night on WXEZ-TV). Video deejay programs combined lip-synch performances, dancers, games, sketches, stunts, and film shorts. Between 1941 and 1947, the Mills Novelty Company produced more than 2,000 promotional jazz and ballad films, or "soundies," for coin-operated machines, and many of these shorts resurfaced on video deejay shows. "Soundies" also were frequently screened between programs to fill airtime, as were the 754 "visual records" that Louis Snader produced in his Hollywood studios between 1950 and 1952. Screen Gems and United Artists produced similar films with a unique twist: silent films were paired with phonograph records, which allowed the clips to be recycled with different songs.

By 1956 local video deejay programs were telecast regularly in nearly 50 markets. These programs were the only significant television programming produced for teenagers and, along with "Top 40" radio, were instrumental in the rising success of rock and roll. The most notable video deejay program debuted on Philadelphia's WFIL-TV as *Bandstand* in September 1952. Dick Clark replaced Bob Horn as host in July 1956, and the following year *American Bandstand* was picked up for national distribution by ABC. The program aired from 3:00 to 4:30 P.M. Monday through Friday afternoons, and Dick Clark had begun to parlay *American Bandstand*'s success into a television empire. More than 100 local imitators of *Bandstand* were on the air by March 1958, and TV had become second only to radio as a means of promoting music. In 1950 standards outnumbered popular tunes on television by four to one, and popular songs on television were already well established on records and radio. Four years later, the ratio of hits to standards was 50/50. "Let Me Go, Lover" was recorded by several artists after its initial success on CBS's *Studio One,* and the "Ballad of Davey Crockett" from Walt Disney's ABC-TV series established TV's importance in making hits.

NBC was the most adventurous network in music programming through the 1950s, particularly through Steve Allen's efforts to present pop, jazz, and classical artists on *The Tonight Show.* Allen also hosted an NBC special, *All-Star Jazz,* in December 1957. Like Allen, Ed Sullivan featured a number of black acts on his *Talk of the Town* variety show in the 1950s. Although most acts were comics and dancers, musical performers included W.C. Handy, Billy Eckstine, Lena Horne, and T-Bone Walker. On April 1, 1949, ABC affiliate WENR in Chicago began airing *Happy Pappy,* a jazz-oriented revue that featured an all-black cast, and three years later an ABC special with Billy Daniels was the first network television program to feature a black entertainer as star. Nat "King" Cole became the first black to host a regular network series (on NBC from 1956 to 1957). The program failed to attract a national sponsor and was boycotted by several stations in the North and South. As a result, blacks were relegated largely to guest shots on variety shows. No black performer would host a network variety series until Sammy Davis Jr. in 1966.

Rhythm and blues and rock and roll originally were objects of ridicule on TV, as exemplified by Sid Caesar's "Three Haircuts" parody skit on *Your Show of Shows,* but programmers began paying closer attention to the burgeoning teenage market in 1956. Ed Sullivan presented a rhythm-and-blues special in November 1955 that featured LaVern Baker, Bo Diddley, and the Five Keys and hosted by radio deejay "Dr. Jive." Attempts at providing a regular network showcase for rhythm and blues failed because of resistance from southern affiliates as well as pressure from ASCAP, which refused to license rhythm-and-blues titles for blatantly racist reasons.

Programmers embraced country music more readily. "Hillbilly," as it was more commonly known, gained its initial video exposure with shows hosted by regional performers in the Midwest, including Earnie Lee at WLW in Cincinnati (1947), Pee Wee King at WAVE in Louisville (1948), and Lulu Belle at WNBQ in Chicago (1949). By 1956, almost 100 live local country-western shows aired on more than 80 stations in 30 states. Eddy Arnold, the "Tennessee Plowboy," was tapped as a summer replacement for Perry Como in 1952, and his program was syndicated through the 1950s. Other network efforts included Red Foley's *Ozark Jubilee* (ABC, 1955–61) and the *Tennessee Ernie Ford Show* (NBC, ABC, 1955–65), and CBS ran a country music program hosted by Jimmy Dean against *Today.* Nevertheless, these programs were largely pop oriented in terms of song selection and guest stars.

Singing personalities increasingly replaced comedians as program hosts in the waning years of the 1950s.

By the fall of 1957, recording stars headlined more than 20 TV shows. Perry Como and Dinah Shore hosted popular series for NBC, and ABC aired efforts by Frank Sinatra, Guy Mitchell, Pat Boone, and Julius La Rosa. Many of these shows suffered poor ratings and were supplanted by westerns in 1958, but the success of Rodgers and Hammerstein's *Cinderella* special on CBS triggered a spate of musical fairy tales on networks in the waning years of the decade. Yet television was decried for unimaginative audio throughout the 1950s. Many productions employed dated music libraries, and dramatic shows often paid little attention to musical scoring (one exception was Richard Rodger's acclaimed score for the documentary series *Victory at Sea,* which NBC aired in late 1952 and early 1953). Another noted production was the *Rodgers and Hammerstein Cavalcade* sponsored by General Foods, which aired simultaneously on all four networks on March 28, 1954.

On January 26, 1956, Elvis Presley made his national television debut on the Dorsey Brothers' CBS *Stage Show* and quickly followed with appearances on the Milton Berle, Steve Allen, and Ed Sullivan shows. The squeals that Presley elicited from teenagers were matched by loathing from parents and critics. Reviewing a September 1956 performance on *The Ed Sullivan Show,* a critic for the *New York Times* noted disapprovingly that Presley "injected movements of the tongue and indulged in wordless singing that were singularly distasteful." Nevertheless, rock and roll would remain a fixture on local and national television, and ABC's *Rock 'n' Roll Show* was the first prime-time network special devoted to rock music. The program aired May 4 and 11, 1957, and was hosted by Alan Freed. In addition to specials and variety shows, rock became integrated into situation comedies. *Ozzie and Harriet* provided a showcase for young Ricky Nelson, who racked up several hits beginning in 1957. The fate of *Your Hit Parade* symbolized Tin Pan Alley's eclipse by rock and roll. The program originated as the *Lucky Strike Hit Parade* on radio in 1935 and retained its popularity after moving to television. As rock and roll began to dominate popular music, *Your Hit Parade* moved from NBC to CBS in 1958 and went off the air on April 24, 1959. An attempt to revive the program in the early 1970s was unsuccessful.

The late 1950s also were marked by a decline in "high culture" musical programming. A 1957 arrangement between Ed Sullivan and Metropolitan Opera led to a brief series of capsule opera performances on Sullivan's variety show. Met impresario Rudolf Bing scotched the deal when Sullivan proposed to divide the opera presentations into two smaller sections, with a ventriloquist act sandwiched in between, to reduce tuning out by viewers. The CBS series *The Seven Lively Arts,* a short-lived series of plays and music, was canceled in 1958, and *The Voice of Firestone* was dropped as a regularly scheduled program in 1959 (it continued as a series of specials until 1962). More successful were CBS's *Young People's Concerts,* which began airing infrequently in the late 1950s and continued until the early 1970s. Leonard Bernstein hosted the concerts, and each telecast was devoted to a single theme; two such concerts were "The Sound of the Hall" in 1962 and "What Is a Melody" the following year. The CBS *Camera Three* arts series ran Sunday mornings from 1956 to 1979, and NBC's *Bell Telephone Hour* presented music "for all tastes" on a semiregular basis from 1959 to 1968.

Jazz enjoyed greater exposure during the waning years of the 1950s. CBS aired Stan Kenton's *Music '55* as a summer replacement series, and the success of the NBC special *All-Star Jazz* in December 1957 led to a jazz boomlet the following year. NBC ran a 13-part series hosted by Gilbert Seldes, *The Subject Is Jazz,* ABC aired *Stars of Jazz* as a summer replacement, and CBS telecast four hour-long excepts from Newport Jazz Festival in July 1958. Still, most jazz programming consisted of standards, swing, and Dixieland. One exception was the widely acclaimed *Jazz Scene USA* (1962), produced by Steve Allen and syndicated by New York's WOR-TV. Television shows increasingly featured jazz background music, particularly tough-guy detective and adventure series such as *Peter Gunn* and *Ellery Queen* (NBC), *77 Sunset Strip* (ABC), and *Perry Mason* and *Route 66* (CBS). Although several of these themes charted on the "Billboard Hot-100," much of the music for establishing moods and providing bridges was imported from Europe. However, musicians and producers began to soften their adversarial stances in 1963 following James Petrillo's dethroning as head of the American Federation of Musicians. In October 1963, all network producers (with the inexplicable exception of the *Mr. Ed* production team) agreed to use live music in telefilms.

The early 1960s continued to see a shift away from musical variety shows. By 1961, only Perry Como, Ed Sullivan, Gary Moore, and Dinah Shore remained on network schedules, and both classical and pop music were relegated largely to specials. One notable exception to this rule was *Sing Along with Mitch,* in which viewers were invited to participate by reading lyrics off the screen. Mitch Miller, record company executive and archenemy of rock and roll, hosted the program, which aired on NBC from 1961 to 1964. Country music continued to figure prominently on television throughout the 1960s. Jimmy Dean hosted a weekly variety show on ABC from 1963 to 1966, and by 1963 more than 130 stations carried local or syndicated country music programs. Among the most popular were Porter Wagoner (whose eye-popping sequined suits rivaled any Liberace creation for sartorial excess), the Wilburn Brothers, and the bluegrass team of Flatt and Scruggs. The latter duo had been performing on television since 1953 but broke out nationally through exposure on *The Beverly Hillbillies* and the subsequent success of their single "The Ballad of Jed Clampett." These programs were joined in 1965 by syndicated efforts from Ernest Tubb and Wanda Jackson. In what surely must have been a surreal viewing experience, Richard Nixon performed a piano duet with Arthur "Guitar Boogie" Smith on the latter's Charlotte, North Carolina–based show. By 1970 almost three-quarters of the stations in the United States featured some form of rural music.

The folk music boom of the early 1960s was represented by ABC's *Hootenanny* (1963), the first regularly scheduled folk music program on network television. Featuring well-scrubbed folk music in the style of the Kingston Trio and Peter, Paul, and Mary, the series was embroiled in controversy from the outset when Pete Seeger and the Weavers were banned from the show for refusing to sign a government loyalty oath. *Hootenanny* was dropped from ABC's schedule in the fall of 1964. *American Bandstand* had switched from daily to weekend-only broadcasts a year earlier, part because of fallout from the payola scandal. Dick Clark had come under congressional investigation during the payola hearings in the late 1950s and early 1960s. Although Clark was never indicted, ABC insisted that Clark divest himself of music publishing and record distribution interests. Local *Bandstand* imitators were down significantly from their peak in 1958, and the music's lack of presence on television reflected a general malaise in rock and roll.

This changed on February 9, 1964, when the Beatles were featured on *The Ed Sullivan Show.* In what arguably is the most influential musical performance ever presented on television, the Beatles were seen in an estimated 73 million homes. The British Invasion was not universally welcomed, however; when the Rolling Stones appeared on *Hollywood Palace,* host Dean Martin openly disparaged their performance and snarled that they "oughta get haircuts." ABC's *Shindig* premiered in September 1964 with the Rolling Stones, the Byrds and the Kinks, and subsequent programs featured a host of English and American "beat groups" surrounded by a cast of writhing dancers. NBC answered with *Hullabaloo* from January 1965 to August 1966.

Until it folded in January 1966, *Shindig* also helped black such as Sam Cooke cross over to white audi-ences. In one particularly memorable broadcast, the headlining Rolling Stones paid homage to their influences by sitting at the feet of the great bluesman Howling Wolf as he performed "Little Red Rooster." The extent of the racial crossover in music was indicated by the fact that *Billboard* dropped its rhythm-and-blues chart in 1964. Efforts at integration were slower in other areas, however; the Chicago branch of the AFM remained segregated until January 1966. Television finally caught up with the civil rights movement in the mid-1960s. By 1968 a growing number of black performers were showcased in network programs, such as an NBC special featuring the Supremes and the Four Tops.

Teen dance shows enjoyed a resurgence in 1965. Some of the most notable syndicated efforts were hosted by Lloyd Thaxton, Casey Kasem (*Shebang,* which originated from KTLA in Los Angeles), Sam Riddle (*Hollywood A Go Go*), Gene Weed (*Shivaree*), and Jerry "The Geater with the Heater" Blavat's *The Discophonic Scene.* The ubiquitous Dick Clark also started a weekday teen show, *Where the Action Is,* on ABC. In addition to records and dancing, these shows often featured filmed performances as well as short "concept" musical films triggered by the success of the Beatles' *A Hard Day's Night.* Mainstream pop music remained the province of variety shows and specials throughout the 1960s. Barbra Streisand and Frank Sinatra aired acclaimed specials in the mid-1960s, and ABC presented an adventurous special, *Anatomy of Pop,* in February 1966, which featured artists as varied as Duke Ellington, Bill Monroe, and the Temptations. Another ABC special, 1967's *Songmakers,* followed the creative process from composition to recording with artists such as the songwriting team of Burt Bacharach and Hal David and the Paul Butterfield Blues Band. The big three networks virtually abandoned classical music to the fledgling NET public network by the late 1960s, although CBS aired a special on Igor Stravinsky in 1966.

Perhaps the greatest rock special in television history, the *T.A.M.I. Show,* was produced by Steve Binder (who later produced Elvis's comeback special and *Pee-wee's Playhouse*) for ABC in late 1964. Shot on video and later transferred to film for theatrical release, the *T.A.M.I. Show* featured Chuck Berry, Bo Diddley, the Rolling Stones, the Beach Boys, the Supremes, and an electrifying performance by James Brown. The program also captured an interracial musical mix conspicuously absent from later rock documentaries, such as *Monterey Pop* and *Woodstock.* Other noteworthy rock specials included a 1965 performance by the Beatles at New York's Shea Stadium (aired by ABC in January 1967) and Elvis Presley's legendary comeback performance on NBC in December 1968. The globalization of television was marked by the June 25, 1967, live telecast of *Our World.* Transmitted by satellite to 34 countries and aired in the United States on NET, the program included a performance by classical pianist Van Cliburn and climaxed with the Beatles warbling "All You Need Is Love."

Television also entered the kid-vid rock market when Beatle cartoons premiered on ABC in September 1965. The most successful cartoon group were the Archies (an assemblage of anonymous studio musicians), who scored a massive hit with "Sugar Sugar" in 1969 and cloned a dozen copies in the late 1960s and early 1970s, such as Josie and the Pussycats, the Bugaloos, the Groovie Goolies (described by critic Lester Bangs as "Munsters dipped in monosodium glutamate"), the Cattanooga Cats, and the Banana Splits. Equally contrived, though in human form, were the Monkees. Former Brill Building pop impresario Don Kirshner recruited four actors to star in a series modeled on "A Hard Day's Night," and *The Monkees* premiered on NBC in September 1966. The "band" racked up several hits of carefully groomed material but shocked their followers in Teenland the following year when they admitted they did not play their own instruments. The series was canceled in 1968. ABC's *The Music Scene* ran for 17 episodes beginning in October 1969 and featured comic sketches interspersed with performances by artists ranging from James Brown to Buck Owens.

The Smothers Brothers also presented some of the more daring "underground" acts of the late 1960s. (The Who's Peter Townshend was nearly deafened by an exploding drum set during one memorable appearance, and the Jefferson Airplane's Grace Slick made a controversial appearance in black face.) Other variety shows hosted by Ed Sullivan and Jonathan Winters presented a variety of alternative acts, each more hirsute and glowering than its predecessors. Sullivan did draw the line at lyrics, however. In a 1967 appearance, with much on-screen eye rolling from Mick Jagger, the Rolling Stones changed the lyrics of their latest hit to "Let's Spend Some Time Together." Other performers were less accommodating. After surveying the set before taping an appearance on *The Tom Jones Show,* Janis Joplin stormed offstage, complaining, "My public don't want to see me in front of no fucking plastic rain drops." Late-night talk shows such as *The Tonight Show* and *The Dick Cavett Show* also featured some rock stars (Joplin was a particular favorite on the latter). The syndicated *Playboy After Dark* also presented a variety of "alternative" artists; in a 1969 taping, the Grateful Dead dosed the unwitting production staff with LSD. Despite (and, in part, because of) the in-

creasingly outré nature of rock music acts on television, country music's video popularity continued unabated in the late 1960s. Johnny Cash was featured in an ABC summer replacement program in 1969, and his guests included the reclusive Bob Dylan. A more enduring success was CBS's *Hee Haw,* which presented a hick version of *Rowan and Martin's Laugh-In* beginning in June 1969. After CBS cleaned its house of "older-oriented" shows, the program continued in syndication until the late 1980s.

The 1970s began with the New Seekers foreshadowing the increasing melding of music, television, advertising, and the global imaginaries of Live Aid and Music Television (MTV) with "I'd Like to Teach the World to Sing." The song was a worldwide hit after airing as a Coca-Cola commercial. Looking backward, ABC introduced *The Partridge Family* with veteran stage and Hollywood musical star Shirley Jones and her son David Cassidy. The half-hour comedy grafted the wacky *Monkees* formula onto the story of the real-life Cowsills to successfully target the teen market. Jones played the single mom of a large musical family with a lovable but inept manager placed in various quirky situations. Musical numbers were performed in rehearsal and in a wrap-up concert setting as the denouement of each episode. The series launched Cassidy, the oldest of the Partridge progeny, as a teen idol. The most traditional outlet for music on the networks in the early 1970s was a host of variety shows: *The Johnny Cash Show, Glen Campbell's Goodtime Hour, This Is Tom Jones,* and *The Carol Burnett Show* featured musical guests lip-synching to their latest hits and sometimes engaging in banal patter with the host. However, reflecting the increasing dominance of market segmentation, ratings for most musical variety shows were plummeting by the mid-1970s. Even so,

The Music Scene, James Brown, 1969–70.
Courtesy of the Everett Collection

The Johnny Cash Show, Johnny Cash, 1969–71.
Courtesy of the Everett Collection

pop duo Captain and Tennille and the Jacksons both entered the variety market in 1976 with their own network shows.

While lip synching remained a common practice, the influence of rock's ideology of authenticity made the presentation of live music more important, and the success of theatrical films of musical events increased the demand for "live" rock shows. In 1973 three network shows featuring live music were introduced. NBC's *Midnight Special* presented 90 minutes of a live concert recorded on a studio soundstage. The show tended to favor more mainstream commercial artists, David Bowie, Marianne Faithfull, and Van Morrison being the limit of its adventurousness. *Midnight Special* was hosted by veteran DJ Wolfman Jack and by Helen Reddy from 1975 to 1977. ABC's *In Concert* combined old film clips by such groups as the Rolling Stones, with footage from concert venues. Produced by Don Kirshner and then taken over by executive producer Dick Clark, the show simulated the bill at the Fillmore Auditorium at which three bands each played a short live. Many of these concerts were shot at the Academy of Music in New York. Kirshner also presented the syndicated *Don Kirshner's Rock Concert.* Again, this featured clips of concert halls around the country interspersed with promotional clips. White rock acts dominated the program.

In a different musical vein, the *Great Performances* series debuted on the Public Broadcasting Service (PBS) in 1974. Produced at WNET in New York, this paved the way for the broadcast of classical music concerts and opera on the Bravo cable network since 1980. Country music found a live showcase in *Austin City Limits,* first broadcast through Austin's PBS station KLRN TV in 1976. The show reflected a return to the roots of country music, away from the saccharine Nashville sound of the period. In its earlier days, musical acts such as the Outlaws—Willie Nelson, Waylon Jennings, and Kris Kristofferson—performed on a stage in front of a small and intimate studio audience. The format remains essentially the same today. Live music has also had a highly visible spot on NBC's *Saturday Night Live* since 1975. A guest star performed one or two live numbers between the program's many skits, and musical choices were often a little more left field than was customary on the networks. On one particular occasion in 1977, Elvis Costello and the Attractions, who had replaced the Sex Pistols at the last minute, launched into their antifascist classic "Less than Zero," then abruptly stopped. Elvis told the band that he had changed his mind, and they then tore into "Radio Radio," running over time and giving producer Lorne Michaels a few nervous palpitations (shades of Jimi Hendrix's legendary appearance on Lulu's British Broadcasting Corporation [BBC] variety show nine years earlier). Sinead O'Connor's appearance on the show in 1994, when she ripped up a photograph of Pope John Paul II after a rendition of Bob Marley's "War," had a similar effect in this prime television showcase for musicians.

Black musical acts found a space for lip-synched performances of soul, funk, and disco hits on *Soul Train.* The creation of Don Cornelius, the show was started in Chicago in 1970 but moved to Hollywood and national syndication in 1971. *Soul Train* featured performers such as Ike and Tina Turner and Al Green, but the real stars were the creative and innovative dancers, who were mainly African-American teens. In many ways, *Soul Train* was a return to the old formula of the teen dance show, except for one major difference: it was black. The show was vital in the popularization of funk and disco music. By 1975 the disco boom was well established, and everyone was trying to get on the bandwagon. Syndicated shows such as *Disco America, Disco Mania,* and *Disco 76* came and went as fast as the latest disco hit. Even James Brown deserted funk for disco with the short-lived syndicated program *Future Shock.* Some journalists and critics feared the end of that discotheque culture was killing live music. But if anything, the real challenge to live performance on television came from music video.

The late 1970s and 1980s saw the video boom that has changed the face of music on television. By 1975 many artists had made promotional film clips for their single releases. Queen's "Bohemian Rhapsody," Rod Stewart's "Hot Legs," and several promotional clips by Swedish quartet Abba had helped their songs become hits in the Euro-American market. In 1975 Manhattan cable TV began showing video clips on a program titled *Nightclubbing.* Rock performers were experimenting with the visual form. New Wave group Devo released *The Men Who Make the Music* in 1979. This anthology was the first long-form video released in the United States. By 1979 *America's Top Ten* played video clips. The Boomtown Rats' "I Don't Like Mondays" was one of the first to make a mark, remembered for the accompanying visuals as much as for its sound recording. The more traditional chart show, *Solid Gold,* debuted in syndication in 1980 and combined a professional cast of dancers with lip-synched performances by various chart-topping pop artists.

The rise of music video is inextricably tied to the ascent of cable television. In 1980 the USA network debuted *Night Flight,* which ran both videos and old movies. The emphasis was on New Wave videos since at this time these artists were more innovative with the nascent form. Another cable network, Home Box Office (HBO), began simulcasting rock concerts, while Showtime and the Playboy channel allotted some time for music videos. Also in 1980, ex-Monkee and Liquid Paper tycoon Mike Nesmith's Pacific Arts Company packaged clips into a half-hour show called *Popclips,* which was sold to Warner Cable and shown on Nickelodeon. The Nashville Network (TNN) and Country Music Television Network, from 1983, also aired music videos. The former maintained some shows that fit the variety format of older country programming.

But during the 1980s and 1990s, the musical stage on television was defined by MTV. Owned by Warner-Amex, MTV began broadcasting in August 1981, prophetically with the Buggles hit, "Video Killed the Radio Star." Robert Pittman, vice president of programming, remarked, "We're now seeing the TV become a component of the stereo system. It's ridiculous to think that you have two forms of entertainment—your stereo and your TV—which have nothing to do with one another. What we're doing is marrying those two forms so that they can work together in unison. We're the first channel on cable to pioneer this." MTV provided a 24-hour service of videos introduced by quirky "veejays." It was a kind of radio for the eyes, mixing different kinds of musical genres in a continuous flow. Many of the early videos were by British "new pop" groups, such as Duran Duran, ABC, Culture Club, and the Human League, who formed what

critics called the "second British invasion;" these performers already had videos ready to air, unlike many U.S. bands, which accounted for MTV's early Anglophilia. By 1982 record companies confidently claimed that MTV increased sales of their top artists by 20 percent.

As MTV became available through cable providers through the country, the music it aired also changed, and programming began to reflect the tastes of a largely white national audience demographic. Heavy metal became the dominant music on the channel. Other cable networks incorporated some of the same strategies as MTV. In June 1983, NBC debuted *Friday Night Videos* in the old *Midnight Special* slot. WTBS began broadcasting the similar *Night Tracks* in June 1983, and Ted Turner launched the ultimately unsuccessful Cable Music Channel in 1984. MTV weathered an antitrust suit from the competing Discovery Network. In 1984 it signed exclusive deals with six major record labels for the broadcast of their artists' videos.

The first American Video Awards took place in 1984, testifying to the emergence of a new cultural form. Meanwhile, more traditional musical fare was on offer in NBC's *Fame,* which began in 1982 and was based on Alan Parker's 1980 film. The program was set in a school of performing arts in New York, with a multiracial cast of talented musicians and dancers who would energetically perform numbers in rehearsal, in class, and at school concerts. The show celebrated traditional showbiz values in a familiar format. It was essentially *The Partridge Family* with angst, Shirley Jones replaced by choreographer and teacher Debbie Allen as guiding hand and maternal motivator.

MTV's impact on network television and the place of music in television could be more directly seen in the NBC police/crime series *Miami Vice* (1984–87), which

Olivia Newton-John, "Let's Get Physical" video, circa 1981–82.
Courtesy of the Everett Collection

had the working title of *MTV Cops.* The show's creator, Michael Mann, later claimed that "the intention of *Miami Vice* was to achieve the organic interaction of music and content." Sometimes an entire episode would be written around a song, such as Glen Frey's "Smuggler's Blues." Frey and other rock musicians would often make cameo appearances as characters in the show. Record companies were obliging with copyrighted material after the success of the pilot and its use of Phil Collins's hit "In the Air Tonight" as the detective partnership of Crockett and Tubbs drove to a climactic shoot-out through the rain-sodden Miami streets.

The visual style of the show owed a great deal to MTV. Film and television narratives incorporated music with the camera angles, lighting, rapid cutting, and polished production values of music videos. Television advertising also became increasingly sensitive to music video aesthetics. In 1984 Michael Jackson appeared in a Pepsi-Cola commercial shot like a music video for one of his songs. Madonna's brief—and eventually banned—Pepsi commercial in 1989 used her song "Like a Prayer."

In the mid- and late 1980s, MTV became less idiosyncratic in its juxtapositions of different kinds of music, moving toward block programming and the development of shows that fit certain musical genres. MTV's programming began to look more like a traditional television schedule. In January 1985, parent company Warner-Amex introduced Video Hits 1 (VH1), whose programming aimed for the pocketbook of older baby boomers. VH1 began with a video of Marvin Gaye singing that old chestnut, "The Star Spangled Banner." In 1986 MTV also indicated its move toward a more traditional television strategy as it began showing old episodes of *The Monkees.*

These developments reflected the segmentation of marketing and targeting of very specific groups of consumers through different channels and shows. This also coincided with Warner-Amex selling its controlling interest in MTV Networks to Viacom International in August 1985. The change in leadership initially brought a more conservative music policy. With criticism of the representation of sex and violence in music videos, there was a brief move away from heavy metal as the central genre. However, the strength of metal in middle America led to its return shortly thereafter.

The biggest triumph of the mid-1980s for MTV and for the music industry in general was the broadcast of the Live Aid concerts in Philadelphia and London in July 1985. The event, designed to raise money for Ethiopian famine relief, proved popular music's sociopolitical value and, like the Beatles' worldwide broadcast of "All You Need Is Love," projected a global imaginary (and market) for popular music culture. In 1987 MTV started MTV-Europe, and the network's rapid movement into further areas of global market continued apace. Live Aid was followed by the 1988 worldwide transmission of an antiapartheid concert in London to celebrate the birthday of Nelson Mandela. However, in the United States, this mammoth rock spectacle did not meet the success of Live Aid, with charges that FOX had delayed the broadcast signal and censored "political" comments made during the event.

Since the early 1980s, critics charged MTV with racism because of its dearth of black music videos. In its early days, the network featured African-American VJ J.J. Johnson and later black British VJ "Downtown" Julie Brown. However, apart from some big names, such as Michael Jackson and Prince, few black acts were found on the video playlist. This changed somewhat in 1989 with the introduction of *Yo! MTV Raps,* a show hosted by hip-hop pioneer Fab Five Freddy. *Yo! MTV Raps* joined other specialist music programs, such as *Headbanger's Ball* (heavy metal) and *120 Minutes* ("alternative" rock), on the network's schedule. Also in 1989, MTV introduced *Remote Control,* a game show that tested viewers' knowledge of television trivia. In the 1990s, the breadth of shows on the network reveals that MTV is now concerned more with the integrated elements of contemporary youth popular culture presented in a more traditional televisual format than with music videos per se. A fashion show (*House of Style*), a *vérité*-style documentary cum soap opera (and harbinger of "reality TV") (*The Real World*), and even a dating game were staples of the network's programming. The *Choose or Lose* and *Rock the Vote* programs contributed to higher voter registration among young citizens during the 1992

Courtesy of the Everett Collection

Luciano Pavarotti in The Three Tenors.
Kraig Geiger/ Everett Collection

presidential election campaign. In all these television formats, music is important as an extra level of commentary (often ironic) on the visual and documentary/news material.

With the exception of *Total Request Live,* music videos are now largely relegated to MTV2 (which is carried by far fewer cable systems), while MTV continues to focus on "reality" series such as *The Osbournes* and game shows. MTV's sister channel, VH1, continues to feature videos, but when its ratings began to founder, VH1 began airing leering "specials," such as one focusing on pornography in rock music, as well as *Behind the Music,* which presented lurid tales of rock star excess in a suitably tabloid fashion. A more family-friendly approach to music was featured in a resurgence of amateur shows such as *American Idol,* whose contestants provided fodder for the star-making machinery as they sought to outdo each other with melismatic vocal contortions.

Though it looks increasingly like other television stations in its programming structure, MTV gives everything from fashion to politics to family crises a musical bent. In this respect, it has "musicalized" television to an unforeseeable extent. Its stylistic repercussions can be found in everything from news programming and station promos to religious broadcasting and drama series, such as *Ally McBeal.* MTV also blurred the distinction between music, programming, and advertising. Alongside such regional and transnational music television networks such as Channel [V], in the 1990s MTV has helped to develop "youth" markets in Europe, Latin America, and Asia for goods other than music. Arguments continue to rage as to whether such globalization under the wing of music television results in Americanization or "glocalization."

With media industries increasingly integrated through technology and business strategies, television music provides cross-marketing opportunities for a variety of sectors. This "convergence" has had aesthetic as well as industrial consequences. Video games are now an important part of music marketing, and feature film directors often gain their training in music video. The sounds of certain music genres, such as hip-hop and techno, incorporate a channel-surfing television aesthetic as they cite and directly sample television texts in a variety of ways. Television arguably now shapes popular music culture as much as the sound recordings themselves.

TOM MCCOURT AND NABEEL ZUBERI

See also American Bandstand; **Clark, Dick; Country Music Television; MTV; MuchMusic;** *Soul Train*

Further Reading

Goodwin, Andrew, *Dancing in the Distraction Factory: Music Television and Popular Culture,* Minneapolis: University of Minnesota Press, 1993

Malone, Bill, *Country Music U.S.A.,* Austin: University of Texas Press, 1985

Mundy, John, *Popular Music on Screen: From Hollywood Musical to Music Video,* Manchester, United Kingdom: Manchester University Press, 1999

Popular Music, 21, no. 3 (2002)

Redd, Lawrence, *Rock Is Rhythm and Blues: The Impact of Mass Media,* East Lansing: Michigan State University Press, 1974

Tosches, Nick, *Country: The Biggest Music in America,* New York: Dell, 1977

Ward, Ed, Geoffrey Stokes, and Ken Tucker, *Rock of Ages: The Rolling Stone History of Rock and Roll,* New York: Summit, 1986

Must-Carry Rules

U.S. Cable Regulation

Must-carry rules, which mandate that cable companies carry various local and public television stations within a cable provider's service area, have a long and dramatic history since their inception in 1972. Designed originally to ensure that local television stations did not lose market share with increased competition from cable networks competing for a limited number of cable channels, must-carry rules have, over time, been ruled unconstitutional and gone through numerous changes.

When first passed in 1972, the must-carry rules required that cable companies provide channels for all local broadcasters within a 60-mile (later changed to 50-mile) radius of the cable company's service area. In the mid-1980s, various cable companies, including superstation WTBS owner Turner Broadcasting, brought suit against the Federal Communications Commission (FCC), claiming that the rules were unconstitutional. In 1985 and 1987, the U.S. Court of Appeals found that must-carry rules did, indeed, violate the First Amendment. From then until 1992, stations were only required to carry public television signals and provide subscribers with an option for an A/B switch to allow access to local broadcast signals. This change bode particularly ill for small UHF (ultrahigh frequency) stations, whose cable carriers could replace them with stronger, more desirable superstations.

The 1992 Communications Act, while still requiring carriage of local commercial and public stations, allowed cable companies to drop redundant carriage of signals, where stations within the service area duplicated programming (e.g., two stations within a 50-mile radius carrying the same network or two college public broadcasting stations both carrying the Public Broadcasting Service [PBS]). More confusion resulted when, in October 1994, the FCC gave stations a choice of being carried under the must-carry rules or under a new regulation requiring cable companies to obtain retransmission consent before carrying a broadcast signal. The retransmission consent ruling gave desirable local stations increased power to negotiate the terms of carriage the cable company would provide, including channel preference.

Must-carry rules were still in effect on passage of the 1996 Telecommunications Act—and still being challenged by cable companies. None of the must-carry rules affects cable retransmission of FM radio signals.

MICHAEL B. KASSEL

See also **Cable Television: United States; Distant Signal; Federal Communications Commission**

Further Reading

Bittner, John R., *Law and Regulation of Electronic Media,* New York: Prentice Hall, 1994

Eastman, Susan Tyler, Sydney W. Head, and Lewis Klein, *Broadcast/Cable Programming Strategies and Practices,* Belmont, California: Wadsworth, 1981; 3rd edition, 1989

Hilliard, Robert L., and Michael C. Keith, *The Broadcast Century,* Boston: Focal, 1992

My Little Margie

U.S. Situation Comedy

The wacky women who dominated 1950s television comedy did not begin with Lucille Ball (Gracie Allen and Imogene Coca pre-dated her TV debut), but the phenomenal success of Ball in *I Love Lucy* surely inspired a grand assortment of imitations on the small screen. Soon after Lucy's TV debut, such programs as *I Married Joan* with Joan Davis, *Life with Elizabeth* with Betty White, and *My Friend Irma* with Marie

My Little Margie, Charles Farrell, Gale Storm, 1952–55.
Courtesy of the Everett Collection

Wilson premiered, all centered around the doings of various "wacky wives" with staid, even dull, husbands. Drawing on similar conventions was one of the most successful sitcoms of the 1950s, *My Little Margie.*

My Little Margie presented 21-year-old Margie Albright, who lived with her widowed father, Vernon, in a New York City penthouse. Mr. Albright worked as an executive for the investment counseling firm Honeywell and Todd and was perpetually in fear of losing "the big account" because of Margie's meddling. Rounding out the cast were Freddie, Margie's "boyfriend"; elderly neighbor Mrs. Odetts; Roberta Townsend, Vern's lady friend; George Honeywell, president of Honeywell and Todd; and Charlie, the black elevator operator (depicted as a sad African-American stereotype, typical of TV at that time).

The program starred Gale Storm (31 years old when she began in the role), a former film actress noted for her roles in westerns playing opposite Roy Rogers. Vernon was played by Charles Farrell, formerly a highly successful leading man in silent films. The program premiered in 1952 as a last-minute summer replacement for *I Love Lucy,* but it proved to be so popular, landing consistently in the top five, that it was renewed for fall and ran for three seasons.

The title *My Little Margie* can certainly be taken in such a way as to be demeaning to women: "my" indicating the possession of someone as if she were a thing, and "little," a somewhat inaccurate and condescending term for a 21-year-old woman. Nevertheless, it has been noted that the premise of *My Little Margie* was in other ways rather progressive. First, Margie was a single woman at a time when most women on television were conventionally married. Second, the Albrights were slightly different from the "normal" nuclear families then being depicted on TV. The widowed father and his daughter were frequently involved in stories designed around the two taking on and exploring roles not their own, duties and responsibilities that conventionally would have been handled by the now absent mother. Additionally, Margie, though "of marrying age," was seldom depicted as eager to walk down the aisle. Although she had a steady boyfriend in neighbor Freddie Wilson, few sparks ever flew between them. Margie was always too busy for her own romance, usually preoccupied with launching schemes to keep gold diggers away from her single dad. Margie's self-chosen single status and irrepressible individuality made her, in some respects, one of TV's prefeminism feminists. Week after week, despite what her father and other men around her wanted or expected her to do, Margie did her own thing, engaging in outrageous acts and everyday rebellions, as Gloria Steinem would later refer to them.

Yet despite the presence of such advanced notions, in practice *Margie* rarely chose to develop them. Produced by the Hal Roach Studios, the series had access to all the studio's haunted-house sets and breakaway props and frequently fell back on the Roach's stock and trade—slapstick. The program got most of its mileage from Storm's enchanting charm, her wardrobe (provided by Junior House of Milwaukee, almost always with a fetching, matching hat), and her frequently performed trademark "Margie gurgle," a rolling of the throat it seemed only Storm could produce.

My Little Margie had absolutely no critical support. From its premier, every newspaper dismissed the show as silly. Yet it had enough fan devotion to secure a highly rated run, making it one of the first shows to survive on audience support alone. Moreover, it was the only television program to reverse the usual media history and make the jump from the small screen to the audio airwaves; an original radio version (also starring Storm and Farrell) aired for two years. The TV series' popularity is also attested to by the fact that *Margie* was one of the most widely syndicated programs of the

1950s and 1960s. It even proved popular enough to air on Saturday mornings, perhaps acquainting a new and loyal audience of children with Margie's near-cartoonish antics.

CARY O'DELL

Cast

Margie Albright	Gale Storm
Vernon Albright	Charles Farrell
Roberta Townsend	Hillary Brooke
Freddie Wilson	Don Hayden
George Honeywell	Clarence Kolb
Mrs. Odetts	Gertrude Hoffman
Charlie	Willie Best

Producer

Hal Roach, Jr.

Programming History

126 episodes

CBS

| June 1952–September 1952 | Monday 9:00–9:30 |
| January 1953–July 1953 | Thursday 10:00–10:30 |

NBC

| October 1952–November 1952 | Saturday 7:30–8:00 |
| September 1953–August 1955 | Wednesday 8:30–9:00 |

Further Reading

Castleman, Harry, and Walter J. Podrazik, *Harry and Walter's Favorite Shows: A Fact-Filled Opinionated Guide to the Best and Worst on TV,* New York: Prentice Hall, 1989

Mitz, Rich, *The Great TV Sitcom Book,* New York: Perigee, 1983

Storm, Gale, *I Ain't Down Yet,* New York: Bobbs-Merrill, 1981

My Three Sons

U.S. Domestic Comedy

Created by Don Fedderson and *Leave It to Beaver* alumnus George Tibbles, *My Three Sons* was one of television's longest-running and most influential domestic comedies. The program was conceived originally as a television vehicle for Fred MacMurray (who owned 50 percent of the program) when Fedderson was approached by Chevrolet to develop a program that was "representative of America." During its 12-year run, the program averaged a respectable but not spectacular 22.2 rating and a 35 percent share and underwent enormous narrative and character changes. The show is most significant for its development of a star-friendly shooting schedule and for its redefinition of the composition of the television family.

Before he agreed to his contract, Fred MacMurray queried veteran television performer Robert Young about Young's workload. On Young's complaint about television's time-consuming schedule, MacMurray insisted on a unique shooting plan that was to be copied by other top actors and christened "the MacMurray method." This so-called writer's nightmare stipulated that all of MacMurray's scenes were to be shot in 65 nonconsecutive days. All other actors had to complete their fill-in shots while MacMurray was on vacation. Practically speaking, this meant that the series had to

stockpile at least half a season's scripts before the season ever began so that MacMurray's role could be shot during his limited workdays. The repercussions of this schedule were enormous. Guest stars often had to return nine months later to finish filming an episode, MacMurray's costars had their hair cut weekly so as to avoid any continuity discrepancies (MacMurray wore a toupee), and any unforeseen event (a sudden growth spurt or a guest star's death) could cause catastrophe. Oftentimes, the producers were forced to film Mac-Murray in scriptless episodes and then construct a script around his very generalized monologues. Frequently, to avoid complication, the writers simply placed his character "out of town," so that there are an inordinate number of episodes in which Steve Douglas communicates to his family only by telephone. Despite the hardship on writers, directors, and costars, the MacMurray method was adapted by a number of film stars (such as Jimmy Stewart and Henry Fonda) as a conditional requirement for their work in a television series.

The program's narrative concept has proven equally influential. Until 1960, most family comedies were centered on strictly nuclear groupings—mom, dad, and biological children. While an occasional program

My Three Sons, William Frawley, Fred MacMurray, Tim Considine, Don Grady, Stanley Livingston, 1960–72.
Courtesy of the Everett Collection

such as *Bachelor Father* or *The Bob Cummings Show* might focus on the comedic exploits of an unmarried adult raising a niece or nephew, most programs, from *I Love Lucy* to *Father Knows Best,* depicted the humorous tribulations of two-parent households and their biological offspring.

My Three Sons initiated what was to become a popular trend in television—that of the widowed parent raising a family. While initial director Peter Tewksbury called the premise a truly depressing one, producers Tibbles and Fedderson chose to ignore the potential for pathos and flung themselves wholeheartedly into the comedic consequences of a male-only household. Ironically (some might even say with more than a touch of misogyny), the bulk of the program's first five years did not focus on the stereotypical male ineptitude for all household chores but instead continually reinforced the notion that males were, in fact, far domestically superior to the "hysterical" female guest stars.

During the course of its 12-year run, *My Three Sons* functioned, in essence, as three successive programs with different casts, writers, and directors. For its first five seasons, the program was shot in black and white and aired on the American Broadcasting Company (ABC). These episodes focus on Steve Douglas (MacMurray), aerospace consultant, who, along with his father-in-law, Bub O'Casey (William Frawley), has struggled to raise Steve's three motherless sons: 18-year-old Mike, 14-year-old Robbie, and seven-year-old Chip. The show was directed and produced by *Father Knows Best* alumnus Peter Tewksbury. The first year of the program is by far the series' darkest, dealing explicitly with how a family survives and even thrives in the event of maternal loss. In its second season, George Tibbles took over, moving the program more toward situation comedy and inserting multiple slapstick-type episodes into the mix. From the third season onward, Ed Hartmann's role as producer redirected the program yet again, this time to a heavily moralistic but lighthearted look at generational and gender conflicts. In addition, Hartmann's longstanding friendship with members of the Asian community contributed to an unusual number of episodes dealing with the Chinese and Japanese friends of the Douglas family, granting television visibility and respect to a previously neglected minority group.

When ABC refused to finance the series' switch to color production, the program moved to the Columbia Broadcasting System (CBS), losing two cast members in an unrelated series of events. First, in the midst of the 1964–65 season, terminally ill William Frawley's $300,000 insurance policy was canceled, and Don Fedderson was forced to replace the character of Bub O'Casey with Uncle Charley, a role played by William

Demarest for the program's remaining seven years. Next, an argument with Don Fedderson over Tim Considine's desire to direct resulted in the actor's departure from the program. As eldest son Mike was written out of the series with a fictionalized "move to California," the producers chose a new third son, Ernie, as a replacement. With no regard for narrative plausibility, the producers created a three-part episode in which Chip's best friend Ernie loses his parents in a car crash, suddenly becomes two years younger, and is adopted by Steve as the youngest member of the Douglas family.

Two years later, the program experienced its third incarnation when the Douglas family moved from the fictional Bryant Park to southern California. Here, Robbie was to romance and wed Katie, and Steve was to end his long-term widowhood by marrying Barbara and adopting her small daughter. For the program's remaining years, the narrative focused on blended families, Chip's romantic escapades and eventual elopement, and Robbie's triplets, where the premise of three sons promised to continue indefinitely.

The series' influence was demonstrated by the quick succession of single-parent households that were to dominate television's comedy schedule for the next decade. *Family Affair, The Courtship of Eddie's Father, Flipper,* and *Nanny and the Professor* all featured eligible bachelors burdened with raising their own (or a relative's offspring) with the help of an adept elderly man or desirable young woman. All these series worked to erase the necessity of the maternal, as the family operated in an emotionally secure and supremely healthy environment without benefit of the long since dead mother. While there were occasional widow-with-children programs (*The Ghost and Mrs. Muir* and *Julia*), these women were not granted the same versatility of their male counterparts and were forced to turn to strong male figures (dead ship captains and doctors, respectively) for continual guidance.

While the 1980s witnessed a regeneration of television's nuclear family, the legacy of *My Three Sons* dominated, and for every *Cosby* there was a *Full House, My Two Dads,* or *Brothers.* By the 1990s, one would be hard pressed to find any family show that was not about a single-parent family, a family with adopted children, or a blended arrangement of two distinct families—all configurations that owe their genesis in some way to *My Three Sons.*

NINA C. LEIBMAN

See also **Family on Television**

Cast

Steve Douglas	Fred MacMurray
Mike Douglas (1960–65)	Tim Considine

Robbie Douglas (1960–71) Don Grady
Chip Douglas Stanley
 Livingston

Michael Francis
 "Bub" O'Casey (1960–65) William Frawley
Uncle Charley O'Casey
 (1965–72) William
 Demarest
Jean Pearson (1960–61) Cynthia Pepper
Mr. Henry Pearson (1960–61) Robert P. Lieb
Mrs. Florence Pearson (1960–61) Florence
 MacMichael
Hank Ferguson (1961–63) Peter Brooks
Sudsy Pfeiffer (1961–63) Ricky Allen
Mrs. Pfeiffer (1961–63) Olive Dunbar
Mr. Pfeiffer (1961–63) Olan Soule
Sally Ann Morrison Douglas
 (1963–65) Meredith
 MacRae
Ernie Thompson Douglas
 (1963–72) Barry Livingston
Katie Miller Douglas (1967–72) Tina Cole
Dave Welch (1965–67) John Howard
Dodie Harper Douglas (1969–72) Dawn Lyn
Barbara Harper Douglas
 (1969–72) Beverly Garland
Steve Douglas, Jr. (1970–72) Joseph Todd
Charley Douglas (1970–72) Michael Todd
Robbie Douglas II (1970–72) Daniel Todd
Fergus McBain Douglas
 (1971–72) Fred MacMurray
Terri Dowling (1971–72) Anne Francis
Polly Williams Douglas
 (1970–72) Ronne Troup

Producers
Don Fedderson, Edmund Hartmann, Fred Henry,
 George Tibbles

Programming History
369 episodes
ABC

September 1960–September 1963	Thursday 9:00–9:30	
September 1963–September 1965	Thursday 8:30–9:00	
CBS		
September 1965–August 1967	Thursday 8:30–9:00	
September 1967–September 1971	Saturday 8:30–9:00	
September 1971–December 1971	Monday 10:00–10:30	
January 1972–August 1972	Thursday 8:30–9:00	

Further Reading

Hamamoto, Darrell Y., *Nervous Laughter: Television Situation Comedy and Liberal Democratic Ideology,* New York: Praeger, 1989

Javna, John, *The Best of TV Sitcoms: Burns and Allen to The Cosby Show, The Munsters to Mary Tyler Moore,* New York: Harmony Books, 1988

Jones, Gerard, *Honey, I'm Home!: Sitcoms, Selling the American Dream,* New York: Grove Weidenfeld, 1992

Leibman, Nina C., *Living Room Lectures: The Fifties Family in Film and Television,* Austin: University of Texas Press, 1995

N

Naked City

U.S. Police Drama

Naked City, which had two incarnations between 1958 and 1963, was one of American television's most innovative police shows, and one of its most important and influential drama series. More character anthology than police procedural, the series blended the urban *policier* a la *Dragnet* with the urban pathos of the *Studio One* school of television drama, offering a mix of action-adventure and Actors' Studio, car chases and character studies, shoot-outs and sociology, all filmed with arresting starkness on the streets of New York.

The series was inspired by the 1948 "semidocumentary" feature *The Naked City* (which borrowed its title from the photographic collection by urban documentarist/crime photographer Weegee). Independent producer Herbert Leonard (*The Adventures of Rin-Tin-Tin, Tales of the 77th Bengal Lancers, Circus Boy*) developed the idea as a half-hour series for Screen Gems, hiring writer Stirling Silliphant for the pilot script. Leonard outlined his plan for the series to *Variety* in 1958 as an attempt to tell anthology-style stories within the framework of a continuing-character show. It was to be "a human interest series about New York," the producer declared, "told through the eyes of two law enforcement officers." Leonard's agenda for the series' setting was equally unique: it would be shot completely on location in New York, duplicating the trendsetting realism of its feature-film progenitor. This was an ambitious, if not radical, move at that moment in television history, for although New York still re-

tained a significant presence as the site of variety shows, a few live anthologies, and the quiz programs, no other telefilm dramas were being produced there at the time.

Naked City's first season on ABC presented 39 taut, noirish half-hours (31 scripted by Silliphant) that mixed character drama, suspense, and action. The characters for the series' two regular detectives were carried over from the feature film: Lt. Dan Muldoon (John McIntire), the seasoned veteran, and his idealistic young subordinate, Detective Jim Halloran (James Franciscus). When creative differences arose between McIntire and Leonard at midseason, Muldoon was written out of the series via a fiery car crash and replaced as the 65th Precinct's father-figure by crusty Lt. Mike Parker (Horace MacMahon). The show's signature was its narrator, who introduced each episode with the assurance that the series was not filmed in a studio, but "in the streets and buildings of New York itself," and returned 30 minutes later to intone the series' famous tag-line (also borrowed from the feature): "There are 8 million stories in the Naked City. This has been one of them."

Despite an Emmy nomination for Best Drama, *Naked City*'s downbeat dramatics did not generate adequate ratings, and it was canceled. Unlike other failed shows, however, *Naked City* was not forgotten. In the fall of 1959, one of the show's former sponsors urged producer Leonard to mount *Naked City* for the follow-

Naked City, Horace McMahon, Paul Burke, Harry Bellaver, 1958–63.
Courtesy of the Everett Collection

ing season in hour-long form. The sponsor's interest led ABC to finance the pilot, and in fall 1960 Leonard was at the helm of two hour-long prime-time drama series (the other being *Route 66* at CBS).

New York itself remained the show's most distinctive star, and extensive location shooting remained its trademark. Horace MacMahon returned as Lt. Parker, but with a different compassionate young colleague, Detective Adam Flint (Paul Burke), who was partnered with good-natured Sgt. Frank Arcaro (Harry Bellaver) and engaged to aspiring actress Libby Kingston (Nancy Malone). Silliphant wrote the pilot and stayed on as executive story consultant, but he wrote fewer scripts due to his heavy involvement with *Route 66.* Leonard brought in anthology veteran Howard Rodman as story editor and frequent scriptwriter and was able to attract other writers with a penchant for social drama, including anthology alumni such as Ernest Kinoy and Mel Goldberg, Hollywood blacklistees such as Arnold Manoff (writing as "Joel Carpenter"), Ben Maddow, and Abram Ginnes—and such budding TV auteurs as Gene Roddenberry.

With a company of serious writers and more time for story and character development, *Naked City*'s anthology flavor became even more pronounced. Stories became more character-driven, with a more central focus on transient characters (that is, "guest stars"), and more extended psychological exploration. This dimension of the show was informed by a distinctive roster of guest stars, from well-known Hollywood performers such as Claude Rains and Lee J. Cobb, and character players like Eli Wallach, Maureen Stapleton, and Walter Matthau, to such up-and-coming talents as Diahann Carroll and Dustin Hoffman. A 1962 *Time* profile called the series' array of stars "the best evidence that *Naked City* is not just another cop show." Its stories provided even stronger evidence. *Naked City*'s structure placed less emphasis on investigation and police work than did police-procedurals in the *Dragnet* mold—and less emphasis on the detectives themselves. As Todd Gitlin has put it, on *Naked City* "the regular cops faded into the background while the foreground belonged to each week's new character in the grip of the city."

With its stories generally emphasizing the points-of-view of the criminals, victims, or persons-in-crisis, *Naked City* exhibited a more complicated and ambiguous vision of morality and justice than traditional *policiers,* where good and bad were clear-cut. Most of the characters encountered by Flint and Arcaro were simply people with problems, who stumbled up against the law by accident or ill fortune; when the occasional hit man, bank robber, or jewel thief was encountered, they too were humanized, their motives and psyches probed. However, sociopaths and career crooks were far outnumbered by more mundane denizens of the naked city, thrust into crisis by circumstance: an innocent ex-con accused of murder; a disfigured youth living in the shadows of the tenements; a Puerto Rican immigrant worn down by poverty and unemployment; a lonely city bureaucrat overcome by suicidal despair; a junior executive who kills over a parking space; a sightless boy on an odyssey through the streets of Manhattan. Eight million stories—or at least 138 as dramatized in this series—rooted in the sociology and psychology of human pain.

Naked City revised the traditional cop-show commitment to crime and punishment. Unlike their primetime counterparts Joe Friday and Eliot Ness, Detectives Flint and Arcaro did not toil in the grim pursuit of "facts" with which to solve cases and incarcerate criminals. Rather, they pondered human puzzles, bore witness to suffering, and meditated on the absurdities of urban existence. With compassion more typical of TV doctors than TV detectives, they brought justice to the innocent, helped lost souls fit back into society, and agonized over broken lives they could not fix. Indeed, as critic David Boroff put it in an essay on "TV's Problem Play," the detectives of *Naked City* were "as much social workers as cops."

Whereas every episode of *Dragnet* ended with the record of a trial (and usually a conviction), *Naked City* was seldom able to resolve its stories quite so easily.

The series offered narrative closure, but no easy answers; it did not pretend to solve social problems, nor did it mute, defuse, or mask them. Although some episodes ended with guarded hope, straightforward happy endings were rare; resolutions were just as likely to be framed in melancholy bemusement or utter despair. *Naked City*'s "solution" was to admit that there are no solutions—at least none that could be articulated in the context of its own dramatic agenda. "One of its strengths," wrote Boroff in 1966, "was that it said nothing which is neatly paraphraseable. It was, in truth, Chekhovian in its rueful gaze at people in the clutch of disaster. *Naked City* was, in essence, a compassionate—not a savage—eye. 'This I have seen,' it said."

Naked City was one of ABC's most prestigious shows during the early 1960s, nominated for the "Outstanding Achievement in Drama" Emmy award every season it was on the air, and winning several Emmys for editing and cinematography. The series was canceled at the end of the 1962–63 season, but its influence was already clear. In its day, it paved the way for the serious, urban dramas that followed, such as *The Defenders,* and *East Side, West Side,* and it sparked a modest renaissance in New York telefilm production in the early 1960s. At a larger level, it experimented with the formal definition of the series, demonstrated that complex drama could be done within the series format, and expanded the aesthetic horizons of the police show. Echoing Weegee's photographic studies, which captured the faces of New York in the glare of a camera flash, television's *Naked City* offered narrative portraits, exposed through the equally revealing light of the writer's imagination. Ultimately, both versions of *Naked City* are less about society or a city than *people,* which is why the portraits are often disturbing, and always fascinating.

MARK ALVEY

See also **Leonard, Herbert; Police Programs; Silliphant, Sterling**

Cast

Detective Lieutenant Dan Muldoon (1958–59)	John McIntire
Detective Lieutenant Jim Halloran (1958–59)	James Franciscus
Janet Halloran (1958–59)	Suzanne Storrs
Patrolman/Sergeant Frank Arcaro	Harry Bellaver
Lieutenant Mike Parker (1959–63)	Horace McMahon
Detective Adam Flint (1960–63)	Paul Burke
Libby (1960–63)	Nancy Malone

Producers

Herbert B. Leonard, Charles Russell

Programming History

138 episodes
ABC

September 1958–September 1959	Tuesday 9:30–10:00
October 1960–September 1963	Wednesday 10:00–11:00

Further Reading

Boroff, David, "Television and the Problem Play," in *TV as Art,* edited by Patrick D. Hazard, Champaign, Illinois: National Council of Teachers of English, 1966

"Case History of a TV Producer," *Variety* (October 14, 1959)

"The City in the Raw," *Newsweek* (December 5, 1960)

Collins, Max Alan, and John Javna, *The Best of Crime and Detective TV,* New York: Harmony, 1988

Gehman, Richard, "Crime and Punishment on the Sidewalks of New York" (part 1), *TV Guide* (June 3, 1961)

Gehman, Richard, "Crime and Punishment on the Sidewalks of New York" (part 2), *TV Guide* (June 10, 1961)

Gelman, Morris J., "New York, New York," *Television* (December 1962)

Gitlin, Todd, *Inside Prime Time,* New York: Pantheon, 1985; revised edition, 1994

"Have Camera, Will Travel," *Variety* (October 12, 1960)

Johnson, B., "Naked City," *TV Guide* (May 16, 1959)

Marc, David, "Eight Million Stories (Give or Take a Mil)," *The Village Voice* (October 15, 1985)

Museum of Broadcasting, *Columbia Pictures Television: The Studio and the Creative Process,* New York: Museum of Broadcasting, 1987 (exhibition catalog)

"*Naked City* Gets New ABC-TV Lease, This Time as a Full-Hour Entry," *Variety* (October 28, 1959)

"*Naked City* More Like a Naked Nightmare (Now It Can Be Told)," *Variety* (June 12, 1963)

"Naked Truth," *Newsweek* (March 4, 1963)

"On the Streets," *Time* (September 7, 1962)

Rosen, George, "Heavy N.Y. Shooting Schedule," *Variety* (March 9, 1960)

Rowan, Arthur, "We Travel Light and We Travel Fast," *American Cinematographer* (August 1959)

"We Can Make 'Em Just as Cheap or Cheaper in N.Y.: Herb Leonard," *Variety* (February 26, 1958)

Naked Civil Servant, The

British Drama

The Naked Civil Servant, adapted from the autobiography of the same title, was a British television biopic of the life and times of the English homosexual Quentin Crisp. Transmitted for the first time on December 17, 1975, it broke new ground in its candid and defiant depiction of homosexuality on British television and shot Crisp himself to overnight notoriety and celebrity. Not merely of interest for its positive treatment of what was then a controversial subject, *The Naked Civil Servant* was compelling television, funny, warm, and moving, and earned John Hurt, as Crisp, a much deserved BAFTA award for Best Actor.

Central to *The Naked Civil Servant*'s critical success and enduring popular (though perhaps cult) appeal is the irreverent wit, flamboyant charm, and tough-minded individualism of Crisp himself. Born Dennis Pratt on Christmas Day 1908 to very ordinary, middle-class parents living in a suburb of London, Crisp went on to cut a larger-than-life figure who openly flouted society's rules in his everyday behavior and demeanor. In hair dyed with henna, and in lipstick and mascara, he risked assault on the streets of London daily to openly flaunt his effeminacy. At times he experienced violence, and though taken before the courts for soliciting, he was never convicted.

Associating with London's more Bohemian set, he passed from job to job, including designing book covers and teaching tap-dancing (even though he was still learning himself). He was also a prostitute for six months, but claimed he did this because he was looking for love rather than for the money. Exempted from military service during World War II due to his homosexuality, he took a job at an art-school as a nude model, becoming a "naked civil servant."

As a model he could simply be himself, and it was being himself that characterized both his homosexuality and his life more generally. He never openly campaigned for gay rights, and was later to be much criticized by activists for his individualistic stance, as well as for perpetuating a homosexual stereotype of campness, rather than showing solidarity with a wider gay movement. In his own view, he just wanted to be accepted for the individual that he was.

His defiance in the face of establishment and social prejudice was marked by mock incredulity, gritty passiveness, and perhaps even pacifism. As an individual,

raconteur, aphorist, and wit, and with nobleness and gentility of manner, Crisp was the quintessential eccentric English gentleman. As such, he lived in a room in London's Chelsea which had, notoriously, never been cleaned. In the autobiography he was commissioned to write in 1968 he stated that "after the first four years the dirt doesn't get any worse."

After the book's publication and modest sales, Crisp attracted some attention and held a one-man stage-show. Around the same time, the dramatist Philip Mackie began to try unsuccessfully to interest producers in making a film based on Crisp's book; he would continue to be unsuccessful for four years. Also turned down by the British Broadcasting Corporation (BBC), the project was finally given the go-ahead by Thames Television, one of the franchised program companies that made up part of the Independent Television (ITV) Network in Britain.

Under the direction of Jack Gold, with Mackie's screenplay, the television production of *The Naked Civil Servant* took an idiosyncratic approach to its unconventional subject matter. Despite the gloom of Edwardian England into which Crisp was born and the austerity of the post-war years, and despite the perpetual menace of violence, the tone of the production is upbeat. Boasting a jaunty score by Carl Davis, and interspersed with ironic intertitles, the episodic narrative is propelled by an all-knowing and wry voice-over by John Hurt playing Crisp. In one memorable scene, a gang of working-class "roughs" run amok after a young Crisp calls their leader a closet "queer" to his face. The subsequent intertitle and epiphanic voice-over notes in mock surprise: "Some roughs are really queer, and some queers are really rough."

Yet despite the humor, the episodic quality of the narrative also provides it with a degree of pathos. Time passes in great leaps, but Crisp remains central in his staunch yet lonely defiance against life's vicissitudes. It is this quality that seems to give Crisp's quest for self-determination a heroic edge. Although cautioned in some quarters against the dangers of playing a gay role—still considered risky to a career at that time—John Hurt, a leading British actor, stated that it was the sense that Crisp was a hero that helped him decide to take the role.

Interestingly, it may have been a combination of humor, individualism and heroism that made *The Naked Civil Servant,* and its potentially controversial subject matter, more palatable to a mainstream television audience. The Independent Broadcasting Authority—at that time Britain's commercial television industry regulator, which awarded television franchises—was so concerned about a possible public backlash against the program that it commissioned a special survey among a representative sample of the national audience on the morning after its first transmission. Ratings indicated that *The Naked Civil Servant* was viewed in about 3.5 million homes, and from its survey sample surmised that 85 percent of the audience did not find the material shocking, while almost half felt they understood and sympathized with Crisp's difficulties.

What viewers may have responded to positively is perhaps not the program's depiction of homosexuality per se. It is an often-cited cliché that the British always like to support the "underdog." In this sense, viewer empathy might lie with Crisp both as an entertaining English eccentric, on the one hand, and on the other, as an "everyman" figure who faces up to life's trials and tribulations with a certain British stoicism, "stiff-upper-lip" determination, and a self-deprecating sense of humor.

Crisp introduced the first transmission of *The Naked Civil Servant* in person, and was subsequently propelled further into the limelight in Britain and abroad; he was essentially famous for being infamous. He moved to New York in 1980 and wrote various books and articles, and appeared in numerous television programs and documentaries. Crisp died on November 21, 1999, on the eve of a sold-out British tour of his one-man show, and he was remembered with much affection in obituaries.

ROB TURNOCK

Cast (selected)

Quentin Crisp	John Hurt
Art student	Patricia Hodge
Mr. Pole	Stanley Lebor
Thumbnails	Colin Higgins

Producer
Barry Hanson

Programming History

ITV	December 17, 1975
Channel 4	September 11, 1986
ITV	August 3, 1989
BBC2	November 16, 1991

Further Reading

"Audience Reactions to *The Naked Civil Servant,*" *Independent Broadcasting* 8 (June 1976)

Crisp, Quentin, *The Naked Civil Servant,* London: Jonathan Cape, 1968

Howes, Keith, *Broadcasting It: An Encyclopedia of Homosexuality on Film, Radio and Television in the UK,* London: Cassell, 1993

Waugh, Thomas, "Films by Gays for Gays," *Jump Cut* 16 (November 1977)

Name of the Game, The

U.S. Adventure/Mystery Series

The Name of the Game occupies a unique place in the history of prime-time television in the United States. Notable for the ambitious scope and social relevance of its stories, and for its innovative 90-minute anthology format, the series was perhaps most influential in its lavish production values, which aimed to recreate the audiovisual complexity of the movies. In 1969, *TV Guide* reported that the show's budget of $400,000 per episode made *The Name of the Game* the most expensive television program in history. The series also functioned as a kind of apprentice field for writers and directors who later achieved great success, including Steven Bochco, Marvin Chomsky, Leo Penn, and Steven Spielberg.

The two-hour pilot film for the series, *Fame Is the Name of the Game,* was broadcast in 1966 as the first *World Premiere Movie,* a weekly series of made-for-television films produced by Universal Studios for NBC. The series itself, which premiered in 1968, retained the fluid, quick-cutting visual texture of the pilot and added a pulsating jazz theme by Dave Grusin. Tony Franciosa, star of the pilot film, returned to the series as Jeff Dillon, ace reporter for *People Magazine,* in a rotation every third week with Gene Barry and

The Name of the Game, 1968–71, Gene Barry, Robert Stack,
Anthony Franciosa.
Courtesy of the Everett Collection

Robert Stack. Barry played a Henry Luce-type media
mogul, Glenn Howard, chief executive officer of
Howard Publications, while Stack—in a role intended
to recall his performance as Eliot Ness, the crime-
fighting hero of *The Untouchables*—played Dan Farrell, a retired FBI agent, now a writer and editor for
Crime Magazine. Providing continuity, Susan St.
James appeared in every episode as Peggy Maxwell,
who remained a research assistant and aide-de-camp to
the male stars through the run of the series despite her
Ph.D. in archaeology and her knowledge of five languages.

Because each episode was essentially a self-
contained film, the series offered a rich venue for performers and served as something of a refuge for movie
actors drawn to television by the breakdown of the
Hollywood studios and the disappearance of the B-
movie. Movie actors who appeared in the series included Dana Andrews, Anne Baxter, Charles Boyer,
Joseph Cotten, Broderick Crawford, Yvonne DeCarlo,
Jose Ferrer, Farley Granger, John Ireland, Van Johnson, Janet Leigh, Ida Lupino, Kevin McCarthy, Ray

Milland, Gene Raymond, Mickey Rooney, and Barry
Sullivan.

One of the first television programs to deal directly
with the increasing social and political turbulence of
the late 1960s, *The Name of the Game* regularly confronted such topics as the counterculture, racial conflict, the sexual revolution, political corruption, and
environmental pollution. Its ideology was a muddled if
revealing strain of Hollywood liberalism, and its rotating heroes, especially Gene Barry's elegant corporate
aristocrat, were enlightened professionals who used
the power of their media conglomerate to right injustice and defend the powerless. If many episodes ended
on a reformist note of muted affirmation for an America shown to be flawed but resilient and ultimately fix-
able, individual scenes and performances often
dramatized social evils, injustice, and moral and political corruption with a vividness and truthfulness rare in
television during this period.

As it continued, the series became more imaginative
and unpredictable, experimenting at times with unusual
and challenging formats. "Little Bear Died Running"
(first broadcast November 6, 1970), written by Edward
J. Lakso, uses a complex strategy of multiple flashbacks
to reconstruct the murder of a Native American by a "legal" posse, in the process powerfully exposing the racist
attitudes of an apparently enlightened white culture.
"Appointment in Palermo" (February 26, 1971), directed by Ben Gazzara, is a zany, affectionate parody of
the godfather genre, its comedy notably sharpened by a
clever use of actors familiar to us from straight gangster
films: Gabriel Dell, Harry Guardino, John Marley and
Joe De Santis. In "Los Angeles 2017" (January 15,
1971), Glenn Howard falls into a nightmare of ecological disaster, in which a vestigial American population
survives beneath the polluted surface of the Earth in
USA, Inc., a regimented society run by a corporate elite.
This notable episode was directed by Steven Spielberg
from a thoughtful screenplay by Philip Wylie.

Even in its less imaginative and intellectually ambitious episodes, *The Name of the Game* held to consistently high standards of production and acting. Both in
its formal excellence and in the intermittent but genuine seriousness of its subject matter, the show brought
a new maturity to U.S. television and deserves recognition as an enabling precursor of the strongest prime-
time programming of the 1970s and 1980s.

DAVID THORBURN

See also **Detective Programs; Movies on Television**

Cast

Glenn Howard	Gene Barry
Dan Farrell	Robert Stack

Jeff Dillon	Tony Franciosa
Peggy Maxwell	Susan St. James
Joe Sample	Ben Murphy
Andy Hill	Cliff Potter
Ross Craig	Mark Miller

Producers

Richard Irving, Richard Levinson, William Link, Leslie Stevens, George Eckstein, Dean Hargrove

Programming History

NBC

September 1968–September 1971   Friday 8:30–10:00

Further Reading

Gianakos, Larry James, *Television Drama Series Programming: A Comprehensive Chronicle, 1959–1975,* Metuchen, New Jersey: Scarecrow, 1978

Perry, Jeb H., *Universal Television: The Studio and Its Programs, 1950–1980,* Metuchen, New Jersey: Scarecrow, 1983

Narrowcasting

In the earlier days of American television, the three major networks (NBC, CBS, and ABC) dominated programming, and each sought to obtain the widest audience possible. They avoided programming content that might appeal only to a small segment of the mass population and succeeded in their goal by between them reaching nearly 90 percent of the television-viewing audience on a regular basis.

The networks maintained their stronghold until competition emerged through the addition of many independent stations, the proliferation of cable channels, and the popularity of videocassettes. These competitors provided television audiences with many more viewing options. Consequently, the large numbers previously achieved through mass-oriented programming dwindled, and "narrowcasting" took hold.

With narrowcasting the programmer or producer assumes that only a limited number of people or a specific demographic group will be interested in the subject matter of a program. In many ways, this is the essence of cable television's programming strategy. Following the format or characteristics of specialized magazines, a cable television program or channel may emphasize one subject or a few closely related subjects. For example, among U.S. cable channels, popular music television is presented on MTV (Music Television), VH1 (Video Hits One), and TNN (The Nashville Network); CNN (Cable News Network) offers 24-hour news coverage; ESPN (Entertainment Sports Network) boasts an all-sports format; and C-SPAN covers the U.S. Congress. Other cable channels feature programming such as shopping, comedy, science-fiction, or programs aimed at specific ethnic or gender groups highly prized by specific advertisers.

For the most part, the major networks continue to gear their programming to the general mass audience. But increasingly, they, too, are engaged in forms of narrowcasting by segmenting similar programs that appeal to specific groups into adjacent time slots. For example, a network might target young viewers by programming back-to-back futuristic space programs on one night, while on a different night, feature an ensemble of programs oriented toward ethnic minorities. This strategy allows the networks to reach the overall mass audience cumulatively rather than simultaneously.

In the United States, then, narrowcasting is driven by economic necessity and competition. In public service systems around the world, where broadcasting is supported by license fee, by tax, or by direct government support, there has never been the same need for each program to reach the largest possible audience. As a consequence, programming for special groups—e.g. children, the elderly, ethnic or religious groups—has been standard practice. Ironically, the same technologies that bring competition to commercial broadcasters in the United States cause similar difficulties for public service broadcasters. In those systems new, commercially supported programming delivered by satellite and cable often draws audiences away from public-service offerings. Government officials and elected officers become reluctant to provide scarce public funds to broadcasters whose audiences are becoming smaller, forcing public service programmers to reach for larger audiences with different types of program content. While multiple program sources—cable, home video—make it unlikely that these systems will move toward "mass audience programming" on the U.S. model, it is the case that the face of broadcasting is changing in these contexts.

KIMBERLY B. MASSEY

See also **Cable Networks; Demographics; Markets; Mass Communication**

Further Reading

Naficy, Hamid, "Narrowcasting and Nationality: Middle Eastern Television in Los Angeles," *Afterimage* (February 1993)

Reitman, Judith, "Narrowcasting Opens Up: Cable is Expanding its Programming to Win Bigger Numbers in the Ratings Game," *Marketing and Media Decisions* (February 1986)

Vane, Edwin T., and Lynn S. Gross, *Programming for TV, Radio, and Cable,* Boston: Focal Press, 1994

Waterman, David, "'Narrowcasting' and 'Broadcasting' on Nonbroadcast Media: A Program Choice Model," *Communication Research* (February 1993)

Nash, Knowlton (1927–)

Canadian Broadcast Journalist

One of the most recognizable personalities in Canadian television, Knowlton Nash inhabits a truly unique space in news and public affairs broadcasting. Nash began his career in journalism at an early age, working in the late 1940s as a copy editor for the wire service British United Press. In three short years, Nash worked in Toronto, Halifax, and later Vancouver, where he assumed the position of writer and bureau chief for the wire service. Soon thereafter, Nash and his young family moved to Washington, D.C. where, after a few years working for the International Federation of Agricultural Producers, he began writing regular copy for the *Windsor Star, Financial Post,* and *Vancouver Sun.*

By 1958 Nash had become a regular correspondent for the Washington bureau of the Canadian Broadcasting Corporation (CBC), where in years to come he would interview key heads of state, including a succession of U.S. presidents. For Canadians, Nash became a familiar face abroad during the heady days of the Cuban missile crisis, the war in Vietnam, and the assassinations of John and Robert Kennedy. Nash's international reports in many respects symbolized the growth and reach of the CBC's news departments around the globe.

In the early 1970s Nash accepted an appointment by the CBC to be head of news and information programming. For many Canadians, Nash is best recognized and most respected for his work as anchor for the CBC's evening news program *The National.* In 1978 Nash played a pivotal role in transforming *The National* into a ratings success for Canada's public broadcaster. Four years later, Nash and *The National* solidified its place in the nation's daily routine when—against all traditions—it moved to the 10:00 P.M. time slot and added an additional half-hour news analysis segment entitled *The Journal.*

In April 1988, after ten years as anchor, Nash retired from *The National.* Benefiting from his unmatched wealth of experience in Canadian television journalism, Nash has taken on a number of projects since his so-called retirement. He has periodically anchored the Friday and Saturday broadcasts of *The National,* as well as the Sunday evening news program *Sunday Report.* Furthermore, Nash anchors both the CBC educational series *News in Review* and the highly acclaimed weekly documentary series *Witness.* On top of his duties in the field of electronic broadcasting and journalism, Nash has written a number of books, some quite controversial, on the history of both private and public-sector broadcasting in Canada.

GREG ELMER

See also **Canadian Programming in English; *National, The/The Journal***

Knowlton Nash. Born in Toronto, Ontario, November 18, 1927. Educated at University of Toronto. Married: 1) Sylvia (died, 1980); 2) Lorraine Thomson, 1982; child: Anne. Began career as newspaper reporter for *Globe and Mail,* Toronto, until 1947; manager, news bureaus for British United Press News Service, 1947–51; worked for International Federation of Agricultural Producers, Washington, D.C., director of information and representative at United Nations, 1951–61; freelance journalist, 1961–64; correspondent, CBC, Washington, D.C., 1964–68; director of information programming, CBC Radio and Television, Toronto, and director of television news and current affairs, 1968–78; chief correspondent and anchor, *The National,* 1978–88; senior correspondent and anchor, *News in Review,* since 1988; host, *Witness,* since 1992. Recipient: Order of Canada, 1988; John Drainie Award, 1995.

Knowlton Nash.
Photo courtesy of Knowlton Nash

Television Series

1960–64   *Inquiry* (expert on American views)
1966–67   *This Week* (host)
1976–78   *CTV National News*
1978–88   *The National* (newsreader)
1988–   *News in Review*
1992–   *Witness*

Publications

History on the Run: The Trenchcoat Memoirs of a Foreign Correspondent, 1984
Times to Remember, 1986
Prime Time at Ten: Behind the Camera Battles of Canadian TV Journalism, 1987
Kennedy and Diefenbaker: Fear and Loathing across the Undefended Border, 1990
Visions of Canada, 1991
Knowlton Nash's The Microphone Wars, 1994
Cue the Elephant!: Backstage Tales at the CBC, 1997
Trivia Pursuit: How Show Business Values are Corrupting the News, 1999
The Swashbucklers: The Story of Canada's Battling Broadcasters, 2001

Further Reading

"Nash Tells All in *Knowlton Nash's The Microphone Wars,*" *Calgary Herald* (November 24, 1994)
"Nash to Get Media Prize: John Drainie Award," *Vancouver Sun* (February 10, 1995)

Nat "King" Cole Show, The

U.S. Musical Variety

The Nat "King" Cole Show premiered on NBC as a 15-minute weekly musical variety show in November 1956. Cole, an international star as a jazz pianist and uniquely gifted vocalist, became the first major black performer to host a network variety series. It was a bruising experience for him, however, and an episode in television history that illuminates the state of race relations in the United States at the dawn of the modern civil rights movement.

Cole's first hit record, "Straighten Up and Fly Right," was recorded with his Nat "King" Cole Trio in

1944. By the mid-1950s he was a solo act—a top nightclub performer with several million-selling records, including "Nature Boy," "Mona Lisa," and "Too Young." A frequent guest on variety programs such as those hosted by Perry Como, Milton Berle, Ed Sullivan, Dinah Shore, Jackie Gleason, and Red Skelton, Cole was in the mainstream of American show business. His performances delighted audiences, and he seemed to be a natural for his own TV show, which he very much wanted.

Although he had experienced virulent racism in his

The Nat "King" Cole Show.
Courtesy of the Everett Collection

life and career, Cole was reluctant to take on the role of a crusader. He was criticized by some for regularly performing in segregated-audience venues in the South, for instance. His bid for a TV show, however, brought with it a sense of mission. "It could be a turning point," he realized, "so that Negroes may be featured regularly on television." Yet, Cole understood, "If I try to make a big thing out of being the first and stir up a lot of talk, it might work adversely."

Cole originally signed a contract with CBS in 1956, but the promise of his own program never materialized on that network. Later in the year, NBC reached an agreement with Cole's manager and agency, which packaged *The Nat "King" Cole Show.* The first broadcast, on November 5, 1956, aired without commercial sponsorship. NBC agreed to foot the bill for the program with the hope that advertisers would soon be attracted to the series. Cole felt confident a national sponsor would emerge, but his optimism was misplaced.

Advertising agencies were unable to convince national clients to buy time on *The Nat "King" Cole Show.* Advertisers were fearful that white Southern audiences would boycott their products. A representative of Max Factor cosmetics, a logical sponsor for the pro-gram, claimed that a "Negro" couldn't sell lipstick for them. Cole was angered by the comment. "What do they think we use?" he asked. "Chalk? Congo paint?" "And what about a corporation like the telephone company?" Cole wondered. "A man sees a Negro on a television show. What's he going to do—call up the telephone company and tell them to take out the phone?" Occasionally, the show was purchased by Arrid deodorant and Rise shaving cream, but it was most often sustained by NBC without sponsorship.

Despite the musical excellence of the program, which featured orchestra leader Nelson Riddle when the show was broadcast from Hollywood and Gordon Jenkins on weeks it originated from New York, *The Nat "King" Cole Show* suffered from anemic Nielsen ratings. Nonetheless, NBC decided to experiment. The network revamped the show in the summer of 1957 by expanding it to 30 minutes and increasing the production budget. Cole's many friends and admirers in the music industry joined him in a determined effort to keep the series alive. Performers who could command enormous fees—including Ella Fitzgerald, Peggy Lee, Mel Torme, Pearl Bailey, Mahalia Jackson, Sammy Davis, Jr., Tony Bennett, and Harry Belafonte—appeared on *The Nat "King" Cole Show* for the minimum wage allowed by the union.

Ratings improved, but still no sponsors were interested in a permanent relationship with the series. Some advertisers purchased airtime in particular markets. For instance, in San Francisco, Italian Swiss Colony wine was an underwriter. In New York the sponsor was Rheingold beer; in Los Angeles, Gallo wine and Colgate toothpaste; and in Houston, Coca-Cola.

This arrangement, however, was not as lucrative to the network as single national sponsorship. So, when the Singer Sewing Machine Company wanted to underwrite an adult western called *The Californians,* NBC turned over the time slot held by *The Nat "King" Cole Show.* The network offered to move Cole's program to a less-expensive and less-desirable place in the schedule, Saturdays at 7:00 P.M., but Cole declined the downgrade.

In the inevitable postmortem on the show, Cole praised NBC for its efforts. "The network supported this show from the beginning," he said. "From Mr. Sarnoff on down, they tried to sell it to agencies. They could have dropped it after the first 13 weeks." The star placed the blame squarely on the advertising industry. "Madison Avenue," Cole said, "is afraid of the dark."

In an *Ebony* magazine article entitled "Why I Quit My TV Show," Cole expressed his frustration:

For 13 months I was the Jackie Robinson of television. I was the pioneer, the test case, the Negro first . . . . On my show rode the hopes and tears and dreams of millions of people.... Once a week for 64 consecutive weeks I went to bat for these people. I sacrificed and drove myself. I plowed part of my salary back into the show. I turned down $500,000 in dates in order to be on the scene. I did everything I could to make the show a success. And what happened? After a trailblazing year that shattered all the old bugaboos about Negroes on TV, I found myself standing there with the bat on my shoulder. The men who dictate what Americans see and hear didn't want to play ball.

Singer and actress Eartha Kitt, one of the program's guest stars, reflected many years later on the puzzling lack of success of *The Nat "King" Cole Show*. "At that time I think it was dangerous," she said, referring to Cole's sophisticated image in an era when the only blacks appearing on television regularly were those on *Amos 'n' Andy* and *Beulah* and Jack Benny's manservant, Rochester. Nat "King" Cole's elegance and interaction with white performers as equals stood in stark contrast. "I think it was too early," Kitt said, "to show ourselves off as intelligent people."

MARY ANN WATSON

See also **Racism, Ethnicity, and Television**

Regular Performers
Nat "King" Cole
The Boataneers (1953)
The Herman McCoy Singers
The Randy Van Horne Singers (1957)
The Jerry Graft Singers (1957)
The Cheerleaders (1957)
Nelson Riddle and His Orchestra

Producer
Bob Henry

Programming History
NBC

November 1956–June 1957	Monday 7:30–7:45
July 1957–September 1957	Tuesday 10:00–10:30
September 1957–December 1957	Tuesday 7:30–8:00

Further Reading

Cole, Nat "King" (as told to Lerone Bennett, Jr.), "Why I Quit My TV Show," *Ebony* (February 1958)

Gourse, Leslie, *Unforgettable: The Life and Mystique of Nat King Cole,* New York: St. Martin's Press, 1991

MacDonald, J. Fred, *Blacks and White TV: Afro-Americans in Television since 1948,* Chicago: Nelson-Hall, 1983; 2nd edition, 1992

Nation, Terry (1930–1997)

British Writer

Terry Nation was one of the most consistent writers of British genre television, having had a lasting impact on the development of science fiction and action-adventure programs. Nation's contributions to such series as *The Saint, Doctor Who, Blake's Seven, The Avengers,* and *MacGyver* built him an international fan following. Although most of his television credits were for hour-long dramas, Nation got his start in comedy. At the age of 25, he made his debut as a stage comedian, receiving a poor response. If his performance skills were found lacking, his original material won an admirer in comedian Spike Milligan, who commissioned him to write scripts for the zany British comedy series *The Goon Show*. Nation soon was developing

material for Peter Sellers, Frankie Howerd, Tony Hancock, and an array of other comic stars. In all, he wrote more than 200 radio comedy scripts before trying his hand on television in the early 1960s.

Some of his first work was for ITV's *Out of This World,* a science fiction anthology series in 1962. The following year Nation was asked to write one of the first storylines for *Doctor Who,* then making its debut at the BBC. Nation's most important contribution to *Doctor Who* were the Daleks, the most popular (and heavily merchandized) villains in the series' history. Citing a childhood spent (in Wales) during World War II, Nation remarked that he modeled the impersonal and unstoppable Daleks after the Nazis, seeing them as embodying "the unhearing, unthinking, blanked-out face of authority that will destroy you because it wants to destroy you." Nation continued to influence the development of the Daleks across a succession of storylines and through two feature-film spin-offs of the series, writing many of the Dalek scripts himself while serving as technical adviser on the others. He was subsequently responsible for the introduction of Davros, the wheelchair-bound mad scientist who created the Daleks to serve his schemes for intergalactic domination.

Building on his success at *Doctor Who,* Terry Nation created two original science fiction series: *The Survivors,* a post-nuclear apocalypse story, and *Blake's Seven,* a popular series about a group of freedom fighters struggling against a totalitarian multi-planetary regime. *Blake's Seven,* which he initially proposed as a science fiction version of *The Dirty Dozen,* remains a cult favorite to the present day, popular for its focus on character conflicts within the Liberator crew, its bleak vision of the future and of the prospects of overcoming political repression, its strongly defined female characters, and the intelligence of its dialogue. The series sought an adult following that contrasted sharply with the *Doctor Who* audience, which the BBC persisted in seeing as primarily composed of children. Nation wrote all 13 of the first season episodes of *Blake's Seven* and continued to contribute regularly throughout its second season, before being displaced as story editor by Chris Boucher, who pushed the series in an even darker and more pessimistic direction.

Nation's contributions to the detective genre are almost as significant as his influence on British science fiction. For a while, it seemed that Nation wrote for or was responsible for many of ITV's most popular adventure series. He wrote more than a dozen episodes of *The Saint,* the series starring Roger Moore as globe-trotting master thief/detective Simon Templar. *The Saint* enjoyed international success and was one of the few British imports to snag a prime-time slot on U.S. television. Nation served as script editor and writer for *The Baron,* another ITV series about a jewel thief that built on *The Saint*'s success. He was script editor for the final season of *The Avengers,* shaping the controversial transition from popular Emma Peel (Diana Rigg) to the less-beloved Tara King (Linda Thorson). He was script editor and associate producer for *The Persuaders,* another successful action-adventure series about two daredevil playboys who become "instruments of justice" under duress. He also contributed regularly to ITV's superhero series *Champions.*

Near the end of his career, Nation shifted his focus onto American television, where he was a producer and writer for the first two seasons of *MacGyver,* an original and imaginative series dealing with a former special forces agent who solves crimes and battles evil through the use of resourceful engineering and tinkering tricks. MacGyver seemed to fit comfortably within the tradition of British action-adventure protagonists whom Nation helped to shape and develop. Nation died of emphysema in March 1997.

Most of the best-known writers of British television are recognized for their original dramas and social realism, but Nation's reputation came from his intelligent contributions to genre entertainment.

HENRY JENKINS

See also **Doctor Who**

Terry Nation. Born in Cardiff, Wales, August 8, 1930. Screenwriter for British and American television; creator of the Daleks, which helped popularize *Doctor Who,* 1963; created *The Survivors,* 1975; created *Blake's Seven,* 1978, writing the entire first season and six later episodes, 1978–81; author. Died in Los Angeles, California, March 9, 1997

Television Series (selected)

1961–69	*The Avengers*
1962–69	*The Saint*
1963–89	*Doctor Who*
1964–65, 1968–69	*The Saint*
1969–71	*Champions*
1971–72	*The Persuaders*
1975–77	*The Survivors*
1978–81	*Blake's Seven*
1985–92	*MacGyver*

Made-for-Television Movies

1974	*Color Him Dead*
1986	*A Masterpiece of Murder*

Film

The House in Nightmare Park (1973; also producer).

Radio

The Goon Show

Publications

Rebecca's World: Journey to the Forbidden Planet, 1975

Survivors, 1976
The Official Doctor Who and the Daleks Book, with
    John Peel, 1988

Further Reading

Haining, Peter, *Doctor Who, the Key to Time: A Year-by-Year
    Record,* London: W.H. Allen, 1984
Tulloch, John, and Manuel Alvarado, *Doctor Who: The Unfold-
    ing Text,* New York: St. Martin's Press, 1983

National, The/The Journal

Canadian News Broadcasts

Since the 1950s the titles *The National News* and *The
National* have been used by the Canadian Broadcasting Corporation (CBC) for its English-language national newscasts. In 1982 CBC management made a
bold decision to create a new, hour-long 10:00 P.M. national news and current-affairs bloc. A new program,
The Journal, provided a nightly current affairs component to the regular news report. By the 1980s, well
over 80 percent of Canadian television households
were cabled, and through their cable systems Canadian viewers had direct access to simultaneous transmission of the prime-time schedules of the U.S.
networks. The CBC's decision to move *The National*
newscast from 11:00 P.M. to 10:00 P.M., along with the
creation of *The Journal,* was controversial in that it
was seen as both an unnecessary disruption of
decades-old Canadian viewing habits, and a risky
counterprogramming strategy in the face of the success of U.S. prime-time dramatic series in the Anglo-
Canadian market.

Nevertheless, the new bloc was introduced in January 1982, with veteran CBC journalist Knowlton
Nash as newsreader for the 22-minute *The National,*
followed by *The Journal,* cohosted by Barbara Frum
and Mary Lou Finlay. Within a very short time, however, the new bloc received positive critical attention
and the counterprogramming strategy seemed successful. The programs saw a substantial improvement in
ratings over the old 11:00 P.M. newscast.

While *The National* continued to be produced by
the same staff within CBC news, *The Journal* was developed by a new unit with CBC Current Affairs, under the direction of Executive Producer Mark
Starowicz. Formally, *The Journal* innovated within
Canadian current affairs television in its mixing of
short- and long-form documentaries and double-ender
interviews with politicians, experts, and commentators. It quickly became the key outlet for political and
social debate in the Anglo-Canadian media. The specific format varied from night to night, sometimes focusing on several stories and issues, sometimes
providing in-depth coverage of single issues, or serving as the site of national policy debates between the
major federal political parties.

While the 10:00 P.M. news and current affairs bloc
remained successful throughout the 1980s, there were
recurrent tensions within the CBC over questions of
news judgment and resource allocation between the
two separate production teams responsible for the
programs. In 1992 Ivan Fecan, the CBC programming executive, introduced a new prime-time schedule to the network, re-creating *The National* and *The
Journal* as the *Prime-Time News,* anchored by Peter
Mansbridge. He also moved the news and current affairs hour to 9:00 P.M. as part of a reprogramming of
CBC prime time into a 7:00–9:00 P.M. "family" bloc
and 10:00–12:00 P.M. "adult" bloc. The production of
the new *Prime-Time News* was reorganized into a single production unit, both to overcome previous organizational antagonisms, and to address budget
constraints in a period of increasing austerity at the
CBC. The move to 9:00 P.M. proved much less successful in ratings, and the initial reformatting of news
and current affairs within one program proved more
difficult than had been anticipated. By 1995 the
scheduling of CBC prime time into "family" and
"adult" blocs was abandoned, and the news and current affairs hour was returned to 10:00 P.M. and renamed *The National,* including the current affairs
coverage under the title of *The National Magazine.*

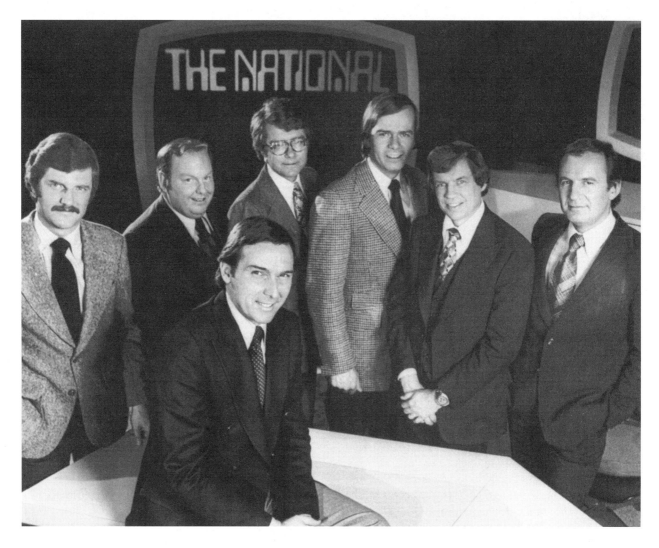

The National.
Photo courtesy of National Archives of Canada/CBC Collection

The return to 10:00 P.M. once again proved successful as a counterprogramming strategy for prime-time competition from U.S. networks.

MARTIN ALLOR

Further Reading

Lockhead, Richard, editor, *Beyond the Printed Word: The Evolution of Canada's Broadcast Heritage,* Kingston, Ontario: Quarry, 1991

Nash, Knowlton, *Microphone Wars: A History of Triumph and Betrayal,* Toronto: McClelland and Stuart, 1994

National Academy of Television Arts and Sciences

U.S. Industry Professional Association

The National Academy of Television Arts and Sciences (NATAS) is a New York-based organization with 19 regional chapters or affiliates in many of the larger television markets. The organization is best known for its Emmy awards, which are bestowed on both programs and individuals in a variety of categories. The "Emmy" is a variation of "Immy," a nickname for the light-sensitive Image Orthicon tube that was the heart of television cameras during the 1950s and 1960s. The award is a statuette of a winged woman holding an electron in her outstretched hands.

NATAS was organized in 1957 as an outgrowth of rivalry between two separate television academies that had been established several years earlier. One was based in Los Angeles, the other in New York. The move to unite the two academies into a single "national" television academy was led by TV variety-show host Ed Sullivan, who was elected its first president. The rival New York and Hollywood academies became "founding chapters" of NATAS and additional chapters were later established in other cities.

The first nationally televised Emmy Awards originated from both New York and Los Angeles in 1955, actually predating the merger of the two academies. These bi-coastal presentations continued through 1971 and mirrored the glamour of the rapidly expanding television industry to the point where the Emmy ceremonies were second only to the Motion Picture Academy Awards in terms of audience interest and recognition. After 1971, separate award ceremonies for prime-time entertainment programs originated from Los Angeles, while New York remained home for the news and documentary awards.

During the 1970s, relations between the Hollywood and New York chapters remained tense. Los Angeles producers of prime-time programs expressed resentment that their programs were being judged by members in New York and the smaller market chapters since they did not consider these individuals to be their peers. They also resented their minority status on a Board of Trustees dominated by the New York and smaller market chapters. After John Cannon of New York defeated Robert Lewine of Hollywood for the presidency of the organization in 1976, the Hollywood chapter left NATAS and created a separate organization: the Academy of Television Arts and Sciences, or ATAS.

ATAS sued for exclusive rights to bestow the Emmy on the grounds that the Los Angeles group had actually given the award several years before NATAS was formed. Litigation by both organizations ended with a compromise: ATAS would retain the Emmy rights for prime-time entertainment programming; NATAS would continue to award Emmys for news and documentary, sports, daytime, and public-service programming, and also for achievements in television engineering.

Initially, NATAS was weakened by the departure of the Los Angeles group. But during the following two decades, NATAS has been strengthened by growing interest in daytime programs (talk shows and soap operas). Each spring, the organization presents a "Daytime at Nighttime" awards ceremony, broadcast during prime time, and showcasing TV's soap-opera stars. The presentation is staged at Radio City Music Hall, Madison Square Garden, or a similar New York location. Separate ceremonies for each of the categories of sports, news, public service, and technology are scheduled on different dates, and sometimes telecast over cable channels.

NATAS has also been strengthened by growth in both the number and size of regional chapters located in many of the major television markets. The nineteen chapters are: Atlanta, Boston, Chicago, Cleveland, Columbus-Dayton-Cincinnati (Ohio Valley), Denver, Detroit, Nashville, New York, Philadelphia, Phoenix, San Diego, San Francisco, Seattle, South Florida, St. Louis, Texas, and Washington, D.C. (A local Los Angeles-area chapter is affiliated with ATAS.)

Each chapter is chartered by the national organization but operates independently in terms of its programs and finances. All 19 chapters conduct Emmy awards presentations to honor television professionals in their respective markets and in adjacent markets that do not have their own chapters. For example, Philadelphia is officially called the Mid Atlantic Chapter and includes Pittsburgh, Scranton, Harrisburg, and several other markets in Pennsylvania. Texas, the newest chapter at this writing, includes Houston, Dallas–Fort Worth, San Antonio, and sixteen smaller markets. It was organized with the assumption that two or more separate chapters might eventually emerge from what is now called the Lone Star Chapter.

At both the national and local levels, considerable emphasis is placed on the peer judging of all entries. The national awards are evaluated by judging panels of individuals working within the respective categories. At the local level, chapters exchange tapes to ensure that judging is performed by qualified professionals in other markets. The local Emmy statuette is a smaller replica of the national Emmy statuettes awarded by NATAS and ATAS for national programming.

Governance of the national organization is the responsibility of a Board of Trustees with individual trustees selected by the chapters. Chapter representation is proportional, with one trustee allocated for every 300 members. Each chapter, in turn, is governed by a Broad of Governors elected by the membership.

John Cannon led NATAS for 25 years, until his death in 2001. After a national search, Peter O. Price, a former newspaper publisher and cable television executive, was named president by the Board of Trustees in 2002.

Under Price, the organization adapted a shorter name, National Television Academy or NTA, which it uses in many of its activities. A redesigned Emmy has also been introduced on letterhead and in many public relations and promotional announcements. However, the full legal name remains the National Academy of Television Arts and Sciences, and the original Emmy statuette remains intact.

Relationships between the two academies (NATAS and ATAS) remain cool, for the most part. Not surprisingly, most of the controversy relates to the awarding of Emmys. For example, ATAS wanted to award an Emmy for the best commercial; NATAS did not. Conversely, NATAS has proposed a separate Emmys awards ceremony for Spanish-language programming, which ATAS opposes.

In addition to the Emmy awards, NATAS publishes *Television Quarterly,* a scholarly journal dealing with the historical development and critical analysis of television programs and the television industry. Three major scholarships, currently $40,000 each, are awarded by the national organization to high school seniors who intend to major in communications in college and pursue a career in television. Also, each of the 19 chapters has its own scholarship program. In 2002, NATAS began National Student Television, a program created to recognize excellence and award special student Emmys to television programs produced by high schools throughout the United States.

NATAS maintains a national office at 70 West 57th Street, New York, NY 10019 and a website at *www. emmyonline.org.* Each of the 19 chapters has offices in their respective cities and all chapters are linked to the national website. The organization and its chapters have 13,000 individual members.

NORMAN FELSENTHAL

See also **Academy of Television Arts and Sciences**

National Asian American Telecommunications Association

U.S. Industry Professional Association

According to the organization's website, the mission of the National Asian American Telecommunications Association (NAATA) is "to present stories that convey the richness and diversity of the Asian Pacific American experience to the broadest audience possible." Since its founding in 1980, the NAATA, based in San Francisco and considered the preeminent Asian-American media arts organizations in the United States, has been bringing award-winning programs by and about Asian Pacific Americans to the public through such venues as national and local television broadcasting, film and video screenings, and educational distribution services.

Through its programming, exhibition, and distribution of works by Asian Pacific Americans, as well as its advocacy and coalition-building efforts, the

NAATA actively serves as both a resource and a promoter for minority communities. Essentially, it coordinates many different realms related to contemporary visual culture—the production of films, videos, and new media works; critical writing and scholarship; distribution and television broadcasting; community and educational outreach; and even legislation and lobbying. In short, it serves as a center of information and human resources.

The NAATA was founded as a conscious and concerted effort on the part of filmmakers and producers in the San Francisco area to address the problem of a lack of equal access to public television and radio. With the guidance and commitment of two older organizations, Visual Communications in Los Angeles and Asian CineVision in New York, both of which emerged out of the movements toward racial and social justice in the 1960s, the NAATA was born out of a three-day conference.

The Association works primarily in three programming areas: television broadcast, exhibition (namely, the annual San Francisco International Asian American Film Festival), and nonbroadcast distribution (more specifically, through their NAATA Distribution Catalog). Through this effort, the organization seeks to support and nurture Asian Pacific American media artists in order to proffer a more accurate representation of their communities to the public. Typically, representations of Asian Americans in American television and film, supporters of the group contend, have led to many false perceptions of this population.

In the 1995 catalog for the San Francisco International Asian American Film Festival, Stephen Gong (film-history scholar and manager of the Pacific Film Archive) argues that the struggles in the career of Sessue Hayakawa (1889–1973, a star of many silent films but perhaps best-known for his role as Colonel Saito in *The Bridge on the River Kwai,* 1957) remain emblematic of the price Asian-American actors pay in order to get some screen time. Referring to the stereotypes of Asian Americans, Gong asks: "Do the commercial constraints that have apparently governed mass media from its earliest days still make it a given that public expectations must be fulfilled before artistic vision can be exercised?" The NAATA attempts to respond to this question by presenting—and more importantly, integrating—alternative and self-proclaimed representations by "marginal" peoples into the mainstream media culture.

The San Francisco International Asian American Film Festival is the NAATA's most dramatic effort to provide the public with self-determined images and stories about Asian and Asian-American experiences. Soliciting new and innovative work from within the United States as well as from Canada and other nations, this festival is a collection of vastly diverse film and video programs as well as installations and panel discussions. For too long, many "cultures, faces, and stories have remained 'in the closet' or simply invisible," as the 1995 festival catalog states. Therefore, the purpose of the festival is to acknowledge the worldwide industry of film and video, which includes and represents many works from the Asian diaspora. "Films submitted to the Asian American film festival reflect the heterogeneous and hybrid cultures of Asian American experience," writes Nerissa S. Balce in her analysis of the 2001 festival. These works "speak to the collective experience of 'Asian/Americans': as people of color, as immigrants, as youth, as queers, as suburbanites, as rural or urban folk, as undocumented workers, as professionals or the working class" (see Balce).

The NAATA's film, video, and audio distribution service has amalgamated a collection of film and video by and about Asian Pacific Americans that serve to challenge the construction and meaning of "Asian American." The intent is to challenge and hopefully change mainstream perceptions of Asian Pacific American identities. Moreover, this service strives not only to foster awareness but also to facilitate discussion, sensitivity, and understanding of cultures that are not one's own. The uses of such a collection include corporate diversity training, high school and university education, and social and political activism. Through the association's website *(www.naatanet.org),* individuals and institutions can order from more than 200 Asian Pacific American films and videos. The online catalog is skillfully organized by topics including media; land/environment; labor; personal stories; health, mental health, and AIDS; sexuality; multiracial/ethnic heritage; youth; art and performance; and U.S. colonialism. The collection is also indexed by title and by ethnicity, and there is a separate index of titles for school-age audiences. In the NAATA's effort to share the work of Asian Pacific Americans and open up discussion on various issues, the distribution service is a helpful and much-needed resource.

The NAATA offers members monthly electronic news bulletins that announce events such as screenings and festivals, and it publishes on its website extensive information about the NAATA's Media Fund, which since 1990 has used funds from the Corporation for Public Broadcasting to sponsor more than 150 Asian Pacific American film and video projects, many of which have aired locally or nationally on public broadcasting stations. The website also keeps readers updated on past, current, and upcoming Asian Pacific American programming on television; presents information for educators; and provides a forum for individuals to make announcements, list job openings, offer assistance, and otherwise participate in the Asian American arts community.

The significance of the NAATA within the media industry is that it sets up a series of connections: it links sponsors to media artists, to distributors, and to larger mainstream venues, all in an attempt to correct the misrepresentation and misperception of minority peoples and histories. The NAATA is both an artistic and a political organization, currently working to ensure that the voices and experiences of people who are often unheard and unknown are made more public and better understood.

LAHN S. KIM

See also **Racism, Ethnicity, and Television**

Further Reading

Asian American Network (Autumn/Winter 1994)
Asian American Network (Spring 1995)
Balce, Nerissa S., *Millennial Narratives: Notes on Viewing Asian American Cinema, 2001,* San Francisco: National Asian American Telecommunications Association, 2001 (available at *www.naatanet.org*)
Leong, Russell, editor, *Moving the Image: Independent Asian Pacific American Media Arts,* Los Angeles: UCLA Asian American Studies Center and Visual Communications, Southern California Asian American Studies Central, 1991

National Association of Broadcasters

U.S. Industry Trade Association

For nearly eight decades, the National Association of Broadcasters (NAB) has represented the interests of most American radio and television stations and networks to Washington policymakers and the public at large. Fiercely protective of broadcasters' First Amendment rights, the NAB has waxed and waned over the years in its political effectiveness, becoming by the early 21st century one of the most important trade associations and lobbying groups in the nation's capital.

Origins

Perhaps fittingly for a commercial business association, the NAB developed as the result of a financial dispute. The American Society of Composers, Authors and Publishers (ASCAP) threatened in mid-1922 to sue radio stations using ASCAP music (virtually all were) if they did not pay royalties. The stations argued they received no income (true at the time) with which to pay such royalties. A half a dozen of them met in a Chicago hotel room to map out a strategy of what to do, and from that came the April 1923 organizational meeting of what became the NAB. Those present agreed to hire a director and create a New York office.

The NAB's initial goals were to overcome the ASCAP demands for royalties while at the same time seeking basic legislation that most radio station operators realized was needed to expand business. Despite early lobbying efforts, the radio broadcasters lost initial battles and agreed to a schedule of payments to ASCAP, in part because so many other issues were impinging on the stations. Facing continuing pressure for ever-higher ASCAP music royalties, the NAB finally decided to found its own music license agency and created Broadcast Music Incorporated (BMI) in 1939–40.

While Congress finally passed a new radio law in 1927 (the NAB had strongly urged such action), attempts to limit commercial time, to control program content, to reserve some channels for educational use, and other issues continually cropped up, requiring an industry-wide response, for which the NAB naturally took up the coordinating role. As public demand for information on the industry increased, so too did NAB publicity and publication efforts—especially in 1933, when colleges and university teams across the country debated whether the U.S. should adopt the features of the British system of public-service broadcasting, a notion the NAB opposed. The association lobbied hard and successfully to resist major policy changes when the Communications Act of 1934 was considered and passed.

Expansion and New Services

As the radio industry grew, so did the NAB. The association's relationship with key government regulators deteriorated for many years in the 1940s and 1950s. Driven in part by strong personalities on both sides, this was unfortunate, as the FCC was developing policies for the new FM radio and television services, and a more cooperative relationship might have eased the entry of both. Initially cool to FM radio, for example, the NAB later supported the service in a variety of ways. NAB was strongly behind the expansion of commercial television from the medium's inception, although it fought a losing battle against educational channel reservations.

From 1951 to 1957, the association took the somewhat clumsy name the National Association of Radio and Television Broadcasters (NARTB) to make clearer the importance of the newer medium. Over the years, the NAB has often absorbed more specialized organizations, including several that have focused on FM radio. At the same time, it has also spawned many more specific organizations, including the Radio Advertising Bureau (RAB), Television Bureau of Advertising (TvB), and the Television Information Office (TIO).

The NAB's annual convention was regularly held each spring in Chicago (Washington, D.C., in presidential inauguration years), attracting hundreds, and later several thousand, broadcasters. Keynote speakers often made news, as new FCC Chairman Newton Minow did in 1961 with his speech describing television programming as a "vast wasteland." The ever-larger technical exhibit helped to showcase expanding technological options such as the introduction of color television technology in the mid-1950s, the arrival of videotape (the star of the 1956 convention), and satellite delivery and reception equipment in the 1970s and 1980s. By the early 1970s, the convention shifted to Dallas, Atlanta, and finally Las Vegas to obtain sufficient exhibit and hotel space.

The NAB produced its first "Code of Ethics" in 1929, in an attempt to preempt the imposition of government program or advertising guidelines. A decade later, again attempting to avoid federal regulation, the NAB issued a more focused "Radio Code" offering programming guidelines and suggested limits on commercial time. NAB added a parallel code of television good practice in 1952, and continued to mod-

Courtesy of NAB

ify both almost annually. Although compliance with the NAB codes was always voluntary, many NAB member stations adhered to them, largely for promotional purposes. When suit was brought against the codes (for raising the cost of radio and television advertising because of their suggested limits on the amount of time stations could sell for advertising), they were dropped in 1982, after a federal district court found the limitations unconstitutional. Today the NAB touts a "Statement of Principles" concerning only program content.

The Modern NAB

Members of the association (stations and networks) set NAB policies through a board of directors. The board is composed of radio and television broadcasters elected by fellow members. This "joint board" is subdivided into a radio and a television board. NAB employs an extensive committee structure to draw on the specialized knowledge of its members and make recommendations to the board. The association publishes a variety of industry reference books and a host of newsletters, many now on-line, representing the broad interests of its station members. These include *Destination Digital TV, RadioWeek, TV Today, Radio TechCheck, TV TechCheck,* and *NAB World,* among others.

Daily operations of the NAB are overseen by a full-time president. Since 1982, Eddie Fritts, a former station owner from Mississippi, has served in that role (longer than any prior NAB leader). With more than 100 full-time employees housed in its own building in downtown Washington, D.C., and an annual budget approaching $50 million, the NAB has in recent years gained a reputation as one of the strongest and most effective lobbies in the nation's capital. Part of this strength comes from the clout inherent in member stations, which provide air time for political candidates and will readily call congressmen to press their views. TARPAC, the industry's political action committee, is operated by the NAB, as is the NAB Educational Foundation, which is designed to foster research into the benefits of broadcasting.

The annual four-day NAB convention and technical exhibit was, by the early 2000s, attracting more than 115,000 attendees to Las Vegas each spring. The industry gathering, increasingly international in tone in recent years, devotes considerable exhibition space to path-breaking technologies such as digital or high-definition television in the early 1990s, and multimedia and Internet technology in the late 1990s and early 2000s. In between conventions, the NAB plays an active role in technical standard setting, such as the long process of developing digital high-definition television and digital audio broadcasting.

The NAB faces growing problems, however, in trying to maintain its role as "the broadcaster's voice before Congress, federal agencies and the Courts," and as an umbrella organization representing the viewpoints of all broadcasters. It has often taken no position on an issue when its members have been divided on the matter at hand. The problem became especially clear when, in 1999–2000, CBS, Fox and NBC withdrew their network and owned-and-operated stations from membership in disagreement over the NAB's position, due to the Association's opposition to a lessening of regulations concerning multiple ownership of television stations (which those networks supported). Of all the national broadcast networks, only ABC remained by mid-2002, which presented a setback to the NAB's usual united-front approach to industry concerns. In-

creasingly, the concerns and interests of radio and television broadcasters, as well as those of smaller stations and large group owners, are diverging, making common agreement within one lobbying organization problematic. At the same time, the NAB is criticized for being short-sighted in its lobbying efforts. The association has to fight the conception of many in government that NAB is on the defensive, protecting single-channel broadcasters in a world increasingly dominated by multi-channel competitors.

CHRISTOPHER H. STERLING

Publications

Broadcast Engineering Conference: Proceedings (annual)
Broadcasting and Government (annual)
Broadcasting in the United States, 1933
NAB Engineering Handbook, 1935, 1960, 1975, 1985, 1992, 1999
NAB Guide to Broadcast Law and Regulations, 1977, 1984, 1998.
Television Financial Report (annual)

Further Reading

Albiniak, Paige, "On a Roll: NAB's Eddie Fritts Expects to Keep on Winning and Prove the Critics Wrong," *Broadcasting & Cable* (April 8, 2002)
Mackey, David R., "The Development of the National Association of Broadcasters," *Journal of Broadcasting* 1/4 (Fall 1957)

National Association of Television Program Executives

U.S.-based Industry Trade Association

The National Association of Television Program Executives (NATPE) began in May 1963 as an organization designed to increase the amount of local programming on television stations, and to help program directors improve their positions within their respective stations.

Since then, NATPE has developed the largest domestic syndication trade show in the United States, and one of the top three international trade shows. Originally dubbed the National Association of Program Directors, the organization later changed its name to NATPE, and finally NATPE International. NATPE's primary function in the television business stems from its annual convention, held in late January, which continues the association's founding missions: providing a space to buy and sell syndicated programming, and educating programmers about the industry.

Social, regulatory, and industry changes led to the formation of NATPE, and more recent changes in those areas threaten the future of the organization. The various broadcast reform movements of the 1960s resulted in broadcasters' increased accountability to their local constituents. Programming executives were typically charged with producing or acquiring programming to fit these local needs, and NATPE provided a venue where syndicators and programmers could trade such programming. Nevertheless, founding member Lew Klein remembers that program directors had little influence in most television stations at the time, and so a secondary role of NATPE was to educate program directors about the industry, and advocate for their professional development. The FCC's 1970 Prime-Time Access Rule contributed significantly to NATPE's growth, as it spurred the creation of a variety of popular, first-run syndicated series. About the same time, the National Association of Broadcasters (NAB) convention, which had served as the main venue for syndication trade, moved program suppliers far away from the main convention floor, prompting many of them to abandon the NAB for the more syndicator-friendly NATPE convention.

In the 1970s, NATPE's membership grew tremendously, from 306 participants in 1970 to 1,891 in 1976. Today, membership includes more than 4,000 media companies. Beginning in 1985, the conference moved to a semi-permanent home in New Orleans, but began in 2001 to alternate between New Orleans and Las Vegas for the convenience of the growing number of syndicators and buyers based on the West Coast. In addition, NATPE has expanded its membership in two key growth areas: new media and international sales. New media first became an important sector for NATPE in 2000, when Internet companies sought out content for their websites and traditional broadcasters and distributors looked for ways to expand their businesses into on-line media. Meanwhile, international sales have been an important part of NATPE's strategy since the late 1980s. In 1993, the association appointed as its president and CEO Bruce Johansen, a well-known international executive with a mandate to increase NATPE's presence as an international trade show. Today, NATPE is one of three premier international television conferences, along with MIP-TV and MIPCOMM.

While the international and new media sectors of NATPE have been growing, the domestic contingent seems to find the convention increasingly unnecessary due to consolidation in television station ownership and the syndication business. Historically, NATPE was the primary site where representatives from hundreds of television stations around the country went to purchase programming from the dozens of syndication companies that attended. With the removal of most broadcasting ownership regulations in the Telecommunications Act of 1996, however, group owners have bought up more and more local stations and consolidated program buying in a single corporate office, which can take advantage of bulk-pricing discounts. Concurrently, the syndication industry has shrunk to less than a dozen large companies, some of which are now part of larger conglomerates that also own television stations. Since the mid-1990s, the major Hollywood studios have threatened to abandon NATPE, claiming they make few significant sales there.

The tensions that currently face NATPE were starkly apparent at the 2002 convention. Due to the economic fallout from the September 11, 2001, terrorist attacks, and the subsequent fall in the advertising market, many of the major distributors abandoned rental of their usual booths on the sales floor for much cheaper hospitality suites at nearby hotels, where a pared-down number of sales representatives met with a handful of important clients. However, the international wings of these same distribution companies were out on the sales floor in force. Their presence reflected the continued relevance of NATPE for international distribution, which continues to expand due to the growth in international distribution outlets and increased competition among distributors selling to international buyers.

The future of NATPE today is uncertain. While the convention will continue for the foreseeable future to have relevance for international syndication, a number of changes have been proposed to try and make the convention more relevant for domestic syndication. One possible future direction is to split the convention into three: one convention, in early April, would include distributors and advertisers; a second, held in November, would include television stations and distributors; while a third, held in January, would cater to international syndication. Whatever the future direction of the organization, NATPE owes its existence to an industry and regulatory era that has now passed, and its continuation depends upon its ability to become relevant to the present era of consolidation and globalization.

TIM HAVENS

See also **National Association of Broadcasters**

Further Reading

Brennan, Steve, "NATPE Moving with the Times," *Hollywood Reporter* (January 24, 2000)

Corvo, Phil, "The 'International' in NATPE," *Broadcasting & Cable* (January 21, 1992)

Dempsey, John, "Blurbsters mull breakaway from NATPE," *Variety* (February 11, 2002)

Freeman, Mike, "NATPE At 30: Charting Syndication's Rising Star," *Broadcasting & Cable* (January 25, 1993)

Mahamdi, Yahia, "Television, Globalization, and Cultural Hegemony: the Evolution and Structure of International Television," Ph.D. dissertation, Austin: University of Texas, 1992

National Broadcasting Company (NBC)

U.S. Network

When General Electric (GE) purchased the National Broadcasting Company (NBC) in 1985, many observers of the media industries were dubious. General Electric was a vast conglomerate based in Fairfield, Connecticut, a manufacturer of medical equipment, power turbines, airplane engines, and appliances that had diversified into such businesses as the financing of commercial and consumer loans. Little in GE's recent history foretold success in programming a television network. NBC's newly appointed chairman, Robert Wright, had risen through the ranks at GE, learning the ropes in the plastics division and, later, in the GE Credit Corporation. He had spent a short time in the cable industry, but had come of age in the corporate culture of GE, famed for its disciplined management and ruthless devotion to the bottom line of corporate earnings. Insiders at NBC questioned whether this outsider, a quintessential corporate manager, had any idea how to run a television network—particularly one that was already at the top of the business, having just swept the prime-time ratings race—or whether this company could make the transition from light bulbs to light comedy.

By the early 21st century, much has changed in the television business, but Robert Wright is still chairman, and NBC has been the dominant network in the United States for much of the past two decades, a model of stability in an otherwise turbulent business. NBC has consistently led all networks in attracting the 18- to 49-year-old adults most coveted by advertisers—winning this demographic in seven of the eight years from 1995 to 2003—and has helped to reorient the entire broadcasting industry toward the pursuit of this segment of the audience. Led by a Thursday night lineup that has launched such hits as *The Cosby Show,* *Cheers,* and *L.A. Law* in the 1980s, and *Seinfeld, Friends,* and *E.R.* in the 1990s, NBC has the highest advertising rates of any broadcast network and has long been the most profitable, generating profits of $700–800 million from its prime-time schedule in the 2002–03 season. NBC's dominance extends to virtually every part of the schedule, where its self-produced entertainment and news programs have led the ratings during much of the past decade: *The Today Show* and *Meet The Press* in the mornings, *NBC Nightly News* among evening newscasts, and *The Tonight Show with Jay Leno, Late Night with Conan O'Brien,* and *Saturday Night Live* in the late-night slot. Over the same period, NBC has been responsible for many of television's most acclaimed series, easily overshadowing the other broadcast networks with a mounting pile of Emmy nominations for *E.R., The West Wing, Law and Order, Homicide: Life on the Streets, Frasier, Seinfeld,* and *Will & Grace.*

Due to the strength of its network programming, NBC's fourteen owned-and-operated television stations contribute another $1 billion in annual advertising revenue. Still, the audience for over-the-air broadcasting continues to shrink in the United States as audiences are dispersed among cable channels and competing forms of home entertainment. Like other media companies, NBC has diversified well beyond its original base in broadcasting in order to reach these elusive viewers. NBC now controls several cable channels, including CNBC, a business news network available in 175 million households worldwide; MSNBC, a 24-hour news network owned jointly with Microsoft; and Bravo, a network targeted at upscale viewers. In order to reach the growing Latino audience in the U.S., NBC purchased Telemundo, the second-largest U.S. Spanish-language broadcast network, in April 2002. With international markets as important as the domestic market to GE's bottom line, NBC programming now reaches viewers in one hundred countries on six continents. All told, NBC Television and Cable operations generate annual revenues of $7.1 billion (still only five percent of GE's annual sales) and operating profits of $1.7 billion.

In September 2003, GE announced its most ambitious expansion for NBC, a plan to acquire Vivendi Universal Entertainment in a deal valued at $14 billion. The purchase would give GE control of Universal movie studio, the USA Network and other cable channels, a television production unit responsible for the network's lucrative *Law and Order* franchise, and Vivendi's interest in the Universal Studios theme parks. By integrating additional cable networks and a major studio with its broadcast network, NBC Universal (as the new company will be known) will compete with the other fully integrated media conglomerates owning broadcast networks: Viacom (CBS and UPN), The Walt Disney Co. (ABC), News Corporation (Fox), and Time Warner (WB).

Throughout its history, the fortunes of the National Broadcasting Company have been closely tied to those of a parent company. Unlike CBS and ABC, which began as independent programming enterprises, NBC came into existence as the subsidiary of an electronics manufacturer, Radio Corporation of America (RCA), which saw programming as a form of marketing, an enticement for consumers to purchase radio and television receivers for the home. The power and influence of a national network aided RCA as it lobbied to see its technology adopted as the industry standard, particularly during the early years of television and in the battle over color television.

RCA, which had begun as a mere sales agent for the other companies in the combine, emerged in the 1930s as a radio manufacturer with two networks (NBC-Red and NBC-Blue), a powerful lineup of clear channel stations, and a roster of stars unequaled in the radio industry. From this position of power, RCA research labs, under the direction of Vladimir Zworykin, set the standard for research into the nascent technology of television. NBC began experimental broadcasts from New York's Empire State building as early as 1932. By 1935, the company was spending millions of dollars annually to fund television research. Profits from the lucrative NBC radio networks were routinely channeled into television research. In 1939, NBC became the first network in the United States to introduce regular television broadcasts with its inaugural telecast of the opening-day ceremonies at the New York World's Fair.

Courtesy of NBC

RCA's dominance of the U.S. broadcasting industry led to government scrutiny in the late 1930s when the FCC began to investigate the legitimacy of networks that linked together hundreds of local stations, or "chain broadcasting" as it was then called. The result was the 1941 publication of the FCC's Report on Chain Broadcasting, which assailed the network's control of a majority of high-powered stations and called for the divorcement of NBC's two networks. RCA challenged the decision in court, but failed to overturn the FCC's findings. In 1943 RCA sold its Blue network to Edward J. Noble, and this network eventually became ABC.

After World War II, RCA moved quickly to consolidate its influence over the television industry. While CBS tried to stall efforts to establish technological standards in order to promote its own color-TV technology, RCA pressed for the development of television according to the existing NTSC technical standards established in 1941. The FCC agreed with RCA, though the two networks continued to battle over standards for color television until the RCA system was finally selected in 1953. Throughout this period, network television played a secondary role at RCA. In the early 1950s NBC accounted for only one-quarter of RCA's corporate profits. NBC's most important role for its parent was in helping to extend the general appeal of television as the market for television sets boomed.

Throughout the 1950s and 1960s, NBC generally finished in second place in the ratings behind CBS. NBC's prime-time schedule relied heavily on two genres: drama, including several of the most acclaimed anthology drama series of the 1950s (such as *Philco/Goodyear Playhouse, Kraft Television Theater*), and comedy/variety, featuring such stars as Milton Berle, Jimmy Durante, Sid Caesar and Imogene Coca, Dean Martin and Jerry Lewis, Bob Hope, and

Perry Como. In spite of its dependence on these familiar genres, NBC was also responsible for several programming innovations.

Several key innovations are credited to Sylvester "Pat" Weaver, who served as the network's chief programmer from 1949 to 1953 and as president from 1953 to 1955. Weaver is credited with introducing the "magazine concept" of television advertising, in which advertisers no longer sponsored an entire series, but paid to have their ads placed within a program, as ads appear in a magazine. Previously, networks had functioned as conduits for programs produced by sponsors; Weaver's move shifted the balance of power toward the networks, which were able to exert more control over their programming and schedules. Weaver expanded the network schedule into the "fringe" time periods of early morning and late night by introducing *Today* and *Tonight*. He also championed "event" programming that broke the routines of regularly scheduled series with expensive, one-shot broadcasts, which he called "spectaculars." Broadcast live, the Broadway production of *Peter Pan* drew a record audience of 65 million viewers in 1955.

Former ABC president Robert Kintner took over programming at NBC in 1956 and served as network president from 1958 to 1965. Kintner supervised the expansion of NBC news, the shift to color broadcasting (completed in 1965), and the network's diversification beyond television programming. Programming under Kintner followed the network's traditional reliance on dramas and comedy/variety. NBC formed a strong alliance with the production company MCA-Universal, whose drama series came to dominate the network's schedule well into the 1970s.

During the late 1970s, after decades spent battling CBS in the ratings, NBC watched as ABC, with a sitcom-laden schedule, took command of the ratings race, leaving NBC in a distant third place. To halt its steep decline, NBC recruited Fred Silverman, the man who had engineered ABC's rapid rise. Silverman's tenure as president of NBC lasted from 1978 to 1981 and is probably the lowest point in the history of the network. Instead of turning around NBC's fortunes, Silverman presided over an era of ratings that declined still further, desertions by the network's affiliate stations, and programs that were often mediocre *(BJ and the Bear)* and occasionally disastrous *(Supertrain)*.

Mired in third place at the depths of its fortunes in 1981, NBC recruited Grant Tinker to become NBC chairman. A cofounder of MTM Enterprises, Tinker had presided over the spectacular rise of the independent production company that had produced *The Mary Tyler Moore Show, Lou Grant,* and *Hill Street Blues.* Tinker led NBC on a three-year journey back to respectability by continuing the commitment to quality programming that had marked his tenure at MTM. He and programming chief Brandon Tartikoff patiently nurtured such acclaimed series as *Hill Street Blues, Cheers, St. Elsewhere, Family Ties,* and *Miami Vice.* The turning point for NBC came in 1984, when Tartikoff convinced comedian Bill Cosby to return to series television with *The Cosby Show.* Network profits under Tinker and Tartikoff climbed from $48 million in 1981 to $333 million in 1985.

By the mid-1980s, NBC generated 43 percent of RCA's $570 million in annual earnings—a hugely disproportionate share of the profits for a single division of a conglomerate. In the merger-mania that swept the corporate world in the 1980s, RCA became a ripe target for takeover, particularly given the potential value of the company when broken into its various components. General Electric purchased RCA, and with it NBC, in 1985 for $6.3 billion. When Tinker stepped down in 1986, GE chairman Jack Welch named Robert E. Wright as network chairman. NBC dominated the ratings until the late 1980s, when its ratings suddenly collapsed, as viewers deserted aging hits like *The Golden Girls* and *L.A. Law.* Just one show, *Cheers,* remained in the Nielsen top ten by 1991, and NBC fell into third place for the first time in over a decade. Network profits plunged from $603 million in 1989 to $204 million in 1992.

The network suffered one public relations debacle after another during this period. The CNBC cable channel, which NBC had launched as a joint venture with cable operator Cablevision, lost $60 million in its first two years, forcing Cablevision to withdraw from the partnership. Wright's appointment of newspaper executive Michael Gartner to head NBC News ended in a highly publicized scandal over a fraudulent news report on the prime-time news magazine, *Dateline.* Attempts to name a successor to the retiring Johnny Carson as host of *The Tonight Show* turned into a public brouhaha as network executives wavered between Jay Leno and David Letterman. Leno eventually ended up in Carson's seat, while Letterman fled to CBS.

Nevertheless, GE held onto NBC, and Robert Wright remained in charge, gradually bringing stability to the network and returning it to prominence starting in 1993. Wright hired Republican public relations guru Roger Ailes to turn around CNBC, and his success was almost immediate; CNBC reported an operating profit of $50 million in 1995. Wright placed Andrew Lack in charge of NBC News, and Lack led *The Nightly News* with Tom Brokaw and *The Today Show* (overhauled by producer Jeff Zucker) into first place. Expanded to three hours, *The Today Show* became an NBC cash cow, generating advertising revenue of $450 million a year. Wright convinced veteran producer Don Ohlmeyer to join the entertainment division, where he and entertainment president Warren Littlefield returned NBC to the top of the prime-time ratings by 1995, with solid hits in *Seinfeld, E.R., Frasier, Friends,* and *Law and Order.* Littlefield passed the torch to Scott Sassa in 1998, and NBC added *The West Wing* and *Will & Grace* to its roster of critical and popular success.

Robert Wright and GE management have adapted to some of the conventions of the television industry, but NBC's accomplishment over the past 10 years is also due to the application of GE's rigorous management strategies to television, where NBC executives dissect audience demographics and measure the advertising potential of each show developed for the network schedule. This has led to NBC's intense focus on the 18- to 49-year-old adult demographic, which rarely wavers across its prime-time schedule. It is the rare NBC series, for instance, that centers on families with children—the sorts of series that appear regularly on CBS and ABC, attracting viewers too young or too old for NBC's desired demographic. This also has led NBC to squeeze every dime out of its Thursday night "Must-See TV" schedule, which has become the most profitable night of television as the movie studios spend heavily on TV advertising for the Friday launch of their blockbusters.

These management strategies also have led NBC to question the economic value of certain types of programming, such as major-league sports, that were considered a network staple just a few years ago. In an initially surprising move, NBC eliminated costly, money-losing sports properties that once defined the power and prestige of a national network, choosing not to renew its contracts with the National Football League, Major League Baseball, and the National Basketball Association.

The competition in prime time has increased over the past several years, as the audience has continued to shrink, the advertising market has flattened, programming costs have risen, new program formats have been introduced, and new networks compete for viewers. There are now six broadcast networks and dozens of cable channels competing for the attention of viewers. Under these conditions it is increasingly difficult to launch a new series, and NBC has not had a breakout hit since *Will & Grace* debuted in 1998. With the exception of *Fear Factor,* NBC has not matched the success of other networks in developing non-scripted series. Therefore, its programmers have been forced to squeeze every ratings point out of the existing hits. Under Scott Sassa, NBC introduced two spin-offs of *Law and Order,* an enduring hit that debuted in 1990

(*Law and Order: SVU* and *Law and Order: Criminal Intent*) and there is talk of a fourth version to follow. Since former *Today Show* producer Jeff Zucker became entertainment president in 2001, he has not launched a hit series, but has kept NBC on top with programming gimmicks, such as "super-sized" episodes of NBC's Thursday night sitcoms, which add extra minutes in order to keep viewers from turning to a competitor's program. He also plans to include short films during the commercial breaks in order to keep viewers, particularly TiVo-empowered viewers, watching the commercials.

The cost of holding together a prime-time schedule has increased dramatically over the past several years, and NBC has been forced to spend lavishly in order to keep in place its most successful series. As it is more difficult than ever to turn a scripted series into a hit, producers of existing series find themselves with considerable bargaining leverage. When *E.R.* came up for renewal in 2000, NBC paid Warner Brothers Television a record $13 million per episode. In order to lure *Friends* back for a final season in 2003–04, NBC paid Warner Brothers $10 million per episode and reduced its order to just eighteen episodes. In spite of sagging ratings, the Emmy-winning *The West Wing* was renewed for $6 million per episode.

While broadcast networks have only a single revenue source—advertising sales—cable networks earn money from advertising and from charging transmission fees to cable and satellite delivery systems, which are passed along to viewers as higher service rates. For the most successful networks, such as Disney's ESPN, these transmission fees can be raised by as much as 20 percent annually. By combining broadcast and cable networks, a company like NBC increases its bargaining leverage over cable and satellite systems when negotiating transmission fees and over advertisers when negotiating advertising rates across a range of networks that can provide access to different sorts of viewers. In addition, a diversified portfolio of broadcast and cable networks allows a company like NBC to reconstitute much of the audience lost by the traditional broadcast networks over the past two decades. Although the audience for the broadcast networks continues to shrink, the five companies that control the broadcast networks still reach more than 80 percent of viewers in prime time, when counting the ratings for their combined broadcast and cable networks. This explains why half of the top 50 cable networks have changed hands since 1990 and why most are now controlled by the five companies that already own broadcast networks.

Cable networks also allow companies to spread operating costs and extend their global reach. NBC has achieved greater efficiency and reach for CNBC by expanding CNBC Europe and CNBC Asia Pacific (both of which are jointly owned with Dow Jones, the publisher of the *Wall Street Journal*) through a range of localized services using the resources of partners in Japan, Australia, Singapore, Hong Kong, Sweden, and several other countries. The 24-hour news network MSNBC uses the resources of NBC News to provide programming for both cable and Internet. Cable networks also lend themselves to the establishment of brand identities and to cross-promotional opportunities, as networks like ESPN, MTV, and Nickelodeon have proven for NBC's competitors. After taking complete ownership of the Bravo cable network in December 2002 by purchasing Cablevision's 50 percent stake for $1.25 billion, NBC spent one-quarter of Bravo's annual marketing budget to launch a signature program, *Queer Eye for the Straight Guy*. With its splashy summer 2003 debut, *Queer Eye* pointed the way toward a future of corporate synergy at NBC. It is relatively inexpensive to produce and loaded with product placements that cannot be ignored by viewers with TiVo. NBC promoted it heavily throughout the network schedule—its cast appeared on the Today and Tonight shows—and has aired episodes in prime time on NBC. Regular episodes on Bravo have drawn as many as 3 million viewers—small by network standards, but the largest in Bravo's 22-year history. In this intensive marketing campaign, one can glimpse the future of corporate synergy and the strategy for transforming a program and a cable network into a marketable brand.

NBC's acquisition of Vivendi's Universal properties follows as a logical step in the network's expansion and should be viewed as a response to two trends: the rising cost of programming, and the value of cable networks. With the support of new GE chairman Jeff Immelt, Robert Wright pursued the Universal assets when they became available after Vivendi CEO Jean-Marie Messier drove the company to the brink of bankruptcy. The movie studio and theme parks may not play a significant role in NBC's long-term plans (and there is speculation that NBC will sell the theme parks in the near future), but they are the cost of acquiring Vivendi's other assets: the television production operation, a library consisting of over 5,000 movies and 34,000 hours of television, and the cable channels USA, Sci-Fi, and Trio. NBC wants its own studio in order to avoid being held hostage in negotiations with producers—or at least to share in the syndication profits of series that achieve success on the network. NBC now owns the *Law and Order* franchise, which reduces many of the headaches involved in negotiating its renewal (though it creates new concerns about potential conflicts of interest) and cuts the network in on its syndication revenues. The real value of the deal for NBC lies in the expansion of its cable holdings through Vivendi's three established cable networks. Over the last half-decade it has often seemed like an episode of *Law and Order* was always on the air, with originals and repeats on NBC or syndicated reruns on A&E, TNT, and USA at virtually any hour of the day. With NBC's newly acquired library of *Law and Order* episodes, and a growing portfolio of cable channels, it is not sheer fantasy to imagine that we have moved one step closer to the day when there will be a cable network that consists of nothing but *Law and Order*, all day, every day.

CHRISTOPHER ANDERSON

See also **Bravo;** *Cosby Show, The;* **Cheers;** *Friends;* **Kintner, Robert E.;** *L.A. Law; Law and Order;* **MSNBC;** *Saturday Night Live; Seinfeld;* **Tartikoff, Brandon; Telemundo; Tinker, Grant;** *Tonight Show, The;* **Weaver, Sylvester (Pat); Wright, Robert C.; Zworykin, Vladimir**

Further Reading

Auletta, Ken, *Three Blind Mice: How the TV Networks Lost Their Way,* New York: Random House, 1991

Barnouw, Erik, *A History of Broadcasting in the United States,* New York: Oxford University Press, 1968

Carter, Bill, "*Law and Order,* A Hot Franchise, Seeks a Rich Deal Early From NBC," *New York Times* (June 2, 2003)

Gunther, Marc, "Jeff Zucker Faces Life Without Friends," *Fortune* (May 12, 2003)

Hirschberg, Lynn, "The Stunt Man," *New York Times Magazine* (September 16, 2001)

Leonard, Devin, "The Unlikely Mogul," *Fortune* (September 29, 2003)

MacDonald, J. Fred, *One Nation Under Television,* New York: Pantheon, 1990

Tinker, Grant, with Bud Rukeyser, *Tinker in Television: From General Sarnoff to General Electric,* New York: Simon and Schuster, 1994

Weaver, Sylvester L. ("Pat"), *The Best Seat in the House: The Golden Years of Radio and Television,* New York: Knopf, 1994

National Cable and Telecommunications Association

U.S. Industry Trade Association

The National Cable and Telecommunications Association (NCTA) is the major trade organization for the U.S. cable television industry, mediating the professional activities of cable system operators, program services (networks), and equipment manufacturers. From its inception, the NCTA has served the dual function of promoting the growth of the cable industry and dealing with the regulatory challenges that have kept that growth in check. The organization's publications and regular meetings have kept members apprised of new technologies and programming innovations, and its legal staff has played a key role in the many executive, legislative, and judicial decisions affecting the cable industry over the years.

The NCTA first was organized as the National Community Television Council on September 18, 1951, when a small group of community antenna television (CATV) operators met at a hotel in Pottsville, Pennsylvania. They gathered in response to concern over the Internal Revenue Service's attempts to impose an 8 percent excise tax on their operations. These businessmen quickly became aware of other common interests, leading to a series of organizational meetings during September and October 1951 and January 1952. On January 28, 1952, the organization's name officially was changed to National Community Television Association.

The NCTA's growth kept pace with the rapidly expanding CATV industry. Within its first year, close to 40 CATV systems joined the organization. Membership then grew into the hundreds by the end of the 1950s and the thousands by the end of the 1960s. In 1968 the term "community antenna television" gave way to the term "cable," reflecting the industry's expanded categories of service, including local news, weather information, and channels of pay television. Accordingly, the NCTA changed its official name to National Cable Television Association. It subsequently changed its name again, in May 2001, to National Cable and Telecommunications Association in order, according to an April 30, 2001, press release, to reflect "cable's transformation from a one-way video provider to a competitive supplier of advanced, two-way services."

Today, the NCTA is headquartered in Washington, D.C. It represents cable systems serving over 80 percent of U.S. cable subscribers, as well as cable program services (networks), hardware suppliers, and other services related to the industry. The organization is divided into departments including: Administration and Finance; Association Affairs; Government Relations; Industry Affairs; Legal; Programming and Marketing; Public Affairs; Research and Policy Analysis; and Science and Technology.

The NCTA hosts an annual industry-wide trade show and produces a number of reports and periodicals. It also maintains an extensive website featuring up-to date cable statistics, addresses, and listings (*www.ncta.com*). From 1979 until 1997 the NCTA recognized outstanding programming for cable television through the National Academy of Cable Programming, which presented the Cable Ace Awards. After that date the Academy of Television Arts and Sciences began to recognize cable programming within the Emmy competition. The NCTA currently presents the Vanguard Awards for personal achievement in a number of categories, including Distinguished Vanguard Awards for

Courtesy of the NCTA

Leadership, Young Leadership, Programmers, Associates and Affiliates, Science and Technology, Cable Operations and Management, Government and Community Relations, and Marketing.

The Association also sponsors Cable in the Classroom, a free service that provides copyright cleared material to schoolrooms. According the NCTA website, the service reaches 81,000 public and private schools, providing materials to 78 percent of K–12 students in the United States.

Throughout the late 1990s and early 2000s, the NCTA has been involved with numerous decisions and controversies surrounding the 1996 Telecommunications Act. More generally, the growing presence of the Internet and other broadband technologies have confronted the cable industry with increasing competition from Direct Broadcast Satellite, and the association has focused efforts on defense of cable modem delivery of high-speed Internet service.

MEGAN MULLEN

See also **Association of Independent Television Stations; Cable Networks; United States: Cable**

Further Reading

Hazlett, Thomas W., "Wired: The Loaded Politics of Cable TV," *New Republic* (May 29, 1989)

McAvoy, Kim, "NCTA's Decker Anstrom: Working around 'Profound Disagreements' with FCC," *Broadcasting and Cable* (May 8, 1995)

Phillips, Mary Alice Mayer, *CATV: A History of Community Antenna Television,* Evanston, Illinois: Northwestern University Press, 1972

Victor, Kirk, "Shifting Sands," *National Journal* (November 20, 1993)

National Educational Television Center

The National Educational Television (NET) Center played the dominant role in building the structure on which the U.S. Public Broadcasting Service (PBS) rests. Funded primarily by Ford Foundation grants, NET was established in 1952 to assist in the creation and maintenance of an educational television service complementary to the entertainment-centered services available through commercial stations. NET initially was designed to function simply as an "exchange center," most of whose programming would be produced at the grassroots level by member stations. This strategy failed to attract a substantial audience because programming produced by the affiliates tended to be overly academic and of poor quality.

By 1958, NET's programming had acquired a well-deserved reputation as dull, plodding, and pedantic. NET officials recognized that if it were to survive and move beyond its "university of the air" status, NET needed strong leadership and a new program philosophy. They hired the station manager of WQED-Pittsburgh, John F. White, to take over the presidency of NET. An extremely ambitious proponent of the educational television movement, White believed that the system would grow and thrive only if NET provided strong national leadership. Consequently, White saw his task as that of transforming NET into a centralized network comparable to the three commercial networks. First, he moved NET headquarters from Ann Arbor, Michigan, to New York City, where it could be associated more closely with its commercial counterparts. Next, he declared his organization to be the "Fourth Network," and attempted to develop program strategies aimed at making this claim a reality. No longer relying primarily on material produced by affiliated stations, NET officials now sought high-quality programming obtained from a variety of sources, including the British Broadcasting Corporation (BBC) and other international television organizations.

In 1964 the Ford Foundation decided to substantially increase their support of NET through a $6 million yearly grant. They believed that only a well-financed, centralized program service would bring national attention to noncommercial television and expand audiences for each local station. The terms of the grant allowed NET to produce and distribute a five-hour, weekly package divided into the broad categories of cultural and public affairs programming. The freedom provided by this funding generated a period of creative risk-taking between 1964 and 1968. Their cultural programming included adult drama such as *NET Playhouse* as well as children's shows like *Mister Rogers' Neighborhood.* But it was through public affairs programming that NET hoped to emphasize its unique status as the "alternative network." Cognizant that the intense ratings war between the three commercial networks had led to a decline in public affairs programming, NET strove to gain a reputation for filling the vacuum left in this area after 1963. NET producers and directors including Alvin Perlmutter, Jack Willis, and Morton Silverstein began to film hard-hitting documentaries rarely found on commercial television. Offered under the series title *NET Journal,* such programs as *The Poor Pay More; Black Like Me; Appalachia: Rich Land, Poor People;* and *Inside North Vietnam* explored controversial issues and often took editorial stands. Although *NET Journal* received positive responses from media critics, many of NET's affiliates, particularly those in the South, grew to resent what they perceived as its "East Coast liberalism."

Despite the fact that John White and his staff believed that NET had been making progress in increasing the national audience for noncommercial television, the Ford Foundation did not share this conviction and began to reevaluate their level of commitment. Between 1953 and 1966, the foundation had invested over $130 million in NET, its affiliated stations, and related endeavors. In spite of this substantial contribution, there was a constant need for additional funding. As Ford looked for ways to withdraw its support, educational broadcasters began to look to the government for financial assistance. Government involvement in this issue led to the passage of the Public Broadcasting Act of 1967, the subsequent creation of the Corporation for Public Broadcasting (CPB), and the eventual demise of NET.

Having been at the center of the educational television movement for 15 years, NET believed it would continue as the distributor of the national network schedule. The CPB initially supported NET's role by allowing NET to serve as the "public television network" between 1967 and 1969. But in 1969 the CPB announced its decision to create an entirely new entity, the Public Broadcasting Service, to take over network operations. The CPB's decision lay not only in its awareness that NET had alienated a majority of the affiliated stations, but also in the corporation's belief that a hopeless conflict of interest would have resulted if NET continued to serve as a principal production center while at the same time exercising control over program distribution. With the creation of PBS in 1969, NET's position became tenuous. NET continued to produce and schedule programming, now aired on PBS, including the well-received BBC productions, *The Forsyte Saga* and *Civilization.* But NET's refusal to end its commitment to the production of hard-hitting controversial documentaries such as *Who Invited US?* and *Banks and the Poor* led to public clashes between NET and PBS over program content. PBS wanted to curb NET's controversial role in the system and create a new image for public television, particularly since NET documentaries inflamed the Nixon administration and imperiled funding. In order to neutralize NET, the CPB and the Ford Foundation threatened to cut NET's program grants unless NET merged with New York's public television outlet, WNDT. Lacking allies, NET acquiesced to the proposed alliance in late 1970 and its role as a network was lost. The final result was WNET-Channel 13.

The legacy that NET left behind included the development of a national system of public television stations and a history of innovative programming. As a testament to this legacy, two children's shows that made their debut on NET, *Sesame Street* and *Mister Rogers' Neighborhood,* continue to air as PBS icons (the production of original episodes of *Mister Rogers' Neighborhood* ceased in 2001 with the retirement of Fred Rogers, but reruns of the program are still broadcast on PBS; *Sesame Street* is still making new shows).

CAROLYN N. BROOKS

See also **Children's Television Workshop; Educational Television**

Further Reading

Barnouw, Erik, *Tube of Plenty: The Evolution of American Television,* New York: Oxford University Press, 1975; 2nd revised edition, 1990

Blakely, Robert J., *To Serve the Public Interest: Educational Broadcasting in the United States,* Syracuse, New York: Syracuse University Press, 1979

Brooks, Carolyn N., "Documentary Programming and the Emergence of the National Educational Television Center as a Network, 1958–1972," Ph.D. dissertation, Madison: University of Wisconsin, 1994

Brown, Les, *Television: The Business behind the Box,* New York: Harcourt Brace Jovanovich, 1971

Gibson, George H., *Public Broadcasting: The Role of the Federal Government, 1912–1976,* New York: Praeger, 1977

Koenig, Allen E., and Ruane B. Hill, editors, *The Farther Vision: Educational Television Today,* Madison: University of Wisconsin Press, 1967

Macy, John W., Jr., *To Irrigate a Wasteland,* Berkeley: University of California Press, 1974

Pepper, Robert M., *The Formation of the Public Broadcasting Service,* New York: Arno, 1979

Powell, John Walker, *Channels of Learning: The Story of Educational Television,* Washington, D.C.: Public Affairs Press, 1962

Stone, David M., *Nixon and the Politics of Public Television,* New York: Garland, 1985

Watson, Mary Ann, *The Expanding Vista: American Television in the Kennedy Years,* New York: Oxford University Press, 1990

Wood, Donald Neal, "The First Decade of the 'Fourth Network': An Historical, Descriptive Analysis of the National Educational Television and Radio Center," Ph.D. dissertation, University of Michigan, 1963

National Telecommunications and Information Administration

U.S. Policy Office

The National Telecommunication and Information Administration (NTIA), an agency within the U.S. Department of Commerce, was established in 1978. In the years preceding the NTIA's inception, the executive branch had established an Office of Telecommunication Policy (headed by Clay T. Whitehead) in order to spearhead administration communication policy in certain areas, notably cable television. The NTIA succeeded this unit and combined the responsibilities and mission of the president's Office of Telecommunication Policy (OTP) and the Department of Commerce's Office of Telecommunications. Its main responsibilities include managing the federal portion of the electromagnetic spectrum and advising and coordinating various agencies within the executive branch on telecommunications and information policy matters. It is the principal adviser to the president on communication policy and also operates a research and engineering Institute for Telecommunication Sciences in Colorado.

An organization like the NTIA seemed necessary to some policy makers in the late 1970s insofar as the Federal Communications Commission (FCC) was (and remains) increasingly burdened by the day-to-day matters of spectrum management and regulating the telephone, other common carrier, television, and cable industries. The commission was hindered by these routine tasks from developing long-range policies that could effectively plan for the increasing range of communication technologies. Moreover, at the same time, the Nixon and Ford administrations were highly critical of the media and desired a more powerful, direct hand in their regulation. The Office of Telecommunications Policy was created in 1970 to satisfy President Richard Nixon's concern in this regard, and under Whitehead the OTP quickly took on duties formerly assumed to be the FCC's jurisdiction. For example, the FCC's 1972 cable rules were largely worked out by Whitehead's office through a consensus agreement crafted among the broadcasting, cable, and program production industry representatives. Under President Jimmy Carter, the OTP's functions were transferred to the NTIA.

Conceived as a planning and policy-generating body within the Department of Commerce, the NTIA maintains its advisory agency status, even though it is capable of mustering strong political support for its positions. Its approximately 250 employees investigate core issue areas that include structuring telecommunications services within a competitive framework, encouraging innovation, and identifying policy adjustments necessary to move efficiently toward a digital era. Some of its reports and position statements have addressed topics such as using spectrum efficiently, smoothing the transition to Third Generation (3G) advanced mobile phone services, promoting e-commerce, advocating public interest considerations in broadcasting's transition to digital signals, and identifying Internet standards.

The NTIA's reports and investigations have yielded information and positions important to some congressional action and to some administration policies regarding communication industries. In the 1990s, for example, the NTIA took a lead role in gathering data and publishing four analyses of the status of the "digital divide" in the United States. The "digital divide" refers to numerous forms of unequal access to a range of Internet service. The most simple "divide" is the gap between those who have computers and those who do not. Even those who have computers, however, do not always have access to Internet service providers. And even among those who have both, a more sophisticated version of the "digital divide" concept refers to user skills, educational opportunities, and class differences." These reports focused a great deal of attention on the role of computers and the Internet in American society. The NTIA has maintained a Public Telecommunications Facilities Program, which helps public broadcasting services cover capital costs associated with endeavors such as upgrading to digital broadcasting. In the 1990s the NTIA also initiated a Technology Opportunities Program (formerly called the Telecommunications and Information Infrastructure Assistance Program, or TIIAP), to assist community-based programs that sought to use advanced telecommunications capabilities for local education and development.

SHARON STROVER

Courtesy of NTIA

See also **Geller, Henry**

Further Reading

Note: Additional information about the National Telecommunications and Information Administration, including various reports on the Digital Divide, are available at the NTIA website: www.ntia.doc.gov/reports.html

National Telecommunications and Information Administration, U.S. Department of Commerce, *NTIA Telecom 2000: Charting the Course for a New Century,* (NTIA Special Publication 88–21), Washington, D.C.: NTIA, October 1988

National Telecommunications and Information Administration, U.S. Department of Commerce, *The NTIA Infrastructure Report: Telecommunications in the Age of Information,* (NTIA Special Publication 91–26), Washington, D.C.: NTIA, October 1991

Stoil, M., "The Executive Branch and International Telecommunications Policy: The Case of WARC '79," in *Communications Policy and the Political Process,* edited by J. Havick, Westport, Connecticut: Greenwood Press, 1983

Nature Programs. *See* **Wildlife and Nature Programs**

Nature of Things, The

Canadian Science Program

One of the longest-running television shows in Canadian history, *The Nature of Things* has aired continuously since November 6, 1960. An hour-long general science program, the show began as a half-hour series—an attempt, as the first press release phrased it, "to put weekly science shows back on North American television schedules." It billed itself as "unique on this continent. On every other television network, the scientist will have stepped aside for the comedian, the gunfighter, or the private-eye." The multi-award-winning show has been broadcast in more than 80 countries, including the United States, where it has aired on the Discovery Channel and PBS.

The first producer of the show was Norman Caton, and the first hosts were Patterson Ivey and his colleague Donald Hume of the University of Toronto. Ivey had cohosted a series in 1959 called *Two for Physics,* and CBC hoped that the time was ripe for a new science series. The series produced shows on the causes of schizophrenia, a review of space technology, a study on how the brain works, and a study of the controlled isolation of human beings. In keeping with the then-lofty aspirations of the CBC, the show was named after a poem by the Roman philosopher Lucretius, "De Rerum Natura" (The Nature of Things).

Since 1979, David Suzuki has been the host of *The*

The Nature of Things.
Photo courtesy of CBC Television

Nature of Things. As a biologist and geneticist, he has been very conscious of the nature of evolution and growth. An ardent and vocal environmental conservationist, Suzuki is a social activist for environmental causes. In the beginning, he appeared an awkward and stilted host, but over the years his manner has relaxed and his delivery improved to the point that the show is practically synonymous with the former fruit-fly geneticist. In fact, its official title is now *The Nature of Things with David Suzuki,* and the host is recognized throughout Canada.

Some of the topics that the show has explored over the years are the disintegration of books in libraries, the logging of old-growth forests, euthanasia, drugs in sports, chaos theory, the history of rubber, the Penan tribe of Malaysia, farmers' use of pesticides, the use of animals in research, forensic science, air crashes, the James Bay hydro-electric project, endangered species, lasers, global warming, children's toys, the pharmaceutical industry, and the reintroduction of Peregrine falcons to the wild. Many individual shows have been produced under the subject headings of endangered species, dimensions of the mind, aspects and diseases of the human body, the global economy, and international issues. *The Nature of Things* repeatedly investigates controversial topics long before they become popular in the general press: in 1972 it did a show on acupuncture and in 1969 one on the dangers of pollution. One show was accused of bias by the forest industry and the Canadian Imperial Bank of Commerce pulled its commercials from the CBC. Another on the global economy and its effect on the environment was also criticized by some groups as being unbalanced. *The Nature of Things,* however, has never been charged with shirking the tough issues.

On the occasion of the 30th anniversary of *The Nature of Things* in 1990, Suzuki wrote in *The Toronto Star* that in the gimmicky world of television-land, where only the new is exciting, "the longevity of a TV series is just like the persistence of a plant or animal species—it reflects the survival of the fittest." In its first 30 years, the program had only three executive producers—John Livingston, James (Jim) Murray, and Nancy Archibald. As of 2002, the executive producer was Michael Adler.

In 1971 Suzuki hosted *Suzuki on Science,* another CBC science show. Suzuki has also been heard for many years on CBC Radio, serving as host of *Quirks and Quarks* from 1974 to 1979 and hosting or contributing to many other programs. In 1979 *Science Magazine,* which Suzuki had hosted since 1974, and *The Nature of Things* were combined into a one-hour show, with Murray again acting as executive producer. Suzuki was an assistant professor at the University of Alberta (Edmonton) and a full professor at the University of British Columbia (Vancouver) before retiring from academia in 2001. In 1977 he was named to the Order of Canada, the country's highest honor.

Ratings for *The Nature of Things* dropped somewhat in 1990, but CBC retained the show. The show has changed with the times, often being the first to explore new subject areas, but the fact that it has been so successful can also be attributed to the ability of its makers to make science understandable, interesting, and entertaining for audiences who vary widely in age, class, race, and cultural background.

JANICE KAYE

Hosts/Presenters
Lister Sinclair
Patterson Ivey
Donald Hume
John Livingston
David Suzuki

Producers
David Walker, John Livingston, James Murray, Nancy Archibald, Norm Caton, Lister Sinclair, Michael Adler

Programming History
CBC
1960–80   Half-hour weekly
1980–   One-hour weekly

Further Reading

Stewart, Sandy, *Here's Looking at Us: A Personal History of Television in Canada,* Toronto: CBC Enterprises, 1986

NBC. *See* National Broadcasting Company

NBC Mystery Movie, The

U.S. Police/Detective Drama

The NBC Mystery Movie aired on the network from 1971 until 1977 and consisted of several recurring programs. Its use of a rotation of different shows under an umbrella title was an NBC innovation during this era. *Mystery Movie* followed on the heels of the network's 1968 umbrella series, *The Name of the Game* (which ran each of its different segments under the same title). In 1969 NBC launched *The Bold Ones* (which included *The New Doctors, The Lawyers, The Protectors,* and, in 1970, *The Senator*), and in 1970 the

NBC Mystery Movie: McCloud, Dennis Weaver.
Courtesy of the Everett Collection

network presented the *Four in One* collection of *Night Gallery, San Francisco International Airport, The Psychiatrist,* and *McCloud.* But the idea behind *Mystery Movie* and similar "wheel format" series had much deeper roots than these NBC versions and can be traced back at least to ABC's *Warner Brothers Presents,* which debuted in 1955.

The original incarnation of *The NBC Mystery Movie* consisted of three rotating series. *McCloud,* starring Dennis Weaver as a modern-day western marshal transplanted from New Mexico to the streets of New York City, was a holdover from NBC's earlier *Four in One* lineup. *McMillan and Wife* starred Rock Hudson and Susan St. James as San Francisco Police Commissioner Stewart McMillan and his wife, Sally. And the most successful *Mystery Movie* segment of all, *Columbo,* featured Peter Falk reprising his role from the highly rated 1968 NBC made-for-television movie, *Prescription: Murder,* as a seemingly slow-witted yet keenly perceptive and doggedly tenacious

Los Angeles Police Department (LAPD) homicide lieutenant.

The new Wednesday night series was an immediate success for NBC, finishing at number 14 in the Nielsen ratings for the 1971–72 season. In addition, *Columbo* was nominated for eight Emmy Awards (including all three nominations for dramatic series writing), winning in four categories. For the next season, NBC attempted to parlay the *Mystery Movie*'s success in two ways. First, it moved the original *Mystery Movie* lineup of *Columbo, McCloud,* and *McMillan and Wife* to the highly competitive Sunday night schedule and, as a fourth installment to this rotation, added *Hec Ramsey,* starring Richard Boone as a turn-of-the-century western crime fighter. Also, NBC initiated a completely new slate of similar shows and moved these into the Wednesday time period formerly occupied by the original *Mystery Movie* lineup. Thus, NBC's 1972 fall schedule contained the original *Mystery Movie* shows, now called *The NBC Sunday Mystery Movie,* plus a completely new set of programs, titled *The NBC Wednesday Mystery Movie.*

NBC continued to achieve commercial and critical success with its *Sunday Mystery Movie* series. The umbrella program finished tied as the fifth-highest-rated series of the 1972–73 season, and *Columbo* garnered four more Emmy nominations to go along with acting nominations for *McMillan and Wife*'s Susan St. James and Nancy Walker. But the *Wednesday Mystery Movie* lineup never was able to realize a similar degree of success. The new Wednesday series included *Banacek,* starring George Peppard as a sleuth who made his living by collecting insurance company rewards for solving crimes and insurance scams (Banacek's Polish-American heritage was also a featured element of the program); *Cool Million,* a segment that featured James Farentino as a high-priced private investigator and former CIA agent; and *Madigan,* starring Richard Widmark as a New York police detective. While the shows' concepts may have sounded similar to those of the original *Mystery Movie* segments, they lacked the novelty and unique characterizations of the originals, and NBC's attempt to clone its *Mystery Movie* format in such a way that it could fill a second block in its prime-time schedule was ultimately unsuccessful. The "knock-off" Wednesday lineup was retooled several times over its two seasons on the air. *Madigan* and *Banacek* were retained for the 1973 fall season, joined in the rotation by *Tenafly,* which featured African-American actor James McEachin as a Los Angeles P.I. (the series title was suspiciously similar to the 1972 "blaxploitation" hit film, *Superfly*), *The Snoop Sisters,* which brought Helen Hayes to prime-time television as half of a mystery-writing/crime-solving team of elderly sisters, and *Faraday and Company,* starring veteran film and television actor Dan Dailey. But after seeing no better results in its second year, the *NBC Wednesday Mystery Movie* was dropped for the 1974 fall season.

NBC was not the only network unable to clone the *Mystery Movie* formula successfully. Both ABC, with its 1972 *The Men* series, and CBS, with its 1973 *Tuesday Night CBS Movie* (which rotated made-for-TV movies with the series *Shaft,* featuring Richard Roundtree reprising the title role from the film of the same name, and *Hawkins,* starring the legendary Jimmy Stewart as a small-town attorney), failed in similar short-lived attempts. But while its imitators struggled, the three original *Mystery Movie* entries remained strong into the mid-1970s. Over these years, NBC continued to try to find a fourth element that could be added to the *Columbo/McCloud/McMillan and Wife* mix, trying out such shows as *Amy Prentiss, McCoy,* and *Lanigan's Rabbi.* Finally, in the fall of 1976, *Quincy, M.E.,* starring Jack Klugman as a Los Angeles medical examiner, joined the rotation. In early 1977 it was spun off as a regular weekly series and would go on to have a successful seven-year run on the network.

By the end of the 1976–77 season, *The Sunday Mystery Movie* had reached the end of its run and was replaced on the NBC schedule by *The Big Event.* But *The NBC Mystery Movie* had left a legacy that would not soon be forgotten, and the series served as an inspiration for a future television trend: the recurring made-for-television movie, featuring regular characters and routine plotlines, which would appear only a limited number of times each season. Ironically, one of the most popular of such recurring programs would be *Mystery Movie's* own *Columbo,* which was revived in the late 1980s by ABC and would go on to garner once again high ratings and still more Emmy Awards for its new network.

DAVID GUNZERATH

See also **Action/Adventure Programs;** *Columbo;* **Detective Programs; Police Programs**

Series Presented As Part of *The NBC Mystery Movie*

1971–72	[Wednesday] *Mystery Movie: Columbo, McCloud, McMillan and Wife*
1972–73	*Sunday Mystery Movie: Columbo, McCloud, McMillan and Wife, Hec Ramsey*
	Wednesday Mystery Movie: Madigan, Cool Million, Banacek
1973–74	*Sunday Mystery Movie: Columbo, McCloud, McMillan and Wife, Hec Ramsey*
	Wednesday Mystery Movie: Madigan, Tenafly, Faraday and Company, The Snoop Sisters (January 1972, series scheduled on Tuesday as *NBC Tuesday Mystery Movie*)
1974–75	*Sunday Mystery Movie: Columbo, McCloud, McMillan and Wife, Amy Prentiss*
1975–76	*Sunday Mystery Movie: Columbo, McCloud, McMillan and Wife, McCoy*
1976–77	*Sunday Mystery Movie: Columbo, McCloud, McMillan and Wife, Quincy, M.E.* (through December 1976), *La nigan's Rabbi* (from January 1977)

Producers
Various

Programming History
NBC

September 1971–January 1974	Wednesday 8:30–10:00
September 1972–September 1974	Sunday 8:30–10:00
January 1974–September 1974	Tuesday 8:30–10:00
September 1974–September 1975	Sunday 8:30–10:30
September 1975–September 1976	Sunday 9:00–11:00
October 1975–April 1977	Sunday various times
May 1977–September 1977	Sunday 8:00–9:30

Further Reading

Brooks, Tim, and Earle Marsh, *The Complete Directory to Prime Time Network TV Shows, 1946–Present,* New York: Ballantine, 1985

Goldberg, Lee, *Television Series Revivals,* Jefferson, North Carolina: McFarland, 1993

Levinson, Richard, and William Link, *Stay Tuned: An Inside Look at the Making of Prime-Time Television,* New York: St. Martin's Press, 1981

Marc, David, and Robert J. Thompson, *Prime Time, Prime Movers: From I Love Lucy to L.A. Law—America's Greatest TV Shows and the People Who Created Them,* Boston: Little, Brown, 1992

Martindale, David, *Television Detective Shows of the 1970s,* Jefferson, North Carolina: McFarland, 1991

O'Neil, Thomas, *The Emmys: Star Wars, Showdowns, and the Supreme Test of TV's Best,* New York: Penguin Books, 1992

NBC Reports

U.S. Documentary

Although not as renowned as *ABC CloseUp, CBS Reports,* or *NBC White Paper, NBC Reports* offered in-depth investigations in the prestige documentary tradition for nearly two decades and is extensively woven into the history of documentaries and newsmagazines on American network television. Introduced in 1972 as a regularly scheduled series, this collection of investigative reports was designed to probe and expose issues of the day. The series is notable as much for its personnel as for its occasionally controversial content. *NBC Reports* was also instrumental in the shift by network news divisions from a long-form documentary commitment to "infotainment" news hours, and eventually the stream of stylish network newsmagazines that proliferated in the 1990s.

NBC Reports initially shared a time slot with the newsmagazine *First Tuesday* and an acclaimed historical documentary series *America,* which was produced by the BBC and Time-Life Films. (*America* moved to PBS for the 1974–75 season.) This scheduling technique became common after 1968 when the networks began experimenting with newsmagazines. News divisions wanted a program format that expanded coverage of the day's headlines but did not warrant the in-depth analysis of a documentary. The newsmagazines were intended to complement the documentary and the evening newscasts. Network executives were also searching for ways to fill programming hours and looked to their news divisions as a source. One solution was to allocate a time slot to the news division, which would fill the period with a combination of newsmagazine and documentary programs, such as *NBC Reports.*

The series arrived after an era of protest against the media that accompanied network television's coverage of the 1968 Democratic National Convention in Chicago and the anti-media sentiment that emanated from the administration of President Nixon. In this hostile climate, the very first documentary offered by *NBC Reports* provoked strong reactions. *Pensions: The Broken Promise,* which aired September 12, 1972, exposed inadequacies in national pension funds that resulted in severe losses for veteran workers. The report won a Peabody Award and praise from the American Bar Association. But it was also investigated by

the Nixon-administration Federal Communications Commission, in response to a complaint from the conservative media watchdog group Accuracy in Media that the report was one-sided and thus violated the Fairness Doctrine. The Supreme Court refused to hear the case and in 1976 let stand a lower court ruling in favor of NBC that the program had achieved reasonable balance.

A number of distinguished producers worked on *NBC Reports,* among them Pam Hill, who did her final work on the series before moving to ABC to produce *ABC CloseUp;* the prolific Robert (Shad) Northshield, who went to CBS News in 1977 and developed the peerless *CBS Sunday Morning;* Lucy Jarvis, who produced NBC documentaries on international and domestic affairs, then left the network in 1976 to become an independent producer; Fred Freed, one of television's outstanding documentarians; and Robert Rogers. Rogers, an award-winning news writer, was a protégé of the documentarian Ted Yates, who was killed in Jerusalem in 1967 while covering the Six-Day War. Rogers continued to produce documentaries and newsmagazines and later became manager of the *NBC White Paper* series.

NBC Reports was later called *NBC Report on America,* an irregularly scheduled documentary series that focused on lifestyle and domestic social issues. In 1987 the series aired two sensationalistic documentaries anchored by correspondent Connie Chung: *Life in the Fat Lane,* a program on overeating and weight control, and *Scared Sexless,* which examined American social mores after the occurrence of AIDS and the decline of the sexual revolution of the 1960s.

These programs, produced by Sid Feders, featured stylish treatments, including computer graphics, popular music, quick pacing, and a minimum of information. They also showcased a celebrity news anchor, Connie Chung, and popular entertainers, such as Alan Alda, Marcus Allen, Nell Carter, Dom Deluise, Jane Fonda, Goldie Hawn, Tommy Lasorda, Danny Sullivan, and Oprah Winfrey.

Although these programs shared characteristics with traditional documentaries—in that they incrementally developed a thesis on a pressing social issue—the decision to team celebrity news reporters with entertainment idols and to evoke an aesthetic look that resembled prime-time entertainment fare was highly successful in attracting large audiences and widespread publicity. Other networks also experimented with this documentary technique, but these *NBC Report on America* broadcasts led the field in 1987 and demonstrated to network management that news divisions could produce profitable programs. By the 1990s the formula evolved into a rush of prime-time news-magazines that showcased glamorous correspondents and popular topics on all the major commercial networks.

TOM MASCARO

See also **Documentary**

Programming History

NBC
September 1972–September
1973 (irregular thereafter)   Tuesday 10:00–11:00

Further Reading

Einstein, Daniel, *Special Edition: A Guide to Network Television Documentary Series and Special News Reports, 1955–1979,* Metuchen, New Jersey: Scarecrow, 1987

Friendly, Fred, *The Good Guys, the Bad Guys, and the First Amendment,* New York: Random House, 1975

Mascaro, Tom, "Documentaries Go Stylish," *Electronic Media* (February 1, 1988)

Mascaro, Tom, "Lowering the Voice of Reason: The Decline of Network Television Documentaries in the Reagan Years," Ph.D. dissertation, Wayne State University, 1995

Yellin, David, *Special: Fred Freed and the Television Documentary,* New York: Macmillan, 1973

NBC-Universal. *See* Universal

NBC White Paper

U.S. News Documentary

Beginning with its premiere in 1960, the long-form documentary series *NBC White Paper* won praise for using the television medium to foster journalistic excellence and an understanding of world affairs. By the 1980s, the program's approach was criticized by some who felt these comprehensive reports chased away viewers and stifled newer documentary forms. This acclaimed series, though, is remembered as one of the prestigious symbols of network news that helped fuel a fierce rivalry between CBS and NBC in the 1960s.

NBC White Paper was spawned, in part, by the need of the networks to heal the damage inflicted by the quiz show scandal. CBS initiated *CBS Reports* to showcase quality nonfiction reporting. Irv Gitlin, a prominent producer for CBS, hoped to head the new series but lost out to Fred Friendly. At NBC, President Robert Kintner sought to bolster the reputation of NBC

News and face CBS head-on. Kintner recruited Gitlin to develop a prestige series, and *NBC White Paper* debuted on November 29, 1960.

Network competition invigorated documentaries. Within a two-week period in 1960, NBC aired *The U-2 Affair,* about government deception regarding a spy mission over the Soviet Union; CBS broadcast the legendary *Harvest of Shame,* which depicted the squalid lives of American migrant workers; and ABC offered *Yanki, No!,* which depicted anti-American sentiment in Central America and Cuba.

Unlike *CBS Reports* in its early years, *NBC White Paper* never had a regular time slot and appeared only a few times each year. Many of its reports, however, were powerful treatments, beginning with the original broadcast. *The U-2 Affair* chronicled the flight and downing of a secret U.S. spy plane over the Soviet

Union, along with denials and subsequent admissions by U.S. officials that such espionage took place. The pilot, Francis Gary Powers, survived the crash. The Soviets distributed film of Powers and the remains of his airplane and forced President Eisenhower to admit the deception.

Chet Huntley, NBC's answer to Edward R. Murrow, was the correspondent for many of the *White Paper* reports. Al Wasserman, formerly of CBS, assisted Gitlin as producer-director. The team was often joined by Fred Freed, Edwin Newman, Frank McGee, Robert Northshield, and others.

Although rival CBS enjoyed a more prominent reputation in the documentary field, the *White Paper* series kept pace in both foreign and domestic affairs coverage and demonstrated an equal willingness to probe controversies. Erik Barnouw recounts how *Sit-In* made NBC filmmaker Robert Young a hero in the black community and led to another report from northern Angola in West Africa. Angola was a colony of Portugal, which was attempting to quell a native uprising. Foreign newsmen were barred from observing the rebellion, but Young persuaded NBC to allow him to go with black camera man Charles Dorkins to the Congo. Armed with letters of reference from prominent African Americans, Young and Dorkins trekked through 300 miles of jungle and shot footage for the 1961 documentary *Angola: Journey to a War.*

The reporters also retrieved fragments of a napalm bomb and shot film of English-language instructions inscribed on the shrapnel. To prevent Soviet use of the report against U.S. interests, Gitlin excised the bomb segment from the final program. The report succeeded, however, in balancing the Portuguese version of events with graphic depictions of native suffering.

With *The Battle of Newburgh, White Paper* employed powerful interview techniques to push the envelope of the editorial function within the documentary form, on a par with CBS's *Harvest of Shame.* A welfare-reform plan by the city manager of Newburgh, New York, intensified debate between liberals who supported children and the underprivileged, and conservatives who decried taxation for "social purposes." An extensive *White Paper* investigation discredited Newburgh's claims about welfare fraud. Although the report illustrated both sides of the argument, a dramatic interview with one needy family had a devastating effect. In a conclusion that straddled editorializing and reportage, narrator Huntley rebuked the charge that Newburgh was riddled with cheats.

Irv Gitlin died in 1967, a year in which there were no *White Paper* reports. Fred Freed assumed the role of executive producer and focused the series on domestic issues, as with the three-part *Ordeal of the American City,* which aired in the 1968–69 season.

In 1980, *White Paper* broadcast *If Japan Can... Why Can't We?,* which explored how that country recovered from World War II to achieve world-class industrial status. NBC was inundated with requests for transcripts and copies of the program, which was studied by major corporations and universities. However, interest began to wane in the *White Paper* approach. In a *Los Angeles Times* interview in 1991, David Fanning, executive producer for the PBS documentary series *Frontline* said, "One of the reasons the documentary declined is that the networks didn't allow the form to grow and be innovative. They didn't sense that people might want something beyond the traditional 'White Paper' approach of throwing a net over an important subject and telling us about our troubles."

TOM MASCARO

See also **Documentary; Freed, Fred; Huntley, Chet**

Producers
Irving Gitlin, Fred Freed

Programming History
NBC
1960–80   various times

Further Reading

Barnouw, Erik, *Tube of Plenty: The Evolution of American Television,* New York: Oxford University Press, 1975; 2nd revised edition, 1990

Bleum, A. William, *Documentary in American Television,* New York: Hastings House, 1965

Carroll, Raymond Lee, "Factual Television in America: An Analysis of Network Television Documentary Programs, 1948–1975," Ph.D. dissertation, University of Wisconsin-Madison, 1978

Einstein, Daniel, *Special Edition: A Guide to Network Television Documentary Series and Special News Reports, 1955–1979,* Metuchen, New Jersey: Scarecrow Press, 1987

Frank, Reuven, *Out of Thin Air,* New York: Simon and Schuster, 1991

Hall, Jane, "Television; The Long, Hard Look: A Producer's Passion for 'Rattling Good Stories' Helps *Frontline* Win Awards—and Preserve a Dying Genre," *Los Angeles Times* (October 13, 1991)

Mascaro, Tom, "Documentaries Go Stylish," *Electronic Media* (February 1, 1988)

Yellin, David, *Special: Fred Freed and the Television Documentary,* New York: Macmillan, 1973

Neighbours

Australian Soap Opera

"Get back to Ramsay Street" was the 1995 promotional line used by the Ten Network, home of *Neighbours* since late 1985. The marketing strategy sought to reorient both the program itself and the audiences who have followed it through uncertain beginnings, extraordinary local and international success, and continuing quiet domestic popularity. The message was clear and reflected a key element in the program's enduring popularity: a decade after it began, after attracting millions of viewers around the world, *Neighbours* is home.

Neighbours is almost without doubt the Australian program with the highest international profile since the 1980s. Well over 2,000 episodes into production, it still commands worldwide audiences of more than 50 million and has helped transform its production company, the Grundy Organisation, into one of the world's most successful television production groups.

The program's success, both in Australia and overseas, has always been attributable to a mix of textual and industry factors. This success lies both in its qualities as a well-developed and well-executed Australian soap opera and in the ways it has been scheduled both in Australia and in the United Kingdom. The premise for the show is the daily interactions of the people living in a middle-class street in a suburb of Melbourne. It is simple in design, yet allows for any number of narrative possibilities. Significantly, it is the limiting of these possibilities to the realms of the ordinary, the unexceptional, and non-melodramatic that has ensured *Neighbours*' success for so long.

Stephen Crofts's detailed analysis of program form and content identifies several key aspects that support these general speculations. These include *Neighbours*' focus on the everyday, the domestic, and the suburban; its portrayal of women as doers; its reliance on teen sex appeal and unrebellious youth; its "feel-good" characters and wholesome neighborliness. Social tension and values conflicts are always resolved, dissolved, or repressed, and the overall ideological tone is of depoliticized middle-class citizenship.

Ramsay Street and its suburb of Erinsborough have provided a pool of characters drawn from the ranks of home owners and small-business people, school kids, and pensioners. Textually, the program firmly roots itself in the domestic—in the family and the home, friends and acquaintances, and the immediate social contexts in which they are located. The mundane nature of the domestic storylines extends to the geographical reach of the show. Erinsborough is a fictional suburb, which constructs the family homes as its hub and the local shops, hotel, surgery, and school as the domain of its characters. While it has been known to send its characters overseas, *Neighbours* has also become notorious for sending its popular players off into the far reaches of Brisbane or the Gold Coast (indeed, it seems that "overseas" is a place from which it is easier to retrieve its characters than from the depths of Queensland). In keeping with the show's philosophy of "the everyday," it is the impact that the characters' interactions with such places produces on other characters that is important to the narrative.

Initially based around three families, the Robinsons, the Ramsays, and the Clarkes, with other local residents thrown in for romance and a touch of conflict, the narrative structures of the program were sufficiently loose to allow for a considerable turnover of characters. In this respect, while the idea of the series is simple, the specifics of the houses in Ramsay Street and the families that inhabit them necessarily change and adapt. The element of continuity lies in the central institutions of the house and home and supporting institutions like small business and public education, and in the performance of small-scale romance and tragedy.

Perhaps one of the most interesting aspects of the show is its foundations in the "neighborliness" of (albeit select segments of) the local community. This means that the households and the living and working arrangements of the residents of Ramsay Street take precedence over the establishment of any strict boundaries that mark out the "family" and the roles of family members. Intergenerational conflict abounds and, while resolution is almost unfailingly the order of the day, the show provides an interesting mix of the nuclear and the non-nuclear family. In its current form, there is not one complete nuclear family unit—a significant reflection on the boundaries for the exploration of the "social" within the program's narrative framework.

Neighbours.
Photo courtesy of Grundy Television Pty Ltd.

These characteristics intertwine with the TV-industry features of the program's success. When the Seven Network axed the show in the second half of 1985—one of the monumental mistakes of Australian network programming—Grundy's managing director, Ian Holmes, offered it to the Ten Network. Ten was able to revive the show with new, sexier characters, and shining, enviable domestic sets. The focus on family and community life continued, this time with a little more glamour and in a later time slot—shifting the program from 5:30 P.M. to 7:00 P.M., Monday to Friday. When the show again ran into trouble in 1986, the new network embarked on a massive selling campaign aimed at reviving flagging Sydney ratings. It worked: ratings in Australia soared along with the developing relationship of its stars, Kylie Minogue and Jason

Donovan. This in turn led the program into the period of its phenomenal success in the United Kingdom.

Clearly, the amiable middle-class "struggles" of the Ramsay Street residents make for a markedly different narrative to those of the *EastEnders* or the residents of *Coronation Street*. *Neighbours* was the first television program in Britain to be screened twice daily and across all five weekdays by the BBC, which had been commanded into greater economic accountability by the Thatcher government of the 1980s. This strategy, followed soon after by another Australian soap opera export, *Home and Away,* was to transform the nature of the program as its cast became international stars: in Australia the already popular Minogue and Donovan, as well as Craig McLachlan and Guy Pierce, were constructed as cultural exports, with the pop-music careers of the first two building a star status unknown by Australian television actors. Morally unproblematic, the program fit well into a conservative U.K. government agenda that sought a new degree of competitiveness from the BBC at the same time that it valorized conservative themes. The BBC found that this product provided a counterpoint to other television drama such as *EastEnders* and *Coronation Street*—and it did so at far less expense. A week's worth of *Neighbours* could be acquired for around £27,000, compared to £40,000 per half-hour episode of *EastEnders*.

While *Neighbours* was winning U.K. audiences of 20 million by the end of 1988 and consistently challenging the two home-grown soaps for the position of highest-rating drama on British television, it was also criticized for its bland representation of life in a sunny, relatively trouble-free, seemingly egalitarian Australian suburb. *EastEnders,* particularly, was attracting commendation for the range of its social and ethnic representation, and, while *Neighbours* had always had its share of strong female characters, it casually overlooked multiculturalism (a phenomenon fundamental to both Australian and British society), as well as other important social subjects such as unemployment. With the U.K.'s growing list of Australian film and television imports, Australian television became the target of arguments addressing issues of British cultural maintenance. And while some of these criticisms may be well-deserved, *Neighbours,* along with *Home and Away,* was in turn important to an Australian film and television industry that was itself accustomed to being seen as an import culture dominated by American and British products. *Neighbours* was the leader in a new wave of audiovisual export successes from the 1980s onward that has invigorated and redirected the local industry.

Finally, the program remains a popular domestic soap opera. *Neighbours* fits well with the Ten Network broadcasting ethos based around the appeal of a global "youth culture." Ten has worked at building a sizeable teen demographic based strictly on ratings, and its success in this respect has contributed to a turn-around in the network's profits—Ten's level of returns to expenditure exceeds that of its long-term rival, the Seven Network. With another cast of sexier young stars, including Blair McDonough (the runner-up in the Ten Network's version of *Big Brother*), and well-chosen older, more experienced actors, *Neighbours* continues as Australia's longest-running soap and one of its most successful television exports.

STUART D. CUNNINGHAM

See also **Australian Programming;** *Coronation Street; EastEnders;* **Grundy, Reg; Soap Opera**

Cast

Max Ramsay (1985–86)	Francis Bell
Maria Ramsay (1985)	Dasha Blahova
Julie Robinson (1985)	Vikki Blanche
Rosemary Daniels (1985–97)	Joy Chambers
Danny Ramsay (1985–86)	David Clencie
Jim Robinson (1985–93)	Alan Dale
Eileen Clarke (1985–88)	Myra De Groot
Paul Robinson (1985–93)	Stefan Dennis
Lucy Robinson (1985–87)	Kylie Flinker
Helen Daniels (1985–97)	Anne Haddy
Des Clarke (1985–90)	Paul Keane
Terri Inglis (1985–86)	Maxine Klibingaitus
Barbara Hill (1985)	Louise Le Nay
Shane Mitchell (1985–88)	Peter O'Brien
Scott Robinson (1985–86)	Darius Perkins
Daphne Clarke (1985–88)	Elaine Smith
Nikki Dennison (1986–87)	Charlene Fenn
Madge Mitchell (1986–92, 1996–2001)	Anne Charleston
Scott Robinson (1986–89)	Jason Donovan
Zoe Davis (1986–87)	Alexandra Fowler
Vicki Gibbons (1986)	Charmaine Gorman
Nell Mangel (1986–89)	Vivian Gray
Jane Harris (1986–89)	Annie Jones
Henry Ramsay (1986–90)	Craig McLachlan
Charlene Mitchell (1986–88)	Kylie Minogue
Clive Gibbons (1986–87, 1989)	Geoff Paine
Mike Young (1986–90)	Guy Pearce
Sally Wells (1987–88)	Rowena Mohr
Rob Lewis (1987–88)	Ernie Bourne
Dan Ramsay (1987–88)	Syd Conabere
Edna Ramsay (1987–88)	Jessica Noad
Tom Ramsay (1987–88, 1991)	Gary Files
Harold Bishop (1987–91, 1996–)	Ian Smith
Tony Romeo (1987–88)	Nick Carrafa
Sue Parker (1987–88)	Kate Gorman
Reverend Sampson (1987–89)	Howard Bell
Lucy Robinson (1987–90)	Sascha Close
Dr. Beverly Marshall (1987–89)	Lisa Armytage
Gail Robinson (1987–89)	Fiona Corke
Katie Landers (1987–89)	Sally Jensen
Hilary Robinson (1987–90)	Anne Scott Pendlebury
Jamie Clarke (1987–90)	S.J. Dey
Emma Gordon (1987–91)	Tamsin West
Todd Landers (1987–92)	Kristian Schmid
Lou Carpenter (1988, 1992–)	Tom Oliver
Malcolm Clarke (1988–89)	Noel Trevarthen

Character	Actor
Bronwyn Davies (1988–90)	Rachel Friend
Toby Mangel (1988–90)	F. Greentree-Keane
Sharon Davies (1988–90)	Jessica Muschamp
Nick Page (1988–90)	Mark Stevens
Joe Mangel (1988–91)	Mark Little
Melanie Pearson (1988–91)	Lucinda Cowden
Sky Bishop (1989–91)	Miranda Fryer
Kerry Bishop (1989–90)	Linda Hartley
Beverley Marshall (1989–90)	Shaunna O'Grady
Melissa Jarrett (1989–91)	Jade Amenta
Matt Williams (1989–91)	Ashley Paske
Jenny Owens (1989)	Danielle Carter
Edith Chubb (1989)	Irene Inescort
Kevin Harvey (1989)	Simon Westaway
Ken Naylor (1990)	Peter Tabour
Josh Anderson (1990–91)	Jeremy Angerson
Gemma Ramsay (1990–91)	Beth Buchanan
Adam Willis (1990–91)	Ian Williams
Cody Willis (1990–92)	Amelia Frid
Doug Willis (1990–94)	Terence Donovan
Pam Willis (1990–96)	Sue Jones
Caroline Alessi (199–93)	Gillian Blakeney
Christina Alessi (1990–93)	Gayle Blakeney
Dorothy Burke (1990–93)	Maggie Dence
Toby Mangel (1990–93)	Ben Geurens
Brad Willis (1991–93)	Scott Michaelson
Gaby Willis (1991–94)	Rachel Blakely
Faye Hudson (1991–92)	Lorraine Bayly
Andrew Robinson (1991–92)	Shannon Holmes
Lucy Robinson III (1991–95)	Melissa Bell
Arthur Bright (1991–92)	Barry Hill
Glen Donnelly (1991–92)	Richard Huggett
Brenda Riley (1991–92)	Genevieve Lemon
Guy Carpenter (1991–92)	Andrew Williams
Phoebe Bright (1991–93)	Simone Robertson
Beth Brennan (1991–93, 1994)	Natalie Imbruglia
Marco Alessi (1992)	Felice Arena
Benito Alessi (1992–93)	George Spartels
Cameron Hudson (1992–93)	Ben Mitchell
Cathy Alessi (1992–93)	Elspeth Ballantyne
Stephen Gottlieb (1992–93)	Lauchie Daddo
Julie Martin (1992–94)	Julie Mullins
Rick Alessi (1992–95)	Dan Falzon
Philip Martin (1992–99)	Ian Rawlings
Hannah Martin (1992–99)	Rebecca Ritters
Debbie Martin (1992–97)	Marnie Reece-Wilmore
Michael Martin (1992–98)	Troy Beckwith
Troy Duncan (1993)	Damian Walshe-Howling

Character	Actor
Mark Gottlieb (1993–96)	Bruce Samazan
Darren Stark (1993)	Scott Major
Wayne Duncan (1993–94)	Jonathan Sammy-Lee
Lauren Carpenter (1993–94)	Sarah Vandenbergh
Annalise Hartman (1993–96)	Kimberley Davies
Cheryl Stark (1993–96)	Caroline Gillmer
Dr. Karl Kennedy (1994–)	Alan Fletcher
Billy Kennedy (1994–2000)	Jesse Spencer
Libby Kennedy (1994–)	Kym Valentine
Susan Kennedy (1994–)	Jackie Woodburne
Malcolm Kennedy (1994–97)	Benjamin McNair
Jesse O'Connor (1994)	James Ryan
Aaron O'Connor (1994)	Greg Stone
Sam Kratz (1994–96)	Richard Grieve
Marlene Kratz (1994–97)	Moya O'Sullivan
Jen Handley (1994–95)	Alyce Platt
Luke Handley (1994–96)	Bernard Curry
Brett Stark (1994–96)	Brett Blewitt
Danni Stark (1994–96)	Eliza Szonert
Luke Foster (1994)	Murray Bartlett
Sassy Patterson-Smythe (1994)	Defah Dattner
Louise Carpenter (1994)	Jiordan Anna Tolli
Kris Hyde (1994)	John Higginson
Len Mangel (1994)	John Lee
Katarina Torrelli (1994)	Josephine Mitchell
Andrew "Macca" MacKenzie (1994)	John Morris
Sally Pritchard (1994)	Brenda Webb
Serendipity Gottlieb (1994–95)	Raelee Hill
Cody Willis (1994–96)	Peta Brady
"Stonefish" Rebecchi (1994–96)	Anthony Engelman
Kev Duve (1994–98)	Brad Wade
Leanne "Packo" Packington (1994, 1995)	Verity McIntyre
Colin Taylor (1995)	Frank Bren
Reuben White (1995)	James Condon
Lance Wilkinson (1995–2001)	Andrew Bibby
Luke Bowers (1995–97)	Jamie Field
Patrick Kratz (1995)	Shane Porteous
Angie Rebecchi (1995–96)	Lesley Baker
Melissa Drenth (1995–96)	Aimee Robertson
Joanna Hartman (1995–97)	Emma Harrison
Rupert Sprod (1995–97)	Tobi Webster
Zoe Tan (1995–98)	Jeuliette Hannafie
Andrew Watson (1996)	Christopher Uhlman
Ruth Wilkinson (1996–99)	Ailsa Piper
Anne Wilkinson (1996–2000)	Brooke Satchwell

Sarah Beaumont (1996–99)   Nicola Charles
Jarrod "Toadfish" Rebecchi
  (1996–)   Ryan Moloney
Steve George (1996)   Alex Dimitriades
Georgia Brown (1996)   Petra Jared
Catherine O'Brien (1996–
  97)   Radha Mitchell
Darren Stark (1996–98)   Todd MacDonald
Ben Atkins (1997–98)   Brett Cousins
Caitlin Atkins (1997–98)   Emily Milburn
Paul McClain (1997–2001)   Jansen Spencer
Amy Greenwood (1997–
  2000)   Jacinta Stapleton
Cassandra (1997–2000)   Elizabeth Shingleton
Geoff Burke (1997–98)   Andrew McKaige
Lisa Elliot (1997)   Kate Straub
Rowan Kendrick (1997)   Paul Zebrowski
Joel Samuels (1998–2002)   Daniel MacPherson
Lily Madigan (1998)   Alethea McGrath
Karen Oldman (1998–99)   Pia Miranda
Pippa Layton (1998–2000)   Natalie Shostak
Drew Kirk (1998–)   Dan Paris
Hilary Grand (1998)   Olivia Hamnett
Mike Healy (1998)   Andrew Blackman
Mickey Dalton (1998)   Trent Fowler
Kenny Hyland (1998)   Jonathan Dutton
Wayne "Tad" Reeves
  (1999–)   Jonathan Dutton
Rose Kirk (1999, 2000)   Diana Greentree
Ron Kirk (1999, 2000)   John Orcsik
Geri Hallett (1999)   Isabella Dunwill
Maurie Ryan (1999)   Neil Fletcher
Teabag Teasdale (1999)   Nathan Phillips
Teresa Bell (1999–2001)   Krista Vendy
Joe Scully (1999–)   Shane Connor
Lyn Scully (1999–)   Janet Andrewartha
Stephanie Scully (1999–)   Carla Bonner
Felicity Scully (1999–)   Holly Valance
Michelle Scully (1999–)   Kate Keltie
Damien Smith (1999–
  2000)   John Ridley
Dione Bliss (2000–)   Madeleine West
Cecile Bliss (2000)   Molly McCaffrey
Patsy Edis (2000)   Anne Moloney
Simone King (2000–)   Denise Briskin
Bianca Nugent (2000–)   Jane Harber
Darcy Tyler (2000–)   Foster (Mark) Raffety
Bernie Samuels (2000–)   Sean Scully

Rachel Bailey (2000)   Carolyn Bock
Merridy Jackson (2000)   Suzy Cato
Connie O'Rourke (2000)   Val Jellay
Carrie Clark (2000)   Vanessa Rossini
Daniel Fitzgerald (2000)   Brett Tucker
Brendan Bell (2000)   Blair Venn
Mick Scully (2000)   Andy Anderson
Dorothy "Allana" Truman
  (2000–01)   Josephine Clark
Larry "Woody" Woodhouse
  (2000–01)   Andrew Curry
Jessica Fielding (2001–)   Elisha Gazdowicz
Matthew Hancock (2001–)   Stephen Hunt
Evan Hancock (2001–)   Nicholas Opolski
Maggie Hancock (2001–)   Sally Cooper
Leo Hancock (2001–)   Anthony Hammer
Emily Hancock (2001–)   Isabella Oldham
Stewart Parker (2001–)   Blair McDonough
Veronica Anderson (2001–)   Monika Isabella
                                                Karwan
Summer Hoyland (2002–)   Marisa Siketa

Programming History

Seven Network	
March 1985–November 1985	Weeknights 6:00–6:30
Ten Network	
November 1985–March 1992	Weeknights 7:00–7:30
March 1992–	Weeknights 6:30–7:00

Producers

The Grundy Organisation

Further Reading

Crofts, Stephen, "Global Neighbours?" in *To Be Continued... : Soap Operas around the World,* edited by Robert C. Allen, London and New York: Routledge, 1995

Cunningham, Stuart, and Elizabeth Jacka, *Australian Television and International Mediascapes,* Melbourne, Cambridge, and New York: Cambridge University Press, 1996

Cunningham, Stuart, and Toby Miller, *Contemporary Australian Television,* Sydney: University of New South Wales Press, 1994

Kingsley, Hilary, *Soap Box: The Australian Guide to Television Soap Operas,* South Melbourne: Sun Books, 1989

Moran, Albert, *Moran's Guide to Australian TV Series,* North Ryde, New South Wales: Allen and Unwin, 1993

Nelson, Ozzie (1907–1975), and Harriet Nelson (1914–1994)

U.S. Actors

During a period that was to last 20 years, the Nelson family—Ozzie, his wife Harriet Hilliard, and their two sons, David and Ricky—were regarded as the preeminent icon of the ideal nuclear family. From his band-leading days of the mid-1930s through his reign, a generation later, as the bumbling patriarch of television's best-known family, Ozzie Nelson was able to conflate, reduce, and transform the professional activities of his family's personal reality into a fictional domestic banality.

Best known for their long-running television series, *The Adventures of Ozzie and Harriet,* the Nelson family began their successful togetherness with the marriage of saxophone-playing Ozzie to his "girl-singer" Harriet in the 1930s. Ozzie's deliberate hesitancy and self-deprecating humor were the perfect foil for the sweet and sassy Harriet, who interrupted her songs with sarcastic banter. During the 1940s, Ozzie, Harriet, and their band were regulars on Red Skelton's radio show, and in 1944 when Red was drafted into the army, they took over his time slot. For Skelton, the Nelsons stuck to their big-band routines with occasional married-couple skits providing nonmusical breaks, but when Ozzie conceived the pilot for his own program he decided to venture more into the realm of domestic comedy, writing a script based on his own family life.

The radio program initially revolved around the trials and tribulations of bandleader Ozzie and his family. There were many references to Ozzie's rehearsals, road tours, and other musical endeavors, and the comedy sketches were balanced with full-length musical numbers. By 1946, however, these musical interludes were eliminated in favor of a more representational narrative. Until 1949 the roles of their two sons were played by child actors, but a guest appearance by Bing Crosby and his sons convinced Ozzie that he should allow the 13-year-old David and 9-year-old Ricky to play themselves. The boys, especially "the irrepressible Ricky," were an enormous success and lent further potency to the verisimilitude of the purely fictional narratives.

Nelson's business skills were unparalleled (he had attended law school at Rutgers University), and he negotiated with ABC for the first "noncancellable ten-year contract," which guaranteed a basic salary for ten years whether the Nelsons worked or not. The family was thus virtually immune from sponsor or network interference (one of the reasons, certainly, that Ozzie and Harriet would be the only television couple allowed a double bed until 1969's *The Brady Bunch*).

While in the middle of this contractual period, ABC expressed interest in a television program. As a test, they had the family star in a movie titled *Here Come the Nelsons* for Universal Studios. The film, costarring Rock Hudson and featuring Ozzie as an advertising executive, was a huge success, and in 1952 the television program began filming at General Service Studios. Interestingly, for the next two years, the radio and television programs continued concurrently, with Nelson insisting on completely different scripts for the television show.

Produced under the banner "Stage Five Productions," which included Ozzie, his brother Don, Bill Davenport, and Ben Gershman, *The Adventures of Ozzie and Harriet* was the result of the uncompromising standards and efforts of perfectionist Ozzie Nelson. He was involved in every one of the program's 435 episodes as head writer, script supervisor, producer, and editor. And, if he did not direct an episode, his son David did. Story meetings were weekly, all-night affairs (with an 11:00 P.M. break for ice cream) and took place at the Nelson home in the Hollywood Hills, with the production staff and auxiliary writers Jay Sommers, Dick Bensfield, and Perry Grant attending.

A stickler for quality, Ozzie was adamant that his program look different from the inferior kinescope products dominating the television schedule, and he hired Academy Award winner William C. Mellor to shoot the program in the finest 35 mm film stock. With preliminary editing complete, Nelson would then rent a Los Angeles theater and screen two or three episodes back-to-back for audiences in order to gauge the placement and intensity of the laugh-track cues.

One of the reasons for the program's tremendous following was that audiences actually believed that the Nelsons were truly playing themselves, a myth the Nelson family helped perpetuate. The exterior of the television house was modeled on the real-life Nelson home, and Ozzie incorporated many real-life events, neighbors, family members, and hobbies into the program. Thus, when David took up motorcycles, or when the boys were interested in the trapeze, these would become the focus for a weekly episode. David's marriage to June Blair and Ricky's to Kris Harmon occurred off-screen, but the new season joyfully "introduced" the "newest members of the Nelson family," to the television viewer.

The most significant example of this blending of fact and fiction resulted from Ricky's interest in rock and roll music. Spurred on by a girlfriend's crush on Elvis Presley, Ricky bragged that he too was about to cut a record, and then quickly enlisted his father to make this boast a reality. In April 1957, the 16-year-old Ricky released a cover version of Fats Domino's big hit "I'm Walkin." As was his habit, Ozzie integrated this latest preoccupation of his son into a television episode, and "Ricky the Drummer" aired concurrently with the record's release. One million records sold in the first week, and for the next six years, Ricky Nelson was to dominate the pop charts with such hits as "Hello, Mary Lou," "Travelin' Man," and "Fools Rush In," all of which benefited from weekly exposure on the television series. With simultaneous promotion in music-trade papers, a new song would "debut" at the end of a completely unrelated episode, tacked on as a pseudo-concert with Ricky singing to a mob of squealing, head-bopping extras. Ricky's impact on the rock world was crucial, and his eventual induction into the Rock and Roll Hall of Fame legitimized his talented contributions. More important than his actual music, perhaps, was the fact that in giving their blessing to Ricky's career, Ozzie and Harriet demonstrated to millions of timid, middle-class Americans that rock and roll was not a satanic threat, but a viable musical alternative. In an unprecedented response to the thousands of irate letters he had received, Ozzie scripted 1956's "Ozzie the Treasurer," in which Harriet extols the tension-releasing benefits of "rhythm and blues music."

Both Nelson boys attempted film careers and found moderate success in some big-budget 1950s films—David in *Peyton Place,* and Ricky in *Rio Bravo.* By the time of the program's end in 1966, however, the Nelson sons were hard-pressed to find a large popular following. Ricky ventured into country music where he had sporadic success until his 1985 death in a plane crash, and David moved into production, working

The Adventures of Ozzie and Harriet, Ricky Nelson, Harriet Nelson, David Nelson, Ozzie Nelson, 1952–66. *Courtesy of the Everett Collection*

mainly in commercials and low-budget features. Their parents, too, seemed unable to capture the magic of the earlier years. A boarding-house sitcom, *Ozzie's Girls,* was canceled during its first season, and the couple semiretired, making the talk show circuit and living together in Laguna Beach until Ozzie's death in 1975.

From the outset, *The Adventures of Ozzie and Harriet* had a nostalgic feel, resembling Ozzie's 1920s youth in New Jersey more than 1950s Los Angeles. The picket-fenced neighborhoods and the corner drugstore and malt shop that were featured weekly in this slow-paced half-hour infiltrated American culture at a time of social unease and quiescent distress. In reality, most 1950s fathers were working ten-hour days and commuting long distances to isolated suburbs. For the Nelsons, however, Ozzie was always home, neighbors still chatted over the back fence, and downtown was a brisk walk away. The Nelsons presented an America that never was, but always wished for, and through their confusion of reality and fantasy worked to concoct an image of American life that is, to this day, mistakenly claimed not only as ideal, but as authentic.

NINA C. LEIBMAN

*See also **Adventures of Ozzie and Harriet, The;
Comedy, Domestic Settings; Family on Television***

Harriet Nelson (Harriet Hilliard). Born Peggy Lou Snyder in Des Moines, Iowa, July 18, 1914. Attended St. Agnes Academy. Married: Ozzie Nelson, 1935; children: David Ozzie and Eric Hilliard. Beauty queen hired as vocalist for Ozzie Nelson's Orchestra, 1932; recording artist for Brunswick, Vocalian, Victor, and Blue Bird; as Harriet Hilliard, was a leading lady in film from 1936; various radio appearances on Red Skelton's radio program in the 1940s, costarred with husband Ozzie in radio series *The Adventures of Ozzie and Harriet,* 1944–54; star of television version of *The Adventures of Ozzie and Harriet,* 1952–66. Recipient: National Family Week Radio citation by the International Council on Christian Family Life, 1947; Radio and TV Women of Southern California Genii Award, 1960; *Los Angeles Times* Woman of the Year; *TV-Radio Mirror* Reader's Poll Best Husband-Wife Team in TV, seven consecutive years. Died in Laguna Beach, California, October 2, 1994.

Television Series

| 1952–66 | *The Adventures of Ozzie and Harriet* |
| 1973 | *Ozzie's Girls* |

Made-for-Television Movies

| 1976 | *Smash-up on Interstate 5* |

Films

Follow the Fleet, 1936; *She's My Everything,* 1936; *Sweetheart of the Campus,* 1941; *Canal Zone,* 1942; *Falcon Strikes Back,* 1943; *Here Come the Nelsons,* 1952.

Radio

Joe Penner's radio show, 1933; Red Skelton's radio show, 1940s; *The Adventures of Ozzie and Harriet,* 1944–52.

Stage

The Impossible Years; State Fair.

Publications

"My Heart Belongs to My Three Men" (with Cameron Shipp), *Woman's Home Companion* (June 1953)

"The Men in My Life" (with Stanley Gordon), *Look* (November 11, 1958)

Ozzie Nelson (Oswald George Nelson). Born in Jersey City, New Jersey, March 20, 1907. Graduated from Rutgers University, 1927, law degree 1930. Married: Harriet Hilliard, 1935; children: David Ozzie and Eric Hilliard. Formed a successful orchestra, 1930; several guest appearances with wife Harriet on Red Skelton's radio program in early 1940s; radio series *The Adventures of Ozzie and Harriet,* 1944–54; starred in ABC-Television's popular *The Adventures of Ozzie and Harriet* 1952–66, also produced, wrote, and directed the series; occasional director of episodes for television series such as *Adam 12.* Recipient: National Family Week Radio citation by the International Council on Christian Family Life, 1947; *TV-Radio Mirror* Reader's Poll Best Husband-Wife Team in TV, seven consecutive years. Died in San Fernando Valley, California, June 3, 1975.

Television Series (star, producer, head writer, and director)

| 1952–66 | *The Adventures of Ozzie and Harriet* |
| 1973 | *Ozzie's Girls* |

Films

Sweetheart of the Campus, 1941; *Hi Good Lookin',* 1944; *People are Funny,* 1945; *Here Come the Nelsons,* 1952; *Love and Kisses* (also writer, producer, and director), 1965.

Radio

Joe Penner's radio show, 1933; Red Skelton's radio show, 1940s; *The Adventures of Ozzie and Harriet,* 1944–52.

Publications

"The Greatest Guy in the World," *Coronet* (July 1949)
Ozzie, 1973

Further Reading

"The Full Nelson," *Time* (February 16, 1948)
Holmes, John R., "The Wizardry of Ozzie: Breaking Character in Early Television," *Journal of Popular Culture* (Fall 1989)
"Mourning in Sitcomville," *New York Times* (October 5, 1994)

Netherlands, The

At first glance, the historical evolution of the broadcasting system in the Netherlands—from a public service broadcasting monopoly to a liberalized dual system of public service and commercial broadcasting—seems in keeping with general developments in Western European broadcasting. However, its embeddedness in Dutch society has equally shaped its specific evolution and contemporary look.

It is impossible to explain the unique structure of Dutch audiovisual media without the concept of "pillarization." This sociocultural phenomenon describes how, from the end of the 19th century on, different religious and ideological groups in Dutch society (Roman Catholics, protestants, socialists, conservatives, liberals) divided society as a whole in segregated microcosms or "pillars." Their networks of organizations encompassed political parties, trade unions, education, and leisure activities. It comes as no surprise, then, that these "pillars" were highly interested in the emerging mass media. This resulted in a system of "pillarized pluralism" whereby the public service broadcasting is not in the hands of the state, but overseen by non-profit associations controlled by religious and ideological currents in society. Although a process of cultural "depillarization" has been ongoing since the 1960s, with a weakening of the societal importance of religious and ideological beliefs, it took much longer for the broadcasting structures to adapt to this change, and even today part of their power remains intact. The irony is that television, although initially confirming pillarization (van der Haak and van Snippenburg), actually contributed to this development since everybody watched everything available, and not only the program of the relevant "pillar" (De Goede).

Dutch television is commonly associated with Hilversum, a city near Amsterdam and since radio days the country's media center. It is in Hilversum that the various radio broadcasting associations were established in the 1920s: the protestant "Dutch Christian Radio Association" (NVRV), the Roman Catholic "Catholic Radio Association" (KRO), the social-democrat "Association of Workers Radio Enthusiasts" (VARA), the progressive protestant "Modern Protestant Radio" (VPRO) and the neutral "General Association of Radio Broadcasting" (AVRO).

The Dutch electronics manufacturer Philips (today a multinational concern) received permission in 1948 to start with experimental television broadcasts for a few hundred viewers in the surroundings of the Philips headquarters in Eindhoven. From the start, government opted for a public-service approach to broadcasting. This is why in 1951, the existing broadcasting associations were granted TV broadcasting licenses under the authority of an umbrella organization, the National Television Foundation (NTS). But the population was slow to adopt television in the 1950s because of the high price of television sets in relation to average incomes at that time, the restricted reach and airtime of the broadcasts, and the strong religious views suggesting television was harmful (van der Haak and van Snippenburg).

In 1964 a commercial "pirate" station, Radio/TV North Sea (REM), began broadcasting from an offshore oil rig in international waters, but was quickly shut down by the government. That same year a second television channel, Nederland 2, was launched. The political pressure to open up the broadcasting system to commercial interests and new public license holders increased in 1965, causing the fall of a Christian-democrat and liberal coalition. The succeeding government soon came up with a white paper on the transformation of the broadcasting system into an "open system."

These plans resulted in the 1967 Broadcasting Act, the first specific broadcasting legislation in the Netherlands since radio's emergence, and a compromise between commercial and public interests. The Act confirmed the existing structure and the ban on commercial television, but accepted the introduction of new players and advertising. Airtime quota and funds were allocated according to the status (A, B, or C) of the broadcasting association. The five existing associations immediately received A-status (with 450,000 members or more), subscribers to the program guide of each association also counting as members. The Netherlands Broadcasting Corporation (NOS) was established to play a coordinating role, provide studios and technical facilities, and produce a joint program of news, weather, and sports. The Foundation for Broadcasting Advertising (STER) was to divide most of the advertising profits among the associations. The existing license fee was thus complemented with advertising revenues. The Television and Radio Broadcasting Corporation (TROS)—in fact a renewed REM—

joined the system that same year. The protestant fundamentalist "Evangelical Broadcasting Corporation" (EO) followed in 1970, as did Veronica Broadcasting Corporation (VOO or Veronica), a former offshore pirate radio station, in 1975.

The new "open system" stimulated competition among associations, thus giving television broadcasting a pseudo-commercial character (De Goede). With two new players, TROS and Veronica, lacking clear identification with a social or cultural group, the associations all promoted themselves in a quest for larger audiences. In combination with a significant schedule enlargement, many felt that the competition was lowering production and programming standards, a phenomenon labeled "Trossification" for the TROS channel, which was the first to introduce this light entertainment strategy. More and more talk shows, sitcoms and other foreign—especially American—series brought a change of diet for an audience used to a public broadcasting mix of "information, education and entertainment" (Manschot, 1993).

The public system came under growing outside threat from foreign cable stations and other developments in the 1980s. A 1983 Christian right-wing coalition white paper on the future of the mass media developed into the 1988 Media Act, a second milestone in Dutch broadcasting policy. Commercial broadcasting remained forbidden. The supervision of compliance with the Media Act was delegated to a Media Authority. And the NOS split off its facilities into the private Dutch Broadcast Production Company (NOB). Broadcasting associations no longer were forced to use NOB facilities, which stimulated the growth of an independent audiovisual production sector. To broaden the airtime, a third channel, Nederland 3, was launched in April 1988.

The overall intentions of the Media Act (keeping the system of pluralism in place, keeping commercial broadcasting out) was clearly out of step with European media developments (van der Haak and van Snippenburg) The paradigm shift from public service broadcasting monopolies to a deregulated commercial broadcasting environment swept across Western Europe in the 1980s. But in the Netherlands, policy was again behind actual developments. In October 1989, RTL Veronica began broadcasting via Astra satellites from its base in Luxembourg using a "U-turn strategy." Although presenting programs in Dutch produced in the Netherlands and clearly aimed at a Dutch audience, it was recognized as a foreign station because it was partly owned by the Luxembourg-based CLT (as well as by the Dutch station Veronica), and therefore admitted on Dutch cable. Veronica was severely punished

for this commercial escapade, had to withdraw from the partnership, and RTL changed into RTL4. The station quickly attracted about a quarter of the Dutch television audience, becoming market leader within a year. The 1980s boom in programming hours created a need for cheap material with a huge popular appeal, which was largely filled with U.S. soaps and other series. *Dallas* and *Falcon Crest,* for instance, were broadcast with great popular success (and the cultural protest of intellectuals). Only in the 1990s would the production of immensely popular domestic soap operas reverse the U.S. dominance.

The last decade of the century was undoubtedly the most dynamic era in terms of new stations, mergers, and policy reforms. As a result, a new Media Act has been permanently "under construction" (van Reenen). At the same time, the development of European Union media regulations gradually reduced the scope of domestic policy to an "exercise in modesty" (De Goede, 1999). The 1990s started with the government commissioning a report from consulting firm, McKinsey & Co., on measures designed to assist public broadcasting to counter commercial television. This 1990 report was to become the basis for several years of television policy. Broadcasting associations were given a fixed space on one of the channels in order to make the three channels equally attractive to audiences and advertisers. The NOS retained its task of broadcasting news, sports, and national events. But the newly founded Netherlands Program Corporation (NPS) became responsible for cultural issues, and minorities and young people's programs. A cabinet of social democrats and liberals continued the move to liberalization in 1994. This led to a new organizational structure for the public system with an independent board of directors in charge. Since then the broadcasting organizations have been represented on a supervisory board charged with the main policy lines. And after more than 20 years, a new broadcasting association, Bart's News Network (BNN) aimed at young people, entered the public system in 1998.

It was in the arena of commercial broadcasting, however, that most thorough changes took place. RTL Launched a second station, RTL 5, in 1992, heavily relying on American series. Veronica left the public system in 1995 to form the Holland Media Group (HMG) with RTL. In 2000 Veronica left HMG and in 2003 is seeking a re-entry in the television market with other partners. HMG has approximately a 40 percent market share. The Arcade Group, a Dutch record company, entered commercial television in 1995 with The Music Factory (TMF) a very popular Dutch version of MTV (and since 2000 owned by MTV), and TV10. TV10 changed its name with consecutive ownership changes, to Fox 8 (FOX), and to V8 (SBS) in 2001. A new channel, SBS6, began in 1995, part of the Swedish-American Scandinavian Broadcasting System (SBS) Group together with *De Telegraaf,* Netherlands largest newspaper. This channel mainly broadcast reality TV, eroticism, and feature films. They launched a second channel, Net5, in 1999, directed at viewers from public broadcasting. Finally, pay-TV, existing since 1984 as Filmnet and Canal Plus, currently owned by Vivendi, has not seemed to catch on. This is not surprisingly considering the huge array of television choices already available.

Since the arrival of the commercial broadcasting companies, the public broadcasting organizations have seen their market share shrink by half, to stabilize at around 40 per cent in 1997. But the market of independent production companies has flourished, the most famous case being Endemol. The 1993 merger of Joop van den Ende and John de Mol Productions, both producing game shows, soaps, talk shows, reality TV, and drama, formed one of the largest audiovisual companies in Europe. Van den Ende's soap format *Goede Tijden, Slechte Tijd*en (GTST) (Good Times, Bad Times) was one of the first domestically produced daily soaps in Europe in 1990. It soon became a key program of RTL4, and remains very popular. Endemol has diversified its output with highly successful and internationally distributed "emotion-TV" formats such as *All You Need is Love* and the by now legendary *Big Brother.* The final episode of *Big Brother* broke all the Dutch ratings records, with 3.5 million viewers (in a population of about 16 million). Endemol, a transnational producer with subsidiaries in more than 15 European countries, turned the Netherlands into a prominent television format exporter. Telefónica, the Spanish telecom giant, acquired Endemol in 2000.

The public sector replied to the commercial competition with yet another reform in 2000, focusing on channel branding, creating diverse and clear channel profiles. Ned 1 is to be the in-depth channel inspired by family values, Ned 2 the most accessible channel, most likely to pinch viewers from commercial channels, and Ned 3 also an in-depth channel, but guided by culturally progressive values and tastes. The NOS became the only licensee, with the associations reduced to participants in the license. The license fee was replaced by a small income-tax rise.

Today, viewers in the Netherlands have a wide range of about 30 television stations, both public and commercial, domestic, foreign, and international, through one of the densest cable networks in Europe. Soccer and other sports programs have become by far the most popular program category, recently joined by reality TV shows.

In the 50 years of its existence, the Dutch broadcasting system has seen its boundaries between government, business, and non-profit associations shifted considerably, the two former gaining in influence, the latter losing power (De Goede, 1999). This resulted in a highly diversified dual landscape of public and commercial broadcasters, with a clear shift toward commercialization, internationalization, and concentration, although the government strongly supports the public broadcasting system.

The coming years of Dutch broadcasting will see digitization and Internet applications, currently in an experimental phase. The introduction of thematic TV channels such as a news channel and a children's channel are under consideration. Looking to future developments in technology, several public and private organizations have joined forces in the consortium Digitenne, with a view to providing digital terrestrial television services.

PHILIPPE MEERS

See also **Big Brother; Public Service Broadcasting**

Further Reading

Beckers, W., "Audience Research in the Netherlands," *Communications: The European Journal of Communication Research* 21/3 (1996)

De Goede, Peter, *Omroepbeleid met en tegen de tijd: interacties en instituties in het Nederlandse Omroepbestel 1919–1999* [Broadcasting Policy in and Out of Time: Interactions and Institutions in the Dutch Broadcasting System, 1919–1999], Amsterdam: Cramwinckel, 1999 (with summary in English)

Noam, Eli, *Television in Europe,* New York and Oxford: Oxford University Press, 1991

van der Haak, Kees, and Leo van Snippenburg, "The Netherlands," in *Western Broadcasting at the Dawn of the 21st Century,* edited by Leen d'Haenens and Frieda Saeys, Berlin and New York: Mouton De Gruyter, 2001

van Reenen, Ben, "The Radio and Television System in the Netherlands," in *Radio and Television Systems in Europe,* edited by Christiane Matzen, Strasbourg: European Audiovisual Observatory, 2000

Wijfjes, Huub, editor, *Omroep in Nederland: vijfenzeventig jaar medium en maatschappij 1919–1994* [Broadcasting in The Netherlands: 75 Years of Medium and Society 1919–1994], Zwolle: Waanders, 1994

Networks: United States

Networks are organizations that produce or acquire the rights to programs, distribute these on systems of interconnection, and secure uniform scheduled broadcasts on a dispersed group of local outlets. In commercial broadcasting, "networking" was recognized at an early date as the clearest path to profitability, because the costs of program production were—and are—fixed, and revenue turned on securing the maximum degree of efficient distribution and exposure to mass audiences.

In the United States, the number of broadcast networks existing at a particular time, and the prospects for entry by new networks, have always been the combined result of the current state of technology, in tension with an extensive role for government regulation. Television broadcasting, tentatively begun prior to the American entry to World War II in 1941, was suspended for the duration of the war, and did not resume until the first wave of station activations in 1946 through 1948. By then, the dynamics of technology and regulation established for radio broadcasting already had shaped the possibilities for television networks.

Beginning in 1920, radio entrepreneurs in the United States had developed an array of informational and entertainment fare, originated in live performances at local stations, and increasingly at network studios in New York City, from which feeds to stations could be disseminated in real time over telephone lines. Commercials, like other copy, were read and performed live. Strong local stations prospered in this system, but the highest return was enjoyed by two major networks, Columbia Broadcasting System (CBS), and the National Broadcasting Company (NBC) unit of a premier radio equipment manufacturer, Radio Corporation of America (RCA). RCA operated dual networks, the Red and Blue. In radio, as was to be the case in television, industry leadership was exercised by a charismatic executive and founder, Robert Sarnoff at NBC, William S. Paley at CBS, Allen B. DuMont, and a few others.

The first comprehensive U.S. radio law, the Radio Act of 1927, did not confer on government any express power to regulate networks directly, but empowered it to regulate stations engaged in "chain broadcasting." This served to consolidate industry control by the network organizations already under-way. The law mandated that radio broadcasting stations be allotted in a manner that equitably served the various states and localities, but withheld actual station ownership of broadcast channels, in favor of renewable licenses for limited periods. It also prohibited the licensing of a person or entity that had been convicted of unfair competition or monopolization. These precepts carried over with the Communications Act of 1934, and shaped the relationship among stations, networks and the government throughout the emergence of television.

At the eve of American entry into World War II, the Federal Communications Commission (FCC), acting under its powers to investigate and regulate stations, concluded a probe of "chain broadcasting" and announced a series of prohibited practices in radio. These included contracts that permitted networks to command and resell advertising time for their own account, or to option time. The rulings also prohibited the specific ownership of dual networks by a single entity, NBC being the singular example. The Supreme Court's decision upholding these actions in 1943 prompted the divestiture of NBC Blue, acquired that year by Lifesaver magnate Edward J. Noble, and became part of the group American Broadcasting Companies, Inc. (*National Broadcasting Co. v. U.S.,* 319 U.S. 190, 1943).

After 1945, as Americans turned to peace-time pursuits, including the development of television, commercial radio already was settled into a pattern, with program fare dominated by two or, generously, perhaps three networks, each of them fortified against hard times by the ownership of a handful of highly-profitable local stations in the largest trading areas. The critical determinant of the number of networks that could be supported was—as it is today—the number of local outlets that could be assured for network audience, by ownership or by contract.

By 1945 the FCC preliminarily had allotted some 19 VHF Channels, numbered 1 through 19, for television broadcasting. Almost immediately Channels 14 through 19 were reallocated to the military, and Channel 1 was put aside for two-way radio. By the end of 1946, seven stations were broadcasting (all on Channels 2 through 6), and approximately 5,000 household receivers were in use. From that point, and even in the absence of detailed technical standards to guard against mutual interference, applications for new stations poured in. The FCC imposed a freeze on new applications on September 30, 1948. Virtually all pre-freeze filers actually built broadcasting facilities, so that by the time the freeze was lifted on 13 April 1952, some 107 VHF stations had been activated in 63 markets, and receivers in use had grown to 15.5 million. Denver led the list of many important markets that had no television at all. During the freeze, NBC moved aggressively to apply for and activate stations in the top markets. CBS got a late start, and proceeded to acquire its first stations by purchase. ABC and a fourth network, DuMont Laboratories, participated actively in the FCC proceedings, but were unable or unwilling to initiate major station investment, pending resolution of the knotty regulatory issues.

The framework adopted by the FCC in 1952 allotted television channels to specific communities throughout the United States, roughly in proportion to market size. VHF Channels 2 through 13 and UHF channels 14 to 83 were utilized, but as of 1952, virtually all TV sets were capable of VHF reception only. The first UHF set-top converter was introduced in March 1952. The decision also sacrificed efficiency, and reduced the potential number of stations, by grandfathering the existing 107 outlets, helter-skelter wherever they had started. Practically speaking, the FCC's allocations provided only enough VHF outlets to provide two-channel service to about 90 percent of the population, and third-channel service to substantially less. NBC and CBS, each emerging with five powerful owned-and-operated stations, and program offerings spun off from their popular radio fare, quickly expanded affiliations.

The Emmy Awards, first presented on January 25, 1949, were an accurate barometer of network emergence. A local station, KTLA in Los Angeles, dominated the awards for year 1948, with the most popular program *(Pantomime Quiz Time)*, most outstanding personality (Shirley Dinsdale and her puppet, Judy Splinters), and the station award. By the second year, with KTLA still prominent, NBC cracked the line-up, jointly with its New York flagship KNBH, winning best kinescope show *(Texaco Star Theater)* and personality (Milton Berle). A network spot for Lucky Strike cigarettes won best commercial. In the third presentation, for 1950, Alan Young and Gertrude Berg were best actor and actress, for CBS jointly with Los Angeles independent KTTV, and their co-produced *Alan Young Show* was recognized for best variety show. Outstanding personality was NBC/KNBH's Groucho Marx. By the end of the FCC's freeze these networks had unqualified leadership of program origination.

In the complex fight over regulation DuMont Laboratories had advocated a plan with a minimum of four VHF frequencies allotted to each of the 140 largest trading areas. Rebuffed at the FCC, DuMont never achieved more than 10 primary or full schedule network affiliates. As the few UHF operators incurred mounting losses, DuMont folded its network in 1955. These by-products of the freeze and subsequent FCC decision to grandfather incumbent stations and intermix VHF and UHF channels have led to harsh criticism of the FCC's decisions.

Throughout this period, ABC was barely operating, and Noble stated that he had never declared a dividend nor taken a salary through 1952. In 1953, however, ABC received FCC approval to merge with United Paramount Theaters. The chain had been spun off from Paramount Pictures Corporation, under court decree that followed the Supreme Court's antitrust decision of 1948, upholding divestment of theatrical production from exhibition. The significance of government involvement could not be more clear, with ABC's very existence jeopardized by one government action, and resolved favorably by another. ABC used its Hollywood connections adroitly, teaming with a studio to co-venture a break-through program, to that date the most expensively produced in history: *Disneyland*.

Collectively the networks could have only as many affiliates as there were stations on the air. Commercial VHF stations grew from 233 in 1954 to 458 in 1962. Commercial UHF stations stood at 121 in 1954, and struggled against the lack of UHF receivers. Many UHFs went dark and returned their licenses for cancellation, and by 1962 their numbers had shrunk to 83. In total, the commercial station universe as it grew roughly from 350 to 550 was adequate to support approximately two-and-a-half national networks. Local stations, in the enviable position of having multiple suitors, frequently left ABC with no local outlet. Congress enacted a law in 1962 mandating that all receivers be capable of UHF tuning, but it was only by the mid-1970s that local stations were plentiful enough for ABC to achieve full comparability.

As the networks consolidated their control of station time during the 1950s, a broad shift occurred in their relationship with the sponsor, enhancing their control even further. In the early part of the decade, shows typically were produced by the sponsor live, or contracted for by the sponsor and delivered to the network on expensive film or kinescope. Production was centered in New York. With the introduction by Ampex of quadruplex videotape recording in 1956, it became possible for programs to be produced and recorded anywhere, and the new orders for entertainment fare shifted to the concentration of expertise in Hollywood studios. Increasingly, the network replaced the sponsor in development, acquisition, and revision to final programming form. From the 1950s can be charted the realization of core concepts in prime-time programming, including the ensemble situation comedy, cop shows, westerns, and regularly scheduled newscasts. This period often is referred to as the Golden Age of television in the United States, perhaps precisely because of its experimental flavor. But while major market stations achieved immediate and impressive profitability, networking was still a gamble, the program performance remained uneven, and in 1961 critic-for-a-day Newton N. Minow described the totality as a "vast wasteland."

The true golden age of three-network hegemony probably dates from 1963, when each network inaugurated a half-hour prime-time newscast, and network television drew the entire nation together in grief after the assassination of President Kennedy. From 1963 until the late 1970s, the networks created a refracted version, shared by all, of the significant events of the day. This cohesion intensified with expanding use of color transmissions and color set sales during the 1960s. One nation resonated with the networks' triune voice, in a manner unparalleled in the past, and likely never again to be seen in the future. ABC, gradually shoring up its group of strong affiliates, and hiring a visionary programmer in Fred Silverman, finally used coverage of the Summer Olympics as the basis for its first full-season ratings victory in 1976–77. The "third network's" potential had been clear for years, but several attempts to acquire ABC during the 1960s were rebuffed, and an attempted buyout by IT&T foundered in 1968, after criticisms were vetted during two years of FCC proceedings.

The membership quota for this elite club of three networks, however, was eventually dismantled by a technology developing quietly during these same years—cable television. The FCC's original framework of 1952 did not assure three-network or *any* network service, to all households, and was particularly deficient where terrain obstacles degraded reception over the air. Community antenna television (CATV) was a local self-help response, tying hilltop repeaters to wires into the home. Because cablers did not utilize the broadcast spectrum, the government was uncertain of its jurisdiction until a Supreme Court decision came down in favor of a broad authority to regulate, *U.S. v Southwestern Cable Co.,* 392 U.S. 157 (1968). Thereafter broadcasters, well aware of the potential competition, leaned on the FCC to retard cable, specifically by forbidding the importation of distant signals that were not available in the local market over-the-air. By 1970,

a regime of anti-cable regulation was firmly in place and for ten years it served to retard competition and preserve the networks' position. A newer technological device again led to significant change in this arrangement.

Domestic communications satellites were authorized in 1972, and by 1975 RCA and Western Union had space satellites launched and working. In 1975 RCA sold time on its Satcom I for Home Box Office, the first program service designed to bypass conventional delivery channels, and offer a unified program lineup directly to cable systems and thus to the home—in the true sense, a network. The following year, uncertainties surrounding the re-sale of broadcast programs to cable were resolved, with passage of a new Copyright Act requiring broadcasters to license to cablers under certain conditions, at below-market rates to be established through a bureaucratic process.

The opportunity presented by the resolution of the two knottiest issues—distribution and rights—was first recognized by Ted Turner, not a cabler but a broadcaster, operator of WTCG in Atlanta (later, WTBS), an independent UHF on Channel 17. By 1978, the FCC had been having second thoughts about the heavy hand it had placed on cable development. Turner approached the agency with a plan to offer Channel 17 to a common carrier he created for the purpose, Southern Satellite Systems. In turn, Southern would deliver the station by satellite to cable headends, charging five cents per household per month. Because embedded in FCC common carrier regulation was the idea of nondiscriminatory rates, for large and small customers (or cable systems) alike, Southern needed a waiver to charge by the number of local subscribers. Astonishingly, the FCC said yes. The debut of Channel 17 as the first "super station" in 1980 assured, year by year, that the three-network share of the program universe would continue to shrivel inexorably. By 1981 the FCC also was in process of a cable "deregulation," abandoning its 10-year folly of attempting to re-bottle the genie of cable program origination. The networks, barred by FCC rules from owning cable systems, began to invest in new cable program services side-by-side with cable companies, Turner, and others.

With President Ronald Reagan taking office in 1981, the deregulatory thrust continued. The former actor, when he thought about such matters, was willing to favor Hollywood studios in their primordial battles with the television networks, and to endorse the expansion of channels for program delivery. A cable television bill, passed in 1984, pre-empted local rate regulation, and so gave the cable industry working capital to continue its strides as program creator and distributor.

These strides were being matched with the opening of a wholly new channel into the home. Sony had introduced a practical, consumer videotape player-recorder, the Beta VCR, in 1976, at a suggested retail price of $1,295. Recording time per tape was one hour. Sony's Japanese rival, Matsushita, which markets under the name Panasonic, followed shortly with an incompatible format that eventually became standard, called VHS. Hollywood studios, led by Universal Pictures and Disney, promptly brought a challenge in Federal Court, claiming that the device inherently was useful only for stealing copyrighted material. The issue oscillated in court until 1984, when the U.S. Supreme Court ruled that home taping for home use was not an infringement of copyright (*Sony Corp. v. Universal City Studios, Inc.,* 464 U.S. 417 [1984], called the "Betamax case"). From that date, sales of home recorders and the rental of tapes exploded. The studios have come to enjoy greater revenue from cassette sales and rentals than from theatrical exhibition, and must look back in wonder at their temporary insanity when the player-recorders first were sighted in North America. But for the networks, this technology presents long-term problems. The rating services have assumed so far that programs can be credited as viewed if they are recorded, but it may become apparent in time that the facts of actual audience behavior are otherwise. In the United States (unlike some other countries, such as Britain), VCRs in their most typical use occupy the household's attention for non-network fare such as movies, just coming off their initial theatrical run.

As cable and cassettes continued to splinter the market, Reagan's FCC abolished many of the rules and policies that had stood in the background of television broadcasting also. In 1984, the rule restricting each television network to the ownership of a maximum five VHF stations, and seven VHF plus UHF, was replaced with a quota of up to twelve VHF so long as the station grouping did not exceed 25 percent of all TV households. While this liberalization was still at the discussion stage at the FCC, Thomas S. Murphy, chairman of the Capital Cities station group, approached ABC about a merger. Once the rule was finalized, Capital Cities in 1986 announced the acquisition of the much larger network, for $3.5 billion, with financing from Warren E. Buffett and Berkshire Hathaway, Inc.

By 1986, RCA was a diminished echo of the industrial giant of the post-war years. Its equipment markets had been overtaken by Japanese manufacturers. Its television network remained competitive and highly

successful, but in no position to refurbish from working capital for the intensified program battles ahead. RCA and its NBC network were sold to General Electric in 1985 for $6.3 billion. General Electric had been instrumental in creating RCA in the 1920s before David Sarnoff's tenure in charge, and now closed the circle in an era more receptive to combinations.

CBS entered this period smarting from a lengthy battle with General William C. Westmoreland over the *CBS Reports* documentary, *The Uncounted Enemy: A Vietnam Deception.* The advocacy group, Accuracy in Media, Senator Jesse Helms, and Ted Turner were each, in 1985, separately talking up plans to acquire the network. CBS beat back these efforts with a $1 billion stock repurchase, but was left with more debt, little working capital, and a reduced stock valuation. The board and the aging founder, Paley, passed effective control of the stock to Loews Corporation and its proprietor, Laurence Tisch. Soon the news division, successors of Edward R. Murrow, was pruned by 230 people. In 1987 CBS dropped to third place in the season ratings for the first time.

Ever since the sputtering start for UHF in the first two decades of television, FCC commissioners had spoken longingly of the desire, first to assure three-network service, and next to realize somehow the dream of a fourth network. By the time the fourth network arrived, family viewing had fractured into discrete-person viewing, multi-set households were common, and broadcast networks had to contend with cable networks, premium cable, home video, even computer games.

Nevertheless, the fabled fourth network did come in 1990, when Rupert Murdoch, an Australian publisher, naturalized as a U.S. citizen to make him eligible for the deal, acquired the strong major-market grouping of Metro Media stations, and placed them under the same roof with the 20th Century-FOX studio. Murdoch eschewed ABC's original 1950s approach—programming mostly cannon fodder against its rivals on a full seven nights—instead making a staged entry with two nights, then three and four. The FOX network finally attained a full-time run, and in less than five years from launch, FOX could first be seen actually winning a prime-time slot here and there. In 1994 FOX purchased rights to the National Football Conference (NFC), building from sports, and luring affiliates in NFC territories, moves taken from the ancient game plan on which ABC's strategy had previously been built.

The rise of FOX placed new pressure on FCC rules intended to adjust the playing field between program suppliers and the networks. These rules imposed a quota on network self-produced fare, by forbidding the networks to own rights for secondary distribution of the programs they originated (called the Fin-Syn Rules), and by keeping an hour of prime time out of the hands of networks, reserved for local stations to program, usually by purchase from syndicators (the Prime-Time Access Rule). Because Fox combined a network with a studio, it sought and obtained waivers, and soon the rules were repealed for all networks.

By 1994, the liberalization of ground rules emboldened three more Hollywood studios to try their hand at networking directly. Warner Brothers launched a network in its own name, and Universal, which had grown to eminence as a prime source for NBC, teamed with Paramount, proud source of the inexhaustible *Star Trek* franchise, to form UPN (United Paramount Network).

In 1995, Capital Cities/ABC agreed to be acquired by Walt Disney Studios for $19 billion in cash and stock. The Disney combination with Capital Cities was the opening round of a new level of consolidation among few great communications trusts equipped to provide multiple channels of information, entertainment, and merchandizing in coordinated fashion throughout the world.

In 1999 Viacom and CBS (acquired earlier by a strong group owner, Westinghouse) merged, in the largest such conglomeration at that time, valued at $50 billion. From the Viacom side, the merged entity included Paramount, Blockbuster Video, television stations, publishing, and other media. Westinghouse/CBS brought to the table its television group, but also from Infinity a major radio group and outdoor advertising. This combination was possible only because the new Telecommunications Act of 1996 abolished the numerical limit on television stations in common ownership, and provided a liberalized cap of 35 percent of national audience for any one station owner. The Viacom/CBS merger also came in the immediate aftermath of an FCC action repealing the "dual network" ban that had divested NBC Blue in 1941. Bill Clinton's arrival in 1993 gradually shifted the partisan striping of the FCC Commissioners. But the bedrock principles in Washington, D.C., did not change much: receptivity to market forces and competition in theory, and receptivity to large media players getting their wish lists in practice.

That power was drifting away from the "club" of three—now four—was evident in the rise of Time Warner, or AOL Time Warner, as it was dubbed at the $183 billion merger in 2000. Without ownership of any one of the "major" networks, Time Warner, with all the growing pains accompanying the initial years, was and remains the most highly capitalized media organization in the world. It has a pervasive impact on televi-

sion through the WB network, HBO, Turner Classic Movies and TNT, CNN and CNN Headline News, Warner Brothers Television, and other program originators, and major footprints in online services, books and magazines, to mention only the highlights.

Since the advent of U.S. television in 1941, there never has been a regulatory change—permitting combinations not previously allowed—that did not trigger moves by the affected parties to the full, lawful outer limits. In 2003 the FCC voted to liberalize most of its remaining restrictions on media ownership, including the phase out of "cross-ownership" restrictions in more than one category of mass media, and an increase in the maximum audience that could be served by network-owned stations, from 35 percent to 45 percent, or higher if the stations broadcast in UHF. But this time the implications appeared obvious to a broad cross-section of the public, from the National Rifle Association to Fairness and Accuracy in Reporting. The proposals created a negative reaction in public comment and meetings when proposed, and then a storm of objections when adopted 3–2 by a sharply divided FCC. Both houses of Congress appeared poised to roll back some or all, unless dissuaded by the Bush administration.

If the latest regulations go into effect they will prompt a new wave of consolidations. For all the heat they have generated, they are but the capstone of a 20-year bi-partisan trend. Another FCC action at the end of 2003 may turn out to have even greater significance. News Corporation, the owner of FOX, was permitted to acquire the ownership of DirecTV, which had a direct satellite feed to eleven million homes, and was the second largest pay-TV provider (after cable TV giant Comcast). No "vertical" combination of program and distribution assets quite like this has been seen at any time since the motion picture combinations were broken up in the 1950s. In blessing this merger, the FCC noted that the new company planned by the end of 2004 to put local TV stations on the satellite—known as local-into-local, for the 100 largest markets.

By 2002, 67 percent of households had cable television, providing at least potential competition for satellites. Eighty-five percent of homes subscribed to a multi-channel video service, so that as few as 15 percent of homes were served by over-the-air broadcast only. The slow emergence of digital television will increase options—eventually—by enabling multicasting of several feeds on a station's video channel. Internet streaming gradually will become more practical, in step with broadband deployment.

Unbound from terrestrial broadcasting, and even from the idea of a single channel, what will a network look like? The answer is already seen on satellite and cable today. The CNN franchise, a Ted Turner legacy acquired by Time Warner, now is seen on cable as CNN, CNN International, CNN en Español, CNN Headline News, CNN fn, and CNN Interactive. CNN Radio is a cable service. All of these can supply news briefs to other channels in the corporate family and can be re-purposed in books, magazines, and elsewhere.

The logical basis for networking in mass media will endure. Production costs are fixed, so the advantage is with those who can achieve the greatest exposure. Exorbitant capital costs in satellite, cable, and high-end digital origination are unlikely to vanish. But the new demand for customization and niche programming points in a very different direction. The large network organizations may have no inherent advantage in reaching a local, specialist, or individualized audience. That provides a possible opening for nimble, adaptive, and small services to endure and even thrive, embracing new technologies as they emerge. In the absence of any governmental brake on consolidation, that would have to be the hope, at least, for any society that depends for its survival on the free flow of information to its citizens.

MICHAEL COUZENS

See also **American Broadcasting Company; Columbia Broadcasting System; FOX Broadcasting Company; National Broadcasting Company; UPN Television Network; WB Network**

Further Reading

Auletta, Ken, *Three Blind Mice: How the TV Networks Lost Their Way,* New York: Random House, 1991

Bagdikian, Ben H., *The Media Monopoly,* Boston, Massachusetts: Beacon, 1992; 6th edition, 2000

Barnouw, Erik, *The Image Empire: A History of Broadcasting in the United States,* vol. 3, New York: Oxford University Press, 1970

Barnouw, Erik, *Tube of Plenty: The Evolution of American Television,* New York: Oxford University Press, 1975; revised edition, 1990

Bedell, Sally, *Up the Tube: Prime Time TV in the Silverman Years,* New York: Viking, 1981

Block, Alex Ben, *Outfoxed: Marvin Davis, Barry Diller, Rupert Murdoch, Joan Rivers, and the Inside Story of America's Fourth Television Network,* New York: St. Martin's Press, 1990

Boddy, William, *Fifties Television: The Industry and Its Critics,* Urbana: University of Illinois Press, 1990

Brown, Les. *Televi$ion: The Business behind the Box,* New York: Harcourt Brace, 1971

Castleman, Harry, and Walter J. Podrazik, *The TV Schedule Book: Four Decades of Network Programming from Sign-on to Sign-off.* New York: McGraw-Hill, 1984

Castleman, Harry, and Walter J. Podrazik, *Watching TV: Four Decades of American Television,* New York: McGraw Hill, 1982

Cooper, R.B., Jr., "The Infamous Television Allocation Freeze of 1948," *Community Antenna Television Journal* (March 1975)

Inglis, Andrew F., *Behind the Tube: A History of Broadcasting Technology and Business,* Boston: Focal, 1990

Kiernan, Thomas, *Citizen Murdoch,* New York: Dodd Mead, 1986

MacDonald, J. Fred, *One Nation under Television,* New York: Pantheon, 1990

Metz, Robert, *CBS: Reflections in a Bloodshot Eye,* Chicago: Playboy, 1975

McChesney, Robert W., *Rich Media, Poor Democracy: Communication Politics in Dubious Times,* New York: New Press, 2000

Owen, Bruce M., *The Internet Challenge to Television,* Cambridge, Massachusetts: Harvard University Press, 1999

Paul, Michael, and James Robert Parish, *The Emmy Awards: A Pictorial History,* New York: Crown, 1970

Sloan Commission on Cable Communications, *On the Cable: The Television of Abundance,* New York: McGraw-Hill, 1971

Wilk, Max, *The Golden Age of Television: Notes From the Survivors,* New York: Delacourte Press, 1976

Government Studies

Federal Communications Commission, *Report on Chain Broadcasting,* Commission order no. 37, docket no. 5060, Washington, D.C.: The Commission May 1941

Federal Communications Commission, *Second Interim Report of the Office of Network Study: Television Network Program Procurement, Part 1,* Washington, D.C.: The Commission, 1965

Federal Communications Commission, Network Inquiry Special Staff, *New Television Networks: Entry, Jurisdiction, Ownership and Regulation,* volume 1: *Final Report;* volume 2: *Background Reports,* Washington, D.C.: The Commission, October, 1980

U.S. House of Representatives (85th Congress, 2nd Session), Committee on Interstate and Foreign Commerce, *Network Broadcasting* [the "Barrow Report"], House Report no. 1297, Washington, D.C.: U.S. Government Printing Office, 1958

U.S. House of Representatives (88th Congress, 1st Session), *Television Network Program Procurement,* House Report no. 281, Washington, D.C.: U.S. Government Printing Office, 1963

U.S. House of Representatives (97th Congress, 1st Session), Committee on Energy and Commerce, *Telecommunications in Transition: The Status of Competition in the Telecommunications Industry,* majority report, Committee Print 97-V, Washington, D.C.: U.S. Government Printing Office, 1981

New Zealand

As observers have noted, there is considerable irony in the fact that New Zealand, the first nation to legislate for state control of radio waves with the Wireless Telegraphy Act of 1903, should have created what the reforming Minister of Broadcasting, Richard Prebble, claimed was "the most open communications market in the world" 86 years later. The development of television has been at the centre of this movement from strong state direction to a competitive marketplace.

In 1935, the first Labour administration set up the National Broadcasting Service as a government department to bring the emerging medium under public control. The following year, 22 private radio stations were nationalized to create a state monopoly.

A government inquiry into the prospects for television was appointed in the 1940s but did not report until 1957. It advocated a public monopoly, and a full service was eventually launched in 1960. Its take-off coincided with a major change in the overall organization of broadcasting when, in 1961, the old National Broadcasting System became the New Zealand Broadcasting Corporation (NZBC), an institution closer to the BBC model.

Because of the country's relatively small population, it was clear that the license fee would not generate sufficient income to cover the costs of the new service, and so advertising was allowed from the outset as a supplementary source of income. Consequently, although the NZBC looked to the BBC as a model, it never enjoyed the same relative independence from commercial pressures, or from political overlordship, as its British counterpart.

As a national monopoly it was expected to reflect and foster national culture and national identity. However, its ability to do this was severely limited by financial constraints. The start-up costs of the new television service were substantial. Constructing a transmitter system across a huge, topographically difficult land area was particularly expensive. Comparatively little funding was therefore available for original program production, and scheduling relied heavily on imported material, particularly from Britain. By the late 1960s, NZBC was the largest purchaser of BBC programs in the world.

In 1972, the organization successfully fought off a bid to introduce a competitive commercial service, and itself launched a second channel. Having more hours of broadcasting time to fill made imported programs even more attractive to cost-conscious executives. They were ten to twenty times cheaper than domestic productions, filling the screen for two days for the price of one hour of home-produced material. By the mid-1980s, imports were providing the majority of programs but taking only 4 percent of the television division's total expenditure. When a UNESCO study calculated local content on television in 1983, Great Britain logged 85 percent, Australia 50 percent, and New Zealand 25 percent—including sports, game shows, news, and current affairs—strong evidence that in a market of only three million people, financial logic worked powerfully against public television's ability to reflect the full diversity of national life.

Despite the rebuff to the private sector lobby in 1972, a limited form of competition was introduced in 1974 when NZBC's two channels became separate operating companies and entered into vigorous competition for viewers and advertising. This pushed programming toward a more populist, entertainment-oriented style. Television viewing increased appreciably.

This fueled renewed pressure from private companies wishing to enter the increasingly lucrative market for television advertising. In 1976, the newly elected (conservative) National Government responded positively with a Broadcasting Act that set up a quasi-judicial Broadcasting Tribunal, with the power to license new stations by issuing broadcasting warrants. However, it took rather longer to break the public monopoly than many early enthusiasts had anticipated. The private consortium that later became the country's first terrestrial commercial service, TV3, lodged an application for a warrant in 1984. It obtained a favorable decision in August 1987 but a judicial review in their favor was not handed down until September 1988. The channel finally went on air in November 1989. It entered a depressed economy encumbered with debts accrued from the protracted tribunal process and went into receivership after only six months. It had also underestimated the public channels' ability to fight their corner.

In addition to establishing the tribunal, the 1976 Act had also replaced the old Broadcasting Service with the Broadcasting Corporation of New Zealand (BCNZ), a publicly owned institution with two major operating divisions: radio, and Television New

Zealand (TVNZ). The two television channels were brought back under unified control and run as complementary services. The government also addressed the organization's mounting deficit produced by the costs of launching the second channel and converting from black-and-white transmissions to color. In 1977, they agreed to retire the debt on the condition that future developments were funded from revenues. To underline the point the license fee was frozen. By 1993 it stood at NZ$110, by which point, if it had been index-linked to inflation since 1975, it would have been NZ$280. Faced with a capped income from the license fee, TVNZ set out to attract more advertising revenue, successfully increasing its overall share of the advertising market from 21 percent to 30 percent in the ten years from 1977. By 1987 advertising accounted for 80 percent of its total revenues, helping it to record a return on equity of close to 20 percent.

This more commercially minded attitude ran counter to the recommendations of the Royal Commission on Broadcasting that had sat between 1984 and 1985. It had advocated a strong public-service system with limits on advertising levels and a local program quota. But even as it reported, it sounded like an echo from the past.

As a division within a public corporation, TVNZ was free to retain any earnings and reinvest them. The treasury, however, favored returning them to the public purse for general use. Its 1984 briefing to the incoming government floated the idea of converting commercially viable public operations into state-owned trading enterprises (SOEs), which would function as private-sector businesses and return a dividend to the government. The process began in 1986. Nine new SOEs in various sectors, including telecommunications, were established, and at the end of 1988 the principle was extended to radio and television broadcasting.

However, TVNZ's capacity to increase its revenues was affected by a radical shift in the terms of competition in the television marketplace initiated by two key pieces of legislation passed in 1989. In response to widespread concern about the costs and delays of the tribunal process for granting new licenses, the government introduced the Radio Communications Act. This allocated radio frequencies by tender, the winning bidder becoming the frequency "manager" for a 20-year term with freedom to pass the license on to another party. The first auction of national and regional UHF frequencies in 1990 opened the market to several new services. They included Sky Network, the country's first pay-TV service, rebroadcasting satellite sports, news, and film services; a regional service based in Canterbury in the South Island; and a racing channel, Action TV.

TVNZ, which had become a separate operating company in December 1988 in preparation for increased competition, responded aggressively in an effort to cut costs and increase revenues. Staffing numbers were cut and employees moved to limited-term individual contracts. Much of the programming formerly made in-house was contracted out to independent producers. Internal subsidiaries looked for outside clients. And the organization moved to spread its interests beyond its traditional business of mass-market national broadcasting. It acquired a 35 percent stake in Sky, formed a partnership with Clear Communications, the second force in the emerging telecommunications market, and entered the burgeoning overseas broadcasting market with a 29.5 percent stake in Asia Business News.

It also retained its dominant position in the national television market. By October 1990, TVNZ's two channels still commanded an 80 percent share of the television audience, as against TV3's 17.3 percent and Sky's 1.5 percent. Its share of television advertising however showed a steeper decline, dropping from 100 percent in 1984, before the advent of competition, to 70 percent ten years later. At the same time, TVNZ lost its monopoly control over the license income.

The 1989 Broadcasting Act transferred responsibility for collecting and distributing the public broadcasting fee to a new body, the Broadcasting Commission, with a particular responsibility for funding local production. It later adopted the title New Zealand on Air (NZOA). Although anyone could bid for funds, TVNZ held on to its dominant position with 76 percent of NZOA's 1992 production budget going to programs made by or for its two channels. A substantial portion of this figure was spent on the medical soap opera *Shortland Street,* NZOA's major prime-time vehicle for representing a changing national culture.

Although the introduction of competition has significantly increased the number of television services available within New Zealand, there is heated debate as to whether it has extended the range of programming on offer.

Critics of the reforms point to the cultural costs of the minimal restrictions on commercial operators, the intensified competition for ratings points, and the shift toward transnational ownership with the removal of all restrictions on foreign holdings in television in 1991. They point to the absence of any quota to protect local programming, to NZOA's inability to compel stations to show the programs it has funded in favorable slots, and to the marked increase in advertising time, which gives more space to commercial speech and less to other voices. Although the figures are contested, one government report suggested that between 1988 and 1991, advertising on the two TVNZ channels increased from an average of 9–10 minutes per hour to 15 minutes.

This eclipse of public-service ideals by commercial imperatives is, critics argue, part of a pattern of change that has produced plurality without diversity. Whether this pattern will be broken or reinforced by current moves towards multimedia convergence and interactivity remains a central question.

GRAHAM MURDOCK

Further Reading

Bell, Avril, "'An Endangered Species': Local Programming in the New Zealand Television Market," *Media, Culture and Society* (April 1995)

Blythe, Martin, *Naming the Other Images of the Maori in New Zealand Film and Television,* Metuchen, New Jersey: Scarecrow Press, 1994

Cross, Iain, *The Unlikely Bureaucrat: My Years in Broadcasting,* Wellington: Allen and Unwin, 1988

Dennis, Jonathan, and Jan Bieringa, editors, *Film in Aotearoa-New Zealand,* Wellington: Victoria University Press, 1992

Harris, Mike, "Kiwis Cotton to Comedies," *Variety* (15 June 1992)

Hawke, G.R., editor, *Access to the Airwaves: Issues in Public Sector Broadcasting,* Wellington: Victoria University Press, 1990

Smith, Paul, and Don Groves, "New Zeal for Kiwi Film, Tube," *Variety* (10 October 1994)

Spoonley, Paul, and Walter Hirsh, editors, *Between the Lines: Racism and the New Zealand Media,* Auckland: Heinemann, 1990

Newhart, Bob (1929–)

U.S. Comedian, Actor

Bob Newhart is one of a few television performers to have starred in two highly successful series. His subtle, ironic humor and deadpan delivery served him well as the star of *The Bob Newhart Show* in the 1970s and *Newhart* in the 1980s. In both programs he had the opportunity to display his greatest strength as an actor: his ability to be a great reactor. While the characters he portrayed were a bit quirky, those surrounding him were so much more bizarre that Newhart seemed an island of sanity as he responded to their zaniness. This calm, controlled style also allowed him to take on some risky subjects (death, for instance) without offending his audience. As Newhart once told an interviewer, this style "has allowed me to say outrageous things with the facade of someone who didn't look like they would be saying outrageous things."

Newhart became a television star in a rather roundabout fashion. In the late 1950s, following college, army service, and a few short-term jobs, he appeared to have settled into an accounting career, but his hobby was performing comedy routines on radio. Some of his demonstration tapes so impressed Warner Brothers' recording division that Warner signed him to record a comedy album, even though he had never performed on the concert stage. His first album, *The Button-Down Mind of Bob Newhart,* was a major hit in 1960. His humor was intelligent and original; some of his now-classic routines involved an inexperienced security guard reporting King Kong's climb up the Empire State Building, Abraham Lincoln's publicist coaching him on the Gettysburg address, and Sir Walter Raleigh's boss hearing about the discovery of tobacco ("You stick it between your lips...you set fire to it?"). Many of these routines were played out as telephone conversations, of which the audience heard only Newhart's side; often he ended the conversation with an indignant "Same to you, fella!"

Newhart was one of several cerebral comedians who found favor in the early 1960s, but he always seemed more accessible than the others, like the kind of guy people would invite into their living rooms. Soon, that is where he was. On the strength of his first album, he was invited to perform on the Emmy Awards telecast in 1960. His appearance went over so well that NBC gave him his first TV series, a comedy/variety program called, like his 1970s sitcom, *The Bob Newhart Show.* It was critically acclaimed and won an Emmy as Best Comedy Series of the 1961–62 season, but it was canceled after that season due to low ratings. (Newhart's subsequent hit series were occasionally nominated for Emmys, but they never won. Newhart himself was twice nominated for Best Actor in a Comedy Series, for *Newhart,* but lost both years to Michael J. Fox in *Family Ties.*)

Throughout the 1960s, Newhart performed with great success in nightclubs and on records, and with less success in films, but he remained familiar to television audiences through frequent guest appearances on *The Tonight Show, The Ed Sullivan Show,* and other variety programs. When Newhart returned to series television in 1972, he won both critical and popular acclaim as Chicago psychologist Dr. Bob Hartley in *The Bob Newhart Show.* The show was one of the best of the ensemble comedies, many of them produced by the MTM company, that became so popular in the 1970s. Its humor was sophisticated, but with a twist: it could laugh at Bob's fixation on death after he nearly fell down an elevator shaft, and it dealt sympathetically with controversial subjects, such as the homosexuality of one of Bob's patients. Unlike programs produced by the Norman Lear organizations, however, *The Bob Newhart Show* was not primarily concerned with social issues, but with human foibles. It was exceptionally well written and had well-drawn supporting characters played by talented actors. Each cast member had an opportunity to shine, but Newhart was the calm center of it all, reacting dryly to strange characters and events, and patiently trying to explain various situations to people who were not interested in his explanations. The program also incorporated some of Newhart's most successful stand-up gimmicks, such as his one-sided telephone conversations.

After six seasons, *The Bob Newhart Show* went off the air voluntarily. Four years later, its star was back with a new series, *Newhart,* in which he played Dick Loudon, a New York writer of "how-to" books who decides to open an inn in Vermont. The premise, in some ways, was not all that different than that of the earlier series. Bob Hartley had to be understanding of all his patients, no matter how difficult they were; Dick Loudon had to be nice to all his guests, despite any pains they caused him. The show had excellent writing and a strong supporting cast, and again Newhart's deadpan, ironic presence was at the center of a universe of eccentric, in some cases truly weird, people.

In the 1990s Newhart again performed primarily in clubs and concerts, but he gave series television two more tries. In 1992 he starred in *Bob,* playing cartoonist Bob McKay. The show had a brief run, was revamped, and had another brief run. Newhart, however, needed stronger supporting characters than this series provided. In 1997 he was teamed with a formidable costar, Judd Hirsh (*Taxi*), in a sitcom titled *George and Leo.* Newhart played George, a staid, mild-mannered bookstore owner on Martha's Vineyard whose life is thrown into chaos when Leo, the father of his son's fiancée and a petty crook from Las Vegas, moves in with him. Although few people realized it, Newhart continued in this series the tradition of using part of his name in the title of the series, because George is his given first name. The leads in *George and Leo* were certainly proven talents and the

Bob Newhart.
Courtesy of the Everett Collection

producers, Rob Long and Dan Staley of *Cheers,* had impressive pedigrees, but the show never took hold with audiences and lasted less than one season. In 2003, Bob Newhart had a guest-star role on three episodes of *ER,* as an architect who is going blind due to macular degeneration, and commits suicide. It is one of the few dramatic roles Newhart has played in his career.

TRUDY RING

*See also **Bob Newhart Show, The; Newhart; Mary Tyler Moore Show, The;** Tinker, Grant*

Bob Newhart. Born George Robert Newhart in Oak Park, Illinois, September 29, 1929. Educated at Loyola University, Chicago, B.Sc., 1952. Married: Virginia Quinn, 1963; children: Robert, Timothy, Jennifer, and Courtney. Served in U.S. Army, 1952–54. Accountant, U.S. Gypsum Company, 1955; copywriter, Fred Niles Films Company, 1958; rose to popularity with phonograph recordings of comedy routines, many of which featured Newhart in one-sided telephone conversations with prominent persons; numerous television guest appearances as stand-up comedian throughout 1960s; starred in two long-running series, *The Bob Newhart Show* and *Newhart*. Recipient: Emmy Award, 1962; Peabody Award, 1962; Sword of Loyola Award,

1975; inducted into the Academy of Television Arts and Sciences Hall of Fame, 1993.

Television Series

1961–62	*The Bob Newhart Show*
1964	*The Entertainers*
1972–78	*The Bob Newhart Show*
1982–90	*Newhart*
1992–93	*Bob*
1997–98	*George and Leo*

Made-for-Television Movies

1974	*Thursday's Game*
1980	*Marathon*
1991	*The Entertainers*

Films

Hell Is for Heroes, 1962; *Hot Millions,* 1968; *On a Clear Day You Can See Forever,* 1970; *Catch-22,* 1970; *Cold Turkey,* 1971; *The Rescuers* (voice), 1977; *Little Miss Marker,* 1980; *First Family,* 1980; *The Rescuers Down Under* (voice), 1990; *In and Out,* 1997; *Rudolph the Red-Nosed Reindeer: The Movie* (1998); *Legally Blonde 2: Red, White, and Blonde* (2003); *Elf* (2003).

Further Reading

Mayerly, Judine, "The Most Inconspicuous Hit on Television: A Case Study of *Newhart,*" *Journal of Popular Film and Television* (Fall 1989)

Sorenson, Jeff, *Bob Newhart,* New York: St. Martin's Press, 1988

Newman, Sydney (1917–1997)

British Programming Executive and Producer

Sydney Newman has been seen as the most significant agent in the development of British television drama. He presided over the transformation of television drama from a dependence on theatrical material and forms to a significant art form in its own right. However, this achievement does not belong to Newman alone; his skill could be located in a successful ability to exploit the best of already favorable circumstances with an incorrigible enthusiasm and clarity of vision.

Born in Toronto in 1917, Newman trained initially as a commercial artist, before joining the National Film Board of Canada as film editor, director, and executive producer. While with the board, he made award-winning documentary films and worked with John Grierson. He subsequently spent a year as a working observer for NBC Television in New York, before becoming supervisor of Drama at the Canadian Broadcasting Corporation (CBC). It was there, working on *General Motors Theatre,* that he developed the policy of working with contemporary dramatists who attempted to confront current issues in their work.

In 1958 he moved to Britain to work for ABC Television Ltd., one of the commercial companies that made up the ITV network. In 1955, commercial television broke the broadcasting monopoly held by the BBC, and ABC was a regional company given the franchise for supplying weekend programming in the North and Midlands. Even before Newman's arrival as head of Drama at ABC, the company had acquired a reputation for some of the best ITV drama. Its *Armchair Theatre* anthology was transmitted every Sunday evening, inheriting a large audience from the highly popular variety show *Sunday Night at The London Palladium,* which preceded it in the schedule.

Newman took over from Dennis Vance as drama head in April 1958. Like Rudolph Cartier at the BBC, Newman arrived in Britain unimpressed with the state of television drama. He also arrived during a sea change in ITV's fortunes; after two years of loss, the new commercial ITV network companies were just beginning to make substantial profits, and by 1958 television audiences for their programs reached over 70 percent. At the same time, the renaissance of British theater was well underway. As Newman admitted to the *Daily Express* on January 5, 1963:

I came to Britain at a crucial time in 1958 when the seeds of *Look Back in Anger* were beginning to flower. I am proud that I played some part in the recognition that the working man was a fit subject for drama, and not just a comic foil in middle-class manners.

Inspired by his experience in drama at the CBC, and unimpressed by the BBC's continuing policy of "mopping up" old theater scripts (according to Newman), he immediately set about organizing a policy of producing plays written for the medium, plays that would reflect and project the experience and concerns of a new working-class audience. As Newman put it in a 1979 interview, "I said we should have an original play policy with plays that were going to be *about* the very people who owned TV sets—which is really a working-class audience."

This explicitly populist "theater of the people" quickly became characterized by the press as "kitchen sink" drama—an unfair appraisal considering the wide variety of plays and genres that Newman's *Armchair Theatre* produced. What the programs did have in common was their ambition to capture contemporary trends and popular experience, and reflect these back to the television audience. To this end, Newman discovered and nurtured new writers, some of whom were to become the best of their generation, including Clive Exton, Alun Owen, and Harold Pinter.

Newman encouraged the transformation of the television landscape not only in terms of subject matter but also in terms of style. If the content of British television drama consisted of bourgeois theater and its limited concerns, then—according to Newman—the shooting style was also limited, constrained by a static respect for theatrical performance conventions. Newman collected a group of young directors from North America, such as Philip Saville, Ted Kotcheff, and Charles Jarrott, as well as poaching directors from the BBC. With these directors—in particular, Saville and Kotcheff—he encouraged stylistic as well as thematic changes, insisting on a new, self-conscious, mobile camera style for the drama productions. As Kotcheff recalled: "We wanted to push against the limitations of the medium, the way it was presently covered—to approach the freedom of film, and not to enslave it to the theatrical tradition in which we found it when we arrived here."

The combination of fresh contemporary material and the freedom Newman gave to his directors (and set designers) to innovate with that material opened up the potential of television drama for all to see. Newman was never far behind them, often photographed on the studio set writing notes, his white-suited swagger suggesting a blazing showbiz evangelist. Contrast the early dramas of Reith's BBC and their "photographed stage plays," respectfully static and distant, with Newman's *Armchair Theatre* drama productions: such plays as "Afternoon of a Nymph" (1961) have an ingenious mobility, with multiple cameras performing a frantic ballet, prodding their lenses into the action, spi-

raling in and between the sets and actors, until their movement itself becomes the significant performance. This new spectrum of theme and style can be seen in other plays such as "The Trouble with Our Ivy" (1961), "A Night Out" (Harold Pinter, 1959), and "No Trams to Lime Street" (Alun Owen, 1958).

Newman's real insight—and the real difference between his work and that of the BBC of the late 1950s—was his estimation of the television audience as discerning, intelligent, and capable of handling new and innovative subject matter. As a producer, he saw himself as a "creative midwife" bringing together the best technical and creative skill.

In fact, Newman's organizational abilities were to find a home at the BBC. In another well-timed move, Newman began work as the head of the BBC Drama Group in January 1963. At this point, the BBC under director-general Hugh Greene was beginning a period of modernization and liberalization. Newman, in a less hands-on, more executive capacity, reorganized the drama department and oversaw the production of the controversial *Wednesday Play* drama anthology. Here Newman was able to draw upon a creative team of writers including Dennis Potter, John Hopkins, Neil Dunn, and David Mercer, and directors such as Don Taylor, Ken Loach, and Gareth Davies. He left the BBC in 1967 and returned to Canada, where he worked again for the National Film Board and the National Film Finance Corporation.

In retrospect, Newman's conscious characterization of BBC drama output as static and middlebrow is unfair. His counterpart at the BBC during the late 1950s, Michael Barry, also attracted new young original writers (including Paul Scott and John Mortimer) and hired young directors such as John Jacobs and Don Taylor. However, it was the newness and innovation that Newman encouraged in his drama output that is most significant: his concentration on the potential of television as television, for a mass, not a middle-brow, audience.

JASON J. JACOBS

See also Avengers, The; **Garnett, Tony; Loach, Ken;** *Wednesday Play*

Sydney Cecil Newman. Born in Toronto, Ontario, April 1, 1917. Attended Ogden Public School, Toronto; Central Technical School, Toronto. Married: Margaret Elizabeth McRae, 1944 (died, 1981); three daughters. Moved to Hollywood, 1938; worked as painter, stage, industrial and interior designer; still and cinema photographer, 1935–41; joined National Film Board of Canada under John Grierson, as splicer-boy, 1941; editor and director, Armed Forces training films and war information shorts, 1942; produced more than 300 documentaries; executive producer for all Canadian government cinema films, 1947–52; assigned to NBC in New York by Canadian government to study U.S. television techniques, 1949–50; director for outside broadcasts, features, and documentaries, Canadian Broadcasting Corporation, 1953; drama supervisor and producer, *General Motors Theatre,* 1954; supervisor and producer of *Armchair Theatre,* ABC-TV, U.K., 1958–62; head of drama, BBC Television, 1963–67; commissioned and produced first television plays of Arthur Hailey, Harold Pinter, and others; special adviser, Broadcast Programmes branch, Canadian Radio and Television Commission, Ottawa, 1970; Canadian Government film commissioner and chair, National Film Board of Canada, 1970–75; trustee, National Arts Center, Ottawa, 1970–75; board member, Canadian Broadcasting Corporation, Canadian Film Development Corporation; director, Canadian Broadcasting Corporation, 1972–75; special adviser on film to Canadian government, 1975–77; chief creative consultant, Canadian Film Development Corporation, 1978–84; president, Sydney Newman Enterprises, 1981; producer, Associated British Pictures; worked as creative consultant to film and television producers. Officer of the Order of Canada, 1981; Knight of Mark Twain (USA). Fellow: Society of Film and Television Arts, 1958; Royal Society of Arts, 1967; Royal Television Society, 1991. Recipient: Ohio State Award for Religious Drama, 1956; Liberty Award for Best Drama Series, 1957; Desmond Davis Award, 1967; Society of Film and Television Arts President's Award, 1969; Writers Guild of Great Britain Zeta Award, 1970; Canadian Pictures Pioneer Award, 1973; Society of Motion Picture and Television Engineers Recognition Award; Venice Award; Canada Award. Died in Toronto, October 30, 1997.

Television Series

1954	*General Motors Theatre* (supervisor and producer)
1954	*Ford Theater* (supervisor and producer)
1954	*On Camera* (supervisor and producer)
1958–62	*Armchair Theatre* (supervisor and producer)
1960	*Police Surgeon* (creator)
1960–61	*Pathfinders*
1961–69	*The Avengers* (creator)
1961–69	*Doctor Who* (creator)
1964–70	*The Wednesday Play* (creator)
1966	*Adam Adamant Lives!* (creator)
1967	*The Forsyte Saga* (creator)

Television Specials (selected; producer)

1960	*O My Lena*
1962	*Dumb Martian*
1963	*Stephen D.*
1965	*The Rise and Fall of the City of Mahagonny*
1965	*Tea Party*
1989	Britten's *The Little Sweep*

Stage (producer)

Flight into Danger; Course for Collision

Publication

Days of Vision, 1990

Further Reading

The Armchair Theatre: How to Write, Design, Direct, Act and Enjoy Television Plays, London: Weidenfeld and Nicolson, 1959

Barry, M., *From the Palace to the Grove,* London: Royal Television Society, 1992

Shubik, I., *Play for Today: The Evolution of Television Drama,* London: Davis-Poynter, 1975

Taylor, D., *Days of Vision,* London: Methuen, 1990

Taylor, J.R., editor, *Anatomy of a Television Play,* London: Weidenfeld and Nicolson, 1962

News Corporation, Ltd.

News Corporation, Ltd. (News Corp), is one of the world's largest media companies. It holds interests in broadcast, satellite, and cable television, film, newspapers, magazines, book publishers, and online services, across four continents. News Corp is headed by its primary shareholder, Rupert K. Murdoch, who built the company from an initial base of two small Australian newspapers in the early 1950s into a global media conglomerate.

News Corp's television properties in the United States include the FOX television network, 20th Century-FOX production studios, numerous owned-and-operated FOX television stations, national cable networks including FX and FOX News Channel, and a string of regional FOX Sports Channels. In addition, News Corp owns a controlling interest in the United Kingdom's direct broadcast satellite television service, British Sky Broadcasting (BSkyB); Europe's Sky Channel television programming service; and Asia's direct broadcast satellite (DBS) service, Star Television.

However, it is impossible to isolate any one form of media as News Corp's core business, because its growth has been fueled by the idea of creating synergies among the company's different components. The resulting economies of scale make the value of the company's whole greater than that of the sum of its parts. A good example of this strategy in action was the combination of News Corp's purchases in the mid-1980s of the 20th Century-FOX studios and Metromedia's large-market U.S. television stations. The combination of production facilities and distribution outlets led directly to the creation of the FOX television network.

The FOX network remains News Corp's most prominent presence in American television. It launched in October 1986, with the premiere of *The Late Show Starring Joan Rivers,* and began its regular schedule of prime-time programming in early 1987. While some of its first shows, such as Rivers's, were critical and commercial disappointments, FOX was slowly able to gain audience share and expand its program schedule. FOX ultimately carved out a solid niche as the fourth broadcast network by targeting the 18- to 34-year-old audience and attracting these viewers through programs that were often offbeat and sometimes audacious. *The Simpsons, Married...With Children,* and *COPS* were among FOX's most prominent early hits and exemplify the unconventional nature of FOX network programming. Indeed, FOX's *COPS* and *America's Most Wanted* were largely responsible for the wide proliferation of a new television genre known as "reality television." Programming on the channel continued to evolve, to produce and respond to new audiences. *Beverly Hills 90210* and *Melrose Place,* "teen" and "young adult" programming from producer Aaron Spelling, found a substantial group of loyal viewers, and major hit *The X-Files* became one of television's most popular and widely discussed programs.

In addition to its regular programs, FOX also made its presence felt in the U.S. television market through a series of bold strategic maneuvers aimed at acquiring special programming and new affiliate stations. As early as 1987, FOX paid a record license fee to telecast the Emmy Awards (the television industry's awards program), which previously had rotated among the "Big Three" networks (ABC, CBS, and NBC). The network also attempted to obtain the rights to the Na-

tional Football League (NFL) *Monday Night Football* television package. Although unsuccessful in the latter effort, FOX was later successful with its record-setting bid for the NFL's National Conference games, wresting the package from longtime rights holder CBS prior to the 1994 NFL season. FOX used the opportunity created by its acquisition of this NFL package to woo new affiliates to the network, which led to the most dramatic realignment of network affiliates in U.S. television history. FOX's agreement with New World Communications, announced in May 1994, represented the largest single affiliate switch ever, but it was considered controversial because many saw the agreement—in which FOX paid New World $500 million and 12 New World stations changed their affiliations to the FOX network—as a vehicle by which FOX was able to circumvent Federal Communications Commission (FCC) limitations on the number of stations a single company is permitted to own.

Another News Corp property that exemplified the company's strategic approach to collecting assets was *TV Guide,* the best-selling weekly magazine in the United States. News Corp purchased *TV Guide,* along with *Seventeen* magazine and *The Daily Racing Form,* in 1988 from Walter Annenberg for a reported price of more than $3 billion. It was News Corp's largest single purchase to that time and represented another instance of the company's willingness to pay a premium price for a unique media property that fits into a synergistic global scheme. While many questioned why News Corp would pay such a price for a mature asset that had seen its circulation decline by about a third since its peak in the late 1970s, *TV Guide*'s merger in 2000 with the Gemstar family of interactive video products placed News Corp at the forefront of the emerging interactive program guide (IPG) market, which promises to exploit fully and build upon *TV Guide*'s tangible assets, as well as its unparalleled brand equity in the television-program-listings marketplace.

News Corp's involvement with DBS service in Europe put the company at great financial risk, but it appears to have been a wise long-term investment. News Corp initially launched a DBS service called Sky Television in 1989, which competed in the United Kingdom with another DBS service, British Satellite Broadcasting (BSB). In 1990 BSB became bankrupt, and Britain's Conservative government, who regarded Rupert Murdoch as a crucial ally, allowed Sky to override concerns about the creation of a satellite broadcasting monopoly and buy BSB's assets; the two satellite broadcasters merged to become the News Corp entity BSkyB. The start-up costs associated with this venture put great strain on News Corp's financial stability, and the losses it encountered in BSkyB's early days, combined with the overwhelming short-term debt load News Corp had accumulated from its years of aggressive acquisitions, nearly forced the company into financial ruin in 1990. However, News Corp was able to negotiate with its creditors for more favorable debt terms and thereby averted disaster. The emergence of BSkyB in the early 1990s as an extremely profitable venture (built, like FOX, on the acquisition of rights to televise sporting events), along with the growing success of FOX in the United States, helped News Corp back to financial health in a relatively short time.

In the latter half of the 1990s, News Corp expanded on its strategy of producing its own content for its distribution channels by aggressively pursuing the acquisition of selected landmark professional sports properties. Its takeover bid for the Manchester United soccer franchise was ultimately blocked by the British government, which cited the unfair advantage that News Corp's BSkyB would have in negotiating for the television rights to the team's games; however, News Corp did successfully purchase the Los Angeles Dodgers Major League Baseball team in 1998. The Dodgers' purchase clearly exemplified News Corp's strategy of owning sports franchises whose popularity extends beyond national borders to other areas of the world where News Corp also owns satellite television distribution services, such as Star TV in Asia and Sky Latin America.

Today, News Corp stands among the foremost media companies in the world and continues to be aggressive in its pursuit of new media and communications properties. Its wide range of media holdings in many countries of the world puts News Corp in a central position among a handful of corporate behemoths that could dominate the global media landscape for many years to come.

DAVID GUNZERATH

See also **Murdoch, Rupert**

Further Reading

Block, Alex Ben, *Outfoxed,* New York: St. Martin's Press, 1990

Cohen, Roger, "Rupert Murdoch's Biggest Gamble," *New York Times* (October 21, 1990)

Consoli, John, "Fox Buys the Henhouse," *Mediaweek* (March 23, 1998)

Fabrikant, Geraldine, "News Corp. Posts Profit in Contrast to '91 Loss," *New York Times* (August 27, 1992)

Fabrikant, Geraldine, "Investors Are Attracted by the News Corporation's Big Picture," *New York Times* (September 3, 1993)

Farhi, Paul, "Murdoch, All Business: The Media Mogul Keeps Making Bets amid Strains in His Global Empire," *Washington Post* (February 12, 1995)

Feder, Barney, "Murdoch's Time of Reckoning," *New York Times* (December 20, 1990)

Gaskell, John, and Sally Malcolm-Smith, "The World According to Murdoch: Empire without Frontiers," *Sunday Telegraph* (September 5, 1993)

Kaplan, Karen, and Sallie Hofmeister, "Gemstar-TV Guide Merger Plan Raises Fear of Monopoly in Interactive TV," *Los Angeles Times* (June 26, 2000)

Shawcross, William, *Rupert Murdoch: Ringmaster of the Information Circus,* New York: Simon and Schuster, 1992

Thomas, Laurie, and Barry Litman, "Fox Broadcasting Company, Why Now?: An Economic Study of the Rise of the Fourth Broadcast 'Network,'" *Journal of Broadcasting and Electronic Media* (1991)

News in the United States, Local and Regional

Local television news in the United States struggles to maintain credibility even as it is increasingly used as a revenue center and promotional tool by an ever-shrinking group of media owners. For broadcasters and cable companies, local and regional newscasts remain the site for occasionally fulfilling the oft-forgotten obligation of public service, earning, to some degree, accolades and audience loyalty. But as the site of intense local competition and substantial advertising revenue, journalism and public service often take second place to ratings-grabbing gimmickry and corporate cross-promotion. Despite taking knocks for its formulaic approach and irresponsible antics, local and regional TV news has grown steadily since the 1950s, and has, with the national cable news networks, contributed to a sharp decline in network news audiences. This entry focuses on news in the United States, though many countries have similarly complementary local and national systems of TV news. Most larger British cities, for example, have both a commercial and public local newscast, though these are far smaller operations than their U.S. counterparts. In Germany, the dominant TV news providers are regional. Intensive promotion of local television journalism and local news celebrities seems to be a purely U.S. phenomenon, however.

Although the earliest experiments with television in the 1930s included simple newscasts, and the first stations licensed provided local news, most local VHF television stations began creating their own newscasts as soon as they went on the air in the 1950s or 1960s. Doing so provided evidence of community involvement and an identity amid otherwise indistinguishable fare. UHF stations neither had the budgets nor the audience ratings to do so. Early local newscasts were brief and non-visual, for videotape technology, debuting in 1956, was too cumbersome to leave the studio and live remotes were all but impossible for their cost and complexity.

Some stations purchased newsfilm from newsreel companies. 16-millimeter film, while an excellent newsgathering medium, was costly and required at least three and a half hours to be processed, edited, and set up for the process of playing it back into a newscast. By the 1970s, as more and more viewers purchased color television sets, color film replaced black and white. Visual coverage of national news increased as the networks trusted their affiliates to cover important stories and send them to New York for the network newscasts. But until the 1980s, quality television news remained the near exclusive domain of the networks, and particularly of CBS. Local stations could not match the look or experience of the networks and rarely profited from news.

Between the mid-1970s and early 1980s came a local news explosion, attributable to a synergy of technology and economics. Sony introduced the 3/4" video cassette recorder, a portable machine capable of recording 20 minutes on each cassette. With it came simple and reliable editing equipment permitting the rapid assembly of stories from the field. Ikegami and RCA produced shoulder-borne television cameras to be used with the field recorders. Electronic News Gathering (ENG) was born, and by 1975, 65 percent of local stations in the United States were using ENG equipment, though many continued to use film into the 1980s. The earliest ENG equipment was expensive and was adopted slowly by all but the wealthiest stations. Field camera and recorder were later combined into the most popular news-gathering tool of the 1980s and 1990s, the Sony Betacam. Stations experimented with many new tape technologies in the 1990s, with many stations opting for smaller and cheaper formats like Sony's Hi-8 or, later, Pansonic's DV.

ENG made more pre-produced material and story "packages" possible, allowing for more news and greater advertising revenue. With the technological revolution came broader conceptions of local news.

News could be more visual, immediate, and exciting. The ability to produce more news—through the expansion of local resources and a plethora of national and international sources—led stations to add newscasts. Those with existing newscasts expanded their operations. With the rapid growth of cable television in the 1980s and 1990s, many cable operators established newscasts of their own, often in towns and cities not well served by broadcasters.

With, at the very least, an early- and late-evening newscast to be filled each day, news directors developed new strategies, and looser standards of journalism, to fill the time and attract viewers. By the 1990s, many stations added morning and midday programs, producing six hours or more of news daily. Newscasts increasingly presented crime or minor tragedy (the fires and accidents which are inexpensive to cover and never in short supply) as news, and made stories shorter and snappier, especially those that were not easily illustrated. Reports on City Hall or problems in the schools offered little visual excitement and so took a back seat to sensational but unimportant news. Local news watchdog Rocky Mountain Media Watch observed that between 1994 and 1999, "violent topics consistently comprise 40 to 50 percent of all the airtime devoted to news" despite the fact that U.S. crimes rates were dropping.

From the mid-1970s to the present, newscasts have been fierce battlegrounds for viewer loyalty. Stations earn a substantial portion of their revenue from their newscasts, and aggressively promote their news. Popular syndicated entertainment programming leading into newscasts is used to deliver viewers to a station's news product, and a popular newscast, in turn, boosts ratings for an entire evening's programming. Stations peddle newscasts and newscasters with billboards and other advertising. But when programming and promotional strategies fail, stations turn from the expertise of their own managers to high paid consultants with a track record of ratings increases and a supposedly scientific approach.

The best known consultants are Frank Magid and Al Primo, but there have been countless imitators. For tens of thousands of dollars their firms conduct viewer surveys and focus groups. The results—a vague indication of what a few viewers think they like—are used to rebuild newscasts from the ground up. Newscasts are made "marketable." The typical gimmicks offered by consultants or newly hired news directors included new or redesigned sets and changes in on-air "talent." Consultants maintain vast nationwide videotape files of news talent, and records of their respective ratings, to help clients find the perfect personalities.

Finally, a new format is usually adopted. The most

grating of these, known as "happy talk" (usually under the "Eyewitness News" designation), in which dual anchors bantered with one another about innocuous matters, has mercifully died away in most markets. Other common formats, some still in evidence, include "Action News," with quick young reporters and barely edited video of the day's highly visual carnage, or "News Center," emphasizing reporting and relevance to viewers. As stations acquired adequate technology to produce live news coverage in the late 1980s, "liveness" was invariably made the newscast's raison d'être. This often puts reporters in ridiculous situations, filing live reports from dark, long-deserted locations, without the depth and quality a pre-produced report would provide.

Despite these variations in theme, local news in the U.S. has maintained an astounding consistency of format from its earliest days. Newscasts are divided into four or more segments, separated by commercials (which are, after all, the reason the newscast is there). Actual news, broadly defined, comes in the first two segments, often including a superficial recap of world and national events when local news is sparse. News is delivered by one or two anchors (usually an older Caucasian male and younger Caucasian female, with limited ethnic diversity in some urban markets), and contains a mix of readers (with an anchor delivering the story), voice-overs (with anchors narrating over videotape), packages (pre-produced stories by reporters), and live reports. One stylistic element has changed in fifty years of local TV news: the average length of soundbites—the time newsmakers are given to explain ideas to viewers—has dropped from an excess of twenty seconds down to seven seconds.

The third and fourth segments are usually sports and weather (with the one of greatest local interest coming first). In smaller cities, much is made of local school sports to lure the parents of schoolchildren to tune in (a sought-after demographic for advertisers). Hour-long news formats and 24-hour regional formats have more segments, but add little in variety apart from extra feature stories, and increasingly (aping CNN and its ilk) lengthy "news analysis" discussions between anchors and hired pundits.

Local television's most urgent task is to persuade audiences of its own relevance to their lives. To ensure its very survival, it attempts to demonstrate that it provides something more or different than national newscasts and other TV fare. But localism alone is no guarantee of relevance, so local news often resorts to exaggeration. Routine storms are presented as threats to life and limb, errant teenagers as deadly gangs. Populist or consumer advocacy stories often pose as news. During the 1990s, some stations merged the content

and aesthetics of tabloid newsmagazine shows with a colloquial reporting style in the hope of attracting a young audience, and desperate efforts to capture the youth market—traditionally the least interested in TV news—continue. Other stations copied the national cable news companies, offering several stories at the same time through the use of an irritating and uninformative "crawl" of words at the bottom of the screen.

But encouragingly, some stations took a new approach, eschewing crime and tragedy except where substantial numbers of viewers are affected, avoiding gimmicks, and focusing on explaining social and political issues. Some replicated the community-service focused "public journalism" model taking hold at many newspapers. Stations going this route—as did Chicago's WBBM for a short time in 2000—remain rare, because those that have done so gained awards and praise, but few rating points.

Quality journalism is not entirely absent in television news, but rarely does it come before economic considerations. As shown by McManus (1994), active discovery of news, especially that which society's powerful prefer hidden, is costly, giving rise to the common allegation that TV news legitimates the status quo. Such journalism requires the allocation of station resources and personnel over long periods to produce a single story.

Excellence in television news does exist, and is recognized in annual awards by the Associated Press and numerous industry organizations. In rare, but remarkable, instances local television news goes on the air full time to report on local disasters or major events, or invests in investigations that bring about needed changes in public policy. When local TV journalists resist sensationalism and premature reporting such coverage can provide a vital public service beyond the means of other media.

Television news operations are fairly autonomous departments within broadcast or cable companies. The senior manager of the news department is the news director, and may be assisted by one or more executive producers. These individuals are responsible for controlling the general look and feel of their newscast while satisfying the demands of their corporate superiors. The successful construction of each newscast is the responsibility of a producer, who in the smallest markets may double as anchor or news director. The producer must ensure that every element of the production is ready at airtime, and deal with problems or changes while the newscast is on the air. In large news departments this involves the coordination of dozens of reporters, videographers, writers, feature producers, tape editors, graphic artists, and other specialized staff. They work with the on-air talent to develop the lineup (story order) of the newscast and write portions of the show not provided by reporters or news writers. Control of day to day newsgathering operations is the domain of the assignment editor who has the unenviable task of ensuring that everything of importance is covered. As the center of incoming information and the dispatcher of a station's news coverage resources, the assignment editor has considerable power to determine "the news."

The technical production of a newscast is accomplished by a staff independent of the news department. Studio production is supervised by a studio director (or newscast director), who works closely with the producers and talent to ensure that each production is flawless. A well-directed newscast is one that calls no attention to its complex technical elements. In larger markets the studio director coordinates a large production team, but in some small markets may perform a remarkable solo ballet of switching, mixing audio, timing, and myriad other tasks. Even the largest news operations, though, are slashing their production staff through the installation of robotic studio cameras and other automation.

Local television news is highly dependent on new technologies, regional news even more so. But while some basic production equipment, like digital cameras and non-linear editing, provide higher quality at lower cost than ever before, other important technologies require massive investment beyond the reach of smaller news departments. The next major development after the field recorder was the rapid increase in the use of microwave systems to transmit live or taped stories from remote locations (also called ENG). Now, all but the smallest stations operate microwave-equipped vehicles.

By the late 1980s, most news departments were using computers to write and archive scripts, at the very least. Many had begun to use integrated news production software designed to simplify writing TV news scripts, arrange them for a newscast, and deliver them to teleprompters for the news anchors to read. Television journalists now make extensive use of computerized information retrieval services and databases, and many television stations have established their own expansive websites to provide updates of stories, special services like highly localized weather forecasts, and to encourage viewer feedback. Increasingly, station websites are being called upon to turn a profit as well, and so most feature extensive advertising and cross-promotion, but little news.

From the late 1980s, Satellite News Gathering (SNG) became the technology to most change the industry. It made regional television news possible, permitted local stations to cover national and international events, and dramatically extended the newsgathering reach of stations. Local TV news was thereby delocalized. An entrepreneur, Stanley Hubbard, is credited with beginning the SNG revolution. Domestic satellites launched in the early 1980s had the new capability of handling signals at a higher, more efficient, frequency band than before—the Ku band. Hubbard began Conus Communications to provide access to these satellites for a "cooperative" group of local stations. The stations would be able to reserve satellite time cheaply in five minute increments to "uplink" a story from the field to their studio and to the rest of the stations in the cooperative. Stations began to purchase sophisticated Satellite News Vehicles (SNV) to transmit localized reports from the scene of major stories anywhere. Not coincidentally, Hubbard also sold SNVs. The networks established plans to help affiliated stations with the cost of purchasing SNVs (at around $300,000 each) in order to create their own cooperatives of live sources and to ensure that they alone would receive any important story from a network-funded SNV. The latest news vehicles have both satellite and microwave transmission capabilities and, due to digital technology, are smaller, lighter, and cheaper.

Stations may receive stories from one or more satellite cooperatives they belong to, their own network (if an affiliate), a national cable news service like CNN or MSNBC, Reuters or Associated Press, other specialized services, public relations firms, and their own news gathering resources. Helicopter news coverage also became common in the 1990s.

The proliferation of sources and the ability to send and receive stories instantly and inexpensively within virtually unlimited geographic areas gave rise to regional news, which has emerged in several forms. An early example of regional television news was an agreement between seven SNG-equipped Florida stations to share resources and personnel, presenting an image of seamless statewide coverage to their audiences. In 1986, News 12 Long Island was started by Cablevision and other investors. Using a mix of ENG and SNG, the cable news channel presents 24-hour news coverage, often live, of the vast Long Island area, which had previously been underserved by the New York stations.

Many other local and regional 24-hour cable news operations have since been created, including some carried by different cable operators spread over a large area, such as New England Cable News and some large city cable operators, most notably Time Warner in New York, have also established twenty-four-hour news stations.

With the flurry of station sales and purchases taking place since the start of extensive broadcast deregulation in the 1980s, station ownership by non-local investors became common. In a sharp contrast to the heavy investment in news of the 1970s, many news departments now run on shoestring budgets to maintain the illusion of community service at little cost to their corporate parents. In many small and medium markets, news departments operate with a staff of a dozen or fewer, and—as with many of the regional news operations—eager young reporters work as "one man bands," acting as videographer and reporter on the several stories they cover daily. Their salaries are among the lowest for college graduates. Owners unwilling to invest in news often close their news departments and more profitably counter the competition's newscasts with syndicated programs. Many news departments are experimenting with new ways to pay their own way. News or weather programs are provided to other stations in the same market that have no news staff of their own. Increasingly, revenue-generating commercials and cross-promotions are presented as news, as when one San Francisco station directed viewers to its website to purchase *Who Wants To Be A Millionaire* board games, as part of a feature news story.

Local television journalists often produce their product with little knowledge or concern about who is watching and why (though they do better in this regard than their national counterparts). When stations do research their audience, what they discover may tend to lead them to ignore the substance of their newscast for the superficialities. It is rarely determined how much viewers actually learn from TV news, but existing research suggests it is very little, and often not what producers intend. Distant ownership makes the lack of connection with audiences more acute. By some accounts, the pressure to sacrifice public-service journalism for corporate financial interests has reached crisis proportions in local TV. The firing of reporters Jane Akre and Steve Wilson by a Florida FOX affiliate in 1997 because their investigative reporting threatened bad publicity for key advertisers has gained the most notoriety, but a national survey in 2000 showed that pressure and intimidation in the newsroom is commonplace, with nearly 40 percent of local broadcast journalists admitting to avoiding stories which might threaten their company's financial interests (Pew).

Other research has shown that contrary to arguments made by the FCC as justification for deregulation, conglomerate-owned stations generally do a poorer job of public service than those owned by smaller companies (Napoli, Project for Excellence in Journalism). And local TV, like its network mentors, continues to ignore vast portions of the population—especially the poor and urban working classes—and present community issues almost exclusively through the eyes of local business owners (when not through the eyes of its corporate parent). While television news has come far, a reorientation toward genuine community service and away from entertainment and profit are desperately needed. As Walter Cronkite observed nearly four decades ago (*Time,* October 14, 1966), a half-hour newscast has fewer words than the first page alone of a decent newspaper, so anyone relying on TV for their news information will never be as well informed as they ought to be.

CHRIS PATERSON

Further Reading

Akre, J., "The Fox, the Hounds, and the Sacred Cows," in *Into the Buzzsaw,* edited by K. Borjessen, New York: Prometheus Books, 2002

Broadcasting and Cable Yearbook, New Providence, New Jersey: R.R. Bowker, annual

Colman, P., "Regional News on a Roll", *Broadcasting and Cable* (August 26, 1996)

Educational Broadcasting Corporation, "Local News Online," 2001, available at *www.pbs.org/wnet/insidelocalnews*

Goedkoop, R., *Inside Local Television News,* Salem, Wisconsin: Sheffield, 1988

Grimes, T., "Encoding TV News Messages Into Memory," *Journalism Quarterly* (Winter 1990)

Hickey, N., "Chicago Experiment—Why it Failed," *Columbia Journalism Review* (January/February 2001), available at *archives.cjr.org/year/01/1/chicago.asp*

Klite, P., "TV News and the Culture of Violence," *Rocky Mountain Media Watch* (1999), available at *www.bigmedia. org/texts6.html*

Lacy, S., "Use of Satellite Technology in Local Television News," *Journalism Quarterly* (Winter 1988)

Lieberman, D., "The Rise and Rise of 24-Hour Local News," *Columbia Journalism Review* (November/December 1998), available at *archives.cjr.org/year/98/6/tvnews3.asp*

McManus, J., *Market Driven Journalism: Let the Citizen Beware?,* Thousand Oaks, California: Sage, 1994

Musburger, R., *Electronic News Gathering,* Boston: Focal Press, 1991

Napoli, P., "Television Station Ownership Characteristics and Local News and Public Affairs Programming: An Expanded Analysis of FCC Data," occasional paper, Washington, D.C.: International Communication Association, 2003

Pew Research Center For The People And The Press, "Self Censorship: How Often and Why—Journalists Avoiding The News," 2000, available at *people-press.org/reports/display. php3?ReportID539*

Postman, N., and S. Powers, *How to Watch TV News,* New York: Penguin, 1992

Powers, R., *The Newscasters,* New York: St. Martin's Press, 1977

Project for Excellence in Journalism, "Does Ownership Matter in Local Television News? A Five-Year Study of Ownership and Quality," 2003, available at *www.journalism.org/ resources/research/reports/ownership/*

Robinson, J., and M. Levy, *The Main Source: Learning from Television News,* Beverly Hills, California: Sage, 1986

Schihl, R., *TV Newscast Processes and Procedures,* Boston: Focal Press, 1992

Stephens, M., *Broadcast News,* Fort Worth, Texas: Harcourt Brace Jovanovich, 1993

Tuggle, C.A.; Carr, F.; Huffman, S., *Broadcast News Handbook,* Boston: McGraw Hill, 2001

Westin, A., *Newswatch,* New York: Simon and Schuster, 1982

News in the United States, Network

As with most forms of television programming, the antecedents to network news in the United States reside in the radio era, beginning as early as 1928, when NBC mounted major coverage of the presidential election race. Yet for a variety of reasons, radio news was slow to develop. It was not until the impending prospect of war in Europe that news programming emerged as a major component of network radio. During the late 1930s, CBS's Edward R. Murrow assembled a team of correspondents scattered across Europe that provided both breaking news and analysis of major events and personalities. The "Murrow Boys"—including Eric Sevareid, Howard K. Smith, and Charles Collingwood—earned renown for their war reporting. In the post-war period, they would come to play a major role in the development of television news as well.

Immediately after the war, few imagined that television news would supersede its radio counterpart. Indeed, most correspondents vied for plum radio postings, and NBC's initial TV news program was hosted not by a journalist but rather by announcer John Cameron Swayze, whose *Camel News Caravan* "hopscotched" the globe, delivering a mere 15-minute sampling of headline stories. Sponsored by Camel cigarettes, the program nevertheless pioneered the use of remote film footage that was shot, processed, and edited under daily deadline conditions. CBS likewise launched *Douglas Edwards with the News,* and late in the 1950s, ABC floated its own nightly news round-up under the leadership of John Daly. Yet the transition from radio to television proved expensive, so all three networks allocated most of their resources to entertainment programming, allowing only occasional opportunities for experimentation in news and information programming.

The leading experimenter was Edward R. Murrow, who had been promoted to vice-president of CBS in recognition for his wartime service. Murrow used his corporate influence and celebrity status to launch television's first news documentary series, entitled *See It Now,* which ranged broadly in its coverage of both domestic and international issues. Produced by Fred Friendly, the program took on prominent social issues and painted vivid portraits of the struggles of everyday citizens. It was also renowned for thought-provoking interviews with such leading figures as Robert Oppenheimer, Jawaharlal Nehru, and Harry Truman. Interestingly, histories of 1950s television less commonly acknowledge *Person to Person,* a companion program developed by Murrow that drew much larger audiences with its interviews of leading show-business personalities in their homes. In television's first venture into infotainment programming, Murrow toured the homes of such stars as Marilyn Monroe and Eddy Fischer, while chatting about celebrity gossip and their personal lives. Both "high-brow" Murrow and "low-brow" Murrow helped to set the early standard for long-form television news.

In 1956, however, NBC began to bid for bragging rights in TV news when its new president, Robert Kintner, took charge. An avowed "news junkie," Kintner expanded the scope and resources of the news division, creating a truly international newsgathering organization during his reign at the network. Most immediately, Kintner parlayed Chet Huntley's and David Brinkley's adroit coverage of the 1956 Democratic and Republican conventions into the *Huntley-Brinkley Report,* a program that would dominate nightly news ratings until 1967. Kintner also nurtured NBC's documentary efforts, overseeing the launch of the distinguished *NBC White Paper* series in 1960. And he was furthermore an advocate of news specials, often breaking away from regularly scheduled entertainment shows in order to provide live coverage of important events, such as spacecraft launches, Congressional hearings, and the Cuban Missile Crisis. Yet Kintner's efforts were motivated by more than *pro bono* professionalism, as he was the first network chieftain to stress the profit potential of news programming. Just as importantly, Kintner, who would later serve in the Johnson administration, understood the public relations value of his news division at a time when government regulators began to press for more news and information programming.

Such growing pressures culminated in the 1961 appointment of Newton Minow, who famously referred to network television as a "vast wasteland" in a speech he delivered shortly after taking office. Like other officials in the Kennedy administration, Minow explicitly put network officials on notice that he considered television a strategic weapon in the struggle against communism, and throughout his two-year term, he prodded and cajoled network officials to expand their news departments and increase their coverage of international issues. TV executives were generally sympathetic to this shift in government policy and news department staffers were especially enthusiastic to see their profession restored to the prominence it had enjoyed during World War II. Indeed, it's important to note that the generation of journalists that filed stories from the battlefronts of WWII were, by the 1960s, in charge of the network news divisions and generally sympathetic to the government's strategic and ideological struggle against communism.

Former war correspondent Walter Cronkite took charge of the *CBS Evening News* in 1962 and Howard K. Smith (one of the "Murrow Boys") anchored ABC's nightly newscast. Both networks furthermore launched prime-time documentary series, *CBS Reports* and *ABC CloseUp,* which shared a similar set of topics and treatments as *NBC White Paper.* Indeed, the early 1960s would prove to be the golden age of the prime-time documentary in the United States, with much of the programming shaped by Cold War concerns. All three networks furthermore competed to provide breaking news coverage of important events, and in 1963, CBS and NBC expanded their nightly news programs from 15 to 30 minutes. By this point, American network news divisions had established bureaus in dozens of cities around the world and had developed a sophisticated infrastructure for the processing, shipment, and editing of news footage, so that visual accounts of important events around the world would find their way to national television screens within 24 hours. In a few short years, news became an integral component of network television and on-camera news professionals became major television personalities, their popularity carefully tracked by audience research services and monitored by network executives.

The growing prominence of television news also encouraged politicians and public officials to play to the camera in an attempt to advance particular causes.

Most capable in this regard was the President Kennedy himself, whose press conferences earned surprisingly strong ratings due in part to his telegenic appearance and his wry humor. Tragically, Kennedy's assassination would also draw record audiences, followed by the capture and on-camera slaying of his assassin, and by live coverage of the visually stunning funeral service beamed from the nation's capital. All three networks suspended commercial advertising and turned the airwaves over to their news divisions for several days, in what many would refer to as the coming of age of television. During those few days, the medium provided a common ground upon which citizens worked through the complex emotions engendered by that historic chain of events.

In the years that followed, however, the news divisions would find that the awesome power invested in them could also prove to be a liability. Although network news now had the authority to direct national attention at specific events and social concerns, it also stirred up controversy and counterattacks when it did so. News programs about the exploitation of migrant laborers angered farmers; criticisms of public education worried parents; and investigations into lung cancer stirred resentments among cigarette companies, then the leading advertisers on network television. Perhaps most significantly, news programs about civil rights elevated African Americans to a level of visibility they had never before enjoyed in the U.S. media. Sympathetic news portrayals of the plight of black citizens stirred both righteous indignation and racist antipathy. As the campaign for civil rights gained momentum in the 1960s, it sometimes skirted conventional politics, appealing directly to national television audiences through a series of carefully orchestrated non-violent protest demonstrations and through the charismatic appeals of black community leaders.

Likewise, as the war in Vietnam heated up, television news became a site of struggle between pro- and anti-war factions. During the early years of the war, Vietnam correspondents rarely challenged the U.S. government's rationale for intervention or its progress reports on the war effort. Yet President Johnson's decision to escalate troop commitments in 1965 greatly expanded the military draft, inciting resistance on American college campuses, within the government, and among military units in the field. Closely monitored by both sides, nightly news divisions juggled the competing claims of the administration and the anti-war movement, as opposing viewpoints began to work their way into regular news coverage. The growing protest movement discouraged Lyndon Johnson from seeking a second presidential term in 1968, and many critics—correctly or not—attributed his political demise in part to television news coverage that was increasingly critical of the war and sympathetic to protestors.

Now widely perceived as a news oligopoly, the networks both influenced public perceptions of key public issues and found themselves called to account for skewing political deliberation. Presidents were especially sensitive to the perceived power of television news: during his time in office, Lyndon Johnson grew increasingly agitated by network reporting, and Richard Nixon was hostile to the three networks from the very moment he entered the Oval Office. Giving voice to the administration's sentiments, Vice President Spiro Agnew publicly lambasted the "effete corps of impudent snobs" that ruled the news media, while officials within the Nixon administration began to advocate the development of cable technology, hoping to undermine the power of the three commercial networks.

Despite these tensions, television would continue to prevail as the public's dominant news source throughout the 1970s, even though the complexion of news organizations would change considerably. At NBC, changes began with the retirement of Chet Huntley in 1970, a vacancy that would stir several years of intense competition to fill the anchor slot. At the same time, executives were reassessing the Kintner legacy that had pushed NBC to a leadership role in TV news. RCA, the parent corporation of NBC, had earlier accepted the costs of an extensive global news operation because it assumed that such programming helped to drive the sale of television sets, both at home and abroad. By the 1970s, however, the sale of sets in the U.S. began to taper off and RCA began to shift its emphasis to informatic, aerospace, and military product lines. Given the importance of government contracts in such fields, and given changing government attitudes toward news, RCA no longer relished the expansive ambitions of the Kintner era. Consequently, NBC News began to trim budgets and close news bureaus. Its nightly news program then began to lag behind its CBS competitor until coverage of the Watergate hearings re-energized the division and catapulted Tom Brokaw to a position of visibility that would eventually earn him the anchor slot on the nightly news in 1976.

Watergate coverage also animated the fortunes of public broadcasting, as Robert McNeil and Jim Lehrer fashioned thoughtful interviews and commentary, providing some of the first regular coverage of national politics on PBS. In 1976, the duo launched the *McNeil-Lehrer Report,* a nightly half-hour program that quickly won a solid audience of opinion leaders and media critics. While earning both criticism and praise

for its emphasis on "talking heads," the program delivered precisely what was lacking in commercial network newscasts. It furthermore addressed two other criticisms often leveled at TV news when in 1983 the anchors bought the production company and expanded their program to an hour-long format, as the *McNeil-Lehrer News Hour.* Ironically, this gave PBS, the network with the most diminutive news resources, the most in-depth and independent nightly newscast.

The resurgent interest in television news could also be measured by the fortunes of the first prime-time newsmagazine, *60 Minutes.* Premiering in 1968, many critics complained that the program represented a softening of the documentary news tradition by emphasizing investigative stories that focused on clearly defined villains, rather than broad-ranging reports on more abstract but pressing social issues. Yet despite the program's calculated tilt toward a narrative style, it failed to attract large audiences and languished at the bottom of the ratings, threatened with cancellation. Ranked 101st among 106 network programs in 1975, *60 Minutes* unexpectedly began a meteoric ascent to become the number 1 ratings draw in 1979. Some attributed its newfound success to a shift in scheduling that moved the program to early prime-time on Sundays, but just as importantly, the reversal of fortune seemed to reflect a growing popular interest in investigative reporting in the wake of Watergate.

ABC soon harnessed this same enthusiasm with the premiere of *20/20* in 1978, a magazine show that balanced tough investigative reports with lighter fare about fads, fashions, and celebrities. Both networks saw benefits to the new programs, since they seemed to fulfill public-service responsibilities while steering clear of government criticism by focusing their attention on unscrupulous crooks rather than hot-button political issues. Moreover, the newsmagazines proved to be money machines, costing only half as much as hour-long dramas, while delivering upscale demographics and premium advertising rates. Just as importantly, they helped to mitigate internal tensions within the news divisions, as they provided showcases for such high-powered talent as Mike Wallace, Barbara Walters, and Ed Bradley. Over the next two decades, both ABC and CBS sought to expand on their successful magazine offerings and NBC tried unsuccessfully to match its competition until finally, in 1992, it too scored a hit with *Dateline.*

For ABC, the growing emphasis on newsmagazines was only part of a larger set of transformations, as Roone Arledge, the architect of the network's successful sports division, moved over to take charge of news in what critics perceived as a shocking triumph of showbusiness over journalistic professionalism.

Arledge, however, proved to be a prodigious booster of news, reformatting the nightly news show and launching *20/20* in 1978. The following year, with the hostage crisis in Iran, ABC was especially aggressive in its coverage, providing regular updates, including the sensationally titled late-night show, *Iran Crisis: America Held Hostage.* The program nevertheless provided sober, in-depth features and interviews, elevating the network's chief diplomatic correspondent, Ted Koppel, to a position of prominence and, after the release of the hostages, allowing him to transform the show into *Nightline,* a commercial counterpart to *McNeil-Lehrer.* In 1981, Arledge also carved out a new home for a disillusioned David Brinkley, who fled NBC to host *This Week with David Brinkley,* a show that would finally bring ABC to a leading position on the Sunday-morning talk circuit. Shortly thereafter, Arledge shrewdly tapped his leading Middle East correspondent, Peter Jennings, to anchor the *ABC World News Tonight.* Thus, in less than a decade, Arledge played a prominent role in transforming ABC into the leading U.S. network news operation with some of the most talented personnel in the profession.

Meanwhile, CBS greeted the 1980s with its own agenda for change. Walter Cronkite, who was often referred to as "the most trusted man in America," retired in 1981 after two decades anchoring the *CBS Evening News.* Dan Rather won out in the struggle to succeed Cronkite, but the ratings of the network's flagship news program began to falter. In response, CBS went through a string of executive producers, trying to restore the luster of the Cronkite years, but the network found itself in an increasingly tight ratings race with its competitors. CBS has other problems, as well. A 1982 documentary, *The Uncounted Enemy: A Vietnam Deception,* stirred up a major libel suit when it re-examined the calculation of combat casualties during the Vietnam War, claiming that military leaders manipulated weekly body counts in an effort to sustain support for the war effort. General William Westmoreland, the retired commander of U.S. forces in Southeast Asia, sued CBS, and the resulting legal settlement sent shock waves through the news department, as an internal investigation sought to rectify dubious journalistic practices, especially standards for editing on-camera interviews.

The biggest problem confronting television news, however, was the steady erosion of ratings, as cable television increasingly siphoned off network viewers throughout the 1980s. Younger audiences were most likely to gravitate to cable channels, and consequently the age demographic for nightly news programs began to drift upward. Cable also posed a direct challenge when in 1980 Ted Turner launched Cable Network News (CNN), a 24-hour news channel, and one year later added *Headline News,* a news update program that rotated on a half-hourly basis. Journalists at the major networks generally dismissed the new challenger, noting that Turner, whom they regarded as a volatile personality, had shown no prior commitment to news, and CNN seemed to be operating on a shoestring budget. Yet the cable network enjoyed certain cost advantages, such as a non-union workforce and a base of operations in Atlanta, where real-estate costs were considerably lower than Manhattan. Turner also enjoyed the counsel of Reese Schonfeld, a veteran news producer who was tapped to lead the news organization during its early years. Schonfeld understood that the key weakness of his competitors was the relatively high cost of maintaining a global news operation in order to produce a half-hour nightly newscast and a few weekly magazine shows. CNN by comparison spread the cost of its news infrastructure across two channels broadcasting around the clock—48 hours of programming per day. In 1985, the cable network went even further, establishing CNN International (CNNI) to manage a collection of distinctive satellite news services targeted at different regions of the globe.

By the mid-1980s, cable TV in the United States was a growing force in both news and entertainment, and Ted Turner's channels emerged as leaders in both cable ratings and advertising. Though still diminutive by comparison to the major broadcast networks, the Atlanta-based upstart began to maneuver for financing that would allow it to mount a hostile takeover of the venerable CBS. Executives at CBS responded by bringing in friendly investors, most prominently Laurence Tisch, who would eventually take control of the network in 1986. Tisch, ironically, proved to be no less disruptive to network operations, and in one of his very first acts as chairman, he toured CBS News bureaus around the world, shuttering operations, laying off staff, and slashing costs. In the same year, Capital Cities Broadcasting took over ABC, and General Electric absorbed NBC. At all three networks, executives suddenly returned their attention to cost controls, seeking to make news operations more efficient and more attractive to advertisers. With only a limited number of programming hours, news divisions sought to develop new prime-time magazine programs and to prop up the sagging ratings of nightly newscasts with more feature-oriented material.

Turmoil within news organizations began to grow, however, as staffers tried to resist what they saw as a further softening of journalistic and public-service standards. Remarkably, they could count on little support from government regulators. Indeed, throughout the Reagan Presidency, the administration aggressively sought to undermine the independence of network news divisions, and the FCC relentlessly rolled back government guidelines regarding the public-service commitments of broadcasters. Chairman Mark Fowler argued that the growing number of available TV channels diluted the government's rationale for regulating broadcasting in the public's interest. According to Fowler, television should enjoy the same First Amendment rights as newspapers and magazines, a position that has increasingly prevailed since the 1980s. Moreover, in its efforts to nurture a multiplication of services, the FCC made a number of rulings that allowed Australian media mogul Rupert Murdoch to launch a fourth commercial broadcast network in 1986, despite the fact that the FOX Network had no immediate plans for news or public-affairs programming. Instead, the channel resolutely focused on entertainment, and its sole forays into news consisted of tabloid-style magazines such as *Inside Edition* and *Hard Copy*. The emergence of FOX, when coupled with changes at the major networks and the increasingly sensational focus of local TV news, fueled criticisms about the growing impact of ratings and entertainment values on the news judgment of television professionals. The word "infotainment" gained widespread currency during the late 1980s, and battles erupted within news organizations over the future of network news. At one point, six of the leading journalists at CBS offered to buy the news division and run it as a separate entity in the hope of protecting it from what they saw as the cynical economic calculations of network executives.

Sobering events at Tiananmen Square, the Berlin Wall, and in the Persian Gulf helped to slow the eroding status of network news operations, however. The Gulf War especially exposed the challenge faced by the down-sized network news divisions, as they seemed to be bested at every turn by CNN, which offered round-the-clock coverage that proved influential not only in the U.S. but also in the Middle East and Europe. CNN furthermore earned kudos for its independent reporting from Baghdad throughout the war, a stark contrast to the pack journalism practiced by its competition. Yet with the luxury of CNN's many hours of programming, it also could swing from the most serious topical news to the most sensational tabloid stories, as it demonstrated with its capacious coverage of domestic stories such as the Menendez murder trial, Tonya Harding's assault on Nancy Kerrigan, and Marina Bobbit's castration of her wayward husband. The apogee of such coverage seemed to arrive with the surreal, slow-motion highway pursuit of O.J. Simpson and his subsequent murder trial, followed shortly thereafter by the Clinton-Lewinsky scandal.

The latter is remarkable on a number of accounts. First of all, the story was broken not by a network news organization, but rather by Matt Drudge, a gossip columnist on the Internet. Several news organizations were already aware of rumors of the President's romantic liaison with a White House intern, but despite intense competitive pressures, each had exercised restraint until Drudge published undocumented assertions on his web page, launching a frenzy of coverage that dominated national news for much of 1998, despite many other pressing social issues. Intense competition among broadcast, cable, and Internet news organizations paradoxically encouraged a growing diversity of electronic sources but also fostered a singular fixation on a story of little consequence in the realm of public policy. Since the networks no longer had a monopoly of airtime, talent, audiences, or advertising revenues they consequently found it difficult to resist the attraction of such a sensational news stories, even if it led to an imbalance in coverage.

Moreover, in a world of multiplying delivery channels, the news organizations that seemed most successful were those that could leverage their news output through as many channels and times of the day as possible, both at home and abroad. Such considerations led NBC to launch two global cable networks in 1995: MSNBC, a joint venture with Microsoft, and CNBC, a financial news channel. CNN took this philosophy to another level when it merged with Time Warner in 1995, hoping to realize synergies with such magazines as *Time, Fortune,* and *Sports Illustrated.* Soon after, News Corporation, the parent company of FOX and the owner of a growing collection of satellite TV services around the world, finally took a plunge into broadcast journalism with the 1996 premier of the FOX News Channel, a service that modeled itself on right-wing talk radio in the U.S., thereby distinguishing it from rivals and helping to push it ahead of CNN in U.S. cable ratings. Interestingly, this put ABC and CBS in a difficult position, since neither news organization enjoyed the same synergies as their competitors and yet both worried that it would be costly to launch yet another cable news service in an already crowded market. Consequently, ABC, now owned by Disney, began to search for strategic partnerships, entering into extended negotiations with CNN. As talks continued, the market value of the two organizations indicated a dramatic reversal of fortune, with CNN reporting profits in 2001 of $200 million on $1.6 billion in revenues and ABC News realizing only $15 million in profits derived from $600 million in revenues. Although at the millennium, the nightly newscasts of the major broadcast networks still drew the largest audiences, the proliferating services of cable television had dramatically redefined the meaning of network news.

MICHAEL CURTIN

See also **Brinkley, David; Brokaw, Tom; Cable News Network; Cronkite, Walter;** *Dateline;* **Huntley, Chet; Murrow, Edward R.; News, Local and Regional; Sevaried, Eric;** *60 Minutes;* **Smith, Howard K.; Walters, Barbara**

Further Reading

Ken Auletta, *Three Blind Mice: How the Networks Lost Their Way,* New York: Random House, 1991

Michael Curtin, *Redeeming the Wasteland: Television Documentary and Cold War Politics,* New Brunswick, New Jersey: Rutgers University Press, 1996

Todd Gitlin, *The Whole World Is Watching: Mass Media in the Making and Unmaking of the New Left,* Berkeley: University of California Press, 1980

Daniel Hallin, *The Uncensored War: Vietnam and the Media,* Berkeley: University of California Press, 1986

Michael D. Murray, editor, *Encyclopedia of Television News,* Phoenix: Oryx Press, 1999

Nichols, Dandy (1907–1986)

British Actor

Dandy Nichols is remembered above all for one role only, that of the long-suffering Else, wife of the appalling Alf Garnett, in the long-running series *Till Death Us Do Part,* and the rather milder follow-up *In Sickness and in Health,* both written by Johnny Speight.

The role of Else Garnett (or Ramsey, as the family was called in the beginning) went first to Gretchen Franklin when a pilot episode of *Till Death Us Do Part* was made in 1965, but Nichols took over when the series got under way and she quickly proved the perfect foil to the bigoted and abusive Garnett, played by Warren Mitchell. The rapport between the two ensured the show's immediate, if controversial, success, and the program was destined to attract top ratings for 10 years before a weary Nichols complained that she could no longer work with Warren Mitchell, and called it a day (in the series it was explained that she had left for Australia to visit her sister). She came back, however, as Else in the sequel, *In Sickness and in Health,* although she was by now confined to a wheelchair because of arthritis and with only months to live.

As Else, Alf Garnett's dimwitted "silly old moo" of a wife, Nichols repeatedly demonstrated the command of technique and timing that she had learned from her long apprenticeship in the theater (she appeared, for instance, in the original Royal Court Theatre cast of David Storey's *Home* in 1970 and acted in the West End with the likes of John Gielgud and Ralph Richardson). She also appeared in some 50-odd films, which ranged from *Carry on Doctor* and *Confessions of a Window Cleaner* to *Nicholas Nickleby* and *Scott of the*

Antarctic. Film directors cast her initially as cockney maids and charwomen, but it was not long before her skills as a character actress were recognized and she was occasionally allowed to extend herself in more varied parts.

Born in Hammersmith, in western London, Nichols was nevertheless quite at home with the East End locale of the Garnett series, and she proved inimitable in the character with which she became most closely identified. Deadpan in the face of Garnett's unforgivable verbal abuse, and resigned to her role as the target of much of her husband's frustration and invective, she could be, by turns, hilarious and pathetic, and she quickly became a firm favorite of the British viewing public. Treasured memories of her performances included the carefully managed moments in which she would bring a careering Alf Garnett to a sudden stop in mid-tirade with some artlessly innocent observation or other, apparently oblivious of the inevitable result that she would draw the full venom of her husband's ire upon herself. Else was a type that many people recognized from real life, and she provided some necessary warmth and pathos to contrast with the monstrous Alf's aggression and viciousness. Without Else, and in a changed climate under the Thatcher government, the later series faltered and failed to resonate with viewers as earlier episodes had done.

Success in the role of Else Garnett, though it came relatively late in her career, brought Nichols the opportunity to play both starring and supporting roles in many other classic television shows. In the sitcom *The Trouble with You, Lillian,* for instance, she was equally

Home, Dandy Nichols, John Gielgud, 1972.
Courtesy of the Everett Collection

effective as Madge, teamed up with the redoubtable Patricia Hayes. Among the other classic series in which she appeared to acclaim were *Emergency-Ward 10, Dixon of Dock Green, No Hiding Place, Mrs. Thursday,* and *Bergerac.* The critics also lavished praise on her performance in a television adaptation of the William Trevor play *The General's Day,* in which she starred opposite Alastair Sim.

DAVID PICKERING

*See also **Till Death Us Do Part***

Dandy Nichols (Daisy Nichols). Born in Hammersmith, London, 1907. Worked for 12 years as a secretary in a London factory, taking acting lessons; professional actor from late 1930s; participated in six-week tour with ENSA during World War II; film debut, 1947; played maids, housewives, and other roles for many years on both stage and screen, before her greatest success opposite Warren Mitchell, as Else in the long-running series *Till Death Us Do Part.* Died February 6, 1986.

Television Series

1965–75	*Till Death Us Do Part*
1971	*The Trouble with You, Lillian*
1985	*In Sickness and in Health*

Films

Hue and Cry, 1947; *Nicholas Nickleby,* 1947; *Woman Hater,* 1948; *Portrait from Life,* 1948; *The Fallen Idol,* 1948; *The Winslow Boy,* 1948; *Here Come the Huggetts,* 1948; *The History of Mr. Polly,* 1948; *Scott of the Antarctic,* 1948; *Don't Ever Leave Me,* 1949; *Now Barabbas was a Robber...,* 1949; *Tony Draws a Horse,* 1950; *Dance Hall,* 1950; *The Clouded Yellow,* 1950; *White Corridors,* 1951; *The Holly and the Ivy,* 1952; *The Happy Family/Mr. Lord Says No,* 1952; *Mother Riley Meets the Vampire/Vampire Over London,* 1952; *Emergency Call/Hundred Hour Hunt,* 1952; *The Pickwick Papers,* 1952; *Woman of Twilight/Twilight Women,* 1952; *Street Corner/Both Sides of the Law,* 1953; *The Wedding of Lili Marlene,* 1953; *Meet Mr. Lucifer,* 1953; *The Intruder,* 1953; *Time Is My Enemy,* 1954; *The Crowded Sky,* 1954; *Mad about Men,* 1954; *Where There's a Will,* 1955; *The Deep Blue Sea,* 1955; *A Time to Kill,* 1955; *Lost/Tears for Simon,* 1955; *Not So Dusty,* 1956; *The Feminine Touch/The Gentle Touch,* 1956; *Yield to the Night/Blonde Sinner,* 1956; *The Strange World of Planet X/Cosmic Monsters,* 1958; *Carry On Sergeant,* 1958; *A Cry from the Streets,* 1958; *Don't Talk to Strange Men,* 1962; *Ladies Who Do,* 1963; *The Leather Boys,* 1963; *Act of Murder,* 1964; *Help!,* 1965; *The Amorous Adventures of Moll Flanders,* 1965; *The Knack...and How to Get It,* 1965; *The Early Bird,* 1965; *Doctor in Clover,* 1966; *Georgy Girl,* 1966; *How I Won the War,* 1967; *Carry On Doctor,* 1968; *Till Death Us Do Part,* 1968; *The Bed Sitting Room,* 1969; *First Love,* 1970; *Home,* 1972; *The Alf Garnett Saga,* 1972; *O Lucky Man!,* 1973; *Confessions of a Window Cleaner,* 1974; *Three for All,* 1974; *Kate the Good Neighbour,* 1980; *The Plague Dogs* (voice only), 1982; *Britannia Hospital,* 1982.

Stage (selected)

The Clandestine Marriage; Plunder; Home.

Nick at Nite/TVLand

U.S. Cable Network

Debuting in 1985, Nick at Nite began as its parent company Nickelodeon's beachhead in primetime, eventually becoming one of the most successful examples of "re-purposing" in the television industry. Looking to establish continuity between Nickelodeon's daytime children's programming and a primetime schedule that would accommodate both children and adults, Nick at Nite mined the extensive vaults at Viacom for "classic" situation comedies with dual appeal. Comprising the kind of sitcoms that had long been used by local programmers in the late afternoon to fill after-school slots for kids (until this timeslot became too lucrative to abandon to children), Nick at Nite also appealed to Baby-Boomer memories of their own favorite television shows from the 1950s, 1960s, and 1970s. The strategy proved so successful that Viacom, after a brief corporate skirmish with MCA, launched a second cable service, TVLand, in 1996. While Nick at Nite continued as an extension of Nickelodeon, TV-Land honed a more ironic style, targeting adults and their love/hate relationship with the world of TV reruns. Series such as *I Love Lucy, The Brady Bunch, The Munsters, Dragnet,* and *The Dick Van Dyke Show* remain staples of both services. TVLand went on to update its schedule to include series of the 1970s and 1980s, such as *The A-Team, Charlie's Angels,* and *Family Ties,* thus tapping into the campy nostalgia of post-Baby-Boomer generations.

Remarkably, both cable services have been extraordinarily successful at revitalizing television series that have long been in syndication and would thus seem to have exhausted their appeal. The key to this success has been a series of innovations in marketing and scheduling. For example, Nick at Nite has attracted a large viewership by packaging these series as "family television," appealing to anxious parents with programs from a more "innocent" time. For parents concerned about the viewing habits of their young children, vintage sitcoms from the network era provide safe material insulated from the often more provocative programming of the post-network system. Appeals to Baby Boomer and Generation X nostalgia are also strong, a strategy epitomized in TV Land's recycling of not only vintage television shows, but vintage commercials.

Along with this "family" appeal, however, Nick at Nite/TV Land has also quite successfully promoted their library of old shows as both "camp" and as a shared TV heritage. Each network surrounds its "timeless" and yet potentially repetitive catalogue of reruns with clever, complex, fast-paced, and ever-changing promotional campaigns, interstitial materials that serve continually to repackage old television for new audiences. Often, these campaigns play on and reward the viewer's familiarity with the programming by parodying certain plot conventions, pointing out inconsistencies and continuity errors in individual episodes, and generally celebrating the naïve "unreality" of vintage television's now increasingly distant and alien worldview. One campaign, for example, tallies the total number of times *Dragnet's* Joe Friday can be seen *not* wearing his trademark gray suit and black tie. Another spot observes how every episode of *The Munsters* includes at least one sequence in "fast-motion," and then considers the comic appeal of this familiar device. These promos have proven so popular and crucial to the networks' profile that the TVLand website allows Internet users to relive their favorite promotional campaigns. The most successful marketing strategy, then, may well be each network's ability to recast the lowly re-run into the collective cultural heritage of TV-Land—a fantasy world where all of television history (or at least, that controlled by Viacom) coalesces into a mythic parallel universe to the real world.

Related to this, Nick at Nite and TVLand have also pioneered a number of innovative scheduling strategies. For example, each network has made extensive use of block programming, adapting it in ways not seen in the network system. In its various "Block Party" promotions, the networks will run ten or twelve episodes of the same series back to back (on at least one occasion, *The Donna Reed Show* ran 24 hours a day for an entire weekend). Such scheduling indulges the dedicated fan (who has an opportunity to tape the series in its original sequence) and creates an "event" around an otherwise shopworn show. Other scheduling schemes have included nights devoted to a common sitcom theme (across several series) and blocks devoted to showcasing a "minor" character on a famous series (such as a "Floyd Night" of *The Andy Griffith Show*).

Courtesy of the Everett Collection

Expanding on its appeal to the TV fan and connoisseur, TV Land in particular has in many ways become television's default historian. Although the network often treats its content as camp, there is also a prominent trend toward according these programs a certain archival and historical respect. Episode numbers and original broadcast dates are now often included in each telecast, as are brief "behind-the-scenes" information about individual episodes. Following a larger trend in cable, TVLand has also produced a series of original documentaries devoted to the development, history, and cultural significance of certain key television programs (including *I Love Lucy, The Dick Van Dyke Show,* and *All in the Family*). Game shows and traveling exhibits based on the mastery of television trivia have also proved central to their marketing agenda. The network's most unusual promotion, however, may well be its plan to unveil bronze sculptures of prominent television characters in geographically relevant locations. A life-size statue of *The Honeymooner's* Ralph Kramden now stands at the Port Authority in Manhattan, with plans for a Mary Richards in Minneapolis and a Joe Friday in Los Angeles. At over $100,000 per sculpture, these TV statues present one of the most unusual examples of "convergence" in contemporary media, but one wholly appropriate to the network's overall public identity as the custodian of television memory.

JEFFREY SCONCE

*See also **All in the Family; Andy Griffith Show, The; Brady Bunch, The; Charlie's Angels; Dick Van Dyke Show, The; Dragnet; Family Ties; Honeymooners, The; I Love Lucy; Mary Tyler Moore Show, The***

Nielsen, A.C. (1897–1980)

U.S. Media Market Researcher

Arthur Charles (A.C.) Nielsen established, and gave his name to, the world's largest market-research organization and the principal U.S. television ratings system. After working as an engineer in the Chicago area, he used investments from former fraternity brothers to establish in 1923 a firm that reported surveys of the performance and production of industrial equipment. A decade later, during the Great Depression, the company was faced with a reduced level of manufacturing on which to study and report, so it launched the Nielsen Food and Drug Index. Begun in 1933 and 1934, these regular reports on the volume and price of packaged goods sales in a national sample of grocery stores and pharmacies became essential to the packaged goods industry. A.C. Nielsen Company became the preeminent U.S. market-research firm.

Because the Depression was also a period of rapid growth for radio, and radio advertising, Nielsen was encouraged to begin measuring radio audiences. In the spring of 1936, he attended a meeting of the Market Research Council in New York, at which the speaker was Robert Elder, an instructor from the Massachusetts Institute of Technology (MIT). Elder described the use of a mechanical recorder that could be attached to the tuning mechanism of a radio receiver, providing a continuous record of the stations to which the set was tuned. The device had been developed independently by Claude Robinson while a student at Columbia University and by Elder with Louis F. Woodruff at MIT. Nielsen quickly acquired the meters that had so far been produced, as well as patent rights and trademark registration for the Audimeter, as the device was

Arthur C. Nielsen.
Photo courtesy of A.C. Nielsen

known. The Nielsen Radio Index (NRI), a series of regular audience surveys conducted with the Audimeter, began in December 1942. The Audimeter became the principal form for measuring radio ratings when in March 1950 Nielsen bought rival C.E. Hooper's radio and television ratings services.

In 1939 the A.C. Nielsen Company Ltd. had been organized in London. The internationalization of the company increased, especially after 1957 when A.C. Nielsen, Jr., became company president.

In 1963 Congressional hearings studying ratings and their influence upon programming in television focused considerable criticism upon the ratings industry and on the reliability of audience-measurement surveys. In that same year Nielsen had discontinued radio Audimeter reports because the increased number of radio stations on the dial made it difficult for the device to distinguish between them. As a stop-gap measure, the company began a diary survey method for radio measurement (Audiologs). Weaknesses in this method attracted unfavorable attention during the hearings. Nielsen Jr. shut down the Audiolog operation, designed what he considered a reliable radio-audience

measurement system and attempted to market it to the radio industry. Finding much resistance, he never brought this service into use.

By 1963 Nielsen was out of the radio ratings business, preferring to concentrate on the relatively young national and local television-audience measurement services—the National Television Index (NTI) and the Nielsen Station Index (NSI), respectively.

In June 1980 A.C. Nielsen, Sr., died in Chicago. In 1984 his company merged with information giant Dunn and Bradstreet. The company has since been split into two entities, Nielsen Media Research and the A.C. Nielson Company; the first was acquired by the Dutch company VNU in 1999; VNU also acquired the second company in 2001.

JAMES E. FLETCHER

See also **A.C. Nielsen Company; Demographics; Ratings; Share; Market**

Arthur Charles Nielsen, Sr. Born in Chicago, Illinois, September 5, 1897. Educated at University of Wisconsin, B.Sc. summa cum laude, 1918. Married: Gertrude B. Smith, 1918; three daughters, two sons. Served in U.S. Naval Reserve, 1918. Worked as electrical engineer, Isko Company, Chicago, 1919–20, and H.P. Gould Company, Chicago, 1920–23; president, 1923–57, and chair, 1957–80, A.C. Nielsen Company; established numerous Nielsen offices in the United States and abroad. Recipient: silver medal, Annual Advertisement Awards Committee, 1936; award for outstanding service, Chicago Federated Advertisements Club, 1941; Paul D. Converse Award, American Marketing Association, 1951 and 1970; elected to Hall of Fame in Distribution, 1953; Knight in Order of Dannebrog, 1961; Parlin Memorial Award, 1963; annual award, International Advertisement Association, 1966; marketing Man of the Year, 1970; elected to National Lawn Tennis Hall of Fame, 1971; elected to the Advertising Hall of Fame, 1986. Died in Chicago, June 1, 1980.

Further Reading

Buzzard, Karen, *Chains of Gold: Marketing the Ratings and Rating the Markets,* Metuchen, New Jersey: Scarecrow Press, 1990
Buzzard, Karen, *Electronic Media Ratings: Turning Audiences into Dollars and Sense,* Boston: Focal, 1992

Nielsen Company. *See* **A.C. Nielsen Company**

Nixon, Agnes (1927–)

U.S. Writer, Producer

Often termed the "queen" of contemporary U.S. soap opera, Agnes Nixon is best known, and most honored, for introducing social issues into the soaps. Like William Bell (creator of *The Young and the Restless* and *The Bold and the Beautiful*), Nixon apprenticed in radio with Irna Phillips, the creator of the first TV soap-operas (adapting the genre from radio), for whom Nixon wrote dialogue for *Woman in White*. In the early 1960s, in her first job as a head writer (on *Guiding Light*), Nixon had the heroine, Bert Bauer (played by Charita Bauer), develop uterine cancer. Typical of this storyteller, Nixon was personally motivated to write this plotline: a friend had died of cancer and Nixon hoped to encourage women to have regular Pap smears.

However, the presentation of social and political issues in television soap opera really began in 1968, with the first show Nixon created, *One Life to Live* (*OLTL*). Nixon developed this soap for ABC, and it reflected the changing social structures and attitudes in the United States of its era. In its early years, *OLTL* was rich in issue stories and characters. It featured leads who were Jewish, as well as up-from-poverty Irish-American and Polish-American characters. In addition, *OLTL* was the first soap to portray African Americans as lead characters (Carla Gray, played by Ellen Holly, and Ed Hall, played by Al Freeman, Jr.). The character of Carla developed from a woman who was "passing as white" to one who embodied black pride, and she had romantic relationships with both black and white men. Ironically, when Holly and Freeman brought Carla and Ed back to *One Life* in the mid 1980s, they seemed out of place in the by-then WASP-ish setting of Llanview, Pennsylvania. "Color" in this era was created not by race, but by style, in the persons of the nouveau riche, *Dallas*-style oil family, the Buchanans. By the mid 1990s, however, interracial and Hispanic families had become central characters on the program.

Nixon created *One Life to Live* for ABC in order to get the opportunity to write her "dream" story, *All My Children* (*AMC*). Launched in 1970, *AMC* placed more emphasis on personal angles than *OLTL*, but the newer soap did tackle social issues such as child abuse and the Vietnam War. In May 1971, *AMC* depicted a character going through the process of abortion—the first this had been done following the legalization of abortion. Assuming the audience would be shocked, *AMC*'s writers gave the character Erica Kane (Susan Lucci) a "bad" motive for seeking the procedure (she wanted a modeling job), and, following the abortion, Erica was afflicted with septicemia (this plot twist being promoted as serving educational ends as well as "poetic justice").

Nixon wrote political nonconformity into scripts, a very rare trait in prime-time television but rarer still in daytime drama. When *All My Children* debuted in 1970, it featured Amy Tyler (Rosemary Prinz) as a peace activist. Nixon then had the young hero Phillip Brent drafted against his will; he was later missing in action in Vietnam. Political pages in U.S. newspapers took note of a speech against the war by the *AMC* character of Ruth Martin (Mary Fickett), who had raised Phillip as her son. Fickett won the first Emmy given to a daytime performer for her work during the 1972–73 season. In 1974 Nixon turned to humanizing the Vietnamese, showing Phillip, in one of the few war scenes on TV soap opera, being rescued by a young Vietnamese, played by a man who had been adopted by one of Nixon's friends.

In the mid-1970s, *All My Children*'s focus on young adult characters included not only romance and sexuality, but also the characters' growing pains. From its ear-

Agnes Nixon.
Courtesy of the Everett Collection

liest days, the soap has revolved around Erica Kane. Initially presented as a willful but winningly vulnerable teenager, Erica has matured over the years, becoming a strong-minded but winningly vulnerable career woman and parent, the always triumphant survivor of rape, the loss of a parent, disastrous love affairs, failed marriages, drug addiction, and innumerable other tragedies.

In the early 1980s, *AMC*'s popularity soared as young people raced home (or to their dormitory lounges) at lunch time to watch the classic star-crossed romance of Jenny Gardner (Kim Delaney) and Greg Nelson (Lawrence Lau). The divisive issue was class: Jenny was from a troubled, lower-class family; Greg's mother, Enid Nelson, was Pine Valley's stereotypical snob. Equally popular were Angie Morgan (Debbi Morgan) and Jesse Hubbard (Darnell Williams), soap opera's first African-American "super couple."

The character of Tad Martin (Michael Knight) epitomized another Agnes Nixon gift to soap opera: humor. Tad's biological parents were an evil father, Ray Gardner (dead since the 1980s), and a loving but ditzy mother, Opal (one of Nixon's most famous comic creations). After Ray abandoned him in a park, Tad was raised by Joe Martin (Ray McConnell) and his wife Ruth. Joe and Ruth were the central father and mother of *AMC,* and in folk-myth terms, they were the good

parents, as steadfast as Tad's blood parents were unreliable and frightening.

Nixon's other archetypal creations on *AMC* include "tent-pole" characters, usually older women such as Erica's mother, Mona Tyler (Frances Heflin), and Myrtle Fargate (Eileen Heckart). Tent-pole characters, says Nixon, are "the Greek chorus, in a sense...telling the audience how to feel."

In addition to folk myth, Nixon also drew on the religious and mystical. One of her favorite tales is from the third soap opera she created (with the late Douglas Marland), *Loving* (ABC, 1983; renamed *The City* in 1995). Archetypal good/bad twins Keith and Jonathan (both played by John Hurley) battled, and the evil Jonathan, after falling from Golden Gate Bridge, returned with supernatural powers. Nixon claimed Jonathan made a pact with the devil, citing *Faust* and C.S. Lewis's *Screwtape Letters* as sources.

After semi-retiring from writing in 1997, Nixon returned to the job of head writer for *All My Children* in 1999, a position she had last held in 1992. Once back at the helm, she launched one more controversial, socially relevant, and precedent-setting storyline, in which the teenage daughter of Erica Kane came out as a lesbian. In 2000 Nixon announced her retirement from writing soap operas. Her involvement with ABC soaps did not end completely, however, as she took a new position as story consultant for all daytime dramas on the network.

CAROL TRAYNOR WILLIAMS

See also **Soap opera**

Agnes (Eckhardt) Nixon. Born in Chicago, Illinois, December 27, 1927. Educated at Northwestern University, Evanston, Illinois. Married: Robert Nixon (died 1996); four children. Freelance writer for radio and television; creator, packager, and head writer for various daytime drama series. Consultant for ABC daytime dramas from 2000. Member: International Radio and TV Society; National Academy of TV Arts and Sciences; Friars Club; Board of Harvard Foundation. Recipient: National Academy of TV Arts and Sciences Trustees Award, 1981; Junior Diabetes Foundation Super Achiever Award; Wilmer Eye Institute Award; American Women in Radio and TV Communicator Award, 1984; American Academy of Achievement Gold Plate Award, 1993; Television Hall of Fame, 1993.

Television Series

1951	*Studio One*
1952–54	*Robert Montgomery Presents*
1957–59	*As the World Turns*
1959–65	*The Guiding Light* (head writer)

1965–68   *Another World* (head writer)
1968   *One Life to Live* (creator, packager)
1970–92,   *All My Children* (creator,
1999–2000   packager, and head writer)
1983–95   *Loving* (called *The City,* 1995;
    creator, packager)

Television Miniseries
1981   *The Mansions of America* (creator)

Television Special
1952–53   *Hallmark Hall of Fame*

Further Reading

Allen, Robert C., *Speaking of Soap Operas,* Chapel Hill: University of North Carolina Press, 1985

Edmondson, Madeleine, and David Rounds, *The Soaps: Daytime Serials of Radio and TV,* New York: Stein and Day, 1973

Intintoli, Michael James, *Taking Soaps Seriously: The World of The Guiding Light,* New York: Praeger, 1984

Wakefield, Dan, *All Her Children,* Garden City, New York: Doubleday, 1976

Williams, Carol T., *"It's Time for My Story"*: *Soap Opera Sources, Structure, and Response,* Westport, Connecticut: Praeger, 1992

North of 60

Canadian Drama Series

Born of the heightened consciousness of the First Nations in the late 1980s, this hour-long CBC series was one of the first in North America to focus almost exclusively on contemporary First Nations characters and situations. Created by Wayne Grigsby and Barbara Samuels, the series aired from 1992 to 1998. Aboriginal writers such as Jordan Wheeler (also a story editor) and novelist and film writer Thomas King provided some of the scripts. The program starred Tina Keeper as Michelle Kenidi, a constable in the Royal Canadian Mounted Police (RCMP). Tom Jackson played her brother, chief (later ex-chief) of the Lynx River community. George Tootoosis portrayed the bootlegger Albert Golo, subsequently chief of the community and the Kenidis' constant antagonist. Dakota House was Teevee Tenia, the restless teenager, new father, and runner for the younger Golos. Other continuing characters included Elsie, Teevee's very direct and widely respected grandmother; Joe, the self-exiled hunter who camped outside of the settlement; Rosie, who was determined to run her own store; her carpenter husband, Leon; Gerry, the exploitative owner of the store; and Harris, the band manager who changed sides but was genuinely in love with Teevee's self-destructive mother, Lois.

In the first two seasons the cast was also headed by John Oliver as Sergeant Eric Olsen, a white, burnt-out RCMP drug cop from Vancouver, who had requested this posting as a change of pace. His (usually inadver-

tent) way of misunderstanding the Cree community of Lynx River provided the early plotlines. As he was educated by the community to the very different values and apparently incomprehensible behavior of the "Indians," so also was the multicultural audience "south of 60." Olsen was followed by a psychotic white "partner" for Michelle and then by an urban Cree partner. Michelle remained the focus for most of the series.

The series raised many sensitive issues: the abuses of the residential schools and the many forms of self-hatred and anger that resulted; the decimation of the aboriginal way of life in the wake of animal-rights protesters; runaways who head south to Vancouver to become street prostitutes; AIDS; land claims (and anthropologists "working" on those lands); interracial marriages. Alcohol abuse, with its effect on the entire community, and unemployment were running motifs. However, *North of 60* was not a series about victims. It was about a community in transition, a community whose core values are threatened but still able to withstand the coming of fax machines and satellite television.

There was truth to the complaint that the series in the early seasons took itself too seriously, lacking the often ambivalent, sometimes oblique, and often very earthy humor characteristic of many First Nations. Subsequent seasons, without Olsen, were a little more lighthearted. Sarah, the white nurse, in a rich and unexpected plot twist, took refuge after a nervous break-

North of 60.
Photo courtesy of CBC Television

sions of a small boy who eventually wounds him with the stone from a slingshot. As Kenidi comes to see, the "boy" is his younger self running away from residential school—but the cut on his forehead is "real." This larger sense of reality offers him a reason to become part of the Lynx River community and to try to find his place in it.

These topics, and others like them, explore difficult cultural concerns. Like *Cariboo Country* in the 1960s and *The Beachcombers* in the 1970s and 1980s, the 90 episodes of *North of 60* used sensitivity and humor to address such issues of cross-cultural contact and conflict, specifically that between mainstream and indigenous cultures. When the series ended, change in the form of oil exploration was on the way. A number of made-for-TV *North of 60* movies have followed, with audiences still enjoying new insights into the characters and their culture.

MARY JANE MILLER

down with Albert, now the chief. Her non sequiturs, together with a generally more confident cast and group of writers, developed a thread of subtle, ironic, and unexpected humor.

The struggles of Michelle, her attempts to befriend her own people while policing them, and her conflicts with her teenage daughter Hannah, created situations any working parent could relate to. Hannah later drowned in a storyline that also introduced Michelle's new love interest, a counselor and bush pilot, Andrew One Sky. However, the series also created unexpected solutions to the usual domestic problems. For example, rather than simply relying on an unchanging, winning combination of characters, Thomas King's script gave Peter Kenidi, even with his master's degree, a reason for staying in Lynx River. An unplanned vision quest is derived from too little sleep, extensive work on the history of the local families and the stories told by the elders, and worry about the offer of a well-paying and influential job in Ottawa. Kenidi has vi-

Cast

Corporal Eric Olsen (1992–94)	John Oliver
Michelle Kenidi	Tina Keeper
Peter Kenidi	Tom Jackson
Sarah Birkett	Tracey Cook
Albert Golo	Gordon Tootoosis
Teevee Tenia	Dakota House
Lois Tenia	Willene Tootoosis
Constable James Harper	Peter Kelly Gaudreault
Gerry Kisilenko	Lubomir Mykytiuk
Harris Miller	Timothy Webber
Ellen Kenidi	Renae Morriseau
Hannah Kenidi	Selina Hanuse
Rosie Deela	Tina Louise Bomberry
Leon Deela	Erroll Kinistino
Elsie Tsa Che	Wilma Pelly
Joe Gomba	Jimmy Herman
Andrew One Sky	Michael Horse
Corporal Brian Fletcher	Robert Bockstael
Sylvie LeBret	Michelle Thrush
Nathan Golo	Michael P. Obey
Rosemary Fletcher	Julie Stewart
Charlie Muskrat	Simon Baker
Inspector Andre Cormier	Yvan Ponton

Producers

Wayne Grigsby, Barbara Samuels, Peter Lauterman, Tom Cox, Doug MacLeod

Programming History
90 episodes
CBC
November 1992–March 1993   Thursday 8:00–9:00
November 1993–March 1994   Thursday 9:00–10:00
November 1994–March 1995   Thursday 9:00–10:00
November 1995–March 1996   Thursday 9:00–10:00
October 1996–January 1997   Thursday 9:00–10:00
September 1997–December
1997   Thursday 9:00–10:00

Northern Exposure

U.S. Dramedy

Northern Exposure, perhaps the best example to date of a crossbred television "dramedy," began inauspiciously as a CBS replacement series in the summer of 1990 but quickly garnered critical acclaim as well as an audience sufficient to warrant its return for a short stint the following year. Its popularity grew, and for its first complete season, 1991–92, *Exposure* received ratings in the top 20, the Emmy for Best Television Drama, and an unusual two-year commitment from the network. During its fourth full year, 1994–95, the show's future appeared questionable. The midseason departure of one of its key players, Rob Morrow, a move from its established Monday night time slot to Wednesday, and the network's mushrooming concern about attracting youthful demographics all contributed to a decline in favor. The program was canceled by the network at the end of the season.

Set in the fictional hamlet of Cicely, Alaska, this unique, contemporary-set, hour-long series was created by Joshua Brand and John Falsey, whose earlier brainchild, *St. Elsewhere,* had also become a surprise hit. Location shooting in and around the towns of Roslyn and Redmond, Washington, offered scenic panoramas invoking cultural images of unspoiled American frontier. Into this haven comes the proverbial "fish out of water," Joel Fleischman (Morrow), compelled to serve as town doctor in order to repay the State of Alaska for his medical school tuition. His initial disdain for Cicely's outwardly unsophisticated inhabitants is exceeded only by his desire to return to his beloved Big Apple where his ambition, cosmopolitan tastes, and Jewishness might have free reign.

The frontier theme is extended and personified in many of the town's multicultural, multigenerational denizens. Former astronaut and wealthy entrepreneur Maurice Minnifield (Barry Corbin) is forever devising ways to exploit Cicely's natural wonders. No-nonsense septuagenarian Ruth-Anne Miller (Peg Phillips) operates Cicely's General Store, where Native American Ed Chigliak (Darren E. Burrows) helps out while aspiring to be a filmmaker and, eventually, a shaman. French-Canadian immigrant Holling Vincoeur (played by Broadway star John Cullum) owns and manages Cicely's watering hole, The Brick. He is assisted by girlfriend-turned-wife Shelly Tambo (Cynthia Geary), an ex-beauty queen some 40 years his junior. Joel's receptionist, Marilyn Whirlwind (Elaine Miles), orients her "boss," a man of science, to her Native American customs and spirituality while keeping him in line with the slightest grimace or glare. Chris Stevens (John Corbett), ex-con and disk jockey for Cicely's KBHR ("Kaybear") radio, peppers the narrative with eclectic musical selections, self-taught philosophy, and Greek chorus-like commentary. Finally, Maggie O'Connell (Janine Turner), a local bush pilot and Joel's landlady, engages him in a tangled romance reminiscent of 1930s and 1940s screwball comedy. When Joel exited the scene during the 1994–95 season, Dr. Phillip Capra (Paul Provenza) and his journalist-spouse Michelle (Teri Polo) were introduced.

It was around intermittent characters that some of *Exposure*'s most groundbreaking episodes and themes emerged. Chris's African-American half-brother Bernard (Richard Cummings, Jr.) and Marilyn's healer cousin Leonard Quinhagak, played by noted film actor Graham Greene *(Dances With Wolves),* deepened and enhanced the show's representation of many cultures. Gender and sexuality were explored through Ron (Doug Ballard) and Erick (Don R. McManus), propri-

Northern Exposure, Rob Morrow, Janine Turner, 1990–96.
Courtesy of the Everett Collection

enced by phenomena such as seasonal winds, Northern Lights, midnight sun, and ice breaking in springtime. The lesson is clear: nature tames human beings—not the other way around.

A cult favorite whose star rose along with that of the Internet, *Northern Exposure* inspired fan clubs, websites, and cyberspace bulletin boards—forums for spirited discussion by an international following. Although its network run was short-lived, the program lived on in syndication and clearly made its mark with innovative, postmodern storytelling, an eclectic musical soundtrack, and character-driven themes crystallizing new and ongoing debates about cultural values weighing heavily on a viewing public facing the uncertainty of a new millennium.

CHRISTINE SCODARI

See also **Dramedy**

Cast

Dr. Joel Fleischman	Rob Morrow
Maggie O'Connell	Janine Turner
Maurice Minnifield	Barry Corbin
Chris Stevens	John Corbett
Ed Chigliak	Darren E. Burrows
Holling Vincoeur	John Cullum
Shelly Tambo	Cynthia Geary
Marilyn Whirlwind	Elaine Miles
Ruth-Anne Miller	Peg Phillips
Rick Pederson (1990–91)	Grant Goodeve
Adam (1991–95)	Adam Arkin
Dave the Cook (1991–95)	William J. White
Leonard Quinhagak (1992–93)	Graham Greene
Bernard Stevens (1991–95)	Richard Cummings, Jr.
Mike Monroe (1992–93)	Anthony Edwards
Walt Kupfer (1993–95)	Moultrie Patten
Eugene (1994–95)	Earl Quewezance
Hayden Keyes (1994–95)	James L. Dunn
Dr. Phillip Capra (1994–95)	Paul Provenza
Michelle Schowdoski Capra (1994–95)	Teri Polo

Producers

Joshua Brand, John Falsey, Charles Rosin, Robert T. Skodis

Programming History

88 episodes
CBS
July 1990–August 1990   Thursday 10:00–11:00

etors of the local inn, whose gay wedding was a primetime first. Ron and Erick's arrival also helped to provide a larger context within which to recollect the town's founding by a lesbian couple, Roslyn and Cicely, later featured in a flashback episode. Eccentric bush couple Adam (Adam Arkin) and Eve (Valerie Mahaffey) allude to the ongoing battle of the sexes rendered center stage by Joel and Maggie, and, with their exaggerated back-to-nature facade and conspicuously consumptive habits, Adam and Eve poke lighthearted fun at *Exposure*'s "yuppie" audience.

The "fish out of water" narrative exemplified by Joel's gradual softening toward Cicely, Cicelians, and small-town life is replicated again and again in episodes about visitors who give of themselves in some fashion while becoming enriched by their interactions with worldly wise, innately intelligent, and accepting locals. Humanity's place within the larger natural environment is another significant thematic thread running through the program's extended text. Behavior and temperament are often seen to be influ-

April 1991–December 1994	Monday 10:00–11:00
January 1995–March 1995	Wednesday 10:00–11:00
July 1995–96	Wednesday 9:00–10:00

Further Reading

Chunovic, L., *The "Northern Exposure" Book,* New York: Citadel, 1993

Crawford, Iain, "Reading TV: Intertextuality in *Northern Exposure,*" *The Mid-Atlantic Almanac: The Journal of the Mid-Atlantic Popular/American Culture Association* (1994)

Dempsey, John, "*Northern* Could Get Double Exposure," *Variety* (30 November 1992)

Di Salvatore, Bryan, "City Slickers: Our Far-Flung Correspondents," *The New Yorker* (22 March 1993)

Kasindorf, Jeanie, "How *Northern Exposure* Became the Spring's Hottest TV Show," *New York Times* (May 27, 1991)

Pareles, J., "Radio Days in Cicely, Alaska: Anything Goes," *New York Times* (May 3, 1992)

Pringle, Mary Beth, and Cynthia L. Shearer, "The Female Spirit of *Northern Exposure*'s Cicely, Alaska," *The Mid-Atlantic Almanac: The Journal of the Mid-Atlantic Popular/American Culture Association* (1994)

Rabkin, Joel, "Their Alaska and Mine," *Television Quarterly* (Winter 1992)

Scodari, Christine, "Possession, Attraction, and the Thrill of the Chase: Gendered Myth-Making in Film and Television Comedy of the Sexes," *Critical Studies in Mass Communication* (1995)

Taylor, Annette M., "Landscape of the West in *Northern Exposure,*" *The Mid-Atlantic Almanac: The Journal of the Mid-Atlantic Popular/American Culture Association* (1994)

Wilcox, Rhonda V., "'In Your Dreams, Fleischman': Dr. Flesh and the Dream of the Spirit in *Northern Exposure,*" *Studies in Popular Culture* (1993)

Williams, Betsy, "'North to the Future': *Northern Exposure* and Quality Television," in *Television: The Critical View,* edited by Horace Newcomb, New York: Oxford University Press, 1976; 5th edition, 1994

Norway

Television in Norway has always been a modest affair. The first television service was not formally opened until 1960, and it was not until the 1990s that the second national channel saw the light of day. The late start and low pace of developments in television can largely be explained with reference to distinct demographic and topographic characteristics. Norway has a small population (4.5 million) scattered over a large area (324,000 sq km or 125,000 sq mi), which works out to only 13 people per square kilometer. Nearly two-thirds of the country is mountainous (a traditional problem for TV transmissions) and uninhabitable. These features make it both expensive and difficult to achieve national distribution for broadcasting, but in Norway, with its strong ethos of social-democratic egalitarianism, the option to leave out non-profitable areas was never seriously considered. The high priority on achieving national distribution has had its price in terms of a more limited program output and large amounts of imported programming. Even today, viewing remains among the lowest in Western Europe, with an average of only two and a half hours per day (2001).

Despite its distinct characteristics, Norway's television history follows a familiar European pattern. The Norwegian Broadcasting Corporation (NRK) was established in 1933 as a license-fee-funded and state-owned radio corporation. NRK had a monopoly on all broadcasting in Norway, and when television came along, the NRK took for granted that it would be responsible for developing the new medium. Like other public broadcasters in the monopoly era, the NRK occupied a singular position as a major component of the national culture. The early years of television was marked by a pervasive social democratic enlightenment ethos inherited from radio. The NRK had from the beginning perceived education as one of its main tasks, and in the 1970s, the policy of enlightenment took on a sharper and more radical edge. News and current affairs became more explicitly geared toward closing the gap between the "information-rich" and the "information-poor," and a wide range of programs—in both the information and entertainment categories—were broadcast with the aim of combating "alienation," "marginalization," and "passive viewing." These ideals were particularly apparent in programs for children and young people, where issues such as racism, third-world poverty, and the environment were central throughout the period. Although the NRK transmitted quite a lot of high culture in the form of classical music and drama, the dominant ideology in the monopoly era was marked more by social-democratic egalitarianism than high-culture elitism. However, the NRK also transmitted highly popular entertainments programs. Norwegian versions of programs such as *Candid Camera* and *The $64,000 Question* were broadcast, although the formats were made more serious and "academic" than in the U.S. originals.

The social-democratic ethos of the NRK was based on an ideology of serving the ordinary man and woman. Many ordinary people were not convinced, however, perceiving the NRK as a self-satisfied, paternalistic and bureaucratic institution. In the polarized social climate of the 1970s, the NRK also became a target of sharp political attacks. Conservatives claimed that the NRK monopoly was controlled by radicals, whereas left-wing and cultural-libertarian interests claimed that their views were not given adequate representation (albeit less strongly). By the end of the 1970s, support for the monopoly was waning, and in 1981, the first moves were made by a conservative government to break up the broadcasting structure. To begin with, a series of experiments were conducted whereby voluntary associations, religious and political groups, and newspapers were authorized to set up local radio and television stations. Permission was also granted to a few cable companies to retransmit programs from Satellite Television Ltd. (later Sky Channel). Once these moves were made there was no turning back, however, and within a few years the conditions for local and satellite broadcasting was permanently liberalized.

The deregulation of broadcasting took place despite substantial political opposition from social-democratic and left-wing interests. These groups remained opposed to the establishment of terrestrial commercial broadcasting services in competition with the NRK, but as satellite services proliferated, the opposition became difficult to sustain. By 1990, almost 40 percent of the population could watch satellite channels, among them two services directed specifically at the Norwegian public. This was the pan-Scandinavian TV3 and the Norwegian cable channel TVNorge (TVN). Both of these came on the air in 1988, and both turned out to be far more popular than the international satellite channels that had been available up to that point. In the end it was the loss of national advertising revenue to services transmitting to Norway from abroad that broke down what remained of the opposition against deregulation. In 1990 the decision was made to allow the establishment of a second "official" Norwegian television channel, a privately owned "public-service" institution licensed by the state.

TV2 began broadcasting in September 1992. The corporation is owned by two of Norway's largest media conglomerates, the Schibsted company and A-pressen, along with the Danish publishing company Egmont. From the beginning, TV2 was organized as a private company, but the political intention was that it should operate as a public-service corporation. There were restrictions on ownership, and there were also stricter regulations concerning advertising than those set out in the European television directive (which applies in Norway even though the country is not a member of the European Union). TV2 (and other commercial channels transmitting from Norway) are not allowed to put advertising breaks in news, current affairs programs, documentaries, and feature films (unless the break lasts 20 minutes or more). Advertising directed at children is also prohibited, and there is a ten-minute ban on advertising before and after children's programs.

Although more channels are now available, the NRK remains a central reference point in Norwegian television. After it lost its monopoly position, the NRK made an effort to build an identity more as an independent media corporation and less of a state enterprise. From the beginning, government and parliament exercised detailed control over organizational and financial matters, but through organizational reforms in 1988 and 1996, the NRK achieved greater autonomy from the state. NRK is now a limited company, and although the state holds all the shares, the reforms have granted the NRK the right to appoint its own Director General and establish new services without going through a lengthy political process. In 1996, the NRK opened a second television channel (NRK2), and in recent years the corporation has been granted the right to fund potential new services (teletext, Internet services, pay-TV, and so on) with advertising. Its basic radio and television services nevertheless remain without advertising, although some forms of sponsorship have been allowed.

In the competitive economic situation of the 1990s and 2000s, the NRK has fought, successfully, to retain its position as the leading television company. In 2001, NRK1 obtained an average market share of 38 percent in the national market, compared with 31 percent for TV2. Although TV2 and NRK both have a set of legally defined public-service obligations, there are important differences between them. TV2 broadcasts far more drama than the NRK, and solely within popular genres. NRK's output include some serious drama and substantially more culture, information, and children and youth programs. In its news service, TV2 has adopted a more tabloid, down-to-earth style than the NRK. Yet NRK continues to hold a strong position within news, entertainment, and sport. Both NRK and TV2 transmit around 50 percent imported programming, mostly from English-speaking countries. While

NRK's main strategy has been to expand early-evening and prime-time programming, and to retain its strong position during evenings and weekends, TV2 is moving toward a 24-hour service. It transmits many more repeats, and its schedule also is more highly structured, with permanent slots for different types of programming and with extensive use of "stripping," the placing of identical programs and series in horizontal strips across the weekly television schedule (that is, broadcasting them at the same time each day). The NRK schedule has traditionally been more loosely structured and resources have been allocated on the basis of "importance" or "relevance," rather than ratings. With the impact of competition, the NRK has also introduced more competitive scheduling policies. Particularly during the weekends, new scheduling principles have been instrumental in retaining viewers.

Although NRK1 remains the biggest channel, it is gradually losing out to TV2 in the younger age groups. Other commercial-service channels broadcasting in Norwegian are also trying to attract young viewers. TvNorge, which commanded a 10 percent market share in 2001, has sustained its position due to successful adaptations of game shows and global reality programs such as *Big Brother* and *Temptation Island.* TvNorge is owned partly by TV2 and partly by Scandinavian Broadcasting Systems (SBS), and is overall a loss-making enterprise. The fourth service broadcasting in Norwegian is TV3-Norway, which is almost wholly owned by the Swedish industrial corporation Kinnevik. TV3 is part of a pan-Scandinavian multichannel operation broadcasting from London, thereby evading Norwegian media law. TV3 operates under far more liberal advertising regulations than the Norwegian-based stations, a fact that has led to loud complaints about unfair competition. TV3 has hardly any factual programming at all and broadcasts mainly drama and "reality" shows. Its market share was 7 percent in 2001. The final national channel is NRK2, which was supposed to help the NRK win back younger viewers and sharpen its cultural profile. It has not been very successful, however, commanding a 3 percent market share in 2001.

As elsewhere, the television debate in Norway in recent years has been focused on the challenges of digitization and convergence. There are presently several digital satellite and cable services available, and there are plans to start building a terrestrial digital net in 2002. There is some doubt about the profitability of this enterprise, due to international experiences and the fact that two-thirds of the population already has access to satellite and cable. Fear that the Norwegian public service channels might lose out to global and commercial competitors has led the NRK and TV2 to join forces, and in January 2002 they announced the formation of a joint venture—Norges Televisjon—that aims to be the leader in terrestrial digital television within the next few years.

The state of Norwegian television in the early years of the new century is one of both stability and turbulence. Audiences for the national channels remain high, although both advertising revenue and the license fee shows signs of stagnation. The political legitimacy of the Norwegian duopoly also appears to be undoubted, as TV2 was awarded a new seven-year license without much public criticism in 2002, and the legitimacy and political support for the NRK has increased remarkably since the monopoly era. There is a broad consensus that the NRK should continue as a license-fee-funded broadcaster, with a broad range of programming. Current financial difficulties have led to claims that the NRK should cease competing against commercial companies for sport and entertainment programs and concentrate on "serious" programming, but this view has not gained support within the political parties nor within the state-appointed Public Service Council.

Regarding the digital future the situation is more uncertain. An important lesson so far in the competitive era is that those services that have limited themselves to low-quality, low-cost international formats have been less successful than those that have made an effort to reflect Norwegian culture and daily life. In Norway, factual programming such as news, documentaries and current affairs, and domestically produced family-entertainment programs still obtain considerably higher ratings than the cheaply made games shows and reality programs available on cable and satellite.

TRINE SYVERTSEN

See also **Convergence; Digital Television; Satellite**

Further Reading

Bastiansen, Henrik, and Trine Syvertsen, "Towards a Norwegian Television History," in *Television in Scandinavia: History, Politics and Aesthetics,* edited by Francesco Bono and Ib Bondebjerg, Luton: University of Luton Press, 1996

Syvertsen, Trine, and Eli Skogerbø, "Scandinavia, Netherlands, and Belgium," in *Television: An International History,* edited by Anthony Smith and Richard Paterson, New York: Oxford University Press, 1998

Syvertsen, Trine, and Gro Maren Mogstad Karlsen, "The Norwegian Television Market in the 1990s," in *Nordicom Review* 21/1 (2000)

Not the Nine O'clock News

British Satirical Review

This fast-paced contemporary satire series launched many successful TV careers and bridged the gap between the surrealist comedy of the *Monty Python* generation and the anarchic new-wave comic revolution of the 1980s. In 1979 radio producer John Lloyd, frustrated that many of the radio shows he had worked on (such as sitcom *To the Manor Born*) had transferred to television without him, approached BBC-TV light entertainment heads and pitched for a TV series. John Howard Davies (head of comedy) and Jimmy Gilbert (head of light entertainment) offered Lloyd a six-show slot with no real brief, but with a stipulation that he collaborate with current affairs expert Sean Hardie, who had been recommended to the comedy department because of a quirky sense of humor that did not always sit comfortably within the confines of current-affairs programming. Lloyd and Hardie found they worked well together and quickly began developing formats. One possible program was called *Sacred Cows,* which each week would have humorously dissected a modern-day trend, such as feminism, similar to the way the *Frost Report* (BBC, 1966–67) had operated. However, they finally settled on a contemporary sketch show that would take a "scatter-gun" approach dealing with all sorts of targets.

A pilot show was produced in March 1979 with a team consisting of Rowan Atkinson, Chris Emmet, Christopher Godwin, John Gorman, Chris Langham, Willoughby Goddard and Jonathan Hyde. The pilot was never transmitted. A general election was imminent, and on viewing the program, the BBC was concerned about its overtly political nature. They sent Lloyd and Hardie back to the drawing board and gave them six extra months, which both agreed was a big advantage. Lloyd and Hardie embarked on forming a new team with only Atkinson and Langham surviving from the pilot. Lloyd in particular was keen to get a woman aboard, but finding a suitable player was proving difficult. They approached comedian Victoria Wood, who felt (rightly) that her future lay as a solo artist, and actresses Alison Steadman and Susan George, to no avail. Finally, John Lloyd met Australian actress Pamela Stephenson at a party and was convinced they had found their woman. Mel Smith was brought in to make up the team, and once they were all together, the shape of the show became clearer. As a bonus, Lloyd found that the cast was willing to become actively involved in molding the material, helping with the selection of sketches and occasionally writing or rewriting pieces.

The first series aired late in 1979 and attracted just enough of an audience overall to convince the BBC to go ahead with a second series the following year. At the end of the first series, it was agreed that Chris Langham did not quite fit in with the rest of the team, and he was replaced by Griff Rhys Jones, who had played some of the extra parts in the first series. Pamela Stephenson had discovered an unexpected talent for mimicry, and her impressions of the female newsreaders of the day proved to be a highlight of the show. Atkinson excelled at visual comedy and verbal gymnastics, and Mel Smith and Griff Rhys Jones brought a natural acting technique to the sketches. The second series firmly established the show, and one episode won the Silver Rose for innovation at the Montreux Festival. The third and fourth series consolidated their success. Some of the written material for the show came from a central team of regular writers, but the show also operated an open-door policy, which meant that virtually anyone could send sketches in and have them read. This policy provided a fertile training ground for new talent, and many budding writers had their first televised work via *Not the Nine O'clock News.* To the writers, the show may have seemed fairly flexible, but Lloyd and Hardie had some firm parameters. The show was contemporary rather than topical, although its recording schedule (taped Sunday evening for transmission the following day) meant that some last-minute material could be added to give an extra edge. Short sketches were preferred (in its entire run, only a handful were over a minute and a half). Although it returned to the idea of using punch lines (a tradition some critics thought had been eradicated for good by the *Monty Python* team), the show was markedly post-*Python* and unashamedly modern. If a sketch took place in a pub, it would be a modern-day pub with Space Invaders machines instead of dominoes; if a sketch took place in a hospital, it would be a

Not the Nine O'clock News.
Copyright © BBC Photo Library

modern understaffed hospital with harassed doctors and nurses. This sensibility, combined with the show's pace, its revoicing of bought-in footage, and its news-style filming and use of new visual equipment and techniques (such as Quantel), created a unique and recognizable look.

Memorable skits included a parody of the then-emerging pop-video industry ("Nice Video, Shame About the Song"); a satirical comment on the religious furor surrounding *Monty Python's Life of Brian,* in which Pythonists accuse the Bible of blaspheming against the Flying Circus; a beauty contest sketch featuring an unusually candid contestant (Host: "And why do you want to be Miss World?" Contestant: "I want to screw famous people"); and an interview with an intelligent and urbane talking gorilla called Gerald (Trainer: "When we captured Gerald he was of course wild." Gerald: "Wild? I was absolutely livid").

In 1982 the team amicably decided to call it a day, feeling that they had gone as far as they could with the format (they had also produced audio recordings of the show which had proved highly popular, and spin-off books which sold in vast numbers). Although it only ran for 28 episodes, the intensity and density of each show, some containing as many as 30 sketches, meant they had used a lot of material and covered a lot of ground. The careers of many of the creative personnel from the show continued to flourish afterwards: Pamela Stephenson worked in Hollywood; Mel Smith and Griff Rhys Jones joined for a number of series of *Alas Smith and Jones* and independently proved very

popular in a number of ventures (Smith has since directed movies in Hollywood). Rowan Atkinson became a household name on both sides of the Atlantic, scoring heavily in the sitcom *Blackadder,* in the irregular series of *Mr. Bean* comic films, and in feature films. Producer John Lloyd went on to initiate many hit series, perhaps the most notable being the satirical puppet caricature series *Spitting Image.* Many of the show's writers went on to further successes, including David Renwick, who wrote the most popular British sitcom of the 1990s, *One Foot in the Grave.* Richard Curtis co-wrote the *Blackadder* series and scripted what became two of the most successful British films in history, *Four Weddings and a Funeral* (1994) and *Notting Hill* (1999). In 1979, although it had finished five years previously, *Monty Python's Flying Circus* was still exerting a huge influence on British TV comedy; *Not the Nine O'clock News* was the first comedy sketch program to shine successfully in the large shadow that *Python* cast.

In 1995 the producers returned to the original shows and began the mammoth task of editing them for retransmission and eventual video release. A U.S. version of the series called *Not Necessarily the News (Not the Network Co. Inc.)* was syndicated in the 1980s.

DICK FIDDY

See also **Atkinson, Rowan**

Performers
Rowan Atkinson
Pamela Stephenson
Mel Smith
Griff Rhys Jones
Chris Langham

Producers
Sean Hardie, John Lloyd

Programming History
28 30-minute episodes
BBC

17 October 1979–20 November 1979	6 episodes
31 March 1980–12 May 1980	7 episodes
27 October 1980–15 December 1980	8 episodes
1 February 1982–12 March 1982	7 episodes

Further Reading

Jeffries, Stuart, "Television: Bog Standards," *The Guardian* (October 28, 1995)

Not Only…But Also…

British Comedy Program

Not Only…But Also… was among the most influential comedy programs seen on British television in the 1960s. Starring former *Beyond the Fringe* partners Peter Cook and Dudley Moore, this fondly remembered comedy-revue series had a considerable impact upon television comedy of the era, with its innovative and often eccentric brand of anarchic humor.

The series, first broadcast on BBC2 in 1965 and then repeated on BBC1, was conceived after Dudley Moore was asked to do a single comedy show for the BBC. Moore recruited Cook to help him write the sketches, and Cook responded with "Pete and Dud," the characters who were destined to become the show's greatest success, and another sketch in which a man explained his life's mission to teach ravens to fly underwater. The resulting show persuaded the BBC to commission a whole series from the duo.

Moore and Cook set about developing sequences of lively comedy sketches linked by musical interludes and other set-piece events featuring themselves or guests. Among the most successful of these latter items was Poets Cornered, in which invited comedians were required to compose (without hesitation) instant rhyming poems, or risk being plunged into a vat of gunge—the first appearance of the so-called gunge tanks that became such a feature of zany quiz shows and children's programs in the 1980s and 1990s. Among those to brave the gunge were Frank Muir, Spike Milligan, and Barry Humphries. Guests in sketches included John Lennon, who appeared in the uniform of a nightclub commissionaire, and Peter Sellers.

Other unique characteristics of the show included its opening sequence, for which the cameras were set up at some unexpected location, such as London's Tower Bridge, to film Moore playing the signature tune on his piano, and the closing song "Goodbye" (which was successfully released as a single in 1965, reaching number 18 in the pop charts).

The highlights of the *Not Only…But Also…* shows were undoubtedly the appearances of Cook and Moore in the roles of "Pete and Dud"—two rather dimwitted characters in long raincoats and cloth caps who mulled over affairs of the day and the meaning of life itself as they sipped pints of beer or munched sandwiches. These hilarious routines were frequently enlivened by bursts of ad-libbing, particularly by Cook, and on several uproarious occasions both men collapsed in fits of giggles, to the delight of audience and viewers.

A second series of *Not Only…But Also…* was broadcast in 1966, and its effect was evident upon many subsequent comedy shows, notably in the head-to-head dialogues of Mel Smith and Griff Rhys Jones in *Alas Smith and Jones* some 20 years later, which harked back unmistakably to the classic "Pete and Dud" format.

DAVID PICKERING

Regular Performers
Dudley Moore
Peter Cook
John Lennon
Barry Humphries
Peter Sellers
Una Stubbs
Eric Sykes
Henry Cooper
Cilla Black
Dusty Springfield
Spike Milligan
William Rushton
Frank Muir
Ronnie Barker

Producers
John McGrath, Dick Clement, John Street, James Gilbert

Programming History
23 episodes
BBC2

January 1965–April 1965	7 45-minute episodes
January 1966–February 1966	7 30-minute episodes
Christmas special	December 25, 1966
February 1970–May 1970	7 45-minute episodes
14 March 1973	Live performance, *Show of the Week*

NYPD Blue

U.S. Police Drama

Amid controversy about Steven Bochco's intent to produce U.S. network television's first "R-rated" series, *NYPD Blue* premiered on ABC in September 1993. This innovative police drama has survived an onslaught of protest to emerge as a popular, long-running, and critically acclaimed series. *Blue* (as it is sometimes promoted) has deliberately tested the boundaries of broadcast restrictions on partial nudity and adult language. Praise for the show's finely crafted storytelling and engaging style soon overtook initial condemnations of its occasional flashes of skin and salty dialogue. After its first season, *NYPD Blue* revived Bochco's reputation as a risk-taking producer of "quality television." For a decade, the series has maintained solid viewership despite a constantly changing cast. Dennis Franz's portrayal of Detective Andy Sipowicz has remained the anchor for a narrative that has added ongoing domestic melodrama to its cops-on-the-job stories.

As a gritty, downbeat cop drama filmed against a backdrop of urban decay, the program has been seen as a return to form for Bochco, who had cocreated the groundbreaking *Hill Street Blues* and *L.A. Law*. Attempts to repeat the success of his law-and-order shows faltered *(Bay City Blues, Cop Rock, Civil Wars)* until *Hill Street* writer-producer David Milch teamed with Bochco to revitalize the genre. Arguing that the networks had to compete with cable TV for the adult audience, the producers persuaded ABC to approve content previously forbidden. The pilot episode concludes with a dimly-lit lovemaking scene. While mild by motion-picture standards, its partial male and female nudity stirred controversy.

Three months before the debut of such "blue" material, ABC screened the pilot for affiliates and advertisers. Although Bochco agreed to trim 15 seconds from the sex scene, adverse reactions threatened the show's broadcast run. Conservative watchdog Reverend Donald Wildmon and his American Family Association (AFA) led a national campaign against *NYPD Blue,* calling on affiliates not to air the program and on citizens to boycott products advertised during the show. A quarter of ABC's 225 member stations preempted the first episode.

Despite the unprecedented number of defections, *Blue* scored well in the ratings. Most blackouts had been in small markets (representing only 10 to 15 percent of potential viewers); Wildmon's campaign provided extra publicity in larger ones. Furthermore, *NYPD Blue* maintained its large audience, leading most advertisers and affiliates to cease their opposition. By the end of its first season, ABC's new hit drama survived a second round of AFA attacks and won endorsements from Viewers for Quality Television, the Emmy Awards (27 nominations), and most reviewers.

After all the hype about sex, violence, and profanity, what viewers discovered was a compelling series that was "adult" in the best, rather than the worst, sense. *NYPD Blue* is mature and sophisticated, not libertine. Instead of inserting racy language and showy sex for the sake of sensation, this story of career cops features complicated human characters. Charges of excessive violence also proved unfounded. As a new round of protests against TV violence circulated in the U.S. in 1993, detractors tagged this latest *bête noire* of television as a prime offender. Yet, particularly for a realistic police show, *NYPD Blue* seldom depicts violent acts. When it does, it tends to dramatize the terrible consequences of such actions. (Eventually, ABC responded to public and congressional pressures by airing a content advisory warning with each episode, although that warning did not mention violence: "This police drama contains adult language and scenes with partial nudity. Viewer discretion is advised.")

Again like *Hill Street, NYPD Blue* excelled with a potent combination of writing, acting, and directing. The look of the show is both realistic and stylized. New York City location shooting make the show's feel for big-city street life palpable, while the jagged editing and nervous, hand-held camera movement (already a convention of the genre) heighten the dramatic tension of scenes in the precinct offices, the place where an ensemble of characters' lives intertwined. Unlike the innovative police drama to which it is often compared—*Homicide: Life in the Streets*—*NYPD Blue* keeps its stylistic flourishes in check, letting actors control scenes. In fact, performers familiar from past

NYPD Blue, Dennis Franz, David Caruso.
©*20th Century Fox/Courtesy of the Everett Collection*

Bochco productions—Charles Haid, Eric Laneauville, Dennis Dugan, Jesus S. Treviño—have directed many episodes.

However, it was another set of alumni from the Bochco stock company who stood out above the ensemble cast. Franz emerged as the scenery-chewing mainstay of the show, reinventing his seedy, sharp-tongued Norman Buntz character from *Hill Street Blues* as Sipowicz. The lesser-known David Caruso quickly became a star and sex symbol playing Sipowicz's partner, John Kelly, a throwback, red-headed Irish cop. Early in the show's run, Caruso received more publicity than Franz, largely because Caruso was the first of the male leads to do a nude scene. However, he departed at the start of the second season. Three other detectives have since been partnered with Sipowicz. *L.A. Law* star Jimmy Smits played Bobby Simone, who wed fellow detective Dianne Russell (Kim Delaney) before dying of heart failure. Young, taciturn Danny Sorenson (played with surprising astuteness by former child star Rick Schroeder) took Simone's place but became a murder victim, and was replaced by second-generation cop John Clark (portrayed by another former child actor, Mark-Paul Gosselaar). The series' smooth transitions through major character changes testifies to the storytelling skills of Milch, Bochco, and their collaborators.

Individual episodes introduce new cases for the detectives of New York's 15th Precinct and blend them with ongoing melodramatic storylines about personal relationships. Entanglements of professional and personal affairs are always imminent as every detective in the precinct has become romantically involved with a co-worker: Kelly with Officer Janice Licalsi; Gregory Medavoy with office secretary Donna Abandando; detectives James Martinez and Adrianne Lesniak with each other, Baldwin Jones with Assistant District Attorney Valerie Haywood. Sipowicz marries District Attorney Sylvia Costas, who is later murdered. After her death, Sipowicz becomes a devoted, sensitive father to their young son Theo, thus countering his own often ugly, violent, struggling alcoholic, on-the-job personality, and again engages in a workplace romance, this time with Detective Connie McDowell.

Even with so many couples, male characters dominate *NYPD Blue*. Their tough-guy machismo, however, is always tempered by a caring side. Rather than playing to good cop/bad cop stereotypes, Sipowicz, Kelly, Simone, and their fraternal colleagues exemplify that emerging archetype of 1990s television: the sensitive man. Like TV cops of the past, they are moral, yet hard enough to crack down on criminals. To this "guy" image, the men of *NYPD Blue* add a dimension of sensitivity. These are sentient cops. The replacement of the Cagneyesque John Kelly with empathetic widower Simone heightened this aspect. The *NYPD Blue* men are working men concerned with emotion. The boys in *Blue* have feelings and discuss them, with both their professional and romantic partners. Women's roles, even nominally feminist ones, have tended only to support men's and lacked depth in early seasons. However, the development of Delaney's character enriched the series. Detective Russell, like Sipowicz, was a complex, edgy, melancholic, recovering alcoholic, who showed the stress of loyalty to "the job." Delaney's portrayal proved strong enough for Bochco to create the law series *Philly* (2001–02) as a star vehicle for her. ABC even moved *Blue* to an earlier hour to serve as a lead-in for the new show; however, *Philly* lasted only one season.

As with other Bochco productions, *NYPD Blue* leavens its mixture of police drama and soap opera with comic relief, often interjecting moments of irreverent, even scatological, humor. The show's uses of nudity and profanity often play at this level. Naked bodies appear in awkward, comic scenes as well as erotic ones. Writers self-consciously invent colorful, funny curse words for Sipowicz to spew at criminals.

Whatever the length of its run, *NYPD Blue* made history with its breakthrough first season. While not a model for commercial imitation, the series proved that risky, adult material could be successfully integrated into network television.

DAN STREIBLE

See also **Bochco, Steven;** *Hill Street Blues;* **Police Programs**

Cast

Detective Andy Sipowicz (1993–)	Dennis Franz
Detective John Kelly (1993–94)	David Caruso
Lieutenant Arthur Fancy (1993–2001)	James McDaniel
Laura Hughes Kelly (1993–94)	Sherry Stringfield
Officer Janice Licalsi (1993–94)	Amy Brenneman
Detective James Martinez (1993–2000)	Nicholas Turturro
Assistant District Attorney Sylvia Costas (1993–99)	Sharon Lawrence
Detective Greg Medavoy (1993–)	Gordon Clapp
Donna Abandando (1994–96)	Gail O'Grady
Detective Bobby Simone (1994–98)	Jimmy Smits
Detective Diane Russell (1995–2001)	Kim Delaney
Detective Jill Kirkendall (1996–2000)	Andrea Thompson
Detective Danny Sorenson (1998–2001)	Rick Schroeder
Detective John Clark (2001–)	Mark-Paul Gosselaar
Detective Baldwin Jones (1999–)	Henry Simmons
P.A.A. John Irvin (1998–)	Bill Brochtrup
A.D.A. Valerie Haywood (2001–)	Garcelle Beauvais
Detective Connie McDowell (2001–)	Charlotte Ross
Lt. Tony Rodriguez (2001–)	Esai Morales
Detective Rita Ortiz (2001–)	Jacqueline Obradors

Producers

Steven Bochco, David Milch

Programming History

ABC

September 1993–August 1994	Tuesday 10:00–11:00
October 1994–May 2001	Tuesday 10:00–11:00
October 2001–	Tuesday 9:00–10:00

Further Reading

"Alan Brydon Reveals Why his Video is Set to Record Every *NYPD Blue* Episode," *Campaign-London* (March 10, 1995)

Auster, Albert, "A Look at Some Contemporary American and British Cop Shows," *Television Quarterly* (Spring 1997)

Brodie, John, "ABC Affils Ponder: How Blue Is *Blue?*" *Variety* (June 21, 1993)

Coe, Steven, "Wildmon Targets *NYPD Blue*," *Broadcasting and Cable* (March 28, 1994)

Cole, Lewis, "NYPD Blue," *The Nation* (October 25, 1993)

Douglas, Susan, "Signs of Intelligent Life on TV," *Ms.* (May–June 1995)

Giles, Jeff, "The Wild Men of Prime Time: Is Bochco's Hot New Cop Series Too Blue?" *Newsweek* (June 28, 1993)

Goodman, Walter, "Good Cop, Bad Cop: Which Is Real?" *New York Times* (February 23, 1995)

Hanczor, Robert S., "Articulation Theory and Public Controversy: Taking Sides over *NYPD Blue*," *Critical Studies in Mass Communication* (March 1997)

Handy, Bruce, "The Real Golden Age Is Now," *Time* (October 30, 1995)

Jensen, Elizabeth, "Crusade against ABC's *NYPD Blue* Goes Local," *Wall Street Journal* (October 6, 1993)

Leonard, John, "NYPD Blue," *New York Times* (September 13, 1993)

Leonard, John, "NYPD Blue," *New York* (January 17, 2000)

McConnell, Frank D., "NYPD Blue," *Commonweal* (October 8, 1993)

McGrath, Charles, and Robert Sullivan, "The Triumph of the Prime-Time Novel," *New York Times Magazine* (October 22, 1995)

Meisler, Andy, "A Writer Moves beyond the Notion of Demons," *New York Times* (October 26, 1993)

Milch, David, and Bill Clark, *True Blue: The Real Stories behind NYPD Blue,* New York: Morrow, 1995

O'Connor, John J., "NYPD Blue," *New York Times* (September 21, 1993)

Rapping, Elayne, "Cops, Crime, and TV," *The Progressive* (April 1994)

Rensin, David, "Steven Bochco," *TV Guide* (August 14–20, 1993)

Schmuckler, Eric, "Bochco Speaks: The Creator of *NYPD Blue* Talks about Why He Made the Show so Racy, and Why He is Unwilling to Make Major Content Changes," *MediaWeek* (August 2, 1993)

Scully, Matthew, "NYPD Blue," *National Review* (September 20, 1993)

Thompson, Robert J., *Television's Second Golden Age,* New York: Continuum, 1996

Weinraub, Bernard, "The Demons That Have Driven *NYPD Blue*," *New York Times* (June 18, 2000)

Wolcott, James, "Untrue Grit," *The New Yorker* (October 4, 1993)

O

O'Connor, Carroll (1924–2001)

U.S. Actor

Best known for his portrayal of cantankerous Archie Bunker on the long-running CBS series *All in the Family,* Carroll O'Connor was one of television's most recognized actors in the late 20th century. For his work on *All in the Family* and *In the Heat of the Night,* the actor received five Emmy Awards, eight Emmy nominations, a Golden Globe Award, and a Peabody Award.

O'Connor's acting career began while he was a student in Ireland in the 1950s. Following experiences in American and European theater, he established himself as a versatile character actor in Hollywood during the 1960s. Between films he made guest appearances on television programs such as the *U.S. Steel Hour, Kraft Television Theatre,* the *Armstrong Circle Theatre,* and many of the filmed series hits of the 1960s. However, O'Connor became a television star with his portrayal of outspoken bigot Archie Bunker, the American archetype whose chair now sits in the Smithsonian Institution.

In 1968, ABC, which had the first rights to the series (which was based on the BBC sitcom *Till Death Us Do Part*), financed production of two pilot episodes of *All in the Family* (then under the title *Those Were the Days*), but the network worried about the program's socially controversial content and rejected the show. Producer Norman Lear then sold the series to CBS, where *All in the Family* was broadcast for the first time on January 12, 1971, with O'Connor as Archie Bunker. By using humor to tackle racism and other sensitive subjects, *All in the Family* changed the style and tone of prime-time programming on television. It may also have opened the door for political and social satires such as *Saturday Night Live* and other controversial programs.

Through its 13 seasons, the show gained immense popularity (in its heyday, it was said to have reached an average of 50 million viewers weekly) and maintained a groundbreaking sense of social criticism. Archie Bunker's regular stream of malapropisms and racial invective catalyzed strong reactions from critics. *All in the Family* was attacked by conservatives, who thought that the show made fun of their views, and by liberals, who charged that the show was too matter-of-fact about bigotry. The show's successor, *Archie Bunker's Place,* was broadcast on CBS from 1979 to 1983, and the earlier show also begat two successful spin-offs, *Maude* and *The Jeffersons,* the latter becoming one of television's longest-running series about African Americans.

From 1988 to 1994, O'Connor starred in and served as executive producer and head writer for the hit prime-time drama *In the Heat of the Night,* based on the characters and scenario of the acclaimed 1967 film of the same title starring Sidney Poitier and Rod Steiger. Set in fictional Sparta, Mississippi, but shot on location in Covington, Georgia, *In the Heat of the Night* may be seen as continuing O'Connor's association with television programs designed to function as social commentary by addressing issues of racism and bigotry. O'Connor played Bill Gillespie (the Steiger role), a

Carroll O'Connor, *All in the Family,* 1971–83.
Courtesy of the Everett Collection

Southern police chief whose top detective (Virgil Tibbs, played by Howard Rollins in the Poitier role) is African American. In its 1993 season, the show also featured the marriage of Chief Gillespie to an African-American city administrator. The series received two National Association for the Advancement of Colored People (NAACP) Image Awards for contributing positive portrayals of African Americans on television. When the series version of *In the Heat of the Night* ended, O'Connor produced several made-for-television movies using the same locations and characters.

In 1995 O'Connor's son and costar on *In the Heat of the Night,* Hugh O'Connor, died of a drug overdose. O'Connor chose to speak out publicly about his grief and his views on the legalization of drugs, giving a number of well-publicized interviews on these topics on television and devoting much of his time to the social problems surrounding drug addiction. Throughout the 1990s he also occasionally appeared in films or as a guest star on such series as *Mad about You* and *Party of Five.* On June 21, 2001, he died of a heart attack in Culver City, California.

DIANE M. NEGRA

See also **All in the Family; Till Death Us Do Part**

Carroll O'Connor. Born in New York City, August 2, 1924. Educated at the University of Montana; National University of Ireland, B.A. 1952; University of Montana, M.A. 1956. Married: Nancy Fields, 1951; child: Hugh (deceased). Stage actor in Ireland, 1950–54; substitute teacher in New York, 1954–56; appeared in plays *Ulysses in Nightown,* 1958, and *The Big Knife,* 1959; character actor in numerous motion pictures, 1961–71, including *Fever in the Blood,* 1961, *Cleopatra,* 1963, and *Kelley's Heroes,* 1970; star of television series *All in the Family,* 1971–79; star of *Archie Bunker's Place,* 1979–83; co-executive producer and star of *In the Heat of the Night,* 1988–94. Recipient: Golden Globe Award; Emmy Awards, 1973, 1977, 1978, 1979, 1989; George Foster Peabody Award, 1980; named to Academy of Television Arts and Sciences Hall of Fame, 1990. Died in Culver City, California, June 21, 2001.

Television Series (Actor)

1971–79	*All in the Family*
1975	*Bronk* (creator and co-executive producer only)
1979–83	*Archie Bunker's Place*
1988–94	*In the Heat of the Night* (also co-executive producer)
1994	*Party of Five*
1996–99	*Mad about You*

Made-for-Television Movies

1969	*Fear No Evil*
1972	*Of Thee I Sing*
1985	*Brass*
1986	*Convicted*
1987	*The Father Clements Story*
1994	*In the Heat of the Night: A Matter of Justice*
1994	*In the Heat of the Night: Who Was Geli Bendl?*
1995	*In the Heat of the Night: Grow Old with Me*
1995	*In the Heat of the Night: By Duty Bound*
1999	*Thirty-Six Hours to Die*

Television Specials

1972	*Of Thee I Sing*
1973	*Three for the Girls*
1977	*The Last Hurrah*
1981	*Man, Myths and Titans* (writer)
1991	*All in the Family 20th Anniversary Special*

Films

Fever in the Blood, 1961; *By Love Possessed,* 1961; *Parrish,* 1961; *Lad: A Dog,* 1961; *Lonely Are the Brave,* 1962; *Cleopatra,* 1963; *In Harm's Way,* 1965; *Hawaii,* 1966; *Not with My Wife, You Don't,* 1966; *Warning Shot,* 1967; *Waterhole #3,* 1967; *Point Blank,* 1967; *What Did You Do in the War, Daddy?,* 1968; *For Love of Ivy,* 1968; *The Devil's Brigade,* 1968; *Marlowe,* 1969; *Death of a Gunfighter,* 1969; *Ride a Northbound Horse,* 1969; *Marlowe,* 1969; *Kelly's Heroes,* 1970; *Doctors' Wives,* 1971; *Law and Disorder,* 1974; *A Different Approach,* 1978; *Gideon's Web,* 1998; *Return to Me,* 2000.

Stage

Ulysses in Nightown, 1958; *The Big Knife,* 1959; *Brothers,* 1983; *Home Front,* 1984.

Further Reading

Bennetts, Leslie, "Carroll O'Connor as Detective Chief," *New York Times* (March 20, 1985)

Du Brow, Rick, "Thriving in the Heat of Adversity despite Heart Bypass Surgery and the Personal Problems of His Co-Star Howard Rollins, Carroll O'Connor Is Happy in His Work," *Los Angeles Times* (March 17, 1990)

Farber, Stephen, "An Actor Stands in as Writer," *New York Times* (January 9, 1989)

Lamanna, Dean, "Carroll O'Connor: These Are the Days," *Ladies' Home Journal* (October 1991)

Odd Couple, The

U.S. Situation Comedy

Although often positioned in the shadow of such groundbreaking series as *The Mary Tyler Moore Show* and *All in the Family, The Odd Couple* is one of the early examples of sophisticated, well-written, character-driven sitcoms that came to dominate the U.S. network output in the 1970s. Like *M*A*S*H,* it is also one of the few successful TV sitcoms to be based on material from another medium, in this case a successful Broadway play and film. Although critically acclaimed, it did not receive popular recognition until syndication.

Originally conceived by Neil Simon, who based the play on his brother Danny's true-life experience, *The Odd Couple* concept is best described in the one-sentence treatment Simon submitted to Paramount, who financed the stage play sight-unseen: "Two men—one divorced and one estranged and neither quite sure why their marriages fell apart—move in together to save money for alimony and suddenly discover they're having the same conflicts and fights they had in their marriages."

The Odd Couple, in all forms, is truly a popular-culture phenomenon. Simon's wildly successful play ran from 1965 to 1967, has been revived on Broadway more than once, and, as Rip Stock notes in his book *Odd Couple Mania,* it is most likely being produced right now by any number of community theater groups across the country. In 1968 the play was made into a successful film starring Walter Matthau as unkempt

sportswriter Oscar Madison and Jack Lemmon as anal-retentive commercial photographer Felix Unger. Naturally, Paramount wanted its TV division to cash in on this success; while Simon had signed away his TV rights, Paramount enlisted *Dick Van Dyke Show* alumni Gary Marshall and Jerry Belson to produce the series for television, which debuted on ABC in September 1970.

The sophisticated style and attention to character that Marshall and Belson had learned during their *Dick Van Dyke* days paid off, and *The Odd Couple* became one of TV's first relevant sitcoms, dealing in an adult fashion with such issues as the generation gap and sex. Of course, the primary focus was on the two main characters. Jack Klugman and Tony Randall made for a perfect Oscar and Felix, and, indeed, the TV actors have become more closely linked than their movie counterparts with these characters. While both actors won Emmy awards for their roles, the series failed to capture a wide audience. Third-placed network ABC had little to lose by airing a marginal show, of course, and remained committed to the sitcom for five seasons before giving it the ax. The series then blossomed in syndication, appearing in major domestic and foreign markets to this day.

The names of those connected with the series, both on and off screen, reads like a *Who's Who* of television. Producer Marshall used the respect he had gained from

The Odd Couple, Tony Randall, Jack Klugman, 1970–75.
Courtesy of the Everett Collection

actors Ron Glass and Demond Wilson in the Felix and Oscar roles. Using many of the same plots from the original episodes, *The New Odd Couple* lasted only one season. In 1992 Klugman and Randall reprised their roles in a special two-hour reunion episode. Given the American public's captivation with the series, it is likely that further versions will continue to surface.

MICHAEL B. KASSEL

See also **Randall, Tony**

Cast (1970–75)

Felix Unger	Tony Randall
Oscar Madison	Jack Klugman
Murray Greshner	Al Molinaro
Speed (1970–74)	Garry Walberg
Vinnie	Larry Gelman
Roger (1973–74)	Archie Hahn
Roy (1970–71)	Ryan McDonald
Cecily Pigeon (1970–71)	Monica Evans
Gwendolyn Pigeon (1970–71)	Carol Shelly
Dr. Nancy Cunningham (1970–72)	Joan Hotchkis
Gloria Unger (1971–75)	Janis Hansen
Blanche Madison	Brett Somers
Myrna Turner (1971–75)	Penny Marshall
Miriam Welby (1972–74)	Elinor Donahue

Cast (1982–83)

Felix Unger	Ron Glass
Oscar Madison	Demond Wilson
Murray	John Schuck
Speed	Christopher Joy
Roy	Bart Braverman
Cecily Pigeon	Sheila Anderson
Gwendolyn Pigeon	Ronalda Douglas
Maria	Liz Torres
Mona	Jo Marie Payton-France

Producers

Garry Marshall, Jerry Belson, Harvey Miller, Sheldon Keller, Tony Marshall, Phil Mishkin

Programming History

114 episodes
ABC

September 1970–January 1971	Thursday 9:30–10:00
January 1971–June 1973	Friday 9:30–10:00
June 1973–January 1974	Friday 8:30–9:00
January 1974–September 1974	Friday 9:30–10:00

the series to create such less critically respected programs as *Happy Days, Mork and Mindy, Laverne and Shirley,* and *Joanie Loves Chachi.* Indeed, it was through his experience with *The Odd Couple* that Marshall learned a valuable lesson—in order to be a major hit, a show must have "kid appeal," a formula Marshall soon had down to an art. While Marshall graduated to feature films, Jerry Belson remained in TV, eventually serving as consultant for *Cybill,* coproducer and cocreator of *The Tracey Ullman Show,* and writer for *The Drew Carey Show.*

Klugman, after his first of several bouts with throat cancer, returned to his dramatic roots by starring in NBC's *Quincy.* Randall moved over to MTM to star in *The Tony Randall Show,* as well as the critically acclaimed NBC series *Love, Sidney.* Penny Marshall, Gary's sister, launched her acting career as Oscar Madison's whining secretary Myrna Turner (a name that rhymed when she pronounced it in her heavy New York accent).

The Odd Couple has enjoyed a number of spin-offs, which included an animated version in 1975 featuring a tidy cat and a sloppy dog. In 1982 Jerry Belson revived the series for prime time, featuring African-American

September 1974–January 1975	Thursday 8:00–8:30
January 1975–July 1975	Friday 9:30–10:00
October 1982–February 1983	Friday 8:30–9:00
May 1983	Friday 8:00–8:30
May 1983–June 1983	Thursday 8:30–9:00

Further Reading

Gross, Edward A., *The 25th Anniversary Odd Couple Companion: Still Odd after All These Years,* Las Vegas, Nevada: Pioneer, 1989

Marc, David, and Robert J. Thompson, *Prime Time, Prime Movers: From I Love Lucy to L.A. Law—America's Greatest TV Shows and the People Who Created Them,* Boston: Little, Brown, 1992

Stock, Rip, *Odd Couple Mania,* New York: Ballantine, 1983

The Office. *See* Comedy, Workplace

Ohlmeyer, Don (1945–)

U.S. Media Executive

Donald W. Ohlmeyer was president of the National Broadcasting Company (NBC), West Coast, a position he held from 1993 until his retirement from the company in 1999. As president of the West Coast division, Ohlmeyer was responsible for the operations of NBC Entertainment and NBC Productions, both of which produce television programs for the network and other venues. American television network production of such internally developed programming has increased since the Federal Communications Commission relaxed its financial-syndication (fin-syn) regulations, which previously limited such self-production.

Ohlmeyer is a veteran television producer-director who won many Emmy Awards from the National Academy of Television Arts and Sciences. He started his career at ABC Sports in 1967, and moved up the career ladder, working on *Wide World of Sports,* a groundbreaking program in terms of technological broadcast innovation and breadth of coverage. At ABC, he directed three Olympic broadcasts in addition to producing *Monday Night Football,* an early ratings success and one of the first U.S. prime-time network sports programs (boxing notwithstanding).

Ohlmeyer moved to NBC in 1977 as Executive Pro-

ducer of Sports and worked on network coverage of the World Series and the Super Bowl. Combining his careers at ABC and NBC, he has produced or directed television coverage of championships in every major sport in the United States.

While at NBC, Ohlmeyer branched out into feature-film production with *The Golden Moment: An Olympic Love Story,* an award-winning made-for-TV movie. He left NBC in 1982 to form his own production company, Ohlmeyer Communications, which produced made-for-TV films, award programs for MTV, and network series. In the latter category, *Lifestories* was an early reality-based series that garnered positive reviews from television critics for its story treatment, but failed to generate a large enough audience for renewal. Ohlmeyer won an Emmy as producer of *Special Bulletin,* a harrowing 1983 depiction of nuclear terrorism that utilized a television news approach for verisimilitude.

Don Ohlmeyer is a rarity among American television executives in that he moved into senior management from the production side of the business. As producer-executive Grant Tinker also demonstrated at NBC, this type of background can be valuable in as-

Don Ohlmeyer.
Courtesy of the Everett Collection

sessing potential projects and encouraging program submissions from producers. Ohlmeyer leveraged his knowledge of sports, feature films, and special-events coverage into a key position managing the production efforts of NBC at a time when the broadcast networks had an economic incentive to develop more of their own programming.

After his retirement from NBC in 1999, Ohlmeyer worked on *Monday Night Football* for ABC for a season, then retired from television management in 2001. He currently teaches at Pepperdine University in the Los Angeles area and is writing a book on broadcast programming.

PETER B. SEEL

See also **Financial Interest and Syndication Rules; National Broadcasting Company; Olympics and Television; Sports and Television; Super Bowl; Tinker, Grant**

Old Grey Whistle Test, The

U.K. Music Show

For nearly 20 years, *The Old Grey Whistle Test (OGWT)* was the British showcase for "grown-up" rock music. The BBC's *Top Of The Pops* showcased hit singles from 1964, but *OGWT* concentrated on albums and live performances. The roots of the series lay in the 1960s and a trendy arts magazine program, *Late Night Line-Up* (1964–1972) one of the most successful offerings from the newly formed BBC 2, the second TV channel of the BBC. Its delvings into modern music proved to be one of the more popular sections of the show; this led to a spin-off program, *Disco 2* (1970–71) which highlighted those artists grouped under the heading "Progressive Rock." The successor to *Disco 2* was *The Old Grey Whistle Test*. The name was derived from a Tin Pan Alley legend that a rough cut of a new song would be played to the gray-haired door-

man of a record company, and if he could whistle the tune after just one hearing, the song had passed "the old grey whistle test" and would therefore be released.

OGWT started modestly on September 21, 1971, introduced by Ian Whitcomb and featuring folk-rock band America and singer-songwriter Lesley Duncan as its live guests. The show had many presenters over the years but it was the period hosted by Bob Harris that is the most fondly remembered segment of the show's history. "Whispering" Bob Harris (so nicknamed because of his low key, almost hushed delivery) was a thoughtful DJ with a wide-eyed enthusiasm for many different sorts of music and artists. His genuine fascination with the subject clicked with the viewing audience, itself mostly formed of knowledgeable rock fans. Harris joined the show in 1972 and introduced the cream of contemporary rock artists including David Bowie, Roxy Music, Todd Rundgren, Steppenwolf, Sparks, Edgar Winter, Crazy Horse, Average White Band, Jim Croce, Ritchie Havens, Captain Beefheart, Elton John, Supertramp, Janis Ian, Golden Earring, The Pretty Things, Dr. Feelgood, Van Morrison, Be Bop De Luxe, Lynryd Skynyrd, Queen, Fleetwood Mac, Ry Cooder, Joni Mitchell, and Emmylou Harris. Artists were filmed in a bare studio, usually presenting two or three songs. Other acts appeared on film, and new album tracks were played regularly and accompanied by old films, usually silent movies or wild cartoons. There was also space for concert news, music updates, and short interviews. The whole mixture was heralded by the catchy bluegrass/rock theme tune "Stone Fox Chase" by Nashville sessionmen band Area Code 615.

When the punk and new-wave movements emerged around 1976 the show was slow to react at first (although uber-punks The New York Dolls had appeared in 1973), but by 1978 the show regularly featured artists that represented the new movements including The Motors, Talking Heads, The Ramones, Patti Smith, Tom Petty and the Heartbreakers, Magazine, The Police, The Only Ones, Bethnal, The Jam, Siouxsie and the Banshees, The Buzzcocks, Devo, Blondie, Ultravox, XTC, Squeeze, Iggy Pop, Lena Lovich, Tubeway Army, and The Damned. This gave the show a new lease of life and enabled it to outlive the many other music programs that were emerging at the time. The punk generation had been catered to by Granada's *So It Goes* (1976–77) and ATV's *Revolver* (1978), and later trends were covered by Channel 4's *The Tube* (1982–87), a lively, irreverent, modern-day version of the classic 1960s pop show *Ready Steady Go*. The BBC had unveiled rivals including live showcase *Rock Goes To College* (1978–81), which was produced by *OGWT* producer Michael Appleton and ran when *OGWT* was off the air; and *Something Else* (1978–82). In 1983 the series dropped the "Old Grey" from its name, becoming just *Whistle Test* for its final years (1983–87), which included a series of live gigs recorded at various venues around the U.K., called *Whistle Test–On The Road* (1983–84).

By 1987 the program was struggling. Although it had changed to reflect the times, its reputation was still largely that of a progressive rock show. It may have dropped the "old" from its title, but it was considered "old hat" in some circles and consequently was put finally to rest. The great majority of the *OGWT* performances have survived, and some footage thought lost has since been returned to the archive by engineers and other program personnel who had kept private copies. The 30th anniversary in 2001 showed an upsurge of interest in the show, with celebratory programming recalling the highlights of the series transmitted on both BBC TV and radio, and the distribution of a fine *OGWT* DVD, featuring many memorable moments and outstanding performances from the show.

DICK FIDDY

See also **Music on Television;** *Ready Steady Go; Top of the Pops*

Programming History
BBC2
Late night airing
1971–87

Presenters
Ian Whitcomb (1971)
Richard Williams (1971)
Bob Harris (1972–79)
Annie Nightingale (1978–82)
Mark Ellen (1980s)
David Hepworth (1980s)
Andy Kershaw (1980s)
Ro Newton (1980s)
Richard Skinner (1980s)

Olympics and Television in the United States

Ever since Walter Cronkite anchored the first U.S. Olympic broadcast in 1960, the games have enjoyed a mutually beneficial relationship with television. TV has popularized the event to the point that the global audience is now estimated to be in the billions. Broadcast sponsorship and revenues have taken the games from a precarious financial position to one of power and prominence in the global media landscape. Over the years, however, U.S. television networks have become mired in a high-stakes bidding war for broadcast rights. The stiff competition has kept rights fees inordinately expensive, so that they now account for some

40 percent of Olympic revenues, making the International Olympic Committee (IOC) increasingly dependent on them.

As a result, U.S. broadcasters contribute much more money than their counterparts in other countries to support the Olympics. For rights to the 1996 Summer games in Atlanta, Georgia, NBC paid $456 million, a figure that did not include the cost of the production itself (estimated at another $150 million). All of the western European nations combined paid $250 million in fees for the same games. Whereas Canada's CBC paid $160 million to broadcast all of the Olympic games between 2000 and 2008, NBC paid $3.5 billion for those same rights, thereby serving as the IOC's largest single financial underwriter.

Consequently, the U.S. networks hold a powerful position in the Olympic arena. Their financial support often allows them a measure of influence in scheduling, especially when determining the time slots for the most popular events. Traditionally, the Winter and Summer Olympics were held in the same year, once every four years, but in 1994 the IOC changed the timing of the games and adopted a two-year staggered schedule, in part to accommodate the U.S. media. Following the 1992 Summer and Winter games, therefore, the next Winter Olympics were held in 1994, in Lillehammer, Norway, followed by the 1996 Summer games in Atlanta, easing the strain on corporations that were beginning to find the price of quality Olympic advertising prohibitive. With 30-second spots selling for hundreds of thousands of dollars during Olympic broadcasts, and companies paying hundreds of millions of dollars for a sponsorship package, neither the IOC nor the networks could afford to lose these important clients. Spacing the Summer and Winter Olympics two years apart thus allowed sponsors to spread out their costs and also to invest in more high-profile packages. The revised schedule also granted the IOC more time to allocate the revenue effectively.

The Olympics first attracted a significant television audience during the 1968 Summer games in Mexico City, when Roone Arledge was at the helm of ABC Sports. Arledge was instrumental in establishing ABC as the dominant network in Olympic television—a legacy that endured for a quarter century, from the Winter games of 1964 in Innsbruck, Austria, through 1988 in Calgary, Alberta. The combination of Arledge's indepth, personalized approach to sports broadcasting (epitomized in ABC's *Wide World of Sports*) and the technological advances in the field, such as satellite feeds and videotape, set the new standard for Olympic telecasts. Utilizing inventive graphics and personal profiles of the athletes, Arledge slated 44 hours of coverage for the Mexico City games, three times as many

hours as the Tokyo Summer games of 1964. He presented the coverage as a dramatic, exciting miniseries for the television audience, and successive producers have continued to expand on this model.

The 1972 Summer Olympics in Munich, West Germany, saw further growth in costs and coverage. However, the drama of the games was overshadowed by the grisly murder of 11 Israeli athletes at the hands of Palestinian terrorists. Viewers watched in horror as the events of the massacre of September 5–6 unfolded, and television turned into an international forum for the extremist politics of the Black September Organization. This event became the worst tragedy in the history of sports broadcasting.

The Olympics have also given television sports some of its most glorious moments and beloved heroes. Few in the United States will ever forget the U.S. ice hockey team's thrilling victory over the Soviet team in 1980, Romanian gymnast Nadia Comaneci's perfect performances, the U.S. women gymnasts winning their first team gold medal ever in 1996, or the dedication and perseverance of such athletes as Mark Spitz, Carl Lewis, or Dan Janssen. In many instances, the top U.S. athletes also become media celebrities, winning lucrative endorsement and commercial deals along with their medals. For the 2002 Olympics in Salt Lake City, Utah, there were advertising campaigns designed around gold medal hopefuls that aired months before the games even began.

Aside from catapulting athletes to media stardom, the Olympic games are usually a ratings boon for their host network. In the United States, that network customarily captures 50 percent of the television audience each night of the Olympic telecast.

The audience drawn to the Olympics often translates into increased ratings for the host network's regularly scheduled programming as well. The tremendous till of advertising revenue and the potential springboard into a new season likely ensures that the Olympic U.S. broadcast rights will remain among the most coveted and expensive in all of television.

Bids for these rights are made knowing that traditionally, networks lose a great deal of money on the Olympics. Consequently, it has been argued that network coverage of the games has expanded to the point of excess in the attempt to recoup spiraling costs by selling more commercial time. However, the games have become such an emotionally charged part of a network's inventory that profit is no longer the chief concern. Broadcasting the Olympics, much like broadcasting professional sports, is more about building a network's reputation than about making business decisions driven solely by the bottom line. The long-range prestige and promotional value for the host network have been deemed far more important than any immediate financial losses incurred by covering the games.

Nevertheless, the expense of televising the Olympics can be quite draining at times, as the 2000 Sydney "Internet Olympics" demonstrated. Faced with an unwieldy 15- to 18-hour time difference between Australia and North America, NBC decided to broadcast all 441.5 hours of the games on tape delay in the United States. The day-old offerings on U.S. television could not compete with the immediacy of results available via the Internet, and NBC's investment of over $800 million in the broadcast resulted in a ratings disaster—the worst Nielsen audience ratings for the Olympics since 1968.

The gamble on Olympic broadcasting only gets riskier as rights fees continue to skyrocket. The Squaw Valley (California) Winter games in 1960 cost CBS only $50,000. Twenty years later, NBC bid an astonishing $87 million for the 1980 Summer games in Moscow. This price was almost four times the fee for the rights to the previous (1976) Summer games in Montreal. Unfortunately for NBC, the U.S. boycott of the Moscow games destroyed hopes of a windfall and sabotaged the scheduled 150 hours of planned coverage. Still, prices have continued to climb. The Summer broadcast rights almost tripled from 1980 to 1984 ($87 million to $225 million), and both Winter and Summer rights have gone for $300 million or more since 1988. In 1995 NBC made its unprecedented $3.5 billion deal for the 2000 through 2008 games, a deal that, despite its overwhelming numbers, was touted as a historic coup giving the network a virtual "monopoly" on the Olympic games.

In the past, these exploding costs have sent networks looking for alternative strategies to ease the financial burden. In 1992 NBC made an ill-fated attempt at utilizing pay-per-view subscriptions for the Summer games in Barcelona. The "Olympic Triplecast" was organized in conjunction with Cablevision and intended to sell packages of commercial-free, extensive programming. The plan was an enormous failure, owing to its complicated, confusing design and viewers' resentment over having to pay for certain events when others were free of charge.

CBS had more success in reducing its outlay by joining forces in 1992 with TNT (Turner Network Television). The Winter Olympics that year (CBS's first Olympic telecast in 32 years) began a collaboration between the two networks that gave TNT 50 hours, or about 25 percent of the total programming time, in exchange for $50 million toward rights fees. The arrangement was so successful that it was renewed in 1994 for the Lillehammer games. The sharing of broadcast duties and costs seemed to hold promise for both the quality and cost of future Olympic coverage, especially when ABC and NBC were negotiating a partnership deal to cover the 2000 Sydney games together. However, NBC instead secured the sole rights to cover the first five Olympics of the new millennium, adding the Olympic logo to their network "brand" for nearly a decade and hoping to strengthen their own image through this unique identification with the games.

JENNIFER HOLT

See also **Arledge, Roone; Ohlmeyer, Don; Sports and Television**

Further Reading

Abrahamson, Alan, and Randy Harvey, "How NBC Got the Gold," *Los Angeles Times* (August 13, 2000)

Farrell, Thomas B., "Media Rhetoric As Social Drama: The Winter Olympics of 1984," *Critical Studies in Mass Communication* (June 1989)

Larson, James F., "A Comparative Analysis of Australian, U.S., and British Telecasts of the Seoul Olympic Opening Ceremony," *Journal of Broadcasting and Electronic Media* (Winter 1991)

Larson, James F., *Global Television and the Politics of the Seoul Olympics,* Boulder, Colorado: Westview Press, 1993

Lawrence, Robert Z., "Fool's Gold: How America Pays to Lose in the Olympics," *Television Quarterly* (Summer 1990)

Rothenbuhler, Eric W., "The Living Room Celebration on the Olympic Games," *Journal of Communication* (Autumn 1988)

Sandomir, Richard, "Play It Again and Again and Again," *New York Times* (February 11, 1992)

Sandomir, Richard, "Lights, Cameras, Psycho-Dramas, Dysfunction! (NBC's Coverage of the 1992 Olympics)," *New York Times* (July 28, 1992)

YEAR	GAMES	LOCATION	NET	HRS.	RIGHTS FEES
1960	Winter	Squaw Valley	CBS	15	$50,000
	Summer	Rome	CBS	20	$394,000
1964	Winter	Innsbruck	ABC	18	$597,000
	Summer	Tokyo	ABC	14	$1.5 million

YEAR	GAMES	LOCATION	NET	HRS.	RIGHTS FEES
1968	Winter	Grenoble	ABC	27	$2.5 million
	Summer	Mexico City	ABC	44	$4.5 million
1972	Winter	Sapporo	NBC	37	$6.4 million
	Summer	Munich	ABC	63	$7.5 million
1976	Winter	Innsbruck	ABC	44	$10 million
	Summer	Montreal	ABC	77	$25 million
1980	Winter	Lake Placid	ABC	54	$15.5 million
	Summer	Moscow	NBC	150	$87 million
1984	Winter	Sarajevo	ABC	63	$91.5 million
	Summer	Los Angeles	ABC	180	$225 million
1988	Winter	Calgary	ABC	95	$309 million
	Summer	Seoul	NBC	180	$300 million
1992	Winter	Albertville	CBS	116	$243 million
	Summer	Barcelona	TNT	50	$50 million
			NBC	161	$401 million
1994	Winter	Lillehammer	CBS	120	$300 million
			TNT	45	$50 million
1996	Summer	Atlanta	NBC	171.5	$456 million
1998	Winter	Nagano	CBS	128	$375 million
2000	Summer	Sydney	NBC	441	$705 million
2002	Winter	Salt Lake City	NBC	373.5	$545 million
2004	Summer	Athens	NBC		$2.3 billion (package with Turin and Beijing)
2006	Winter	Turin	NBC		
2008	Summer	Beijing	NBC		

Omnibus

U.S. Cultural Series

Omnibus was the most successful cultural magazine series in the history of U.S. commercial television and a prototype for the development of programming on educational television. Developed by the Television-Radio Workshop of the Ford Foundation, *Omnibus* generated both corporate sponsorship and a loyal, but limited, network audience for intellectual programming over nine years (1952–61) on all three networks.

Omnibus was the vision of Robert Saudek, a former ABC vice president of public affairs who became director of the Workshop in 1951. Commissioned to devise an innovative series for network television, Saudek created a variety show for the intellect, a compendium of the arts, literature, science, history, and even some pure entertainment. Saudek hired journalist Alistair Cooke to serve as master of ceremonies.

Cooke was known for his literate commentary on *Letter from America,* a BBC radio series heard throughout Great Britain. With initial underwriting from the Ford Foundation, which *TV Guide* called "risk capital" for the untried, Saudek also secured financing from advertisers to produce a weekly, 90-minute series, first airing from 4:30 to 6:00 on Sunday afternoons. *Omnibus* premiered on November 9, 1952, on CBS. The first installment featured a short drama with Rex Harrison and Lilli Palmer as Henry VIII and Anne Boleyn; William Saroyan narrating an adaptation of his short story "The Bad Men"; and the first images of X-ray movies, an inside look at the working human digestive system.

Saudek and his producers, among them Fred Rickey, William Spier, and Mary V. Ahern, deftly interwove the high and popular arts into a cultural smorgasbord. Their definition of "culture" was flexible enough to encompass Orson Welles's triumphant return from Europe to star in Peter Brook's production of *King Lear;* a production of William Inge's *Glory in the Flower* with Jessica Tandy, Hume Cronyn, and a still very green James Dean; S.J. Perelman's paean to burlesque with Bert Lahr; several appearances by Agnes DeMille, including the performance of her ballet *Three Virgins and the Devil* ("Virgins" becoming "Maidens" because of network censors); Jack Benny recreating his notorious role as an avenging angel in *The Horn Blows at Midnight;* and Peter Ustinov in his U.S. television debut as Dr. Samuel Johnson. *Omnibus* also gave air time to artists new to the mass media: William Faulkner gave a tour of Oxford, Mississippi; James Agee contributed a five-part docudrama on the life of Abraham Lincoln, now considered one of the first miniseries; Frank Lloyd Wright discussed architectural forms with Cooke; and painter Thomas Hart Benton gave a tour of his studio. In addition, individuals who would later become fixtures in prime time received a career boost on *Omnibus,* including Mike Nichols and Elaine May, who brought their sardonic humor to an edition entitled "Suburban Revue"; Les Ford and Mary Ford, who demonstrated multitrack recording with a madrigal-singing Cooke; and Jacques Cousteau, who screened his first undersea adventure on U.S. television.

Beginning with Leopold Stokowski conducting Benjamin Britten's *Young Person's Guide to the Orchestra,* Saudek linked pedagogy with showmanship to produce a series of visual lectures that became a model for educational television. The most stimulating and original of the electronic teachers was Leonard Bernstein, who single-handedly enlarged the possibilities of musical analysis and performance on television. Commencing with his dissection of Beethoven's Fifth Symphony in 1954, Bernstein brought an intellectual passion of excitement and discovery to his subject and later explored musical comedy, jazz, grand opera, and modern music with the same vigor. Gene Kelly in his video lecture compared the art and choreography of ballet dancers to the movements of professional athletes, exemplified by his tap dance with boxer Sugar Ray Robinson.

For most of its run, *Omnibus,* nearly always broadcast live, graced the "ghetto" of weekend programming, Sunday afternoon. As that day-part became more valuable, beginning on CBS with the success of professional football, *Omnibus* shifted to other networks. The series was seen on CBS from 1952 to 1956; on ABC from 1956 to 1957; and NBC from 1957 to 1961. During the final season, *Omnibus* appeared as a series of irregular specials, concluding with a look at the future of the western hemisphere. In all, Saudek and his team assembled 166 editions totaling more than 230 hours of entertaining enlightenment. The series was revived by producer Martin Starger as a series of specials on ABC in 1981. In 1999 PBS distributed the first-ever retrospective of *Omnibus* on television for its December pledge drive.

The artistic concerns and approaches to production of *Omnibus* provided a road map for public television. The Ford Foundation, citing *Omnibus*'s struggle for ratings, questioned whether commercial broadcasters were dedicated to "the development of mature, wise, and responsible citizens," and began to fund educational television projects. Without the foundation's support, Saudek formed his own production company in 1955 to create and gain network sponsorship for the series. The *Omnibus* sensibility has been felt throughout the history of public television in the United States. During the National Educational Television years, *NET Playhouse* (1966–72) and *NET Festival* (1967–70) were direct descendants. Since the formation of the Public Broadcasting Service, *Great Performances* (1974–) has partaken of the *Omnibus* ethos to share a cultural mélange with a discriminating audience. And, of course, the ringmaster of *Omnibus,* Alistair Cooke, became a PBS icon for over 20 years as host of *Masterpiece Theatre.*

RON SIMON

See also **Cooke, Alistair; Educational Television**

Host
Alistair Cooke

Producers
Robert Saudek, Fred Rickey, William Spier, Mary V. Ahern

Programming History

CBS

October 1952–April 1956   Sunday 4:30–6:00

ABC

October 1956–March 1957   Sunday 9:00–10:30

NBC

April 1957–April 1961   Sunday irregular
                            schedule

Further Reading

Beck, Kirstin, *Cultivating the Wasteland,* New York: American Council for the Arts, 1983

Bernstein, Leonard, *The Joy of Music,* New York: Fireside, 1963

Henderson, Amy, *On the Air: Pioneers of American Broadcasting,* Washington, D.C.: Smithsonian Institution Press, 1988

Jones, William M., and Andrew Walworth, "Saudek's *Omnibus:* Ambitious Forerunner of Public TV," *Current* (December 13, 1999)

Leonard Bernstein: The Television Work, New York: Museum of Broadcasting, 1985

Rose, Brian, *Television and the Performing Arts,* Westport, Connecticut: Greenwood Press, 1986

Rose, Brian, *Televising the Performing Arts,* Westport, Connecticut: Greenwood Press, 1992

One Day at a Time

U.S. Domestic Comedy

Although the series was created by Whitney Blake (formerly an actor on TV's *Hazel*), *One Day at a Time* showed the unmistakable imprint of Norman Lear, its powerhouse producer. The series, like other Lear comedies, strove to be topical, progressive, even controversial, and to mix serious issues with more comical elements. At times the mix was less than even, yet it proved to be very popular, and *One Day at a Time* was one of the most successful series of the 1970s and 1980s, outlasting many of Lear's other, more highly praised series.

The program centered around Ann Romano, a television character who found herself struggling through many of the same experiences facing real American women. Married at 17, Romano was now divorced, raising two teenagers more or less on her own, and entering the job market for the first time since her marriage. Played by Bonnie Franklin, Romano was not TV's first divorced woman or mother (Diana Rigg in *Diana* preceded her, as did Vivian Vance on *The Lucy Show*), but she was probably—to that time—the most realistic. Romano struggled with money, fighting for every penny of the child support that was supposed to come from her frequently deadbeat ex-husband. She struggled with finding a job. And she struggled to be both father and mother to her two children, Julie (Mackenzie Phillips) and Barbara (Valerie Bertinelli).

Just as the portrayal of Ann was without romanticism, so was the depiction of her two children.

Throughout the series, Barbara and particularly Julie dealt with issues of birth control, sexuality, virginity, alcohol, and drugs with an honesty and forthrightness that Gidget and other previous TV teens never dreamed of.

Rounding out the cast was apartment-building superintendent Schneider (his first name was hardly ever used), who, over the course of the series, played an increasingly important role in both the program's plots and the lives of the girls. In this role, actor Pat Harrington, Jr., also frequently supplied some much-needed comic relief in the midst of the ongoing exploration of serious topics.

One Day at a Time went through many cast changes during its run and developed various, almost convoluted, plot twists and turns. When the show began, Ann was working for an advertising agency, then later founded her own company. One season she became engaged, only to have her fiancé killed by a drunk driver. Then, for a time following his death, she became legal guardian to his teenage son. Daughter Julie married and had a baby, only later to abandon her new family. Ann's mother (played by veteran actor Nanette Fabray) eventually became a series regular, appearing in almost every episode. Finally, daughter Barbara married (having remained a virgin until her wedding night) and the next season Ann married Barbara's father-in-law. The series ended with Ann, now remarried, moving to London with her new husband to take an exciting new job.

One Day at a Time, Richard Masur, Pat Harrington Jr., Valerie Bertinelli, Bonnie Franklin, Mackenzie Phillips, 1975–84.
Courtesy of the Everett Collection

For all the problems that were played out in front of the cameras, just as many occurred behind the scenes. Phillips was fired from the series in 1980 because of her ongoing drug addiction. She would later return to the series, only to be written out again when she suffered other health problems.

In some ways, one of the first television shows in the "dramedy" genre (a hybrid of drama and comedy to be later embodied by series such as *The Days and Nights of Molly Dodd*), *One Day at a Time* made extensive use of multipart episodes (one three-parter dealt with Julie running away from home), focused on contemporary issues (one episode dealt with teen suicide), and incorporated political messages into its stories. Nothing was ever easy or dealt with offhandedly on *One Day at a Time*. The decision not to shy away from difficult themes in the series' portrayal of contemporary life, especially of women's lives and of female adolescence, set the program apart from others of its time. Thus, the series helped expand the dimensions and role of U.S. television comedy.

Less brash and politically explicit than Lear's other feminist comedy heroine, Maude Finley, Ann Romano (who took back her maiden name after her divorce and preferred to be referred to as "Ms.") was more "middle of the road" and therefore easier for audiences to accept as a realistic type of character. This wide appeal, along with the popularity of series' stars Franklin, Harrington, and Bertinelli, allowed the show to endure for an eventful and trendsetting nine-year run.

CARY O'DELL

Cast

Ann Romano (Royer)	Bonnie Franklin
Julie Cooper Horvath (1975–78, 1981–83)	Mackenzie Phillips
Barbara Cooper Royer	Valerie Bertinelli
Dwayne Schneider	Pat Harrington, Jr.
David Kane (1975–76)	Richard Massur
Ginny Wrobliki (1976–77)	Mary Louise Wilson
Mr. Jerry Davenport (1976–79)	Charles Siebert
Max Horvath (1979–80, 1981–84)	Michael Lembeck
Katherine Romano (1979–84)	Nanette Fabray
Nick Handris (1980–81)	Ron Rifkin
Alex Handris (1980–83)	Glenn Scarpelli
Francine Webster (1981–84)	Shelley Fabares
Mark Royer (1981–84)	Boyd Gaines
Sam Royer (1982–84)	Howard Hessman
Annie Horvath (1983–84)	Lauren/Paige Maloney

Producers

Norman Lear, Mort Lachman, Norman Paul, Jack Elinson, Alan Rafkin, Bud Wiseman, Dick Bensfield, Perry Grant, Allan Mannings, Patricia Fass Palmer, Katherine Green

Programming History

205 episodes
CBS

December 1975–July 1976	Tuesday 9:30–10:00
September 1976–January 1978	Tuesday 9:30–10:00
January 1978–January 1979	Monday 9:30–10:00
January 1979–March 1979	Wednesday 9:00–9:30
March 1979–September 1982	Sunday 8:30–9:00
September 1982–March 1983	Sunday 9:30–10:00
March 1983–May 1983	Monday 9:30–10:00
June 1983–February 1984	Sunday 8:30–9:00
March 1984–May 1984	Wednesday 8:00–8:30
May 1984–August 1984	Monday 9:00–9:30
August 1984–September 1984	Sunday 8:00–8:30

Further Reading

Castleman, Harry, and Walter J. Podrazik, *Harry and Walter's Favorite Shows: A Fact-Filled Opinionated Guide to the Best and Worst on TV,* New York: Prentice Hall, 1989
Mitz, Rick, *The Great TV Sitcom Book,* New York: Perigee, 1983

One Foot in the Grave

British Situation Comedy

One Foot in the Grave, like so many of Britain's most enduring and well-liked situation comedies, took three seasons to establish itself before suddenly becoming the most popular program on television, with 18 million viewers. Six series of the program, and numerous specials, were aired between 1990 and 2000.

The show was writer David Renwick's first situation comedy after having spent a number of years writing sketches for the likes of the Two Ronnies and Alexei Sayle. Renwick created the lead character, Victor Meldrew, with Scottish actor Richard Wilson in mind, but Wilson initially turned down the role because he felt he was too young to play a 60-year-old man. Luckily, he reconsidered and a new hero for the 1990s made his debut on January 4, 1990.

The first episode, "Alive and Buried," introduced Victor Meldrew just as he was about to be made redundant from his job as a security guard, and replaced by a computer chip. From then on Victor's life is portrayed as a never-ending battle against the rest of the world. Everything conspires against him, from his neighbors, to shop assistants, to God. The series showed that elderly people did not have one foot in the grave, but wanted to lead lives actively like anybody else. However, Renwick cleverly created situations which would anger anyone but which, bizarrely, could only happen to Victor Meldrew. In "Valley of Sleep," for example, Victor finds himself in hospital with suspected appendicitis. It is only when the male nurse who is shaving him begins discussing the price of property on the moon that we, along with Victor, gradually become aware that the nurse is, in fact, a mental patient. In "The Worst Horror of All" Victor is convinced that the skip (dumpster) he has hired will have an old mattress dumped in it in the morning. When he wakes, his familiar cry of "I don't believe it" reveals that someone has in fact dumped a Citroen 2CV into the skip. Renwick skillfully returns to his original joke, however, for when Victor opens the car door, out falls the mattress which he had so feared he would find.

The program's other constant character is Victor's long-suffering wife Margaret, played by the often underrated Annette Crosbie. She has to bear the brunt of most of Victor's grumpiness, and, although he some-times irritates her immensely, we are never left in any doubt that she loves him dearly. It is to Renwick's credit that he has occasionally been able to insert some moments of great pathos in which we learn a little more about Margaret and come to understand why she and Victor may be unable to live without each other. Although they are childless, we do learn in "Timeless Time" that they had a son who died as a baby, but we never learn how.

The series has not been without controversy. Some viewers objected when Margaret found a dead cat nestling among the fish-sticks in her freezer, and others when an old lady got trapped overnight in their loft. The program was censured for content in the "Hearts of Darkness" episode. In one scene, set in an old peoples' home, a resident was abused and kicked, actions that offended a number of elderly viewers. The scene was cut slightly when the episode was repeated.

In addition to his two main characters, Renwick also created an idiosyncratic supporting cast: Margaret's friend Mrs. Warbouys (Doreen Mantle), to whom Victor can barely be civil; Nick Swainey, the social worker who lives next door and constantly refers to his (unseen) bedridden mother; and Patrick and Pippa, next-door neighbors, whose lives are made a misery from the moment they first meet the Meldrews.

Renwick has constantly tried to extend the boundaries of situation comedy, not only with the situations his characters have to face, but also within the confines of the 30-minute program. In "Timeless Time" the whole episode is devoted to a sleepless night, in which Victor and Margaret toss and turn, agonizing over life, and during which no other characters are involved and we never leave the bedroom. The first ten minutes of "Heart of Darkness" contain virtually no dialogue; the only sound is a musical accompaniment. "The Beast in the Cage" sees the Meldrews stuck in a traffic jam for the whole episode. This daring culminated in "Trial," when Victor was given an entire episode to himself as he waited at home to be called for jury service. As many newspapers pointed out, this was the first time any actor had been given this comedy accolade since the great Tony Hancock.

Renwick finally decided to write one last series, and

in November 2000, Victor was killed in a road accident—ironically by a new friend of his wife. It was a sad and tragic end for one of Britain's greatest comic heroes, and even Meldrew himself would have railed against the injustice of his final moment being upstaged by ITV, which screened the first millionaire winner of *Who Wants To Be A Millionaire* as a spoiler on the same night. It was probably a fitting end, as Victor Meldrew was the comic hero of his time, and just as much a part of it as were Harold Steptoe and Basil Fawlty of theirs.

PAMELA ROSTRON

Cast

Victor Meldrew	Richard Wilson
Margaret Meldrew	Annette Crosbie
Mrs. Warbouys	Doreen Mantle
Patrick Trench	Angus Deayton
Pippa Trench	Janine Duvitski
Nick Swainey	Owen Brenman

Producer

Susan Belbin

Programming History

BBC 1
35 episodes and 9 specials

Season One: January 4–February 9, 1990	Thursday 9:30
Season Two: October 4–November 15, 1990	Thursday 9:30
Special: December 27, 1990	Thursday 9:30
Special: December 30, 1991	Monday 9:30
Season Three: February 2–March 8, 1992	Sunday 9:05
Season Four: January 31–March 7, 1993	Sunday 8.55
Short special, Comic Relief: March 12, 1993	Friday 10.30
Special, *One Foot In The Algarve:* December 26, 1993	Sunday 9.05
Special: December 25, 1994	Sunday 9:00
Season Five: January 1–January 29, 1995	Sunday 9:00
Special: December 25, 1995	Monday 9:00
Special: December 26, 1996	Thursday 9:00
Special: December 25, 1997	Thursday 9:00
Season Six: October 16–November 20, 2000	Monday 9:00
Short special, Comic Relief: March 16, 2001	Friday 8.30

Further Reading

Bedell, Geraldine, "What's Gone Wrong?," *The Independent* (February 28, 1993)
"Funny but Serious," *Sunday Telegraph* (December 24, 1995)
Rampton, James, "Interview: Can You Believe It?," *The Independent* (April 27, 1996)

Only Fools and Horses

British Situation Comedy

Only Fools and Horses, a long-running situation comedy series concerning the misadventures of a cockney "wide boy" and his naive younger brother, was first screened by the BBC in 1981, and over the next decade became the most popular and acclaimed sitcom on British television. Reflecting the capitalist fervor of Thatcherite Britain in the 1980s, a time of contrasting economic fortunes, the series celebrated the proverbial optimism of the archetypal cockney street trader, with his dreams of a wealthy future and aspirations for a better life.

The program began as an idea by writer John Sullivan, who constructed the first scripts under the title *Readies* and finally persuaded the BBC to risk making a whole series based on the dubious dealings of a personable cockney "fly-pitcher," who made a precarious living selling shoddy goods and—quite without malice—duping customers (including his own family and friends) at every opportunity. Retitled *Only Fools and Horses* after the time-honored proverb "only fools and horses work," the first series failed to attract much attention, but the quality of the scripts and the excellence of the actors gradually won a huge and devoted audience, and by the mid-1980s, special festive episodes topped the BBC's Christmas ratings.

The leading role of the brash, streetwise Derek "Del

Boy" Trotter, decked out with chunky gold jewelry and well versed in cockney rhyming slang, was developed to perfection by David Jason, who deftly realized the character's combination of sentimentality and scheming unscrupulousness. Determined to improve his place in the world in the face of every setback, his Del Boy—like *Minder*'s Arthur Daly—became a byword for shady practices, although his endearing incompetence (embodied in the rusty, yellow three-wheeled van he drove) and his breezy vulgarity ensured that he always remained sympathetic. Time and again, Del Boy's ambitious plans had to be abandoned in order to extricate another of the Trotter clan (or himself) from trouble. Often he was his own worst enemy, even when his motives were at their most pure. When he felt moved to touch up his mother's monument in the churchyard, for instance, he used his own supply of suspiciously acquired paint, and when night fell found out to his horror that it was luminous.

Del Boy's foil was his younger brother Rodney Trotter, gauche and easily misled ("a right plonker" according to his sibling, who used, or rather misused him) and played with pained indignation by former child actor Nicholas Lyndhurst. The relationship between Del Boy and Rodney lay at the heart of the series' success, veering as it did from conflict and petty deceptions to pathos and genuine warmth and mutual reliance. The premise was that Rodney had never known his father and could not remember his mother, who had died when he was a baby, thus leaving him in the care of his scornful but devoted brother. The Trotter trio was completed by dotty old Grandad, played by Lennard Pearce, and, after Pearce's unexpected death from a heart attack in 1984, by Grandad's brother, Uncle Albert (played by Buster Merryfield).

The format changed little over the years, nor did the tasteless decor of the Trotter flat in high-rise Nelson Mandela House, Peckham, or the memorable clientele of the East End pub where the brothers congregated with such "business associates" as the shady but often fooled Boycie, nicknamed Jaffa (because he was sterile, thus like a Jaffa seedless orange), and the even more dimwitted road-sweeper Trigger (so named because he looked like a horse). There were, however, some changes in the Trotter household, notably Rodney's disaster-strewn romance and eventual marriage to city banker Cassandra and Del Boy's liaison with the actress Raquel, which led ultimately to the birth of the first of a future generation of Trotter entrepreneurs, the ominously named Damien.

After a glorious run of some ten years, with both Jason and Lyndhurst successfully involved in various other television projects, the series petered out with the exception of occasional specials, which effortlessly proved that the tried and tested formula still worked.

The achievement of the series was recognized by a BAFTA Best Comedy prize in 1989 (the year of Rodney's wedding to Cassandra). In a final, forgivably sentimental outing, Del Boy's dreams of riches were unexpectedly realized by winning the lottery, although the viewers' last sight of the Trotter trio was of the incorrigible Del Boy, Rodney, and Albert walking into the sunset discussing schemes to become even richer.

DAVID PICKERING

See also **Jason, David; Lyndhurst, Nicholas**

Cast

Del Trotter	David Jason
Rodney	Nicholas Lyndhurst
Grandad	Lennard Pearce
Uncle Albert	Buster Merryfield
Trigger	Roger Lloyd Pack
Boycie	John Challis
Micky Pearce	Patrick Murray
Mike	Kenneth MacDonald
Marlene	Sue Holderness
Denzil	Paul Barber
Alan	Dennis Lill
Cassandra	Gwyneth Strong
Raquel	Tessa Peake-Jones

Producers
Ray Butt, Gareth Gwenlan

Programming History
49 episodes (variable lengths); 14 specials
BBC

September 1981–October 1981	6 episodes
December 28, 1981	Christmas special
October 1982–December 1982	7 episodes
December 27, 1982	Christmas special
November 1983–December 1983	7 episodes
December 25, 1984	Christmas special
February 1985–April 1985	7 episodes
December 25, 1985	Christmas special
August 1986–October 1986	6 episodes
December 25, 1986	Christmas special
December 25, 1987	Christmas special
December 25, 1988	Christmas special
January 1989–February 1989	6 episodes
December 25, 1989	Christmas special
December 25, 1990	Christmas special
December 1990–February 1991	6 episodes
December 24, 1991	Christmas special
December 25, 1991	Christmas special
December 25, 1992	Christmas special
December 25, 1993	Christmas special
December 1996	4 episodes

Open University

Britain's Open University is an innovative and highly successful distance-learning program that utilizes a variety of media, including television and online computer resources, to extend college and graduate-level education to nontraditional, non-local students. Founded in 1969 with financial support from the government and a commitment of airtime from the BBC, the Open University offered its first televised courses in January 1971. Targeted at working adults who had not continued on to higher education, it was an immediate success: more than 40,000 people applied for 24,000 places. With more than 200,000 students enrolled, it is Britain's largest university. It has served as the model for other distance-education programs in more than 30 countries worldwide, including the Netherlands, Spain, Germany, and Australia.

The Open University is "open" in several senses. First, it is open to applicants of any age or background. Unlike conventional universities in England, there are no entrance requirements of any kind. It has also been especially useful for traditionally underserved populations, such as people with disabilities. Second, it is open in the sense that it utilizes an array of educational methods, including television and radio broadcasts, video and audio tapes, mailed correspondence lessons, email and electronic conferencing, web-based courses, and multimedia CD-ROM materials, as well as locally based tutors, regional study centers, and on-campus summer-school sessions. Third, it is open in the sense of place. It has no campus of its own, and is equally accessible to students from even the most remote locations. (Administrative offices and production facilities are maintained in Milton Keynes, England.) Fourth, it is open in terms of time. Students can set their own schedule and progress at their own pace; there is also no time limit for completion of a degree.

Originally to be called "University of the Air," television played a key role in the Open University concept from the beginning. It was felt that television served as a crucial bridge to the "average" nonacademic person. It also provided a human dimension to the prevailing distance-education model then known as correspondence study; through television, students could "meet" their faculty. Lastly, and perhaps most importantly, television offered the most cost-effective means for delivering higher education content to a mass public.

Open University courses are developed by teams of academic, education, and media specialists. Television-based course materials generally consist of printed booklets that contain the lessons, supplementary readings, and specially designed broadcast notes and exercises to accompany the television programs. Televised lessons are approximately 30 minutes in length, aired during non-peak viewing times on BBC 2, and usually repeated during the same week. Videocassette recorders enable many students to time-shift their viewing to more convenient times. The Open University contracts with the BBC for production of the programs. Initially, most were studio productions (in black and white), but location shooting was increasingly added as more experience was gained in the educational qualities of the medium. In addition, some courses utilize archive footage from the BBC. Because the Open University pays for production costs, the programs are produced solely for use in coursework and not for wider commercial appeal. Nevertheless, some programs are no doubt watched by incidental viewers, who may develop an interest and end up taking a course. In one year, 36,000 "study packs" were sold to people who wanted to audit an Open University course without enrolling.

Television brings a number of unique abilities to the teaching/learning experience: it can broadcast an interview with a leading authority in the field under study; illustrate abstract mathematical and economic concepts through animation; show demonstrations of scientific experiments, speeding them up or slowing them down; and provide tours of actual sites of sociological, anthropological, or historical interest.

Great care is taken in course planning and execution to attain quality standards equivalent to conventional universities. An Open University degree has become well respected, and credits received are transferable to regular universities. Indeed, many Open University students, perhaps as many as two-thirds, already have the academic credentials to attend regular universities but have chosen not to for a variety of personal or logistical reasons.

JERRY HAGINS

See also **British Television; Educational Television**

Further Reading

Bates, W.A., editor, *The Role of Technology in Distance Education,* New York: St. Martin's Press, and London: Croom Helm, 1984

Ferguson, John, *The Open University from Within,* New York: New York University Press, 1976

Gardiner, Jo, "Pipe-dream That Opened Up Learning," *Times Educational Supplement* (April 29, 1994)

Garrison, D.R., *Understanding Distance Education,* London: Routledge, 1989

Legge, Derek, *The Education of Adults In Britain,* Milton Keynes, England: Open University Press, 1982

Perry, Walter, *Open University,* Milton Keynes, England: Open University Press, 1976

Tunstall, Jeremy, *The Open University Opens,* London: Routledge and Kegan Paul, 1974

Walker, David, "Britain's Pioneering Open University Begins Its Third Decade with a New Vice-Chancellor and Big Expansion Plans," *Chronicle of Higher Education* (June 19, 1991)

Original Amateur Hour, The

U.S. Amateur Talent, Performance, and Variety Contest

The Original Amateur Hour was first heard on New York radio in 1934 as *Major Bowes' Original Amateur Hour.* The following year it was programmed on CBS Radio, where it remained until 1946 when Major Bowes, the program's creator and host, died. Two years later, the program was revived on ABC Radio and on DuMont Television, hosted in both media by Ted Mack, a talent scout and director of the series under Bowes. The radio and television programs were originally sponsored by Old Gold Cigarettes, represented on television by the famous dancing cigarette box. During its first season, *Original Amateur Hour* was a ratings sensation, and although it never equaled its initial success, its longevity is testament to its ability to attract a consistently profitable audience share.

Original Amateur Hour lasted on radio until 1952 and on television until 1970. The television version was ultimately broadcast over all four major networks during its long run, eventually settling in as a Sunday afternoon CBS feature during its final decade of production.

The format of the program remained virtually unchanged from its premiere in early network radio. The show was essentially an amateur talent contest, the nonprofessional status of contestants thus distinguishing *Original Amateur Hour* from *Arthur Godfrey's Talent Scouts,* which also ran during the late 1940s and early 1950s. Contestants traveled to New York's Radio City from all parts of the United States to sing, dance, play music, and participate in various forms of novelty entertainment. Those who passed an initial screening were invited to compete on the program. Winners were determined by viewers who voted via letters and phone calls, and winning contestants returned to compete against a crop of new talent on the next program. Between amateur acts, Mack conducted rambling interviews and shared corny jokes with contestants. Contestants who won three times earned cash prizes, scholarships, or parts in a traveling stage show associated with the program. In 1951 five such shows traveled about the United States.

While most contestants fell back into obscurity following their appearance on the program, others went on to successful professional careers. Stars who first appeared on television's *Original Amateur Hour* include ventriloquist Paul Winchell and pop singers Teresa Brewer, Gladys Knight, and Pat Boone.

Original Amateur Hour offered a shot at fame and fortune to thousands of hopeful, would-be professional entertainers. As such, it represented a permeable boundary between everyday viewers and the national entertainment industry. The program's general appeal, reliable ratings, simple format, and low production costs have inspired many imitators in television, including the *Gong Show* (which resurrected the notorious rejection gong, not heard since the Major Bowes's radio broadcasts) and, more recently, *Star Search.*

WARREN BAREISS

See also **Variety Programs**

Emcee
Ted Mack

Announcers
Dennis James
Roy Greece

Producers
Ted Mack, Lou Goldberg

Programming History
DuMont Television Network

January 1948–September 1949	Sunday 7:00–8:00
NBC	
October 1949–January 1952	Tuesday 10:00–11:00
January 1952–September 1952	Tuesday 10:00–10:45
April 1953–September 1954	Saturday 8:30–9:00
ABC	
October 1955–December 1955	Sunday 9:30–10:00
January 1956–February 1956	Sunday 9:30–10:30
March 1956–September 1956	Sunday 9:00–10:00
October 1956–March 1957	Sunday 7:30–8:30
April 1957–June 1957	Sunday 9:00–10:00
NBC	
July 1957–September 1957	Monday 10:00–10:30
September 1957–December 1957	Sunday 7:00–7:30
February 1958–October 1958	Saturday 10:00–10:30
CBS	
May 1959–June 1959	Friday 8:30–9:00
July 1959–October 1959	Friday 10:30–11:00
ABC	
March 1960–September 1960	Monday 10:30–11:00

Further Reading

Brooks, Tim, and Earle Marsh, *The Complete Directory to Prime Time Network TV Shows; 1946–Present,* New York: Ballantine, 1988

Dunning, J., *Tune in Yesterday: The Ultimate Encyclopedia of Old-Time Radio,* Englewood Cliffs, New Jersey: Prentice Hall, 1976

McNeil, Alex, *Total Television: A Comprehensive Guide to Programming from 1948 to 1980,* Harmondsworth, England, and New York: Penguin Books, 1980; fourth edition as *Total Television: A Comprehensive Guide to Programming from 1948 to the Present,* New York: Penguin Books, 1996

"Ted Mack," in *Current Biography: Who's News and Why, 1951,* edited by A. Rothe, New York: H.W. Wilson, 1951

Ouimet, Alphonse (1908–1988)

Canadian Broadcasting Executive

Alphonse Ouimet was one of a small, quixotic band of public broadcasters who dreamed that television could make a truly Canadian culture. He played a commanding role as engineer, manager, and eventually administrator in the formation and maintenance of a Canadian television system during the 1950s and 1960s. But his hopes were never realized, a lesson that demonstrates the limits of the cultural power of television.

Ouimet was first employed in 1932 by a Montreal firm then experimenting with television. He joined the engineering staff of Canada's public broadcaster, soon called the Canadian Broadcasting Corporation (CBC), in 1934. After World War II, he became the CBC's television specialist. In 1946 he began work on an international report on the technology of television; three years later he was appointed both coordinator of television and chief engineer, and in January 1953 he became general manager. Thus, he was the chief operating officer of CBC-TV (which had commenced broadcasting in September 1952) during the years it spread across the country. In one forum after another,

Ouimet, CBC chairman Davidson Dunton, and other managers sold the idea of public television, supported by both tax and advertising revenues, as a tool of cultural nationalism that could counter the sway of New York and Hollywood. In the next 6 years the initial 2 stations expanded to 36 (as of March 31, 1995), 8 owned and operated by the CBC and the rest private affiliates, reaching well over 80 percent of the population. On Dominion Day, July 1, 1958, the opening of a microwave relay system from Victoria, British Columbia, on the west coast to Halifax, Nova Scotia, on the east gave the CBC the longest television network in the world. It was a great triumph of engineering and a source of national pride—although the most popular English-language shows carried on the network were nearly always American in origin.

Ouimet became president of the CBC in 1958, which made him one of few high-ranked French Canadians in the service of the federal government at that time. Ironically, his first crisis involved Radio-Canada, as the French-language service of the CBC was (and is) known. Early in 1959 a labor dispute involving French-language producers in Montreal and English-language managers in Ottawa eliminated most of the popular local programming in Quebec for over two months. The partial shutdown excited nationalist passions in Quebec and left behind a legacy of bitterness that Ouimet could never dispel.

The crisis strengthened the presumption that Ouimet's sympathies were on the side of authority, not creativity. Before long, he was portrayed as a distant ruler, more interested in "housekeeping" than "program content," to borrow the terminology of one government commission that severely criticized the CBC for waste, inefficiency, and bureaucracy. Finally, in 1966 Ouimet ran afoul of the producers in Toronto, the center of English-language television. Ottawa management had tried to impose its authority over the extraordinarily successful public affairs show *This Hour Has Seven Days* (1964–66), whose bold opinion and sensational style had captured a mass audience. That upset Ouimet, who adhered to a creed of public broadcasting in which the CBC was neutral, educational, and never partisan. When the *Seven Days* crew declared war on management, they won the support of Toronto producers, many journalists, and much of the public. Eventually, after three months of agitation, including a parliamentary inquiry, the appointment of a federal mediator, even an attempt to secure a new president, Ouimet had his way: *Seven Days* disappeared from the airwaves. It was a pyrrhic victory, however, since public affairs broadcasting in Canada would not recover a similar kind of significance until the appearance of *The Journal* in the 1980s.

Ultimately much more significant was what had happened to the television system in Canada. The 1958 Broadcasting Act led to the end of the CBC's network monopoly and a partial privatization of the system. The new independent stations, especially the affiliates of the Canadian Television Network (CTV) in English Canada, used cheap U.S. programs to win audience share. Ouimet and his managers believed they had to compete by offering their own imports in order to retain viewers and boost advertising revenues. Indeed, these revenues were necessary to support the production of less-popular Canadian content. The annual parliamentary grant of funds was never sufficient.

Late in 1967, Ouimet retired from the presidency, though he would continue in public service as head of Telesat Canada (1969–80), a crown corporation in the field of telecommunications. He left broadcasting just before the onset of a new act that further reduced the stature of the CBC. His legacy was decidedly mixed. Public television still won the attention of nearly half the Canadian audience for its mix of popular and de-

manding programming. But the English-language service offered only a few Canadian examples of storytelling, the great staple of popular television, and specialized much more in sports coverage, news and public affairs, and minority programming. The promise of a cultural renaissance had never materialized. Direct U.S. competition had secured nearly one-quarter of the Canadian audience outside of Quebec by 1967. Only in French Canada was the CBC able to create a continuing series of local dramas, known as *téléromans,* that proved enormously popular with audiences. Television merely built upon the fact that in English Canada tastes were emphatically American, whereas in French Canada there was a strong tradition of homegrown entertainment.

PAUL RUTHERFORD

See also **This Hour Has Seven Days**

[Joseph-]Alphonse Ouimet. Born in Montreal, Quebec, June 12, 1908. Educated at McGill University, Montreal, degree in electrical engineering, 1932. Built TV set and did broadcast experiments for Canadian Television Ltd., 1933–34; engineer, Canadian Radio Broadcasting Corporation (CRBC), 1934 and assistant chief engineer, Canadian Broadcasting Corporation (CBC) when it replaced CRBC, 1946; coordinator of TV, chief engineer and adviser to the board, CBC, 1949; general manager, CBC, 1953; named the "father of Canadian television" for building the world's most geographically widespread TV system when CBC pioneered Canadian TV, 1950s; president, CBC, 1958, retired, 1967; chair, Telesat Canada, 1969–80; in retirement worked with UNESCO, served on committees and task forces; wrote on communication technology and the erosion of Canadian sovereignty. Died December 20, 1988.

Publication

"The Future Role of CBC," *CBC Times* (January 30–February 3, 1960)

Further Reading

Koch, Eric, *Inside Seven Days,* Scarborough, Ontario: Prentice-Hall, 1986

Peers, Frank, *The Public Eye: Television and the Politics of Canadian Broadcasting 1952–1968,* Toronto: University of Toronto Press, 1979

Raboy, Marc, *Missed Opportunities: The Story of Canada's Broadcasting Policy,* Kingston, Ontario: McGill-Queens University Press, 1990

Rutherford, Paul, *When Television Was Young: Primetime Canada 1952–1967,* Toronto: University of Toronto Press, 1990

Our Friends in the North

British Drama Serial

Our Friends in the North was British television's most ambitious, and in many respects most important, drama production of the 1990s. It was BBC 2's most expensive-ever production at £7.5 million, and one of its longest commissions in terms of running time. It also showed that television drama could engage both the brain and the heart at a time when it seemed that British television drama had sunk into a morass of formulaic police and doctor shows.

Our Friends in the North followed the lives of four friends from the industrial city of Newcastle-upon-Tyne, in the northeast of England, between 1964 and 1995. Each episode was set in a year during this period, mainly those in which there was a general election in the U.K. This emphasized the serial's primary theme: the relationship between people and power.

The four friends followed very different paths leading away from their shared working-class backgrounds in the mid-1960s. Dominic "Nicky" Hutchinson was a political radical, desperate to change the world and impatient with the restrictions and corruption of the political process. Mary Soulsby believed that the solution to these problems could be found in improving the mainstream parties and the system. In contrast, Terry "Tosker" Cox became a self-made businessman with little time for concerns beyond profit and pleasure. George "Geordie" Peacock had no interest in politics, but his life was constantly affected by those in power as he turned to crime and alcoholism.

The series had a tortured history before it finally reached the television screen. The author, successful playwright Peter Flannery, originally devised it in the early 1980s but the BBC hesitated to air it, as political drama was no longer fashionable. The corporation was also wary of legal action, as some of the plots affecting the characters were obviously drawn from real-life events. In the mid-1960s, Nicky worked for city boss Austin Donohue, only to discover that he corruptly organized housing contracts for a builder, John Edwards, who was aided by the Home Secretary. This referred to the scandal of the time involving an architect, John Poulson, the leader of Newcastle City Council, T. Dan Smith, and the Conservative Home Secretary, Reginald Maudling. In the late 1960s, Geordie worked in London's red-light district of Soho for a pornographer, and was involved with corrupt detectives. This was based on true events involving the Vice Squad, and the anti-corruption investigation, Operation Countryman, in the 1970s.

The characters also found themselves in the thick of other events drawn from contemporary British history. Nicky joined a terrorist organization similar to the urban guerrilla group The Angry Brigade of the early 1970s. Tosker made money from the credit boom of the 1980s, and many characters were involved in the miners' strike of 1984–85. Even the minor hurricane that buffeted southeast England in 1987 made an appearance.

"Seize the power" was the phrase with which Geordie teased Nicky. The series explored whether it is possible to obtain any kind of power over one's own life, and posed this concern not only in the encounters with the police, organized crime, the Labour Party, or the political establishment, but also in the interactions between the characters and their families. Mary married Tosker after she became pregnant by him, but her real love was Nicky, whom she married in the 1980s, only to see the marriage founder over his coldness. Nicky and Geordie both had troubled relationships with their fathers, respectively distant and cynical and violently alcoholic, only to become just like them. Mary had problems with her angry, unhappy policeman son, Anthony.

Fascinating though the political plots were, it was the personal dramas that really engaged the viewer, as the show refused to provide easy answers to complex problems. The characters, viewed over thirty years of their lives, exhibit numerous personality flaws, and illustrate the difficulty of resisting compromise with society's rules and restrictions, or one's own worst tendencies.

This all comes together in the marvellous final episode, which is marked by scenes of intense beauty and emotion. These included Nicky weeping in isolation at his mother's funeral and his doomed attempts to earn his senile father's respect; Anthony telling Mary that she was not a good mother because "she was never happy"; and Geordie's attempts to stop a father who is abusing a son. However, some hope is offered as well. Tosker is much improved by the love of a good woman, Elaine, and finally gets to fulfill his dream of playing in a rock band. Nicky and Mary put disappointment and bitterness behind them and resolve to be reconciled. Only Geordie, damaged by his years of drink and prison, cannot be wholly redeemed. The closing shot was of him walking past the camera over Newcastle's famous Tyne Bridge, toward an uncertain future.

Our Friends in the North was both a critical and popular success for BBC2. The series was marked by strong acting from all four primary figures, as well as the actor Peter Vaughan who played Nicky's father, Felix.

PHIL WICKHAM

Cast

Dominic "Nicky" Hutchinson	Christopher Eccleston
George "Geordie" Peacock	Daniel Craig
Mary Soulsby	Gina McKee
Terry "Tosker" Cox	Mark Strong
Austin Donahue	Alun Armstrong
Felix Hutchinson	Peter Vaughan
Florrie Hutchinson	Freda Dowie
Eddie Wells	David Bradley
Benny Barrett	Malcolm McDowell
Elaine Cox	Tracey Wilkinson
Anthony Cox	Daniel Casey

Writer
Peter Flannery

Directors

Pedr James	1964, 1967, 1970, 1974
Stuart Urban	1966
Simon Cellan Jones	1979, 1984, 1987, 1995

Producer
Charles Pattinson

Programming History
9 episodes, each lasting between 65 and 75 minutes, broadcast at 9:00 on BBC 2
Dates aired:
January 15, 1996
January 22, 1996
January 29, 1996
February 5, 1996
February 12, 1996
February 19, 1996
February 26, 1996
March 4, 1996
March 11, 1996

Further Reading

Dessau, Bruce, "Tyneside Story," *Time Out* (January 10–17, 1996)

Jeffries, Stuart, "Away the Lads," *The Guardian* (March 12, 1996)

Paterson, Peter, "Peter was the Best of Friends," *Daily Mail* (March 12, 1996)

Smith, Rupert, "Four Friends and 30 Stormy Years," *Radio Times* (January 13, 1996)

Our Miss Brooks

U.S. Situation Comedy

The heart and soul of the successful 1950s sitcom *Our Miss Brooks* was actor Eve Arden. A Hollywood film and New York stage veteran, Arden specialized in playing the wisecracking friend to the heroine. She often did it better than anyone else, achieving her greatest success with an Oscar nomination for *Mildred Pierce* (1945). However, Arden's skill with the wicked one-liner and acid aside was beginning to lead to typecasting. To find a new image, she signed on for the radio comedy role of Connie Brooks, English teacher at fictional Madison High School, a smart and sharp-witted—but ever-likable—character. Unlike most of her film roles, radio offered her the lead.

Beginning on radio in 1948, *Our Miss Brooks* was successfully transferred to television beginning in 1952 (it ran on both media, with largely the same cast, for several months in 1952). Between gentle wisecracks, Miss Brooks doted on nerdish student Walter Denton and frequently locked horns with crusty, cranky principal Mr. Conklin. Many of the program's episodes revolved around Miss Brooks's unrequited desire for Philip Boynton, the school's biology teacher. In this way Miss Brooks was the beginning of a long list of female TV characters of a certain type, like Sally Rogers (Rose Marie) on *The Dick Van Dyke Show* and Jane Hathaway (Nancy Kulp) on *The Beverly Hillbillies*.

Our Miss Brooks, Richard Crenna, Eve Arden, 1952–56.
Courtesy of the Everett Collection

Our Miss Brooks enjoyed good ratings on radio and enlarged its audience when it moved to TV. While some professional educators criticized the series, others celebrated Miss Brooks and Arden's work: she received teaching job offers, and fan letters from educators; she was made an honorary member of the National Education Association; in 1952 she was given an award from the Alumni Association of the Teachers College of Connecticut for "humanizing the American Teacher." Said Arden of her on-screen alter ego: "I tried to play Miss Brooks as a loving person who cared about the kids and kept trying to keep them out of trouble, but kept getting herself in trouble."

Obviously, Miss Brooks encountered enough trouble to sustain the series for more than 150 episodes, but unlike many other female comics on TV at that time, Miss Brooks's forte was not the wild antics of Lucy or the lopsided logic of Gracie Allen. Instead, Miss Brooks's humor was achieved by her own sharp, observing wit and by her centered presence in the midst of a group of eccentric supporting players, including dimwitted, squeaky-voiced student Walter and pompous Conklin. Miss Brooks was always the source of the jokes, not the butt of them.

In 1955 ratings for the program were beginning to wane, and the series was overhauled. Miss Brooks and Mr. Conklin were moved out of Madison High to Mrs. Nestor's Private Elementary School. For a time, there was no Mr. Boynton for whom Miss Brooks would pine, but there was a muscle-bound teacher of physical education, Mr. Talbot, who longed for Miss Brooks. This was an important turn-about in the overall premise of the show: now Miss Brooks was the pursued rather than the pursuer. (Mr. Boynton did turn up again in early 1956, just as the series was about to be canceled; in a film version of the series released by Warner Brothers in 1956, Miss Brooks and Mr. Boynton finally did tie the knot and presumably lived happily ever after.)

Connie Brooks was one of TV's noblest working women; she was the center of a highly successful show, toiling in a realistically portrayed and unglamorous career (Miss Brooks often made mention of how low her wages were), and rewarded and honored by real workers whom she represented. While she was not quite as "no nonsense," nor as tough, as film's prominent working women (such as the characters played by Rosalind Russell and Joan Crawford), Connie Brooks, with her tart tongue, brisk manner, sharply cut jackets, and slim skirts, was just about as savvy as women were allowed to be on TV in the 1950s. Despite Miss Brooks's desire to become "Mrs." Something—and despite the fact that she was never promoted to school principal—*Our Miss Brooks*'s legacy in television history is that it dared to depict a funny, attractive, wise, competent woman, beyond the realms of the home, marriage, and children.

CARY O'DELL

Cast

Connie Brooks	Eve Arden
Osgood Conklin	Gale Gordon
Philip Boynton	Robert Rockwell
Walter Denton (1952–55)	Richard Crenna
Mrs. Margaret Davis	Jane Morgan
Harriet Conklin (1952–55)	Gloria McMillan
Stretch Snodgrass (1952–55)	Leonard Smith
Miss Daisy Enright (1952–54)	Mary Jane Croft
Mrs. Martha Conklin (1952–53)	Virginia Gordon
Mrs. Martha Conklin (1953–56)	Paula Winslowe
Superintendent Stone (1953–55)	Joseph Kearns
Angela (1954–56)	Jesslyn Fax
Ricky Velasco (1954–55)	Ricky Vera
Mr. Oliver Munsey (1955–56)	Bob Sweeney
Mrs. Nestor (1955)	Nana Bryant
Mrs. Nestor (1955–56)	Isabel Randolph
Gene Talbot (1955–56)	Gene Barry
Clint Albright (1955–56)	William Ching
Benny Romero (1955–56)	Ricky Vera
Mr. Romero (1956)	Hy Averback

Producer
Larry Berns

Programming History
154 episodes
CBS
October 1962–June 1953   Friday 9:30–10:00
October 1953–June 1955   Friday 9:30–10:00
October 1955–September 1956   Friday 8:30–9:00

Further Reading

Arden, Eve, *The Three Phases of Eve,* New York: St. Martin's Press, 1985
Castleman, Harry, and Walter J. Podrazik, *Harry and Walter's Favorite Shows: A Fact-Filled Opinionated Guide to the Best and Worst on TV,* New York: Prentice Hall, 1989
Mitz, Rick, *The Great TV Sitcom Book,* New York: Perigee, 1983

Ovitz, Michael (1946–)

U.S. Media Executive

As leader of the Creative Artists Agency (CAA) from 1975 to 1995, Michael Ovitz succeeded in increasing the importance of talent agents in the film and television industries during a key period of technological change and economic expansion in Hollywood. After a brief period as president of the Walt Disney Company (1995–96), Ovitz has been involved in talent management, as well as television and film production.

According to a fellow agent, Ovitz "redefined what an agent was" while at CAA. Ovitz modeled CAA on the legendary Music Corporation of America (MCA) talent agency led by Jules Stein and Lew Wasserman. Emphasizing teamwork, professionalism, and aggressiveness, Ovitz reshaped CAA from a small television agency that packaged programs such as *The Rich Little Show* and *The Jackson Five Show,* into a major film agency that corralled top stars, directors, and writers, including Tom Cruise, Dustin Hoffman, Barbra Streisand, Michael Douglas, Steven Spielberg, Barry Levinson, and Sydney Pollack, among others. During the early 1980s, Ovitz and his teams of agents courted contacts with access to new scripts, such as literary agent Morton Janklow, whose clients included authors Jackie Collins and Danielle Steele. These efforts resulted in successful television miniseries packaged by CAA, including *Rage of Angels, Princess Daisy,* and *Hollywood Wives.* Having signed major screenwriters, such as Joe Eszterhaus, CAA then attracted and signed top film talent with the promise that it would "package" script and talent into projects, shopping those projects around to studios for financing and production. This activist approach to securing work for clients resulted in films such as *Rain Man* (1988),

Cliffhanger (1993), and *Jurassic Park* (1993), as well as flops such as *Legal Eagles* (1986). Although studio executives complained that CAA was superseding their producing prerogatives and raising the price for talent, the studios also benefited from CAA's efficient packaging. In effect, CAA exploited the studios' need for more product in the face of increasing demand due to the proliferation of multiplex theaters, home video recorders, and premium-movie cable services.

CAA's film packaging tactic simply mirrored common agency practice in television. Since the 1950s, talent agencies have packaged program concepts, scripts, actors, and directors from their stables of clients and shopped these packages around to networks for financing and production, in return for fees representing percentages of the program's production budget and syndication revenues. If the program is a hit, packaging fees are far more lucrative for the agency than single-client commissions because the fees are paid for the life of the program, on and off network. For example, the William Morris Agency earned at least $50 million for packaging *The Cosby Show,* a network and syndication hit.

Having successfully addressed the studios' need for film and television projects, Ovitz began to focus on Hollywood's increasing need for capital investment as well. Ovitz acted as broker between film studios and investors during several transactions that helped reshape Hollywood's ownership structure, including Sony's 1989 purchase of Columbia Pictures, the French bank Credit-Lyonnais's rescue of MGM in 1993, Matsushita's purchase of MCA/Universal in 1990, and its sale to Seagram in 1995. Seeking to apply his expertise to other fields, Ovitz also helped shape Coca-Cola's "Always Coca-Cola" advertising campaign in the early 1990s and consulted with the "Baby Bells" (telephone and telecommunications companies) on their unsuccessful video-on-demand service, Tele-TV. By the mid-1990s, Ovitz was being hailed in the press as the "King of Hollywood" for his precedent-breaking involvement in its reshaping.

In 1995 Ovitz rattled the power structure of Hollywood by accepting a position as president of the Walt Disney Company to work with his then-friend, CEO Michael Eisner. Having just acquired Capital Cities/ABC, Eisner announced that Ovitz would help integrate the divisions of the rapidly growing entertainment conglomerate. After barely 14 months, however, Ovitz's Disney presidency ended, and his reputation as a power broker was severely undercut.

Ovitz returned to the talent business in 1998 by founding Artists Management Group (AMG), whose clients included Leonardo DiCaprio, Cameron Diaz, Martin Scorsese, Michael Crichton, and Tom Clancy. Talent managers, unlike talent agents, are allowed to own equity stakes in their clients' productions in addition to earning 10 percent commissions on clients' earnings. Managers are not allowed to procure work for clients, which is the agents' job, but only advise them as to which work to accept. In keeping with his strategy at CAA to generate work for his clients, Ovitz also started sister film and television production companies, Artists Television Group (ATG) and Artists Production Group (APG). The plan was to use the star power of the management group to drive production projects in which the stars (as well as Ovitz) would have ownership stakes despite having no distribution control.

ATG surprised the television industry by selling four of its programs to four different networks for the fall 2000 season: *The $treet* (FOX), *Grosse Pointe* (WB), *The Weber Show* (NBC), and *Madigan Men* (ABC). Although most television programs are produced by integrated film and television companies (such as Warner, FOX, and Disney) with deep pockets to absorb losses caused by the high failure rate of network programs, Ovitz decided to self-finance the independent ATG, and he signed numerous expensive pacts with talent to facilitate their participation. However, episode costs of $2 million each for the critical hit *The $treet* were not covered fully by network license fees (under the deficit financing system, networks pay 80 percent of production costs for the right to broadcast a program twice). ATG soon ran up huge deficits, cushioned only by Ovitz's personal investment of an estimated $100 million. ATG produced 23 television pilots in two years, in the hope that one would emerge as a

hit and in syndication generate the profits necessary to offset the failures. Unfortunately, all seven ATG programs that made it on to network schedules were canceled. In August 2001, despite having promised to produce *The Ellen Show* for CBS and *Lost in the USA* for the WB network, ATG closed its doors and sold off its assets, having succumbed to the 95 percent failure rate for new network programs. In 2002, after losing the support of major investors, Ovitz also sold control of the talent management company, AMG.

Ovitz's efforts as a talent agent to leverage his clients' star power into greater control over film and television projects as well as larger shares of revenues were successful from the late 1980s until the mid-1990s. Ovitz and CAA were able to take advantage of Hollywood's relatively decentralized production process, which—coupled with the rising demand for blockbuster, star-driven film and television vehicles in the 1980s and 1990s—allowed CAA's agents to operate as "de facto producers" for a time. By the 2000s, however, no single talent agency retained that kind of clout. Although Ovitz subsequently followed the typical career path of former agents, working as a studio executive, talent manager, and film/television producer, his post-1995 efforts have been far less successful.

CYNTHIA B. MEYERS

See also **American Broadcasting Company**

Michael Ovitz. Born in Chicago, Illinois, December 14, 1946. Graduated from University of California, Los Angeles, 1968; briefly attended law school. Married Judy Reich, 1969; children: Christopher, Kimberly, and Eric. Worked for William Morris Agency, first as trainee, then as agent, 1969–75; cofounder of Creative Artists Agency, 1975–95; president of the Walt Disney Company, 1995–96; cofounder of Artists Management Agency, 1998–2002, Artists Television Group, 1999–2001, and Artists Production Group 1999–2001.

Further Reading

Grover, Ronald, "Ovitz: How Many Fields Can the King of Hollywood Conquer?" *Business Week* (August 9, 1993)

Hirschberg, Lynn, "Michael Ovitz Is on the Line," *New York Times Magazine* (May 9, 1999)

Singular, Stephen, *Power to Burn: Michael Ovitz and the New Business of Show Business,* Secaucus, New Jersey: Carol Publishing Group, 1996

Slater, Robert, *Ovitz: The Inside Story of Hollywood's Most Controversial Power Broker,* New York: McGraw Hill, 1997

Zeman, Ned, "Michael Ovitz, Take Two," *Vanity Fair* (April 2001)

Ownership

U.S. Regulatory Policy

Private ownership of the airwaves is prohibited under U.S. law. Unlike in many countries that have maintained direct ownership of broadcasting frequencies by the sovereign government, the U.S. Congress has asserted that ownership of the radio spectrum resides with the people of the United States. Users are assigned portions of the spectrum through a licensing mechanism. Control of radio licensing was first assigned to the Secretary of Commerce and Labor under the Radio Act of 1912. Subsequently communication legislation transferred licensing authority first to the Federal Radio Commission and finally its successor, the Federal Communications Commission (FCC) in 1934. Today, although no person or entity can own part of the radio spectrum, control of broadcast licenses is an issue of increasing concern both within the industry and among the general viewing public.

The FCC licenses all non-governmental broadcasting stations in the United States. Broadcast licenses are assigned to specific locales or regions of the United States, related to allocation tables that show coverage areas and areas of potential interference. Applicants must make a license application after determining whether a frequency is available for the desired community. For many years, the Commission was obliged to determine the character of the applicant, ascertaining qualifications such as citizenship, character, civic involvement in the community of license, prior experience in broadcasting, and other related factors. During the 1990s, the FCC streamlined the licensing and renewal process. Today, while the FCC still needs to determine the suitability of the applicant, rules concerning licensing have been relaxed. When there are competing applications for the same frequency assignment the Commission resolves the difficulty by means of an auction process, as mandated in the Telecommunications Act of 1996.

Historically, the FCC asserted a "scarcity theory" rationale for limiting the number of licenses that any entity could own. For example, the FCC imposed national limits on television station ownership and promulgated various rules designed to limit media companies from co-owning a television license and other media property such as a cable company, a news-paper, or a telephone service in the same market. During the 1960s, the Commission placed limits on ownership and restricted group licenses to a maximum of 5 VHF stations; later rules were relaxed to include 7 stations, then increased to 12 stations or 25 percent of the national audience. The FCC also promulgated the "duopoly rule" that limited a single owner to one AM, one FM and one TV license in a single local market. When the Commission instituted this rule in 1964, the U.S. television marketplace consisted only of 649 television stations and a small number of cable systems, which retransmitted the signals of over-the-air broadcast stations. Numerical limits were coupled with cross-ownership restrictions as a means of ensuring that the viewing public would be exposed to the widest variety of viewpoints within the local community.

Since its earliest days, the FCC has acted on the belief that diversification of media ownership generally served the public interest. Originally, numerical restrictions limiting ownership were developed to ensure that no one entity gained control of too many broadcasting stations. Additionally, limiting the number of stations that a broadcast entity could own effectively limited the power of the three original networks (ABC, CBS, and NBC) to reach into the local community. In 1975, the Commission adopted regulations prohibiting cross-media ownership between television stations and co-located newspapers. Although the FCC permitted a number of markets to continue with a co-owned newspaper-television station combination under a grandfather clause, the Commission asserted a public interest in enforcing a policy of diversification of media ownership. Even though the number of commercial television stations doubled in the thirty year period between 1966 and 1996, restrictive ownership policies remained a basic tenet of FCC policy.

The Telecommunications Act of 1996 fundamentally changed U.S. communications policy by abolishing the numerical restrictions on ownership, although it placed a maximum on national audience penetration of 35 percent. Terms for licenses changed as well. Until 1981, broadcast licenses were granted for a period of three years. During the 1980s the FCC eased license restrictions somewhat, but the Act increased license terms to 8 years. Additionally, section 202 of the Act required the Commission to execute a biennial review of rules and regulations with the presumption favoring the repeal or modification of unnecessary rules.

Growth of the industry, coupled with Congress's legislative mandate in the 1996 Act to ease national ownership restrictions, have changed the media landscape in the United States, particularly in the area of radio ownership and operation. As the new millennium began, the use of the "scarcity" argument, originally offered by the Commission as the rationale for licensing and limiting ownership, has come under increasing scrutiny, particularly as the growth of broadcast outlets, cable, and satellite outlets spawned an unprecedented growth of new video services during the late 1980s and 1990s. With the passage of the 1996 Act, the FCC eased some rules and restrictions regarding local television ownership and local management agreement rules. The industry petitioned the Commission to make sweeping reforms during the 1998 biennial review, but the FCC declined to make broad changes to the rules at that time.

In 2001, Chairman Michael Powell created the Media Ownership Working Group. The group undertook a number of studies that focused on determining whether various broadcast ownership rules needed to be changed or modified under section 202 of the 1996 Act. Also, two significant cases, FOX TV Stations v. FCC and Sinclair Broadcast Group v. FCC, left the Commission with the task of either defending the current rules with substantive evidence or modifying some or all of the various ownership rules.

During the later part of 2002 the Commission released 12 studies conducted by the Media Ownership Working Group on various aspects of the ownership rules. The various ownership rules under consideration included:

(1) newspaper/broadcast cross-ownership prohibition
(2) local radio ownership
(3) national television ownership limits
(4) local TV multiple ownership rules
(5) radio/TV cross-ownership restrictions
(6) dual television network restrictions

Public comment was invited and the Commission set early 2003 as the time for reply. During this period various outside groups, reflecting both industry and consumer viewpoints, filed a voluminous number of comments regarding the status of the FCC rules. In June, voting along partisan lines, Powell and two other Commissioners voted to increase the ownership cap from 35 percent to 45 percent and to relax cross-ownership restrictions for newspaper ownership in all but the smallest TV markets. The Commission also lifted local ownership rules, allowing dual and triple ownership of stations in medium and large-sized television markets.

Following the Commission's announcement, a firestorm of protests moved Congress to form a bipartisan coalition aimed at repealing the ownership caps. In the autumn of 2003, a compromise raising the cap to 39 percent was announced in the Senate. However, as the rules were set to be implemented, a federal appeals court in Philadelphia suspended all the FCC-adopted ownership changes. As this publication went to press, it was unclear whether the courts would sustain the FCC rule changes.

Proponents of relaxing ownership rules point to the increasing competition from cable and the Internet as the reason changes are necessary, but the increasing convergence of media properties has many media critics worried that the number of diverse voices in the local marketplace is decreasing. Critics of the proposed rule changes have pointed to a sharp decrease in the number of independent newspaper and television owners over the last quarter century. Some claim that relaxation in ownership rules will allow large media conglomerates to fortify their market power, although television network owners say that changes are necessary to sustain current standards of programming. Due to economies of scale and the convergence of new digital media, consolidation of television ownership may be inevitable.

FRITZ MESSERE

See also **Federal Communications Commission; U.S. Policy: Telecommunications Act of 1996**

Further Reading

Baer, Walter S., *Concentration of Mass Media Ownership: Assessing the State of Current Knowledge,* Santa Monica, California: Rand Corporation, 1974

Ho, David, "FCC Votes to Ease Media Ownership Rules," *Associated Press* (June 2, 2003)

Kahn, Frank J., editor, *Documents in American Broadcasting,* 4th edition, New York: Appleton-Century-Crofts, 1984

Levin, Harvey J., "U.S. Broadcast Deregulation: A Case of Dubious Evidence," *Journal of Communication* 36/1 (Winter 1986)

Sterling, Christopher H., and John Michael Kittross, *Stay Tuned: A History of American Broadcasting,* 3rd edition, Mahwah, New Jersey: Lawrence Erlbaum Associates, 2002

Walker, James R., and Douglas Ferguson, *The Broadcast Television Industry,* Boston: Allen and Bacon, 1998

P

Paar, Jack (1918–2004)

U.S. Talk Show Host

Jack Paar was one of television's most intriguing and enigmatic talk show hosts. He served as the host of *The Tonight Show* from 1957 through 1962 and headed his own NBC variety series from 1962 to 1965. Both series were stamped with Paar's volatile and unpredictable personality and were often a haven for witty, literate conversation.

Although Paar is considered one of the key talents uniquely suited to the cool medium of television, he worked extensively in other areas of show business. Leaving school at 16, he first worked as a radio announcer and later as a humorous disc jockey. During World War II Paar entertained troops in the South Pacific with his wry impersonations of officers, sometimes in concert with his army colleague Jackie Cooper. After the war, he returned to radio, serving as a fill-in for Don MacNeill on the *Breakfast Club* and as a panelist on *The $64 Question*. In 1947 he was the summer replacement for Jack Benny, a comedian whose mannerisms Paar would later emulate. Paar was signed to a contract at Howard Hughes's RKO pictures and had his first significant role in *Walk Softly, Stranger* (1950) with Joseph Cotten. In 1951 he made *Love Nest* for Twentieth Century Fox, playing the sexy boyfriend opposite an emerging starlet, Marilyn Monroe.

Paar was first employed in television as a host of game shows, notably *Up to Paar* (1952) and *Bank of Stars* (1953). In November 1953 he hosted his own daytime variety series for CBS and assembled a cast of regulars, including Edith Adams, Richard Hayes, Jack Haskell, and pianist Jose Melis. In August 1954 he took over the *Morning Show* from Walter Cronkite and became a competitor of Dave Garroway and the *Today* show. During this morning experience, Paar developed his conversational skills and an appreciation for a relaxed program with no rigid guidelines. When CBS again changed formats, Paar was given another variety series, this time in the afternoon.

Because of several well-received guest appearances on NBC's *Tonight,* Paar ascended to the permanent host slot on July 29, 1957. For several months before, the late-night series had floundered when original host Steve Allen moved permanently to prime time. Paar was given free rein to restore the show's luster and assembled his own freewheeling staff, including writers Jack Douglas and Paul Keyes, to give the show an extemporaneous quality. The new creative team emphasized the importance of the opening monologue as a vehicle to transmit Paar's singular, often emotional view of the world. Unlike any other host of *The Tonight Show,* Paar had no talent for sketches, so his writers created a persona through his words, always leaving space for the host to improvise verbally.

Called a "bull in his own china shop," Paar gained notoriety by creating feuds with others in the show business community, including Ed Sullivan, Walter Winchell, William Paley, and most television critics. To salve his often bruised ego, he surrounded himself

Jack Paar.
Photo courtesy of Jack Paar

with a salon of eccentrics whose ranks included pianist and professional hypochondriac Oscar Levant, the outspoken Elsa Maxwell, the irreverent Alexander King, and British raconteurs Robert Morley, Bea Lillie, and Peter Ustinov. He resurrected the careers of performers on the entertainment fringe, inviting back on a regular basis the folksy Cliff "Charley Weaver" Arquette, music-hall veteran Hermione Gingold, French chanteuse Genevieve, and acerbic Hans Conreid. More in keeping with *The Tonight Show* ethos, Paar also nurtured young comic talent, and among his discoveries were Bob Newhart, the Smothers Brothers, Dick Gregory, Godfrey Cambridge, and Bill Cosby.

Paar also moved the talk show out of the controlled studio and began to intermingle politics and entertainment. He and author Jim Bishop journeyed to Cuba and prepared a special report, "The Background of the Revolution." Paar's unexplained embrace of Castro was vehemently questioned by Batista supporters and even the U.S. House of Representatives. Paar also became friendly with the Kennedys and invited Robert Kennedy, then serving as chief counsel of the Senate Labor-Management Relations Committee, to discuss his investigation of organized crime in the unions. The head of the Teamsters, Jimmy Hoffa, responded with a

$1 million lawsuit against Kennedy and Paar, which was eventually thrown out of court. Paar was also the first entertainer to originate a program from the Berlin Wall, which he did less than a month after its construction at the height of cold war tension.

Paar became the most successful presence in late night, expanding his affiliate base from the 46 stations with which he started out to 170. In 1957 his talk show's title was changed to *The Jack Paar Tonight Show,* and the next season the show was taped early in the evening instead of being broadcast live. Beginning in July 1959, Paar broadcast only four nights a week; Friday night became "The Best of Paar," inaugurating a tradition of *Tonight Show* reruns. At the height of his fame, he objected to NBC censoring a joke about a water closet (a British euphemism for a bathroom). Incensed, he walked out at the beginning of the following evening's show, leaving announcer Hugh Downs to finish the program. His walk-off and subsequent disappearance dominated news for five weeks until he returned after an extended stay in Hong Kong.

Paar's roller-coaster ride on *The Tonight Show* continued until March 30, 1962, when he retired from late night, having hosted more than 2,000 hours. In September 1962 Paar returned to the variety format and produced a weekly Friday night series, borrowing the most successful elements of his talk show. Each telecast was ignited by a monologue, and the core of each program was an in-depth conversation with some of Hollywood's most voluble personalities, including Judy Garland, Tallulah Bankhead, Richard Burton, and Jonathan Winters. Paar also spiced the series with home movies of his family trips, with his wife, Miriam, and daughter, Randy, also becoming celebrities.

Paar continued to make headlines with newsworthy segments. He ventured into Gabon, Africa, to interview Nobel Prize recipient Dr. Albert Schweitzer. Richard Nixon made his first public appearance after his defeat in the gubernatorial race in California and entertained Paar's audience with a piano solo. Paar also presented the first footage of the Beatles in prime time, a performance he openly derided as the downfall of British civilization.

Paar retired from the network grind in 1965 to manage a television station in Maine. In March 1973 he was persuaded to return to late night to compete against the inheritor of *The Tonight Show* mantle, Johnny Carson. This time he was reduced to one week every month, as part of *ABC's Wide World of Entertainment.* The format that he had fostered had changed considerably, and Paar retired five months later, this time for good. In 1997 Paar was the subject of an *American Masters* profile on public television, a program that achieved record audience numbers for the series.

Paar was an integral part of a new generation of television personalities. Unlike an older generation trained in vaudeville and Broadway, Paar and such 1950s contemporaries as Garry Moore, Arthur Godfrey, and Dave Garroway had no specific show-business talents. They could not act, sing, or dance. They were products of an intimate electronic technology that allowed for a personalized connection with the audience. As a talk show and variety host, Paar created a complex, unpredictable character, whose whims and tantrums created national tremors.

RON SIMON

See also **Talk Shows;** *Tonight Show*

Jack Paar. Born in Canton, Ohio, May 1, 1918. Married: 1) Irene, late 1930s; 2) Miriam Wagner, 1943; child: Randy. Served as a noncombatant soldier in the U.S. Army with the 28th Special Service Company during World War II. Actor in motion pictures, 1948–52; appeared in radio and television shows, including *The $64 Question, Up to Paar,* and *CBS Morning Show,* 1947–57; star of NBC's *The Tonight Show,* 1957–62, and of various other programs. Died in Greenwich, Connecticut, January 27, 2004.

Television Series (selected)

1952	*Up to Paar*
1953	*Bank on the Stars*
1953–54	*The Jack Paar Show*
1957–62	*The Tonight Show* (renamed *The Jack Paar Tonight Show,* 1959)
1962–65	*The Jack Paar Program*
1973	*ABC's Wide World of Entertainment*

Television Specials

1960	*Jack Paar Presents*
1967	*A Funny Thing Happened on the Way to Hollywood*
1967	*Jack Paar and a Funny Thing Happened Everywhere*
1969	*Jack Paar and His Lions*
1970	*Jack Paar Diary*
1986	*Jack Paar Comes Home*
1987	*Jack Paar Is Alive and Well*

Films

Variety Time, 1948; *Easy Living,* 1949; *Walk Softly, Stranger,* 1950; *Love Nest,* 1951; *Footlight Varieties,* 1951; *Down among the Sheltering Palms,* 1952.

Publications

I Kid You Not, with John Reddy, 1960
My Saber Is Bent, with John Reddy, 1961
Three on a Toothbrush, 1965
P.S. Jack Paar, 1983

Further Reading

Galanoy, Terry, *Tonight!,* Garden City, New York: Doubleday, 1972

Henderson, Amy, *On the Air: Pioneers of American Broadcasting,* Washington, D.C.: Smithsonian Institution Press, 1988

Metz, Robert, *The Tonight Show,* New York: Playboy Press, 1980

Paik, Nam June (1932–)

U.S. Video Artist

Nam June Paik—composer, performer, and video artist—played a pivotal role in introducing artists and audiences to the possibilities of using video for artistic expression. His works explore the ways in which performance, music, video images, and the sculptural form of objects can be used in various combinations to question our accepted notions of the nature of television.

Growing up in Korea, Nam June Paik studied piano and composition. When his family moved, first to Hong Kong and then to Japan, he continued his studies in music while completing a degree in aesthetics at the University of Tokyo. After graduating, Paik went to Germany to pursue graduate work in philosophy. There he became part of the Fluxus group of artists, who were challenging established notions of what constituted art. Their work often found expression in per-

Nam June Paik with "Piano Piece," 1993.
Courtesy of the Holly Solomon Gallery

formances and happenings that incorporated random events and found objects.

In 1959 Paik performed his composition *Hommage a John Cage.* This performance combined a prerecorded collage of music and sounds with "onstage" sounds created by people, a live hen, a motorcycle, and various objects. Random events marked this and other Paik compositions. Instruments were often altered or even destroyed during the performance. Most performances were as much a visual as a musical experience.

As broadcast television programming invaded the culture, Paik began to experiment with ways to alter the video image. In 1963 he included his first video sculptures in an exhibition, *Exposition of Music—Electronic Television.* Twelve television sets were scattered throughout the exhibit space. The electronic components of these sets were modified to create unexpected effects in the images being received. Other video sculptures followed. *Distorted TV* used manipulation of the sync pulse to alter the image. *Magnet TV* used a large magnet that could be moved on the outside of the television set to change the image and create abstract patterns of light. Paik began to incorporate television sets into a series of robots. The early robots were constructed largely of bits and pieces of wire and metal; later ones were built from vintage radio and television sets refitted with updated electronic components.

Some of Paik's video installations involve a single monitor, others use a series of monitors. In *TV Buddha* a statue of Buddha sits facing its own image on a closed-circuit television screen. For *TV Clock* 24 monitors are lined up. The image on each is compressed into a single line with the lines on succeeding monitors rotated to suggest the hands of a clock representing each hour of the day. In *Positive Egg* the video camera is aimed at a white egg on a black cloth. In a series of larger and larger monitors, the image is magnified until the actual egg becomes an abstract shape on the screen.

In 1964 Paik moved to New York City and began a collaboration with classical cellist Charlotte Moorman to produce works combining video with performance. In *TV Bra for Living Sculpture,* small video monitors became part of the cellist's costume. With *TV Cello* television sets were stacked to suggest the shape of the cello. As Moorman drew the bow across the television sets, images of her playing, video collages of other cellists, and live images of the performance area combined.

When the first consumer-grade portable video cameras and recorders went on sale in New York in 1965, Paik purchased one. Held up in a traffic jam created by Pope Paul VI's motorcade, Paik recorded the parade and later that evening showed it to friends at Café a Go-Go. With this development in technology, it was possible for the artist to create personal and experimental video programs.

Paik was invited to participate in several experimental workshops, including one at WGBH in Boston and another at WNET in New York City. *The Medium Is the Medium,* his first work broadcast by WGBH, was a video collage that raised questions about who is in control of the viewing experience. At one point in a voice-over, Paik instructed the viewers to follow his directions, to close or open their eyes, and finally to turn off the set. At WGBH Paik and electronics engineer Shuya Abe built the first model of Paik's video synthesizer, which produced nonrepresentational images. Paik used the synthesizer to accompany a rock-and-roll sound track in *Video Commune* and to illustrate Beethoven's Fourth Piano Concerto. At

WNET Paik completed a series of short segments, *The Selling of New York,* which juxtaposed the marketing of New York and the reality of life in the city. *Global Groove,* produced with John Godfrey, opened with an explanation that it was a "glimpse of a video landscape of tomorrow when you will be able to switch to any TV station on the earth and TV guides will be as fat as the Manhattan telephone book." What followed was a rapid shift from rock-and-roll dance sequences to Allen Ginsberg, to Charlotte Moorman with the TV cello, to an oriental dancer, to John Cage, to a Navaho drummer, to a Living Theatre performance. Throughout, the video image was manipulated by layering images, reducing dancers to a white line outlining their form against a wash of brilliant color, creating evolving abstract forms. Rapid edits of words and movements, and seemingly random shifts in the backgrounds against which the dancers performed, created a dreamlike sense of time and space.

Paik continues to innovate. In 2000 the Guggenheim Museum in New York mounted an important retrospective of his work, entitled "The Worlds of Nam June Paik." In addition to displaying notable pieces from other decades in Paik's career and numerous videos of his collaborations with other artists, the exhibit featured two new installations: 3-D laser light sculptures (described as "postvideo" art on the exhibition's website) surrounded by 100 upturned television monitors showing a variety of images and emitting musical excerpts, as well as by video projections on the walls of the museum.

Nam June Paik pioneered the development of electronic techniques to transform the video image from a literal representation of objects and events into an expression of the artist's view of those objects and events. In doing so, he challenges our accepted notion of the reality of televised events. His work questions time and memory, the nature of music and art, even the essence of our sensory experiences. Most significantly, perhaps, that work questions our experience, our understanding, and our definitions of "television."

LUCY A. LIGGETT

See also **Experimental Video**

Nam June Paik. Born in Seoul, Korea, July 20, 1932. Educated at the University of Tokyo, 1952–56; studied music with Stockhausen at Darmstadt; studied art history and philosophy in Germany, 1956–58. Worked as video artist in electronic music studio for Radio Cologne, 1958–61; associated with the Fluxus group, New York, 1960s; artist-in-residence, WGBH-TV, 1969; artist-in-residence, WNET-TV, New York, 1971; has worked closely with Japanese artist Shigeko Kubota and other collaborators.

Television Projects (selected)
1970	*Video Commune*
1972	*The Selling of New York*
1974	*Tribute to John Cage*

Publications

"Expanded Education for the Paperless Society," *Interfunktionen* (1971), reprinted in *Flash Art* (May/June 1972)

An Anthology of Nam June Paik (exhibition catalog), 1984

Further Reading

Atkins, Robert, "Two Years On," *Horizon* (April 1987)

Baker, Kenneth, "Currents," *Art News* (February 1985)

Carr, C., "Beam Me Up, Nam June," *The Village Voice* (October 14, 1986)

Denison, D.C., "Video Art's Guru," *New York Times* (April 25, 1982)

Gardner, Paul, "Tuning in to Nam June Paik: After Twenty Years of Tinkering with TV Sets, Paik Is at His Peak," *ARTnews* (May 1982)

Hanhardt, John G., *The Worlds of Nam June Paik,* New York: Guggenheim Museum, 2000

Hanhardt, John G, editor, *Nam June Paik,* New York: Norton, 1982

Hoberman, J., "Paik's Peak," *Village Voice* (May 25, 1982)

Hughes, Robert, "Electronic Finger Painting: A Flickering Retrospective for Nam June Paik at the Whitney," *Time* (May 17, 1982)

Nam June Paik: Mostly Video (exhibition catalog), Tokyo: n.p., 1984

Robinson, Walter, "Nam June Paik at Holly Solomon," *Art in America* (June 1987)

Serwer, Jacquelyn D., "Nam June Paik: Technology," *American Art* (Spring 1994)

Silver, Kenneth E., "Nam June Paik: Video's Body," *Art in America* (November 1993)

Sloane, Patricia, "Patricia Sloane Discusses the Work of Nam June Paik," *Art and Artists* (March 1972)

Smith, Roberta, "Out of the Wasteland: An Avant-Gardist's Obsession with Television," *Newsweek* (October 13, 1986)

Solomon, Holly, "Nam June Paik," *ARTnews* (December 1986)

Spotnitz, Frank, "The Future Belongs to Video," *American Film* (January/February 1989)

Stoos, Toni, and Thomas Kellein, editors, *Nam June Paik: Video Time, Video Space,* New York: Abrams, 1993

Tomkins, Calvin, "Profiles: Video Visionary," *The New Yorker* (May 5, 1975)

Paley, William S. (1901–1990)

U.S. Media Executive

William S. Paley developed the CBS radio and television networks and ran them for more than a half century. "A 20th-century visionary with the ambitions of a 19th-century robber baron," as the *New York Times* described him, Paley took over a tiny failing network with only 16 affiliate stations and developed it into a world-class communications empire. Delegating management details to others, he had a seemingly unfailing sense of popular taste and a resultant flair for programming.

Radio's commercial potential came to fascinate Paley early on. Using funds from his father's cigar company shares, Paley purchased working control of the struggling CBS network in September 1928. He was just turning 27. A year later, family purchase of additional shares gave him majority control.

Paley's insights helped to define commercial network operations. At the start of his CBS stewardship, he transformed the network's financial relationship with its affiliates so that the latter agreed to carry sustaining programs free, receiving network payments only for commercially supported programs. Paley enjoyed socializing and negotiating with broadcast stars. In the late 1940s, his "talent raids" hired top radio stars (chiefly away from NBC) by offering huge prices for rights to their programs and giving them, in return, lucrative capital gains tax options. The talent pool thus developed helped to boost CBS radio ratings just as network television was beginning. At the same time, he encouraged development of CBS News before and during World War II, as it developed a stable of journalistic stars soon headed by Edward R. Murrow.

During World War II he served as deputy chief of the psychological warfare branch of General Dwight Eisenhower's staff. Paley became chair of the CBS board in 1946, turning the network's presidency over to Frank Stanton, who held the post until his own retirement in 1973. The television network first showed a profit in 1953, and from 1955 through 1976, CBS television consistently led in prime-time network ratings. Network profits helped expand CBS into many other lines of entertainment and education—including the Broadway musical *My Fair Lady* in 1956—as Paley acquired other businesses.

There were technical opportunities as well. CBS Laboratories' Peter C. Goldmark developed a mechanical system of color television that was briefly (1950–53) the nation's first standard, before being pushed aside by a superior all-electronic RCA system. By then, CBS had traded a quarter of its stock to buy Hytron, a TV receiver manufacturer later sold for a huge loss. More successfully, Goldmark also pioneered the long-playing (LP) record, introduced in 1948, which revolutionized the recording industry and made CBS Records (sold in 1987 to Sony for $2 billion) the leading record company in the United States for both classical and popular records.

As he stayed beyond CBS's compulsory (for others) retirement age of 65, Paley sought to delay his inevitable passing of control to others. Paley worked through several short-lived potential heirs in the late 1970s; he stepped down as chief executive officer in 1977 but retained the powerful chairmanship. Finally he hired Pillsbury's Thomas H. Wyman to become president in 1980. Wyman succeeded Paley as the network's second chair in 1983. Concerned with some of Wyman's decisions in the aftermath of an unsuccessful attempt by Ted Turner to acquire CBS in 1985, Paley allied himself with Laurence Tisch (who was by then holding the largest single block of company shares) to oust Wyman and install Tisch as chief executive officer in 1986. Paley returned as a figurehead chair until his death in late 1990.

Paley is important for having assembled the brilliant team that built and expanded the CBS "Tiffany Network" image over several decades. For many years he had an innate programming touch, which helped keep the network on top in annual ratings wars. He blew hot and cold on network news, helping to found and develop it, but willing to cast much of that work aside to avoid controversy or to increase profits. Like many founders, however, he stayed too long and unwittingly helped weaken his company.

Paley was very active in New York art and social circles throughout his life. He was a key figure in the Museum of Modern Art from its founding in 1929. He prompted construction of the Eero Saarinen–designed "Black Rock" headquarters into which the network moved in 1965. His was the primary donation that helped to create in 1976 what is now the Museum of

William S. Paley, Founder of CBS, photo dated 04/15/50.
Courtesy of the Everett Collection/CSU Archives

Television and Radio in New York City. The middle "S" in his name stood for nothing—Paley added it in his early business years. He had no formal middle name.

CHRISTOPHER H. STERLING

See also **Columbia Broadcasting System; Murrow, Edward R.; Stanton, Frank**

William S. Paley. Born in Chicago, Illinois, September 28, 1901. Graduated from Western Military Academy, Alton, Illinois, 1918; studied at the University of Chicago, 1918–19; University of Pennsylvania, B.S. 1922. Married: 1) Dorothy Hart Hearst, 1932 (divorced, 1947); one son and one daughter; 2) Barbara Cushing Mortimer, 1948 (died, 1978); one son, one daughter, one stepson, and one stepdaughter. Served as colonel, U.S. Army, World War II; deputy chief, psychological warfare division, Supreme Headquarters, Allied Powers (Europe); deputy chief, information control division, USGCC. Vice president, Congress Cigar Company, Philadelphia, 1922–28; president, CBS, Inc., New York City, 1928–46, chair of the board,

1946–83, founder and chair, 1983–86, acting chair, 1986–87, chair and director, 1987–90; partner, Whitcom Investment Company, 1982–90; founder, and member of board of directors, Genetics Institute, 1980–90; Thinking Machines Corp., 1983–90; cochair, *International Herald Tribune,* 1983–90; president and director, William S. Paley Foundation, Greenpark Foundation, Inc. Trustee: Museum of Modern Art, 1937–90, president, 1968–72, chair, 1972–85, chair emeritus, 1985–90, life trustee; trustee, Columbia University, 1950–73, trustee emeritus, 1973–90; North Shore University Hospital, 1949–57, cochair, board of trustees, 1954–73; life trustee, Federation Jewish Philanthropies of New York. Member: board of directors, W. Averill Harriman Institute for Advanced Study of Soviet Union, Columbia University; Commission for White House Conference on Education, 1954–56; chair, President's Materials for Policy Commission, which produced "Resources for Freedom," 1951–52; executive committee, Resources for the Future, 1952–69, chair, 1966–69, honorary member, board of directors, 1969–90; chair, New York City Task Force on Urban Design, which prepared "The Threatened City" report, 1967; Urban Design Council City, New York, 1968–71; founding member, Bedford-Stuyvesant D and S Corp., director, 1967–72; Commission on Critical Choices for America, 1973–77, Commission for Cultural Affairs, New York City, 1975–78; founder and chair of the board, Museum of Broadcasting, from 1976; Council on Foreign Relations; Academy of Political Sciences; National Institute for Social Sciences; Royal Society of the Arts (fellow). Honorary degrees: LL.D.: Adelphi University, 1957, Bates College, 1963, University of Pennsylvania, 1968, Columbia University, 1975, Brown University, 1975, Pratt Institute, 1977, Dartmouth College, 1979; L.H.D.: Ithaca College, 1978, University of Southern California, 1985, Rutgers University, 1986; Long Island University, Southampton, 1987. Military honors: Decorated Legion of Merit; Medal for Merit; officer, Legion of Honor, France; Croix de Guerre with Palm, France; commander, Order of Merit, Italy; associate commander, Order of St. John of Jerusalem. Recipient: Gold Achievement Medal, Poor Richard Club; Keynote Award, National Association of Broadcasters; George Foster Peabody Awards, 1958 and 1961; Broadcast Pioneers, special award; Concert Artists Guild Award, 1965; Skowhegan Gertrude Vanderbilt Whitney Award; National Planning Association, Gold Medal; David Sarnoff Award, University of Arizona, 1979; Society of Family of Man Gold Medallion, 1982; Joseph Wharton Award, Wharton School Club, New York, 1983; *TV Guide* Life Achievement Award, 1984; Center for Communications Award, 1985; co-recipient, Walter

Cronkite Award, Arizona State University, 1984; City of New York Medallion of Honor; First Amendment Freedoms Award, Anti-Defamation League, B'nai B'rith; Robert Eunson Distinguished Service Award, Association of Press Broadcasters; named to Junior Achievement National Business Hall of Fame, 1984. Died in New York City, October 26, 1990.

Publication

As It Happened: A Memoir, 1979

Further Reading

Halberstam, David, *The Powers That Be,* New York: Knopf, 1979

Metz, Robert, *CBS: Reflections in a Bloodshot Eye,* Chicago: Playboy Press, 1975

Paper, Lewis J., *Empire: William S. Paley and the Making of CBS,* New York: St. Martin's Press, 1987

Slater, Robert, *This…Is CBS: A Chronicle of 60 Years,* Englewood Cliffs, New Jersey: Prentice-Hall, 1988

Smith, Sally Bedell, *In All His Glory: The Life of William S. Paley, the Legendary Tycoon and His Brilliant Circle,* New York: Simon and Schuster, 1990

Palin, Michael (1943–)

British Comedian, Actor

Michael Palin is best known for his performances as a member of the six-man British comedy troupe Monty Python. Although it is surely the case that some of Palin's most memorable work was with Monty Python, both in the group's TV series, *Monty Python's Flying Circus,* and in its films and live performances, the versatile comedian-actor also has done much notable television work on his own, including *Ripping Yarns* and *Around the World in 80 Days.*

Palin's comedy career began at Oxford University, where he wrote and performed comedic revues with classmate and future Python Terry Jones. After graduating with a history degree in 1965, Palin moved to London, where his first TV job was as host of *Now!,* a teenage pop music show broadcast by the now-defunct Television West Wales. In his spare time, he continued to write with Jones, who was working for the BBC. The team wrote scripts for *The Ken Dodd Show, The Billy Cotton Bandshow,* and other BBC shows.

Palin and Jones first worked with fellow Pythons Graham Chapman, John Cleese, and Eric Idle in 1966, writing for *The Frost Report.* Palin also worked with various future Pythons on *Do Not Adjust Your Set* (1968–69) and *The Complete and Utter History of Britain* (1969), a Jones and Palin production.

In 1969 Palin, Jones, Chapman, Cleese, Idle, and Terry Gilliam (the group's lone American) created *Monty Python's Flying Circus,* after rejecting other possible titles such as "Owl Stretching Time," "Vaseline Parade," and "Bunn, Wackett, Buzzard, Stubble, and Boot." The show ran on the BBC for 45 episodes,

from 1969 to 1974, and took on a life of its own, spawning five films, a series of stage shows, and numerous books, records, and videos.

Some of Palin's most memorable performances on *Monty Python's Flying Circus* include a man who believes he is qualified to be a lion tamer because he already has the hat; Arthur Pewtie, who suspects his wife is being unfaithful and goes for marriage counseling, only to watch the counselor make love to his wife; a lumberjack who, in his spare time, "puts on women's clothing and hangs around in bars" (and sings about it, backed by a chorus of Mounties); a cheese-shop owner whose shop is "completely uncontaminated by cheese."

With a kindly face and gentle demeanor, Palin is frequently cast as a sweet, unassuming man (such as the cheated-upon Arthur Pewtie, or the stuttering animal-lover Ken in the film *A Fish Called Wanda*). But he is equally good in more outrageous characters (like the transvestite lumberjack, or, in another *Python* sketch, a high court judge who removes his robe, revealing that he's wearing only ladies' underwear beneath).

After the TV series *Monty Python's Flying Circus* ended, Palin continued to perform with the group in films, stage shows, and a series of Secret Policeman's Balls, benefit concerts for Amnesty International that featured several comedians and musicians. Palin also hosted four episodes of NBC's *Saturday Night Live* from 1978 to 1984.

In 1976 the BBC began airing one of Palin's most memorable efforts, *Ripping Yarns.* Conceived, written,

Pole To Pole, Michael Palin, 1992.
Courtesy of the Everett Collection

and performed with Jones, *Ripping Yarns* consisted of two series, one of six shows and one of three shows. Each show had its own plot, and the plots were not interrelated; the stories were based on English tales of the early 20th century.

For the next several years, Palin appeared mostly in films. He returned to television in 1989's *Around the World in 80 Days,* a six-hour documentary of his attempt to re-create Phileas Fogg's fictional journey, retracing Fogg's route using only transportation that would have been available in Fogg's day. Followed by a five-man BBC crew, Palin traveled on trains, hot-air balloons, dogsleds, and garbage barges through Greece, Africa, India, Asia, the United States, and back to England.

Palin has since starred in a number of similar travelogues. In *Pole to Pole* (1993), he and a BBC crew traveled from the North Pole to the South Pole, through Finland, Russia, and Africa. *Full Circle with Michael Palin* (1997) took Palin around the Pacific rim, whereas *Michael Palin's Hemingway Adventure*

(1999) recorded his encounters in the places Ernest Hemingway described in his writings, from Spain to Africa to Cuba. Palin also appeared in a variety of roles in a 2001 series written and hosted by fellow Python Cleese, *The Human Face,* an entertaining exploration of beauty and human expression.

JULIE PRINCE

See also **Cleese, John;** *Monty Python's Flying Circus*

Michael (Edward) Palin. Born in Sheffield, Yorkshire, England, May 5, 1943. Educated at Birkdale School, Sheffield; Brasenose College, Oxford, B.A. in modern history. Married: Helen M. Gibbins, 1966; children: Rachel, Thomas, and William. Performed in plays and revues while at Oxford and formed writing partnership with Terry Jones; subsequently wrote for such television shows as *The Frost Report;* became member of the Monty Python comedy team, 1969; later wrote and starred in television series *Ripping Yarns;* host of acclaimed travel documentaries; director, Meridian Television. President, Transport 2000. Recipient: British Academy of Film and Television Arts Award for Best Supporting Actor, 1988; Travel Writer of the Year Award, British Book Awards, 1993.

Television Series

1966–67	*The Frost Report* (writer only)
1966–67	*The Late Show* (writer only)
1967	*A Series of Bird's* (writer only)
1967	*Twice a Fortnight*
1968–69	*Do Not Adjust Your Set*
1969	*The Complete and Utter History of Britain*
1969–74	*Monty Python's Flying Circus* (also co-writer)
1975	*Three Men in a Boat*
1976–80	*Ripping Yarns* (also writer)
1983	*Secrets*
1989	*Around the World in 80 Days*
1991	*GBH* (performer only)
1992	*Palin's Column*
1993	*Pole to Pole*
1993	*Tracey Ullman: A Class Act*
1997	*Full Circle with Michael Palin*
1999	*Michael Palin's Hemingway Adventure*
2001	*The Human Face* (performer only)

Television Specials

1980	*Great Railway Journeys of the World*
1986	*East of Ipswich* (writer)
1987	*Number 27* (writer)

1995   *Three Men in a Boat* (actor)
1995   *Wind in the Willows* (voice)

Films

And Now for Something Completely Different (also co-writer), 1970; *Monty Python and the Holy Grail* (also co-writer), 1975; *Jabberwocky*, 1976; *Pleasure at Her Majesty's* (U.S. title, *Monty Python Meets beyond the Fringe*), 1976; *Monty Python's Life of Brian* (also co-writer), 1979; *The Secret Policeman's Ball*, 1979; *Time Bandits* (also co-writer), 1980; *The Secret Policeman's Other Ball*, 1982; *Confessions of a Trainspotter*, 1981; *The Missionary* (also co-writer and coproducer), 1982; *Monty Python Live at the Hollywood Bowl*, 1982; *Monty Python's The Meaning of Life* (also co-writer), 1983; *A Private Function*, 1984; *The Secret Policeman's Private Parts*, 1984; *Brazil*, 1985; *The Dress*, 1986; *Troubles*, 1987; *A Fish Called Wanda*, 1988; *American Friends* (also co-writer), 1991; *The Secret Policeman's Biggest Ball*, 1991; *Splitting Heirs*, 1993; *Fierce Creatures*, 1997.

Stage

Hang Down Your Head and Die; Aladdin; Monty Python's First Farewell Tour; Monty Python Live at Drury Lane; Monty Python Live at City Center; The Secret Policeman's Ball; The Weekend, 1994.

Publications (selected)

Monty Python's Big Red Book, with others, 1970
Monty Python's Brand New Book, with others, 1973
Ripping Yarns, 1978
More Ripping Yarns, 1980
Small Harry and the Toothache Pills, 1982
The Missionary, 1983
Dr. Fegg's Encyclopedia of All World Knowledge, 1984
Limericks, 1985
Cyril and the Dinner Party, 1986
Cyril and the House of Commons, 1986
The Mirrorstone, 1986
Around the World in 80 Days, 1989
Pole to Pole, 1992
Pole to Pole: The Photographs, 1994
The Weekend, 1994
Hemingway's Chair (novel), 1995
Full Circle, 1997

Further Reading

Hewison, Robert, *Monty Python: The Case against Irreverence, Scurrility, Profanity, Vilification, and Licentious Abuse,* New York: Grove, 1981
Johnson, Kim, *The First 20 Years of Monty Python,* New York: St. Martin's Press, 1989
Johnson, Kim, *Life (before and) after Monty Python: The Solo Flights of the Flying Circus,* New York: St. Martin's Press, 1993
McCall, Douglas L., *Monty Python: A Chronological Listing of the Troupe's Creative Output, and Articles and Reviews about Them,* Jefferson, North Carolina: McFarland, 1991

Palmer, Geoffrey (1927–)

British Actor

Geoffrey Palmer is one of British television's most reliable supporting actors, appearing in several of the most popular situation comedies of the last 20 years or so, and on occasion taking the lead role himself.

With his bloodhound features and lugubrious voice and manner, Palmer is instantly familiar in whatever role he plays. Not only is his face at once recognizable from the situation comedies in which he has appeared, but his voice is doubly well known from his frequent employment as a voice-over artist for television commercials (notably for Audi cars). After serving his apprenticeship as an actor in the theater, Palmer emerged as an accomplished performer in television situation comedy through his casting as the absentminded eccentric Jimmy, brother-in-law to Leonard Rossiter's Perrin in *The Rise and Fall of Reginald Perrin.* Forever apologizing for turning up at the Perrin household in search of a meal after yet another "cock-up on the catering front," Palmer's Jimmy was manifestly appealing, although divorced from reality and patheti-

As Time Goes By, Geoffrey Palmer and Judi Dench,
1992–2002.
Courtesy of the Everett Collection

cally woebegone. These qualities were clearly ideal for situation comedy, and soon after the end of the Perrin series, Palmer was back on the screen on a regular basis playing Wendy Craig's other half in Carla Lane's hit series *Butterflies.* As manic-depressive dentist Ben Parkinson, Palmer provided extremely sturdy support to Craig herself, alternately bewildered at his wife's outbursts and endearingly patient and clumsy in his efforts to understand her frustrations—although he could also be stubborn, tactless, and impervious to suggestion when he chose.

Palmer returned to the dottiness of Jimmy in the Perrin series when he went on to play the comically unhinged Major Harry Kitchener Wellington Truscott, the central character in *Fairly Secret Army.* Convinced that the country was on the brink of chaos due to the machinations of the political left, Truscott was committed to forming his own army to counter the revolution that he feared was just around the corner. Thanks

largely to Palmer's performance as Truscott, this seemingly unpromising scenario fared reasonably well, with the dotty major proving surprisingly lovable in his futile attempts to muster a competent force, despite his reactionary views and rabidly bigoted attitude toward those of differing political opinions.

His subsequent series, *Executive Stress* and *As Time Goes By,* both saw Palmer back in more familiar sitcom territory, playing belligerently adorable partners in support of strong female stars—in the first instance, Penelope Keith (in the role of her husband, Donald Fairchild) and in the latter case, Judi Dench (in the role of her old flame, Lionel Hardcastle). *Executive Stress* proved a mixed success, although Palmer gave good value as always, but *As Time Goes By* settled in well as the plot traced the reunion of the two erstwhile lovers. Palmer played a returned colonial planning to write his memoirs, to be typed up by Dench's secretarial agency. This led to the gradual rebirth of their romance, culminating in their marriage in the 1995 series.

Palmer has occasionally ventured out of the sitcom territory with which he is usually associated. Notable examples of experiments in other fields of comedy have included guest appearances in such acclaimed shows as *Fawlty Towers* and *Blackadder Goes Forth,* in which he played Field Marshall Haig.

DAVID PICKERING

*See also **Fall and Rise of Reginald Perrin, The***

Geoffrey Palmer. Born in London, June 4, 1927. Attended Highgate School, London. Married: Sally Green, 1963; children: Charles and Harriet. Began career as unpaid trainee assistant stage manager, Q Theatre, London; subsequently became popular star of situation comedies; has also appeared on stage, in films, and on the radio.

Television Series

1976–79	*The Fall and Rise of Reginald Perrin*
1978–82	*Butterflies*
1984–86	*Fairly Secret Army*
1986	*Executive Stress*
1986–88	*Hot Metal*
1992–	*As Time Goes By*

Made-for-Television Movie

1991	*A Question of Attribution*

Films

O Lucky Man!, 1973; *The Riddle of the Sands,* 1978; *The Outsider,* 1979; *The Honorary Consul,* 1983; *A Zed and Two Noughts,* 1985; *Clockwise,* 1985; *A*

Fish Called Wanda, 1988; *Christabel,* 1989; *The Madness of King George,* 1994; *Mrs. Brown,* 1997; *Tomorrow Never Dies,* 1998; *Anna and the King,* 1999; *Rat,* 2001.

Stage (selected)

Difference of Opinion; West of Sussex, 1971; *Private Lives,* 1973; *Eden End,* 1974; *Saint Joan,* 1977; *Tishoo,* 1979; *Kafka's Dick,* 1986; *Piano,* 1990.

Panorama

British Public-Affairs Program

The longest-running current affairs program anywhere in the world, *Panorama* has long been among the most influential of all British political commentaries. The first program was broadcast in 1953, but the format was quite different then, with a magazine-style approach. The original presenter was newspaper journalist Patrick Murphy, although he was soon replaced by Max Robertson. Alongside them were roving interviewer Malcolm Muggeridge, art critic Denis Mathews, book reviewer Nancy Spain, and theater critic Lionel Hale, who all made their varied contributions to the fortnightly program.

Everything changed in 1955, when the program was relaunched under the slogan "window on the world." With the new look came a new anchorman, Richard Dimbleby, who over the next few years did much to establish *Panorama*'s reputation for determined investigation into important political and social matters on behalf of the viewing public. Politicians were suddenly obliged to take the program seriously, and senior members of the government soon learned that their standing in the polls could very easily depend on their performance on this show, the BBC's current affairs flagship.

In 1961 *Panorama* achieved a notable first when Prince Philip agreed to be interviewed by Dimbleby, thus becoming the first member of the royal family to make such a television appearance. Dimbleby was impeccably courteous but nonetheless extracted from the royal guest the sort of things the viewing public wanted to hear.

The show has had its lighter moments, however. Perhaps the most memorable of these was the April Fool hoax perpetrated by Richard Dimbleby when he delivered a straight-faced report on the state of the Swiss spaghetti harvest, delivered while walking between trees festooned with strings of spaghetti. Many viewers were taken in and rang the program to ask how they may obtain their own spaghetti plants; the producer suggested that planting a tin of spaghetti in tomato sauce might do the trick.

The late 1950s and early 1960s are sometimes looked upon as the "golden era" for the program, but this view belittles *Panorama*'s continuing achievement, which has kept it at the forefront of investigative programs despite the burgeoning of often very competent rival programs on other networks. It remains the case that the headlines on the morning after the program often reflect what has been discussed on *Panorama* the night before, and prominent politicians freely admit that appearances on the program have played a key role in furthering or hindering their careers and even in deciding the results of both local and national elections over the years. In view of the influence wielded by the program, any political bias that has been perceived in its editorial approach has led to furious rows in Parliament, and to repeated affirmations by the BBC that this, perhaps still their best-known current affairs program, will remain resolutely nonaffiliated.

Among the most notable of Richard Dimbleby's successors in the chair of *Panorama* have been his son David Dimbleby; Robin Day, who set a new standard in the hostile interviewing of such reluctant political guests as Alastair Burnet; Charles Wheeler; and Robert Kee.

The removal of the program to a Sunday-night slot in the 1990s was opposed by many who feared for the show's future, but it remains a significant feature in the schedule.

DAVID PICKERING

See also **Dimbleby, Richard; Royalty and Royals on Television**

Presenters (selected)
Patrick Murphy
Max Robinson

Richard Dimbleby
Nancy Spain
Denis Matthews
Lionel Hale
Christopher Chataway
John Freeman
Michael Barratt
Michael Charlton
Trevor Philpott

Leonard Parkin
Robin Day
David Dimbleby
Robert Kee
Charles Wheeler

Programming History
BBC1
1953–

Park, Nick (1958–)

British Animator, Animation Director

The name of Nick Park is synonymous with that of Aardman Animations, the Bristol-based company founded in the early 1970s by Peter Lord and David Sproxton that has been responsible for a highly successful series of 3-D stop-frame animation shorts made for British television. The most celebrated of these shorts have been the three films featuring the adventures of Wallace, a nondescript northerner with a flair for ramshackle invention, and his perspicacious but put-upon dog, Gromit. The first, *A Grand Day Out,* started out as Park's graduation project at the National Film and Television School (NFTS), where he studied animation from 1980 to 1983, and was finally completed in 1989. *The Wrong Trousers* was screened on BBC 2 at Christmas 1993: the highest-rated program over the two-day holiday period, it went on to become one of BBC Worldwide's most valuable properties both for video sales and merchandising. It also brought Park his second Academy Award for Best Animated Short, the first having been picked up for another Aardman film, *Creature Comforts,* in 1991. The third in the Wallace and Gromit trilogy, *A Close Shave,* also won an Oscar in 1996.

Park's work with Aardman Animations is a popular manifestation of the wider, if less frequently reported, success enjoyed by British animation since the 1980s, much of which has been nurtured by Channel 4 and its commissioning editor for animation. Aardman's highly successful work on commercials—particularly the captivating "Heat Electric" campaign, a stylistic and thematic development of *Creature Comforts*—has also allowed the company to spread its wings, a reminder of the importance of this area of television production as a source of funding and creative experiment in a country bereft of a subsidized film industry.

Park began making puppet animations in his parents' attic at the age of 13, using the family's Bell and Howell 8 mm camera. He was persuaded to show his work at school, and in 1975 his entry in the European Young Filmmaker of the Year Competition, *Archie's Concrete Nightmare,* was shown on BBC Television. He completed a B.A. in Communication Arts at the Sheffield Arts School before going on to study animation at the NFTS. His work shows the signs of his early fascination with science fiction and monster films and the special effects of Ray Harryhausen, as well as his later admiration for the imaginative animated puppetry of Ladislaw Starewicz, Jiri Trnka, and Jan Svankmajer. However, it is the influence of a childhood filled with Heath Robinson inventions (his parents once fashioned a caravan from a box and set of wheels, fitting it out with makeshift furniture and decoration) that seems to permeate the world of Wallace and Gromit, a world of handmade objects, idiosyncratic domestic details, and, above all, enterprising mechanical contraptions.

Park's stop-frame animation of plasticine models has developed into a distinctive and highly sophisticated technique and is often perceived as the Aardman house style, although the company has used a number of other processes—in the Peter Gabriel "Sledgehammer" pop promo, for example, on which Park collaborated with several independent animators, including the Brothers Quay. The method grew out of Aardman's work in the 1970s on sequences for BBC Children's Television featuring Morph, a plasticine character capable of metamorphosing into a multitude of shapes. Park's first job with the company was on the Morph production line. By this time, Aardman had also made two series, *Animated Conversations* for the BBC and *Lip Synch* for Channel 4, in which plasticine characters were animated to a sound track built from "fly-on-the-wall" recordings of real conversations and interviews. This became the basis of Park's award-winning *Creature Comforts,* in which a range of vox-pop interviews about people's living conditions provide the speech for animals commenting on their life behind bars in a zoo. It was here that the subtle psychological and sociological characterization and carefully observed facial and gestural expressiveness that are the features of Wallace and Gromit were developed. For all their farcical playfulness, these narratives are shot through with stinging moments of poignancy, as the animated figures momentarily betray the pain, longing, and regret behind a life of repressed British ordinariness.

Although particularly televisual in its domestic intimacy and attention to psychological detail, Park's work has also brought a sophisticated level of film literacy into the process of animation. With their larger budgets, *The Wrong Trousers* and *A Close Shave* are not only technically more accomplished than *A Grand Day Out* but also are more cinematic in their use of lighting, framing, and camera movement. Both later pieces are also full of film allusion and pastiche, with references to a number of popular genres and stock sequences, as well as specific British and American movies. It was no surprise, therefore, when Park and his collaborators were offered the opportunity to try their hand at feature filmmaking. The result was the farmyard comedy *Chicken Run,* released in 2000 and based on a long-held idea of Park's himself: *The Great Escape,* enacted with chickens.

JEREMY RIDGMAN

Nick Park. Born in Preston, Lancashire, England, 1958. Educated at the Sheffield Polytechnic, Faculty of Art and Design, B.A. 1980; National Film and Television School, Beaconsfield, 1980–83. Animator since the age of 13; has worked at Aardman Animation, Bristol, since 1985; projects include Peter Gabriel's "Sledgehammer" video, 1986; numerous commercials for Access credit cards and Duracell batteries; creator of claymation stars Wallace and Gromit. Recipient: three Academy Awards, three BAFTA Awards. Commander of the Order of the British Empire, 1997.

Made-for-Television Movies (selected)

1989   *War Story* (animator)
1989   *A Grand Day Out* (animator/director)
1989   *Creature Comforts* (animator/director)
1993   *The Wrong Trousers* (animator/director)
1996   *A Close Shave* (animator/director)
1996   *Wallace and Gromit: The Best of Aardman Animation* (animator/director)

Film
Chicken Run, 2000.

Further Reading

Adair, Gilbert, "That's My Toon," *Sunday Times* (June 19, 1994)
Macdonald, Kevin, "A Lot Can Happen in a Second" (interview), in *Projections 5,* edited by John Boorman and Walter Donohue, London: Faber, 1996
Thompson, Ben, "Real Lives" (interview), *Independent on Sunday* (March 10, 1992)

Parker, Everett C. (1913–)

U.S. Media Activist

Everett C. Parker played a leading role in the development of public interest of American television. He served as director of the Office of Communication of the United Church of Christ from 1954 until 1983. In that position, he was at the forefront of Protestant communications, overseeing the public media activities of one of the leading mainline Protestant religious groups. He is better known, however, for two other contributions: his leadership in the development of an influential media reform and citizen action movement in broadcasting; and his activism directed at improved broadcast employment prospects for women and minorities. Near the end of his career, he was named one of the most influential men in broadcasting by the trade publication *Broadcasting Magazine.*

Parker had an early career in radio production. After a year at NBC in New York, he founded and became head of an interdenominational Protestant Church broadcasting organization, the Joint Religious Radio Committee (JRRC). The JRRC was formed to serve as a counterbalance to the dominance of the Federal Council of Churches in public-service religious broadcasting. Besides its impact on programming, the JRRC also addressed the impact of media on society and public-interest issues in broadcasting. The JRRC was an early vocal supporter of reserved FM frequency assignments for educational use, for example.

While a lecturer in communication at Yale Divinity School, from 1949 until 1954, he headed the Communication Research Project, the first major study of religious broadcasting. This project resulted in the definitive work on religious broadcasting for nearly two decades, *The Television-Radio Audience and Religion,* coauthored by Parker, David Barry, and Dallas Smythe.

In 1954 he founded the Office of Communication of the United Church of Christ, the first such agency to combine press, broadcasting, film, research, and educational functions in one unit. The office pioneered programs to improve the communication skills of ministers, to improve the communication activities of local churches, and to use television for education. It also participated in the production of some landmark television programs, including *Six American Families,* a nationally syndicated documentary series produced in collaboration with Westinghouse Broadcasting Company and the United Methodist Church.

The work of Parker and the office took an important turn in the 1960s, as the civil rights movement was gaining momentum. After reviewing the civil rights performance of television stations in the South, the office identified WLBT-TV in Jackson, Mississippi, as a frequent target of public complaints and Federal Communication Commission (FCC) reprimands regarding its public service. In 1963 the office filed a "petition to deny renewal" with the FCC, initiating a process that had far-reaching consequences in U.S. broadcasting. The FCC's initial response to the petition was to rule that neither the United Church of Christ (UCC) nor local citizens had legal standing to participate in its renewal proceedings. The UCC appealed, and in 1966 Federal Appeals Court Judge Warren Burger granted such standing to the UCC and to citizens in general. After a hearing, the FCC renewed WLBT's license, resulting in another appeal by the UCC. Burger declared the FCC's record "beyond repair" and revoked WLBT's license in 1969.

Based on this new right to participate in license proceedings, Parker's office began to work with other reform and citizens' groups to monitor broadcast performance on a number of issues, including employment discrimination and fairness. In 1967 the office's petition to the FCC dealing with employment issues led to the commission's adoption of Equal Employment Opportunity (EEO) rules for broadcasting. In 1968 it participated as a "friend of the court" in the landmark *Red Lion* case, which confirmed and expanded the Fairness Doctrine.

Parker and the office continued to play a central role in the developing media reform movement throughout the 1970s and 1980s, in cooperation with organizations such as Citizens' Communication Center, the Media Access Project, the National Citizens' Committee for Broadcasting, Ralph Nader's Public Citizen organization, and a variety of other religious and civic groups. The attention of this movement broadened in subsequent years to include cable television and telecommunications and telephone policy. These organizations became active in the developing change in regulation and eventual breakup of AT&T during the period from 1978 to 1984.

In his later years, Parker devoted more attention to issues of employment in broadcasting and the communication industries. In 1974 he established Telecommunications Career Recruitment, a program for the recruitment and training of minority broadcasters, with the cooperation and support of the Westinghouse Broadcasting and Capital Cities Broadcasting companies.

Upon his retirement in 1983, *Broadcasting Magazine* somewhat grudgingly hailed him as "the founder of the citizen movement in broadcasting" who spent "some two decades irritating and worrying the broadcast establishment." He went on to found the Donald McGannon Communication Research Center at Fordham University, where he teaches graduate courses in Communication Policies and Practices, Critical Issues in Electronic Communication, and Public-Service Communication.

STEWART M. HOOVER AND GEORGE C. CONKLIN

See also **Religion and Television**

Everett C(arlton) Parker. Born in Chicago, Illinois, January 17, 1913. Educated at University of Chicago, A.B. 1935; Chicago Theological Seminary, B.D. magna cum laude 1943, Blatchford Fellow, 1944–45, D.D. 1964; Catawba College, Salisbury, North Carolina, D.D. 1958. Married: Geneva M. Jones, 1939; children: Ruth A., Eunice L., and Truman E. Began career as assistant public-service and war program manager, NBC, 1943–45; lecturer in communication, Yale Divinity School, 1945–57; founder and director, Protestant Radio Communications, 1945–50; founder and director, Office of Communication, United Churches of Christ, 1954–1983; editor-at-large, *Channels of Communication Magazine,* 1983–84; professor, Fordham University, from 1983; founder, Foundation for Minority Interests in Media, 1985. Honorary degrees: L.H.D., Fordham University, 1978; L.H.D., Tougaloo College, 1978. Recipient: Alfred I. Dupont-Columbia University Award; Human Relations Award, American Jewish Committee, 1966; Faith and Freedom Award, Religious Heritage Broadcasting, 1969; Roman Catholic Broadcasters Gabriel Award for public service, 1970; Lincoln University Award for significant contributions to human relations, 1971; Racial Justice Award, Committee for Racial Justice, United Christian Church, 1973; Public Service Award, Black Citizens for a Fair Media, 1979; Pioneer Award, World Associate for Christian Communications, 1988.

Television (producer)

1956 *Off to Adventure*
1965 *Tangled World*
1977 *Six American Families* (series)

Films

The Pumpkin Coach, 1960; *The Procession,* 1961; *Tomorrow?,* 1962.

Publications

Religious Radio: What to Do and How, 1948
Film Use in Church, 1953
The Television-Radio Audience and Religion, with David W. Barry and Dallas W. Smythe, 1955
Religious Television: What to Do and How, 1961
Television, Radio, Film for Churchmen, 1969
"Old Time Religion on TV—Blessing or Bane?" *Television Quarterly,* Fall 1980
"Social Responsibility of Television in the United States," with Eli Noam and Alfred Schnieder, 1994

Further Reading

Austin, Charles, "After 30 Years, This Media Watchdog Still Vigilant," *New York Times* (August 28, 1983)
Brown, Les, *Keeping Your Eye on Television,* New York: Pilgrim Press, 1979
Ellens, J. Harold, *Models of Religious Broadcasting,* Grand Rapids, Michigan: Eerdmans, 1974
Jennings, Ralph, "Policies and Practices of Selected National Religious Bodies as Related to Broadcasting in the Public Interest," Ph.D. diss., New York University, 1969
Soukup Paul, *Christian Communication: A Bibliographic Survey,* New York: Greenwood, 1989
"U.C.C.'s Parker to Step Down," *Broadcasting* (March 14, 1983)

Parkinson

U.K. Talk Show

The benchmark for British chat shows on television since its inception in 1971, *Parkinson*—under the nononsense, gruff Yorkshire control of host Michael Parkinson (born 1932)—successfully embraced almost every legendary colossus from Hollywood's Golden Age. Michael Parkinson's laudable obsession with the richness of 1930s and 1940s glamour gave these unforgettable encounters an affectionate and endearing aura of wide-eyed fan meeting unattainable hero.

Indeed, unlike his contemporaries and later wannabe successors to the throne, Parkinson's original run of high-profile chat encounters relied not on the subject attempting to remorselessly plug his or her latest book, film, or marriage, but rather on a relaxed career overview in the guest's autumn years. It was the 1970s, when vintage films were gradually being ac-cepted as something more than cheap television time fillers on a Sunday afternoon. Parkinson reunited veteran gangster pals James Cagney and Pat O'Brien, showcased a laid-back singing set from Fred Astaire, chatted with awe with a typically ebullient Orson Welles, and sat back openmouthed as Bing Crosby, on his final trip to Europe, reflected on years in the limelight, and more. Only Frank Sinatra seemed to elude this one-stop London chat shop for visiting American entertainment gurus.

Parkinson also had—and has—a fondness and familiarity with comedians, both established and upcoming. Most famously, he was the first to champion and promote Billy Connolly south of the Scottish border, with Connolly delighting the presenter and eventually becoming the most oft-repeated and warmly greeted guest. Reunions are always good television, and for admirers of anarchic British comedy none was more welcome than the special "Parkinson Meets the Goons" edition, so popular that the BBC released the sound track as a record. Manic architect of the Goonish movement, Spike Milligan, was ill in Australia and joined the show via television link, while Harry Secombe and Peter Sellers joined Parkinson in the studio. Parkinson also delighted in the unpredictable insanity of Tommy Cooper and the flamboyant camp of Kenneth Williams, who was once beautifully partnered by his friend Maggie Smith in a solemn and moving poetry reading.

It was often Parkinson's love of incongruous gatherings of interviewees that made even the most average or uninspiring guest list literally come alive with tension, admiration, or a mixture of both. The very first program presented the tennis ace Arthur Ashe on the same bill as comedian Terry-Thomas. Later in the run, Peter Cook, with his almost estranged cohort Dudley Moore, sat back and waited for the comic inroads as British boxer John Conti explained the need for sexual abstinence before a big fight. Beloved British comedians Eric Morecambe and Ernie Wise were pitted alongside a stunningly attractive, lowcut-gown-wearing Raquel Welch, who, initially straight-faced, described the time when her famous "equipment" (her shapely figure) arrived. Violin virtuoso Stefan Grappelli, from the jazz school, and Yehudi Menuhin, from the classical school, delivered a mesmerizing rendition of "Honeysuckle Rose."

However, in 1987 *Parkinson* the show and Parkinson the man were ousted from British television. Various suggestions—ranging from a lackluster attitude on the part of the BBC to Parkinson's own disinterested reactions to the so-called stars who joined him in the same studios that once hosted the now-departed Hollywood royalty he adored—could not fully explain why the program was pulled from the air. ITV tried to resurrect the format, first with *Parkinson One-to-One* and then with *Parky* in the late 1980s.

Then, in a climate of chat show slump and "personality" overload, a glut of classic Parkinson-hosted compilation repeats proved ratings winners. Therefore, after a successful and ongoing *Sunday Supplement* program for BBC Radio 2 (which allowed Parkinson to play his favorite music and, once a show, interview a famous guest), the BBC television show was resurrected for a new generation. Parkinson's hair may have become grayer, his suits slightly more trendy, and the format a bit more commercially minded, but very little else had changed in the decade-long hiatus. Whole programs were now devoted to the great and the good of show business, with the elusive John Cleese, the charmingly reticent Woody Allen, the beguiling Victoria Wood, and the omnipotent Sir Paul McCartney gracing the program, itself an almost sainted and revered part of the British national consciousness. Cocky rocker Robbie Williams summed it up when, with gleeful amazement, he turned to the camera, addressed his watching mother, and exclaimed, "Look, I'm on *Parky!*"

Comedy was still crucial to the mix. Paul Merton (lately of *Have I Got News for You*) was the first guest on the brand-new programs, while Connolly made a clutch of appearances with his world-weary and energetic observations on life very much intact. The guest mixtures were as effective as ever, with old alternative comedian chums Ben Elton (plugging his latest novel) and Robbie Coltrane (fresh from creating the role of Hagrid for the *Harry Potter* series) sharing the stage with Hollywood hard-hitter Samuel L. Jackson.

However, the overshadowing demons of Parkinson's own reluctance to continue were unintentionally but pointedly embraced with one particular edition of the show. Football (soccer) legend George Best and extravagant pop musician Sir Elton John were juxtaposed with new-millennium football hero David Beckham and his Spice Girl wife, Victoria. The contrast and unspoken contradiction was typically electric.

In the long interim between the show's runs, the replacements and pretenders to the Parkinson chat throne (from Terry Wogan to Jonathan Ross) all seemed to be bigger personalities than the guests they were trying to hype. In contrast, Parkinson did not try to justify his name as the star attraction of the program; he was more than happy to sit back and be entertained with familiar or unfamiliar anecdotes from the worlds of film, music, and sports.

Still, as an elder statesman with his hands still very much on the steering wheel, Parkinson has passed beyond criticism into that reassuringly and untouchable bracket of national treasure. Even the brilliant lampooning of Parkinson on Alistair McGowan's *Big Impression,* which superbly highlights Parkinson's often brusque, unrelenting, and incoherent interviewing style, cannot damage him. It may well be that arguably his greatest interview, with Muhammad Ali on October 17, 1971, will remain the chat benchmark, as Parkinson bristled and shone opposite the erudite fighter, who with menace sweetened with tenderness muttered, "You can't beat me mentally nor physically!" Parkinson, for all his faults and foibles, remains the best of the bunch for one simple reason—he lets his guests talk.

ROBERT ROSS

See also **Parkinson, Michael; Talk Show**

Programming History
BBC 1
First broadcast June 19, 1971
Over 350 shows until 1982
Currently airs Saturday 10:30–11:30 P.M.
First new series:
January 9–March 13, 1998
January 8–April 2, 1999
June 27–September 17, 1999
December 3, 1999 (Sir Paul McCartney Special)
January 21–April 7, 2000
September 8–November 12, 2000
February 17–April 21, 2001

September 22, 2001–December 1, 2001
Christmas Eve special, 2001
February 23, 2002–May 18, 2002
September 21, 2002–November 30, 2002
Christmas Eve special, 2002
February 22, 2003–May 3, 2003
September 20, 2003–November 22, 2003

Further Reading

Parkinson: Selected Interviews from the Television Series, London: Elm Tree Books/Hamish Hamilton, 1975

Parkinson, Michael (1935–)

British Television Personality, Host

Michael Parkinson was the most successful of the British chat show hosts who proliferated in the 1970s and earned a lasting reputation as a viewers' favorite. He subsequently exploited his role in a variety of other television series.

A Yorkshireman to the core, Michael Parkinson started out as a newspaper journalist but later moved to Granada Television, where he worked on current affairs programs, and then to the BBC, where he joined the *24 Hours* team and also indulged his enduring love of sport, producing sports documentaries for London Weekend Television.

Priding himself on his Yorkshireman's "gift of the gab," he made his debut as a chat show host with his own *Parkinson* show in 1971. Broadcast every Saturday night for the next 11 years, the show became an institution and set the standard for all other television chat show hosts to meet. Relaxed, well groomed, and attentive to his guests' feelings, Parkinson nonetheless proved adept at getting the best out of the celebrities who were persuaded to come on the show, without causing offense. The questions he asked were often innocuous and served as invitations to the guest to assume the central role. The best interviews were with those who had a tale to tell and the confidence to tell it without much prodding from the host; Parkinson was sensible enough not to interrupt unless it was absolutely necessary. At the top of the list of dynamic guests Parkinson interviewed were Dr. Jacob Bronowski, Di-

ana Rigg, Shirley MacLaine, the muppet Miss Piggy, Dame Edith Evans, the inimitable raconteur Peter Ustinov, comedian Billy Connolly, and boxer Mohammad Ali, who responded magnificently to the geniality and flattery that the devoted Parkinson lavished on him.

If Parkinson took a personal dislike to a guest, he tried not to let it show (though viewers were quick to detect any animosity). Among those he later confessed to finding most difficult were comedian Kenneth Williams, who appeared a total of eight times on the show and was quick to use Parkinson as a verbal punching bag, and Rod Hull's Emu, the ventriloquist-dummy bird who wrestled an unusually disheveled Parkinson to the floor to the delight of the audience and the barely concealed fury of the host himself.

After the long run of *Parkinson* came to an end in the early 1980s, after 361 shows and 1,050 guests, Parkinson worked for a time as a chat show host on Australian television, then busied himself with helping to set up the troubled TV-AM organization in the United Kingdom in 1983. After the collapse of TV-AM, he returned to the roles of sportswriter, radio presenter, and host of a range of popular television shows, ranging from quizzes to the antiques program *Going for a Song*. In 1998 he revised his role as host of *Parkinson,* attracting return visits by many of the guests he had last interviewed in the 1970s and 1980s. The show continues to air Saturday nights at 10:30 on BBC 1.

DAVID PICKERING

Michael Parkinson. Born in Cudworth, Yorkshire, England, March 28, 1935. Attended Barnsley Grammar School. Married: Mary Heneghan; children: Andrew, Nicholas, and Michael. Began career as newspaper journalist, local papers and *The Guardian, The Daily Express,* and *The Sunday Times;* reporter and producer, Granada Television; executive producer and presenter, London Weekend Television, 1968; leading chat show host, from the 1970s; presented sporting documentaries among other programs; chat show host, Channel 10, Australia, 1979–84; director, Pavilion Books, 1980–97; cofounder, TV-AM, 1983; presenter, LBC Radio, 1990; revived popular *Parkinson* chat show, 1998. Recipient: Sports Feature Writer of the Year, 1995; Sony Radio Award, 1998; Sports Writer of the Year, 1998; Media Personality of the Year, Variety Club, 1998; Most Popular Talk Show, National TV Award, 1998, 1999; Best Light Entertainment, BAFTA, 1999; Media Society Award, 2000. Fellow, British Film Institute, 1998. Commander of the British Empire, 2000.

Television Series

1969–71	*Cinema*
1971	*Tea Break*
1971	*Where in the World*
1971	*The Movie Quiz*
1971–82	*Parkinson*
1979–84	*Parkinson in Australia*
1983–84	*Good Morning Britain*
1984–91	*Give Us a Clue*
1984–86	*All Star Secrets*
1987–88	*Parkinson One to One*
1991–92	*The Help Squad*
1993	*Surprise Party*
1995–99	*Going for a Song*
1998–	*Parkinson*

Television Specials

1981	*The Boys of '66*
1985	*The Skag Kids*
1992	*Ghostwatch*
1995	*A League Apart: 100 Years of Rugby League*

Radio

Start the Week; Desert Island Discs, 1986–888; *Parkinson on Sport,* 1994–97; *Parkinson's Sunday Supplement,* 1996– .

Publications

Football Daft, 1968
Cricket Mad, 1969
A to Z of Soccer, with Willis Hall, 1970
A Pictorial History of Westerns, with Clyde Jeavons, 1972
Sporting Fever, 1974
Football Classified, with Willis Hall, 1974
Best: An Intimate Biography, 1975
Bats in the Pavilion, 1977
The Woofits' Day Out, 1980
Parkinson's Lore, 1981
The Best of Parkinson, 1982
Sporting Lives, 1996
Sporting Profiles, 1996
Michael Parkinson on Golf, 1999

Parliament, Coverage by Television

At present almost 60 sovereign states provide some television coverage of parliamentary bodies. Among them are countries as diverse in political organization as Australia, Germany, and Japan, Hungary, Bulgaria, and Russia, China, Denmark, and Egypt. With varying allocations of control of the coverage between media entities and chamber officials, countries provide this form of televised information to citizens in response to three related perceptions on the part of governmental institutions: a lack of public familiarity with Parliament and its distinctness from the executive; a lack of public knowledge of citizenship; and the desire to form channels of communication between the public and politicians that can avoid the mediation of media owners and professionals.

In 1944 the British War Cabinet argued that "proceedings in Parliament were too technical to be understood by the ordinary listener who would be liable to get a quite false impression of the business transacted." It favored professional journalists as expert

Prime Minister Tony Blair.
Photo courtesy of C-SPAN

mediators between public and politics. Winston Churchill regarded television as "a red conspiracy" because it had a robotic component that combined undifferentiated mass access with machinelike reproduction. But debates over televising proceedings in Britain were common from 1965, with 12 separate parliamentary proposals discussed between 1985 and 1988. Arguments for TV rested on the medium's capacity both to involve the public in making politicians accountable and to involve politicians in making the public interested. Arguments against coverage centered on the intrusiveness of broadcasting equipment, the trivialization through editing of the circumstance and pomp integral to British politics, the undue attention to the major parties and to adversarial division that TV would encourage, and the concern that established procedures and conduct would change to suit television. Channel 4 screened a program called *Their Lordships' House* from 1985. The Lower House rejected a proposal for coverage that year, but trial Commons telecasts commenced in late 1989, despite the then prime minister's opposition. The public had become an audience that must be made into a citizen. Consider the position enunciated by contemporary British Conservative politician Norman St. John-Stevas: "To televise parliament would, at a stroke, restore any loss it has suffered to the new mass media as the political education of the nation."

This was already a given elsewhere. In postwar Germany, televising the Bundestag was said to be critical for democratizing the public. Proceedings came to Netherlands television in 1962, via three types of coverage: live for topical issues, summaries of less important debates, and "flashes" on magazine programs. The

first years of the system saw considerable public disaffection because Members of Parliament (MPs) tended toward dormancy, absence, novel-reading, and jargon on-camera. Over time, MPs came to attend at the same time as producers, viewer familiarity with procedural norms grew, and ratings increased on occasions of moment. In France, it was two years after President Pompidou resignedly intoned that "Whether one likes it or not, television is regarded as the Voice of France" that a clutch of broadcasting reforms required certain stations to cover the National Assembly. It is no surprise, similarly, that during the extraordinary events in Czechoslovakia at the end of 1989, the opposition Civic Forum made the televising of Parliament one of its principal demands.

Sometimes such moves have amounted to a defensive reaction, at others to a positive innovation. The European Parliament was directly elected from 1979. It has used TV coverage for the past decade in search of attention and legitimacy. Recordings and live material are available to broadcasters without cost, to encourage a stronger image for the new Europe. Second-order coverage of the Parliament had always been minimal, due to lack of media interest, but it increased markedly with live TV material. The rules on coverage are more liberal than elsewhere, even encouraging reaction shots and film of the public gallery. When Ian Paisley, a Northern Ireland member, pushed in front of Margaret Thatcher to display a poster in 1986, and interrupted the pope's speech in 1988, his demonstration was broadcast and made available on tape. One thinks here of the chariots that go into the Indian countryside with video recordings of political rallies and speeches to be shown on screens to five thousand at a sitting. Direct TV politics can be a special event. Uganda adopted color television to coincide with a meeting of the Organisation of African Unity, and the first live broadcast of the Soviet Union's new Congress of People's Deputies in 1989 attracted a record 200 million viewers across a dozen time zones, a 25 percent increase on the previous figure. A side effect was assisting in the formation of a new image overseas. For American journalists, televising parliamentary sessions helped to bring the USSR into the field of political normalcy.

In the United States, despite the introduction of a bill in 1922 providing for electronic media coverage of Congress, with a trial the following year, there were no regular radio broadcasts of proceedings until the signing of the Panama Canal Treaties of 1978. The opening of the Eightieth Congress in 1947 was carried on television, but this was mostly proscribed until 1971. The major drive for change stemmed from the results of public opinion polls from the early 1970s suggesting that politicians were held in low esteem. Regular closed-circuit trials were instituted in 1977. Following successful coverage of the Connecticut and Florida State legislatures, the House of Representatives allowed routine broadcasts from 1979. After extensive tests, the Senate agreed to the same in 1986. The service is available via Cable-Satellite Public Affairs Network (C-SPAN and C-SPAN2), which also broadcasts House and Senate committees, Prime Minister's Question Time from the British House of Commons, and an array of public-policy talkfests.

The political process has also been modified by the use made of new communications technologies, designed to break down mediation between politicians and publics in the United States. Direct contact between congresspeople and their constituents has positioned them at the leading edge of applications of cable, satellite, videocassette recording, and computer-aided interaction. Alaska, for example, has a Legislative Teleconferencing Network that permits committees to receive audio and computer messages from citizens. Ross Perot linked six U.S. cities by satellite in 1992 to convene a "nationwide electronic rally," a metonym for the "electronic town hall," which was to administer the country should he become president; he would debate policies with Congress and have citizens respond through modem or telephone.

The most spectacular recent examples of U.S. parliamentary coverage are the Senate Judiciary Committee's Judge Thomas confirmation hearing of 1991 and the appearance of Oliver North before a congressional committee in the 1987 hearings into funding the Contras in Nicaragua. The evidence about Clarence Thomas and Anita Hill was so "popular" that its competition, Minnesota versus Toronto, drew the lowest ratings ever for a baseball play-off. North's evidence had five times as many viewers as *General Hospital,* its closest daytime soap opera competitor. Most commentators on that hearing clearly read it intertextually, referring to acting, entertainment, and stars in their analysis. CBS actually juxtaposed images of North with Rambo and Dirty Harry, emphasizing the lone warrior against an establishment state that would not live up to its responsibilities. North assisted this process in his promise "to tell the truth, the good, the bad and the ugly." Much media attention was given to Reagan's words of admiration to North: "This is going to make a great movie one day." The reaction of the public was similarly remarkable. Polls that showed that years of government propaganda still found 70 percent of Americans opposed to funding the Contras saw a 20 percent switch in opinion after the hearings. Once the policy issue became personalized by North, and opposition to him could be construed as the work

of a repressive state, congressional television viewing became popular and influential.

Conversely, rules enunciated by the British Select Committee on Televising the Commons prohibit cutaway reaction shots, other than of those named in debate. Close-ups and shots of sleeping members are also proscribed. Disruptions lead to a cutaway to the Speaker. These restrictions persuaded Channel 4 to abandon plans for live telecasts, although the House decided to permit wide-angle shots in 1990 in order to increase the televisuality of the occasion. How should one read instructions that insist that: "Coverage should give an unvarnished account of the proceedings of the House, free of subjective commentary and editing techniques designed to produce entertainment rather than information"? Such a perspective contrasts starkly with the response to falling public interest in watching convention politics made by Roone Arledge, network news president of the American Broadcasting Company: "The two political parties should sit down on their own, or maybe with the networks, to come up with something more appealing to the American people."

For the most part, parliaments want to control coverage. Guidelines on the use of file footage of proceedings issued by Australia's Joint Committee on the Broadcasting of Parliamentary Proceedings, for example, are concerned about the unruly gazes of directors and publics. They insist on maintaining continuity, avoiding freeze frames, and receiving guarantees that material will not "be used for the purposes of satire or ridicule." After the first day of *Question Time TV* in Britain, a Conservative member stated that "some of the men—I happen to know—are carrying powder-puffs in their pockets to beautify their sallow complexions." And who can forget former U.S. House Speaker Tip O'Neill's sensational findings on TV coverage of Democratic and Republican Party conventions: "If a delegate was picking his nose, that's what you'd see.... No wonder so many of us were skittish"? Satire can never be kept far apart from pomposity.

TOBY MILLER

See also **British Programming; Hill-Thomas Hearings; Political Processes and Television; U.S. Congress and Television; U.S. Presidency and Television**

Further Reading

Abramson, Jeffrey B., F. Christopher Arterton, and Gary R. Orren, *The Electronic Commonwealth: The Impact of New Media Technologies on Democratic Politics,* New York: Basic, 1988

Arterton, F. Christopher, *Teledemocracy: Can Technology Protect Democracy?* Beverly Hills, California: Sage, 1987

Franklin, Bob, editor, *Televising Democracies,* London: Routledge, 1992

Garber, Marjorie, "Character Assassination: Shakespeare, Anita Hill, and JFK," in *Media Spectacles,* edited by Marjorie Garber, Jann Matlock, and Rebecca L. Walkowitz, New York: Routledge, 1993

Golding, Peter, Graham Murdock, and Philip Schlesinger, editors, *Communicating Politics,* Leicester: Leicester University Press, 1986

Hetherington, A., K. Weaver, and N. Ryle, *Cameras in the Commons,* London: Hansard Society for Parliamentary Government, 1990

Hutchinson, Jenny, *The Big Picture on the Small Screen* (Papers on Parliament 5), Canberra: Department of the Senate, 1989

Kline, Susan L., and Glenn Kuper, "Self-Presentation Practices in Government Discourse: The Case of US Lt. Col. Oliver North," *Text* (1994)

Lamb, Brian, *C-SPAN: America's Town Hall,* Washington: Acropolis, 1988

Miller, Toby, *The Well-Tempered Self: Citizenship, Culture, and the Postmodern Subject,* Baltimore, Maryland, and London: Johns Hopkins University Press, 1993

Morrison, Toni, editor, *Race-ing Justice, Engendering Power: Essays on Anita Hill, Clarence Thomas and the Construction of Social Reality,* New York: Pantheon, 1992

Schulte-Sasse, Linda, "Meet Ross Perot: The Lasting Legacy of Capraesque Populism," *Cultural Critique* (Fall 1993)

Smith, Anthony, editor, *Television and Political Life: Studies in Six European Countries,* London: Macmillan, 1979

Tomasulo, Frank P., "Colonel North Goes to Washington," *Journal of Popular Film and Television* (1989)

Partridge Family, The

U.S. Situation/Domestic Comedy

The Partridge Family was broadcast on ABC from 1970 to 1974. A modest ratings success, the show peaked at number 16 in the ratings for the 1971–72 season. Although *The Partridge Family* never attracted huge audiences, it was a major hit with younger viewers. The series was also distinguished for spawning highly successful, if short-lived, commercial tie-ins. Children's mystery books and comic books featured the Partridges; their musical albums were heavily promoted; and David Cassidy, one of the actors, became a teen idol.

The Partridges were a fatherless family of six who decided, in the premier episode, to form a rock band and tour the country in a psychedelically painted school bus. Most episodes began at the family home in California. Under the leadership of 1970s supermom Shirley Partridge (Shirley Jones), the five Partridge kids survived various capers that almost always culminated in successful concerts. Mom covered lead vocals. Teenage son Keith (David Cassidy) helped keep the family in line. Keith sometimes clashed with sister Laurie (Susan Dey), and everyone clashed with ten-year-old brother Danny (Danny Bonaduce), the freckle-faced drummer who was always looking for the big score. Danny's special nemesis was band manager Reuben Kinkaid (David Madden), an irritable man with a knack for getting the family into trouble when the plot needed fresh complications. Two younger Partridges, Chris and Tracy, rounded out the cast, along with a next-door neighbor, Ricky, and

Reuben's nephew Alan, who joined the show in 1973.

The show was not a sustained hit in syndication. During the 1990s, however, a retro vogue endowed *The Partridge Family* with minor cult status. With their shag hairdos, flair pants, and polyester outfits, the Partridges epitomized the early 1970s. MTV vee-jay Pagan Kennedy praised the show for having made rock 'n' roll culture seem both exciting and benign: "*The Partridge Family* took drug culture, made it square, and added kids. It was hipness for the under-10 crowd."

The dramatic formula of the show—something between *The Brady Bunch* and *Scooby Doo*—rarely receives scholarly attention. References occasionally note Shirley Partridge's status as a supermother in the Donna Reed mold. For the most part, the show is remembered for its successful commercial tie-ins. Several Partridge Family songs became genuine hits, including the theme, "Come On, Get Happy," and "I Think I Love You," which sold 4 million copies. On the Partridge Family albums, Jones and Cassidy sang their own parts, but studio artists supplied background vocals and music. The family never toured (since they did not play their own music), but Cassidy had a brief and wildly successful career as a pop singer. At the heights of his popularity, he could fill stadiums with prepubescent girls.

In 1973–74 *The Partridge Family* was switched from Friday nights to Saturday nights, opposite *All in the Family* and *Emergency.* The ratings quickly fell and the show was canceled before the next season. A

The Partridge Family, Susan Dey, David Cassidy, Dave Madden, Shirley Jones, Jeremy Gelbwaks, Danny Bonaduce, Suzanne Crough, 1970–74.
Courtesy of the Everett Collection

cartoon sequel, *Partridge Family: 2200 AD,* brought the Partridges back to life in space. The show played Saturday mornings for one season (1974–75), featuring voices from the prime-time cast.

J.B. BIRD

Cast

Shirley Partridge	Shirley Jones
Keith Partridge	David Cassidy
Laurie Partridge	Susan Dey
Danny Partridge	Danny Bonaduce
Christopher Partridge (1970–71)	Jeremy Gelbwaks
Christopher Partridge (1971–74)	Brian Forster
Tracy Partridge	Suzanne Crough
Reuben Kinkaid	David Madden
Ricky Stevens (1973–74)	Ricky Segall
Alan Kinkaid (1973–74)	Alan Bursky

Producers

Bob Claver, Paul Junger Witt, Mel Swope, William S. Bickley, Michael Warren

Programming History

96 episodes
ABC

September 1970–June 1973	Friday 8:30–9:00
June 1973–August 1974	Saturday 8:00–3:30

Further Reading

Brooks, Tim, and Earle Marsh, *The Complete Directory To Prime-Time Network TV Shows; 1946–Present,* New York: Ballantine, 1992

Kennedy, Pagan, "I Think I Love You," *The Village Voice Literary Supplement* (December 10, 1991)

Mitz, Rick, *The Great TV Sitcom Book,* New York: Perigree, 1988

Steinberg, Cobbet, *TV Facts,* New York: Facts on File, 1985

Pauley, Jane (1950–)

U.S. Broadcast Journalist

Jane Pauley is best known as longtime morning broadcaster for NBC's *Today,* an NBC news reporter, and, most recently, as a cohost for NBC's popular newsmagazine, *Dateline.* Her career began at the age of 21, when she was hired as daytime and weekend caster at WISH-TV in Indianapolis. Four years later she was appointed as the first woman to anchor the evening news at WMAQ, Chicago. Despite low ratings, Pauley was selected in 1976 to interview as a possible successor to Barbara Walters as Tom Brokaw's cohost on NBC's *Today.* Competing with well-known reporters Linda Ellerbee and Betty Rolin, Pauley was chosen for the position, shocking the industry and disappointing critics who found her too cheery, young, and pretty. Though fans embraced Pauley for these qualities, NBC News president Dick Wald defended Pauley's hire based on her poise and control. Her honest address and family commitment, radically different from the more reserved Diane Sawyer, made Pauley popular with female baby boomers. Pauley spent the next 13 years cohosting *Today.* Her team ushered the program past ABC's *Good Morning America,* to become the number one morning show in the United States.

When NBC hired Bryant Gumbel, a sportscaster with no news experience, to succeed Tom Brokaw as head anchor, a compliant Pauley remained in the coanchor seat. Her career seemed to flounder further when renowned Washington reporters Chris Wallace and Judy Woodruff joined the morning group, pushing Pauley to the periphery. Finally, in 1989, NBC brought 31-year-old Debra Norville to the *Today* team, to attract a youthful audience. Sensing she would soon be replaced, Pauley threatened to break her $1.2 million *Today* contract two years early, to which NBC responded with the offer of Pauley's own prime-time magazine show. Despite the fact that she had prevailed in a long, hard-nosed battle and achieved a notable appointment, the media cast Pauley as a spurned wife, to the mistress Norville. Nevertheless, Pauley departed gracefully with a sincere, on-air good-bye to Norville, leaving the show's ratings to tumble 22 percent during sweeps week, and ultimately losing its number one spot to *Good Morning, America.*

Following this media soap opera, Pauley herself became the news item of the day, appearing on talk shows, featured in magazines and on *Life* magazine's cover, in December 1989, which proclaimed, "How Jane Pauley Got What She Wanted: Time for Her Kids, Prime Time for Herself." Pauley became deputy anchor to Tom Brokaw on the *NBC Nightly News,* and in 1989, her magazine pilot, *Changes,* received the highest ratings in its prime-time slot. Her subsequent 1991 show, *Real Life with Jane Pauley,* featuring human interest reports for her traditional audience, aired five successful summer segments. In pursuit of a broader audience, the magazine was revamped in 1992 as

Jane Pauley, *Dateline NBC,* November, 1998.
©*NBC/Courtesy of the Everett Collection*

Dateline NBC, adding investigative reporting, and reporter Stone Philips aboard as cohost. *Dateline* suffered a huge press attack on its ethics when it was discovered that producers staged the explosion of a General Motors truck for an auto safety report; viewers, however, stayed tuned, and by 1995 *Dateline* was a consistent ratings winner.

By calling NBC's bluff, Pauley was catapulted to the ranks of other women investigative TV reporters such as Maria Shriver, Connie Chung, and Diane Sawyer. Nevertheless, Jane Pauley continues to be framed by the mass media and NBC as the maternal, baby-boom, career heroine of television news fame.

Pauley is a trustee of the Radio and Television News Directors Foundation and a fellow with the Society for Professional Journalists (SPJ).

PAULA GARDNER

Jane Pauley. Born in Indianapolis, Indiana, October 31, 1950. Educated at Indiana University, B.A. in political science 1971. Married: Gary Trudeau (*Doonesbury* cartoonist); three children. Began career as TV reporter, WISH-TV, Indianapolis, 1972–75; various positions as reporter and anchor with NBC News programs, since 1975. Recipient of numerous awards, including the Edward R. Murrow Award; multiple Emmy Awards; the Radio and Television News Directors Foundation's Leonard Zeidenberg First Amendment Award; and the first national Matrix Award from the Association for Women in Communications. Inducted into the Broadcasting and Cable Hall of Fame, 1998. Honorary degrees: DePauw University, Indiana University, Notre Dame University, Providence College.

Television

1976–	*NBC News* (correspondent)
1976–90	*Today* (correspondent),
1980–82	*NBC Nightly News* (reporter/principal writer)
1982–83	*Early Today* (coanchor)
1990–	*NBC Nightly News* (substitute anchor)
1990–91	*Real Life with Jane Pauley* (principal correspondent)
1992–	*Dateline NBC* (cohost)

Publication

"Defending Dateline," *The Quill* (November–December 1994)

Further Reading

Geimann, Steve, "Pauley Seeds Project: Task Force's Goal to Help Education," *The Quill* (March 1995)

Henry, William A. III, "Will NBC Make Jane an Anchor?," *Time* (June 18, 1990)

Hoban, Phoebe, "The Loved One (Jane Pauley)" (interview), *New York Times* (July 23, 1990)

"Morning Becomes Pauley," *Broadcasting* (June 2, 1986)

Waters, Harry F., "If It Ain't Broke, Break It," *Newsweek* (March 26, 1990)

Zoglin, Richard, "Surviving Nicely, Thanks: When She Thought NBC Wanted Her Out, Jane Pauley Prepared to Go Quietly, But the Public Uproar Provided Revenge She Is too Ladylike to Savor," *Time* (August 20, 1990)

PAX Television

PAX Television (also known as PAX-Net) was launched in 1998 by West Palm Beach, Florida, media magnate Christian Lowell White "Bud" Paxson. PAX-TV is now considered to be the seventh network (joining ABC, CBS, NBC, FOX, UPN, and WB). Currently reaching 88 percent of Nielsen households, PAX is the largest owned and operated network of stations in the country. On basic cable PAX-TV reaches more homes than Lifetime, Turner Network Television, or USA Network. Previously the owner of cable television's Christian Network, The Home Shopping Network, and multiple radio stations, Bud Paxson conceived of PAX-TV as an "antinetwork network" that would challenge existing broadcasters in two central ways: PAX-TV would invert the traditional model of network-affiliate business practices; and it would depart from the "mainstream" in its network branding, programming, and audience address. PAX-TV's fairly rapid growth and gradually increasing ratings success was initially premised on these " antinetwork" practices. However, by 2004, commitment to this corporate strategy had led to contentious struggles with business partners and legislators that suggested PAX-Net would have to reinvent itself to remain a force after the U.S. television industry's mandated transition to digital television in 2006.

Courtesy of Pax Television

The bulk of PAX stations are low-power, UHF outlets (only 4 of the network's 96 affiliates are VHF outlets). Each station has, typically, fewer than five personnel. No PAX station has a news division or produces its own local news. Essentially, each PAX station serves purely as a distribution site for national programming. The few staff members at each station are dedicated to local and regional advertising sales that form the majority of PAX-TV's revenue stream. In prime time, particularly, this emphasis raises the cost-per-point to an immensely profitable level that allows PAX to endure and prosper in spite of relatively low ratings compared with its competitors.

In terms of network identity and audience appeals, while most early press surrounding PAX-TV's emergence referred to it as a "Christian network," Paxson does not consider his stations to be explicitly Christian. Rather, Paxson, his executives, and network promotions and programming all posit PAX-Net as a national family network representing a nondenominational yet spiritually uplifting haven for viewers presumed to feel alienated by mainstream media. In this regard, the former chief executive officer, Jeff Sagansky, has described PAX-Net's brand as "upbeat, positive, family-friendly," characterized by "no sex, no violence, no profanity," and featuring "values-based spirituality" with "no cynicism."

In spite of its antinetwork focus, PAX-TV has succeeded largely due to strategic alliances with traditional networks that have allowed PAX to marshal capital, extend market penetration, and procure program product. PAX-TV started broadcasting in 1998 with programs that, while clearly fitting its professed brand ethic, were also almost exclusively former CBS program fare, particularly programming owned and distributed by CBS Films (a film production and distribution studio separate from though related to the CBS television network). Such programs included *Touched by an Angel* (which remains, at this writing, the most popular program on PAX network), *Dr. Quinn, Medicine Woman, Diagnosis Murder, Christy, Dave's*

World, Life Goes On, and *Promised Land.* In its first year, PAX's entire weeknight prime-time schedule consisted of series that had aired or were concurrently airing on CBS (i.e., syndicated on PAX while in first run on CBS). Further, PAX-TV's day-to-day operations were overseen by former CBS Entertainment executive Jeff Sagansky (who resigned in August 2003 after five years at the helm). By the year 2000, PAX expanded its "PAX Originals" programming to include a range of original dramatic series and reality and game-show series. Examples include *Doc* (featuring country and western singer Billy Ray Cyrus as a country doctor transplanted to New York City), *The Ponderosa* (a prequel to *Bonanza*), *Miracle Pets, Twice in a Lifetime, Supermarket Sweep,* and *Next Big Star.* PAX currently features one or more original series six nights a week in prime time. The network also continues to program syndicated shows formerly on CBS, such as *Diagnosis Murder* and *Touched by an Angel,* as well as to rebroadcast programming that originated on NBC, including the game show *The Weakest Link* and the drama *Mysterious Ways.*

In relation to the growing "family values" media niche, PAX remains distinct because it is arguably more accessible to interested viewers than family-oriented channels available only via cable or through a direct broadcast satellite dish. Unlike the family-oriented Hallmark Channel, or ABC Family and its sister network the Disney Channel, PAX stations remain available in most markets via traditional over-air broadcast delivery (though the quality of these signals is often compromised due to their origination on UHF).

PAX's institutional growth and development largely was staked on provisions of the Telecommunications Act of 1996. The Telecommunication Act's significance for PAX-Net was twofold: it upheld must-carry rules that require cable franchises to carry all local broadcast channels, including the low-power UHF stations that make up the 92 of the 96 stations in the PAX network chain. This provided PAX-TV with a much larger start-up audience than it might have otherwise been able to attract. The 1996 Act also relaxed restrictions that limited the number and types of local stations individual companies could own which enabled the development of duopolies in major television markets. In 1999 this enabled Paxson to sell 32 percent of his company to NBC at a cost of $415 million. The terms of the NBC-PAX partnership gave NBC the option to purchase PAX television stations as well as first-refusal rights on sales of PAX-TV stations located in the top-70 U.S. television markets. Paxson retained the option to buy out the cash value of NBC's ownership stake as of September 2004. The PAX-NBC partnership was originally designed to allow the networks to share programming and to enable programs pre-empted by local NBC affiliates to be aired within that same market on PAX. In most markets, PAX affiliates also "repurpose" or rerun the local NBC affiliate's local late newscast, a half hour after its first airing on NBC. And yet recent FCC rules changes, proposed legislation regarding UHF spectrum auctions, and PAX-Net's professed "family values" orientation have led to uneasy relations with media industry critics, some legislators, and strained relations with NBC.

Initially, PAX-TV's start-up was marred by an up-roar over its explicitly conservative promotions in major news and television industry trade papers condemning the major networks for "promoting 'alternative lifestyles'"—a phrase often invoked in the press to refer to gay and lesbian populations. Later, PAX battled NBC over its Memphis station's refusal to broadcast *Will & Grace* (a program that features two homosexual characters in its ensemble cast) because of PAX executives' perceptions that the highly rated NBC program conflicted with PAX's family-friendly programming mission. Because local Memphis affiliate WMC-TV was contractually obligated to carry a Memphis Grizzlies basketball game, Memphis's PAX affiliate, WPXX, was slated to air NBC's entire Thursday night lineup that night. WPXX agreed to air only the first and last hour of the prime-time bloc, thus excising *Will & Grace* and *Just Shoot Me* from the Memphis market area.

More recently, the PAX-NBC partnership has been jeopardized by NBC's purchase of the Spanish-language network Telemundo. While Bud Paxson entered into the NBC partnership with hopes that PAX-Net would one day be a full-fledged member of the NBC network "family," he has stated that NBC's acquisition of Telemundo suggested NBC's lack of commitment to PAX on three fronts: the potential pur-chase by NBC of PAX stations; NBC's commitment to strengthen PAX's business; and as regards the development of shared NBC-PAX programming. As ownership rules restrict operation of more than two stations in major markets, PAX-Net affiliates were now placed at risk in cities such as Los Angeles, New York, Chicago, and Miami, where NBC and Telemundo both have a strong presence. Finally, pending legislation proposed by the George W. Bush White House—in anticipation of U.S. TV's transition from analog to digital—would require clearing television broadcasters from channels 60 to 69 to be auctioned for wireless radio use. This would have a potentially devastating impact on PAX because over 17 percent of its network affiliates are located in the UHF spectrum at channel 60 or above. As of fall 2003, the PAX-Net station group was opening discussion with potential buyers in anticipation of the likely conclusion of its partnership with NBC, set for renegotiation in 2004 (at which point Paxson has the option to buy out NBC's large stake in his network).

VICTORIA E. JOHNSON

See also **Religion on Television;** *Touched by an Angel*

Further Reading

Grappi, Michelle, "What Went Wrong with Paxson, NBC," *Electronic Media* (December 10, 2001)

Halonen, Doug, "Let the Duopolies Begin," *Electronic Media* (August 9, 1999)

Higgins, John M., and Sara Brown, "Paxson Renders Unto TCI," *Broadcasting and Cable* (May, 1998)

Motavalli, John. "Pittman Seeking Stations," *Television Week* (July 7, 2003)

Paxson, Lowell, and Gary Templeton, *Threading the Needle: The Pax Net Story,* New York: HarperBusiness, 1998

Schneider, Michael, "Paxson Learns Politically Correct Lesson," *Electronic Media* (July 27, 1998)

Pay Cable

Pay or premium cable is a cable television service that supplements the basic cable service. Most cable system operators carry one or more pay-cable services (called "multipay") on their systems and make them available to customers for a monthly fee that is added to the basic fee. Cable customers who choose not to subscribe to pay cable receive a scrambled signal on the pay-cable channel or channels. The monthly pay-cable fee is subject to unit discounts whenever a customer subscribes to two or more pay-cable services.

Pay-per-view (PPV) and video-on-demand (VOD) are two additional forms of pay cable that require cable television customers to pay for individual programs rather than a program package. PPV customers order movies, sports, or other event programs from their cable system and view the programming at a time determined either by the system operator or the event scheduler. VOD customers, via a more sophisticated digital delivery technology than is required for PPV, are able to order recorded programming for viewing at a time determined by the customers themselves. The cable customer's monthly bill reflects the total cost of each PPV and/or VOD program or event viewed during the preceding month.

Subscription video-on-demand (SVOD) is yet another kind of pay-cable service that several cable systems were providing customers by late 2001. SVOD could best be described as a hybrid of pay cable and VOD whereby a cable customer pays a monthly fee (about $10 in 2001 figures) to access selections from the SVOD program library for viewing at a time convenient to the customer. The same digital delivery technology required for VOD also is required for SVOD.

Since pay-cable services are supported by subscriber fees, they carry no commercials. Pay-cable programmers usually schedule programs that are unique and that may never be seen on basic cable or broadcast television. These include sports events; musical concerts; first-run, uncut movies; and program series produced by or for a particular pay-cable service. Some movies carried on pay cable are especially produced by the pay-cable service; others were released originally for theatrical viewing prior to their availability for a pay-cable audience.

Some 48 million U.S. households (accounting for nearly 72 percent of all cable television households in the United States) subscribed to a pay-cable service by early 2001. Pay-cable subscribers typically pay about $10 per month (in 2001 figures) above their basic cable service charge. Any cost figure above or below the average depends on the total number of pay-cable services in the subscriber's package and the package discount allowed by the subscriber's cable system operator. The operator keeps approximately 50 percent of the fees collected from pay-cable subscribers. The other 50 percent goes to the company or companies originating the pay-cable service.

Pay cable predates the cable industry by several years. The first known pay television or subscription television (STV) service in the United States was a short-lived experimental effort by Zenith Radio Corporation in 1951 called Phonevision. During its 90-day life span, Phonevision offered daily movies carried by a special telephone line to some 300 Chicago households. Two other experimental STV services, one in New York City and one in Los Angeles, followed the Phonevision lead in 1951 but met with a similar fate.

The Federal Communications Commission (FCC) enacted rules in 1957 that severely limited STV program acquisition. The rules prevented STV from "siphoning" movies and special events such as sports from "free" television to pay television. In 1969 FCC rules were revised to limit any STV service to a single channel, available only in communities already served by at least five commercial television stations. Such restrictions for STV and, by then, pay cable were eliminated by a 1977 U.S. Court of Appeals decision that declared that the FCC's pay television rules infringed on the cable television industry's First Amendment rights.

The court of appeals decision was especially important to the Home Box Office (HBO) pay-cable service. The idea behind HBO was conceived by Charles F. Dolan. Financial assistance from Time-Life Cable to launch HBO was followed by agreements with Madison Square Garden and Universal Pictures allowing HBO to carry live sports events and recent movies. HBO was launched on November 8, 1972, providing pay-cable programming (a professional hockey game and a movie) to 365 Service Electric Cable subscribers in Wilkes-Barre, Pennsylvania. In less than one year, HBO's service was carried by 14 cable television systems to more than 8,000 cable customers.

New ground was broken in pay-cable distribution in 1975, when HBO first carried its service via satellite to UA Columbia Cablevision subscribers in Fort Pierce and Vero Beach, Florida, and to American Television and Communications Corporation subscribers in Jackson, Mississippi. The first satellite distributed (via RCA's Satcom) pay-cable programming was the Muhammad Ali–Joe Frazier championship boxing match from Manila. A nationally distributed pay-cable network was in the making but would not be a reality until HBO managed to convince prospective cable system affiliates to spend nearly $100,000 to purchase the necessary satellite receiving dish and accompanying hardware.

By 2001, 30 companies had launched national pay-cable services in the United States. HBO remained the largest, with 33 million subscribers receiving the service from more than 9,300 cable systems. In 2001 other leading national pay-cable services (with subscribership numbers that exceeded 1 million) were Cinemax, Showtime, the Movie Channel, Encore, Starz, and the Sundance Channel. One regional pay-cable service, The New England Sports Network, was carried by 169 cable systems and reached some 1.5 million subscribers in 2001. Several national pay-cable services also had subdivided themselves by 2001 in order to serve a more specific group of viewers. For example, HBO provided programming via the HBO Family and HBO Latino channels

Since their inception pay-cable services have struggled to satisfy subscribers, who frequently choose to disconnect from pay cable after a brief sampling period. According to surveys of subscribers, such "churn" occurs because low-quality movies are repeated too often, making pay cable a poor entertainment value.

The pay-cable industry is at a disadvantage in combating this criticism because of the preference (based on financial considerations) that the movie industry has for pay cable's chief rival—home video. Production companies whose movies score particularly well at the box office generally follow the movies' theatrical run by release to the home video market. The movies are then available for rental or purchase on videocassettes and DVDs and sometimes may be released to air on PPV cable services several weeks or months before they appear on pay cable. Pay-cable services that are best able to compete with home video in coming years may be those that have the financial resources to produce their own movies and original series.

Pay cable has therefore focused greater attention in recent years on airing original programming. HBO, in particular, has achieved critical success with such program series as *The Sopranos* and *Sex and the City*. Several pay-cable services have turned to boxing as the most popular choice for their sports-minded viewers. Also, many pay-cable services have begun airing a heavier schedule of programs during late evening hours aimed primarily at adult viewers.

RONALD GARAY

See also **Cable Networks; Pay-per-View Cable; Pay Television; United States: Cable**

Further Reading

Note: *Broadcasting and Cable* (a weekly), *Multichannel News* (a biweekly), and *Cablecasting* (a monthly) carry numerous articles and updated statistics regarding all facets of the cable TV industry.

Applebaum, Simon, "Video on the Move," *Cablevision* (August 14, 2000)

Dominick, Joseph R., Barry L. Sherman, and Gary A. Copeland, *Broadcasting, Cable, and Beyond,* New York: McGraw-Hill, 1990; 4th edition, by Dominick, Sherman, and Fritz Messere, as *Broadcasting, Cable, the Internet, and Beyond,* 2000

Eastman, Susan Tyler, *Broadcast/Cable Programming: Strategies and Practices,* Belmont, California: Wadsworth Publishing Co., 1981; 6th edition, by Eastman and Douglas A. Ferguson, as *Broadcast/Cable/Web Programming,* 2002

Garay, Ronald, *Cable Television: A Reference Guide to Information,* Westport, Connecticut: Greenwood Press, 1988

Iler, David, "VOD Shining Brightly in Cable Universe," *Broadband Week* (August 6, 2001)

Messina, Ignazio, "Premium Values," *Cablevision* (July 3, 2000)

Picard, Robert G., editor, *The Cable Networks Handbook,* Riverside, California: Carpelan, 1993

Pay-per-View/Video-on-Demand

Pay-per-view (PPV) is a pay-cable offshoot that allows cable television subscribers to access movies and special one-time-only events and to pay a preannounced fee only for the single movie or event viewed. Most cable system operators offer two or more PPV channels to their customers. The signal on each PPV channel is scrambled until the cable subscriber chooses to view programming on one of the channels. At such time, the subscriber contacts the cable system headend, either by phone or with an interactive handheld remote control, to order the PPV programming. Following the initial order, a computer at the headend activates a device near the subscriber's television set called an "addressable converter," which unscrambles the ordered PPV program signal for the program's duration. All PPV "buys" are totaled by computer and added to the cable subscriber's monthly bill.

Video-on-demand (VOD) is a relatively new program-delivery service akin to PPV. VOD allows cable customers equipped with addressable converters to order recorded programming whose start time can be determined by the customers themselves. An array of program titles are digitally stored in a server located at the cable system headend and distributed to cable customers as ordered. Billing procedures for VOD buys is the same as that for PPV buys.

The history of PPV and pay cable shared a parallel course until 1974, when Coaxial Communication inaugurated the first true PPV service in Columbus, Ohio. The service, called Telecinema, provided movies priced at $2.50 per title. Telecinema shortly succumbed to pay cable's better revenue stream. Warner Cable introduced Columbus to another short-lived PPV service via its interactive QUBE system in 1978.

Pay-per-view event, *WWF Smackdown,* Vince McMahon, The Rock (aka Dwayne Johnson).
Courtesy of the Everett Collection

Not until late 1985 did two satellite-distributed national PPV services appear. Viewer's Choice was launched on November 26, 1985, and Request Television was launched a day later. By 2001, 13 PPV networks were in operation in the United States. The In Demand network led its competitors in cable-system carriage as well as subscriber potential. More than 1,750 systems carried In Demand to over 24 million addressable subscriber households. By 2000, in the United States there were more than 52 million addressable cable households (75 percent of all cable households) capable of receiving PPV programming. VOD deployment was just beginning to gather steam at the beginning of the 21st century. By the end of 2001, some 36 VOD services were either operating or preparing for launch. In all, these services were meant to reach more than 6 million cable households.

PPV programming falls into two broad categories: movies and events. Movies occupy most PPV network schedules. However, following their initial theatrical run, most movies that perform well at the box office are released to home video before they are accessible through PPV. Only after videocassette or DVD versions of the movies have been available for rental or purchase for a period (called a "window") ranging from 30 to 90 days are they then available for PPV. VOD programming also consists primarily of movies, with a growing number of customers—PPV and VOD alike—preferring adult (i.e., sexually explicit) movies and associated adult fare such as "call-in" programs.

The PPV event category may be subdivided primarily into sports and concerts. Sports, especially professional boxing and wrestling, occupies a commanding share of the category. Professional baseball, football, basketball, and hockey, as well as several college football teams, all make some of their games available to PPV subscribers.

Pricing PPV events is a matter of what the market will bear. In 2001 PPV prices for professional boxing matches ranged from $40 to $50. Rock concerts and other musical events during the same period ranged in price from $10 to $20. Movies generally cost between $3 and $4 per title. It is risky to predict what PPV subscribers will pay for an event and what the buy rate (the percentage of PPV subscribers who choose to buy a movie or event) might be. For instance, NBC bet that 5 million subscribers would pay between $95 and $170 apiece for access to daily live events of the 1992 Summer Olympics from Barcelona. The so-called Triplecast—for the three PPV channels that carried the events—proved a failure, however, and NBC eventually tallied its Triplecast loss at nearly $100 million.

Apart from such failures as the Triplecast, PPV revenues have continued to rise. PPV revenues for 2000 stood at more than $2 billion. Most of that revenue came from the purchase of movies, but roughly one-fifth was generated by sports and musical events and another one-fifth was generated by adult movies and associated programming. Wrestling events such as "Wrestlemania" led other sports events in total buy rates. Also, cable system operators were finding that in terms of adult PPV services, the more explicit the content, the higher the buy rate. Buy rates for VOD customers were highest (roughly 70 percent) in the hit movie category. About 20 percent of VOD buys were in the adult programming category. Program buying characteristics that were emerging in 2001 showed that fewer than 20 percent of PPV customers accounted for nearly 80 percent of all PPV buys, and the buy rate for VOD movies was nearly triple that of PPV movies.

The success of PPV cable has been and continues to be a function of promotion. One cable executive labeled PPV a "marketing-intensive business" that relies on an "impulse buy" strategy to attract subscribers. The PPV industry's future appears firmly in place, however, with predictions that nearly one-quarter of the 500-channel cable system of tomorrow will be occupied by PPV program networks.

VOD was still a relatively new service at the beginning of the 21st century. Nonetheless, cable system operators were hoping that customer embrace of VOD would help build digital-cable penetration, which had reached nearly 14 million households (accounting for roughly 20 percent of all U.S. cable households) by the end of 2001. Cable operators also were counting on VOD to help stem the number of persons who were choosing direct broadcast satellite (DBS) services over cable. By the end of 2001, new DBS subscribers led new cable subscribers by a 3-to-1 ratio. Another delivery system that stood poised to compete with cable was computer-based streaming video. A service launched by Microsoft in late 2001 provided its high-speed Internet customers in selected markets with the opportunity to download VOD movies at a cost comparable to that charged for video rentals. However, any advantage that one delivery system might have over another eventually may depend less on technology than on the deals that VOD providers make with movie producers for their product.

RONALD GARAY

Further Reading

Dominick, Joseph R., Barry L. Sherman, and Gary A. Copeland, *Broadcasting, Cable, and Beyond,* New York: McGraw-Hill, 1990; 4th edition, by Dominick, Sherman, and Fritz Messere, as *Broadcasting, Cable, the Internet, and Beyond,* 2000

Donohue, Steve, "Movies, Porn Up; Events Down: SET," *Multichannel News* (December 11, 2000)

Eastman, Susan Tyler, *Broadcast/Cable Programming: Strategies and Practices,* Belmont, California: Wadsworth Publishing, 1981; 6th edition, by Eastman and Douglas A. Ferguson, as *Broadcast/Cable/Web Programming,* 2002

Keefe, Bob, "Video-on-Demand Debuts on Computers," *The Atlanta Journal and Constitution* (October 18, 2001)

Stump, Mel, "Quietly, Cable VOD Efforts Head toward Critical Mass," *Multichannel News* (November 5, 2001)

Umstead, R. Thomas, "Adult PPV Looks Hot in 2001," *Multichannel News* (January 1, 2001)

Umstead, R. Thomas, "Saturday Was Super for PPV," *Multichannel News* (February 5, 2001)

Pay Television

Advertiser support has been the foundation for American broadcast television since the industry's beginnings. It is worth noting, however, that many experiments with direct viewer payment for television programs also have taken place throughout television history. The idea for pay television (also known variously as "toll" or "subscription" television) actually dates to television experiments of the 1920s and 1930s (at which point the method of financing a national television system had not yet been determined) and can be traced through various developmental stages leading up to modern satellite-carried pay-cable program services.

Many pay-TV systems have been proposed over the years. Some have been designed to transmit programming to subscribers' homes over the air, typically on underutilized UHF frequencies. Other systems have been designed to transmit by wire, sometimes wires shared by community antenna or cable TV systems. Various methods have been tested for ordering pay-TV programming and unscrambling the electronic signals.

Until the proliferation of modern satellite-delivered pay program services (both pay-cable and direct satellite), only a small portion of the many planned pay-TV systems ever reached the experimentation stage. Fewer still were used commercially. Economics certainly have had an impact on the fortunes of pay-TV, as has the recurring hesitation of the Federal Communications Commission (FCC) to approve the systems. Even when the commission actually granted permission for testing, final approval for commercial use tended to take many years. Furthermore, no fewer than six major FCC rulings on pay-TV have been handed down over the years, only to be amended in subsequent decisions. Regulators have been aware of ongoing opposition to the various forms of pay-TV on the part of commercial broadcasters and networks, movie theater owners, citizens groups, and other constituencies.

In 1949 Zenith Radio Corporation petitioned the FCC for permission to test an over-the-air pay system called Phonevision. The test was run over a period of 90 days in 1951 with a group of 300 households in Chicago. Phonevision was a system of pay television that used telephone lines for both program ordering and decoding of its scrambled broadcast signal.

In 1953 Skiatron Electronics and Television Corporation tested a different over-the-air system, "Subscriber-Vision," that used IBM punch cards for billing and unscrambling. The programming was transmitted on New York independent station WOR during off-hours.

Also in 1953 the International Telemeter Corporation, partly owned by Paramount Pictures, launched a combination community antenna/wired pay-TV operation in Palm Springs, California. Broadcast signals from Los Angeles were delivered without charge, and subscribers paid for additional programming through coin boxes attached to their television sets. This system lasted through 1955.

The Telemovies system was launched in 1957 in Bartlesville, Oklahoma, by Video Independent Theatres (VIT). Telemovies offered a first-run movie channel and a rerun movie channel. The movies originated from a downtown studio and, in the case of the first-run selections, were shown concurrently in VIT's local movie theaters. Telemovies charged a flat monthly rate rather than a per-program fee. After undergoing several changes, including the addition of community antenna service, the system ceased operations in summer 1958.

In the late 1950s, in the wake of the much-publicized failure of the Bartlesville system, International Telemeter announced its latest coin-box system—designed to use either wires or broadcast signals to transmit programming. The site chosen for a test of a wired version of the system was Etobicoke, Ontario, a suburb of Toronto, under the auspices of Paramount's Canadian movie theater subsidiary. Service began there on February 26, 1960, with 1,000 subscribers, and continued through 1965.

On June 29, 1962, two years after its petition for an experimental license had been filed with the FCC, a Phonevision system was launched in Hartford, Connecticut. By this point, Phonevision had become a joint venture between RKO and Zenith. Phonevision programming was broadcast on WHCT, a UHF station licensed specifically for the Phonevision trial. Although it never made a profit, the Hartford experiment ran through January 31, 1969, and the system won FCC approval for nationwide use in 1970.

Subscription Television Inc. (STV) was launched in July 1964 and continued through November of that year—a short-lived but nonetheless highly touted pay-TV system. STV was the heir (through a complicated series of stock transactions) to Skiatron's over-the-air system. The two major figures behind STV were Skiatron's Matthew Fox and former adman and NBC executive Sylvester L. (Pat) Weaver. STV had built wire networks in San Francisco and Los Angeles, and the company planned eventually to wire major cities as well as to incorporate existing CATV systems. Although STV's three channels offered a mixture of sports, movies, children's programs, and theatrical performances (typical of most pay-TV systems), it was baseball that provided the foundation for its programming.

Both wired and over-the-air pay-TV systems were launched in the 1970s. In 1977 over-the-air systems were started in Newark, New Jersey, by Wometco-Blonder-Tongue (over station WWHT) and in Corona (Los Angeles), California, by Chartwell Communications (over station KBSC). By 1980, 8 others were in operation, with an additional 16 stations authorized and ready to launch. These over-the-air systems were developing concurrently with satellite-delivered cable program services, however, and were not able to compete with the wired medium once it became available in major urban areas.

By the early 1970s cable had become the preferred vehicle for pay television, with most start-up pay ventures seeking to run their services on local cable systems. Since the early 1950s cable operators had been experimenting with channels of locally originated programming for their systems. While not directly a form of pay-TV, these experiments suggested the possibility that cable could offer more than simply retransmitted broadcast signals—a potential not lost on pay-TV entrepreneurs.

The most notable early pay-cable operation was Home Box Office, which launched in 1972 by providing cable systems with pay programming via microwave relays in the northeastern United States. When HBO took its program service to satellite in 1975, it gained the potential to reach virtually any cable system in the United States. Other pay-cable program services were to follow, including Showtime, the Movie Channel, and others.

During the 1990s cable began to face serious competition from direct broadcast satellite technology. As the new delivery technology began enticing consumers with multiple premium and pay-per-view services, traditional cable also began to make multiple versions of popular premium channels available—aided by the increased use of fiber optics and digital compression.

Pay-cable's programming has developed as well. In the early 2000s, premium cable channels such as HBO and Showtime boast some of television's most highly acclaimed programming. In addition to made-for-cable movies, this includes original series such as *Oz, Sex and the City,* and *The Sopranos* on HBO, and *Queer As Folk* on Showtime.

MEGAN MULLEN

See also **Cable Networks: Home Box Office (HBO); Pay-per-View Cable; Showtime Network; United States: Cable**

Further Reading

Note: *Broadcasting and Cable* (a weekly), *Multichannel News* (a biweekly), and *Cablecasting* (a monthly) carry numerous articles and updated statistics regarding all facets of the cable TV industry.

Gould, Jack, "Pay-As-You-See TV: The ABC's of the Controversy," *New York Times* (June 19, 1955)

Howard, H.H., and S.L. Carroll, *Subscription Television: History, Current Status, and Economic Projections,* Knoxville: University of Tennessee, 1980

Peck, Bob (1945–1999)

British Actor

The British actor Bob Peck shot to television stardom in 1986 in the acclaimed BBC drama serial, *Edge of Darkness.* His performance as the dour Yorkshire policeman Ronald Craven, inexorably drawn by his daughter's sudden and violent death into a passionate quest for the truth behind a series of incidents in a nuclear processing facility, won him Best Actor Awards from the Broadcasting Press Guild and the British Academy of Film and Television, as well as establishing an image of brooding diffidence that was to set the seal on a number of subsequent roles. His aquiline, yet disconcertingly ordinary, countenance was to become familiar to television audiences even if his name did not always spring to mind. Following the success of *Edge of Darkness,* and particularly toward the end of his life, Peck was much in demand for voice-overs and documentaries, to which his distinctive bass tones lent a potent mixture of assurance and mystery, as well as an association with the integrity of purpose that characterized his performance as Craven. Success in *Edge of Darkness* also brought him film roles, notably in the British productions *The Kitchen Toto* and *On the Black Hill* in 1987, then, most famously, as the doomed game warden Muldoon in *Jurassic Park* (1993).

Peck received no formal training as an actor but studied art and design at Leeds College of Art, where, in an amateur dramatic company, he was spotted by the writer-director Alan Ayckbourn, who recruited Peck to his new theater company in Scarborough. After stints in the West End and regional repertory, Peck joined the Royal Shakespeare Company, where he stayed for nine years, playing a wide range of parts in classical and contemporary work. One of his final appearances for the company was in the double role of John Browdie and Sir Mulberry Hawke in the epic dramatization of *The Life and Adventures of Nicholas Nickleby,* subsequently televised on Channel 4 in 1982. Along with Anthony Sher, Bernard Hill, and Richard Griffiths, Peck was one of a number of established stage actors in the early 1980s to be brought into television for roles in major new drama serials by BBC producer Michael Wearing.

Peck's performance in *Edge of Darkness* embodied the paradox that is at the heart of the drama. Just as the labyrinthine plot remorselessly exposed the apocalyptic vision behind a veneer of English restraint, so Craven was depicted as a detached loner, whose mundane ordinariness hid long-repressed emotions and whose enigmatic composure exploded into bursts of grief, passion, and—in the closing moments—primal anguish. In this sense, Peck's was also a performance that, like other work of this period (such as Hill's Yosser Hughes in *Boys from the Blackstuff*), brought to the surface the expressionistic subcurrents of a new wave of British television drama realism. Peck was cast as Craven partly because an unknown actor was wanted for the role and because it was written for a Yorkshireman, yet there are mystic and mythic elements in the quest conducted by this seemingly ordinary character that ultimately assume epic proportions. The plot called for long sequences of physical activity and energy, but Peck's real achievement was a granite-like impassivity that just managed to hold back the pain and possible madness behind the character's stoic endurance. This tension was cleverly offset by the puckish outlandishness of Joe Don Baker's performance as the CIA agent Jedburgh.

The figure of Craven was partly reprised in the serial *Natural Lies* (BBC, 1992), where Peck played an advertising executive, Andrew Fell, accidentally stumbling across a conspiracy to cover up a BSE-like scare in the British food industry. In *Centrepoint* (Channel 4, 1992), another dystopian drama, Peck played Armstrong, a surveillance expert, this time with far-right security connections. In a serialization of Catherine Cookson's *The Black Velvet Gown* (Tyne Tees, 1991), Peck brought his brooding presence to the role of the reclusive former teacher Percival Miller. He also played a real-life police officer in the drama-documentary *Who Bombed Birmingham?* (1990); a member of the Securitate state police in a semifictional account of the Romanian revolution, *Shoot the Revolution* (1990); and the role of the detective sergeant in the psychological crime thriller *The Scold's Bridle* (1998).

Peck's range, however, was wider than the image of the tormented hard man might suggest. Perhaps his most highly acclaimed performance after *Edge of Darkness* was as the mild-mannered, accident-prone academic James Westgate, who falls victim to his childhood sweetheart's psychopathic desires, in Simon Gray's Prix Italia–winning television play *After Pilkington* (BBC, 1987). Like many actors of his generation, Peck also was able to bring his stage experience to bear on a variety of classical roles, from Gradgrind in the BBC serialization of *Hard Times* (1994) and Shylock in a Channel 4 production of *The Merchant of Venice* (1996) to Nicias in *The War That Never Ends* (BBC, 1991)—a drama-documentary account of the Peloponnesian Wars written by former Royal Shakespeare Company director John Barton—and Dante in Peter Greenaway and Tom Phillips's *A TV Dante: The Inferno Cantos I-VIII* (Channel 4, 1989).

In the stage play *In Lambeth*, transposed to television in 1993, Peck played the role of Thomas Paine in an imaginary encounter with the poet William Blake, and, in the same year, he renewed his relationship with the work of Edward Bond in Bond's play for the *Crime and Punishment* season, *Tuesday* (1993). "It's nice to be able to sympathize with what you're having to say," Peck remarked when playing Paine. Much of his later voice-over work, from ecological series to documentaries on Britain's clandestine support for Francisco Franco during the Spanish Civil War or the sugar trade in the Dominican Republic, reflected that quiet social commitment. Peck's last work for television was in two British/Russian animated programs, as the voice of Chaucer in *The Canterbury Tales* and Joseph of Arimathea in *The Miracle Worker*.

JEREMY RIDGMAN

Bob (Robert) Peck. Born in Leeds, England, August 23, 1945. Educated at Leeds College of Art, diploma in Art and Design, 1967. Married: Gillian Mary Baker, 1982; children: Hannah Louise and George Edward. Member of repertory theaters in Birmingham, Scarborough, and Exeter, 1969–74; Royal Shakespeare Company, 1975–84; appeared in numerous television

programs and films, from 1974. Recipient: Broadcasting Press Guild Award; BAFTA Award. Died in London, April 4, 1999.

Television Series (selected)

1982	*The Life and Adventures of Nicholas Nickleby*
1984	*Birds of Prey II*
1985	*Edge of Darkness*
1991	*The Black Velvet Gown*
1992	*Natural Lies*
1992	*Centrepoint*
1992	*Children of the Dragon*
1994	*Hard Times*
1998	*The Scold's Bridle*

Television Plays (selected)

1974	*Sunset across the Bay*
1979	*Macbeth*
1981	*Bavarian Knight*
1986	*The Disputation*
1986	*After Pilkington*
1989	*One Way Out*
1989	*A TV Dante: The Inferno Cantos I–VIII*
1990	*Shoot the Revolution*
1990	*Who Bombed Birmingham?*
1990	*Screen Two: "Children Crossing"*
1991	*The Prodigal Son*
1991	*The War That Never Ends*
1992	*An Ungentlemanly Act*
1993	*Tuesday*
1993	*In Lambeth*
1996	*The Merchant of Venice*
1997	*Deadly Summer*
1997	*Hospital*
1998	*The Canterbury Tales* (voice)
2000	*The Miracle Worker* (voice)

Television Documentary

1991	*Beside Franco in Spain* (*Timewatch*)

Films

Royal Flash, 1975; *Parker*, 1985; *On the Black Hill*, 1987; *The Kitchen Toto*, 1987; *Slipstream*, 1989; *Ladder of Swords*, 1989; *Lord of the Flies*, 1990; *Hard Times*, 1991; *Jurassic Park*, 1993; *Surviving Picasso*, 1996; *Fairytale: A True Story*, 1997; *Smilla's Sense of Snow*, 1997.

Stage

Life Class, 1974; *Henry IV, Parts One and Two*, 1975–76; *King Lear*, 1976; *A Winter's Tale*, 1976;

Man Is Man, 1976; *Destiny*, 1976–77; *Schweyk in the Second World War*, 1976–77; *Much Ado about Nothing*, 1977; *Macbeth*, 1976–78, 1983; *Bandits*, 1977; *The Bundle*, 1977; *The Days of the Commune*, 1977; *The Way of the World*, 1978; *The Merry Wives of Windsor*, 1978; *Cymbeline*, 1979; *Othello*, 1979;

The Three Sisters, 1979; *The Accrington Pals*, 1981; *The Life and Adventures of Nicholas Nickleby*, 1981; *Anthony and Cleopatra*, 1983; *The Tempest*, 1983; *Maydays*, 1983; *A Chorus of Disapproval*, 1985; *The Road to Mecca*, 1985; *In Lambeth*, 1989; *The Price*, 1990; *Rutherford and Son*, 1995.

Pee-wee's Playhouse

U.S. Children's Program

Pee-wee's Playhouse, a half-hour CBS-TV Saturday morning live-action "children's show," aired from 1986 until 1991 and was enormously popular with both children and adults. The program won six Emmy Awards and a host of other accolades during its first season. Incorporating clips from vintage cartoons and old educational films, newly produced 3-D animation, hand puppets, marionettes, and a cast of endearingly eccentric characters led by a gray-suited and red-bow-tied Pee-wee Herman (Paul Reubens), *Pee-wee's Playhouse* might best be described as a flamboyant takeoff on the genre of children's educational TV—a sort of *Mister Rogers' Neighborhood* meets MTV. Each week the childlike Pee-wee welcomed viewers into his Technicolor fantasyland and led them through a regimen of crafts and games, cartoon clips, "secret words," and "educational" adventures via his Magic Screen. Yet, in stark contrast to the high moral seriousness of its predecessors, *Pee-wee's Playhouse* was marked from its outset by a campy sensibility and frequent use of double entendre, allowing different types of viewers to enjoy the show in many different ways. As *The Hollywood Reporter* put it, *Pee-wee's Playhouse* was "TV gone Dada...skillfully balanc[ing] the distinction between low-camp and high performance art."

Pee-wee Herman was the brainchild of Reubens, an actor who developed the rather nasal-voiced and somewhat bratty character through routines and skits in comedy clubs. Reubens as Pee-wee (the ruse was to present Pee-wee as a "real" person and not just a character) appeared on comedy and talk shows and in a successful Los Angeles theater production, *The Pee-wee Herman Show*, which quickly developed a cult following after it was taped and aired on Home Box Office. In 1985 the character starred in Tim Burton's debut feature film, *Pee-wee's Big Adventure*, and the

next year *Pee-wee's Playhouse* premiered on CBS. Based on *The Pee-wee Herman Show*, the Saturday morning series was considerably less "adult" than the theater piece had been, although it incorporated many of the same supporting characters, including lusty seaman Captain Carl (Phil Hartman in his pre-*Saturday Night Live* days) and the magical genie Jambi (co-writer John Paragon), the latter a disembodied head in a box who granted Pee-wee's wishes. Other (human) characters appearing on the TV show included Reba the mail lady (S. Epatha Merkerson), the pretty girl-next-door Miss Yvonne (Lynne Stewart), the King of Cartoons (William Marshall and Gilbert Lewis), Cowboy Curtis (Larry Fishburne), Tito the lifeguard (Roland Rodriguez), Ricardo the soccer player (Vic Trevino), and the obese Mrs. Steve (Shirley Stoler). Puppetry was employed to create the characters of bad-boy Randy, the Cowntess, Pteri the Pterodactyl, Conky the Robot, Globey the Globe, Chairy the Chair, and many others. Newly produced animated sequences focused on a young girl named Penny, a family of miniature dinosaurs who lived in the walls of the Playhouse, and a refrigerator full of anthropomorphized food. Music for the shows was provided by cutting-edge artists such as Mark Mothersbaugh, Todd Rundgren, Danny Elfman, and Van Dyke Parks. Dolls and toys of both Pee-wee and other Playhouse denizens were successfully marketed, and something of a Pee-wee craze spread through popular culture. Episodes of the series were aired in prime time in November of 1987, and another feature film, *Big Top Pee-wee*, was released in 1988. That same year *Pee-wee's Playhouse Christmas Special* aired in prime time, featuring most of the regular characters plus a plethora of special guest stars, including k.d. lang, Zsa Zsa Gabor, Little Richard, the Del Rubio Triplets, Cher, Grace Jones,

Pee-wee's Playhouse, Paul Reubens, Chairie, 1986–90.
Courtesy of the Everett Collection

Dinah Shore, Joan Rivers, Annette Funicello, and Frankie Avalon.

From its debut, *Pee-wee's Playhouse* attracted the attention of media theorists and critics, many of whom championed the show as a postmodernist collage of queer characters and situations that seemed to fly in the face of dominant racist, sexist, and heterosexist presumptions. (Some accounts of the show were less celebratory and criticized the show's regular use of comic fat women as sexist.) The show was forthrightly multicultural in cast and situation: the "mailman" was an African-American mail lady; Latino soccer player Ricardo often spoke Spanish without translation; the white Miss Yvonne went on a date with African-American Cowboy Curtis; tough-as-nails cab driver Dixie (Johann Carlo) was a possible lesbian; and Jambi was played as a dishy gay man. Pee-wee himself often poked fun at heterosexist conventions: he once "married" a bowl of fruit salad. The smirking irony, the campy double entendre ("Is that a wrench is your pocket?"), and the use of icons from gay and lesbian culture (perhaps most infamously on the Christmas special, which, aside from its guest stars, featured two muscular and shirtless workmen building a "blue boy" wing to the playhouse out of fruitcakes) furthered this interpretation. This apparent outbreak of playful queerness during the politically reactionary Reagan-Bush/Moral Majority years was a key factor in many adults' enjoyment of the show. Yet that same queerness lurked in the realm of connotation, where it was just as easily ignored or dismissed by other, more mainstream critics. Some parents objected to the show's polymorphous and anarchic approach to childhood (encouraging children to "scream real loud" or jump around the house).

When Paul Reubens was arrested inside an adult movie theater in August 1991, the Pee-wee craze came to an abrupt end. The show was canceled, and in many toy stores Pee-wee merchandise was removed from the shelves. A few years later, Reubens as Pee-wee made an appearance at an MTV event, but it seemed as if his days as a television host of a "children's show" were over, despite the fact that his pre-(hetero)sexualized antics and progressive social attitude had captured the United States' imagination so strongly—for a few years, at least.

HARRY M. BENSHOFF

Cast

Pee-wee Herman	Paul Reubens
Miss Yvonne	Lynne Stewart
Dixie	Johann Carlo
King of Cartoons	Gilbert Lewis/William Marshall
Conky the Robot	Gregory Harrison
Reba	S. Epatha Merkerson
Jambi	John Paragon
Elvis	Shawn Weiss
Cher	Diane Yang
Opal	Natasha Lyonne
Captain Carl	Phil Hartman
Cowboy Curtis	Larry Fishburne
Tito	Roland Rodriguez
Ricardo	Vic Trevino
Mrs.Steve	Shirley Stoler

Programming History

CBS

September 1986–August 1991   Saturday mornings

Further Reading

Balfour, Ian, "The Playhouse of the Signifier," *camera obscura* (May 1988)

Bryan, Bruce, "Pee-wee Herman: The Homosexual Subtext," *CineAction* (Summer 1987)

Doty, Alexander, *Making Things Perfectly Queer: Interpreting Mass Culture,* Minneapolis: University of Minnesota Press, 1993

Jenkins, Henry, "'Going Bonkers!': Children, Play, and Pee-wee," *camera obscura* (May 1988)

Penley, Constance, "The Cabinet of Dr. Pee-wee: Consumerism and Sexual Terror," *camera obscura* (May 1988)

Pennies from Heaven

British Drama Series

Pennies from Heaven, a six-part drama series written by Dennis Potter, received great popular and critical acclaim, including the BAFTA Award for Outstanding Drama, when it was first transmitted on BBC TV in 1978. This was the first six-part drama by Potter after some 16 single television plays, and in its format and mixture of popular music and dance sequences, it anticipated such later works as *The Singing Detective* (1986) and *Lipstick on your Collar* (1993). Potter's ironic handling of music and dance in the television serial was a landmark in British television and his own career. He uses these forms of expression to both disrupt the naturalism of the narrative and to show unconscious desires of individuals and of society (the MGM feature film version failed to capture the seamless flow from conscious to unconscious desires, treated the story as a conventional musical, and was a flop).

The play tells the story of Arthur Parker, a sheet-music salesman in 1930s Britain who is frustrated by his frigid wife, Joan, and by the deafness of the shop-keepers to the beauty of the songs he sells. Although, as Potter has recalled, Arthur is "an adulterer, and a liar and was weak and cowardly and dishonest…he really wanted the world to be like the songs" (see Potter, 1993). When he falls in love with a young schoolteacher named Eileen, Arthur connects the beauty of the songs with his sexual longings. When she becomes pregnant, she has to abandon her schoolteaching career and flee to London, where she takes up prostitution to earn a living. After making contact with Arthur once more, she abandons her pimp, Arthur abandons Joan, and they set off for the country for a brief experience of happiness. The rural idyll is breached by two murders: Arthur is wrongly pursued for the rape and murder of a blind girl; while seeking a hideaway from pursuers, Eileen murders a threatening farmer. The two return to London where Arthur is apprehended, charged, and hanged for the blind girl's murder. Eileen, significantly, is not pursued.

The disturbing realities that punctuate the narrative (rape, murder, prostitution, the grinding poverty of the Depression era) are counterbalanced by the naive optimism of Arthur, expressed through the sentimental love songs of the period. Daydreams and reality are constantly juxtaposed, but Potter does not provide easy evaluations. It is possible to laugh at the simplicity of Arthur's belief in the "truth" of the popular love songs he sells, but scorn the shallow cynicism of his salesmen companions. Arthur's naïveté has to be balanced against his duplicity: although he loves Eileen and promises to help her, he scribbles down a wrong address and creates enormous complications for them. Yet, however sentimental the songs are, they point to a world of desire that, in some form, human beings need and that is otherwise unrecognized in popular discourse. Although Potter used popular music and Busby Berkeley–type choreography, *Pennies* is not a conventional musical: the music is not contemporary and thus arrives with a freight of period nostalgia. Moreover, the music is dubbed and the actors lip-synch (on occasion across gender lines) so that the effect is comic or ironic as well as enticingly nostalgic.

If the songs and dance routines are used to express unconscious desires or those beyond the characters' ability to articulate, another device that provides access to the unconscious and interferes with any naturalistic reading is the use of doubles. Although physically and in terms of class distinctly different, Arthur and the accordion man, and Joan and Eileen, are potential versions of the same identity. While the accordion man is presumed to have raped and killed a blind girl (significantly, not shown), Arthur's barely suppressed wish to rape her shows his equivalence. Similarly, Joan and Eileen, though opposites in terms of sexual repression, share a similar shrewd awareness of social reality. The main difference is that Eileen is led to defy social conventions while Joan is content to work within them, recognizing their power. Arthur's limited understanding is compensated for by his naive passion for music and love, which offers a truth about how the world might be.

Pennies from Heaven can be seen as a development from the 1972 play *Follow the Yellow Brick Road,* in which the hero Jack Black, a television actor, shuns the real world in favor of the ideal world of television ads in which families are happy, the sun shines, and everybody is optimistic. The earlier play expresses a bleaker Manichean universe of good and evil, while the later work acknowledges the internal nature of good and

Pennies from Heaven, Bob Hoskins, 1978.
Courtesy of the Everett Collection

evil and suggests the possibility of redemption, if not accommodation, between our lower and higher impulses. At a further remove, *Pennies from Heaven* can be seen to pick up the themes of the life-affirming power of transgressive behavior, and the comic/musical presentation of them, found in John Gay's *Beggar's Opera* (1728).

BRENDAN KENNY

See also **Potter, Dennis;** *Singing Detective, The*

Cast

Arthur Parker	Bob Hoskins
Eileen Everson	Cheryl Campbell
Joan Parker	Gemma Craven
Accordion Man	Kenneth Colley
Mr. Warner	Freddie Jones
Tom Hywel	Bennett
Major Archibald Paxville	Ronald Fraser
Police Inspector	Dave King
Sergeant	John Ringham
Conrad Baker	Nigel Havers
Bank Manager	Peter Cellier
Marjorie	Rosemary Martin
Barrett	Arnold Peters
Dave	Philip Jackson
Irene	Jenny Logan
Maurice	Spencer Banks
Dad	Michael Bilton
Blind Girl	Yvonne Palfrey
Miner	Frederick Radley
Mrs. Corder	Bella Emberg
Barman	Will Stampe
Farmer	Philip Locke
Judge	Carleton Hobbs
Jumbo	Robert Putt
Woman Patient	Maryann Turner
Cafe Proprietor	Tony Caunter
Estate Agent	Roger Brierley
Will	Keith Marsh
Police Constable	Roger Forbes
Customer	Tudor Davies
Michael	Nigel Rathbone
Constable	Tim Swinton
Betty	Tessa Dunne
Alf	Bill Dean
Detective Inspector	John Malcolm
Doctor	Vass Anderson
Tramp	Paddy Joyce
Clerk of the Court	Stanley Fleet
Carter	Wally Thomas
Youth	Tony London
Man on Bridge	Alan Foss
Foreman of the Jury	Hal Jeayes
Pianist	Sam Avent
Street Whore	Phyllis MacMahon
Busker	Ronnie Ross
Mike Savage	Arnold
Olwen Griffiths	First Pub Whore
Maggy Maxwell	Second Pub Whore
Reg Lever	Man in Queue
Roy Boyd	Horace
Laurence Harrington	Inspector
Noel Collins	Chaplain
David Webb	Shop Manager
Roger Heathcott	Executioner
Robin Meredith	Customer
Steve Ubels	Pedestrian
Betty Hardy	Railway Passenger #1
Frank Lazarus	Railway Passenger #2
Norman Warwick	Railway Passenger #3
David Rowlands	Railway Passenger #4

Programming History
6 episodes
BBC
March 7, 1978–April 11, 1978

Further Reading

Potter, Dennis, *Pennies from Heaven,* London: Quartet Books, 1981

Potter, Dennis, *Waiting for the Boat,* London: Faber and Faber, 1984

Potter, Dennis, *Potter on Potter,* edited by Graham Fuller, London and Boston: Faber and Faber, 1993

Potter, Dennis, *Seeing the Blossom,* London and Boston: Faber and Faber, 1994

Stead, Peter, *Dennis Potter,* Bridgend: Seren Books, 1993

Wu, Duncan, *Six Contemporary Dramatists: Bennett, Potter, Gray, Brenton, Hare, Ayckbourn,* New York and London: St. Martin's Press, 1995

Wyver, John, "Paradise Perhaps," *Time Out* (March 3, 1978)

Perry Mason

U.S. Legal Drama/Mystery

Perry Mason was the longest-running lawyer show in American television history. Its original run lasted nine years, and its success in both syndication and made-for-television movies confirm its impressive stamina. Mason's fans include lawyers and judges who were influenced by this series to enter their profession. The Mason character was created by mystery writer Erle Stanley Gardner and delivered his first brief in the novel *The Case of the Velvet Claws* (1933). From 1934 to 1937, Warner produced six films featuring Mason. A radio series also based on Mason ran every weekday afternoon on CBS radio from 1944 to 1955 as a detective show/soap opera. When the CBS television series was developed as an evening drama, the radio series was changed from *Perry Mason* to *The Edge of Night,* and the cast renamed, so as not to compete against the television series.

The title character is a lawyer working out of Los Angeles. Mason, played on TV by Raymond Burr, is teamed with two talented and ever-faithful assistants: trusty and beautiful secretary Della Street, played by Barbara Hale, and the suave but boyish private detective Paul Drake, played by William Hopper. In each episode, this trio works to clear their innocent client of the charge of murder, opposing the formidable district attorney Hamilton Burger, played by William Talman. Most episodes follow this simple formula: the guest characters are introduced and their situation shows that at least one of them is capable of murder. When the murder happens, an innocent person (most often a woman) is accused, and Mason takes the case. As evidence mounts against his client, Mason pulls out a legal maneuver in-

volving some courtroom "pyrotechnics." This act not only proves his client innocent but identifies the real culprit. These scenes are easily the best and most memorable. It is not because they are realistic. On the contrary, they are hardly that. What is so engaging about them is the combination of Mason's efforts to free his client, perhaps a surprise witness brought in by Drake in the closing courtroom scene, and a dramatic courtroom confession. The murderer being in the courtroom during the trial and not hiding out in the Bahamas provides the single most important image of each episode. The murderer forgoes the Fifth Amendment and admits his/her guilt in an often tearful outburst of "I did it! And I'm glad I did!" This pronouncement happens under the shocked, amazed eyes of district attorney Burger and the stoic, sure face of defense attorney Mason.

Although it is often identified with other lawyer dramas such as *L.A. Law* and *The Defenders, Perry Mason* was more of a detective series. Each episode was a carefully structured detective puzzle that both established and perpetuated a number of conventions associated with most television detective series. *Perry Mason* used the legal profession and the trial situation as a forum for detective work. Although strictly formulaic, each episode was guided by the elements of the variations that distinguish one episode from another. For example, since nearly every episode began with the guest characters rather than with the series regulars, these guest characters set the tone for the rest of the episode. If the show were going to be youth oriented, these characters were young. If it were going to be a contested will, the heirs were introduced.

Perry Mason, Raymond Burr, Barbara Hale, 1957–66.
Courtesy of the Everett Collection

The credit for the series' success should be split equally between Burr, the *Perry Mason* production style, and the series' creator Gardner. Burr provided the characterization of a cool, calculating attorney, while the production style built tension in plots at once solidly formulaic and cleverly surprising, and Gardner, as an uncredited executive story editor, made sure each episode carefully blended legal drama with clever detective work. In all, the series won three Emmys, two for Burr and one for Hale.

The series made a brief return in 1973, with the same production team as the original series but a new cast. Monte Markham replaced Burr. That this version did not survive 15 episodes reveals that one of the key draws of the original series was its casting. It is interesting to note, however, that Markham's Mason was closer to the one featured in the original novels. Both were brash, elegant, and coolly businesslike in their dealings with clients, something Burr never was. But it was Burr's coolness and control that became so identified with the character that, for the television audience, there was no other Mason than Burr.

Beginning with *Perry Mason Returns*, Burr returned to his role in 1985 for an almost 10-year run of made-for-television movies. *Perry Mason Returns* was followed by *The Case of the Notorious Nun* (1986). Burr was back as Mason, albeit a bit older, grayer, and bearded, with Barbara Hale as his executive secretary. Since William Hopper had died in 1970, William Katt (who is the real-life son of Barbara Hale) was featured in the first nine episodes as Paul Drake, Jr. In *The Case of the Lethal Lesson* (1989), Katt was replaced by a graduating law student, Ken Malansky, played by William R. Moses. Each plot developed over two hours instead of one, and the extra time was spent on extended chases and blind alleys. However, the basic formula stayed the same.

This newest version of *Perry Mason* took an interesting twist in the spring of 1994. After Burr's death in the fall of 1993, executive producers Fred Silverman and Dean Hargrove followed the wishes of the estate of Erle Stanley Gardner and kept the character alive but off-screen. First to replace him as visiting attorney was Paul Sorvino as Anthony Caruso in *The Case of the Wicked Wives* (1993) and then Hal Holbrook starred as "Wild Bill" McKenzie in *The Case of the Lethal Lifestyle* (1994). In each movie, Mason was conveniently absent. But Street and Malansky were still available as assistants for the "visiting" attorney, and the series was still called *A Perry Mason Mystery,* so that, production after production, the character could live on. However, after the last appearance of Holbrook as the visiting attorney, the TV movie series was canceled.

J. DENNIS BOUNDS

See also **Burr, Raymond; Detective Programs**

Cast (1957–66)

Perry Mason	Raymond Burr
Della Street	Barbara Hale
Paul Drake	William Hopper
Hamilton Burger	William Talman
Lieutenant Arthur Tragg (1957–65)	Ray Collins
David Gideon (1961–62)	Karl Held
Lieutenant Anderson (1961–65)	Wesley Lau
Lieutenant Steve Drumm (1965–66)	Richard Anderson
Sergeant Brice (1959–66)	Lee Miller
Terrence Clay (1965–66)	Dan Tobin

Cast (1973–74)

Perry Mason	Monte Markham
Della Street	Sharon Acker
Paul Drake	Albert Stratton

Lieutenant Arthur Tragg   Dane Clark
Hamilton Burger   Harry Guardino
Gertrude Lade   Brett Somers

Producers
Gail Patrick Jackson, Arthur Marks, Art Seid, Sam
  White, Ben Brady

Programming History
245 episodes
CBS
September 1957–September
  1962   Saturday 7:30–8:30
September 1962–September
  1963   Thursday 8:00–9:00
September 1963–September
  1964   Thursday 9:00–10:00

September 1964–September
  1965   Thursday 8:00–9:00
September 1965–September
  1966   Sunday 9:00–10:00
September 1973–January
  1974   Sunday 7:30–8:30

Further Reading

Fugate, Francis L., and Roberta B. Fugate, *Secrets of the World's Best Selling Writer: The Storytelling Techniques of Erle Stanley Gardner,* New York: Morrow, 1980
Hughes, Dorothy B., *Erle Stanley Gardner: The Case of the Real Perry Mason,* New York: Morrow, 1978
Kelleher, Brian, and Diana Merrill, *The Perry Mason Show Book,* New York: St. Martin's Press, 1987
Martindale, David, *The Perry Mason Casebook,* New York: Pioneer, 1991
Meyers, Richard, *TV Detectives,* San Diego, California: Barnes, and London: Tantivy Press, 1981

Person to Person

U.S. Talk/Interview Program

Person to Person developed out of Edward R. Murrow's belief that human beings are innately curious. That curiosity was intense regarding the private lives of public people, or visiting the extraordinary in the most ordinary environment—the home. For his television program, then, Murrow, sitting comfortably in the studio, informally greeted two guests a week, who gave 15-minute interviews from their homes, talking about the everyday activities of their lives. The interviews avoided politics, detailed discussion of current events, and a line of questioning that delved deeper into one or two issues. The more general the question, and more frequent the change of topic, the more satisfying the process of revealing different facets of the private figure. On *Person to Person,* people conversed with Murrow and, starting in the fall of 1959, with Charles Collingwood, as host. Almost every year for nine years, informal chats positioned the show in the top-ten network programs. But the series increasingly became the battleground, inside and outside CBS, over the function of television news, the ethics of peering into private lives for profit, Murrow's journalistic integrity, and the organizational control of the network's image.

From 1953 through 1956, CBS News aired *Person to Person,* but it was independently owned and produced by John Aaron, Jesse Zousmer, and Murrow. Tensions inside CBS began when Fred Friendly, Murrow's producer of *See It Now,* accused Murrow of capitalizing on the remote, in-home, investigative news interviews done with political leaders, and pioneered by Friendly, on *See It Now.* Although the remote, in-home interview was not new, *Person to Person*'s approach differed substantially from other CBS projects. Murrow anticipated criticism of the series' lack of news-directed discussion. But that was not, in fact, its intended purpose.

Murrow wanted the series to "revive the art of conversation." But the image was as significant as the conversation. Employing from two to six cameras, a program opened up different parts of an individual's home. This was a historical step to building the cult of the personality in news programs. The personalities were divided into two camps, with the entertainment and sports figures in one; the second camp included all others, such as artists, writers, politicians, lawyers, scientists, and industrialists.

Given the period in which it was produced, the series' success was as much technological as human. Regardless of the series' news value, it took time and effort to reach people who were otherwise inaccessible. Murrow's "guests" lived in different locations marked by distinctive terrain. Thus, in a time of presatellite technology, a prerequisite to introducing them to Americans via television was a line-of-sight transmission from the guest home to a telephone microwave transmission tower. The production crew always conquered terrain barriers. Although the crew received notoriety for shearing off part of a hill to achieve line of sight, they most frequently broke records for building tall relay towers for onetime remotes, the first adjacent to the Kutcher's Hotel in Monticello, New York, enabling interviews with boxers-in-training Rocky Marciano and Ezzard Charles.

The guests were maintained in constant visual and aural contact through advance placement of large video cameras in different rooms. It was also necessary to obtain FCC approval for a special high-frequency wireless microphone that could be attached to the guests. Each program periodically used a split-screen image, a new experience for many television viewers.

For the live program to proceed smoothly in real time, some rehearsal was required. From 1953, interviews and statements by Murrow made it common knowledge that cue questions were used before the show so that guests could be "talked through" the movements to be made from room to room. Thus, certain questions were prepared, but answers were spontaneous. The visit to Marlon Brando's home, for example, began outside at night, with a stunning view of Los Angeles. From there it moved to his living room, and finally, to a downstairs area where friends waited to play some music with Brando. A home's content was part of a guest's personality, so the camera frequently stopped to reveal a picture on the wall, vases, and other objects of interest. In the early days of the series, guests pointing out possessions of special value interrupted discussion, sometimes making the series more of a gallery of art objects. And many times a show's success depended on how comfortable both the guest and the host were with the arrangement. Inevitably, the spontaneous nature of the discussion or awkwardness of a situation generated embarrassing moments, such as Julie Harris folding diapers as she spoke, or Maria Callas throwing Murrow off guard by innocently noting she liked the quality of lingerie in the United States. Perhaps for these reasons, the producers valued those infrequent visits to "homes" that had more news value, such as the warden's home on Alcatraz Island, or an old lighthouse.

The series and Murrow received frequent criticism. Respected television critics, including Harriet Van Horne, Philip Mintoff, Gilbert Seldes, and John Lardner, pointed to Murrow's petty, aimless chatter, arguing that television demanded more substance and depth, especially from someone of Murrow's journalistic background. For Murrow's colleagues, the series diverted his valuable time and energy from other projects and added an unnecessary burden. When Collingwood took over as host, these critics quietly accepted the series for what it purported to be.

But Murrow steadfastly defended the series. When an author, such as Walter White, mentioned a new book, book sales increased. Thousands of viewers requested a one-sentence, 57-word Chinese proverb read by Mary Martin, which she had engraved in a rug. If two or three children committed themselves to piano lessons after seeing Van Cliburn, Murrow believed the criticism to be worth taking. Moreover, the range and variety of people interviewed was unprecedented for network television at the time. One three-week period in 1957 included interviews with the political cartoonist Herbert Block, media market researcher A.C. Nielsen, and Robert F. Kennedy, chief council of the Senate's Select Committee.

In 1956 CBS Television bought the series from Murrow, at that time its sole owner. However, because *Person to Person* with Murrow made a large profit for CBS, it continued to be the center of conflict between Murrow and management. *Person to Person* elevated its host to celebrity status with the public, and some at the network resented the fact that the series placed Murrow in a powerful position. Frank Stanton accused *Person to Person*'s production practices of deceit and dishonesty, claiming guests were coached in questions. This charge, coming after the quiz show scandals and directly attacking Murrow's integrity, resulted in a public airing of personality conflicts that hurt CBS's image and further estranged Murrow from the executive branch at the network. A public respectful of Murrow as host, however, did not rush to condemn him for taking risks on other shows, such as his methodical criticism of Senator McCarthy. Fidel Castro's appearance on *Person to Person* had the potential to alienate viewers who considered him a communist dictator, and the program attracted government criticism of CBS, but Murrow survived the resulting criticism. *Person to Person*'s success in the ratings translated to Collingwood as host, continuing to feed the public's appetite for the celebrity interview. When Collingwood began, the series added the attraction of overseas interviews, filmed or taped.

Person to Person first generated many of the arguments still lodged by critics of today's talk shows, arguments questioning the primacy of the individual in news and the role of a voyeuristic camera as a compelling approach to news. But before the series began, Murrow insisted on a thorough respect for the home of guests "invaded" by the camera. Unlike the series to follow, Murrow and the camera did not confront guests with questions constituting an inquiry. Both Murrow and Collingwood permitted their guests to direct the conversations, which accounted for a meandering pace. The hosts' respect for the public figure in a private setting and avoidance of emotional confrontations created a unique ambiance in this programming genre, and *Person to Person* stands as a vital example of television's potential for personal, individualized communication.

RICHARD BARTONE

See also **Friendly, Fred W.; Murrow, Edward R.; Talk Shows**

Hosts
Edward R. Murrow
Charles Collingwood

Producers
John Aaron, Jesse Zousmer, Charles Hill, Robert Sammon, Edward R. Murrow

Programming History
CBS
October 1953–June 1959   Friday 10:30–11:00

October 1959–September
1960   Friday 10:30–11:00
September 1960–December
1960   Thursday 10:00–10:30
June 1961–September
1961   Friday 10:30–11:00

Further Reading

Bliss, Edward Jr., editor, *In Search of Light: The Broadcasts of Edward R. Murrow, 1939–1961,* New York: Knopf, 1967
Cloud, Stanley, and Lynne Olson, *The Murrow Boys: Pioneers on the Front Lines of Broadcast Journalism,* New York: Houghton Mifflin, 1996
Friendly, Fred, *Due to Circumstances Beyond Our Control …,* New York: Random House, 1967
Friendly, Fred, "Edward R. Murrow's Legacy and Today's Media," *Educational Broadcasting Review* (August 1971)
Gates, Gary Paul, *Air Time; The Inside Story of CBS News,* New York: Harper and Row, 1978
Gould, Jack, "CBS Revises TV Policy to End Program Deceits," *New York Times* (October 20, 1959)
Kendrick, Alexander, *Prime Time: The Life of Edward R. Murrow,* Boston: Little, Brown, 1969
Kuralt, Charles, "Edward R. Murrow," *North Carolina Historical Review* (1971)
Merron, J., "Murrow on TV: See It Now, Person to Person, and the Making of a 'Masscult Personality,'" *Journalism Monographs* (1988)
"Murrow's Indictment of Broadcasting," *Columbia Journalism Review* (Summer 1965)
Persico, Joseph E., *Edward R. Murrow: An American Original,* New York: Dell, 1990
Sperber, A.M., *Murrow: His Life and Times,* New York: Freundlich, 1986

Pertwee, Jon (1919–1996)

British Actor

Jon Pertwee was a British comedy character actor credited with an extensive list of stage, screen, radio, and cabaret appearances. The onetime spouse of *Upstairs, Downstairs* star Jean Marsh, Pertwee is best known for his turn from 1970 to 1974 as the Doctor in the long-running BBC program, *Doctor Who.* A master of accents, voices, sounds, and comical walks, Pertwee perfected his multiple comedic personae on the radio series *The Navy Lark* and in supporting roles in various films, beginning with his appearance in 1937's *Dinner at the Ritz.*

Recruited by *Doctor Who* producer Peter Bryant in

1969 to take over as the Doctor from Patrick Troughton, Pertwee brought to the program a radically different interpretation of the title character. Aired initially in 1963, *Doctor Who* was produced by the drama department at the BBC and—contrary to many reports—was not intended primarily for children. The first Doctor, as portrayed by William Hartnell, was a renegade Time Lord from the planet of Gallifrey who exhibited a strong moral sense, an aggressive and curmudgeonly attitude, and impatience with his various earthly companions' comparative mental slowness. Hartnell was replaced in 1966 by Patrick Troughton,

Jon Pertwee as Doctor Who.
Courtesy of the Everett Collection

who played the part as a "cosmic hobo" in the tradition of Charlie Chaplin's Little Tramp.

As Sean Hogben asserted in "Doctor Who: Adventure with Time to Spare" in *TV Week,* however, "*Doctor Who* won its reputation as a top science fiction series during Jon Pertwee's time in the role." Reacting to the popularity of the early James Bond films, and determined to move away from the clownish depiction Troughton gave the Doctor, Pertwee played the character as an action-based interplanetary crusader exhibiting the characteristics of a folk hero. Pertwee was thus able to draw on his considerable ability to perform his own stunts—resulting from his love of skin diving and waterskiing, along with his habit of driving fast vehicles—which gave a harder edge to his interpretation.

The Pertwee era began with the serialization of "Spearhead from Space," which also introduced the program's fans to the series' first broadcasts in color, after 17 years of black-and-white shows. Pertwee's adoption of his grandfather's evening suits as the foundation of the Doctor's garb allowed him to switch among different colored velvet smoking jackets to mark each passing season of episodes. With this change in the Doctor's apparel, the producers began to publicize the series as providing "adventure in style," alluding to Pertwee's penchant for a similar type of life outside the studio while partly cashing in on the liberated "Swinging Sixties" ambiance still prevalent in Great Britain during the early 1970s. The fact that the program was attracting a considerable audience among upscale 17- to 19-year-olds also contributed to this change in character depiction and promotion.

Pertwee's love of fast vehicles and gadgets prompted him to suggest that the Doctor travel from trouble spot to trouble spot in an Edwardian four-seat roadster eventually named "Bessie." During most of Pertwee's term, the Doctor was banished to Earth by the Time Lords of Gallifrey, thus necessitating a different mode of transportation than his predecessors enjoyed with the Tardis, the Doctor's police-box-styled time machine. Thus, "Bessie" and (in 1974) the "Who-mobile," a flying-saucer-shaped, custom three-wheel car built for Pertwee by Peter Faries, became the Doctor's primary transportation during the four years Doctor Number 3 assisted UNIT (United Nations Intelligence Taskforce) and its indefatigable leader, Brigadier Lethbridge-Stewart (Nicholas Courtney), as they saved the Earth from a variety of monsters, aliens, megalomaniacs, and other menaces.

In early 1974 Pertwee announced he would step down from his stint as the Doctor following that season's shooting, in order to resume his stage career in *The Breadwinner.* His final appearance came in "The Planet of the Spiders," which dovetailed with the initial episode the following season, "Robot," during which Tom Baker took over as the regenerated Time Lord. Pertwee returned in 1983 to share top billing with his fellow Doctors in "The Five Doctors," a 20th-anniversary celebration and one of the stories best received by the series' fans. The plot found all five incarnations of Doctor Who taking on their most memorable enemies, who attempted, but failed, to destroy the five Doctors for good.

Jon Pertwee returned briefly to British television in 1979 for the short-lived comedy series *Worzel Gummidge.* His post-Doctor years found him performing primarily onstage and in motion pictures. He continued his association with the Doctor Who character from time to time with appearances at *Doctor Who* conventions worldwide. While on vacation in the United States, Pertwee died unexpectedly at the age of 77 on May 20, 1996.

ROBERT CRAIG

See also **Doctor Who**

Jon Devon Roland Pertwee. Born in London, July 7, 1919. Attended Royal Academy of Dramatic Art (expelled). Married: 1) Jean Marsh, 1955 (divorced, 1960); 2) Ingeborg Rhosea, 1960; children: Dariel and Sean. Toured with the Arts League of Service Travelling Theatre, prior to World War II; film debut, 1937; after service with the Royal Navy, worked in BBC radio comedy and also appeared in films; achieved fame as television performer as third actor to star in *Doctor Who,* 1970–74; also starred in *Worzel Gummidge* and made many other television appearances. Died May 20, 1996.

Television Series

1970–74, 1983	*Doctor Who*
1975–78	*Whodunnit?* (host)
1979–81	*Worzel Gummidge*
1987	*Worzel Gummidge Down Under*

Films (selected)

A Yank at Oxford, 1937; *Murder at the Windmill,* 1948; *Mr. Drake's Duck,* 1951; *Will Any Gentleman?,* 1953; *A Yank in Ermine,* 1956; *It's a Wonderful World,* 1956; *Carry On Cleo,* 1964; *Carry on Cowboy,* 1965; *I've Gotta Horse,* 1965; *Carry On Screaming,* 1966; *A Funny Thing Happened on the Way to the Forum,* 1966; *The House That Dripped Blood,* 1970; *One of Our Dinosaurs Is Missing,* 1975; *Adventures of a Private Eye,* 1977; *Wombling Free* (voice only), 1977; *The Water Babies* (voice only), 1978; *The Boys in Blue,* 1983; *Carry On Columbus,* 1992.

Radio

Up the Pole; The Navy Lark.

Recordings

Worzel's Song, 1980; *Worzel Gummidge Sings,* 1980.

Stage

HMS Waterlogged, 1944; *Waterlogged Spa,* 1946; *Knock on Wood,* 1954; *There's a Girl in My Soup; Oh Clarence; Irene.*

Further Reading

Bentham, Jeremy, *Doctor Who: The Early Years,* London: Allen, 1986

Dicks, Terrance, and Malcolm Hulke, *The Making of Doctor Who,* London: Allen, 1980

Haining, Peter, *Doctor Who, the Key to Time: A Year-by-Year Record,* London: Allen, 1984

Nathan-Turner, John, *Doctor Who: The Tardis Inside Out,* New York: Random House, 1985

Peter Gunn

U.S. Detective Program

Peter Gunn, a top-rated detective drama, ran on NBC from 1958 to 1960, and then on ABC in 1960 and 1961. The television series was distinguished for its stylish and sophisticated lead character, Peter Gunn, and is also remembered for the jazz-influenced music of Henry Mancini. Created and produced by then-neophyte filmmaker Blake Edwards, *Peter Gunn* was typical of the male private-eye genre of the late 1950s and early 1960s. The lead character was handsome, dashing, and consistently well dressed in tailored suits, which never seemed to wrinkle even after the usual scuffles with the bad guys. Edwards clearly modeled the character of Peter Gunn on Cary Grant, considered one of Hollywood's most debonair leading men. The actor chosen to play Gunn, Craig Stevens, even bore a close resemblance to Grant.

The series was set in Los Angeles and, more often than not, inside a jazz club called Mother's. The story-line essentially centered around Gunn solving his client's problems, which always involved his having to deal with an assortment of hit men, hoodlums, and as-sorted "hip" characters found on the jazz scene. He was often aided by his personal friend and confidant, police Lieutenant Jacoby (Herschel Bernardi). Although Gunn often had to endure many thrown fists, he himself did not advocate brutality, and violence was not a feature of the series. In the end, the crime was always solved, the criminals were behind bars, and Gunn was shown relaxing at Mother's, where his girlfriend, the vocalist Edie Hart (Lola Albright), was the main attraction.

The style of *Peter Gunn* has been described by some viewers as borderline parody. The dialogue was delivered in a hip, deadpan fashion, and at times the series seemed to be poking fun at more conventional private-eye series. Blake Edwards attributed the critical success of *Peter Gunn* to the series' tendency to be somewhat over the top. The success of the show spawned many similar private detective dramas in the late 1950s and early 1960s, such as *Philip Marlowe* and *Richard Diamond.*

An important ingredient in the show, one that pro-

Peter Gunn, Craig Stevens, Lola Albright, 1958–61, episode
Spell of Murder aired 1/11/60.
Courtesy of the Everett Collection

show's action, and here too it set the precedent for shows that were to follow.

The show lasted for only three seasons, but by stressing style and sophistication *Peter Gunn* caught the attention of many viewers. The combination of the main character's smooth, stoic demeanor, together with Henry Mancini's outstanding jazz themes, worked to leave a lasting impression in the minds of fans.

GINA ABBOTT AND GARTH JOWETT

See also **Detective Programs**

Cast

Peter Gunn	Craig Stevens
Edie Hart	Lola Albright
Lieutenant Jacoby	Herschel Bernardi
"Mother" (1958–59)	Hope Emerson
"Mother" (1959–61)	Minerva Urecal

Producers

Blake Edwards, Gordon Oliver

Programming History

114 episodes	
NBC	
September 1958–September 1960	Monday 9:00–9:30
ABC	
October 1960–September 1961	Monday 10:30–11:00

Further Reading

Collins, Max Allan, *The Best of Crime and Detective TV: Perry Mason to Hill Street Blues, The Rockford Files to Murder She Wrote,* New York: Harmony, 1988

Larka, Robert, *Television's Private Eye: An Examination of Twenty Years Programming of a Particular Genre, 1949 to 1969,* New York: Arno, 1979

Meyers, Richard, *TV Detectives,* San Diego, California: A.S. Barnes, and London: Tantivy, 1981

vided its unique character, was the music of Henry Mancini. He provided a new score for each episode, and when released on the RCA label, the two albums *The Music of Peter Gunn* and *More Music from Peter Gunn* became best sellers. (The "Peter Gunn Theme" continues to be played on mainstream radio and has even been used as the vehicle for modern rock versions.) Mancini's music was an integral part of the

Peter Pan

U.S. Special Presentation

First broadcast on NBC in March 1955 and repeated annually for many years thereafter, *Peter Pan* was a popular melding of American television and Broadway theater. It formed part of an ongoing series titled *Pro-*

ducers' Showcase, a loose rubric for high-quality dramatic presentations put together by producer Fred Coe for the network about once a month between 1954 and 1957.

The impetus for the telecast was the popular Broadway musical *Peter Pan,* starring Mary Martin in the title role and costarring Cyril Ritchard as Pan's nemesis Captain Hook. Based on the 1904 J.M. Barrie play of the same name, the Broadway production was staged by Jerome Robbins. When it ended its theatrical run, Coe arranged to run a version of it, modified for the small screen, on NBC on March 5, 1955.

The production fitted neatly into two of NBC's strategies for establishing its identity as a network. First, *Peter Pan* was what NBC vice president (and programming chief) Pat Weaver called a "spectacular"—a special, high-quality event that publicized the network and drew programming power away from individual sponsors, which generally could not afford to foot the entire bill for these expensive shows. Second, the show was hailed by the network and by critics as a splendid forum for the color television system the network and its parent company, RCA, were hawking.

The teleplay loosely followed the familiar original Barrie play, moving from the nursery of the Darling family in London to the island of Neverland, a magical and mythical place to which the eternally young Peter Pan lured the Darling children. He was especially interested in Wendy, whom he and the other "lost boys" wished to adopt as their mother. Before the play's end, Peter had to defeat the dastardly Captain Hook, a humorously effeminate villain played with panache by Ritchard, and return Wendy and her brothers to their home.

The program's sets, particularly the Neverland set, were simple yet colorful, and audiences and critics enjoyed the close-up view of the Broadway play provided by the television production. Robbins's staging blended lively and tender moments, engaging the audience from the play's beginning. The production gained prestige not just from its famous stars but also from the addition of Lynn Fontaine as the program's narrator.

Peter Pan proved an immediate and spectacular success, garnering an overnight rating of 48 and inspiring Jack Gould of the *New York Times* to speculate that the program had provided "perhaps television's happiest hour." The production was remounted, live, in January 1956 and was rebroadcast annually for years thereafter. It was singled out in the 1955 Emmys as the best single program of the year, and Martin was named best actress in a single performance.

It is easy to account for the teleplay's popularity. It presented a charming and imaginatively staged version of a classic children's tale, drawing in both adult and youthful viewers. It also gave Americans a fantasy-filled forum in which to debate gender in the postwar years.

The teleplay's message about adult manhood and womanhood, that they were states to be avoided at all

Peter Pan, Mary Martin, Maureen Bailey, Kent Fletcher, Joey Trent, 1960 TV special.
Courtesy of the Everett Collection

costs (Peter did not want to grow up, and Wendy was unhappy when she did), played into a growing discomfort with preset gender roles. And both its hero and its villain were highly androgynous.

The message and the androgyny were, of course, present in the original Barrie play. They were enhanced, however, by script changes and by the intimacy of the medium on which the play was broadcast. *Peter Pan* on television resonated with the color and the confusion of its era—and encouraged audiences to fly to Neverland for years to come.

TINKY "DAKOTA" WEISBLAT

See also **Coe, Fred; Special/Spectacular**

Cast

Peter Pan	Mary Martin
Captain Hook/George Darling	Cyril Ritchard
Mary Darling	Margalo Gillmore
Wendy Darling	Kathleen Nolan
John Darling	Robert Harrington
Michael Darling	Joseph Stafford
Liza	Hellen Halliday
Smee	Sondra Lee

Peter Pan

Slightly	David Bean	**Director**
Tootles	Ian Tucker	Jerome Robbins
Ostrich	Joan Tewkesbury	
Crocodile	Norman Shelly	
Wendy (as adult)	Ann Connolly	**Programming History**
Nibs	Paris Theodore	NBC
Noodler	Frank Lindsay	Two hours; March 7, 1955

Executive Producer
Richard Halliday

Further Reading

Hanson, Bruce K., *The Peter Pan Chronicles: The Nearly 100-Year History of the "Boy Who Wouldn't Grow Up,"* Secaucus, New Jersey: Carol, 1993
Martin, Mary, *My Heart Belongs,* New York: Quill, 1984
Rivadue, Barry, *Mary Martin: A Bio-Bibliography,* New York: Greenwood, 1991

Producer
Fred Coe

Peyton Place

U.S. Serial Melodrama

When it appeared on ABC, at that time still the third-ranked U.S. network, *Peyton Place,* a prime-time program based on the Grace Metalious novel, was an experiment for American television in both content and scheduling. Premiering in the fall of 1964, *Peyton Place* was offered in two serialized installments per week, Tuesday and Thursday nights, a first for American prime-time television. Initially drawing more attention for its moral tone than for its unique scheduling, the serial was launched amid an atmosphere of sensationalism borrowed from the novel's reputation. ABC president Leonard Goldenson defended the network's programming choice as a bread-and-butter decision for the struggling network, and the moral outcry settled down once the program established itself as implying far more sensation than it would deliver. This prototype of what came to be known in the 1980s as the prime-time soap opera initially met with great success: a month after *Peyton Place* premiered, ABC rose in the Nielsen ratings to number one for the first time. At one point, the program was so successful that a spin-off serial was considered. Both CBS and NBC announced similar prime-time serials under development.

Executive producer Paul Monash rejected the "soap opera" label for *Peyton Place,* considering it instead a "television novel." (His term is, in fact, the one applied in Latin America, *telenovela,* and Francophone Canada, *teleroman.*) Set in a small New England town, *Peyton Place* dealt with the secrets and scandals of two generations of the town's inhabitants. An unmarried woman, Constance MacKenzie, and her daughter, Allison, were placed at the dramatic center of the story. Constance (played by 1950s film melodrama star Dorothy Malone) eventually married Allison's father, Elliott Carson, when he was released from prison, though his rival Dr. Michael Rossi was never entirely out of the picture. Meanwhile, Allison (Mia Farrow) was caught up in a romantic triangle with wealthy Rodney Harrington (Ryan O'Neal) and Betty Anderson (Barbara Parkins), a girl from the wrong side of the tracks. Over the course of the series, Betty tricked Rodney, not telling him until after they were married that she had miscarried their child; Rodney fled and found love with Allison, but Allison disappeared; Betty was married briefly to lawyer Steven Cord but finally remarried Rodney. Other soap-operatic plotlines involved Rodney's younger brother, Norman Harrington, and his marriage to Rita Jacks.

The production schedule was closest to that of daytime soap opera, with no summer hiatus, no repeats, unlike any prime-time American series before or since. Within the first year, the pace was increased to three episodes per week rather than two, going back to two

Peyton Place, Mia Farrow, Ryan O'Neal, Dorothy Malone, Chris Connelly, Barbara Parkins, 1964–69.
©*20thCentury Fox/Courtesy of the Everett Collection*

Peyton Place, Barbara Parkins, Dorothy Malone, Ryan O'Neal, 1964–69.
Courtesy of the Everett Collection

episodes per week in the 1966–67 season as the craze for the show declined. Several of the show's plot twists were necessitated by cast changes. Most notably, Allison MacKenzie's disappearance occurred when Mia Farrow left the series in 1966 for her highly publicized marriage to Frank Sinatra. The program never fully recovered from Farrow's departure, though news of the distant Allison kept the character alive. Some two years after Farrow left, a young woman appeared with a baby she claimed was Allison's, a development that timed with the release of Farrow's theatrical film, *Rosemary's Baby.*

In 1968 *Peyton Place* underwent a transformation. Some storylines were developed to accommodate more cast changes (Dorothy Malone left the show), but many of the changes in the final season seem to have been in response to Goldenson's call for more youthful, "relevant" programming. One of the youthful additions was the leader of a rock group. Most significant, however, an African-American family—Dr. Harry Miles (Percy Rodriguez), his wife, Alma (Ruby Dee), and their teenage son, Lew (Glynn Turman)—assumed a central position in the heretofore

all-white *Peyton Place.* Cut back to one half-hour episode per week, the show also was scheduled a half hour earlier to appeal further to youthful audiences.

These drastic changes did nothing to revive ratings for the serial, which lasted through the spring of 1969. ABC brought it back for two years in the 1970s as a daytime serial, and in 1985 nine of the original cast members appeared in a made-for-TV movie, *Peyton Place: The Next Generation.*

SUE BROWER

See also **Melodrama; Soap Opera**

Cast

Constance MacKenzie/Carson (1964–68)	Dorothy Malone
Allison MacKenzie (1964–66)	Mia Farrow
Dr. Michael Rossi	Ed Nelson
Matthew Swain (1964–66)	Warner Anderson
Leslie Harrington (1964–68)	Paul Langton
Rodney Harrington	Ryan O'Neal

Norman Harrington	Christopher Connelly	Eddie Jacks (1967–68)	Dan Duryea
Betty Anderson/Harrington/		Carolyn Russell (1968–69)	Elizabeth "Tippy"
Cord/Harrington	Barbara Parkins		Walker
Julie Anderson	Kasey Rogers	Fred Russell (1968–69)	Joe Maross
George Anderson (1964–65)	Henry Beckman	Marsha Russell (1968–69)	Barbara Rush
Dr. Robert Morton (1964–65)	Kent Smith	Rev. Tom Winter (1968–69)	Bob Hogan
Steven Cord	James Douglas	Susan Winter (1968–69)	Diana Hyland
Hannah Cord (1965–67)	Ruth Warrick	Dr. Harry Miles (1968–69)	Percy Rodriguez
Paul Hanley (1965)	Richard Evans	Alma Miles (1968–69)	Ruby Dee
Elliott Carson (1965–68)	Tim O'Connor	Lew Miles (1968–69)	Glynn Turman
Eli Carson	Frank Ferguson	Jill Smith/Rossi (1968)	Joyce Jillison
Nurse Choate (1965–68)	Erin O'Brien-Moore	Joe Rossi (1968)	Michael Christian
Dr. Claire Morton (1965)	Mariette Hartley		
Dr. Vincent Markham (1965)	Leslie Nielsen		
Rita Jacks/Harrington (1965–		**Producers**	
69)	Patricia Morrow	Paul Monash, Everett Chambers, Richard Goldstone,	
Ada Jacks (1965–69)	Evelyn Scott	Felix Feist, Richard DeRoy	
David Schuster (1965–66)	William Smithers		
Doris Schuster (1965)	Gail Kobe		
Kim Schuster (1965)	Kimberly Beck	**Programming History**	
Theodore Dowell (1965)	Patrick Whyte	514 episodes	
Stella Chernak (1965–68)	Lee Grant	ABC	
Joe Chernak (1965)	Dan Quine	September 1964–June 1965	Tuesday and Thursday
Gus Chernak (1965–66)	Bruce Gordon		9:30–10:00
Dr. Russ Gehring (1965–66)	David Canary	June 1965–October 1965	Tuesday, Thursday, and
John Fowler (1965–66)	John Kerr		Friday 9:30–10:00
Marian Fowler (1965–66)	Joan Blackman	November 1965–August	Monday, Tuesday, and
Martin Peyton (1965–68)	George Macready	1966	Thursday 9:30–10:00
Martin Peyton (temporary		September 1966–January	Monday and Wednes-
replacement, 1967)	Wilfred Hyde-White	1967	day 9:30–10:00
Sandy Webber (1966–67)	Lana Wood	January 1967–August 1967	Monday and Tuesday
Chris Webber (1966–67)	Gary Haynes		9:30–10:00
Lee Webber (1966–68)	Stephen Oliver	September 1967–September	Monday and Thursday
Ann Howard (1966)	Susan Oliver	1968	9:30–10:00
Rachael Welles (1966–67)	Leigh Taylor-Young	September 1968–January	Monday 9:00–9:30 and
Jack Chandler (1966–67)	John Kellogg	1969	Wednesday 8:30–9:00
Adrienne Van Leyden (1967)	Gena Rowlands	February 1969–June 1969	Monday 9:00–9:30

Phil Silvers Show, The

U.S. Situation Comedy

The Phil Silvers Show, a half-hour comedy series, first ran on CBS from September 1955 to September 1959. The show's original title was *You'll Never Get Rich,* but this name was dropped shortly after its debut. Since its inception the series has also been commonly referred to as "Sergeant Bilko."

The program's 138 episodes trace the minor victories and misfortunes of the scheming, fast-talking Master Sergeant Ernie Bilko (Phil Silvers), head of the motor pool at the mythical U.S. Army station of Fort Baxter in Roseville, Kansas. In his relentless pursuit of personal gain and physical comfort, Bilko attempts to manipulate

The Phil Silvers Show (aka *Sgt. Bilko/You'll Never Get Rich*), Harvey Lembeck, Phil Silvers, Allan Melvin, 9/20/55.
Courtesy of the Everett Collection

those around him through the selective use of flattery, false naïveté, pulling rank, and a canny ability to identify and stimulate desires, weaknesses, and emotions in others. Although his reputation for masterful chicanery is well known around the base, the other characters in the show prove no match for Bilko's complex mental designs and are ultimately unable to avoid following the course of action he desires. In his attempts to buck the system, Bilko is aided by members of his platoon: a motley collection of blue-collar, "ethnic" Americans whose own distaste for military discipline is displayed through their visible admiration for their brilliant leader.

Aside from money and favors won in poker games and elaborate rackets, however, Bilko never benefits at the expense of others. Faced with innocent victims, the sergeant's conscience kicks in and he expends every

mental resource to resolve the problem. Bilko's one redeeming moral quality, therefore, is his heart of gold, which prevents him both from truly prospering or losing his humanity.

Frequently, unforeseen obstacles to Bilko's strategies arise out of a misunderstanding between the principal characters. Much of the program's humor derives from Bilko's incomplete knowledge of a situation—the audience watches as he unwittingly makes matters worse for himself, before realizing his error and having to employ his quick thinking in order to make amends. Sharp dialogue and tightly woven plotlines (involving absurd, but believable, situations), combined with a heavy emphasis on visual comedy, made *The Phil Silvers Show* one of the most popular and critically acclaimed sitcoms of the 1950s.

The series developed as a collaboration between Silvers, a Brooklyn-born veteran of vaudeville, Broadway, and motion pictures, and Nat Hiken, the show's unassuming head writer, producer, and stage director. Hiken had already earned a reputation for superb radio and TV comedy writing for such celebrities as Fred Allen and Martha Raye. Silvers and Hiken were given tremendous creative license by CBS to devise and cast the show. The two creators experimented with numerous settings and narrative structures before deciding on a military location, a Bilko-centered narrative trajectory, and a colorful coterie of supporting characters. In the spring of 1955, filming began at the DuMont studios in New York. CBS confidence in the production was such that 20 episodes were produced prior to the show's broadcast debut in the fall. The network's magnanimity is understandable, given that "Bilko" neatly fit the successful formula upon which CBS had built its television reputation: a half-hour situation comedy series written as a vehicle for an established performer.

The Phil Silvers Show was initially recorded live on film, using a three-camera setup. Postproduction was minimal, giving the final program a spontaneous, no-frills appeal despite its celluloid status. As the series developed, the storylines often incorporated outside characters who were portrayed by guest celebrities. Mike Todd appeared in one 1958 episode, insisting that it be shot using a movie-style, one-camera production process. The more relaxed shooting schedule engendered by this approach appealed to cast and crew, and the show subsequently adopted this filming technique permanently. This meant that the scenes would be shot throughout the week and later edited together in order. Consequently, the studio audience disappeared, requiring the recording of a laugh track at a weekly screening of the final program.

Despite being scheduled against NBC's Tuesday-night powerhouse Milton Berle, *The Phil Silvers Show* quickly attracted viewers and passed Berle in the ratings within a few months. The show's popularity was matched by great critical acclaim. Along with a bevy of other awards, the series won five Emmys in its first season on the air, and more were to follow over the next couple of years. Nevertheless, the drain of weekly programming eventually began to take its toll. Hiken's total commitment to the show proved physically and creatively exhausting for him, and he left the series in 1957 to pursue less hectic projects. By the spring of 1959, when CBS announced its forthcoming cancellation of the series, Silvers too was complaining of fatigue induced by the show's grueling routine. Bending under the weight of the 22 cast members' salaries, CBS canceled the still-popular series in order to maximize its syndication price and potential.

Following the show, Hiken and Silvers collaborated on several hour-long musical specials for CBS at the end of the 1950s. While the actor then returned to the stage and big screen, Hiken achieved another TV comedy hit with *Car 54, Where Are You?* In 1963, attracted by a lucrative financial offer from CBS, Silvers attempted to recapture his earlier television success with *The New Phil Silvers Show.* This series transferred the Bilko scenario to a civilian setting: Silvers played Harry Grafton, a crafty, wheeling-dealing maintenance superintendent at an industrial plant. Grafton lacked Bilko's magical presence and any of his redeeming values; the series floundered in the ratings and was canceled in its first season. The Bilko formula was more successfully reinvoked in the early 1960s in the form of the ABC cartoon *Top Cat.* This prime-time animated series featured the voice of Maurice Gosfield—who had played the slothful audience favorite Duane Doberman in *The Phil Silvers Show*—as Benny the Ball.

Over the decades since its original broadcast, "Sergeant Bilko" has inspired a whole genre of male-dominated, uniformed, nondomestic sitcoms. Such series as *McHale's Navy, Hennesey, M*A*S*H,* and *At Ease* (a banal, short-lived 1980s imitation), to name only a few, have clearly attempted to emulate *The Phil Silvers Show*'s successful blend of distinctive, engaging characters and first-class writing. A 1996 movie named *Sergeant Bilko* starred Steve Martin in the title role.

MATTHEW MURRAY

See also **Silvers, Phil**

Cast

Master Sergeant Ernie Bilko	Phil Silvers
Corporal Rocco Barbella	Harvey Lembeck
Private Sam Fender	Herbie Faye
Colonel John Hall	Paul Ford
Private Duane Doberman	Maurice Gosfield
Sergeant Rupert Ritzik	Joe E. Ross
Corporal Henshaw	Allan Melvin
Private Dino Paparelli	Billy Sands
Private Zimmerman	Mickey Freeman
Nell Hall	Hope Sansberry
Sergeant Grover	Jimmy Little
Sergeant Joan Hogan (1956–58)	Elisabeth Fraser

Producers

Edward J. Montagne, Aaron Ruben, Nat Hiken

Programming History

138 episodes
CBS
September 1955–October 1955   Tuesday 8:30–9:00

November 1955–February 1958   Tuesday 8:00–8:30
February 1958–September 1959   Friday 9:00–9:30

Further Reading

Drury, Michael, "Backstage with Phil Silvers," *Colliers* (May 11, 1956)

Freeman, Mickey, and Sholom Rubinstein, "But Sarge...Behind the Lines with Sgt. Bilko," *Television Quarterly* (1986)

Freeman, Mickey, and Sholom Rubinstein, *Bilko: Behind the Lines with Phil Silvers,* London: Virgin Publishing, 2000

Silvers, Phil, with Robert Saffron, *This Laugh Is on Me: The Phil Silvers Story,* Englewood Cliffs, New Jersey: Prentice Hall, 1973

Philbin, Regis (1933–)

U.S. Television Personality

Regis Philbin is one of the most recognized individuals in American television. Finally, after more than 45 years in the business, he won two Emmys in 2001 as Best Game Show Host for ABC's blockbuster *Who Wants to Be a Millionaire?* and Best Talk Show Host for syndicated, top-rated daytime talker *Live with Regis & Kelly.*

The eldest child of Frank and Florence Philbin, an Irish-Italian/ Catholic couple, Philbin was named after his father's alma mater, Regis High School, a Manhattan Jesuit boys' school. Regis was raised in the South Bronx section of New York City and graduated from Cardinal Hayes High School in 1949. He earned his B.A. in Sociology at Notre Dame University in 1953. Philbin secretly wanted to major in broadcasting but could not find the courage to do it.

After two years in the navy, where he became a lieutenant, Philbin interviewed unsuccessfully in 1955 with L.A.'s KCOP-TV. He returned to New York and worked as an NBC page/usher for Steve Allen's *The Tonight Show.* Three months later, KCOP-TV hired him as a stagehand and then writer, researcher, and producer. After substituting once on-air in sports, Philbin wanted to be on-air permanently and became frustrated with behind-the-scenes work. In 1957 he switched to radio news at San Diego's KSON, where he developed unremarkable but quirky "Philbinesque" stories. In 1960 San Diego's KFMB-TV news hired him specifically to do "Philbinesque" stories. Within a year, he was anchor at San Diego's KOGO-TV and host of *The Regis Philbin Show.* The Saturday late-night show enabled Philbin to emulate Jack Paar and to develop the trademark "host chat" he still uses on *Live.*

In October 1964 Philbin replaced Steve Allen on Westinghouse's nationally syndicated late-night talk show. Philbin, whose live ad-libbing about daily events was created out of necessity on KOGO-TV, could not function on *That Regis Philbin Show* in a highly structured, taped format shown on a two-week delay. Canceled after 26 weeks, Philbin resumed KOGO-TV's *The Regis Philbin Show* in 1965 and commuted to L.A.'s KTTV for a weekday show.

Philbin ascended to network television as sidekick on ABC's *The Joey Bishop Show,* launched April 17, 1967, to compete with NBC's *The Tonight Show Starring Johnny Carson.* Philbin tried to suppress his ego but tired of Bishop's jokes and insults. One night, Philbin walked out on-air, but he returned a week later. It remains unclear if it was a publicity stunt. He also recorded *It's Time For Regis!,* an album for Mercury records rereleased on CD in 1998. He ventured into acting, appearing on NBC's *Get Smart* on March 23, 1968.

Philbin held a variety of jobs until 1975. On L.A.'s KHJ-TV, he hosted *Philbin's People* and *Tempo,* a three-hour news and information morning show. Once a month he commuted to St. Louis to do one live and three taped installments of *Regis Philbin's Saturday Night in St. Louis,* a variety show on CBS affiliate KMOV. Philbin debuted on film in 1972's *Everything You Always Wanted to Know About Sex* as a celebrity game show guest. In November 1974 L.A.'s KABC-TV hired him as movie reviewer. In 1975 he also co-hosted KABC's *A.M. Los Angeles* with Sarah Purcell. Joy Senese, whom he married in 1970, frequently substituted for Purcell. Purcell joined NBC's *Real People* in 1979, and Cyndy Garvey replaced her.

Philbin also hosted ABC's daytime *The Neighbors* (1975–76), in which five neighbors gossiped about one another and were awarded prizes. In 1976 Philbin was on-field correspondent for ABC's *Almost Anything Goes,* a one-hour game show shot on location with

American small towns competing against one another. He continued occasional TV and movie appearances.

In November 1981 NBC aired *The Regis Philbin Show,* a 30-minute daily national morning show co-hosted by Mary Hart. Just half of NBC's affiliates carried the taped show. It received an Emmy for Outstanding Daytime Variety Series but was canceled after four months. In 1982 Philbin created a magazine show for Cable Health Network (now Lifetime), called *Regis Philbin's Celebrity Health Styles.* It moved to prime time as *Regis Philbin's Lifestyles,* focusing on cooking, health, and fitness, and became Lifetime's highest-rated program ever, lasting until 1988.

In January 1983 New York's WABC-TV hired Philbin for *The Morning Show.* Until 1985 his cohost was again Cyndy Garvey, until Kathie Lee Gifford replaced her in June 1985. The chemistry between Philbin and Gifford sent ratings skyrocketing, and the show was nationally syndicated in September 1988 as *Live with Regis & Kathie Lee. Live* showcased the cohosts' abilities to talk with guests and to each other about anything. Philbin and Gifford coauthored 1993's *Cooking with Regis & Kathie Lee* and 1994's *Entertaining with Regis & Kathie Lee,* hosted the Miss America pageant, and appeared together and separately in concert to sold-out crowds. Philbin's 1993 angioplasty led to his own exercise video: *Regis, My Personal Workout.* He has also written his autobiography, *I'm Only One Man* (1995), and *Who Wants to Be Me?* (2000).

In 1999 ABC's ratings were slumping. Philbin was hired to host a new game show, based on a British program, called *Who Wants to Be a Millionaire?* Originally slated for a two-week sweeps run, it became the highest-rated prime-time game show in history and was permanently placed in ABC's lineup, taking the network back to the top. In February 2000 ABC's corporate owner, Disney, signed Philbin to a salary of $20 million per year, a record for a game show host. He also introduced the popular catchphrase "Is that your final answer?" into national popular culture.

Gifford left *Live* in 2000 to pursue other interests. Proving Philbin's popularity, the ratings rose dramatically. After a much-publicized search for a new cohost, Philbin introduced soap opera star Kelly Ripa and renamed the show *Live with Regis & Kelly* in February 2001.

W.A. KELLY HUFF

See also **Allen, Steve; Paar, Jack**

Regis Philbin. Born Regis Francis Xavier Philbin in New York City, August 25, 1933. Married: 1) Kay Faylan, 1957 (divorced, 1968); children: Amy (1961) and Daniel (1967); 2) Joy Senese, 1970; children: Joanna (1973) and Jennifer (1974). Graduated from Cardinal Hayes High School, Bronx, New York; B.A. Sociology, University of Notre Dame, 1953 and honorary doctor of laws degree, 1999. Served in U.S. Navy. Started career as page/usher for NBC's *The Tonight Show,* New York (1955); worked as stagehand and as writer, researcher, and producer at KCOP-TV, Los Angeles (1955–57); worked in radio news at KSON, San Diego (1957–60) and TV news at KFMB-TV, San Diego (1960). Has hosted *The Regis Philbin Show* on KOGO-TV, San Diego (1961–63) and Westinghouse's Nationally Syndicated *That Regis Philbin Show* (1964–65); cohosted ABC's *The Joey Bishop Show* (1967–69); hosted *Philbin's People* and *Tempo* on KHJ-TV, Los Angeles (1970–73); *A.M. Los Angeles* on KABC-TV (1975–81); hosted ABC's *The Neighbors* (1975–76); on-the-field correspondent for ABC's *Almost Anything Goes,* (1976); hosted NBC's *The Regis Philbin Show* (1981–82); cohosted with Joy Philbin *Regis Philbin's Celebrity Health Styles* aka *Regis Philbin's Lifestyles* on Cable Health Network/Lifetime (1982–88); cohosted WABC-TV New York's *The Morning Show* (1983–88); cohosted nationally syndicated *Live with Regis & Kathie Lee* (1989–2000); hosts ABC's *Who Wants to Be a Millionaire?* (1999–2002; became *Who Wants to Be a Super Millionaire?,* 2004–); hosted *Live with Regis* (2000–01); hosts nationally syndicated *Live with Regis & Kelly* (2001–present). Eleven-time Emmy Award nominee (ten as cohost of *Live* and one as host of *Who Wants to Be a Millionaire?*) and two-time winner in 2001 for Best Talk Show Host and Best Game Show Host. Honored by New York City mayor Rudolph Giuliani with Crystal Apple Award for contributions to New York TV industry.

Television

1961–63	*The Regis Philbin Show* (KOGO-TV, San Diego)
1964–65	*That Regis Philbin Show* (Westinghouse, Nationally Syndicated)
1967–69	*The Joey Bishop Show* (ABC)
1970–73	*Tempo* and *Philbin's People (KHJ-TV, Los Angeles)*
1972–75	*Regis Philbin's Saturday Night in St. Louis* (KMOV-TV, St. Louis)
1975–81	*A.M. Los Angeles* (KABC-TV, Los Angeles)
1975–76	*The Neighbors* (ABC)
1976	*Almost Anything Goes* (ABC)

1981–82	*The Regis Philbin Show* (NBC)
1982–88	*Regis Philbin's Celebrity Health Styles,* aka *Regis Philbin's Lifestyles* (Cable Health Network/ Lifetime)
1983–88	*The Morning* Show (WABC-TV, New York)
1989–2000	*Live with Regis & Kathie Lee* (nationally syndicated)
1999–2002	*Who Wants to Be a Millionaire?* (ABC)
2000–01	*Live with Regis*
2001–present	*Live with Regis & Kelly* (nationally syndicated)
2004–present	*Who Wants to Be a Super Millionaire?*

Videotape

Regis: My Personal Workout, 1993

Films

Everything You Always Wanted to Know About Sex (but Were Afraid to Ask), 1972; *The Bad News Bears Go to Japan,* 1978; *Sextette,* 1978; *The Man Who Loved Women,* 1983; *Malibu Express,* 1985; *Funny About Love,* 1990; *Night and the City,* 1992; *Open Season,* 1996; *Dudley Do-Right,* 1999; *Little Nicky,* 2000; *Pinocchio* (voice only), 2002.

Made-for-Television Movies

SST: Death Flight, 1977; *Mad Bull,* 1977; *Mirror, Mirror,* 1979; *California Girls,* 1985; *Perry Mason: The Case of the Telltale Talk Show Host,* 1993.

Recording

It's Time For Regis!, 1998.

Publications

Cooking with Regis & Kathie Lee, 1993
Entertaining with Regis & Kathie Lee, 1994
I'm Only One Man (autobiography), 1995
Who Wants to Be Me?, 2000

Further Reading

Allen, Steve, *Hi-Ho Steverino: My Adventures in the Wonderful Wacky World of TV,* Fort Lee, New Jersey: Barricade Books, 1992

Bauder, David, "Philbin's Ratings Shoot Up After Kathie Lee Gifford Leaves," *The Associated Press* (September 9, 2000)

Farache, Emily, "Regis (Finally) Wins Emmy!" *E! Online* (April 19, 2002)

King, Norman, *Regis and Kathie Lee: Their Lives Together and Apart,* New York: A Birch Lane Press Book, 1995

McNeil, Alex, *Total Television: A Comprehensive Guide to Programming from 1948 to the Present,* 3rd ed., New York: Penguin Books, 1991

Tracy, Kathleen, *Regis! The Unauthorized Biography,* Toronto: ECW Press, 2000

Philco Television Playhouse

U.S. Anthology Drama

Philco Television Playhouse was one of the most distinguished of the many "live" anthology dramas that aired during the so-called Golden Age of television. The first episode of the *Philco* program was broadcast over NBC on Sunday October 3, 1948, between 9:00 and 10:00 P.M. *Philco Television Playhouse* remained on the air for just over seven seasons, until 1955. At the beginning of its fourth season in 1951, *Philco Television Playhouse* acquired an alternating sponsor, the Goodyear Tire and Rubber Company. From 1951 until it went off the air, the program shared its Sunday night slot with *Goodyear Playhouse*.

For a short period between August 28, 1955, and February 12, 1956, *Philco Television Playhouse* alternated with *The Alcoa Hour* in addition to *Goodyear Playhouse.* Following the end of the *Philco Television Playhouse* in 1955, *The Alcoa Hour* and *Goodyear Playhouse* continued in alternation with broadcasts of one-hour live dramas until September 29, 1957.

Under the guidance of producer Fred Coe (who also served as one of the program's several directors), *Philco Television Playhouse* became known for its high-quality adaptations of plays, short stories, and novels. It was also the first anthology drama to encourage the writing of original plays exclusively for television.

Philco Television Playhouse: The Joker
Photo courtesy of Wisconsin Center for Film and Theater Research

During its first season, *Philco Television Playhouse* emphasized adaptations. The first broadcast was a television version of *Dinner at Eight,* a play by George S. Kaufman and Edna Ferber. Directed by Coe, the production starred Peggy Wood, Dennis King, Judson Laire, Mary Boland, and Vicki Cummings.

Other adaptations from plays that first season included *Counselor-at-Law* with Paul Muni, *The Old Lady Shows Her Medals,* and a version of the Edmund Rostand play *Cyrano de Bergerac* starring Jose Ferrer. Among the novels adapted were Daphne du Maurier's *Rebecca,* Alexandre Dumas's *Camille,* and Jane Austen's *Pride and Prejudice.* On December 19, 1948, *Philco Television Playhouse* broadcast an adaptation of the Charles Dickens's story *A Christmas Carol.* The program included a filmed rendering of "Silent Night" sung by Bing Crosby.

Although it continued to produce adaptations of plays and novels, *Philco Television Playhouse* began to air original scripts toward the end of the first season. These became more important in subsequent seasons. A number of young writers, including Paddy Chayef-

sky, Horton Foote, Tad Mosel, Alan Arthur, Arnold Schulman, and Gore Vidal, began their careers writing teleplays for the program.

Chayefsky wrote several scripts for *Philco/Goodyear.* Among them were *Holiday Song* (*Goodyear,* September 14, 1952), *The Bachelor Party* (*Philco,* October 11, 1953), *The Mother* (*Philco,* April 4, 1954), *Middle of the Night* (*Philco,* September 19, 1954), and *The Catered Affair* (*Goodyear,* May 22, 1955). *The Bachelor Party, Middle of the Night,* and *The Catered Affair* were later made into feature films.

Chayefsky's most famous *Philco* script was *Marty,* aired on May 24, 1953. Directed by Delbert Mann, the production starred Rod Steiger in the title role. It became the most renowned production from the Golden Age of television anthologies and marked a turning point for television drama because of the considerable amount of critical attention paid to it by the press.

According to Delbert Mann, *Marty* was inspired by the ballroom of the Abbey Hotel on the corner of Fifty-third Street and Seventh Avenue in New York City. A meeting place for single people during the evening hours, the ballroom was the site of *Philco Television Playhouse* rehearsals during the day. Chayefsky had originally planned to have the main character be a woman but then changed the role into that of the lonely butcher, Marty. The story is a simple one, focused on character and emotion rather than excessive dramatic action. After many unsuccessful attempts to find a girl, Marty visits the ballroom one evening and meets a homely young teacher. Against the objections of his mother and his bachelor friends, Marty finally stands up for himself and calls the young woman back for a date.

Mann believed that Rod Steiger gave the best performance of his life in the role of Marty, and Steiger became so moved by the story that he wept openly on the set. Mann's last direction to Steiger before air was to "hold back the tears." Mann also directed the 1956 film version of *Marty,* which won four Academy Awards—for Best Picture, Best Screenplay, Best Director, and Best Actor (given to Ernest Borgnine for his portrayal of Marty).

Other important productions broadcast on the *Philco Television Playhouse* were Gore Vidal's *Visit to a Small Planet* (*Goodyear,* May 8, 1955), which later became a Broadway play and a feature film; Vidal's *The Death of Billy the Kid* (*Philco,* July 24, 1955), which became the 1958 film *The Left-Handed Gun;* and Horton Foote's *A Trip to Bountiful,* later staged on Broadway in the 1950s and reshot in the 1980s as a film, with actress Geraldine Paige winning an Academy Award for Best Actress for her performance in the film.

Fred Coe, a graduate of the Yale Drama School, was active as a director and producer for the *Philco Television Playhouse* for six years. Coe and other staff directors including Gordon Duff, Delbert Mann, Vincent Donehue, and Arthur Penn shared directing responsibilities on a rotating basis. Usually, they worked three weeks ahead with one show in preparation, one in rehearsal, and one on the studio floor ready for telecasting.

During its long tenure, the *Philco Television Playhouse* became a breeding ground for an entire generation of young directors, actors, and writers who later became famous in motion pictures and on Broadway. The program won a Peabody Award in 1954 for its "superior standards and achievements." Some of the best-known actors who appeared on the series were Joanne Woodward, Steve McQueen, Rod Steiger, Eva Marie Saint, Grace Kelly, Kim Stanley, Jack Klugman, and Walter Matthau.

HENRY B. ALDRIDGE

See also **Advertising, Company Voice; Anthology Drama; "Golden Age" of Television;** *Goodyear Playhouse*

Host
Bert Lytell (1948–49)

Producers
Fred Coe, Gordon Duff, Garry Simpson

Programming History
NBC
October 1948–October 1955   Sunday 9:00–10:00

Further Reading

Hawes, William, *The American Television Drama: The Experimental Years,* Tuscaloosa: University of Alabama Press, 1986
Kindem, Gorham, editor, *The Live Television Generation of Hollywood Film Directors: Interviews with Seven Directors,* Jefferson, North Carolina: McFarland, 1994
MacDonald, J. Fred, *One Nation under Television: The Rise and Decline of Network TV,* New York: Pantheon, 1990
Saalbach, Louis Carl, "Jack Gould: Social Critic of the Television Medium," Ph.D. diss., University of Michigan, 1980
Skutch, Ira, *Ira Skutch: I Remember Television: A Memoir,* Metuchen, New Jersey: Scarecrow Press, 1989
Stempel, Tom, *Storytellers to the Nation: A History of American Television Writing,* New York: Continuum, 1992
Sturcken, Frank, *Live Television: The Golden Age of 1946–1958 in New York,* Jefferson, North Carolina: McFarland, 1990
Wicking, Christopher, and Tise Vahimagi, *The American Vein: Directors and Directions in Television,* New York: Dutton, 1979
Wilk, Max, *The Golden Age of Television: Notes from the Survivors,* New York: Delacorte Press, 1976

Phillips, Irna (1901–1973)

U.S. Writer

The universally recognized originator of one of television's most enduring—and profitable—television genres, Irna Phillips is responsible for the daytime drama as we know it today. Her contributions to one format are unprecedented in television history. Television comedy had many parents—Ernie Kovacs, Jackie Gleason—and TV drama was initially shaped by such figures as Paddy Chayefsky, Rod Serling, Reginald Rose, and others. The soap opera, however, had only one "mother," and Phillips was it. She founded an entire industry based on her techniques and beliefs, and the ongoing, interlocking stories that she dreamed.

Born in Chicago in 1901, the youngest of ten children, legend has it that Phillips endured her poverty-stricken, lonely childhood by reading and concocting elaborate lives for her dolls. When she started college, she dreamed of an acting career, but school administrators doubted that her looks would get her far so she turned to teaching. After graduation, she taught in Missouri and Ohio for several years before returning to Chicago.

There she fumbled her way into a job with radio station WGN as a voice-over artist and actress. Soon after, the station asked her to concoct a daily program "about a family." Phillips's program *Painted Dreams* premiered on October 20, 1930. *Dreams* is usually recognized as radio's first soap opera. It ran with Phillips both writing and acting in it until 1932, when she left WGN because of dispute between her and the owners about the future of the program. At WGN's competi-

Irna Phillips, 1935.
Courtesy of the Everett Collection

tion, WMAQ, Phillips created *Today's Children,* which aired for seven years. Other highly successful dramas followed: *The Guiding Light* in 1937, *The Road of Life* in 1938, and *The Right to Happiness* in 1939. By this time, Phillips had given up acting to devote her time to writing. She had also sold the shows to national networks.

By 1943, just over ten years from her beginning, Phillips had five programs on the air. Her yearly income was in excess of $250,000 and her writing output was around 2 million words a year. It was at this phase that she developed the need for assistants to create dialogue for the stories she created. To keep her scripts accurate she also kept a lawyer and doctor on retainer.

Not one to put pen to paper, Phillips created her stories by acting them out as a secretary jotted down what she spoke. Her process of creating by assuming the identities of her characters was so successful it was later adopted by many of Phillips's protégés, including Bill Bell, who went on to create *The Young and the Restless.*

Phillips pioneered in radio many of the devices she would later put to successful (eventually clichéd) use in television. She was the first to use organ music to blend one scene into the next. She was the first to employ Dickensian cliff-hanger endings to keep audiences coming back and to develop the casual pace of these shows—she wanted the busy housewife to be able to run to the kitchen or see to the baby and not miss anything. She was the first to address social concerns in her storylines. She was also the first to shift the focus of serials from blue-collar to white-collar characters; under Phillips, doctors and lawyers became soap staples. In fact, hospital settings and stories about illness were vintage Phillips; a hypochondriac who visited doctors daily, Phillips brought her fascination with medicine to her work.

In other ways, the serials she created did not mirror Phillips's life. For example, although her shows were eventually all produced in New York, Phillips refused to leave Chicago; instead, she stayed involved in all aspects of her programs with frequent phone calls to the East. Also, Phillips, who based her stories on nuclear families, never married, although late in her life she adopted two children.

When Phillips brought her creations to television (somewhat reluctantly), she brought all her devices with her. *The Guiding Light* premiered on TV in 1952. *The Brighter Day* and *The Road of Life* came to the small screen in 1954.

In the early 1950s Phillips began a long association with Procter and Gamble, longtime sponsors of soap operas. All of Phillips's shows at that time, and all she would create in the future, would be under the umbrella of Procter and Gamble Productions.

On April 2, 1956, Phillips premiered what was to become her most successful (and some say favorite) show, *As the World Turns.* Until the 1980s phenomenon of *General Hospital,* it was the most successful soap in history. At its ratings peak in the 1960s, it was regularly viewed by 50 percent of the daytime audience. *As the World Turns* has broken much historical ground during its existence. It was daytime's first half-hour soap (previous shows lasted 15 minutes), and it was the first to introduce a scheming female character, Lisa Miller (played by Eileen Fulton), using feminine wiles to catch unavailable men and generate havoc. The show's popularity even inspired a prime-time spin-off, *Our Private World,* which aired for a few months in 1965.

In 1964 Phillips created daytime's *Another World,* TV's first hour-long soap and the first to broach the subject of abortion. (Phillips never shied away from controversy: when writing for the soap *Love Is a Many-Splendored Thing,* she attempted to introduce an interracial romance. When the network balked, Phillips quit the show.)

Also in 1964, Phillips began working as a consultant

on the prime-time soap *Peyton Place*. Phillips now had control over shows running on all three U.S. networks. In 1965 she created another long-lasting daytime drama, *Days of Our Lives*.

Despite Phillips's legendary golden touch and her importance to the daytime drama, by the 1970s the times and the genre were leaving her behind. Soaps were important profit centers for networks, whose executives concluded that the serials needed to become more sensational in order to keep ratings. Phillips's simpler stories were now out of fashion. She was fired by Procter and Gamble in 1973 and died in December of that year.

Today, daytime is populated with programs she created: *As the World Turns, Days of Our Lives*, and *Guiding Light*. The latter has now set the record as the longest-running series in broadcasting history. Many other soaps on the air were created by those who began their careers working for Phillips: Bill Bell and *All My Children* creator Agnes Nixon.

Phillips believed her success was based on her focus on character, rather than on overly complicated plots, and her exploration of universal themes: self-preservation, sex, and family. She said in 1965, "None of us is different, except in degree. None of us is a stranger to success and failure, life and death, the need to be loved, the struggle to communicate."

CARY O'DELL

See also **Peyton Place; Soap Opera**

Irna Phillips. Born in Chicago, Illinois, July 1, 1901. Educated at University of Illinois, B.S. in education 1923. Children: Thomas Dirk and Katherine Louise. Began career as junior college speech and drama instructor, Fulton, Missouri, 1924; teacher, Dayton, Ohio, 1924–29; first writing job with WGN, Chicago radio station, hired to create ten-minute family drama,

Painted Dreams, 1930; launched the soap *Guiding Light*, 1937; *Guiding Light* switched to TV, 1952; consultant, *Peyton Place*, first successful evening serial, 1964; continued writing soaps until just before her death. Died in Chicago, December 22, 1973.

Television Series

1952–	*Guiding Light*
1954–65	*The Brighter Day*
1954–55	*The Road of Life*
1956–	*As the World Turns*
1964–99	*Another World*
1964–69	*Peyton Place* (consultant)
1965	*Our Private World*
1965–	*Days of Our Lives*
1967–73	*Love Is a Many-Splendored Thing*

Radio

Painted Dreams, 1930–32; *Today's Children*, 1932–38; *Masquerade*, 1934–35; *Guiding Light*, 1937–52; *The Road of Life*, 1938–54; *Woman in White*, 1938–48; *The Right to Happiness*, 1939–60; *Lonely Women*, 1942 (renamed *Today's Children*, 1943); *The Brighter Day*, 1948–56.

Further Reading

Allen, Robert C., *Speaking of Soap Opera*, Chapel Hill: University of North Carolina Press, 1985

LaGuardia, Robert, *Soap World*, New York: Arbor House, 1983

Matelski, Marilyn J., *The Soap Opera Evolution: America's Enduring Romance with Daytime Drama*, Jefferson, North Carolina: McFarland, 1988

O'Dell, Cary, *Women Pioneers in Television*, Jefferson, North Carolina: McFarland, 1996

Soares, Manuela, *The Soap Opera Book*, New York: Harmony, 1978

Pierce, Frederick S. (1933–)

U.S. Media Executive, Producer

Frederick S. Pierce began working at ABC Television 13 years after the company's birth. Starting as an analyst in television research in 1956, Pierce held over 14 positions until resigning as vice chairman of Capital Cities/ABC in January 1986. Pierce's period of greatest accomplishment came from 1974 through 1979, when he served as president of ABC Television. However, he began formulating policies and strategies during the 1950s and 1960s as ABC defined its path in network broadcasting.

Frederick S. Pierce.
Photo courtesy of Frederick S. Pierce

Before ABC's programming department built momentum, CBS and NBC were already entrenched, funneling talent from their established artist bureaus in radio to television affiliates. Both networks had money and leverage, which were an attraction to advertisers, and had independent producers ready to invest. ABC, relying on inexpensive and varied programs, targeted different audiences; Leonard H. Goldenson, ABC's founder and ex-owner of United Paramount Theaters, sought product and collaborative efforts in Hollywood. In this programming environment, Pierce moved up through research, sales, development, and planning until becoming president of ABC Television in October 1974.

On a daily basis, Goldenson phoned the research and sales development department, requesting sales and rating numbers from Pierce, a practice that started a professional and personal bond between them. In the 1950s and 1960s, ABC pursued the youth market with programs such as *American Bandstand* and *Maverick* and relied on a mixture of programs, hoping to find a niche in the diversity of *Bewitched, Mod Squad,* and

Marcus Welby, M.D. The network experimented with violent program content, such as *Bus Stop,* and stressed nontraditional sports, including rodeo and wrestling. Pierce's singular characteristic of persevering within these boundaries made ABC an industry power. Reaching number one in prime time in 1976–77, and maintaining the position for two more seasons, Pierce captured the young, urban viewer with comedy and action, produced longer and more elaborate miniseries and special programs, offered glossy production values in sports programming, and even redirected afternoon soaps toward youth. As president of the Television Division, Pierce introduced three megahits, *Happy Days, Taxi,* and *Mork and Mindy.* The violence and tame sexual content of *The Rookies, Baretta, S.W.A.T.,* and *Charlie's Angels* that angered critics was a natural progression of ABC under Pierce's leadership, the outcome of taking risks and looking—for more than a decade—for any different approach.

Pierce brought passion and dauntless optimism to the conception, development, and scheduling of ABC programming. The news programs *Nightline, 20/20,* and *Good Morning, America* were introduced under his leadership. The network's strategy stemmed from innovation, experimentation, risk, and diversity—words Pierce frequently employed. He introduced the "living schedule," the practice of testing five to eight new series in late winter and the spring, each for a month or more, in preparation for fall scheduling. Pierce also referred to this practice, to be adopted by the other networks, as "investment spending," and he thought of it as a way of respecting and responding to audience feedback. When the "family-viewing hour" was instituted, Pierce scheduled comedies and other fare from 8:00 to 9:00 P.M. and followed with action-adventure programs, Monday through Friday. The strategy, called " clotheslining" or "ridgepoling," succeeded in holding viewers.

Before and after ABC's hold on first place, Pierce brought a new perspective. If an ABC program ranked third in its time slot, it was a failure by industry standards. In his view, though, and therefore the view of ABC, even a third-place program was a success if its rating with a specific target audience was large, for these numbers could translate into value to the advertiser. The other networks soon followed Pierce's view of program assessment and focused attention and efforts on material developed with specific demographic groups in mind.

In the drive for success, Pierce programmed "events" that could draw critical attention and viewership. The miniseries was transformed into such a television event, at times lasting, as in the cases of *Roots* and *The Winds of War,* more than seven nights. Under the supervision of Roone Arledge as president of ABC Sports, sports coverage became a central source of revenue for ABC. The quest for a hit sports event meant Pierce's approval of large outlays of money for programming such as the Olympics and championship boxing matches. When one event was a success, it justified Pierce's spending but kept the company in a precarious position for the long term.

The news division received the least amount of attention from Pierce until he convinced Goldenson to appoint Arledge president of ABC News in 1977. Pierce believed sports and news held a conceptual common ground. Arledge agreed and successfully applied engaging production techniques with commentators seeking celebrity status in American homes. Although Pierce believed Arledge could assist the news division, Pierce also made the dramatic move of hiring Barbara Walters as an additional safeguard.

Since Pierce was driven by a lifelong commitment to ABC, he expected the same loyalty in return. He stated publicly that he sought the presidency of ABC, but in January 1974 Goldenson first appointed him executive vice president in charge of ABC Television, with the added responsibilities of developing the company's cable, pay-per-view, and video projects, before naming him president of ABC Television in October of that year, responsible for five divisions: entertainment, finance and planning, the TV network, ABC-owned stations, and sports. However, Pierce had difficulty positioning ABC in the larger media puzzle with some of the projects he initiated. From 1978 through 1980, Pierce baffled the industry with his statements against cable, calling for the protection of free television and criticizing cable's unrestricted content. But other statements soon followed, describing cable as a tool for diverse programming. Pierce's credibility began to be questioned.

In the 1970s Pierce was surrounded at different times by such prominent figures as Arledge, Fred Silverman, Barry Diller, and Michael Eisner. He pursued Silverman for the position of president of ABC Entertainment, and they worked efficiently together. But upon Silverman's departure, Pierce became highly critical of Silverman's limitations, minimizing his contributions to ABC's turnaround. Pierce was self-consciously basking in the glory of establishing ABC as a powerful network. The situation began to change. Pierce all but abandoned action-adventure series by 1980, when they were partly responsible for securing young, urban male viewers. He did not recognize the changes developing in television's collaborative arrangements with Hollywood. He continued to depend on the "living schedule," with its rush to find a hit within four weeks, and in so doing alienated producers whose programs were removed from the schedule without time for the series to develop an audience. As president of ABC, Inc., he surrounded himself with allies, including Tony Thomopoulous, president of ABC Television, Pierce's most cherished area.

Pierce reached the top of ABC as numerous ventures stalled in development, when money was already committed to major events, and shareholders were demanding fiscal prudence. After ABC was purchased by Capital Cities, Pierce needed Tom Murphy, the new chair and chief executive officer, to position ABC for the future. Pierce, however, had no inclination of what the future held. CapCities' assessment of ABC and what needed to be done significantly excluded him. By the time of his resignation in 1986, he expressed amazement and disbelief at the turn of events, suggesting an inability to perceive the complex and unstable structure he helped build.

Since leaving ABC Pierce has continued to be active in the entertainment industry. With his two sons, Richard and Keith, he founded the Frederick S. Pierce Company, dedicated to quality films and television programs. The company's projects included the four-part *20,000 Leagues Under the Sea* (ABC, 1997) and the Emmy-winning *The Positively True Adventures of the Alleged Texas Cheerleader-Murdering Mom* (HBO, 1993). Since 1998 Pierce has been an executive producer of the American Film Institute's centennial salute to American cinema, including the institute's *100 Years, 100 Passions* in June 2002. Pierce comes to this yearly project after serving as chairman of the American Film Institute's Board of Trustees from 1992 to 1996.

RICHARD BARTONE

See also **American Broadcasting Company; Arledge, Roone; Diller, Barry; Eisner, Michael; Goldenson, Leonard; Programming; Silverman, Fred**

Frederick S. Pierce. Born in New York City, April 8, 1933. Educated at Bernard Baruch School of Business Administration, City College of New York, B.A., 1953. Served with U.S. Combat Engineers, Korean War. Married: Marion; children: Richard, Keith, and Linda. Began career as analyst in TV research, ABC, 1956; director of sales planning, ABC, 1962; vice president of planning, 1970; vice president in charge, ABC-TV planning and development, and assistant to president, 1974, president of ABC TV, 1974; president and chief operations officer, ABC, Inc., 1983, resigned from ABC, Inc., 1986; founder, Frederick Pierce Company, 1988, and Pierce/Silverman Company with Fred Silverman, 1989. Chairman of the Board of Trustees, American Film Institute, 1992–96.

Made-for-Television Movies

1992	*Deadlock*
1993	*The Positively True Adventures of the Alleged Texas Cheerleader Murdering Mom*
1994	*Witness to the Execution*
1994	*The Substitute Wife*
1997	*The Absolute Truth*

Television Miniseries

1997	*20,000 Leagues under the Sea*

Television Specials

2000	*AFI's 100 Years, 100 Laughs: America's Funniest Movies*
2001	*AFI's 100 Years, 100 Thrills: America's Most Heart-Pounding Movies*
2002	*AFI's 100 Years, 100 Passions*

Film

Money Train, 1995.

Further Reading

Auletta, Ken, *Three Blind Mice: How the TV Networks Lost Their Way,* New York: Random House, 1991

Bedell, Sally, *Up the Tube: Prime Time TV and the Silverman Years,* New York: Viking, 1981

Goldenson, Leonard H., *Beating the Odds: The Untold Story Behind the Rise of ABC,* New York: Scribner's, 1991

Gunther, Marc, *The House That Roone Built: The Inside Story of ABC News,* Boston: Little, Brown, 1994

Mermigas, Diane, "Q and A: Fred Pierce," *Electronic Media* (September 30, 1985)

"The Pierce Persona," *Broadcasting* (January 17, 1983)

"Pierce-Silverman: Former Top ABC Executives Team Up," *Broadcasting* (March 27, 1989)

Quinlan, Sterling, *Inside ABC: American Broadcasting Company's Rise to Power,* New York: Hastings House, 1979

Williams, Huntington, *Beyond Control: ABC and the Fate of the Networks,* New York: Macmillan, 1989

Pilot Programs

During the first four months of the year, U.S. television studios and production companies (and, increasingly, similar organizations in other nations) immerse themselves in the annual rite of spring known as "pilot season." The television pilot program is a sample episode of a proposed television show, which may be chosen by networks for the following fall's schedule. Pilot season is a frenetic, competitive time in Hollywood; prominent producers, reputable writers, and experienced directors design and showcase their wares for network executives, with each "player" hoping for the next hit series.

Pilots are expensive to produce, and shows that are not purchased by a network have no value. Since the new season is planned using pilots, and the entire offering of a network is usually in place by mid-May, the careful selection of pilots is crucial for designing a competitive lineup of shows. Shows made as pilots during this period are frequently the culmination of long-term preparation, sometimes spanning years. A pilot concept deemed unacceptable by network executives in one year may later become suitable as tastes and mores change. Writers and producers may also design potential shows based on the popularity of programming from a previous season. For example, the final fall 1995–96 season contained several programs resembling the 1994–95 sleeper hit, *Friends* (NBC). Youth-oriented, nighttime soaps such as *Melrose Place* (FOX, 1992) and *Central Park West* (CBS, 1995) traced their lineage to the unexpected popularity of *Beverly Hills, 90210* (FOX, 1990). Another source for pilot concepts comes from cycles of popular genres in motion pictures or television. In some cases, networks derive pilots by developing "spin-offs," which use characters or guest stars from television shows or movies to establish a new program. In 2000 CBS considered a pilot starring talking Baby Bob, a character originally developed to pitch FreeInternet.com.

The process begins when a writer or producer "pitches" an idea to the networks. Pitches may occur year-round, but most occur in autumn, shortly after the fall season premieres. By then, network executives have already begun to consider the success or failure of new programming and have charted trends in topics, types of characters, and other information pertinent to development. If a pitched concept is given a "green light," the network will commission a script, to be written by the series' creator or by a well-known writer. After reading the completed script, the interested network offers extensive notes on changes as well as positive elements. Few scripts are commissioned, and fewer still lead to the production of a pilot; estimates suggest that out of 300 pitches, approximately 50 scripts are commissioned, and of those, only 6 to 10 lead to the production of a pilot.

Because pilots may take months or years to develop, casting becomes a primary concern during the actual pilot-making process. The first quarter of the year is often the busiest, most lucrative time for actors, agents, producers, and casting directors. Networks like projects that come with a known star attached and are willing to pay a studio more if a potential program contains an actor with a following or name recognition. A pilot that is also a star vehicle generates more publicity: the press increases its commentary and gossip about the star or show; fans of the star already exist, thereby building a core audience for the show's debut; and the presence of a star gives a show an advantage over competition in similar genres or opposing time slots.

Network executives are aware, however, that known stars often fail to carry shows and lesser-known performers can quickly build audiences. A 1990s trend involved the casting of stand-up comedians. Unknown to most viewers, but with solid track records in clubs or other venues, such actors cost less initially but have enhanced potential for becoming successes. Roseanne, Jerry Seinfeld, and Tim Allen illustrated the intelligence of this strategy.

The choice of leading players also influences later casting of supporting actors. Appealing, marketable pilots may sell based on the "chemistry" between the star and members of the supporting cast. In the case of situation comedies (sitcoms), such interplay is often a deciding factor in choosing one pilot over another.

Producers spend a disproportionate amount of money on pilots relative to series' regular episodes. By the early 1990s, the average cost for a half-hour pilot ranged from $500,000 to $700,000, and hour-long pilot program costs have soared beyond $2 million, with James Cameron's pilot for *Dark Angel* reportedly costing close to $10 million. If a show is not contracted (or "picked up") by a network, then producers or studios are not reimbursed for costs.

A trend that began in the mid-1990s, designed to cut costs, is the production of shorter presentation tapes, called "demos." Instead of making a standard-length, 22-minute sitcom using new sets, original music, and complete titles, producers create a partial episode, 15 minutes in length. The presentation tape provides a sample of the show's premise, writing, and cast. Studios rely on preexisting sets, furniture, and props from other shows; titling and new music are limited. If a network buys the series, presentation tapes may be ex-

panded to episode format by adding music, titles, and new footage. If not contracted, the presentation format helps offset costs. Comparable techniques are used in preparing hour-long presentation tapes.

Producers screen finished pilots for network representatives; if the show receives favorable opinions, it will be shown to a test audience, which comments on its qualities. Based on screenings and other criteria, a network decides whether to reject or purchase the series intact, or change cast, location, premise, or other elements, and rescreen. Another decision involves purchase and scheduling; executives must decide whether to contract for "one bite" or "two bites." A one-bite show gets a tryout during the fall schedule; if a show is being contemplated for two bites, its producers know that it may be chosen in the fall, or also as midseason replacement programming, giving it two chances to be selected. Once decisions are made, networks place orders for a number of episodes. Traditionally, at least 13 to as many as 23 episodes were ordered for production; recent changes have led to as few as 7. For actors, "pickup" means a contractual commitment to the show for five to seven years; if the show is not renewed after three years of production, the actor is not paid for the remainder of the contract. Such contracts safeguard a producer's interests: the actor is available for an extended run of the series, increasing the likelihood that at least 100 episodes will be made—the minimum number usually needed for domestic syndication. However, the networks often revise pilots after purchase, recasting stars or replacing producers.

The addition of new networks, cable stations, and premium channels is altering the process of pilot production and sales, by creating more outlets for programs—even those rejected by other networks. A record 42 new series appeared in U.S. prime time during the 1995 fall season, in part because of the previous year's addition of the United Paramount Network (UPN) and the Warner Brothers (WB) Network. These joined relative newcomer FOX Broadcasting Company as a venue for new pilots and subsequent programming. During the pilot season for the 1998–99 schedule, the six major networks commissioned approximately 150 pilots for potential new shows but chose to purchase only 37.

Although pilots and presentation tapes remain essential in the process of program development, new regulations and strategies may eliminate the pilot-producing season. HBO has initiated new programs in June, and more channels are in development for series and movies all year long. It is clear that as the marketing and distribution strategies and capabilities of entertainment television continue to shift and change, so, too, will the process by which programs come to be created and viewed.

KATHRYN C. D'ALESSANDRO

See also **Programming**

Further Reading

Bond, Paul, "Baby Bob Bouncing to CBS Primetime Pilot," *The Hollywood Reporter* (August 4, 2000)

Carter, Bill, "Networks Tuning Out Pilots As a Way to Develop Shows," *New York Times* (January 20, 1992)

Paisner, Daniel, *Horizontal Hold: The Making and Breaking of a Network Television Pilot,* New York: Carol, 1992

Terrace, Vincent, *Fifty Years of Television: A Guide to Series and Pilots,* New York: Cornwall, 1991

Vest, David, "Prime-time Pilots: A Content Analysis of Changes in Gender Representation," *Journal of Broadcasting and Electronic Media* (Winter 1992)

Pittman, Robert W. (1953–)

U.S. Media Executive

Robert W. Pittman was listed in *Advertising Age*'s spring 1995 special issue on the 50th anniversary of television as one of "50 Who Made a Difference" in the history of television. Known as "the father of MTV," at age 27 he created the Music Television cable network. MTV revitalized the music business and spawned the music video industry, which in turn influenced an entire new generation of television programming, production, and commercials that appealed to the so-called MTV generation of young viewers.

Pittman began his remarkable career at age 15 as a radio disc jockey in his hometown of Jackson, Mississippi. From there he went to Milwaukee, then Detroit, and at 18 got his first job in programming, as the program director for WPEZ-FM in Pittsburgh, Pennsylvania. He took the contemporary-music-format radio station to the top of the ratings in its younger target demographic area. He then moved to Chicago and, at the age of 20, programmed country music on NBC-owned WMAQ-AM, where the station shot up from 22nd to 3rd. WMAQ's success is considered one of the major programming turnaround success stories in radio history.

Pittman duplicated the phenomenal success of WMAQ-AM when he was given the responsibility of programming WMAQ's co-owned FM station, WKQX, late in 1975, when he was 22. In one rating book he beat the longtime album-oriented-rock (AOR) leader in the market and made a debut near the top of the target demographic ratings. In 1977 NBC sent Pittman to New York to program the floundering WNBC-AM. Once again the "Boy Wonder," as he was known in radio circles, led the contemporary-music-and-personality-format station, WNBC, to the top of the ratings in its target groups. Many knowledgeable radio programmers and historians consider Pittman to have been the most successful radio program director ever, primarily because of his spectacular success in a variety of formats.

His unusual combination of creative and analytic brilliance made him a rare programmer. A research-oriented manager, he also understood and interacted well with the creative talents and egos of people in the music industry, disk jockeys, and personalities such as Don Imus (whom Pittman was instrumental in firing and then rehiring at WNBC-AM). Pittman's varied talents led John Lack, the executive vice president of Warner Satellite Entertainment Company (WASEC), to hire Pittman as the programmer for the Movie Channel in 1979, giving him his first job in television. Although Lack had conceived of doing an all-music channel filled with related programs, it was Pittman who developed the concept of an all-video channel, where record company-produced videos would be programmed in the same fashion as records on a radio station.

As much as—and perhaps more—than the music, it was the image, attitude, and style that made MTV an instant hit with the antiestablishment, antiauthoritarian, under-30 audience it targeted. The network became a cultural icon, the first network expressly designed to target young audiences. From the beginning, Pittman's genius was in positioning MTV to be different from the traditional networks (ABC, CBS, and NBC). He hired cutting-edge, avant-garde production houses to create logos that would be instantaneously recognizable because they were not network logos, not traditional graphics, symbols, or icons, and thus not connected with the traditional networks in any way. He made sure it would be impossible for any young person to click by MTV on a television set and mistake it for any other network or station; immediate recognition and a unique look were his goals.

Another facet of Pittman's brilliance was his ability to conceptualize programming. He postulated a new theory to explain how young people who grew up with television consumed it differently from their parents. The older generation, he suggested, watched TV as they read books, in a linear way. The new television generation, he believed, processed TV in a nonlinear manner, processing visual information much faster than previous generations. Younger viewers processed television in a nonsequential and nonlinear manner, and they were not disoriented by brief, disjointed images. From this insight came the distinct style of MTV.

Pittman's business savvy was also notable. MTV was the first basic cable network to become profitable. The record companies paid for the programming (the videos) just as they gave radio stations their records. MTV's programming content was virtually free.

This combination of business acumen and programming astuteness led to Pittman's being named CEO of the MTV networks in 1983. In this capacity, he oversaw the redesign and relaunch of Nickelodeon, the creation of VH1 and Nick at Nite, the expansion of MTV into global markets (Europe, Australia, and Japan), and the company's 1984 initial public offering on the stock market.

In 1987 Pittman left MTV after an unsuccessful attempt to buy out the network, cofounding Quantum Media with MCA. Quantum Media produced *The Morton Downey Jr. Show,* a television talk show, and the innovative police documentary *The Street.* Quantum Media was sold to Time Warner in 1989, and Pittman became an executive assistant to Steve Ross. In 1990 he was named CEO of Time Warner Enterprises and took over the additional responsibilities of being chief executive of Six Flags amusement parks, majority-owned by Time Warner. As he did at radio stations and cable networks, he revitalized Six Flags and made the company extremely profitable. When Time Warner sold Six Flags in 1995, Pittman decided to take his payoff from the sale and look for new challenges. He joined Century 21 at the urging of his close friend and investor Henry Silverman and joined the board of directors of America Online.

In 1996 Steve Case, the CEO of America Online, hired Pittman to operate a company that was struggling with outsized growth and expenses. As he had with radio stations, television programs, and amusement parks, Pittman used his marketing acumen and operational expertise to turn around AOL, as he led a spectacular growth spurt in subscriber and advertising revenue. When Case engineered the largest merger in U.S. business history with Time Warner to create the world's largest media company, Pittman became co-chief operating office along with Richard Parsons under CEO Gerald Levin. When the AOL Time Warner board forced Levin to retire, it named Parsons chief executive office to replace Levin, and Pittman chief operating officer of the entire company. However, the dot.com bubble burst, which partially led to AOL Time Warner stock plummeting at the same time that America Online's growth was slowing. Pittman agreed to take on the additional duties of being CEO of AOL in an attempt to help the struggling unit regain its early glory. However, he resigned in exhaustion in July 2002.

CHARLES WARNER

See also **AOL Time Warner; MTV**

Robert Pittman. Born in Jackson, Mississippi, December 28, 1953. Attended Millsaps College, Jackson, Mississippi. Married: 1) Sandy (divorced); child: Bo; 2) Veronique; children Andrew and Lucy. Started as a 15-year-old disk jockey, Jackson, Mississippi, 1968; worked in radio in Milwaukee and Detroit; program director, WPEZ-FM, Pittsburgh, 1971; program director, WMAQ-AM, Chicago, 1973; program director, WKQX-FM, 1975; program director, WNBC-AM, 1977; producer and host, weekly video music show for NBC-owned television stations, 1978; program director, the Movie Channel, 1979; head of programming, Warner Amex Satellite Entertainment; created programming for Music Television (MTV), 1981; president and chief executive officer, MTV Networks, 1983–87; cofounder of Quantum Media (with MCA), 1987; sold Quantum Media to Warner Communications, 1989; president and chief executive officer, Time Warner Enterprises, 1988–91; president and chief executive officer, Six Flags Entertainment, 1990–95; chief executive officer, Century 21 Real Estate, 1995–96; president, America Online, 1996–2000; Co-chief operating officer AOL Time Warner 2000–01; chief operating officer AOL Time Warner, 2001–02.

Television Series

1988–89	*The Morton Downey Jr. Show* (syndicated)
1989–92	*Totally Hidden Video*

Pittman, Robert W.

Television Special

1988   *The Street*

Publication

"We're Talking the Wrong Language to 'TV Babies,'"
New York Times (January 24, 1994)

Further Reading

"Bob Pittman," *Time* (January 7, 1985)
"50 Who Made a Difference," *Advertising Age* (Spring 1995)
Lewis, Lisa, *Gender Politics and MTV: Voicing the Difference,*
    Philadelphia: Temple University Press, 1990
Powers, Ron, "The Cool, Dark Telegenius of Robert Pittman,"
    GQ—Gentleman's Quarterly (March 1989)
Powers, Ron, *The Beast, The Eunuch and the Glass-Eyed Child:*
    Television in the '80s, New York: Harcourt Brace Jo-
    vanovich, 1990

Playhouse 90

U.S. Anthology Drama

A relative latecomer to the group of live anthology dramas, *Playhouse 90* was broadcast on CBS between the fall of 1956 and 1961. Its status as a "live" drama was short-lived in any case, since the difficulties in mounting a 90-minute production on a weekly basis required the adoption of the recently developed videotape technology, which was used to prerecord entire shows from 1957 onward. Both the pressures and the costs of this ambitious production eventually resulted in *Playhouse 90* being cut back to alternate weeks, sharing its time slot with *The Big Party* between 1959 and 1960. The last eight shows were aired irregularly between February and May 1960, with repeats broadcast during the summer weeks of 1961.

Despite its late entry into the field of anthology dramas, many considered, and still consider, *Playhouse 90* as the standard against which all other drama anthology programs are to be judged. Although its debut show, a Rod Serling adaptation of the novel *Forbidden Area,* failed to garner much critical interest, the following week's presentation of an original teleplay by Serling, *Requiem for a Heavyweight,* was quite notable, with the story becoming an enormous success both in this initial television broadcast and later as a feature film. *Requiem* swept the 1956 Emmys, winning awards in all six categories in which it was nominated, including Best Direction, Best Teleplay, and Best Actor. *Playhouse 90* established its reputation with this show and continued to maintain it throughout the remainder of its run.

The success of *Playhouse 90* continued into the 1957–58 season with productions of *The Miracle Worker, The Comedian,* and *The Helen Morgan Story.* Although these shows, along with *Requiem* and *Judg-*

ment at Nuremberg, were enough to ensure the historical importance of *Playhouse 90,* the program also stood out because of its emergence in the "film era" of television broadcasting evolution. By 1956 much of television production had moved from the East to the West Coast, and from live performances to filmed series. Most of the drama anthologies, a staple of the evening schedule to this point, fell victim to the newer types of programs being developed. *Playhouse 90* stands in contrast to the prevailing trend, and its reputation benefited from both the growing nostalgia for the waning live period and a universal distaste for Hollywood on the part of New York television critics. It is also probable that since the use of videotape (not widespread at the time) preserved a "live" feel, discussion of the programs could be easily adapted to the standards introduced by the New York television critics.

It has been argued that *Playhouse 90* in fact contributed to the demise of live television drama by making the genre too expensive to produce. The program's lavish budget was undoubtedly a factor in the quality of its productions, but its cost was enormous when compared with that of filmed series, against which it could not compete in the newly introduced ratings system. *Playhouse 90* stood out as an anomaly in its time, and its short run of less than four seasons suggested that a program of its kind could not survive in a changing production environment, regardless of its acclaim. Although *Playhouse 90* was an outstanding program, and representative of the best that drama anthology programs could offer, it was also the last of its genre to be shown as part of a regular network schedule.

KEVIN DOWLER

Playhouse 90 1956–60: Requiem for a Heavyweight, Ed Wynn, Jack Palance, Keenan Wynn, 1956.
Courtesy of the Everett Collection

See also **Anthology Drama; Coe, Fred; "Golden Age" of Television; Mann, Abby; Robinson, Hubbell; Serling, Rod**

Producers
Martin Manulis, John Houseman, Russell Stoneman, Fred Coe, Arthur Penn, Hubbell Robinson

Programming History
133 episodes
CBS

October 1956–January 1960	Thursday 9:30–11:00
July 1961–September 1961	Tuesday 9:30–11:00

Further Reading

Hawes, William, *The American Television Drama: The Experimental Years,* Tuscaloosa: University of Alabama Press, 1986

Kindem, Gorham, editor, *The Live Television Generation of Hollywood Film Directors: Interviews with Seven Directors,* Jefferson, North Carolina: McFarland, 1994

MacDonald, J. Fred, *One Nation under Television: The Rise and Decline of Network TV,* New York: Pantheon, 1990

Skutch, Ira, *Ira Skutch: I Remember Television: A Memoir,* Metuchen, New Jersey: Scarecrow Press, 1989

Stempel, Tom, *Storytellers to the Nation: A History of American Television Writing,* New York: Continuum, 1992

Sturcken, Frank, *Live Television: The Golden Age of 1946–1958 in New York,* Jefferson, North Carolina: McFarland, 1990

Wicking, Christopher, and Tise Vahimagi, *The American Vein: Directors and Directions in Television,* New York: Dutton, 1979

Wilk, Max, *The Golden Age of Television: Notes from the Survivors,* New York: Delacorte Press, 1976

Poland

For much of its early existence, Polish television remained in radio's shadow. Only in the 1960s did the postwar communist regime begin to take it seriously and recognize its usefulness as an instrument of propaganda. Despite developing in a totalitarian system, the medium was never completely politicized; since the fall of communism and subsequent deregulation of the media landscape, politicians have sought closely to control its development.

Preliminary experiments date back to the 1930s. Although limited in scope, and centered in Warsaw, they encouraged Polish Radio to plan a custom-built television studio (1940) and to inaugurate a regular service by 1941, but the German occupation set back progress by nearly a decade. It was 1947 before the State Telecommunications Institute resumed trials. In late 1951 the exhibition "Radio in the Struggle for Progress and Peace" demonstrated television's capabilities to some 100,000 visitors. A half-hour test broadcast in October 1952 from the Ministry of Communications marked the official launching of Polish television (TVP) and regular transmissions of up to an hour's duration, usually every Friday, soon followed (January 1953). The medium's onerous working conditions, together with its limited range, militated against serious treatment by the party. Therefore, the criterion of political reliability played little part in appointments.

Rapid technological advances and the start of domestic set production (the Soviet-based *Wisła* and *Belweder* models) in 1956 accelerated television's expansion in the late 1950s. Prime Minister Józef Cyrankiewicz formally opened the Warsaw Television Centre in May 1956, but television would no longer remain the capital's preserve. In line with the general tendency to decentralize cultural offerings, television centers quickly emerged in other cities. Simultaneously, the number of Polish license fee payers rose exponentially: from 5,000 in 1957 (when registration became compulsory) to 6.5 million by the mid-1970s. From 1957, television was on the air for several hours, five days a week; in February 1961 this increased to seven days. Indicative of television's growing importance, the Committee for Radiophonic Affairs was renamed the Radio and TV Committee (December 1960).

Under Jerzy Pański (director of programming, 1957–63), TVP established a reputation for its cultural and entertainment schedule, which, unlike many other Eastern Bloc countries, also included nonsocialist films (*Rashomon, Wages of Fear*) and television serials (*Dr. Kildare, Alfred Hitchcock Presents*). *Teatr Telewizji,* one of its greatest achievements, began in 1958, and at the height of its popularity would be watched by almost half the available audience. TVP branched out into school programming (March 1961), and children's bedtime television (1962), but its political and informational programs, particularly the main evening news (*Dziennik TV,* 1958–90), assumed increasing importance in the propagation of ideology. By the end of the decade fraternal socialist productions outnumbered Western imports. Traditionally hostile to communist ideology, Poles could enjoy popular domestic series with pro-Soviet messages (such as *Stawka większa niż życie—A Stake Greater Than Life Itself,* 1968) while ignoring their partisan overtones. Television steadfastly promoted the official government line during crises (although events in 1968 saw the dismissal of 150 employees) yet also immortalized historic moments, such as First Secretary Edward Gierek's personal appeal to strikers on the Baltic Coast (1971) to return to work.

During the 1970s, when Gierek attempted a great economic leap forward (funded by Western credits that ultimately condemned Poland to chronic indebtedness), television played a crucial role in promoting his "propaganda of success." Under his crony, Maciej Szczepański (Radio and TV Committee Chairman, 1972–80), television was subjected to much more rigorous controls; Szczepański himself oversaw production of Gierek's speeches, and "live" interviews were prerecorded and thoroughly vetted, with presenters and guests learning their scripts by rote. It was the party leadership that took the major decisions—the Main Censorship Office (1945–90) played only an ancillary role. Television news, especially, presented an unswervingly positive image of contemporary life, in stark contrast to most Poles' experience.

New technology and the industry's expansion at the turn of the decade greatly facilitated this process. In 1969 massive studios opened in Warsaw, and the introduction of the Ampex system allowed prerecording. TVP2, designed to provide more high-brow programming, started in December 1970, while color broadcasts (like Soviet television, using the Secam system) commenced in time for the VI Party Congress (December 1971). Television schedules offered a mélange of mindless entertainment, propaganda, foreign imports, and high culture. Bergman and Fellini films ran alongside *Columbo* and *Kojak,* popular domestic soaps (*Czterdziestolatek—Forty-Year-Old*) and, with Poland's growing international success in soccer (1974) and athletics, extensive sports coverage.

The massive turnout to greet Pope John Paul II's first visit (June 1979) presented a major challenge, and the government permitted television to transmit only heavily manipulated reports. Not even TVP, however, resisted the emergence of Solidarity (the regional Interenterprise Strike Committee, August 1980). The party leadership tolerated programs such as *Listy o gospodarce* (*Letters on the Economy,* November 1980), where viewers wrote in to criticize the economic and political situation. From March 1981, officials appeared on *Monitor Rządowy* (*Government Monitor*), every Friday after the main evening news, to justify their activities. The declaration of martial law (December 13, 1981) ushered in a sharp, but brief, political freeze. TVP2 went off-air until February 1982, presenters appeared in military uniform to read out official announcements, and the secret police took over television's upper echelons. Seventy employees were interned for pro-Solidarity sympathies. Television news displayed an extreme antiopposition bias. In protest, many actors mounted an effective boycott of television, lifting it only in the more liberal climate of the mid-1980s.

The last decade of communist rule initiated several key changes in TVP's profile. The rise of Latin American soaps (*Isaura the Slave-Girl*), the introduction of erotic movies (the so-called pink series) and more chic news programs (such as *Teleexpress* [1986], and *Panorama dnia* [1987]), and commercials indicated a shift toward capitalism. The government, lacking credibility in society at large, realized it could not reform the economy without Solidarity's assistance and brokered the Round Table talks of February to April 1989. Here, a special subcommittee dealt with media issues. Solidarity's demands included access to TVP, the transformation of state television into a public broadcaster, and the reinstatement of journalists sacked during martial law. Prior to the first semifree elections of May 1989, it duly received television slots (*Studio Solidarność*) to promote its candidates. Its other demands would be met in the months that followed electoral "victory" (near total control of the newly established Senate, and all the seats available in the lower house). The creation of the first postcommunist government under the Catholic intellectual Tadeusz Mazowiecki (August 1989), followed by the dissolution of the party

(January 1990), heralded the end of the party's audio-visual monopoly.

The need to create democratic institutions often from scratch also had a profound impact on television. It played a key role in those changes by providing an important forum for political candidates in local, presidential (1990), then parliamentary elections (1991). In the chaos of transformation, politicians, reluctant to expose TVP to competition before it had the chance to transform, delayed much-needed new legislation. The December 1992 law established a nine-member National Radio and TV Council (KRRT) as the supreme body in audiovisual media affairs and transformed state television into a joint stock company as of January 1, 1994, its single shareholder being the Treasury. The KRRT was further charged with defining the criteria for license allocation over two rounds of bidding (1994, 1997). The law limited the share of foreign capital in Polish terrestrial broadcasters to one-third, but evoked most controversy for an ill-defined clause requiring programmers to respect "Christian values."

Public television, meanwhile, implemented internal changes, creating a Biuro Reklamy (Advertising Bureau) (by 1994, advertising would provide 51 percent of TVP's total income) and embarking on a massive expansion from 1992. Breakfast programming (*Kawa czy herbata—Coffee or Tea*) extended the daily schedule while TVP's autonomous regional centers (eventually 12 in number and known collectively as TVP3) commenced their own local production, a move that required enormous financial investment. TV Polonia, a satellite channel for Polish communities abroad, launched in 1993, and a dedicated digital music channel, *Tylko Muzyka* (April 1997–February 1998), broke more new ground. As of January 1, 1995, TVP started using the PAL system, the Western European norm. The increasing share of revenue from advertising made public television highly sensitive to commercial competition and its resultant downmarket shift laid it open to charges of "dumbing down." TVP successfully adopted Western formats: game shows (*Blind Date, Wheel of Fortune*), fly-on-the-wall documentaries, chat shows, and more relaxed news programming (a multipresenter *Wiadomości* replacing *Dziennik*). TVP2, traditionally more high-brow, also reflected these trends, showing American police high-speed pursuits alongside the minilectures of the philosopher Leszek Kołakowski. Despite such activity, TVP remains hamstrung by its comparatively low funds (amounting to only one-sixth of French public television's) and shows a tendency—most evident in program quality—to spread those funds thinly. Attempts at restructuring have largely failed.

Piracy characterized private broadcasting in the

early 1990s, since the Ministry of Communications granted a license to only one new station (Echo, 1990). Small private stations mushroomed across Poland, many of which eventually joined Polonia 1, established by the Italian media magnate Nicolo Grauso in 1993. When he failed to win a franchise, Grauso withdrew from the scene, and Polonia 1 moved to Italy. TV Odra (1994) now serves as an umbrella for about a dozen stations broadcasting in the west and north of Poland. Somewhat surprisingly, given its lack of capital, the Franciscan Order's TV Niepokalanów (1995) received a nationwide license in 1994 on condition that advertising did not exceed 2 percent of its schedule. In 2001, it managed to raise this to 15 percent, paying a larger fee for its franchise; and TV Puls, which then started broadcasting on its frequencies, supplemented its largely religious programming with family entertainment (*The Cosby Show, Little House on the Prairie*).

The greatest challenge to TVP comes from two private stations—Zygmunt Solorz's Polsat (1992), the only totally commercial station with a nationwide franchise, and Mariusz Walter's TVN (1997), which began as a supraregional station but has since expanded. Solorz won a ten-year franchise in 1994, and, in addition to his major cable interests (Dami) and media investments in all three Baltic states, has developed his terrestrial holdings—adding TV4, formerly the debt-ridden Nasza Telewizja (*Our Television,* 1997)—and extended into satellite (Polsat 2, 1997), and digital (Polsat Cyfrowy, 2000). TVN became an exclusively Polish concern after the withdrawal of its American partner CME in 1998. Its original license gave access to northern Poland, Warsaw, and Łódź, but Walter bought TV Wisła (1994) in 1997, thereby extending TVN's coverage to the south. Its presence was further enhanced by inclusion in the pay-per-view digital platform Wizja TV. In September 2001 TVN started broadcasting the first news channel, TVN 24, loosely modeled on CNN.

Polsat has occasionally achieved higher ratings than TVP1 (up to 30 percent audience share in 1998), but like TVN is generally seen as being more downmarket. Both have gained notoriety for their reality shows: TVN launched *Big Brother* in Spring 2001, which the KRRT condemned as "socially harmful," but proved enormously popular with the audience (70 percent/8.4 million viewers watched the final episode). Its other key programs include *Milionerzy* (*Who Wants to Be a Millionaire?,* autumn 1999) and *Fakty,* its main evening news program, which is almost as popular as *Wiadomości.* The poaching of several TVP star presenters (including Tomasz Lis, Krzysztof Ibisz) boosted its profile. Polsat's soaps enjoy greater success; it owns

the rights to the lucrative European Champions League and broadcast the 2002 World Cup. Together, TVP, TVN, and Polsat currently dominate television advertising (90 percent of all ad spend/US$1.45 billion in 2001).

Cable and digital television are growing in importance. Cable's origins lie in the early 1990s: key operators today are Polska Telewizja Kablowa (PTK: founded 1989, license 1995) with networks in most cities, and Aster City Cable (license 1997). Digital has been an arena of major struggle between American-backed operations—HBO (1996) and Wizja TV (launched 1998; taken over by the Dutch-owned United Pan-Europe Communications in 1999)—and the French Canal+ Cyfrowy (license 1997). The former broadcast from outside Poland (from Hungary and the United Kingdom, respectively) to circumvent restrictions on foreign capital, which caused Canal+ to complain about unfair competition. However, in December 2001, Wizja and Canal+ merged to form a single company, Telewizja Korporacja Partycypacyjna (25 and 75 percent shares, respectively). Further concentration of cable and digital television looks likely.

Controversy dogged both licensing rounds, with the Supreme Court challenging nearly every award on procedural grounds. In each case the KRRT has confirmed its original decision. Politicians often intervene in the workings of television: President Wałęsa, dissatisfied with the 1994 licensing round, sacked the KRRT head, Marek Markiewicz, although his authority to do so was doubtful. The political composition of the Council remains a contentious issue, with all parties seeking to advance their own agendas. These problems particularly affect TVP, one of whose most dynamic directors, Wiesław Walendziak, resigned in protest at political interference in February 1996. His successor, Ryszard Miazek, declared that TVP journalists should seek to inform viewers about, rather than comment on, politicians' statements, which seemed to presage a return to communist practices.

A new media bill, designed to bring Poland (a member of the European Broadcasting Union since 1992) into line with EU legislation, is creating a major furor. The bill lifts restrictions on foreign capital for European businesses and relaxes them for others, proposes strict limits on cross-media ownership (no nationwide newspaper can simultaneously own a national station), and greatly bolsters TVP's position by allowing it to launch unlimited channels. President Kwaśniewski has promised to exercise his veto. The Polish television industry nonetheless constitutes one of the great success stories of postcommunist Central and East European broadcasting.

JOHN BATES

Further Reading

Dziadul, Chris, "New Channels pop up in Poland," www. tvinsite.com/television-europe (February 14, 2002)

Giorgi, Liana, *The Post-Socialist Media: What Power the West? The Changing Media Landscape in Poland, Hungary, and the Czech Republic,* Avebury, Aldershot, Vermont: Ashgate Publishing, 1995

Goban-Klas, Tomasz, *The Orchestration of the Media. The Politics of Mass Communications in Communist Poland and the*

Aftermath, Boulder, San Francisco, Oxford: Westview Press, 1994

Jakobowicz, Karol, "Improving on the West—the Native Way: Poland," in *The Development of the Audiovisual Landscape in Central Europe since 1989,* Luton: ULP/John Libbey Press, 1998

Jung, Bohdan, "Media Consumption and Leisure in Poland in the 1990s," *The International Journal on Media Management* (Summer 2001)

Karpiński, Jakub, "Politicians Endanger Independence of Polish Public TV," *Transition* (April 1996)

Poldark

British Historical Drama

Poldark is one of the most successful British television dramas of all time. The popularity of the first series in 1975 was matched by enthusiastic reception of the 1993 video release. As a costume drama, scheduled for early evening family viewing, *Poldark* was not unusual, but its exterior sequences, cast, and immense popularity have made it ultimately memorable. The first episode, opening to Ross Poldark's ride across the Cornish landscape on his return from the U.S. War of Independence, was seen by an audience of 5 million. As the series continued, this figure rose to an average of 15 million viewers. The two BBC Poldark series sold to more than 40 countries, and in 1996 a made-for-television movie sequel aired on ITV.

The *Poldark* series are all closely based on the novels of Winston Graham, well known for his thrillers and for the screen adaptations of his later nonhistorical books, the British film noir *Fortune Is a Woman* (1956) and *Marnie* (1964), directed by Alfred Hitchcock. In 1969 Associated British Picture bought an option on the Poldark best sellers and commissioned a four-hour Cornish equivalent to *Gone With the Wind*. However, the film project was dropped during the EMI takeover of the company. The option was taken over by London films, who eventually collaborated with the BBC.

The first BBC series dramatizes the original four novels Graham wrote at the end of World War II. Graham had initially planned a trilogy set in 18th-century Cornwall, which would explore the love triangle between the war hero Captain Poldark, his less-exciting cousin Francis Poldark, and the aristocratic Elizabeth Chynoweth. However, as the narrative developed, Graham became more interested in the social situation in

Cornwall at that time and the dramatic contrast between the oppressed poor and the new landowning classes. Graham added the engaging urchin Demelza, who marries Ross out of her class, and a fourth book focused on the villain, the nouveau riche George Warleggan.

The first series established Ross Poldark as a character at war with his own class. After his return to Cornwall and his failure to win back Elizabeth, Ross attempts to restore Nampara, his father's ruined estate. He shocks his neighbors by marrying Demelza, the daughter of a brutal miner, and interesting himself in the affairs of those who work for him. His legitimate business deals and mining company ventures bring him into direct competition with George Warleggan. Illegal activities, such as the false charge of incitement to riot and, later smuggling, also bring Poldark into conflict with the Warleggans. In this feud, Poldark is portrayed as the forward-looking, benevolent landowner and entrepreneur, whereas Warleggan is seen as a tyrannical arriviste, whose grand house is burnt to the ground by dispossessed miners and tenants.

The house-burning scene and climax to the first series was a radical departure from Graham's novels. Although the author felt that the first series was marred by the use of a different writer for every episode, Graham wrote a further trilogy for adaptation and became closely involved with the second series made in 1977. This series follows the fortunes of four different marriages: that of the Poldarks; Elizabeth's marriage to Warleggan; Caroline's union with the progressive doctor Dwight Enys; and the marriage of Elizabeth's un-

Poldark, Angharad Rees, Robin Ellis, 1975.
Courtesy of the Everett Collection

happy cousin Morwenna. All are affected by the intense rivalry between Poldark and Warleggan. Ross Poldark and George Warleggan continue their feud in London as well as Cornish society by becoming opposing members of Parliament.

The outdoor locations set the first series apart from other studio-based costume dramas. Scenes such as the dramatic rescue of Dr. Enys from a prisoner of war camp in revolutionary France; the wrecking of the Warleggan ship; and action set in mines, against seascapes, and on coastal paths all created a spectacular backdrop for the vicissitudes of Poldark's marital and financial dilemmas. The contrast between the theatrical approach to studio production and the spontaneity engendered by location filming gave the historical drama a unique, fresh quality.

Not surprisingly, the BBC expressed an interest in making a third series, but at that time Graham did not feel that he could write the books required for the source material. However, Graham did come to write

additional books dealing with a second generation of Poldarks, continuing the Warleggan feud and introducing the industrial revolution to Cornwall. The 1996 TV movie based on some of this material, and featuring new actors in the lead roles, was not as well received as the 1970s series.

NICKIANNE MOODY

Cast

Ross Poldark	Robin Ellis
George Warleggan	Ralph Bates
Jud Paynter	Paul Curran
Mark Daniel	Martin Fisk
Francis Poldark	Clive Francis
Caroline Penvenen Enys	Judy Gleason
Demelza Poldark	Angharad Rees
Verity Poldark (1975)	Norma Streader
Elizabeth Warleggan Poldark	Jill Townsend
Prudie	Mary Wimbush
Francis Poldark (1975)	Clive Francis
Sir Hugh Bodrugan (1975)	Christopher Benjamin
Lady Bodrugan (1975)	Cynthia Grenville
Jeremy Poldark (1977)	Thomas Grady
Sam Carne (1977)	David Delve
Drake Carne (1977)	Kevin McNally
Zacky Martin	Forbes Collins
Geoffrey Charles	Stefan Gates
Morwenna	Jane Wymark
Dwight Enys (1975)	Richard Morant
Dwight Enys (1977)	Michael Caldman

Producers
John McRae, Morris Barry, Tony Coburn

Programming History
BBC
1975	16 episodes
1977	13 episodes

Further Reading

Clarke, D., *Poldark Country,* St. Teath, England: Bossiney Books, 1977

Ellis, R., *Making Poldark,* St. Teath, England: Bossiney Books, 1978

Graham, W., *Poldark's Cornwall,* London: Chapmans, 1994

Westland, E., *Cornwall: The Cultural Construction of Place,* Newmill, England: Pattern Press, 1996

Police Programs

Since its beginnings in the late 1940s the U.S. police procedural genre has continued to bring together a variety of social issues with physical action. It is unabashedly a genre of car chases and gun battles and fistfights, but it is also imbued with values critical to the fabric of a society: justice, social order, law. More than any other TV genre, the police program brings into sharp relief the conflicts between individual freedom and social responsibility in a democratic society. Although the police are closely related to the private detective in their pursuit of criminals, they are ultimately an employee of the state, not a private individual, and are sworn "to protect and to serve." In theory, this means the police officer is expected to enforce society's laws and maintain order (unlike the private eye, who can be more flexible in his/her obedience to the rule of law). In practice, though, policing figures can also be disruptive forces, violating the letter of the law in order to enforce a "higher" moral code. As times change and ideology shifts, so does the police drama.

Although 1949's *Stand by for Crime* and *Chicagoland Mystery Players* provided television's first police detectives, neither was as influential as their long-running successor, *Dragnet,* which had two separate TV incarnations, from 1952 to 1959 and then from 1967 to 1970. *Dragnet* defined the genre during the 1950s. Jack Webb produced and starred as Sergeant Joe Friday, who doggedly worked his way through official police procedures. *Dragnet* drew its stories from California court cases and prided itself on presenting "just the facts," as Friday frequently reminded witnesses. Friday was an efficient bureaucrat with a gun and a badge, a proud maintainer of police procedure and society's rules and regulations. Producer Webb had such success with this formula that he returned to the police procedural program in the 1970s with *Adam 12.*

The police procedural strain dominated the genre during the 1950s, but its dry presentational style and endorsement of the status quo came under attack in the 1960s. Webb's programs seemed anachronistic and out of touch with many viewers' reality during that turbulent decade. New issues, imagery, and character types revived the genre in programs such as *Ironside* and *The Mod Squad.*

Ironside, in contrast to the Webb programs, attempted to pour a liberal politics into the mold of the police drama. *Ironside*'s team of crime fighters cobbled together representatives of society's disenfranchised groups (women, African Americans, and the young) under the guidance of a liberal patriarch, the wheelchair-bound Robert Ironside (Raymond Burr). Ironside was an outsider who understood the workings of police procedure but chose not to function within the system. Instead, he formed an alliance of sharply defined individuals outside the bounds of the police organization proper. *Ironside* did not challenge the status quo, but neither did it fully endorse it.

In *The Mod Squad,* the policing characters were drawn from Hollywood's vision of 1960s countercul-

Inspector Maigret, Michael Gambon, 1991.
Courtesy of the Everett Collection

Police Woman, Angie Dickinson, 1974–78.
Courtesy of the Everett Collection

ture: "one white, one black, one blond," the advertising promised. Although actual members of the counterculture spurned the program as fake and inaccurate, *The Mod Squad* illustrated how policing figures can adopt an antisocial patina, how they can come to resemble the rebellious and anarchic forces they are supposed to contain.

The 1970s saw a flood of police programs (approximately 42 premiered during the decade) and their protagonists became increasingly individualistic and quirky. They came closer and closer to the alienated position of the private detective and moved farther and farther from the *Dragnet*-style police procedural. The title figures of *McCloud, Columbo,* and *Kojak* were police detectives marked as much by personal idiosyncrasies as by concerns with proper procedure or the effectiveness of law enforcement. McCloud (Dennis Weaver) was a deputy from New Mexico who brought western "justice" to the streets of Manhattan. Columbo (Peter Falk) dressed in a crumpled raincoat and feigned lethargy as he lured suspects into a false sense of confidence. And Kojak (Telly Savalas) was as well known for his bald head and constant lollipop sucking as for problem solving.

The 1970s inclination toward offbeat police officers peaked in detectives that spent so much time undercover (and masqueraded so effectively as criminals) that the distinction between police and criminals became less and less clear. *Toma* (a ratings success even though it lasted just one season) and *Baretta* led the way in this regard, drawing their inspiration from *Serpico,* a popular Peter Maas book that eventually evolved into a film and a low-rated TV series. These unorthodox cops bucked the police rulebook and lived unconventional lives, but, ultimately, they existed on a higher moral plane than the regular police officer.

The genre was also fortified in the 1970s through other strategies: incorporating a medical discourse (*Quincy, M.E.*), setting policemen astride motorcycles (*CHiPs*—a term, incidentally, that was fabricated by the program and is not used by the California Highway Patrol), or casting younger, hipper actors (*Starsky and Hutch*).

By the 1980s the police drama was a well-established genre, possibly in danger of stagnation from the glut of programs broadcast during the previous decade. With remarkable resiliency, however, the genre continued to evolve through a series of programs that took its basic conventions and thoroughly reworked them. *Hill Street Blues, Cagney and Lacey,* and *Miami Vice* were very different programs, but each of them was seen as an iconoclastic, rule-breaking police program.

Police programs have always invoked realism and claimed authenticity, as was apparent in the genre's archetype, *Dragnet.* But there are different forms of realism, and *Hill Street Blues* altered the prevailing understanding of realism. Among its innovations were documentary-film techniques (such as the handheld camera), fragmented and disjointed narrative structure (actions kept happening without conventional motivation and/or explanation), and morally ambiguous characterizations (mixing good and evil in a single individual). *Hill Street Blues* also altered the usually all-white, usually all-male composition of the police force by including women and minorities as central figures—a trend that had begun in the 1970s.

Cagney and Lacey took the inclusion of women characters and women's concerns much further than *Hill Street Blues* or *Ironside.* Indeed, it challenged the genre's patriarchal underpinnings in fundamental, unprecedented ways. There had been women-centered police programs as early as 1974's *Get Christie Love* and *Police Woman,* but these programs were more concerned with exploiting Teresa Graves's or Angie Dickinson's sexual desirability than presenting a feminist agenda. *Cagney and Lacey,* in contrast, confronted women's issues that the genre had previously ignored: breast cancer, abortion, birth control, rape (particularly acquaintance rape), and spousal abuse.

That *Cagney and Lacey* disrupted the male-dominated genre is evidenced by the battles that had to be fought to keep it on the air. In the most notorious incident, the role of detective Christine Cagney was recast after the first, low-rated season because, according to an unnamed CBS executive quoted in *TV Guide,* "The American public doesn't respond to the bra burners, the fighters, the women who insist on calling manhole covers peoplehole covers.... We perceived them [actors Tyne Daley and Meg Foster] as dykes." Consequently, a more conventionally feminine actor (Sharon Gless) assumed the Cagney role. (Gless was actually

Hawaii Five-O, Jack Lord, Khigh Dhiegh, 1968–80.
Courtesy of the Everett Collection

the third actor to play the part; Loretta Swit played Cagney in the made-for-TV movie version.) Despite this ideological backpedaling, *Cagney and Lacey* went on to establish itself as one of the most progressively feminist programs on television.

The third 1980s police program to unsettle the conventions of the genre was *Miami Vice.* This immensely popular show featured undercover cops who were so far "under" that they were almost indistinguishable from the criminals: quite a far cry from Sergeant Friday. In *Miami Vice,* good and evil folded back over each other in impenetrable layers of disguise and duplicity. James "Sonny" Crockett (Don Johnson) and Ricardo "Rico" Tubbs (Philip Michael Thomas) usually found their way out of the urban jungle they patrolled, but not always. In one season, Crockett was stricken with amnesia and actually believed himself to be a hoodlum. The clearly demarcated moral universe of *Dragnet* had become hopelessly ambiguous.

However, moral ambiguity was not entirely new to the genre. This territory was frequently traveled by previous programs such as *Baretta.* What was truly innovative in *Miami Vice* was the style of its sound and image, rather than its themes. *Miami Vice* borrowed its imagery from *film noir*: high contrast, imbalanced lighting, dissymmetrical compositions, extreme low and high camera angles, foreground obstructions, black-and-white set design, and so on. These images were often edited together into elusive, allusive, music-video-style segments incorporating music by Tina Turner, Glenn Frey, Suicidal Tendencies, and many others. This led some critics to nickname the show "MTV cops."

Hill Street Blues and *Miami Vice* paved the way for further experimentation with the genre. Stephen Bochco, the producer of *Hill Street Blues,* began the 1990s with *Cop Rock,* a bold, but ultimately failed, effort to blend the police program with the musical. Unlike *Miami Vice*'s musical segments, which drew upon music video, *Cop Rock*'s episodes more resembled *West Side Story* or an operetta, as police officers, criminals, and attorneys sang about life on the streets. It only lasted three months, but it stands as one of the most unconventional programs within the genre.

Bochco fared better in more familiar surroundings when he developed *NYPD Blue,* a program about police detectives that resembles *Hill Street Blues* in its serialized, unstable narrative development and cinema verité visual style. Although the program raised some controversy in its use of partial nudity and more flavorful language than was common on television at the time, it actually has broken little new ground as far as the genre's conventions were considered. More unconventional in its narrative structure is *Law and Order,* in which the program is strictly divided between the first

and second halves. In the former, the police investigate a crime, and in the latter the district attorney's office prosecute that crime. Like *NYPD Blue, Law and Order* is set in New York City and it presents its urban environment through conventions of "realism" that evolved from *Hill Street Blues.*

The legacy of *Miami Vice*'s visual stylization was most apparent in *Homicide: Life on the Street,* which may well have been the most stylized police drama of the 1990s. *Homicide* broke many of television's most sacred rules of editing and narrative continuity. Jump cuts were numerous, as the program came to resemble a French New Wave film from the 1960s. Wild camera movements and unpredictable shifts in narrative development marked it as one of the most unconventional programs in the genre.

Another anomalous 1990s police program was David E. Kelley's *Picket Fences.* Although many of the central characters were police officers (thus possibly qualifying it for the genre), *Picket Fences* did not adhere to the central police-program convention of an urban environment. Instead, the program was set in a small town, which consequently avoided the pressures of city life. Moreover, *Picket Fences* dealt with many topics previously unknown to the genre (such as spontaneous combustion of a human being). Perhaps because of its quirkiness, this program has not had much impact on the genre. It was, however, a significant antecedent to Kelley's series about lawyers, *The Practice* and *Ally McBeal,* both of which continue his fascination with the idiosyncrasies of the U.S. legal system.

One program that has influenced the police genre is the documentary program *COPS,* produced by John Langley. *COPS* presents handheld, videotape footage of actual police officers apprehending criminal perpetrators. There is no host introducing this footage and the only explanation of what is happening is provided by the participants themselves (principally, the police men and women). In a sense, *COPS* is merely the logical extension of *Hill Street Blues*' shooting style and disjointed narratives—and is much cheaper to produce. There have been a number of *COPS* parodies, including an episode of *The X-Files* shot in the *COPS* style and following the pursuit of a monster.

As the 1990s ended, the police drama waned slightly. Don Johnson of *Miami Vice* returned to the genre in *Nash Bridges,* which managed to last six seasons despite mediocre ratings. Innovative programs such as *Homicide, NYPD Blue,* and *Law and Order* were canceled (*Homicide*) or settled into conventional patterns (*NYPD Blue*). Even iconoclastic producer Bochco's latest attempt at a police drama, *Brooklyn South,* seemed all too familiar and was soon taken off the air. There are signs, however, that the genre may reinvigorate itself. *Law and Order,* for example, has proven quite successful with audiences, who seem to enjoy the format in which each crime is solved in a single episode, and private lives of the principal characters remain unexplored. The original series has led to three spin-offs. *Law and Order SVU (Special Victims Unit)* focuses on crimes dealing with sexually related offenses. *Law and Order CI (Criminal Intent)* examines crimes by exploring the perspectives of the criminals involved. *Crime and Punishment,* the most recent production, presents itself as a "dramamentary" and follows real-life cases as they are prosecuted by the San Diego, California, district attorney's office.

Another innovative program, *C.S.I.: Crime Scene Investigation,* has recast the police detective as a forensic scientist. The series' high-tech gadgetry and stylized visuals have attracted a sizable audience and has also spun off a related program, *C.S.I. Miami.* These developments suggest that the genre can still find new ways to present issues of crime, justice, and the preservation of social order.

JEREMY G. BUTLER

See also **Cagney and Lacey; Columbo; Dixon of Dock Green; Dragnet; Homicide; Inspector Morse; La Plante, Lynda; Miami Vice; Naked City; NBC Mystery Movie; NYPD Blue; Police Story; Prime Suspect; Starsky and Hutch; Sweeney; Untouchables; Webb, Jack; Z Cars**

Further Reading

Auster, Albert, "Did They Ever Catch the Criminals Who Committed the Armed Robbery On People's Drive: *Hill Street Blues* Remembered," *Television Quarterly* (Summer 1988)

Bochco, Steven, "Interview," *American Film* (July–August 1988)
Butler, Jeremy G., "Miami Vice: The Legacy of Film Noir," *Journal of Popular Film and Television* (Fall 1985)
Christensen, Mark, "Bochco's Law," *Rolling Stone* (April 21, 1988)
Collins, Max Allen, *The Best of Crime and Detective TV: Perry Mason to Hill Street Blues, The Rockford Files to Murder She Wrote,* New York: Harmony Books, 1989
Crew, B. Keith, "Acting Like Cops: The Social Reality of Crime and Law on TV Police Dramas," in *Marginal Conventions: Popular Culture, Mass Media, and Social Deviance,* edited by Clinton R. Sanders, Bowling Green, Ohio: Popular Culture Press, 1990
D'Acci, Julie, *Defining Women: Television and the Case of Cagney and Lacey,* Chapel Hill: University of North Carolina Press, 1994
Douglas, Susan, "Signs of Intelligent Life on TV," *Ms.* (May–June 1995)
Fiske, John, and John Hartley, "A Policeman's Lot," in *Reading Television,* edited by John Fiske and John Hartley, New York: Methuen, 1978
Grant, Judith, "Prime-Time Crime: Television Portrayals of Law Enforcement," *Journal of American Culture* (Spring 1992)
Hurd, Geoffrey, "The Television Presentation of the Police," in *Popular Television and Film,* edited by Tony Bennett et al., London: British Film Institute, 1981
Inciardi, James A., and Juliet L. Dee, "From the Keystone Cops to *Miami Vice:* Images of Policing in American Popular Culture," *Journal of Popular Culture* (Fall 1987)
Kaminsky, Stuart, and Jeffrey H. Mahan, *American Television Genres,* Chicago: Nelson-Hall, 1985
O'Connor, John J., "When Fiction Is More Real Than 'Reality,'" *New York Times* (February 7, 1993)
Weber, Bruce, "New York City Police: TV's Archetypes of Toughness," *New York Times* (October 28, 1994)
Zynda, Thomas H., "The Metaphoric Vision of *Hill Street Blues,*" *Journal of Popular Film and Television* (Fall 1986)

Police Story

U.S. Police Anthology

Police Story is a title shared by two unrelated police anthology programs. The first *Police Story* aired on CBS during 1952. The live, half-hour program dramatized actual crimes lifted from the files of law enforcement agencies across the United States. The series anticipated "reality" crime programs such as *Rescue 911* with its emphasis on casting actors who resembled the actual participants and use of the real names of police officers. Norman Rose narrated the series.

The better-known *Police Story* series ran from 1973 to 1977 on NBC. In 1988 four made-for-television movies based on the original's script aired on ABC. Los Angeles police officer and writer Joseph Wambaugh created the series after his first two police novels, *The Blue Knight* and *The New Centurions,* made the best-seller lists. (*The Blue Knight* was also adapted into a series for CBS.)

Airing during a network television era rife with

crime dramas, *Police Story* distinguished itself from other programs in the genre through its anthology format and emphasis on a more realistic depiction of police officers. Set in 1970s Los Angeles, *Police Story* focused on officers from various divisions of the Los Angeles Police Department. While the series had its share of car chases and psycho killers, Wambaugh and series producer David Gerber primarily concentrated on making police officers more three-dimensional and human. The series presented the job of police officer as challenging, dangerous, and at times mundane. Undercover detectives spent their lives on stakeouts; rookie cops faced tough street educations; SWAT sharpshooters hit innocent bystanders. Problems such as corruption and racism on the police force and tensions between ethnic communities were frequently explored. The personal lives of the characters were also examined, most often in the context of the pressures police work put on all members of the cop's family.

Although the visual and aural style of *Police Story* episodes were on the whole indistinguishable from other crime dramas of the era, the series introduced and concluded episodes with simple recurring motifs that asserted the series' verisimilitude. Each episode opened with the brief *Police Story* title and then leapt into its story. Episodes ended with a blurry freeze frame of the last bit of action. The audio of the scene fell silent and was replaced by the chillingly efficient voice and static of police dispatchers making a radio call, "Eleven-Mary-six, call the station. Thirteen-zero-five, John-Frank-William, eight-nine-nine."

The result of these narrative and aesthetic conventions was an at times disturbing picture of police officers operating on the edge of society and their own personal sanity. While episodes consistently started stronger than they finished, the anthology format and the ever-present influence of documentary film conventions helped *Police Story* to stand out from more familiar cops-and-robbers fare. These stylistic factors suggest that the series was, in various ways, the predecessor of later police programs such as *Hill Street Blues, NYPD Blue,* and *Homicide: Life on the Street.* The series received wide critical praise and Emmy nominations for Outstanding Dramatic Series every year during its 1970s run.

Although most episodes in *Police Story* were unrelated, a few actors reprised their characters across several episodes. Don Meredith and Tony LoBianco appeared as partners or separately in six episodes from 1973 to 1975. Two *Police Story* episodes also served as spin-offs for the police dramas *Police Woman* and *Joe Forrester.* Gerber produced these series as well.

STEPHEN LEE

Producers

Stanley Kallis, David Gerber, Liam O'Brien, Christopher Morgan, Hugh Benson, Mel Swope, Larry Broder, Carl Pingitore

Programming History

84 episodes
NBC
October 1973–September
  1975   Tuesday 10:00–11:00
September 1975–October
  1975   Tuesday 9:00–10:00
November 1975–August
  1976   Friday 10:00–11:00
August 1976–August 1977   Tuesday 10:00–11:00

Further Reading

Collins, Max Allen, *The Best of Crime and Detective TV: Perry Mason to Hill Street Blues, The Rockford Files to Murder, She Wrote,* New York: Harmony Books, 1989

Crew, B. Keith, "Acting like Cops: The Social Reality of Crime and Law on TV Police Dramas," in *Marginal Conventions: Popular Culture, Mass Media, and Social Deviance,* edited by Clinton R. Sanders, Bowling Green, Ohio: Popular Culture Press, 1990

Grant, Judith, "Prime-Time Crime: Television Portrayals of Law Enforcement," *Journal of American Culture* (Spring 1992)

Inciardi, James A., and Juliet L. Dee, "From the Keystone Cops to *Miami Vice:* Images of Policing in American Popular Culture," *Journal of Popular Culture* (Fall 1987)

Kaminsky, Stuart, and Jeffrey H. Mahan, *American Television Genres.* Chicago: Nelson-Hall, 1985

Political Processes and Television

Since its beginnings television in the United States has been intertwined with political processes of every type, covering major political events and institutions and affecting the direction of campaigns and elections. From its early position as a new medium for political coverage in the 1950s, television quickly supplanted radio and newspapers to become, by the early 1960s, the major source of public information about politics.

Televised Coverage of Major Political Events

Television's influence grew quickly by providing audiences with the chance to experience major political events live or with little delay. For instance, observers have long discussed the fact that television coverage of the famous 1954 McArthur Day Parade in Chicago communicated more excitement and a greater sense of immediacy to television viewers than to those participating in the live event. The televised hearings in conjunction with Senator Joseph McCarthy's search for communist sympathizers in the early 1950s also captured the attention of the public.

Probably no political event in the history of television coverage so mesmerized television audiences as the coverage of the assassination of President John F. Kennedy in 1963. Film of the actual tragedy in Dallas, Texas, was played and replayed, and Jack Ruby's subsequent assassination of suspect Lee Harvey Oswald occurred on live television.

By the 1970s the live coverage of major political events had become almost commonplace, but television's ability to lend drama and intimacy to political events continues to this day. Through television, Americans have been eyewitness to state funerals and foreign wars; a presidential resignation; hearings on scandals such as Watergate, Iran-Contra, and Whitewater; triumphs of presidential diplomacy and negotiation; and innumerable other political events.

Television and Political Campaigns/Elections

No aspect of the political process has been affected more by television than political campaigns and elections. The first presidential election to see extensive use of television was the 1952 race between Dwight D. Eisenhower and Adlai Stevenson. In that campaign, Richard M. Nixon, as Eisenhower's vice presidential candidate, "took his case to the people" to defend himself on television against corruption charges in his famous "Checkers" speech. However, the most significant innovation related to the role of television in the 1952 campaign was undoubtedly Eisenhower's use of short-spot commercials to enhance his television image. The Eisenhower campaign utilized the talent of successful advertising executive Rosser Reeves to devise a series of short spots that appeared, just like product ads, during commercial breaks in standard television programming slots. Not only did this strategy break new ground for political campaigning, but many observers have credited the spots with helping Eisenhower to craft a friendly,

charming persona that contributed to his eventual electoral success.

Stevenson made it easier for the Eisenhower campaign by refusing to participate in this type of electronic campaigning. Although Stevenson did produce television commercials for the 1956 campaign, he was never able to overcome Eisenhower's popularity.

This early use of television for political advertising was the beginning of a trend that has grown so dramatically that televised political advertising is now the major form of communication between candidates and voters in the American electoral system. Every presidential campaign since 1952 has relied heavily on political television spots. In the 2000 election, Al Gore and George W. Bush and their national parties spent over $200 million on the production and airing of television spots. Even below the presidential level, spots now dominate most major statewide (particularly gubernatorial and U.S. Senate) and congressional races in the United States, accounting for 50 to 75 percent of campaign budgets.

Several reasons account for the preeminence of television advertising in politics. First, television spots and their content are under the direct control of the candidate and his/her campaign. Second, the spots can reach a much wider audience than other standard forms of electoral communication. Third, the spots, because they occur in the middle of other programming fare, have been shown to overcome partisan selectivity (i.e., the spots are generally seen by all voters, not just those whose political party is the same as that of the candidate). Finally, research has shown that voters actually learn more (particularly about issues) from political spots than they do from television news or television debates.

The use of television advertising in political campaigns has often been criticized of lowering the level of political discourse. Observers bemoan that television fosters drama and visual imagery, leading to an emphasis on a candidate's image or appearance, instead of policy issues. However, scholarly research has shown that television spots for campaigns at all levels are much more likely to concentrate on issues than on images.

Many observers also blame the rise of negative campaigning on the extensive reliance upon television for campaign communication. Scholars and journalists alike have noted that more and more political campaigns rely on negative television spots to attack opponents. Although even Eisenhower's original spot campaign in 1952 contained a large number of critical or negative messages and Lyndon Johnson's 1964 campaign spots attacking Barry Goldwater are considered classic negative ads (particularly the "Daisy Girl" spot), the news media labeled the 1980s as the heyday of negative spots. Over the history of political spot use, about one-third of all spots for presidential campaigns have been negative spots.

One of the causes of increased negative spot use has been the growth in "independent expenditures" by political action committees (PACs) and other special-interest groups. Campaign finance regulations (the Federal Election Campaign Acts of 1971 and 1974 and amendments) and related Supreme Court decisions in the 1970s (*Buckley v. Valeo* [1976]) declared that, while limits on individual contributions to campaigns were legal, constitutional free-speech provisions prohibited limits on the amount individuals or groups could spend independently to advocate for or against a given candidate. Spending by independent individuals or groups on television spots has mushroomed since the 1980s, and often such television spending has been concentrated on negative attacks on candidates (usually incumbents).

Other than the federal election laws just noted, which created the Federal Election Commission to oversee campaign finance and expenditure reporting, there are very few regulations in the United States that affect television's role in the political process. The Federal Communications Act of 1934 contained the Equal Time Rule, which obligates television and radio stations that give or sell time to one candidate to do the same for all legally qualified candidates for federal office. The Fairness Doctrine, which has been retained only with regard to political campaigns and related attacks, provides for a prescribed right of response to attacks contained in broadcast programming. However, because of free speech concerns, neither the Federal Election Commission nor the Federal Communications Commission imposes any restrictions on the content of political-message broadcasts, except to require sponsor identification.

Television News Coverage of Political Campaigns

Politics provide a great deal of natural content for television news programming. During political campaign periods, the national networks, as well as many local stations, devote substantial amounts of time to covering the candidates and their campaigns. So important has television news coverage of politics become that some observers suggest its growth has been accompanied by, and perhaps caused, the demise of political parties in U.S. politics. Media producer Tony Schwartz has commented that in the past, "political parties were the means of communication from the candidate to public. The political parties today are ABC, NBC, and CBS."

Because more people get their campaign news from television than from any other news source, there has been great concern about how television actually covers a political campaign. Studies have shown that television's predispositions to drama and visual imagery have resulted in television news coverage that concentrates more on candidate images, "horse-race" journalism (who is winning, who is losing, opinion poll results), and campaign strategy than on issue concerns.

Television news coverage of campaigns has also come to rely extensively on "sound bites," snippets of candidate messages or commentary excerpts. By the late 1980s the average sound bite on national television news covering political campaigns was only about nine seconds. In addition to reliance on short sound bites, television news coverage of campaigns has been characterized by reliance on "spin doctors," individual experts who interpret events for viewers by framing, directing, and focusing remarks to favor one side or the other.

Since television coverage is so important to campaigns and politicians, the question of potential bias in coverage has been raised repeatedly. Former Vice President Spiro Agnew is often credited with raising the salience of potential bias in his 1969 speeches accusing television of political, liberal-leaning bias. Early studies of political bias in television, focused initially on the 1972 presidential campaign, concluded that there was little evidence of such bias. Scholars suggested instead that differences among media in their attention to particular candidates and issues might be attributed to structural characteristics of the media (e.g., television needs visuals more than newspapers do, television has a predisposition to drama, etc.). However, more recent investigations have led to less complacency, suggesting that there may be unexplained differences in coverage of Republican and Democratic, and conservative and liberal, political candidates.

In addition to outright political bias, television news has also been criticized for placing too much emphasis on coverage of candidate personalities, particularly the personal lives of candidates. Examples often cited as evidence of extremes in this regard are the scrutiny of the prior treatment for mental illness of McGovern's original vice presidential choice, Thomas Eagleton, and 1988 primary presidential candidate Gary Hart's extramarital affairs. Both were forced from the political arena by the surrounding media frenzy. This media fascination with personal issues reached new heights during the presidency of Bill Clinton, whose administration was plagued with a series of scandals investigated by an independent prosecutor and covered widely by the media. The media frenzy reached its greatest heights when Clinton's sexual involvement with White House intern Monica Lewinsky was revealed. The media focus was intense and comprehensive, culminating in live coverage of congressional debates in which Clinton was eventually impeached by the U.S. House of Representatives in late 1998. Although the U.S. Senate acquitted the president, these events and the memorable media attention defined Clinton's presidency.

Television news also plays a major role in the coverage of the presidential candidate selection process before the national party conventions. By covering and scrutinizing candidates in state primaries and caucuses, television coverage can help determine which candidates are perceived by the electorate as viable and which might be dismissed as unlikely to succeed. This ability to give and withhold attention has been seen by many as making television's role in the political process a decisive one, since a candidate who does not do well in early primaries faces not only an uphill battle in subsequent contests but may have difficulty raising funds to continue at all. Coverage of primaries has also provided opportunities for coverage of events that have continued to be influential on through the general election. For instance, George H.W. Bush's unprecedented, hostile encounter with Dan Rather on the *CBS Evening News* in January 1988 is often credited with erasing Bush's "wimp" image and giving him momentum for the contests ahead. Conversely, Edmund Muskie was forever diminished when television cameras caught tears in his eyes at a New Hampshire primary rally early in the 1972 campaign.

News media coverage to politics is not limited to simple reporting on candidates and campaign activities, however. Television news has also played a large role in other aspects of the political process. In 1952 television covered its first series of national party conventions. While it was originally believed that such attention would bring the party process into the open and help voters better understand the political selection process, parties quickly learned to "script" their conventions for television. National television networks no longer provide gavel-to-gavel coverage of national party conventions, furnishing only convention highlights to viewers.

Televised campaign debates provide other fodder for the television news operation. The first televised debates in the 1960 Kennedy-Nixon campaign were viewed as important, perhaps decisive, in Kennedy's victory. Kennedy's success has often been attributed to his impressive appearance on television in these debates. The next set of presidential debates did not occur until the 1976 contest between Gerald Ford and Jimmy Carter, but there has been some type of single or multiple debate encounter in every subsequent presidential election. All of these cases have been noteworthy for the attention television news has focused on the events. In some instances, such as the second 1976 Ford-Carter debate, researchers have shown that television's emphasis on Ford's famous misstatement about Soviet domination of Poland and the Eastern bloc changed the interpretation and significance of the event to many viewers.

Presidential campaigns are defining moments for media involvement in the political process, and the 2000 campaign gave every indication of following a similar path, with media attention focused on the candidates' campaigns, their ads, and a series of debates. However, even the media were taken by surprise when a contest that was labeled "too close to call" on election eve could not be decided for several weeks. As the votes were counted on election night, the television networks first declared Gore the winner, then reversed to declare George W. Bush the president-elect, then eventually placed the race back in limbo. The uncertainty came down to Florida, where Bush held a slight lead that many speculated might disappear if various counties with possible voting irregularities were allowed to recount their ballots. As other states' voting totals were firmed up, the Florida votes remained in doubt. The media found new life for postcampaign coverage as they converged on Florida to watch and interpret for the public a series of legal challenges. When the U.S. Supreme Court eventually called a halt to the recount process on equal protection grounds in December, Florida's electoral votes went into the Bush column, making him the winner. However, for the first time in over a century, the presidential winner had won the contest on electoral votes, while losing the popular vote. The aftermath of the 2000 election experience led to a serious examination of the media's use of polling to project vote winners and its use of these data during election broadcasts.

Several innovations in television coverage of political campaigns were apparent in the last decades of the 20th century. One such innovation was the attention paid by the television news media to coverage of political television spots. News media personnel, in conjunction with their print journalist counterparts, decided that candidate-controlled spots should be scrutinized and critiqued by the news media. Beginning with the 1988 presidential contest, the television networks, as well as local stations, began to devote increased amounts of time to analyzing candidate spots in what came to be known as "ad watches." Television stations, particularly local ones, also began to take advantage of satellite technology and other remote-feed capabilities to provide more on-the-spot coverage of campaigns and candidates. Traditional television news formats, however, have found themselves challenged by another innovation, the frequent appearance of political candidates on television talk shows and personality interview programs. These shows have provided candidates with new ways to pitch their messages, often with the benefit of direct voter call-in questions. The potential influence of such shows has been enhanced by the proliferation of cable channels offering multiple distribution systems. Another recent challenge to television's half-century-long dominance of the political process appears to be the increased use of the Internet for political information.

Television and the Rise of Political Professionals

The increased importance of television to political campaigning is also largely responsible for the growth of political or media "handlers." The need to perform well on television (in controlled paid advertising, in debates, on talk shows, in news interviews, and on pseudoevents planned for television news coverage) has created a great demand for professional campaign consultants. Joe McGinniss's 1969 book, *The Selling of the President 1968,* brought new public visibility to the process by which media consultants mold and manage candidates for television by chronicling the media strategies and packaging of Nixon in his 1968 presidential bid. Dan Nimmo's *The Political Persuaders* (1970) helped a whole generation of political students and scholars understand this new partnership between candidates and media specialists. By the 1980s it was possible to point to particular philosophies and schools of consulting thought and to identify the specific strategies used by consultants to manipulate candidate images for television.

Television and the Governing Process

While television's role in political campaigns and elections is difficult to overestimate, television's significance in the political process carries over to the governing of the nation. Television monitors government institutions and the governing process. Every branch of government is affected by this watchdog.

The president of the United States probably bears the greatest weight of this scrutiny. It is rare to see any national television newscast that does not contain one or more stories centered on the executive branch of government. In addition, presidents generally have the ability to receive free network television time for national addresses and for frequent press conferences. Their inaugural addresses and State of the Union addresses are covered live and in full. In *Presidential Television* (1973), Newton Minow, John Bartlow Martin, and Lee M. Mitchell first called attention to the tremendous advantage this coverage might yield for the president, suggesting that it gave the president the ability to command public attention and overpower the more divided and less-visible branches of the federal government, Congress and the Supreme Court. Certainly, the White House has been a plum assignment for television journalists, who have often been accused of being co-opted by the aura of power that surrounds the presidency. This unique situation has been characterized as leading, not to a traditional adversarial relationship between press and president, but to a symbiotic relationship in which journalist and politician need to use each other in order to prosper.

However, since the introduction of cameras into Congress in 1969 and the creation of the C-SPAN network to cover political affairs, there has been some leveling of the presidential advantage in television coverage. Although sometimes accused of "playing to the cameras" in their legislative work, congressional leaders believe this opening up of the governing process to the television audience has provided new understanding of and visibility for the legislative branch of government. The Supreme Court nonetheless continues to function outside the realm of day-to-day television coverage.

Television and International Political Processes

As television's role in the U.S. political system has developed, increasing attention has been focused on the interrelationship between television and politics in many international political environments. Although often characterized by parliamentary and multiparty systems and government-owned media, many other democracies have been influenced by American styles of television campaigning and coverage. This "Americanization" of the media and political process can be seen in the growth of American-style political advertising and journalistic coverage. Britain, France, Germany, Italy, Israel, many Latin American countries, and others have seen this trend, and newly developing democracies in East and Central Europe are also being affected. These countries have not only seen the growth of television advertising and American patterns of media coverage of politics, but a corollary lessening of emphasis on political parties in favor of candidate-centered politics.

Media faced a new challenge to both domestic and international coverage when terrorists struck the World Trade Center in New York City and the Pentagon in Washington, D.C., on September 11, 2001. The aftermath of these horrific events and the challenges of live coverage brought the media into the center of serious world events. The U.S. "war on terrorism" offered new opportunities for the media to demonstrate their ability to help the public understand complex events, while seeking to ensure that freedom of information and rights of free expression are preserved.

Theories and Perspectives on Television and Politics

Early research into the effects of messages delivered through the mass media, particularly television, posited the so-called direct-effects theory: that television messages have direct effects on the behavior of recipients. However, the early research did not fully support this thesis, and scholars for a time tended to discount the notion that such messages directly affected the behavior of recipients such as voters. Recent studies of a more sophisticated design have tended to show that the media do affect behavior, although not necessarily in the most obvious ways initially anticipated.

Television has been proven to have sufficiently identifiable effects to justify a belief in some direct effect of the medium in the political process. While the foregoing discussion clearly implies some direct effects of television's participation in the political process, it is important to note that there are many different theories and interpretations about the role television and other media really play in affecting voter knowledge, opinions, and behavior. Dan Nimmo and Keith Sanders's classic treatment of political communication in *The Handbook of Political Communication* (1981) provides a good overview of the theories that have guided research in this area. Early theorists did assume a kind of direct effect from media exposure but were later cautioned to view the media as having a more limited role. Agenda-setting researchers were the first to break with the limited-effects model and to suggest that media coverage of particular issues in political campaigns affected the agenda of issues judged to be important by voters. Agenda-setting theory—the idea that the media does not tell us what to think, but what to think *about*—remains an important theory of media effects, and researchers have demonstrated that the agenda of issues and candidate characteristics stressed by television and other media may become the voters' agenda as well.

Researchers interested in the political effects of the television have also espoused a "uses and gratifications" theory suggesting that voters attend to various political media messages in order to use the information in various ways. Jay Blumler and his colleagues first proposed this theory as an explanation for why voters in Britain watch or avoid political party broadcasts.

Many other theories and perspectives on television's possible effects on political processes have been advocated. Researchers have demonstrated, for instance, that television may play an important role in political socialization, helping both children and adults to acquire knowledge about the political system and how it operates; however, exposure to television may increase voter cynicism and feelings of inefficacy. Others have suggested that we can best understand television's role in politics by viewing it as a medium through which fantasies "chain out" among the public, shaping views of events and political actors in a dramatist-like fashion. Critical and interpretive views also provide perspective on the interrelationship between governing philosophies, societal values, and television culture. All these approaches and orientations will be essential in the future, as television continues to play a central role in the political processes that touch the lives of citizens throughout the world.

LYNDA LEE KAID

See also **Kennedy, John F.: Assassination and Funeral; Kennedy, Robert F.: Assassination; Kennedy-Nixon Presidential Debates, 1960; 2000 Presidential Election Coverage**

Further Reading

Blumler, Jay G., and Denis McQuail, *Television in Politics: Its Uses and Influence,* London: Faber, 1968; Chicago: University of Chicago Press, 1969

Bormann, E.G., "Fantasy and Rhetorical Vision: The Rhetorical Criticism of Social Reality," *Quarterly Journal of Speech* (1972)

Clancey, M., and M. Robinson, "General Election Coverage: Part I," *Public Opinion* (December/January 1985)

Devlin, L.P., "Contrasts in Presidential Campaign Commercials of 1992," *American Behavioral Scientist* (1993)

Frank, Robert S., *Message Dimensions of Television News,* Lexington, Massachusetts: Lexington Books, 1973

Graber, Doris A., "Press and Television As Opinion Resources in Presidential Campaigns," *Public Opinion Quarterly* (1976)

Graber, Doris A., *Mass Media and American Politics,* Washington, D.C.: Congressional Quarterly Press, 1980; 6th edition, 2002

Gurevitch, M., and Jay G. Blumler, "Comparative Research: The Extending Frontier," in *New Directions in Political Communication,* edited by David L. Swanson and Dan D. Nimmo, Newbury Park, California: Sage, 1990

Hofstetter, C. Richard, *Bias in the News: Network Television Coverage of the 1972 Election Campaign,* Columbus: Ohio State University Press, 1976

Joslyn, R.A., "The Content of Political Spot Ads," *Journalism Quarterly* (1980)

Kaid, Linda Lee, "Political Advertising," in *Handbook of Political Communication,* edited by Dan D. Nimmo and Keith R. Sanders, Beverly Hills, California: Sage, 1981

Kaid, Lynda Lee, "Political Advertising in the 1992 Campaign," in *The 1992 Presidential Campaign: A Communication Perspective,* edited by R.E. Denton, Westport, Connecticut: Praeger, 1994

Kaid, Lynda Lee, and A. Johnston, "Negative Versus Positive Television Advertising in U.S. Presidential Campaigns, 1960–1988," *Journal of Communication* (1991)

Kaid, Lynda Lee, Dan D. Nimmo, and Keith R. Sanders, *New Perspectives on Political Advertising,* Carbondale: Southern Illinois University Press, 1986

Kaid, Lynda Lee, et al., "Television News and Presidential Campaigns: The Legitimization of Televised Political Advertising," *Social Science Quarterly* (1993)

Kaid, Lynda Lee, Jacques Gerstlé, and Keith R. Sanders, editors, *Mediated Politics in Two Cultures: Presidential Campaigning in the United States and France,* New York: Praeger, 1991

Kaid, Lynda Lee, and C. Holtz-Bacha, editors, *Political Advertising in Western Democracies.* Newbury Park, California: Sage, 1995

Kern, Montague, *30-Second Politics: Political Advertising in the Eighties,* New York: Praeger, 1989

Klapper, Joseph T., *The Effects of Mass Communication,* Glencoe, Illinois: Free Press, 1960

Kraus, S., editor, *The Great Debates: Background, Perspectives, Effects,* Bloomington: Indiana University Press, 1962

Lichter, S. Robert, Daniel Amundson, and Richard Noyes. *The Video Campaign: Network Coverage of the 1988 Primaries,* Washington, D.C.: American Enterprise Institute for Public Policy Research, 1988

McCombs, M.E., and D.L. Shaw, "The Agenda-Setting Function of Mass Media," *Public Opinion Quarterly* (1972)

McGinniss, Joe, *The Selling of the President, 1968,* New York: Trident Press, 1969

Minow, Newton N., John Bartlow Martin, and Lee M. Mitchell, *Presidential Television,* New York: Basic Books, 1973

Nimmo, Dan D., *The Political Persuaders,* Englewood Cliffs, New Jersey: Prentice Hall, 1970

Nimmo, Dan D., and Keith R. Sanders, editors, *Handbook of Political Communication,* Beverly Hills, California: Sage, 1981

Patterson, Thomas E., and Robert D. McClure, *The Unseeing Eye: The Myth of Television Power in National Politics,* New York: Putnam, 1976

Sabato, Larry J., *The Rise of Political Consultants: New Ways of Winning Elections,* New York: Basic Books, 1981

Sabato, Larry J., editor, *Overtime: The Election 2000 Thriller,* New York: Longman, 2002

Schwartz, Tony, *Media: The Second God,* New York: Random House, 1981

Semetko, H.A., et al., *The Formation of Campaign Agendas: A Comparative Analysis of Party and Media Roles in Recent American and British Elections,* Hillsdale, New Jersey: Lawrence Erlbaum, 1991

Steeper, F.T., "Public Response to Gerald Ford's Statements on Eastern Europe in the Second Debate," in *The Presidential Debates: Media, Electoral, and Policy Perspectives,* edited by George F. Bishop, Robert G. Meadow, and Marilyn Jackson-Beeck, New York: Praeger, 1978

West, Darrell M., *Air Wars: Television Advertising in Election Campaigns, 1952–1992,* Washington, D.C.: Congressional Quarterly Press, 1993; 3rd edition, as *Air Wars: Television Advertising in Election Campaigns, 1952–2000,* 2001

Politically Incorrect with Bill Maher

Dubbed by some critics the "McLaughlin Group on Acid," *Politically Incorrect with Bill Maher* offered viewers of Comedy Central (1993–96) and later ABC (1997–2002) a unique twist on political talk on television. Hosted by comedian Bill Maher, the half-hour program featured four guests, selected in part for their status as "nonexperts on politics," who discussed political and social matters of the day. Designed to resemble a televised cocktail party, this hybrid political discussion/entertainment show featured a no-holds-barred approach to political talk designed to live up to the show's name.

The brainchild of stand-up comedian Maher, the show first appeared on Comedy Central in 1993. The cable channel was looking for original programming that would bring much-needed recognition and ratings to the young network, which had begun in 1991. *Politically Incorrect* (P.I.) was the first signature show for Comedy Central, helping define the channel as more

than simply a site for stand-up comedy routines and stale B movies.

Owned and produced by Brillstein-Grey Entertainment and HBO Downtown Productions, the show began its first season with 24 episodes. Taped in Manhattan, the weekly program featured Maher and an eclectic array of comedians, actors, and actresses, but also public personalities such as authors, politicians, journalists, activists, and sports and music stars. With the group sitting in a semicircle discussing politics, the show's early production values resembled those of a local cable access show. Still, it offered a serious but entertaining reformulation of both the entertainment and pundit talk show genres. The novelty lay in the concept: famous people, few of whom were political experts, talking about something other than their latest project. This format was generally considered the show's primary attraction for both audiences and the guests who increasingly requested to be on the show.

The discussions and arguments could seem glib and ironic, yet they offered viewers honest and passionate exchanges—a very different approach to political talk on television.

After producing 45 episodes and winning a Cable Ace Award in its second season, the show added Maher's name to the title and began appearing nightly during the third season. This allowed Maher and producers to include more topical discussions based on issues of the day. The show also appeared in the 11 P.M. (EST) time slot, going head-to-head with late-night network programming. Each show began with Maher offering a brief stand-up routine before launching into the panel discussions. In January 1996 the show moved its production to Los Angeles amid talk of the program becoming a post-*Nightline* companion show for the ABC network. In its last season on Comedy Central, *P.I.* produced *Indecision '96,* a satirical take on the 1996 presidential elections that included sending its own "correspondents" to both major party conventions for reports and interviews with politicians and delegates.

After producing 411 shows for Comedy Central, *Politically Incorrect* moved to ABC in January 1997, one of the first successful migrations from cable to network television. Though ABC had not competed in the "late-night comedy entertainment wars" since 1991, network executives thought the show would work well as a topical companion to *Nightline.* The show also enabled the network to appeal to the 18–49 demographic so desired by advertisers. By moving to ABC, *P.I.* was able to reach ten times the audience it had on Comedy Central while offering essentially the same show in the same format with little to no interference from network censors.

Like other cable news and talk channels, *P.I.*'s ratings were best when breaking news or controversial issues were available for discussion. The Oklahoma City bombing and the O.J. Simpson murder trial were favorite discussion topics for many shows on Comedy Central, but it would be the presidential scandal of Bill Clinton's affair with White House intern Monica Lewinsky that would comprise the show's most frequented topic during its early years at ABC. Maher was a persistent and aggressive supporter of Clinton during the controversy and impeachment proceedings, and the subject's mixture of sex and politics proved perfect for entertaining late-night discussions. The deliberations on *P.I.* were distinctive, however, more closely resembling public opinion on the scandal than views expressed on most pundit-staffed political talk shows (Jones, 2001).

During slow news periods, *P.I.* offered numerous thematic gimmicks to increase viewership. From

Politically Incorrect, Bill Maher.
Photo courtesy of ABC Photo Archives

1999–2000, the show began sporadically featuring a "Citizen Panelist." Maher and his staff visited affiliate stations in various cities across the nation, conducting tryouts for a local citizen to win a guest spot on the show, thus fulfilling a top request from viewers—for a "regular" citizen to appear on the panel. The stunt may also have been designed to improve affiliate relations and clearance issues in these cities as well as to garner publicity and ratings points. To attract more politicians as panelists, the show was occasionally taped in Washington, D.C. To attract more intellectuals, it would be taped in New York. The show also taped episodes in London, in a prison in Arizona, and with mobsters as panelists in New York (to capitalize on the popularity of HBO's *The Sopranos*).

The show's defining moment, perhaps, occurred due to discussions about the terrorist attacks on the World Trade Center in New York and the Pentagon in Washington, D.C., on September 11, 2001. Upon the show's return to the air after the attacks, Maher and panelist

Dinesh D'Souza began a discussion of whether the Bush administration's designation of the terrorists as "cowards" was an appropriate label. When D'Souza argued that the word was misplaced, Maher agreed saying, "We have been the cowards, lobbing cruise missiles from 2,000 miles away. That's cowardly. Staying in the airplane when it hits the building, say what you want about it, it's not cowardly." Maher was referring to American military conduct during the Clinton administration, but radio talk show hosts used the statement the following day to excoriate him as an unpatriotic traitor. Though the network supported the show and Maher attempted to clarify his statements in the days and weeks ahead, 17 affiliates eventually dropped the program—with 9 still refusing to show it six months later. Two major advertisers, Sear's & Roebuck and Federal Express, dropped their advertising. The comment even elicited a rebuke from White House ress secretary Ari Fleischer, who said Americans "need to watch what they say." Maher and others have suggested that this event was the final step in the show's demise. In March 2002 Maher was honored along with George Carlin, Dick Gregory, and the Smothers Brothers at the U.S. Comedy Arts Festival with a Freedom of Speech Award. Maher's contract was not renewed, and the show went off the air in December 2002.

Politically Incorrect began with a cable channel's need for an identity in a competitive environment and as a comedian's jab at sanitized public discourse in an era of political correctness. But throughout its decade-long run, the show proved that political talk on television was no longer the exclusive domain of news agencies and broadcast networks, and that elite sources of political commentary did not necessarily speak for or to many audience members. The show radically challenged traditional boundaries and generic conceptions of entertainment programming on the one hand, and serious public-affairs programming on the other. Indeed, *P.I.* represents the television talk show as a truly combinatory form with its blend of politics and social issues, humor and serious discourse, comedic monologues and group discussions, celebrities and less well-known public personalities, and layperson versus elite discourse.

JEFFREY P. JONES

See also **Political Processes and Television; Talk Show**

Further Reading

Carter, Bill, "Lots of Political Humor, and No Morton Kondracke," *New York Times* (February 27, 1994)

Jones, Jeffrey P., "Forums for Citizenship in Popular Culture," in *Politics, Discourse and American Society: New Agendas,* edited by R.P. Hart and B.H. Sparrow, Boulder: Rowman and Littlefield, 2001

Jones, Jeffrey P., "Talking Politics in Post-Network Television: The Case of Politically Incorrect," Unpublished diss., University of Texas at Austin, 1999

Mifflin, Lawrie, "Mix Comedy and Politics with Strange Bedfellows, Then Hope for Sparks," *New York Times* (February 4, 1997)

"'Politically Incorrect' Thriving on Lewinsky Situation," *The Associated Press* (March 5, 1998)

Pool Coverage

Pool coverage involves the combined resources of media outlets to report on a major news event. Such resources include funds, supplies, equipment, and humanpower. Members of the media pool often share news stories and photographic images of the event with other news outlets outside of the pool. Each news outlet may use the pool feed at its discretion.

In the United States, press pools often are associated with war efforts. Indeed, the free press always has been considered a little too free for the Pentagon. The Vietnam War represented the first instance when press coverage brought significant numbers of negative images of U.S. military action into American homes. Since this war the first example of military "guidance" of what the press could and could not cover occurred during the U.S. invasion of Grenada in October 1983. Outcries from the press against the military's virtual blackout of the media's information-gathering efforts in that action brought the establishment of the Department of Defense's National Media Pool.

The Pentagon chooses members of the National Media Pool by lottery. Members of the press take turns serving in the pool. Pool reporters write accounts of the activities they view and share their information with other members. To be included in the National Media Pool, news organizations must demonstrate a familiarity with U.S. military affairs and maintain a correspondent who regularly covers military affairs and Pentagon press conferences; maintain a Washington, D.C., staff; be able to participate in the pool on standby and be able to deploy a reporter within a minimum of four hours; agree to adhere to pool ground rules; and be U.S. owned and operated.

The National Media Pool is designed to represent all news organizations and to serve as the eyes and ears of Americans when the U.S. military is active. However, pool reports often have a uniform quality because all reporters are given access to the same information. Moreover, many journalists claim that military officials often make it hard to provide objective, firsthand coverage of events.

In 1992 representatives from the military and news organizations developed nine principles for pool coverage. As outlined by D. Gersh, these principles embrace open and independent reporting. Furthermore, pools should not be the standard means of coverage; pools may be necessary for specific events and should be disbanded when needed; journalists will be given credentials by the U.S. military and must abide by security rules; journalists will be provided access to all major military units, although special operation restrictions may limit some access; military officials will act as liaisons; field commanders will permit journalists to ride on military vehicles and aircraft when feasible; and materials will be provided to ensure timely, secure, and compatible transmission of pool material (see Gersh, 1992).

According to Mark Thompson (2002), the National Media Pool "came to life on July 19, 1987, when a ban of ten reporters took off from Andrews Air Force Base for its first real-world deployment" (to witness U.S. military operations in the Persian Gulf). In theory, such pool coverage would provide independent press coverage to journalists while maintaining the safety and security of the nation's most sensitive military operations. However, Thompson contends that military resistance has prevented the National Media Pool from reaching this potential. In one notable example, although pool reporters were notified to stand by after the September 11, 2001, terrorist attacks on the World Trade Center and the Pentagon, the pool was not officially deployed during the U.S. attack in Afghanistan in the months that followed.

Media resources also have been pooled to reduce the unnecessary clutter of camera crews at the scene of an event. Pools have been implemented to cover the Republican and Democratic national conventions, presidential primaries, and high-profile elections. They also are utilized to provide coverage of individual political candidates. According to Dan Nimmo and James E. Combs, each day on the campaign trail, a couple of members of the pool reporters are in close contact with the candidate. These members may be "on the candidate's private plane, at small enclaves, during motorcades, and so forth." These reporters write accounts of the candidate's activities, which are then made available to pool journalists who cannot be with the candidate. In presidential elections, pool members are elite press members. Nimmo and Combs explain that there is a pecking order for pool members: "At the top are national political reporters—experienced correspondents of prestigious newspapers, the wire services, national newsmagazines, and television networks. At the bottom are the representatives of smaller newspapers and organizations." Regardless of status, pool coverage often is similar. Timothy Crouse (1974) writes, "After a while, they [pool journalists] began to believe in the same rumors, subscribe to the same theories, and write the same stories."

Recently, pools have been enlisted to organize coverage of high-profile criminal trials. According to Gersh (1991), when serial killer Jeffrey Dahmer was tried for 17 murders allegedly involving cannibalism, more than 450 journalists flocked to Milwaukee, Wisconsin, from around the world to cover the bizarre story. Daniel Patrinos, media coordinator for the Wisconsin court, set up a pool system to handle coverage of the proceedings. In addition to utilizing advisories from Associated Press, United Press International, and Reuters wire services, Patrinos saw to it that local community papers (including black and gay newspapers) were well informed. The judge in this case allowed 23 pool journalists into the courtroom and allowed others to watch from a media center.

Likewise, reporters, photographers, and camera crews turned out in record numbers on January 23, 1995, for the opening statements of the trial of O.J. Simpson on double murder charges. Judge Lance Ito allowed only pool journalists into the courtroom, and a media room was set up for other journalists. In spite of these controls, the term most often used to describe the situation was "media circus."

Whether pool coverage is used to report on military combat, to cover political races, or to control coverage in high-profile legal cases, the goal of pool coverage is the same. Pool coverage, while providing journalists access to events, offers those who employ it a way to manage media coverage.

LORI MELTON MCKINNON

See also **News, Network**

Further Reading

Boot, William (pseud. for Christopher Hanson), "What We Saw, What We Learned," *Columbia Journalism Review* (May/June 1991)

Crouse, Timothy, *The Boys on the Bus,* New York: Ballantine Books, 1974

Gersh, D., "Coordinating Coverage for a Media Trial," *Editor and Publisher* (1991)

Gersh, D., "Press Pool Inclusion Rules Proposed," *Editor and Publisher* (1992)

Lowther, W., "Counting the Hidden Costs," *MacLean's* (January 22, 1990)

Nimmo, Dan, and James E. Combs, *Mediated Political Realities,* New York: Longman, 1983; 2nd edition, 1990

O'Sullivan, G., "Against the Grain: The Free Press—Every Military Should Own One," *The Humanist* (May/June 1991)

Stein, M.L., "Media Circus Begins Again," *Editor and Publisher* (1995)

Thompson, Mark, "The Brief, Ineffective Life of the Pentagon's Media Pool," *Columbia Journalism Review* (March/April 2002)

Porridge

British Sitcom

Porridge was a prison-based sitcom in which sparkling dialogue and tight plots combined to create a funny, sometimes touching, show that became a huge hit with the viewing public. The setting was Slade Prison, a grim edifice, isolated on a moor in an unspecified area in northern England. In the pilot episode ("Prisoner and Escort") the viewer meets the "hero," Norman Stanley Fletcher, a serial offender being escorted by two guards to begin his latest incarceration for five years. Fletcher is a nonviolent petty criminal whose regular capture and conviction suggests he's not as bright as he thinks he is. Nevertheless, Fletcher is quick-witted and spirited, and he refuses to let the system grind him down. Once at the prison Fletcher enters the daily routine of prison life determined to "keep his nose clean" and survive on the regular minor victories he enjoys over the prison wardens, or "screws." His cellmate is Lennie Godber, a first-time offender who is terrified of prison life. Fletcher has no wish to play nursemaid to the lad and puts on a front of being indifferent to Godber's welfare. However, Fletcher is an essentially decent person and soon finds himself acting as a surrogate father to the newcomer, showing him the ropes and generally keeping him out of harm's way. The two main wardens in Fletcher and Godber's life are MacKay, a dour, militaristic Scotsman with a jaundiced view of his charges, and Barrowclough, a sensitive man with a soft spot for the inmates in general and Fletcher in particular. Barrowclough is as optimistic about the men being rehabilitated as MacKay is pessimistic. MacKay is a no-nonsense, by-the-book veteran of the prison service and he is not easy to fool. Barrowclough, on the other hand, is much kinder and fairer to the inmates, but human nature being what it is (and criminal nature being even worse) the prisoners are quick to take advantage of Barrowclough's soft approach and simplistic naïveté.

Although these four are the main protagonists, several regular characters make up the mix, notably the effete prison governor, various inmates, and, most frighteningly, Harry Grout, who runs a criminal empire from within the prison and who has as much sway within the walls as the governor himself. It is the plots where Fletcher and Godber find themselves caught between the wardens and Harry Grout that feature the most rewarding twists and turns.

Porridge was the brainchild of veteran sitcom writers Dick Clement and Ian La Frenais, who had first shone in the genre with their 1960s comedy *The Likely Lads* (BBC 1964–66). In the 1970s they perfected their technique with two comedy classics, *Whatever Happened to the Likely Lads* (BBC 1973–74) and *Porridge.* The banter between Fletcher and Godber was vibrant, funny, and superbly constructed. It also helped that the scripts were played by two skilled actors doing their best work. Ronnie Barker, already a major TV comedy star with a string of sitcom successes and a popular sketch show (*The Two Ronnies* BBC 1971–97, with comedy partner Ronnie Corbett), played Fletcher. Richard Beckinsale, a likable young actor who had already made a splash playing a confused suitor in an earlier sitcom, *The Lovers* (Granada 1970–71), played Godber. The series was attracting huge audience figures shortly after its debut, regularly topping the ratings (during its repeat run in the 1980s, it placed even higher in the ratings).

Clement and La Frenais toyed with calling the series *Bird* (London East End rhyming slang for a prison sentence: Bird Lime–Time) before settling on *Porridge,* another slang word for doing time (from the ubiquitous prison breakfast). Eventually, they penned 21 episodes of the series before Fletcher had done his time and left to join the outside world. But the story did not end there. The writers decided to see how Fletcher would fare "outside," and his adventures were continued in *Going Straight* (BBC 1978), which also featured Lennie Godber, likewise released and now courting Fletcher's daughter, Ingrid. The series failed to sparkle like its predecessor and only ran to one season of six episodes. The character, however, had one last bow, this time on the big screen in the 1979 movie spin-off *Porridge,* which featured the original cast in a caper wherein Fletcher and Godber are unwittingly involved in a jail break and, desperate not to ruin their chances of parole, strive to break back into the prison before their absence is noticed. Tragically, the young Richard Beckinsale died of a heart attack before the feature film was released.

There was a U.S. version of *Porridge: On The Rocks* (ABC 1975–76) with Jose Perez in the lead as Latino Hector Fuentes incarcerated in Alamesa Minimum Security Prison. It failed to duplicate the resonance of the U.K. version, however, and bowed out after a few months. It spawned a pilot, *I'll Never Forget What's Her Name* (ABC 1976), featuring Rita Moreno as Hector's cousin Rosa, but this failed to graduate to a series. The British *Porridge* remains a mainstay of the schedules, and Norman Fletcher has taken his place in the British sitcom hall of fame alongside such characters as Alf Garnett, Basil Fawlty, Edmund Blackadder, and Victor Meldrew.

DICK FIDDY

See also **La Frenais, Ian;** *Likely Lads, The*

Cast

Norman Stanley Fletcher	Ronnie Barker
Lennie Godber	Richard Beckinsale
Mr. MacKay	Fulton MacKay
Mr. Barrowclough	Brian Wilde

Producer

Sydney Lotterby

Writers

Dick Clement, Ian La Frenais

Programming History

Pilot: *Seven of One:* "Prisoner and Escort"
20 Episodes
BBC
Pilot: April 1, 1973
September 1974–March 1977

Further Reading

Ableman, Paul, *Porridge: The Inside Story,* London: Pan Books, 1979

Barker, Ronnie, *Fletcher's Book of Rhyming Slang,* London: Pan Books, 1979

Clement, Dick, and Ian La Frenais, *Porridge,* London: B.B.C. Paperback, 1975

Clement, Dick, and Ian La Frenais, *Another Stretch of Porridge,* London: B.B.C. Paperback, 1976

Clement, Dick, and Ian La Frenais, *A Further Stir of Porridge,* London: B.B.C. Paperback, 1977

Lewisohn, Mark, *The Radio Times Guide to TV Comedy,* London: BBC, 1998, 2002

Webber, Clement, and Ian La Frenais, *Porridge: The Inside Story,* London: Headline, 2001

Post, Mike (1945–)

U.S. Composer

Mike Post, one of the most successful composers in television history, has written music for television since the 1970s. He has won five Grammy Awards and one Emmy for his theme songs and, by his own count, has scored more than 2,000 hours of film. Post has produced the signature melodies for programs such as *Hill Street Blues, L.A. Law,* and *NYPD Blue*. His distinct themes often have intense, industrial rock music cross-cut with smooth jazz sounds. These compositions are noted for their unique blending of styles as well as for the dramatic manner in which they complement a show's narrative.

Post is regarded as the youngest musician to be appointed as musical director for a television program; he assumed that role in 1969, at age 24, on *The Andy Williams Show.* Prior to that appointment, Post worked

Post, Mike

Mike Post.
Photo courtesy of Mike Post

primarily as a session musician for a number of major artists including Sammy Davis Jr., Dean Martin, and Sonny and Cher (he played guitar on the duo's "I Got You Babe" in 1965). He was also a successful producer and arranger, winning a Grammy at age 22 for Best Instrumental Arrangement on Mason Williams's "Classical Gas."

Post began his career in Los Angeles with the country-rock band First Edition, featuring Kenny Rogers. In the late 1960s he joined forces with Pete Carpenter, trombonist, arranger, and veteran of television theme scoring, and began to write music for television. Post and Carpenter began working for producer Stephen J. Cannell and first wrote the theme for Cannell's cop show *Toma* in 1973. *The Rockford Files* theme, however, was their breakthrough assignment. The whimsical synthesizer melodies seemed perfectly suited to the ironic character of James Garner's Rockford. The score sealed their reputations and won Post his second Grammy Award for Best Instrumental Arrangement in 1975.

Hill Street Blues brought more accolades and continued success. The theme song, an elegant composition of simple, poignant piano music, struck a chord

with audiences and soared onto the pop charts. It also impressed his peers and the critics and brought Post two more Grammys in 1981: one for Best Pop Instrumental Performance and one for Best Instrumental Composition.

Hill Street Blues also marked the beginning of Post's long-running creative collaboration with Steven Bochco. One of the most prolific producers of successful dramatic series in the 1980s and 1990s, Bochco hired Post to write the *Hill Street Blues* theme and has worked closely with him ever since. The composer's career was largely established by the music he composed for Bochco's police or law dramas, and their enduring relationship has continued to push the boundaries of television music.

Post's work is wholly devoted to compelling a program's storyline and contributing to its overall tone. The slick, polished opening sounds of *L.A. Law* and the aggressive, chaotic drumbeats punctuating the segments of *NYPD Blue* episodes are examples of talent for melding images, emotions, and sounds. He is also exceptionally resourceful in orchestrating his award-winning melodies. To achieve the unique sound of the *NYPD Blue* theme, for example, he used, among other effects, 1,000 men jumping up and down on a wooden floor, a cheese grater, and a subway horn. All these ideas are largely inspired by the program's script, and Post's ability to encompass a show's character in his music is what has landed him atop the elite class of Hollywood composers. Only Pat Williams, Henry Mancini, and Dave Grusin have attained comparable levels of success and respect in this field.

Ironically, some of his music has become so popular that the themes play on pop radio, a medium wholly disconnected from the visual drama he is committed to enhancing. One of his songs, "The Greatest American Hero," is among the few TV themes ever to reach the number one spot on the pop singles charts. Others, such as the themes for *Hill Street Blues* and *The Rockford Files,* have reached the top ten.

His popular and unique compositions are not Mike Post's only enduring legacy to television, however. He can also be credited with elevating television scoring to a fine art, and creating a new dimension of drama with his "ear for the visual."

JENNIFER HOLT

See also **Music on Television**

Mike Post. Born in San Fernando, California, 1945. Married; children: Jennifer and Aaron. Began career as member of Kenny Rogers's country-rock band First Edition; went on to play for Sammy Davis Jr., and Dean Martin; musical director, *The Andy Williams*

Show, 1969; produced numerous television scores, including *The Rockford Files, Hill Street Blues, L.A. Law, Doogie Howser,* and *NYPD Blue;* arranged various Ray Charles records; record producer, Dolly Parton's *9 to 5,* among others. Recipient: five Grammy Awards and one Emmy.

Television (selected scoring)
(Note: Dates indicate the year in which the program debuted.)

1971	*The NBC Mystery Movie*
1971	*Two on a Bench*
1971	*Make Your Own Kind of Music*
1972	*Gidget Gets Married*
1973	*Griff*
1973	*Needles and Pins*
1973	*Toma*
1974	*Locusts*
1974	*The Morning After*
1974	*The Rockford Files*
1974	*The Texas Wheelers*
1975	*The Bob Crane Show*
1976	*The Invasion of Johnson County*
1976	*Richie Brockelman: Missing 24 Hours*
1976	*Scott Free*
1976	*Baa Baa Black Sheep* (renamed *The Black Sheep Squadron,* 1977)
1977	*CHiPs*
1977	*Charlie Cobb: Nice Night for a Hanging*
1977	*Off the Wall*
1978	*Doctor Scorpion*
1978	*Richie Brockelman: Private Eye*
1978	*The White Shadow*
1979	*Big Shamus, Little Shamus*
1979	*Captain America*
1979	*Captain America II*
1979	*The Duke*
1979	*The 416th*
1979	*The Night Rider*
1979	*Operating Room*
1979	*240-Robert*
1980	*Magnum, P.I.*
1980	*Tenspeed and Brown Shoe*
1980	*Scout's Honor*
1980	*Hill Street Blues*
1980	*Coach of the Year*
1981	*The Greatest American Hero*
1982	*Palms Precinct*
1982	*The Quest*
1982	*Tales of the Gold Monkey*
1982	*Will, G. Gordon Liddy*
1983	*The A-Team*
1983	*Bay City Blues*
1983	*Big John*
1983	*Hardcastle and McCormick*
1983	*Riptide*
1983	*The Rousters*
1983	*Running Brave*
1984	*Four Eyes*
1984	*Hadley's Rebellion*
1984	*Hard Knox*
1984	*No Man's Land*
1984	*The Return of Luter Gillie*
1984	*The River Rat*
1984	*Welcome to Paradise*
1984	*Hunter*
1985	*Brothers-in-Law*
1985	*Heart of a Champion*
1985	*Stingray*
1986	*Adam: His Song Continues*
1986	*L.A. Law*
1986	*The Last Precinct*
1987	*Beverly Hills Buntz*
1987	*Destination America*
1987	*Hooperman*
1987	*Sirens*
1987	*Wiseguy*
1988	*Murphy's Law*
1988	*Sonny Spoon*
1989	*Booker*
1989	*The Ryan White Story*
1989	*B.L. Stryker: The Dancer's Touch*
1989	*Doogie Howser, M.D.*
1989	*Quantum Leap*
1990	*Cop Rock*
1990	*Law and Order*
1990	*Unspeakable Acts*
1990	*Without Her Consent*
1991	*Silk Stalkings*
1991	*The Commish*
1991	*Blossom*
1992	*Renegade*
1993	*NYPD Blue*
1994	*The Byrds of Paradise*
1995	*News Radio*
1995	*Murder One*
1997	*Players*
1997	*Brooklyn South*
1997	*Total Security*
1998	*Martial Law*
1999	*Law and Order: Special Victims Unit*
2000	*Arrest and Trial*
2000	*Deadline*
2000	*City of Angels*
2001	*Law and Order: Criminal Intent*
2001	*PBS Hollywood Presents*
2001	*Philly*
2002	*Law and Order: Crime and Punishment*

2002	*Dead Above Ground*
2002	*Inside NYPD Blue: A Decade on the Job*
2003	*Dragnet*
2003	*The Gin Game*

Further Reading

Borzillo, Carrie, "TV Composer Mike Post Takes BMI Award (Lifetime Achievement)," *Billboard* (May 28, 1994)

Fink, Edward J., "Episodic's Music Man: Mike Post" (interview), *Journal of Popular Film and Television* (Winter 1998)

Harris, Steve, *Film and Television Composers: An International Discography, 1920–1989,* Jefferson, North Carolina: McFarland, 1992

Olsen, David C., editor, *Best of the 80's: TV Songbook: A Prime Time Anthology,* Miami, Florida: CPP/Belwin, 1988

Wescott, Steven D., *A Comprehensive Bibliography of Music for Film and Television,* Detroit, Michigan: Information Coordinators, 1985

Potter, Dennis (1935–1994)

British Writer

Dennis Potter is arguably the most important creative figure in the history of British television. From 1965 until his death in 1994, he constructed a personal oeuvre of such remarkable character and consistency that it will probably never be equaled in the medium. The most prolific yet also most controversial of television playwrights, he remains the undisputed figurehead of that peculiarly British phenomenon of writers who expend much of their working lives and passions attempting to show that television can be just as powerful a vehicle for artistic expression as cinema or theater.

Potter was raised in what he later described as the "tight, enclosed, backward" world of the Forest of Dean; a remote rural idyll nestling between two rivers, the Severn and the Wye, on the aggressively English side of the border with Wales. The product of a remote, God-fearing community, he attended chapel at least twice every Sunday, and the vividness of that institution's language and metaphors formed a powerful influence on his writing.

After an earlier career in journalism and politics, Potter came to prominence in 1965, when his first plays were all transmitted by the BBC within the space of a year, as part of *The Wednesday Play*'s groundbreaking policy of introducing radical new writers to television. The most successful of these productions were *The Nigel Barton Plays*—a pair of semiautobiographical dramas that expertly dissected the effects of social class upon the psyche of its eponymous hero. The *Barton* plays won notable awards and helped to seal Potter's reputation as a major new playwright of passion and ideas. However, as the 1960s wore on and

Potter continued to write for *The Wednesday Play* and its successor *Play for Today,* it gradually became clear that underlying the broadly political attacks in his earlier work was an older chapel sensibility: Potter represented a personality molded by biblical teaching and imagery, yet now in desperate search of answers in the face of acute spiritual crisis.

In 1969 *Son of Man* was transmitted; it is a gospel play in which Potter audaciously created the messiah in his own image, as a human, suffering Christ, racked by doubts over his own mission and plagued by the fear that he has been forsaken by God. With this and other titles that followed—such as *Angels Are So Few* (1970), *Where Adam Stood* (1976), and, most controversially of all, *Brimstone and Treacle* (originally intended for transmission in 1976 but banned by the BBC for 11 years on account of a scene where the devil rapes a mentally handicapped girl)—it became clear that Potter had discovered his true vocation as a dramatist of religious or spiritual themes, albeit one highly unorthodox and sometimes offensive to the political and moral establishment.

Central to Potter's quest for spiritual answers was his own personal affliction of psoriatic arthropathy: a painful combination of psoriasis enflaming the skin and arthritis crippling the joints, which he had suffered from since the age of 26 and which had necessitated his withdrawal from the public worlds of politics and current affairs into the more private realm of life as a television playwright. This inwardness was also manifested in Potter's famous "nonnaturalistic" style: his determination to challenge the dominant British television drama tradition of "dreary" naturalism, through

Writer/director Dennis Potter with Alan Bates and Gina Bellman, 1991.
Courtesy of the Everett Collection

an alternative emphasis on inner, psychological reality. He successfully customized a whole series of nonnaturalistic devices—including flashback and fantasy sequences; direct-to-camera address by characters; the use of adult actors to play children—all of which he believed represented more truthfully "what goes on inside people's heads."

In 1978 Potter showcased what became his most famous technique when Bob Hoskins burst into song, miming to an old 78 rpm recording in the BBC TV serial *Pennies from Heaven*. The international success of *Pennies* transformed Potter's career, leading to a lucrative spell as a Hollywood screenwriter, which included a disastrous movie remake of the serial in 1981. Throughout the 1980s and early 1990s, however, Potter continued to produce original work for television, although he now wrote serials rather than one-off plays. Among his most notable programs from this era is *The Singing Detective* (1986), in which his famous device of characters miming to popular song is used to punctuate a narrative as complex and layered as any work of serious literature; this program that will un-

doubtedly endure as Potter's monument to the creative possibilities of the medium.

The rapturous plaudits that greeted *The Singing Detective* in Britain and the United States may have elevated Potter to the rare status of a genuine TV auteur, but the period after 1986 was not an easy one for Potter. In 1989, after a falling out with his erstwhile producer Kenith Trodd, Potter decided to direct a television adaptation of his "feminist" novel *Blackeyes*. The result was a critical bloodbath in the United Kingdom, with the director accused of precisely the misogyny and sexual exploitation he claimed he had been trying to expose on-screen. Nor was *Lipstick on Your Collar* (1993), a six-part "drama with songs" set in the 1950s, the resounding popular success he had desired.

In February 1994 Potter was diagnosed with terminal cancer of the pancreas. He died four months later but not before giving an extraordinary television interview in which he talked movingly about his imminent death, revealing his plans to complete two final television serials to be uniquely coproduced by rival national channels BBC 1 and Channel 4. Defying the medical odds, he succeeded in completing the works, *Karaoke* and *Cold Lazarus,* and, in accordance with his wishes, these were transmitted posthumously by both channels in the spring of 1996. Although critical reaction to the programs was somewhat mixed in Britain, the very fact of the joint production seemed to confirm Potter's creative legacy as the practitioner who, above all others, aspired to raise television to an art form and whose pioneering nonnaturalism had indeed been successful in opening up the medium's drama to the landscape of the mind.

JOHN COOK

See also **Pennies from Heaven; Singing Detective, The; Wednesday Play**

Dennis (Christopher George) Potter. Born in Joyford Hill, Coleford, Gloucestershire, England, May 17, 1935. Educated at Christchurch Village School; Bell's Grammar School, Coleford; St. Clement Danes Grammar School, London; New College, Oxford, B.A. 1959. Married: Margaret Morgan, 1959; one son and two daughters. Member of the Current Affairs Staff, BBC Television, 1959–61; television critic for various publications, 1961–78; contributed to *That Was the Week That Was,* 1962; Labour candidate for Parliament, East Hertfordshire, 1964; first plays televised, 1965; first screenplay, 1981. Honorary fellow, New College, Oxford, 1987. Recipient: Writers Guild Awards, 1965 and 1969; Society of Film and Television Arts Award, 1966; British Academy of Film and Television Arts Award, 1979 and 1980; Prix Italia, 1982; San Francisco Film Festival Award, 1987; Broadcasting Press Guild Award, 1987. Died in Ross-on-Wye, Herefordshire, June 7, 1994.

Television Series

1971	*Casanova*
1978	*Pennies from Heaven*
1985	*Tender Is the Night*
1986	*The Singing Detective*
1988	*Christabel*
1989	*Blackeyes* (writer, director)
1993	*Lipstick on Your Collar*

Television Plays

1965	*The Wednesday Play: The Confidence Course*
1965	*Alice*
1965	*Cinderella*
1965	*Stand Up, Nigel Barton*
1965	*Vote Vote Vote for Nigel Barton*
1966	*Emergency Ward 9*
1966	*Where the Buffalo Roam*
1967	*Message for Posterity*
1968	*The Bonegrinder*
1968	*Shaggy Dog*
1968	*A Beast with Two Backs*
1969	*Moonlight on the Highway*
1969	*Son of Man*
1970	*Lay Down Your Arms*
1970	*Angels Are So Few*
1971	*Paper Roses*
1971	*Traitor*
1972	*Follow the Yellow Brick Road*
1973	*Only Make Believe*
1973	*A Tragedy of Two Ambitions*
1974	*Joe's Ark*
1974	*Schmoedipus*
1975	*Late Call*
1976	*Double Dare*
1976	*Where Adam Stood*
1978	*The Mayor of Casterbridge*
1979	*Blue Remembered Hills*
1980	*Blade on the Feather*
1980	*Rain on the Roof*
1980	*Cream in My Coffee*
1987	*Visitors*
1987	*Brimstone and Treacle*
1996	*Karaoke*
1996	*Cold Lazarus*

Films

Pennies from Heaven, 1981; *Brimstone and Treacle,* 1982; *Gorky Park,* 1983; *Dreamchild,* 1985; *Track 29,* 1988; *Blackeyes,* 1990; *Secret Friends* (writer, director), 1991.

Stage

Sufficient Carbohydrate, 1983.

Publications

The Glittering Coffin, 1960

The Changing Forest: Life in the Forest of Dean Today, 1962

The Nigel Barton Plays: Stand Up, Nigel Barton, Vote Vote Vote for Nigel Barton: Two Television Plays, 1968

Son of Man (television play), 1970

Hide and Seek (novel), 1973

Brimstone and Treacle (television play), 1978

Pennies from Heaven (novel), 1981

Sufficient Carbohydrate (play), 1983

Waiting for the Boat: Dennis Potter on Television, 1984

The Singing Detective (television series), 1986
Ticket to Ride (novel), 1986
Blackeyes (novel), 1987
Christabel (television series), 1988
Potter on Potter (edited by Graham Fuller), 1993
Seeing the Blossom: Two Interviews, a Lecture, and a Story, 1994
Karaoke and Cold Lazarus (television plays), 1996

Further Reading

Aitken, Ian, "Shout to the Top," *New Statesman and Society* (April 22, 1994)
Bell, Robert H., "Implicated without Choice: The Double Vision of *The Singing Detective*," *Literature-Film Quarterly* (July 1993)
Bragg, Melvin, "The Present Tense" (interview), *New Left Review* (May–June 1994)
Cantwell, Mary, "Dennis Potter's Last Interview: Dying, He Was Brilliantly Alive," *New York Times* (July 30, 1994)
Carpenter, Humphrey, *Dennis Potter: The Authorized Biography,* London: Faber and Faber, 1998; as *Dennis Potter: A Biography,* New York: St. Martin's Press, 1999
Cook, John R., *Dennis Potter: A Life on Screen,* Manchester, England: Manchester University Press, and New York: St. Martin's Press, 1995
Creeber, Glen, *Dennis Potter: Between Two Worlds: A Critical Reassessment,* New York: St. Martin's Press, 1998
Fuller, Graham, "Dennis Potter," *American Film* (March 1989)
Fuller, Graham, *Potter on Potter,* London and New York: Faber and Faber, 1993
Gilbert, W. Stephen, *Fight and Kick and Bite: The Life and Work of Dennis Potter,* London: Hodder and Stoughton, 1995; as *The Life and Work of Dennis Potter,* Woodstock, New York: Overlook Press, 1998
Gras, Vernon W., and John R. Cook, editors, *The Passion of Dennis Potter: International Collected Essays,* Basingstoke, England: Macmillan, and New York: St. Martin's Press, 2000
Lichtenstein, Therese, "Syncopated Thriller: Dennis Potter's *Singing Detective*," *Artforum* (May 1990)
Simon, Ron, "The Flow of Memory and Desire: Television and Dennis Potter," *Television Quarterly* (Spring 1993)
Stead, Peter, *Dennis Potter,* Bridgend, England: Serend, 1993
Yentob, Alan, "Dennis Potter" (obituary), *Sight and Sound* (July 1994)

Powell, Dick (1904–1963)

U.S. Actor, Producer

Dick Powell may be best remembered as a movie star, a boyish crooner in dozens of Hollywood musicals of the 1930s, and later, a hard-boiled, film noir tough guy. Like many stars of the studio era, Powell turned his dramatic talents to television in the 1950s, but he did so as an adjunct to his most significant television role, as an independent telefilm producer. Between 1952 and his death in 1963, Powell served as the head of Four Star Television, which became, under his leadership, one of Hollywood's leading suppliers of prime-time network programming.

As the star of numerous Warner Brothers musicals, Powell was one of Hollywood's top box-office draws during the 1930s (and quickly became just as popular on radio). By mid-decade, the young singer was lobbying to break into more serious roles, but his efforts were rebuffed by Jack Warner. The parts became somewhat more varied after a 1940 move to Paramount, but the actor's dramatic ambitions were blocked there as well. The turning point came in 1944, when Powell convinced RKO to cast him as private eye Philip Marlowe in *Murder, My Sweet* (regarded by many as the definitive rendition of Raymond Chandler's fictional sleuth). Thereafter the singing roles stopped, and Powell began a new career as a hard-boiled antihero in such films as *Cornered, Pitfall, Johnny O'Clock,* and *Cry Danger,* in the process remaking his radio persona as well, with a stint as gumshoe Richard Rogue in *Rogue's Gallery,* and three seasons as *Richard Diamond, Private Detective.*

Still eager to broaden his creative horizons, Powell set his sights on movie directing in the late 1940s, but he once again met with resistance from studio powers. Finally, in 1952 RKO studio head Howard Hughes gave Powell a chance to direct the thriller *Split Second,* and the success of that film led Hughes to offer Powell a producing job. Although there was some speculation in Hollywood that Powell would become head of production at RKO, he was able to complete only one feature, *The Conqueror,* before Hughes sold the company in 1955. Powell went on to helm three more features in as many years at other studios.

Dick Powell in *Four Star Playhouse, The House Always Wins,* 1952–56.
Courtesy of the Everett Collection

Although the leadership of RKO had eluded him, Powell had already begun his rise as a television mogul. On the heels of his first feature assignment, Powell had formed an independent telefilm production company with actors Charles Boyer and David Niven. Four Star Films derived its name from its first project, the half-hour anthology *Four Star Playhouse,* in which one of the three partners would rotate with a different weekly guest star. In its second season, the partners invited guest Ida Lupino to become the show's permanent "fourth star." Although she did not become a stockholder in the firm, Lupino went on to direct many episodes of *Playhouse* and other Four Star series, in addition to her acting duties.

Boyer and Niven each owned a healthy share of Four Star, but Powell ran the company. A 1962 *Television* magazine profile of Powell called him the company's "principal architect of policy as well as the most valuable performer and production executive" and noted that the firm's fortunes moved in direct proportion to the time the boss devoted to it. A "workaholic" in today's parlance, Powell was notoriously driven and closely involved with both the financial and creative aspects of Four Star. He not only managed operations but was active in developing story properties,

oversaw script conferences, and, when needed, used his charm—and the weight of his celebrity—to close a program sale.

Four Star's stock-in-trade early on was anthologies. Powell followed up *Four Star Playhouse* in 1954 with the short-lived *Stage 7,* and two years later *Dick Powell's Zane Grey Theater,* hosted by, and occasionally starring, the Four Star chief executive officer himself. Powell and company also produced one season of *Alcoa Theatre* in 1958 and in subsequent years crafted anthologies around one of Powell's partners (*The David Niven Theater*), and his wife (*The June Allyson Show*), both featuring the requisite array of Hollywood stars.

Zane Grey Theater ran for seven years, at once feeding and riding the crest of the phenomenal surge of western programs on television in the late 1950s. Four Star generated its share of the stampede, scoring its biggest hits in the genre with *The Rifleman, Wanted: Dead or Alive,* and *Trackdown,* as well as less-successful entries like *Johnny Ringo, Black Saddle, Law of the Plainsman, Stagecoach West,* and the highly regarded but extremely short-lived Sam Peckinpah project, *The Westerner.*

Four Star's western output highlights the creative economy of program development under Powell. Anthologies were the perfect vehicles by which to generate new program pilots at a network or sponsor's expense. Most of the Four Star westerns, for example, were born as installments of *Zane Grey Theater* (*Wanted: Dead or Alive* had its trial run as an episode of *Trackdown*). *Four Star Playhouse* spawned two crime series featuring gambler Willy Dante: eight *Four Star* installments starring Powell as Dante were repackaged as a 1956 summer replacement series (*The Best in Mystery*), and a new *Dante* series was hatched in 1960 with Howard Duff in the title role. Another spin-off of sorts came in 1957 when Powell revived his *Richard Diamond* radio vehicle for television, with young David Janssen as the suave P.I. *Michael Shayne, Private Detective* was a less-successful Four Star entry in the private-eye cycle of the late 1950s.

Four Star was one of the busiest telefilm suppliers in the business in 1959, when Powell hired Thomas McDermott away from the Benton and Bowles ad agency to be executive vice president of production. The following year the newly renamed Four Star Television marked its peak in prime time with a remarkable 12 series on the networks. Even after dropping to six shows in 1962, Four Star was producing more programming than any other Hollywood independent, surpassed only by MCA-Revue and Columbia-Screen Gems, leading *Broadcasting* magazine to dub the firm a "TV major." More literally "independent" than most of his producing counterparts, Powell resisted the increasingly common practice of ceding control of off-network distribution to the networks themselves. Although Four Star often had to cut the broadcasters in on series profits, the firm retained syndication rights to all its shows, starting its own syndication division, rather belatedly, in 1962.

Powell the executive was sensitive to the creative process as well as profits, no doubt due to his own experiences as a performer and later a director. "Four Star was a paradise for writers," according to Powell biographer Tony Thomas, and many Four Star alumni have attested to their boss's sensitivity and support. Powell personally fielded ideas from writers, interceded with sponsors to protect controversial scripts from censorship, and would support any story—even if it conflicted with his own political conservatism—if the writer were passionate enough about it. Powell mentored writer-producers such as Sam Peckinpah, Blake Edwards, Bruce Geller, and Aaron Spelling and signed young writers like Christopher Knopf, Richard Levinson and William Link, Leslie Stevens, and Robert Towne early in their careers. By all accounts, Powell was universally respected by his creative personnel.

With the western on the wane in the early 1960s, Four Star diversified its product, turning out situation comedies like *The Tom Ewell Show, Peter Loves Mary, McKeever and the Colonel, The Gertrude Berg Show,* and *Ensign O'Toole,* as well as a courtroom drama (*The Law and Mr. Jones*), an organized crime saga (*Target: The Corrupters*), and an unusual anthology, *The Lloyd Bridges Show.* Only *The Detectives, Starring Robert Taylor* constituted even a modest success. In early 1961 Powell reduced his involvement in the overall operations at Four Star and focused his attentions on producing *The Dick Powell Show,* a star-studded anthology featuring Powell as host and frequent star. The new anthology presented even more pilots than *Zane Grey*—over a dozen in two years—yielding the newspaper series *Saints and Sinners* in 1962, and *Burke's Law* the following year (among the unsold projects was *Luxury Liner*—produced by future *Love Boat* creator Aaron Spelling). One of television's few remaining anthologies, the Powell show received an Emmy nomination for Outstanding Dramatic Achievement for both of its seasons on the air.

After Powell's death in January 1963, Four Star continued operation under McDermott's leadership, but Four Star's reign as a "TV major" was over. With six series on the fall schedule for 1962, a year later *Burke's Law* was the firm's only prime-time entry. The change in Four Star's fortunes probably had as much to do with ratings as anything else. The company had not had a major hit since *The Rifleman,* and its attempts to exploit the sitcom were unsuccessful. The firm's continued resistance to network control of syndication may have cost it prime-time sales. Certainly the loss of Powell's leadership, his formidable salesmanship powers, and indeed his reputation could not have helped matters. With declining network program sales, more flops (e.g., *Honey West, The Rogues*), and the disappointing performance of the company's own (belated) syndication division, Four Star's ledgers were awash in red ink by 1966. *The Big Valley* was the last series being produced under the Four Star banner when the firm was sold in 1967.

The bulk of Four Star's output reflected Powell's own history in motion pictures, turning out solid, unpretentious entertainment. If Powell and company did not assay social realism or topical drama with the same panache as, say, Stirling Silliphant or Reginald Rose, neither did they pursue the radical self-imitation characterized by Warner Brothers' western and detective series. Rather, Four Star products reflected the relative diversity necessary to survive in an uncertain entertainment marketplace. Even Four Star's genre-bound series exhibited the kind of conventional innovation, and occasional quirkiness, that defines American commercial television at its most fascinating, and Powell was pursuing anthologies long after the conventional wisdom had abandoned the form.

Of all the Four Star products from Powell's tenure, only *The Rifleman* remains a syndication staple today, although *Zane Grey Theater* and *Wanted: Dead or Alive* survive on commercial video, and *Burke's Law* was revived for the 1990s by its star (and co-owner) Gene Barry. Aficionados of Hollywood film can, on cable, video, or at the occasional retrospective screening, still enjoy Powell's innocent grin and golden tones in *Gold Diggers of 1933,* and his stubbled smirk and grim wisecracks in *Murder, My Sweet.* His final dramatic roles, on *Zane Grey* and *Dick Powell,* are the purview of collectors of TV ephemera, until their resurrection on video. It remains for historians to cite Dick Powell the independent producer, the telefilm pioneer, the "TV major," and to emphasize that by the early 1960s he was a more successful producer of motion pictures—for the small screen—than any of the old-line Hollywood studios. One wonders what Jack Warner must have thought.

MARK ALVEY

Dick (Richard) Ewing Powell. Born in Mountain View, Arkansas, November 14, 1904. Attended Little Rock College, Arkansas. Married: 1) M. Maund (divorced); 2) actress Joan Blondell, 1936 (divorced, 1945); children: Ellen and Norman; 3) actress June

Allyson, 1945, one daughter and one son. Began career as singer with his own band, 1921; singer, comedian, and master of ceremonies, Stanley Theatre, Pittsburgh, Pennsylvania, 1930; film debut, *Blessed Event*, 1932; cofounder, Four Star Productions, 1952; first directed film, *Split Second*, 1953; host and producer, various shows, and film producer. Died in Hollywood, California, January 2, 1963.

Television

1952–56	*Four Star Playhouse*
1956–62	*Dick Powell's Zane Grey Theater*
1961–63	*The Dick Powell Show*

Films

Blessed Event, 1932; *Too Busy to Work*, 1932; *The King's Vacation*, 1933; *42nd Street*, 1933; *Gold Diggers of 1933*, 1933; *Footlight Parade*, 1933; *College Coach*, 1933; *Convention*, 1933; *Dames*, 1934; *Wonder Bar*, 1934; *Twenty Million Sweethearts*, 1934; *Happiness Ahead*, 1934; *Flirtation Walk*, 1934; *Gold Diggers of 1935*, 1935; *Page Miss Glory*, 1935; *Broadway Gondolier*, 1935; *A Midsummer Night's Dream*, 1935; *Shipmates Forever*, 1935; *Thanks a Million*, 1935; *Colleen*, 1936; *Hearts Divided*, 1936; *Stage Struck*, 1936; *The Gold Diggers of 1937*, 1936; *On the Avenue*, 1937; *The Singing Marine*, 1937; *Varsity Show*, 1937; *Hollywood Hotel*, 1937; *Cowboy from Brooklyn*, 1938; *Hard to Get*, 1938; *Going Places*, 1938; *Naughty but Nice*, 1939; *Christmas in July*, 1940; *I Want a Divorce*, 1940; *Model Wife*, 1941; *In the Navy*, 1941; *Happy Go Lucky*, 1942; *Star Spangled Rhythm*, 1942; *True to Life*, 1943; *Riding High*, 1943; *It Happened Tomorrow*, 1944; *Meet the People*, 1944; *Murder, My Sweet*, 1944; *Concerned*, 1945; *Johnny O'Clock*, 1947; *To the Ends of the Earth*, 1948; *Pitfall*, 1948; *Station West*, 1948; *Rogue's Regiment*, 1948; *Mrs. Mike*, 1949; *The Reformer and the Redhead*, 1950; *Right Cross*, 1950; *Cry Dangers*, 1951; *The Tall Target*, 1951; *You Never Can Tell*, 1951; *The Bad and the Beautiful*, 1952; *Susan Slept Here*, 1954.

Films (director)

Split Second, 1953; *The Conqueror*, 1956; *You Can't Run Away from It*, 1957; *The Enemy Below*, 1957; *The Hunters*, 1958.

Radio (selection)

Rogue's Gallery, 1945–46; *Richard Diamond, Private Detective*, 1949–50.

Further Reading

"Dialogue on Film: Aaron Spelling," *American Film* (May 1984)

Simmons, Garner, *Peckinpah: A Portrait in Montage*, Austin: University of Texas Press, 1982

Stempel, Tom, *Storytellers to the Nation: A History of American Television Writing*, New York: Continuum, 1992

Thomas, Tony, "Dick Powell," *Films in Review* (May 1961)

Thomas, Tony, *The Dick Powell Story*, Burbank, California: Riverwood Press, 1993

Power without Glory

Australian Serial Drama

Power without Glory is probably among the two or three finest drama series to have been produced in Australia. The series was, in effect, a local equivalent to *The Forsyte Saga* and told the story of John West, and his wife and family, from the 1890s when he was an impoverished youth in the depression-stricken city of Melbourne to his death around 1950. By that time, he had become a millionaire, although he was tainted by shady political and business dealings. The series was based on the novel of the same name by Australian author Frank Hardy, which had been published in 1949.

At the time, it was widely believed that Hardy had based the figure of John West on the real-life Australian businessman John Wren. The Wren family took legal action against Hardy, accusing him of libel. Hardy successfully defended the case, however, on the basis that his novel was fiction. Subsequently, the book sold extremely well, no doubt because the public believed that it was in fact based on the Wren story. *Power without Glory* should have been a natural adaptation for either radio or television in the 1950s or 1960s, but no broadcast producer was willing to take

Power without Glory.
Courtesy of Australian Broadcasting Corporation

began on-air nationally on the ABC in June 1976. *Power without Glory* starred Martin Vaughan as West and Rosalind Spiers as his wife. Other well-known Australian actors in the series included Terence Donovan, George Mallaby, and Michael Pate. Like many television miniseries, especially those with such a long screen-time, *Power* went well beyond the domestic drama of the couple and included the developing lives and careers of their children and acquaintances. These mostly private dramas were stitched onto a larger historical canvas that included political and national events such as the formation of the Australian Labour Party, the conscription debates of World War I, and the impact of the Great Depression and World War II.

The quality and integrity of the production—most especially its writing and the performance of the large cast—effectively sustained audience interest over the serial's 26 hours. *Power* proved enormously popular and prestigious for the ABC. In 1977 it won a host of industry awards, including nine Sammys and four Penguins. The series was repeated in 1978, and in 1981 it was sold to Network Ten, where it was to receive two further screenings. *Power without Glory* was arguably the finest drama series ever made at the ABC. Its production and screening were watershed events, coinciding with the 20th anniversary of the first ABC television transmission, and also highlighting the fact that, with a change in federal government and a downturn in the Australian economy, the circumstances that had made such a production possible were now a thing of the past.

ALBERT MORAN

on the material for fear of further legal action from the Wren family. It was not until 1974 that such a project was undertaken.

That year Oscar Whitbread, veteran producer with the public-service television broadcaster, the Australian Broadcasting Corporation (ABC), decided that the novel should be brought to the television screen. After all, despite the timidity of ABC management, the court case had happened more than 20 years earlier and had, in any event, been lost by Wren. Moreover, under a federal Labour Party government, the ABC was expected to be progressive and innovative in its productions; its revenue, coming directly from the government, was, in real terms, at an all-time high. Whitbread judged that the time was right for such a massive undertaking, and he and script editor Howard Griffiths set to work on adapting the novel. The book was split into 26 hour-long episodes, and a series of ABC and former Crawford Production writers, including Tony Morphett, Sonia Borg, and Phil Freedman, were set to work to develop scripts. Writing and filming took place over the next 18 months, and the series

Cast

John West	Martin Vaughan
Nellie Moran	Rosalind Spiers
Mrs. Moran	Heather Canning
Mrs. West	Irene Inescort
Piggy Lewis	Michael Aitkens
Barney Robinson	George Mallaby
Eddie Corrigan	Sean Scully
Mick O'Connell	John Bowman
Paddy Cummins	Tim Connor
Jim Tracey	Alan Hardy
Detective Sgt. O'Flaherty	Peter Cummins
Sergeant Devlin	David Ravenswood
Mr. Dunn	Carl Bleazby
Constable Brogan	Burt Cooper
Sergeant Grieve	Terry Gill
Alec	Les James
Arthur West	Tim Robertson
Mrs. Tracey	Marnie Randall
Father O'Toole	John Murphy
Brendan	Richard Askew

Sugar Renfrey
Bob Standish
Florrie Robinson
David Garside
Mrs. Finch
Frank Ashton
Tom Trumbleward
Jim Francis
Dick Bradley
Rev Joggins
Martha Ashton
Commissioner Callinan
Constable Baddson
Detective Roberts
Constable Harris
Constable Logan
Dolly West
Frank Lammence
Lou Darby
Dr. Malone
Ron Lassiter
Snoopy Tanner
Mr. Johnstone
Harriet
T.J. Real
Turner
Smith
Margaret
Kate
Marjorie
Mary
Brendan
Jim Morton
Ned Horan
Maurice Blackwell
Mary West
Marjorie West
Brendon West
Luke Carson
Peter Monton
Hugo
Andy Mackenzie
Paul Andreas

John Wood
Reg Evans
Sheila Hayes
Leon Lissek
Esme Melville
Barry Hill
Frank Wilson
Telford Jackson
Gerard Kennedy
Jonathon Hardy
Elaine Baillie
Keith Aden
Stephen Oldfield
Tony Hawkins
Hugh Price
Matthew King
Kerry Dwyer
Terence Donovan
Gil Tucker
Michael Pate
Terry Norris
Graham Blundell
Byron Williams
Rowena Wallace
Carl Bleazby
Lou Brown
Iain Merton
Joan Letch
Sue Jones
Lisa Crittenden
Andrea Butcher
Stewart Fleming
Norman Hodges
Norman Kaye
Tony Barry
Wendy Hughes
Fay Kelton
Tony Bonner
Fred Betts
Tristan Rogers
David Cameron
Kevin Colebrook
Warwick Sims

Bill Tinns
Graham Kennedy
Keith Burkett
Ted Thurgood
Jimmy Summers
Smollett
Lygon
Monton
Mrs. Granger
Brenda
Ben Worth
Vera Maguire
Egon Kisch
Jock McNeil
Watty
Paddy Kelleher
Vincent Parelli
Michael Kiely
Dr. Bevan
Tony Grey

Gus Mercurio
Clive Parker
Charles Tingwell
Ken Wayne
Peter Aanensen
Garay Files
John Nash
Arthur Barradell-Smith
Margaret Reid
Camilla Rowntree
Ben Garner
Patsy King
Kurt Ludescher
Michael Duffield
Fred Culcullen
Jonathan Hardy
Alan Bickford
Bobby Bright
Michael Duffield
Peter Cox

Producer
Oscar Whitbread

Programming History
26 one-hour episodes
Australian Broadcasting Corporation
June 21, 1976–December 13, 1976

Further Reading

Cunningham, Stuart, Toby Miller, and David Rowe, *Contemporary Australian Television,* Sydney: University of New South Wales Press, 1994
Hardy, Frank J., *The Hard Way,* Port Melbourne: Mandarin Australia, 1961
Moran, Albert, *Images and Industry: Television Drama Production in Australia,* Sydney: Currency Press, 1985
O'Regan, Tom, *Australian Television Culture,* St. Leonard's New South Wales: Allen and Unwin, 1993
Tulloch, John, and Graeme Turner, editors, *Australian Television: Programs, Pleasures, Politics.* Sydney and Boston: Allen and Unwin, 1989

Practice, The. *See* **Workplace Programs**

Premium Cable. *See* **Pay Cable**

President. *See* **United States Presidency and Television (Historical Overview)**

Presidential Nominating Conventions

In the United States the Democratic and Republican political parties, as well as numerous smaller parties, hold conventions every four years to nominate candidates for president and vice president and to adopt party platforms. For the two major parties, these conventions are four-day events held during the summer of each presidential election year. The first national political conventions emerged in the 1830s as a reform to the caucus system, which had been heavily controlled by party machines and party bosses. Although the key functions of the nominating conventions have not changed in the past 160 years, advances in communication technologies during the 20th century have had great influence on the nature of the meetings. The most dramatic of these alterations have come from television coverage.

The first experiments in televising the nominating conventions began in Philadelphia, Pennsylvania, in 1948; by 1952 both the Democratic and Republican conventions were broadcast nationwide on television. The impact of the medium, eventually networked into a truly national phenomenon, was immediate. After watching the first televised Republican convention in 1952, Democratic party officials made last-minute changes to their own convention in attempts to maintain the attention of viewers at home.

By 1956 both parties further amended their convention programs to fit better the demands of television coverage. Party officials condensed the length of the convention, created uniform campaign themes for each party, adorned convention halls with banners and patri-

otic decorations, placed television crews in positions with flattering views of the proceedings, dropped daytime sessions, limited welcoming speeches and parliamentary organization procedures, scheduled sessions to reach a maximum audience in prime time, and eliminated seconding speeches for vice presidential candidates. Additionally, the presence of television cameras encouraged parties to conceal intraparty battling and choose host cities amenable to their party.

Until the early 1950s conventions actually selected as well as nominated the party's candidates. Today the presidential nominees of the major parties are generally determined before the convention takes place. The prevalence of state political primaries, the increased power of television as a source of political news, the trend of early presidential campaigning, and the prominence of political polling almost ensure that each party's candidates are selected prior to the nominating convention. Indeed, since 1952 only two presidential nominees have not competed in the primary season (Aldai Stevenson in 1952 and Hubert Humphrey in 1968). And, in all but the Democratic convention of 1952, the Democratic and Republican nominees were chosen on the first ballot. Therefore, the conventions broadcast on television are no longer geared toward selecting nominees but staged to celebrate candidates and attract television coverage.

Television coverage of the convention has assigned new roles to political parties, candidates, and television news divisions in the presidential selection process. Today political parties must share the convention

Chicago Mayor Richard J. Daley at the 1968 Democratic Convention.
Photo courtesy of Chicago Historical Society

stage with aspiring candidates and prominent journalists. Nominating conventions are no longer controlled by party bosses making decisions in smoke-filled rooms. Contemporary conventions are planned by professional convention managers and consultants who see the nominating convention as an unequaled opportunity for the party to obtain free, rehearsed exposure on television newscasts. Thus, parties use nominating conventions to project a desirable party image and inspire party loyalty.

For presidential candidates, the televised convention has brought freedom from the party establishment. Today it is not uncommon for presidential candidates to rise to prominence without party help. State political primaries and television news and advertising allow a greater number of candidates to seriously contest for their party's nomination. Jimmy Carter's nomination in 1976 provides an example of an outsider with little national political experience benefiting from television and the primary season. The candidacies of Democrat Jesse Jackson and Republican Pat Robertson also profited from political primaries and the televised convention. Television coverage does, of course, ensure that today's conventions are well attended by prominent politicians. Many high-profile political leaders use the televised convention to launch their own future presidential bids, promote their current legislative efforts, or support other causes, groups, or programs.

To the television news divisions, the national conventions are the biggest extended political media events of the election year. The networks (ABC, CBS, FOX, and NBC), as well as the cable channels CNN and C-SPAN, allocate prime-time coverage and assign their top personnel to the conventions. Foote and Rimmer refer to convention coverage as the "'Olympics of television journalism' where the networks have a rare opportunity to go head-to-head on the same story."

Waltzer contends presidential election years are unmatched showcases for the rival networks to exhibit their competing talents. Internetwork rivalry manifests itself in several ways: (1) the networks engage in extensive advertising to capture the eye of the viewer; (2) the conventions are used to introduce new items of television equipment; (3) the networks compete in marshaling political consultants and analysts to augment their coverage staffs; (4) the networks compete for superiority in content, completeness, and depth of coverage—it is a race for "exclusives," "scoops," and "firsts," and for the unusual "features" of a convention; (5) the networks compete to make news with their coverage as well as to report the news of the conventions; (6) the networks seek to overcome the enormity and confusion of the convention and their coverage by personalizing coverage with anchor correspondents; and (7) the networks compete for audiences and audience ratings.

These factors indicate why television has made a commitment to broadcasting the convention over the years, and why the networks strive continually to create the "right" formats to attract audiences. From 1956 through 1976, for example, the networks covered conventions in their entirety. Although ABC cut back its broadcast in 1968, the other networks continued gavel-to-gavel coverage through 1976. Since 1980 all news outlets have cut back on their coverage. Future airtime is expected to depend on the "newsworthiness" of the convention, largely determined by the perceived competitiveness between the two party tickets as well as potential conflict or infighting within one party's nominating process.

Parties much prefer to control the visual images broadcast to voters themselves, as the Republicans did in 1984. In that year, the Republicans aired Ronald Reagan's campaign film, *A New Beginning,* a film that celebrated the Reagan presidency, transformed the art of political filmmaking, and, according to Joanne Morreale, established the televisual campaign film as a centerpiece of the presidential campaign.

At times, however, no one is able to control the conventions; political officials and network executives and technicians alike are caught up in events beyond their control. This was certainly the case in the 1968 Democratic convention, perhaps the most famous of all televised events of this sort. On that occasion, antiwar protesters demonstrated outside the Chicago Convention Center, drawing down the wrath of the Chicago police. Inside, the conflict was reflected in charges and countercharges, name-calling, and recrimination. Much of this activity was caught on camera, but the sense was that even the TV cameras were reacting rather than controlling. Few conventions since that time have been so dramatically bound to television, and most are tightly controlled events exhibiting small moments of spontaneity.

Viewership for nominating conventions has decreased over the years. According to the Harvard University's Shorenstein Center on the Press, Politics, and Public Policy, television networks aired 60 hours of each party convention in 1952, and 80 percent of the households in the United States watched about 10 to 13 hours of this coverage. Forty-four years later, network coverage of the 1996 conventions averaged eight hours, and just 10 percent of households reported tuning into the coverage. In 2000 roughly 20 percent of Americans tuned in to two hours or more of the conventions, according to the Annenberg Public Policy Center, Annenberg School for Communication, University of Pennsylvania.

At the close of the 20th century, strategies for increasing the audience for conventions took at least three forms. Parties attempted to plan the conventions with "star power," scheduling political personalities at key moments to attract viewers. In 2000 cable channels (such as CNN, Fox News, CNBC) offered extensive in-depth coverage to attract viewers desiring extended or non-prime-time reporting, while Internet sites experimented with interactive activities to accompany or replace television viewing of the conventions, including alternative camera angles, gavel-to-gavel streaming video, web-exclusive commentary, 24-hour chat rooms and related message boards, up-to-the-minute polls and interactive quizzes, and opportunities to chat with delegates. While the hype surrounding such efforts was notable, actual traffic on these Internet sites was modest.

Advocates of the current system contend televised conventions inspire party loyalty and enthusiasm and allow the selection of a candidate who represents the political middle rather than the extremes. Critics allege today's nominating conventions are undemocratic spectacles and propose replacing them with a national presidential primary system. Despite these critiques and aforementioned efforts to increase viewership, substantial convention reform is unlikely. Today's streamlined conventions continue to attract an audience for television networks and cable channels, political parties, and presi-

dential candidates alike. Although television coverage has brought cosmetic changes to the convention, it has not interfered with its basic functions. As in earlier days, contemporary conventions honor presidential nominees, create party enthusiasm, and present party platforms.

SHARON JARVIS

See also **Political Processes and Television; U.S. Presidency and Television**

Further Reading

Adams, W.C., "Convention Coverage," *Public Opinion* (1985)
Davis, James W., *U.S. Presidential Primaries and the Caucus-Convention System: A Sourcebook,* Westport, Connecticut: Greenwood Press, 1997
Fant, C.H., "Televising Presidential Conventions, 1952–1980," *Journal of Communication* (1980)
Farrell, T.B., "Political Conventions As Legitimation Ritual," *Communication Monographs* (1978)
Foot, J., and R. Rimmer, "The Ritual of Convention Coverage in 1980," in *Television Coverage of the 1980 Presidential Campaign,* edited by William C. Adams, Norwood, New Jersey: Ablex, 1983
Henry, D., "The Rhetorical Dynamic of Mario Cuomo's 1984 Keynote Address: Situation, Speaker, Metaphor," *Southern Speech Communication Journal* (1988)
Morreale, Joanne, *A New Beginning: A Textual Frame Analysis of the Political Campaign Film,* Albany, New York: State University of New York Press, 1991
Morreale, Joanne, *The Presidential Campaign Film: A Critical History,* Westport, Connecticut: Praeger, 1993
National Party Conventions, 1831–1996, Washington, D.C.: Congressional Quarterly, 1997
Paletz, David L., and M. Elson, "Television Coverage of Presidential Conventions: Now You See It, Now You Don't," *Political Science Quarterly* (1976)
Reinsch, James Leonard, "Broadcasting the Conventions," *Journal of Broadcasting* (1968)
Sautter, R. Craig, and Edward M. Burke, *Inside the Wigwam: Chicago Presidential Conventions, 1860–1996,* Chicago: Loyola Press, 1996
Shafer, Byron E., *Bifurcated Politics: Evolution and Reform in the National Party Convention,* Cambridge, Massachusetts: Harvard University Press, 1988
Smith, Larry David, "Narrative Styles in Network Coverage of the 1984 Nominating Conventions," *Western Journal of Speech Communication* (1988)
Smith, Larry David, and Dan Nimmo, *Cordial Concurrence: Orchestrating National Party Conventions in the Telepolitical Age,* New York: Praeger, 1991
Waltzer, H., "In the Magic Lantern: Television Coverage of the 1964 National Conventions," *Public Opinion Quarterly* (1966)
Womack, D., "Live ABC, CBS, and NBC Interviews during Three Democratic Conventions," *Journalism Quarterly* (1985)
Womack, D., "Status of News Sources Interviewed During Presidential Conventions," *Journalism Quarterly* (1986)
Womack, D., "Live TV Interviews at the 1984 GOP Convention," *Journalism Quarterly* (1988)
Womack, D., "Live Television Interviews at the 1988 Democratic Convention," *Journalism Quarterly* (1989)

Press Conference

President Dwight D. Eisenhower held the first televised presidential press conference in January 1955. Although Eisenhower regularly used television as a means to address the American electorate, President John F. Kennedy was the first to utilize television as a direct means of communication with voters via the live press conference. As Richard Davis explains, "John Kennedy enjoyed press conferences because of his skill in bantering with reporters; his press conferences reinforced the image of a president in command of the issues." Kennedy's successors have been measured against his performance and have scheduled press conferences less frequently. They also have employed variations to the live press conference format. The administrations of Jimmy Carter, Ronald Reagan, and George H.W. Bush held mini press conferences. President George Bush Sr., relied on impromptu, daytime televised press conferences rather than formal, prime-time gatherings. President Clinton used a variation of the press conference: his televised "town meetings." With these conferences, Clinton managed to sidestep the White House press corps and address questions asked by average citizens. One such meeting featured children and was moderated by PBS's Fred Rogers of *Mister Rogers' Neighborhood.*

President George W. Bush's administration has held press conferences more frequently than his recent predecessors did. This administration also is known for joint press conferences with national political leaders and with foreign heads of state and government. In a press conference of February 22, 2001, Bush informed journalists, "One of my missions has been to change the tone here in the nation's capital to encourage civil discourse." Indeed, press conferences provide a forum for dialogue between the president and the public.

As a general category of media strategy, press conferences involve the communication of news about an individual or organization to the mass media and specialized media outlets. The objective is favorable news coverage of the sponsor's actions and events. Since the mid-20th century, most press conferences have centered on the orchestrated use of television, although various print and broadcast media outlets usually are invited to attend. According to Jerry Hendrix, press conferences are classified as uncontrolled media. Thus, with press conferences, media decision makers become the target audience members. These gatekeepers then determine what information to communicate to the public.

Professionals generally agree that, as a public relations tool, press conferences should be used sparingly, reserved for circumstances that truly are newsworthy. Such occasions often call for a personal presentation by the organization's chief executive officer, a celebrity, a dignitary, or similarly positioned person. In the general realm of business affairs, some organizations have used press conferences to announce the introduction of major corporate changes such as new product lines, takeovers, or mergers. Press conferences also have been used to organize and manage information in crisis situations or to respond to accusations of wrongdoing.

Although in the business sector press conferences are not viewed as a routine means of public relations, major government agencies employ them on a more regular basis. Indeed, press conferences are a principal component of political communications. Politicians rely on them as a way of providing important information to the public and shaping public opinion. For correspondents, they serve as a means of obtaining such information and examining the opinion-shaping process.

In the United States the press and politicians have traditionally enjoyed an adversarial relationship. Even as political press conferences are used to provide information to the public, the goal for the politician is persuasion or news management. Thus, the political figure wants to control the release of information. Conversely, the press relies on such conferences as a means for ensuring that the politician is held accountable for his or her policies and actions. Media outlets also rely on press conferences as a way of obtaining new information so it can be released as quickly as possible.

Even prior to television, press conferences were essential in the United States to communications between the executive branch of government and the public. According to Carolyn Smith, Theodore Roosevelt was one of the first U.S. presidents to use the press as a frequent means of communicating with the public. Although he did not hold formal press conferences in their contemporary sense, he realized that the media could be used to shape public opinion and established close relationships with journalists. Woodrow

Wilson was the first president to hold regular and formal press conferences. Not only did he view the press as a means of influencing public opinion, but he also believed that communication via the press was a chief duty of democratic leaders.

Although presidents are not bound by law to hold them, presidential press conferences have become somewhat institutionalized. As Smith contends, a sense of "public contract has evolved to such a degree that the general occasion of the press conference cannot be avoided with political impunity." Since the Wilson administration, all presidents have held formal press conferences. However, the decision to grant a press conference is always made by the White House, not by the media, and press conferences have varied in frequency and format with each administration.

Not surprisingly, presidents are most likely to hold press conferences when the conferences serve their best advantage. Ultimately, the president can control the time, place, and setting for a press conference. To some extent, they also control the participants. In the contemporary era, journalists at presidential press conferences have traditionally included representatives of ABC, CBS, and NBC, the wire services, national newsmagazines; and national newspapers such as the *New York Times* and the *Washington Post.* They also

usually include a selection of reporters from other news organizations, such as regional newspapers or news syndicates, who may be more likely to pose questions the president will find favorable.

In general, press conferences often are criticized for their theatrical nature. However, for individuals, organizations, and government branches, press conferences serve an important public relations function. They are an effective means of organizing and disseminating newsworthy information to the public.

LORI MELTON MCKINNON

See also **Political Processes and Television; Pool Coverage; U.S. Presidency and Television**

Further Reading

Davis, Richard, *The Press and American Politics: The New Mediator,* Upper Saddle River, New Jersey: Longman, 1992; 3rd edition, 2001
Hanson, C., "Mr. Clinton's Neighborhood," *Columbia Journalism Review* (1993)
Hendrix, Jerry A., *Public Relations Cases,* Belmont, California: Wadsworth, 1988; 5th edition, 2001
Kernell, Samuel, *Going Public: New Strategies of Presidential Leadership,* Washington, D.C.: Congressional Quarterly Press, 1986; 3rd edition, 1997
Smith, Carolyn, *Presidential Press Conferences: A Critical Approach,* New York: Praeger, 1990

Prime Suspect

British Crime Series

In 1991 *Prime Suspect* was broadcast on British television to great critical and public acclaim. The production received numerous awards for its writer Lynda La Plante and star Helen Mirren, including a rather controversial BAFTA Award for Best Drama Serial. *Prime Suspect*'s importance to the development of the police drama series as a genre in Britain is great. By installing a woman as the head of a murder squad, *Prime Suspect* broke new ground in terms of both gender and the authenticity in the portrayal of the internal dynamics of the police as an organization.

Almost six years earlier, La Plante brought to the television audience the formidable Dolly Rawlins as the single-minded leader of a group of disparate but gutsy women criminals in her successful television crime drama *Widows*. With *Prime Suspect* and the cre-

ation of DCI Jane Tennison, La Plante continued to elaborate on her predilection for problematic heroines, but this time her central character is not a criminal but a woman both shaped and defined by her role as an officer of the law.

By being positioned as the head of a murder squad hunting for a sadistic serial killer, Tennison transcends many of the traditions of the British police series. It is interesting to note that La Plante did not put Tennison forward primarily as a woman police officer who does her job the feminine way. In terms of the British police series, Tennison's female predecessors such as Kate Longton (*Juliet Bravo*) and Maggie Forbes (*The Gentle Touch*) had been deliberately represented as bringing the nurturing and compassionate aspects associated with femininity to the role of senior police

Prime Suspect.
Photo courtesy of Frank Goodman Associates

officer. In fact, it would be true to say that central to programs such as *Juliet Bravo, The Gentle Touch,* and, indeed, the American police series *Cagney and Lacey* was the exploration of the contradictions inherent between the institutionalized masculinity of the police and the presence of femininity. The dramatic resolution, however, was usually to endorse the compassionate compromise made by the female characters between being a good police officer and being a "real" woman. The fascination of Tennison as a character was the powerful and compelling focus on the internal and external confrontations and contradictions faced by a leading female character who was in most circumstances a police officer first and a woman second.

It is, in fact, the Tennison character, and Mirren's performance, that unify and act as the reference for the programs in the series. And although La Plante has only written *Prime Suspect I* and *II,* her creation of Tennison, her exacting original script, and Mirren's own compelling performance have generated a successful and repeatable legacy and framework.

Symptomatically, the subtext for each individual drama in the series has some kind of social issue as its basis and could be read, in order, as sexism, racism, homosexuality, young male prostitution, the results of physical abuse in childhood, class, and institutional conformity in the police. Equally symptomatically, it could be noticed that each drama contains a character who has a particular investment in the chosen subtext: for example, one of the officers is black; in the next drama, one is gay; in the next, one has suffered childhood abuse; and so on. In a rather obvious, sometimes crude manner, this device has been used to situate and contextualize the tensions of the internal police dynamics within those of the larger society. It is our fascination with Tennison that spawns a more integrated and sophisticated involvement with the drama. Because of Tennison's place in the text, the issue of gender in the police force is never far away, as evidenced by the fact that masculinity and male relationships are also always under inspection.

Above all, no matter the focus of a case on a particular social problem, it is the institutionalized performance of masculinity and femininity within the police force that dictates the often considerable dramatic tension. In Tennison's pursuit of serial killer George Marlowe in *Prime Suspect I,* for example, not only must she prove she is an exceptional detective and win the support of her male colleagues, but the narrative is shot through with her compulsive need to succeed in her job at any cost. Her obsession with her police career even becomes tinged with perversity when the interrogation sessions between Tennison and Marlowe are used to generate a fake, yet compelling, sexual tension. The fact that she will get out of bed at night to interview a serial killer but will not make time to see to the needs of the man in her life heightens the idea of perversity and obsession.

In a culture still guided by the binary divisions of active masculinity and passive femininity, the fact that Tennison is a woman means that her sexuality and sexual practices are subject to much more dramatic scrutiny than if she were a man. Tennison does not, however, stray much from the sexual conduct expected from the male officer in the television police genre. As Geoffrey Hurd explains, "the main characters...are either divorced, separated, widowed, or unmarried, a trail of broken and unmade relationships presented as a direct result of the pressures and demands of police work."

The focus on sexuality, however, is dramatically changed by Tennison's pregnancy in *Prime Suspect III* and her consequent abortion in *Prime Suspect IV.* This moment marks the watershed in her personal and career conflict, and it is interesting that the following programs (not written by La Plante) then seem to devote themselves to saving Tennison's soul. No moral judgment is made about the abortion; in fact, it is not even discussed. The imperative is clearly to establish Tennison's reputation and stature within the police (she is promoted to the rank of superintendent) and to reestablish her and contain what femininity remains within a heterosexual relationship with a professional equal, the psychologist played by Stuart Wilson.

In *Prime Suspect V,* an interesting intertextual exercise is carried out when the Marlowe case is reopened, with the investigation now centered on Tennison's own police practices. Apart from one long-standing loyal male colleague, the male ranks are again seen to close in the face of this unsympathetic woman who remains insistent on her infallibility and methodical detection. Her ultimate triumph in the case casts her in a new but recognizable mold, that of maverick cop, where gender is even less of an issue. *Prime Suspect VI: The Last Witness* aired in November 2003.

ROS JENNINGS

See also **British Programming; La Plante, Lynda; Mirren, Helen; Police Programs**

Prime Suspect

Cast

Jane Tennison	Helen Mirren
DS Bill Otley	Tom Bell
DCS Michael Kiernan	John Benfield
DCI John Shefford	John Forgeham
Terry Amson	Gary Whelan
DI Frank Burkin	Craig Fairbrass
DI Tony Muddyman	Jack Ellis
WPC Maureen Havers	Mossie Smith
DC Jones	Ian Fitzgibbon
DC Rosper	Andrew Tiernan
DC Lillie	Phillip Wright
DC Haskons	Richard Hawley
DC Oakhill	Mark Spalding
DS Eastel	Dave Bond
Commander Trayner	Terry Taplin
DC Avison	Tom Bowles
DC Caplan	Seamus O'Neill
DI Caldicott	Marcus Romer
George Marlow	John Bowe
Moyra Henson	Zoe Wanamaker
Mrs. Marlow	Maxine Audley
Felix Norman	Bryan Pringle
Willy Chang	Gareth Tudor Price
Tilly	Andrew Abrahams
Joyce	Fionnuala Ellwood
Lab Assistant	Maria Meski
Lab Assistant	Martin Reeve
Lab Assistant	John Ireland
Peter	Tom Wilkinson

Prime Suspect

Marianne	Francesca Ryan
Joe	Jeremy Warder
Major Howard	Michael Fleming
Mrs. Howard	Daphne Neville
Karen	Julie Sumnall
Michael	Ralph Fiennes
Mr. Tennison	Wilfred Harrison
Mrs. Tennison	Noel Dyson
Pam	Jessica Turner
Tony	Owen Aaronovitch
Sergeant Tomlins	Rod Arthur
Carol	Rosy Clayton
Linda	Susan Brown
Painter	Phil Hearne
Helen Masters	Angela Bruce
Mrs. Salbanna	Anna Savva
Arnold Upcher	James Snell
Mr. Shrapnel	Julian Firth

Producer
Don Leaver

Programming History
2 2-hour episodes
Granada TV
April 7–8, 1991

Prime Suspect II

Cast
DCI Jane Tennison	Helen Mirren
Sgt. Robert Oswald	Colin Salmon
D. Supt. Michael Kernan	John Benfield
DI Tony Muddyman	Jack Ellis (III)
DI Frank Burkin	Craig Fairbrass
DS Richard Haskons	Richard Hawley
DC Lillie	Philip Wright
DC Jones	Ian Fitzgibbon
DC Rosper	Andrew Tiernan
Commander Traynor	Stafford Gordon
Sgt. Calder	Lloyd Maguire
DCI Thorndike	Stephen Boxer
Asian PC	Nirjay Mahindru
Esme Allen	Claire Benedict
Vernon Allen	George Harris (II)
Tony Allen	Fraser James
Cleo Allen	Ashley James
David Allen	Junior Laniyan
Sarah Allen	Jenny Jules
Esta	Josephine Melville
David Harvey	Tom Watson (I)
Eileen Reynolds	June Watson

Jason Reynolds	Matt Bardock
Nola Cameron	Corinne Skinner-Carter
Oscar Bream	David Ryall

Producer
Paul Marcus

Programming History
Granada TV
1992

Prime Suspect III

Cast
DCI Jane Tennison	Helen Mirren
Vera Reynolds	Peter Capaldi
Edward Parker-Jones	Ciarán Hinds
James Jackson	David Thewlis
Sergeant Bill Otley	Tom Bell
Chief Superintendent Kernan	John Benfield
Jessica Smythie	Kelly Hunter
Margaret Speel	Alyson Spiro
DC Lillie	Philip Wright
DI Brian Dalton	Andrew Woodall
WPC Norma Hastings	Karen Tomlin
Supt. Halliday	Struan Rodger
Red	Pearce Quigley
Anthony Field	Jonny Lee Miller
DS Richard Haskons	Richard Hawley
John Kennington	Terence Harvey
Commander Chiswick	Terrence Hardiman
Jason Baldwin	James Frain
DI Ray Hebdon	Mark Drewry
Mrs. Kennington	Rowena Cooper
Disco Driscoll	Jeremy Colton
Billy Matthews	Andrew Dicks

Producer
Paul Marcus

Programming History
Granada TV
1993

Prime Suspect IV: "The Lost Child," "Inner Circles," and "The Scent of Darkness"

Cast
Supt. Jane Tennison	Helen Mirren
Chris Hughes	Robert Glenister ("The Lost Child")

Susan Covington	Beatie Edney ("The Lost Child")	Derek Palmer	Alan Perrin ("Inner Circles")
Anne Sutherland	Lesley Sharp ("The Lost Child")	Len Sheldon	Pip Donachy ("The Scent of Darkness")
DI Richard Haskons	Richard Hawley ("The Lost Child")	Chief Inspector Finlay	Hugh Simon ("The Scent of Darkness")
DI Tony Muddyman	Jack Ellis ("The Lost Child")	Supt. Howell	Alan Leith ("The Scent of Darkness")
Doctor Gordon	Graham Seed ("The Lost Child")	Dr. Elizabeth Bramwell	Penelope Beaumont ("The Scent of Darkness")
Chief Supt. Kernan	John Benfield ("The Lost Child")	Anthony Bramwell	Christopher Ashley ("The Scent of Darkness")
WPC Maureen Havers	Mossie Smith ("The Lost Child")	Wayne	Glen Barry ("The Scent of Darkness")
Dr. Patrick Schofield	Stuart Wilson ("The Lost Child")	Policewoman 1	Rebecca Thorn ("The Scent of Darkness")
Oscar Bream	David Ryall ("The Lost Child")	Geoff	Scott Neal ("The Scent of Darkness")
Geoff	Tom Russell ("Inner Circles")	DC Catherine Cooper	Caroline Strong ("The Scent of Darkness")
Paul Endicott	James Laurenson ("Inner Circles")		
Lynne Endicott	Helene Kvale ("Inner Circles")		
Maria Henry	Jill Baker ("Inner Circles")		
Polly Henry	Kelly Reilly ("Inner Circles")		
Denis Carradine	Gareth Forwood ("Inner Circles")		
James Greenlees	Anthony Bate ("Inner Circles")		
Micky Thomas	Jonathan Copestake ("Inner Circles")		
Olive Carradine	Phillada Sewell ("Inner Circles")		
Sheila Bower	Julie Rice ("Inner Circles")		
DCI Raymond	Ralph Arliss ("Inner Circles")		
DS Cromwell	Sophie Stanton ("Inner Circles")		
DC Bakari	Cristopher John Hale ("Inner Circles")		
DI Haskons	Richard Hawley ("Inner Circles")		
Club Manager	Albert Welling ("Inner Circles")		
Hamish Endicott	Nick Patrick ("Inner Circles")		
Superintendent Mallory	Ian Flintoff ("Inner Circles")		
Chief Supt. Kernan	John Benfield ("Inner Circles")		

Executive Producer
Sally Head

Producers
Paul Marcus (*The Lost Child* and *Inner Circles*); Brian Park (*The Scent of Darkness*)

Programming History
Granada TV
1995

Prime Suspect V: Errors of Judgment

Cast

Supt. Jane Tennison	Helen Mirren
DCS Martin Ballinger	John McArdle
DI Claire Devanny	Julia Lane
DS Jerry Rankine	David O'Hara
DC Henry Adeliyeka	John Brobbey
The Street	Steven Mackintosh
Michael Johns	Ray Emmet Brown
Toots	Paul Oldham
Radio	Joe Speare
Campbell Lafferty	Joseph Jacobs
Janice Lafferty	Marsha Thomason
Noreen Lafferty	Gabrielle Reidy
DC Skinner	Anne Hornby
Desk Sergeant	Steve Money
Nazir	Chris Bisson
DC Growse	Antony Audenshaw
DS Pardy	Martin Ronan
Willem	Kevin Knapman

Paramedic	Paul Warriner
Outboard	Paul Simpson
Deborah	Sarah Jones

Producers
Rebecca Eaton, Lynn Horsford

Programming History
1996
Granada TV

Further Reading

Ansen, David, "The Prime of Helen Mirren," *Newsweek* (May 16, 1994)
Carter, Bill, "A British Miniseries with Many Lives," *New York Times* (May 2, 1994)
Dugdale, John, "Intruder in a Man's World," *New Statesman and Society* (December 11, 1992)
Jennings, Ros, "The Prime of DCI Tennison: Investigating Notions of Feminism, Sexuality, Gender and Genre in Relation to Lynda La Plante's *Prime Suspect*," *Iris* (Autumn 1998)
Rennert, Amy, editor, *Helen Mirren: Prime Suspect: A Celebration,* San Francisco, California: KQED Books, 1995

Prime Time

Prime time is that portion of the evening when the U.S. audience levels for television viewing are at their highest. In the Eastern and Pacific time zones, prime time is 7:00 to 11:00 P.M.; in the Central and Mountain time zones, prime time is 6:00 to 10:00 P.M. The 9:00 P.M. hour (Eastern and Pacific) and the 8:00 P.M. hour (Central and Mountain) have the highest homes-using-television (HUT) level.

The commercial broadcast networks have always attracted the largest portion of the prime-time viewing audience. Through the 1960s, it was not unusual for the three networks (ABC, CBC, and NBC) to attract 85 to 90 percent of the available prime-time audience. The remaining 10 to 15 percent of the audience would be watching programming available on independent television stations or on public television stations.

Broadcast networks pay their affiliated stations in each local market to air the network offerings (this is called "network compensation"). In return, the networks retain the bulk of the commercial time for sale to national advertisers. This arrangement works well for both parties, as the networks attract audiences in each local market for their programming, which enables them to sell commercial time during such programs to advertisers wanting to reach a national audience. The local affiliated television stations receive high-quality programming, payment from the network, and the opportunity to sell the remaining commercial time (usually about one minute each hour) to local advertisers. However, with the increased costs involved in producing and securing prime-time programming and with smaller audience shares due to in-

creased competition from cable, the networks have been reducing compensation payments to affiliates. In fact, some network programming is distributed sans compensation.

In the mid-1990s, the average 30-second prime-time network television advertising spot cost about $100,000. By the 2001–02 broadcast season, the average 30-second, prime-time network television advertising spot cost about $125,000. These same spots on a top-rated series average about $325,000, and such spots on low-rated network prime-time programs average about $50,000. Top-rated prime-time spots in local television markets cost as much as $20,000.

Because of network dominance in prime time, independent television stations (those not affiliated with a major broadcast network) have found it difficult to compete directly with network-affiliated television stations during these most desirable hours. In an attempt to allow independents to compete somewhat more fairly, during at least a portion of prime time, the Federal Communications Commission (FCC) enacted the Prime Time Access Rule (PTAR). The rule limits the amount of time a local affiliate can broadcast programming provided by the network. The most recent version of PTAR became effective in September 1975. It basically limited network-affiliated television stations in the 50 largest markets to no more than three hours of network (or off-network syndicated) programming during the four hours of prime time. The three-hour limit could be exceeded if the additional programming was public-affairs programming, children's programming, or documentary programming, or if the additional programming was a network newscast that was adjacent to a full hour of local newscasts. Other exceptions to the three-hour limit included runover of live sporting events, and feature films on Saturday evenings. The FCC ended the PTAR in 1996; however, network offerings continue to be limited, now by convention, to three hours.

The growth of cable television in the 1980s resulted in a plethora of viewing options for the audience. Where audiences once had a choice of up to five, perhaps six options at any point in time, the new multichannel environment provided viewers with more than 50 programming choices at once. Meanwhile, the development of the FOX network in the late 1980s, and on a slightly smaller scale, the Warner Brothers (WB) Network and the United Paramount Network (UPN) in the early 1990s, raised the prime-time status and visibility of independent stations. In addition, the advent of the videocassette recorder (VCR) also enabled viewers to rent prerecorded tapes, or to time-shift (watch programs that were recorded at an earlier time). The result of all this increased competition is that the networks' share of the audience declined throughout the 1980s and 1990s. This was most evident in the prime-time hours. By the 2001–02 season, the networks' share of the audience had dropped from previous heights of 80 to 90 percent to 50 to 60 percent. And as cable and VCR penetration levels (70 percent and 84 percent, respectively, in 2001) continue to grow, the fate of network television in prime time may decline still further.

Although prime-time programming has changed much during the history of television, three main trends continue: (1) the continued growth of the situation comedy; (2) the continued decline and perhaps death of the variety show; and (3) the consistent appeal of drama.

As new technologies, increased competition, and decreased regulation of television systems have developed throughout the world in recent decades, the notion of prime time has become more and more prevalent in systems outside the United States. Where television programming in other countries was once a special activity, often a limited number of hours roughly equivalent to American prime time, the move toward 24-hour programming has added new significance to the evening hours. Prime time is now a common marker in the days of citizens around the globe and this televisual "clock" has become part of everyday experience in almost every society.

MITCHELL E. SHAPIRO

Further Reading

Bedel, Sally, *Up the Tube: Prime-time TV and the Silverman Years,* New York: Viking, 1981

Blum, Richard A., and Richard D. Lindheim, *Primetime: Network Television Programming,* Boston, Focal, 1987

Brooks, Tim, and Earle Marsh, *The Complete Directory to Primetime Network TV Shows, 1946–Present,* New York: Ballantine, 1992

Cantor, Muriel G., *Prime-time Television: Content and Control,* Beverly Hills, California: Sage, 1980

Castleman, Harry, and Walter Podrazik, *Watching TV: Four Decades of American Television,* New York: McGraw-Hill, 1982

Eastman, Susan Tyler, and Robert Klein, *Strategies in Broadcast and Cable Promotion: Commercial Television, Radio, Cable, Pay-Television, Public Television,* Belmont, California: Wadsworth, 1981; 5th edition, by Eastman and Douglas A. Ferguson, as *Broadcast/Cable Programming: Strategies and Practices,* 1997

Gitlin, Todd, *Inside Prime Time,* New York: Pantheon, 1985; revised edition, 1994

Goldstein, Fred P., and Stan Goldstein, *Prime-time Television: A Pictorial History from Milton Berle to "Falcon Crest,"* New York: Crown, 1983

Head, Sydney W., *Broadcasting in America: A Survey of Television and Radio,* Boston: Houghton Mifflin, 1956; 9th edition, with Thomas Spann and Michael A. McGregor, as *Broadcasting in America: A Survey of Electronic Media,* 2001

Lichter, S. Robert, *Prime Time: How TV Portrays American Culture,* Washington, D.C.: Regnery, 1994

Marc, David, and Robert J. Thompson, *Prime Time, Prime Movers: From I Love Lucy to L.A. Law—America's Greatest TV Shows and the People Who Created Them,* Boston: Little Brown, 1992

McCrohan, Donna, *Prime Time, Our Time: America's Life and Times through the Prism of Television,* Rockin, California: Prima Publication and Communication, 1990

Montgomery, Kathryn, *Target: Prime Time: Advocacy Groups and the Struggle over Entertainment Television,* New York: Oxford University Press, 1989

Sackett, Susan, *Prime-time Hits: Television's Most Popular Network Programs, 1950 to the Present,* New York: Billboard Books, 1993

Selnow, Gary W., "Values in Prime-time Television," *Journal of Communication* (Spring 1990).

Shapiro, Mitchell E., *Television Network Prime-Time Programming, 1948–1988,* Jefferson, North Carolina: McFarland, 1989

Prime Time Access Rule

The Prime Time Access Rule (PTAR) was established by the U.S. Federal Communications Commission (FCC) to limit network domination of prime-time programming throughout the United States. Prime time is normally from 7:00 P.M. to 11:00 P.M. in the Eastern and Pacific time zones, and from 6:00 P.M. to 10:00 P.M. in the Central and Mountain time zones.

The "Big Three" networks, ABC, CBS, and NBC, dominated prime-time programming of their own network-affiliated stations nationally in the 1960s. Reruns of old network shows also dominated the schedules of independent (non-network-affiliated) television stations. The FCC began an investigation of this virtual monopoly in 1965 and issued its initial PTAR in 1970. The rule was modified in 1973, rewritten in 1975, and finally rescinded in 1996. Paraphrasing the rule itself, the PTAR basically limited network-affiliated stations in the 50 largest television markets to airing only three hours of network entertainment programming during prime time. Exceptions were made for some program genres, such as news, public affairs, education, and children's shows.

This rule meant that the Big Three networks regularly provided 22 hours of prime-time shows weekly, 4 hours on Sunday and 3 hours on the other six evenings each week. Sunday included an extra hour because feature films, newsmagazines, and family shows qualified as exceptions to the PTAR. Other exceptions included fast-breaking news events and the running over of live broadcasts of sporting events. In markets where local television stations scheduled the half-hour network newscast immediately following the local newscast, this was also considered an exception. In actual practice, the networks now provided only three hours of programming to all their affiliate stations in every market, not just the top 50, and established what became known as the "Access Hour" nationally.

The PTAR also prohibited top-50 market network-affiliated stations from airing off-network rerun programs during the access hour, while encouraging local independent stations to do so as well. This aspect of the rule gave independent stations the exclusive right to broadcast reruns of successful network situation comedies such as *I Love Lucy* during the first hour of prime time, while forcing the network-affiliated stations to provide alternative programming.

The FCC wanted to encourage community-oriented local programming by network stations, as well as provide small, independent programming producers expanded marketing opportunities. Prior to the PTAR, almost all network programming was produced by major studios or the networks themselves.

With respect to the development of community-oriented local programming, the PTAR was a dismal failure, as most local television stations opted to purchase inexpensive syndicated entertainment programming, such as game shows, to fill the access hour rather than developing their own public-affairs programs. The PTAR was a resounding success in providing independent producers with more than 200 local television markets and over 600 local stations as potential customers for their original programming. The result was a plethora of game shows and other programs in inexpensive-to-produce genres. Along with the Financial Interest and Syndication Rule (Fin-Syn), the PTAR prevented the Big Three networks from monopolizing the television production industry and limited them to distribution and exhibition of prime-time entertainment programming for 16 years.

The creation of FOX, the fourth major network, as well as the variety of other channels introduced as the cable and satellite industries developed, provided television audiences in the United States with many more viewing options. This shift eroded the Big Three networks' share of the audience from over 90 percent in 1970 to less than 50 percent in the mid-1990s. It also gave independent program producers many more venues to which they could sell programming and basically eliminated a need for restrictions on network programming such as the PTAR. The FCC finally eliminated the rule in August 1996.

Since the PTAR's demise there has been virtually no change in the number of hours of prime-time programming that networks provide their affiliates. Now, affiliate stations' access hours are highly profitable time slots for selling local advertising spots at premium rates, and affiliate stations therefore have no desire to give up the access hour to the networks for programming. Even network newscasts typically no longer appear during the access hour.

ROBERT G. FINNEY

See also **Allocation; Federal Communications Commission; License; Syndication**

Further Reading

Carter, T. Barton, Marc A. Franklin, and Jay B. Wright, *The First Amendment and the Fifth Estate: Regulation of Electronic Mass Media,* Mineola, New York: Foundation Press, 1986; 5th edition, New York: Foundation Press, 1999

Creech, Kenneth C., *Electronic Media Law and Regulation,* Boston: Focal Press, 1993; 3rd edition, 2000

Eastman, Susan Tyler, Sydney W. Head, and Lewis Klein, *Broadcast Programming: Strategies for Winning Television and Radio Audiences,* Belmont, California: Wadsworth,

1981; 6th edition, by Eastman and Douglas A. Ferguson, as *Broadcast/Cable Programming: Strategies and Practices,* 2002

Ginsburg, Douglas H., *Regulation of the Electronic Mass Media: Law and Policy towards Radio, Television, and Cable Communications,* St. Paul, Minnesota: West Publications, 1979; 3rd edition, by Michael Botein, as *Regulation of the Electronic Mass Media: Law and Policy for Radio, Television, Cable, and the New Video Technologies,* St. Paul, Minnesota: West Group, 1998

Primetime Live

U.S. Newsmagazine Show

In 1989 the American Broadcasting Company (ABC) added a second newsmagazine, *Primetime Live,* to accompany *20/20* on its prime-time schedule. Straying from the lackluster tradition of network news, the look of *Primetime Live* was better characterized as glitzy and glamorous. ABC launched a huge promotional campaign and on August 3 the highly publicized *Primetime Live* debuted. The show featured numerous segments, from the secretary of state on American hostages in Lebanon to an interview with Roseanne Barr. It incorporated comments from a studio audience, as well as live location feeds that were frequently uninspiring. Booed by critics and parodied by *Saturday Night Live, Primetime Live*'s ratings continually declined. Industry journals were replete with accounts of difficulties plaguing the show, but none discussed cancellation.

A handful of factors contributed to the staying power of *Primetime Live.* Generally speaking, reality programming was recognized as a cost-effective alternative in comparison with the expense and risk of developing fictional series. But despite trailing its competition, *Primetime Live* was rated considerably higher than the traditional entertainment previously scheduled in its time slot. Furthermore, programming a newsmagazine improved the audience draw for network affiliates that followed the broadcasts with their local news.

More specifically, and perhaps most pivotal to the eventual success of the show, was ABC's stated commitment to stand by the show for at least two years. This allowed executive producer Richard Kaplan to modify the program and reshape the still-emerging

newsmagazine genre. First to disappear was the studio audience. Ironically, *Primetime Live* then phased out the "live" aspects of the program. Following its recognized coverage of the crash of Pan American Flight 103 and the fall of the Berlin Wall, the show's producers reduced the number of segments for each episode and focused instead on more in-depth journalism. *Primetime Live* evolved into an award-winning newsmagazine with its own distinct signature. Central to establishing this distinctiveness was the use of undercover investigations and hidden cameras that documented everything from racial discrimination to political scandal and corporate corruption.

Although their formats and often their content can be similar, *Primetime Live* was distinguished as a news rather than a tabloid magazine show because it was produced under the umbrella of the ABC News division. But as a prime-time show the entertainment value of the program was at least as important as its information value, inspiring the critical label "infotainment." Rather than reporting facts, newsmagazine journalists were expected to be on-air personalities or celebrities for audience members to identify with. They packaged segments of dramatic narrative, but also needed to communicate professional legitimacy. Therefore, coanchors Diane Sawyer and Sam Donaldson were vital to *Primetime Live.* Both were praised as talented and well-respected journalists when they joined the show. Donaldson, a White House correspondent, and Sawyer, lured to ABC following five years as a reporter for *60 Minutes,* lent an air of credibility to the fledgling newsmagazine.

For the 1998 season ABC merged *Primetime Live*

Primetime Live, Charles Gibson and Diane Sawyer.
Photo courtesy of ABC Photo Archives

with the more preferred *20/20,* which expanded to three (and eventually four) nights a week. The strategy was in keeping with the trend toward stripping one recognizable brand across the network's weekly schedule. The Wednesday, 10:00 P.M. broadcast was planned to maintain the flavor of *Primetime Live.* Sawyer remained as coanchor of *20/20* on Wednesday night, along with Charles Gibson, who had replaced Donaldson. David Westin, president of ABC News, revealed this was part of his hope to expand *20/20* to run seven nights a week. Economic concerns motivated the increased pervasiveness of newsmagazine programming, which cost as much as 50 percent less to produce than an episode of scripted comedy or drama. Additionally, newsmagazine content, though rarely syndicated, could be repurposed for other ABC news programming and for media outlets aligned through corporate synergies.

Soon, however, network executives decided that stripping their newsmagazines as one franchise reduced audience anticipation. To generate more demand for a product perceived as uniform ABC separated the multiple broadcasts of *20/20* into inde-

pendently titled shows. For the 2000 season the Wednesday broadcast of *20/20* was moved to Thursday night, reincarnating *Primetime Live* as *Primetime Thursday.* Sawyer and Gibson remained coanchors of the program. The goal was to reassociate the show with its previous success.

ABC News's metamorphosis over the years can be traced through the history of *Primetime Thursday.* The unsuccessful attempt to expand the *20/20* franchise has resulted instead in a deeper branding of ABC News when it becomes clear that it is the organizational franchise, rather than a program franchise, that has been most strengthened. In the process, the way network news is produced has also changed. Today, *Primetime Thursday* is able to draw on the resources of the entire ABC News organization. And as the show's staffers, from producers to correspondents, are no longer to dedicated to one show, they now contribute to an array of the news division's programming. Rather than following an entrenched formula, the spirit and legacy of *Primetime Live* endure precisely because the concept has been so adaptable to change.

JENNIE PHILLIPS

See also **News, Network ; Sawyer, Diane**

Coanchors
Diane Sawyer (1989–)
Sam Donaldson (1989–98)
Charles Gibson (1998–)

Executive Producers
Richard Kaplan (1989–94)
Phyllis McGrady (1994–98)
Victor Neufeld (merged with *20/20,* 1998–2000)
David Doss (reincarnated as *Primetime Thursday,* 2000–)

Senior Producers, *Primetime Thursday*
Jennifer Grossman
Robert Lange
Victor Neufeld
Marc Robertson
Ira Rosen
Lisa Soloway
Jessica Velmans

Correspondents, ABC News
Bob Brown
Juju Chang
Christopher Cuomo
Arnold Diaz

Jami Floyd
Tom Jarriel
Timothy Johnson
Cynthia McFadden
John Quinones
Brian Ross
Jay Schadler
Lynn Sherr
Joel Siegel
John Stossel
Nancy Snyderman
Elizabeth Vargas
Chris Wallace

Programming History
ABC

August 1989–September 1994	Thursday 10:00–11:00
September 1994– September 1998	Wednesday 10:00–11:00
September 1998– September 2000 (merged with *20/20*)	Wednesday 10:00–11:00
September 2000–	Thursday 10:00–11:00 (reincarnated as *Primetime Thursday*)

Further Reading

Baker, Russ W., "Truth, Lies, and Videotape: PrimeTime Live and the Hidden Camera," *Columbia Journalism Review* (July/August 1993)

Bernstein, Paula, "Doss Is Ready for 'Primetime,'" *Variety* (November 28, 2000)

Consoli, John, "All the News That Fits: Television News in Prime Time," *Adweek* (June 1, 1998)

Grabe, Mary Elizabeth, "Tabloid and Traditional Television News Magazine Crime Stories: Crime Lessons and Reaffirmation of Social Class Distinctions," *Journalism & Mass Communication Quarterly* (Winter 1996)

Gunther, Marc, *The House Tthat Roone Built: The Inside Story of ABC News.* Boston: Little, Brown, 1994

McClellan, Steve, "Cutting Edge at ABC News," *Broadcasting & Cable* (September 21, 1998)

Mifflin, Lawrie, "Network News Magazine Shows May Look Similar but Each Has Its Own Personality Traits," *New York Times* (May 24, 1999)

Spragens, William C., *Electronic Magazines: Soft News Programs on Network Television,* Westport, Connecticut: Praeger, 1995

Princess Diana: Death and Funeral Coverage

The sudden death of Diana, Princess of Wales, following a car accident in Paris in the early hours of Sunday August 31, 1997, sparked a dramatic week of intense television coverage and high public emotion in the United Kingdom and sent shock waves through international media circles.

At the age of 36, the princess cut a figure of glamour and beauty and, despite the years of controversy and acrimonious dispute with the royal family, she still commanded much public popularity and international interest. In the week leading up to the accident, the tabloid press in Britain had been filled with pictures of her relaxing in the south of France with her new boyfriend, Dodi Al Fayed. Her death in a car crash, apparently while being chased by press photographers, seemed as shocking as it was unexpected.

That Sunday, British terrestrial television channels suspended their scheduled programming and ran live rolling news for all or most of the day. The news coverage was dramatic and emotive, combining news narratives associated with disaster and crisis with what

TV critic Mark Lawson has described as "memorial broadcasting," where praise is heaped upon the recently deceased. Tributes were relayed from eminent politicians and personages around the world, and cameras started to focus on members of the public, some angry and emotional, leaving flowers outside palaces in London. A bitter and scathing statement vilifying the press was read by Earl Spencer, the princess's brother in South Africa, and television commentators and journalists distanced themselves from the print media and discussed the potential implications of the accident on press regulation.

The future of the royal family was also discussed, and over the afternoon the coverage was intercut with scenes of Prince Charles and Diana's two sisters flying to Paris to collect her body. Scenes of their return, with the aircraft departing Paris, flying into the sunset and then landing at an air force base just outside London, were particularly poignant and moving.

Yet a disorientating air of unreality hung over the day's coverage, especially when television broadcast images of the car wreckage alongside footage of the princess while still alive, attending gala functions, meeting the sick and poor, and accompanying her two sons on visits to a theme park.

In the following days, television news followed events as revelations emerged that the princess's French chauffeur may have been driving drunk, preparations were made for the funeral, and cameras relayed extraordinary scenes of people lining up for hours to leave flowers and sign books of condolence in London. These images were read as evidence of public mourning and helped fuel criticism in the tabloid press, which was repeated on television, of the royal family's apparent neglect of the princess when alive. The royal family was also accused of being out of touch, for not displaying a response in keeping with the wave of public sympathy after her death. So stinging was the criticism that the queen was effectively forced to make a live address to the nation across all the terrestrial channels in memorial of the princess on the Friday night before the funeral.

The princess's funeral, on Saturday, September 6, was described by a Buckingham Palace press spokesman as "a unique event for a unique person." It had been a focus of speculation throughout the week and was, in the end, a triumph of organization for both the authorities and the broadcasters. With very little time for preparation, permission from the princess's family to film the funeral service live inside Westminster Abbey was only granted to the British Broadcasting Corporation (BBC) and Independent Television News (ITN) on Tuesday evening. Agreement was made with both the Spencer and royal families that there would be no television close-ups of any of the mourners in the Abbey.

The funeral was televised live across four out of five of the U.K. terrestrial channels, with both the BBC and ITN providing live relays to broadcasters around the world. It is estimated that a possible 2.5 billion people watched the funeral globally. Live coverage commenced at 9 A.M. in the U.K. as the funeral cortege, consisting of a horse-drawn gun-carriage bearing the princess's coffin, and a small escort of guardsmen and mounted policemen, left Kensington Palace in London. The coverage followed the cortege every step of the way as it made its two-hour journey, on a sunny morning, through streets lined with people, past Buckingham Palace and Whitehall to Westminster Abbey. On the BBC, historical continuity was provided by the

solemn commentary of David Dimbleby, son of the famous broadcaster Richard Dimbleby who had commentated for television at the queen's coronation in 1953 and the funeral of Winston Churchill in 1965.

The coverage continued through the hour-long service, which was marked by hymns, prayers, and readings and included an address by Earl Spencer and a live rendition of the song "Candle in the Wind" rewritten for the occasion and sung by the pop star Elton John. After the service and a national minute of silence, the main broadcasters continued to follow events as the princess's coffin was taken by hearse back through London streets, lined with crowds applauding and throwing flowers, and then onto the motorway to make its last journey to Althorp in Northamptonshire. There the coverage ended as the princess was finally buried, out of the public gaze, at a private family service in the late afternoon.

Undoubtedly a poignant event that gripped and moved a large British and international audience, the funeral was considered the kind of television event at which the British excel. The BBC's then-director general, John Birt, was to describe the week as "one of the most demanding in the BBC's history."

A year later, television's response to the first anniversary of the princess's death was a more muted affair. Several reports and books began to be published that suggested that not everyone had been caught up in the wave of public emotion, and some were critical of the press and media for orchestrating the apparent public response, and for perpetuating what some came to refer to as "grief fascism."

ROB TURNOCK

See also **Birt, John; Political Processes and Television**

Further Reading

Dayan, Daniel, and Elihu Katz, *Media Events: The Live Broadcasting of History,* Cambridge, Massachussetts: Harvard University Press, 1992

Liebes, Tamar, "Television's Disaster Marathons: A Danger for Democratic Process?" in *Media, Ritual and Identity,* edited by Tamar Liebes and James Curran, London and New York: Routledge, 1998

Merck, Mandy, editor, *After Diana: Irreverent Elegies,* London and New York: Verso, 1998

Turnock, Rob, *Interpreting Diana: Television Audiences and the Death of a Princess,* London: British Film Institute, 2000

Walter, Tony, editor, *The Mourning for Diana,* Oxford and New York: Berg, 1999

Prinze, Freddie (1954–1977)

U.S. Actor

Freddie Prinze is one of only a handful of Puerto Rican Americans to earn national prominence as a popular entertainer—in his case, as a stand-up comedian. Prinze was born in Washington Heights, a working-poor, multiethnic neighborhood on the Upper West Side of New York City. His father was a Hungarian immigrant who worked as a tool and die maker, his mother a Puerto Rican immigrant who worked in a factory. Playing on the name "Nuyorican," as many New York Puerto Ricans identify themselves, Prinze called himself a "Hungarican."

Prinze came from a diverse religious as well as ethnic background. His father was part Jewish, his mother Catholic, and they chose to send him to a Lutheran elementary school. On Sundays he attended Catholic Mass. "All was confusing," he told *Rolling Stone* in 1975, "until I found I could crack up the priest doing Martin Luther." Prinze was also overweight when he was a young boy, which further heightened his anxiety about his "mixed" identity. "I fitted in nowhere," he continued. "I wasn't true spic, true Jew, true anything. I was a miserable fat schmuck kid with glasses and asthma." Like many comedians, Prinze used humor to cope with the traumas of his childhood. "I started doing half-hour routines in the boys' room, just winging it. Guys cut class to catch the act. It was, 'What time's Freddie playing the toilet today?'" His comedic talents paid off, as he was selected to attend the prestigious High School of the Performing Arts in New York.

Prinze did not graduate from the High School of the Performing Arts, although after his later professional successes, school administrators awarded him a certificate. The young comedian skipped many of his morning classes, most commonly economics, because he often worked as late as 3:00 A.M. in comedy clubs perfecting his routine and style. Of his time spent in these clubs, Prinze would later say, "My heart doesn't start till 1:00 P.M." One of his favorite spots was the Improvisation on West Forty-fourth Street, a place where aspiring comics could try out their material on receptive audiences.

Prinze called himself an "observation comic," and his routines often included impressions of ethnic minorities and film stars such as Marlon Brando. One of his most famous impressions was of his Puerto Rican apartment building superintendent who, when asked to fix a problem in the building, would say with a thick accent: "Eez not mai yob." The line became a national catchphrase in the early 1970s. His comedy also had a political edge that was poignant and raw, perhaps best illustrated by his line about Christopher Columbus: "Queen Isabelle gives him all the money, three boats, and he's wearing a red suit, a big hat, and a feather—that's a pimp." Prinze's comic wit, based in the tradition of street humor pioneered by such comics as Lenny Bruce and Richard Pryor, landed him a number of television appearances, including *The Tonight Show Starring Johnny Carson* in 1973. His performance there was a major success and the start of his television career.

Indeed, James Komack, a television producer, liked what he saw in Prinze's routine and cast him to play the part of Chico Rodriquez, a wisecracking Chicano, in a situation comedy called *Chico and the Man.* Komack told *Time* magazine that Prinze "was the best comic to come along in 20 years." *Chico and the Man* also starred veteran actor Jack Albertson as "the Man," a crusty old-timer, owner of a run-down garage in a Chicano barrio of East Los Angeles. Among the supporting cast were Scatman Crothers, who played Louie the garbageman, and Della Reese, who played Della the landlady. In the style of other situation comedies such as *All in the Family* and *Sanford and Son,* most of the plots involved ethnic conflicts between Chico, who worked in the garage, and the Man, the only Caucasian living in the mostly Latino neighborhood. "Latin music sounds like Mantovani getting mugged," the Man says to Chico in one episode. Chico would often respond to the old-timer's bigoted statements with the line, "Looking good," which also became a national catchphrase. Premiering on NBC-TV in September 1974, *Chico and the Man* quickly rose to the top of the Nielsen ratings. *Time* reported that Prinze was "the hottest new property on prime-time TV," and the comedian literally became an overnight star: the first and, to date, only Puerto Rican comedian to command a nationwide audience. He began working in Las Vegas for a reported $25,000 a night. He bought himself a new Corvette and his parents a home in the Hollywood hills. He was only 20 years old.

Freddie Prinze, *Chico and the Man,* 1974–78.
Courtesy of the Everett Collection

Chico and the Man faced criticism and protests from the Los Angeles Chicano community, who protested the use of Prinze, a New York Puerto Rican, to play a Los Angeles Chicano. Citing dialect and accent differences, and the fact that network television rarely employed Chicano actors, Chicano groups picketed NBC's Burbank studios and wrote protest letters. Prinze responded with his usual irreverent humor: "If I can't play a Chicano because I'm Puerto Rican, then God's really gonna be mad when he finds out Charlton Heston played Moses." Nonetheless, the network and producers of the show buckled under the pressure, changing the character to half-Puerto Rican and half-Chicano brought up in New York City. The shift in the character's ethnic identity apparently did not bother television audiences, for *Chico and the Man* never slipped below sixth place in the ratings when Prinze was its star.

Prinze, however, had a difficult time adjusting to the pressures of his overnight success and stardom, and during this period, he experienced many personal problems. His wife of 15 months, Katherine Elaine Cochran, filed for divorce and Prinze was now less able to see his adored 15-month-old son. Early in the show's run, Prinze was arrested for driving under the influence of prescription tranquilizers, fueling speculation of a drug problem. Indeed, friends reported that Prinze turned to drugs to cope with the pressures of fame and the breakup of his marriage. "Freddie was into a lot of drugs," comedian Jimmy Walker said to

the *New York Times,* "not heroin, as far as I know, but coke and a lot of Ludes. The drug thing was a big part of Freddie's life. It completely messed him up."

On January 28, 1977, after a night of phone calls to his secretary, business manager, psychiatrist, mother, and estranged wife, Freddie Prinze shot himself in the head in front of his business manager. He was rushed to the hospital, where he was pronounced dead. He was 22 years old. A note found in his apartment read: "I can't take any more. It's all my fault. There is no one to blame but me." According to the *New York Times,* Prinze had previously threatened suicide in front of many of his friends and associates, often by holding a gun to his head and pulling the trigger while the safety was on. It is not known whether the young comedian actually intended to kill himself that night or merely suggest that he might, as he had done in the past, but it is clear that he was critically depressed.

The death of Freddie Prinze is an American success story turned tragedy. His streetwise insight and raw wit is surely missed, perhaps most by the Puerto Rican American community, who have yet to see another politically minded Puerto Rican comedian grab national attention.

DANIEL BERNARDI

Freddie Prinze. Born in New York City, June 22, 1954. Educated at the High School of the Performing Arts, 1970. Married: Katherine Cochran, 1975; one son, Freddie Prinze Jr. Performed in Manhattan comedy nightclubs; appeared on Jack Paar's television show, 1972; appeared on *The Tonight Show Starring Johnny Carson,* 1973; starred in television show *Chico and the Man,* 1974–77. Died in Los Angeles, California, January 28, 1977.

Television Series

1974–77   *Chico and the Man*

Further Reading

Burke, Tom, "The Undiluted South Bronx Truth about Freddie Prinze," *Rolling Stone* (January 30, 1975)
Kasindorf, Jeanie, "'If I Was Bitter, I Wouldn't Have Chosen Comedy,'" *New York Times* (February 9, 1975)
Nordheimer, Jon, "Freddie Prinze, 22, Dies after Shooting," *New York Times* (January 30, 1977)
Pruetzel, Maria, *The Freddie Prinze Story,* Kalamazoo, Michigan: Master's Press, 1978.

Prisoner

Australian Prison Melodrama

Prisoner, which aired from 1979 to 1986 in Australia and was broadcast in other countries as *Cell Block H,* is a triumph of the Australian television industry, a classic of serial melodrama. *Prisoner* was conceived by the Grundy Organisation for Network Ten. Reg Watson, in the senior ranks of Grundy, had just returned from Britain, where he had been one of the originators of the long-running serial *Crossroads.* In 1978 Watson set out to devise a serial set in a women's prison, in the context of considerable public attention being given in Australia to prison issues generally and to the position of female prisoners in particular. Women Behind Bars had been founded in 1975 and had successfully campaigned for the eventual release of Sandra Willson, Australia's longest-serving female prisoner. The combination of an active women's movement, prisoner action groups, and an atmosphere of public inquiry and media attention, stimulated by gaol riots and a royal commission, laid a basis for an interest in the lives of women in prison. Watson and his team at Grundy, in their extensive research for the new drama, interviewed women in prison as well as prison officers (the "screws," as they are always called in *Prisoner*), and later some of the actors also visited women's prisons. Notice was taken of prison reform groups, whose desire for a halfway house for women was incorporated into the program. The result was a very popular long-running serial, shown from 8:30 to 10:30 P.M., which only in its eighth year revealed signs of falling ratings.

Prisoner became as controversial as it was popular. In its frequent grimness, pathos, sadness, toughness of address, occasional violence, and atmosphere of threat, it appeared very decidedly to be adult drama, its "look" spare, hard, dynamic. Yet ethnographic research pointed to *Prisoner*'s consistent appeal to schoolchildren, not least schoolgirls, perhaps identifying the harsher screws with cordially disliked teachers. It was not the favorite text of school principals and was the subject of complaint by them.

With *Prisoner,* the audience is invited to sympathize and empathize with a particular group of prisoners, in particular, mother figure Bea Smith, aunt figure Judy Bryant, grandmother figure Lizzie Birdsworth, as well as some young prisoners, the acting daughters and granddaughters, Doreen and Maxie and Bobby. Often this group is shown at work in the prison laundry, where Bea rules as "top dog," having the right to press the clothes. Here Bea and her "family" resist the oppression of a labor process the prison management forces on them by taking smokes, having fun, exercising cheek and wit, chatting, planning rituals such as birthday celebrations, or being involved in dramas of various kinds that distract them from the boredom of work.

Such "kinship" relationships, often remembered rather wistfully by ex-prisoners who are having a hard time of it alone on the outside, offer the possibility of close friendship, fierce loyalty, cooperation, genuine concern for each other: an image of *communitas,* inversionary since it is this community of "good" prisoners, not those in authority, whom the text continually invites us to sympathize and empathize with. Opposed to the powerful resourceful figure of Bea are various other women, also powerful personalities, such as Kate or Nola MacKenzie or Marie Winters, individualistic and ruthlessly selfish, manipulative and wily, who scheme and plot (sometimes with harsh screws like Joan Ferguson, known as the Freak, who is also corrupt, or Vera Bennett, known as Vinegar Tits) to topple Bea and destroy her authority and influence.

In *Prisoner,* however, relationships of all kinds are always complicated, shifting, and often uncertain. Not all screws are harsh; there is, for example, Meg, more a social worker, though still suspected by the women. The struggle between those who take a more permissive, helping approach, such as Meg, and the advocates of rigid discipline like Ferguson and Bennett and, to a lesser degree, Colleen Powell goes on and on and is never resolved, as each approach is alternately seen to result in further tension, restlessness, and disorder. As the women's leader, Bea is particularly ambivalent. She possesses impressive wisdom about human relations, which she shrewdly uses for the benefit of the prisoners as a whole. She dislikes and tries to counter or sometimes punish actions that are self-seeking and competitive at the expense of what she perceives as a family group. But if Bea is a kind of moral center in *Prisoner,* she is an unusual and complex one, drawn as she is to exerting her control through violence or the

Prisoner.
Photo courtesy of Grundy Television Pty Ltd.

threat of it: after killing her, she brands "K" (for killer) on Nola MacKenzie's chest with a soldering iron (Nola had tried to drive Bea insane over the memory of her dead daughter Debbie).

Prisoner relies very little on conventional definitions of masculinity and femininity, beyond the basic point that sympathy generated for the women rests on the perception that women are not usually violent or physically dangerous. Many of the women are very strong characters indeed, active and independent. Bea, Nola, Marie Winters, the Freak are most unusual in the gallery of characters of television drama. They are not substitute men, but active strong women. Strength and gentleness are not distributed in *Prisoner* on male-female lines. The binary image of the powerful man and the weak or decorative woman is simply not there. Nor are the women in *Prisoner* in the least glamorized. They are usually dressed in shabby prison uniforms, while those on remand usually appear in fairly ordinary clothes. Their faces suggest no makeup, and they range in bodily shape from skinny wizened old Lizzie (loving, concerned, and kind, yet also a mischievous old lag rather like a child, liable to get herself into trouble) to the big girls like Bea, Doreen, and Judy. Their faces, luminously featured as in so much serial melodrama, are shown as grainy and interesting, faces full of character, with signs of hardship and suffering, alternately soft and hard, happy and depressed, angry or bored. The women are not held up voyeuristically as sexual objects but present themselves as human, female, subjects.

Although *Prisoner* talks to very contemporary, historically specific concerns, it also draws on much wider, longer, older cultural histories. *Prisoner* can be located in a long female tradition of inversion and inversionary figures in popular culture, from the "unruly" or "disorderly" women of early modern Europe evoked by Natalie Zemon Davis as Women on Top to the rebellious Maid Marian's important in Robin Hood ballads and associated festivities of the May-games, to the witches of 17th-century English stage comedy. In such "wise witch" figures, we perhaps approach the female equivalent of the male mythological tradition of Robin Hood, Dick Turpin, Rob Roy—outlaws and tricksters who, like Bea in *Prisoner,* inspire fear as well as admiration.

In addition to drawing from such carnivalesque traditions of world upside-down, misrule, and charivari, *Prisoner* speaks to and takes in new directions dramas of crime on television where private passions erupt into public knowledge, debate, contestation, judgment. As dramaturgy, *Prisoner* revels in the possibilities of the TV serial form, of cliff-hangers at the end of episodes, intensifying melodrama as (in Peter Brooks's terms in *The Melodramatic Imagination*) an aesthetic of excess. *Prisoner* is already a classic of serial melodrama, yet, in world television, there is and has been nothing else quite like it.

ANN CURTHOYS AND JOHN DOCKER

Cast

Doreen May Anderson/Burns	Colette Mann
Freida "Franky" Doyle	Carol Burns
Vera "Vinegar Tits" Bennett	Fiona Spence
Lizzie Birdworth	Sheila Florance
Monica Ferguson	Lesley Baker
Marilyn Mason	Margaret Laurence
Bea Smith	Val Lehman
Karen Travers	Peta Toppano
Lynn Warner	Kerry Armstrong
Stud Wilson	Peter Lindsay
Jim Fletcher	Gerard Maguire
Erica Davidson	Patsy King
Colleen Powell	Judith McGrath
Bob Moran	Peter Adams (II)
Tammy Fisher	Gloria Adjenstrat
Officer Green	John Allen
Jean Vernon	Christine Amor
Camilla Wells	Annette Andre
Di Hagen	Christine Andrew
Reb Kean	Janet Andrewartha
Valarie Jacobs	Barbara Angell
Meg Morris	Elspeth Ballantyne

Susan Rice
Andrew Fry
Sarah West
Matthew "Matt" Delaney
Lisa Snell
Randi Goodlove
Tracy Belman
Harry Grovesnor
Toni McNally
Evy Randel
Judy Bryant
Mervin "Merv" Pringle
Dennis Cruckshank
Jill Clarke
Merle Jones
Ida Brown
Sonya Stevens
Sandra Williams
Barbara Davidson
Deirdre Kean
Linda Gorman
Anne Yates
Fay Donnally
Bella Abrecht
Edie Warren
Margo Gaffney
Alice Jenkins/"Lurch"
Head of Department: James
    Dwyer
Bongo Connors
Jenny Armstrong
Alan Farmer
Anita Selby
Diane Henley
Maxine Daniels
Carol Lewis
Glynis Ladd
Ian Marhoney
Pat Slattery
Roxanne Bradshaw
Hazel Kent
Frances Harvey
Ruth Ballinger
Wendy Stone
Geoff McCrae
Bev Baker
Peter
Andrea Radcliff
Vicki McPherson
Joanna Jones
Lorili Wilkinson
Jock Stewart
Janet Williams
Scott Collins

Briony Behets
Howard Bell
Kylie Belling
Peter Bensley
Liza Bermingham
Zoe Bertram
Alyson Best
Mike Bishop
Pat Bishop
Julia Blake
Betty Bobbit
Ernie Bourne
Nigel Bradshaw
Katy Brinson
Rosanne Hull Brown
Paddy Burnet
Tina Bursill
Andrea Butcher
Sally Cahill
Anne Charleston
Mary Charleston (II)
Kirsty Child
Maud Clark
Liddy Clarke
Collene Clifford
Jane Clifton
Lois Collinder

James Condon
Shane Connors
Sally Cooper
Michael Cormick
Diana Craig
Ellen Cressley
Lisa Crittenden
Liz Crosby
Debs Cummings
Peter Curtin
Dorothy Cuts
Peppie D'Or
Belinda Davey
Wanda Davidson
Lindy Davies
Vivean Davies
Les Dayman
Maggie Dence
Sue Devine
Marrian Dimmick
Rebecca Dines
Nichole Dixon
Paula Duncan
Tommy Dysart
Christine Earl
Tim Elston

Jessie Wyndem
Len Murphy
Lainie Dobson
Kerryn Davies
Angela "Angel" Adams
Jennifer Bryant
Cindy Moran
Brandy Carter
Mo Maquire
Samantha "Sam" Greenway
Vivienne Williams
Detective Inspector Grace
Helen Smart
Kevin Burns
Gloria Payne
Suzy Driscoll
Kay White
Edna Preston
Barbara Fields
"Auntie" May Collins
Dr Kate Peterson
Terry Harrison
Pippa Reynolds
Sally Dempster
Roach Walters
Bob Morris
Gail Summers
Leigh Templar
Jennie Baxter
Steve Ryan
Barbie Cox
Tina Murry
Syd Humphries
Sheila Brady
Kath Maxwell
Wally Wallace
Paddy Lawson
Rodney Adams
Stan Dobson
Steve Faulkner
Martha Ives
Sarah Higgens
Ros Fisher
Kathy Hall
Lorna Young
Denise Crabtree
Alison Page
Gerri Googan
Frank Burke
Philip Clary
Joan Ferguson (The Freak)
Bobbie Mitchell
Sharon Gilmour
Noelene Burke

Pat Evison
Maurie Fields
Marina Findley
Jill Forster
Kylie Foster
Susannah Fowle
Robyn Frank
Roslyn Gentle
Browyn Gibbs
Robyn Gibbs
Bernadette Gibson
Terry Gill
Caroline Gillmer
Ian Gilmour
Tot Goldsmith
Jacqui Gordon
Sandy Gore
Vivean Grey
Susan Gurin
Billie Hammerberg
Olivia Hamnett
Brian Hannan
Christine Harris
Liz Harris
Linda Hartley
Anthony Hawkins
Susanne Haworth
Virginia Hay
Leila Hayes
Peter Lind Hayes
Jayne Healey
Hazel Henley
Edward Hepple
Colleen Hewet
Kate Hood
Alan Hopgood
Anna Hruby
Philip Hyde
Brian James (I)
Wayne Jarrett
Kate Jason
Nell Johnson
Marinia Jonathon
Sue Jones
Barbara Jungwirth
Lynda Keane
Fay Kelton
Deborah Kennedy
Trevor Kent
Steve Khun
Maggie Kirkpatrick
Maxine Klibingaitus
Margot Knight
Jude Kuring

Michelle Parkes
Daphne Graham
David Andrews
Sandy Edwards
Tony Bernum
Andrea Hennesey
Marlene "Rabbit" Warren
Rita Conners
Jenny Hartley
Faye Quinn
Clara Goddard
Janice Grant
Petra Roberts
Debbie Pearce
Georgie Baxter
Meryl King
Jonathon Edmonds
Nicki Lennox
Pat O'Connell
Pixie Mason
Rosie Hudson

Dot Farrow
Catherine Roberts
Cass Parker
Tom Lucas
Ernest Craven
Ray Proctor
Irene Zervos
Yamille Bacartta
Marie Winter
Trixie Mann
Eddie Cooke
Chrissie Latham
Michelle "Brumby" Tucker
Hannah Simpson
Heather Rogers
Anne Reynolds
Joyce Martin
Ken Pierce
Helen Masters
Sara Webster
Lisa Mullins
Philis Hunt
Anna Geltschmidt
Myra Desmond
Melinda Cross
Minnie Donovan
Lucy Furgusson
Greg Miller
Ethel May "Ettie" Parslow
Agnus Forster
Sandy Hamilton
Leone Burke

Nina Landis
Debra Lawrence
Serge Lazareff
Louise Le Nay
Alan David Lee
Bethany Lee
Genevieve Lemon
Glenda Linscott
Jenny Lovell
Anne Lucas
Betty Lucas
Jenny Ludlam
Penny Maegraith
Dina Mann
Tracey Mann
Marilyn Maquire
Bryan Marshall
Vicki Mathios
Monica Maughton
Judy McBurney
Anne Maree
  McDonald
Althea McGrath
Margo McLennan
Babs McMillan
John McTernan
Ray Meagher
Alex Menglet
Maria Mercedes
Maria Mercedes
Maggie Miller
Anna Mizza
Richard Moir
Amanda Muggleton
Sheryl Munks
Julienna Newbold
Victoria Nicholls
Gerda Nicolson
Judy Nunn
Tom Oliver
Louise Pajo
Fiona Paul
Nicki Paul
Ray Pearce
Agnieska Perpeczko
Anne Phelan
Lulu Pinkus
Wendy Playfair
Yoni Prior
Barry Quinn
Lois Ramsay
Lois Ramsay
Candy Reymond
Tracy Jo Riley

Zara Moonbeam
Queenie Marshall
Spike Marsh
Janet Dominguez
Kath Deakin
Pamela Madigan
Dan Moulton
Janet Conway
Angie Dobbs
Lou Kelly
Nola McKenzie
Delia Stout
Ted Douglas
Mighty Mouse
Caroline Simpson
May Worth
Kath Leach
Eve Wilder
Spider Simpson
Ben Fulbright
Shane Monroe
Nora Flynn
Roslyn Coulson
Mr. Hudson
Rachael Millson
Lexie Patterson
Lisa Mullins
Anne Griffin
David Bridges
Jeanette Mary "Mum" Brooks
Joyce Barry
Maggie May Kennedy
Donna Mason
Janice Young
Marty Jackson
Julie "Chook" Egbert
Neil Murray
Joanne Slater
Rosmary Kay

Ilona Rodgers
Marilyn Rodgers
Victoria Rowland
Deidre Rubenstein
Michelle Sargent
Justine Saunders
Sean Scully
Kate Sheil
Gonza Sheils
Louise Siversen
Carol Skinner
Desiree Smith
Ian Smith
Jentah Sobott
Ros Spiers
Adair Stagg
Penny Stewart
Lynda Stoner
Tyra Stratton
Kevin Summers
Robert Summers
Sonja Tallis
Sigrid Thornton
Bud Tingwell
Kim Trentgrove
Pepe Trevor
Terrie Waddell
Rowena Wallace
David Walters
Mary B. Ward
Joy Westmore
Davina Whitehouse
Arkie Whitely
Catherine Wilken
Michael Winchester
Jackie Woodburne
Adrian Wright
Carole Yelland
Jodi Yemm

Producers
Philip East, John McRae, Ian Smith, Marie Trevor

Programming History
692 episodes
Ten Network

February 1979–November 1980	Tuesday and Wednesday 8:30–9:30
February 1981–June 1981	Tuesday and Wednesday 7:30–8:30

June 1981–November 1981	Tuesday and Wednesday 8:30–9:30
February 1982–November 1982	Tuesday and Wednesday 7:30–8:30
February 1983–December 1986	Tuesday and Wednesday 8:30–9:30

Further Reading

Bakhtin, Mikhail, *The Dialogic Imagination,* Austin: University of Texas Press, 1981

Curry, Christine, and Christine O'Sullivan, *Teaching Television in Secondary Schools,* Sydney: New South Wales Institute of Technology Media Papers, 1980

Curthoys, Ann, and John Docker, "Melodrama in Action: *Prisoner,* or *Cell Block H,*" in *Postmodernism and Popular Culture: A Cultural History,* by Docker, Cambridge and New York: Cambridge University Press, 1994

Curthoys, Ann, and John Docker, "In Praise of *Prisoner,*" in *Australian Television: Programs, Pleasures and Politics,* edited by John Tulloch and Graeme Turner, Sydney: Allen and Unwin, 1989

Hodge, Robert, and David Tripp, *Children and Television: A Semiotic Approach,* Cambridge: Polity, 1986

Kingsley, Hilary, *Prisoner: Cell Block H: The Inside Story,* London: Boxtree, 1990

Moran, Albert, *Moran's Guide to Australian TV Series,* Sydney: AFTRS/Allen and Unwin, 1993

Palmer, Patricia, *The Lively Audience: A Study of Children around the TV Set,* Sydney: Allen and Unwin, 1986

Stern, Lesley, "The Australian Serial: Home Grown Television," in *Nellie Melba, Ginger Meggs, and Friends,* edited by Susan Dermody, John Docker, and Drusilla Modjeska, Melbourne: Kibble, 1982

Thomas, Claire, "Girls and Counter-School Culture," in *Melbourne Working Papers 1980,* edited by David McCallum and Uldis Ozolins, Melbourne: University of Melbourne, 1980

Willson, Sandra, "Prison, Prisoners and the Community," in *Women and Crime,* edited by S.K. Mukherjee and J. Scutt, Sydney: Allen and Unwin, 1981

Prisoner, The

British Spy and Science Fiction Series

The Prisoner, an existential British spy and science fiction series, was first aired in England in 1967. Actor Patrick McGoohan conceived of the idea for the series, wrote some of the scripts, and starred in the central role. McGoohan had become bored with his previous series, *The Secret Agent,* and wanted something very different. The new series comprised 17 "adventures," each self-contained, but each also carrying the story forward to its remarkable, highly ambiguous conclusion.

The series has attained cult status because it is so complex, so filled with symbolism, with dialogue and action working at several levels of meaning, that the entire story remains open to multiple interpretations. *The Prisoner* was shot in the Welsh village of Portmeirion, whose remarkable architecture contributes to the rich, mysterious atmosphere of the series. In many ways an allegory, the adventures within *The Prisoner* can be read as commentaries on contemporary British social and political institutions.

The hero of the series is an unnamed spy, who is first shown resigning his position. He leaves the bureaucratic office building housing his agency, goes to his apartment, starts packing—and is gassed—presumably by those for whom he used to work. He wakes up in "The Village," a resortlike community on what seems to be a remote island. The Village, however, is actually a high-tech prison, and the spy is a prisoner, along with others, men and women, who were, it is understood, spies. All have been sent to the Village to be removed from circulation in any circumstances where their secret knowledge might be discovered.

Every member of the Village is known only by a number. The McGoohan character becomes Number Six and finds himself engaged in constant intellectual, emotional, and sometimes physical struggles with Number Two. But each episode presents a different Number Two. With a few exceptions, each episode begins with a repetition of some of the opening sequence from the first episode—McGoohan resigns; his file is dropped by a mechanical device into a filing cabinet labeled "Resigned"; he is gassed; he wakes in the Village and confronts (the new) Number Two. This beginning is followed by a set piece of dialogue:

Prisoner:	Where am I?
Number Two:	In the Village.
Prisoner:	What do you want?

Number Two:	Information.
Prisoner:	Which side are you on?
Number Two:	That would be telling. We want information, information, information ... .
Prisoner:	You won't get it.
Number Two:	By hook or by crook we will.
Prisoner:	Who are you?
Number Two:	The new Number Two.
Prisoner:	Who is Number One?
Number Two:	You are Number Six.
Prisoner:	I am not a number. I am a free man.
Number Two:	Ha, ha, ha, ha ... .

Some fans of the series argue that there is a slight gap between the words "are" and the "Number Two" in this exchange ("You are. Number Six"), which would mean that Number Six is also Number One, a character who remains unseen until the final episode. Number Two pushes the inquiry. He wants to know why Six resigned. Six says he will not tell him, then vows to escape from the Village and destroy it.

Each episode in the series consists of an attempt by a new Number Two and his or her associates to find out why Six resigned and of measures taken by Six to counter these attempts. Every possible method, from drugs to sex, from the invasion of his dreams to the use of supercomputers, is used to get Number Six to reveal why he resigned. In some episodes Six shifts his focus from escape attempts to schemes for bringing down the administration of the Village, though it is always understood that escape is his ultimate goal.

The concluding episode, written by McGoohan, was extremely chaotic, confusing, and very controversial. Number Six has defeated and killed Number Two in the previous episode, "Till Death Do Us Part." When Number Six finally gets to see Number One, he turns out to be a grinning ape. But when Number Six strips off the ape mask, we see what appears to be a crazed version of Number Six, suggesting that Number One was, somehow, a perverted element of Number Six's personality. Six, aided by several characters also deemed "revolutionaries" by the administration (including the Number Two of the previous episode, somehow brought back to life), does destroy the Village. He escapes with his associates in a truck driven by a midget, who may have been the servant of all previous Number Two figures. They blast through a tunnel just before the Village is destroyed and find themselves, surprisingly, on a highway near London.

The Prisoner is continually rebroadcast, usually presented as a science fiction program, though it is probably best described as a spy series filled with technological gadgetry. Each program and every aspect of the series has been subjected to scrutiny by its fans. Dealing with topics ranging from the nature of individual identity to the power of individuals to confront totalitarian institutions, The Prisoner remains one of the most enigmatic and fascinating series ever produced for television.

ARTHUR ASA BERGER

See also **Spy Programs**

Cast

The Prisoner	Patrick McGoohan
Number Two	Guy Doleman
	George Baker
	Leo McKern
	Colin Gordon
	Eric Portman
	Anton Rodgers
	Mary Morris
	Peter Wyngarde
	Patrick Cargill
	Derren Nesbitt
	John Sharpe
	Clifford Evans
	David Bauer
	Georgina Cookson
	Andre Van Gysegham
	Kenneth Griffith
The Kid/Number 48	Alexis Kanner
The Butler	Angelo Muscat
The Supervisor	Peter Stanwick
Shopkeeper	Denis Show

Producer

David Tomblin

Programming History

17 50-minute episodes
ITC/Everyman Films for ITV
September 1967–February 1968

Further Reading

Disch, Thomas, *The Prisoner,* New York: Ace, 1970
McDaniel, David, *Who Is Number Two?,* New York: Ace, 1969
Rogers, Dave, *The Prisoner and Danger Man,* London: Boxtree, 1989
Stine, Hank, *The Prisoner: A Day in the Life,* New York: Ace, 1970
White, Matthew, and Jaffer Ali, *The Official Prisoner Companion,* New York: Warner, 1988

Producer in Television

Although the medium's technical complexity demands that any television program is a collective product involving many talents and decision makers, in American television it is the producer who frequently serves as the decisive figure in shaping a program. Producers assume direct responsibility for a show's overall quality and continued viability. Conventional wisdom in the industry consequently labels television "the producer's medium"—in contrast to film, where the director is frequently regarded as the key formative talent in the execution of a movie.

In fact, producers' roles vary dramatically from show to show or organization to organization. Some highly successful producers, such as Quinn Martin and Aaron Spelling, are primarily business executives presiding over several programs. They may take an active role in conceiving new programs and pitching (presenting them for sale) to networks, but once a show is accepted they are likely to concentrate on budgets, contracts, and troubleshooting, handing over day-to-day production to their staffs, and exercising control only in a final review of episodes. Other producers are more intimately involved in the details of each episode, participating actively in screenwriting, set designs, and casting and—like James Burrows—serving as a frequent director for their programs. Still others serve as enabling midmanagers who delegate crucial activities to directors, writers, and actors, but who choose such personnel carefully, and enforce critical standards, while working to insulate the creative staff from outside pressures. Many producers dispatch their duties within studio hierarchies, while others own independent companies, sometimes contracting space, equipment, and personnel from studios.

Some scholars consider the producer television's auteur, suggesting that shows should be considered above all extensions of the producer's individual, creative sensibility (Marc, 1989; Marc and Thompson, 1992). Rather than creators freely following a vision, however, producers typically function as orchestrators of television programs, applying the resources available within an organization to the problem of mounting a show each week. Those resources—and deeper cultural presumptions about television's social roles and limits—may shape the producer's ambitions as much as he shapes them (Gitlin, 1983).

Beginning in the mid-1970s, Hollywood embraced an auteurist theory of its own, when the success of well-written comedies produced by small, writer-centered independent companies led to the presumption that the literate writer-producer was the single most indispensable creative resource for generating new shows attractive to demographically desirable audiences. Both studios and networks began an escalating trend of signing promising writer-producers to long-term, concessionary contracts. The most notorious—and arguably the most successful—was ABC and Twentieth Century Fox's 1988 agreement with Steven Bochco to underwrite and air the next ten shows he conceived—a decision that offered Bochco room to experiment, sometimes disastrously, with shows like *Cop Rock,* an attempt to bring opera to prime time. The emphasis on the producer-as-author marked the culmination of a concerted shift from 1950s industry procedure, which regarded the networks' relationships with particular studios as the most decisive aspect in generating new programming. Arguably, the shift represented a move away from a factory system whose emphases were standardization and cost containment, and whose most desirable TV producer was an effective employee or bureaucrat, toward an arts and crafts model of TV whose emphasis was differentiation and variety, and whose most desirable producer was a talented visionary with a track record. (The shift manifests the transformation of filmmaking from studio-centered Hollywood to the talent packages of the New Hollywood.)

The expanding syndication market ensured that producers—who can negotiate part-ownership of their shows—could enjoy not only creative scope but considerable financial reward as well. By the 1990s observers within the industry noted that college graduates once eager to become network executives or studio employees now arrived hoping to become producers—a shift in the sociology of television production with potential import to the comparatively new medium.

Respect for producers' creativity, however, did not mitigate Hollywood's strong inclination to treat producers as specialists in specific genres. When, for example, the successful action-adventure producer Stephen Cannell tried to diversify into comedy in the early 1980s, the networks were unreceptive, on the grounds that Cannell had no demonstrated skill in comedy. As with many commercial artists, then, the television producer's scope of innovation is generally delimited by convention and often amounts to a variation in formula rather than a dramatic break with practices or expectations held by the industry or the producer's audiences (Newcomb and Alley, 1983; Selnow and Gilbert, 1993).

One sign that the producer is not an individual auteur is the multiplication of producer credits seen on American shows since the mid-1980s. Programs may identify an "executive producer" (sometimes a financial underwriter, sometimes the conceiver of the show's premise), an associate producer, a supervising producer (who usually serves as head writer), or a line producer (who oversees day-to-day production), or they may list any combination of these titles (which hardly comprise an exhaustive list), all in addition to the regular "producer." Such credits may reflect a complex division of labor established by the organization or packagers producing a show. They can also reflect the growing negotiating power of participants in a highly successful show, who, no longer content simply to write or act, wish to have contractual control over the assembly of entire episodes, and perhaps, eventually, develop a measure of artistic and financial independence by forming their own production companies. In any case, the proliferating credits suggest that "producerly" authority is divisible and negotiable, not individual and singular—a construction emerging from institutional pressures and politics (though individual talents and preferences of course affect how a given person executes any institutionally defined role).

The first television producers were studio personnel in local stations across the country. They included advertising agency employees who put together shows in the years of sponsor-controlled programming. Somewhat later, the Hollywood executives assigned to the first television divisions of the studios were known as producers (Anderson, 1994). All, in turn, may have owed elements of their jobs to precursors in radio (Hilmes, 1990). But the TV producer's definition as a uniquely creative figure was probably initiated by Desi Arnaz and Lucille Ball, who, in 1950, formed Desilu expressly to produce I Love Lucy on their own terms. Their crucial innovation of shooting shows on film in front of a studio audience combined the excitement of live performance with the quality control of film and enabled reruns and syndication, thus transforming television economics, as well as the struggle for creative control (Schatz, 1990).

Desilu serves as an important example of the simultaneously artistic and commercial role of the producer.

Given the series format of most television programming, the producers—much more than are film directors—ultimately are faced with operating an economically, logistically, and theatrically successful assembly line, and so their influence on a program stems from their entrepreneurial, as well as their formal, ingenuity. Like so much else about television, the producer's role combines traditionally conceived realms of "artistic" and "managerial" decision making into a hybrid activity in which artistic criteria and commercial calculation impinge on each other.

Two examples from the late 1990s and into the 2000s illustrate these interactions in distinctive ways. David E. Kelley began his television career as a writer for Steven Bochco. A lawyer by education and early experience, Kelley wrote and later produced L.A. Law. He soon created his own program, Picket Fences, again drawing on legal experience. This quirky series established him as an outstanding, perhaps "auteurist" producer, and he exemplified this role with Ally McBeal, almost a cult favorite that grew into a legitimate "hit" on the FOX network. At one time Kelley had several shows on the air, on different networks, at the same time, and he was famous for writing "all" the episodes of his series by himself. He was permitted considerable freedom from many of television's famous industrial constraints. He brought characters from different shows together in "crossover" episodes. He experimented with "re-editing" Ally McBeal into a half-hour sitcom (a notable failure). But by 2003 the declining ratings for one of his series, The Practice, forced him to take a rather drastic step and fire many of the principal actors in order to cut costs and continue the series on ABC.

A contrasting success story is offered in the work of Dick Wolf, creator of the Law and Order "franchise." Like Kelley, Wolf also wrote on Bochco series, in his case Hill Street Blues. Law and Order, however, is the antithesis of the continuing narratives that distinguished Bochco's work. Each episode, following the commission of a crime, the capture of the criminal, and the subsequent trial of the criminal, is completed in one hour. Law and Order was largely unnoticed for many years but maintained a loyal audience. Finally recognized with awards and heavily programmed on cable television in reruns, Wolf created "different" versions of the series—Law and Order SVU (Special Victims Unit dealing with sex crimes), and Law and Order CI (Criminal Intent), presenting, in some ways, the crimes from the criminal's perspective. Other versions were less successful, but from a financial and programming perspective, these programs were enormous successes. Any "auteurist" efforts on Wolf's part came in the creation of a basic concept rather than in the stamp of a distinctive sensibility.

Significantly, changes in the television industries caused by expansion of distribution through cable, consolidation of ownership, and the increased use of personal video recorders has led to an interesting development in the role of the producer. By the early 2000s, "nonwriting producers" had returned to prominence in some parts of the industry. These individuals took on the business role of the producer in a manner not unlike producers in the early years of the medium. Their primary work is to make deals, not television programs, and their efforts in the latter arena extend to locating and hiring the best writer-producers they can attract to those deals. Combined with the increasing participation by advertisers and underwriters in the processes of creating television programs and the industry bears more and more features that would have been familiar to executives in the 1950s. In many ways, opportunities for the most "creative" producers were found in "premium" or "subscription" television venues such as HBO, or on the more innovative and risk-taking cable channels, such as the FX cable network.

MICHAEL SAENZ

See also **Bochco, Steven; Burrows, James; Spelling, Aaron**

Further Reading

Cantor, Muriel G., and Joel Cantor, *The Hollywood TV Producer: His Work and His Audience,* New Brunswick, New Jersey: Transaction, 1988

Gitlin, Todd, *Inside Prime Time,* New York: Pantheon, 1983

Hilmes, Michelle, *Hollywood and Broadcasting: From Radio to Cable,* Champaign: University of Illinois Press, 1990

Levinson, Richard, and William Link, *Stay Tuned: An Inside Look at the Making of Prime-time Television,* New York: St. Martin's Press, 1981

Marc, David, *Comic Visions: Television Comedy and American Culture,* Boston: Unwin Hyman, 1989

Marc, David, and Robert Thompson, *Prime Time, Prime Movers,* Boston: Little, Brown, 1992

Newcomb, Horace, and Robert Alley, *The Producer's Medium: Conversations with Creators of American TV,* New York: Oxford University Press, 1983

Schatz, Thomas, "Desilu, I Love Lucy, and the Rise of Network TV," in *Making Television: Authorship and the Production Process,* edited by Robert Thompson and Gary Burns, New York: Praeger, 1993

Selnow, Gary, and Richard R. Gilbert, *Society's Impact on Television: How the Viewing Public Shapes Television Programming,* Westport, Connecticut: Praeger, 1993

Professional Wrestling. *See* **Wrestling on Television**

Programming

The term *programming* refers both to television content and to strategies of content selection and presentation. Yet shifts in the medium over the past two decades have called into question the apparently obvious nature of both. Modern television, after all, goes beyond the broadcast-based mode of operation that shaped the medium for so many years. Today a television is not just a set for receiving entertainment, but also a device for viewing videotapes, playing computerized games, or going channel surfing. Increasingly, it is also a means of telecommunication, of accessing dedicated information services, or of transacting home shopping. These events leave a single obvious definition of television programming—whatever appears on a television set—unwieldy and highly mutable.

Another definition of television programming might turn on the formal aspects of content appearing on the tube. But in fact, many elements of television programming have never been limited exclusively to television. Historically, television programming has borrowed liberally from other media. In addition, Hollywood promotion, sponsor marketing, and the self-promotion of the television industry have long ensured that the imaginative worlds of television characters and stories are also available through T-shirts, toys, or other products. Much television programming, in fact, serves as part of the staged release of products by horizontally integrated entertainment companies like Paramount, Time Warner, or Disney.

The essential point in these processes is that television programming rarely appears in discrete, isolable units or displays an innately "televisual" form. Instead programming is often part of a broader set of commercial or cultural trends that are being drawn upon, commented upon, or manipulated.

Moreover, these trends are continually being reconfigured by the appearance of new technologies and businesses that establish new potential forms and forums for programming. U.S. television programming may once have been defined by Hollywood studios and U.S. television networks, but increasingly it seems likely to be defined by AT&T, Microsoft, Netscape, or America Online—companies bringing different business agendas, technical expertise, and marketing strategies to newly reconceived "texts" and "audiences."

This tie to larger sequences of events is one of the major reasons that television programming provokes broader cultural analysis and evaluation by viewers, regulators, and critics. Certainly contemporary television programming—in whatever form—seems to be more socially significant, and more revelatory of general cultural dialogue, than, say, contemporary opera, or even contemporary written literature. The idea of programming, indeed, might be better served by abandoning narrow definitions based on content or form and focusing on a set of social processes organized under the rubric of television programming. From this view, ultimately, television programming is a historically developed, changing cultural system for circulating and transforming meaning and value—a system collectively shared and supported by television producers, distributors, and users, who subscribe to and bend its priorities through their participation.

Programming, then, is a process for imbuing public value that—advertisers, celebrities, government officials, cultural monitors, and program producers all hope—can be traded in later for cash or the political power to continue their specific forms of program production and distribution. Treating programming as a processual cultural system for the circulation of meaning and value is to focus on television programming as always organized but always changing. Any examination of television programming must ultimately analyze such a system institutionalized through an array of activities.

Programming as Industrialized Commodity

The variety of television formats—and the continuing fluidity of television genres within this social process—stem from programming's status as a malleable form that can be developed for profit in often divergent ways. They stem, in short, from programming's status as a commodity.

Yet television programming is a complex and expensive product, and profitability demands standardization and routinization as much as it requires entrepreneurial experimentation or market differentiation. Programming standards and routines—and the scope for innovation—depend intimately on the financial and political configuration of the medium at any moment. And so programming emerged as a fluid commodity form whose diversity, mode of address, and regularity are delimited, at any given time, by television's industrial underpinnings.

In the first five decades of television, for example, the difficulties of developing the new medium typically meant that television lay in the hands of institutions that could weather high start-up costs and that would benefit from crucial economies of scale in the medium's use. The result was early broadcasting's distinctive mode of address: wide audiences were typically exposed to a handful of channels centrally programmed by institutions seeking large audiences, institutions like national commercial networks in the United States, or the state in the Soviet systems, or to sets of certain cultural expectations, as in the Reithian version of the British Broadcasting Corporation (BBC). Programming had to conform respectively to the dramatic expectations and financial investments provided by advertisers, to the ideological goals and prescriptions of government bureaucracies, or to the standards of cultural guardians and tutors.

Over the decade of the 1990s, however, the nature of programming was profoundly renovated. New institutions put forward a different set of economic, technological, and organizational arrangements and sought to profit from television in ways that diverged from the centralized broadcasting model. The commodity of programming was accordingly complicated and differentiated.

These developments suggest how specifically early television programming focused on wide, simultaneous presentation of a limited number of information and entertainment formats. And they suggest that programming is not a static collection of texts or conventions, but rather a flexible notion, a locus of potential commodities whose capacity to convey meaning or particular kinds of social exchange can be redefined as the institutions profiting from them alter their strategies.

Though it is familiar enough to seem simple, then, television programming is a complicated cultural phenomenon establishing a shared speculative reality among wide audiences. The next section focuses on the specific ways in which television programming developed as a commodity under the U.S. broadcast network model. The focus on the United States is limiting, but instructive, since U.S. television programming, like U.S. filmmaking, has enjoyed a disproportionate influence on television worldwide—an advantage not coincidentally related to U.S. television's elaboration of effective means for attracting unprecedented investment, controlling risk, and developing efficiencies of production, distribution, and exhibition of its commodity texts. Despite the considerable strictures of its commodity form, however, U.S. television programming has also experienced considerable development and elaboration, as changing institutional relationships have altered the financial strategies behind programming.

Historical Changes in U.S. Programming

For the first three years, television programming was all live, since there existed no feasible means of recording the signal produced by television cameras. Shows were confined to studios or to on-location programs. In the United States, studios were located in network headquarters in New York—yet in the medium's first five years, from 1948 to 1953, the networks did not produce much of their programming. Instead, sponsors hired advertising agencies to design, budget, and produce shows that fit their marketing needs. Sponsor-controlled production suited the new networks, which could not afford to produce the quantity of programming they had promised affiliates, particularly in such an experimental and trouble-prone medium. Sponsors were encouraged to purchase the time slot they wished and think of it as their franchise, to develop as they so desired. In the words of David Sarnoff, the president of RCA, NBC's holding company, the network existed simply as a "pipeline" for sponsors.

After 1953, however, television became less uncertain, and networks began to suspect they could maximize profits by undertaking their own program production, centralizing control over the schedule, and extending the still-haphazard programming day to new time slots. Under president Sylvester Weaver, NBC ejected recalcitrant sponsors and advertising agencies and launched new network-produced live programs— *Today, Tonight,* and *Home,* a failed afternoon program—which made programming an ever-present commodity. Weaver also undertook a concerted effort to popularize television through expensive, attention-grabbing, variety show "spectaculars." His expensive strategies were effective, so much so that by 1955 they were no longer needed, and he was succeeded, quickly, by a new generation of executives who boosted profitability through routinization.

In 1954 and 1955 the U.S. networks turned to a new program source that would become a central part of modern television worldwide: Hollywood. The first routinely filmed television show, *I Love Lucy,* had begun in 1951, but filming remained the exception rather than the rule. By 1955 Hollywood—as part of its long-term response to the Paramount Decree of 1948, an antitrust agreement that forced the studios to sell their highly lucrative theater chains—was ready to consider television a crucial new client and point of exhibition. The result of the partnership was a new standard of television programming, the telefilm mass-produced by newly formed divisions of the Hollywood studios.

The concerted move to products of the Hollywood factory system altered the look and production of programming. The plays that had composed much of earlier television programming drew frequently on writers and actors available from Manhattan theater, radio, and literary circles. Live television, moreover, had frequently depended on "anthology" programs that could vary considerably from week to week. The telefilm's use of recurrent actors, sets, stock footage, and dramatic formulas, by contrast, helped establish the recurring series as the basis of television programming and emphasized programming's standardization. The results prompted many critics to consider earlier live TV a "Golden Age" of television drama. Others have subsequently questioned the aesthetic superiority of live TV, granting its spontaneity and occasional dramatic ambitions, but pointing to the persistent incursion of ads within sponsor-produced shows, and questioning, ironically, the consistency of its achievements.

Programming in the 1960s reflected a stabilizing network oligopoly. Series had longer average runs than shows in later decades. The number of cancellations per season declined steadily. Even the networks' relative position remained fixed: CBS continued building a remarkable (and given later events, a decidedly induplicable) 20 years as the number one network in television ratings. ABC, the smallest and youngest network, remained the perennial third; NBC in the middle. Throughout the decade, however, all three networks' ratings converged. Their programming philosophy was summed up by NBC's Paul Klein, who articulated a policy: Least Objectionable Programming. Viewers, the philosophy assumed, will watch anything unless they are offended into changing the channel. Many critics have consequently regarded 1960s programming—characterized by the most popular show in television history, *The Beverly Hillbillies*—as assembly line, escapist TV, though others are reexamining the presumed homogeneity of programming in the period. The perennial third-place network, ABC, was in some respects the most interesting, introducing shows that titillated (*Bracken's World, Love American Style*), sought out young audiences (*The Flying Nun*), or highlighted the spectacular (*ABC's Wide World of Sports*).

A decisive break in programming came in 1970. That year, three milestone developments—the cigarette ad ban, the Prime Time Access Rule, and the Financial Interest and Syndication Rules—prompted the networks to address an inevitable question: how could continued network growth come from the finite amount of advertising time available on television, and the inevitable plateauing of demand by advertisers. The primary answer was to develop finer demographic targeting, a strategy that could make some shows more expensive than the prevailing norm. The consequence was a new emphasis on programming that would attract varying demographics. Differentiation rather than standardization, and active attraction rather than innocuousness, became the basis of network strategies. In 1969 CBS president Robert Wood canceled 13 shows appealing to older and rural audiences in favor of a more urban, higher-income audience. Among the replacements were the three innovative sitcoms that served as the basis for what later critics have called the "Television Renaissance": *The Mary Tyler Moore Show, All in the Family,* and *M*A*S*H,* programs that ultimately found broad appeal, yet did so through ambitious character development, topical controversy, and innovative production styles. "Quality" television had emerged as a desirable, even necessary commodity for the networks to develop.

CBS's move contradicts a common tenet that the last-place network in the oligopoly was the most likely to experiment with innovative programming in an effort to raise its standing. Third-place standing could be a powerful motive for some innovations, but it was probably only the perennial first-place network, CBS, that could have risked such an abrupt and wholesale change in programming philosophy.

Not only did television programming develop a more complex hierarchy of quality after 1970, it became less of an anonymous, industrial product. Some producers, like Norman Lear, Stephen Cannell, Aaron Spelling, and Steve Bochco, became household names and were credited with functioning as television authors. At the same time, the first generations of TV children were achieving adulthood and brought to their viewing a cumulative, retrospective acquaintance with the history of programming. Producers and viewers alike became more self-conscious about television programming's variety, its capacities as an expressive medium, and its historical depth.

For producers, these developments marked a codification of unstated industry practices, into more self-consciously assumed production "styles," "authorial"

qualities, and, increasingly, "innovative" distribution and mode of exhibition. Independent producer Stephen Cannell, for example, began to develop an entire menu of programs—some for prime time, some for syndication, some exclusively for cable, each with different target appeals, and each observing different budgetary constraints according to expected income. Yet all bore the Cannell imprimatur—made explicit by a trailer following each show, in which Cannell flourishingly ripped a script from a typewriter. In one show designed for fringe-hour cable, Cannell appeared personally as host, using his name recognition to attract audiences to a highly tongue-in-cheek suspense anthology reminiscent of the old *Alfred Hitchcock Presents.* The show's appeal—actively dwelling on its divergence from prime-time budgets, topics, and taste—presumed a much more complex sense of televisual position and quotation than would have been normal in 1960s programming.

By 1988 the networks, surrounded by new competition, were in the historically unique position of having to react to program trends, rather than working to select and cultivate them. The emergence of the FOX broadcast network in 1986—the Big Three's first viable competition—was based in programming that parodied or transgressed the oligopoly's genres. It used irreverence to target and imply a savvy, urban, youthful audience. When FOX did use more routine forms, it put in a twist by featuring black characters, assuring disproportionately large and loyal black audiences. Prime-time television on the Big Three—which, despite falling audiences, still constituted the industrial, financial, and aesthetic point of reference—began to reflect the influence of FOX, music videos, syndicated tabloid shows, and producers (often arriving from filmmaking) whose projects were conceived for multiple distribution. From 1988 to 1990, the networks actively experimented with new generic hybrids and outre programming with shows like *Twin Peaks, Bagdad Cafe,* and *Northern Exposure.*

Accompanying these changes was a profound shift in the cultural role of programming. Given the medium's persistent popularity, the finite amount of programming available under the three-network oligopoly had served as a prominent and recognizable social touchstone, a set of social facts that most Americans acknowledged and shared as part of their national culture. In the days before videotape, such programming had also been ephemeral, assuming the aspect of an occasion or experience; and programming's simultaneous broadcast nationwide made that ephemeral experience a uniquely collective one. Programming, then, possessed the attributes of a public ritual, through which viewers collectively attended to experiences constituting a sense of social connection through the establishment of collective representations.

Just as pronounced was the sense of comparative propriety and circumspection in programming prevailing under the network oligopoly. Aware that their most unique commodity was widespread acceptance by audiences—and that the U.S. regulatory framework defined broadcasting as a public resource serving the public interest—networks used censors to enforce what they regarded as prevailing public mores of sexuality, violence, and sensationalism. Individual networks occasionally sought to boost ratings through titillation or scandal, but these attempts were measured departures from conventional TV standards that remained far more circumscribed than the license taken routinely in films or novels.

As television programming began to expand beyond the three-channel network system, its ritual aspects and its highly conventionalized moral circumspection began to dissolve. Shows were no longer singular, punctual experiences, once they could be recorded, viewed later the same day in syndication, or bought at a video store. Audiences were no longer collective and mass, but fragmented according to the particular time and venue they chose to engage a program. Moreover, viewers choosing from many, rather than just three, options were arguably less of a public, and more of a self-elected fractional interest group, likely to be watching programming that could diverge dramatically from "mainstream" interests or values. With the decline of the three networks, then, programming became less of a central social ritual attended by wide audiences, and more of a varied, highly differentiated medium circulating commodities that could be more casually engaged by viewers. Scholars of the 1970s had identified television programming as a public forum and a modern bard. By the 1990s television programming arguably constituted a variegated cultural "newsstand."

This alteration has intensified throughout the 1990s and into the new century. One major contributing factor has been the growth of cable and satellite television systems, especially those enhanced with digital delivery capability. These systems regularly offer more than 100 channels, many of them highly specialized, targeted toward specific demographic groups (witness the growth in offerings for children) or particular interests—sports programming morphs into The Golf Channel and multiple channels for sports news and information; MTV spins off channels specializing in particular musical genres and faces competition from multiple channels focused on music; 24-hour news programming expands; and some channels offer spe-

cific appeals to audiences with particular political interests.

Many of the new channels were owned or co-owned by networks or studios producing television content for broadcast, and new strategies developed to make maximum financial use of programs. "Repurposing" described a procedure in which a program would appear in one venue only to be presented in another during the same week. Local broadcasters protested the use of network material on cable or satellite, arguing that the practice reduced the size of their audiences, thereby reducing potential advertising revenue. They were less concerned, however, when programming flowed in the other direction. When Bravo, the NBC-owned cable network, discovered a bona fide hit with *Queer Eye for the Straight Guy*, broadcasters profited from the migration of the show to the network.

Other new technologies intensified the capability of viewers to act as their own programmers. Digital video recorders such as TiVo and RePlay made recording television programs much simpler than videocassette recorders had allowed, even making it possible for viewers to collect an entire "season" of a single title, playing back episodes at will—and fast-forwarding through commercials. In a somewhat related development, some popular television shows began to be available for rental on VHS and DVD formats. Viewers without access to premium distribution channels such as HBO could rent *The Sopranos* or *Sex and the City*, or even earlier programs such as *The Prisoner* and view them on home video systems.

The profound alterations outlined here have been paralleled by an equally important set of institutional arrangements and developments designed to best control television programming at any given time.

Institutional Changes in Broadcast Programming

As a commodity, commercial programming is produced following familiar priorities of standardization (to control costs), differentiation (to penetrate markets), and innovation conceived largely as variation within repetition (to contain risk). Although some critics regard these attributes as evidence of programming's lamentable role in manifesting the values of the marketplace, others see them as "enabling conditions" establishing some of television programming's most unique and recognizable pleasures.

Perhaps the strongest symptom of commercial programming's commodity status is its common organization into recurrent daily or weekly series. U.S. television is not generally filled with unique, onetime programs. Such programming would frustrate not only producers and networks, who are trying to extract reliably continuous income from television, but viewers too, who (many commentators would argue) are accustomed by consumer society to pleasure that is organized around a continual but measured introduction of novelty. Unlike a painting or a novel, a television show that appears once is unsatisfyingly ephemeral, while a show that is exactly reproduced is just a rerun. The series format, in which episodes invoke familiar settings and characters in slightly varied situations, satisfies ambitions both for more of the same and for something new. The series allows producers to develop long-term elaborations and complications of characters and situations that (most notoriously in the case of the soap opera) can make a program's fictional world part of the viewer's own. Such involvement also makes viewers' loyalty to the show into a reliable commodity that networks can either sell to advertisers or use to secure reliable subscriber fees. At the same time, the series routinizes production schedules and standardizes the costs that producers and networks must expect to pay to produce a new week of programming.

The seasonal schedule long prevalent in the United States also served to routinize production, viewing, and advertising sales not just week to week, but on a yearly calendar, which concentrated the industry's introduction of novelty in a single spectacular moment. The impending fall season could foment substantial bidding wars for the coming years' commercial slots, by advertisers involved in active speculation over the popularity of future programs. Definite seasons were a strong fixture of the industry when it was dominated by the oligopoly of ABC, NBC, and CBS, but new developments such as overnight ratings systems, competition from cable and syndication, and the rise of new networks such as FOX have blurred the outlines of these markers.

Conventions like the length of a series and the integrity of the season alter, in fact, with changing pressures within the industry. In the 1960s, during the height of a stable three-way network monopoly, U.S. TV functioned on a reliable calendar inherited from radio, in which a 39-week season was interrupted by a 13-week summer rerun period (the lack of new summer production costs enhanced profits for networks). As competition for network growth became more intense after 1970, and as viewers began to abandon network television for cable and syndication after 1976, networks became more reluctant to make long-term mistakes and tried routinely to contract a minimum of episodes—as few as four at a time in 1990.

If series programming forms a major part of the schedule in order to regularize viewership and cultivate loyalty over the long term, shorter-run formats like the docudrama, miniseries, the sports special, and feature film introduce a sense of novelty and occasion, of divergence from one's own routine and that of competitors. Often they represent attempts to capitalize on timely, singular events—a sports championship, a scandalous murder, political intrigue—which are likely to have sufficient recognition to ensure a large immediate audience. (Here entertainment blurs indissolubly into information.) Historically, the most persistent complement to standard series programming have been feature films licensed from Hollywood studios and run under titles such as the *Wednesday Movie of the Week.*

The commodity form of television programming is evident not just in the rhythm of seasons and the length of series, but in the specific distribution of shows among eight "dayparts." Scheduling strategies and purchases of advertising time vary with dayparts, each of which fosters unique genres in an effort to attract the presumably distinctive audiences available at different times of the day. Many critics suggest that television's dayparts ultimately represent the penetration of rationalized economic organization into the most mundane, casual, and intimate activities of domestic life; others suggest that they form the basis for familiar pleasures and ease of use. The composition of dayparts has changed historically, but since the mid-1980s typical dayparts for an ideal typical U.S. network affiliate station have remained relatively stable.

Early Morning (7:00–10:00 A.M.)
Audience: adults preparing for work; preschool children. Programming: news, talk; local or network

Daytime (10:00 A.M.–6:00 P.M.)
Audience: midmorning until midafternoon, "housewives." Programming: talk, fiction (soap operas) networks, syndicated. Audience: midafternoon until early evening, children. Programming: cartoons and light drama; local, network, and syndicated.

Early Fringe (6:00–7:00 P.M.)
Audience: elders and adults returning from work. Programming: news; local and network

Prime Access (7:00–8:00 P.M.)
Audience: busy adults in the home, children. Programming: "infotainment," game shows, comedies; syndicated, local.

Prime Time (8:00–11:00 P.M.)
Audience: first hour, "family"; progressively "adult." Programming: comedy, into melodrama, action-adventure, etc.; network.

Late Fringe (11:00–11:30 P.M.)
Audience: Adults. Programming: news; local.

Late Night (11:30 P.M.–12:30 A.M.)
Audience: Adults, "liminal adults" (maturing adolescents). Programming: talk shows, fiction; network, syndicated.

Overnight (12:30–7:00 A.M.)
Audience: Adults, liminal adults. Programming: syndicated talk, comedy, drama, and "old movies"; network, syndicated.

Though these conventionally labeled audiences reflect the hoped-for targets of advertisers, from the viewer's perspective they constitute modes of address that do not necessarily conform with actual identities. Many teenagers, for example, probably indulge in late-night programming explicitly to feel more like liminal adults; while many single adults enjoy the warm and fuzzy feelings of early-evening shows "aimed" at children.

The highly familiar succession of genres and implied audiences associated with dayparts reflects the U.S. medium's priority on maximizing available viewership at all times, in order to maximize the fees advertisers will pay. Important dayparts accrue an identifiable tone: early morning, a hale, nationwide conviviality that orients viewers to the day; early fringe, a local-community focus supported by the plethora of local ads sold by affiliates; prime access, the netherworld of syndicated tabloid and game shows. Prime time, of course, is the costliest, most watched period of television, featuring the most elaborately produced dramas, comedies, or films, and harboring the greatest sense of public event. Late night engages in moral license for off-color humor in the part of the day most distant from work and school, and having a presumably adult audience.

Systems with less stake in appealing to audiences often develop a less-differentiated programming day. Even within the United States, the tendency to target dayparts remains most pronounced on the major networks and their affiliates and is less consistent on cable and independent channels whose appeal may already lie in a particular audience segment, programming genre, or for that matter, in programming against the norm set by broadcast television.

In the United States between 1950 and 1984, the overwhelming majority of profitable stations were affiliates of one of the three major networks. New network shows were the most ambitious production on television, and their contractually secured prominence in favored dayparts made them the most familiar to audiences. All network programs, however, eventually lost enough of their popularity to be removed from network schedules. The most successful then entered into circulation in the piecemeal syndication market that sold programs for rebroadcast on U.S. stations during dayparts not filled by network feeds—or to international markets. Syndication was thus responsible for a distinctive kind of programming based on the reuse of proven commodities: the rerun.

Syndication of network programs was highly profitable, since it involved the recycling of commodities whose production costs had been almost entirely paid for by network fees. Originally, U.S. networks tried to secure syndication profits by demanding part ownership of a show as a condition for airing it, but this became illegal because of antitrust concerns in 1970. As product suppliers assumed control, syndication quickly became less of an appendage to network programming, and more of a competitor. When the number of television stations in the United States increased dramatically in 1984 (because of relaxed regulation of television licenses), a wholly alternative market for syndicated programming suddenly emerged. Demand for additional shows was sufficient to stimulate a boom in first-run syndication—programs produced exclusively for individual bidding stations and never intended for network release. The syndication market was a somewhat poorer one than the traditional network oligopoly, and so first-run syndication frequently constituted a kind of B-grade programming.

As networks audiences continued to decline throughout the 1980s, suppliers became less concerned with a long-standing convention governing reruns. Networks had typically preferred their programming to be exclusive and had discouraged early episodes of a current program from airing in syndication while the show still remained part of the network lineup. In the mid-1980s, offers from independent stations and cables channels for network-quality programming became too lucrative to ignore, and so it became common for viewers to be able to see a show on the same day from two radically different perspectives: as the wholly novel experience of a new network episode, and as a reencounter with syndicated episodes from the show's past. This accentuated the series nature of programming and made retrospective evaluation of dramatic characters and situations a routine part of viewing. It also undermined the networks' sense of exclusive venue by emphasizing the independence of shows from particular channels.

In sum, syndication—the attempt to increase profits through reuse of old programming or to develop cheaper alternatives to network programming—complicated and enriched the body of television programming, introducing historical depth; a new "low end" of programming inviting self-conscious irony in viewing; multiple, simultaneous views of individual series; and a divorce of specific shows from previously inevitable network lineups. Changes that demanded that programming serve as a commodity in new ways also altered how programming would be used as a text. As indicated earlier, expansion of cable and satellite delivery systems, new digital recording systems, and the commercial sale and rental of television series directly to viewers modified all the conventions of television's first three decades. Seasons became more erratic. Dayparts continued to be targeted by demography, but even more so by age, as "aging down" to younger audiences affected categories and forms such as talk shows and soap operas. As audiences "fragmented" or "segmented" into smaller groups, the difficulty of creating a "hit" show that could last for many years became more and more difficult. Thus, while expanding delivery systems demanded more and more syndicated material, fewer and fewer programs achieved the longevity associated with the practice. More "first-run" syndication emerged as original programming, and cable networks, like the conventional broadcast networks, joined the search for creative talent capable of producing original programming.

Programming Strategies

Commercial television generally profits from advertising revenues, which increase with audience size. Both local stations and networks thus devote considerable effort to structuring their programming to hold the largest desirable audiences possible.

The premium on holding audiences leads to one of the most identifiable characteristics of commercial U.S. television: its continual interruption by commercials. The industry has long presumed that viewers are alienated by commercials and will only watch them if they are interspersed with other programming. The length, frequency, and grouping of ads is a constantly renegotiated aspect of the television ad market. Networks try to limit ads to keep prices high and viewers tuned in, while advertisers try to secure many commercials—short, cheap, and well separated from those of the competition. In the long term, advertisers' demands have steadily decreased the length, increased the frequency, and fragmented the grouping of ads, making commercial television seem increasingly like a cluttered "flow" of programming.

Programming strategies are not, of course, limited to the distribution of advertisements. Station and network programmers work concertedly not just to select attractive programming, but to sequence shows in a way that will hold audiences once they have tuned in. A number of tactics have been developed to build a profitable schedule.

"Block programming" involves scheduling a series of related shows that are likely to attract and hold a given audience for an entire daypart. U.S. stations and networks, for example, have traditionally filled Saturday mornings with cartoons aimed at children, and Sunday afternoons with (presumably) male-oriented sports. A block may be defined by particular demographics, but its definition can take other forms. From 1984 to 1987 NBC scheduled a famous Thursday evening lineup featuring five critically acclaimed series in a row: *Cosby, Family Ties, Cheers, Night Court,* and *Hill Street Blues.* The first four were sitcoms that attracted such inclusive audiences that they ended most years in the top 20. The last program was an innovative drama with a much smaller, but quite exclusive audience whose demographics made *Hill Street Blues'* advertising rates the highest of the season. Despite their differences, all five programs were treated as an identifiable block of programming because they fostered NBC's strategy of offering a night of high-quality television.

Block programming has become increasingly overt, and now it is quite common for cable or broadcast networks to package particular nights of programming as blocks devoted to "Our Television Heritage," "Bette Davis Night," on "All Comedy Night." Such promotions potentially highlight aspects of shows that viewers may not have conceived alone: as in the case of reruns, programming's nature as a commodity that can be packaged can affect the public's appreciation of shows.

"Counterprogramming" involves running an attractive alternative to competitors' shows. CBS, for example, has tried several times to develop Monday night as a lineup of shows attractive to women, whom they presume are alienated by ABC's ratings-leading *Monday Night Football.*

"Hammocking" refers to scheduling a new or comparatively unpopular show between two established popular programs, on the theory that audiences are less likely to change channels for a single time slot. Hammocking has historically been a reliable strategy, raising the ratings of the middle show, if not always making it into a hit. The risk is that the weak show will diminish audiences that would have stayed if the two popular programs had formed a block. "Lead-ins" and "lead-outs," like hammocking, try to achieve success through association, lead-ins by placing a popular program right before a lower-rated one, lead-outs by placing the popular program immediately after the less-successful show. Historically, lead-ins have proved more successful. "Bridging" staggers the start of a long-format program so that viewers would have to abandon it in the middle in order to tune in to the beginning of the competitor's show. "Ridgepoling" distributes the individual shows comprising a successful block across different nights of the week, where they can serve as lead-ins (or -outs) for additional programming.

New or ailing stations and networks have frequently reversed their fate by combining these strategies: after establishing a minimal block of two or three programs, they will extend the block by hammocking a new show. Then each of the shows in the block will be ridgepoled to establish a foothold on several nights of the week.

"Stunting" refers to a variety of exceptional tactics used to boost viewership during key weeks of the season, or when a network, station, or program is in special trouble. Frequent stunts involve programming a highly promoted miniseries or feature film to attract concentrated viewer attention; having one show's star appear on another program; or mounting highly promoted, end-of-season weddings, births, or cliffhangers. More dramatic stunts involve delaying the season debut of a highly popular program a few weeks in order to build suspense—and, hopefully, steal audiences decisively away from competitors' just-rolling season. In 1990 CBS pulled a stunt that experimented with long-held presumptions about the acceptable frequency and amount of repetition allowed on network prime time. Following the example of syndication and cable channels, it ran each episode of a new series (*The Flash*) in two different time slots each week. The idea was both to save money and to give the show twice the chance for its audience to discover it and build loyalty. The experiment failed. The seeming incongruity of such an attempts attests to how strongly the conventional season and schedule format organizes producers' and viewers' expectations for different varieties of television programming: what works for syndication did not work for network prime time.

Programming in Other National Contexts

This history of programming in the U.S. television system should serve to emphasize its differences from other national systems, which are grounded in different forms of financial support and different regulatory circumstances. In the public-service tradition, for example, most closely identified with the British Broadcasting Corporation, programmers are mandated to provide diversity. Free of the advertiser's necessary search for the largest audience or the audience with the most purchasing power, alternative forms of programming may be provided to minority audiences. More attention may be paid to children and elder groups. Linguistic distinctions can be more readily recognized and honored. Moreover, programming schedules need not be so regularized and routinized; "seasons" and "dayparts" need not be so rigidly applied. As a result, expectations of creative communities, industries, and audiences may all be different from those attached to the U.S. system.

In the Soviet model, also free from advertiser demands, programming took on yet other configurations, more closely aligned to state agendas and more overtly ideological goals. Here again, the routines and patterns were easily altered by fiat.

Throughout the world, mixtures of these systems have been developed, often forged in specific relationships to neighboring nations and almost always in some relation to the U.S. television industry, which often supplied supplemental programming, even in systems constructed along lines of the Soviet model. But as ideological, technological, economic, and regulatory shifts have spread, more and more the patterns of industrial and programming arrangements seem to converge. The "newsstand" model is now expanded by satellites to a global level, and it has become possible to acquire "information" and "entertainment" in many languages and forms or to observe changes within specific nations and regions that are the direct result of new technological configurations.

In India, for example, the publicly operated state broadcast channels long offered an "official" version of news. As household videotape machines became more common, however, alternative monthly video newsmagazines emerged, supported by subscribers. These video magazines offered fuller exposés into important events. Because they were directed at those wealthy enough to own videotape machines, they also served to constitute a self-conscious elite, newly defined by its well-informedness. Here programming is again tied to the shifting institutional arrangements that enable production, distribution, and exhibition, and the specific kind of commodity formed by programming delimits, not just its financial viability, but its historical aesthetic, social, and cultural import.

In this process the struggles of nations and regions to maintain forms of aesthetic, social, and cultural autonomy and distinction—to place their own items on the global newsstand or to construct a continuing local identity—are now carried out in relation to international media conglomerates. These organizations make use of new technologies that blur national boundaries as easily as they blur program genres and once again throw television programming into a process of significant redefinition. All the technological developments and industrial practices described are increasingly common throughout much of the world. Multiple channels, increasing commercialization, 24-hour schedules, new devices for recording and programming in the home—all these have altered the meanings and uses of television programming in some ways while maintaining received practices in others. Even when new developments appear radical or startling, the old patterns often lie just beneath the surface. Television programming has become a familiar feature of social experience and is likely to remain so for some time.

MICHAEL SAENZ

See also **Arledge, Roone; Australian Programming; British Programming; Canadian Programming; Dann, Michael; Family Viewing Time; Goldenson, Leonard; Genre; Independent Production Companies; Paley, William S.; Prime Time; Reruns/Repeats; Sarnoff, David; Silverman, Fred; Syndication; Tartikoff, Brandon; United States: Networks; Weaver, Sylvester (Pat)**

Further Reading

Allen, Robert, *Speaking of Soap Opera,* Chapel Hill: University of North Carolina Press, 1985

Anderson, Christopher, *Hollywood TV,* Austin: University of Texas Press, 1994

Barker, David, "Television Production Techniques as Communication," in *Television: The Critical View,* edited by Horace Newcomb, New York: Oxford University Press, 1976; 4th edition, 1987

Bergreen, Laurence, *Look Now, Pay Later,* Garden City, New York: Doubleday, 1980

Boddy, William, *Fifties Television: The Industry and Its Critics,* Urbana: University of Illinois Press, 1990

Feuer, Jane, "The Concept of Live TV: Ontology as Ideology," in *Regarding Television,* edited by E. Ann Kaplan, Frederick, Maryland: American Film Institute and University Publications of America, 1983

Feuer, Jane, Paul Kerr, and Tise Vahimagi, editors, *MTM "Quality Television,"* London: British Film Institute, 1984

Fiske, John, and John Hartley, *Reading Television,* London: Methuen, 1978

Gitlin, Todd, *Inside Prime Time,* New York: Pantheon, 1983

Gitlin, Todd, "Prime Time Ideology: The Hegemonic Process in Television Entertainment," in *Television: The Critical View,* edited by Horace Newcomb, New York: Oxford University Press, 1976; 4th edition, 1987

Jameson, Frederic, *Signatures of the Visible,* New York: Routledge, 1992

Kepley, Vance Jr., "From 'Frontal Lobes' to the 'Bob-and-Bob' Show: NBC Management and Programming Strategies, 1949–65," in *Hollywood in the Age of Television,* edited by Tino Balio, Cambridge, Massachusetts: Unwin-Hyman, 1990

Newcomb, Horace, and Paul Hirsch, "Television as a Cultural Forum," in *Television: The Critical View,* edited by Horace Newcomb, New York: Oxford University Press, 1976; 4th edition, 1987

Thorburn, David, "Television Melodrama," In *Television: The Critical View,* edited by Horace Newcomb, New York: Oxford University Press, 1976; 4th edition, 1987

Williams, Raymond, *Television: Technology and Cultural Form,* New York: Schocken, 1974

PROMAX

PROMAX International (formerly Broadcast Promotion and Marketing Executives, or BPME) is the trade organization for media promotion and marketing professionals. Founded in the United States in 1956 as the Broadcast Promotion Association (BPA), its name changes tellingly reflect the substantial changes experienced by the electronic media industries since the mid-20th century.

Initially, "broadcast promotion" was the term for media efforts conducted by television and radio stations to maximize the size of audiences and the numbers of advertisers. These efforts largely consisted of date/time program announcements on the station's own air coupled with print advertisements in the local media (particularly *TV Guide* in the case of television

promotion). More elaborate promotion campaigns were usually handled by the networks. Sweeping industry changes in the 1970s and 1980s—including the lessening of the dominance of the commercial networks, the growing importance of locally produced news, the rise of cable and pay-TV services, increases in program production costs, and the growth of syndicated programming—resulted in a significantly more complex media environment and led to the need for more-sophisticated promotion techniques. Consequently, in 1985 the organization changed its name to Broadcast Promotion and Marketing Executives to reflect the increasing importance of marketing principles such as the use of consumer research, competitive positioning, long-range planning, and audience segmentation. An ever-more-rapidly changing media scene in the late 1980s and early 1990s—including the growth of nonbroadcast program distribution channels and increasingly international webs of participation—led to a second major name change, to PROMAX International, in 1993.

PROMAX, a loose acronym for Promotion and Marketing Executives in the Electronic Media, employs a full-time paid president and staff and receives oversight from a volunteer board of directors composed of industry personnel. Focusing on the fields of television (including broadcast, cable, and satellite), radio, and digital media, the organization supports a wide range of related activities including promotion, marketing, advertising, public relations, design, sales, and community service. Among its services to members are the electronic magazine *PROMAX Online,* which reports on industry events and developments, key issues, notable campaigns, and new products, services, and techniques (available on the Web and via e-mail); an annual directory/promotion planner listing members and suppliers, as well as key industry dates and events; the Resource Center, located in the organization's Los Angeles headquarters, which houses an extensive collection of videotapes, printed materials, and publications; and a Job Line, which provides information on available positions and job seekers (a key service in a field noted for advancement across, rather than within, markets). Perhaps the most notable service is the organization's annual seminar, where members meet for workshops, demonstrations, presentations, and general network-ing. Suppliers of promotion materials demonstrate their products and services in an exhibit hall, and networks, group owners, and other industry organizations host suites for special presentations. The culmination of the seminar is an awards ceremony recognizing creative excellence.

In addition to ongoing member services, PROMAX awards several academic scholarships in cooperation with sponsoring industry groups. In 1980 the organization published a college text, *Broadcast Advertising and Promotion: A Handbook for Students and Professionals.* It has also conducted numerous surveys over the years on salaries, budgets, staff size, and other departmental measures, which help promotion executives gauge their status and performance according to industry standards.

PROMAX is organizationally linked with the Broadcast Designers' Association (BDA), an association of graphic designers who specialize in creating promotion materials for electronic media. In addition, PROMAX has increasingly expanded its activities to include international affiliations, with branch associations in Australia/New Zealand, Asia, Europe, Latin America, and the United Kingdom.

JERRY HAGINS

Further Reading

Eastman, Susan Tyler, and Robert A. Klein, *Strategies in Broadcast and Cable Promotion,* Belmont, California: Wadsworth, 1982

Webster, Lance, "The Growth Years: BPA to BPME," *BPME Image* (April 1991)

Pryor, Richard (1940–)

U.S. Comedian, Actor

Richard Pryor, comic, writer, and television and film star, was the first African-American stand-up comedian to speak candidly and successfully to integrated audiences using the language and jokes blacks previously only shared among themselves when they were most critical of the United States. His career really began as a high school student, when his teacher persuaded him to discontinue cutting and disrupting class by offering him the opportunity to perform his comic routine once a week for his classmates. Nevertheless, Pryor dropped out of high school, completed a tour of duty in the army, then began playing small clubs and bars, anywhere he could secure a venue. His keen and perceptive observation of people, especially his audiences, enabled him to develop into a gifted monologist, mimic, and mime.

The first phase of his career began in the 1960s, when as a clean-cut imitator of Bill Cosby, Pryor played New York clubs. His material, best suited for an integrated audience, did not contain the cutting-edge

Richard Pryor, May 1974.
Courtesy of the Everett Collection

dialogue for which he later became most noted. By 1970, tired of the constant comparisons to Cosby and feeling disgusted with himself for the direction of his career, he walked off the Las Vegas Aladdin Hotel stage in the middle of a performance. After a two-year hiatus in Berkeley, California, where he spent time reading Malcolm X's work, visiting bars, clubs, and street corners to observe people, and collaborating with a group of African-American writers later known as the "Black Pack," Pryor returned to performing. A metamorphosis took place during those two years, and Pryor offered his audiences a new collection of characters, earthy metaphors, and the tough, rough profane language of the streets. No longer did he mimic Cosby, for he now spoke on behalf of the underclass, and his monologues and jokes reflected their despair and disillusionment with life in the United States.

His performances, enhanced by his use of body language, captured the personalities of the numerous black characters he created to ridicule and comment upon the circumstances under which African Americans lived. It was revolutionary humor. Pryor's characters introduced to his audiences persons from black folklore as well as characters from the streets of Anytown, U.S.A. He integrated his personal style of comedy with commentary on the social condition. His popularity skyrocketed, and his career as a stand-up comedian expanded to that of a television and film star.

The Richard Pryor Show premiered on NBC in 1977 and rocked the censors until, after only five shows, the series was canceled. Television was not ready for his explosive talent, and Pryor was not ready to alter the content of his program. He portrayed the first African-American president of the United States and, in another skit, used costumes and visual distortion to appear nude. Simultaneously, his concert films—full of his impersonations, cockiness, and assertiveness and balanced by his perceptive vulnerability—achieved wide audience appeal and became legendary in their content. *Richard Pryor: Live in Concert* (1979), considered by critics to be one of his best concert films and his first concert released to theaters, showcased Pryor and his unique ability to capture ethnic humor and make it acceptable to a mainstream audience. Pryor appeared on numerous television programs and served as a co-writer for *Blazing Saddles* and as a writer for *Sanford and Son, The Flip Wilson Show,* and *The Lily Tomlin Special,* for which he won an Emmy in 1973.

Even though his early movie roles are forgettable, film served as another venue for Pryor's dangerous and uncontrollable personality. *Lady Sings the Blues* was the turning point. As the Piano Man, Pryor proved he was capable of sustaining a supporting role in a dramatic film. He added life and vitality to the role and to the film. After *Lady Sings the Blues,* he starred or costarred in *The Mack* (1973), *Hit* (1973), *Uptown Saturday Night* (1974), *Car Wash* (1976), *The Bingo Long Traveling All-Stars and Motor Kings* (1976), and *Silver Streak* (1976). Costarring in *Silver Streak* served as another breakthrough for Pryor, and he soon received starring roles in *Which Way Is Up?* (1977) and *Greased Lightning* (1977), among others. His record albums, full of his special humor and street-wise characters, topped the charts: *That Nigger's Crazy* (1974); *Is It Something I Said?* (1975); *Bicentennial Nigger* (1976); and *Wanted, Richard Pryor Live and in Concert* (1979).

In 1980 Pryor sustained third-degree burns over most of his body while, it was reported, he was free-basing cocaine. The response to this tragedy was overwhelming, and Pryor received attention from the media as well as from citizens throughout the United States. He returned to the large screen to complete *Bustin' Loose,* then went on to receive rave reviews for his concert films *Richard Pryor: Live on Sunset Strip*

(1982) and *Richard Pryor: Hear and Now* (1983). The autobiographical film *Jo Jo Dancer, Your Life is Calling* (1986) offered his audiences some insight into his troubled personal life.

After his accident, Pryor's other starring roles in movies did not portray the comic as the dynamic, controversial storyteller he became after his exile in Berkeley. The roles in his latter films presented a meeker, more timid person; and, in *The Toy* (1982), he literally played the toy for a spoiled white child. This character and his dialogue were a far cry from the Pryor persona most admired by his audiences.

Stricken with multiple sclerosis in the 1990s, Pryor appeared on television talk shows and toured infrequently. He still played to sold-out audiences, but the old fire and cutting-edge rhetoric evident in his monologues of the 1970s were missing. Pryor in the 1970s would never allow a heckler to intrude on his story and ruin his timing. The Pryor of the 1990s, weak and deeply affected by his disease, did not give the quick, biting, and sarcastic comeback that would always silence a brave heckler from the audience. He did, however, guest star on the popular situation comedies *Martin* (1993) and *Malcolm and Eddie* (1996).

Richard Pryor and his comic style emancipated African-American humor, and his influence and ascendancy crushed boundaries and opened frontiers in comedy unheard of until he appeared on the concert stage. A testament to his influence was evident in a September 1991 televised gala tribute to Pryor presented by comic stars. In 1998 he was selected as the first recipient of the Mark Twain Award for Humor, presented by the John F. Kennedy Center for the Performing Arts.

BISHETTA D. MERRIT

Richard Pryor. Born Franklin Lenox Thomas in Peoria, Illinois, December 1, 1940. Married numerous times; children: Elizabeth Ann, Richard, Rain, Renee. Served in the U.S. Army, 1958–60. Began career as a stand-up comic in the 1960s; recorded hit comedy album, 1974; co-wrote and starred in motion pictures, since 1974; star of television's *The Richard Pryor Show,* 1977. Member: National Academy of Recording Arts and Sciences; Writers Guild of America. Recipient: Emmy Award, 1973; two American Academy of Humor Awards, 1974; American Writers Guild Award, 1974; Grammy Awards, 1974, 1976; Mark Twain Award for Humor, 1998.

Television

1973	*The Lily Tomlin Special* (co-writer)
1977	*The Richard Pryor Show* (writer, star)
1984–85	*Pryor's Place*

Television Specials (selected)

1973	*The Lily Tomlin Show* (guest)
1973	*Lily* (guest)
1977	*The Richard Pryor Special*
1982	*The Richard Pryor Special*
1982	*Hollywood: The Gift of Laughter* (cohost)
1993	*The Apollo Hall of Fame* (honoree)

Films (selected)

The Busy Body, 1967; *The Green Berets,* 1968; *Wild in the Streets,* 1968; *The Phynx,* 1970; *Dynamite Chicken,* 1970; *Lady Sings the Blues,* 1972; *Hit,* 1973; *Wattstax,* 1973; *The Mack,* 1973; *Some Call It Loving,* 1973; *Blazing Saddles* (co-writer only), 1974; *Adios Amigos* (also writer), 1976; *Car Wash* (also writer), 1977; *Silver Streak* (also writer), 1976; *Greased Lightning,* 1977; *Which Way Is Up?,* 1977; *Blue Collar* (also writer), 1978; *The Wiz,* 1978; *Wholly Moses,* 1980; *In God We Trust,* 1980; *Stir Crazy* (also writer), 1980; *Bustin' Loose* (also producer), 1981; *Live on Sunset Strip,* 1982; *Some Kind of Hero,* 1982; *The Toy* (also director), 1982; *Superman III,* 1983; *Brewster's Millions,* 1985; *Jo Jo Dancer, Your Life Is Calling* (also writer, producer, director), 1986; *Critical Condition,* 1987; *Moving,* 1988; *See No Evil, Hear No Evil,* 1989; *Harlem Nights,* 1989; *Another You,* 1991.

Recordings

That Nigger's Crazy, 1974; *Is It Something I Said?,* 1975; *Bicentennial Nigger,* 1976; *Wanted: Richard Pryor Live and in Concert,* 1979.

Publication

Pryor Convictions, and Other Life Sentences, with Todd Gold, 1995

Public Access Television

Public access television has been one of the most interesting and controversial developments in the intersection between media and democracy within the past several decades. Beginning in the 1970s, cable systems began to offer access channels to the public, so that groups and individuals could make programs for other individuals in their own communities. Access systems began to proliferate, and access programming has been cablecast regularly in such places as New York, Los Angeles, Boston, Chicago, Atlanta, Madison, Urbana, Austin, and perhaps as many as 4,000 other towns or regions (Linder, 1999).

When cable television began to be widely introduced in the early 1970s, the Federal Communications Commission (FCC) mandated in 1972 that "beginning in 1972, new cable systems [and after 1977, all cable systems] in the 100 largest television markets be required to provide channels for government, for educational purposes, and most importantly, for public access." This mandate suggested that cable systems should make available three public access channels to be used for state and local government, education, and community public access use, which collectively came to be referred as PEG access.

"Public access" was construed to mean that the cable company should make available equipment and airtime so that literally anybody could make noncommercial use of the access channel, and say and do anything they wished on a first-come, first-served basis, subject only to obscenity and libel laws. The result was an entirely different sort of programming, reflecting the interests of groups and individuals usually excluded from mainstream television.

The rationale for public access television was that, as mandated by the Federal Communications Act of 1934, the airwaves belong to the people, that in a democratic society it is useful to multiply public participation in political discussion, and that mainstream television severely limited the range of views and opinion. Public access television, then, would open television to the public; it would make possible community participation and thus would be in the public interest of strengthening democracy.

Creating an access system required, in many cases, setting up a local organization to manage the access channels, though in other systems the cable company itself managed the access center. In the beginning, however, few, if any, cable systems made as many as three channels available, but some systems began offering one or two access channels in the early to mid-1970s. The availability of access channels depended, for the most part, on the political clout of local governments and committed, and often unpaid, local groups to convince the cable companies, almost all privately owned, to make available an access channel. A 1979 Supreme Court decision, however, struck down the 1972 FCC ruling on the grounds that the FCC had no authority to mandate access, an authority that supposedly belongs to the U.S. Congress alone. Nonetheless, cable was expanding so rapidly and becoming such a high-growth competitive industry that by the 1980s city governments considering cable systems were besieged by companies making lucrative offers (20- to 80-channel cable systems) and were able to demand access channels and financial support for public access systems as part of their contract negotiations.

Consequently, public access grew significantly during the 1980s and 1990s and the Cable Communications Policy Act of 1984 and the Cable Television Consumer Protection and Competition Act of 1992 provided language that allowed local governments to require public access cable channels as part of their negotiated agreements (Linder, 1999).

Not surprisingly, public access television has been controversial from the beginning. Early disputes revolved around explicit sexuality and obscenity, particularly in New York City where public access schedules with programs like *Ugly George* and *Midnight Blue* drew attention and provoked criticism. Focus then turned to controversial political content when extremist groups such as the Ku Klux Klan and Aryan Nation began distributing programs nationally. Many groups like the American Atheists, labor groups, and a diverse number of political groups began producing programs for syndication, and debates emerged over whether access systems should show programming that was not actually produced in the community where it was originally cablecast.

Despite the controversy, public access television has thrived in many parts of the United States. A few systems charge money for use of facilities, or charge a fee for use of airtime, but due to competitive bidding among cable systems in the 1980s and 1990s for the most lucrative franchises, many cable systems offer free use of equipment, personnel, and airtime, and occasionally even provide free videotapes. In these situations, literally anyone can make use of public access facilities without technical expertise, television experience, or financial resources.

Many public access systems also offer a range of conceptual and technical training programs designed to instruct groups or individuals who wish to make their own programs from conception through final editing. As video equipment costs have rapidly declined it has even become possible for some groups to purchase their own equipment.

In the 1990s, following the trends of talk radio, many talk television access shows emerged. Individuals fielded calls from members of the community and discussed current political problems, or, in some cases, personal problems. In many ways, this "conversational" mode exemplified the community focus and personal orientation of access television, again moving away from mainstream TV designed to reach the largest possible audiences, while creating a host of highly idiosyncratic conversations.

But various actions moving toward greater media deregulation in the 1990s and into the new millennium threaten the continued survival of access, as do the Internet and other new communications technologies. In a highly competitive environment, cable systems may very well close down access systems if there is insufficient government pressure to keep them open, though competitive market pressures might promote the survival of popular access channels. And although the Internet and other emerging delivery systems could render obsolete the relatively low-tech access systems, these same forms of communication may even multiply access television, en-

abling literally any group or individual to make their own television programs and distribute them over the Internet. Whether a more democratic communications system emerges or dissolves is up to citizens who are interested in communicating with other citizens and nourishing instruments of democratic communication such as public access TV. Present trends toward concentration of media ownership, commercialization, and tabloidization of news and information threaten the integrity of the public sphere and the possibilities for democratic communication. If U.S. democracy is to survive and thrive, citizens need to use all instruments of democratic communication such as community radio, public access television, and now the Internet.

DOUGLAS KELLNER

See also **Activist Television; Cable Television: United States**

Further Reading

Alvarez, Sally M., "Reclaiming the Public Sphere: A Study of Public Access Television Programming by the U.S. Labor Movement," Ph.D. diss., University of North Carolina, 1995

Frederiksen, H. Allan, *Community Access Video,* Menlo Park, California: Nowells, 1972

Fuller, Linda K., *Community Television in the United State,.* Westport, Connecticut: Greenwood Press, 1994

Kellner, Douglas, *Television and the Crisis of Democracy,* Boulder, Colorado: Westview Press, 1990

Linder, Laura R., *Public Access Television. America's Electronic Soapbox,* Westport, Connecticut: Praeger, 1999

Phillips, Mary Alice Mayer, *CATV: A History of Community Antenna Television,* Evanston, Illinois: Northwestern University Press, 1972

Ryan, Charlotte, *Prime-Time Activism,* Boston: South End Press, 1991

Public Interest, Convenience, and Necessity

U.S. Broadcasting Policy

Originally contained in U.S. public utility law, the "public interest, convenience, and necessity" provision was incorporated into the Radio Act of 1927 to become the operational standard for broadcast licensees. This act contained a regulatory framework that ensured broadcasters operated within their assigned frequencies and at the appropriate time periods. It not only specified technical requirements, but programming and licensing ones as well. The Communications Act

of 1934 expanded on the Radio Act of 1927 to include the telephone and telegraph industries, and the 1934 law has in turn been amended to accommodate subsequent telecommunications technologies, such as television and cable.

The obligation to serve the public interest is integral to the "trusteeship" model of broadcasting, the philosophical foundation upon which broadcasters are expected to operate. The trusteeship paradigm is used to justify government regulation of broadcasting. It maintains that the electromagnetic spectrum is a limited resource belonging to the public, and only those most capable of serving the public interest are to be entrusted with a broadcast license. The Federal Communications Commission (FCC) is the U.S. government body responsible for determining whether applicants for broadcast licenses meet the requirements to obtain them, and the FCC also further regulates those to whom licenses have been granted.

Interpretation of the "public interest, convenience, and necessity" clause has been a continuing source of controversy. Initially, the Federal Radio Commission (FRC) implemented a set of tests, criteria that would loosely define whether the broadcasting entity was fulfilling its obligation to the listening public. Specifications included program diversity, quality reception, and "character" evaluation of licensees. These initial demands set a precedent for future explications of the public interest.

The pretelevision "Blue Book," as the set of criteria was popularly known, was developed by the FCC in 1946 to evaluate the discrepancy between the programming "promise" and "performance" of radio broadcasters. Since license renewal was dependent on serving the public interest, program content became a significant consideration in this procedure. The "Blue Book" required licensees to promote the discussion of public issues, serve minority interests, and eliminate superfluous advertising. Unpopular with commercial broadcasters, the "Blue Book" was rendered obsolete after five years because of the economic threat it posed.

In its "1960 Program Policy Statement," the FCC echoed similar sentiments pertaining to television broadcasters. In response to assorted broadcasting scandals, the FCC issued this statement to "remind" broadcasters of how to serve the public interest. Although previous tenets of the "Blue Book" were rejected, this revised policy included the "license ascertainment" stipulation, requiring broadcasters to determine local programming needs through distribution and analysis of surveys. However, adherence to such programming policies has never been strictly enforced.

The deregulatory fervor of the 1980s seriously challenged the trusteeship model of broadcasting. Obviously, this same move toward deregulation subsequently challenged the means by which satisfaction of the "public interest, convenience, and necessity" should be determined. The rise of cable television undermined the "scarcity of the spectrum" argument because of the newer system's potential for unlimited channel capacity. The trusteeship model was replaced with the "marketplace" model (which had always undergirded commercial broadcasting in the United States). It was now argued that the contemporary, commercially supported telecommunications environment could provide a multiplicity of voices, eradicating the previous justification for government regulation. Under this model, the public interest would be defined by "market forces." A broadcaster's commercial success would be indicative of the public's satisfaction with that broadcaster.

Advocates of the marketplace argument reject the trusteeship model of broadcasting. It is no surprise that the Cable Act does not contain a "public interest, convenience, and necessity" stipulation. However, because cable also falls under the regulatory scrutiny of the FCC, serving the public interest is encouraged through the PEG (public, educational, and government) access requirement related to the granting of cable franchises.

Among the deregulatory policies implemented during the 1980s were the relaxation of ownership and licensing rules, eradication of assorted public-service requirements, and the elimination of regulations limiting the amount of commercial advertising in children's programming. Perhaps most detrimental to the legal justification for the trusteeship model of broadcasting, however, was the abolition of the Fairness Doctrine. This action altered future interpretations of the "public interest, convenience, and necessity" clause.

In 1949 the FCC established the Fairness Doctrine as a policy that guaranteed (among other things) the presentation of both sides of a controversial issue. This concept is rooted in the early broadcast regulation of the Federal Radio Commission. In 1959 Congress declared the doctrine part of the Communications Act in order to safeguard the public interest and First Amendment freedoms. The U.S. Supreme Court upheld the constitutionality of the Fairness Doctrine in the case of *Red Lion Broadcasting Co. v. FCC* (1969). Although the Fairness Doctrine was enacted to promote pluralism, it eventually produced an opposite effect. Concerned that advertising time would be squandered by those who invoked the Fairness Doctrine, broadcasters challenged its constitutionality, claiming that it promoted censorship instead of diversity. Declared in violation of the First Amendment, the Fairness Doctrine was repealed, and in 1987 President Ronald Reagan vetoed attempts to provide constitutional protection for the doctrine.

The 1996 Telecommunication Act, the most sweeping revision of U.S. policies in history, confirmed the dominance of the "marketplace" model. Taking note of a wider range of communication technologies no longer reliant on the limited electromagnetic spectrum, the act was presumably designed to encourage "competition" among media suppliers, thereby enhancing and increasing options available to the "public." In practice, the act enabled a round of massive mergers, placing ownership of distribution devices as well as content production under control of fewer and fewer entities. By 2002 many of these large companies foundered, and the "marketplace" was in a precarious state.

The obligation to serve the "public interest, convenience, and necessity" is demonstrated through myriad broadcast policies. Licensing requirements, the equal-time and candidate access rules, the Fairness Doctrine, and the Public Broadcasting and Cable Acts are just some examples of U.S. regulations that were implemented to safeguard the public from the possible selfish motives of broadcasters. History has proven, however, that interpretation of the "public interest, convenience, and necessity" is subject to prevailing political forces. The development of new technologies continues to test the trusteeship model of broadcasting and what defines the public interest. Yet despite its ambiguity and the difficulties encountered in its application, this phrase remains the stated regulatory cornerstone of telecommunications policy in the United States.

SHARON ZECHOWSKI

See also **Allocation; Federal Communications Commission; License; Local Television; Prime Time Access Rule; Ownership; Station and Station Group**

Further Reading

Ford, Frederick W., "The Meaning of the Public Interest, Convenience, or Necessity," *Journal of Broadcasting* (Summer 1961)

Head, Sydney W., *Broadcasting in America: A Survey of Television and Radio,* Boston: Houghton Mifflin, 1956; with Thomas Spann and Michael A. McGregor, as *Broadcasting in America: A Survey of Electronic Media,* 9th edition, 2001

Kahn, Frank J., editor, *Documents of American Broadcasting,* Englewood Cliffs, New Jersey: Prentice Hall, 1969; 3rd edition, 1978

Krugman, Dean M., and Leonard E. Reid, "The Public Interest As Defined by FCC Policy Makers," *Journal of Broadcasting* (Summer 1980)

Pember, Don R., *Mass Media Law,* Madison, Wisconsin: Brown and Benchmark, 1977; 9th edition, Boston: McGraw-Hill, 1998

Public-Interest Groups. *See* Advocacy Groups

Public-Service Announcement

In the United States a public-service announcement (PSA) is defined by the Federal Communications Commission (FCC) in a formal and detailed manner. A PSA is any announcement (including network) for which no charge is made and which promotes programs, activities, or services of federal, state, or local governments (e.g., recruiting, sale of bonds, etc.) or the programs, activities, or services of nonprofit organizations (e.g., United Way, Red Cross blood donations, etc.) and other announcements regarded as serving community interests, excluding time signals, routine weather announcements, and promotional announcements.

PSAs came into being with the entry of the United States into World War II. Radio broadcasters and advertising agencies offered their skills and facilities to aid the war effort and established the War Advertising Council, which became the official home front propaganda arm of the Office of War Information. Print media, outdoor advertising, and especially radio became the carriers of such messages as "Loose lips sink ships," "Keep 'em Rolling," and a variety of exhortations to buy war bonds.

By the end of the war, the practice of volunteering free airtime had become institutionalized, as had the renamed Advertising Council, which now served as a

U.S. Department of Transportation PSA.
Photo courtesy of Advertising Council

facilitating agency and clearinghouse for nationwide campaigns that soon became a familiar part of daily life. "Smokey the Bear" was invented by the Ad Council to personify its "Only You Can Prevent Forest Fires" campaign; "A Mind Is a Terrible Thing to Waste" has raised millions of dollars for the United Negro College Fund; the American Cancer Society's "Fight Cancer with a Checkup and a Check" raised public awareness as well as funds for research and patient services.

The ultimate demonstration of the effectiveness of PSAs came in 1969. Two years earlier, a federal court upheld the FCC's application of the Fairness Doctrine to cigarette advertising on radio and television and ordered stations to set aside "a significant amount of time" for the broadcast of antismoking messages. This effectively meant one antismoking PSA would air for every three tobacco commercials. The PSAs proved so effective that smoking rates began to decline for the first time in history; the tobacco industry withdrew all cigarette advertising; and Congress made such advertising illegal after 1971. With the passage of that law, however, the bulk of the antismoking messages also disappeared and cigarette consumption rose again for a while. On balance, however, public health professionals credit the PSAs with having saved many millions of lives by initiating the decline in smoking by Americans.

During the 1960s and 1970s, as media access became an issue, the Advertising Council—and to some extent the very concept of PSAs—came under criticism as being too narrow in focus. As David Paletz points out in *Politics in Public Service Advertising on Television,* campaigns such as "Only you can stop pollution" were seen as distracting attention from the role of industry in creating demands for excessive energy and in creating dangerous waste products. Other cam-

paigns struck critics as too eager to build consensus around seemingly inconsequential but carefully nonpartisan concerns. The networks sought to distance themselves from the Ad Council, and to set their own agendas, by dealing directly with the organizations themselves. Local stations were under additional pressure from innumerable new community-based organizations seeking airtime; many stations created and produced announcements in an effort to meet local needs, especially once the FCC came to require that stations report how many PSAs they presented and at what hour.

In the 1980s a number of stations long held by their founders' families went public or changed hands. The resulting debt load, mounting costs, as well as increased competition from the new media, all resulted in demands for greater profitability. Most unsold airtime was devoted to promoting the station or network. Moreover, deregulation saw government relinquishing the model of trusteeship of a scarce national resource in favor of a marketplace model.

Offsetting this trend to some extent were growing concerns about the illicit drug problem. The Advertising Media Partnership for a Drug-Free America (famous for the PSA intoning "This is your brain..." over a shot of an egg; "This is your brain on drugs. Any questions?" over a shot of an egg frying) was set up by a group of media and advertising agency executives, spearheaded by Capital Cities Broadcasting Company, then completing the takeover of ABC. Rallying unprecedented support, the organization mounted the largest public-service campaign ever. Indeed, at its height, with more than $365 million worth of print lineage and airtime annually, it rivaled the largest advertising campaigns. Consistent with contemporary thinking about the nature of social marketing, the campaign was solidly grounded in McGuire's paradigm of behavioral change: awareness of a problem by a number of people will result in a smaller number who undergo a change of attitude toward the problem; an even smaller number from this second group will actually change their behavior. During the first years of the campaign, its research team documented considerable difference in attitudinal and behavioral change among young people. Later evidence led to less-optimistic conclusions about the antidrug campaign, as a number of societal factors changed and media time and space became less readily available.

Other recent developments include two distinctive strategies. The Entertainment Industries Council combined high-profile film, television, and recording stars doing network PSAs with depiction efforts—producers, writers, and directors incorporating seatbelt use, designated drivers, AIDS education, and antidrug references in storylines. The other major development, championed and often carried out by consultants, was the appearance of the Total Station Project. Stations would adopt a public-service theme and, often after months of planning and preparation, coordinate PSAs with station editorials, heavily promoted public-affairs programs, and features in the local news broadcasts. Total Station Projects most frequently are aired during sweeps periods, the months when the station's ratings determine the next year's commercial time prices.

GEORGE DESSART

Further Reading

Atkin, Charles, and Lawrence Wallack, editors, *Mass Communication and Public Health: Complexities and Conflicts,* Newbury Park, California: Sage, 1990

Dessart, George, *More than You Want to Know about PSA's: A Guide to Production and Placement of Effective Public Service Announcements on Radio and Television,* Boston: National Broadcast Association for Public Affairs, 1982

Fritschler, A. Lee, *Smoking and Politics: Policy Making and the Federal Bureaucracy,* Englewood Cliffs, New Jersey: Prentice Hall, 1969; with James M. Hoefler, 5th edition, Upper Saddle River, New Jersey: Prentice Hall, 1996

Ginsburg, Douglas H., Michael H. Botein, and Mark K. Director, *Regulation of the Electronic Mass Media: Law and Policy for Radio, Television, Cable, and the New Technologies.* St. Paul, Minnesota: West Publishing, 1979; by Botein only, 3rd edition, 1998

Gunther, Albert C., "Perceived Persuasive Effects of Product Commercials and Public Service Announcements: Third-Person Effects in New Domains," *Communication Research* (October 1992)

Lorch, Elizabeth Pugzles, "Program Context, Sensation Seeking, and Attention to Televised Anti-drug Public Service Announcements," *Human Communication Research* (March 1994)

Paletz, David L., Roberta E. Pearson, and Donald L. Willis, *Politics in Public Service Advertising on Television,* New York: Praeger, 1977

Public-Service Broadcasting

Public-service broadcasting is based on the principles of universality of service, diversity of programming, provision for minority audiences (including the disadvantaged), sustaining an informed electorate, and cultural and educational enrichment. The concept was conceived and fostered within an overarching ideal of cultural and intellectual enlightenment of society.

The roots of public-service broadcasting are generally traced to documents prepared in support of the establishment of the British Broadcasting Corporation (BBC) by Royal Charter on January 1, 1927. This corporation grew out of recommendations of the Crawford Committee appointed by the British postmaster general in August 1925. Included in those recommendations was the creation of a public corporation that would serve as a trustee for the national interest in broadcasting. It was expected that as public trustee, the corporation would emphasize serious, educational, and cultural programming that would elevate the level of intellectual and aesthetic tastes of the audience. The BBC was to be insulated from both political and commercial influence. Therefore, the corporation was a creation of the Crown rather than Parliament, and funding to support the venture was determined to be derived from license fees on radio (and later television) receivers rather than advertising. Under the skillful leadership of the BBC's first director general, John Reith, this institution of public-service broadcasting embarked on an ethical mission of high moral responsibility to utilize the electromagnetic spectrum (a scarce public resource) to enhance the quality of life of all British citizens.

Within the governance of national authorities, public-service broadcasting was re-created in various forms in other democracies in Western Europe and beyond. At the core of each plan was a commitment to operating radio and television services in the public good. The principal paradigm adopted to accomplish this mission was the establishment of a state-owned broadcasting system that functioned either as a monopoly or at least as the dominant broadcasting institution. Funding came in the form of license fees, taxes, or similar noncommercial options. Examples of these organizations include the Netherlands Broadcasting Foundation, Danish Broadcasting Corporation, Radiodiffusion Television Française, Swedish Television Company, Radiotelevisione Italiana, Canadian Broadcasting Corporation, and Australian Broadcasting Corporation. The ideals on which these and other systems were based suggested services that were characterized by universality and diversity; however, there were notable violations to these ideals, especially in Germany, France, and Italy. In some cases the state-owned broadcasting system became the political mouthpiece for whomever was in power. Such abuse of the broadcasting institutions' mandate made public-service broadcasting the subject of frequent political debates.

Contemporary accounts of public-service broadcasting worldwide often include the U.S. Public Broadcasting Service (PBS) and National Public Radio (NPR) as American examples. However, unlike the British model that was adopted across Europe, the U.S. system came into being as an alternative to the commercially financed and market-driven system that has dominated U.S. broadcasting from its inception. Whereas 1927 marked the beginning of public-service broadcasting in Britain, the United States Radio Act of 1927 created the communication-policy framework that has enabled advertiser-supported radio and television to flourish. Language contained within this act explicitly mandated broadcasting stations to operate "in the public interest, convenience, and necessity," but the public-service ideals of raising the educational and cultural standards of the citizenry were marginalized in favor of capitalistic incentives. When the Radio Act was replaced by the Communications Act of 1934, the Federal Communications Commission (FCC) recommended to Congress that "no fixed percentages of radio broadcast facilities be allocated by statute to particular types or kinds of non-profit radio programs or to persons identified with particular types or kinds of non-profit activities." It was not until 1945 that the FCC created a license for "noncommercial educational" radio stations. These stations were envisioned to be the United States' answer to the ideals of public-service broadcasting, but the government's failure to provide any funding mechanism for noncommercial educational stations for nearly 20 years resulted in a weak and undernourished broadcasting service. Educational radio in the United States was referred to as the "hidden medium."

Educational television was authorized by the FCC's Sixth Report and Order adopted on April 14, 1952, but the creation of a mechanism for funding educational radio and television in the United States had to wait for passage of the Public Broadcasting Act on November 7, 1967. Funding levels never approached the recommendations set forth by the Carnegie Commission on Educational Television in its report *Public Television: A Program for Action,* in which the term "public television" first appeared.

During the 1970s and 1980s public-service broadcasting worldwide came under attack, as the underlying principles on which it was based were called into question. The arrival of new modes of television delivery—cable television, satellites, videocassettes—had created new means of access to broadcast services and thus changed the public's perception about the importance and even legitimacy of a broadcasting service founded on the principle of spectrum scarcity. Ideological issues also came into play. Conservative critics raised questions about the very notion of a public culture, whereas some liberals charged that public-service broadcasting was a closed, elitist, inbred, white-male institution.

Furthermore, movement toward a global economy was having an ever-increasing impact on the way policymakers saw the products of radio and television. The free-market viability of educational and cultural programming as successful commercial commodities seemed to support the arguments of critics contending that public-service broadcasting was no longer justified. Deregulation of communication industries was a necessary prerequisite to the breakdown of international trade barriers, and the shift toward increased privatization brought new players into what had been a closed system. The growing appeal of economic directives derived from consumer preferences favored the substitution of the U.S. market-forces model for the long-standing public-trustee model that had been the backbone of public-service broadcasting. Adding to the appeal of the U.S. paradigm was the growing realization that program production and distribution costs would continue to mount within an economic climate of flat or decreasing public funding.

By the early 1990s, the groundswell of political and public dissatisfaction with the privileged position of public-service broadcasting entities had reached new heights. Studies were revealing bureaucratic bungling, cost overruns, and the misuse of funds. One commission after another was recommending at least the partial dismantling or reorganization of existing institutions. New measures of accountability demanded more than idealistic rhetoric, and telecommunication policymakers were turning a deaf ear to public-service broadcasting advocates.

Communication scholars, who for the most part had been reticent on these issues, began to mount an intellectual counterattack, based largely on the experiences of public broadcasting in the United States. Critics of U.S. communications policy underscored concerns about the evils of commercialization and the influence of the open marketplace. Studies pointed to the loss of minority voices and a steady decline in programs for segmented populations. Scholars also challenged the illusion that new television delivery systems such as 500-channel cable networks and direct broadcast satellites would offer unlimited program choices. Content analyses revealed program duplication, not diversity, across the channels, and the question of just how far commercial broadcasters would venture away from the well-proven formulas and formats received public attention. A concerned electorate was beginning to ask whether the wide-scale transformation of telecommunications was not without considerable risk. Many worried that turning over the electronic sources of culture, education, and political discourse to the ever-shifting forces of the commercial marketplace might have profound negative consequences.

By the mid-1990s, telecommunications policy issues ranged from invasion of privacy to depictions of violence on television, the manufacturing of parent-controlled TV sets, revisions in technological standards, and finding new funding alternatives to sustain public-service broadcasting in some form. These issues were also firmly embedded in the public discourse. Communication corporations appeared and disappeared daily. The environment of electronic communications was in a state of flux as companies selling new technologies vied for a piece of a quickly expanding and constantly evolving marketplace. Public-service broadcasters reassessed their missions and began building new alliances with book publishers, computer software manufacturers, and commercial production houses. In the United States, public radio and television stations experimented with enhanced underwriting messages that looked and sounded more and more like conventional advertising.

In June 2000 a group of scholars assembled at the University of Maine to assess the merits of public-service broadcasting worldwide, and to develop plans for media reform within the United States. At this occasion the formation of a new organization, Citizens for Independent Public Broadcasting, was announced, with the association aiming to restore U.S. broadcasting to its original mission of public service. Despite all the fanfare and high hopes of those assembled in Maine, however, issues related to growing commercialization and the inability to get Congress to create an insulated trust fund to support public broadcasting remained unresolved in the early part of the 21st century. A ruling by the FCC that permitted public broadcasters to use a portion of their newly assigned space on the digital spectrum for commercial ventures seemed to signal that the trend toward an increased blurring of the line between commercial and noncommercial licenses would continue. Other U.S. efforts to create increased citizen access to the airwaves were largely thwarted when Congress minimized the potential impact of new low-power FM radio stations, an innovation that had been devised by the FCC as a way to deal with growing numbers of so-called pirate radio stations that were operating illegally.

In the early 2000s telecommunications policy worldwide seemed increasingly tied to the opportunities afforded by a new global economy shaped by market forces and privatization. Whether public-service broadcasting ideals could survive within this evolving political and economic environment remained a topic for robust debate.

ROBERT K. AVERY

Further Reading

Avery, Robert K., editor, *Public Service Broadcasting in a Multichannel Environment: The History and Survival of an Ideal,* White Plains, New York: Longman, 1993

Blumler, Jay G., and T.J. Nossiter, editors, *Broadcasting Finance in Transition: A Comparative Handbook,* Oxford and New York: Oxford University Press, 1991

Burns, Tom, *The BBC: Public Institution and Private World,* London: Macmillan, 1979

Carnegie Commission on Educational Television, *Public Television: A Program for Action,* New York: Bantam, 1967

Carnegie Commission on the Future of Public Broadcasting, *A Public Trust,* New York: Bantam, 1979

Day, James, *The Vanishing Vision: The Inside Story of Public Television,* Berkeley: University of California Press, 1995

Emery, Walter B., *National and International Systems of Broadcasting: Their History, Operation, and Control,* East Lansing: Michigan State University Press, 1969

Engelman, Ralph, *Public Radio and Television in America: A Political History,* Newbury Park, California: Sage, 1996

McChesney, Robert W., *Telecommunications, Mass Media, and Democracy: The Battle for the Control of U.S. Broadcasting, 1928–1933,* New York and Oxford: Oxford University Press, 1994

Raboy, Marc, *Missed Opportunities: The Story of Canada's Broadcasting Policy,* Montreal: McGill-Queen's University Press, 1990

Tracey, Michael, *The Decline and Fall of Public Service Broadcasting,* Oxford and New York: Oxford University Press, 1998

Witherspoon, John, Roselle Kovitz, Robert K. Avery, and A.G. Stavitsky, *A History of Public Broadcasting,* Washington, D.C.: Current Publishing, 2000

Public Television

U.S. public television is a peculiar hybrid of broadcasting systems. Neither completely a public-service system in the European tradition, nor fully supported by commercial interests as in the dominant pattern in the United States, it has elements of both. Although the Public Broadcasting Service (PBS) is emerging as a national image for U.S. public TV, at its base, this system consists of an ad hoc assemblage of stations united only by the fluctuating patronage of the institutions that fund them, and in the relentless grooming of various constituencies. The future of public broadcasting in the United States may in fact be assured by the range of those constituencies and by public TV's malleable self-definition. As technologies to permit both storage and interaction with viewers expand, public TV may come to be as much an electronic public library as a broadcaster. It staked a claim to a unique role in an increasingly diversified televisual environment by its early-21st-century campaign to generate "social capital," identified as networks of mutually rewarding social relationships in a community.

Since it became a national service in 1967 public TV has had a significant cultural impact—an especially impressive achievement given its perpetually precarious arrangements. Through its programming choices, it has not only introduced figures such as Big Bird and Julia Child into national culture, and created a home for sober celebrities such as Bill Moyers and William Buckley, but it has also pioneered new televisual technologies. Early achievements included closed captioning and distance learning. More recently, public TV has pioneered original digital programming, particularly using high-definition technology, and led in the development of web-based extensions of television programs.

U.S. public TV programming evolved to fill niches that commercial broadcasters had either abandoned or not yet discovered. Children's educational programming (especially for preschoolers), "how-to" programs stressing the pragmatic (e.g., cooking, home repair, and painting and drawing), public-affairs news and documentaries, science programs, upscale drama, experimental art, educationally tilted reality and docusoap programming, and community-affairs programming all contribute to the tapestry of public TV. In the course of a week, half the television-viewing homes in the United States turn to a public TV program for at least 15 minutes, and, overall, the demographics describing viewers of public TV more or less match those of the nation as a whole. However, based on an annual average, public TV's prime-time rating hovers at 2 percent of the viewing audience, a rating on par with some popular cable services but far below network television ratings. Demographics for any particular program are narrowly defined; overall, they are weakest for young adults. Less heralded, but increasingly important in public TV's rationale, is its extensive instructional programming and information-networking, most of which is nonbroadcast.

In the critical design period of American broadcasting (1927–34), which resulted in the Communications Act of 1934, public-service broadcasting had been rejected out of hand by legislators and their corporate mentors. A small amount of spectrum space on the more poorly received ultra-high frequency (UHF) band was set aside for educational television in 1952. This decision was modeled after the 1938 set-aside for educational (not public or public-service) radio stations, a regulation that had been implanted in response to the rampant commercialization of radio. In TV, as in radio, much of that spectrum space went unused, and most programming was low cost and local (e.g., a lecture).

After World War II, "educational television" evolved into "public television," around the concerns of cold war politics and the corporate growth of the television industry. The Public Broadcasting Act of 1967 reflected, in part, the renewed emphasis placed on mass media by major foundations such as Carnegie and Ford, as well as the concern of liberal politicians and educators, and, in part, it demonstrated an interest in communications technology by the nation's military-industrial strategists. The historic 1965 Carnegie Commission on Educational Television, willed into being by President Lyndon Johnson in search of a televisual component to the Great Society program, claimed that a "Public Television" could "help us see America whole, in all its diversity," and "help us know what it is to be many in one, to have growing maturity in our sense of ourselves as a people." Many legislators and conservatives, however, openly feared the specter of a fourth network dominated by eastern liberals. Commercial broadcasters did not want real rivals, although they supported the notion of a service that could complement theirs and relieve their public-interest burden.

The service was thus deliberately created as the "lemon socialism" of mass media, providing what commercial broadcasters did not want to offer. The only definition of "public" was "noncommercial." Token start-up funds were provided, and the system was not merely decentralized but balkanized. The current complex organization of public TV reflects its origins. The station, the basic unit of U.S. public TV, operates through a nonprofit entity, most commonly a nonprofit community organization, through the state's government (which provides mininetworks for all stations in a state), or through a university. Of the approximately 1,660 stations in the United States, there are about 350 public TV stations, although less than 200 independently program for their communities (the others mostly retransmit signals). Almost everyone in the United States can receive a public TV signal. About two-thirds of the public TV stations are UHF, still a significant limiting factor in reception. At the turn of the 21st century, about 40 stations also broadcast on digital channels, as a result of the requirement of the 1996 Telecommunications Act to use new spectrum given to each station for digital transmission.

Stations are fiercely independent, cultivating useful relationships with local elites, although the stations often form consortia for program production and delivery and to shape more general policy for public TV as a whole. A handful of wealthy, powerful producing stations contrasts with a great majority of small stations that produce no programming. In most major markets, there are several stations, with much duplication of PBS programming, but occasionally "overlap" stations establish some distinctive services catering to minorities and showcasing independent or experimental productions.

The 1967 Public Broadcasting Act also created the Corporation for Public Broadcasting (CPB) as a private entity, to provide support to the stations. The governing board of the CPB is politically appointed and balanced along partisan lines, and it is funded by tax dollars. The CPB was designed to assist stations with research, policy direction, grants to upgrade equipment and services, and, eventually, a small programming fund. However, the CPB was specifically banned from distributing programs. This was designed to inhibit the creation of a national network. Over the years, the corporation has acted as the lightning rod for congressional discontent, since the CPB is a funnel for federal tax dollars. Congress has usually removed the board's discretionary authority over funds rather than cut its budget. As a result, most of CPB's funds are now set up to flow directly to local stations.

Despite governmental intent to keep public broadcasting local, centralized programming services of several kinds quickly sprang up. Public-affairs services centered, just as political conservatives had feared, on the eastern seaboard. Resulting programs enraged President Richard Nixon, who tried to abolish the service and did succeed in weakening it.

Out of this conflict grew, by 1973, today's Public Broadcasting Service, the first and still premier national programming service for public TV. Shaped in part by station owners who, like Nixon, disliked eastern liberals, PBS is a membership organization of television stations. Member stations pay dues to receive up to three hours of prime-time programming at night, several hours of children's programming during the day, and other recommended programs. Since 1990 stations have accepted a programming schedule designed by a PBS executive. This policy replaced a previous system in which programs were selected through a system driven by majority vote. Stations were persuaded to cede power because overall ratings for public TV were declining. Although not obliged to honor the prime-time schedule, stations are urged to do so, and they are increasingly constrained by contract conditions to devote larger sections of their programming to a common national schedule. This version of a common schedule assists in enlarging the audience and enables stations to benefit from national advertising. Other programming services abound, both regionally and nationally, but none has the imprimatur of PBS.

CPB and PBS both provide funds for the development and purchase of programming, but they do not make most programs. Producing television stations, especially in New York, Boston, Los Angeles, and Washington, D.C., have historically produced the bulk of programming. Public TV also depends heavily on a few production houses, both commercial and noncommercial. Canadian production houses have risen in importance, with favorable exchange rates lowering production costs there, and smaller stations are increasingly producing individual programs and series, and working in producing consortia. Smaller television and film producers, historically frozen out of commercial broadcast television and typically constrained within formats on cable, chronically complain that public TV—their last resort and the only venue for authorial filmmaking—slights them. They argue that their work exemplifies the diversity of viewpoints and perspectives celebrated in the Constitution's First Amendment. Their complaints, coordinated over a decade, finally convinced Congress in 1988 to create the Independent Television Service, as a wing of the CPB, with the specific mission to fund innovative work for underserved audiences.

Public TV's funds come from a variety of sources, each of which comes with its own set of strings. Funding sources include (for fiscal year 1999) the federal government (15 percent), state and local governments (17 percent), public and private universities (11 percent), and private funders: subscribers (26 percent) and corporations (15 percent). The federal appropriation brings controversy virtually on an annual basis. Even so, the CPB's budget has, with few exceptions (notably, during the first Reagan presidency, and in 1995, when a new Republican congressional majority took office), been regularly increased to keep its total amount roughly steady with 1976 levels measured in 1972 dollars. The content of public-affairs programming has consistently been the target of Republican and conservative legislators' ire, and such anger has caused public TV to be hypercautious about such programs. This may explain why public TV has not developed an institutional equivalent of National Public Radio's around-the-clock news reporting.

About half the funds for public TV come from the private sector. Viewers are the single largest source of funding; their contributions come, effectively, without strings and so are especially valuable. These funds are often raised during "pledge drives" in which special, highly popular programming is presented in conjunction with heartfelt pleas for funds from station staff, prominent local supporters, and other celebrities. Programs aired during pledge drives (shows hosted by self-help celebrities, operas sung by stars such as Placido Domingo, a *Harry Potter*–themed program) reflect the genteel image of the service. Stations have also found some success with Internet pledging, another indication of the upscale tilt of public TV and its viewers. These pledge drives are supplemented, in many markets, with other fund-raising efforts, such as auctions or special performances. The 10 percent of all public TV viewers who become donors tend to be culturally and politically cautious, and the need to cultivate them skews public TV programming to what venerable broadcast historian Erik Barnouw called the "safely splendid."

Business contributes about a sixth of the funding, but its contributions have disproportionate weight in shaping programming decisions, because business dollars are usually given in association with a particular program. Public broadcasters openly market their audience to corporations as an upscale demographic, one that businesses are eager to capture in what is known as "ambush marketing": catching the attention of a listener or viewer who usually resists advertising. The hallmark PBS series *Masterpiece Theatre* was designed, from logo to host, by a Mobil Oil Corporation executive looking to create an image for Mobil as "the thinking man's gasoline." Conflict-of-interest issues ensue from corporate underwriting, as do questions about allowing corporations to set programming and production priorities. (If stations had not aired *Doing Business in Asia,* a series sponsored by Northwest Airlines, which has Asian routes, what else might they have been able to do with their time and money?)

These pressures have combined to make the service vulnerable to political attack from both the left and right as elitist. After Nixon accused the service of being dangerously liberal, many broadcasters scanted public affairs and presented "safe" cultural programming, only to be accused by the Reagan administration in 1981 of providing "entertainment for a select few." Reagan's attempt to cut funds also failed, although the administration succeeded in rescinding advance funding that had been designed as a political "heat shield" after Nixon's attack. In 1992 Republican Senator Bob Dole of Kansas threatened to hold up funding for public broadcasting on charges that it was too liberal, and he succeeded in making broadcasters nervous and forcing CPB to spend $1 million on surveys and studies that changed nothing. In 1994, following on the Republican victory in Congress, both Dole and Speaker of the House Newt Gingrich of Georgia targeted the CPB for rescission, on grounds that it was both elitist and liberal.

At the same time, the variety of funding sources, along with the decentralized structure of public TV, militated against mission-focused planning, in the prolonged industry turmoil that marked the last years of the 20th century. Multichannel, satellite, and cable television successfully eroded much of public TV's traditional niche, although public TV continued to hold as a unique audience the 30 percent of the population that does not receive pay television. Commercial investors, hungry for content, increasingly invested in public TV, and public TV entities have searched out commercial partners. New technologies posed hypothetical opportunities while requiring extensive experiment and innovation. Stations were forced to invest in digital technology without business plans or public subsidies for programming, as a result of a push largely by commercial broadcasters for expanded spectrum. In 2001 the Federal Communications Commission permitted stations to carry advertising on, and make money from, ancillary (nonbroadcast) services on digital channels, such as voice messaging and data transmission.

At the beginning of the 21st century, economic, political, and technological forces finally converged to refocus public TV's role. PBS attained a clearer agenda-setting role within the diffuse bureaucracies involved in public TV, effectively controlling the national schedule and radically revising its prime-time lineup for the first time in two decades. It aggressively branded the public TV environment as "PBS" by such measures as creating websites for all programs but refusing to cite competing websites on air; carrying the PBS "bug" on channel feeds; outreach and educational campaigns and materials; and public relations with opinion makers. The ascension of Pat Mitchell, a veteran of commercial cable TV, as PBS president in 2000, brought crisper decision making and more direct competition for programs with commercial channels, as well as the "social capital" campaign. Producers within and for public TV more frequently entered into international coproductions, with both public-service and commercial partners, and worked harder to retain intellectual property rights. The challenge of developing and programming digital channels has created new financial pressures and new business plans. At the same time, stations have individually experimented with local partners, with extended educational services (including distance learning), and with becoming nodes of community networks.

The September 11, 2001, terrorist attacks on the United States proved a test of the role of public TV in national culture, and it demonstrated public TV's strengths and weaknesses. In the immediate aftermath, the service demonstrated its inability to cover news thoroughly, since few stations had any ability to cover events live. However, in the days that followed, public TV turned out to be the place to go for thoughtful, well-researched documentaries about topics related to the terrorism, with some of this programming being rerun to high ratings, after low-rated debuts. The teams that produced these documentaries demonstrated the value of deep investment in the subject matter and were able to draw on contacts and outtakes to produce more public affairs quickly. PBS created an information-rich website with a page for storytelling that expanded quickly and many links to local stations' websites, where users could contribute to charities and support organizations. Thus, the service's functions as high-quality programmer, educational resource, and community network node were showcased.

An improbable, many-headed creature, public TV is unlikely to disappear even under political assault. It is also unlikely suddenly to become a service that a plurality of Americans would expect to turn to on any given evening. It is likely to become more commercial in its broadcast services and more entrenched (and defensible as taxpayer-funded) in its infrastructure and instructional services.

PATRICIA AUFDERHEIDE

Further Reading

Aufderheide, Patricia, *The Daily Planet: A Critic on the Capitalist Culture Beat,* Minneapolis: University of Minnesota Press, 2000

Avery, R., and R. Pepper, "The Evolution of the CPB-PBS Relationship 1970–1973," *Public Telecommunications Review* (1976)

Baker, William F., and George Dessart, *Down the Tube: An Inside Account of the Failure of American Television,* New York: Basic Books, 1998

Bullert, B.J., *Public Television: Politics and the Battle over Documentary Film,* New Brunswick, New Jersey: Rutgers University Press, 1997

Carnegie Commission on Educational Television, *Public Television: A Program for Action,* New York: Harper and Row, 1967

Engelman, Ralph, *Public Radio and Television in America: A Political History,* Thousand Oaks, California: Sage, 1996

Gibson, George H., *Public Broadcasting: The Role of the Federal Government, 1912–1976,* New York: Praeger, 1977

Horowitz, D., "The Politics of Public Television," *Commentary* (December 1991)

Hoynes, William, *Public Television for Sale: Media, the Market and the Public Sphere,* Boulder, Colorado: Westview, 1994

Katz, H., "The Future of Public Broadcasting in the U.S.," *Media, Culture, and Society* (April 1989)

Konigsberg, E., "Stocks, Bonds, and *Barney:* How Public Television Went Private," *Washington Monthly* (September 1993)

Lapham, L., "Adieu, Big Bird: On the Terminal Irrelevance of Public Television," *Harper's* (December 1993)

Lashley, Marilyn, *Public Television: Panacea, Pork Barrel, or Public Trust?,* New York: Greenwood, 1992

Ledbetter, James, *Made Possible By...: The Death of Public Broadcasting in the United States,* London and New York: Verso, 1997

Macy, John W. Jr., *To Irrigate a Wasteland: The Struggle to Shape a Public Television System in the United States,* Berkeley: University of California Press, 1974

McChesney, Robert, *Telecommunications, Mass Media, and Democracy: The Battle for the Control of U.S. Broadcasting, 1928–1935,* New York: Oxford University Press, 1993

Ouellette, L., *Viewers Like You: The Cultural Contradictions of Public TV,* New York: Columbia University Press, 2002

Pepper, Robert M., *The Formation of the Public Broadcasting Service,* New York: Arno Press, 1976

Rowland, W., "Public Service Broadcasting: Challenges and Responses," in *Broadcasting Finance in Transition: A Comparative Handbook,* edited by Jay G. Blumler and T.J. Nossiter, Oxford and New York: Oxford University Press, 1991

Schmertz, Herb, and William Novak, *Good-bye to the Low Profile: The Art of Creative Confrontation,* Boston: Little, Brown, 1986

Somerset-Ward, R., *Quality Time? The Report of the Twentieth Century Fund Task Force on Public Television,* New York: The Twentieth Century Fund, 1993

Starr, Jerold M., *Air Wars: The Right to Reclaim Public Broadcasting,* Boston: Beacon Press, 2000

Stone, David M., *Nixon and the Politics of Public Television,* New York: Garland, 1985

Puerto Rico

The U.S. Federal Communications Commission (FCC) regulates television in Puerto Rico. Its jurisdiction over the Puerto Rican communication industry is identical to that over the United States and the other U.S. territories. It oversees most aspects pertaining to the television industry, including the assignment of frequencies, the granting of licenses and their renewal, the evaluation and approval of construction permits, and requests for changes in frequencies, potency, and ownership. Following passage of the Telecommunications Act of 1996, all facets of the telecommunication industry in Puerto Rico, like those throughout the United States, have been rapidly changing. Mergers and acquisitions, convergence of industries, and economic distress have affected many telecommunication sectors. Although actions of the FCC remained uncertain as of 2002, it was clear that Puerto Rican television would be altered in the near future.

History and Trends

Television could not develop in Puerto Rico as early as it did in other areas of the region, due to Puerto Rico's condition as a territory of the United States, which put the communication industry under the overriding control of the FCC. When the FCC implemented the television freeze and "ordered applications for new TV stations placed in the pending file" on September 29, 1948, Puerto Rico had no choice but to postpone its incursion into the new medium.

The agency renewed the process for the issuance of broadcasting licenses on April 12, 1952, and soon thereafter, on July 24, 1952, it granted the first permit for the construction of a commercial television station in a U.S. territory to El Mundo Broadcasting Company. WKAQ-TV, Telemundo, was founded by Angel Ramos, who also owned *El Mundo* newspaper and WKAQ radio (Radio el Mundo), the first radio station in Puerto Rico (established in 1922). Telemundo received its FCC license to transmit over Channel 2 in San Juan on February 12, 1954, and went on the air with regular programming on March 28, 1954. The second permit for the construction of a commercial television station was granted to Ramón Quiñónez, owner of WAPA Radio on August 12, 1952. WAPA-TV received its FCC license to transmit over Channel 4 in San Juan on March 15, 1954. It started regular

transmission on May 1, 1954. Programming at both TV stations extended from 4:30 P.M. to 10:30 P.M. and included varied genres such as live comedy and drama, variety shows, women's programs (cooking shows), news programs, and films (mostly Mexican).

Competition has always been fierce among these two broadcasters, which have alternated in their success at being the first to offer videotape technology (1966), color television (1968), and satellite broadcasting (1968)—many times achieving these accomplishments within a week of each other. They have also alternated in obtaining the largest share of the audience and the top programs. Due to their early successes, these two stations attracted the attention of mainland corporations. A succession of sales took place and continues to this day; in fact, changes in ownership have accelerated since approval of the Telecommunications Act of 1996.

WKAQ-TV, Telemundo, was first sold to John Blair and Company, a diversified, publicly traded U.S. company on April 14, 1983. Blair and Company then sold the station in October 1987 to Reliance Inc., the owners of Telemundo, the Spanish-language television network in the United States. Thus, Telemundo of Puerto Rico became part of the large network of Hispanic TV stations on the mainland. In October 2001 NBC, a division of General Electric, acquired Telemundo Communications Group, which includes Telemundo of Puerto Rico, in a package deal worth $2.7 billion. Regulatory approval by the Federal Trade Commission (FTC) has been granted; FCC approval was expected shortly.

WAPA-TV, or Televicentro, has changed ownership several times since 1975. It was acquired first by Western Broadcasting in the United States; later sold to Screen Gems, a subsidiary of Columbia Pictures; and acquired in 1980 by Pegasus Inc., a subsidiary of General Electric. In December 1999 WAPA-TV was sold to LIN Television, a subsidiary of diversified media company Chancellor Media Corporation, which also owns and operates eight FM radio stations in Puerto Rico through Primedia Broadcast Group.

In the early 1950s the Department of Education, headed by Mariano Villalonga, lobbied for the establishment of public broadcasting. On June 25, 1954, the Puerto Rican Legislature approved Joint Resolution Number 94, which authorized and assigned the funding for the creation of the Public Radio and Television Service and the installation and operation of public TV and radio stations. After obtaining approval by the FCC to transmit over Channel 6, WIPR-TV went on the air on January 6, 1958, thus becoming the first educational TV station in Latin America. Offering educational and cultural fare unavailable in commercial broadcasting, it initially transmitted from 3:30 P.M. to 9:00 P.M. on weekdays and for only three hours on weekends. Its affiliation with the National Educational Television and Radio Association in 1961 increased its programming. Also in 1961, a second station, Mayagüez's WIPM-TV (an affiliate of WIPR-TV), retransmitted programs to the west coast over Channel 3. Trailing the commercial stations, WIPR-TV first offered regular programming in color on May 12, 1971. By 1979 WIPR-TV and WIPM-TV joined the Public Broadcasting Service (PBS), further increasing their offerings and bringing English-language programs from the United States to Puerto Rican viewers. On January 21, 1987, radio and TV broadcasting was transferred from the Department of Education to a newly created state venture, named Corporación para la Difusión Pública (Corporation for Public Broadcasting). An increased budget has since allowed improvements in physical facilities, equipment, and programming, with airtime gradually extended to 24 hours a day. The public TV stations created a news department in November 1995, and two editions of its newscast are presented daily. Export of local productions to some U.S. markets has been intermittent.

WRIK-TV was established in Ponce, on the south coast of Puerto Rico, after receiving an FCC permit to go on the air on Channel 7 on February 2, 1958. Its owner was Alfredo Ramírez de Arellano, and, lacking its own programming, the station retransmitted Telemundo's fare. By 1970 it was bought by United Artists, moved to San Juan, renamed Rikavisión, and started to produce its own programming without much success. In 1979 it was acquired by Puerto Rican producer Tommy Muñiz and became WLUZ-TV. Economic problems forced Muñiz to sell the station in 1985 to Malrite Communications Group. The station became WSTE-TV, and in 1991 it was sold to Jerry Hartman, a Florida entrepreneur. Known locally as SuperSiete, it is a limited outlet for independent producers, who buy time to present their programs during periods other than the 57 weekly hours contracted through a long-term marketing agreement to transmit Channel 11 programming.

In 1960 Rafael Pérez Perry received authorization to start WKBM-TV and transmit over Channel 11. At the time, he owned one of the most successful radio stations on the island (WKBM-AM). However, his suc-

cess in radio did not extend to television. As has happened to Channel 7, Channel 11's competition with Channels 2 and 4 was never effective, and, after Perry's death, the station's economic problems worsened, leading it to declare bankruptcy, and close in 1981. In 1986 Lorimar Telepictures acquired the station from Bankruptcy Court and renamed it WSII-TV. It was subsequently sold to Malrite Communications Group in 1991. Called Teleonce, Channel 11 has achieved great success, and since 1995 it has been capable of truly competing with Channels 2 and 4, obtaining equal or better shares and ratings in several time periods. In 1998 it was sold to Montgomery, Alabama–based Raycom Media, only to be sold again in June 2001 to Univisión Communications, the leading Spanish-language media company in the United States. Through their subsidiary Univisión Radio, they also own and operate four radio stations acquired in 2003 in Puerto Rico's lucrative radio market.

During the 1980s and early 1990s, other commercial stations, all lesser players, struggled without much success. WPRV-TV, Channel 13; WSJU-TV, Channel 18 (the oldest of this group dating back to the mid-1960s); WSJN-TV, Channel 24; and WRWR-TV, Channel 30, were all unable to effectively compete with the older, more solidly established stations. Serious economic problems forced some into bankruptcy, and all went off the air. In recent years, all of these stations started to transmit again, albeit with changes in ownership, call letters, and programming.

WPRV-TV, Channel 13, was bought by the Catholic Church, Archdiocese of San Juan, in January 1995. Known locally as Teleoro, it is a commercial station built around social, religious, and cultural programming.

WSJU-TV, Channel 18, was acquired in December 1990 and belongs to International Broadcasting Corporation. This Puerto Rican enterprise catered to independent producers, had scarce programming, and mostly played Spanish-language music videos. Its call letters changed to WAVB-TV and most recently to WTCV-TV. In February 2001 Channel 18 entered into a local marketing agreement with the Home Shopping Network to carry the network's Spanish-language edition. WVEO-TV, Channel 44, and WIEC-TV, Channel 48, are affiliate stations retransmitting to the west and south, respectively.

WSJN-TV, Channel 24, was bought by S&E Network, a Puerto Rican venture that went on the air on November 1994 and produced some 50 hours a week of sports programs and studio-based talk shows. The station's call letters were changed to WJPX-TV, and in 1997 it was sold to Paxson Communications, a Florida-based TV and radio company, together with two affiliate stations (WKPV-TV, Channel 20, and WJWN-TV, Channel 38). In July 2001 the network, known as Telenet, was acquired by LIN Television, which has put Channel 24 and its affiliate stations under the control of Televicentro. This has increased the reach of WAPA-TV, Channel 4, to areas of weak signals.

With new call letters, WSJU-TV, Channel 30, was launched in March 2000, when its license was granted to the Puerto Rican firm Aerco Broadcasting Corporation. WSJU plays only Spanish-language music videos.

Other TV stations—educational, commercial, and religious—have emerged since the mid-1980s. WMTJ-TV, Channel 40, is an educational station belonging to the Ana G. Méndez Foundation, a private university. It was inaugurated in 1985 as a PBS affiliate, and, besides PBS programming, it also offers its own news, current affairs programs, and televised college courses. Its affiliate station, WQTO-TV in Ponce, retransmits to the southern coast over Channel 26. WZDE-TV, Channel 52, is an independent commercial station broadcasting music videos. It belongs to Puerto Rican firm R&F Broadcasting, Inc. and started transmission early in 2003 after a long battle with a cable television franchise over the mandated FCC must-carry rule. WELU-TV, Channel 32; WDWL-TV, Channel 36; WCCV-TV, Channel 54; WUJA-TV, Channel 58; and WECN-TV, Channel 64, all are religious stations belonging to diverse Protestant groups. Programming on these stations includes religious services, revivals, testimonials, interviews, fundraising, and news programs.

With the exception of a limited number of programs, all stations transmit in Spanish. Commercial television content mostly consists of Puerto Rican productions, particularly comedy, children's programs, news, talk shows, and variety shows. Dubbed American TV series and movies, and Mexican, Colombian, and Venezuelan soap operas, comprise the rest of the offerings. Teleonce's acquisition by Univisión in 2001 initiated a move toward more canned programming from their stateside studios that was directed to the Hispanic-American population in the United States. This is now standard fare and is altering the offerings of Puerto Rico's television. The amount of local programming is diminishing while imported programs are on the rise. The other commercial stations, following a global trend, have emulated this. Reality TV, both imported and locally produced, is also a new and rapidly increasing trend. There are very limited European or Canadian offerings, except for BBC or CBC specials carried over PBS stations WIPR-TV and WMTJ-TV. Interestingly, public television has increased the amount of local productions during this same timeframe but still command a minuscule number of the television audience.

An estimated 1,325,610 households exist in Puerto Rico, of which 1,313,223 have at least one television set, for a penetration of 99.1 percent (Mediafax, June 2003). A number of affiliate stations exist on the island, which means that TV signals of major stations reach all geographic areas. Channels 2, 4, and 11 consistently get the largest share of the audience, with all other channels trailing far behind. Television audience measurements are an important element for marketing and programming decisions, and, through the years, several companies have performed this function. The earliest measurements took place in September 1956, but it was not until the 1970s that companies like Clapp and Mayne and Stanford Klapper made inroads into a field that was rapidly developing and which determined where the advertising dollar would go. Mediafax is the only company offering television audience measurements, with television stations and local advertising agencies subscribing and paying a fee for these services. Kantar Media Research, a subsidiary of British global company WPP Group, acquired Mediafax in July 2001.

Cable Television

The cable television industry has transformed the landscape of television in Puerto Rico. Plagued by problems in the beginning, it is now an evolving alternative to local television and its programming strategies. Since 1996 the Junta Reglamentadora de Telecomunicaciones (Telecommunication Regulatory Board) has overseen operations of cable TV in Puerto Rico; it now authorizes franchises, a responsibility previously held by the Public Service Commission. In the mid-1960s, the availability of Puerto Rico Cablevision, a subsidiary of International Telephone and Telegraph, was limited to major San Juan hotels. The first franchise for residential service for the area of San Juan was granted in 1970 to the Cable Television Company of Puerto Rico. By 1976 the company was bankrupt, and Cable TV of Greater San Juan took over the franchise in March 1977. It was bought by Century Communications in 1986, and major investments in infrastructure took place. Other cable TV operators were granted franchises to offer cable service on the rest of the island.

In the early 21st century, four cable companies covered the ten franchise areas that serviced more than 90 percent of the island and reached an estimated 407,979 subscribers (Mediafax, June 2003). Current cable companies are Adelphia Communications, which in October 1999 completed its acquisition of Century Communications and is now the parent company of Cable TV of Greater San Juan and Community Cablevision; Centennial Cable TV of Puerto Rico, which since September 2000 has bought Pegasus Communications of Puerto Rico (two franchise areas), Teleponce Cable, and Cable TV del Noroeste; Liberty Media, which acquired TCI Cablevision of Puerto Rico (three franchise areas) in February 2000; and Digital TV One (previously Telecable of Puerto Rico), the only remaining Puerto Rican company.

The expansion of the cable industry is indicated by the steady growth in the number of subscribers. In 1980 there were 35,000 subscribers, increasing to 127,400 by 1985, 218,900 in 1990, 352,000 in 2001, and 408,000 in 2003 (PR Cable Subscriber History, 1994; Mediafax, 2001; June 2003). A conservative estimate puts their yearly billing at over $300 million. Expansion is expected to continue, although not as fast as previously thought because of the inroads made by satellite television since 2001. Still, cable penetration is only about 31 percent compared to around 70 percent in the United States (Caribbean Business, September 14, 2000; Mediafax, June 2003). Additional consolidation and convergence of services is anticipated and will further transform the cable TV industry.

Cable TV systems carry all local stations and more than 150 North American channels via satellite. A move to digital cable is well advanced among all providers. Their fare is mostly in English and includes all major networks such as ABC, CBS, NBC, and FOX, as well as channels specializing in sports (ESPN, ESPN2), news (CNN), finance (CNBC), music (MTV, VH1), movies (American Movie Classics, HBO, HBO2, Showtime, Cinemax, The Movie Channel), cartoons (Cartoon Network), children's programs (Nickelodeon, The Disney Channel), science (The Discovery Channel, The Learning Channel), arts (A&E, Bravo!), public affairs (C-Span, C-Span2), comedy, (Comedy Central), religion (EWTN), shopping (HSC, HSN, QVC, QVC2), weather (The Weather Channel), and many other areas. There are also some 70 pay-per-view channels offering movies, sports, and adult fare as well as 45 satellite music channels. Channels featuring programming in Arabic, Chinese, Hindi, Italian, French, and Japanese, although limited, are available. Few Spanish-language channels are available through cable TV. Among these are TV Chile, Venevisión, TV3, and Spanish TVE.

The Telecommunications Act of 1996 allows cable companies to become integrated providers of the full spectrum of interactive broadband network services. This is rapidly changing the nature and reach of cable companies, as well as the services they offer. The convergence of services now permitted has allowed cable companies in Puerto Rico recently to start launching cable modem service, by which cable subscribers are able to access the Internet at very high speeds through the cable TV network. While not all cable systems offer this service yet, and those that do do not have it available in all areas they control, this is a rapidly changing situation. Cable companies have most of the required infrastructure ready, and with the completion of the Americas II submarine fiber-optic cable, all will further diversify their offerings.

Satellite Television

Unregulated by local agencies, the operations of satellite television in Puerto Rico are overseen by the FCC. As with cable TV, satellite television had its share of problems in the beginning. Initially, small mom-and-pop operators sold and installed deep-dish antennas, from the late 1970s. These never operated any sort of large-scale enterprise and were mostly unreliable. The island's first taste of organized satellite TV came with the Alphastar service launched in 1997. Alphastar went dark, however, after falling into bankruptcy problems.

Direct-to-home satellite television was again made available through DirecTV Puerto Rico, which was established in mid-1999. It is a subsidiary of DirecTV Latin America (formerly Galaxy Latin America), a multinational company owned by Hughes Electronics Corporation and Darlene Investments, an affiliate of the Cisneros Group of Companies. DirecTV has grown rapidly and aggressively in Puerto Rico. It offers 130 video and audio channels, has 470 employees, and in late 2003 claimed to have 165,000 clients (DirecTV, January 2004). The other provider of satellite television is Dish Network, a subsidiary of EchoStar Communications Corporation, which predates DirecTV, operates only through dealerships, and has no offices locally. Independent information about this industry is still unavailable. Unverified data points to a conservative estimate of 300,000 subscribers to satellite television services at the end of 2003. If accurate, this would imply a penetration of about 23 percent for satellite services and a total penetration of close to 54 percent for both satellite and cable TV services combined. Since data available for satellite services is unverifiable and does not allow knowing whether the same households subscribe to both services or not, and if so, in which percentage they do, these last two statistics are only notional. Mediafax has plans to include audience measurements of satellite television homes in the near future.

Conclusion

The trends seen in Puerto Rico's television industry suggest that further expansion and acquisitions, mergers, and realignments will take place. Minor players unable to compete will either disappear or be taken over. The post-1996 era has proven Puerto Rico to be an important market of interest to global players. Already major U.S. media companies such as NBC, LIN Television, and Univisión have obtained control of the principal television networks, and everything points to a continuation of this trend. Educational broadcasters enjoy relative success in that their audience share, although small, is steady, and investment in infrastructure and programming is increasing. Insufficient data exists to speculate about the future of religious channels. As for cable and satellite television, undoubtedly growth will continue in a still-developing market that has consolidated amid acquisitions by major U.S. and global media companies.

RODOLFO B. POPELNIK

Q

Quatermass

British Science Fiction Series

Years before the English Sunday supplements ever discovered the "Angry Young Man," jazz, science fiction, and other "marginal" art forms began to gather adherents among those who formerly might have quickly passed by them. Postwar British culture had entered a self-conscious period of transition, and science fiction suddenly seemed much more important both to pundits such as Kingsley Amis and to readers in general, who made John Wyndham's novels (beginning with *The Day of the Triffids* [1951]) surprising best sellers.

The 1950s were also a period of adjustment for the BBC, which lost its television monopoly midway through the decade with the dreaded debut of the Independent Television Authority (ITA)—the invasion of commercial TV. Classical works and theatrical adaptations suddenly seemed insufficient to secure the BBC's popular support. Perhaps not surprisingly, the corporation turned to science fiction: in 1953 the drama department put its development budget behind one writer, Nigel Kneale, who in exchange produced the script for the BBC's first original, adult work of science fiction, a serial to be produced and directed by Rudolph Cartier and titled *The Quatermass Experiment.* The summer of that year, its six half-hour episodes aired, and with them began a British tradition of science fiction television that runs in various forms from *Quatermass* to *A Is for Andromeda* to *Blake's Seven,* and from *Doctor Who* to *Red Dwarf.* Kneale himself went on to adapt George Orwell's *Nineteen Eighty-Four* for Cartier's controversial 1954 telecast. Later in the decade, Kneale adapted John Osbourne's *Look Back in Anger* and *The Entertainer* for the screen.

Yet Kneale's first major project was quite possibly his most elegant as well. The story of *The Quatermass Experiment* is fairly simple: a British scientist, Professor Bernard Quatermass, has launched a rocket and rushes to the site of its crash. There he discovers that only one crew member, Victor Carroon, has returned with the ship. Carroon survived only as a host for an amorphous alien life-form, which is not only painfully mutating Carroon's body but also preparing to reproduce. Carroon escapes and wreaks havoc on London, until Quatermass finally tracks the now unrecognizably human mass to Westminster Abbey. There Quatermass makes one final appeal to Carroon's humanity.

Years before, H.G. Wells had inaugurated contemporary science fiction with warnings in *War of the Worlds* about Britain's failure to advance from its colonial self-satisfaction. *The Quatermass Experiment*'s depiction of an Englishman's transformation into an alienated monster dramatized a new range of gendered fears about Britain's postwar and postcolonial security. As a result, or perhaps simply because of Kneale and Cartier's effective combination of science fiction and poignant melodrama, audiences were captivated.

With a larger budget and better effects, Kneale and Cartier continued the professor's story with *Quatermass II* (1955), an effectively disturbing story of alien

Quatermass.
Photo courtesy of Robert Dickinson

possession and governmental conspiracies prefiguring *Invasion of the Body Snatchers* (1956). Perhaps fittingly, *Quatermass II* provided early counterprogramming to the BBC's new commercial competition.

That same year, the small, struggling Hammer Films successfully released its film adaptation of *The Quatermass Experiment* in Britain. The next year the film (retitled *The Creeping Unknown*) performed unexpectedly well in the lucrative U.S. market, providing the foundation for the company's subsequent series of Gothic horror films. Hammer released its film adaptation of the second serial (retitled *The Enemy Within* for the United States) in 1957.

Kneale and Cartier's third serial in the series, *Quatermass and the Pit,* combined the poetic horror of the first serial and the paranoia of the second. In it, Quatermass learns that an archaeological discovery made during routine subway expansion means nothing less than humanity itself is not what we have believed it to be. The object discovered in that subway "pit" is an ancient Martian craft, and its contents indicate humans are their genetically engineered offspring. By the conclusion of the serial, London's inhabitants have been inadvertently triggered into a programmed mode of rioting, and the city lies mostly in ruins. "We're all Martians!" became Quatermass's famous cry, and the serial's ample references to escalating racial and class tensions give his words an ominous power.

It is this grim, elegant ending, filmed by Hammer in 1967 (and released in the United States as *Five Million Years to Earth*), that Greil Marcus used in his history of punk to describe the emotional experience of a Sex Pistols concert. If nothing else, Marcus's reference in *Lipstick Traces* (1989) suggests that Quatermass, like those repressed Martian memories, may return at the most cu-

rious moments. Even in less-unexpected contexts than Marcus's, the name Quatermass may still operate as a certain sort of cultural code word; for example, in his extensive science fiction history *Trillion Year Spree* (1986), Brian Aldiss uses "the Quatermass school" as if every reader should automatically understands its meaning.

By the late 1970s the BBC was no longer willing to commit itself to the budget necessary for Kneale's fourth and final Quatermass serial, simply titled *Quatermass.* Commercial television was ready, however, and in 1979, at the conclusion of a 75-day ITV strike, the four-part *Quatermass* debuted with John Mills starring as the now elderly professor in his final adventure.

Only the serial's opening sequence, involving Quatermass deriding a U.S.-USSR "Skylab 2," displays the force of the earlier series: a moment after Quatermass blurts out his words in a live television interview, the studio monitors are filled with the image of Skylab 2 blowing to pieces. Subsequent episodes are less successfully provocative. Concerning a dystopic future Britain where hippielike youth are being swept up by aliens, the serial's narrative was recognized as somewhat stale and unconvincing. Yet even in the late 1970s, despite the last serial's lukewarm reviews, *Quatermass* remained a source of fan preoccupation reminiscent of the commitment of many to *Star Trek.*

Unlike the three earlier serials, *Quatermass* was not adapted for the screen. It was simply edited and repackaged as *The Quatermass Conclusion* for theatrical and video distribution abroad. Of the earlier serials, only *Quatermass and the Pit* has had a video release, although most of the first serial and all of the second have been preserved by the British Film Institute.

ROBERT DICKINSON

See also **Cartier, Rudolph; Lambert, Verity; Science Fiction Programs**

The Quatermass Experiment

Cast

Professor Bernard Quatermass	Reginald Tate
Judith Carroon	Isabel Dean
John Paterson	Hugh Kelly
Victor Carroon	Duncan Lamont
James Fullalove	Paul Whitsun-Jones

Producer
Rudolph Cartier

Programming History
6 30-minute episodes
BBC
July 18, 1953–August 22, 1953

Quatermass II

Cast

Quatermass	John Robinson
Paula Quatermass	Monica Grey
Dr. Leo Pugh	Hugh Griffiths
Captain John Dillon	John Stone
Vincent Broadhead	Rupert Davies
Fowler	Austin Trevor

Producer

Rudolph Cartier

Programming History

6 30-minute episodes
BBC
October 22, 1955–November 26, 1955

Quatermass and the Pit

Cast

Quatermass	Andre Morrell
Dr. Matthew Roney	Cec Linder
Barbara Judd	Christine Finn
Colonel Breen	Anthony Bushell
Captain Potter	John Stratton
Sergeant	Michael Ripper
Corporal Gibson	Harold Goodwin
Private West	John Walker
James Fullalove	Brian Worth
Sladden	Richard Shaw

Producer

Rudolph Cartier

Programming History

6 35-minute episodes
BBC
December 22, 1958–January 26, 1959

Quatermass

Cast

Quatermass	John Mills
Joe Kapp	Simon MacCorkindale
Clare Kapp	Barbara Kellerman
Kickalong	Ralph Arliss
Caraway	Paul Rosebury
Bee	Jane Bertish
Hettie	Rebecca Saire
Marshall	Tony Sibbald
Sal	Toyah Wilcox
Guror	Brewster Mason
Annie Morgan	Margaret Tyzack

Producers

Verity Lambert, Ted Childs

Programming History

4 60-minute episodes
ITV
October 24, 1979–November 14, 1979

Further Reading

Briggs, Asa, *The History of Broadcasting in the United Kingdom,* vol. 4, Oxford: Oxford University Press, 1979

Fulton, Roger, *The Encyclopedia of TV Science Fiction,* London: Boxtree, 1990

Kneale, Nigel, *The Quatermass Experiment; Quatermass II; Quatermass and the Pit,* London: Penguin, 1960

Kneale, Nigel, *Quatermass,* London: Hutchinson, 1979

Leman, Joy, "Wise Scientists and Female Androids: Class and Gender in Science Fiction," in *Popular Television in Britain,* edited by John Corner, London: British Film Institute, 1991

Marcus, Greil, *Lipstick Traces: A Secret History of the Twentieth Century,* Cambridge, Massachusetts: Harvard University Press, 1989

Pirie, David, *A Heritage of Horror: The English Gothic Cinema, 1946–1972,* London: Gordon Fraser, 1973

Quebecor Media Inc.

Quebecor Media is a leading global multimedia conglomerate based in Quebec, Canada, with large holdings in newspaper, magazine, and commercial publishing; television production, broadcasting, and distribution; and cable, Internet, and interactive television services. While the company has already captured a large part of the French-Canadian market, its corporate vision is global in scope. Quebecor has benefited from a relaxed regulatory environment in Canada, which has allowed the company to vastly expand its holdings both within and across media and to pursue a strategy that emphasizes convergence and economies of scale as well as achieve vertical integration of its print and television services. Like other multimedia conglomerates such as Time Warner or Universal-Vivendi, Quebecor has largely acquired its holdings through corporate buyouts and mergers. Quebecor's television holdings have largely resulted from the company's purchase of Groupe Videotron Ltee. in October 2000, although its exploitation of the television medium dates back to the early 1950s.

Publishing magnate Pierre Peladeau founded Quebecor in 1965. Peladeau had begun his career in 1950 as a publisher of community newspapers in Montreal. In 1955 Peladeau launched *Nouvelles et Points,* the first of a series of weekly entertainment magazines, which focused heavily on the burgeoning Francophone television industry and its celebrities. Over the years, Peladeau's magazines and newspapers would carve out a niche in Quebec by devoting significant coverage to French-Canadian stars and TV series. In 1964 Peladeau started *Le Journal de Montreal,* which would become the largest French-language daily in North America. The newspaper emulated local television news by using an abundance of colorful and sensational photographs accompanied by short articles and by devoting a significant amount of space to local sports and culture.

Over the years, Quebecor's publishing empire grew, expanding beyond Quebec into the rest of Canada and the United States and eventually the world. Today, Quebecor is the world's largest commercial printer, operating 160 plants in 17 countries and employing 39,000 people worldwide. The corporation also owns Sun Media, the second-largest newspaper group in Canada with eight metropolitan dailies, eight community dailies, and 175 weekly newspapers, and it remains the largest magazine publisher in Quebec. Additionally, Quebecor owns Videotron, the largest cable TV provider in Quebec with an estimated 1.4 million subscribers as of 2003. Videotron is also one of the largest Internet service providers in Canada. Videotron subsidiary SuperClub Videotron is the leading video rental and sales chain in Quebec with over 170 locations. Finally, Quebecor also owns and operates TVA, the top general-interest network in Quebec, maintaining a market share of approximately 35 percent.

With the purchase of Videotron Ltee. in 2000, Quebecor not only expanded into the world of cable and Internet services but also acquired a major stake in the development of interactive television. Videotron operates the illico digital interactive television system, which currently has 114,000 subscribers. Illico allows subscribers to access e-mail and surf the Internet through their television set, as well as participate in specially designed chat rooms and newsgroups unique to the interactive service. It also provides easy access to home shopping, creating new synergies between television programs and ancillary markets for the products they feature. Viewers are alerted to the availability for purchase of particular fashions, furniture, and accessories shown on select programs. Quebecor has identified interactive television as key to its media convergence strategy. According to Quebecor's website, "[interactive television] will crystallize the synergies among the company's media properties, giving advertisers a multitude of cross-promotion opportunities and customers a host of innovations and value-added interactive services."

In September 2001 Quebecor added the TVA group to its conglomerate. In order to own the lucrative television channel, Quebecor was first required to sell off its holdings in TQS, which it had owned since 1997. Under Canadian law, companies cannot own more than one broadcast channel in the same market, though they can own multiple newspapers and operate various services within a single market. TVA is the largest private-sector producer and broadcaster of French-language programming in North America. Ten stations reaching the majority of French-speaking households in Quebec as well as the rest of Canada carry TVA's signal. The TVA network owns six of those ten stations. Additionally, TVA International was founded in 1997 when the TVA group bought Motion International, which has since become the leading distributor of Canadian programming in Canada. With the addition of TVA International, the company has achieved full vertical integration of its television holdings. Finally, TVA has a significant interest in specialty cable channels, launching *Le Canal Nouvelles TVA,* a 24-hour all-news station, in 1998, and partnering to create *Canal Evasion,* a French-language travel and tourism specialty channel, and *Canal Indigo,* a French-language pay-per-view channel. TVA also owns 50 percent of HSS Canada, a leading producer of infomercials, and has launched *Club TVAchat,* a French-language equivalent of the Home Shopping Network.

AVI SANTO

Queer as Folk

British Drama Series (adapted in U.S.)

This British television drama, by Russell T. Davies, was first aired on public television from February to April 1999, causing equal measures of controversy and delight. The original eight-part series was followed by the two-part *Queer as Folk 2: Same Men. New Tricks.* In 2000 the program idea transferred to the U.S. cable channel Showtime as a 20-episode series. Writers Ron Cowen and Daniel Lipman relocated the action from Manchester to Pittsburgh, and it aired its fourth season in the autumn of 2003. Davies went on to irk some gay viewers by writing *Bob and Rose* (ITV 2001), a drama about a gay man who falls in love and sleeps with a woman, questioning the absolute nature of his homosexuality. He has been commissioned to write the relaunching of the camp BBC sci-fi TV series, *Dr. Who,* thereby regaining, in the eyes of some, his "gay-friendly" reputation. *Queer as Folk* was, and remains, controversial because it challenged accepted modes of screening homosexuality on television, and because Davies rejects the "gay writer" tag. Produced by Channel 4 TV in the United Kingdom, the program expressed the channel's remit to screen challenging material, even though it was scheduled at a cautious 10:30 P.M. time slot.

The program's title plays on the northern English aphorism that "there's nowt [nothing] as queer as folk," innocently meaning that there is no accounting for the behavioral surprises that people will spring on you. But it also suggests a politicized use of the word: the provocatively postgay slogan "Queer as Fuck" associated with radical activist groups that emerged in the late 1980s. "Queer" activists sought to reappropriate the abusive term *queer* for subversive uses: to counter prejudices against HIV, and to protest against the culture of arcane legislative iniquities in Britain (namely, but not solely, Section 28, which prohibits local authorities from the "promotion of homosexuality" and forbids presenting homosexuality in government-funded schools as an acceptable or appropriate aspect of family life). But more significantly, "queer politics" tried to forge a sexual politics beyond the simple binary of gay/straight, and to disrupt the liberal progressive identity politics associated with gay reform groups Stonewall or GLAAD (Gay and Lesbian Alliance Against Defamation). Davies wrote *Queer as Folk* as a counter to most mainstream TV portrayals of homosexual characters as incidental or associated with misery or villains. All the main characters in *Queer as Folk* are gay, but instead of attempting to create an imagined gay world that represented a politically correct diversity, Davies focused his setting on Manchester's Canal Street gay scene. It was filmed on location in a colorful, vibrant style with an upbeat, partying theme and club music sound track.

The three main characters were hardly all likable. They had faults and behaved foolishly, selfishly, or naively. The most striking, Stuart (Aiden Gillen), a late-20s advertising executive, is a pill-popping sexually voracious "scene queen"; for most of the series, he is not "out" to his family. Vince (Craig Kelly), his long-suffering best friend and secret admirer, is the manager of a supermarket. Finally, Nathan (Charlie Hunnam), a 15-year-old boy, is seduced on his first time out in Canal Street by the predatory Stuart and proceeds to fall in love with him. The sequel, *Queer as Folk 2,* ended by whisking the boys off in their jeep in a magical, surrealistic finale, the audiovisual excess of which broke any links that the series had tentatively kept with the long tradition of British TV social realism.

The strength of *Queer as Folk* was that it created an entirely credible world for the characters, with their priorities and emotional landscape brilliantly captured in the dialogue and the scenarios depicted. Life in this gay scene was exhilarating, highly pleasurable, and marked by excessive alcohol consumption and drug-fueled sex. It was also misogynistic, exploitative, and deeply materialistic. It unashamedly showed the intimate lives of a few affluent gay men in the 1990s enjoying a consumer-led hedonism that captured the spirit of "scene gays," and also of many young heterosexual adults living in Britain.

The worth of the series is signified both by its initial disruptive impact, its enduring "after-life" qualities, and its commercial abilities to travel well across the world. Banned from Australian public TV, it spawned the U.S. adaptation, another series, called *Metrosexuality* (Channel 4, 2001), that featured black gay characters, DVD and music collections, and academic writing and conferences devoted to it. *Queer as Folk* has become a media phenomenon, sustaining itself as a product of the consumerism that it represented on-screen. The program was critically divisive within a majority, heterosexual society, some hating it, some loving it. Interestingly, it divided gay people and their community representatives in Britain.

Press releases, media commentary, and trailers ensured that viewers expected taboos to be broken: over 4 million of them were not disappointed. The opening ten minutes of the first episode showed 15-year-old Nathan (under the legal age for sex) and Stuart engaged in graphically depicted oral-anal and anal sex. This set a record number of complaints to the ITC, independent television's regulatory body. These official complaints were not upheld, but the ITC did disapprove of the program's "celebratory tone" and castigated it for its lack of a moral framework or posttransmission advice about safer sex. Angela Mason of Stonewall, the gay reform group, condemned the program and distanced her organization from the series because it propagated the idea that gay people were sexually promiscuous; Stonewall believed that the program would damage its campaign to lobby the new Labour government (1997) to push its equality and decriminalization laws through Parliament. The program's sponsor (Beck's beer) withdrew its support.

The U.S. version is a polished, well-acted, and credible transatlantic version that has worked very successfully for its own constituency, although its wider social impact is restricted since Showtime is a pay-to-view channel. Post-*Ellen,* it provides a much-needed antidote to the wisecracking but anodyne and inoffensive U.S. sitcom *Will & Grace.*

LANCE PETTITT

See also Ellen; **Sexual Orientation and Television**

Program Notes

U.K. version

Cast

Stuart Alan Jones	Aidan Gillen
Nathan Maloney	Charlie Hunnam
Vince Tyler	Craig Kelly

Writer
Russell T. Davies

Executive Producer
Nicola Shindler

Programming History
Channel 4
8 episodes
February–April 1999   Tuesday 10:30

Queer as Folk 2: Same Men. New Tricks.
2-part special:
February 15, 2000–February 22, 2000

U.S. version

Cast

Brian Kinney	Gale Harold
Michael Novotny	Hal Sparks
Justin Taylor	Randy Harrison
Emmett Honeycutt	Peter Paige
Ted Schmidt	Scott Lowell
Melanie Marcus	Michelle Clunie
Lindsay Peterson	Thea Gill

Developers for U.S. Version
Ron Cowen, Daniel Lipman

Executive Producers
Ron Cowen, Tony Jonas, Daniel Lipman

Programming History
Showtime
49 episodes (as of winter 2003)
Season 1: December 3, 2000–June 24, 2001
                                                Sunday 10:00
Season 2: January 6, 2002–June 16, 2002
Season 3: March 2, 2003–June 22, 2003

Further Reading

Almighty Records, *Queer as Folk: The Whole Love Thing. Sorted,* ALMYCD28, 1999
Davies, R.T., *Queer as Folk: The Scripts,* Channel 4 Books, 1999
Davies, R.T., "Transmission was madness. Honestly," *The Guardian* (September 16, 2003): 16–17
Cooke, L., *British Television Drama,* British Film Institute, 2003
Munt, S.R., "Shame/Pride Dichotomies in Queer as Folk," *Textual Practice* 14:2 (2000): 531–46
Showtime, *Queer as Folk: The Complete First Season,* VHS, SHO2001, 2001
Tobin, R., "Showtime's *Queer as Folk,*" *Film and History* 31:2 (2001): 75–77

Queer Eye for the Straight Guy.

See **Bravo; Sexual Orientation and Television**

Quentin Durgens, M.P.

Canadian Drama Series

One of the first hour-long Canadian drama series produced by the CBC, *Quentin Durgens, M.P.,* began as six half-hour episodes entitled *Mr. Member of Parliament* in the summer of 1965 as part of *The Serial,* a common vehicle for Canadian dramas. The program starred a young Gordon Pinsent as a naive rookie member of Parliament who arrives in Ottawa and quickly learns that the realities behind public service can be alternately humorous, overwhelming, and frustrating.

Consciously designed to be an absolutely distinctive Canadian drama series, *Quentin Durgens, M.P.,* contrasted the private struggles and controversies faced by politicians with the more sedate, pompous image presented by Parliament. Many of its plots were inspired by real-life issues and situations. Pornography, violence in minor-league hockey, gender discrimination, and questions of religious tolerance were topics addressed among its episodes. In all of them, however, the inner workings of power, with its backroom deals and interpersonal struggles, remained the backbone of the series.

The regular series of *Quentin Durgens, M.P.,* began in December 1966 as a winter season replacement. It followed the popular series *Wojeck* in a Tuesday 9:00 P.M. time slot, and, like *Wojeck, Quentin Durgens* was hailed as an example of Canadian television, distinct and set apart from Hollywood drama. The show still carried its imprint as a serial with open narratives, unresolved psychological conflicts, and the freedom to construct stories around topical issues. Frequent allusions to actual social events and a great deal of subtext were interwoven in plots that juxtaposed rational and

emotional behavior. The result made for what its director and producer David Gardner called an "ironic drama." Documentary techniques grounded in the tradition of the National Film Board of Canada also added to the "behind-the-scene" feel of the series and reflected, according to Canadian television critic Morris Wolfe, a Canadian tradition of "telling it like it is." Despite these claims, other Canadian television critics and historians such as Paul Rutherford have questioned the uniqueness of these "made-in-Canada" dramas, arguing instead that many of the characteristics attributed to Canadian drama series such as *Wojeck, Quentin Durgens, M.P.,* and *Cariboo Country* were already to be found in some U.S. and, especially, British dramas.

Although *Quentin Durgens, M.P.,* was part of a formidable lineup, it was never popular with Canadian viewers. With fewer funds and resources than *Wojeck,* the show had to be videotaped (on location and in the studio) for its initial two seasons. The flattened, taped images and sometimes awkward edits detracted from the documentary feel. Nor were its scripts consistently strong. Despite the increased support in its third season (after the end of *Wojeck*), when all 17 episodes were filmed and in color, *Quentin Durgens* failed to hold the large audiences *Wojeck* had won for the evening. Canadian viewers, it seemed, did not share the CBC's and producers' interest in developing a distinctive Canadian perspective. Parliamentary intrigues were not fascinating enough to attract a large following, and *Quentin Durgens, M.P.,* simply lacked the excitement of cop shows.

MANON LAMONTAGNE

Quentin Durgens, M.P.

Quentin Durgens, M.P.
Photo courtesy of National Archives of Canada/CBC Collection

Cast

Quentin Durgens, M.P.	Gordon Pinsent
His Secretary	Suzanne Levesque
Other Members of Parliament	Ovila Legere,
	Franz Russell,
	Chris Wiggins

Producers

David Gardner, Ron Weyman, John Trent, Kirk Jones

Programming History

41 episodes (including 6 as *Mr. Member of Parliament* on *The Serial,* summer 1965)

December 1966–January 1967	Tuesday 9:00–10:00
February 1967–April 1967	Tuesday 9:00–10:00
September 1968–January 1969	Tuesday 9:00–10:00

Further Reading

Miller, Mary Jane, *Turn Up the Contrast: CBC Television Drama since 1952,* Vancouver: University of British Columbia Press, 1987

Rutherford, Paul, *When Television Was Young: Primetime Canada, 1952–1967,* Toronto: University of Toronto Press, 1990

Wolfe, Morris, *Jolts: The TV Wasteland and the Canadian Oasis,* Toronto: James Lorimer, 1985

Quiz and Game Shows

Prior to the quiz show scandals in 1958, no differentiation existed between quiz shows and game shows. Programs that relied mainly on physical activity and had no significant quiz element to them, such as *Truth or Consequences* or *People Are Funny,* were called "quiz shows," as was an offering like *The $64,000 Question,* which emphasized factual knowledge. The scandals mark an important turning point because in the years following, programs formerly known as "quiz shows" were renamed "game shows." This change coincided with a shift in content, away from high culture and factual knowledge common to the big-money shows of the 1950s. However, the renaming of the genre also represents an attempt to distance the programs from the extremely negative connotations of the scandals, which had undermined the legitimacy of the high-cultural values that quiz shows (the term and the genre) embodied. Thus, the new name, "game shows," removed the genre from certain cultural assumptions and instead creates associations with the less-sensitive concepts of play and leisure. Nevertheless, the historical and material causes for this renaming still fail to provide a sufficient basis for a definition of this genre as a whole.

In *Television Culture,* John Fiske suggests more satisfactory definitions and categories with which to distinguish among different types of shows. One of the main appeals of quiz shows is that they deal with issues such as competition, success, and knowledge—central concerns for American culture. It makes sense, then, to follow Fiske in defining this genre according to its relation to knowledge. He begins by suggesting a basic split between "factual" knowledge and "human" knowledge. Factual knowledge can be further divided into "academic" knowledge and "everyday" knowledge. Human knowledge consists of knowledge of "people in general" and of specific "individuals." While Fiske does not clearly distinguish between the terms *game show* and *quiz show,* his categories reflect a significant difference in program type. All shows that deal with competitions between individuals or groups, and based primarily on the display of factual knowledge, may be considered quiz shows. Shows dealing with human knowledge (knowledge of people or of individuals), or that are based primarily on gambling or on physical performances, fall in the category of game shows. Thus, *The Gong Show* or *Double Dare* are not

considered quiz shows, since they rely primarily or completely on physical talents, whereas *Family Feud* and *The Newlywed Game,* which rely entirely on knowledge of people or of individuals, would also be considered game shows. *Jeopardy!,* however, with its focus on academic, factual knowledge, is clearly a quiz show.

Many early television quiz shows of the 1940s were transferred or adapted from radio, the most prominent among them being *Information Please, Winner Take All,* and *Quiz Kids.* These shows also provided a professional entry point for influential quiz show producers such as Louis Cowan, Mark Goodson, and Jack Barry. Although a number of early radio and television quiz shows were produced locally and later picked up by networks, this trend ended in the early 1950s, when increasing production values and budgets led to the centralization of the production of quiz shows under the control of networks and sponsors. Nevertheless, the relatively low production costs, simple sets, small casts, and highly formalized production techniques have continually made quiz shows an extremely attractive television genre. Quiz shows are more profitable and faster to produce than virtually any other form of entertainment television.

In the late 1940s and early 1950s, most quiz shows were extremely simple in visual design and the structure of the games. Sets often consisted of painted flats and a desk for an expert panel and a host. The games themselves usually involved a simple question-and-answer format that displayed the expertise of the panel members. An important characteristic of early quiz shows was their foregrounding of the expert knowledge of official authorities. A standard format (used, e.g., on *Americana* or *Information Please*) relied on home viewers to submit questions to the expert panel. Viewers were rewarded with small prizes (money or consumer goods) for each question used, and with larger prizes if the panel failed to answer their question. Some programs relied on the audience to send in questions and challenge the intellectual authority of the expert panel. *Information Please,* for example, played with the appeal of reversing educational hierarchies and challenged its viewers to "stump the experts." While the expert-panel format dominated the 1940s, it was slowly replaced by audience-centered quizzes in the early 1950s. In this period, "everyday people" from the studio audience became the subjects of the show. The host of the show, however, remained the center of attention and served as a main attraction for the program (e.g., Bert Parks and Bud Collyer in *Break the Bank* and James McClain in *Doctor I.Q.*).

At this point, the visual style of the shows was still fairly simple, often re-creating a simple theatrical proscenium or using an actual theater stage. The Mark Goodson–Bill Todman production *Winner Take All* was an interesting exception. Although it also used charismatic hosts, it introduced the concept of a returning contestant who faced a new challenger for every round. Thus, the attention was moved away from panels and hosts and toward the contestants in the quiz.

A 1954 U.S. Supreme Court ruling created the impetus for the development of a new type of program when it removed "jackpot" quizzes from the category of gambling and made it possible to use this form of entertainment on television. At CBS, producer Cowan, in cooperation with Revlon Cosmetics as sponsor, developed the idea for a new "jackpot" quiz show based on the radio program *Take It or Leave It*. The result— *The $64,000 Question*—raised prize money to a spectacular new level and also changed the visual style and format of quiz shows significantly. *The $64,000 Question,* its spin-off *The $64,000 Challenge,* and other imitations following between 1955 and 1958 (e.g., *Twenty-One, The Big Surprise*) all focused on high-culture and factual, often academic, knowledge. These programs were part of television's attempts in the 1950s to gain respectability and, simultaneously, a wider audience. They introduced a much more elaborate set design and visual style and generally created a serious and ceremonious atmosphere. *The $64,000 Question* introduced an IBM sorting machine, bank guards, an isolation booth, and neon signs, while other shows built on the same ingredients to create similar effects. In an effort to keep big-money quiz shows attractive, the prize money was constantly increased and, indeed, on a number of shows, became unlimited. *Twenty-One* and *The $64,000 Challenge* also created tense competitions between contestants, so that audience identification with one contestant could be even greater. Consequently, the most successful contestants became celebrities in their own right, perhaps the most prominent among them being Dr. Joyce Brothers and Charles Van Doren.

However, this reliance on popular returning contestants, on celebrities in contest, also created a motivation for program makers to manipulate the outcome of the quizzes. Quiz show sponsors in particular recognized that some contestants were more popular than others, a fact that could be used to increase audience size. These sponsors required or advocated the rigging

of the programs to create a desired audience identification with these popular contestants.

When these practices were discovered and made public, the ensuing scandals undermined the popular appeal of big-money shows and, together with lower ratings, led to the cancellation of all of these programs in 1958–59. Entertainment Productions Inc. (EPI), a production company founded by Cowan, was particularly involved in and affected by the scandals. EPI had produced a majority of the big-money shows and was also most actively involved in the riggings. Following the scandals, the networks used the involvement of sponsors in the rigging practices as an argument for the complete elimination of sponsor-controlled programming in prime-time television.

Still, not all quiz shows of the late 1950s were canceled due to the scandals. A number of programs that did not rely on the huge prizes (e.g., *The Price Is Right, Name That Tune*) remained on the air and provided an example for later shows. Even these programs, however, were usually removed from prime time, their stakes significantly reduced, and the required knowledge made less demanding. In the early 1960s, very few new quiz shows were introduced, and most were game shows focusing less on high culture and more on gambling and physical games. Overall, the postscandal era was marked by a move away from expert knowledge to contestants with everyday knowledge. *College Bowl* and *Alumni Fun* still focused on "academic" knowledge without reviving the spectacular qualities of 1950s quiz shows, but *Jeopardy!*, introduced by Merv Griffin in 1964, is the only other significant new program developed in the decade following the scandals. It reintroduces "academic" knowledge, a serious atmosphere, elaborate sets, and returning contestants, but offers only moderate prizes. The late 1960s were marked by even more cancellations (CBS canceled all of its shows in 1967) and by increasing attempts of producers to find alternative distribution outlets for their products outside the network system. Their hopes were realized through the growth in first-run syndication.

In 1970 the Federal Communications Commission (FCC) introduced two new regulations, the Financial Interest and Syndication Rules (Fin-Syn) and the Prime Time Access Rule (PTAR), that had a considerable effect on quiz/game show producers and on the television industry in general. Fin-Syn limited network ownership of television programs beyond their network run and increased the control of independent producers over their shows. The producers' financial situation and their creative control were significantly improved. Additionally, PTAR gave control of the 7:00 to 7:30 P.M. time slot to local stations. The intention of this change was to create locally based programming, but the time period was usually filled with syndicated programs, primarily inexpensive quiz shows and tabloid-news offerings. The overall situation of quiz/game show producers was substantially improved by the FCC rulings.

As a result, a number of new quiz shows began to appear in the mid-1970s. They were, of course, all in color and relied on extremely bright and flashy sets, strong primary colors, and a multitude of aural and visual elements. In addition to this transformation to the traditionally solemn atmosphere of quiz shows, the programs were thoroughly altered in terms of content. Many of the 1970s quiz shows introduced an element of gambling to their contests (e.g., *The Joker's Wild, The Big Showdown*) and moved them further from a clear "academic" and serious knowledge toward an everyday, ordinary knowledge. A number of shows, such as *Card Sharks* and *Family Feud,* not only emphasize the everyday character of their contestants but also ask players to guess the most popular responses to questions asked in small polls. Contestants are thus rewarded for understanding or representing "average" people.

Blatant consumerism began to play an important role in quiz shows such as *The Price Is Right* and *Sale of the Century,* as the distinctions between quiz and game shows became increasingly blurred in this period. As Graham points out in *Come on Down!!!,* quiz shows had to change in the 1970s, adapting to a new cultural environment that included flourishing pop culture and countercultures. On *The Price Is Right,* Goodson answered this challenge by creating a noisy, carnival atmosphere that challenged cultural norms and assumptions represented in previous generations of quiz shows.

The same type of show remained prevalent in the 1980s, although most examples now appeared primarily in syndication and, to a lesser extent, on cable channels. Both *Wheel of Fortune* and a new version of *Jeopardy!* were extremely successful as syndicated shows in the prime-time-access slot (7:00–8:00 P.M.) and remain popular in that time period even though the PTAR was rescinded in 1996.

In what may become a trend, Lifetime Television introduced two quiz shows combining everyday knowledge (of consumer products) with physical contests (shopping—and spending—as swiftly as possible). These shows, *Supermarket Sweep* and *Shop 'Til You Drop,* also challenge assumptions about cultural norms and the value of everyday knowledge. In particular they focus on "women's knowledge" and thus effectively address the predominantly female audience of this cable channel. In September 2000 these two

highly consumerist programs moved to the PAX network, where they exemplify family-friendly programming that, according to PAX's mission, features strong values and positive role models. This shows the status of many quiz shows as wholesome entertainment and the ability of the genre to adapt to a wide variety of programming demands. One area of growth for quiz shows in the era of cable television, then, seems to be the creation of this type of "signature show," which appeals to the relatively narrowly defined target audience of specific cable channels.

The unexpected success of ABC's *Who Wants to Be a Millionaire?* in the summer of 1999 gave quiz shows a new presence on prime-time television and focused a significant degree of public attention on the genre. Adapted from a British program of the same name, *Millionaire* incorporated both traditional, educational knowledge and trivia and often emphasized the presumed mental prowess of its winners. Additionally, it provided several devices for contestants to receive assistance from the home or studio audience, thus creating a link between program and viewers that tended to encourage increased viewer identification. Several other prime-time game shows premiered in the following fall and spring season, including *Greed* on FOX and a new version of *Twenty-One* on NBC, both of which lasted less than a season. Although faced with a number of competing programs, *Millionaire* was the most successful of the quiz shows premiered from 1999 on. For a time, it dominated the ABC schedule, with episodes airing several nights a week and consistently ranking among the top-10 rated programs. However, perhaps because of overexposure, its rating plummeted in the 2001–02 season, and *Millionaire* was not renewed as a regular series for the 2002–03 season (though occasional specials were anticipated). The *Millionaire* concept continues to thrive in adaptations shown around the world. In 2004 Regis Philbin introduced "Who Wants to Be a Super Millionaire" on ABC.

Following the wave of new shows initiated by *Millionaire,* the premiere on CBS of *Survivor* in May 2000 introduced to the United States a new type of hybrid programs, often termed "reality shows," which quickly started to gain popularity. *Survivor, Big Brother, Fear Factor, Boot Camp, Lost,* and *The Amazing Race* all have structured their competition like an extended game show. Contestants have to perform a variety of physically and, less frequently, mentally challenging tasks; earn different types of rewards; and get eliminated one by one until the winner of the game is identified. What has changed from traditional game shows is mainly the use of a manipulated exterior or nonstudio ("real") space in which much of the extended competition takes place. Following the example of *Millionaire,* the level of prize money on these shows is extremely high, often ranging from $500,000 to $1 million. While the hybridization of game shows into reality shows has generated a significant amount of new programming, these shows also stand out for their excessive abuse of contestants and their inconsiderate use of the countries and landscapes in which they are set. One of the striking characteristics of many reality game shows is that they entice their contestants to do literally anything to win. On several shows, contestants ate insects, rotten food, or animal innards; were exposed to starvation and injury; and displayed various forms of antisocial behavior to stay ahead in the game. It seems that more than ever, game shows tend to legitimize greed and ruthless competitive behavior as the genre develops in new directions.

OLAF HOERSCHELMANN

See also **Goodson, Mark, and Bill Todman; Griffin, Merv; Grundy, Reg;** *I've Got A Secret;* **Moore,** **Garry; Quiz Show Scandals;** *Sale of the Century;* ***$64,000 Question, The/The $64,000 Challenge***

Further Reading

Barnouw, Erik, *A History of Broadcasting in the United States,* volume 3, *The Image Empire, from 1953,* New York: Oxford University Press, 1970

Boddy, William, *Fifties Television: The Industry and Its Critics,* Urbana: University of Illinois Press, 1990

Fabe, M., *TV Game Shows,* Garden City, New York: Doubleday, 1979

Fiske, John, *Television Culture,* London: Routledge, 1987

Graham, J., *Come on Down!!!: The TV Game Show Book,* New York: Abbeville Press, 1988

Schwartz, D., S. Ryan, and F. Wostbrock, *The Encyclopedia of Television Game Shows,* New York: Zoetrope, 1987; 3rd edition, New York: Facts on File, 1999

Shaw, P., "Generic Refinement on the Fringe: The Game Show, *Southern Speech Communication Journal* 52 (1987)

Stone, J., and T. Yohn, *Prime Time and Misdemeanors: Investigating the 1950s TV Quiz Scandal—A D.A.'s Account,* New Brunswick, New Jersey: Rutgers University Press, 1993

Quiz Show Scandals

No programming format mesmerized television viewers of the 1950s with more hypnotic intensity than the "big-money" quiz show, one of the most popular and ill-fated genres in U.S. television history. In the 1940s a popular radio program had awarded top prize money of $64. The new medium raised the stakes a thousandfold. From its premiere on CBS on June 7, 1955, *The $64,000 Question* was an immediate sensation, racking up some of the highest ratings in television history up to that time. Its success spawned a spin-off, *The $64,000 Challenge,* and a litter of like-minded shows: *The Big Surprise, Dotto, Tic Tac Dough,* and *Twenty-One.* When the Q-and-A sessions were exposed as elaborate frauds, columnist Art Buchwald captured the national sense of betrayal with a glib name for the producers and contestants who conspired to bamboozle a trusting audience: the Quizlings.

Broadcast live and in prime time, the big-money quiz show presented itself as a high-pressure test of knowledge under the heat of klieg lights and the scrutiny of 55 million participant-observers. Set design, lighting, and pure hokum enhanced the atmosphere of suspense. Contestants were put in glass isolation booths, with the air conditioning turned off to make them sweat. Tight close-ups framed faces against darkened backgrounds, and spotlights illuminated contestants in a ghostly aura. Armed police guarded "secret" envelopes and impressive-looking contraptions spat out precooked questions on IBM cards. The big winners—such as Columbia University student Elfrida Von Nardroff, who earned $226,500 on *Twenty-One,* or warehouse clerk Teddy Nadler, who earned $252,000 on *The $64,000 Challenge*—took home a fortune.

By the standards of the game shows of a later epoch, the intellectual content of the 1950s quiz shows was erudite. Almost all the questions involved some demonstration of cerebral aptitude: retrieving lines of poetry; identifying dates from history; or reeling off scientific classifications, the stuff of memorization and canonical culture. Since victors returned to the show until they lost, risking accumulated winnings on future stakes, individual contestants might develop a devoted following over a period of weeks. Matching an incongruous area of expertise to the right personality was a favorite hook, as in the cases of Richard McCutchen, the rugged marine captain who was an expert on French cooking, or Dr. Joyce Brothers (not then an icon of pop psychology), whose encyclopedic knowledge of boxing won her $132,000.

If the quiz shows made celebrities out of ordinary folk, they also sought to engage the services of celebrities. Orson Welles claimed to have been approached by a quiz show producer looking for a "genius type" and guaranteeing him $150,000 and a seven-week engagement. Welles refused, but bandleader Xavier Cugat won $16,000 as an expert on Tin Pan Alley songs in a rigged match against actress Lillian Roth on *The $64,000 Challenge.* "I considered I was giving a performance," he later explained guilelessly. Twelve-year-old Patty Duke won $32,000 against child actor Eddie Hodges, then the juvenile lead in *The Music Man* on Broadway. Teamed with a personable marine flyer named John Glenn, Hodges had earlier won the $25,000 grand prize on *Name That Tune.*

Far and away the most notorious Quizling was Charles Van Doren, a contestant on NBC's *Twenty-One,* a quiz show based on the game of blackjack. Scion of the prestigious literary family and a lecturer in English at Columbia University, Van Doren was an authentic pop phenomenon, whose video charisma earned him $129,000 in prize money, the cover of *Time* magazine, and a permanent spot on NBC's *Today,* where he discussed non-Euclidean geometry and recited 17th-century poetry.

From the moment Van Doren walked onto the set of *Twenty-One,* on November 28, 1956, for his first face-off against a high-IQ eccentric named Herbert Stempel, he proved himself a telegenic natural. In the isolation booth, Van Doren managed to engage the spectators' sympathy by sharing his mental concentration. Apparently muttering unself-consciously to himself, he let viewers see him think: eyes alert, hand on chin, then a sudden bolt ("Oh, I know!"), after which he delivered the answer. Asked to name the volumes of Winston Churchill's wartime memoirs, he muttered, "I've seen the ad for those books a thousand times!" Asked to come up with a biblical reference, he said self-deprecatingly, "My father would know that." Van Doren's was a remarkable and seductive performance.

Twenty-One's convoluted rules decreed that, in the event of a tie, the money wagered for points doubled, from $500 a point to $1,000 (and so on). Thus, contestants needed to be coached not only on answers and acting but on the amount of points they selected in the gamble. A tie meant double financial stakes for each successive game with a consequent ratcheting up of the tension. By pregame arrangement, the first Van Doren–Stempel face-off ended with three ties; hence, the next week's game would be played for $2,000 a point, and publicized accordingly.

On Wednesday, December 5, 1956, at 10:30 P.M., an

Charles Van Doren.
Photo courtesy of Wisconsin Center for Film and Theater Research

estimated 50 million Americans tuned in to *Twenty-One* for what host and coproducer Jack Barry called "the biggest game ever played in the program." The first category was boxing, and Van Doren fared poorly. Ahead 16 points to Van Doren's 0, Stempel was given the chance to stop the game. Supposedly, only the audience knew he was in the lead and, if he stopped the game, Van Doren would lose. At this point, on live television, Stempel could have reneged on the deal, vanquished his opponent, and won an extra $32,000. But he opted to play by the script and continue the match. The next category, movies, proved more Van Doren-friendly. Asked to name Brando's female costar in *On the Waterfront,* Van Doren teased briefly ("she was that lovely frail girl") before coming up with the correct answer (Eva Marie Saint). Stempel again had the chance to ad-lib his own lines, but he did not. Asked to name the 1955 Oscar Winner for Best Picture, he hesitated and answered *On the Waterfront.* The correct answer was *Marty.*

But another tie meant another round at $2,500 a point. The next round of questions was crucial. Van Doren was asked to give the names and the fates of the third, fourth, and fifth wives of Henry VIII. As Barry led him through the litany, Van Doren took the audience with him every step of the way. ("I don't think he beheaded her.... Yes, what happened to her?") Given the same question, Stempel successfully named the wives, and Barry asked him their fates. "Well, they all died," he cracked to gales of laughter. Van Doren stopped the game and won the round.

In August and September 1958 disgruntled former contestants went public with accusations that the results were rigged and the contestants coached. First, a standby contestant on *Dotto* produced a page from a winner's crib sheet. Then, the bitter Herbert Stempel told how he had taken a dive in his climatic encounter with Van Doren. An artist named James Snodgrass had taken the precaution of mailing registered letters to himself with the results of his appearances on *Twenty-One* predicted in advance. Most of the high-drama matchups, it turned out, were carefully choreographed. Contestants were drilled in Q-and-A before airtime and coached in the pantomime of nail-biting suspense (stroke chin, furrow brow, wipe sweat from forehead).

By October 1958, as a New York grand jury convened by prosecutor Joseph Stone investigated the charges and heard closed-door testimony, quiz show ratings had plummeted. For their part, the networks played damage control, denying knowledge of rigging, canceling the suspect shows, and tossing the producers overboard. Yet it was hard to credit the innocence of executives at NBC and CBS. A public relations flack for *Twenty-One* best described the implied contract: "It was sort of a situation where a husband suspects his wife but doesn't want to know because he loves her."

Despite the revelations and the grand jury investigation, the quiz show producers, Van Doren, and the other big-money winners steadfastly maintained their innocence. Solid citizens all, they feared the loss of professional standing and the loyalty of friends and family as much as the retribution of the district attorney's office. Nearly 100 people committed perjury rather than own up to activities that, though embarrassing, were not illegal. Prosecutor Stone lamented that "nothing in my experience prepared me for the mass perjury that took place on the part of scores of well-educated people who had no trouble understanding what was at stake."

When the judge presiding over the New York investigations ordered the grand jury report sealed, Washington smelled a cover-up and a political opportunity. Through October and November 1959 the House Subcommittee on Legislative Oversight, chaired by Oren Harris (Democrat, Arkansas), held standing-room-only hearings into the quiz show scandals. A renewed wave of publicity recorded the testimony of the now-repentant network bigwigs and star contestants whose minds, apparently, were concentrated powerfully by federal intervention. At one point, committee staffers came upon possible communist associations in the background of a few witnesses.

Meanwhile, as newspaper headlines screamed "Where's Charlie?," the star witness everyone wanted to hear from was motoring desperately through the back roads of New England, ducking a congressional subpoena. Finally, on November 2, 1959, with tension mounting in anticipation of Van Doren's appearance to answer questions (the irony was lost on no one), the chastened former English professor confessed. "I was involved, deeply involved, in a deception," he told the Harris Committee. "The fact that I too was very much deceived cannot keep me from being the principal victim of that deception, because I was its principal symbol." In another irony, Washington's made-for-TV spectacle never made it to the airwaves due to the opposition of House Speaker Sam Rayburn, who felt that the presence of television cameras would undermine the dignity of Congress.

The firestorm that resulted, claimed *Variety*, "injured broadcasting more than anything ever before in the public eye." Even the sainted Edward R. Murrow was sullied when it was revealed that his celebrity interview show, CBS's *Person to Person*, provided guests with questions in advance. Perhaps most significantly in terms of the future shape of commercial television, the quiz show scandals made the networks forever leery of "single sponsorship" programming. Henceforth, they parceled out advertising time in 15-, 30-, or 60-second increments, wrenching control away from single sponsors and advertising agencies.

THOMAS DOHERTY

Further Reading

Anderson, Kent, *Television Fraud: The History and Implications of the Quiz Show Scandals,* Westport, Connecticut: Greenwood Press, 1978

Karp, Walter, "The Quiz-show Scandal," *American Heritage* (May–June 1989)

Real, Michael, "The Great Quiz Show Scandal: Why America Remains Fascinated," *Television Quarterly* (Winter 1995)

Stone, Joseph, and T. Yohn, *Prime-Time and Misdemeanors: Investigating the 1950s TV Quiz Scandal: A D.A.'s Account,* New Brunswick, New Jersey: Rutgers University Press, 1992

R

Racism, Ethnicity, and Television

Until the late 1980s, whiteness was consistently naturalized in U.S. television—social whiteness, that is, not the "pinko-grayishness" that British novelist E.M. Forster identified as the "standard" skin hue of Europeans. This whiteness has not been culturally monochrome. Irish, Italian, Jewish, Polish, British, French, German, and Russian people, whether as ethnic entities or national representatives, have dotted the landscape of TV drama, providing the safe spice of white life, entertaining trills and flourishes over the *basso ostinato* of social whiteness.

In other words, to pivot the debate on race and television purely on whether and how people of color have figured, on or behind the screen or in the audience, is already to miss the point. What was consistently projected, without public fanfare, but in teeming myriads of programs, news priorities, sportscasts, movies, and ads, was the naturalness and normalcy of social whiteness. Television visually accumulated the heritage of representation in mainstream U.S. science, religion, education, theater, art, literature, cinema, radio, and the press. According to television representation, the United States was a white nation, with some marginal "ethnic" accretions that were at their best when they could simply be ignored, like well-trained and deferential maids and doormen. This was even beyond being thought a good thing. It was axiomatic, and self-evident.

Thus, American television in its first two genera-

tions inherited and diffused, on an hourly and daily basis, a mythology of whiteness that framed and sustained a racist national self-understanding. U.S. television was not alone in this respect. Nations as different as Australia, Brazil, Britain, France, and Mexico shared in common a television representation of people of color that rather systematically excluded them or was content to stereotype them, and a set of news values that privileged whiteness as normal. Joel Zito Araújo has provided an absorbing account of the painful struggle to represent Afro-Brazilians (50 percent of the population) in Brazil's hugely popular *telenovelas*. Nonetheless, none of these television systems had anything like the global reach of American TV. The implications of American TV for helping cement racially prejudicial attitudes elsewhere in the world, for normalizing certain levels of white racism, would make a fitting topic for international communication research.

There is a second issue in American television, which has become increasingly significant at the beginning of the 21st century. Insofar as the televisual hegemony of social whiteness has been critiqued, either on television itself, or on video, or in print, it has most often tended to focus on African-American issues. Yet, in reviewing racism and ethnicity in U.S. television, we need not downplay four centuries of African-American experience and contribution in order to recognize as well the importance of Native American nations, Latinos, and Asian Americans in all their variety. Thus, in this essay, attention will be paid, so far as research permits, to each one of these four groupings, although there will not be space to treat the important subgroupings (Haitians, Vietnamese, etc.) within each. The discussion will commence with representation, mainstream and alternative, and then move on to employment patterns in the TV industry, broadcast and cable. The conclusion will introduce the so far underresearched question of racism, ethnicity, and TV audiences. Before doing so, however, a more exact definition is needed of racism in the U.S. context.

First, racism is expressed along a connected spectrum, from the casual patronizing remark to the sadism of the prison guard, from avoidance of skin contact to the starving of public education in inner cities and reservations, or to death rates among infants of color higher than in some Third World countries. Racism does not have to take the form of lynching, extermination camps, or slavery to be systemic and virulent—yet simultaneously dismissed as of minor importance or even as irrelevant by the white majority.

Second, racism may stereotype groups differently. Class is often pivotal here. Claimed success among Asian Americans and Jews is attacked just as is the alleged inability to make good among Latinos and African Americans. Multiple Native American nations with greatly differing languages and cultures are lumped together in a generic "Indian" category. Gender plays a role too: white stomachs will contract at supposedly truculent and violence-prone men of color, but ethnic minority women get attributed with pliancy—even, for white males, to presuming their special eagerness for sexual dalliance.

Third, racism in the United States is binary. People of mixed descent are not permitted to confuse the issue but belong automatically to a minority group of color; witness the public debate around the appropriateness of a "multiple" category for racial/ethnic self-identification in the 2000 census. Ethnic minority individuals whose personal cultural style may be read as emblematic of the ethnic majority's are quite often responded to as traitors, and thus they are either warmly regarded as the "good exception" by the white majority or derisively labeled as "self-hating" by the minority.

Lastly, as Robert Entman and Andrew Rojecki have argued, racist belief has changed to being more supple, and "modern" racism has shed its biological absolutism. In the "modern" version, the civil rights movement won, racial hatred is past, and talented individuals now make it. Therefore, continuing ethnic minority poverty is solely the minority's overall cultural/attitudinal fault.

Mainstream Representation

In discussing mainstream representation, it is vital to note three issues. One is the importance of historical shifts in the representation of these issues, especially since the mid-1980s, but also at certain critical junctures before then. The second is the importance of taking into account the entire spectrum of what television provides, including ads (perhaps 20 percent of U.S. TV content), weathercasting, sitcoms, documentaries, sports, MTV, non-English-language programming, religious channels, old films, breaking news, reality programs, and talk shows. Too many studies have zeroed in on one or another format and then taken it as representative of the whole. Here we will try to engage with the spectrum, although space and available research will put most of the focus on whites and blacks in mainstream television news and entertainment. The third is the strong concentration of African Americans in comedy and crime scenarios. Quality of representation is as important as quantity.

Historically, as J. Fred MacDonald has shown, U.S. television perpetuated patterns established in U.S. cinema, radio, theater, and other forms of public communication and announced people of color overwhelmingly by their absence. It was not that these people were malevolently stereotyped or denounced. They simply did not appear to exist. If they surfaced, it was almost always as wraiths, silent black butlers smiling deferentially, Latino field hands laboring sweatily, or Indian braves whooping wildly against the march of history. Speaking parts were rare, heavily circumscribed, and typically an abusive distortion of actual modes of speech. But the essence of the problem was virtual nonexistence.

Thus, the TV industry collaborated to a marked degree with the segregation that has marked the U.S. nation, once legally and residentially, now residentially. Programs and advertisements that might have inflamed white opinion in the South were strenuously avoided, partly in accurate recognition of the militancy of some opinions that might lead to boycotts of advertisers, but partly yielding simply to inertia in defining that potential as a fact of life beyond useful reflection.

The programs shunned were rarely in the slightest degree confrontational, or even suggestive of interracial romance. The classic case was *The Nat "King" Cole Show*, which premiered on NBC in November 1956, and which was eventually taken off for good in December of the following year. A *Who's Who* of distinguished black as well as white artists and performers virtually gave their services to the show, and NBC strove to keep it alive. But the program could not find a national sponsor, at one point having to rely on no less than 30 sponsors in order to be seen nationwide. Cole himself explicitly blamed the advertising agencies' readiness to be intimidated by the White Citizens Councils, the spearhead of resistance to desegregation in southern states.

This was not the only occasion that African Americans were seen on the TV screen in that era. A number of shows, notably *The Ed Sullivan Show,* made a point of inviting black performers on to the screen. Yet entertainment was only one thin slice of the spectrum. Articulate black individuals, such as Paul Robeson, with a clear critique of the racialization of the United States, were systematically excluded from expressing their opinions on air (in his case, on the pretext he was a communist).

This generalized absence, and univocal whiteness, was first punctured by TV news coverage of the savage handling of civil rights demonstrators in the latter 1950s and early 1960s. Images of police dogs, fire hoses, and billy clubs being unleashed against unarmed black demonstrators in Montgomery, Alabama, and white parents—with their children standing by their side—spewing obscenities and hurling rocks at Martin Luther King, Jr.'s march through Cicero, Illinois, may still have portrayed African Americans as largely voiceless victims, but the coverage was nonetheless able to communicate the activists' dignity under fire, whereas their white persecutors communicated their own monstrous inhumanity. The same story repeated itself in the school desegregation riots in New Orleans in 1964 and Boston in 1974.

U.S. television since then has made sporadic attempts to address these particular white-black issues, with such shows as *Roots, The Cosby Show,* and *Eyes on the Prize,* and through a proliferation of black newscasters at the local level, but all the while cleaving steadfastly to three traditions. First, there is the continuing virtual invisibility of Latinos, Native Americans, and Asian Americans. Indeed, some studies indicate that for decades Latinos have hovered around 1 to 2 percent of characters in TV drama, very substantially less than their percentage of the population. Darrell Hamamoto similarly charges that, "By and large, TV Asians are inserted in programs chiefly as semantic markers that reflect upon and reveal telling aspects of the Euro-American characters." Second, the tradition of color-segregating entertainment has changed but little. Even though black shows began to multiply considerably from the latter 1980s, casts have generally been white or black (and never Latino, Native, or Asian). Third, the few minority roles in dramatic TV have frequently been of criminals and drug addicts. This pattern has intensively reinforced, and seemingly been reinforced by, the similar racial stereotyping

In Living Color, Keenen Ivory Wayans, Damon Wayans, 1990–94.
©*20th Century Fox/Courtesy of the Everett Collection*

common in "reality TV" police shows and local TV news programs. The standard alternative role for African Americans has been comic actor (or stand-up comic in comedy shows). Commenting upon the wider cinematic tradition of Latino portrayals, Charles Ramírez-Berg has identified the bandit/greaser, the mixed-race slut, the buffoon (male and female), the Latin lover, and the alluring Dark Lady, as five hackneyed and offensive tropes.

Roots (1977) and *Roots: The Next Generations* (1979) confounded the TV industry's prior expectations, with up to 140 million viewers for all or part of the first miniseries, and over 100 million for *The Next Generations.* For the first time on U.S. television, some of the realities of slavery—brutality, rape, enforced deculturation—were confronted over a protracted period, and through individual characters with whom, as they fought to escape or survive, the audience could identify. Against this historic first was the individualistic focus on screenwriter Alex Haley's determined family, presented as "immigrants-times-ten" fighting an exceptionally painful way over its generations toward the American Dream myth of all U.S. immigrants. Against it, too, was the emphasis on the centuries and decades before the 1970s, which the ahistorical vector in U.S. culture easily cushions from application to the often devastating here and now. Nonetheless, it was a signal achievement.

The Cosby Show (1984–92) was the next milestone. Defeating industry expectations just as *Roots* had, the series scored exceptionally high continuing ratings right across the nation. The show attracted a certain volume of hostile comment, some of it smugly supercilious. The fact it was popular with white audiences in the South, and in South Africa, was a favorite quick shot to try to debunk it. Some critics claimed it fed the mirage that racial injustice could be overcome through individual economic advance; others posited that it primly fostered Reaganite conservative family values. Both of the analyses were indeed easily possible readings of the show within contemporary U.S. culture.

Herman Gray, one of the few critics to acknowledge the role of the show in opening the gate to a large number of black television shows and to new professional experience and openings for many black media artists, is also correct in characterizing *The Cosby Show* as assimilationist. It hardly ever directly raised issues of social equity, except in interpersonal gender relations. Nonetheless, in the context of the nation's and the industry's history, the show could have been exquisitely correct—and never once have hit the screen.

Eyes on the Prize (1987; 1990) allows a much more straightforward discussion. A documentary series on the American civil rights movements from 1954 to 1985, it too marked a huge watershed in U.S. television history. Partly, its achievement was to bring together historical footage with movement participants, some very elderly, who could supply living oral history. Partly, too, its achievement was that producer-director Henry Hampton consistently included in the narrative the voices of segregationist foes of the movement, on the ground that the story was theirs, too. This gave the opportunity for self-reflection within the white audience, rather than easy self-distancing.

However, the series was on PBS and thus never drew the kind of audience *Roots* did. In the United States the public appetite for documentaries was also at something of a low toward the end of the century, as opposed to Europe and Russia, where the documentary form was much more popular. *Eyes'* influence would be slower than *Roots* or *Cosby* achieved, though significant through video rentals and college courses. Its primary significance for present purposes is its demonstration of what could be done televisually, but what was never contemplated to be undertaken by the commercial TV companies.

In 1996, PBS screened a similar four-part series, *Chicano!*, by documentarist Héctor Galán on the Chicano social movements in the southwest, a story much less known even than the civil rights movements.

These then were turning points, not in the sense of an instantaneous switch, but in terms of setting a high-water mark that expanded the definition of the possible in U.S. TV. The other turning point was the proliferation, mostly locally, of black and other ethnic minority group individuals as newscasters. Although newscasters rarely had the clout to write their own bulletin scripts, let alone decide on news priorities for reporting or investigation, they had the cachet of a very public, trusted role. To that extent, this development did carry considerable symbolic prestige for the individuals concerned. As of 2001, the Radio-Television News Directors Association found 10 percent of general managers and 14 percent of TV news directors were people of color. This was a move in the right direction but still left minorities vastly underrepresented in these key authority positions.

Only as time went on and racial news values and priorities remained the same or similar despite the change in faces, did the limits of this development begin to become more apparent. At about the same time, most news bulletins, especially local ones, were deteriorating into "infotainment," with lengthy weather and sports reports incorporated into the half hour. The latter trend continues in the early 2000s. With news audiences highly concentrated in the over-50 age group, programmers expend much effort to make news still more entertaining to younger audiences.

Alternative Representations

Alternative representation became somewhat more frequent after *The Cosby Show*'s success. In part, this change was also due to the steadily declining price of video cameras and editing equipment, to support from federal and state arts commissions, and to developments in cable TV, especially public access, which opened up more scope for independent video makers to develop their own work, some of which could be screened locally and even nationally.

From the mid-1990s, first FOX and then imitators WB and UPN sought to challenge the dominance of the "Big Three" networks (ABC, CBS, and NBC) by offering fresh programming, including a series of shows with African-American content. Kristal Brent Zook suggests that while this was a rare and exciting moment in a number of instances, the fundamental impetus was competitive rather than inclusive, and that once the new networks began to establish themselves with advertisers their innovative programming began to tail off, especially with regard to shows featuring African Americans. On cable, Nickelodeon and the expensive premium channels (HBO, Showtime) also offered some innovation, such as the children's series *The Brothers Garcia* (Nickelodeon), the Latino-themed *Resurrection Boulevard* (Showtime), and some strong documentaries and docudramas with African-American themes (HBO). Quite often too, HBO's casting and scripting met the "quality" test by having minority-ethnic characters in nonstereotypical roles, such as the Puerto Rican mortician and the gay black cop played by Freddy Rodriguez and Mathew St. Patrick, respectively, in *Six Feet Under.*

A further development was the emergence of black and Latino cable and UHF channels such as Black Entertainment Television (BET), Univision, and Telemundo, together with leased ethnic-group program slots in metropolitan areas. With respect to the latter, Hamid Naficy has explored the world of expatriate Iranian programming in Los Angeles and thereby opened up a whole new perspective on migration, ethnicity, and "American-ness" as they play out in television. These new developments were often contradictory. The often cheap-shot satirization of racial issues on *In Living Color;* the question Gray and others raise concerning BET programming as often simply a black reproduction of white televisual tropes; the role of black sitcoms and stand-up comics as a new version of an older tradition in which blackness is acceptable as farce—each of these highlights in some way the tensions in television's representations of race.

Another contradictory example is Univision, effectively dominated by Mexico's near-monopoly TV giant, Televisa. Its entertainment programs are mostly a secondary market for Televisa's products, and while they are certainly popular, they have had little direct echo of Chicano or other Latino life in the United States. At the same time, as América Rodríguez has shown, Univision's news program has cultivated, for commercial reasons of mass appeal, pan-ethnic Spanish that over time may arguably contribute to a pan-Latino U.S. cultural identity, rather than the Chicano, Caribbean, Central and South American fragments that constitute the Latino minority.

MacDonald goes so far as to forecast cable TV's multiple channels as an almost automatic technical solution to the heritage of unequal access for African Americans. However, the "technological fix" he envisages would not of itself address the urgent national need for dialogue on race and whiteness in television's public forum, because a multichannel environment may resemble a Babel of voices mutually insulated from each other rather than engaged with each other. Nor does his proposal seem to bargain with the huge costs of generating mostly new product for even a single cable channel.

Scattered as they are over multiple tiny distributors or self-distributed, it is difficult to generalize about the profusion of single features and documentaries generated by video artists of color and/or on ethnic themes. Suffice it to say that distribution—cable channels notwithstanding—is the largest single problem that such work encounters. (Sources of information on these videos include Asian-American CineVision and the Black Filmmakers Foundation, both in New York City, and Facets Video in Chicago.)

In examining alternatives, finally, we need to take stock of some of the mainstream alternatives to segregated casts, such as one of the earliest, *Hawaii Five-O,* and the later *Miami Vice* and *NYPD Blue.* The first was definitely still within the "Tonto" tradition insofar as the ethnic minority cops were concerned ("Yes, boss" seemed to be the limit of their vocabulary). *Miami Vice*'s tri-ethnic leads were less anchored in that tradition, although Edward James Olmos as the police captain often approximated Captain Dobey in *Starsky and Hutch,* apparently only nominally in charge. *NYPD Blue* carried over some of that tradition as regarded the African-American Lieutenant Fancy's role, but it actually starred Latinos in key police roles.

A central issue on *NYPD Blue,* however, raised once more the question of "modern" racism. A repetitive feature of the show was the skill of the police detectives in pressuring people they considered guilty to sign confessions and not to avail themselves of their legal rights. Two comments are in order here. One is that a police team is shown at work, undeflected by racial animosity, strenuously task-driven. It is a theme with its roots in many World War II movies, although in those films, ethnicity was generally the focus rather than race. The inference plainly to be drawn was that atavistic biases should be laid aside in the face of clear and present danger, with the contemporary "war" being against the constant tide of crime.

Second, it is a fact that the number of U.S. prisoners who are African Americans and Latinos is vastly disproportionate to the size of these subpopulations relative to the U.S. population as a whole. On *NYPD Blue* we see firm unity among white, black, and Latino police professionals in defining aggressive detection and charge practices as legitimate and essential, even though it is procedures like those that, along with racially differential sentencing and parole procedures, have often helped create that huge racial imbalance in U.S. prisons.

The Television Industry and Race Relations

Except for a clutch of public figures led by Bill Cosby, CNN's political analyst Bernard Shaw (who retired in 2001), talk show hosts Oprah Winfrey and Geraldo Rivera; moderately influential behind-the-camera individuals such as Susan Fales, Charles Floyd Johnson, Ralph Farquhar, Thomas Carter, and Suzanne de Passe; and local newscasters, the racial casting of television organizations has been distinctly leisurely in changing. Cable television has the strongest ratio of minority personnel, but this should be read in connection with its lower pay scales and its minimal original production schedules. Especially in positions of senior authority, television is still largely a white enterprise.

The Federal Communications Commission's (FCC) statistics are often less than helpful in determining the true picture and represent a classic instance of bureaucratic response to the demand to collect evidence by refusing to focus with any precision on the matter in hand. In the National Association of Minorities in Communication survey of cable TV, the same phenomenon was evident, with a number of multiple system operators (MSOs) including not only executives with direct influence over programming (e.g., marketing) in their minority/ethnic headcount but also human resources personnel. Given the undoubted intelligence of those who communicate these statistics, it is hard to see other than a pattern of deliberate obfuscation at work. The FCC's two top cable and broadcast employment categories, for example (Officials and Managers, and Professionals), are extremely broad and render completely foggy the degree of real authority entailed over the process. Drawing meaningful conclusions from minority/ethnic percentages within those categories is consequently impossible. Unless and until cable and broadcast organizations see fit to reveal clearly the holders of significant executive power and their ethnic status, it is logical to assume that television boardrooms are as white as U.S. corporate boardrooms in general, and yet those boardrooms are, to belabor the obvious, where the fundamental television decisions are made. Whether or not this exclusion of racial minorities from the corridors makes immediate market sense, the implications of the television industry's decision-making process for the immediate future of American life and culture are very disturbing ones.

Data from 2001 indicated 47 TV stations, 75 percent of which were UHF, had minority/ethnic owners. Eight of these stations were in California; seven in Puerto Rico; seven in Texas; two each in Connecticut, Illinois, Indiana, Mississippi, New Jersey, New York, and Wisconsin; and one each in Arizona, Colorado, Hawaii, Louisiana, Michigan, Vermont, Virginia, and Washington, D.C. This was a higher number than five years previously, but still a pathetic coda when 30 percent of the U.S. population is identified as minority/ethnic. As of early 2001, a Federal Appeals Court, responding to a case brought by three broadcast associations, actually struck down FCC rules promoting the hiring of people of color and women in the broadcast industry. A CBS spokeswoman announced that CBS's "commitment to diversity is as strong as ever," which was hardly reassuring.

The question then at issue is to what degree this absence of minorities from positions of TV authority determines the mainstream representation patterns surveyed above. One might argue that if no customary formats or tropes were changed, and if none of the legal, financial, and competitive vectors vanished, then a television executive stratum composed entirely of ethnic minority individuals would likely proceed to reproduce precisely the same patterns of representation.

However, this position is an abstract one and only helps to shed light on the pressures to conform faced by the few ethnic minority individuals scattered through the TV hierarchy. Sociologically, were the percentage of executive positions held by minorities to increase to within even hailing distance of their percentage of the national population, a much wider internal dialogue would be feasible concerning the very limits of the possible in television. We come back, in a sense, to *Cosby*.

At the time that program aired, the proportion of blacks and Latinos who watched TV was higher than the national average, and these two minority groups accounted in 1995 for at least $300 billion in consumer spending a year. Therefore, by the mid-1990s, the economic logic of advertising seemed to point toward increasing inclusiveness on TV. How this clash between economic logic and inherited culture would work out remained to be seen. The efforts of advocacy groups, such as the National Association for the Advancement of Colored People (NAACP), the National Council of La Raza, Children Now, and others, became more intensive from 1993 onward, and in 2000 many joined the Multi-Ethnic Coalition, monitoring and publicly critiquing failures of representation.

Audience and Spectatorship

The most complex issue centers on how viewers process televisual content related to race and ethnicity. It has already been argued that decades of daily programs have mostly underwritten the perception of the United States as, at its core, a white nation with a white culture, rather than a multicultural nation beset by entrenched problems of ethnic inequity. Television fare has obviously not been a lone voice in this regard, nor has it been anything resembling a steady opposition voice. This judgment clearly transcends interpretations of particular programs or even genres. It is sufficiently loose in formulation to leave its plausible practical consequences open to extended discussion. However, given the ever greater dominance of television in U.S. culture, TV's basic vision of the world can hardly be dismissed as impotent.

Historically, it has been a vision likely to reassure the white majority that it has little to learn or benefit from people of color. Rather, TV coverage of immigration and crime has made it much easier to be afraid of ethnic and racial minorities. George H.W. Bush's manipulation of the Willie Horton case for a 1988 campaign commercial (with Horton representing the specter of the vicious black rapist aided and abetted by a liberal Democrat—Bush's opponent, Michael Dukakis) had even the nation's vice president (and president-to-be) drawing on, and thus endorsing, the standard tropes of local TV news. Particularly following the September 11, 2001, terrorist assaults on New York and Washington, D.C., but also for some 20 years before that, television coverage of Arabs and Muslims, while often maintaining an abstract theme of tolerance and civil rights, did much at the same time to encourage many members of the U.S. public to distrust as potential terrorists and enemies anyone who answered to (or appeared to answer to) those identities. The suspicious reaction and backlash was reminiscent of the anti-Asian culture that formed the backdrop for hostility toward Japanese Americans following the Pearl Harbor attack 60 years previously.

Naturally, not all of the white majority have endorsed or believed that vision. However, it has been difficult to muster a coherent and forward-looking public debate about race, whiteness, and the nation's future, given TV's continuing refusal, in the main, to squarely face the issue. This medium was not the only institution with that responsibility, nor the unique forum available. But TV was and is crucial to any solution.

The detailed analysis of audience reception of particular shows or series is a delicate business, linking as it will into the many filaments of social and cultural life for white audiences and for audiences of color. It is, however, a sour comment on audience researchers that so little has been done to date to explore how TV has been appropriated by various ethnic minority audiences, or how majority audiences handle ethnic themes. Commercial research has been content simply to register viewer levels by ethnicity, whereas academic research, with a scattering of exceptions, has rarely troubled to explore ethnic diversity in processing TV, despite the outpouring of ethnographic audience studies in the 1980s and 1990s.

JOHN D.H. DOWNING

See also **Allen, Debbie;** *Amen; Amos 'n' Andy; Beulah;* **Black Entertainment Network; Cosby, Bill;**

Cosby Show, The; Different World, A; Eyes on the Prize; Frank's Place; Flip Wilson Show, The; Goldbergs, The; Good Times; **Haley, Alex;** *I Spy; Jeffersons, The; Julia; Nat "King" Cole Show, The;* **National Asian Americans in Telecommunications Association; Pryor, Richard;** *Room 222;* **Social Class and Television; Telemundo;** *227;* **Univision; Winfrey, Oprah**

Further Reading

Araújo, Joel Zito, *A Negação do Brasil: o Negro na Telenovela Brasileira,* São Paulo: Editora SENAC, 2000

Bobo, Jacqueline, *Black Women As Cultural Readers,* New York: Columbia University Press, 1995

Corea, Ash, "Racism and the American Way of Media," in *Questioning the Media: A Critical Introduction,* 2nd edition, edited by John Downing, Ali Mohammadi, and Annabelle Sreberny-Mohammadi, Thousand Oaks, California: Sage, 1995

Cosby, Camille O., *Television's Imageable Influences: The Self-Perceptions of Young African-Americans,* Lanham, Maryland: University Press of America, 1994

Dates, Jannette L., and William Barlow, editors, *Split Image: African Americans in the Mass Media,* Washington, D.C.: Howard University Press, 1993

Downing, John, "The Cosby Show and American Racial Discourse," in *Discourse and Discrimination,* edited by Teun A. Van Dijk and Geneva Smitherman-Donaldson, Detroit, Michigan: Wayne State University Press, 1988

Entman, Robert M., and Andrew Rojecki, *The Black Image in the White Mind: Media and Race in America,* Chicago: University of Chicago Press, 2000

Fiske, John, *Media Matters: Everyday Culture and Political Change,* Minneapolis: University of Minnesota Press, 1994

Gray, Herman, *Watching Race: Television and the Struggle for "Blackness,"* Minneapolis: University of Minnesota Press, 1995

Hamamoto, Darrell Y., *Monitored Peril: Asian Americans and the Politics of TV Representation,* Minneapolis: University of Minnesota Press, 1994

Heider, Don, *White News: Why Local News Programs Don't Cover People of Color,* Mahwah, New Jersey: Lawrence Erlbaum, 2000

hooks, bell, *Black Looks: Race and Representation,* Boston: South End Press, 1992

Hunt, Darnell M., *Screening the Los Angeles "Riots": Race, Seeing, and Resistance,* Cambridge and New York: Cambridge University Press, 1997

Jhally, Sut, and Justin Lewis, *Enlightened Racism: The Cosby Show, Audiences, and the Myth of the American Dream,* Boulder, Colorado: Westview, 1992

MacDonald, J. Fred, *Blacks and White TV: Afro-Americans in Television Since 1948,* Chicago: Nelson-Hall, 1983; 2nd edition, 1992

Naficy, Hamid, *The Making of Exile Cultures: Iranian Television in Los Angeles,* Minneapolis: University of Minnesota Press, 1993

Navarrete, Lisa, and Charles Kamasaki, *Out of the Picture: Hispanics in the Media,* Washington, D.C.: National Council of La Raza, 1994

Noriega, Chon, *Shot in America: Television, the State, and the Rise of Chicano Cinema,* Minneapolis: University of Minnesota Press, 2000

Ramírez-Berg, Charles, *Latino Images in Film: Stereotypes, Subversion, and Resistance,* Austin: University of Texas Press, 2002

Rodríguez, América, *Making Latino News: Race, Language, Class,* Thousand Oaks, California: Sage, 1999

Waterston, Alisse, et al., *A Look Towards Advancement: Minority Employment in Cable,* La Palma, California: National Association of Minorities in Communication, 1999

Zook, Kristal Brent, *Color by Fox: The Fox Network and the Revolution in Black Television,* New York: Oxford University Press, 1999

Radio Corporation of America

U.S. Radio Company

In 1919, General Electric (GE) formed a privately owned corporation to acquire the assets of the wireless radio company American Marconi from British Marconi. The organization, known as the Radio Corporation of America (RCA), was formally incorporated on October 17 of that year. Shortly thereafter, American Telephone and Telegraph (AT&T) and Westinghouse acquired RCA assets and became joint owners of RCA. In 1926, RCA formed a new company, the National Broadcasting Company (NBC), to oversee operation of radio stations owned by RCA, General Electric, Westinghouse, and AT&T.

In the early 1930s, the Justice Department filed an antitrust suit against the company. In a 1932 consent decree, the organization's operations were separated, and GE, AT&T, and Westinghouse were forced to sell their interests in the company. RCA retained its patents and full ownership of NBC. Shortly after becoming an independent company, RCA moved into new headquarters in the Rockefeller Center complex in New York City, into what later became known as Radio City.

While other American companies were cutting back on research expenditures during the depression years, David Sarnoff, president of RCA since 1930, was a staunch advocate of technological innovation. He expanded RCA's technology research division, devoting increased resources to television technology. Television pioneer Vladimir Zworykin was placed in charge of RCA's television research division. RCA acquired competing and secondary patents related to television technology, and once the organization felt that the technology had attained an appropriate level of refinement, it pushed for commercialization of the new medium.

In 1938, RCA persuaded the Radio Manufacturers Association (RMA) to consider adoption of its television system for standardization. The RMA adopted the RCA version, a 441-line, 30-pictures-per-second system, and presented the new standard to the FCC on September 10, 1938. Upon the recommendation of the RMA, the Federal Communications Commission (FCC) scheduled formal hearings to address the adoption of standards. The hearings, however, did not take place until January 1940.

In the interim, RCA began production of receivers and initiated a limited schedule of television programming from the New York transmitters of NBC, basing their service upon the RMA-RCA standards. The service was inaugurated in conjunction with the opening of the New York World's Fair on April 30, 1939, and continued throughout the year. At the commission's hearing addressing standards on January 15, 1940, opposition to the proposed RMA standards emerged. The two strongest opponents of the standard were DuMont Laboratories and Philco Radio and Television. One of the criticisms voiced by both organizations was the assertion that the 441-line standard did not provide sufficient visual detail and definition. Given the lack of a clear industry consensus, the Commission did not act on the proposed RMA standards.

Despite the absence of official approval, RCA continued to employ the RMA standards and announced plans in early 1940 to increase production of television receivers, cut the price to consumers by one-third, and double its programming schedule. While some commentators saw this as a reasonable and progressive action, the Commission perceived it as a step toward prematurely freezing the standards in place and, as a consequence, scheduled another set of public hearings for April 8, 1940. At these hearings, opponents argued that the action taken by RCA was stifling research and development into other alternative standards. As a result of the hearings, the Commission eliminated commercial broadcasting until further development and refinement had transpired. Furthermore, the Commission asserted that commercialization of broadcasting would not be permitted until there was industry consensus and agreement on one common system. To marshal industry-wide support for a single standard, the RMA formed the National Television System Committee (NTSC). The NTSC standards, a 525-line, 60-fields-per-second system, were approved by the FCC in 1941.

Several years later, RCA also became a major participant in the establishment of color television standards. In 1949, the organization proposed to the FCC that its dot sequential color system, which was compatible with existing black and white receivers, be adopted as the new color standard. Citing shortcomings in the compatible systems offered by RCA and other organizations, the FCC opted to formally adopt an incompatible color system offered by the Columbia Broadcasting System as the color standard. RCA appealed this decision all the way to the Supreme Court, while simultaneously refining its color system. A second NTSC was formed to examine the color issue. In 1953, the FCC reversed itself and endorsed a modified version of the RCA dot sequential compatible color system offered by the NTSC.

In the 1950s, RCA continued the military and defense work in which it had been heavily engaged during World War II. In the late 1950s and early 1960s, the company became involved with both satellite technology and the space program. During the 1960s, RCA began to diversify as the company acquired such disparate entities as the publishing firm Random House and the car rental company Hertz. Throughout the 1970s and early 1980s, RCA began to divest itself of many of its acquired subsidiaries. In June 1986, RCA was acquired by General Electric, the organization that had originally established it as a subsidiary. GE retained the brand name RCA, established NBC as a relatively autonomous unit, and combined the remainder of RCA's businesses with GE operations.

DAVID F. DONNELLY

See also **National Broadcasting Company; Sarnoff, David; Sarnoff, Robert; Silverman, Fred; Tartikoff, Brandon; Tinker, Grant; United States: Networks**

Further Reading

Barnum, Frederick O., "His Master's Voice," in *America: Ninety Years of Communications Pioneering and Progress,* Camden, New Jersey: Victor Talking Machine Company, Radio Corporation of America, and General Electric, 1991

Bilby, Kenneth M., *The General: David Sarnoff and the Rise of the Communications Industry,* New York: Harper and Row, 1986

Graham, M., *RCA and the VideoDisc: The Business of Research,* Cambridge: Cambridge University Press, 1986

Lewis, Thomas S.W., *Empire of the Air: The Men Who Made Radio,* New York: Edward Burlingame Books, 1991

Lyons, Eugene, *David Sarnoff, A Biography,* New York: Harper and Row, 1966

Sarnoff, David, *Looking Ahead; The Papers of David Sarnoff,* New York: Wisdom Society for the Advancement of Knowledge, Learning, and Research in Education, 1968

The Wisdom of Sarnoff and the World of RCA, Beverly Hills, California: Wisdom Society for the Advancement of Knowledge, Learning, and Research in Education, 1967

Radio Television News Directors Association

U.S. Professional Organization

The Radio Television News Directors Association (RTNDA) is the trade organization representing broadcast news professionals in the United States. Founded in 1946, when radio was the dominant broadcast news medium, the association now serves all electronic media, with the bulk of its membership comprised of local television news professionals. Its primary focus is on the needs of broadcast news managers. While membership is open to all electronic journalists as well as students, educators, suppliers, and other interested parties, only members who exercise significant editorial supervision of news programming are allowed to vote.

Among the organization's services to members are a monthly magazine, *RTNDA Communicator,* and an annual convention held in the fall and featuring training sessions, notable speakers, technology demonstrations, and an exhibit area for suppliers of news products and services. Augmenting its printed magazine is the RTNDA website (*http://www.rtnda.org*), which provides such member services as job listings, a talent bank for posting résumés, and a membership directory. Other ongoing member services include a resource catalog of related books and tapes, and industry research projects that examine pertinent issues such as salaries, staff size, and profitability.

The number and scope of RTNDA services reflect the dramatic changes experienced by the broadcast news industry in recent years. Among such developments have been the growing profitability and expansion of local television news; the emergence of new outlets such as Cable News Network, MSNBC, C-SPAN, and online information services; and advances in the technology of news gathering, particularly in live remote broadcast capabilities and satellite transmission. In addition, local TV news operations, unlike their newspaper counterparts, are generally locked in fierce three-way competition with other local news programs in the same market. The pressure to maximize ratings often puts the news manager in the precarious situation of having to decide between news values and entertainment values. The nature of a commercial medium such as television generally makes such conflict unavoidable.

Through its ongoing activities and services, RTNDA strives to set and promote professional standards for electronic journalists. The RTNDA Code of Ethics is published in each issue of the organization's monthly magazine. The code states that "the responsibility of radio and television journalists is to gather and report information of importance and interest to the public accurately, honestly, and impartially," and provides guidelines for fair, balanced reporting that respects the dignity and privacy of subjects and sources, avoiding deception, sensationalism, and conflicts of interest.

RTNDA honors professional excellence through its Edward R. Murrow Awards in the areas of spot news coverage, feature reporting, series, investigative reporting, and overall newscast (awarded separately for small- and large-market stations). The organization's top honor is the Paul White Award, given each year to an individual for lifetime achievement in the field of broadcast journalism. RTNDA also sponsors the Radio Television News Directors Foundation, a nonprofit organization that engages in research, education, and training activities related to such topics as journalistic ethics, the impact of technology on electronic news gathering, the role of electronic journalism in politics and public policy, environmental news coverage, and cultural diversity in the profession.

JERRY HAGINS

See also **National Broadcasting Company; Sarnoff, David; Sarnoff, Robert; Silverman, Fred; Tartikoff, Brandon; Tinker, Grant; United States: Networks**

Further Reading

Cook, Philip S., Douglas Gomery, and Lawrence W. Lichty, *The Future of News: Televisions, Newspapers, Wire Services, Newsmagazines,* Washington, D.C.: Woodrow Wilson Center Press, 1992

Fields, Howard, "RTNDA at 40: Major Lobbying Role," *Television-Radio Age* (August 18, 1986)

Jacobs, Jerry, *Changing Channels: Issues and Realities in Television News,* Mountain View, California: Mayfield Publishing, 1990

Kaniss, Phyllis C., *Making Local News,* Chicago: University of Chicago Press, 1991

McManus, John H., *Market-Driven Journalism: Let the Citizen Beware?* Thousand Oaks, California: Sage, 1994

"RTNDA and the State of Electronic Journalism," *Broadcasting* (December 12, 1988)

Randall, Tony (1920–2004)

U.S. Actor

Tony Randall, an Emmy Award-winning television and film actor, was most noted for his role as the anal-retentive Felix Unger in the ABC sitcom *The Odd Couple.* A popular guest on numerous variety and talk shows, Randall was connected with all three major broadcast networks, as well as with PBS.

Randall began his career in radio in the 1940s, appearing on such shows as the *Henry Morgan Program* and *Opera Quiz.* From 1950 to 1952, Randall played Mac on the melodramatic TV serial *One Man's Family.* He then went on to play Harvey Weskit, the brash, overconfident best friend of Robinson Peepers (Wally

Tony Randall, 1987.
©*Stockline/Courtesy of the Everett Collection*

Cox) in the live sitcom *Mr. Peepers* (1952–55). After finding a niche in films, including numerous roles in romantic comedies, Randall won the part of Felix Unger in the ABC television version of *The Odd Couple* (1970–75).

Randall played Unger in a Chicago stage version of *The Odd Couple,* but the Broadway and film versions of *The Odd Couple* became established hits with different stars in the role. Nevertheless, Randall lent numerous additions to the Felix character. Drawing upon his interest in opera, Randall had Felix become an opera lover. Randall also added the comedic honking noises that accompanied Felix's ever-present sinus attacks. Much like television costar Jack Klugman's close connection to the Oscar Madison role, Randall became synonymous with Unger.

Despite low ratings for the series, ABC, the third-place network, allowed *The Odd Couple* a five-season run. In 1975, Randall won an Emmy for Best Lead Actor for his role as Felix. A popular guest on numerous variety shows, Randall was present on two Emmy

Award-winning variety show episodes, *The Flip Wilson Show* (1970) and *The Sonny and Cher Show* (1971). Randall's frequent appearances as a guest on the *Tonight Show* won him a role playing himself in Martin Scorsese's *King of Comedy* (1983).

Beginning in 1976, Randall starred in the CBS sitcom *The Tony Randall Show.* Randall played Walter Franklin, a judge who deliberated over his troubled family as much as he did over the cases presented to him in his mythical Philadelphia courtroom. In 1981, Randall returned to television playing Sidney Shorr in NBC's *Love, Sidney,* a critically acclaimed yet commercially unsuccessful sitcom canceled in 1983. The series did attract some criticism from religious and culturally conservative communities. In *Sidney Shorr,* the made-for-television movie that preceded the series, Randall's character was presented as homosexual. In the series, this aspect of the role was simply dropped.

Randall reprised his Felix Unger role in a 1993 TV-movie version of *The Odd Couple.* He has also hosted the PBS opera series *Live from the Met* and continued to appear frequently on such talk shows as *The Late Show with David Letterman.* However, from 1991, Randall focused his professional efforts primarily on the National Actors Theatre, a classical repertory company he founded and with which he frequently acted.

MICHAEL B. KASSEL

See also *Odd Couple, The*

Tony Randall. Born Leonard Rosenberg in Tulsa, Oklahoma, February 26, 1920. Educated at Northwestern University, Chicago; Columbia University, New York; the Neighborhood Playhouse School of the Theatre, New York City, 1938–40; and the Officer Candidate School at Fort Monmouth, New Jersey. Married: 1) Florence Gibbs (died, 1992); 2) Heather Harlan, 1995; two children. Served as private and first lieutenant, U.S. Army Signal Corps, 1942–46. Announcer and actor in radio soap operas; New York debut as stage actor, *A Circle of Chalk,* 1941; various theater and radio work, 1947–52; television actor, from 1952. Member: Actors' Equity Association; Screen Actors Guild; American Federation of Television and Radio Artists; Association of the Metropolitan Opera Company; founder and artistic director of the National Actors Theatre in New York City. Recipient: Emmy Award, 1975. Died in New York City, May 17, 2004.

Television Series

1949–55	*One Man's Family*
1952–55	*Mr. Peepers*
1970–75	*The Odd Couple*
1976–78	*The Tony Randall Show*
1981–82	*Love, Sidney*

Made-for-Television Movies

1978	*Kate Bliss and the Ticker Tape Kid*
1981	*Sidney Shorr: A Girl's Best Friend*
1984	*Off Sides*
1985	*Hitler's SS: Portrait in Evil*
1986	*Sunday Drive*
1988	*Save the Dog*
1989	*The Man in the Brown Suit*
1993	*The Odd Couple: Together Again*

Television Specials (selected)

1956	*Heaven Will Protect the Working Girl* (host)
1960	*Four for Tonight* (costar)
1960	*So Help Me, Aphrodite*
1962	*Arsenic and Old Lace*
1967	*The Wide Open Door*
1969	*The Littlest Angel*
1977	*They Said It with Music: Yankee Doodle to Ragtime* (cohost)
1981	*Tony Randall's All-Star Circus* (host)
1985	*Curtain's Up* (host)
1987	*Walt Disney World Celebrity Circus* (host)

Films

Oh Men, Oh Women, 1957; *Will Success Spoil Rock Hunter?*, 1957; *The Mating Game*, 1959; *Pillow Talk*, 1959; *Let's Make Love*, 1960; *Lover Come Back*, 1962; *Send Me No Flowers*, 1964; *The Brass Bottle*, 1964; *Fluffy*, 1965; *Bang, Bang, You're Dead*, 1966; *Hello Down There*, 1969; *Everything You Always Wanted to Know About Sex...*, 1972; *Huckleberry Finn*, 1974; *Scavenger Hunt*, 1979; *Foolin' Around*, 1980; *The King of Comedy*, 1983; *My Little Pony*, 1986; *That's Adequate*, 1989; *Gremlins 2: The New Batch* (voice), 1990; *Fatal Instinct*, 1993; *Down with Love*, 2003.

Stage (selected)

Circle of Chalk, 1941; *Candida*, 1941; *The Corn Is Green*, 1942; *The Barretts of Wimpole Street*, 1947; *Anthony and Cleopatra*, 1948; *Caesar and Cleopatra*, 1950; *Oh Men, Oh Women*, 1954; *Inherit the Wind*, 1955–56; *Oh Captain*, 1958; *UTBU*, 1966; *Two Into One*, 1988; *M. Butterfly*, 1989; *A Little Hotel on the Side*, 1992; *The Master Builder* (director), 1992; *Three Men on a Horse*, 1993; *The Government Inspector*, 1994; *The Odd Couple*, 1994; *The School for Scandal*, 1995; *Inherit the Wind*, 1995; *The Sunshine Boys*, 1998.

Radio

I Love a Mystery; *Portia Faces Life*; *When a Girl Marries*; *Life's True Story.*

Publication

Which Reminds Me (with Michael Mindlin), 1989

Rather, Dan (1931–)

U.S. Broadcast Journalist

In a career in journalism that is now in its fifth decade, Dan Rather has established himself as a crucial figure in broadcast news. Anchor of the *CBS Evening News* since 1981, Rather has enjoyed a long and sometimes colorful career in broadcasting. Rather has interviewed every U.S. president from Dwight D. Eisenhower to Bill Clinton, and international leaders from Nelson Mandela to Boris Yeltsin. In 1990, he was the first American journalist to interview Saddam Hussein after Iraq's invasion of Kuwait. Rather's hard-hitting journalistic style has sometimes been as much discussed as the content of his reporting, particularly in the case of well-publicized contretemps with Richard Nixon and George Bush.

Rather began his career in journalism in 1950 as an Associated Press reporter in Huntsville, Texas. He subsequently worked as a reporter for United Press International, for KSAM Radio in Huntsville, for KTRH Radio in Houston, and at the *Houston Chronicle*. He became news director of KTRH in 1956 and a reporter for KTRH-TV in Houston in 1959. He was news director at KHOU-TV, the CBS affiliate in Houston, before joining CBS News in 1962 as chief of the southwest bureau in Dallas.

In 1963, Rather was appointed chief of CBS's southern bureau in New Orleans, responsible for coverage of news events in the South, Southwest, Mexico, and Central America. He reported extensively on southern racial strife, becoming well acquainted with Dr. Martin Luther King, Jr. On November 22, 1963, in Dallas, Rather broke the news of the death of President John F. Kennedy. A few weeks after the assassination, he became CBS's White House correspondent.

Rather attracted notice in 1974 for an exchange with Richard Nixon. At a National Association of Broadcasters convention in Houston, Rather was applauded when he stood to ask a question, drawing Nixon's query, "Are you running for something?" Many saw Rather's quick retort, "No, sir, Mr. President. Are you?" as an affront to presidential dignity.

A year later, Rather was selected to join the roster of journalists on CBS's *60 Minutes,* and in 1981, after lengthy negotiations with the network, Rather became the successor to Walter Cronkite, anchoring the *CBS Evening News.* During Rather's tenure, he has sometimes been associated with striking, even bizarre, moments of news coverage. For one week in September 1986, Rather concluded his nightly broadcast with the solemn, ominous-sounding, single-word sign-off "Courage." The line, seen as an attempt to respond to or replace audience familiarity with Cronkite's "And that's the way it is," attracted widespread media coverage and more than a little satire. In October 1986, Rather was attacked outside the CBS building by thugs reportedly demanding "What's the frequency, Kenneth?" and he subsequently appeared on the air with a swollen and bruised face. In September 1987, Rather walked off the *CBS Evening News* set in protest over the network's decision to allow U.S. Open tennis coverage to cut into the broadcast. His action on this occasion left CBS with a blank screen for more than six minutes. This moment was recalled in an explosive live interview Rather conducted with Vice President George Bush in January 1988. When Rather pressed Bush about his contradictory claims regarding his involvement in the Iran-Contra scandal, the vice president responded by asking Rather if he would like to be judged by those minutes resulting from his decision to walk off the air.

Connie Chung joined Rather on the *CBS Evening News* in a dual anchor format in 1993 amid constant speculation that he did not approve of the appointment. When Chung left the *Evening News* spot in 1995, he did not seem displeased. Rather also continues to anchor and report for the CBS News broadcast *48 Hours* (which premiered in 1988). He was the first network journalist to anchor an evening news broadcast and a prime-time news program at the same time, a practice which has since been adopted by other networks.

Dan Rather, anchorman of *The CBS Evening* News, 3/10/85. *Courtesy of the Everett Collection*

Rather's career reflects the passing of the era in which one anchor, Walter Cronkite, was unproblematically "the most trusted man in America." Along with Tom Brokaw and Peter Jennings, Rather is one of a triumvirate of middle-aged white male anchors who dominate the U.S. national nightly news. The three network news broadcasts continue to be locked in a tightly contested ratings race, and these highly paid anchors are decidedly valuable properties, the "stars" of television news. CBS, cognizant of this state of affairs, offered Rather a new three-year contract in 2002, which he signed.

DIANE M. NEGRA

See also **Anchor; Columbia Broadcasting System; News, Network;** *60 Minutes*

Dan Rather. Born in Wharton, Texas, October 31, 1931. Educated at Sam Houston State College, Huntsville, Texas, B.A. in journalism 1953; attended University of Houston and South Texas School of Law. Married: Jean Goebel; children: Dawn Robin and

Daniel Martin. Journalism instructor, Sam Houston State College; worked for the *Houston Chronicle;* news writer, reporter, and news director, CBS radio affiliate KTRH, Houston, mid- to late 1950s; director of news and public affairs, CBS television affiliate KHOU, Houston, late 1950s to 1961; chief, CBS's southwestern bureau, Dallas, 1962–64; CBS White House correspondent, 1963; chief, CBS's London bureau, 1965–66; war correspondent, Vietnam, 1966; returned to position as CBS White House correspondent, 1966–74; anchor-correspondent, *CBS Reports,* 1974–75; correspondent and co-editor, *60 Minutes,* 1975–81; anchor, *Dan Rather Reporting,* CBS Radio Network, since 1977; anchor and managing editor, *CBS Evening News with Dan Rather,* since 1981; anchor, *48 Hours,* since 1988; anchored numerous CBS news specials. Recipient: Texas Associated Press Broadcasters' Awards for spot news coverage, 1956, 1959; numerous Emmy Awards.

Television

1974–75	*CBS Reports*
1975–81	*60 Minutes*
1981–	*CBS Evening News with Dan Rather*
1988–2002	*48 Hours*
1998–	*60 Minutes II*

Publications

America at War: The Battle for Iraq: A View from the Frontlines, 2003

The American Dream: Stories from the Heart of Our Nation, 2001

The Camera Never Blinks: Adventures of a TV Journalist (with Mickey Herskowitz), 1977

The Camera Never Blinks Twice: Further Adventures of a Television Journalist, 1994

Further Reading

Corliss, Richard, "Broadcast Blues," *Film Comment* (March–April, 1988)

Goldberg, Robert, and Gerald Jay Goldberg, *Anchors: Brokaw, Jennings, Rather, and the Evening News,* New York: Birch Lane, 1990

Jones, Alex S., "The Anchors: Who They Are, What They Do, The Tests They Face," *New York Times* (July 27, 1986)

Matusow, Barbara, *The Evening Stars,* Boston: Houghton Mifflin, 1983

Westin, Av, *Newswatch: How TV Decides the News,* New York: Simon and Schuster, 1982

Zelizer, Barbie, "What's Rather Public About Dan Rather: TV Journalism and the Emergence of Celebrity," *Journal of Popular Film and Television* (Summer 1989)

Ratings

Ratings are a central component of the television industry, almost a household word. They are important in television because they indicate the size of an audience for specific programs. Networks and stations then set their advertising rates based on the number of viewers of their programs. Network revenue is thus directly related to the ratings. The word "ratings," however, is actually rather confusing because it has both a specific and a general meaning. Specifically, a rating is the percentage of all the people (or households) in a particular location tuned to a particular program. In a general sense, the term is used to describe a process (also referred to as "audience measurement") that endeavors to determine the number and types of viewers watching TV.

One common rating (in the specific sense) is the rating of a national television show. This calculation measures the number of households—out of all the households in the United States that have TV sets—watching a particular show. There are approximately 100 million households in the United States, and most of them have TV sets. If 20 million of those households are watching NBC at 8:00 P.M., then NBC's rating for that time period is 20 (20 million / 100 million = 20). Another way to describe the process is to say that one rating point is worth 1 million households.

Ratings are also taken for areas smaller than the entire nation. For example, if a particular city (Yourtown) has 100,000 households and 15,000 of them are watching the local news on station KAAA, that station would have a rating of 15. If Yourtown has a population of 300,000 and 30,000 people are watching KAAA, the station's rating would be 10. And because television viewing is becoming less and less of a group activity with the entire family gathered around the living-room TV set, most ratings are expressed in terms of people rather than households.

Many calculations are related to the rating. Sometimes people, even professionals in the television business, confuse them. One of these calculations is the *share*. This figure reports the percentage of households (or people) watching a show out of all the households (or people) *who have the TV set on*. So if Yourtown has 100,000 households but only 50,000 of them have the TV set on and 15,000 of those are watching KAAA, the share is 30 (15,000 / 50,000 = 30). Shares are always higher than ratings unless, of course, everyone in the country is watching television.

Another calculation is the *cume*, which reflects the number of different persons who tune in a particular station or network over a period of time. This number is used to show advertisers how many different people hear their message if it is aired at different times such as 7:00 P.M., 8:00 P.M., and 9:00 P.M. If the total number of people available is 100, five of them view at 7:00, those five still view at 8:00, but three new people watch, and then two people turn the TV off, but four new ones join the audience at 9:00, the cume would be 12 (5 + 3 + 4 = 12). Cumes are particularly important to cable networks because their ratings are very low. Two networks with ratings of 1.2 and 1.3 cannot really be differentiated, but if the measurement is taken over a wider time span, a greater difference will probably surface.

Average quarter hours (AQH) are another measurement. This calculation is based on the average number of people viewing a particular station (network, program) for at least 5 minutes during a 15-minute period. For example, if, out of 100 people, 10 view for at least 5 minutes between 7:00 and 7:15, 7 view between 7:15 and 7:30, 11 view between 7:30 and 7:45, and 4 view between 7:45 and 8:00, the AQH rating would be 8 (10 + 7 + 11 + 4 = 32; 32 / 4 = 8).

Many other calculations are possible. For example, if the proper data have been collected, it is easy to calculate the percentage of women between the ages of 18 and 34, or of men in urban areas, who watch particular programs. Networks and stations gather as much information as is economically possible. They then try to use the numbers that present their programming strategies in the best light.

The general ratings (audience measurement) process has varied greatly over the years. Audience measurement started in the early 1930s with radio. A group of advertising interests joined together as a nonprofit entity to support ratings known as "Crossleys," named after Archibald Crossley, the man who conducted them. Crossley used random numbers from telephone directories and called people in about 30 cities to ask them what radio programs they had listened to the day before his call. This method became known as the re-

call method, because people were remembering what they had listened to the previous day. Crossleys existed for about 15 years but ended in 1946 because several for-profit commercial companies began offering similar services that were considered better.

One of these, the Hooper ratings, was begun by C.E. Hooper. Hooper's methodology was similar to Crossley's, except that respondents were asked what programs they were listening to at the time of the call—a method known as the coincidental telephone technique. Another service, the Pulse, used face-to-face interviewing. Interviewees selected by random sampling were asked to name the radio stations they had listened to over the past 24 hours, the past week, and the past five midweek days. If they could not remember, they were shown a roster containing station call letters to aid their memory. This was referred to as the roster-recall method.

Today the main radio audience measurement company is Arbitron. The Arbitron method requires people to keep diaries in which they write down the stations they listen to at various times of the day. In these diaries, they also indicate demographic features—their age, sex, marital status, etc.—so that ratings can be broken down by subaudiences.

The main television audience measurement company is the A.C. Nielsen Company. For many years Nielsen used a combination of diaries and a meter device called the Audimeter. The Audimeter recorded the times when a set was on and the channel to which it was tuned. The diaries were used to collect demographic data and list which family members were watching each program. Nielsen research in some markets still uses diaries, but for most of its data collection, Nielsen now attaches Peoplemeters to TV sets in selected homes. Peoplemeters collect both demographic and channel information because they are equipped with remote control devices. These devices accommodate a number of buttons, one for each person in the household and one for guests. Each person watching TV presses his or her button, which has been programmed with demographic data, to indicate viewing choices and activities.

There are also companies that gather and supply specialized ratings. For example, one company specializes in data concerning news programs and another tracks Latino viewing.

All audience measurement is based on samples. At present, there is no economical way of finding out what every person in the entire country is watching. Diaries, meters, and phone calls are all expensive, so sometimes samples are small. In some cases, no more than .004 percent of the population is being surveyed. However, the rating companies try to make their samples as representative of the larger population as possible. They consider a wide variety of demographic features—size of family, gender and age of head of household, access to cable TV, income, education—and try to construct a sample comprising the same percentage of the various demographic traits as in the general population.

In order to select a representative sample, the companies attempt to locate every housing unit in the country (or city or viewing area), mainly by using readily available government census data. Once all the housing units are accounted for, a computer program is used to randomly select the sample group in such a way that each location has an equal chance of being selected. Company representatives then write or phone people in the households that have been selected, trying to secure their cooperation. About 50 percent of those selected agree to participate. People are slightly more likely to allow meters in their house and to answer questions over the phone than they are to keep diaries. Very little face-to-face interviewing is now conducted because people are reluctant to allow strangers into their houses. When people refuse to cooperate, the computer program selects more households until the number needed for the sample have agreed to volunteer.

Once sample members have agreed to participate, they are often contacted in person. In the case of a diary, someone may show them how to fill it out. In other cases, the diary and instructions may simply be sent in the mail. For a meter, a field representative goes to the home (apartment, dorm room, vacation home, etc.) and attaches the meter to the television set. This person must take into account the entire video configuration of the home—multiple TV sets, VCRs, satellite dishes, cable TV, and anything else that might be attached to the receiver set. The field representative also trains family members in the use of the meter.

People participating in audience measurement are usually paid, but only a small amount, such as five dollars. Ratings companies have found that paying people something makes them feel obligated, but paying them a large amount does not make them more reliable.

Ratings companies try to see that no one remains in the sample very long. Participants become weary of filling out diaries or pushing buttons and cease to take the activities seriously. Soliciting and changing sample members is expensive, however, so companies do keep an eye on the budget when determining how to update the sample.

Once the sample is in order, the data must be collected from the participants. For phone or face-to-face interviews, the interviewer fills in a questionnaire and the data are later entered into a computer. For meters,

the data collected are sent over phone lines to a central computer. People keeping diaries mail them back to the company, and employees then enter the data into a computer. Usually, only about 50 percent of diaries are useable; the rest are never mailed back or are so incorrectly filled out that they cannot be used.

From the data collected and calculated by the computer, ratings companies publish reports. These vary according to what was surveyed. Nielsen covers commercial networks, cable networks, syndicated programming, public broadcasting, and local stations. Other companies cover more limited aspects of television. Reports on each night's prime-time national commercial network programming, based on Nielsen Peoplemeters, are usually ready about 12 hours after the data are collected. It takes considerably longer to generate a report based on diaries. The reports dealing with stations are published less frequently than those for prime-time network TV. Generally, station ratings are undertaken four times a year—November, February, May, and July—periods that are often referred to as "sweeps." The weeks of the sweeps are very important to local stations because the numbers produced then determine advertising rates for the following three months. Most reports give not only the total ratings and shares but also information broken down into various demographic categories—age, sex, education, income. The various reports are purchased by networks, stations, advertisers, and any other companies with a need to know audience statistics. The cost is lower for small entities, such as TV stations, than for larger entities, such as commercial networks. The latter usually pay several million dollars a year to receive a ratings service.

While current ratings methods may be the best yet devised for calculating audience size and characteristics, audience measurement is far from perfect. Many of the flaws of ratings should be recognized, particularly by those employed in the industry who make significant decisions based on ratings.

Sample size is one aspect of ratings that is frequently questioned in relation to rating accuracy. Statisticians know that the smaller the sample size the more chance there is for error. Ratings companies admit to this and do not claim that their figures are totally accurate. Most of them are only accurate to within 2 or 3 percent. This was of little concern during the times when ratings primarily centered around three networks, each of which was likely to have a rating of 20 or better. Even if CBS's 20 rating at 8:00 P.M. on Monday was really only 18, this was not likely to disturb the network balance. In all likelihood, CBS's 20 rating at 8:00 Tuesday evening was really a 22, so numbers evened out. Now that there are many sources of programming, however, and ratings for each are much lower, statistical inaccuracies are more significant. A cable network with a 2 rating might actually be a 4, an increase that might double its income.

Audience measurement companies are willing to increase sample size, but doing so would greatly increase their costs, and customers for ratings do not seem willing to pay. In fact, Arbitron, which had previously undertaken TV ratings, dropped them in 1994 because they were unprofitable.

As access to interactive communication increases, it may be easier to obtain larger samples. Wires from consumer homes back to cable systems could be used to send information about what each cable TV household is viewing. Many of these wires are already in place. Consumers wishing to order pay-per-view programming, for example, can push a button on the remote control that tells the cable system to unscramble the channel for that particular household. Using this technology to determine what is showing on the TV set at all times, however, smacks of a "Big Brother" type of surveillance. Similarly, by the 1970s, a technology existed that enabled trucks to drive along streets and record what was showing on each TV set in the neighborhood. This practice, perceived as an invasion of privacy, was quickly ended.

Sample composition, as well as sample size, is also seen as a weakness in ratings procedures. When telephone numbers are used to draw a sample, households without telephones are excluded and households with more than one phone have a better chance of being included. For many of the rating samples, people who do not speak either English or Spanish are eliminated. Perhaps one of the greatest difficulties for ratings companies is caused by those who eliminate themselves from the sample by refusing to cooperate. Although rating services make every attempt to replace these people with others who are similar in demographic characteristics, the sample's integrity is somewhat downgraded. Even if everyone originally selected agreed to serve, the sample cannot be totally representative of a larger population. No two people are alike, and even households with the same income and education level and the same number of children of the same ages do not watch exactly the same television shows. Moreover, people within the sample, aware that their viewing or listening habits are being monitored, may act differently than they ordinarily do.

Other problems rise from the fact that each rating technique has specific drawbacks. Households with Peoplemeters may suffer from "button pushing fatigue," thereby artificially lowering ratings. Additionally, some groups of people are simply more likely to push buttons than others. When the Peoplemeter was first introduced, ratings for sports viewing soared while those for children's program viewing decreased significantly. One explanation held that men, who were watching sports intently, were very reliable about the button pushing, perhaps, in some cases, out of fear that the TV would shut off if they didn't push that button. Children, on the other hand, were confused or apathetic about the button, thereby underreporting the viewing of children's programming. Another theory held that the women of the household had previously kept the diaries and although they were not always aware of what their husbands were actually viewing, they were quite conscious of what their children were watching. Under the diary system, in this explanation, sports programming was underrated.

But diaries have their own problems. The return rate is low, intensifying the problem of the number of uncooperative people in the sample. Even the diaries that are returned often have missing data. Many people do not fill out the diaries as they watch TV. They wait until the last minute and try to remember details—perhaps aided by a copy of *TV Guide*. Some people are simply not honest about what they watch. Perhaps they do not want to admit to watching a particular type of program.

With interviews, people can be influenced by the tone or attitude of the interviewer or, again, they can be less than truthful about what they watched out of embarrassment or in an attempt to project themselves in a favorable light. People are also hesitant to give information over the phone because they fear the person calling is really a salesperson.

Beyond sampling and methodological problems, ratings can be subject to technical problems: computers that go down, meters that function improperly, cable TV systems that shift the channel numbers of their program services without notice, station antennas struck by lightning.

Additionally, rating methodologies are often complicated and challenged by technological and sociological changes. Videocassette recorders, for example, have presented difficulties for the ratings companies. Generally, programs are counted as being watched if they are recorded. However, many programs that are recorded are never watched, and some are watched several times. In addition, people replaying tape often skip through commercials, destroying the whole purpose of ratings. And ratings companies have yet to decide what to do with sets that show four pictures at once.

Another major deterrent to the accuracy of ratings is the fact that electronic media programmers often try to manipulate the ratings system. Local television stations program their most sensational material during ratings periods. Networks preempt regular series and present star-loaded specials so that their affiliates will fare well in ratings and can therefore adjust their advertising rates upward. Cable networks show new programs as opposed to reruns. All of this, of course, negates the real purpose of determining which electronic media entities have the largest regular audience. It simply indicates which can design the best programming strategy for sweeps week.

Because of the possibility for all these sampling, methodological, technological, and sociological errors, ratings have been subjected to numerous tests and investigations. In fact, in 1963, the House of Representatives became so skeptical of ratings methodologies that it held hearings to investigate the procedures. Most of the skepticism had arisen because of a cease-and-desist order from the Federal Trade Commission (FTC) requiring several audience measurement companies to stop misrepresenting the accuracy and reliability of their reports. The FTC charged the rating companies with relying on hearsay information, making false claims about the nature of their sample populations, improperly combining and reporting data, failing to account for nonresponding sample members, and making arbitrary changes in the rating figures.

The main result of the hearings was that broadcasters themselves established the Electronic Media Rating Council (EMRC) to accredit rating companies. This group periodically checks rating companies to make sure their sample design and implementation meet preset standards that electronic media practitioners have agreed upon, to determine whether interviewers are properly trained, to oversee the procedures for handling diaries, and in other ways assure the ratings companies are compiling their reports as accurately as possible. All the major rating companies have EMRC accreditation.

The EMRC and other research institutions have continued various studies to determine the accuracy of ratings. These studies have shown that people who cooperate with rating services watch more TV, have larger families, and are younger and better educated than those who will not cooperate; telephone interviewing gets a 13 percent higher cooperation rate than diaries; Hispanics included in the ratings samples watch less TV and have smaller families than Hispanics in general.

Both electronic media practitioners and audience measurement companies want their ratings to be accurate, so both groups undertake testing to the extent they can afford it. In 1989, for example, broadcasters initiated a study to conduct a thorough review of the Peoplemeter. The result was a list of recommendations to Nielsen that included changing the amount of time people participate from two years to one year to eliminate button-pushing fatigue, metering all sets including those on boats and in vacation homes, and simplifying the procedures by which visitors log into the meter.

Still, the weakest link in the system, at present, seems to be how the ratings are used. Networks tout rating superiorities that show .1 percent differences, differences that certainly are not statistically significant. Programs are canceled because their ratings fall one point. Sweeps weeks tend to become more and more sensationalized. At stake, of course, are advertising fees that can translate into millions of dollars. Advertisers and their agencies need to remain vigilant so that they are not paying rates based on artificially stimulated ratings that bear no resemblance to the programs in which the sponsor is actually investing.

At this time all parties in the system seem invested in some form of audience measurement. So long as the failures and inadequacies of these systems are accepted by these major participants, the numbers will remain a valid type of "currency" in the system of television.

LYNNE SCHAFER GROSS

See also **A.C. Nielsen Company; Advertising; Advertising, Company Voice; Cost-Per-Thousand/Cost-Per-Point; Demographics; Market; Nielsen, A.C.; Programming; Share**

Further Reading

Buxton, William J., and Charles R. Acland, "Interview with Dr. Frank Stanton: Radio Research Pioneer," *Journal of Radio Studies,* Vol. 8 (Summer 2001)

Buzzard, Karen, *Electronic Media Ratings,* Boston: Focal, 1992

Gross, Lynne S., *Telecommunications: An Introduction to Electronic Media,* New York: McGraw-Hill, 2000

Webster, James G., Patricia Phalen, and Lawrence W. Lichty, *Ratings Analysis: The Theory and Practice of Audience Research* (Lea's Communication Series) (2nd edition), Mahwah, New Jersey: Lawrence Erlbaum Associates, 2000

Ready Steady Go!

Ready Steady Go! was a seminal 1960s pop show that featured the top music acts of the time. The British pop scene had begun to evolve with the solo teenage singing stars (Billy Fury, Tommy Steele, Marty Wilde, Adam Faith) giving way to female solo singers (Dusty Springfield, Lulu, Sandie Shaw) and groups, many from the Merseyside area round Liverpool (The Beatles, Gerry and the Pacemakers, Billy J. Kramer and the Dakotas, etc.). With the pop scene becoming ever bigger and the British sound in particular so globally successful, it was obvious that television producers had to invent new style shows to cover this phenomenon. *Ready Steady Go!* began in 1963 on the independent TV station Associated Rediffusion, and the BBC's *Top of the Pops* debuted the following year. These two shows dominated the TV music coverage of the 1960s in the United Kingdom. Whereas *Top of the Pops* followed the simple (but highly durable) format of simply featuring artists performing their hits in the charts, *Ready Steady Go!* featured a mixture of live performances, interviews, dance instructions, and competitions.

Ready Steady Go! was first broadcast on August 9, 1963, and initially ran 30 minutes. Billy Fury was on the first show, but more representative of the upcoming guests were Brian Poole and the Tremoloes, who were currently popular thanks to their version of "Twist and Shout." The following year the show expanded to a 50-minute slot and entered a golden period. Top acts were booked every week, and they performed to a studio audience of 200 or so teenagers. Initially located at the Kingsway Studios in London, it soon outgrew its home, and production moved to the airier Wembley Studios. The show's main presenters were Keith Fordyce, an established TV face who came across like an affable uncle, and Cathy McGowan, a fashionable, pretty ingénue who quickly struck a chord with the viewing audience. The producers of *Ready Steady Go!* were determined to find a new face to front the show and advertised in the music press for potential presenters. McGowan's sister sent in an application on her behalf and, despite the fact that she had no experience whatsoever in the field (she was a secretary at the time), she landed the job and enjoyed virtual overnight success. McGowan was understandably nervous on screen at first and a little overawed by her surroundings, but she quickly got a handle on the job. Fordyce may have been more professional, but McGowan was younger (roughly the same age as the fans) and far trendier. She was someone with whom the audience could identify. The fact that she was on screen talking to the likes of Mick Jagger and John Lennon resonated with the home viewers, who could almost imagine themselves doing the same job. Such was her impact that in 1964 she was named TV personality of the year by the Variety Club of Great Britain, a prestigious honor. Cathy McGowan's presence in the show was one of the factors that made *Ready Steady Go!* such a success.

Of even more importance, though, were the ramshackle, fast-paced style of the show and the consistently good lineup of acts, chosen mainly because of the individual tastes of the creative crew rather than any chart position. A spin-off magazine was launched to cash in on the success of the program, which was also ideally situated to cover the emergence of "mods" and their music. This meant that, apart from local bands, the show also featured American artists (including many African-American artists). A Motown special in 1965 was hosted by show regular Dusty Springfield and featured all the leading Motown acts of the day (Stevie Wonder, Smokey Robinson, Marvin Gaye, The Supremes, Temptations, Martha Reeves and the Vandellas).

The last edition of the series (headlining The Who and subtitled *Ready Steady Gone!*) aired December 23, 1966. The show had been groundbreaking and influential, and the surviving footage provides a priceless archive of some memorable moments and important performances. The rights to tapes of the series were acquired by pop artist-turned-entrepreneur Dave Clark in the 1980s.

DICK FIDDY

See also **Music on Television;** *Top of the Pops*

Reagan, Ronald (1911–2004)

U.S. Actor, Politician

Ronald Reagan lived in the public eye for more than 50 years as an actor and politician. He appeared in 53 Hollywood movies, from *Love Is in the Air* (1937) to *The Killers* (1964). Never highly touted as an actor, his most acclaimed movie was *Kings Row* (1942), while his favorite role was as George Gipp in *Knute Rockne—All American* (1940). He served as president of the Screen Actors Guild from 1947 to 1952 and again in 1959, where he led the fight against communist infiltration in the film industry and brokered residual rights for actors.

Reagan made his debut on television on December 7, 1950, as a detective on the CBS *Airflyte Theater* adaptation of an Agatha Christie novel. After a dozen appearances over the next four years on various shows, Reagan's big television break came when Taft Schreiber of MCA acquainted him with *General Electric Theater.* Reagan hosted this popular Sunday evening show from 1954 to 1962, starring in 34 episodes himself. Reagan was one of the first movie stars to see the potential of television, and, as host, he introduced such Hollywood notables as Joan Crawford, Alan Ladd, and Fred Astaire in their television debuts. He also became a goodwill ambassador for General Electric (GE), plugging GE products, meeting GE executives, and speaking to GE employees all over the United States. These activities proved fine training for his future political career as he honed his speaking skills, fashioned his viewpoints, and gained exposure to middle America.

In 1965, Reagan began a two-season stint as host of *Death Valley Days,* which he had to relinquish when he announced his candidacy for governor of California, in January 1966. During his terms as governor (1966–74), Reagan made frequent televised appearances on *Report to the People.*

The hinge between Reagan's acting and political careers swung on a nationally televised speech, "A Time for Choosing," on October 27, 1964. This speech for Barry Goldwater, which David Broder hailed as "the most successful political debut since William Jennings Bryan electrified the 1896 Democratic convention with his 'Cross of Gold' speech," brought in over $1 million for the Republican candidate and marked the beginning of Reagan's reign as the leading conservative for the next 25 years.

By 1980, the year Reagan was elected president for the first of his two terms, more people received their political information from television than from any other source. Reagan's experience as an actor in film and on television gave him an enormous advantage as politics moved fully into its television era. His mastery of the television medium earned for him the title "the great communicator." He perfected the art of "going public," appealing to the American public on television to put pressure on Congress to support his policies. The rhetoric of this "prime-time president" suited television perfectly. Whether delivering a State of the Union address, eulogizing the crew of the space shuttle *Challenger,* or speaking directly to the nation about his strategic defense initiative, he captured the audience's attention by appealing to shared values, creating a vision of a better future, telling stories of heroes, evoking memories of a mythic past, exuding a spirit of can-do optimism, and converting complex issues into simple language that people could understand and enjoy.

Reagan understood that television is more like the oral tradition committed to narrative communication than like the literate tradition committed to linear, factual communication. As Robert E. Denton puts it, in video politics "how something is said is more important than what is said." Reagan surmounted his numerous gaffes and factual inaccuracies until the Iran-Contra affair, when it became apparent that his style could not extricate him from the suspicion that he knew more than he was telling the American public.

Reagan's administration also greatly expanded the Office of Communication to coordinate White House public relations, stage important announcements, control press conferences, and create visual productions such as *That's America,* shown at the 1984 Republican convention. Image management and manipulation increased in importance because of television. Reagan's aides perfected a new political art form, the visual press release, whereby Reagan could take credit for new housing starts while visiting a construction site in Fort Worth, Texas, or announce a new welfare initiative during a visit to a nursing home.

Ronald Reagan was an average television actor but a peerless television politician. Both Reagan and his

Ronald Reagan in the 1960s.
Courtesy of the Everett Collection

staff set the standard by which future administrations will be judged. As Robert Schmuhl argues in *Statecraft and Stagecraft,* Reagan represented not only the rhetorical presidency, but the theatrical presidency as well.

D. JOEL WIGGINS

See also **General Electric Theater; U.S. Presidency and Television (Historical Overview)**

Ronald (Wilson) Reagan. Born in Tampico, Illinois, February 6, 1911. Educated at Eureka College, Illinois, B.A. in economics and sociology, 1932. Married: 1) Jane Wyman, 1940 (divorced, 1948); children: Maureen and Michael; 2) Nancy Davis, 1952; children: Patti and Ron. Served in U.S. Army Air Force, 1942–45. Wrote sports column for Des Moines, Iowa, newspaper; sports announcer, radio station WOC, Davenport, Iowa, 1932–37; in films, 1937–64; contract with Warner Brothers, 1937; first lead role in big-budget film was in *Kings Row,* 1942; president, Screen Actors Guild, 1947–52, and 1959; in television, 1953–66, starting as host of *The Orchid Awards,* 1953–54; governor of California, 1966–74; U.S. president, 1980–88. Died June 5, 2004, in Bel-Air, California.

Television Series

1953–54   *The Orchid Awards* (host)
1953–62   *General Electric Theater* (host and program supervisor)
1965–66   *Death Valley Days* (host)

Made-for-Television Movie

1964   *The Killers* (released as theatrical feature due to violent content)

Films

Love Is in the Air, 1937; *Hollywood Hotel,* 1937; *Swing Your Lady,* 1938; *Sergeant Murphy,* 1938; *Accidents Will Happen,* 1938; *The Cowboy from Brooklyn,* 1938; *Boy Meets Girl,* 1938; *Girls on Probation,* 1938; *Brother Rat,* 1938; *Going Places,* 1939; *Secret Service of the Air,* 1939; *Dark Victory,* 1939; *Code of the Secret Service,* 1939; *Naughty but Nice,* 1939; *Hell's Kitchen,* 1939; *Angels Wash Their Faces,* 1939; *Smashing the Money Ring,* 1939; *Brother Rat and a Baby,* 1940; *An Angel from Texas,* 1940; *Murder in the Air,* 1940; *Knute Rockne—All American,* 1940; *Tugboat Annie Smith Sails Again,* 1940; *Santa Fe Trail,* 1940; *The Bad Men,* 1941; *Million Dollar Baby,* 1941; *Nine Lives Are Not Enough,* 1941; *International Squadron,* 1941; *Kings Row,* 1941; *Juke Girl,* 1942; *Desperate Journey,* 1942; *This Is the Army,* 1943; *Stallion Road,* 1947; *That Hagen Girl,* 1947; *The Voice of the Turtle,* 1947; *John Loves Mary,* 1949; *Night unto Night,* 1949; *The Girl from Jones Beach,* 1949; *It's a Great Feeling,* 1949; *The Hasty Heart,* 1950; *Louisa,* 1950; *Storm Warning,* 1951; *Bedtime for Bonzo,* 1951; *The Last Outpost,* 1951; *Hong Kong,* 1952; *She's Working Her Way Through College,* 1952; *The Winning Team,* 1952; *Tropic Zone,* 1953; *Law and Order,* 1953; *Prisoner of War,* 1954; *Cattle Queen of Montana,* 1954; *Tennessee's Partner,* 1955; *Hellcats of the Navy,* 1957; *The Young Doctors* (narrator), 1961; *The Killers,* 1964.

Publications

Where's the Rest of Me? (with Richard Hubler), 1965
The Reagan Wit (edited by Bill Adler), 1981
Ronald Reagan: An American Life, 1990

Further Reading

Barilleaux, Ryan J., *The Post-modern Presidency: The Office After Ronald Reagan,* New York: Praeger, 1988
Cannon, Lou, *Reagan,* New York: Putnam, 1982
Deaver, Michael, *A Different Drummer: My Thirty Years with Ronald Reagan,* New York: HarperCollins, 2001

Deaver, Michael, with Mickey Herskowitz, *Behind the Scenes: In Which the Author Talks About Ronald and Nancy Reagan…and Himself,* New York: William Morrow, 1987

Denton, Robert E., Jr., *The Primetime Presidency of Ronald Reagan,* New York: Praeger, 1988

D'Souza, Dinesh, *Ronald Reagan: How an Ordinary Man Became an Extraordinary Leader,* New York: Free Press, 1997

Erickson, Paul D., *Reagan Speaks: The Making of an American Myth,* New York: New York University Press, 1985

Gold, Ellen Reid, "Ronald Reagan and the Oral Tradition," *Central States Speech Journal* (1988)

Jamieson, Kathleen Hall, *Eloquence in an Electronic Age: The Transformation of Political Speechmaking,* New York: Oxford University Press, 1988

Kernal, Samuel, "Going Public," *Congressional Quarterly Press* (1986)

Kiewe, Amos, and Davis W. Houck, *A Shining City on a Hill: Ronald Reagan's Economic Rhetoric, 1951–1989,* New York: Praeger, 1991

Leamer, Laurence, *Make-believe: The Story of Nancy and Ronald Reagan,* New York: Harper and Row, 1983

McClelland, Doug, *Hollywood on Ronald Reagan: Friends and Enemies Discuss Our President, the Actor,* Winchester, Massachusetts: Faber and Faber, 1983

McClure, A.F., C.D. Rice, and W.T. Stewart, editors, *Ronald Reagan: His First Career: A Bibliography of the Movie Years,* Lewiston, New York: Edwin Mellen, 1988

Morris, Edmund, *Dutch: A Memoir of Ronald Reagan,* New York: Random House, 1999

Pearce, Barnett, and Michael Weiler, *Reagan and Public Discourse in America,* Tuscaloosa: University of Alabama Press, 1992

Schmuhl, Robert, *Statecraft and Stagecraft: American Politics in the Age of Personality,* Notre Dame, Indiana: University of Notre Dame Press, 1990

Stuckey, Mary E., *Getting into the Game: The Pre-presidential Politics of Ronald Reagan,* New York: Praeger, 1989

Stuckey, Mary E., *Playing the Game: The Presidential Rhetoric of Ronald Reagan,* New York: Praeger, 1990

Stuckey, Mary E., *The President As Interpreter-in-Chief,* Chatham, New Jersey: Chatham House, 1991

Thomas, Tony, *The Films of Ronald Reagan,* Secaucus, New Jersey: Citadel, 1980

Real World, The

U.S. Reality Series

Beginning in the spring of 1992, *The Real World* tested the supposition of what would happen if seven strangers lived together for several months before video cameras and had most aspects of their lives taped for later editing and broadcast. The ultimate appeal for viewers, as the show suggests in its opening, is watching what happens "when people stop being polite, and start getting real." As is made clear at the beginning of the program, the format for *The Real World* consists of hand-selecting seven young adults (ages 18 to 28), plopping them in a plush, rent-free home for four to five months, and observing their interactions. While living in this fishbowl environment the "cast" is videotaped 24 hours a day, seven days a week. Finally, the videotape—over 2,000 hours of footage—is edited into 22 or 23 half-hour episodes.

Each season *The Real World* sets up in a new city, with a new cast of seven young adults, picked from thousands of applicants reflecting a diverse set of backgrounds, ideologies, and stereotypes. *The Real World Chicago* (season 11) is typical, and includes a biracial lesbian; a recovering alcoholic; a homosexual male; an all-American, football-playing Princeton student; a sexually fixated black male who is determined

to sleep with the house lesbian; and a religious woman who is intimidated by blacks and believes homosexuality is a sin. As a result of the selective casting, drama between the roommates inevitably ensues, especially when placed in *The Real World* environment. For example, no televisions or radios are allowed in *The Real World* household. As a result of this and other devices, cast members must interact with each other instead of zoning out on music or television.

Episodes of *The Real World* cover the day-to-day activities of the cast. They are usually required to perform some volunteer work with a local organization. Snippets of the roommates' activities are highlighted by "confessionals," allowing cast members, in solitude, to directly address a video camera in a manner similar to a video diary. The "confessional" is a *Real World* invention that dozens of other reality shows, including *Survivor, Boot Camp, Making of the Band, Big Brother,* and *The Real World's* sister show, *Road Rules,* have adopted. By allowing the audience to listen to a cast member explain his or her thoughts or give context to events they are witnessing, the viewer has an even closer look at the lives and individual thoughts of cast members.

In some ways, then, *The Real World* combines the soap opera format with elements of documentary film to create a distinctive reality television experience. The cast and their reactions to events are real. However, through the magic of editing, storylines and sensational moments are pulled from the material to build an ongoing saga. It is no surprise to learn that the creators of *The Real World,* Mary-Ellis Bunim and Jonathan Murray, previously worked with soap operas and documentary films, respectively.

Since its inception, *The Real World* has continued to garner impressive ratings in the highly coveted young adult market. In addition, the success of *The Real World* has launched a home-video market. These videos primarily feature content—nudity or other "adult-oriented" material—that could not be shown on basic cable television. *The Real World*'s spin-off, *Road Rules,* is similar to *The Real World,* but instead of living in a lavishly decorated house, the *Road Rules* cast lives on a huge, traveling bus and competes in challenges to win money and prizes. The producers of *The Real World* and *Road Rules* have tapped the combined drawing power of the shows to create television specials such as *The Road Rules/Real World Challenge,* which features cast members from the two shows competing against each other for prizes and cash. Other *Real World* specials include cast reunions, love specials (featuring cast members who engaged in romantic relationships), and fight specials (featuring the worst—or best—arguments). There are even specials devoted to examining the "rejects" of the show, splicing together in comical fashion clips of audition tapes from the thousands of *Real World* wannabes who did not make the cut.

The Real World's commercialism and synergy extends beyond home-video sales and television specials. Fans of the show are prompted at the end of each episode to purchase a CD of the music featured on *The Real World.* Additionally, *Real World* enthusiasts can visit the show's website, buy *Real World* merchandise, and even bid on items from the current *Real World* house that are auctioned off to the highest bidder. In this manner *The Real World* blends nicely with the basic programming format of the Music Television network (MTV), which is designed essentially to sell music and music-related merchandise through the advertising potential grounded in airing music videos and music-related programming.

The Real World served as an important foundation for other reality series to follow. It was instrumental in popularizing the voyeuristic, real-life soap-opera format and was the first to utilize the "confessional," which has become a mainstay for many reality television programs. Its popularity has spread to the creation of hundreds of websites maintained by and engaging

thousands of fans, to sales of videos and merchandise, and to the creation of *Real World* auctions, specials and spin-offs. As a result, *The Real World* can be viewed as the grandfather of the contemporary reality television genre.

LISA JONIAK

*See also **Big Brother; MTV; Reality Programming; Survivor***

Cast

Season 1:	Andre, Becky, Eric, Heather, Julie, Kevin, and Norman
Season 2:	Aaron, Beth, David, Dominic, Irene, Jon, and Tami
Season 3:	Cory, Judd, Mohammed, Pam, Pedro, Puck, and Rachel
Season 4:	Jacinda, Jay, Kat, Lars, Michael, Neil, and Sharon
Season 5:	Cynthia, Dan, Flora, Joe, Melissa, Mike, and Sarah
Season 6:	Elka, Genesis, Jason, Kameelah, Montana, Sean, and Syrus
Season 7:	David, Irene, Janet, Lindsey, Nathan, Rebecca, and Stephen
Season 8:	Amaya, Collin, Justin, Kaia, Matt, Ruthie, and Teck
Season 9:	Danny, David, Jamie, Julie, Kelly, Matt, and Melissa
Season 10:	Coral, Kevin, Lori, Malik, Mike, Nicole, and Rachel
Season 11:	Aneesa, Cara, Chris, Keri, Kyle, Theo, and Tonya
Season 12:	Alton, Arissa, Brynn, Frank, Irulan, Steven, and Trishelle
Season 13:	Ace, Adam, Chris (CT), Christina, Leah, Mallory, and Simon

Creators/Excutive Producers
Jonathan Murray and Mary-Ellis Bunim

Programming History

1992	Season 1, New York, 13 episodes
1993	Season 2, Los Angeles, 23 episodes
1994	Season 3, San Francisco, 23 episodes
1995	Season 4, London, 22 episodes
1996	Season 5, Miami, 23 episodes
1997	Season 6, Boston, 23 episodes
1998	Season 7, Seattle, 23 episodes
1999	Season 8, Hawaii, 23 episodes
2000	Season 9, New Orleans, 23 episodes
2001	Season 10, Back to New York, 22 episodes

2002	Season 11, Chicago, 23 episodes
	(note: start of two seasons per year)
2002	Season 12, Las Vegas, 28 episodes
2003	Season 13, Paris, 23+ episodes

Music Television (MTV)
June 1992–
present   Tuesday 10:00–10:30

Further Reading

Collins, Monica, "MTV's Risqué 'Real World' Is Twisted, Sleazy Fun," *Boston Herald* (January 29, 2002)
Joniak, Lisa, "Understanding Reality Television: A Triangulated Analysis," Ph. D. diss., University of Florida, 2001
Kloer, Phil, "We Got Our MTV," *Atlanta Constitution* (August 1, 2001)
Real World Casting Special, produced by Mary-Ellis Bunim and Jonathan Murray, on Music Television Network, New York: MTV, 2000

Reality Television (U.S.)

"Reality television" is a label that encompasses a wide range of nonfiction formats, including gamedocs, makeover programs, talent contests, docusoaps, dating shows, court programs, tabloid newsmagazine shows, and reality-based sitcoms. Yet, the genre's overarching characteristic is its claim to "the real," which it works to underscore through its aesthetic strategies (use of cinema verité techniques, surveillance video, low-end production values, or "natural settings"), its relentless obsession with the intimate, and its tendency to focus on ordinary people in extraordinary circumstances. And it is these very traits that have helped make reality TV one of the most talked about, reviled, and popular genres on television.

The summer of 2000 is often considered the starting point of the reality television phenomenon in the United States, since it marked the initial appearance and unexpected popularity of *Survivor* and *Big Brother*. Yet, the roots of the genre stretch back to television's early years with programs that delved into the personal lives of game contestants (*Queen for a Day* and *Bride and Groom*) or used hidden cameras to catch people in compromising or embarrassing situations (*Candid Camera*). Nevertheless, there have been distinct periods in television history wherein reality programs have swelled in numbers or developed in novel and significant ways.

During the 1980s, the networks' financial and labor troubles contributed to a proliferation of reality-based programs. Already burdened by rising production costs, debts incurred by the mid-decade sale of three networks to new owners, and a loss of viewers to burgeoning cable channels, the broadcast industry faced a writers' strike in 1988. In the midst of what would become a 22-week walk-off, networks came to depend on their existing lineup of reality programs (which did-

n't depend on writers or other above-the-line talent) and produced new reality shows in order to fill the gap left by their fictional counterparts. From this, the networks learned reality programming was not only cheap, but also strike-proof, and they consequently added more of such programs to their prime-time lineups. Some of the most successful of the shows that came out of this period were *COPS, America's Most Wanted, Unsolved Mysteries, America's Funniest Home Videos* and *Rescue 911.* But reality programs were not just confined to prime time. Syndicated talk shows such as *Geraldo, Oprah,* and *Donahue* began to take over the daytime programming slots, while tabloid magazine programs like *Inside Edition, A Current Affair,* and *Entertainment Tonight* were populating afternoon and early evening slots.

The fact that these programs tended to focus on the personal problems of both ordinary people and celebrities led many to decry them as exploitative and sensational and to eventually group them under the derogatory heading, "trash TV." According to many critics, one producer in particular seemed to represent the very worst tendencies of this type of reality production. Mike Darnell, a former child star, produced a series of controversial specials for FOX during the mid-1990s—such as *World's Scariest Police Chases* and *When Good Pets Go Bad*—which were amped-up collections of recycled home movie and news footage that were described by the *New York Times* as "gross-out shockumentaries and socially unreedeming freak shows." In 1999, FOX's decision to air Darnell's *Who Wants To Marry a Multimillionaire?* (a combination beauty contest and dating show met with almost universal scorn) appeared to be the death knell for both Darnell's career and, perhaps, reality programming in general. However, at that very moment, CBS executives and producer Mark Burnett were creating a new model of reality in the form of an expensively produced game show/documentary hybrid. That program, *Survivor,* would air the following summer and give rise to an unprecedented number of reality programs in prime-time television.

Like the wave of reality in the 1980s, the proliferation of reality in the early 2000s was driven, in part, by financial concerns and the threat of more strikes by writers and actors. However, this most recent surge was also pushed along by both the promise and threat posed by new technologies. The appearance of digital video recorders like TiVo and Replay, which allowed consumers to not only record up to 90 hours of their favorite shows, but to also skip over commercial spots during real-time broadcasts, threatened to upend the long-standing relationship between networks and advertisers. However, a re-envisioned version of reality programming, as exemplified by *Survivor,* allowed for sponsorship and product placement, enabling networks a way around the commercial-skipping feature.

Other technologies offered the potential for audience participation and worked well to increase viewer interest in the gamedoc format of many of these new reality programs. They also significantly increased the potential for profits. Phone numbers set up to take viewer votes to expel contestants often charged callers for the privilege. Websites were set up to provide extra footage or updates for a price, like the *Big Brother* site that charged $19.95 for access to 24-hour live streaming video of the contestants in the house. While not a popular strategy for American television, European versions of reality programs sold a service that would keep fans on top of program developments with regular text message updates sent to their cell phones. These technologies not only gave networks new financing opportunities, but also offered viewers rather unique ways to engage with a reality narrative that seemed to extend outside the boundaries of traditional textual installments.

But it was not only networks that were investing in reality TV. Basic and premium cable channels also found the genre to be a cheap and popular programming alternative that they could easily gear toward the interests of their target audiences. MTV, whose long-standing *Real World* program had prefigured many of the characteristics of the new wave of reality programming a decade before *Survivor* came on the air, developed reality shows that featured teenagers, sorority girls, and rock stars. *The Osbournes,* a reality sitcom that centered on the domestic life of Ozzy Osbourne and his wife, children, and innumerable pets, became the most successful (and expensive) of such shows of 2002. Premium channels Showtime and HBO also

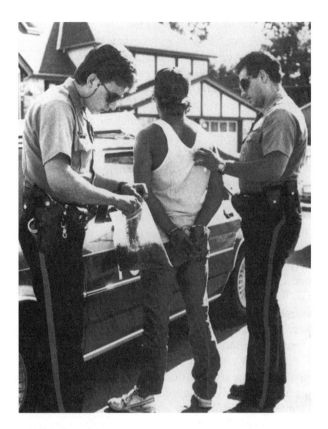

COPS.
Photo courtesy of Fox Broadcasting Company

added more risqué or raw versions of reality to their schedules with series like *Freshman Diaries* and *America Undercover.* The Learning Channel found its reality niche with makeover and lifestyle shows that often were packaged with an "educational" or family bent. Expanding upon its success with *A Wedding Story/A Baby Story* series, it filled its daytime schedule with *A Makeover Story, A Personal Story, A Dating Story,* and added shows like *Maternity Ward* and *Resident Life* to its prime-time lineup. It also Americanized a number of British imports such as *Changing Rooms* (which it renamed *Trading Spaces)* and *What Not To Wear.*

Reality TV has become a decidedly global phenomenon that has involved a reversal of the usual flow of programming across international borders. Instead of theUnited States being the major television exporter, European companies were the originators of many of the formats that have become the most popular reality programs in the United States The Dutch production company Endemol is one of the most successful producers of such formats, selling basic elements of shows like *Big Brother* and *Fear Factor* to not only the United States but also markets in Africa, Latin America, Asia, and Europe. British exporters have also done well for themselves selling programs that found their initial success on the BBC and Channel 4 to U.S. cable stations and networks. The practice of selling formats instead of providing already-produced programs for international distribution is relatively new industrial practice, and is considered yet another financial advantage of the genre. Believing that a program can be evacuated of its cultural particulars and then refilled with new ones once it arrives in another country, production companies assume that the basics of reality programming maintain a universal appeal.

Although many critics in the United States predicted the genre's rapid decline or demise just a year or two after its rise, reality TV continued to dominate the airwaves. In fact, in early 2003, ABC announced that one-seventh of all its programming was reality-based and was planning to add even more to its schedule in upcoming seasons. The staying power of the genre and the success of new shows like *American Idol* and *The Bachelorette* convinced networks to make long-term plans for reality TV and its accompanying business strategies. In a front-page story on the topic in the *New York Times*, president of CBS television, Leslie Moonves, proclaimed rather melodramatically that, "The world as we knew it is over." A few months later, development plans

for an all-reality cable channel were revealed, and *The Real Cancun*, the first "reality movie" was released in theaters. Surprisingly, even Darnell and FOX overcame the taint of the *Multimillionaire* disaster and came out with two new and softer marriage programs, *Joe Millionaire* and *Married by America*, which had followed ABC's success with *The Bachelor*.

SUSAN MURRAY

See also **America's Most Wanted; Big Brother; Candid Camera; COPS; Real World; Survivor**

Further Reading

Andrejevic, Marc, *Reality TV: The Work of Being Watched,* New York: Rowan and Littlefield, 2003

Brenton, Sam, and Reuben Cohen, *Shooting People: Adventures in Reality TV,* New York: Verso, 2003

Calvert, Clay, *Voyeur Nation: Media, Privacy and Peering in Modern Culture,* New York: Westview Press, 2000

Friedman, James, *Reality Squared: Televisual Discourses on the Real,* New Brunswick, New Jersey: Rutgers University Press, 2002

Glynn, Kevin, *Tabloid Culture: Trash Taste, Popular Power and the Transformation of American Television,* Durham, North Carolina: Duke University Press, 2000

Murray, Susan, and Laurie Ouellette, *Reality TV: Remaking Television Culture,* New York: New York University Press, 2004

Red Green Show, The

Canadian Comedy Program

The Red Green Show is a half-hour comedy series targeted to family audiences. *The Red Green Show* is the creation of Steve Smith (S & S Productions) and debuted on CHCH-TV in Hamilton, Ontario, Canada, in 1990 and featured on the Public Broadcasting System (PBS). The low-budget variety show is a spinoff of the *Smith & Smith* variety show that featured Smith and his wife, Morag, and served as a debut for the Green character. *The Red Green Show* features Smith as Red Green, a gentle, handy, outdoorsman with a laid-back sense of humor. *The Red Green Show* is set at the fictitious Possum Lodge, Chapter 13, known as the hangout of "the last real men on the planet." The cast consists mostly of incompetent outdoorsmen in plaid shirts who unwittingly work right into Green's bizarre sense of humor. *The Red Green Show* is intended as a

spoof on male bonding in the outdoors and gives an intentionally hilarious insight into the dreams and obsessions of men. Regular segments include the "Handyman's Corner" (where Red's philosophy of "if women don't find you handsome, they should at least find you handy" is played out with innovative, yet unseemly construction adaptations using duct tape, the "handyman's secret weapon"); "The Experts" (featuring a panel of Possum Lodge, Chapter 13 members who answer viewer mail and find any way to respond without the words, "I don't know"); and "Adventures with Bill" (a klutzy outdoors and nature segment hosted by Possum Lodge's resident naturalist and narrated by Red and shot in black and white).

Other Lodge members and characters include nerdy nephew Harold Green (Pat McKenna); clumsy naturalist Bill Smith (Rick Green); compulsive liar Hap Shaughnessy (Gordon Pinsent); bush pilot and hippie Buzz Sherwood (Peter Wildman); Monster Truck driver Dougie Franklin (Ian Thomas); natural resources enthusiast and golfer Bob Stuyvestant (Bruce Hunter); vacationless fire watch tower warden Ranger Gord (Peter Kelleghan); penny-pinching Dalton Humphries (Bob Bainborough); sales-without-the-service marina owner Glen Braxton (Mark Wilson); sweet but not innocent repeat offender Mike Hammer (Wayne Robson); dynamite-loving Edgar Montrose (Graham Greene); septic-sucking motivator Winston Rothschild III (Jeff Lumby); and big-city land developer Kevin Black (Paul Gross). Mythical characters include Red's wife, sweet Bernice; the cranky, old, senile, and mean Old Man Sedgewick; the large, stupid, and strong Moose Thompson; the smelly and unclean Stinky Peterson; and the unlucky in love Junior Singleton. Co-writers are Rick Green and Peter Wildman.

The Red Green Show was been honored with Canada's 1999 Gemini Award for Best Performance in a Comedy Program or Series (awarded to Steve Smith and Patrick McKenna), and the Rockie Award of the Sir Peter Ustinov Endowment. Smith is a successful fundraiser for PBS; his supporters and fans pledge millions of dollars to PBS.

MARGARET MILLER BUTCHER

Red Skelton Show, The

U.S. Comedy/Variety Program

The Red Skelton Show, which premiered on September 30, 1951, was not only one of the longest-running variety series on television but also one of the first variety shows to make the successful transition from radio to television. Despite his popularity as an entertainer in nightclubs, vaudeville, radio, and 26 feature films, Skelton was unsure of the new medium. Consequently, he continued his weekly radio broadcasts while simultaneously working on the first two seasons of his television show.

The series originally aired in a half-hour format on NBC. Despite an outstanding first year, in which his show was ranked fourth in the Nielsens and won two Emmy Awards, the series' ratings toppled in its second season. When NBC canceled the show, it was immediately picked up by CBS, and *The Red Skelton Show* became a Tuesday night staple from 1954 to 1970, garnering a total of 16 Emmy nominations.

The format of the series was similar to Skelton's radio program. Each show began with Skelton performing a monologue based on topical material, followed by a musical interlude. Next would follow a series of blackout sketches featuring one or more of his characters. The sketches were a mixture of new material and old routines perfected over the years in vaudeville and in nightclubs (including his popular "Guzzler's Gin" sketch). At the end of the program, Skelton would turn serious, expressing his gratitude to his audience for their love and laughter. His signature closing line became "Good night, and may God bless."

The Red Skelton Show, unlike other variety series, did not rely on guest stars every week. Skelton had a strong group of support players, most of whom had worked with him on radio, including Benny Rubin, Hans Conried, Mel Blanc, and Verna Felton.

Most of Skelton's characters were first developed for radio and worked equally well on television. Among the best known were Junior the Mean Widdle Kid (who was famous for his expression, "I dood it"), country boy Clem Kadiddlehopper, Sheriff Deadeye, boxer Cauliflower McPugg, drunkard Willy Lump-Lump, and con man San Fernando Red. Skelton had a reputation for his extensive use of "headware"—each character had his own specific hat, which Skelton used as a means to find the center of each personality. The only television addition to his repertoire of characters was Freddie the Freeloader, a hobo who never spoke. A special "silent spot" featuring the hobo character was added to the program and provided Skelton the opportunity to demonstrate his talents as a pantomimist.

Skelton's forte was his use of slapstick. He appeared oblivious to physical punishment and often ended his vaudeville act by falling off the stage into the orchestra pit. One of his most popular pieces was created for his premiere show. At the end of his monologue, while

Red Skelton Show, Eve Arden, Red Skelton as George Appleby, 1951–71; 1961 episode.
Courtesy of the Everett Collection

During the run of his variety series, Skelton was also able to demonstrate his dramatic abilities. He played punch-drunk fighter Buddy McCoy in *Playhouse 90*'s *The Big Slide* (CBS, November 8, 1956), for which he was nominated for an Emmy Award as best actor. He died in Rancho Mirage, California, on September 17, 1997.

SUSAN R. GIBBERMAN

See also **Skelton, Red; Variety Programs**

Regular Performers
Red Skelton
David Rose and His Orchestra
Carol Worthington (1970–71)
Chanin Hale (1970–71)
Jan Arvan (1970–71)
Bob Duggan (1970–71)
Peggy Rea (1970–71)
Brad Logan (1970–71)
The Burgundy Street Singers (1970–71)

Producers
1951–70: Nat Perrin, Cecil Barker, Freeman Keyes, Ben Brady, Gerald Gardner, Bill Hobin, Seymour Berns; 1970–71: Guy Della Cioppa, Gerald Gardner, Dee Caruso

Programming History
NBC

September 1951–June 1952	Sunday 10:00–10:30
September 1952–June 1953	Sunday 7:00–7:30
CBS	
September 1953–June 1954	Tuesday 8:30–9:00
July 1954–September 1954	Wednesday 8:00–9:00
September 1954–December 1954	Tuesday 8:00–8:30
January 1959–June 1961	Tuesday 9:30–10:00
September 1961–June 1962	Tuesday 9:00–9:30
September 1962–June 1963	Tuesday 8:30–9:30
September 1963–June 1964	Tuesday 8:00–9:00
September 1964–June 1970	Tuesday 8:30–9:30
NBC	
September 1970–March 1971	Monday 7:30–8:00
June 1971–August 1971	Sunday 8:30–9:00

Further Reading

Busch, N.F., "Red Skelton: Television's Clown Prince," *Reader's Digest* (March 1965)
Castro, Peter, "Good Night and God Bless: Despite Grievous Losses, TV's Clown Prince Red Skelton Made Laughter His Life's Work," *People Weekly* (October 6, 1997)
Chassler, S., "Helter Skelton," *Colliers* (March 29, 1952)

Skelton was taking a bow, two hands reached out from under the curtain, grabbed him by the ankles, and swept him off the stage.

Many stars got their start on *The Red Skelton Show*. In 1954, Johnny Carson, one of Skelton's writers, was called upon to fill in for the star when Skelton injured himself during a rehearsal. The Rolling Stones made one of their earliest U.S. appearances on the show in 1964.

Critics often chastised Skelton for breaking into laughter at his own material on the air. But, no matter how many times he succumbed to his giggles, took another pratfall, mugged for the camera, or made asides to the audience, his popularity only increased.

Although the series remained among the top-20 rated shows, CBS canceled it in 1970, citing high production costs. However, it was also the case that Skelton's main audience was very young viewers, and it is more likely that the network wanted shows that would increase its audience share of young adults. The next season, Skelton returned to NBC in a half-hour format on Monday night, but the new show lasted only one season.

"Clown of the Year," *Newsweek* (March 17, 1952)

Gehring, Wes D., "Red Skelton and Clem Kadiddlehopper," *Indiana Magazine of History* (March 1, 1996)

Gehring, Wes D., *Seeing Red: The Skelton in Hollywood's Closet: An Analytical Biography,* Davenport, Iowa: Robin Vincent Publishing, 2001

Marceau, Marcel, "Red Skelton: America's Clown," *TV Guide* (October 11, 1997)

Marx, Arthur, *Red Skelton,* New York: E.P. Dutton, 1979

Pryor, Thomas M., "Impromptu Comic: In TV, Red Skelton Is a Free-Wheeling Clown," *New York Times* (March 2, 1952)

Tschopp, Henry W., "Six Radio Comedians: An Introduction and Investigative Study," Ph.D. diss., University of New Mexico, 1977

Redmond, Phil (1949–)

British Producer

Phil Redmond is the most well-known drama producer in Britain, recognized as the creator of the long-running children's school drama *Grange Hill* and the soap opera *Brookside*. Redmond rose from a council estate childhood in north Liverpool to become a media celebrity and owner of a large private production company. As for most working-class children, a career in the media lay outside his reach, and in 1968 he left his local comprehensive school to train as a quantity surveyor in the building trade. However, by 1972, he had abandoned this, having resolved instead to become a writer, and to take a university degree in social studies to help him in the task. The course had a profound effect on his career, and his writing and programs continually draw on forms of social observation.

The producer's career in television began as a scriptwriter for comedy programs, but his major breakthrough came in 1978, when his proposals for a new children's drama series were adopted by the BBC. What set *Grange Hill* apart from other high school dramas was the program's realism and its interweaving of serious moral and social issues, such as truancy, teenage sex, heroin addiction, and racism, into the story lines. The program's unsentimental approach to school and controversial subject matter has frequently provoked complaints from pressure groups. Despite the objections, however, the series has always been hugely popular with young people, and successive generations of school students have grown up with the program and enjoyed exposure to the problems of the "real" world.

Redmond wrote over 30 episodes for *Grange Hill* in its first four seasons, but his ambitions were driving him toward becoming a producer in his own right and following up the opportunities created by the advent of the fourth channel in Britain. He approached the head of Channel 4, Jeremy Isaacs, and its commissioning editor for fiction, David Rose, and succeeded in convincing them that they should adopt his proposals for *Brookside,* a twice-weekly soap opera focusing on social issues based around family life on a new private housing estate. Channel 4 brought a new style of television production to Britain by commissioning independent production companies to make programs. In 1981, Redmond secured a £4 million investment from Channel 4 to establish his own company, Mersey Television, and to begin work on *Brookside*. Much of the money was spent purchasing and fitting out the real Liverpool housing estate that was to serve both as the production and company base.

The development of Redmond's soap opera is of considerable importance to the history of British television. For many years following its launch in 1982, *Brookside* provided Channel 4 with by far its most popular program and played a major role in establishing the viability of the channel. The setting up of Mersey Television in Liverpool to produce the program represented a considerable innovation, for it created not only the largest independent production company in Britain, with over 100 full-time jobs for the local workforce, but also significantly extended the opportunities for television production outside London.

Redmond has always contended that the audience of popular drama will respond positively to challenging subject matter. With *Brookside* he was to prove his point. After a slightly shaky start, the program's realist aesthetics, pioneering single-camera video production on location, and focus on major social issues such as unemployment, rape, drug use, and gay rights has won over an up-market audience group not normally interested in soaps. The program helped to raise the stakes

Phil Redmond, creator of "*Brookside,*" "*Hollyoaks,*" and "*Grange Hill.*"
Photo courtesy of Phil Redmond

of production design, and has added a new seriousness to popular drama. A new generation of realist drama programs, including top shows such as *EastEnders* and *Casualty,* have followed *Brookside*'s example and explored contemporary social problems.

Redmond's wider business activities provide a conspicuous example of the entrepreneurial spirit that has pervaded broadcasting in Britain following deregulation. In 1991, he was at the center of the £80 million consortium bid for the new ITV franchise in northwest England, which had been held by Granada since 1956. Though the bid was unsuccessful, the additional premises that had been acquired to substantiate it have strengthened the power base of Mersey Television and enabled it to extend its production. In 1990, the output of *Brookside* was increased to three episodes a week and its audience peaked at 8 million viewers in 1993. In 1995, Redmond successfully bid for a new youth

soap opera, and *Hollyoaks* was introduced into Channel 4's early evening schedule.

Redmond and his company have ridden the recession in British commercial TV at the start of the new century with more limited success. The proliferation of new digital and terrestrial channels drew away large numbers of viewers from Channel 4, and by 2002 *Brookside*'s audience had dropped to less than a million. Audience tastes, too, were changing, moving away from realist fictions to reality television and lifestyle shows *Brookside* was closed down in November 2003. However, *Hollyoaks* has moved from strength to strength in its niche as an upbeat, lifestyle soap, and output has been increased to five episodes a week. At the same time, Redmond has also resumed executive control of *Grange Hill*. The move of the production from London to Mersey Television has taken up some of the company's spare capacity brought about by the loss of *Brookside*.

Redmond remains the chair of the largest independent drama production company in Britain, which over the years has launched the careers of some of the most well-known actors, writers, directors, and producers in British television. He continues to play an active role in television training.

BOB MILLINGTON

See also **Brookside; Channel 4; Grange Hill**

Phil Redmond. Born in Liverpool, Lancashire, England, 1949. Began career as a television scriptwriter, contributing to *Z Cars* and other series; established reputation with the realistic school series *Grange Hill,* BBC; subsequently moved into independent television, setting up Mersey Television and creating *Brookside* soap opera for Channel 4.

Television Series

1978–	*Grange Hill*
1982–2003	*Brookside*
1995–	*Holly Oaks*

Further Reading

Cooke, Lez, *British Television Drama, A History,* London: British Film Institute, 2003

Geraghty, Christine, *Women and Soap Opera,* London: Polity, 1990

Redmond, Phil, *Brookside, The Official Companion,* London: Weidenfeld and Nicolson, 1987

Tunstall, Jeremy, *Television Producers,* London: Routledge, 1993

Redstone, Sumner (1923–)

U.S. Media Mogul

Sumner Redstone is one of the most powerful media moguls of the early 21st century. In his capacity as chairman of the board and chief executive officer of Viacom, Redstone controls Hollywood's Paramount Pictures television and motion picture factory; the CBS and UPN networks; a handful of cable TV networks, including MTV, the Movie Channel, Showtime, Black Entertainment Television, The Nashville Network, Comedy Central, Country Music Television, Nickelodeon, and VH-1; several radio and TV stations; and a TV production and syndication business that owns the lucrative syndication rights to *Roseanne, A Different World, I Love Lucy, Perry Mason, The Twilight Zone,* and *The Cosby Show.* Viacom has also produced such prime-time fare as *Matlock* and *Jake and the Fatman.*

Redstone's father, Michael, first sold linoleum from the back of a truck, later became a liquor wholesaler, and finally purchased two nightclubs and set up one of the original drive-in movie operations in the United States. By the time Sumner Redstone graduated from Harvard University in 1943, his father was concentrating on the movie industry. One of a number of struggling owners in the fledgling drive-in business, he was unable to book first-run films because the vertically integrated Hollywood giants promoted their own movie theaters.

Sumner Redstone graduated first in his class from the prestigious Boston Latin School and then finished Harvard in less than three years. Upon graduation, he was recruited by Edwin Reischauer, a future U.S. ambassador to Japan, for an ace U.S. Army intelligence unit that would become famous for cracking Japan's military codes. After three years of service, during which he received two Army commendations, Redstone entered Harvard Law School.

After graduating from Harvard Law in 1947, he began to practice law, first in Washington, D.C., and then in Boston, but he soon was lured into the family movie-theater business. Two decades later, Redstone became president and chief executive officer of the family firm, National Amusements, Inc. (NAI) and he took on the additional role of chairman of the NAI board in 1986. Indeed, even with his move to Viacom,

Redstone has continued in the movie-exhibition business. At the end of the 20th century, National Amusements operated 1,350 screens across the United States, the United Kingdom, and Latin America.

Redstone is a physically tough individual. In 1979, he survived a Boston hotel fire by clinging to a third-floor window with one severely burned hand. Doctors never expected him to live through 60 hours of surgery, but he did. Medical experts told him he would never walk again, yet Redstone began to exercise daily on a treadmill and to play tennis regularly, wearing a leather strap that enabled him to grip his racquet. Those who know the Boston tycoon say that his recovery spurred his ambition to succeed in the motion-picture and later television business.

As he recovered from his burns, Redstone used his knowledge of the movie business to begin selectively acquiring stock in Hollywood studios. In a relatively short time, he made millions of dollars buying and selling stakes in Twentieth Century Fox, Columbia Pictures Entertainment, MGM/UA Entertainment, and Orion. At first, Viacom represented simply another stock market investment, but soon Redstone realized that the company needed new management, and, in 1987, he resolved to take over and run the operation.

Redstone's acquisition proved difficult. The company had rebuffed an earlier takeover attempt by financier Carl Icahn, and Viacom executives had sought to buy and protect their own company. Redstone became embroiled in a bitter, six-month corporate raid that forced him to raise his offer three times. Upon final acquisition, rather than break up Viacom and sell off divisions to pay for the deal as his bankers advised, Redstone slowly and quietly built the company into one of the world's top TV corporations.

Redstone hired former Home Box Office chief executive Frank Biondi to build on Viacom's diversity. For example, by the mid-1990s, Viacom had expanded its MTV music network far beyond its original base in the United States to reach more than 200 million households in approximately 80 countries in Europe, Latin America, and Asia. Redstone felt that his networks needed a Hollywood studio to make new products, and in 1993 he decided to acquire Paramount. He soon

Sumner Redstone, 2000.
©*Robert Bertoia/Everett Collection*

decision maker. Thus, Redstone brought together the CBS and UPN television networks and Viacom's cable channels under one roof, making Redstone one of the handful of the world's most powerful media moguls. But as the advertising market soured at the commencement of the 21st century, the synergy of the merger did not increase profits. Overall, advertising sales were down, and it was uncertain whether Redstone, as he neared his 80th birthday, would spin off subsidiaries he deemed unnecessary for Viacom's future.

DOUGLAS GOMERY

See also **Cable Networks; MTV; Syndication**

Sumner Murray Redstone. Born Sumner Murray Rothstein in Boston, Massachusetts, May 27, 1923. Educated at Harvard University, B.A., 1944, L.L.B., 1947. Married: Phyllis Gloria Raphael, 1947; children: Brent Dale and Shari Ellin. Served as first lieutenant, U.S. Army, 1943–45. Admitted to the Massachusetts Bar, 1947; instructor of law and labor management, University of San Francisco, 1947; law secretary, U.S. Court of Appeals for 9th Circuit, San Francisco, 1947–48; admitted to U.S. Court of Appeals (1st and 9th Circuits), 1948; special assistant to U.S. Attorney General, Washington, D.C., 1948–51; admitted to U.S. Court of Appeals (8th Circuit), 1950; admitted to Washington, D.C., Bar, 1951; partner in firm of Ford, Bergson, Adams, Borkland, and Redstone, Washington, D.C., 1951–54; admitted to U.S. Supreme Court, 1952; executive vice president, Northeast Drive-In Theater Corporation, 1954–68; president, Northeast Theater Corporation; assistant president, Theater Owners of America, 1960–63, president, 1964–65; chair of the board, National Association of Theater Owners, 1965–66; president and chief executive officer, National Amusements, Inc., Dedham, Massachusetts, since 1967, chair of the board, since 1986; chair of the board, Viacom International, Inc. and Viacom, Inc., New York City; professor, Boston University Law School, 1982, 1985–86. Member: American Bar Association; National Association of Theatre Owners; Theatre Owners of America; Motion Picture Pioneers; Boston Bar Association; Massachusetts Bar Association; Harvard Law School Association; American Judicature Society. Recipient: Army Commendation Medal; William J. German Human Relations Award, American Jewish Committee Entertainment and Communication Division, 1977; Silver Shingle Award, Boston University Law School, 1985; Man of the Year, Entertainment Industries Division of United Jewish Appeal Federation, 1988; Variety New England Humanitarian Award, 1989; Pioneer of the Year, Motion Picture Pioneers, 1991.

found himself in a battle with QVC Network, Inc., and in time he joined forces with video rental empire Blockbuster Entertainment to cement the deal.

Owning more than two-thirds of Viacom's voting stock (as of 2002) means that Redstone controls a vast media empire second only to that of Rupert Murdoch. Through the 1990s and early 2000s, *Forbes* ranked Redstone among the richest persons in the United States, with a net worth in excess of $4 billion. Yet Redstone has never "gone Hollywood." At the start of the 21st century, he continues to operate his collection of enterprises, not from Paramount's sprawling studio on Melrose Avenue in Hollywood, but from his long-time NAI headquarters in Dedham, Massachusetts.

On September 7, 1999, Redstone announced the capstone deal of his life by taking over CBS Corporation for $37.3 billion. He was able to bend the Federal Communications Commission ownership rules, and the deal sailed past government regulators. Mel Karmazin of CBS became the chief operating officer of the whole company, but with Redstone owning controlling interest in the stock, it was clear who was the boss, the final

Publication

A Passion to Win (with Peter Knobler), 2001

Further Reading

Auletta, Ken, "The Last Studio in Play," *The New Yorker* (October 4, 1993)

Bart, Peter, "Owners Take Over the Asylum: Murdochian Moguls Become Hands-on," *Variety* (February 26, 1995)

Gallese, Liz Roman, "'I Get Exhilarated by It,'" *Forbes* (October 22, 1990)

Greenwald, John, "The Man with the Iron Grasp," *Time* (September 27, 1993)

Landler, Mark, "The MTV Tycoon: Sumner Redstone Is Turning Viacom into the Hottest Global TV Network," *Business Week* (September 21, 1992)

Landler, Mark, "Sumner at the Summit," *Business Week* (February 28, 1994)

Lenzer, Robert, "Late Bloomer," *Forbes* (October 17, 1994)

Leonard, Devin, "Who's the Boss?" *Fortune* (April 16, 2000)

Maney, Kevin, *Megamedia Shakeout: The Inside Story of the Leaders and Losers in the Exploding Communications Industry,* New York: John Wiley, 1995

Matzer, Marla, "Winning Is the Only Thing," *Forbes* (October 17, 1994)

Parker, Jim, "The CBS-Viacom Merger: Impact on Journalism," *Federal Communications Law Journal* (May 2000)

Schwartzman, Andrew Jay, "Viacom-CBS Merger: Media Competition and Consolidation in the New Millennium," *Federal Communications Law Journal* (May 2000)

Stern, Christopher, "Ready to Take On the World" (interview), *Broadcasting and Cable* (September 20, 1993)

"Sumner Redstone: A Drive to Win," *Broadcasting* (November 14, 1988)

Waterman, David, "CBS-Viacom and the Effects of Media Mergers: An Economic Perspective," *Federal Communications Law Journal* (May 2000)

Rees, Marian

U.S. Producer

After graduating with honors in sociology from the University of Iowa, Marian Rees moved to Los Angeles in 1952, where she began her television career as a receptionist-typist at NBC. By 1955, she had joined the Norman Lear-Bud Yorkin company, Tandem Productions, and in 1958, she served as an associate producer of the much-honored *An Evening with Fred Astaire.* She continued to advance in the organization, and by the early 1970s, she served as associate producer of the pilots of *All in the Family* and *Sanford and Son.* In 1972, however, she was told by Tandem that she would be happier elsewhere, and was given two weeks' notice. It was a stunning blow, but as she told an interviewer in 1986, she used the firing to grow.

Rees assumed a new position at the independent production company Tomorrow Entertainment, where she broadened her knowledge of development, preproduction, and postproduction. At Tomorrow, Rees was associated with a variety of quality productions, including *The Autobiography of Miss Jane Pittman.* She then spent two years as vice president of the NRW Company, where she was the executive producer of *The Marva Collins Story,* a *Hallmark Hall of Fame* presentation starring Cicely Tyson. In 1982, Rees formed her own company, Marian Rees Associates. Anne Hopkins joined the company as a partner and has continued to work with Rees ever since.

In order to fund her first independent productions, Rees initially mortgaged her home and car, facing demands for financial qualification far more extensive than would have been required for a man. She pressed for months to gain network approval for her first production, *Miss All-American Beauty,* but resistance continued, and she finally learned that the male executive she had to convince simply did not want to trust a woman. Finally, with funds running extremely low, approval for the project came from CBS. Rees completed the production under budget, and her company at last found itself on solid footing.

In the succeeding years, Rees has garnered 11 Emmy Awards and 38 Emmy nominations. In 1992, just ten years after her company began, she saw her film for NBC, *Miss Rose White,* garner four Emmys out of ten nominations, a Golden Globe nomination, and the Humanitas Award. Ten of her productions have been aired as part of the *Hallmark Hall of Fame* series.

Rees has remained faithful to her vision of excellence, even in times of financial difficulty. She examines potential stories to ascertain whether they speak to her personally, and whether they will make her proud to be associated with the final product. These same concerns are reflected in the meticulous attention she and her partner give to each project once it is in production. While filming *Miss Rose White* in spring 1992

Marian Rees.
Photo courtesy of Marian Rees

in Richmond, Virginia, for example, both Rees and Hopkins supervised details at every stage and personally examined each location shot for authenticity. Such care has meant that their work is usually focused on a single film at a time. Rees and Hopkins form a remarkable team, taking considerable risks, and always delivering quality products, a task made more difficult in today's U.S. television industry.

In 1997, the partners joined with Stephen Kulczycki to form ALT Films, a nonprofit production company that in 1999 won a grant to produce five films based on American literary works for *ExxonMobil Masterpiece Theatre's American Collection* on PBS. The adapted works were Esmeralda Santiago's *Almost a Woman,* James Agee's *A Death in the Family,* Eudora Welty's *The Ponder Heart,* Willa Cather's *The Song of the Lark,* and Langston Hughes's *Cora Unashamed.* These five films aired from 2000 to 2002.

A champion for women's rights in the U.S. television industry throughout her career, Marian Rees served two terms as president of Women in Film. Her service to her profession also includes board membership at the American Film Institute and the Producer's

Guild of America, where she has served as vice president. "Producer" may be an easy title to acquire in the modern television age. Few earn it, and certainly none deserve it more than Marian Rees.

ROBERT S. ALLEY

*See also **All in the Family; Hallmark Hall of Fame; Sanford and Son***

Marian Rees. Worked in live television, New York City, from 1950s; associate producer, Tandem Productions, 1955–72; executive, Tomorrow Entertainment, First Artists Television, EMI Television, and NRW Company's features division, 1972–82; founder, Marian Rees Associates, 1982, ALT Films, 1997; producer, numerous made-for-television movies. Member: Women in Film (twice elected president); board of directors, American Film Institute; Producers Guild of America (vice president, 1996).

Television Series (selected)

1971–79	*All in the Family*
1972–77	*Sanford and Son*
2000–02	*ExxonMobil Masterpiece Theatre's American Collection*

Made-for-Television Movies (selected)

1979	*Orphan Train*
1981	*The Marva Collins Story*
1981	*Angel Dusted*
1982	*Miss All-American Beauty*
1983	*Between Friends*
1984	*License to Kill*
1984	*Love Is Never Silent*
1986	*Christmas Snow*
1986	*Resting Place*
1987	*The Room Upstairs*
1987	*Foxfire*
1988	*Little Girl Lost*
1989	*The Shell Seekers*
1989	*Home Fires Burning*
1990	*Decoration Day*
1992	*Miss Rose White*
1995	*In Pursuit of Honor*
1995	*When the Vows Break*
1998	*Ruby Bridges*
2000	*Cora Unashamed*
2000	*Papa's Angels*
2000	*The Song of the Lark*
2001	*Almost a Woman*

Television Special

1958	*An Evening with Fred Astaire*

Reid, Tim (1944–)

U.S. Actor, Writer, Producer

Tim Reid is an accomplished television actor and producer whose critically acclaimed work has, unfortunately, often failed to meet with sustained audience acceptance. As an African American, Reid has tried to choose roles and projects that help effect a positive image for the black community. Through both his acting and writing, he has provided important insights regarding black-white relationships and bigotry.

Being a part of show business was one of Reid's childhood dreams. Not content with simply being an actor, he hoped to play a vital role behind the scenes, as well. Like many young actors, he began his career as a stand-up comedian, working with Tom Dreesen as part of the comedy duet "Tim and Tom." It was during this experience that Reid began exploring the dynamics of black-white relationships. In 1978, after performing in various episodic series, he received the role of Venus Flytrap in Hugh Wilson's *WKRP in Cincinnati*. From the beginning, Reid made it clear to Wilson that he was not interested in playing just another "jive-talking" black character. Wilson agreed, eventually giving Reid control over his character's development, which culminated in a story that revealed a much deeper character than the Flytrap persona first presented.

It was during *WKRP* that Reid gained experience as a writer, contributing several scripts to the series. One episode, "A Family Affair," dealt with the underlying tones of bigotry that plague even the best of friends. He also worked closely with Wilson on the script "Venus and the Man," in which Venus helped a young black gang member decide to return to high school. Teacher's organizations applauded the effort, and scenes from the show were reproduced, in comic book form, in *Scholastic* magazine.

After *WKRP*, Reid landed a recurring role in the detective drama *Simon and Simon*, for which he also wrote a number of scripts. In 1987, he again joined forces with Wilson to coproduce *Frank's Place*, which starred Reid as a Boston professor who took over his deceased father's bar in a predominately black section of New Orleans. While critics raved about the rich writing (Wilson won an Emmy for the *Frank's Place* script "The Bridge"), acting, and photography, the se-

ries was canceled after its first season. Reid contends that this cancellation was due to the constant schedule changes that afflicted the series (a problem he and Wilson experienced previously with *WKRP*), as well as CBS's overall dismal ratings at the time.

In 1989, Reid became executive producer of *Snoops,* a drama in which he starred with his wife, Daphne Maxwell Reid, as a sophisticated husband-and-wife detective team in the tradition of the *Thin Man* series. Just as with *Moonlighting* and *Remington Steele, Snoops* placed character development over mystery. Once again, despite quality scripts and performances, the show failed to find an audience. Reid's best-known television role of the 1990s was the father on *Sister, Sister* (ABC then WB; 1994–99).

In 1997, Reid established New Millennium Studios in Petersburg, Virginia. The studio features a soundstage and postproduction facilities and has allowed him to produce his own work as well as contract with other producers in search of a location for television and film projects. Reid has personally used the studio as creator and producer of the 1998 series *Linc's,*

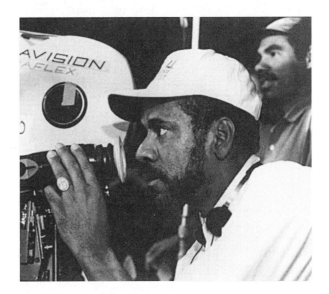

Tim Reid.
Photo courtesy of Tim Reid Productions

shown on the Showtime cable channel, and as producer of feature and made-for-television films.

MICHAEL B. KASSEL AND ELIZABETH NISHIURA

See also **Frank's Place; Racism, Ethnicity, and Television**

Tim Reid. Born in Norfolk, Virginia, December 19, 1944. Educated at Norfolk State College, B.B.A., 1968. Married: Daphne Maxwell, 1982; children: Tim II, Tori LeAnn, Christopher Tubbs. Marketing representative for Dupont Corporation, 1968–71; actively involved in anti-drug movement, since 1969; stand-up comedian, Tim and Tom comedy team, 1971–75; actor in series television, from 1976; founded Timalove Enterprises, 1979; creator, producer, anti-drug video *Stop the Madness,* 1986; founded Tim Reid Productions, 1989; cofounded, with Black Entertainment Television, United Image Entertainment Enterprises, 1990; founder and president, New Millennium Studios, since 1997. Also co-chair; organizer, and sponsor, Annual Tim Reid Celebrity Tennis Tournament, Norfolk State University campus. Member: Writers Guild of America; Screen Actors Guild; board of directors, Phoenix House of California; board of trustees, Norfolk State University, Commonwealth of Virginia; board of directors, National Academy of Cable Programming; AFTRA; life member, NAACP. Recipient: Emmy Award; Critics Choice Award, 1988; NAACP Image Award, 1988; Viewers for Quality Television Best Actor in a Comedy Award, 1988; National Black College Alumni Hall of Fame, 1991.

Television Series

1976	*Easy Does It...Starring Frankie Avalon*
1977	*The Marilyn McCoo and Billy Davis, Jr. Show*
1977	*The Richard Pryor Show*
1978–82	*WKRP in Cincinnati*
1983	*Teachers Only*
1983–87	*Simon and Simon*
1987–88	*Frank's Place* (also co-executive producer)
1989–90	*Snoops* (also co-creator, executive producer)
1994–99	*Sister, Sister* (also creator, producer)
1998	*Linc's* (also creator and producer)

Made-for-Television Movies

1979	*You Can't Take It with You*
1990	*Perry Mason: The Case of the Silenced Singer*
1991	*Stephen King's It*
1991	*The Family Business*
1992	*You Must Remember This*
1994	*Race to Freedom: The Underground Railroad* (producer)
1995	*Simon and Simon: In Trouble Again*
1998	*About Sarah* (executive producer)
2000	*Alley Cats Strike*

Films

Dead Bang, 1989; *The Fourth War,* 1990; *Once Upon a Time...When We Were Colored* (director), 1995; *Mu Sa Do,* 2002; *For Real,* 2003 (director and actor); *On the One,* 2004.

Further Reading

Gray, Herman, *Watching Race: Television and the Struggle for "Blackness,"* Minneapolis: University of Minnesota Press, 1995

Reiner, Carl (1922–)

U.S. Comedian, Writer, Producer

Carl Reiner is one of the few true Renaissance persons of 20th-century mass media. Known primarily for his work as creator, writer, and producer of *The Dick Van Dyke Show,* Reiner has also made his mark as a comedian, actor, novelist, and film director. From Reiner's "Golden Age" TV connection with Sid Caesar to his later film work with Steve Martin, the Emmy Award-winning Reiner has touched three generations of American comedy.

According to Vince Waldron's *Official "Dick Van Dyke Show" Book* (1994), Reiner began his career as a sketch comedian in the Catskill Mountains. After serving in World War II, he landed the lead role in a national touring company production of *Call Me Mister,* which he later reprised on Broadway. Reiner's big break came in 1950, when producer Max Leibman, whom he had met while working in the Catskills, cast Reiner as a comic actor in Sid Caesar's *Your Show of Shows.* Drawn to the creative genius of the show's writers, which included Mel Brooks and Neil Simon, Reiner ended up contributing ideas for many of the series' sketches. The experience undoubtedly provided Reiner with a good deal of fodder for his later *Dick Van Dyke Show.* While he never received credit for his writing efforts on *Your Show of Shows,* in 1955 and 1956 he received his first two of many Emmy Awards, these for his role as supporting actor. In 1957, Reiner conquered another medium when he adapted one of his short stories into *Enter Laughing,* a semi-autobiographical novel focusing on a struggling actor's desire to break into show business. In 1963, the book became a hit play.

By the summer of 1958, after Caesar's third and final series was canceled, Reiner spent the summer preparing for what many consider his greatest accomplishment—writing the first 13 episodes of "Head of the Family," a sitcom featuring the exploits of fictional New York comedy writer Rob Petrie. Originally intended as an acting vehicle for himself, Reiner's pilot failed to sell. However, Danny Thomas Productions' producer Sheldon Leonard liked the idea and said it had potential if it were recast—which was Leonard's nice way of saying, "Keep Reiner off camera." When Reiner's Rob Petrie was replaced with TV newcomer Dick Van Dyke (who had just enjoyed a successful Broadway run in *Bye, Bye Birdie*), *The Dick Van Dyke Show* was born.

As with *Enter Laughing,* Reiner's sitcom was autobiographical. Like Petrie, Reiner was a New York writer who lived in suburban New Rochelle. Like Petrie, Reiner spent part of his World War II days at Camp Crowder in Joplin, Missouri, a fact that was brought out in several flashback episodes. Even Petrie's 148 Bonny Meadow Road address was an allusion to Reiner's own 48 Bonny Meadow Road home.

Perhaps it was this realism that contributed to the series' timelessness, making it a precursor for such sophisticated and intelligent sitcoms as *The Mary Tyler Moore Show* and *The Bob Newhart Show.* Just as with these later works, Reiner's series placed character integrity over raw laughs. By being the first to combine both the home and work lives of the series' main character, Reiner also provided interesting insights regarding both sedate suburbia and urbane New York. *The Dick Van Dyke Show* also serves as an early example of the "coworkers as family" format, which has become a staple relationship in modern sitcoms.

Carl Reiner was one of the first "auteur producers,"

with his first 13 episodes becoming the "bible" upon which consequent episodes were based. He continued to write many of the series' best episodes, as well as portray recurring character Alan Brady, the egomaniacal star of the variety program for which Petrie and crew wrote. After a tough first season in 1961, Leonard was able to convince CBS executives, who had canceled the series, to give it a second chance. The series became a top hit in subsequent years, enjoying five seasons before voluntarily retiring. The reruns have never left the air, and it, along with *I Love Lucy,* comprises some of the most-watched programs in syndication history. Those series, along with *The Mary Tyler Moore Show,* also became the flagship programs of U.S. cable's classic-TV powerhouse Nick at Nite.

While many view *The Dick Van Dyke Show* as the high point of Reiner's career, his films cannot be ignored. After directing *Enter Laughing* in 1967, Reiner went on to do several critically acclaimed films such as *The Comic* (1969), a black comedy starring Dick Van Dyke as an aging silent-film comedian, and *Where's Poppa?* (1970). Reiner also directed the wildly successful George Burns vehicle *Oh, God!* (1977). Reiner is also significant for his role as straight man in "The 2,000 Year Old Man" recordings, which he began with Mel Brooks in 1960.

In the 1970s, Reiner and Van Dyke re-entered television with *The New Dick Van Dyke Show.* While Reiner had hoped to break new ground, he became frustrated with the network's family-standard provisions that hampered the series' sophistication. It was not until 1976 that Reiner returned to series television as actor and executive producer of the short-lived ABC sitcom *Good Heavens.*

Just as *The Dick Van Dyke Show* had represented a departure from the standard sitcom fare of the 1960s, *Saturday Night Live* and its famous guest host Steve Martin forged their own type of late-1970s humor. Once again on the cutting edge, Reiner joined forces with Martin as the "wild and crazy" comedian made the transition to film, with Reiner directing Martin in *The Jerk* (1979), *The Man with Two Brains* (1983), and *All of Me* (1984).

In a 1995 episode of the NBC comedy series *Mad About You,* Reiner reprised his role as Alan Brady and won an Emmy Award for outstanding guest appearance in a comedy series for this program. In the fictional world of the newer sitcom, *The Dick Van Dyke Show* is "real," as is the Brady character. Reiner's performance drew on the entire body of his work, from his days with Sid Caesar through his work as writer, director, and producer, and the portrait he presented in this new context echoed with references to the television history he has lived and to which he has so fully contributed. He remains active as a writer and as an actor in both film and television—for example, writing novels and short stories; reviving the 2,000-year-old man character with Mel Brooks in 1997; lending his voice to episodes of the animated TV series *King of the Hill* (FOX, 1997) and *Disney's Hercules* (1998); guest-starring on two episodes of the CBS legal drama *Family Law* (1999 and 2000); and playing a featured role in the film *Ocean's Eleven* (2001). For his career achievements, he has been honored by the Kennedy Center in Washington, D.C., and inducted into the Academy of Television Arts and Sciences Hall of Fame.

MICHAEL B. KASSEL

See also **Caesar, Sid;** *Dick Van Dyke Show, The*

Carl Reiner. Born in the Bronx, New York, March 20, 1922. Educated at the School of Foreign Service, Georgetown University, 1943. Married: Estelle Lebost, 1943; children: Robert, Sylvia, and Lucas. Served in the U.S. Army, attached to Major Maurice Evans's Special Services Unit, 1942–46. Worked in Broadway shows, 1946–50; character actor and emcee, television show *Your Show of Shows,* 1950–54; appeared in *Caesar's Hour,* 1954–57; appeared in short-lived *Sid Caesar Invites You,* 1958; emcee, *Keep Talking,* 1958–59; writer, actor, and producer, various TV series, from 1960; director and star, numerous motion pictures, since 1959. Recipient: 12 Emmy Awards, since 1965; Kennedy Center Mark Twain Prize for American Humor, 2000. Inducted in Academy of Television Arts and Sciences Hall of Fame, 1999.

Television Series

1950–54	*Your Show of Shows*
1954–57	*Caesar's Hour*
1956–63	*The Dinah Shore Chevy Show*
1958–59	*Keep Talking*
1961–66	*The Dick Van Dyke Show* (producer and writer)
1971–74	*The New Dick Van Dyke Show* (producer and writer)
1976	*Good Heavens* (actor and producer)
2003	*The Alan Brady Show*

Television Specials

1967	*The Sid Caesar, Imogene Coca, Carl Reiner, Howard Morris Special*
1968	*The Fabulous Funnies* (host)
1969	*The Wonderful World of Pizzazz* (cohost)
1970	*Happy Birthday Charlie Brown* (host)
1984	*Those Wonderful TV Game Shows* (host)
1984	*The Great Stand-Ups: 60 Years of Laughter* (narrator)
1987	*Carol, Carl, Whoopi, and Robin*

Films (selected)

Happy Anniversary, 1959; *The Gazebo,* 1960; *Gidget Goes Hawaiian,* 1961; *It's A Mad, Mad, Mad, Mad World,* 1963; *The Russians Are Coming!,* 1966; *Enter Laughing* (director), 1967; *Where's Poppa?,* 1970; *Heaven Help Us* (coproducer), 1976; *Oh, God!* (director), 1977; *The End,* 1978; *The One and Only* (director), 1978; *The Jerk* (director), 1979; *Dead Men Don't Wear Plaid,* 1982; *The Man with Two Brains* (codirector), 1983; *All of Me* (director), 1984; *Summer Rental* (director), 1985; *Summer School* (director), 1987; *Bert Rigby, You're a Fool* (director), 1989; *The Spirit of '76,* 1990; *Basic Instinct,* 1993; *The Slums of Beverly Hills,* 1998; *The Adventures of Rocky and Bullwinkle,* 2000; *Ocean's Eleven,* 2001; *The Majestic* (voice), 2001; *Good Boy!,* 2003; *Ocean's Twelve,* 2004.

Stage

Call Me Mister, 1947–48; *Inside U.S.A.,* 1948–49; *Alive and Kicking,* 1950; *Enter Laughing,* 1963; *Something Different* (writer and director), 1968; *So Long 147th Street* (writer), 1976; *The Roast* (director), 1980.

Publications

Enter Laughing (novel), 1958
The 2,000 Year Old Man (with Mel Brooks), 1981
All Kinds of Love (novel), 1993
Continue Laughing (novel), 1995
The 2,000 Year Old Man in the Year 2000 (with Mel Brooks), 1997
How Paul Robeson Saved My Life, and Other Mostly Happy Stories, 1999

Reith, John C.W. (1889–1971)

British Media Executive

John Reith, the founding director general of the British Broadcasting Corporation (BBC) from 1922 to 1938, was aptly designated by the *New York Times* as "the single most dominating influence on British broadcasting." Reith developed strong ideas about the educational and cultural public-service responsibilities of a national radio service, ideas subsequently pursued by many broadcasting systems around the world.

Reith was born the fifth son of a Scottish minister and trained in Glasgow as an engineer. After service in World War I, where he was severely wounded (his face carried the scars), and a growing boredom with engineering, he answered a 1922 advertisement for a post at the new BBC, then a commercial operation. He knew nothing of radio or broadcasting and did not even own a receiver. He was hired and a year later was promoted to managing director.

Learning on the job, Reith soon defined public-service broadcasting as having four elements, which he described in his book *Broadcast over Britain* (1924). Such a system, he argued, operated on a public-service rather than commercial motive, offered national coverage, depended upon centralized control and operation rather than local outlets, and developed high-quality standards of programming. He held broadcasting to high moral—almost religious—standards and rather quickly identified the BBC (which became a public corporation early in 1927) with the political establishment, just as he also insisted on BBC operational independence from any political pressures.

Reith directed the expanding BBC operations from Broadcasting House, the downtown London headquarters he initiated, which opened in 1932 and remains a landmark. His primary interest was in radio, however, and the BBC was slow to cooperate with John Logie Baird and other TV experimenters. With the development of effective all-electronic television, Reith's BBC inaugurated the world's first regular public schedule of television broadcasts from November 1936 until Britain entered World War II in September 1939.

Reith felt increasingly underutilized at the BBC by the late 1930s; the system he had built and the key people he had selected were all doing their jobs well and the system hummed relatively smoothly. He was both revered and somewhat feared in the organization he had shaped. In a mid-1938 managerial coup, however, Reith was eased out as director general by the BBC's Board of Governors (acting in consort with the government), which had grown weary with his self-righteous inflexibility within the organization as well as his political stance. He left the BBC after 16 years, with considerable bitterness that remained for the rest of his life.

Reith's remaining three decades were a disappointment to him and others. After a brief period (1938–40) heading Imperial Airways as it became the British Overseas Airways Corporation (the government-owned predecessor of British Airways), he held a number of minor cabinet posts in wartime and postwar governments and served as chair of several companies. Reith's strong views, conviction that he was nearly always right, and dour personality made it difficult for him to readily get along in the rapidly changing postwar British scene. He wrote an autobiography, *Into the Wind* (1949), and complained he had never been "fully stretched." Indeed, he saw his entire life as one of failure. He argued strongly in the House of Lords against the inception of commercial television in 1954. He felt the BBC had long since given way to social pressures and lowered its standards. It was no longer his child.

Reith was an obsessive keeper of diaries all his life—excerpts published in 1975 showed him to be a man with strong convictions, powerful hatreds, considerable frustration, and an immense ego.

CHRISTOPHER H. STERLING

See also **British Television; Public Service Television**

John Charles Walsham Reith. Born in Stonehaven, Grampian, Scotland, July 20, 1889. Attended Glasgow Academy; Gresham's School, Holt. Married Muriel Odhams; one son and one daughter. Served in World War I; also uniformed service as officer in Royal Navy Reserve, 1942–44, assigned to the Admiralty. Engineer, Coatbridge; first general manager, BBC, 1922; director general, 1927–38, pioneering public-service broadcasting; chair, Imperial Airways, 1938; elected member of Parliament, Southampton, 1940; appointed minister of information, 1940, later minister of works and public buildings, 1940–42. Elected a director of Cable & Wireless, 1943; Commonwealth Communications Council, 1944–45; chair, Commonwealth Telecommunications Board, 1946–50, and Colonial Development Corporation, 1946–57. Annual Reith lectures inaugurated in his honor, 1948. Knighted, 1927; created Baron Reith of Stonehaven, 1940; member of House of Lords. Died June 16, 1971.

Publications

Broadcast over Britain, 1924
Into the Wind (autobiography), 1949
Wearing Spurs, 1966
The Reith Diaries (edited by Charles Stuart), 1975

Further Reading

Allighan, Garry, *Sir John Reith,* London: Stanley Paul, 1938
BBC Annual, London: BBC, 1935–37
BBC Handbook, London: BBC, 1938
BBC Yearbook, London: BBC, 1928–34
Boyle, Andrew, *Only the Wind Will Listen: Reith of the BBC,* London: Hutchinson, 1972
Briggs, Asa, *The History of Broadcasting in the United Kingdom: The Birth of Broadcasting,* Oxford: Oxford University Press, 1961
Briggs, Asa, *The Golden Age of Wireless,* Oxford: Oxford University Press, 1965
Briggs, Asa, *Governing the BBC,* London: BBC, 1979
McIntyre, Ian, *The Expense of Glory: A Life of John Reith,* London: Harper Collins, 1993
Milner, Roger, *Reith: The BBC Years,* Edinburgh: Mainstream Publishing, 1983

Religion on Television

American television has had a long, uneasy relationship with religion. Television has always broadcast programs with religious themes, but more often to fulfill regulatory obligations or sell undesirable air time than to attract viewers. Still, although American television tolerates religious faith more than embraces it, religious programs and commercial programs with religious themes have been constants on television.

Until the 1960s, religion on television followed the pattern devised earlier by radio broadcasters. Broadcasters provided time and production facilities free of charge for programs produced by mainline Protestants (the National Council of Churches and, in the South, the Southern Baptist Convention); Catholics (the United States Catholic Conference); and Jews (New York Board of Rabbis). This arrangement enabled broadcasters to satisfy their license requirement to donate time for "public interest" programs, while allowing them to choose religious programmers whose material would not motivate viewers to change the channel. The result was programming with ecumenical appeal, including the award-winning *Lamp Unto My Feet* (CBS) and *Frontiers of Faith* (NBC).

Fundamentalist and evangelical groups wishing to express their unique perspectives received neither time nor access to production facilities. They had to produce their own programs and buy air time, usually purchasing the little-viewed hours of Sunday morning. Nevertheless, the evangelical imperative and the persuasive power of television compelled pioneering televangelists forward. *The Lutheran Hour* and *Youth on the March* both debuted in 1949, and the first of Billy Graham's prime-time crusades aired in 1957.

The cozy relationship between the networks and mainline Protestants, Catholics, and Jews began to erode in 1960, when the Federal Communications Commission (FCC) ruled that broadcasters need not give away time to earn public interest credit. Once paid, religious broadcasts counted as much as donated religious broadcasts in the FCC's public interest accounting, broadcasters lost their incentive to give time away. When the mainline groups chose not to include expensive television productions in their budgets, the non-denominational, Christian evangelical direction of paid religious programming was set: American religious television would be dominated by personality-driven "television ministries" such as *Oral Roberts and You,* Jerry Falwell's *Old Time Gospel Hour,* and Pat Robertson's *700 Club.* These three programs were so remunerative that their founders were able to create universities with their proceeds. Oral Roberts University began in 1963; Falwell established Liberty University in 1971; and Pat Robertson founded Regent University, originally CBN University, in 1977.

In the 1980s, critics worried that powerful televangelists were reducing church attendance and income and influencing national politics, but these fears subsided after academic studies showed that the audience for televangelism was a small subset of churchgoers, news reports exposed the sexual misdeeds of Jim Bakker and Jimmy Swaggart, and a Republican primary ended Pat Robertson's bid for president. The lesson many televangelists learned was to spend more time on ministry and less on politics and fund raising.

Televangelism continues to dominate religious programming today, whether in individual programs or in cable services like the Family Channel, which mixes G-rated network reruns and movies with straightforward evangelical programs. The leader is Trinity Broadcasting Network, a 24-hour, commercial-free service founded in 1973 that appears on thousands of television stations and cable systems as well as dozens of satellites around the world. TBN far overshadows its mainline Christian and Jewish counterpart, Faith & Values Media, whose programming appears on cable's Hallmark Channel mostly on Sunday and early morning, or in some prime-time holiday specials.

But religion has not simply been relegated to fringe time and the odd televangelism cable channel; from the beginning of television, it has appeared in the popular hours of commercial prime time. Most notable in this regard is Bishop Fulton Sheen's *Life Is Worth Living* (1952–57), the only explicitly religious program ever to be commercially viable. For most dramas and comedies, however, the principle of least-objectionable material applied in the first few decades of television. In order not to offend any viewers, God was seldom mentioned, and even more seldom connected to any particular faith. Characters sometimes attended church or participated in weddings or funerals, but religious specifics were glossed over. A priest may have worn a collar and a nun a habit, but their clothing rarely communicated more than vague humanitarianism.

This blandness began to disappear in the 1980s, when the broadcast television networks began to compete with cable and then satellite channels. Programmers began to look for distinct characters and themes to set them apart from run-of-the-mill competition, and one underused source was religion. NBC found success in *Highway to Heaven,* in which an angel is assigned to help people through tough times. CBS followed with *Touched by an Angel,* in which three angels help human beings understand that God wants to be involved in their lives. Other shows explored religious themes in particular episodes. UPN's *Star Trek: Deep Space Nine* delved into the religion of the planet Bajor; CBS's *Picket Fences* took up the issues of biblical literalism, miracles, and prayer; and HBO's *Oz* portrayed complex questions of faith faced by a Muslim leader and a prison chaplain. On the WB network *7th Heaven* is a family melodrama constructed around a

The Hour of Power with Robert Schuller.
Courtesy of the Everett Collection

family in which the father is a minister. Significantly, the series, which began in 1996, continues to be one of the most popular programs among teenagers, often attracting more teens than any other program airing at the same time. At the beginning of the autumn 2003 television season, *Joan of Arcadia* was among the very few new programs to attract a substantial audience. In this series God appears to Joan, a high school student, in the personae of "ordinary" people she encounters in everyday settings. Their exchanges, in conventional conversational manner, usually lead to the exploration of some generally "religious" aspect of personal or social engagement.

Network news sometimes addresses religious topics and issues. *ABC World News Tonight* hired Peggy Wehmeyer as a full-time religion news correspondent from 1994 until 2001. *Religion & Ethics News Weekly,* a weekly half-hour of news about religion and ethics, began on PBS in 1997. And in 2002, PBS's *Frontline* broadcast the provocative *Faith and Doubt at Ground Zero,* in which a number of clergymen and -women explored the question of God's presence or absence during the terrorist attacks of September 11, 2001.

However attentive television can be to religious issues and practices, most Americans view these treatments of religion only occasionally, a situation not likely to change with a medium governed by visual appeal and commerce.

JOHN P. FERRÉ

See also **Landon, Michael; Robertson, Pat;** *Touched by an Angel*

Further Reading

Bruce, Steve, *Pray TV: Televangelism in America,* New York: Routledge, 1990

Forbes, Bruce David, and Jeffrey H. Mahan, editors, *Religion and Popular Culture in America,* Berkeley: University of California Press, 2000

Hoover, Stewart M., and Lynn Schofield Clark, editors, *Practicing Religion in the Age of the Media: Explorations in Media, Religion, and Culture,* New York: Columbia University Press, 2002

Robertson, C.K., editor, *Religion as Entertainment,* New York: Peter Lang, 2002

Remote Control Device

The remote control device (RCD) is a central technological phenomenon of popular culture. Though many cartoons, anecdotal accounts, and even television commercials trivialize the RCD, they also reflect its ubiquity and importance in everyday life. For better or for worse, the RCD has permanently altered television viewing habits by allowing the user to exercise some of the functions once the exclusive province of program and advertising executives. The RCD has altered viewing styles by increasing activities such as "zapping" (changing channels during commercials and other program breaks), "zipping" (fast forwarding through pre-recorded programming and advertising), and "grazing" (the combining of disparate program elements into an individualized programming mix).

Although wired RCDs existed in the "Golden Age" of radio, their history is more directly tied to the television receiver manufacturing industry and, more recently, to the diffusion of videocassette recorders (VCRs) and cable television. Zenith Radio Corporation engineer Robert Adler developed the Space Command, the first practical wireless RCD in 1956. Although other manufacturers would offer both wired and wireless RCDs from the mid-1950s on, the combination of high cost (RCDs typically were available only on more expensive "high end" receivers), technological limitations, and, most critically, the limited number of channels available to most viewers made the RCD more a novelty than a near-standard feature of television receivers until the 1980s.

The rapid increase in the number of video distribution outlets in the 1980s was instrumental in the parallel mass diffusion of RCDs. The RCD, in essence, was the necessary tool for the use of cable, VCRs, and more complex television receivers. Without the RCD, the popularity and impact of these programming conduits would have been much less. In the 1990s, a converging television/telecommunications industry redefined the RCD as a *navigational tool* whose design is essential to the success of advanced and interactive consumer services such as DVDs, personal video recorders (PVRs), and Internet/television hybrids (e.g., Microsoft's Ultimate TV; AOLTV). RCD manufacturers continue to introduce more advanced models to control the expanding number of media devices in U.S. homes.

While some industry figures see the RCD as a key to the success of future services, the same elements that allow viewers to find and use specific material from the many channels available also enables them to avoid content that they find undesirable. Both academic and industry studies have identified two types of gratification derived by viewers from RCD use that cause particular concern for the industry: advertising avoidance and "getting more out of television." These rewards are evidence of a generation of "restless viewers" who challenge many of the conventional practices of the television industry.

The industry has coped with the RCD "empowered" viewer by implementing changes in programming and advertising. Examples include "seamless" scheduling, where one program immediately segues into the following program; the reduction or elimination of opening themes; shorter and more visually striking commercials; increasing advertising-program integration, and more emphasis on television brand promotion. Although not solely a result of RCD diffusion, the ongoing economic consolidation of the world televi-

Zenith print ad for remote control television (c. 1957).
Photo courtesy of Zenith Electronics Corporation

sion/telecommunications industry; the continuing shift of costs to the television viewer/user through cable, pay-per-view, and emerging interactive services; and the increased emphasis on integrated marketing plans that treat traditional advertising spots as only one element of the selling process can all be regarded in part as reactions to restless and RCD-wielding television viewers.

ROBERT V. BELLAMY, JR.

See also **Zapping**

Further Reading

Bellamy, Robert V., Jr., and James R. Walker, *Grazing on a Vast Wasteland: The Remote Control and Television's Second Generation,* New York: Guilford Press, 1996

Ferguson, Douglas A., "Channel Repertoire in the Presence of Remote Control Devices, VCRs, and Cable Television," *Journal of Broadcasting and Electronic Media,* Vol. 38 (1992)

Walker, James R., and Robert V. Bellamy, Jr., editors, *The Remote Control in the New Age of Television,* Westport, Connecticut: Praeger, 1993

Reruns/Repeats

A television program that airs one or more times following its first broadcast is known as a rerun or a repeat. In order for a program to be rerun, it must have been recorded on film or videotape. Live telecasts, obviously, cannot be rerun. The use of reruns is central to the programming and economic strategies of television in the United States and, increasingly, throughout the world.

In the early days of U.S. television, most programming was live. This necessitated the continuous production of new programs, which, once aired, were gone. Certain program formats, such as variety, talk, public affairs, quiz, sports, and drama, dominated the airwaves. With the exception of variety and drama, each of these formats is relatively inexpensive to produce, so the creation of live weekly or daily episodes worked fairly well for broadcasters. Even the production costs for variety shows could be reduced over time with the repeated use of sets and costumes.

Production of dramatic programming, however, was more expensive. Most dramatic series were "anthologies"; a different story was broadcast each week, with different characters and, often times, different talent. The costs involved in creating each of these plays was considerable and could rarely be reduced, as the cost of variety programs could be, by repeated use of the durable properties. Because of the expense, the number of dramatic programs decreased, and the number of other less-expensive types of programs increased, during the first decade of television.

During the early 1950s, several weekly prime-time series, most notably *I Love Lucy,* began filming episodes instead of airing live programs. This allowed producers to create fewer than 52 episodes a year, yet still present weekly episodes throughout the year. They could produce 39 new episodes and repeat 13 of those, usually during the summer months when viewership was lower. While some expenses, for additional payments to creative personnel, are involved in airing reruns, the cost is almost 75 percent less than that incurred in presenting a new first-run episode. The practice proved so successful that by the end of the 1950s there was very little live entertainment programming left on U.S. television, and the television industry, which had been well established in New York, had shifted its center to Hollywood, the center of U.S. film production.

By the 1970s, most network prime-time series were producing only 26 new episodes each year, repeating each episode once (the 26/26 model). By the 1980s, the standard prime-time model was 22/22, with specials or limited series occupying the remaining weeks.

The shift to film or videotape as the primary form of television production also turned out to have benefits far exceeding the reduction of production costs and modifications of the programming schedule. Reruns and repeats are not used merely to ease production schedules and cut costs. By contractual arrangement, episodes usually return to the control of the producer after two network showings. They may then be licensed for presentations by other television distributors. This strategy is financially viable only after several years of a successful network run, when enough episodes of a television program are accumulated to make the series valuable to other programmers. It does lead to the possibility, however, that reruns of a program can be in syndication forever and almost anywhere. A common industry anecdote claims—and it may be true—that *I Love Lucy* is playing somewhere in the world at any given moment of the day.

The development of the rerun system, particularly as it supports syndication, has become the economic foundation on which the U.S. television industry does business. Because networks, the original distributors of television programs, rarely pay the full production costs for those programs, independent producers and/or studios must create programs at a deficit. That deficit can only be recouped if the program goes into syndication (not a foregone outcome). If the program is sold into syndication, the profits may be great—sufficient to pay off the cost of deficit financing for the original production and support both the development of other series and the programming of less-successful programs that may never be syndicated. This entire system is dependent on a sufficient market for rerun programs, a market traditionally composed of independent television stations and the international television systems, and on an economical means of reproduction.

Initially, film was more desirable than videotape as a means of storing programs because film production contracts called for lower residual payments (the payments made to performers in the series when episodes are repeated). Programs produced on film were under the jurisdiction of the Screen Actors Guild, which required lower residual payments than did the American Federation of Television and Radio Artists, which oversaw programs produced on videotape. By the mid-1970s, residual costs for film and taped performances evened out, and more and more programs are now produced on or transferred to videotape for syndication.

In addition to their use in prime time, reruns are scheduled by networks in all other time periods. Several unions have petitioned the Federal Communications Commission (FCC) in an attempt to restrict network use of reruns, claiming that the use of reruns results in a loss of jobs because it leads to less original production. All of these attempts have failed.

With the tremendous growth of television distribution outlets throughout the world in the 1980s—growth often founded on the expansion of cable television systems and the multichannel environment—additional markets for reruns of old network series were created. In the 1990s, cable networks, such as, Nickelodeon's TV Land and Nick at Nite, found success putting together entire schedules consisting of reruns of old network series. In addition, new partnerships between broadcast and cable networks were established to help defray initial production costs of a new series. Reruns of new episodes of prime-time series such as *Law & Order: \Special Victims Unit* (NBC) and *Once and Again* (ABC) have aired on cable networks as soon as ten days after the initial network broadcast. So long as these venues continue to increase, the financial basis for U.S. television production will continue to be stable. And, as more and more countries establish large programming systems of their own, the amount of material available for second, third, and continuing airings will continue to grow.

Mitchell E. Shapiro

See also **Prime Time Access Rule; Programming; Syndication**

Further Reading

Boddy, William, *Fifties Television: The Industry and Its Critics,* Urbana: University of Illinois Press, 1990

"Brits Bank on Rerun Bonanza with U.S. Help," *Variety* (September 28, 1992)

Eastman, Susan T., *Broadcast/Cable Programming: Strategies and Practices,* Belmont, California: Wadsworth, 1981; 4th edition, 1993

Godfrey, Donald G., *Reruns on File: A Guide to Electronic Media Archives,* Hillsdale, New Jersey: Lawrence Erlbaum, 1992

Moore, Barbara, "The *Cisco Kid* and Friends: The Syndication of Television Series from 1948 to 1952," *Journal of Popular Film and Television* (1980)

Nelson, Jenny L., "The Dislocation of Time: A Phenomenology of Television Reruns," *Quarterly Review of Film and Video* (October 1990)

Robins, J. Max, "Rerun Resurrection: Webs Favor Old Shows, Newsmags, to Summer Startups," *Variety* (June 27, 1994)

Shales, Tom, "The Re Decade," *Esquire* (March 1985)

Simon, Ronald, "The Eternal Rerun: Oldies but Goodies," *Television Quarterly* (1986)

Story, David, *America on the Rerun: TV Shows That Never Die,* Secaucus, New Jersey: Carol, 1993

Williams, Phil, "Feeding off the Past: The Evolution of the Television Rerun," *Journal of Popular Film and Television* (Winter 1994)

Reynolds, Gene (1925–)

U.S. Actor, Producer, Director

From a child movie actor in *Boy's Town,* Gene Reynolds grew into a respected producer-director identified with thoughtful television dramas reflecting complex human situations. The programs Reynolds is associated with often possess an undercurrent of humor to entertain, but without softening socially significant story lines.

As producer-director of *Room 222* (1969–74), Reynolds found a supportive, kindred spirit in the series' creator James L. Brooks. Exploring life among high school teachers, administrators, and students, their program featured African-American actor Lloyd Haynes as a revered, approachable teacher. A lighter touch in dialogue and situations helped keep the stories attractive to casual viewers. Still, the central characters were involved each week in matters of personal and social import such as drugs, prejudice, self-worth, and dropping out of school.

Again aligning himself with a congenial, creative associate for a TV version of the novel and motion picture *M*A*S*H,* Reynolds sought out respected "comedy writer with a conscience" Larry Gelbart. Together they fleshed out a sensitive, probing, highly amusing, and wildly successful series about the foibles and aspirations of a military surgical team in the midst of warfare. Raucous, sometimes ribald comedy acted as counterpoint to poignant human dilemmas that are present when facing bureaucratic tangles amid willful annihilation. Though intended as comedy-drama commentary on the devastating absurdities of war in general, and the Vietnam conflict in particular, Reynolds and Gelbart pushed the time period of their show back to Korea in the 1950s in order to be acceptable to the network and stations, and to a deeply divided American public. Gelbart left the series early on, and Reynolds eventually became executive producer, turning the producer's role over to Burt Metcalf. The ensemble cast only grew stronger as new actors replaced departing ones through the decade. The acclaimed series earned awards from all sectors during its 11-year run (1972–83), including the Peabody Award in 1975, Emmy Awards for outstanding comedy series in 1974; many other Emmys for outstanding writing, acting, and direction; Emmys twice for best directing by Gene Reynolds (1975, 1976); and the Humanitas Prize.

The public voted, too; their sustained viewing kept the program among the top-ranked five or ten pro-grams every year *M*A*S*H* aired. The concluding two-and-one-half-hour "farewell" episode (February 28, 1983) still stands as the single-most-watched program in American TV history, attracting almost two out of every three homes in America (60.3 rating). More than 50 million families tuned in that evening to watch the program.

Reynolds left *M*A*S*H* in 1977. He teamed up again with James L. Brooks and Allan Burns, all as executive producers of *Lou Grant.* This series explored the combative turf of a major metropolitan newspaper. It dealt with the constitutional and ethical issues found in pitting journalists against politicians, corporate executives, courts, and the general public. Reynolds's creative team avoided cliché-driven plots, focusing instead on complex, unresolved issues and depicting their impact on a mix of vulnerable personalities. The series (1977–82) received critical acclaim, including Peabody, Emmy, and Humanitas Awards, for exploring complicated challenges involving media and society.

Gene Reynolds's modus operandi for producing a television series is to thoroughly research the subject area by extended visits to sites—schools, battlefields (Vietnam to replicate Korean field hospitals), and newspaper offices. There he interviews at length those engaged in career positions. He and his creative partners regularly returned to those sites armed with audiotape recorders to dig for new story ideas, for points of view, for technical jargon and representative phrases, and even for scraps of dialogue that would add verisimilitude to the words of studio-stage actors recreating an incident. Reynolds and his associates always strive for accuracy, authenticity, and social significance. They present individual human beings caught up in the context of controversial events, but affected by personal interaction.

A thoughtful, serious-minded creator with a quiet sense of humor, Gene Reynolds's ability to work closely with colleagues earns the respect of both actors and production crews. He often directs episodes, regularly works with writers on revising scripts, and establishes a working climate on the set that invites suggestions from the actors for enhancing dialogue and action.

Reynolds directed pilots for potential TV series and movies for television, including *People Like Us*

Director Gene Reynolds, Stanley Livingston on the set of *My Three Sons*, 1962.
Courtesy of the Everett Collection

Gene Reynolds. Born in Cleveland, Ohio, April 4, 1925. Married: Bonnie Jones. Began career as film actor, debut in *Thank You, Jeeves,* 1936; producer and director of numerous television series, from 1968. Recipient: five Emmy Awards, Directors Guild of America Award, Peabody Award.

Television (producer, director)

1968–70	*The Ghost and Mrs. Muir* (pilot)
1969–74	*Room 222* (executive producer)
1972	*Anna and the King*
1972–83	*M*A*S*H* (also director)
1973–74	*Roll Out*
1975	*Karen*
1977–82	*Lou Grant*
1984	*The Duck Show*
1988–95	*In the Heat of the Night*
1989	*Studio 5-B*
1993–97	*Lois & Clark: The New Adventures of Superman*
1994–95	*Christy*
1994–2003	*Touched by an Angel*
1996–99	*Promised Land*

Made-for-Television Movies (selected)

1976	*People Like Us* (producer, director)
1983	*In Defense of Kids* (director)
1986	*Doing Life* (director)
1991	*The Whereabouts of Jenny* (director)
1999	*How To Get There* (director)

Films

Thank You, Jeeves (actor) 1936; *In Old Chicago* (actor), 1937; *Boys Town* (actor), 1938; *They Shall Have Music* (actor), 1939; *Edison, the Man* (actor), 1940; *Eagle Squadron* (actor), 1942; *The Country Girl* (actor), 1954; *The Bridges at Toko-Ri* (actor), 1955; *Diane* (actor), 1955.

(1976), *In Defense of Kids* (1983), and *Doing Life* (1986). He continued to produce and direct throughout the 1990s and early 2000s, notably the television series *In the Heat of the Night* and *Touched by an Angel.* In 1993, having served actively in organizations and on committees in the creative community for many years, he was elected president of the Directors Guild of America, a role in which he served until 1997.

JAMES A. BROWN

*See also **Lou Grant; M*A*S*H; Room 222; Touched by an Angel***

Rich Man, Poor Man

U.S. Miniseries

One of the first American television miniseries, *Rich Man, Poor Man* aired on ABC from February 1 to March 15, 1976. Adapted from the best-selling 1970

Irwin Shaw novel, *Rich Man, Poor Man* was a limited 12-part dramatic series consisting of six two-hour prime-time made-for-television movies. The televised

Rich Man, Poor Man, Nick Nolte, Susan Blakely, Peter Strauss, 1976.
Courtesy of the Everett Collection

1924

novel chronicles the lives of the first-generation immigrant Jordache family. The story focuses on the tumultuous relationship between brothers, Rudy (Peter Strauss) and Tom Jordache (Nick Nolte), as they suffer through 20 years (1945–65) of conflict, jealousy, and heartbreak.

The serial was enormously successful, leading the weekly ratings and ending as the second-highest-rated show for the 1976–77 television season. Along with its enormous audience popularity, it also garnered critical praise, reaping 20 Emmy nominations and winning four Emmy Awards—two for acting achievement, one for directing, and one for musical score.

The success of *Rich Man, Poor Man* hinged on its employment of several innovative techniques. The narrative struck a unique combination that contained the lavish film-style production values of prestigious special-event programming while at the same time relying upon the "habit viewing" characteristic of a weekly series. Also, by setting the plots in the historical context of such developments as McCarthyism, the Korean War, campus riots, and the Civil Rights Movement, *Rich Man, Poor Man* suggested larger circumstances than those usually found in a traditional soap opera. However, the limited series also liberally took on a range of risqué melodramatic topics, including adultery, power struggles, and alcoholism. Another inventive concept introduced by *Rich Man, Poor Man* was the use of multiple, revolving guest stars throughout the series. While the three principal cast members were relatively unknown at the time, shuffling better-known actors throughout the series was a way to maintain interest and achieve some form of ratings insurance on the $6 million venture.

By invigorating the concept of adapting novels into television miniseries, *Rich Man, Poor Man* began a rapid proliferation of similar prime-time programming, including a sequel. The continuation, *Rich Man, Poor Man: Book II,* was a 21-part weekly series that began airing in the fall of 1976. Although the sequel was not as successful as its predecessor, the idea of extended televised adaptations of popular novels quickly became a component of network schedules. In the season following the debut of *Rich Man, Poor Man,* each of the major networks scheduled at least one miniseries, including an adaptation of Harold Robbins's *The Pirates* and Alex Haley's historical epic *Roots.*

Although eclipsed by the record-breaking 1977 miniseries *Roots* (aired January 1 through 30 on ABC), *Rich Man, Poor Man* nonetheless has staked a spot in television history. It helped to create a special niche for televised novels as an economically viable miniseries genre.

LIZA TREVIO

See also **Adaptation; Miniseries**

Rich Man, Poor Man

Cast

Rudy Jordache	Peter Strauss
Tom Jordache	Nick Nolte
Julie Prescott Abbott Jordache	Susan Blakely
Axel Jordache	Edward Asner
Mary Jordache	Dorothy McGuire
Willie Abbott	Bill Bixby
Duncan Calderwood	Ray Milland
Teddy Boylan	Robert Reed
Virginia Calderwood	Kim Darby
Sue Prescott	Gloria Grahame
Asher Berg	Craig Stevens
Joey Quales	George Maharis
Linda Quales	Lynda Day George
Nichols	Steve Allen
Smitty	Norman Fell
Teresa Sanjoro	Talia Shire
Marsh Goodwin	Van Johnson
Irene Goodwin	Dorothy Malone
Kate Jordache	Kay Lenz
Sid Gossett	Murray Hamilton
Arnold Simm	Mike Evans
Al Fanducci	Dick Butkus
Clothilde	Fionnula Flanagan
Brad Knight	Tim McIntire
Bill Denton	Lawrence Pressman
Claude Tinker	Dennis Dugan
Gloria Bartley	Jo Ann Harris
Pete Tierney	Roy Jenson
Lou Martin	Anthony Carbone
Papadakis	Ed Barth
Ray Dwyer	Herbert Jefferson, Jr.
Arthur Falconetti	William Smith
Col. Deiner	Andrew Duggan
Pinky	Harvey Jason
Martha	Helen Craig
Phil McGee	Gavan O'Herlihy
Billy	Leigh McCloskey
Wesley	Michael Morgan

Producers

Harve Bennett, Jon Epstein

Programming History

6 2-hour episodes
ABC

February 1976–March 1976	Monday 10:00–11:00
May 1977–June 1977	Tuesday 9:00–11:00

Rich Man, Poor Man: Book II

Cast

Senator Rudy Jordache	Peter Strauss
Wesley Jordache	Gregg Henry
Billy Abbott	James Carroll Jordan
Maggie Porter	Susan Sullivan
Arthur Falconetti	William Smith
Marie Falconetti	Dimitra Arliss
Ramona Scott	Penny Peyser
Scotty	John Anderson
Charles Estep	Peter Haskell
Phil Greenberg	Sorrell Brooke
Annie Adams	Cassie Yates
Diane Porter	Kimberly Beck
Arthur Raymond	Peter Donat
Claire Estep	Laraine Stephens
Senator Paxton	Barry Sullivan
Kate Jordache	Kay Lenz
John Franklin	Philip Abbott
Max Vincen	George Gaynes
Al Barber	Ken Swofford
Senator Dillon	G.D. Spradlin

Producers

Michael Gleason, Jon Epstein

Programming History

21 episodes
ABC
September 1976–March
  1977   Tuesday 9:00–10:00

Rigg, Diana (1938–)

British Actor

After shooting her first 12 episodes in the role of Mrs. Emma Peel in *The Avengers,* Diana Rigg discovered that her weekly salary as the female lead in an already highly successful series was £30 less than what the show's cameraman earned. Rigg had not even been the first choice to replace the popular Honor Blackman as secret agent John Steed's accomplice; the first actress cast had been sacked after two weeks. The role then fell to Rigg, whose television résumé at the time consisted only of a guest appearance on *The Sentimental Agent* and a performance of Donald Churchill's *The Hothouse.*

Rigg's stage experience, however, was solid. After joining the Royal Shakespeare Company in 1959, the same year as Vanessa Redgrave, Rigg had steadily amassed a strong list of credits, including playing Cordelia to Paul Schofield's Lear. Years later, Rigg described the rationale for her turn to television: "The trouble with staying with a classical company is that you get known as a 'lady actress.' No one ever thinks of you except for parts in long skirts and blank verse."

Rigg's salary complaints were quickly addressed, and American audiences, who had never been exposed to Blackman's *Avengers* episodes (which did not air in the United States until the early 1990s), quickly embraced Rigg's assertive, upper-class character. Peel's name may have been simply a play upon the character's hoped-for "man appeal," but Rigg's embodiment of the role suggested a much more utopian representation of women. Peel demonstrated that women can be intelligent, independent, and sexually confident. After three seasons and an Emmy nomination, Rigg left the series in 1968, claiming "Emma Peel is not fully emancipated." Still, Rigg resisted publicly associating herself with feminism; to the contrary, she flippantly claimed to find "the whole feminist thing very boring."

Following Blackman into James Bond films (in 1964 Blackman had been *Goldfinger*'s Pussy Galore), Rigg's presence in *On Her Majesty's Secret Service* (1969) as the tragic Mrs. James Bond added intertextual interest to the film. Paired with the unfamiliar George Lazenby as Bond, it was Rigg who carried the film's spy genre credentials, even though her suicidal, spoiled character displayed few of Peel's many abilities. However, the British spy genre had already begun to collapse, followed by the rest of the nation's film industry, and Rigg's career as a movie star never soared.

Rigg did not immediately return to series television. In fact, she publicly attributed her problems on film to having learned to act for television only too well; she had become too "facile" before film cameras, a trait necessitated by the grueling pace of series production.

Apparently, her stage skills remained unaffected, and Rigg went on to a wide range of both classical and contemporary roles as a member of the Royal Shakespeare Company and the National Theatre, and on Broadway. However, while Rigg has originated the lead roles in such stylish works as Tom Stoppard's *Jumpers* (1972), the stage work she performed for television broadcast tended to fit more snugly into familiar Anglophilic conventions. In the United States, her television appearances in the 1960s included *The Comedy of Errors* (1967) and *Women Beware Women* (1968) for *NET Playhouse;* in the 1980s, they included *Hedda Gabler, Witness for the Prosecution,* Lady Dedlock in a multipart adaptation of *Bleak House* (1985), and Laurence Olivier's *King Lear* (1985).

During the decade between, however, NBC attempted to capitalize upon what Rigg jokingly called her "exploitable potential" following *The Avengers.* After one failed pilot, the network picked up *Diana* (1973–74), a *Mary Tyler Moore Show*-inspired sitcom, and Rigg returned to series television as a British expatriate working in New York's fashion industry. As if to acknowledge the sexual daring of her first series, Rigg's character became American sitcom's first divorcée (Moore's character had been initially conceived as divorced, but that scenario was altered before *The Mary Tyler Moore Show* aired). In *Diana,* Rigg's comedic talents, which television critics had once praised as wry and deliberately understated, did not shine; instead, she appeared rather bland, and the series provided no Steed for verbal repartee. (Perhaps even more damning, *Diana* showed few traces of *The Avengers'* always dashing fashion sense.) NBC programmed *Diana* during what had once been *The Avengers'* time slot, but the sitcom shortly disappeared.

A year later, Rigg successfully played off both her previous roles and her sometimes bawdy public persona in a sober religious drama, *In This House of Brede* (1975). Portraying a successful businesswoman entering a convent, Rigg's combination of restraint and technique seemed quintessentially British and earned her a second Emmy nomination.

In 1989, Rigg succeeded Vincent Price in hosting the PBS series *Mystery!,* and in 1990 she impressed American audiences as the star of an Oedipal nightmare, *Mother Love,* a multipart British import presented on that program. In her role as the series' host, Rigg has in a sense become that "lady actress" she had once entered television to avoid: ensconced in finely tailored suits and beaded gowns, her performance as host displays all the genteel, ambassadorial authority of a woman now entitled to be addressed as Dame Rigg (having been named Dame Commander, Order of the British Empire, in 1994).

Avengers, Diana Rigg, 1961–69.
Courtesy of the Everett Collection

In addition to her hosting duties on *Mystery!,* Rigg was busy in the 1990s playing a range of notable stage roles, including the leads in *Medea* (for which she won a 1994 Tony Award), *Mother Courage* (1995–96), and *Who's Afraid of Virginia Woolf* (1996–97). She also took on a number of character roles on television. These latter parts were frequently villainous to some degree, whether in bodice-rippers (*A Hazard of Hearts,* 1987), light comedy (*Mrs. 'arris Goes to Paris,* 1992), or edgy comedy such as the Holocaust farce *Genghis Cohn* (1994). For her portrayal of Mrs. Danvers in the miniseries *Rebecca* (shown in the United States in 1997 on *ExxonMobil Masterpiece Theatre*), she won an Emmy Award for outstanding supporting actress in a miniseries. Since 1998, she has also played the title role in *The Mrs. Bradley Mysteries,* a crime drama set in the 1920s, which debuted on the BBC and has since aired in the United States (on *Mystery!* and the cable channel BBC America) and Australia (on ABC).

ROBERT DICKINSON AND ELIZABETH NISHIURA

See also **Avengers, The**

Diana Rigg. Born in Doncaster, Yorkshire, England, July 20, 1938. Attended Fulneck Girls' School, Pudsey; Royal Academy of Dramatic Art (RADA), London. Married: 1) Menachem Gueffen, 1973 (divorced, 1974); 2) Archibald Stirling, 1982 (divorced); child: Rachel. Began career as stage actor, making debut with RADA during the York Festival at the Theatre Royal, York, 1957; made London stage debut, 1961; member, Royal Shakespeare Company (RSC), 1959–64; made London debut with RSC, Aldwych Theatre, 1961; toured Europe and the United States with RSC, 1964; made television debut as Emma Peel in *The Avengers,* 1965; film debut, 1967; joined National Theatre Company, 1972; has since continued to appear in starring roles both on screen and on stage; director, United British Artists, from 1982; vice president, Baby Life Support Systems, from 1984. Companion of the Order of the British Empire, 1988; Dame Commander of the Order of the British Empire, 1994. Chair: Islington Festival; MacRoberts Arts Centre. Recipient: *Plays and Players* Award, 1975, 1979; Variety Club Film Actress of the Year Award, 1983; British Academy of Film and Television Arts Award, 1989; *Evening Standard* Drama Award, 1993, 1996; Tony Award, 1994; Emmy Award, 1997.

Television Series (selected)

1965–67	*The Avengers*
1973–74	*Diana*
1989–	*Mystery!* (host)
1999–	*The Mrs. Bradley Mysteries*

Made-for-Television Movies (selected)

1975	*In This House of Brede*
1980	*The Marquise*
1982	*Witness for the Prosecution*
1986	*The Worst Witch*
1987	*A Hazard of Hearts*
1994	*Genghis Cohn*
1994	*Running Delilah*
1995	*The Haunting of Helen Walker*
1995	*Danielle Steele's Zoya*
1996	*Chandler and Co.*
1996	*Samson and Delilah*
2001	*The American*
2001	*Victoria and Albert*

Television Miniseries (selected)

1979	*Oresteia*
1985	*Bleak House*
1989	*Mother Love*
1996	*The Fortunes and Misfortunes of Moll Flanders*
1997	*Rebecca*
2000	*In the Beginning*
2003	*Charles II*

Television Specials (selected)

1964	*The Hothouse*
1968	*Women Beware Women*
1981	*Hedda Gabler*
1984	*King Lear*
1986	*Masterpiece Theatre: 15 Years*
1992	*The Laurence Olivier Awards 1992* (host)

Films (selected)

A Midsummer Night's Dream, 1968; *The Assassination Bureau,* 1969; *On Her Majesty's Secret Service,* 1969; *Married Alive,* 1970; *Julius Caesar,* 1970; *The Hospital,* 1971; *Theatre of Blood,* 1973; *A Little Night Music,* 1977; *The Serpent Son,* 1979; *Hedda Gabler,* 1980; *The Great Muppet Caper,* 1981; *Evil Under the Sun,* 1982; *Little Eyolf,* 1982; *Held in Trust,* 1986; *Snow White,* 1986; *A Good Man in Africa,* 1994; *Parting Shots,* 1998.

Stage (selected)

The Caucasian Chalk Circle, 1957; *Ondine,* 1961; *The Devils,* 1961; *Beckett,* 1961; *The Taming of the Shrew,* 1961; *Madame de Tourvel,* 1962; *The Art of Seduction,* 1962; *A Midsummer Night's Dream,* 1962; *Macbeth,* 1962; *The Comedy of Errors,* 1962; *King Lear,* 1962; *The Physicists,* 1963; *Twelfth Night,* 1966; *Abelard and Heloise,* 1970; *Jumpers,* 1972; *'Tis Pity She's a Whore,* 1972; *Macbeth,* 1972; *The Misanthrope,* 1974; *Pygmalion,* 1974; *Phaedra Britannica,* 1975; *The Guardsman,* 1978; *Night and Day,* 1979; *Colette,* 1982; *Heartbreak House,* 1983; *Little Eyolf,* 1985; *Antony and Cleopatra,* 1985; *Wildfire,* 1986; *Follies,* 1986; *Love Letters,* 1990; *All for Love,* 1991; *Berlin Bertie,* 1992; *Medea,* 1992; *Mother Courage,* 1995–96; *Who's Afraid of Virginia Woolf,* 1996–97.

Publications

No Turn Unstoned (editor), 1982
So Too the Land (editor), 1994

Further Reading

Jenkins, Henry, *Textual Poachers: Television Fans and Participatory Culture,* New York and London: Routledge, 1992
Nathan, David, "Heavy-Duty Lightweight," *The Times* (London; April 20, 1991)
Rogers, Dave, *The Avengers,* London: ITV Books, 1983
Story, David, *America on the Rerun: TV Shows That Never Die,* New York: Citadel Press, 1993

Riggs, Marlon (1957–1994)

U.S. Filmmaker

Before his death in 1994, African-American film-maker, educator, and poet Marlon Riggs forged a position as one of the more controversial figures in the recent history of public television. He won a number of awards for his creative efforts as a writer and video producer. His theoretical-critical writings appeared in numerous scholarly and literary journals and professional and artistic periodicals. His video productions, which explored various aspects of African-American life and culture, earned him considerable recognition, including Emmy and Peabody Awards. Riggs will nonetheless be remembered mostly for the debate and contention that surrounded the airing of his highly charged video productions on public television stations during the late 1980s and early 1990s. Just as art photographer Robert Mapplethorpe's provocative, homo-erotic photographs of male nudes caused scrutiny of government agencies and their funding of art, Marlon Riggs's video productions similarly plunged public television into an acrimonious debate, not only about funding but about censorship as well.

Riggs's early works received little negative press. His production *Ethnic Notions* aired on public television stations throughout the United States. This program sought to explore the various shades of mythology surrounding the ethnic stereotyping of African Americans in various forms of popular culture. The program was well received and revolutionary in its fresh assessment of such phenomena as the mythology of the Old South and its corresponding caricatures of black life and culture.

The video *Color Adjustment,* which aired on public television stations in the early 1990s, was an interpretive look at the images of African Americans in 50 years of American television history. Using footage from such shows as *Amos 'n' Andy, Julia,* and *Good Times,* Riggs compared the grossly stereotyped caricatures of blacks contained in early television programming to those of more recent, and presumably more enlightened, decades.

By far the most polemical of Riggs's work was his production *Tongues Untied.* This 55-minute video, which "became the center of a controversy over censorship" as reported *The Independent* in 1991, was aired as part of a series entitled *P.O.V. (Point of View),* which aired on public television stations and featured independently produced film and video documentaries on various subjects ranging from personal reflections on the Nazi Holocaust to urban street life in the contemporary United States.

Tongues Untied is noteworthy on at least three accounts. First, Riggs chose as his subject urban, African-American gay men. Moving beyond the stereotypes of drag queens and comic-tragic stock caricatures, Riggs offered to mainstream America an insightful and provocative portrait of a distinct gay subculture—complete with sometimes explicit language and evocative imagery. Along with private donations, Riggs had financed the production with a $5,000 grant from the National Endowment for the Arts (NEA), a federal agency supporting visual, literary, and performing arts. News of the video's airing touched off a tumult of debate about the government funding of artistic creations that to some were considered obscene. While artists argued the basic right of free speech, U.S. government policymakers, especially

Marlon Riggs.
Photo courtesy of Signifyini Works/Andy Stern

those of a conservative bent, engaged in a hotly contentious debate regarding the use of taxpayer money for the funding of such endeavors.

The second area of consternation brought on by the *Tongues Untied* video concerned the issue of funding for public broadcasting. The *P.O.V.* series also received funding from the NEA, in the amount of $250,000, for its production costs. Many leaders of conservative television watchdog organizations labeled the program as obscene (though many had not even seen it). Others ironically heralded the program's airing, in the hope that U.S. taxpayers would be able to watch in dismay how their tax dollars were being spent.

Lastly, the question of censorship loomed large throughout the debate over the airing of *Tongues Untied.* When a few frightened station executives decided not to air the program, the fact of their self-censorship was widely reported in the press. As mentioned, *Tongues Untied* was not the first *P.O.V.* production to be pulled. Arthur Kopp of People for the American Way noted in *The Independent,* "the most insidious censorship is self-censorship.... It's a frightening sign when television executives begin to second guess the far right and pull a long-planned program before it's even been attacked."

Riggs defended *Tongues Untied* by lambasting those who objected to the program's language and imagery, stating in a 1992 *Washington Post* interview, "People are far more sophisticated in their homophobia and racism now...they say 'We object to the language, we have to protect the community'...those statements are a ruse."

Tongues Untied was awarded Best Documentary of the Berlin International Film Festival, Best Independent Experimental Work by the Los Angeles Film Critics, and Best Video by the New York Documentary Film Festival.

Before his death, Riggs began work on a production entitled *Black Is, Black Ain't.* In this video presentation, Riggs sought to explore what it meant to be black in the United States, from the period when "being black wasn't always so beautiful" to the 1992 Los Angeles riots. This visual reflection on gumbo, straightening combs, and Creole life in New Orleans was Riggs's own personal journey. It also unfortunately served as a memorial to Riggs. Much of the footage was shot from his hospital bed as he fought to survive the ravaging effects of AIDS. The video was finished posthumously and was aired on public television during the late 1990s.

PAMALA S. DEANE

See also **Public Service Broadcasting; Racism, Ethnicity, and Television**

Marlon Riggs. Born in Ft. Worth, Texas, February 3, 1957. Graduated from Harvard University, magna cum laude, B.A. in history, 1978; University of California, Berkeley, M.A. in journalism, 1981. Taught documentary film, Graduate School of Journalism, University of California, Berkeley, from 1987; produced numerous video documentaries, from 1987. Honorary doctorate, California College of Arts and Crafts, 1993. Recipient: Emmy Awards, 1987 and 1991; George Foster Peabody Award, 1989; Blue Ribbon, American Film and Video Festival, 1990; Best Video, New York Documentary Film Festival, 1990; Erik Barnouw Award, 1992. Died in Oakland, California, April 5, 1994.

Television Documentaries

1987   *Ethnic Notions*
1988   *Tongues Untied*
1989   *Color Adjustment*
1992   *Non, Je Ne Regrette Rein (No Regret)*
1994   *Black Is, Black Ain't*

Publications (selected)

"Black Macho Revisited: Reflections of a Snap! Queen," *Black American Literature Forum* (Summer 1991)
"Notes of a Signifying Snap! Queen," *Art Journal* (Fall 1991)

Further Reading

Becquer, M., "Snap-Thology and Other Discursive Practices in *Tongues Untied," Wide Angle: A Quarterly Journal of Film History, Theory, and Criticism* (1991)
Berger, M., "Too Shocking to Show," *Art in America* (July 1992)
Creekmur, Corey K., and Alexander Doty, *Out in Culture: Gay, Lesbian, and Queer Essays on Popular Culture,* Durham, North Carolina: Duke University Press, 1995
Grundmann, R., "New Agendas in Black Filmmaking: An Interview with Marlon Riggs," *Cineaste* (1992)
Harper, Phillip Brian, "Marlon Riggs: The Subjective Position of Documentary Video," *Art Journal* (Winter 1995)
Maslin, Janet, "Under Scrutiny: TV Images of Blacks," *New York Times* (January 29, 1992)
Mercer, Kobina, "Dark and Lovely Too: Black Gay Men in Independent Film," in *Queer Looks: Perspectives on Lesbian and Gay Film and Video,* edited by Martha Gerver et al., New York: Routledge, 1993
Mills, David, "The Director with Tongue Untied; Marlon Riggs, A Filmmaker Who Lives Controversy," *Washington Post* (June 15, 1992)
Prial, Frank J., "TV Film About Gay Blacks Is Under Attack," *New York Times* (June 25, 1991)
Scott, Darieck, "Jungle Fever? Black Gay Identity Politics, White Dick, and the Utopian Bedroom," *GLQ: A Journal of Lesbian and Gay Studies* (1994)

Rintels, David W. (1939–)

U.S. Writer, Producer

Writer-producer David W. Rintels has worked in a variety of dramatic television forms, including series, made-for-television movies, and miniseries. He began his television career in the early 1960s, writing episodes for the critically acclaimed CBS courtroom drama series *The Defenders*. He continued his series involvement writing episodes for *Slattery's People* (1964–65), a CBS political drama, and became head writer for the ABC science fiction series *The Invaders* (1967–68) before concentrating his energies on writing and producing made-for-television movies and miniseries. His work has been honored with two Emmy Awards for outstanding writing (*Clarence Darrow*, 1973, and *Fear on Trial*, 1975); Writers Guild of America Awards for outstanding scripts ("A Continual Roar of Musketry," parts 1 and 2 of the series *The Senator*, 1970; *Fear on Trial*, 1975; and *Gideon's Trumpet*, 1980); and a cable ACE Award for writing (*Sakharov*, 1984). Rintels's achievements also include the sole story and joint screenplay credits for the feature film *Scorpio* (1972).

Rintels's television work in the genres of fictional history (using novelistic invention to portray real historical figures and events) and historical fiction (placing fictional characters and events in a more or less authentic historical setting) has been praised by *Los Angeles Times* television critic Howard Rosenberg, who noted that Rintels's "fine record for using TV to present history as serious entertainment is probably unmatched by any other present dramatist." Some critics have argued, however, that while his faithfulness to historical detail and accuracy is commendable, Rintels's use of lengthy expository sequences has, on occasion, diminished the stories' dramatic power.

Following his involvement as an episode writer for *The Defenders*, the Emmy Award-winning drama series featuring a father and son legal team defending people's constitutional rights, Rintels returned to the subject of the courts in *Clarence Darrow* (NBC, 1973) and *Gideon's Trumpet* (CBS, 1980), the latter a *Hallmark Hall of Fame* production he both wrote and produced. Based on Anthony Lewis's book, *Gideon's Trumpet* was the real-life story of Clarence Earl Gideon (played by Henry Fonda), a drifter with little education, who was arrested in the early 1960s for "breaking and entering." The U.S. Supreme Court held that Gideon was entitled to an attorney, although he could not afford to pay for one; this case established the constitutional right to legal representation, now guaranteed to all U.S. citizens.

Rintels has also frequently focused on the political sphere, and especially on idealistic individuals who become ensnared in the nefarious webs woven by those seeking power or influence. In "A Continual Roar of Musketry," he developed the character of Hayes Stowe, an idealistic U.S. senator (played by Hal Holbrook).

In the 1975 CBS docudrama *Fear on Trial,* starring George C. Scott and William Devane, Rintels told the story of John Henry Faulk, a homespun radio personality who wrote a book about the blacklisting in television in the 1950s. Upon publication of this book, Faulk suddenly found his own name appearing in the AWARE bulletin, a blacklisting sheet created by two communist-hunting businessmen who proclaimed themselves protectors of the entertainment industry.

Washington: Behind Closed Doors (1977), a 12-and-one-half-hour ABC miniseries co-written (with Eric Bercovici) and co-produced by Rintels, was a provocative examination of the Nixon administration, including a striking psychological portrait of Nixon, fictionalized as President Richard Monckton. Played to perfection by Jason Robards, Monckton is described by Michael Arlen as "nervous and disconnected...insecure, vengeful, riddled with envy, and sublimely humorless." Although loosely based on *The Company* (the novel by Nixon administration insider John Erlichman) the Rintels and Bercovici script transcended Erlichman's one-dimensional characterizations to bring to the small screen "an intelligent and well-paced scenario of texture and character." Yet working in the genre of historical fiction was not without its pitfalls. In a foreshadowing of the heated debate surrounding Oliver Stone's 1995 feature film *Nixon,* Arlen questioned the production's mixing of fiction with fact:

> There should be room in our historical narratives for such a marvelously evocative (though not precisely factual) interpretation as Robards' depiction of Nixon-Monckton's strange humorous humorouslessness, where an actor's art gave pleasure, brought out character, and took us closer to truth. At the same time, for major tele-

David W. Rintels, 1980.
Courtesy of the Everett Collection/CSU Archives

vision producers...to be so spaced out by the present Entertainment Era as to more or less deliberately fool around with the actual life of an actual man, even of a discredited President...seems irresponsible and downright shabby.

Rintels turned his attention to political repression abroad in *Sakharov* (HBO, 1984), the moving story of the courageous Soviet scientist Andrei Dmitrievich Sahkarov (played by Robards) and his second wife Yelena G. Bonner (Glenda Jackson). *Sakharov* chronicles the 1975 Nobel Peace Prize winner's painful journey into dissent, and his outspoken advocacy of human rights. Because so much information about affairs in the Soviet Union was cloaked in secrecy, it would have been tempting to invent much of Sakharov's tale. Rintels, however, was loath to do this. Rather, in order to present the personal side of Sakharov, Rintels compiled information from extensive interviews with Sakharov's children and their spouses, who had emigrated to the United States, and with Yelena Bonner's mother. Rintels also drew upon Sakharov's own accounts and those of his friends, and on reports from journalists stationed in Moscow. As the story unfolded for Rintels, he decided to use, as a primary framing de-

vice, Sakharov's "growing awareness—through his personal relationship with Yelena—of his moral duty." Rintels was careful to avoid painting the Soviet bureaucrats and security police as "evil" in simplistic melodramatic terms in order to glorify Sakharov. The script attempted to explain why the Soviet officials perceived Sakharov as an internal threat and was circumspect regarding his motivations when the facts (or lack thereof) warranted.

In two other efforts, *Day One* (AT&T Presents/CBS, 1989) and *Andersonville* (TNT, 1996), Rintels examined the United States at war. *Day One* was a three-hour drama special detailing the history of the Manhattan Project to build an atomic bomb during World War II. Based on Peter Wyden's book *Day One: Before Hiroshima and After,* the program was written and produced by Rintels and won an Emmy Award for outstanding drama special. The story began with the flight of top European scientists, who feared Nazi Germany was progressing toward developing an atomic bomb, to the United States. Near the program's conclusion, a lengthy, balanced, and soul-searching debate transpires among scientists, military leaders, and top civilian government officials, including President Truman, regarding whether to drop the bomb on Japan without prior notice or to invite Japanese officials to a demonstration of the bomb in hopes that they would surrender upon seeing its destructive power. Throughout the piece, Rintels explores the symbiotic relationship that developed between the two key players in the Manhattan Project: the intellectual scientist and project leader, J. Robert Oppenheimer, and the military leader charged with overall coordination of the effort, General Leslie R. Groves.

Andersonville, a four-hour, two-part drama written and produced by Rintels, recounts the nightmare of the Civil War Confederate prison camp in southwest Georgia—a 26-acre open-air stockade designed for 8,000 men, which at peak operation contained 32,000 Union Army prisoners of war. Of the 45,000 Union soldiers imprisoned there between 1864 and 1865, nearly 13,000 died, mostly from malnutrition, disease, and exposure. Not only were the Confederate captors cruel; there also existed in the camp a ruthless gang of prisoners, the Raiders, who intimidated, beat, and even killed fellow prisoners for their scraps of food. The other prisoners eventually revolted against the Raiders, placing their six ring leaders on trial and hanging them with the Confederates' blessing. Rintels places the blame for the squalid conditions in the camp both on the camp's authoritarian German-Swiss commandant, Henry Wirz, the only person tried and executed for war crimes following the Civil War, and on larger forces that were the products of a devastating four-year war:

shortages of food, medicine, and supplies that plagued the entire Confederacy and forced it to choose between supplying its own armies or the Union prisoners. To Rintels, the Andersonville camp, unlike the Nazi concentration camps, seemed less the result of a conscious evil policy than the tragic result of a brutal war.

The Holocaust and the people responsible for it were the subject of Rintels's miniseries *Nuremberg* (TNT, 2000), which earned the highest ratings to date for any miniseries aired on U.S. basic cable. Starring Alec Baldwin (who also coproduced the four-hour miniseries) as the lead U.S. prosecutor, *Nuremberg* chronicles the International Military Tribunal proceedings against Nazi officers after World War II, focusing not only on the horrible crimes committed but also on the challenges faced in this first effort to establish standards for the international prosecution of war crimes.

Rintels tackled a somewhat less weighty subject in his next for-cable project, a biography of Indiana University's volatile head basketball coach, Bobby Knight. *A Season on the Brink* (2002) is notable for two reasons: it represents the first effort by the sports cable channel ESPN to air an original drama, and it was aired simultaneously on ESPN, with dialogue heavily peppered with profanity, and ESPN2, where the offending words were covered by "bleeps."

In addition to his creative work, Rintels has also been active in the politics of television. As president of the Writers Guild of America (1975–77), he coordinated the successful campaign, led by the Guild and producer Norman Lear, to have the courts overturn the Federal Communications Commission's 1975 "family-viewing" policy, which designated the first two hours of prime time (7:00–9:00 P.M.) for programs that would be suitable for viewing by all age groups. Rintels and Lear argued that the policy violated the First Amendment, forcing major script revisions of more adult-oriented programs appearing before 9:00 P.M. and the rescheduling of series such as *All in the Family.*

Since the early 1970s, Rintels has been a vocal critic of television networks' timidity in their prime-time programming. In 1972, he condemned commercial television executives for rejecting scripts dealing with Vietnam draft evaders, the U.S. Army's storing of deadly nerve gas near large cities, antitrust issues, and drug companies' manufacture of drugs intended for the illegal drug market. In a 1977 interview, Rintels criticized the bulk of prime-time entertainment television: "That's the television most of the people watch most of the time—75 to 80 million people a night. And it is for many people a source of information about the real world. But the message they are getting is, I think, not an honest message."

HAL HIMMELSTEIN AND ELIZABETH NISHIURA

See also Defenders, The; Writer in Television

David W. Rintels. Born in Boston, Massachusetts, 1939. Educated at Harvard University, B.A. magna cum laude, 1959. Journalist, *Boston Herald,* 1959–60; news director, WVOX-Radio, New Rochelle, New York, 1959; researcher, National Broadcasting Company, 1961; television writer, since the early 1960s. Member: Writers Guild of America, West, president, 1975–77; chair, Committee on Censorship and Freedom of Expression; advisory board, Death Penalty Focus. Recipient: ACE Award, George Foster Peabody Award, 1970; Silver Gavel Award from the American Bar Association, 1971; Writers Guild of America Awards, 1970, 1975, 1980; Emmy Awards, 1973, 1975.

Television Series

1961–75	*The Defenders*
1964–65	*Slattery's People*
1965–68	*Run for Your Life*
1967–68	*The Invaders*
1970–71	*The Senator*
1970–71	*The Young Lawyers*

Made-for-Television Movies

1973	*Clarence Darrow*
1975	*Fear on Trial*
1980	*Gideon's Trumpet*
1980	*The Oldest Living Graduate*
1981	*All the Way Home*
1982	*The Member of the Wedding*
1984	*Choices of the Heart*
1984	*Mister Roberts*
1984	*Sakharov*
1985	*The Execution of Raymond Graham*
1989	*Day One* (also producer)
1990	*The Last Best Year* (also producer)
1992	*A Town Torn Apart*
1994	*World War Two: When Lions Roared*
1995	*My Antonia*
2002	*A Season on the Brink*

Television Miniseries

1977	*Washington: Behind Closed Doors* (co-producer, co-writer)
1996	*Andersonville*
2000	*Nuremberg*

Films

Scorpio (co-writer), 1972; *Not Without My Daughter,* 1992.

Rintels, David W.

Stage

Clarence Darrow, 1975.

Further Reading

Arlen, Michael J., "The Air: Getting the Goods on Pres. Monckton," *The New Yorker* (October 3, 1977)

Nordheimer, Jon, "How the Ordeal of Sakharov Was Re-created for Cable TV," *New York Times* (June 17, 1984)

Rintels, David W., "Not for Bread Alone," *Performance 3* (July/August 1972)

Rosenberg, Howard, "Civil War POWs' Tale of Horror," *Los Angeles Times* (March 1, 1996)

Wertheimer, Ron, "*A Season the Brink:* A Movie on Two Channels, One with Cussing," *New York Times* (March 9, 2002)

Rising Damp

British Situation Comedy

Rising Damp, the Yorkshire Television situation comedy series set in a run-down northern boarding house, was originally screened on ITV between 1974 and 1978 and has continued to be revived on British television at regular intervals ever since, always attracting large audiences (many of whom were no doubt lodgers at one time or another in similarly seedy houses). Created by writer Ernie Chappell, the series depicted the comic misadventures and machinations of Rupert Rigsby, the embittered, down-at-heel landlord, who constantly spied on the usually very innocent private lives of an assortment of long-suffering tenants.

The success of *Rising Damp* depended largely upon the considerable comic talent of its star, Leonard Rossiter, who played the snooping and sneering Rigsby. Rossiter had first demonstrated his impeccable comic timing in the same role (though under the name Rooksby) in the one-off stage play *Banana Box,* from which the television series was derived. Rossiter rapidly stamped his mark upon the money-grubbing, lecherous, manneristic landlord, making him at once repulsive, vulnerable, paranoid, irrepressible, ignorant, cunning, and above all hilarious. Sharing his inmost fears and suspicions with his cat Vienna, he skulked about the ill-kempt house, bursting in on tenants when he thought (almost always mistakenly) that he would catch them *in flagrante,* and impotently plotting how to seduce university administrator Miss Jones, the frustrated spinster who was the reluctant object of his desire.

Rigsby's appalling disrespect for the privacy of his lodgers and his irrepressible inquisitiveness were the moving force behind the storylines, bringing together the various supporting characters who otherwise mostly cut lonely and inadequate, even tragic, figures. The supporting cast was in fact very strong, with Miss

Jones played in highly individualistic style by the respected stage actress Frances de la Tour; the confused, naive medical student Alan played by an ingenuous but appealing Richard Beckinsale; and Philip, the proud but smug son of an African tribal chief, played by Don Warrington. Only Beckinsale had not appeared in the original stage play. Other lodgers later in the series were Brenda (Gay Rose) and Spooner (Derek Newark).

The frustrations and petty humiliations constantly suffered by the various characters, coupled with their dingy surroundings, could easily have made the series a melancholy affair, but the deft humor of the scripts, married to the inventiveness and expertise of the performers, kept the tone light, if somewhat hysterical at times, and enabled the writers to explore Rigsby's various prejudices (concerning sex, race, students, and anything unfamiliar) without causing offense. In this respect, the series was reminiscent of the techniques employed in *Steptoe and Son,* and by Johnny Speight and Warren Mitchell in the "Alf Garnett" series, although here there was less emphasis on invective and more on deliberately farcical comedy. One occasion on which the series did come unstuck was when fun was had at the expense of an apparently fictional election candidate named Pendry, who was described as crooked and homosexual. Unfortunately, there was a real Labour member of Parliament of the same name, and Yorkshire Television was obliged to pay substantial damages for defamation as a result.

The success of the television series led to a film version in 1980, but this met with mixed response, lacking the conciseness and sharpness of the television series and also lacking the presence of Beckinsale, who had tragically died of a heart attack at the age of 31 the previous year. Rossiter himself went on to star in the equally popular series *The Fall and Rise of Reginald Perrin* before his own premature death from heart failure in 1984.

DAVID PICKERING

Cast

Rupert Rigsby	Leonard Rossiter
Alan Moore	Richard Beckinsale
Ruth Jones	Frances de la Tour
Philip Smith	Don Warrington
Spooner	Derek Newark
Brenda	Gay Rose

Producers

Ian MacNaughton, Ronnie Baxter, Len Luruck, Vernon Lawrence

Programming History

28 episodes
Yorkshire Television (ITV)

September 2, 1974	pilot episode
December 1974–January 1975	five episodes
November 1975–December 1975	eight episodes
December 27, 1976	Christmas special
April 1977–May 1977	seven episodes
April 1978–May 1978	six episodes

Rivera, Geraldo (1943–)

U.S. Journalist, Talk Show Host

The name of journalist and talk show host Geraldo Rivera has become synonymous with more sensational forms of talk television. His distinctive style, at once probing, aggressive, and intimate, has even led, at times, to parodies of him in a variety of print and broadcast media. He has seemed to contribute to this high-profile identification by playing himself (or a close approximation) in fictional settings, such as an episode of *thirtysomething,* a 1992 *Perry Mason* TV movie, the finale of *Seinfeld,* and the theatrical films *The Bonfire of the Vanities* (1990) and *Primary Colors* (1998). Yet, ironically, his fear of going too far with his public image led him to turn down an offer to play the role of an over-the-top tabloid reporter in Oliver Stone's *Natural Born Killers* (1994). A master of self-promotion, Rivera's drive has taken his career in directions he may not have predicted. Despite having won ten Emmys and numerous journalism awards (including the Peabody), Rivera is still primarily known for the more public nature of both his personal life and his talk show.

Rivera was discovered while working as a lawyer for the New York Puerto Rican activist group the Young Lords. During the group's occupation of an East Harlem church in 1970, Rivera had been interviewed on WABC-TV local news and caught the eye of the station's news director Al Primo, who was looking for a Latino reporter to fill out his news team. In 1972, Rivera gained national attention with his criti-

cally acclaimed and highly rated special on the horrific abuse of mentally retarded patients at New York's Willowbrook School. He then went on to work for ABC national programs, first as a special correspondent for *Good Morning, America,* and then, in 1978, for the prime-time investigative show *20/20.* However, his brashness led to controversies with the network, and in 1985 he was fired after publicly criticizing ABC for canceling his report on an alleged relationship between John F. Kennedy and Marilyn Monroe.

Rivera was undaunted by his altercation with the network, and he moved to boost his visibility with an hour-long special on the opening of Al Capone's secret vault in April 1986. The payoff for the audience was virtually nil, since the vault contained only dirt, but the show achieved the highest ratings for a syndicated special in television history. Rivera wrote in his autobiography, "My career was not over, I knew, but had just begun. And all because of a silly, high-concept stunt that failed to deliver on its titillating promise."

The same high-concept approach became the base for Rivera's talk show *Geraldo,* which debuted in September 1987. The first guest was Marla Hanson, a model whose face had been slashed on the orders of a jilted lover. Many critics attacked the show, and Rivera, for his theatrics and "swashbuckling bravado," but *Geraldo* garnered a respectable viewership. However, Rivera has pointed out that it was his 1987 show, "Men in Lace Panties and the Women Who Love

Them," which turned the talk format in a more sensational direction. The following year, he broke talk show rating records with a highly publicized show on Nazi skinheads. During the show's taping, a brawl had broken out between two of the guests—a 25-year-old leader of the White Aryan Resistance Youth and black activist Roy Innis. A thrown chair hit Rivera square in the face, breaking his nose. The show was news before it even aired. The press jumped on this opportunity to use Rivera as an example of television's new extremes. A November 1988 cover of *Newsweek* carried a close-up of his bashed face next to a headline reading, "Trash TV: From the Lurid to the Loud, Anything Goes."

Throughout the late 1980s and early 1990s, *Geraldo* (which was eventually renamed *The Geraldo Rivera Show*) continued to capitalize on the sensational aspects of Rivera's reputation. He inserted himself into the talk show narrative, often using his own exploits and bodily desires to fill out the issue at hand. In a show on plastic surgery, Rivera had fat sucked from his buttocks and injected into his forehead in a procedure to reduce wrinkles. A few years later, in another procedure, he had his eyes tucked on the show. The publication of his autobiography, *Exposing Myself,* in the fall of 1991 caused a major stir due to Rivera's revelations of his numerous affairs.

In a 1993 interview, Rivera offered an analysis of his own place in American life:

> I'm so much a part of the popular culture now. I'm a punch line every night on one of the late-night shows.... I'm used as a generic almost in all the editorials and commentaries and certainly all the books about whether the news media has gone too far. It's just that, what is a review going to do to me? They either like me or don't like me, but I'm always interesting to watch.

By mid-1994 Rivera had begun working to recoup his former role as a "serious" journalist. While still taping episodes of his daytime talk show, he began hosting his own legal affairs program, *Rivera Live,* on CNBC and became a regular contributor to the *Today Show.* Although many at NBC News were uncomfortable with Rivera's tabloid image, *Rivera Live* became one of the cable network's highest-rated programs and Rivera won critical praise for his coverage of the O.J. Simpson trial in 1997. In early 1998, Rivera signed a lucrative new six-year contract with NBC, and in May he taped the last original episode of *The Geraldo Rivera Show.* In the fall of that year, Rivera became host of a second CNBC show, *Upfront Tonight.*

Yet Rivera could not completely shake the controversy that seemed to follow him. In 2001, he left CNBC with two years left on his contract for a position as war correspondent at the cable channel FOX News; a few months later he was lambasted for one of his reports from the U.S.-led war against terrorism in Afghanistan. After the deaths of three American soldiers in Kandahar by "friendly fire" in early December 2001, Rivera (dressed in flak jacket and carrying a pistol) reported that he had "walked over the spot where the friendly fire took so many of our men.... I said the Lord's Prayer and really choked up." Newspapers quickly pointed out that the "hallowed" ground of which he spoke was actually hundreds of miles away from where he was standing during his report. Rivera, admitting his mistake, blamed "the fog of war." More criticism followed, as he acted as a swaggering patriot in many of his reports about events following the September 11, 2001, terrorist attacks on the United States. When Rivera promised that if he ever found Osama bin Laden, he would "kick his head in, then bring it home and bronze it," many wondered if this "new" Geraldo Rivera was all that different from the old.

Susan Murray

See also **Talk Shows**

Geraldo Rivera. Born Jerry Rivers in New York City, July 4, 1943. Educated at University of Arizona, B.S., 1965; Brooklyn Law School, J.D., 1969; postgraduate work at University of Pennsylvania, 1969; attended School of Journalism, Columbia University, New York, 1970. Married: 1) Edith Bucket "Pie" Vonnegut, 1971; 2) Sherryl Raymond, 1976; 3) C.C. Dyer, 1987 (divorced); children: Gabriel Miguel, Isabella, Simone. Member, antipoverty neighborhood law firm Harlem Assertion of Rights and Community Action for Legal Services, New York City, 1968–70; admitted to New York Bar, 1970; in television, from 1970, beginning at *Eyewitness News,* WABC-TV, New York City; host, numerous television specials and talk shows; reporter for FOX News, since 2001. Member: Puerto Rican Legal Defense and Education Fund; Puerto Rican Bar Association. Recipient: Smith Fellowship, University of Pennsylvania, 1969; three national and seven local Emmy Awards; two Robert F. Kennedy Awards; Peabody Award; Kennedy Journalism Awards, 1973 and 1975.

Television Series

1970–75	*Eyewitness News*
1973–76	*Good Morning, America*
1974–78	*Geraldo Rivera: Goodnight, America*
1978–85	*20/20* (correspondent and senior producer)
1987–98	*Geraldo* (host; show's title later changed to *The Geraldo Rivera Show*)

1991–92	*Now It Can Be Told*
1994–2001	*Rivera Live*
1998–2001	*Up Front Tonight*

Made-for-Television Movie

1992	*Perry Mason: The Case of the Reck less Romeo*

Television Specials (selected)

1986	*The Mystery of Al Capone's Vault*
1986	*American Vice: The Doping of a Nation*
1986	*American Vice: The Real Story of the Doping of a Nation*
1987	*Modern Love: Action to Action*
1987	*Innocence Lost: The Erosion of American Childhood*
1987	*Sons of Scarface: The New Mafia*
1988	*Murder: Live from Death Row*

Films

The Bonfire of the Vanities, 1990; *Grumpier Old Men*, 1995; *Meet Wally Sparks*, 1997; *Contact*, 1997; *Copland*, 1997; *Primary Colors*, 1998.

Publications (selected)

A Special Kind of Courage: Profiles of Young Americans, 1977
Exposing Myself (with Daniel Paisner), 1991

Further Reading

Heaton, Jeanne Albronda, and Nona Leigh, *Tuning in Trouble: Talk TV's Destructive Impact on Mental Health*, San Francisco: Jossey-Bass, 1995

Leershen, Charles, "Sex, Death, Drugs, and Geraldo," *Newsweek* (November 14, 1988)

Levine, Art, "Blitzed: Ed Murrow, Meet Geraldo," *The New Republic* (January 9, 1989)

Littleton, Cynthia, "Geraldo Takes the Pledge," *Broadcasting and Cable* (January 8, 1996)

Livingstone, Sonia, and Peter Lunt, *Talk on Television: Audience Participation and Public Debate*, London: Routledge, 1994

Munson, Wayne, *All Talk: The Talkshow in Media Culture*, Philadelphia, Pennsylvania: Temple University Press, 1993

Priest, Patricia Joyner, *Public Intimacies: Talk Show Participants and Tell-All TV*, Creskill, New Jersey: Hampton, 1995

Silverman, Art, "Network McNews: The Brave New World of Peter, Dan, Tom…and Geraldo," *ETC.: A Review of General Semantics* (Spring 1990)

Timberg, Bernard, "The Unspoken Rules of Television Talk," in *Television: The Critical View*, edited by Horace Newcomb, New York: Oxford University Press, 1994

Road to Avonlea

Canadian Family Drama

Road to Avonlea, one of English Canada's most successful dramatic series, aired on CBC (the Canadian Broadcasting Corporation network) for seven seasons, from 1990 to 1996. In addition to this domestic success, the series has been among the most widely circulated Canadian programs in international markets; it was sold in more than 140 countries by the end of its domestic run. The series was both a popular and a critical success and is a singular example of the adaptation of "national" Canadian fiction for the generic constraints of both domestic and international televisual markets. This singularity is evident in both the production context of the series and in its narrative development across the seven seasons. The program was produced by Sullivan Entertainment in association with the Disney Channel in the United States and was supported with the participation of Telefilm Canada. Thus, from the beginning of its production run, the series was developed in relation to both domestic and international markets. In addition, the program was plotted in relation to the considerations of both a national broadcasting service and a specialty cable service.

The narrative was developed from the novels of Lucy Maud Montgomery, following the previous success of Sullivan Entertainment's miniseries adaptation of Montgomery's best-known novel, *Anne of Green Gables*. Set in the Atlantic province of Prince Edward Island (P.E.I.) in the first decades of the 20th century, *Avonlea* opens with the move of young Sara Stanley (Sara Polley) from Montreal to the small P.E.I. town of Avonlea to live with two aunts, Hetty King (Jackie Burroughs) and Olivia King (Mag Ruffman). Over the

Road to Avonlea.
Photo courtesy of Sullivan Entertainment/Marni Grossman

seven seasons, the narrative traces the coming of age of Sara and the other children of the town as well as the adjustments of the adults in the community to the increasing changes that 20th-century modernization brings to rural island life. The series is situated simultaneously within the genres of period-costume drama and children's, or family, drama—on the CBC, the series ran in the 7:00 P.M. family hour.

The dramatic formula for the series was relatively stable. Episode plots built upon the development of the children's interrelationships and their increasing entrance into the "adult" world of family and community life. At the same time, the shape of the community was developed through the interactions of series regulars with "outsiders" who instigated disruptions into both family and kinship ties, and who served as indices of the invasive modernity encroaching on town life. The dramatic formula therefore intertwined the coming-of-age incidents and the character development of a traditional children's series with an idealized and nostalgic accounting of rural forms of community life. The fact that the series' narrative ends on the eve of World War I serves to reinforce this linking of childhood, family, and community in an earlier, more innocent period.

The episodic use of outsider characters also integrated well with the series development in relation to both domestic and foreign markets. Over the years the producers succeeded in recruiting for these roles a number of internationally known Canadian guest stars (for example, Kate Nelligan, Colleen Dewhurst) and international guest stars (Michael York, Stockard Channing), a production decision that greatly aided in the international marketing of the series. *Road to Avonlea,* therefore, is a prime example of the adaptation of a national popular culture narrative to the constraints of the international television culture of the 1990s. At the same time, it demonstrates one possible strategy for series finance within relatively "small" national television industries.

MARTIN ALLOR

See also **Canadian Programming in English**

Cast

Sara Stanley (1990–94)	Sara Polley
Aunt Hetty King	Jackie Burroughs
Janet King	Lally Cadeau
Alec King	Cedric Smith
Olivia King Dale	Mag Ruffman
Jasper Dale	R.H. Thompson
Felicity King	Gema Zampogna
Felix King	Zachary Bennett
Rachel Lynde	Patricia Hamilton

Producers
Kevin Sullivan, Trudy Grant

Programming History
91 episodes
CBC
January 1990–March 1996   Sunday 7:00–8:00

Further Reading

Miller, Mary Jane, "Will English Language Television Remain Distinctive? Probably," in *Beyond Quebec: Taking Stock of Canada,* edited by Kenneth McRoberts, Montreal: McGill Queen's Press, 1995

Robertson, Pat (1930–)

U.S. Religious Broadcaster

Pat Robertson is the leading religious broadcaster in the United States. His success has made him not only a television celebrity but also a successful media owner, a well-known philanthropist, and a respected conservative spokesman. Robertson experienced a religious conversion while running his own electronics company in New York, and he became increasingly certain that God wanted him to buy a television station to spread the gospel. Robertson brought his family to Portsmouth, Virginia, in November 1959, with only $70 in his pocket, and a year later he bought a bankrupt UHF station in Portsmouth for a mere $37,000 (the station was valued at $500,000). The station he bought was given the call letters WYAH-TV, for "Yahweh," the Hebrew word for "God," and Robertson called his enterprise the Christian Broadcasting Network (CBN). CBN went on the air on October 1, 1961, with an evangelistic religious format.

In the fall of 1963, CBN held its first telethon asking 700 supporters to join the "700 Club" by pledging $10 a month to help meet the station's monthly operational budget of $7,000. In 1966, after another successful telethon, Robertson started *The 700 Club* as a daily broadcast of prayer and ministry that encouraged a telephone response; toll-free 800 numbers were always displayed, and viewers could ring in for advice and prayer.

Robertson's genius was to recognize early the importance of an Earth station that could uplink and downlink his programs to local cable operators; he made an application to the Federal Communications Commission (FCC) and then signed an agreement with Scientific Atlanta to purchase CBN's satellite Earth station, and he also bought substantial air time on one of the U.S. domestic satellites. On April 29, 1977, CBN began 24-hour Christian and family programming; this was the beginning of the Family Channel. By December 1977, the CBN Satellite Network had become the largest syndicator of satellite programs in the United States. Two years later, in October 1979, CBN opened its new International Communications Center in Virginia Beach, Virginia. CBN has since expanded its broadcasts internationally, and in 2002 it broadcast to 180 nations in 71 languages.

CBN also affiliated with 33 U.S. Christian television stations to form the Home Entertainment Network in 1989. A year later CBN decided to sell its 24-hour Family Channel, whose most important function was to carry *The 700 Club* three times a day. The new company, called International Family Entertainment, was launched on the New York Stock Exchange and sold in 1997 to Fox Kids Worldwide for $1.8 billion, with CBN receiving $136.1 million from the sale. Under the terms of the sale, Fox carried *The 700 Club* twice a day, and the same conditions applied when in 2001 Fox Kids Worldwide was sold to Disney. The cable network is now called ABC Family, and it continues to carry *The 700 Club* daily.

Robertson, an ordained minister of the Southern

David Frost interviewing Pat Robertson.
Courtesy of the Everett Collection

Baptist church, resigned his ordination in 1986 in order to make a bid for the presidency of the United States. As a result of Robertson's actions, CBN lost nearly 40 percent of its gift income in 1988, but upon Robertson's return to *The 700 Club* in 1988, finances were restored. Robertson's conservative political commentaries became an ever more important aspect of his program.

Robertson can claim to have built the popularity of the religious talk show format, a format that has proved consistently popular for more than 30 years. The 2002 version of *The 700 Club* talk show remains a mixture of news; in-depth feature reports on current ethical and moral issues such as school prayer; stories and commentary asserting the agenda of the new Christian right; and Christian evangelism with a charismatic flavor. The program is an important indicator of what evangelicals and Pentecostals believe about current moral and political issues.

In 2002, Pat Robertson retired from the leadership of the Christian Coalition and from active politics, announcing that he intended to spend his remaining years concentrating on the leadership of CBN and Regent University, which he founded in 1978, and which has provided many of his best broadcasting executives. His younger son Gordon is now the principal host of *The 700 Club* and is expected to continue if and when his father retires.

ANDREW QUICKE

See also **Religion on Television**

Pat Robertson. Born Marion Gordon Robertson in Lexington, Virginia, March 22, 1930. Educated at Washington and Lee University, B.A., 1950; Yale University, J.D., 1955; New York Theological Seminary, MDiv, 1959. Married: Adelia Elmer; children: Timothy, Elizabeth, Gordon, and Ann. Founder and president,

Christian Broadcasting Network, Virginia Beach, from 1960; ordained minister, Southern Baptist Convention, 1961–86; author of numerous books, from 1972; on board of directors, National Broadcasters, from 1973; founder and president, CBN (now Regent) University, 1978; started relief organization Operation Blessing, 1978; founder and president, Continental Broadcasting Network, from 1979; cofounded Freedom Council foundation, 1981; member, Presidential Task Force on Victims of Crime, Washington, D.C., 1982; candidate for Republican nomination for U.S. president, 1988. ThD. (honorary), Oral Roberts University, 1983. Recipient: National Council of Christians and Jews Distinguished Merit citation; Knesset Medallion; Religious Heritage of America Faith and Freedom Award; Southern California Motion Picture Council Bronze Halo Award; Religion in Media's International Clergyman of the Year, 1981; International Committee for Goodwill's Man of the Year, 1981; Food for the Hungry Humanitarian Award, 1982; Freedoms Foundation George Washington Honor Medal, 1983.

Television Series

1963–   *The 700 Club* (host)

Publications (selected)

The Secret Kingdom, 1982; revised edition, 1992
Beyond Reason, 1984
Answers to 200 of Life's Most Probing Questions, 1985
Shout It from the Rooftops, 1986
America's Date with Destiny, 1986
The New World Order, 1991
The Turning Tide, 1993
The End of the Age: A Novel, 1995

Further Reading

Boston, Rob, *The Most Dangerous Man in America?: Pat Robertson and the Rise of the Christian Coalition,* Amherst, New York: Prometheus, 1996
Donovan, John B., *Pat Robertson: The Authorized Biography,* New York: Macmillan, and London: Collier Macmillan, 1988
Foege, Alec, *The Empire God Built: Inside Pat Robertson's Media Machine,* New York: John Wiley and Sons, 1996
Green, John Clifford, and James L. Guth, "The Christian Right in the Republican Party: The Case of Pat Robertson's Supporters," *Journal of Politics* (February 1988)
Harrow, David Edwin, *Pat Robertson: A Personal, Religious, and Political Portrait,* New York: Harper and Row, 1987
Hertzke, Allen D., *Echoes of Discontent: Jesse Jackson, Pat Robertson, and the Resurgence of Populism,* Washington, D.C.: Congressional Quarterly Press, 1992
Peck, Janice, *The Gods of Televangelism,* Crosskill, New Jersey: Hampton, 1993
Straub, Gerard Thomas, *Salvation for Sale: An Insider's View of Pat Robertson,* Buffalo, New York: Prometheus, 1988

Robinson, Hubbell (1905–1974)

U.S. Writer, Producer, Network Executive

Hubbell Robinson was active in American broadcasting as a writer, producer, and network programming executive for over 40 years. As the CBS executive who championed the 1950s anthology drama *Playhouse 90,* his efforts to develop high-quality programming that he described as "mass with class" contributed to CBS's long-lived reputation as the "Tiffany" network.

Robinson's broadcasting career began in 1930, when he became the first head of the new radio department at the advertising agency Young and Rubicam. In the era of early commercial broadcasting, when corporate clients sought new radio programs to sponsor, many advertising agencies helped develop program genres, such as the soap opera, that encouraged habitual listening. At Young and Rubicam, Robinson created and wrote scripts for General Foods' soap opera *The Second Mrs. Burton.* The program's success was based, according to Robinson, on "four cornerstones": simple characterizations, understandable predicaments, the centrality of the female characters, and the soap opera's philosophical relevance.

During the late 1930s and early 1940s, Young and Rubicam became an important radio program provider, simultaneously producing *The Jack Benny Show,* Fred Allen's *Town Hall Tonight,* and *The Kate Smith Hour,* among others. As did other radio executives at the agency, Robinson wrote many scripts and commercials, in addition to producing programs.

By the time Robinson joined CBS Television in 1947, his extensive background in radio programming had prepared him well for the new medium. Indeed, in his autobiography, *As It Happened,* then-CBS chairman William Paley referred to Robinson as "the all-around man in our programming department." As executive vice president in charge of television programming at CBS, Robinson championed and oversaw the development of such popular programs as *I Love Lucy, You'll Never Get Rich* (with Phil Silvers as Sergeant Bilko), and *Gunsmoke.*

However, according to Paley, "Culturally, [Robinson's] interests were levels above many of his colleagues. . . . His special flair was for high-quality programming." Robinson organized and championed the 90-minute dramatic anthology series, *Playhouse 90,* which featured serious dramas written by Paddy

Chayevsky, Reginald Rose, and Rod Serling, among others. During its run from 1956 to 1961, *Playhouse 90*'s plays included *Requiem for a Heavyweight, A Sound of Different Drummers, The Miracle Worker,* and *Judgment at Nuremberg.* Robinson was credited with bringing serious television drama to its peak with *Playhouse 90.*

For Paley and others at CBS, however, the anthology drama format was a drawback: its lack of continuity from week to week did not seem to encourage regular television viewing habits. But the networks' increasing reliance on filmed episodic programs was disparaged by many admirers of live anthology drama. Referring to critics' concerns that network programming quality was declining, Robinson openly criti-

Hubbell Robinson in the 1960s.
Courtesy of the Everett Collection

cized the television industry's "willingness to settle for drama whose synonym is pap." Paley, on the other hand, expressed concern that, as a network executive, Robinson "may have lacked the common touch." Still, it was Robinson's stance that helped CBS deal with federal regulators when questions were raised about whether CBS programs served the (loosely defined) public interest.

Robinson returned to CBS briefly from 1962 to 1963 and later joined ABC as executive producer of the *Stage 67* series and the on-location series *Crisis!* from 1966 to 1969. In the early 1960s, he was credited with helping erode stereotyping of African Americans on television by distributing a memorandum calling for producers to cast blacks in a greater variety of roles. Robinson's contributions as a producer and programmer spanned the crucial decades of radio's maturity and television's early growth. As the executive responsible for the programming of both popular and innovative television programs in the 1950s, he helped CBS establish and maintain its reputation as the network with the highest ratings and best programming, a reputation that endured for several decades.

CYNTHIA MEYERS

See also **Anthology Drama; "Golden Age" of Television;** *Playhouse 90*

Hubbell Robinson. Born in Schenectady, New York, October 16, 1905. Graduated from Phillips Exeter Academy, 1923; Brown University, B.A., 1927. Married: 1) Therese Lewis, 1940 (divorced, 1948); 2) Margaret Whiting (divorced); 3) Vivienne Segal (legally separated, 1962). Drama critic, *Exhibitors Herald*, 1927; reporter, *Schenectady Union Star*, Albany Knickerbocker Press, 1929; radio producer, Young and Rubicam, 1930, vice president and radio director, 1942; vice president and program director, ABC radio, New York City, 1944–45; vice president, Foote, Cone, and Belding advertising agency, 1946; vice president and program director, CBS, 1947–56; executive vice president, CBS-TV, 1956–59; organized Hubbell Robinson Productions, 1959; senior vice president, television programs, CBS, 1962–63; executive in charge of various productions, ABC-TV, 1966–69; contributing critic, *Films in Review,* 1971–74; film critic, CATV Channel 8, New York City, 1969–72. Recipient: Emmy Awards, 1958 and 1959; two TV Digest Awards, 1960; Producers Guild Award, 1962; Fame Award, 1967; Television Academy's Salute Award, 1972. Died in New York City, September 4, 1974.

Television Series (executive producer)

1956–61	*Playhouse 90*
1966–69	*Crisis!*
1967	*Stage 67*

Radio

The Second Mrs. Burton; The Jack Benny Show; Fred Allen's Town Hall Tonight; The Kate Smith Hour.

Further Reading

Boddy, William, *Fifties Television: The Industry and Its Critics,* Urbana: University of Illinois Press, 1990
Metz, Robert, *CBS: Reflections in a Bloodshot Eye,* Chicago: Playboy Press, 1975
Paley, William S., *As It Happened,* Garden City, New York: Doubleday, 1979

Rockford Files, The

U.S. Detective Drama

The Rockford Files is generally regarded (along with *Harry O*) as one of the finest private eye series of the 1970s, and indeed of all time, consistently ranked at or near the top in polls of viewers, critics, and mystery writers. The series offered superbly plotted mysteries, with the requisite amounts of action, yet it was also something of a revisionist take on the hard-boiled detective genre, grounded more in character than crime, and infused with humor and realistic relationships. Driven by brilliant writing, an ensemble of winning characters, and the charm of its star, James Garner, the series went from prime-time Nielsen hit in the 1970s to a syndication staple with a loyal cult following in the 1980s, before spawning several made-for-TV movie sequels in the 1990s.

The show was created by producer Roy Huggins

and writer Stephen J. Cannell. Huggins originally sketched the premise of a private eye who took on only closed cases (a conceit quickly abandoned in the series), at one point intending to introduce the character in an episode of the cop show *Toma*. Huggins assigned the script to Cannell—a professed aficionado of the hard-boiled detective tradition—who decided to have fun with the story by flouting the genre's clichés and breaking its rules. After the *Toma* connection crumbled, James Garner signed on to the project, NBC agreed to finance the pilot, and *The Rockford Files* was born.

Cannell was largely responsible for the character and the concept that finally emerged in the pilot script and the series. Jim Rockford did indeed break the mold set by television's earlier two-fisted chivalric P.I.s. His headquarters was a mobile home parked at the beach rather than a shabby office off Sunset Boulevard; in lieu of a gorgeous secretary, an answering machine took his messages; he preferred to talk, rather than slug, his way out of a tight spot; and he rarely carried a gun. (When one surprised client asked why, Rockford replied, "Because I don't want to shoot anybody.") No troubled loner, Jim Rockford spent much of his free time fishing or watching TV with his father, Joe Rockford (Noah Beery, Jr.), a retired trucker with a vocal antipathy to "Jimmy's" chosen profession. Inspired by an episode of *Mannix* in which that tough-guy P.I. took on a child's case for some loose change and a lollipop, Cannell decided to make his creation "the Jack Benny of private eyes." Rockford always announced his rates up front: $200 a day, plus expenses (which he itemized with abandon). He was tenacious on the job, but business was business—and he had payments on the trailer.

For all of its ostensible rule-breaking, however, *The Rockford Files* hewed closely to the hard-boiled tradition in style and theme. The series' depiction of Los Angeles's sun-baked streets and seamy underbelly rivals the novels of Raymond Chandler and Ross MacDonald. Chandler, in his essay "The Simple Art of Murder," could have been writing about Jim Rockford when he describes the hard-boiled detective as a poor man, a common man, a man of honor, who talks with the rude wit of his age. Rockford's propensity for wisecracks, his fractious relationship with the police, and his network of shady underworld connections, lead straight back to Dashiell Hammett by way of Chandler and Rex Stout. As for his aversion to fisticuffs, Rockford was not a coward, but a pragmatist, different only by degree (if at all) from Philip Marlowe; when violence was inevitable, Rockford was as tough as nails. Most tellingly of all, he shared the same code as his Los Angeles predecessors Marlowe and

The Rockford Files, James Garner, 1974–80.
Courtesy of the Everett Collection

Lew Archer: an unwavering sense of morality, and an almost obsessive thirst for the truth. Thus, despite his ostensible concern for the bottom line, in practice Rockford ended up doing at least as much charity work as any fictional gumshoe (as in "The Reincarnation of Angie," when the soft-hearted sleuth agrees to take on a distressed damsel's case for his "special sucker rate" of $23.74).

Ultimately—perhaps inevitably—all of Cannell's generic revisionism served to make his hero more human, and the stories that much more realistic. Jim Rockford could be the Jack Benny of private eyes precisely because he was the first TV private eye—perhaps the first literary one—to be created as a fully credible human being, rather than simply a dogged, alienated purveyor of justice. *The Rockford Files* was as much about character and relationships as it was about crime and detection. The presence of Rockford's father was more than a revisionist or comic gimmick. Although "Rocky" and Jim's wrangling was the source of much humor, that humor was credible and endearing; their relationship was the emotional core of the show, underlining Jim's essential humanity—and subtly, implicitly, sketching in a history for the detective. By the same token, a tapestry of supporting and recurring characters gave Rockford a life beyond the case at hand: Los Angeles Police Department Sergeant Dennis Becker (Joe Santos), Jim's buddy on the force, served a stock genre function as a source of favors and threats, but their friendship, which played out apart from the precinct and the crime scene, added another dimension of character. Likewise, Jim's attorney and sometimes girlfriend Beth Davenport (Gretchen Corbett) further fleshed out the details of his personal life, and served as an able foil for Becker and his more ill-tempered superiors (in the process imparting a dash of 1970s feminism to the show). Angel Martin (Stuart Margolin), Rockford's San Quentin cellmate, the smallest of small-time grifters, the weasel's weasel, at once hilarious and pathetic, evoked Rockford's prison past, evinced his familiarity with Los Angeles's seamier side and balanced Rocky's homeliness with an odious measure of sleaze. These regular members of the Rockford family, and a host of distinctive recurring characters—cops, clients, crooks, con men, ex-cons— helped create, over time, a web of relationships that grounded *Rockford,* investing it with a more intense and continuing appeal than would a strict episodic focus on crime and detection.

As the preceding might suggest, *The Rockford Files* was underlined with a warmth not usually associated with the private eye genre. Much of the show's distinctiveness was its emphasis on humor, exploiting Garner's comic gifts (and his patented persona of "reluctant hero") and the humor of the protagonist's often prickly relationships with his dad, Becker, Angel, and his clients. In later seasons the series occasionally veered into parody—especially in the episodes featuring dashing, wealthy, virtuous detective Lance White (Tom Selleck), and bumbling, pulp-fiction-addled, would-be private eye Freddie Beamer (James Whitmore, Jr.)—and even flirted with self-parody, as the show's signature car chases became more and more elaborate and (sometimes) comical (as when Rockford is forced to give chase in a Volkswagen beetle with an enormous pizza adorning the top). Even so, the series was faithful to its hard-boiled heritage. Yet the series also brought a contemporary sensibility to the hard-boiled tradition's anti-authority impulses, assailing political intrigue, official corruption, and bureaucratic absurdity with a distinctly post-Watergate cynicism.

Rockford's most profound homage to the detective tradition was first-rate writing and a body of superbly realized mysteries. Cannell and Juanita Bartlett wrote the bulk, and most of the best, of the series' scripts, with writer-producer David Chase (*I'll Fly Away, Northern Exposure, The Sopranos*), also a frequent contributor of top-notch work. Mystery author Donald Westlake, quoted in *The Best of Crime and Detective*

TV, captures the series' central strengths in noting that "the complexity of the plots and the relationships between the characters were novelistic." John D. MacDonald, critiquing video whodunits for *TV Guide,* proposed that in terms of "believability, dialogue, plausibility of character, plot coherence, *The Rockford Files* comes as close to meeting the standards of the written mystery as anything I found." During its run, the series was nominated for the Writers Guild Award and the Mystery Writer's of America "Edgar" Award, in addition to winning the Emmy for outstanding drama series in 1978.

The Rockford Files ran for five full seasons, coming to a premature end in the middle of the sixth, when Garner left the show due to a variety of physical ailments brought on by the strenuous demands of the production. Yet *Rockford* never really left the air; not only has the series remained steadily popular in syndication and on cable, eight made-for-television movies reuniting the original cast aired on CBS between 1994 and 1999. In addition, a loyal cult following continues to celebrate the series on various *Rockford File* websites. The show's rather rapid canonization as a touchstone of the private eye genre is evinced by subsequent series, including *Magnum, P.I., Detective in the House,* and *Charlie Grace,* consciously imitating or directly quoting it.

The Rockford Files marked a significant step in the evolution of the television detective, honoring the traditional private eye tale with well-crafted mysteries, and enriching the form with what television does best: fully developed characters and richly drawn relationships. In musing on the hard-boiled detective whose tradition he helped shape, Raymond Chandler wrote, "I do not care much about his private life." In *Rockford,* Cannell and company embraced and exploited their detective's private life. Television encourages, even demands this intimacy. For all the gritty realism of Spade and Marlowe's mean streets, they were, in their solitary asceticism, figures of romantic fantasy. Jim Rockford was no less honorable, no less resolute in his quests; he was, however, by virtue of his trailer, his dad, his gun in the cookie jar, just that much more real.

MARK ALVEY

See also **Cannell, Stephen; Detective Programs; Garner, James; Huggins, Roy**

Cast

Jim Rockford	James Garner
Joseph "Rocky" Rockford	Noah Beery, Jr.
Detective Dennis Becker	Joe Santos
Beth Davenport (1974–78)	Gretchen Corbett
Evelyn "Angel" Martin	Stuart Margolin

John Cooper (1978–79)   Bo Hopkins
Lieutenant Alex Diehl
  (1974–76)   Tom Atkins
Lieutenant Doug Chapman
  (1976–80)   James Luisi

Producers

Meta Rosenberg, Stephen J. Cannell, Charles Floyd
  Johnson, Juanita Bartlett, David Chase

Programming History

114 episodes
NBC

September 1974–May 1977	Friday 9:00–10:00
June 1977	Friday 8:30–9:30
July 1977–January 1979	Friday 9:00–10:00
February 1979–March 1979	Saturday 10:00–11:00
April 1979–December 1979	Friday 9:00–10:00
March 1980–April 1980	Thursday 10:00–11:00
June 1980–July 1980	Friday 9:00–10:00

Further Reading

Chandler, Raymond, *The Simple Art of Murder*, New York: Houghton Mifflin, 1950

Collins, Max, and John Javna, *The Best of Crime and Detective TV: Perry Mason to Hill Street Blues, The Rockford Files to Murder She Wrote*, New York: Harmony, 1988

Grillo, Jean, "A Man's Man and a Woman's Too," *New York Daily News TV Week* (June 10, 1979)

Kane, Hamilton T., "An Interview with Stephen J. Cannell," *Mystery* (January 1981)

MacDonald, John D., "The Case of the Missing Spellbinders," *TV Guide* (November 24, 1979)

Martindale, David, *The Rockford Phile*, Las Vegas, Nevada: Pioneer, 1991

Randisi, Robert J., "The Best TV Eyes of the 70s," *Mystery* (January 1981)

Robertson, Ed, *"This Is Jim Rockford…": The Rockford Files*, Beverly Hills, California: Pomegranate, 1995

Torgerson, Ellen, "James Garner Believes in Good Coffee— And a Mean Punch," *TV Guide* (June 2, 1979)

Vallely, Jean, "The James Garner Files," *Esquire* (July 1979)

Wicking, Christopher, and Tise Vahimagi, *The American Vein: Directors and Directions in Television*, New York: Dutton, 1979

Roddenberry, Gene (1921–1991)

U.S. Writer, Producer

Gene Roddenberry, who once commented, "No one in his right mind gets up in the morning and says, 'I think I'll create a phenomenon today,'" is best known as the creator and executive producer of *Star Trek,* one of the most popular and enduring television series of all time.

A decorated B-17 pilot during World War II, Roddenberry flew commercially for Pan American Airways after the war while taking college writing classes. Hoping to pursue a career writing for the burgeoning television industry, Roddenberry resigned from Pan Am in 1948 and moved his family to California. With few prospects, he followed in his father's and brother's footsteps and joined the Los Angeles Police Department (LAPD), where he served for eight years. During his career as a police officer, the LAPD was actively involved with Jack Webb's *Dragnet* series, giving technical advice on props, sets, and story ideas based on actual cases, many of which were submitted by police officers for $100 in compensation. Roddenberry submitted treatments based on stories from friends and colleagues.

Roddenberry's first professional television work was as technical adviser to Frederick Ziv's *Mr. District Attorney* (1954). The series also gave him his first professional writing work. In addition to creating episodes for *Mr. District Attorney,* Roddenberry also wrote the science fiction tale "The Secret Weapon of 117," which was broadcast on the syndicated anthology series *Chevron Hall of Stars* (March 6, 1956). As he gained increasing success in his new career, he decided to resign from the LAPD in 1956 to pursue writing full time.

Roddenberry continued working on Ziv's new series, *The West Point Story* (CBS, 1956–57; and ABC, 1957–58), and eventually became the show's head writer. For the next few years, he turned out scripts for such series as *Highway Patrol* (syndicated), *Have Gun—Will Travel* (CBS), *Jane Wyman Theater* (NBC), *Bat Masterson* (NBC), *Naked City* (ABC), *Dr. Kildare* (NBC), and *The Detectives* (ABC and NBC). Even at this furious pace, Roddenberry continued to develop ideas for new series.

Gene Roddenberry, *Star Trek,* 1973–75.
Courtesy of the Everett Collection/CSU Archives

The first series created and produced by Roddenberry was *The Lieutenant* (NBC, 1963–64). Set at Camp Pendleton, *The Lieutenant* examined social questions of the day in a military setting. Coincidentally, the show featured guest performances by three actors who later played a large role in *Star Trek:* Nichelle Nichols, Leonard Nimoy, and Majel Barrett, whom he later married. Casting director Joe D'Agosta and writer Gene L. Coon would also work with Roddenberry on *Star Trek.*

A lifelong fan of science fiction, Roddenberry developed his idea for *Star Trek* in 1964. The series was pitched to the major studios and finally found support from Desilu Studios, the production company formed by Lucille Ball and Desi Arnaz. The original $500,000 pilot received minor support from NBC executives, who later commissioned an unprecedented second pilot. The series premiered on September 8, 1966.

Like *The Lieutenant, Star Trek* episodes comment on social and political questions in a military (albeit futuristic) setting. Roddenberry described *Star Trek* as a *"Wagon Train* to the stars" because, like that

popular series, its stories focused on the "individuals who traveled to promote the expansion of our horizons." *Star Trek* was the first science fiction series to depict a peaceful future, and Roddenberry often credited the enduring success of the series to the show's positive message of hope for a better tomorrow. It was also the first series to have a multicultural cast. *Star Trek* received little notice during its three-year run and was canceled after the third season due to low ratings. However, it gained worldwide success in syndication.

In addition to producing the *Star Trek* feature films, Roddenberry continued to write and produce for television, but without the same degree of success. His pilot for *Assignment: Earth* (NBC) was incorporated as an episode of *Star Trek* (March 29, 1968). Later pilots included *Genesis II* (CBS, March 23, 1973), *The Questor Tapes* (NBC, January 23, 1974), *Planet Earth* (ABC, April 23, 1974), and *Spectre* (May 21, 1977). Roddenberry also served as executive consultant on an animated *Star Trek* series (NBC, 1974–75). A second *Star Trek* series, *Star Trek: The Next Generation,* premiered as a syndicated series in 1987 and had a successful seven-year run.

Star Trek: The Next Generation was the last series on which Roddenberry had an active role. Since his death in 1991, three new *Star Trek* series based on Roddenberry's original concept have been created: *Star Trek: Deep Space Nine* (1993–99), *Star Trek: Voyager* (1995–2001), and *Star Trek: Enterprise* (2001–). Two other science fiction series based on Roddenberry's earlier writings have also been televised: *Earth: Final Conflict* (1997–2002) and *Andromeda* (2000–).

Known affectionately to *Star Trek* fans as "the Great Bird of the Galaxy," Roddenberry was the first television writer to be honored with his own star on the Hollywood Walk of Fame, on September 4, 1985. In 1992, with the permission of Roddenberry's widow, Majel Barrett, the late producer's ashes were carried aboard a flight of the space shuttle *Columbia.* In 1993, Roddenberry was posthumously awarded NASA's Distinguished Public Service Medal for his "distinguished service to the nation and the human race in presenting the exploration of space as an exciting frontier and a hope for the future."

SUSAN R. GIBBERMAN

*See also **Star Trek***

Gene (Eugene Wesley) Roddenberry. Born in El Paso, Texas, August 19, 1921. Educated at Los Angeles City College; University of Miami; Columbia University; University of Southern California. Married: 1) Eileen Anita Rexroat, 1943 (divorced, 1969); 2) Majel Leigh Hudec (Majel Barrett), 1969; child: Eugene Wesley. Served in U.S. Army Air Force, World War II. Pilot for Pan American Airways, 1946–49; worked for Los Angeles Police Department, 1949–51; television scriptwriter, 1951–62; wrote first science fiction script, "The Secret Defense of 117," episode for *Chevron Theater*, 1952; created and produced several television series. D.H.L., Emerson College, 1973; D.Sc., Clarkson College, 1981. Recipient: Distinguished Flying Cross; Emmy Award; Hugo Award. Died in Santa Monica, California, October 24, 1991.

Television Series

1952   "The Secret Defense of 117," *Chevron Theatre* (writer)
1955–58   *Jane Wyman Theater* (writer)
1955–59   *Highway Patrol* (writer)
1956–58   *The West Point Story* (writer)
1957–63   *Have Gun—Will Travel* (writer)
1958–63   *Naked City*
1959–61   *Bat Masterson*
1959–62   *The Detectives*
1961–66   *Dr. Kildare*
1963–64   *The Lieutenant* (creator and producer)
1966–69   *Star Trek* (creator and producer)
1973–74   *Star Trek* (animated show)
1987–91   *Star Trek: The Next Generation* (executive producer)

Made-for-Television Movies (pilots; producer)

1973   *Genesis II*
1974   *Planet Earth*
1974   *The Questor Tapes*

1975   *Strange New World*
1977   *Spectre* (director)

Films

Pretty Maids All in a Row (producer and writer), 1971; *Star Trek: The Motion Picture* (producer), 1979; *Star Trek II: The Wrath of Khan* (executive consultant), 1982; *Star Trek III: The Search for Spock*, 1984; *Star Trek IV: The Voyage Home*, 1986; *Star Trek V: The Final Frontier*, 1989.

Publications

The Making of "Star Trek" (with Stephen E. Whitfield), 1968
Star Trek: The Motion Picture, 1979
The Making of "Star Trek: The Motion Picture" (with Susan Sackett), 1980
Star Trek: The First Twenty-Five Years (with Susan Sackett), 1991
Gene Roddenberry: The Last Conversation: A Dialogue with the Creator of Star Trek (with Yvonne Fern), 1994

Further Reading

Alexander, David, *Star Trek Creator: The Authorized Biography of Gene Roddenberry*, New York: ROC, 1994
Barrett, Majel, *The Wit and Wisdom of Gene Roddenberry*, New York: HarperCollins, 1995
Engel, Joel, *Gene Roddenberry: The Myth and the Man Behind Star Trek*, New York: Hyperion, 1994
Paikert, Charles, "Gene Roddenberry: American Mythmaker," *Variety* (December 2, 1991)
Van Hise, James, *The Man Who Created Star Trek: Gene Roddenberry*, Las Vegas, Nevada: Movie Publisher Services, 1992

Rogers, Fred McFeely (1928–2003)

U.S. Children's Television Host, Producer

Fred McFeely Rogers, better known to millions of American children as Mr. Rogers, was the creator and executive producer of the long-running children's program on public television, *Mister Rogers' Neighborhood*. While commercial television most often offers children animated cartoons, and many educational programs employ the slick, fast-paced techniques of commercial television, Rogers's approach was as unique as his content. He simply talks with his young viewers. Although his program provided a great deal of information, the focus was not upon teaching specific facts or skills, but upon acknowledging the

Fred Rogers.
Photo courtesy of Family Communications, Inc.

only a meager budget, their public television show was not a slick production, but Rogers did not view this as a detriment. He wanted children to think that they could make their own puppets, no matter how simple, and create their own fantasies. The important element was to create the friendly, warm atmosphere in the interactions of Josie and the puppets (many of whom remained a part of *Mister Rogers' Neighborhood*), which became the hallmark of the program.

In 1963, the Canadian Broadcasting Corporation (CBC) in Toronto provided Rogers another opportunity to pursue his ministerial charge through a 15-minute daily program called *Mister Rogers*. This was his first opportunity to develop his on-camera style: gentle, affirming, and conversational. The style was grounded in Rogers's view of himself as an adult who took time to give children his undivided attention, rather than as an entertainer.

Rogers returned to Pittsburgh in 1964, acquired the rights to the CBC programs, and lengthened them to 30 minutes for distribution by the Eastern Educational Network. When production funds ran out in 1967 and stations began announcing the cancellation of the show, an outpouring of public response spurred the search for new funding. As a result of support by the Sears, Roebuck Foundation and National Educational Television, a new series entitled *Mister Rogers' Neighborhood* began production for national distribution. New episodes were taped from 1979 to 2001 and broadcast along with the original 460 episodes.

Mister Rogers' Neighborhood was unique because it provided a warmth and intimacy seldom found in mass media productions. The show was designed to approximate a visit between friends, and was meticulously planned in consultation with psychologists at the Arsenal Family and Children's Center. The visit began with a model trolley that traveled through a make-believe town to Rogers's home. He entered, singing "Won't You Be My Neighbor?," an invitation for the viewer to feel as close to him as to an actual neighbor. He also created a bond with his audience by speaking directly to the camera, always in an inclusive manner about things of interest to his viewers. As he spoke, he changed from his sport coat to his trademark cardigan sweater, and from street shoes to tennis shoes, to further create a relaxed, intimate atmosphere.

The pacing of the program also approximated that of an in-depth conversation between friends. Rogers spoke slowly, allowing time for children to think about what he said and to respond at home. Psychologists studying the show have verified that children do respond. He also took time to examine objects around him or to do simple chores such as feed his fish. Although he invited other "neighbors," such as pianist

uniqueness of each child and affirming his or her importance.

Rogers did not originally plan to work in children's television. Rather, he studied music composition at Rollins College in Florida, receiving a bachelor's degree in 1951. He happened to see a children's television program, and felt it was so abysmal that he wanted to offer something better. While he worked in television, however, he also pursued his dream of entering the ministry, continuing his education at Pittsburgh Theological Seminary. In 1962, Rogers received a bachelor of divinity degree, and was ordained by the United Presbyterian Church with the charge to work with children and their families through the mass media.

Rogers began his television career at NBC, but joined the founding staff of America's first community-supported television station, WQED in Pittsburgh, as a program director in 1953. His priority was to schedule a children's program; however, when no one came forward to produce it, Rogers assumed the task himself and, in April 1954, launched *The Children's Corner*. He collaborated with on-screen hostess Josie Carey on both the scripts and music to produce a show that received immediate acclaim, winning the 1955 Sylvania Award for the best locally produced children's program in the country. Rogers and Carey also created a separate show with similar material for NBC network distribution on Saturday mornings. With

Van Cliburn, to share their knowledge, the warm rapport also allowed him to tackle personal subjects, such as fears of the dark or the arrival of a new baby.

Recognizing the importance of play as a creative means of working through childhood problems, he also invited children into the Neighborhood of Make Believe. Because Rogers wanted children to clearly separate fantasy from reality, this adjacent neighborhood could only be reached via a trolley through a tunnel. The Neighborhood of Make Believe was populated by a number of puppets who were kindly and respectful but not perfect. King Friday XIII, for example, was kind but also somewhat pompous and authoritarian.

Human characters also inhabited this neighborhood and engaged the puppets on an equal level. Since Rogers was the puppeteer and voice for most of the puppets, it was difficult for him to interact in this segment. This movement away from "center stage," however, was a conscious choice. His lack of visible participation underscored the separation between the reality he created in his "home" and these moments of fantasy. The trolley then took the children back to Rogers's home, and the visit ended as he changed back into his street clothes and left the house, inviting the children back at a later date.

In 1971, Rogers formed Family Communications, Inc., a nonprofit corporation of which he was president, to produce *Mister Rogers' Neighborhood* and other audiovisual, educational materials. Many of these productions, such as the prime-time series *Mister Rogers Talks with Parents* (1983), and his books *Mister Rogers Talks with Parents* (1983) and *How Families Grow* (1988), are guides for parents. He also recorded six albums of children's songs. However, these activities were viewed as educational endeavors rather than profit-generating enterprises, and most of the funding for his productions came from grants.

Fred Rogers succeeded in providing something different for children on television, and in acknowledgment of his accomplishments he received two Peabody Awards, a first for noncommercial television. Rather than loud, fast-paced animation or entertaining education, he presented a caring adult who visits with children, affirming their distinction and value, and understanding their hopes and fears. Fred Rogers passed away due to stomach cancer on February 27, 2003.

SUZANNE WILLIAMS-RAUTIOLLA

See also **Children and Television**

Fred McFeely Rogers. Born in Latrobe, Pennsylvania, March 20, 1928. Educated at Dartmouth College, 1946; Rollins College, Winter Park, Florida, B.A. in music, 1951; Pittsburgh Theological Seminary, bachelor of divinity, 1962. Married: Sara Joanne Byrd, 1952; children: James Byrd and John Frederick. Assistant television producer and network floor director, NBC, 1951–53; program director, producer, writer, and performer, WQED, Pittsburgh, 1953–62; producer and television host, Canadian Broadcasting Corporation, Toronto, Ontario, 1963–64; producer and host, PBS show *Mister Rogers' Neighborhood,* 1967–2001; producer and host, *Old Friends, New Friends,* 1979–81; producer of videocassettes, CBS, 1987–88. Founder and president, Family Communications, Inc., 1971. Member: Esther Island Preserve Association; Luxor Ministerial Association; board of directors, McFeely-Rogers Foundation; honorary chair, National PTA, 1992–94. Numerous honorary degrees. Recipient: Peabody Awards, 1969 and 1993; Emmy Awards, 1980 and 1985; Ohio State Awards, 1983 and 1986; ACT Award, 1984; Christopher Award, 1984; Educational Press Association of America's Lamplighter Award, 1985; Children's Book Council Award, 1985; Gold Medal at the International Film and TV Festival, 1986; Parent's Choice Award, 1987–88; PBS Award in recognition of 35 years in public television, 1989; Eleanor Roosevelt Val-Kill Medal, 1994; Joseph F. Mulach, Jr., Award, 1995. Died February 27, 2003.

Television Series

1954–61	*Children's Corner*
1963–67	*Misterogers*
1967–2001	*Mister Rogers' Neighborhood*
1979–81	*Old Friends, New Friends*

Television Special (selected)

1994	*Fred Rogers' Heroes*

Recordings

Won't You Be My Neighbor?, 1967; *Let's Be Together Today,* 1968; *Josephine, The Short-Necked Giraffe,* 1969; *You Are Special,* 1969; *A Place of Our Own,* 1970; *Bedtime,* 1992; *Growing,* 1992.

Publications (selected)

Mister Rogers Talks with Parents, 1983.
The New Baby, 1985.
Making Friends, 1987.
Mister Rogers: How Families Grow, 1988.
You Are Special, 1994.

Rogers, Fred McFeely

Further Reading

Barringer, Felicity, "Mister Rogers Goes to Russia," *New York Times* (September 21, 1987)

Berkvist, Robert, "Misterogers Is a Caring Man," *New York Times* (November 16, 1969)

Blau, Eleanor, "Rogers Has New TV Series on School," *New York Times* (August 20, 1979)

Briggs, Kenneth A., "Mr. Rogers Decides It's Time To Head for New Neighborhoods," *New York Times* (May 8, 1975)

Collins, Glenn, "TV's Mr. Rogers—A Busy Surrogate Dad," *New York Times* (June 19, 1983)

Fischer, Stuart, "Children's Corner," *Kids TV: The First Twenty-Five Years,* New York: Facts on File, 1983

"Fred M(cFeely) Rogers," in *Current Biography,* edited by Charles Moritz, New York: H.W. Wilson, 1970

"Fred McFeely Rogers," *Broadcasting and Cable* (July 26, 1993)

Lewin, Tamar, "A Lifetime of Beautiful Days," *New York Times* (March 2, 2003)

"The Man Kids Believe," *Newsweek* (May 12,1969)

McCleary, Elliott H., "Big Friend to Little People," *Today's Health* (August 1969)

O'Connor, John J., "An Observer Who Bridges the Generation Gap," *New York Times* (April 12, 1978)

O'Connor, John J., "Mr. Rogers, a Gentle Neighbor," *New York Times* (February 15, 1976)

"TV: On Superheroes," *New York Times* (February 4, 1980)

Ziaukas, Tim, "Kid Video," *Pittsburgh* (July 1986)

Rogers, Ted (1933–)

Canadian Media Executive

The founder and chief executive officer of Rogers Communications, Inc., Ted Rogers has become Canada's undisputed new-media mogul. A tireless worker, over the last 35 years Rogers has ceaselessly expanded his business undertakings by plunging head-long into each new communication technology. He has compared his corporate machinations to the likes of Rupert Murdoch's News Corporation and Time-Warner, maintaining that only by building Canadian companies of comparable size and diversity can Canadians be assured of a distinctive voice at the forefront of the electronic highway.

Established in 1967, Rogers Communications has grown into one of Canada's largest media conglomerates. Rogers Communications is the largest cable television business in Canada, with more than 30 percent of all Canadian cable subscribers. As a broadcaster and television content provider, Rogers Communications owns more than 40 radio stations, CFMT in Toronto (a multicultural television station), the cable channel Sportsnet, and the Canadian Home Shopping Channel. It also owns a chain of video stores. In telecommunications, Rogers Communications held a major stake in Unitel Communications, a long-distance telephone company, from 1989 to 1995, and has been in the wireless telephone business since 1985. As of 2002, Rogers Communications owned 51 percent of Rogers AT&T Wireless, a Canada-wide cellular phone service. As a result of its 1994 takeover of Maclean-Hunter Ltd., Rogers Communications became the majority share-holder of the Toronto Sun Publishing Corporation, publisher of newspapers across Canada, and is also the owner of dozens of periodicals in Canada, Britain, the United States, and Europe. In 1993, Rogers Communications generated revenues of $1.34 billion; the addition of the assets from Maclean-Hunter bring the annual revenues of Rogers Communications to more than double that figure.

Ted Rogers's interest in broadcasting continues a family tradition. His father, Edward Samuel Rogers, Sr., was the first amateur radio operator in Canada to transmit successfully a signal across the Atlantic. In 1925, he invented the radio tube that made it possible to build "battery-less" alternating current receiving sets, and in the same decade he founded Rogers Majestic Corporation to build them. Until then, neither radio receivers nor transmitters could utilize existing household wiring or power lines, and the batteries that powered radio receivers were cumbersome, highly corrosive, and required frequent changing. Rogers's radio greatly increased the popularity of broadcasting. The elder Rogers also established a commercial radio station, CFRB (with the call letters signifying Canada's First Radio Batteryless), in Toronto, which grew to command Canada's largest listening audience. In 1935, Rogers Sr. was granted the first Canadian license to broadcast experimental television. He died eight years later at the age of 38, when Ted Rogers was five. After Rogers Sr.'s death, the Rogers family lost control of CFRB.

Ted Rogers.
Photo courtesy of Ted Rogers

In 1960, while still a student at Osgoode Hall Law School in Toronto, Ted Rogers bought all the shares in CHFI-FM, a small, 940-watt Toronto radio station that pioneered the use of frequency modulation (FM) at a time when only 5 percent of Toronto households had FM receivers. By 1965, Rogers was in the cable TV business. In 1979 and 1980, he bought out two competitors, Canadian Cablesystems and Premier Cablevision (both were larger than his own operation), and, by 1980, Rogers Communications had taken over UA-Columbia Cablevision in the United States, to become for a time the world's largest cable operator, with more than 1 million subscribers.

Rogers has since sold his stake in U.S. cable operations to concentrate on the Canadian market. His forays into long-distance and cellular telephone service, his ownership of cable services such as the Home Shopping Network and specialty channels such as Sportsnet, and the acquisition of Maclean-Hunter's publishing interests, with more than 60 magazine and trade periodicals, make Rogers a key player in virtually all of Canada's media markets.

Although the Canadian Radio-television and Telecommunication Commission has generally given its assent to Rogers's corporate maneuvers, there are many who believe that the commission has neither the regulatory tools nor the will to monitor or control adequately the activities of Rogers Communications and other large cable operators, especially with regard to pricing and open network access. While cable rates rose an average of 80 percent between 1983 and 1993, Rogers Communications was busy adding to its corporate empire and upgrading its technical infrastructure.

As some cable operators tremble at the prospect of competition from direct-to-home satellites and telephone companies, Ted Rogers has ensured that Rogers Communications is well positioned for life after the era of local cable monopolies. Taking his cue from corporate strategists south of the border, Rogers has added a sports property to his holding with his purchase of the Toronto Blue Jays, and his wireless venture now accounts for more operating revenue than his cable assets. From humble beginnings, Rogers has built a company that seems destined to travel in the fast lane.

TED MAGDER

See also **Canadian Production Companies**

Ted (Edward Samuel) Rogers. Born in Toronto, Ontario, Canada, May 27, 1933. Educated at the Upper Canada College, Toronto; University of Toronto, Trinity College, B.A., 1956; Osgoode Hall Law School, LL.B., 1961. Married: Loretta Anne Robinson, 1963; children: Lisa Anne, Edward Samuel, Melinda Mary, and Martha Loretta. Read law for Tory, Tory, DesLauriers, and Binnington; called to bar of Ontario, 1962; founder, Rogers Communications, 1967; president and chief executive officer. Director: Toronto-Dominion Bank, Canada Publishing Corporation, Hull Group, Wellesley Hospital, Junior Achievement of Canada.

Further Reading

Dalglish, Brenda, "Shifting Ground: Changes in Canada and U.S. Rulings Give Rogers Second Thoughts on His Bid for Maclean Hunter," *Maclean's* (March 7, 1994)

Dalglish, Brenda, "King of the Road," *Maclean's* (March 21, 1994)

Fotheringham, Allan, "The Revenge of Mila Mulroney," *Maclean's* (February 14, 1994)

Newman, Peter C., "Life in the Fast Lane," *Maclean's* (March 21, 1994)

Newman, Peter C., "The Ties That Bind: Ted Rogers' Past Is Shaping His Future," *Maclean's* (February 21, 1994)

Room 222

U.S. High School Drama

Room 222 was a half-hour comedy-drama that aired on ABC from 1969 to 1974. While seldom seen in syndication today, the show broke new narrative ground that would later be developed by the major sitcom factories of the 1970s, Grant Tinker's MTM Enterprises and Norman Lear's Tandem Productions. Mixing dramatic elements with traditional television comedy, *Room 222* also prefigured the "dramedy" form by almost two decades.

The series was set at an integrated high school in contemporary Los Angeles. While the narrative centered on a dedicated and student-friendly African-American history teacher, Pete Dixon (Lloyd Haynes), it also depended upon an ensemble cast of students and other school employees. The optimistic idealism of Pete, guidance counselor Liz McIntyre (Denise Nicholas), and student-teacher Alice Johnson (Karen Valentine) was balanced by the experienced, somewhat jaded principal, Seymour Kaufman (Michael Constantine). These characters and a handful of other teachers would spend each episode arguing among themselves about the way in which to go about both educating their students and acting as surrogate parents.

A season and a half before Norman Lear made "relevant" programming a dominant genre with the introduction of such programs as *All in the Family* and *Maude, Room 222* was using the form of the half-hour comedy to discuss serious contemporary issues. During its five seasons on the air, the show included episodes that dealt with such topics as racism, sexism, homophobia, dropping out of school, shoplifting, drug use among both teachers and students, illiteracy, cops in school, guns in school, Vietnam War veterans, venereal disease, and teenage pregnancy.

Most importantly, *Room 222* served as a prototype of sorts for what would become the formula that MTM Enterprises would employ in a wide variety of comedies and dramas during the 1970s and 1980s. When Grant Tinker set up MTM, he hired *Room 222*'s executive story editors James L. Brooks and Allan Burns to create and produce the company's first series, *The Mary Tyler Moore Show*. This series eschewed issue-oriented comedy, but it picked up on *Room 222*'s contemporary and realistic style as well as its setting in a "workplace family." Treva Silverman, a writer for *Room 222,* also joined her bosses on the new show, and Gene Reynolds, another *Room 222* producer, produced *The Mary Tyler Moore Show* spin-off *Lou Grant* several years later.

Room 222 was given a number of awards by community and educational groups for its positive portrayal of important social issues seldom discussed on television at the time. It won an Emmy Award for outstanding new series in 1969.

ROBERT J. THOMPSON

See also **Brooks, James L.; Burns, Allan; Dramedy; Tinker, Grant**

Room 222, Denise Nicholas, Michael Constantine, Karen Valentine, Lloyd Haynes, 1969–74.
©20th Century Fox/Courtesy of the Everett Collection

Cast

Pete Dixon	Lloyd Haynes
Liz McIntyre	Denise Nicholas
Seymour Kaufman	Michael Constantine
Alice Johnson	Karen Valentine
Richie Lane (1969–71)	Howard Rice
Helen Loomis	Judy Strangis
Jason Allen	Heshimu
Al Cowley (1969–71)	Pendrant Netherly
Bernie (1970–74)	David Jollife
Pam (1970–72)	Te-Tanisha
Larry (1971–73)	Eric Laneuville

Producers

Gene Reynolds, William D'Angelo, John Kubichan, Ronald Rubin

Programming History

112 episodes
ABC

September 1969–January 1971	Wednesday 8:30–9:00
January 1971–September 1971	Wednesday 8:00–8:30
September 1971–January 1974	Friday 9:00–9:30

Further Reading

Eisner, Joel, and David Krinsky, *Television Comedy Series: An Episode Guide to 153 TV Sitcoms in Syndication,* Jefferson, North Carolina: McFarland, 1984

Feuer, Jane, Paul Kerr, and Tise Vahimagi, editors, *MTM: "Quality Television,"* London: British Film Institute, 1984

MacDonald, J. Fred, *Blacks and White TV: Afro-Americans in Television Since 1948,* Chicago: Nelson-Hall, 1983; 2nd edition, 1992

Newcomb, Horace, and Robert S. Alley, *The Producer's Medium: Conversations with Creators of American TV,* New York: Oxford University Press, 1983

Tinker, Grant, and Bud Rukeyser, *Tinker in Television: From General Sarnoff to General Electric,* New York: Simon and Schuster, 1994

Roots

U.S. Miniseries

Roots remains one of television's landmark programs. The 12-hour miniseries aired on ABC from January 23 to January 30, 1977. For eight consecutive nights it riveted the United States. ABC executives initially feared that the historical saga about slavery would be a ratings disaster. Instead, *Roots* scored higher ratings than any previous entertainment program in history. It averaged a 44.9 rating and a 66 audience share for the length of its run. The seven episodes that followed the opener earned the top seven spots in the ratings for their week. The final night held the single-episode ratings record until 1983, when the finale of *M*A*S*H* aired on CBS.

The success of *Roots* has had lasting impact on the television industry. The show defied industry conventions about black-oriented programming: executives simply had not expected that a show with black heroes and white villains could attract such huge audiences. In the process, *Roots* almost single-handedly spawned a new television format—the consecutive-night miniseries. (Previous miniseries, such as the 1976 hit *Rich Man, Poor Man,* had run in weekly installments.)

Roots also validated the docudrama approach of its executive producer, David Wolper. The Wolper style, blending fact and fiction in a soap opera package, influenced many subsequent miniseries. Finally, *Roots* was credited with having a positive impact on race relations and expanding the nation's sense of history.

Adapted for television by William Blinn and based on Alex Haley's best-selling novel about his African ancestors, *Roots* follows several generations in the lives of a slave family. The saga begins with Kunta Kinte (LeVar Burton), a West African youth captured by slave raiders and shipped to America in the 18th century. Kunta receives brutal treatment from his white masters and rebels continually. An older Kunta (John Amos) marries and his descendants carry the story after his death. Daughter Kizzy (Leslie Uggams) is raped by her master and bears a son, later named Chicken George (Ben Vereen). In the final episode, Kunta Kinte's great-grandson Tom (Georg Stanford Brown) joins the Union Army and gains emancipation. Over the course of the saga, viewers saw brutal whip-

Roots, LeVar Burton, 1977.
Courtesy of the Everett Collection

pings and many agonizing moments: rapes, the forced separations of families, slave auctions. Through it all, however, *Roots* depicted its slave characters as well-rounded human beings, not merely as victims or symbols of oppression.

Apprehensions that *Roots* would flop shaped the way that ABC presented the show. Familiar television actors such as Lorne Greene were chosen for the white, secondary roles, to reassure audiences. The white actors were featured disproportionately in network previews. For the first episode, the writers created a conscience-stricken slave captain (Ed Asner), a figure who did not appear in Haley's novel but was intended to make white audiences feel better about their historical role in the slave trade. Even the show's consecutive-night format allegedly resulted from network apprehensions. ABC programming chief Fred Silverman hoped that the unusual schedule would cut his network's imminent losses—and get *Roots* off the air before sweeps week.

Silverman need not have worried. *Roots* garnered

phenomenal audiences. On average, 80 million people watched each of the last seven episodes. More than 100 million viewers, almost half the United States, saw the final episode, which still claims one of the highest Nielsen ratings ever recorded, a 51.1 with a 71 share. A stunning 85 percent of all U.S. television homes saw all or part of the miniseries. *Roots* also enjoyed unusual social acclaim for a television show. Vernon Jordan, former president of the Urban League, called it "the single most spectacular educational experience in race relations in America." Today, the show's social effects may appear more ephemeral, but at the time they seemed widespread. More than 250 colleges and universities planned courses on the saga, and during the broadcast, more than 30 cities declared *Roots* weeks.

The program drew generally rave reviews. Black and white critics alike praised *Roots* for presenting African-American characters who were not tailored to suit white audiences. The soap opera format drew some criticism for its emphasis on sex, violence, and romantic intrigue. A few critics also complained that the opening segment in Africa was too Americanized—it was difficult to accept such television regulars as O.J. Simpson as West African natives. On the whole, however, critical acclaim echoed the show's resounding popular success. *Roots* earned more than 30 Emmy Awards and numerous other distinctions.

The program spawned a 1979 sequel, *Roots: The Next Generations.* The sequel did not match the original's ratings but still performed extremely well, with a total audience of 110 million. Overall, *Roots* had a powerful and diverse impact, as a cultural phenomenon, an exploration of black history, and the crown jewel of historical miniseries.

J.B. BIRD

See also **Adaptation; Haley, Alex; Miniseries; Racism, Ethnicity, and Television**

Producer
Stan Margulies

Cast

Kunta Kinte (as a boy)	LeVar Burton
Kunta Kinte (Toby; adult)	John Amos
Binta	Cicely Tyson
Omoro	Thalmus Rasula
Nya Boto	Maya Angelou
Kadi Touray	O.J. Simpson
The Wrestler	Ji-Tu Cumbuka
Kintango	Moses Gunn
Brimo Cesay	Hari Rhodes
Fanta	Ren Woods
Fanta (later)	Beverly Todd

Capt. Davies	Edward Asner
Third Mate Slater	Ralph Waite
Gardner	William Watson
Fiddler	Louis Gossett, Jr.
John Reynolds	Lorne Greene
Mrs. Reynolds	Lynda Day George
Ames	Vic Morrow
Carrington	Paul Shenar
Dr. William Reynolds	Robert Reed
Bell	Madge Sinclair
Grill	Gary Collins
The Drummer	Raymond St. Jacques
Tom Moore	Chuck Connors
Missy Anne	Sandy Duncan
Noah	Lawrence-Hilton Jacobs
Ordell	John Schuck
Kizzy	Leslie Uggams
Squire James	Macdonald Carey
Mathilda	Olivia Cole
Mingo	Scatman Crothers
Stephen Bennett	George Hamilton
Mrs. Moore	Carolyn Jones
Sir Eric Russell	Ian McShane
Sister Sara	Lillian Randolph
Sam Bennett	Richard Roundtree
Chicken George	Ben Vereen
Evan Brent	Lloyd Bridges
Tom	Georg Stanford Brown
Ol' George Johnson	Brad Davis
Lewis	Hilly Hicks
Jemmy Brent	Doug McClure
Irene	Lynne Moody
Martha	Lane Binkley
Justin	Burl Ives

Programming History

eight episodes on consecutive nights

ABC

January 1977	9:00–11:00, or 10:00–11:00

Further Reading

Adams, Russell L., "An Analysis of the *Roots* Phenomenon in the Context of American Racial Conservatism," *Presence Africaine: Revue Culturelle du Monde Noir/Cultural Review of the Negro World* (1980)

Blayney, Michael Steward, "*Roots* and the Noble Savage," *North Dakota Quarterly* (Winter 1986)

Bogle, Donald, "*Roots* and *Roots: The Next Generations,*" in *Blacks in American Television and Film: An Encyclopedia,* New York: Garland, 1988

Brooks, Tim, and Earle Marsh, *The Complete Directory to Prime-Time Network TV Shows: 1946–Present,* New York: Ballantine, 1979; 5th edition, 1992

Gray, Herman, *Watching Race: Television and the Struggle for "Blackness,"* Minneapolis: University of Minnesota Press, 1995

Gray, John, *Blacks in Film and Television: A Pan-African Bibliography of Films, Filmmakers, and Performers,* New York: Greenwood, 1990

Haley, Alex, *Roots,* Garden City, New York: Doubleday, 1976

Journal of Broadcasting, special issue on *Roots* (1978)

Kern-Foxworth, Marilyn, "Alex Haley," in *Dictionary of Literary Biography,* Detroit: Gale, 1985

Tucker, Lauren R., and Hemant Shah, "Race and the Transformation of Culture: The Making of the Television Miniseries *Roots,*" *Critical Studies in Mass Communication* (December 1992)

Winship, Michael, *Television,* New York: Random House, 1988

Woll, David, *Ethnic and Racial Images in American Film and Television,* New York: Garland, 1987.

Rose, Reginald (1920–2002)

U.S. Writer

Reginald Rose was one of the outstanding television playwrights to emerge from the "Golden Age" of television drama anthology series. Like his acclaimed contemporaries—Paddy Chayefsky, Tad Mosel, and Rod Serling, for example—Rose takes a place in history at the top of the craft of television writing. In addition to other accolades, Rose was nominated for six Emmy Awards during his career, and won three. Although most of Rose's fame derived from his teleplays for the live drama anthologies, he also wrote a number of successful plays for screen and stage. Additionally, he created and wrote scripts for *The Defenders* at CBS, and he won recognition for the revived *CBS Playhouse* in the late 1960s.

Rose's first teleplay to be broadcast was *The Bus to Nowhere,* which appeared on *Studio One* (CBS) in

Author Reginald Rose, on stage with Harry Bergman (L), and Rene Auberjonois (R).
Courtesy of the Everett Collection

1951. It was the 1954–55 season, however, that gave Rose his credentials as a top writer—that year has been referred to as "*the* Reginald Rose season" at *Studio One*. His contributions included the noted plays *12:32 A.M., An Almanac of Liberty, Crime in the Streets,* as well as the play that opened the season and became perhaps Rose's best-known work, *Twelve Angry Men*. In addition to winning numerous awards and undergoing transformation into a feature film, *Twelve Angry Men* undoubtedly established Rose's reputation almost immediately as a major writer of drama for television.

What distinguished Rose's teleplays from those of his colleagues, such as Chayefsky and Serling, was their direct preoccupation with social and political issues. Although the other writers were perhaps equally concerned with the larger social dimensions of their work, they concentrated on the conflicts that emerge in

private life and the domestic sphere, and the problems of society as a whole remain implicit in their writing. Rose, in contrast, tackled controversial social issues head-on.

In one of his best-known and most contentious plays, *Thunder on Sycamore Street* (*Studio One,* 1953), Rose aimed to confront the problem of social conformity. In this story, an ex-convict moves to an upscale neighborhood in an attempt to make a new beginning. When the man's past is discovered, one of his neighbors organizes a community march to drive the ex-convict out of his new home. Rose dealt directly with the issues of mob anger and difference from the norm, issues of general concern in a time when the pressures of conformity were overwhelming and the memory of fascism still prevalent. This play was controversial from the outset, since the central character was originally written to be an African American. Rose was forced, under pressure from *Studio One* sponsors fearful of offending (and losing) audiences in the South, to change the character into an ex-convict. This controversy, perhaps more than anything, was indicative of his ability to touch on the most sensitive areas of American social life of that time.

Although Rose kept his sights directed at the scrutiny of social institutions and mechanisms, his characters were as finely drawn as those of writers who focused on domestic struggles. Exemplary in this regard is the tension created by exhausting deliberations within the confined closeness of the jury room in which *Twelve Angry Men* occurs. The remake of this powerful drama and Paddy Chayefsky's teleplay *Marty* (*Goodyear Playhouse*, 1953) into successful feature films marked the breakthrough of the television drama aesthetic into Hollywood cinema. Rose was responsible in part for the creation of this new approach. This gritty realism that became known as the "slice of life" school of television drama was for a time the staple of the anthology shows and reshaped the look of both television and American cinema.

KEVIN DOWLER

See also **Defenders; Playhouse 90; Studio One; Writing for Television**

Reginald Rose. Born in New York City, December 10, 1920. Studied at City College (now of the City University of New York), New York, 1937–38. Married: 1) Barbara Langbart, 1943 (divorced); children: Jonathan, Richard, Andrew, and Steven; 2) Ellen McLaughlin, 1963; children: Thomas and Christopher. Served in U.S. Army, 1942–46. Writer in television, from 1951, starting with CBS, eventually working for all the major networks; wrote CBS-TV's *Studio One* episode *Twelve Angry Men,* 1954; wrote and coproduced *Twelve Angry Men* film version, 1957, and wrote stage version, 1964; writer of films, from 1956; author of books, from 1956; wrote CBS pilot for series *The Defender,* as episode of *Studio One,* 1957; wrote Emmy-nominated *The Sacco-Vanzetti Story,* NBC-TV's *Sunday Showcase,* 1960; president, Defender Productions, from 1961; created series and with others wrote *The Defenders,* 1961–65; wrote Emmy-nominated *Dear Friends* for *CBS Playhouse,* 1967; wrote multiple-award-winning CBS miniseries *Escape from Sobibor,* 1987. President of Reginald Rose Foundation. Recipient: Emmy Awards, 1954, 1962, 1963 (with Robert Thom), 1968; Edgar Allan Poe Award, 1957; Berlin Film Festival Golden Berlin Bear Award, 1957; Writers Guild of America Award, 1960; Writers Guild of America Laurel Award, 1958 and 1987. Died in Norwalk, Connecticut, April 19, 2002.

Television Series (various episodes)

1948–55	*Philco Television Playhouse/Goodyear Playhouse*
1948–58	*Studio One*
1951	*Out There*
1954–55	*Elgin Hour*
1955–57	*The Alcoa Hour/Goodyear Playhouse*
1956–61	*Playhouse 90*
1959–60	*Sunday Showcase*
1961–65	*The Defenders* (creator and writer)
1967	*CBS Playhouse*
1975	*The Zoo Gang* (creator and writer)
1977	*The Four of Us* (pilot)

Miniseries

1979	*Studs Lonigan*
1987	*Escape from Sobibor*

Made-for-Television Movies

1982	*The Rules of Marriage*
1986	*My Two Loves* (with Rita Mae Brown)

Films

Crime in the Streets, 1956; *Dino,* 1957; *Twelve Angry Men* (also co-produced), 1957; *Man of the West,* 1958; *The Man in the Net,* 1958; *Baxter!,* 1972; *Somebody Killed Her Husband,* 1978; *The Wild Geese,* 1978; *The Sea Wolves,* 1980; *Whose Life Is It, Anyway?* (with Brian Clark), 1981; *The Final Option,* 1983; *Wild Geese II,* 1985.

Stage

Black Monday, 1962; *Twelve Angry Men,* 1964; *The Porcelain Year,* 1965; *Dear Friends,* 1968; *This Agony, This Triumph,* 1972.

Publications

Six Television Plays, 1957
The Thomas Book, 1972

Further Reading

Hawes, William, *The American Television Drama: The Experimental Years,* University: University of Alabama Press, 1986

Sturcken, Frank, *Live Television: The Golden Age of 1946–1958 in New York,* Jefferson, North Carolina: McFarland, 1990

Wilk, Max, *The Golden Age of Television: Notes from the Survivors,* New York: Delacorte Press, 1976

Roseanne (1952–)

U.S. Actor, Comedian

Roseanne (née Roseanne Barr, formerly Roseanne Arnold) is best known as the star of the situation comedy *Roseanne,* for several years the most highly rated program on American television and the centerpiece of ABC comedy programming. She was also one of the more controversial and outspoken television stars of the 1980s and 1990s. Her public statements, appearances on celebrity interview shows, and feature articles about her life in magazines and tabloid newspapers have often overshadowed her work as an actress and comedian.

When Roseanne created the lead character for the series *Roseanne,* it was based on her own comic persona, a brash, loud-mouthed, working-class mother and wife who jokes and mocks the unfairness of her situation and who is especially blunt about her views of men and sexism. First revealed to a national television audience in the mid-1980s in her stand-up routines on such late-night programs as *The Tonight Show* and in two HBO specials, Roseanne's humor aggressively attacks whomever and whatever would denigrate fat, poor women: husbands, family and friends, the media, or government welfare policies. She has often stated that her life experiences were the basis for the TV character and her comedy. Critics have described the persona as a classic example of the "unruly" woman who challenges gender and class stereotypes in her performances.

Roseanne's published self-disclosures, in her two autobiographies, provide a detailed public record of her life. She grew up in Salt Lake City, Utah, in a working-class Jewish family she has defined as "dysfunctional," a description that includes her assertions of having been sexually molested by family members. A high-school dropout, she reports getting married while still in her teens in order to get away from her family. She worked as a waitress, and, according to *People Weekly* magazine, began her comedy by being rude to her customers. Her career as a stand-up comic began in Denver, Colorado, where her club appearances gained a following among the local feminist and gay communities. She toured nationally on the comedy club circuit and made well-received appearances on late-night talk shows before starring in her own comedy specials on HBO. In 1986, the Carsey-Werner

Company approached her with a proposal for developing a situation comedy based on her stand-up routines. The show would be an antidote to the upper-middle-class wholesomeness of the previous Carsey-Werner hit, *The Cosby Show.* The popularity of her sitcom *Roseanne,* which aired from 1988 to 1997, broadened the audience for Roseanne as a public persona and greatly increased her power within show business (she has been compared to Lucille Ball in this regard).

There have been missteps, however. One highly publicized gaffe was Roseanne's off-key performance of the national anthem at a professional baseball game, a performance that ended with a crude gesture. Still, the resulting flurry of outraged criticism from public officials and in the media did not diminish the popularity of the *Roseanne* show. In another exercise of industry clout, Roseanne threatened to move her sitcom to a different network when ABC decided to cancel the low-rated *The Jackie Thomas Show,* which starred her then-husband Tom Arnold. The threat created real jitters among network executives until it was discovered that Roseanne did not own the rights to the show (only Carsey-Werner could make such a decision). Roseanne also pushed boundaries by having her series take a number of risks by raising issues of gender, homosexuality, and family dysfunction. The forthrightness of these dramatic moments is rare in prime-time sitcoms. Despite such frankness, the series continued to appeal to a wide segment of the viewing audience during its nine-year run.

The show's treatment of such charged issues was consistent with Roseanne's stated political and social views. While she did not write the scripts (for a time, Arnold was heavily involved in writing), Roseanne retained a good deal of artistic control. Many of the plots drew on aspects of her life prior to her success or referred to contemporaneous events in her "real" life. Other episodes included entire dialogues proposed by Roseanne to address specific themes or issues. The show occasionally strayed from the sitcom formula of neatly tying up all the plotlines by the end of the episode. As Kathleen Rowe notes, one year saw Darlene (Sara Gilbert), the younger daughter character, going through an early adolescent depression that continued for the entire season.

Roseanne.
Courtesy of the Everett Collection

Although the program continued to be extremely popular as it grew older, with some critics arguing that later seasons improved over earlier ones, Roseanne herself faced greater media exposure for details of her personal life (cosmetic surgery, divorce, remarriage, pregnancy) than for her political views or her career as an actor. In almost every case, she seemed able to turn such public discussions into more authority and control within the media industries. After the sitcom concluded, however, Roseanne's next major television venture, a talk show titled *The Roseanne Show,* suggested that there were limits to her power; afflicted with poor ratings and reviews, the syndicated series was canceled after less than two years on the air.

In 2003, Roseanne contributed to the reality television trend with *The Real Roseanne Show,* a "behind-the-scenes" look at another television show she was working on, a cooking and lifestyle series entitled *Domestic Goddess. The Real Roseanne Show* followed the development of *Domestic Goddess* in the studio, as

well as Roseanne's personal life during the production, with some segments filmed in her home. However, the premiere of *Domestic Goddess* was delayed when Roseanne had to undergo a hysterectomy. Under these circumstances, *The Real Roseanne Show,* already widely panned by critics and plagued with low ratings, was forced to suspend production after only two weeks on the air.

KATHRYN CIRKSENA

See also **Comedy, Domestic Settings; Family on Television; Gender and Television;** *Roseanne*

Roseanne (also known as Roseanne Barr and Roseanne Arnold). Born in Salt Lake City, Utah, November 3, 1952. Married: 1) Bill Pentland, 1974 (divorced, 1989); children: Jessica, Jennifer, Brandi, and Jake; 2) Tom Arnold, 1990 (divorced, 1994); 3) Ben Thomas, 1994 (divorced, 2002); child: Buck. Cocktail waitress in Denver, Colorado, and comedy performer in local clubs, including the Comedy Store in Los Angeles, 1985; appeared in or starred in several TV specials; star of television series *Roseanne,* 1988–97; co-executive producer, *The Jackie Thomas Show,* 1992; host of *The Roseanne Show* talk show, 1998–2000; executive producer, *The Real Roseanne Show,* 2003. Has acted in motion pictures since 1989. Recipient: Cable Ace Award, 1987; Best Comedy Special, 1987; Emmy Award, 1993.

Television Series

1988–97	*Roseanne*
1990	*Little Rosie* (voice)
1992	*The Jackie Thomas Show* (coproducer)
1998–2000	*The Roseanne Show* (host and executive producer)
2003	*The Real Roseanne Show*

Made-for-Television Movies

1991	*Backfield in Motion*
1993	*The Woman Who Loved Elvis* (also coproducer)

Television Specials

1985	*Funny*
1986	*Rodney Dangerfield: It's Not Easy Bein' Me*
1987	*Dangerfield's*
1987	*On Location: The Roseanne Barr Show*
1990	*Mary Hart Presents Love in the Public Eye*
1992	*The Rosey and Buddy Show* (voice; coproducer)
1992	*Class Clowns*

Films

She-Devil, 1989; *Look Who's Talking Too* (voice),
1990; *Freddy's Dead,* 1991; *Even Cowgirls Get the
Blues,* 1994; *Blue in the Face,* 1995; *Meet Wally
Sparks,* 1997; *Cecil B. DeMented,* 2000; *15 Minutes,* 2001.

Publications

Roseanne: My Life As a Woman, 1989
"What Am I, a Zoo?" *New York Times,* July 31, 1989
"I Am an Incest Survivor: A Star Cries Incest," *People
Weekly,* October 7, 1991
My Lives, 1994

Further Reading

Cole, Lewis, "Roseanne," *The Nation* (June 21, 1993)
Klaus, Barbara, "The War of Roseanne," *New York Times* (October 22, 1990)
Murphy, Mary, and Frank Swertlow, "The Roseanne Report," *TV Guide* (January 4, 1992)
Rowe, Kathleen, *The Unruly Woman: Gender and the Genres of Laughter,* Austin: University of Texas Press, 1995
Van Buskirk, Leslie, "The New Roseanne: The Most Powerful Woman in Television," *Us* (May 1992)
Wolcott, James, "On Television: Roseanne Hits Home," *New Yorker* (October 1992)

Roseanne

U.S. Domestic Comedy

Roseanne evolved from the stand-up comedy act and HBO special of its star and executive producer, Roseanne (formerly Roseanne Barr). In the act, Roseanne deemed herself a "domestic goddess" and dispensed mock cynical advice about child-rearing: "I figure by the time my husband comes home at night, if those kids are still alive, I've done my job." *Roseanne,* the program, built a working-class family around this matriarchal figure and became an instantaneous hit when it premiered in 1988 on ABC.

Roseanne's immediate success may well have been in reaction to the dominant 1980s domestic situation comedy, *The Cosby Show.* Like *The Cosby Show,* *Roseanne* starred an individual who began as a stand-up comic, but the families in the two programs were polar opposites. Where *The Cosby Show* portrayed a loving, prosperous family with a strong father figure, *Roseanne*'s Conner family was discordant, adamantly working class, and mother-centered.

The Conner family included Roseanne, her husband Dan (John Goodman), sister Jackie (Laurie Metcalf), daughters Darlene (Sara Gilbert) and Becky (played alternately by Lecy Goranson [1988–92, 1995–96] and Sarah Chalke [1993–95, 1996–97]), and son D.J. (Michael Fishman). Over the years the household expanded to include Becky's husband Mark (Glenn Quinn) and Darlene's boyfriend David (Johnny Galecki) and, in 1995, a

new infant for Roseanne and Dan, Jerry Garcia Conner (Cole and Morgan Roberts).

The Conners are constantly facing money problems, as both Roseanne and Dan work in blue-collar jobs: in factories; hanging sheetrock; running a motorcycle shop; and eventually owning their own diner, where they serve "loose-meat" sandwiches. Their parenting style is often sarcastic, bordering on scornful. In one episode, when the kids leave for school, Roseanne comments, "Quick. They're gone. Change the locks." But caustic remarks such as these are always balanced by scenes of affection and support, so that the stability of the family is never truly in doubt. Much as in its working-class predecessor, *All in the Family,* the Conner family is not genuinely dysfunctional, despite all the rancor.

Roseanne often tested the boundaries of network standards and practices. One episode deals with the young son's masturbation. In others, Roseanne frankly discusses birth control with Becky and explains her (Roseanne's) choice to have breast reduction surgery. The program also featured gay and lesbian characters, which made ABC nervous, especially when a lesbian character kissed Roseanne. The network initially refused to air that episode until Roseanne, the producer, demanded they do so.

Roseanne became increasingly quirky as the years went by. The final season was filled with strange episodes in which Roseanne won the lottery and lived

Roseanne, Glenn Quinn, Sarah Chalke, Roseanne, Michael Fishman, John Goodman, 1993.
Courtesy of the Everett Collection

out numerous fantasies (including one in which she imagines herself as an action figure named Roseambo). Then, in the program's last episode, Roseanne spoke directly to the viewers as the program's producer and denied the reality of the entire season, explaining that Dan had died the season before, even though he had appeared to survive a heart attack. The final season had been the character Roseanne's reveries as she struggled to deal with his death. It was a controversial, and, for some critics, an unsatisfying, way to end the program's nine-year run.

Controversy attended the program off screen as well as on. During its first season, there were well-publicized squabbles among the producing team, which led to firings and Roseanne assuming principal control of the program. Subsequently, Roseanne battled ABC over its handling of her then-husband Tom Arnold's sitcom, *The Jackie Thomas Show.* Dwarfing these professional controversies was the strife in Roseanne's publicly available personal life. Among the events that were chronicled in the tabloid press were her tumultuous marriage to and divorce from Arnold (amid accusations of spousal abuse), her reconciliation with the daughter she put up for adoption (an event that was forced by a tabloid newspaper's threat to reveal the story), her charges of being abused as a child, her struggles with addictions to food and other substances, and her misfired parody of the national anthem at a baseball game in 1990.

JEREMY G. BUTLER

See also **Comedy, Domestic Settings; Family on Television; Gender and Television**

Cast

Roseanne Conner	Roseanne
Dan Conner	John Goodman
Becky Conner (1988–92, 1995–96)	Lecy Goranson
Becky Conner (1993–95; 1996–97)	Sarah Chalke
Darlene Conner	Sara Gilbert
D.J. (David Jacob) Conner (pilot)	Sal Barone
D.J. Conner	Michael Fishman
Jackie Harris	Laurie Metcalf
Crystal Anderson (1988–92)	Natalie West
Booker Brooks (1988–89)	George Clooney
Pete Wilkins (1988–89)	Ron Perkins
Juanita Herrera (1988–89)	Evalina Fernandez
Sylvia Foster (1988–89)	Anne Falkner
Ed Conner (1989–97)	Ned Beatty
Bev Harris (1989–97)	Estelle Parsons
Mark Healy (1990–97)	Glenn Quinn
David Healy (1992–97)	Johnny Galecki
Grandma Nanna (1991–97)	Shelley Winters
Leon Carp (1991–97)	Martin Mull
Bonnie (1991–92)	Bonnie Sheridan
Nancy (1991–97)	Sandra Bernhard
Fred (1993–95)	Michael O'Keefe
Andy	Garrett and Kent Hazen
Jerry Garcia Conner	Cole and Morgan Roberts

Producers
Marcy Carsey, Tom Werner, Roseanne

Programming History
ABC

October 1988–February 1989	Tuesday 8:30–9:00
February 1989–September 1994	Tuesday 9:00–9:30
September 1994–March 1995	Wednesday 9:00–9:30
March 1995–May 1995	Wednesday 8:00–8:30
May 1995–September 1995	Wednesday 9:30–10:00
September 1995–May 1997	Wednesday 8:00–8:30

Further Reading

Arnold, Roseanne, *My Lives,* New York: Ballantine, 1994

Dresner, Zita Z., "Roseanne Barr: Goddess or She-Devil," *Journal of American Culture* (Summer 1993)

Dworkin, Susan, "Roseanne Barr: The Disgruntled Housewife as Stand-up Comedian," *Ms.* (July–August 1987)

Givens, Ron, "A Real Stand-up Mom," *Newsweek* (October 31, 1988)

Klaus, Barbara, "The War of the *Roseanne:* How I Survived Three Months in the Trenches Writing for TV's Sitcom Queen," *New York Times* (October 22, 1990)

Lee, Janet, "Subversive Sitcoms: Roseanne as Inspiration for Feminist Resistance," *Women's Studies: An Interdisciplinary Journal* (1992)

Mayerle, Judine, "Roseanne—How Did You Get Inside My House? A Case Study of a Hit Blue-Collar Situation Comedy," *Journal of Popular Culture* (Spring 1991)

Rich, Frank, "What Now My Love," *New York Times* (March 6, 1994)

Rowe, Kathleen, *The Unruly Woman: Gender and Genres of Laughter,* Austin: University of Texas Press, 1995

Volk, Patricia, "Really Roseanne," *New York Times Magazine* (August 8, 1993)

Rosenthal, Jack (1931–)

British Writer

As one of British television's most successful dramatists, Jack Rosenthal has received British Academy of Film and Television Arts Awards for *The Evacuees, Bar Mitzvah Boy, P'tang Yang Kipperbang,* and *Ready When You Are, Mr. McGill,* an Emmy Award for *The Evacuees,* and the Prix Italia for *Spend, Spend, Spend,* and *The Knowledge.* He has written for the big screen with *The Chain* and *The Knowledge,* and has also authored five plays for the live stage, notably *Smash!*

Rosenthal learned the craft of writing for the medium of television in the 1960s, at a time when television drama in Britain (particularly on the BBC) was still dominated by writers schooled in theatrical conventions and overly concerned with being taken seriously. This resulted in a preoccupation with adaptations of theatrical successes, revivals of classics (e.g., Shakespeare, Dickens), and writing that exploited literary rather than visual resources. Independent television in the late 1950s was looking to develop more popular forms of drama to attract wider audiences and brought in Sydney Newman from Canada, who fostered new dramatists and initiated new series. It was against this background that Rosenthal started work in Granada, where he served his apprenticeship by creating more than 150 scripts for the popular TV soap *Coronation Street.* The experience of writing for a popular genre prepared him for originating such comedy serials as *The Dustbinmen, The Lovers,* and *Sadie, It's Cold Outside.* His growing reputation in the 1970s as a reliable professional writer led to his being entrusted with the prestigious single play: a form that Rosenthal himself prefers because of the freedom it offers the artist to explore his own vision.

Rosenthal was born in Manchester to Jewish parents, and he drew on his experiences to write *Bar Mitzvah Boy* and *The Evacuees.* But his interest lies in observing the interactions of individuals in diverse social networks, and the Jewish community is merely one of the many institutions that he explores: schools (*P'tang Yang Kippperbang*), taxi drivers (*The Knowledge*), the army (*Bootse and Snudge*), fire fighters (*London's Burning*), and TV drama (*Ready When You Are, Mr. McGill*). He is also interested in the common experiences that many face at particular moments in life: moving (*The Chain*), growing up (*Bar Mitzvah Boy, P'tang Yang Kippperbang*), falling in love (*The Lovers*), and forgetfulness and old age (*A Day to Remember*).

The strength of Rosenthal's comedy lies in its closeness to tragedy; from another perspective, the petty cruelties of the stepmother in *The Evacuees* could have blighted the lives of the children, but both plot and psychological insight combine to restore harmony and recognize the cruelty as misplaced possessiveness. So too,

Jack Rosenthal.
Photo courtesy of Jack Rosenthal

in *A Day to Remember,* the terror and pain of short-term memory loss, attendant on a stroke in old age, are contained and balanced by the comic presentation of the gaps and imperfections that beset the middle-aged. If the comic vision is shown as perceptive about the frailties of the human condition, it is not sentimentalized. The insight that comes through comedy is one that is often painfully achieved. The schoolboy hero of *P'tang Yang Kipperbang* is only able to kiss his first love; he enters upon adult sexuality by recognizing the fantasy element of that anticipated delight. To fulfill his desire means abandoning private fantasy and entering the real world in which people are both less than we would wish and more diverse than we could expect. Similarly, when the aspirant cabby in *The Knowledge* finally achieves his ambition to be a London taxi driver, he discovers his girlfriend, the initial driving force behind his application, has fallen for somebody else. He neglected her to focus on the discipline of acquiring "the knowledge" (learning by heart the streets and landmarks of London by perpetually driving around them). Knowledge of chaps rather than maps turns out to be that which is most difficult to acquire.

Although the comedy of Jack Rosenthal is invariably rooted in a recognizable social setting that has been carefully researched, the characters are not deeply explored. The story is, instead, focused on the themes: in *Another Sunday and Sweet FA,* the frustrations of refereeing a football match provide the opportunity for a comic disquisition on the competing claims of power and justice; in *P'tang Yang Kipperbang,* imagination and reality struggle for an accommodation; in *The Chain,* the seven deadly sins provide the motivation for Fortuna's wheel of house-hunting. If there is a thread that underlies most of Rosenthal's work, it is that our desire as individuals to do good in order to be liked and admired is at variance with our role as social beings to impose order, our order, on others. Wisdom comes when we learn to accommodate these competing demands and accept responsibility for fulfilling our desires.

BRENDAN KENNY

See also **Coronation Street; That Was the Week That Was**

Jack Morris Rosenthal. Born in Manchester, England, September 8, 1931. Attended Colne Grammar School; Sheffield University, B.A. in English language and literature; University of Salford, M.A., 1994. Married: Maureen Lipman, 1973; one son and one daughter. Writer for television; subsequently consolidated reputation with comedy series and one-off dramas, several of which were pilots for series. Commander of the Order of the British Empire, 1994. D.Litt., University of Manchester, 1995. Recipient: British Academy of Film and Television Arts Writer's Awards; Emmy Award; Prix Italia; Royal Television Society Writer's Award, 1976; British Academy of Film and Television Arts Best Play Awards, 1976, 1977.

Television Series

1960–	*Coronation Street*
1962–63	*That Was the Week That Was*
1965	*Pardon the Expression*
1969–70	*The Dustbinmen*
1970–71	*The Lovers*
1975	*Sadie, It's Cold Outside*
1994	*Moving Story*

Television Specials

1963	*Pie in the Sky*
1963	*Green Rub*
1968	*There's a Hole in Your Dustbin, Delilah*
1972	*Another Sunday and Sweet FA*
1974	*Polly Put the Kettle On*
1974	*Mr. Ellis Versus the People*
1974	*There'll Almost Always Be an England*
1975	*The Evacuees*
1976	*Ready When You Are, Mr. McGill*
1976	*Bar Mitzvah Boy*
1977	*Spend, Spend, Spend*
1979	*Spaghetti Two-Step*
1979	*The Knowledge*
1982	*P'tang Yang Kipperbang*
1985	*Mrs. Capper's Birthday*
1986	*Fools on the Hill*
1986	*London's Burning*
1986	*A Day to Remember*
1989	*And a Nightingale Sang*
1989	*Bag Lady*
1991	*Sleeping Sickness*
1992	*'Bye, 'Bye, Baby*
1993	*Wide-Eyed and Legless*
1996	*Eskimo Jim*
2003	*Lucky Jim*

Films

Lucky Star, 1980; *Yentl* (with Barbra Streisand), 1983; *The Chain,* 1985; *Captain Jack,* 1999.

Stage (selected)

Smash!, 1981.

Publications

The Television Dramatist (with others), 1973
*Three Award Winning Television Plays: Bar Mitzvah
Boy, The Evacuees, Spend, Spend, Spend,* 1978

First Loves: Stories (anthology), 1984
The Chain, with *The Knowledge,* and *Ready When
You Are, Mr. McGill,* 1986.

Route 66

U.S. Drama

Route 66 was one of the most unique American television dramas of the 1960s, an ostensible adventure series that functioned, in practice, as an anthology of downbeat character studies and psychological dramas. Its 1960 premiere launched two young drifters in a Corvette on an existential odyssey in which they encountered a myriad of loners, dreamers, and outcasts in the small towns and big cities along U.S. Highway 66 and beyond. And the settings were real; the gritty social realism of the stories was enhanced by location shooting that moved beyond the Hollywood hills and studio back lots to encompass the vast face of the country itself. *Route 66* took the anthology on the road, blending the dramaturgy and dramatic variety of the *Studio One* school of TV drama with the independent filmmaking practices of the New Hollywood.

Route 66 was the brainchild of producer Herbert B. Leonard and writer Stirling Silliphant, the same creative team responsible for *Naked City.* The two conceived the show as a vehicle for actor George Maharis, casting him as stormy Lower East Side orphan Buz Murdock, opposite Martin Milner as boyish, Yale-educated Tod Stiles. When Tod's father dies, broke but for a Corvette, the two young men set out on the road looking for "a place to put down roots." Amid a dispute with the show's producers, Maharis left the show in 1963 and was replaced by Glenn Corbett as Linc Case, a troubled Vietnam vet also seeking meaning on the road.

Like *Naked City,* which producer Leonard had conceived as an anthology with a cop-show pretext, the picaresque premise of *Route 66* provided the basis for a variety of weekly encounters from which the stories arose. Episodes emphasized the personal and psychological dramas of the various troubled souls encountered by the guys on their stops along the highway. Guest roles were filled by an array of Hollywood

faces, from such fading stars as Joan Crawford and Buster Keaton to newcomers such as Suzanne Pleshette, Robert Duvall, and Robert Redford. The show's distinct anthology-style dimension was symptomatic of a trend *Variety* dubbed "the semi-anthology," a form pioneered by *Wagon Train* and refined by such shows as *Bus Stop* and *Route 66.* The series' nomadic premise, and its virtual freedom from genre connections and constraints, opened it up to a potentially limitless variety of stories. While the wandering theme was hardly new in a television terrain overrun with westerns, for a contemporary drama the premise was quite innovative. *Route 66* was consistent in tone to the rest of TV's serious, social-realist dramas of the period, but it was unencumbered by any predetermined dramatic arena or generic template—setting it apart from the likes of *The Defenders* (courtroom drama), *Dr. Kildare* (medical drama), *Saints and Sinners* (newspaper drama), or *Mr. Novak* (blackboard drama). Indeed, the show's creators met initial resistance from their partner/distributor Screen Gems for this lack of a familiar "franchise," with studio executives arguing that no one would sponsor a show about two "bums." Of course, Chevrolet proved them wrong.

Perhaps even more startling for the Hollywood-bound telefilm industry was the program's radical location agenda. Buz and Tod's cross-country search actually was shot across the country, in what *Newsweek* termed "the largest weekly mobile operation in TV history." Remarkably, by the end of its four-season run, the *Route 66* production caravan had traveled to 25 states—as far from Los Angeles as Maine and Florida—as well as Toronto. The show's stark black-and-white photography and spectacular locations provided a powerful backdrop to its downbeat stories and yielded a photographic and geographical realism that has never been duplicated on American television.

Route 66, Martin Milner, George Maharis, 1960–64.
Courtesy of the Everett Collection

The literate textures and disturbing tones of *Route 66*'s dramas were as significant as its visual qualities. The wandering pretext provided both a thematic foundation and a narrative trajectory upon which a variety of psychological dramas, social-problem stories, and character studies could be played out. The nominal series "heroes" generally served as observers to the dramas of others: a tormented jazz musician, a heroin addict, a washed-up prizefighter, migrant farm workers, an aging RAF pilot (turned crop-duster), a runaway heiress, Cajun shrimpers, a weary hobo, an eccentric scientist, a small-time beauty contest promoter, drought-stricken ranchers, Cuban-Basque jai-alai players, a recent ex-con (female and framed), a grim Nazi-hunter, a blind dance instructor, a dying blues singer—each facing some personal crisis or secret pain.

The show's continuing thread of wandering probed the restlessness at the root of all picaresque sagas of contemporary American popular culture. The search that drove *Route 66* was both a narrative process and a symbolic one. Like every search, it entailed optimism as well as discontent. The unrest at the core of the series echoed that of the Beats—especially Jack Kerouac's *On the Road,* of course—and anticipated the

even more disaffected searchers of *Easy Rider.* The show's rejection of domesticity in favor of rootlessness formed a rather startling counterpoint to the dominant prime-time landscape of home and family in the 1960s, as did the majority of the characters encountered on the road. The more hopeful dimension of *Route 66* coincided with the optimism of the New Frontier circa 1960, with these wandering Samaritans symbolic of the era's new spirit of activism. Premiering at the dawn of a new decade, *Route 66* captured in a singular way the nation's passage from the disquiet of the 1950s to the turbulence of the 1960s, expressing a simultaneously troubled and hopeful vision of the United States.

Despite its uniqueness as a contemporary social drama, and its radical break from typical Hollywood telefilm factory practice, *Route 66* has been largely forgotten amid the rhetoric of 1960s' TV-as-wasteland. When the series is cited at all by television historians, it is as the target of CBS-TV president James Aubrey's attempts to inject more "broads, bosoms, and fun" into the series ("the Aubrey dictum"). Aubrey's admitted attempts to "lighten" the show, however, only serve to underscore its dominant tone of seriousness. What other American television series of the 1960s could have been described by its writer-creator as "a show about a statement of existence, closer to Sartre and Kafka than to anything else"? (see "The Fingers of God," *Time*). Silliphant's hyperbole is tempered by critic Philip Booth, who suggested in a *Television Quarterly* essay that the show's literacy was "sometime spurious," and that it could "trip on its own pretensions" in five of every ten stories. Still, Booth wrote, of the remaining episodes, four "will produce a kind of adventure like nothing else on television, and one can be as movingly universal as Hemingway's 'A Clean, Well-Lighted Place.'"

How often *Route 66* matched the power of Ernest Hemingway (or the existential insight of Jean-Paul Sartre) is debatable. That it was attempting something completely original in television drama is certain. Its footloose production was the antithesis of the claustrophobic stages of the New York anthologies of old, yet many of the program's dramatic and thematic concerns—even certain of its stories—echoed those of the intimate character dramas of the *Philco Playhouse* era. Indeed, one of Aubrey's CBS lieutenants, concerned with the show's "downbeat" approach to television entertainment, protested to its producers that *Route 66* should not be considered "a peripatetic *Playhouse 90*"—capturing, willingly or not, much of the show's tenor and effect. *Route 66* was trying to achieve the right mix of familiarity and difference, action and angst, pathos and psychology, working innovative elements into a commercial package keyed to the demands of the industry context. Even with its gleaming roadster, jazzy theme song, obligatory fistfights, and occasional romantic entanglements, *Route 66* was far removed indeed (both figuratively and geographically) from the likes of *77 Sunset Strip.*

In 1993, the Corvette took to the highway once more in a nominal sequel, a summer series (on NBC) that put Buz's illegitimate son at the wheel with a glib Generation-X partner in the passenger seat. Although the new *Route 66* lasted only a few weeks, by reviving the roaming-anthology premise of the original, it evinced television's continuing quest for narrative flexibility (and Hollywood's inherent penchant for recycling). From *The Fugitive* to *Run For Your Life* to *Highway to Heaven* to *Quantum Leap* to *Touched by an Angel,* television has continued to exploit the tradition of the wandering Samaritan, to achieve the story variety of an anthology within a series format. *Route 66* established the template in 1960, launching a singular effort at contemporary drama in a nonformulaic series format. That the series mounted its dramatic agenda in a Corvette, on the road, is to its creators' everlasting credit.

MARK ALVEY

See also **Silliphant, Stirling**

Cast

Tod Stiles	Martin Milner
Buz Murdock (1960–63)	George Maharis
Linc Case (1963–64)	Glenn Corbett

Producers
Herbert B. Leonard, Jerry Thomas, Leonard Freeman, Sam Manners

Programming History
116 episodes
CBS
October 1960–September 1964   Friday 8:30–9:30

Further Reading

Barnouw, Erik, *Tube of Plenty: The Evolution of American Television,* New York: Oxford University Press, 1975; 2nd revised edition, 1990

Bergreen, Laurence, *Look Now, Pay Later: The Rise of Network Broadcasting,* Garden City, New York: Doubleday, 1980

Booth, Philip, "*Route 66*—On the Road Toward People," *Television Quarterly* (Winter 1963)

Castelman, Harry, and Walter Podrazik, *Watching TV: Four Decades of American Television,* New York: McGraw-Hill, 1982

Chandler, Bob, "Review of *Route 66,*" *Variety* (October 12, 1960)

Dunne, John Gregory, "Take Back Your Kafka," *New Republic* (September 4, 1965)

"The Fingers of God," *Time* (August 9, 1963)

"Have Camera, Will Travel," *Variety* (October 12, 1960)

"The Hearings that Changed Television," *Telefilm* (July–August 1962)

Jarvis, Jeff, "The Couch Critic," *TV Guide* (June 12, 1993)

Jenkins, Dan, "Talk About Putting a Show on the Road!" *TV Guide* (July 22, 1961)

"A Knock Develops on *Route 66,*" *TV Guide* (January 26, 1963)

"Rough Road," *Newsweek* (January 2, 1961)

Seldes, Gilbert, "Review of *Route 66,*" *TV Guide* (February 10, 1962)

Rowan and Martin's Laugh-In

U.S. Comedy-Variety Program

Rowan and Martin's Laugh-In was an NBC comedy-variety program that became an important training ground for a generation of comic talent. If *The Smothers Brothers Comedy Hour* captured the political earnestness and moral conscience of the 1960s counterculture, *Laugh-In* snared the decade's flamboyance, its anarchic energy, and its pop aesthetic, combining the blackout comedy of the vaudeville tradition with a 1960s-style "happening."

In an age of "sit-ins," "love-ins" and "teach-ins," NBC was proposing a "laugh-in" that somehow bridged generational gaps. Originally a one-shot special, *Laugh-In* was an immediate hit and quickly became the highest-rated series of the late 1960s. In a decade of shouted slogans, bumper stickers, and protest signs, *Laugh-In* translated its comedy into discrete one-liners hurled helter-skelter at the audience in hopes that some of them would prove funny. Many of

Rowan and Martin's Laugh-In.
Photo courtesy of George Schlatter Productions

them became catchphrases: "Sock it to me," "Here come de judge," "You bet your sweet bippy," and "Look that up in your *Funk and Wagnalls.*" In this frenetic and fragmented series, comic lines were run as announcements along the bottom of the screen, printed in lurid colors on the bodies of bikini-clad go-go girls, and shouted over the closing credits. The humor was sometimes topical, sometimes nonsensical, sometimes "right on" and sometimes right of center, but it largely escaped the censorship problems that besieged the Smothers Brothers. Its helter-skelter visual style stretched the capabilities of television and videotape production, striving for the equivalent of the cutting and optical effects Richard Lester brought to the Beatles movies.

Laugh-In broke down the traditional separation of comedy, musical performance, and dramatic interludes that had marked most earlier variety shows and decentered the celebrity hosts from their conventional position as mediator of the flow of entertainment. Dan Rowan and Dick Martin, successful Las Vegas entertainers, sought to orchestrate the proceedings but were constantly swamped by the flow of sight gags and eccentric performances that surrounded them. Similarly, guest stars played no privileged role here. For a time, everyone seemed to want to appear on *Laugh-In,* with guests on one memorable episode including Jack Lemmon, Zsa Zsa Gabor, Hugh Hefner, and presidential candidate Richard Nixon. But no guest appeared for more than a few seconds at a time, and none received

the kind of screen time grabbed by the program's ensemble of talented young clowns.

The comic regulars—Gary Owens's overmodulated announcer, Ruth Buzzi's perpetually frustrated spinster, Arte Johnson's lecherous old man, Goldie Hawn's dizzy blonde, Jo Anne Worley's anti-Chicken-Joke militant, Henry Gibson's soft-spokenly banal poet, Lily Tomlin's snorting telephone operator, Pigmeat Markham's all-powerful Judge, and countless others—dominated the program. Many of these comics moved almost overnight from total unknowns to household names, and many became important stars for the subsequent decades. Not until *Saturday Night Live* would another television variety show ensemble leave such a firm imprint on the evolution of American comedy. These recurring characters and their associated shtick gave an element of familiarity and predictability to a program that otherwise depended upon its sense of the unexpected.

While *Laugh-In* lacks the satirical bite of later series such as *Saturday Night Live* or *In Living Color,* or of *That Was the Week That Was* (to which it was often compared by contemporary critics), *Laugh-In* brought many minority and female performers to mainstream audiences, helping to broaden the composition of television comedy. Its dependence upon stock comic characters and catchphrases was clearly an influence on the development of *Saturday Night Live,* which by comparison, has a much more staid visual style and more predictable structure. Unfortunately, *Laugh-In*'s topicality, even its close fit with 1960s aesthetics, has meant that the program has not fared well in reruns, being perceived as dated almost from the moment it was aired. However, the ongoing success of *Laugh-In* alums such as Hawn, Tomlin, or even game show host Richard Dawson point to its continued influence.

HENRY JENKINS

See also **Variety Programs**

Regular Performers
Dan Rowan
Dick Martin
Gary Owens
Ruth Buzzi
Judy Carne (1968–70)
Eileen Brennan (1968)
Goldie Hawn (1968–70)
Arte Johnson (1968–71)
Henry Gibson (1968–71)
Roddy-Maude Roxby (1968)
Jo Anne Worley (1968–70)
Larry Hovis (1968, 1971–72)
Pigmeat Markham (1968–69)

Charlie Brill (1968–69)
Dick Whittington (1968–69)
Mitzi McCall (1968–69)
Chelsea Brown (1968–69)
Alan Sues (1968–72)
Dave Madden (1968–69)
Teresa Graves (1969–70)
Jeremy Lloyd (1969–70)
Pamela Rodgers (1969–70)
Byron Gilliam (1969–70)
Ann Elder (1970–72)
Lily Tomlin (1970–73)
Johnny Brown (1970–72)
Dennis Allen (1970–73)
Nancy Phillips (1970–71)
Barbara Sharma (1970–72)
Harvey Jason (1970–71)
Richard Dawson (1971–73)
Moosie Drier (1971–73)
Patti Deutsch (1972–73)
Jud Strunk (1972–73)
Brian Bressler (1972–73)

Sarah Kennedy (1972–73)
Donna Jean Young (1972–73)
Tod Bass (1972–73)
Lisa Farringer (1972–73)
Willie Tyler and Lester (1972–73)

Producers
George Schlatter, Paul W. Keyes, Carolyn Raskin

Programming History
124 episodes
NBC
January l968–May 1973   Monday 8:00–9:00

Further Reading

Castleman, Harry, and Walter J. Podrazik, *Watching TV: Four Decades of American Television,* New York: McGraw-Hill, 1982
Rowan, Dan, *A Friendship: The Letters of Dan Rowan and John D. McDonald, 1967–1974,* New York: Knopf, 1986
Waters, Harry R., "Laugh-In," *Newsweek* (February 8, 1993)

Royal Canadian Air Farce, The

Canadian Satirical Review

On December 9, 1973, the first radio show by the Royal Canadian Air Farce comedy troupe was broadcast coast-to-coast on CBC Radio and CBC Stereo. After a ten-episode series in 1981 and several specials in the 1980s, *The Royal Canadian Air Farce*—a Canadian institution for political commentary, social satire, and general nonsense—became a weekly CBC television series in the fall of 1993. Like the radio show, the television *Air Farce* is topical, on the edge of controversy, and performed in front of a live audience. The group consists of Roger Abbot, Don Ferguson, and Luba Goy. John Morgan performed with the troupe until retiring in 2001, at the end of the series' eighth television season. Dave Broadfoot was a member of the troupe for 15 years before moving on to a solo career; he has continued to make guest appearances since leaving the troupe. Two nonperforming writers, Rick Olsen and Gord Holtam, have been with the troupe since 1977.

In 1992, the group became the first Canadian in-ductees into the International Humour Hall of Fame. The editors of *Maclean's* (Canada's national news magazine) chose the *Air Farce* for the 1991 Honour Roll of Canadians who make a difference. The group has won 15 ACTRA Awards (Association of Canadian Television and Radio Artists) for radio and television writing and performing, and a Juno Award (Canadian recording award) for best comedy album. In 1993, Abbott, Ferguson, and Goy were each awarded honorary doctor of law degrees by Brock University in St. Catharines.

The *Air Farce* keeps in touch with Canadians and ensures that the troupe's humor remains relevant by performing and recording in all ten provinces and two territories. For several years the troupe worked on both radio and television. "We're reluctant to give up radio," Ferguson told *Toronto Star* journalist Phil Johnson. "Radio allows us to showcase new acts and characters." However, after 24 years, the troupe broadcast its last radio program on May 25, 1997. They generally play in halls that hold 2,000 or 2,500 people, and did so even when taping for radio. This approach creates the need for more visual interest. "I did [former Prime Minister] Brian Mulroney for 20 years—the worst years of my life I might add," Ferguson told *Globe and Mail* columnist Liam Lacey. "On-stage, I'd have a long walk over to the microphone, so I'd start from the side of the stage with just the chin first, and then the stuck-out bum would follow. The audiences would be roaring before I reached the microphone. Then we'd edit all that out, and cut to the voice."

When the Air Farce first tried a television show in 1981, it was shot in advance and produced with canned laughter. The lack of live performance and topicality destroyed the spontaneity that is at the heart of the *Farce,* and the show failed. Then in 1993, a New Year's Eve special was made, raking in 2 million viewers, almost 10 percent of the entire Canadian population. Network executive Ivan Fecan approved a series. It became one of the top-20 Canadian shows and one of the CBC's top five.

Rather than leaning toward a particular point of view, the Farce points fingers at all parties. Skewered politicians and media figures regularly show up in person to do sketches on the show. Individual performers do not even know how the other members of the group vote and would not dream of discussing it. As Liam Lacey wrote in noting that the *Farce* receives indirect governmental support (by virtue of its airing on the public network CBC), "One would be hard-pressed to imagine another country in the world where purveyors of official disrespect would be regarded with such widespread affection." Dave Broadfoot used to say, "Do you know what they'd call us in the Soviet Union? Inmates."

JANICE KAYE

See also **Canadian Programming in English**

Regular Performers
Roger Abbot
Don Ferguson
Luba Goy
John Morgan (retired 2001)
Dave Broadfoot (left 1988)

Programming History (television only)
CBC
1980	one-hour special
February–April 1981	ten episodes
January 31, 1992	"1992 Year of the Farce Special"
October 8, 1993–	weekly series

Further Reading

Turbide, Diane, "The Air Farce Is Flying High," *Maclean's* (February 26, 1996)

Royalty and Royals on Television

The relationship between television and the royalty of the United Kingdom and other states has always been uneasy, albeit generally mutually respectful, as the perceived dangers to both sides have been immense. With television audiences of grand royal occasions and major documentaries running into many millions around the globe, the impact of a mishandled interview could have serious political repercussions for any monarchy, as well as huge public relations problems for television networks anxious not to outrage public opinion.

The idea that members of the British royal family might allow themselves to be seen on television in any capacity other than at the end of a long-range lens in the course of a formal state occasion or fleetingly in newsreel footage was once considered unthinkable. In the early days, immediately after World War II, television was regarded by many in the establishment as too trivial to be taken seriously, and it was argued that it was inappropriate for heads of nations to appear on TV. In Britain Sir Winston Churchill was in the vanguard of those who considered television a vulgar plaything and beneath the dignity of the crown.

The crunch came in 1953, when it was suggested that television cameras be allowed to film the coronation of Elizabeth II. Churchill, the archbishop of Canterbury, the earl marshal, and various members of the British cabinet strongly opposed the idea, but, to their surprise, the 26-year-old Princess Elizabeth, in a decision subsequently hailed for its sagacity, insisted upon the rest of the nation being able to witness her enthronement via television, and the cameras were allowed in. The resulting broadcast, expertly narrated by the BBC's anchorman Richard Dimbleby, was a triumph, bringing the monarchy into the television age and cementing the image of Elizabeth II as a "people's monarch."

Following the 1953 coronation experiment, it became accepted that the television cameras would be permitted to film grand royal occasions, including weddings, the state opening of Parliament, and the trooping of the color, as well as jubilee celebrations, visits by the royal family to local businesses, and so forth. Coverage of royal events, however, remained a sensitive area in broadcasting, and many rows erupted when it was felt cameras had intruded too far or, conversely, that too much deference had been shown. Certain presenters, including ITV's Alistair Burnet and the BBC's Raymond Baxter, specialized in coverage of royal stories or spectacles, but found they had to tread a very thin line between being accused of sycophancy or charged with gross insensitivity.

The British queen is sheltered from more intrusive interrogation on television by necessity: there is a constitutional imperative that the monarch should not comment personally on the policies of her government because of the implications this might have in terms of party politics, and because of this rule, Buckingham Palace, in concert with the government of the day, closely controls the style and content of all broadcasts in which she appears. In 1969, an attempt was made for the first time, in the joint BBC and ITV production *Royal Family,* to portray Queen Elizabeth as a private person rather than as a constitutional figurehead. The program attracted an audience of 40 million in the United Kingdom alone, and similarly large audiences have watched her celebrated annual Christmas broadcasts, which have over the years become more relaxed in tone, inspiring further occasional documentaries inviting the cameras "behind the scenes" (though, again, only under strict direction from the palace).

There is more leeway in television coverage of other members of the royal family; however, this has been exploited with increasing vigor since the 1980s, in response to changing public attitudes toward royalty. Prince Philip's hectoring manner during rare appearances on chat shows did little to endear television audiences, and he was henceforth discouraged from taking part in such programs. Princess Anne developed a similarly tempestuous relationship with the media as a whole, though she was better received after her good works for charity won public recognition. Prince Andrew came over as bluff and hearty, and Prince Edward was considered affable enough—though there were adverse comments about loss of dignity in 1987 when

The Prince and Princess of Wales.
Courtesy of the Everett Collection

the three youngest of the queen's children attempted to sound a populist note by appearing in a special *It's a Knockout* program for charity (royal guests stormed out of press meetings when the questioning became hostile, and the experiment was not repeated).

After years of carefully treading the line between deference and public interest, television's relationship with the British royals was stretched to the limit in the 1990s during the furor surrounding the break-up of several royal marriages, notably that of the heir-apparent, Prince Charles (whose wedding to Lady Diana Spencer had been seen by 700 million people worldwide in 1981). A notorious interview with Princess Diana that was broadcast on *Panorama,* when it was becoming clear that the rift was irreparable (though many still hoped the marriage could be saved), provoked howls of protest from many quarters—not least from the palace itself. Charles was given his own program in which to tell his side of the story, but he only succeeded in drawing more fire upon himself and his family. For many viewers, both interviews were enthralling, though to others they were distasteful and reflected badly both on the individuals themselves and on the institution of the monarchy.

A severe test of the relationship between television and the British royal family came in 1997, when Diana, Princess of Wales, died in a car accident in Paris. The media's coverage of the tragedy and of the national trauma that ensued provoked intense debate. The fact that, initially at least, press photographers pursuing the princess's car were blamed for the crash heightened the feeling that all members of the media should behave more responsibly when covering the royal family. From the moment that the first shots of the tangled wreckage of the princess's car were transmitted, it became clear that broadcasters would have to behave with the utmost sensitivity. As the extent of public sympathy for the dead princess emerged, it was quickly realized that Buckingham Palace's wishes would have to take second place to national sentiment. The accident and its aftermath received blanket coverage on all channels, and the royal family itself was obliged, with evident reluctance, to obey the dictates of the cameras.

The failure of the queen to sanction any immediate public expression of grief over the disgraced princess's death was a public relations mistake, although the parading of the princess's sons before the cameras at their mother's funeral did something to deflect hostility. The impression of most viewers was that the palace had mishandled things badly and needed to overhaul its public relations policy. With the funeral over and schedules back to normal, the verdict on how television covered events was that it had faced the challenge rather better than the royals, managing to avoid insensitive sensationalization of the tragedy while still reflecting the public mood.

In the wake of Diana's death, there has been some reform of the relationship between the royal family and the media, but there is still tension. In 2001, with press attention to Diana's son Prince William escalating, the royal family was caused particular embarrassment when a video company in which Prince Edward had an interest was accused of breaking an embargo on filming William while at university. The company was severely criticized and subsequently announced it would no longer undertake filming of the royal family.

Other monarchies have experienced not dissimilar difficulties in their relations with television and other organs of the media. For a number of years, the Rainiers of Monaco, for instance, seemed to live their lives in the constant glare of the cameras. Some, however, have protected themselves by insisting that the cameras remain at a discreet distance (as in Japan, where the emperor is only rarely filmed), despite the demands imposed by unflagging public interest.

Television's fascination with royalty has expressed itself in other forms besides coverage of contemporary royals, notably in the field of drama. The BBC in particular won worldwide acclaim in the late 1960s and 1970s for lavish costume series dealing with Henry VIII, Elizabeth I, Edward VII, and, rather more controversially, Edward VIII. More recently, a documentary series in which Prince Edward delved into the lives of some of his royal ancestors was also well received.

DAVID PICKERING

See also **Parliament, Coverage by Television; Political Processes and Television**

Royle Family, The

British Sitcom

Just when critics in the United Kingdom were pronouncing that the British sitcom was dead, *The Royle Family* restored faith in the genre. Not only was it critically acclaimed, but ratings were high, with around ten million viewers at its peak. In its brief run between 1997 and 2000, the show managed to become part of the fabric of British culture, much like the best sitcoms of the past, such as *Till Death Us Do Part* and *Whatever Happened to The Likely Lads?* Part of the success

of *The Royle Family* lay in its contradictions. It was that most traditional of TV staples, the family sitcom, but was it hugely innovative. It showed modern Britain, but remained strangely old-fashioned. It said something about the world, but hardly ever moved away from one living room in Manchester.

The series was created by Caroline Aherne and Craig Cash, who drew on their own backgrounds to forge a new kind of family sitcom. Aherne was already a big name in British comedy through her persona as Mrs. Merton, a deceptively sweet old lady who interviewed and frequently humiliated minor celebrities. Instead of the usual weary plots, she based the new series firmly on the characters and their interactions, saying "I knew that if you strip it bare and have funny characters and love in it, it would work."

Nothing special happens in *The Royle Family,* and that is the point of the show. There are a few major life events, such as weddings or births, but mostly the Royles just sit round the television and talk. Dad Jim is coarse, miserly, and hypocritical, while the mother, Barbara, is kind, loyal, and slightly dim. Daughter Denise (played by creator Aherne) is idle, while the nice son Anthony, is put upon and long suffering. Son-in-law Dave lends a constant air of dull stupidity to the proceedings, as does Barbara's whining mother Norma. Occasionally friends, like the Carrolls who live next door, visit. For the audience, the lack of action quickly ceases to be a problem because it becomes the expectation. The audience understands that the pleasures of the series are in magnifying humdrum reality.

Executives originally insisted on a studio audience, but a test episode proved disastrous, so it was dropped. Also out are harsh studio lighting and the theatrical performance conventions of television sitcom. The Royles' sitting room, the center of all the episodes, is beautifully shot on film in a documentary style. The actors rely on laughs from the smallest facial expression or verbal quirk, which allows the complexities of the characters to be gradually revealed to the audience. Unlike many sitcoms, the quality of acting is as good in minor roles (such as Jessica Stevenson as Denise's friend Cheryl) as it is in the leads. Perhaps as a result of the success of *The Royle Family,* these innovations are becoming the norm in U.K. TV comedy.

The Royle Family is also important in its understanding of the role the media plays in our lives. Previously TV programs existed in a parallel universe, where people never watched TV themselves nor were affected by it. Here the characters are not only watching television, they are also talking about it. The audience at home is watching a show about a family watching television. The mirror image is constantly there to challenge the viewer.

For all the formal innovation and self-reflection, however, the success of the series is also a result of its affirmation of traditional British sitcom virtues. There is an air of melancholy underlying the laughter. People are held back by their flaws, by bad luck, and by society, but they have the strength to endure.

In many ways *The Royle Family* echoes the classic 1960s program *Till Death Us Do Part.* Like Alf Garnett, Jim Royle captured the mood of the nation.

The Royle Family, Caroline Aherne, Craig Cash, Ralf Little, Ricky Tomlinson, Sue Johnston, 1998–2000.
Courtesy of the Everett Collection

Ricky Tomlinson's portrayal of an obnoxious but witty slob ("with more faces than the town hall clock") was hugely popular. British audiences treasured him as a wry comment on what they suspected they had become.

The family became popular at a time when some claimed the English working class no longer existed, or had become reactionary. Aherne is affectionate but not uncritical about the reality of life in the north of England. Inevitably a few critics (invariably middle class themselves) accused her of being condescending, but she was speaking from her own experience. Only on very rare occasions (the baby's middle name is Keanu) is there a false note.

The general critical consensus was that the program declined over the three series. The show could feel repetitive, but even so it still dared to challenge its audience. In the third series, for example, Denise's neglect of her baby and Jim's bullying of Anthony were highlighted. Aherne was brave enough to give these actions a comic aspect, but there is also a deep sense of unease. Even so, at no time does she moralize or go for cheap laughs.

Eventually, and probably wisely, Caroline Aherne pulled the plug on the show. Tired of media intrusion into her private life, she announced her retirement from performing and moved to Australia.

The Royle Family imparted a much-needed freshness to the sitcom genre and proved it could be popular once more. It reminded us that sitcoms could be profound about the human condition and command the highest quality in writing, camera work, and performance. It also offered a shared pleasure at a time when the viewing public seemed irredeemably fragmented.

PHIL WICKHAM

*See also **Till Death Do Us Part***

Cast

Jim Royle	Ricky Tomlinson
Barbara Royle	Sue Johnston
Denise Royle/Best	Caroline Aherne
Anthony Royle	Ralf Little
Dave Best	Craig Cash
Norma	Liz Smith
Cheryl Carroll	Jessica Stevenson
Mary Carroll	Noreen Keogh
Joe Carroll	Peter Martin
Twiggy	Geoffrey Hughes
Emma	Sheridan Smith

Writers

Caroline Aherne and Craig Cash with Henry Normal (series 1) and Carmel Morgan (1999 Christmas Special)

Directors

Series 1	Mark Mylod
Series 2	Steve Bendelack
Series 3	Caroline Aherne

Producers

Series 1	Glenn Wilhide
Series 2	Kenton Allen
Series 3	Kenton Allen and Caroline Aherne

Executive Producer

Andy Harries

Programming History

18 episodes and two Christmas specials
The program started on BBC 2 but after the success of the first series was switched to BBC 1. The second series premiered on BBC 1 with a repeat on BBC 2 later in the week.

Series 1 (six episodes)	BBC 2 September–October 1998
Series 2 (six episodes)	BBC 1 September–October 1999
Christmas special 1999 (40 minutes)	
Series 3 (six episodes)	BBC 1 October–November 2000
Christmas special 2000 (30 minutes)	

Further Reading

Aherne, Caroline, Craig Cash, and Henry Normal, *The Royle Family Scripts: Series 1,* London: Granada Media, 1999
Christiansen, Rupert, "Comedy of a Different Class," *Daily Telegraph* (London; December 20, 1999)
Lewis-Smith, Victor, "Royles Have the Last Laugh," *Evening Standard* (London; February 10, 2000)
Parker, Ian, "They Shout 'Arses' Don't They," *Observer* (London; September 20, 1998)
Raven, Charlotte, "Class of '98," *Guardian* (London; September 17, 1998)

Rule, Elton (1916–1990)

U.S. Media Executive

Elton Rule took the ABC TV network from a struggling operation in 1968 to top of the television network world a decade later. Under Rule's leadership, ABC-TV expanded its number of affiliates from 146 to 214 stations, and revenues increased from $600 million to $2.7 billion. The "alphabet network" began turning a profit in 1972; by 1976, it was the highest rated network in prime time; a year later Rule was presiding

Elton Rule.
Courtesy of the Everett Collection

over a television empire that was collecting more money for advertising time than any media corporation in the world.

The key to this extraordinary success was Rule's ability to find top programming. During the 1970s, Rule helped introduce such innovations as the made-for-television movie, the miniseries, and *Monday Night Football.* One of his first moves as network president was to sign the Hollywood producer Aaron Spelling, who through the 1970s added a string of top-ten hits to ABC's line-up, including *Mod Squad, Family, Starsky and Hutch, Love Boat,* and *Charlie's Angels.* Rule pioneered the presentation of made-for-television movies as a regular part of network schedules, billing them as ABC's Movie of the Week, and producing such early hits as *Brian's Song* and *That Certain Summer.* In 1974, Rule approved the miniseries *QB VII.* Three years later, a week of *Roots,* from Alex Haley's best-selling book, set ratings records, earned Rule wide acclaim, and generated for ABC vast sums of advertising dollars.

During the 1970s, Rule made ABC the leading sports network, centered on *Monday Night Football* and the Olympics. Rule must also be credited with making the ABC news division the industry leader. He moved sports producer Roone Arledge over to head a languishing network operation, approved hiring reporters from major newspapers, and expanded the locus of the network's foreign news bureaus. By the mid-1980s, ABC News was the leading broadcast journalism operation in the United States.

When Rule retired in January 1984, he was properly hailed as a corporate savior. Through the remainder of the 1980s, he bought and sold television stations, becoming a multimillionaire. He is remembered, and heralded, for creating a television network empire, an economic, political, social, and cultural force second to none in the history of television.

DOUGLAS GOMERY

See also **American Broadcasting Company; Networks; United States**

Elton (Hoerl) Rule. Born in Stockton, California, June 13, 1916. Graduated from Sacramento College, Sacramento, California, 1938. Married: Betty Louise Bender; children: Cindy Rule Dunne, Christie, James. Served in the U.S. Army Infantry, 1941–45. Worked at KROY, Sacramento, 1938–41; radio sales account executive, 1946–52; assistant sales manager, KECA-TV (now KABC-TV), 1952; general sales manager, 1953–60; general manager, 1960–61; vice president and general manager, 1961–68; president, California Broadcasters Association, 1966–67; president, ABC-TV, 1968–70; group vice president, ABC, 1969–72; president, ABC division, 1970–72; director, ABC, 1970–84; president, chief executive officer, and member of executive committee, ABC, 1972–83; vice chair, ABC, 1983–84; president, chair, investment funds with I. Martin Pompadur; co-chair, National Center of Film and Video Preservation. Member: advisory board, Institute of Sports Medicine and Athletic Trauma, Lenox Hill Hospital, 1973–84; board of visitors, University of California, Los Angeles, School of Medicine, 1980–84. Recipient: Purple Heart; Bronze Star with Oak Leaf Cluster; International Radio and TV Society Gold Medal Award, 1975; Academy of TV Arts and Sciences Governor's Award, 1981. Died in Beverly Hills, California, May 5, 1990.

Further Reading

Brown, Les, *Televi$ion: The Business Behind the Box,* New York: Harcourt Brace Jovanovich, 1971

Goldenson, Leonard H., *Beating the Odds,* New York: Scribner's, 1991

Gunther, Marc, *The House That Roone Built: The Inside Story of ABC News,* Boston: Little, Brown, 1994

Quinlan, Sterling, *Inside ABC: American Broadcasting Company's Rise to Power,* New York: Hastings's House, 1979

Williams, Huntington, *Beyond Control: ABC and the Fate of the Networks,* New York: Atheneum, 1989

Rumpole of the Bailey

British Legal/Mystery Comedy

Rumpole of the Bailey, a mix of British courtroom comedy and drama, first aired on Thames Television in 1978. The program made a successful transatlantic voyage and has been popular in the United States as part of PBS's *Mystery!* anthology series.

All episodes feature the court cases of Horace Rumpole (Leo McKern), a short, round, perennially exasperating, shrewd, lovable defense barrister. His clients are often caught in contemporary social conflicts: a father accused of devil worshipping; the Gay News Ltd. sued for blasphemous libel; a forger of Victorian photographs who briefly fooled the National Portrait Gallery; a pornographic publisher. Rumpole's deep commitment to justice leads him to defend wholeheartedly hopeless cases and the spirit of the law, as opposed to his fellow barristers who stubbornly defend the letter of the law. Rumpole is given to frequent oratorical outbursts from the *Oxford Book of English Verse* and manages to aim the elegant passages at upper-class hypocritical trumpeters, buffoons, and other barristers and at prosecution-inspiring justices. He comments on the phenomenon of "judgitis [pomposity] which, like piles, is an occupational hazard on the bench." His suggested cure is "banishment to the golf course."

Rumpole is married to Hilda (played at various times by Joyce Heron, Peggy Thorpe-Bates, and Marion Mathie), to whom he refers as "She Who Must Be Obeyed." Hilda—whose father was head of chambers—aspires for a more prestigious position for her husband and a bit more luxurious lifestyle for herself, but she continues to support her husband's brand of justice rather than that sought by egotistical or social-climbing royal counsels. Rumpole revels in lampooning his fellow colleagues, whom he believes to be a group of twits. They include the dithery and pompous Claude Erskine-Brown (Julian Curry), the full-of-himself Samuel Ballard (Peter Blythe), and the variety of dour judges who preside in court—the bumbling Justice Guthrie Featherstone (Peter Bowles), the blustering "mad bull" Justice Bullingham (Bill Fraser), the serious and heartless Justice Graves (Robin Bailey), and the almost kindly Justice "Ollie" Oliphant (James Grout). Among Rumpole's colleagues, he favors Claude's wife, the savvy and stylish Phillida Neetrant

Erskine-Brown (Patricia Hodge), a feminist voice for the series, and the endearing Uncle Tom (Richard Murdoch), an octogenarian waiting to have the good sense to retire, who, in the meantime, practices his putting in chambers.

The prolific writer John Mortimer is creator of the Rumpole stories and has exclusive rights in writing the television series, for which he continues to write new scripts. Mortimer draws upon both his 36 years of experiences as queen's counsel and his life with his father, a blind divorce lawyer. Much like Rumpole, Mortimer adores good food, enjoys a bottle of claret before dinner, loves Dickens, and fights for liberal causes. He is much revered in England, and in 1988 the queen awarded him a knighthood.

In addition to the quick-witted dialogue among characters, Mortimer's series is distinguished by its social commentary. Specifically, the program is a cleverly entertaining vehicle for tweaking the legal profession and the general state of British mores and manners. In chambers and during court cases, Rumpole provides viewers with grumbling commentaries and under-the-breath critiques of pomposity and the all-too-frequent soulless application of strict legalism. Yet, even though these comments on various social issues such as gay rights, censorship, and the treatment of children in court are quite serious, Mortimer never allows the issues to get in the way of the story. Meticulous attention to detail, well-written scripts, and top-notch actors contribute to have made *Rumpole* fine television without the formula-driven action/adventure genres typically associated with drama programming.

The program's charm is particularly enhanced by the superb casting of Leo McKern, who was the very embodiment of the fictional Rumpole. Robert Goldberg, a television critic from the *Wall Street Journal,* compares this match to other strokes of casting genius: "Every once in a while a character and an actor fit together so precisely that is becomes hard to imagine one without the other (Sean Connery and James Bond, Jeremy Brett and Sherlock Holmes)." McKern's jowls, bulbous nose, and erratic eyebrows were made to fit the eccentric, irrepressibly snide barrister who is, in Goldberg's words, as "lovable as a grumpy old panda."

Rumpole of the Bailey, Leo McKern as Horace Rumpole, 1978–92.
Courtesy of the Everett Collection

Rumpole of the Bailey is a cherished series in the United States. According to Boston public television station WGBH's senior producer Steven Ashley, *Rumpole* has enjoyed solid ratings and can be regarded as one of the most popular titles in the *Mystery!* schedule, having attracted a healthy audience even when faced with stiff competition from commercial networks. Approximately 300 public television stations have carried the *Rumpole* series on an ongoing basis, representing 95 percent of all PBS stations. In the San Francisco Bay Area, some of the show's more active fans formed the "Rumpole Society" with over 450 members; they have featured principal actors or John Mortimer as guest speakers at their annual fete and have visited the Rumpole studios in London.

LYNN T. LOVDAL

See also **British Programming; McKern, Leo**

Cast

Horace Rumpole	Leo McKern
Guthrie Featherstone	Peter Bowles
Erskine-Brown	Julian Curry
Phillida	Patricia Hodge
George Frobisher	Moray Watson
Uncle Tom	Richard Murdoch
Hilda Rumpole (1975)	Joyce Heron
Hilda Rumpole (1978–83)	Peggy Thorpe-Bates
Hilda Rumpole (1987–92)	Marion Mathie
Justice Bullingham	Bill Fraser
Fiona Allways	Rosalyn Landor
Henry	Jonathan Coy
Diane	Maureen Derbyshire
Marigold Featherstone	Joanna Van Gysegham
Nick Rumpole	David Yelland
Liz Probert	Abigail McKern
Judge Graves	Robin Bailey
Samuel Ballard	Peter Blythe

Producers

Irene Shubik, Jacqueline Davies

Programming History

44 episodes
BBC 1

As an installment of *Play for Today*	December 16, 1975
Thames	
April 1978–May 1978	six episodes
May 1979–June 1979	six episodes
December 1980	special: *Rumpole's Return*
October 1983–November 1983	six episodes
January 1987–February 1987	six episodes
November 1988–December 1988	six episodes
October 1991–December 1991	six episodes
October 1992–December 1992	six episodes

Further Reading

Gussow, Mel, "The Man Who Put Rumpole on the Case," *New York Times* (April 13, 1995)

Mortimer, John Clifford, *The First Rumpole Omnibus,* Harmondsworth, England, and New York: Penguin, 1983

Mortimer, John Clifford, *The Best of Rumpole,* New York: Viking, 1993

Rushton, William (1937–1996)

British Author, Actor, Artist

A versatile cartoonist, broadcaster, author, and actor, William Rushton's range of talent emerged early, while a student at Shrewsbury School. There he edited the school magazine, *The Salopian,* and regularly illustrated its issues. The public school friendships and joint contributions for *The Salopian* led to the idea of a satirical publication, *The Private Eye,* cofounded by Rushton and first published in 1962. With its comprehensive attack on the establishment, who were presented as running England in the manner of a private club, *The Private Eye* pioneered a style of satire that was to become fashionable in the early 1960s.

In 1962, Rushton moved on to television to take part in BBC's satirical program, *That Was the Week That Was (TW3).* Under director Alasdair Milne and producer Ned Sherrin, the crew put together their best work to express doubts about the old order in Britain. In an even more practical step, *The Private Eye* team, upset by the possibility of Sir Alec Douglas Home's further career in politics, posted Rushton to run against him in the Kinross by-election. Rushton's failed candidacy and his Macmillan impersonation on *TW3* made his name, but the irreverent show, anchored by David Frost, deeply divided the public, and the resulting controversy led to its removal from television screens.

In the 1964–65 season, Rushton cohosted the follow-up to *TW3,* called *Not So Much a Programme, More a Way of Life.* This show had less clear direction and was at its most successful when it approached the impertinence of *TW3.* Even this milder satirical program, however, faced political criticism that put an end to its existence.

The success of *TW3* opened the way to the cinema for Rushton. Director Clive Donner incorporated three of the show's presenters into *Nothing but the Best* (1964). The film featured a young opportunist and provided a brash criticism of affluent Britain through a mocking celebration of its values. Rushton also played a role in *Those Magnificent Men in Their Flying Machines* (1965), a humorous take on the early days of aviation.

The slightly overweight Rushton, who described his hobbies as "gaining weight, losing weight, and parking," served as presenter for *Don't Just Sit There* (1973), a BBC series on healthy living. He also took part in the television show *Up Sunday* (1975–78) and entertained the viewers in *Celebrity Squares* (1979–80), a popular game show based on the idea of the U.S. syndicated program *Hollywood Squares.* In addition, he did voice-overs for the BBC's *Jackanory* and *Asterix* series. On radio he appeared in 27 series of the popular anarchic game show, *I Am Sorry I Haven't a Clue.*

As a stage actor, Rushton made his debut in Spike Milligan's *The Bed-Sitting Room* in Canterbury in 1961. After a number of smaller parts, he returned to stage in a full-length role in Eric Idle's play *Pass the Butler* (1982). This witty black comedy, written by a member of the offbeat *Monty Python* team, played suc-

William Rushton.
Courtesy of the Everett Collection/CSU Archives

cessfully in Britain. Later, he returned to stand-up comedy, presenting "Two Old Farts" with Barry Cryer on nationwide tours.

Rushton wrote and illustrated a number of books, including *William Rushton's Dirty Book* (1964), *Superpig* (1976), *The Filth Amendment* (1981), and *Marylebone Versus the Rest of the World* (1987). He also provided illustrations and cartoons for many others, including a number of children's books.

After his early success in the 1960s, Rushton continued to work for *The Private Eye* and drew cartoons for the *Literary Review* and the *Daily Telegraph*'s "Way of the World" column until his death in December 1996. Known particularly for his humorous cartoons and funny personal presentations, he was a fine performer, a versatile and interesting artist for whom television provided a continuing opportunity for comic invention.

RITA ZAJÁCZ

See also That Was the Week That Was

William George Rushton. Born in London, August 18, 1937. Attended Shrewsbury School, Shropshire. Married: Arlene Dorgan, 1968; children: Tobias, Matthew, and Sam. After National Service, worked as solicitor's articled clerk, freelance cartoonist, and satirist; cofounder and editor, *The Private Eye*, 1961; stage debut, 1961; made television debut as one of *That Was the Week That Was* team, 1962; comic performer on radio, film, and television, appearing on numerous panel shows. Died December 11, 1996.

Television Series (selected)

1962–63	*That Was the Week That Was*
1964–65	*Not So Much a Programme, More a Way of Life*
1969–72	*Up Pompeii!*
1975–78	*Up Sunday*
1979–80	*Celebrity Squares*
1980	*Rushton's Illustrated*

Films

It's All Over Town, 1963; *Nothing but the Best*, 1964; *Those Magnificent Men in Their Flying Machines*, 1965; *The Mini-Affair*, 1968; *The Bliss of Mrs. Blossom*, 1968; *The Best House in London*, 1969; *Monte Carlo or Bust/Those Daring Young Men in Their Jaunty Jalopies*, 1969; *Flight of the Doves*, 1971; *The Adventures of Barry McKenzie*, 1972; *Keep It up Downstairs*, 1975; *The Chiffy Kids*, 1976; *Adventures of a Private Eye*, 1977; *Adventures of a Plumber's Mate*, 1978; *The Blues Band*, 1981; *The Magic Shop*, 1982; *Consuming Passions*, 1987.

Radio

I'm Sorry I Haven't a Clue, 1976– ; *Trivia Test Match*.

Stage

The Bed-Sitting Room, 1961; *Gulliver's Travels*, 1971, 1979; *Pass the Butler*, 1982; *Tales from a Long Room*, 1988.

Publications (selected)

William Rushton's Dirty Book, 1964
How to Play Football: The Art of Dirty Play, 1968
The Day of the Grocer, 1971
The Geranium of Flüt, 1975
Superpig, 1976
Pigsticking: A Joy for Life, 1977
The Reluctant Euro, 1980
The Filth Amendment, 1981
W.G. Grace's Last Case, 1984
Willie Rushton's Great Moments of History, 1985
The Alternative Gardener: A Compost of Quips for the Green-Fingered, 1986
Marylebone Versus the Rest of the World, 1987
Spy Thatcher (editor), 1987
Every Cat in the Book, 1993

Further Reading

Marnham, Patrick, *The Private Eye Story: The First 21 Years*, London: Andre Deutsch, 1982
Murphy, Robert, *Sixties British Cinema*, London: British Film Institute, 1992

Russell, Ken (1927–)

British Filmmaker

Ken Russell is best known in the United States as director of such feature films as *Women in Love* (1969), *The Music Lovers* (1970), *Tommy* (1975), and *Altered States* (1980). Although his television work is less well known outside the United Kingdom, it has had a major impact on the development of the television genre of fictional history, described by historian C. Vann Woodward as the portrayal of "real historical figures and events, but with the license of the novelist to imagine and invent." Russell's special province in the genre (a psycho-biographical form he terms the "biopic") has been music composers and other artists such as dancers and poets. His imaginative interpretations of the lives of artists have, on occasion, outraged both critics and the general public.

After a brief career as a ballet dancer, and later as a successful commercial photographer, Russell turned his attention to film directing. On the basis of a portfolio of three low-budget short films, he was hired by the British Broadcasting Corporation (BBC) in 1959, at the age of 32, to work as a director on its arts series *Monitor.* Most of the *Monitor* pieces (10- to 15-minute short subjects) focused on contemporary artists working in British music, dance, and literature. Russell noted that, at the time, there was no real experimental film school in Britain, except for *Monitor. Monitor* producer Huw Wheldon, who later became managing director of BBC-TV, encouraged experimentation (within limits), and Russell took full advantage of this.

The two most important productions from Russell's *Monitor* period were *Elgar* (1962) and *The Debussy Film* (1965). *Elgar,* Russell's attempt to counter British music critics' negative assessments of the British composer Edward Elgar, was his first full-length *Monitor* film, lasting 50 minutes. It also marked the celebration of the 100th *Monitor* program. In *Elgar,* Russell advanced the idea of using actors to impersonate historical characters, which he had introduced the previous year on *Monitor* in the short film *Portrait of a Soviet Composer,* on the life of Sergei Prokofiev. Prior to this, the BBC had prohibited the use of actors in the portrayal of historical personages. In the Prokofiev film, Russell used an actor to show the composer's hands, a so-called anonymous presence. In *Elgar,* Russell took the concept a step further, allowing Elgar to be seen (but still not heard). Five different actors, mostly amateurs, portrayed the composer at various stages of his life. Most of the scenes with the actors were shot in medium-shot. According to Russell, the viewer was "not aware of a personality; just a figure." Russell skillfully combined silent footage of the actors, stock footage of English life at the turn of the century, and photographs of Elgar and his family, all of which were enhanced by Elgar's compositions. Russell focused his interpretation on Elgar's reverence for the English countryside—his "return to the strength of the hills" (a theme of great importance in Russell's own life). That theme would reemerge in many subsequent Russell biopics. *Elgar* was extremely popular with the audience, in large measure because of Russell's romantic use of Elgar's music; the show was repeated at least three times. As John Baxter points out, this work launched Russell's national reputation.

After an unsuccessful feature film, *French Dressing,* Russell returned to the BBC to direct *The Debussy Film: Impressions of the French Composer* (1965). Here, Russell broke through the BBC's last remaining prohibition against using actors in speaking roles in historical drama. According to Russell, as quoted in Gene D. Phillips's *Ken Russell,* Wheldon thought the film "a bit esoteric" and insisted on beginning the film "with a series of photographs of Debussy along with a spoken statement assuring viewers they were about to see a film based on incidents in Debussy's life and incorporating direct quotations from Debussy himself." The BBC feared that viewers might believe they were watching newsreels of real people. To circumvent this potential problem, Russell created an intriguing "film-within-a-film," in which the framing story depicts a French film director coming to England to shoot a film on Debussy. In the script, actors were clearly identified as actors playing the various historical figures. Russell, and writer Melvyn Bragg (who would collaborate with Russell on several films and later become the editor and presenter of *The South Bank Show*), conceived Debussy as "a mysterious, shadowy character"—an unpredictable and sensual dreamer. This is accentuated by Russell's evocative use of macabre physical comedy.

Isadora Duncan: The Biggest Dancer in the World (1966) is the most celebrated and least factual of Russell's BBC biopics. The film used a mix of classical music and popular tunes (from Beethoven to "Bye, Bye, Blackbird") and featured a nude dance, suicide attempts, and wild parties to depict Duncan's sensational life and her death wish. Excerpts from Leni Riefenstahl's *Olympia* were intercut with original footage, Ken Hanke reports, to convey the "ideal of German perfection" Duncan sought to emulate. Duncan was at once "sublime" and "vulgar," if not grotesque. Interestingly, some of Russell's more hostile critics have accused the director of the same tendencies.

Song of Summer (BBC, 1968) chronicles the last years of the life of composer Frederick Delius, who, blind and crippled with syphilis, is living in a French village with his wife, Jelka, and his amanuensis, Eric Fenby. Fenby, who advised Russell on the film, is portrayed as a young man who sacrificed his own career out of love and respect for Delius. In the end, according to Russell, as quoted by Phillips, Fenby feels "robbed of his own artistic vision" (see Phillips). The ultimate irony, says Russell, is that much of Delius's music is second-rate. In *Song of Summer,* Russell is able to express an understanding and even compassion for a composer whose basic personality and music he clearly dislikes. The theme, evident in *Isadora,* of what Hanke refers to as "the artist's unfortunate need to debase himself and his art," reemerges here. As in *Elgar,* Russell highlights the artist's obsession with nature. According to Hanke, in *Song of Summer,* Russell exhibited his "ability to work in a restrained manner if the subject matter calls for it."

The last film Russell would make for the BBC, the infamous *The Dance of the Seven Veils: A Comic Strip in Seven Episodes on the Life of Richard Strauss* (1970), exhibited no such restraint. The complete title reveals Russell's intention to create a satirical political cartoon on the life of the German composer, whom Russell saw as a "self-advertising, vulgar, commercial man...[a] crypto-Nazi with the superman complex underneath the facade of the distinguished elderly composer." Although, according to Russell, "95 percent of what Strauss says in the film he actually did say in his letters and other writings," many critics and viewers found Russell's treatment of the venerated composer itself to be vulgar. Hanke's assessment is that in the film, Russell contends that Strauss "betrayed himself and his art through his lack of personal responsibility," which included his currying favor with the Nazis during World War II. The most objectionable sequences in the film were Strauss conducting "Der Rosenkavalier," and exhorting his musicians to play ever louder to drown out the screams of a Jew being tortured in the audience by SS men, who were carving a Star of David on the man's chest with a knife; and the playing of Strauss's "Domestic Symphony" over shots of Strauss and his wife making love, their climax being mirrored by the orchestra. The film concludes with Russell himself portraying a wild-haired orchestra conductor bowing and walking away from the camera as his director's credit appears on the screen (perhaps signaling his own farewell to the BBC). The film aired once, leading to mass protests and questions raised in Parliament. As Russell put it, "all hell broke loose." Huw Wheldon, head of BBC-TV, defended Russell. At the same time, the BBC tried to placate critics, including Strauss's family and his publisher, by presenting a roundtable discussion in which music critics and conductors denounced both Russell and the film. By the time *The Dance of the Seven Veils* aired on the BBC, Russell's feature film *Women in Love* had assured him a reputation in feature-film circles, and the BBC experience convinced him it was time to abandon the small screen.

Russell would return to television, but not to the BBC. In 1978, Russell directed *Clouds of Glory* for British independent television's Grenada-TV. This program was actually two one-hour episodes. The first, *William and Dorothy,* was a biopic on the love of William Wordsworth for his sister Dorothy. The second episode, *The Rime of the Ancient Mariner,* was a biopic on the life of Samuel Taylor Coleridge.

In the 1990s, Russell continued to make television films about composers and music: *The Strange Affliction of Anton Bruckner* (1990), *The Secret Life of Sir Arnold Bax* (1992), *The Mystery of Doctor Martinu* (1993), *Classic Widows* (1995), and *In Search of the English Folk Song* (1997). Other television projects by Russell in this decade included a historical drama about the Dreyfus case, *Prisoners of Honor* (1991); literary adaptations (the miniseries *Lady Chatterley* [1993] and *Ken Russell's Treasure Island* [1995]), and a prison drama, *Dogboys* (1998). He also directed a television documentary on Russia and Russians entitled *Alice in Russialand* (1995), and in 2001 he offered a TV documentary on women soccer players, *The Brighton Belles,* which aired as part of the BBC 2 series *Southern Eye.* Russell also remains active as a feature filmmaker and director of operas.

HAL HIMMELSTEIN AND ELIZABETH NISHIURA

See also **Bragg, Melvyn; British Programming; Wheldon, Huw**

Ken (Kenneth Alfred) Russell. Born in Southampton, Hampshire, England, July 3, 1927. Educated at Pangbourne Nautical College, 1941–44; Walthamstow Art School; International Ballet School. Married: 1) Shirley Ann Kingdon, 1957 (divorced, 1978); five children; 2) Vivian Jolly, 1984 (divorced, 1991); children: Molly and Rupert; 3) Hetty Baines, 1992; 4) Lisi Tribble, 2001. Served in Merchant Navy, 1945, and Royal Air Force, 1946–49. Dancer, Ny Norsk Ballet, 1950; actor, Garrick Players, 1951; photographer, 1951–57; amateur film director; documentary filmmaker, BBC, 1958–66; debut as professional film director, 1963; established reputation on television with series of biographical films about great composers for the arts program *Omnibus,* from 1966, and the *South Bank Show,* from 1983; freelance film director, also staging opera and directing pop videos, since 1966. Recipient: Screen Writers Guild Awards, 1962, 1965, 1966, 1967; Guild of Television Producers and Directors Award, 1966; Desmond Davis Award, 1968; Emmy Award, 1988.

Television Series
1993   *Lady Chatterley*

Television Documentaries
1959   *Poet's London*
1959   *Gordon Jacob*
1959   *Variations on a Mechanical Theme*
1959   *Robert McBryde and Robert Colquhoun*
1959   *Portrait of a Goon*
1960   *Marie Rambert Remembers*
1960   *Architecture of Entertainment*
1960   *Cranks at Work*
1960   *The Miners' Picnic*
1960   *Shelagh Delaney's Salford*
1960   *A House in Bayswater*
1960   *The Light Fantastic*
1961   *Old Battersea House*
1961   *Portrait of a Soviet Composer*
1961   *London Moods*
1961   *Antonio Gaudi*
1962   *Pop Goes the Easel*
1962   *Preservation Man*
1962   *Mr. Chesher's Traction Engines*
1962   *Lotte Lenya Sings Kurt Weill*
1962   *Elgar*
1963   *Watch the Birdie*
1964   *Lonely Shore*
1964   *Bartok*
1964   *The Dotty World of James Lloyd*
1965   *The Debussy Film: Impressions of the French Composer*
1965   *Always on Sunday*
1966   *The Diary of a Nobody*

1966   *Don't Shoot the Composer*
1966   *Isadora Duncan: The Biggest Dancer in the World*
1967   *Dante's Inferno*
1968   *Song of Summer*
1970   *The Dance of the Seven Veils: A Comic Strip in Seven Episodes on the Life of Richard Strauss*
1978   *Clouds of Glory, Parts I and II*
1983   *Ken Russell's View of the Planets*
1984   *Elgar*
1984   *Vaughan Williams*
1988   *Ken Russell's ABC of British Music*
1989   *Ken Russell: A British Picture*
1990   *Strange Affliction of Anton Bruckner*
1992   *The Secret Life of Sir Arnold Bax*
1993   *The Mystery of Doctor Martinu*
1995   *Classic Widows*
1995   *Alice in Russialand*
1997   *In Search of the English Folk Song*
2001   *Brighton Belles*
2002   *Elgar: Fantasy of a Composer on a Bicycle*

Made-for-Television Movies
1991   *Prisoners of Honor*
1995   *Ken Russell's Treasure Island*
1996   *The Insatiable Mrs. Kirsch* (short shown as part of *Tales of Erotica*)
1998   *Dogboys*

Films (director)
Amelia and the Angel, 1957; *Peep Show,* 1958; *Lourdes,* 1958; *French Dressing,* 1963; *Billion Dollar Brain,* 1967; *Women in Love,* 1969; *The Music Lovers* (also producer), 1970; *The Devils* (also writer and co-producer), 1971; *The Boy Friend* (also writer and producer), 1971; *The Savage Messiah* (also producer), 1972; *Mahler* (also writer), 1974; *Tommy* (also writer and co-producer), 1975; *Lisztomania* (also writer), 1975; *Valentino* (also co-writer), 1977; *Altered States,* 1980; *Crimes of Passion,* 1984; *Gothic,* 1986; *Aria* (episode), 1987; *Salomé's Last Dance,* 1988; *The Lair of the White Worm,* 1988; *The Rainbow,* 1989; *Whore,* 1991; *The Russia House* (actor), 1991; *Mindbender* (also co-writer), 1995; *Lion's Mouth* (short), 2000; *The Fall of the Louse of Usher,* 2002; *Charged: The Life of Nikola Tesla,* 2003.

Radio
The Death of Scriabin, 1995.

Stage (operas)

The Rake's Progress, 1982; *Die Soldaten,* 1983; *Madame Butterfly,* 1983; *La Bohème,* 1984; *The Italian Girl in Tangiers,* 1984; *Faust,* 1985; *Mefistofoles,* 1989; *Princess Ida,* 1992; *Salomé,* 1993; *Weill and Lenya,* 2000.

Publications

A British Picture: An Autobiography, 1989

Fire over England: British Cinema Comes Under Friendly Fire, 1993

The Lion Roars: Ken Russell on Film, 1993

Directing Film: From Pitch to Premiere, 2000; published in United States as *Directing Film: The Director's Art from Script to Cutting Room Floor,* 2001

Further Reading

Atkins, Thomas, *Ken Russell,* New York: Monarch, 1976

Baxter, John, *An Appalling Talent: Ken Russell,* London: Joseph, 1973

Dempsey, Michael, "The World of Ken Russell," *Film Quarterly* (Spring 1972)

Dempsey, Michael, "Ken Russell, Again," *Film Quarterly* (Winter 1977–78)

Farber, Stephen, "Russellmania," *Film Comment* (November/December 1975)

Fisher, Jack, "Three Paintings of Sex: The Films of Ken Russell," *Films Journal* (September 1972)

Gilliatt, Penelope, "Genius, Genia, Genium, Ho Hum," *The New Yorker* (April 26, 1976)

Gomez, Joseph, "*Mahler* and the Methods of Ken Russell's Films on Composers," *Velvet Light Trap* (Winter 1975)

Gomez, Joseph, *Ken Russell: The Adaptor As Creator,* London: Muller, 1976

Hanke, Ken, *Ken Russell's Films,* Metuchen, New Jersey: Scarecrow, 1984

Jaehne, Karen, "Wormomania: Ken Russell's Best Laid Planaria," *Film Criticism* (1988)

Kolker, Robert, "Ken Russell's Biopics: Grander and Gaudier," *Film Comment* (May/June 1973)

Phillips, Gene D., *Ken Russell,* Boston: Twayne, 1979

Rosenfeldt, Diane, *Ken Russell: A Guide to Reference Sources.* Boston: Hall, 1978

Woodward, C. Vann, *The Future of the Past,* New York: Oxford University Press, 1989

Yacowar, M., "Ken Russell's *Rabelais,*" *Literature/Film Quarterly* (1980)

Russia

Russia was the largest and the culturally predominant republic of the U.S.S.R., and the history of Russian television up to the disintegration of that country in 1991 is inseparable from that of Soviet television. Moreover, in spite of the changes that have taken place since then, Russian television remains the principal inheritor of the traditions (as well as the properties) of its Soviet predecessor.

Regular television broadcasting began in Moscow in 1939, although the service was interrupted for the duration of World War II (1941–45). Broadcasting was always given a high priority by the Soviet authorities, and television expanded rapidly in the postwar years, so that by the late 1970s there were two general channels that could be received over most of the country and two other channels (one local and one educational) in certain large cities. There were also television stations in the constituent republics and studios in most large cities. Apart from a gradual extension of the coverage of the two national channels until the first, at least, could be received in virtually the whole of the country, this situation remained little changed until

1991. Because of its size, the Soviet Union was a pioneer of satellite transmission: by the mid-1980s both national channels were broadcast in four time-shifted variants to eastern parts of the country, while the first channel was among the earliest television programs to be made available worldwide. Regular color transmissions began in 1967, using the SECAM system.

Administratively, television was the responsibility of the All-Union Committee for Television and Radio (generally known as Gosteleradio), the chairman of which was a member of the Council of Ministers and of the Central Committee of the Soviet Communist Party. Equivalent committees existed in the constituent republics, with the exception, owing to a quirk of the system, of Russia itself. Only in May 1991, after sustained pressure from the Russian Parliament, did a separate Russian organization start its own television transmissions; its programs, broadcast for six hours per day on the second channel, were in the summer of that year a focus of opposition to President Mikhail Gorbachev. Broadcasting was financed out of the state budget, the receiving license having been replaced in

1962 by a notional addition to the retail price of television sets.

The social, political, and economic upheavals that accompanied the collapse of the Soviet system have led to major changes in Russian television. The period since 1991 has been characterized by a rapid growth of commercialization and a continuing debate concerning the roles of both the state and private businesses in owning, financing, and controlling the content of the electronic media. There has also been continuous disagreement between the executive and legislative branches of power over which of them should exercise control over broadcasting. Up to now, this question has invariably been resolved in favor of the former, and the entire structure of Russian television has in effect been put into place by a series of presidential decrees.

As in most of Europe, Russian television is provided by a combination of publicly and privately owned organizations. The All-Russian State Television and Radio Company (VGTRK), founded in 1991 and wholly owned by the state, operates two channels: RTR (general interest) and Kul'tura (more "highbrow"). A second state company, Ostankino, which was created out of the former Gosteleradio when the Soviet Union disintegrated, was abolished in 1995. Its functions were taken over by Obshchestvennoe rossiiskoe televidenie (Russian Public Television, known as ORT), owned 51 percent by the state and 49 percent by private interests. ORT is largely a commissioning company. Publicly owned broadcasting organizations continue to exist in each of the regions of Russia; one of these, TV-Tsentr, mostly owned and financed by the Moscow city government, uses franchising arrangements to have its programs broadcast in other large cities. In the private sector, there is one national company, NTV, while another, TV-6, is available in many large cities, thanks to franchising agreements; both NTV and TV-6 commenced operations in 1993. There are also several hundred local stations, and cable television exists in many cities. Most national channels have international versions, aimed principally at Russian-speaking audiences in Israel.

The changes since 1991 have had an equally profound effect on programs and their content. In Soviet times, television was first and foremost an instrument of propaganda, serving the interests of party and state, and this purpose was reflected in all news bulletins and political programs. The main evening news program, *Vremia* (Time), was shown simultaneously on all channels and often ran far beyond its allotted 40 minutes (a cavalier attitude toward the published schedules has been a characteristic of both Soviet and Russian television). All programs were in effect, if not formally, subject to censorship, and caution usually prevailed: the popular student cabaret KVN was taken off the air in the 1971 for being too daring, and a high proportion of the nonpolitical programs consisted of high culture (opera, ballet, or classical drama), films made for the Soviet cinema, and sport, all of which could be guaranteed in advance to be inoffensive.

Because of television's importance as a means of propaganda, the effects of *glasnost* were felt more slowly in that medium than in the print media. By the late 1980s, however, a certain liberalization could be discerned: KVN returned to the screens, and previously taboo topics began to be discussed in programs such as *Vzgliad* (View) and *Do i posle polunochi* (Before and After Midnight). These were followed by a range of lively and innovative productions originated by the semi-independent production company ATV, as well as by attempts to liven up news presentation. However, as late as the 1990–91 season, all of these programs were liable to suffer cuts imposed by the censors or even to disappear altogether; the suspension of *Vzgliad* in January 1991 was a particular cause célèbre. Under the circumstances, it is not surprising that the removal of all restrictions after the collapse of the August 1991 putsch led to a brief flowering of creative talent (and the emergence of long-forbidden programs) that may prove to have been something of a "golden age" for Russian television.

The 1990s and 2000s have witnessed a gradual Westernization of Russian television with the appearance of genres hitherto eschewed. Among these are game shows, such as *Pole chudes* (Field of Miracles), which is based on *Wheel of Fortune* and which is one of Ostankino/ORT's most popular programs; more recently, the Russian version of *Who Wants to Be a Millionaire* has attracted many viewers. Other newly adopted genres include talk shows, such as *Tema* (Theme) and *My* (We), which likewise have clear ancestral links with their American counterparts, and soap operas. These are almost invariably imported from the United States or Latin America; home-grown versions have been few in number and short-lived. One genre to which Russian television has remained immune is situation comedy, although in the area of satire it is worth mentioning NTV's *Kukly* (Puppets), which uses the format of the British program *Spitting Image* and which has occasionally succeeded in annoying the authorities. Films made in the United States and other Western countries are now widely shown, although since the mid-1990s, presumably in response to complaints from viewers, there has been a marked increase in the number of Russian/Soviet films being broadcast. There is a limited amount of religious broadcasting, mostly in connection with festivals of the Russian Orthodox Church. Literature, classical music, and serious drama, which at one time had almost totally disappeared from the screens, have regained a tenuous foothold on the Kul'tura channel.

This Westernization has by no means met with universal approval, although it is not only a reaction to Soviet isolationism but also a response to commercial pressures. The financing of Russian television is heavily opaque, but it may be assumed that the state makes a modest contribution to the running costs of VGTRK, though not to ORT. This means that all channels except Kul'tura are now heavily dependent on advertising, and with the relationship between audience ratings and the prices charged for advertising becoming as sophisticated as in the West, there is a requirement to show programs that will attract viewers. Advertising is lightly regulated and takes many forms, including spots between and during programs and sponsorship. It tends to be unpopular, partly because of the unfamiliar intrusiveness (the amount of advertising is much greater than in most European countries), but also because in the early days a high proportion of the ads were either for foreign goods not widely available or (especially from 1992 to 1994) for disreputable financial institutions that subsequently collapsed. Nevertheless, while some transnational companies have preferred to recycle advertisements previously used in their older markets, the best Russian-produced examples of the form will bear comparison to anything shown in the West. The rapid growth of advertising has led to widespread allegations of corruption, and the murkier side of Russian television received prominence in March 1995 with the still unsolved murder of Vladislav List'ev, originator and presenter of several popular programs and director-general-designate of ORT. In some cases additional financial support for television may come from owners or patrons. However, the costs of running the national channels have for some years exceeded income, and all the main channels, whether public or private, are heavily in debt. In 2001, the Duma approved a law banning foreign citizens or companies from owning more than 50 percent of a national television company; given the financial and political uncertainties, it is perhaps not surprising that there has been little or no foreign investment in Russian television.

Commercial pressures have not, however, entirely succeeded in supplanting political pressures, although until recently the latter have been incomparably more subtle than in Soviet times. The mass media under Boris Yeltsin were by historical standards surprisingly free and pluralistic, partly because the president was himself relaxed about criticism, but partly because the ramshackle nature of the state made effective control problematic. Nevertheless, in both areas the long-established Soviet practice of "telephone law" (whereby a person in power uses that instrument to convey his or her wishes/instructions) continued to prevail, and Ostankino and its successor ORT acquired a reputation for being "pro-presidential," but this was principally because of the perceived slant of their news coverage. At the same time, however, certain programs produced for these channels by independent production companies were accused, somewhat contradictorily, of giving opponents of the president too much air time, and it is generally considered that the demagogic nationalist Vladimir Zhirinovskii largely owes his political career to television. In the 1996 presidential election, self-interest and political pressure ensured that all television channels supported the re-election of Yeltsin; NTV was rewarded for its support by significant improvements to the terms of its license, albeit at some cost to its reputation for independence and lack of bias.

The period after 1996 saw the growth of informal power networks involving politicians and businessmen and the appearance of "oligarchic television," where channels were controlled by tycoons with political ambitions. In particular, ORT was controlled by Boris Berezovskii, its main financier, while NTV was run by Vladimir Gusinskii, alternately Berezovskii's ally and rival. During the 1999/2000 elections, the two channels were on opposite sides: ORT supported Vladimir Putin and his allies; NTV displayed a demonstrative coolness toward the future president. Campaigning methods were remarkably robust, and this period saw the emergence of the phenomenon of the "telekiller," presenters of news-analysis programs (notably NTV's Sergei Dorenko), who indulged in vicious character assassinations of their patrons' opponents.

With Putin safely elected, a reckoning followed, the results of which were not entirely predictable. If the series of legal and extralegal measures taken against NTV and Gusinskii had a certain obvious logic, the easing-out of Berezovskii was more surprising. The latter sold, or was made to sell his shares, in ORT, and in April 2001 NTV came under the effective control of Gazprom, the partly state-owned gas monopoly, which had previously been a minority shareholder in NTV. The ostensible reason for the takeover was the inability of NTV to repay its debts, but it seems clear that the incident was engineered by the presidential administration to reign in an increasingly recalcitrant broadcaster. The events of 2000–01 were carried out with a curious mixture of scrupulously observed legal procedures and naked blackmail. The result has not been a re-Sovietization of Russian television, but a certain success in resetting the boundaries of pluralism rather more narrowly than in Yeltsin's time.

Russian television operates in a climate where the structures of a civil society have been only partially created and where politics in terms of being the determining factor both in interchannel rivalry and in viewer affections plays a role similar to that played by association football in western Europe. In the absence of a clear legal framework and of an agreed definition of "public service broadcasting," commercial pressures may offer the best available guarantees of maintaining some degree of freedom of speech. With the problems and opportunities associated with digitization still destined to have a significant impact, the creation of a stable and financially secure structure of broadly based channels aimed at a national audience is likely to remain the main issue in Russian television in the near future.

J.A. DUNN

Further Reading

Graffy, Julian, and Geoffrey A. Hosking, editors, *Culture and Media in the USSR Today,* London: Macmillan, 1989

McNair, Brian, "From Monolith to Mafia: Television in Post-Soviet Russia," *Media, Culture, and Society* (July 1996)

McNair, Brian, *Glasnost, Perestroika, and the Soviet Media,* London: Routledge, 1991

Mickiewicz, Ellen, *Split Signals: Television and Politics in the Soviet Union,* Oxford and New York: Oxford University Press, 1988

Mickiewicz, Ellen, *Changing Channels: Television and the Struggle for Power in Russia,* Oxford and New York: Oxford University Press, 1997; 2nd edition, Durham, North Carolina: Duke University Press, 1999

Paasilinna, Reino, *Glasnost and Soviet Television, Research Report 5,* Helsinki: Ylesradio (Finnish Broadcasting Company), 1995

Siefert, Marsha, editor, *Mass Culture and Perestroika in the Soviet Union,* Oxford and New York: Oxford University Press, 1991